The ADVENTURES IN LITERATURE Program

ADVENTURES FOR READERS: BOOK ONE

Annotated Teacher's Edition
Teacher's Manual
Tests

ADVENTURES FOR READERS: BOOK TWO

Annotated Teacher's Edition
Teacher's Manual
Tests

ADVENTURES IN READING

Annotated Teacher's Edition
Teacher's Manual
Tests

ADVENTURES IN APPRECIATION

Annotated Teacher's Edition
Teacher's Manual
Tests

ADVENTURES IN AMERICAN LITERATURE

Annotated Teacher's Edition
Teacher's Manual
Tests

ADVENTURES IN ENGLISH LITERATURE

Annotated Teacher's Edition
Teacher's Manual
Tests

CURRICULUM AND WRITING

Francis Hodgins
University of Illinois
Urbana, Illinois

Kenneth Silverman
New York University
New York, New York

Milton R. Stern
University of Connecticut
Storrs, Connecticut

Rolando R. Hinojosa-Smith
University of Texas at Austin
Austin, Texas

ADVENTURES
in American Literature

P E G A S U S   E D I T I O N

 HBJ **Harcourt Brace Jovanovich, Publishers**
Orlando   San Diego   Chicago   Dallas

ACKNOWLEDGMENTS

For permission to reprint copyrighted material, grateful
acknowledgment is made to the following sources:

Margaret Walker Alexander: "Childhood" from *For My People*
by Margaret Walker Alexander. Copyright 1942 by the Yale
University Press.

Atheneum Publishers, Inc., a division of Macmillan, Inc.:
"Marsyas" from *The Country of a Thousand Years of Peace*
(1959) in *FROM THE FIRST NINE: Poems 1946 – 1976* by
James Merrill. Copyright © 1982 by James Merrill.

James Baldwin: "The Creative Process" from *Creative America*
by James Baldwin. Published by Ridge Press.

Elizabeth Barnett, Literary Executor: "God's World" and "On
Hearing a Symphony of Beethoven" from *Collected Poems*
by Edna St. Vincent Millay. Copyright © 1913, 1921, 1928,
1940, 1948 by Edna St. Vincent Millay; copyright © 1955
by Norma Millay Ellis. Published by Harper & Row,
Publishers, Inc.

Bilingual Review/Press: "Braulio Tapia" from *The Valley* by
Rolando Hinojosa. © 1983 by Bilingual Press/Editorial
Bilingue.

Brandt & Brandt Literary Agents, Inc.: "The Devil and Daniel
Webster" from *The Selected Works of Stephen Vincent Benét.*
Copyright 1936 by The Curtis Publishing Company;
copyright renewed © 1964 by Thomas C. Benét, Stephanie
B. Mahin, and Rachel B. Lewis.

Gwendolyn Brooks: "The Explorer" from *The World of Gwen-
dolyn Brooks* by Gwendolyn Brooks. Copyright © 1959 by
Gwendolyn Brooks. "In Honor of David Anderson Brooks,
My Father—July 30, 1883 – November 21, 1959" from
Selected Poems by Gwendolyn Brooks. Copyright © 1960 by
Gwendolyn Brooks.

Dodd, Mead & Company, Inc.: "Douglass" and "Life's Trag-
edy" from *The Complete Poems of Paul Laurence Dunbar.*
"Trifles" from *Plays* by Susan Glaspell. Copyright 1920 by
Dodd, Mead & Company, Inc.; copyright renewed 1948 by
Susan Glaspell.

Elizabeth H. Dos Passos: "Tin Lizzie" from *U.S.A.* by John Dos
Passos. Copyright by Elizabeth H. Dos Passos.

Doubleday & Company, Inc.: "Elegy for Jane" and "The Pike"
from *The Collected Poems of Theodore Roethke.* Copyright ©
1938, 1940, 1950 and 1963 by Theodore Roethke.

Farrar, Straus & Giroux, Inc.: "The Ball Poem" from *Short
Poems* by John Berryman. Copyright 1948 by John Ber-
ryman; copyright renewed © 1976 by Kate Berryman. "The
Fish" from *The Complete Poems 1927 – 1979* by Elizabeth
Bishop. Copyright © 1940, 1969 by Elizabeth Bishop. "The
Death of the Ball Turret Gunner" from *The Complete Poems*
by Randall Jarrell. Copyright 1941 by Mrs. Randall Jarrell;
copyright renewed © 1968 by Mrs. Randall Jarrell.
"Hawthorne" and "Water" from *For the Union Dead* by
Robert Lowell. Copyright © 1956, 1960, 1961, 1962, 1963 by
Robert Lowell. "The First Seven Years" from *The Magic
Barrel* by Bernard Malamud. Copyright © 1950, 1958 by
Bernard Malamud; copyright renewed © 1978 by Bernard
Malamud. "Lost" from *A Crown of Feathers* by Isaac Bashevis
Singer. Copyright © 1970, 1971, 1972, 1973 by Isaac
Bashevis Singer. Originally published in *The New Yorker.*

David R. Godine, Publisher, Inc., Boston: From pp. 61 – 64 in
Hunger of Memory by Richard Rodriguez. Copyright © 1981
by Richard Rodriguez.

Rodolfo Gonzales: From "I Am Joaquín" by Rodolfo Gonzales. Copyright © 1967 by Rodolfo Gonzales; copyright © 1972 by Bantam Books, Inc.

Harcourt Brace Jovanovich, Inc.: "pity this busy monster,manunkind" copyright 1944 by E. E. Cummings,
renewed 1972 by Nancy T. Andrews and "anyone lived in
a pretty how town" copyright 1940 by E. E. Cummings, renewed 1968 by Marion Morehouse Cummings from *Complete Poems 1913 – 1962* by E. E. Cummings. Commentary on
"Stopping by Woods on a Snowy Evening" by Robert Frost
from *100 American Poems of the Twentieth Century.* Copyright
© 1966 by Laurence Perrine and James M. Reid. "The Life
You Save May Be Your Own" from *A Good Man Is Hard to
Find and Other Stories* by Flannery O'Connor. Copyright

CRITICAL READERS

CONTENTS

REALISM AND NATURALISM (1890–1914)

LITERATURE IN MODERN AMERICA

MODERN FICTION

MODERN NONFICTION

MODERN DRAMA

READING AND WRITING ABOUT LITERATURE

READING LITERATURE

WRITING ABOUT LITERATURE

C A N A D A

WASHINGTON

Bear Paw Mountain
Chief Joseph surrenders

MONTANA

NORTH DAKOTA

Wallowa Valley
Chief Joseph's birthplace

OREGON

IDAHO

SOUTH DAKOTA

Hailey
Pound's birthplace

WYOMING

NEBRASKA

NEVADA

Carson City
Twain's *Roughing It*

Calaveras County
Twain's *Jumping Frog*

UTAH

Denver
Gonzales' birthplace

Red Cloud
Cather's childhood

The Sierras
Harte's *The Outcasts of Poker Flat*

COLORADO

Cather's *The
Sculptor's Funeral*

San Francisco
London's birthplace

KANSAS

Carmel
Jeffers' poetry

Hutchinson
Stafford's birthplace

Monterey
Steinbeck's *Flight*

CALIFORNIA

OKLAHOMA

Oklahoma City
Ellison's birthplace

Albuquerque
Silko's birthplace

ARIZONA

NEW MEXICO

Wichita Range
Momaday's *The Way
to Rainy Mountain*

**PACIFIC
OCEAN**

**YUKON
TERRITORY**
London's *To Build a Fire*

M E X I C O

TEXAS

Indian Creek
Porter's birthplace

Honolulu
Twain's *Roughing It*

Brownsville
Paredes' birthplace

ALASKA

HAWAII

Mercedes
Hinojosa-Smith's birthplace

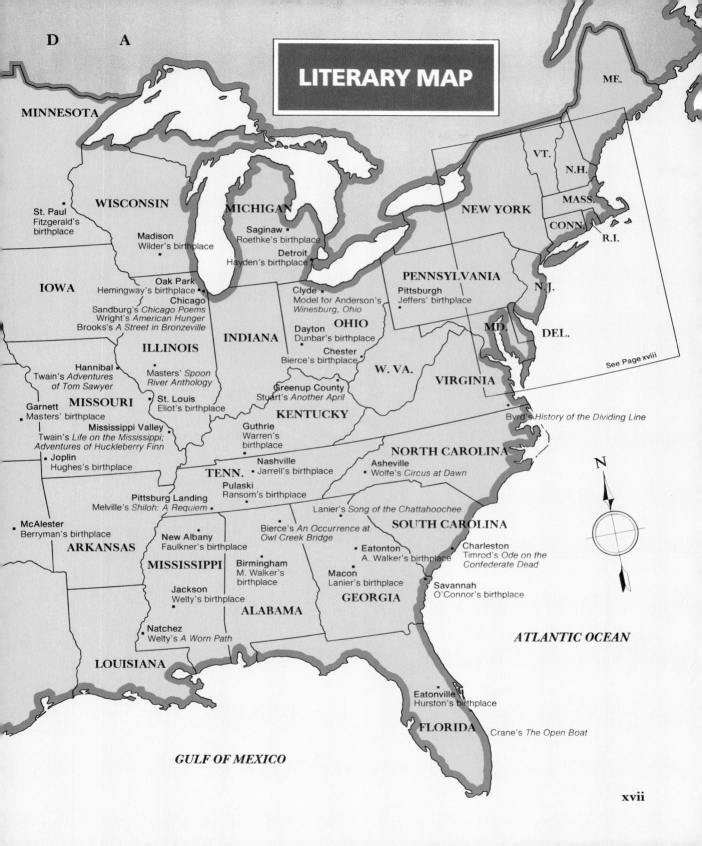

LITERARY MAP

D A

MINNESOTA

ME.

VT.

N.H.

WISCONSIN

MICHIGAN

NEW YORK

MASS.

CONN.

R.I.

St. Paul
Fitzgerald's
birthplace

Madison
Wilder's birthplace

Saginaw
Roethke's birthplace

Detroit
Hayden's birthplace

PENNSYLVANIA

Pittsburgh
Jeffers' birthplace

N.J.

IOWA

Oak Park
Hemingway's birthplace

Clyde
Model for Anderson's
Winesburg, Ohio

MD.

DEL.

Chicago
Sandburg's *Chicago Poems*
Wright's *American Hunger*
Brooks's *A Street in Bronzeville*

OHIO

Dayton
Dunbar's birthplace

INDIANA

Chester
Bierce's birthplace

W. VA.

See Page xviii

ILLINOIS

Hannibal
Twain's *Adventures
of Tom Sawyer*

Masters' *Spoon
River Anthology*

Greenup County
Stuart's *Another April*

VIRGINIA

Garnett
Masters' birthplace

St. Louis
Eliot's birthplace

KENTUCKY

Byrd's *History of the Dividing Line*

MISSOURI

Mississippi Valley
Twain's *Life on the Mississippi;
Adventures of Huckleberry Finn*

Guthrie
Warren's
birthplace

NORTH CAROLINA

N

Joplin
Hughes' birthplace

Nashville
Jarrell's birthplace

Asheville
Wolfe's *Circus at Dawn*

TENN.

Pulaski
Ransom's birthplace

McAlester
Berryman's birthplace

Pittsburg Landing
Melville's *Shiloh: A Requiem*

Lanier's *Song of the Chattahoochee*

SOUTH CAROLINA

ARKANSAS

New Albany
Faulkner's birthplace

Bierce's *An Occurrence at
Owl Creek Bridge*

Eatonton
A. Walker's birthplace

Charleston
Timrod's *Ode on the
Confederate Dead*

MISSISSIPPI

Birmingham
M. Walker's
birthplace

Macon
Lanier's birthplace

Savannah
O'Connor's birthplace

Jackson
Welty's birthplace

GEORGIA

ALABAMA

ATLANTIC OCEAN

Natchez
Welty's *A Worn Path*

LOUISIANA

Eatonville
Hurston's birthplace

FLORIDA

Crane's *The Open Boat*

GULF OF MEXICO

xvii

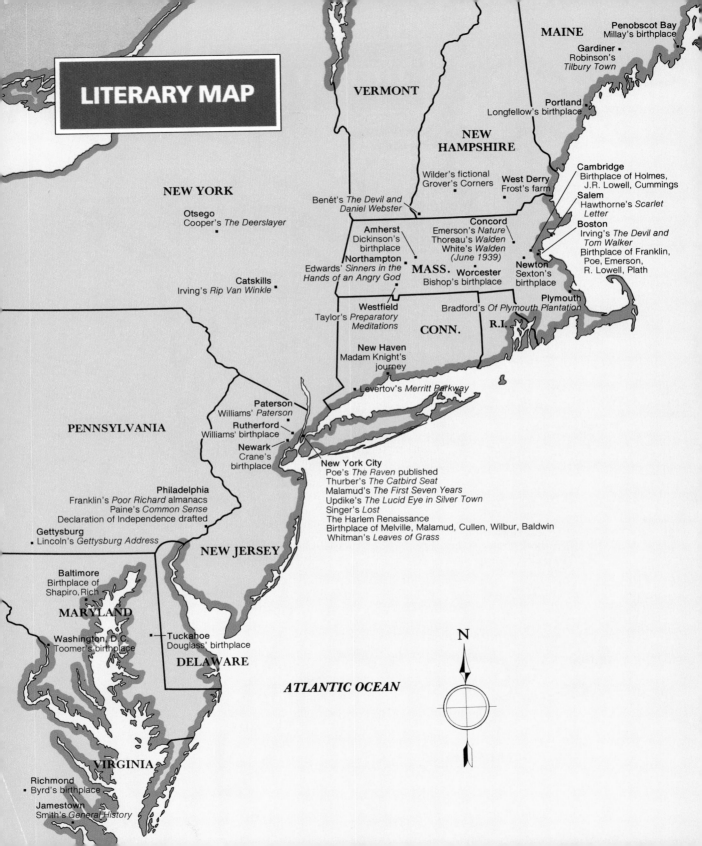

LITERARY MAP

MAINE

Penobscot Bay
Millay's birthplace

Gardiner
Robinson's
Tilbury Town

Portland
Longfellow's birthplace

VERMONT

NEW HAMPSHIRE

Wilder's fictional
Grover's Corners

West Derry
Frost's farm

NEW YORK

Otsego
Cooper's *The Deerslayer*

Benét's *The Devil and
Daniel Webster*

Cambridge
Birthplace of Holmes,
J.R. Lowell, Cummings

Salem
Hawthorne's *Scarlet
Letter*

Boston
Irving's *The Devil and
Tom Walker*
Birthplace of Franklin,
Poe, Emerson,
R. Lowell, Plath

Amherst
Dickinson's
birthplace

Concord
Emerson's *Nature*
Thoreau's *Walden*
White's *Walden*
(June 1939)

Northampton
Edwards' *Sinners in the
Hands of an Angry God*

MASS.   Worcester
Bishop's birthplace

Newton
Sexton's
birthplace

Catskills
Irving's *Rip Van Winkle*

Plymouth
Bradford's *Of Plymouth Plantation*

Westfield
Taylor's *Preparatory
Meditations*

CONN.

R.I.

New Haven
Madam Knight's
journey

Levertov's *Merritt Parkway*

PENNSYLVANIA

Paterson
Williams' *Paterson*

Rutherford
Williams' birthplace

Newark
Crane's
birthplace

Philadelphia
Franklin's *Poor Richard* almanacs
Paine's *Common Sense*
Declaration of Independence drafted

New York City
Poe's *The Raven* published
Thurber's *The Catbird Seat*
Malamud's *The First Seven Years*
Updike's *The Lucid Eye in Silver Town*
Singer's *Lost*
The Harlem Renaissance
Birthplace of Melville, Malamud, Cullen, Wilbur, Baldwin
Whitman's *Leaves of Grass*

Gettysburg
Lincoln's *Gettysburg Address*

NEW JERSEY

Baltimore
Birthplace of
Shapiro, Rich

MARYLAND

Washington, D.C.
Toomer's birthplace

Tuckahoe
Douglass' birthplace

DELAWARE

ATLANTIC OCEAN

N

VIRGINIA

Richmond
Byrd's birthplace

Jamestown
Smith's *General History*

ADVENTURES
in American Literature

THE BEGINNINGS OF THE AMERICAN TRADITION
TO 1760

John Cotton bids farewell to his parishioners on the *Arbella*, the ship that brought Anne Bradstreet to the New World in 1630. Stained glass, 1944.

Christopher Columbus by unknown artist.
Civic Museum, Como, Italy

The New World

A journal written five hundred years ago reports: "The admiral, at ten o'clock in the night, being on the sterncastle, saw a light. . . . it was like a small wax candle, which was raised and lowered."

The night was that of Thursday, October 11–12, 1492. The "sterncastle" was the raised back deck of the ship *Santa María,* which had left Spain on August 2. The admiral was Christopher Columbus, and the light—which he probably only imagined seeing—turned out to be an island. The native inhabitants, he learned when he landed the next day, called the island *Guanahaní,* but he renamed it San Salvador.

Having set sail for Asia, Columbus believed himself to be somewhere near Japan. It did not occur to him that the oceans west of Europe, separating it from the Orient, contained a stupendous land mass—indeed contained a New World. Only six years later did he begin to realize that he had reached a place whose existence he had never suspected. "I believe that this is a very great continent," he wrote on his third voyage to America, "which until today has been unknown."

Emblem of Columbus, Frontispiece of book naming privileges ceded to Columbus by Ferdinand and Isabella.
Naval Museum, Pegli, Italy

Exploration and Settlement

The desire to explore and describe the new continent accidentally discovered by Columbus inspired many of the earliest works of American literature. For fifty years after his voyages, Europeans explored the New World actively. Some hoped to find a faster trade route to China; others hoped to find the fabled Earthly Paradise containing a cure for all diseases, rivers filled with gold, and the Fountain of Youth. Both hopes came to nothing. But the explorers brought back remarkable and often grim stories, particularly about the more than two thousand Indian tribes they discovered already living on the continent. Books soon told of Cortés, who besieged Mexico City for ninety-three days until he destroyed it and exterminated the Aztec inhabitants. They told of Cabeza de Vaca, marooned with a few other men in Florida, who in searching for a European settlement walked across nearly two-thirds of North America. Other stories about the New World were less grim but more fanciful. They told about a land where people slept under water, about a king who became a giant by having his bones stretched, about people with hard tails.

Near the end of the sixteenth century, interest in the New World began changing from exploration to settlement. Desire for adventure and gold remained, but Europeans now began to see America also as a place where food was plentiful and where poor people might own land. Like the earlier explorations, the new interest in settlement produced literature. Inexpensive pamphlets and poems appeared throughout Europe advertising the attractions of life in America, much as today's brochures advertise some vacation spot or retirement village. Typical was *News from Virginia*, published in London in 1610:

> To such as to Virginia, do purpose to repair,
> And when that they shall thither come, each man shall have his share.
> Day wages for the Laborer, and for his more content,
> A house and garden plot shall have. . . .

The promise of land, good wages, or some other benefit brought permanent settlers to America, first to the South, shortly afterward to the North. Their settlements shaped the future not only of American history but also of American literature.

The North: Puritanism

In 1620 a hundred or so English men and women settled in Plymouth, Massachusetts, to be followed ten years later by about another thousand who settled around Boston. Most of these settlers came not so much seeking the New World as fleeing from the Old. For decades, they had battled with English authorities over the right to practice their religion, known as Puritanism. One Puritan published a pamphlet proposing drastic reforms in the Church of England. Authorities put him in jail—and also fined him, whipped him, cut off the tops of his ears, burned his forehead with a hot iron, and slit his nose. Although eager to escape such trials, most Puritans left the Old World reluctantly. If settlement in America meant an end to harassment, it also meant leaving friends and relatives and facing a wilderness.

Puritanism was a way of life and cannot be summarized in a few words. Yet three beliefs pervade Puritan writing and deeply influenced later American culture. First, Puritans wished to have their feelings radically changed, an experience they called *grace*. They wished to cleanse themselves of envy, vanity, and lust so as to love God and God's creation wholeheartedly. But they recognized that people cannot simply decide to convert their feelings; no amount of prayer, churchgoing, or Bible reading can make people love what they do not love. Puritans believed that feelings could be changed only through grace, the miracle by which God grants some people the ability to love truly. They spent much of their lives examining their feelings for signs of grace.

Second, Puritans valued *plainness*, especially in religion. They desired to return Christianity to the simple forms of worship described in the New Testament. This meant eliminating whatever religious practices had come into being since the time of Christ, which the Puritans regarded not as God-given commands but as human decorations. In striving for plainness, they met for worship not in ornate cathedrals with stained-glass windows, but in square wooden buildings, painted white and stripped of ornament.

Cotton Mather (1727)
by Peter Pelham.
Mezzotint engraving.

Third, the Puritans' conviction that they were carrying to America true Christianity as decreed by God led them to see their lives in the New World as a *divine mission.* They believed that America was a place specially appointed by God to be an example to the rest of the world, a "city upon a hill."

Like others before and after them, the Puritans wrote about their encounter with America in a variety of forms. Many Puritans kept diaries, attempting to trace the rise of grace in their souls. Puritans who achieved grace often told of their experiences in a form called the *spiritual autobiography.* Among the several Puritan histories, the most impressive is the long, learned *Magnalia Christi Americana* (*The Great Works of Christ in America*) (1702) by the famous minister Cotton Mather. It contains accounts of the lives of the leaders of New England, of the Puritans' conflict with the Indians, and of the notorious witchcraft trials at Salem.

Puritans also wrote a great deal of poetry. Later you will read verse by Anne Bradstreet and Edward Taylor, the two outstanding Puritan poets. But two works not included in this anthology deserve mention.

1492	Columbus reaches the "New World"

Emblem of Columbus

1513	Balboa reaches the Pacific
1519–1522	Magellan's ships circle the earth
1539	De Soto begins exploration of North America; reaches the Mississippi River 1541
1607	Settlement at Jamestown, Virginia

JOHN SMITH (1579 or 1580–1631)
A True Relation of Virginia (1608)

The rescue of John Smith

1620	Mayflower Compact; Settlement at Plymouth, Massachusetts

SMITH
The General History (1624)

1630	Massachusetts Bay Colony founded at Salem

WILLIAM BRADFORD (1590–1657)
History of Plymouth Plantation (1630–1647)

1635	First public school in America (Boston Latin School)
1636	Harvard, first college in America, founded

The Mayflower

Anne Bradstreet

Cotton Mather

Jonathan Edwards

1639 First printing press in America
(Cambridge, Massachusetts)

Bay Psalm Book (1640)

EDWARD TAYLOR (1642?–1729)
Poetical Works (published 1939)

ANNE BRADSTREET (1612–1672)
The Tenth Muse Lately Sprung Up in America (1650)

MICHAEL WIGGLESWORTH
The Day of Doom (1662)

1670 Charleston founded

1673 Joliet and Marquette explore upper Mississippi River

1682 La Salle descends Mississippi River to its mouth;
Philadelphia founded

New England Primer (1683?)

1693 William and Mary College founded

1701 Yale University founded

COTTON MATHER (1663–1728)
Magnalia Christi Americana (1702)

1704 First newspaper in America, Boston *News-Letter*

SARAH KEMBLE KNIGHT (1666–1727)
The Journal of Madam Knight (1704)

EBENEZER COOK
The Sot-Weed Factor (1708)

1718 New Orleans founded

1729 Baltimore founded

WILLIAM BYRD (1674–1744)
The History of the Dividing Line (1729)

JONATHAN EDWARDS (1703–1758)
"Sinners in the Hands of an Angry God" (1741)

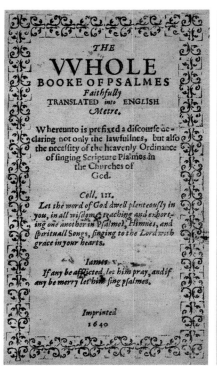

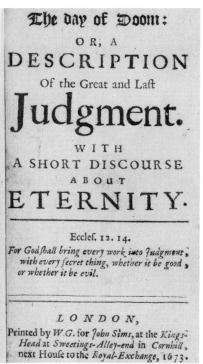

The Bay Psalm Book (1640)—a translation of the Biblical book of
Psalms—was the first book published in America. Its authors believed
that "God's altar needs not our polishing." That is, they considered
God's word sacred, and so powerful in itself as to need no artistic
reshaping. In making their translation, they wished simply to reproduce in English the exact meaning of the original Hebrew text. So
although they used rhyme and meter, their version of the psalms
lacks the poetic quality of the familiar version in the King James
Bible:

Psalm 23
A Psalm of David

The Lord is my shepherd; I shall not want.
He maketh me to lie down in green pastures:
he leadeth me beside the still waters.
He restoreth my soul: he leadeth me in the
paths of righteousness for his name's sake.
Yea, though I walk through the valley of the
shadow of death, I will fear no evil: for thou
art with me; thy rod and thy staff they
comfort me. . . .

(King James Version, 1611)

23 A Psalm of David

The Lord to me a shepherd is,
*   want therefore shall not I.*
He in the folds of tender grass,
*   doth cause me down to lie:*
To waters calm me gently leads,
*   restore my soul doth he:*
he doth in paths of righteousness
*   for his name's sake lead me.*
Yea though in valley of death's shade
*   I walk, none ill I'll fear:*
because thou art with me, thy rod
*   and staff my comfort are.*

(*The Bay Psalm Book,* 1640)

In its stiff simplicity, *The Bay Psalm Book* is a classic expression of the Puritan plain style.

The second notable work is a long poem called *The Day of Doom* (1662) by a minister named Michael Wigglesworth (1631–1705). Like the translators of *The Bay Psalm Book,* he used simple verse, perhaps so that his poem could be easily read by children. We might not consider it children's reading today, for Wigglesworth depicted the awful punishments awaiting the wicked on Judgment Day. He began by describing the fierce light that would appear at midnight, wakening sinners from their sleep. With tears and dread they run to their windows:

Mean men lament, great men do rent
*   their Robes, and tear their hair:*
They do not spare their flesh to tear
*   through horrible despair.*
All Kindreds wail: all hearts do fail:
*   horror the world doth fill*
With weeping eyes, and loud outcries,
*   yet knows not how to kill.*

Some hide themselves in Caves and Delves,
*   in places under ground:*
Some rashly leap into the Deep,
*   to 'scape by being drown'd:*
Some to the rocks (O senseless blocks!)
*   and woody Mountains run,*
That there they might this fearful sight,
*   and dreaded Presence shun.*

Despite its gruesome subject, *The Day of Doom* became immensely popular, and is sometimes called "the first American best seller." It was owned by about one out of thirty-five people in New England—roughly equivalent to a poem selling six million copies today.

Puritanism as a way of life lasted only about a century in America. The zeal of the first settlers began to fade as the villages of New England grew into towns and cities, as religion itself came under attack in the new Age of Reason, and as the founders died and were replaced by generations born in America who had not had to risk slit noses for their beliefs. Puritanism revived briefly in the 1740s during the Great Awakening, when grace seemed to seize masses of people throughout New England. But many of these religious conversions proved short-lived. By the time of the American Revolution, few Americans would have called themselves Puritans.

The South: Gentlemen Planters

The Southern settlements and those of New England were different in several ways. The two regions differed in climate, in manner of settlement, in religion, and in ideals of behavior. The South had warmer weather and richer soil. Whereas the typical Puritan settlement was a village community, populated by friends and acquaintances who had come to America together, the typical Southern settlement was a plantation of several hundred acres, managed by a single planter with the help of numerous black slaves. (Many Puritans owned slaves too, but the number of slaves in the North was fewer than in the South.) The often long distances between plantations forced each planter to become a civilization unto himself. Each planter had to do his own farming, weaving, and baking, and had to provide his own medical care and entertainment. Occasionally he traveled to Williamsburg, Charleston, or some other urban center to conduct business and have a say in political life. The dominant religion of the South was the Church of England, the same church whose forms of worship the Puritans defied. The Southern ideal of conduct, moreover, was represented not by the zealous, soul-searching believer, but by the generous, self-controlled gentleman, attentive to manners and keenly aware of his obligation to serve the public.

These qualities are reflected in early Southern literature. Southerners turned their attention not so much inward as outward. They wrote less than Northerners did on religion and more on nature and society. It is in Southern literature that we find some of the most detailed descriptions in early American writing of the wilderness and frontier life, such as William Byrd's *History of the Dividing Line* (page 50). Whereas Puritans usually wrote for instruction or inspiration, Southerners often wrote for amusement or diversion. One of the earliest Southern poems, Ebenezer Cook's *The Sot-Weed Factor* (1708), tells the comic adventures of a tobacco merchant in colonial Maryland. The Puritans detested plays and even passed laws against their performance; but around 1716, Southerners erected in Williamsburg, Virginia, the first known theater in America.

The Beginnings of American Literature

Explorers seeking the Fountain of Youth, Puritans longing for grace, Southern planters describing the wilderness—all introduced into American culture ideas and ideals that have endured. Although Puritanism as a way of life vanished, its emphasis on examining and purifying one's feelings lingers in Ralph Waldo Emerson's call for Americans to see the world not through the eyes of the past, but freshly, as if reborn. The Puritans' insistence on plainness, too, resounds in the spare poetry of Emily Dickinson and the undecorated prose of Ernest Hemingway. The Puritan vision of America as a divinely appointed place pervades later American concepts of an "American Mission," a "Manifest Destiny," or "The American Dream." Similarly, the Southern gentleman's ideal of public service survives in Washington, Jefferson, and the other Southern Revolutionary leaders; and the planter's closeness to the land lives on in the works of modern Southern writers like William Faulkner.

What the explorers, Puritans, and early Southerners share with later American writers most of all is a desire to convey the special quality of life in America, to show how they felt living in a New World, facing new experiences. From Columbus to the present, in various ways, nearly all American writers have been discovering America.

Review

1. Where did Columbus believe himself to be when he reached the New World?
2. Name three myths associated with the New World.
3. How did Europeans learn about the benefits of settling in the New World?
4. What were the chief forms of writing among the Puritans?
5. Who wrote a history including accounts of the Salem witchcraft trials?
6. Name the first book published in America.
7. Which poem was the most popular literary work of its day?
8. What is the name given to the revival of Puritanism in the 1740s?
9. What tended to be the ideal of conduct among Southern plantation owners?
10. Where was the first known theater in America erected?

Spanish Explorers in the New World

During the sixteenth century Spain sent several expeditions to explore, conquer, and colonize the New World. Fortunately, narratives of these expeditions have survived. The *Relación* of Álvar Núñez Cabeza de Vaca (äl'vär nōō'nyäth kä-bä'thä dä vä'kä) (1490?–1557?), first published in 1542, is an extraordinary document of American exploration. Cabeza de Vaca was a member of an expedition that set sail in June, 1527, for Florida. The journey was dogged by misfortunes: two ships were wrecked; men deserted; many died. Finally, Cabeza de Vaca and a small party were shipwrecked on a narrow island off the coast of Texas. His narrative reveals the great hardships these men endured between 1528 and 1536 as they walked across Texas, New Mexico, and Arizona before reaching Mexico.

For several years Cabeza de Vaca and his companions lived among the Indians as slaves. In the following excerpt, he tells of the extreme privations they suffered while they were living among the Avavares. The text given here is based on the translation by Thomas Buckingham Smith (1851), which was edited by John Shea and published with additions in 1871.

I have already stated that throughout all this country we went naked, and as we were unaccustomed to being so, twice a year we cast our skins like serpents. The sun and air produced great sores on our breasts and shoulders, giving us sharp pain; and the large loads we had, being very heavy, caused the cords to cut into our arms. The country is so broken and thickset, that often after getting our wood in the forests, the blood flowed from us in many places, caused by the obstruction of thorns and shrubs that tore our flesh wherever we went. At times, when my turn came to get wood, after it had cost me much blood, I could not bring it out either on my back or by dragging. In these labors my only solace and relief were in thinking of the sufferings of our Redeemer, Jesus Christ, and in the blood He shed for me, in considering how much greater must have been the torment He sustained from the thorns, than that I there received.

I bartered with these Indians in combs that I made for them and in bows, arrows, and nets.

We made mats, which are their houses, that they have great necessity for; and although they know how to make them, they wish to give their full time to getting food, since when otherwise employed they are pinched with hunger. Sometimes the Indians would set me to scraping and softening skins; and the days of my greatest prosperity there, were those in which they gave me skins to dress. I would scrape them a very great deal and eat the scraps, which would sustain me two or three days. When it happened among these people, as it had likewise among others whom we left behind, that a piece of meat was given us, we ate it raw; for if we had put it to roast, the first native that should come along would have taken it off and devoured it; and it appeared to us not well to expose it to this risk; besides we were in such condition it would have given us pain to eat it roasted, and we could not have digested it so well as raw. Such was the life we spent there; and the meager subsistence we earned by the matters of traffic which were the work of our hands.

The Caribbean, Central America, and Portions of North and South America.
From the Portolan Atlas by Pierre Desceliers, M. 506, f. 2, French (c. 1545).
The Pierpont Morgan Library, New York

Between 1539 and 1542 Hernando de Soto led an expedition through the Gulf States. An eyewitness account of this expedition was written by a gentleman from Elvas, a town in Portugal, and first published in 1557. In the following passage he records the crossing of the Mississippi, the "River Grande." Members of the expedition included Juan de Guzmán (hwän dä gōōs-män') and Francisco Maldonado (frän-sē'skō mäl-dō-nä'thō).

There was little maize in the place, and the Governor moved to another town, half a league from the great river, where it was found in sufficiency. He went to look at the river, and saw that near it there was much timber of which piraguas[1] might be made, and a good situation in which the camp might be placed. He directly moved, built houses, and settled on a plain a crossbow-shot from the water,

bringing together there all the maize of the towns behind, that at once they might go to work and cut down trees for sawing out planks to build barges. . . .

During the thirty days that were passed there, four piraguas were built, into three of which, one morning, three hours before daybreak, the Governor ordered twelve cavalry to enter, four in each, men in whom he had confidence that they would gain the land notwithstanding the Indians, and secure the passage

1. **piraguas** (pī-rä'gwəz): flat-bottomed sailing boats.

Spanish Explorers in the New World **13**

or die: he also sent some crossbowmen of foot with them, and in the other piragua, oarsmen, to take them to the opposite shore. He ordered Juan de Guzmán to cross with the infantry, of which he had remained captain in the place of Francisco Maldonado; and because the current was stiff, they went up along the side of the river a quarter of a league, and in passing over they were carried down, so as to land opposite the camp; but, before arriving there, at twice the distance of a stone's cast, the horsemen rode out from the piraguas to an open area of hard and even ground, which they all reached without accident.

So soon as they had come to shore the piraguas returned; and when the sun was up two hours high, the people had all got over.[2] The distance was near half a league: a man standing on the shore could not be told, whether he were a man or something else, from the other side. The stream was swift, and very deep; the water, always flowing turbidly, brought along from above many trees and much timber, driven onward by its force. . . .

2. **got over:** This crossing was made some miles below Memphis, either at Council Bend or Walnut Bend in Mississippi.

Between 1540 and 1542 Francisco Vásquez de Coronado (frän-thēs′kō väs′käth dā kō′rō-nä′dō) led an expedition from Mexico into the Southwest, in search of the Seven Cities of Cíbola, fabled for their great wealth. Coronado reached the Pueblo tribes of the Southwest, the Grand Canyon, and the Great Plains. A record of this expedition was kept by Pedro de Castañeda (pĕ′drō dā käs-tä-nyā′thä), a soldier in Coronado's army, whose narrative was not published until the nineteenth century. In the following excerpt, he describes the Indian villages of the Pueblos.

In general, these villages all have the same habits and customs, although some have some things in particular which the others have not. They are governed by the opinions of the elders. They all work together to build the villages, the women being engaged in making the mixture and the walls, while the men bring the wood and put it in place. They have no lime, but they make a mixture of ashes, coals, and dirt which is almost as good as mortar, for when the house is to have four stories, they do not make the walls more than half a yard thick. . . .

The young men live in the estufas,[1] which are in the yards of the village. They are underground, square or round, with pine pillars. Some were seen with twelve pillars and with four in the center as large as two men could stretch around. They usually had three or four pillars. The floor was made of large, smooth stones, like the baths which they have in Europe. They have a hearth made like the binnacle or compass box of a ship, in which they burn a handful of thyme[2] at a time to keep up the heat, and they can stay in there just as in a bath. The top was on a level with the ground. Some that were seen were large enough for a game of ball. When any man wishes to marry, it has to be arranged by those who govern. The man has to spin and weave a blanket and place it before the woman, who covers herself with it and becomes his wife. The houses belong to the women, the estufas to the men. If a man repudiates his woman, he has to go to the estufa. It is forbidden for women to sleep in the estufas, or to enter these for any purpose except to give their husbands or sons something to eat. The men spin and weave. The women bring up the children and prepare the food. . . .

1. **estufas** (ĕ-stoō′fəz): chambers in which sacred fires are kept burning.

2. **thyme:** here, sagebrush.

JOHN SMITH
1579 or 1580–1631

Captain John Smith, detail from Smith's map of Virginia (1616).

The first man to promote the permanent settlement of America, and the first to attempt it successfully, was the English soldier and adventurer Captain John Smith. Before he was twenty-five years old he had battled in the Netherlands and Hungary, fought at sea off the African coast, and been captured and taken as a slave to Constantinople.

When Smith sailed late in 1606 for America, trouble and excitement awaited him. Captured by Indians in Virginia, he was brought to their leader, Powhatan, and threatened with death. He was rescued by Powhatan's daughter, Pocahontas (her real name was Matoaka), and he was made Powhatan's son. Badly burned in an explosion in 1609, he went back to England, only to return to America five years later—this time to New England, where he explored the coasts of Maine and Massachusetts.

Smith contributed more to the settlement of America than colorful adventures. He founded Jamestown, Virginia, the first English colony; he gave New England its name; he made excellent maps that continued to be used for two hundred years. Like many others, he also wrote about his experiences in the New World. His writings include the first English book on America, *A True Relation of Virginia* (1608). The selection that follows comes from Smith's longest and most important work, *The General History of Virginia, New England, and the Summer Isles* (1624). He partly wrote the book himself and partly compiled it from accounts by others. While describing the founding of Jamestown for readers across the Atlantic, he also encouraged them to settle in America, appealing to their sense of personal and national glory and to their hope of economic advancement. He also described at length his "cat-and-mouse" relationship with the Indians; each looked for an advantage, so that "we sometimes had peace and war twice in a day."

But Smith's deeper intention in his *General History* was to clear away European myths about America. To those back home who insisted on finding gold where there was none, or uncovering a route to the South Seas when none existed, he answered: "I know no reason but to believe my own eyes before any man's imagination." Europeans idealized America, but he had been there. He had learned that to make America thrive required not fantasies but patience, a sense of glory, an experienced commander, and, above all, hard work.

Smith's encounter with America ended in disappointment. The company that sponsored his voyage to Virginia replaced him as commander, and for his efforts awarded him "Smith's Isles." They consisted, he said, "of barren rocks, the most overgrown with such shrubs and sharp whins [thorns] you can hardly pass them."

The General History

In his *General History,* John Smith tells of the difficult early days of the Jamestown colonists after the ship that had brought them departed. The supplies that the ship had left eventually gave out. Exhausted and sick, the colonists nonetheless labored to build defenses against Indian attacks. But Smith records that, at the height of the colonists' misery, the Indians seemed to have a change of heart, and "brought such plenty of their fruits, and provision, as no man wanted." Smith criticizes the president of the colony for his poor judgment and indolence. Referring to himself in the third person, he tells how he gradually assumed most of the responsibility for organizing the colony.

What Happened Till the First Supply

Being thus left to our fortunes, it fortuned that within ten days scarce ten amongst us could either go[1] or well stand, such extreme weakness and sickness oppressed us. And thereat none need marvel, if they consider the cause and the reason, which was this.

Whilst the ships stayed, our allowance was somewhat bettered, by a daily proportion of biscuit,[2] which the sailors would pilfer to sell, give, or exchange with us, for money, sassafras, furs, or love. But when they departed, there remained neither tavern, beer house, nor place of relief but the common kettle.[3] Had we been as free from all sins as gluttony and drunkenness, we might have been canonized for saints; but our President[4] would never have been ad-

mitted, for engrossing to his private[5] oatmeal, sack,[6] oil, aqua vitae,[7] beef, eggs, or what not, but the kettle; that indeed he allowed equally to be distributed, and that was half a pint of wheat, and as much barley boiled with water for a man a day, and this having fried some twenty-six weeks in the ship's hold, contained as many worms as grains, so that we might truly call it rather so much bran than corn; our drink was water, our lodgings castles in the air.

With this lodging and diet, our extreme toil in bearing and planting pallisadoes[8] so strained and bruised us, and our continual labor in the extremity of the heat had so weakened us, as were cause sufficient to have made us as miserable in our native country, or any other place in the world.

---

1. **go:** be active.
2. **biscuit:** hardtack, a kind of hard bread.
3. **the common kettle:** the communal cooking pot.
4. **our President:** the head of the colony, Wingfield.

5. **engrossing to his private:** taking for his private use.
6. **sack:** a kind of dry white wine.
7. **aqua vitae** (ä′kwə vī′tē): strong liquor.
8. **pallisadoes** (păl′ə-sād′ōz): palisades, large pointed stakes set in the ground as a means of defense.

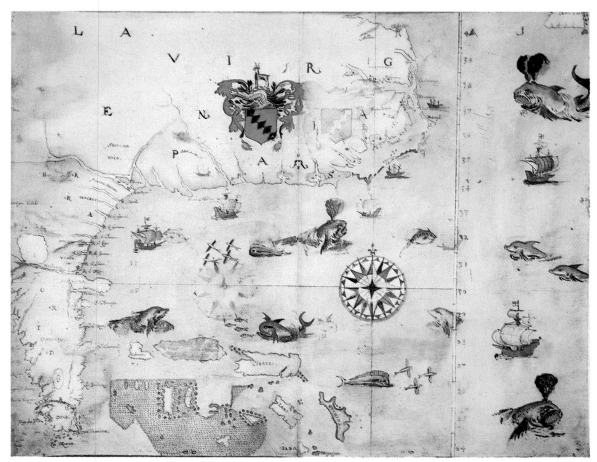

Manuscript map of North America from Florida to Chesapeake Bay (c. 1585) by John White. White, who was governor of the Lost Colony of Roanoke Island, did a number of watercolors of Indian life.

From May to September, those that escaped lived upon sturgeon and sea crabs; fifty in this time we buried; the rest, seeing the President's projects to escape these miseries in our pinnace[9] by flight (who all this time had neither felt want nor sickness), so moved our dead spirits as we deposed him, and established Ratcliffe in his place. . . .

But now was all our provision spent, the sturgeon gone, all helps abandoned, each hour expecting the fury of the savages; when God, the patron of all good endeavors, in that desperate extremity so changed the hearts of the savages that they brought such plenty of their fruits, and provision, as no man wanted.

And now where some affirmed it was ill done of the Council[10] to send forth men so badly provided, this uncontradictable reason will show them plainly they are too ill-advised to nourish such ill conceits:[11] first, the fault of our going was our own; what could be thought

9. **pinnace** (pĭn′ĭs): small sailing ship.

10. **Council:** the group of seven men who had charge of the expedition in Virginia.
11. **conceits:** flights of the imagination.

The Manner of Their Fishing. Drawing
by John White.
Photographed at the British Museum by
Lee Boltin

Such actions have ever since the world's beginning been subject to such accidents, and everything of worth is found full of difficulties; but nothing so difficult as to establish a commonwealth so far remote from men and means, and where men's minds are so untoward[12] as neither do well themselves nor suffer others. But to proceed.

The new President, and Martin,[13] being little beloved, of weak judgment in dangers, and less industry in peace, committed the managing of all things abroad to Captain Smith: who by his own example, good words, and fair promises, set some to mow, others to bind thatch, some to build houses, others to thatch them, himself always bearing the greatest task for his own share, so that in short time, he provided most of them [with] lodgings, neglecting any for himself.

With a small party, Captain Smith set out to explore the Chickahominy River. During the expedition, he and his men were unexpectedly attacked by the Indians, and he was taken prisoner.

The manner how they used and delivered him is as followeth.

The savages having drawn from George Cassen whither Captain Smith was gone, prosecuting[14] that opportunity they followed him with three hundred bowmen, conducted by the King of Pamaunkee,[15] who in divisions searching the turnings of the river, found Robinson and Emry[16] by the fireside: those they shot full of arrows and slew. Then finding the Captain, as is said, that used the savage that was his guide as his shield (three of them being slain and divers[17] others so galled), all the rest would not come near him. Thinking thus to have returned to his boat, regarding them, as he marched, more than his way, [he] slipped

12. **untoward:** stubborn or unruly.
13. **Martin:** the colonist John Martin.
14. **prosecuting:** taking advantage of.
15. **Pamaunkee:** the Pamunkey River.
16. **Robinson and Emry:** colonists John Robinson and Thomas Emry.
17. **divers** (dī′vərz): several.

fitting or necessary we had; but what we should find, or want, or where we should be, we were all ignorant, and supposing to make our passage in two months, with victual to live, and the advantage of the spring to work; we were at sea five months, where we both spent our victual and lost the opportunity of the time and season to plant, by the unskillful presumption of our ignorant transporters, that understood not at all what they undertook.

up to the middle in an oozy creek and his savage with him; yet durst they not come to him till being near dead with cold, he threw away his arms. Then according to their composition[18] they drew him forth and led him to the fire, where his men were slain. Diligently they chafed his benumbed limbs.

He demanding for their Captain, they showed him Opechankanough, King of Pamaunkee, to whom he gave a round ivory double compass dial. Much they marveled at the playing of the fly and needle,[19] which they could see so plainly, and yet not touch it because of the glass that covered them. But when he demonstrated by that globelike jewel the roundness of the earth and skies, the sphere of the sun, moon, and stars, and how the sun did chase the night round about the world continually; the greatness of the land and sea, the diversity of nations, variety of complexions, and how we were to them antipodes,[20] and many other such like matters, they all stood as amazed with admiration.

Notwithstanding, within an hour after, they tied him to a tree, and as many as could stand about him prepared to shoot him: but the King holding up the compass in his hand, they all laid down their bows and arrows, and in a triumphant manner led him to Orapaks, where he was after their manner kindly feasted and well used. . . .

At last they brought him to Werowocomoco, where was Powhatan, their Emperor. Here more than two hundred of those grim courtiers stood wondering at him, as he had been a monster; till Powhatan and his train had put themselves in their gravest braveries. Before a fire upon a seat like a bedstead, he sat covered with a great robe, made of raccoon skins, and all the tails hanging by. On either hand did sit a young wench of sixteen or eighteen years, and along on each side the house, two rows of men, and behind them as many women, with all their heads and shoulders painted red, many of their heads bedecked with the white down of birds, but everyone with something; and a great chain of white beads about their necks.

At his entrance before the King, all the people gave a great shout. The Queen of Appamatuck was appointed to bring him water to wash his hands, and another brought him a bunch of feathers, instead of a towel, to dry them. Having feasted him after their best barbarous manner they could, a long consultation was held, but the conclusion was, two great stones were brought before Powhatan: then as many as could laid hands on him, dragged him to them, and thereon laid his head, and being ready with their clubs to beat out his brains, Pocahontas, the King's dearest daughter, when no entreaty could prevail, got his head in her arms, and laid her own upon his to save him from death: whereat the Emperor was contented he should live to make him hatchets, and her bells, beads, and copper; for they thought him as well of all occupations as themselves. For the King himself will make his own robes, shoes, bows, arrows, pots; plant, hunt, or do anything so well as the rest.

Two days after, Powhatan having disguised himself in the most fearfulest manner he could, caused Captain Smith to be brought forth to a great house in the woods, and there upon a mat by the fire to be left alone. Not long after, from behind a mat that divided the house, was made the most dolefulest noise he ever heard; then Powhatan, more like a devil than a man, with some two hundred more as black[21] as himself, came unto him and told him now they were friends, and presently he should go to Jamestown, to send him two great guns and a grindstone, for which he would give him the country of Capahowosick, and forever esteem him as his son Nantaquoud.

So to Jamestown with twelve guides Powhatan sent him. That night they quartered in the

---

18. **composition:** ways.
19. **fly and needle:** parts of a compass. The needle moves over the fly, on which the compass points are marked.
20. **antipodes** (ăn-tĭp′ə-dēz′): two places opposite one another on the earth.

21. **black:** painted black.

Pocahontas (oil on canvas) by unidentified artist, after Simon van de Passe's 1616 engraving.

woods, he still expecting (as he had done all this long time of his imprisonment) every hour to be put to one death or other, for all their feasting. But almighty God (by his divine providence) had mollified the hearts of those stern barbarians with compassion. The next morning betimes they came to the fort, where Smith having used the savages with what kindness he could, he showed Rawhunt, Powhatan's trusty servant, two demiculverins[22] and a millstone to carry [to] Powhatan: they found them somewhat too heavy; but when they did see him discharge them, being loaded with stones, among the boughs of a great tree loaded with icicles, the ice and branches came so tumbling down that the poor savages ran away half dead with fear. But at last we regained some conference with them, and gave them such toys, and sent to Powhatan, his women, and children such presents, as gave them in general full content.

22. **demiculverin** (dĕm′ē-kŭl′vər-ĭn): a type of cannon.

Now in Jamestown they were all in combustion,[23] the strongest preparing once more to run away with the pinnace; which with the hazard of his life, with saker falcon[24] and musket shot, Smith forced now the third time to stay or sink.

Some no better than they should be, had plotted with the President, the next day to have put him to death by the Levitical law,[25] for the lives of Robinson and Emry, pretending the fault was his that had led them to their ends: but he quickly took such order with such lawyers that he laid them by the heels till he sent some of them prisoners for England.

Now every once in four or five days, Pocahontas, with her attendants, brought him so much provision that saved many of their lives that else for all this had starved with hunger.

His relation of the plenty he had seen, especially at Werowocomoco, and of the state and bounty of Powhatan (which till that time was unknown), so revived their dead spirits (especially the love of Pocahontas) as all men's fear was abandoned.

Thus you may see what difficulties still crossed any good endeavor; and the good success of the business being thus oft brought to the very period of destruction; yet you see by what strange means God hath still delivered it.

23. **combustion:** tumult.
24. **saker** (sā′kər) **falcon:** a light cannon.
25. **Levitical law:** from the Bible, Leviticus 24:17, a law stating that anyone responsible for another person's death should be put to death as punishment.

Reading Check

1. Why did the colonists depose Wingfield, the head of the colony?
2. List three of the reasons Smith gives for the colonists' hardships.
3. Who kept the colonists from starving?
4. What presents did Smith give to King Powhatan?
5. What charge was brought against Smith when he returned to Jamestown?

Analyzing and Interpreting the Selection

1a. What contrast does John Smith draw between the other colonists and himself? **b.** What motives might he have had for drawing such a contrast?

2. We rarely react to experience with simple approval or disapproval. Usually we like one feature of a person or place and dislike another. The quality of feeling different ways about the same thing is called *ambivalence*. Ambivalence appears in John Smith's account of the Indians. **a.** What did Smith like about the Indians? **b.** What did he dislike?

3. From the writings of Smith to the latest Western movie or television show, American culture has been concerned with violence. This is not surprising if one considers that Americans have often found themselves in wilderness conditions outside the reach of the law. **a.** What violent episodes does Smith relate in this selection? **b.** What is his attitude toward violence?

Close Reading

Paraphrasing a Passage

When the language or structure of a passage is difficult to understand, it often helps to *paraphrase* individual sentences or whole paragraphs. To paraphrase a work means to restate its language and ideas in your own words. Compare the following passage from Smith's *General History* with the paraphrase on the right:

Original

Had we been as free from all sins as gluttony and drunkenness, we might have been canonized for saints; but our President would never have been admitted, for engrossing to his private oatmeal, sack, oil, aqua vitae, beef, eggs, or what not, but the kettle; that indeed he allowed equally to be distributed, and that was half a pint of wheat, and as much barley boiled with water for a man a day, and this having fried some twenty-six weeks in the ship's hold, contained as many worms as grains, so that we might truly call it rather so much bran than corn; our drink was water, our lodgings castles in the air.

Paraphrase

Had we been as free from all other sins as we were free from gluttony and drunkenness, we might have been pronounced saints, but our President would never have been included because he was guilty of taking for his own use oatmeal, wine, oil, liquor, beef, eggs, or anything else except what went into the communal cooking pot. He allowed only the communal food to be distributed equally. The rations for each man consisted of half a pint of wheat and half a pint of barley boiled with water. Because the grain had been kept in the ship's hold at high temperatures for twenty-six weeks, it was full of worms so that what we had was the husks rather than the grain itself. Our drink was nothing but water; our lodgings merely daydreams, not likely to be realized.

Paraphrase the following passage so that the content is clear:

And now where some affirmed it was ill done of the Council to send forth men so badly provided, this uncontradictable reason will show them plainly they are too ill-advised to nourish such ill conceits: first, the fault of our going was our own; what could be thought fitting or necessary we had; but what we should find, or want, or where we should be, we were all ignorant, and supposing to make our passage in two months, with victual to live, and the advantage of the spring to work; we were at sea five months, where we both spent our victual and lost the opportunity of the time and season to plant, by the unskillful presumption of our ignorant transporters, that understood not at all what they undertook.

Literary Elements

Forms of Discourse: Persuasion, Exposition, Description, Narration

Writing can be classified according to four types: persuasion, exposition, description, and narration. **Persuasion** tries to make its audience adopt an opinion or perform an action, or both—as do political speeches and television commercials. **Exposition** presents information; it explains related facts or ideas—as does the paragraph you are reading now. **Description** shows how something strikes the senses, how it looks, smells, feels, tastes, or sounds; Smith's account of how Powhatan's Indians appeared when seated around their chief is description. Finally, **narration** tells about a series of events; Smith's story of his famous rescue by Pocahontas is narration. A writer rarely uses one type of discourse alone. For instance, Smith uses description to show how the Indians are dressed, and narration to show how they behaved toward him.

The types of discourse are different ways of talking about the same things. "You should read the book" is persuasion; "the book was written fifty years ago" is exposition; "the book is blue" is description; "I took the book to the country" is narration.

1. Find passages of description in which Smith reveals his keen powers of observation. Which details are particularly effective?

2. Find details or incidents that Smith uses to persuade us of his good judgment and leadership.

Language and Vocabulary

Finding Origins of Words

John Smith mentions that Powhatan, at their first meeting, was sitting before a great fire, robed in the skins of raccoons. The word *raccoon* is so familiar to us that we may not recognize it as an Indian word that was brought into English by the early explorers and settlers. In fact, the more than two hundred separate Indian languages have added many words to our everyday speech: names for objects—*canoe, hammock, hurricane, moccasin;* names for plants and vegetables—*potato, tomato, tobacco, squash;* names for animals—*moose, chipmunk, skunk.* (One Indian word that did not make its way into English is the former name of Webster Lake in Connecticut— Charuggogagaugmanchaugagoggchaubunagungamaugg.)

Pocahontas asks her father to spare Smith's life. Engraving from *The General History* (1624).

Choose three of the italicized words and look them up in a dictionary. What are their specific origins? Can you think of any other words that may have come from an Indian language? If you are unsure of their origins, check them in a dictionary.

Writing About Literature

Developing a Thesis Statement

Using the excerpt in your anthology, develop this thesis statement: In *The General History* Smith distinguishes between the qualities that are desirable and those that are undesirable in a colonist, in order to emphasize the qualities necessary for successful colonization of the New World. For assistance in developing your paper, see the section called *Writing About Literature* at the back of this textbook.

Descriptive, Narrative, and Expository Writing

Keeping a Diary

Keep a diary for three days, writing a paragraph each day. The first day, describe a thing or place you saw (description). The second day, tell about something you did (narration). The third day, discuss a feeling or idea that occurred to you (exposition).

In his upbringing and his devotion to God, William Bradford typified most of the first settlers of New England. The son of an English farmer, he began to read the Bible seriously at the age of twelve. While still a boy, he joined with a group of Puritans for prayer and religious discussion. The act took courage, for members of Bradford's family urged against it, and Puritans in England were often, in Bradford's words, "taken and clapped up in prison" or "had their houses beset and watched night and day. . . ." Such hounding by authorities led many Puritans to flee to Holland. Bradford was among them. Uneasy in Holland as well, he and some other Puritans decided to come to America.

Bradford's life in America began tragically, and in this too he typified many of the first settlers. With about a hundred other English emigrants, Bradford reached Plymouth, Massachusetts, in December 1620, aboard the *Mayflower*—a tiny ship with a cracked beam that barely weathered the crossing. While the ship stood in Cape Cod harbor considering where to land, Bradford's wife fell—or jumped—overboard and drowned. Many of those who landed were no luckier. In their first, fierce winter ashore in America, about half of them died.

If Bradford's experience was typical, it was also in two ways special: he became the governor of Plymouth, and he wrote its history. In their yearly voting, the settlers elected and reelected him governor some thirty times. In 1630 he wrote down his recollections of the founding of Plymouth, and began keeping a record of annual events in the settlement, a practice he continued until 1647. His manuscript, containing about two hundred seventy pages, was consulted by other Puritan historians. But it stayed unpublished for two hundred years, during which time it somehow made its way back to England.

Bradford's work, *Of Plymouth Plantation* (published for the first time in 1856 as *History of Plymouth Plantation*), is pervaded by an enduring vision of America as a nation dedicated to and sustained by God. The book also relates some of the best-remembered episodes in American history. It describes the Puritans' flight from England to Holland where, fearing the corruption of their children by foreign customs, they planned their desperate second remove to America. It tells of such trials as the terrible first winter in the "hideous and desolate wilderness, full of wild beasts and wild men." The Indians themselves appear often in Bradford's history: Samoset and Squanto, who not only tell the Pilgrims about the surrounding country but also do so, to the Pilgrims' astonishment, in English (see page 30); the bloody Pequot War, climaxed by the killing of about six hundred Indian men, women, and children during the deliberate burning of their village—"a fearful sight," Bradford wrote, "to see them thus frying in the fire and the streams of blood quenching the same. . . ."

Begun in tragedy, Bradford's life in America closed in disappointment. As his book nears the end of its story of the twenty-five-year effort to settle Plymouth, its tone grows mournful. Having fled a corrupt Europe, the settlers themselves began to commit crimes and live immorally. Having survived the wilderness, war with the Indians, and financial exploitation by profiteers in England, many of the settlers began moving away from Plymouth. To Bradford, the place seemed "like an ancient mother grown old and forsaken of her children. . . ."

In his disappointment Bradford once again proves typical. He would not be the last American writer to feel that the divinely guided nation had fallen short of its promise.

FROM

Of Plymouth Plantation

Of Their Voyage, and How They Passed the Sea; and of Their Safe Arrival at Cape Cod

September 6. These troubles[1] being blown over, and now all being compact together in one ship, they put to sea again with a prosperous wind, which continued divers days together, which was some encouragement unto them; yet, according to the usual manner, many were afflicted with seasickness. And I may not omit here a special work of God's providence. There was a proud and very profane young man, one of the seamen, of a lusty,[2] able body, which made him the more haughty; he would alway be contemning the poor people in their sickness and cursing them daily with grievous execrations; and did not let[3] to tell them that he hoped to help to cast half of them overboard before they came to their journey's end, and to make merry with what they had; and if he were by any gently reproved, he would curse and swear most bitterly. But it pleased God before they came half seas over, to smite this young man with a grievous disease, of which he died in a desperate manner, and so was himself the first that was thrown overboard. Thus his curses light on his own head, and it was an astonishment to all his fellows for they noted it to be the just hand of God upon him.

After they had enjoyed fair winds and weather for a season, they were encountered many times with crosswinds and met with many fierce storms with which the ship was shroudly[4] shaken, and her upper works made very leaky; and one of the main beams in the midships was bowed and cracked, which put them in some fear that the ship could not be able to perform the voyage. So some of the chief of the company, perceiving the mariners to fear the sufficiency of the ship as appeared by their mutterings, they entered into serious consultation with the Master and other officers of the ship, to consider in time of the danger, and rather to return than to cast themselves into a desperate and inevitable peril. And truly there was great distraction and difference of opinion amongst the mariners themselves; fain[5] would they do what could be done for their wages' sake (being now near half the seas over) and on the other hand they were loath[6] to hazard their lives too desperately. But in examining of all opinions, the master and others affirmed they knew the ship to be strong and firm under water; and for the buckling of the main beam, there was a great iron screw the passengers brought out of Holland, which would raise the beam into his place; the which being done, the carpenter and master affirmed that with a post put under it, set firm in the lower deck and otherways

---

1. **troubles:** the unseaworthiness of one of their ships.
2. **lusty:** strong.
3. **let:** omit.

4. **shroudly:** severely.
5. **fain:** gladly.
6. **loath** (lōth): reluctant.

Colored engraving of the *Mayflower* approaching the coast of Massachusetts in 1620.

bound, he would make it sufficient. And as for the decks and upper works, they would caulk them as well as they could, and though with the working of the ship they would not long keep staunch, yet there would otherwise be no great danger, if they did not overpress her with sails. So they committed themselves to the will of God and resolved to proceed.

In sundry of these storms the winds were so fierce and the seas so high, as they could not bear a knot of sail, but were forced to hull[7] for divers days together. And in one of them, as they thus lay at hull in a mighty storm, a lusty young man called John Howland, coming upon some occasion above the gratings was, with a seele[8] of the ship, thrown into sea; but it pleased God that he caught hold of the top-sail halyards[9] which hung overboard and ran out at length. Yet he held his hold (though he was sundry fathoms under water) till he was hauled up by the same rope to the brim of the water, and then with a boat hook and other means got into the ship again and his life saved. And though he was something ill with it, yet he lived many years after and became a profitable member both in church and commonwealth. In all this voyage there died but one of the passengers, which was William Butten, a youth, servant to Samuel Fuller, when they drew near the coast.

But to omit other things (that I may be brief) after long beating at sea they fell with that land which is called Cape Cod; the which being made and certainly known to be it, they were not a little joyful. After some deliberation had amongst themselves and with the Master of the ship, they tacked about and resolved to stand for the southward (the wind and weather being fair) to find some place about Hudson's River for their habitation. But after they had sailed that course about half the day, they fell amongst dangerous shoals and roaring breakers, and they were so far entangled therewith

as they conceived themselves in great danger; and the wind shrinking upon them withal,[10] they resolved to bear up again for the Cape and thought themselves happy to get out of those dangers before night overtook them, as by God's good providence they did. And the next day they got into the Cape Harbor,[11] where they rid in safety. . . .

Being thus arrived in a good harbor, and brought safe to land, they fell upon their knees and blessed the God of Heaven who had brought them over the vast and furious ocean, and delivered them from all perils and miseries thereof, again to set their feet on the firm and stable earth, their proper element. . . .

But here I cannot but stay and make a pause, and stand half amazed at this poor people's present condition; and so I think will the reader, too, when he well considers the same. Being thus passed the vast ocean, and a sea of troubles before in their preparation (as may be remembered by that which went before), they had now no friends to welcome them nor inns to entertain or refresh their weather-beaten bodies; no houses or much less towns to repair to, to seek for succor. It is recorded in Scripture as a mercy to the Apostle and his shipwrecked company,[12] that the barbarians showed them no small kindness in refreshing them, but these savage barbarians, when they met with them (as after will appear), were readier to fill their sides full of arrows than otherwise. And for the season it was winter, and they that know the winters of that country know them to be sharp and violent, and subject to cruel and fierce storms, dangerous to travel to known places, much more to search an unknown coast. Besides, what could they see but a hideous and desolate wilderness, full of wild beasts and wild men—and what multitudes there might be of them they knew not. Neither

7. **hull:** drift.
8. **seele:** rolling movement.
9. **halyards** (hăl′yərdz): ropes for hoisting or lowering sails.

10. **withal:** also.
11. **Cape Harbor:** now Provincetown Harbor.
12. **Scripture . . . company:** Acts 28 in the Bible records the kindness shown to Saint Paul and his shipwrecked companions by the natives of the island of Malta.

could they, as it were, go up to the top of Pisgah[13] to view from this wilderness a more goodly country to feed their hopes; for which way soever they turned their eyes (save upward to the heavens) they could have little solace or content in respect of any outward objects. For summer being done, all things stand upon them with a weather-beaten face, and the whole country, full of woods and thickets, represented a wild and savage hue. If they looked behind them, there was the mighty ocean which they had passed and was now as a main bar and gulf to separate them from all the civil parts of the world. If it be said they had a ship to succor them, it is true; but what heard they daily from the master and company? But that with speed they should look out a place (with their shallop[14]) where they would be, at some near distance; for the season was such as he would not stir from thence till a safe harbor was discovered by them, where they would be, and he might go without danger; and that victuals consumed apace but he must and would keep sufficient for themselves and their return. Yea, it was muttered by some that if they got not a place in time, they would turn them and their goods ashore and leave them. Let it also be considered what weak hopes of supply and succor they left behind them, that might bear up their minds in this sad condition and trials they were under; and they could not but be very small. It is true, indeed, the affections and love of their brethren at Leyden[15] was cordial and entire towards them, but they had little power to help them or themselves; and how the case stood between them and the merchants at their coming away hath already been declared.

What could now sustain them but the Spirit of God and His grace? May not and ought not the children of these fathers rightly say: "Our fathers were Englishmen which came over this great ocean, and were ready to perish in this wilderness; but they cried unto the Lord, and He heard their voice and looked on their adversity,"[16] etc. "Let them therefore praise the Lord, because He is good: and His mercies endure forever." "Yea, let them which have been redeemed of the Lord, shew how He hath delivered them from the hand of the oppressor. When they wandered in the desert wilderness out of the way, and found no city to dwell in, both hungry and thirsty, their soul was overwhelmed in them. Let them confess before the Lord His lovingkindness and His wonderful works before the sons of men."[17]

The Starving Time

But that which was most sad and lamentable was, that in two or three months' time half of their company died, especially in January and February, being the depth of winter, and wanting houses and other comforts; being infected with the scurvy[18] and other diseases which this long voyage and their inaccommodate[19] condition had brought upon them. So as there died sometimes two or three of a day in the foresaid time, that of one hundred and odd persons, scarce fifty remained. And of these, in the time of most distress, there was but six or seven sound persons who to their great commendations, be it spoken, spared no pains night nor day, but with abundance of toil and hazard of their own health, fetched them wood, made them fires, dressed them meat, made their beds, washed their loathsome clothes, clothed and unclothed them. In a word, did all the homely and necessary offices for them which dainty and queasy stomachs cannot endure to hear named; and all this willingly and cheerfully, without any grudging

13. **Pisgah** (pĭz′gə): the mountain in Jordan from which Moses viewed the Promised Land.
14. **shallop:** small, open boat.
15. **brethren at Leyden** (līd′n): the Puritan community in Holland.

16. **Our fathers . . . adversity:** an allusion to the plight of the Israelites in Egypt (Deuteronomy 26:5–8).
17. **Let them . . . sons of men:** from Psalm 107:1–5, 8.
18. **scurvy:** a disease caused by vitamin C deficiency, resulting in weakness, anemia, and bleeding.
19. **inaccommodate:** unfit.

William Bradford **27**

Hooded wicker cradle of Peregrine White, born aboard the *Mayflower*.

(Page 29) Meeting House built at Plymouth in 1683.

in the least, showing herein their true love unto their friends and brethren; a rare example and worthy to be remembered. Two of these seven were Mr. William Brewster, their reverend Elder, and Myles Standish, their Captain and military commander, unto whom myself and many others were much beholden in our low and sick condition. And yet the Lord so upheld these persons as in this general calamity they were not at all infected either with sickness or lameness. And what I have said of these I may say of many others who died in this general visitation, and others yet living; that whilst they had health, yea, or any strength continuing, they were not wanting to any that had need of them. And I doubt not but their recompense is with the Lord.

But I may not here pass by another remarkable passage not to be forgotten. As this calamity fell among the passengers that were to be left here to plant, and were hasted ashore and made to drink water that the seamen might have the more beer, and one in his sickness desiring but a small can of beer, it was answered that if he were their own father he should have none. The disease began to fall amongst them also, so as almost half of their company died before they went away, and many of their officers and lustiest men, as the boatswain, gunner, three quartermasters, the cook and others. At which the Master was something strucken and sent to the sick ashore and told the Governor he should send for beer for them that had need of it, though he drunk water homeward bound.

But now amongst his company there was far another kind of carriage[20] in this misery than amongst the passengers. For they that before

20. **carriage:** manner of behaving.

had been boon[21] companions in drinking and jollity in the time of their health and welfare, began now to desert one another in this calamity, saying they would not hazard their lives for them, they should be infected by coming to help them in their cabins; and so, after they came to lie by it, would do little or nothing for them but, "if they died, let them die." But such of the passengers as were yet aboard showed them what mercy they could, which made some of their hearts relent, as the boatswain (and some others) who was a proud young man and would often curse and scoff at the passengers. But when he grew weak, they had compassion on him and helped him; then he confessed he did not deserve it at their hands, he had abused them in word and deed. "Oh!" (saith he) "you, I now see, show your love like

Christians indeed one to another, but we let one another lie and die like dogs." Another lay cursing his wife, saying if it had not been for her he had never come this unlucky voyage, and anon[22] cursing his fellows, saying he had done this and that for some of them; he had spent so much and so much amongst them, and they were now weary of him and did not help him, having need. Another gave his companion all he had, if he died, to help him in his weakness; he went and got a little spice and made him a mess of meat once or twice. And because he died not so soon as he expected, he went amongst his fellows and swore the rogue would cozen[23] him, he would see him choked before he made him any more meat; and yet the poor fellow died before morning.

21. **boon:** close.

22. **anon** (ə-nŏn′): soon.
23. **cozen** (kŭz′ən): cheat.

William Bradford **29**

Plaster bust of *Squanto*.
Pilgrim Hall Museum, Plymouth, Massachusetts

Indian Relations

All this while the Indians came skulking about them, and would sometimes show themselves aloof off, but when any approached near them, they would run away; and once they stole away their tools where they had been at work and were gone to dinner. But about the sixteenth of March, a certain Indian came boldly amongst them and spoke to them in broken English, which they could well understand but marveled at it. At length they understood by discourse with him, that he was not of these parts, but belonged to the eastern parts where some English ships came to fish, with whom he was acquainted and could name sundry of them by their names, amongst whom he had got his language. He became profitable to them in acquainting them with many things concerning the state of the country in the east parts where he lived, which was afterwards profitable unto them; as also of the people here, of their names, number and strength, of their situation and distance from this place, and who was chief amongst them. His name was Samoset. He told them also of another Indian, whose name was Squanto, a native of this place, who had been in England and could speak better English than himself.

Being, after some time of entertainment and gifts dismissed, a while after he came again, and five more with him, and they brought again all the tools that were stolen away before, and made way for the coming of their great Sachem,[24] called Massasoit. Who, about four or five days after, came with the chief of his friends and other attendance, with the aforesaid Squanto. With whom, after friendly entertainment and some gifts given him, they made a peace with him (which hath now continued this twenty-four years) in these terms:

1. That neither he nor any of his should injure or do hurt to any of their people.
2. That if any of his did hurt to any of theirs, he should send the offender, that they might punish him.
3. That if anything were taken away from any of theirs, he should cause it to be restored; and they should do the like to his.
4. If any did unjustly war against him, they would aid him; if any did war against them, he should aid them.
5. He should send to his neighbors confederates to certify them of this, that they might not wrong them, but might be likewise comprised in the conditions of peace.
6. That when their men came to them, they should leave their bows and arrows behind them.

After these things he returned to his place called Sowams, some forty miles from this

---

24. **Sachem** (sā′chəm): chief of a tribe or confederation.

place, but Squanto continued with them and was their interpreter and was a special instrument sent of God for their good beyond their expectation. He directed them how to set their corn, where to take fish, and to procure other commodities, and was also their pilot to bring them to unknown places for their profit, and never left them till he died.

Reading Check

1. Who was the first person to die on the *Mayflower* voyage?
2. What danger did the crew and passengers face from the main beam?
3. Why did the *Mayflower* return to Cape Cod?
4. During the first winter, how many of the pilgrims survived?
5. Which Indian became an interpreter for the settlers?

For Study and Discussion

Analyzing and Interpreting the Selection

1. Like many Americans after him, Bradford had a *providential* view of history. That is, he believed that whatever happens in history happens because God wants it to happen. In which episodes does Bradford see signs that God is directing the history of the Pilgrims?
2. Bradford wrote his history not only to record events. He also hoped to make younger Puritans feel respect and obligation toward the older generation for having overcome great difficulties in settling New England. **a.** What difficulties did the first settlers encounter from nature? **b.** What difficulties did they encounter from human nature?
3. Although the Puritans were individualistic, they also felt a strong sense of community. Notice that Bradford writes not so much about "I" or "he" or "she," as about "they"—about the settlers as a group. What episode illustrates the Puritans' concern for each other?
4. Read over the terms of peace between the Indians and the settlers. **a.** In what ways did the two groups promise to aid each other? **b.** Were the peace terms more favorable to the settlers or to the Indians?

Writing About Literature

Comparing Two Colonial Figures
Captain John Smith and William Bradford were important figures in colonizing the New World. Write an essay comparing the two men. In your essay, consider each man's relationship to his fellow settlers, his sense of community (or lack of it), and his view of the role providence played in his affairs and the affairs of his colony.

The Plain Style and the Ornate Style

Bradford's writing may in places seem hard to read. But that is only because of changes in the English language over the last three hundred years. Actually, Bradford wrote his history in the *plain style,* a style favored by many Puritans because it was easily understood.

The plain style is marked by simple words in clear order. A writer should, of course, use whatever language fully expresses his or her meaning, even if this calls for difficult words and complex order. But the meaning most Puritans wished to express called for a plain style. They believed themselves to be the correct interpreters of God's commandments as revealed in the Bible. They wrote plainly because God's word could not be improved by human decoration, and because they wished to make the meaning of the divine commandments clear to people of every level of intelligence. Some Puritans also considered the plain style particularly suited to the rawness of the New World. One minister asked his readers to remember that if his writing seemed "homely," it was because settlers had to concentrate on essentials: "It comes out of the wilderness, where curiosity is not studied. Planters if they can provide cloth to go warm; they leave the cuts [fancy style] and lace to those that study to go fine."

The virtues of the plain style can be appreciated by sampling its opposite, the *ornate style.* Below is a paragraph from a history of New England written seventy-five years after Bradford by the famous Puritan leader Cotton Mather. By Mather's time, many Puritans had given up the plain style, just as places like Boston were changing from wilderness clearings into cities. The paragraph appears in a discussion of history writing, in which Mather states that the historian gives a sort of life to the dead. His entire long paragraph consists of one sentence. Reading it aloud makes one gasp for breath:

If such a Renowned Chemist, as *Quercetanus,* with a whole Tribe of *Laborers in the Fire,* since that Learned Man, find it no easy thing to make the common part of Mankind believe, that they can take a *Plant* in its more vigorous Consistence, and after a due *Maceration, Fermentation* and *Separation,* extract the *Salt* of that *Plant,* which, as it were, in a *Chaos,* invisibly reserves the *Form* of the whole, with its vital Principle; and, that keeping the *Salt* in a *Glass* Hermetically sealed, they can, by applying a *Soft Fire* to the *Glass,* make the *Vegetable* rise by little and little out of its *Ashes,* to surprise the Spectators with a notable Illustration of that *Resurrection,* in the Faith whereof the *Jews* returning from the Graves of their Friends, pluck up the *Grass* from the Earth, using those Words of the Scripture thereupon, *Your Bones shall flourish like an Herb:* 'Tis likely, that all the Observations of such Writers, as the Incomparable *Borellus,* will find it hard enough to produce our Belief, that the

Essential Salts of *Animals* may be so Prepared and Preserved, that an Ingenious Man may have the whole *Ark of Noah* in his own Study, and raise the fine *Shape* of an *Animal* out of its Ashes at his Pleasure: And, that by the like Method from the *Essential Salts of Human Dust,* a Philosopher may, without any Criminal *Necromancy,* call up the *Shape* of any *Dead* Ancestor from the Dust whereinto his Body has been Incinerated.

Mather's meaning is simple: People find it hard to believe that dead things can be revived. Yet his idea is buried under the decorations of the ornate style: learned references ("the Incomparable *Borellus*"); odd sentence structure (the subject of the sentence does not appear for about one hundred fifty words); parallelisms (*"Maceration, Fermentation* and *Separation"*). To be a bit unfair to Mather, who was often a brilliant writer, compare his style in this passage to Bradford's plain style in introducing the famous Indian who befriended the Pilgrims: "His name was Samoset."

Perhaps the best definition of the plain style comes from Benjamin Franklin, who said that writing should be "smooth, clear, and short." Franklin wrote in the style himself, as, in various degrees, have such later American writers as Mark Twain, Emily Dickinson, and Ernest Hemingway. The plain style has never disappeared from American literature, perhaps because it appeals to American ideals of democracy and straightforwardness. It is a style that can be understood by all, and that tries not to adorn the naked truth.

Close Reading

Rendering Sentences into Modern English

Though Bradford's style is clear and simple by early seventeenth-century standards, a twentieth-century reader must find modern equivalents for a number of obsolete expressions. For example, "perceiving the mariners to fear the sufficiency of the ship" should be understood to mean "noticing that the mariners were worried about the condition of the ship."

Rewrite the following four sentences as a modern author might write them. On the basis of changes you have made, be prepared to discuss differences between Bradford's English and contemporary English.

1. Thus his curses light on his own head, and it was an astonishment to all his fellows for they noted it to be the just hand of God upon him.

2. In sundry of these storms the winds were so fierce and the seas so high, as they could not bear a knot of sail. . . .

3. But here I cannot but stay and make a pause, and stand half amazed at this poor people's present condition. . . .

4. For summer being done, all things stand upon them with a weather-beaten face, and the whole country, full of woods and thickets, represented a wild and savage hue.

ANNE BRADSTREET
1612–1672

By permission of the Vicar and Church Wardens, St. Botolph's Church, Boston, England

In London, in 1650, there appeared a volume of poems entitled *The Tenth Muse Lately Sprung Up in America.* In two ways the book was remarkable. It was the first volume of poems published by an American—a Puritan living in a still-unsettled wilderness. And it was one of the first volumes of poetry in English written by a woman—Anne Bradstreet.

Born in Northampton, England, Bradstreet grew up in the house of a Puritan nobleman. Her father, Thomas Dudley, worked for the nobleman, as did a graduate of Cambridge University named Simon Bradstreet, whom she married when she was sixteen. Both her husband and her father were destined for higher rank: both men became governors of Massachusetts. In 1630, Anne sailed with them from England to Boston. About ten years later, the Bradstreets moved to the small village of Andover. There, Anne spent the rest of her life, caring for her eight children, but frequently ill. Six years after her death, a revised edition of her works was published in Boston.

Appearing twenty-eight years apart, Bradstreet's two volumes differ greatly in style and content. The differences indicate how the American wilderness affected a well-bred young Englishwoman. The first edition contains very long poems written in a learned style on such subjects as medicine, history, and the qualities of fire. The second edition contains far shorter poems, written in a simpler style, about children, husband, and home. It is as if the wilderness forced Anne Bradstreet to devote herself to private matters of immediate concern and to speak about them plainly. The later poems express her deep attachment to her family and her deep sense of loss when her husband is called away on business, when her grandchildren die, and when her house burns to the ground. They also express, again and again, her Puritan belief that one must not become too attached to things of this world.

If it seems striking that the author of *The Tenth Muse* was a woman, Anne Bradstreet was good-humoredly conscious of the fact herself, and a bit

Stained glass window of St. Botolph's Church showing Anne Bradstreet holding a nest of birds, an image suggested by a line in one of her poems: "I had eight birds hatched in one nest."

apologetic. She clearly liked to write, yet she apparently felt it improper for a woman to appear in print. As a proper Puritan wife, she was quick to assert the superiority of men:

> *Let Greeks be Greeks, and Women what they are,*
> *Men have precedency, and still excel,*
> *It is but vain, unjustly to wage war,*
> *Men can do best, and Women know it well.*

Whether or not "men can do best," men did not. The person who deserves to be called the first American poet was a woman.

To My Dear and Loving Husband

If ever two were one, then surely we.
If ever man were loved by wife, then thee;
If ever wife was happy in a man,
Compare with me, ye women, if you can.
I prize thy love more than whole mines of gold   5
Or all the riches that the East doth hold.
My love is such that rivers cannot quench,
Nor ought° but love from thee, give recompense.
Thy love is such I can no way repay,
The heavens reward thee manifold, I pray.   10
Then while we live, in love let's so persevere°
That when we live no more, we may live ever.

8. **ought:** an archaic word meaning "anything whatever."   11. **persevere:** here, pronounced pər-sĕv′ər.

Upon the Burning of Our House
July 10th, 1666

In silent night when rest I took
For sorrow near I did not look
I wakened was with thund'ring noise
And piteous shrieks of dreadful voice.
That fearful sound of "Fire!" and "Fire!"   5
Let no man know is my desire.
I, starting up, the light did spy,
And to my God my heart did cry
To strengthen me in my distress
And not to leave me succorless.   10
Then, coming out, beheld a space
The flame consume my dwelling place.
And when I could no longer look,
I blest His name that gave and took,
That laid my goods now in the dust.   15
Yea, so it was, and so 'twas just.
It was His own, it was not mine,
Far be it that I should repine;
He might of all justly bereft
But yet sufficient for us left.   20
When by the ruins oft I past
My sorrowing eyes aside did cast,
And here and there the places spy

Where oft I sat and long did lie:
Here stood that trunk, and there that chest,   25
There lay that store I counted best.
My pleasant things in ashes lie,
And them behold no more shall I.
Under thy roof no guest shall sit,
Nor at thy table eat a bit.   30
No pleasant tale shall e'er be told,
Nor things recounted done of old.
No candle e'er shall shine in thee,
Nor bridegroom's voice e'er heard shall be.
In silence ever shall thou lie,   35
Adieu,° Adieu, all's vanity.
Then straight I 'gin my heart to chide,
And did thy wealth on earth abide?
Didst fix thy hope on mold'ring dust?
The arm of flesh didst make thy trust?   40
Raise up thy thoughts above the sky
That dunghill mists away may fly.
Thou hast an house on high erect,
Framed by that mighty Architect,
With glory richly furnished,   45
Stands permanent though this be fled.
It's purchased and paid for too
By Him who hath enough to do.
A price so vast as is unknown
Yet by His gift is made thine own;   50
There's wealth enough, I need no more,
Farewell, my pelf,° farewell my store.
The world no longer let me love,
My hope and treasure lies above.

36. **Adieu** (ə-dyōō'): French for "goodbye."   52. **pelf** (pĕlf): a contemptuous term for wealth.

For Study and Discussion

Analyzing and Interpreting the Poems
1. Anne Bradstreet's poems deal with two important Puritan themes: domestic life and God. "To My Dear and Loving Husband" concerns a happy marriage. It describes the greatness of the poet's love for her husband and of his love for her. Through what details does Bradstreet suggest the intensity of their love and the fact that the love is mutual?
2. "Upon the Burning of Our House" insists that wordly goods should not be loved too intensely, for they perish or must be given up.   **a.** Where in the poem does Bradstreet remind herself not to have too much affection for earthly things?   **b.** What does Bradstreet refer to in lines 43–47 when she speaks of a "house on high"?   **c.** How does her awareness of this "house" help console her for her loss of the first house?
3. The kinds of words a poet chooses—long, short, common, uncommon—are called the poet's **diction.** Bradstreet's diction is characteristic of the plain style: short, homely words ordinarily used in conversation, such as "roof," "table," "candle," "price."

Like William Bradford and most other Puritans, however, Bradstreet allowed for a bit of adornment. Find three words in the poems that show Bradstreet ornamenting her homely diction.

Literary Elements

The Iambic Couplet

"To My Dear and Loving Husband" is written in one of the most often used forms of English verse, the **iambic couplet. Iambic** refers to the rhythmic pattern—an unaccented syllable followed by an accented syllable: "If éver wífe was háppy ín a mán." (If you beat out the accents mentally, the rhythmic pattern would sound like ta-túm, ta-túm, ta-túm, ta-túm, ta-túm.) **Couplet**—as its resemblance to the word *couple* suggests—refers to two successive lines that rhyme. Below are some other couplets from Anne Bradstreet's poetry. Pick out the two that are iambic couplets.

> *Within this Tomb a Patriot lies*
> *That was both pious, just and wise.* . . .
>
> *Alas slain is the Head of Israel,*
> *Illustrious Saul whose beauty did excel.* . . .
>
> *My head, my heart, mine eyes, my life, nay more*
> *My joy, my magazine of earthly store.* . . .

Both of Anne Bradstreet's poems are written in iambic couplets. Browse through the book and see what other examples of iambic couplets you can find.

Writing About Literature

Responding to an Interpretation

You have seen that in "Upon the Burning of Our House," Bradstreet tells herself not to have too much affection for earthly things. Some critics feel that Bradstreet's reminders occur so frequently as to suggest that she does not really want to give up earthly things. In a brief composition, tell whether you agree or disagree with this view.

Chair cover embroidered by Anne Bradstreet.
Museum of Fine Arts, Boston, gift of Samuel Bradstreet

EDWARD TAYLOR
1642?–1729

It took two hundred years for the best poems written in early America to be published. Although their author, Edward Taylor, wrote thousands of lines of poetry, he allowed only two stanzas of one poem to be published during his long life, and asked his heirs not to publish any more. Written in the late seventeenth and early eighteenth centuries, his poems were not printed until the twentieth century.

Like most American Puritan writers, Taylor was a minister. He came to Boston in 1668 after losing a teaching position in England because he refused to take an oath contrary to his religious beliefs. He already had a degree from an English university, but he took a second degree at Harvard. After graduation he accepted a post as minister to the tiny frontier town of Westfield, Massachusetts. He wrote that the hundred-mile journey there in November 1671 proved difficult, "the snow being mid-leg deep, the way unbeaten, or the track filled up again, and over rocks and mountains. . . ."

Difficulties persisted during the nearly sixty years Taylor spent in Westfield. The town was under constant threat of attack during King Philip's War, the great Indian war of the 1670s in which two-thirds of the villages of Massachusetts Bay were damaged or destroyed. Taylor's first wife bore eight children, five of whom died as infants. A conservative and seemingly irritable man, he also quarreled with tenants on his property and with his own congregation and other ministers on religious matters.

Taylor wrote a good deal. No one knows how much, for poems by him are still being discovered. Some turned up not long ago stuffed in the bindings of books in his library. Almost all of his known poetry concerns religion. Taylor tried to defend the original faith of the Puritans against newer, more liberal religious ideas. He believed that only persons who had had the mystical experience of grace should be allowed to become full members of a

Gravestone from Old Burying Ground, Deerfield, Massachusetts.

church—at a time when many other Puritans wished to eliminate grace as a requirement for church membership in hopes of keeping the churches filled. His poetic style also differs from that of most other Puritan poets, being often difficult and intricate. His chief poetic work is a group of more than two hundred poems entitled *Preparatory Meditations*, which he wrote on and off for forty-four years. Here, he explored the mystery of grace, trying to understand how a human being, a "crumb of dust," could be joined to God, "Might Almighty."

Taylor wrote little directly about his life in the New World. Yet his poems testify to the intensity of Puritan religious life in wilderness America, and their publication after two hundred years contributes to American literature a powerful and original imagination.

Needlework showing pastoral scene with lady (c. 1750–1760).

Huswifery°

Make me, O Lord, thy Spinning Wheel complete.
  Thy Holy Word my Distaff make for me.
Make mine° Affections° thy Swift Flyers neat
  And make my Soul thy holy Spool to be.
  My Conversation make to be thy Reel   5
  And Reel the yarn thereon spun of thy Wheel.

Make me thy Loom then, knit therein this Twine:
  And make thy Holy Spirit, Lord, wind quills:°
Then weave the Web thyself. The yarn is fine.
  Thine Ordinances° make my Fulling Mills.°   10
  Then dye the same in Heavenly Colors Choice,
  All pinked° with Varnished° Flowers of Paradise.

Then clothe therewith mine Understanding, Will,
  Affections, Judgment, Conscience, Memory,
My Words and Actions, that their shine may fill   15
  My ways with glory and thee glorify.
  Then mine apparel shall display before ye
  That I am Clothed in Holy robes for glory.

°**Huswifery:** housewifery; the work of a housewife. Also thrift, making the most of something. 3. **mine:** my. **Affections:** emotions. 8. **quills:** spools on a loom. 10. **Ordinances:** sacraments. **Fulling Mills:** mills for cleansing cloth. 12. **pinked:** decorated. **Varnished:** bright, shining.

Edward Taylor **39**

Commentary

"Huswifery" develops out of an intricate comparison between cloth making and God's granting of grace. Such an extended comparison between two startlingly different things—a lowly household task and salvation—is a type of metaphor called a *conceit*. (For a discussion of *metaphor* see page 333.)

Conceits are associated mostly with the writing of seventeenth-century English poets such as John Donne and George Herbert. They introduced into their poetry many images that are not usually considered poetic. For example, Donne compared the union of a man and a woman to a flea that, having bitten them both, unites their blood within itself. Herbert compared the relationship between humanity and God to that between a tenant and a rich lord. Part of the pleasure in reading such poems lies in recognizing the surprising, yet meaningful, way in which the poet has worked out an involved comparison between things that at first seem to have nothing in common.

In religious poetry a conceit may serve a deeper purpose than surprise. It can emphasize the underlying unity among all things in God's creation—high and low, familiar and strange. As a Puritan, Taylor believed that the miracle of grace consisted in mighty God consenting to join with lowly human beings. Thus, it was natural for him to compare the granting of grace to a housewife making homespun clothes.

"Huswifery" is a kind of prayer in which the poet asks God for grace. The conceit begins in the first stanza, as the poet compares himself to a spinning wheel. The "Holy Word" (the Bible) is like the distaff—a stick on which raw wool is placed before spinning. The basic meaning of this complex comparison is that one cannot receive grace without having some knowledge of Scripture. The poet's emotions are like the "Flyers" that twist and carry the raw wool; his soul is like the spool that gathers the thread from the wheel; his conversation, or social behavior, is like the reel to which the finished thread is transferred from the spinning wheel.

The second stanza compares the poet to a loom, on which the thread or yarn is turned into cloth. God appears now as a weaver meshing the threads into cloth ("the Web"). Once the cloth is woven, it is to be cleansed by such sacraments or ordinances as communion (the "Fulling Mills"), dyed, and decorated. In the last stanza Taylor asks that the colorful material be fashioned into beautiful robes to clothe his thoughts, feelings, and behavior. If God will thus glorify the poet, say the final lines of the poem, the poet will then be able to glorify God through the beauty of his being.

In his imaginative conceit, Taylor expresses a key Puritan belief. Grace is a miraculous transformation of oneself from coarse imperfections to shining purity, a transformation as total and dramatic as turning fuzzy wool into majestic robes.

For Study and Discussion

Analyzing and Interpreting the Poem

1. An important question in Puritanism was, Can one achieve religious grace through one's own efforts? Or must it come simply as a gift from God? **a.** Given the poet's relation to God in "Huswifery," how do you suppose Taylor might have answered this question? **b.** Note how often the word *make* appears in the poem. Can you justify Taylor's repetition of this word?

2. Despite his homely images, Taylor can be difficult to read, in part because he deals with complicated religious ideas. Critics themselves often disagree about the meaning of Taylor's lines or words, some of which have not one but several meanings. How would you interpret the following words in "Huswifery": *complete* (line 1); *neat* (line 3); *fine* (line 9)?

Creative Writing

Developing an Intricate Comparison

Write a brief composition in which, as if you were composing a poetic conceit, you compare in detail two quite different things, ideas, or experiences, and show unexpected similarities between them. You might, for example, compare a baseball game to a can opener, or a telephone conversation to a fire engine. At their most successful, such comparisons can be pleasurable and imaginative experiences in themselves, while revealing subtle features of the things or ideas being compared.

Reading the eighteenth-century Bostonian Sarah Kemble Knight, we may recall the intelligence and ability of Anne Bradstreet fifty years earlier. Madam Knight managed to be both a schoolteacher and a businesswoman. She not only taught writing (one of her pupils may have been young Benjamin Franklin), but also took in lodgers at her house, apparently ran a stationery store, and later became the owner of several farms and an inn.

This unusual woman remains known today for an unusual feat. Early in October, 1704, at the age of thirty-eight, she took a business trip from Boston to New York and back. The fact may not seem remarkable. But at the time travel by land meant wearying hours on horseback through dense woods, and swift streams to cross by night—"enough," as she wrote, "to startle a more masculine courage." With stops for rest, work, and sightseeing, her journey took five months, twice as long as it took Columbus to reach America from Spain.

Madam Knight found the crude state of civilization scarcely more friendly to her than nature. The few poor inns along the way allowed her no choice of where to stay or what to eat. She was forced to spend one night in a collapsing house whose door was tied on with cord and whose floor was the bare earth. Other times she had to sleep on mattresses stuffed with corncobs, and dine on some strange "twisted thing like a cable" topped by mysterious purple sauce. When she found the food completely inedible, she paid for it but left it, so that her dinner was "only smell."

However weary, frightened, or hungry, Madam Knight enjoyed observing how other people lived, and she recorded her trip in a journal. It describes the customs and manners of small rural communities and solitary settlers in the backwoods, as well as of aspiring cities like New Haven and New York. The liveliness of her journal comes not only from what she sees but also from her way of seeing it. Her courage and practicality allowed her to deal with and report on the dangers of the frontier. But her literary education and an element of romance in her character led her also to feel and remark on its appeal to her imagination. As a well-bred inhabitant of the growing city of Boston, too, she was fascinated and amused by what seemed to her the coarseness of life in the wilderness and the provinces. The combination in her of the keen social observer, the romantic traveler, and the urbanite, makes her journal by turns realistic, poetic, and funny.

A seventeenth-century trunk.
Pilgrim Hall Museum, Plymouth, Massachusetts

FROM

The Journal of Madam Knight

On a Journey from Boston to New York, in the Year 1704

Tuesday, October the third. About eight in the morning, I with the post[1] proceeded forward without observing anything remarkable, and about two, afternoon, arrived at the post's second stage, where the western post met him and exchanged letters. Here having called for something to eat, the woman brought in a twisted thing like a cable, but something whiter; and laying it on the board, tugged for life to bring it into a capacity to spread; which having with great pains accomplished, she served in a dish of pork and cabbage, I suppose the remains of dinner. The sauce was of a deep purple, which I thought was boil'd in her dye kettle. The bread was Indian, and everything on the table service agreeable to these. I, being hungry, got a little down; but my stomach was soon cloy'd, and what cabbage I swallowed serv'd me for a cud[2] the whole day after.

Having here discharged the ordinary[3] for myself and guide (as I understood was the custom), about three, afternoon, went on with my third guide, who rode very hard; and having crossed Providence Ferry, we came to a river which they generally rode thro'. But I dared not venture. So the post got a lad and canoe to carry me to t'other side, and he rid thro' and led my horse. The canoe was very small and shallow, so that when we were in, she seem'd ready to take in water, which greatly terrified me, and caused me to be very

circumspect, sitting with my hands fast on each side, my eyes steady, not daring so much as to lodge my tongue a hair's breadth more on one side of my mouth than t'other, nor so much as think on Lot's wife,[4] for a wry thought would have overset our wherry.[5] But I was soon put out of this pain, by feeling the canoe on shore, which I as soon almost saluted with my feet, and rewarding my sculler,[6] again mounted and made the best of our way forwards. The road here was very even and the day pleasant, it being now near sunset. But the post told me we had nearly fourteen miles to ride to the next stage (where we were to lodge). I asked him of the rest of the road, foreseeing we must travel in the night. He told me there was a bad river we were to ride thro', which was so very fierce a horse could sometime hardly stem[7] it; but it was but narrow, and we should soon be over. I cannot express the concern of mind this relation set me in: no thoughts but those of the dangerous river could entertain my imagination, and they were as formidable as various, still tormenting me with blackest ideas of my approaching fate—sometimes seeing myself drowning, otherwhiles drowned, and at the best like a holy sister just come out of a spiritual bath in dripping garments.

Now was the Glorious Luminary,[8] with his

1. **post:** mail carrier.
2. **cud:** something to chew on.
3. **discharged the ordinary:** paid for the food.

4. **Lot's wife:** In the Old Testament, Lot's wife looked back as the city of Sodom was being destroyed, and was turned into a pillar of salt (Genesis 29:1–26).
5. **a wry thought . . . wherry:** that is, our small rowing boat would have been overturned by so much as an out-of-the-way thought.
6. **sculler:** rower.
7. **stem:** make headway against.
8. **Glorious Luminary . . . :** that is, the sun had set.

swift coursers, arrived at his stage, leaving poor me with the rest of this part of the lower world in darkness, with which we were soon surrounded. The only glimmering we now had was from the spangled skies, whose imperfect reflections rendered every object formidable. Each lifeless trunk, with its shatter'd limbs, appear'd an armed enemy, and every stump like a ravenous devourer. Nor could I so much as discern my guide, when at any distance, which added to the terror.

Thus, absolutely lost in thought, and dying with the very thoughts of drowning, I came up with the post, who I did not see until even with his horse. He told me he stopped for me, and we rode on very deliberately a few paces, when we entered a thicket of trees and shrubs, and I perceived by the horse's going, we were on the descent of a hill, which, as we came nearer the bottom, was totally dark with the trees that surrounded it. But I knew by the going of the horse we had entered the water, which my guide told me was the hazardous river he had told me of; and he, riding up close to my side, bid me not fear—we should be over immediately. I now rallied all the courage I was mistress of, knowing that I must either venture my fate of drowning, or be left like the children in the wood.[9] So, as the post bid me, I gave reins to my nag, and sitting as steady as just before in the canoe, in a few minutes got safe to the other side, which he told me was the Narragansett country.

Here we found great difficulty in traveling, the way being very narrow, and on each side the trees and bushes giving us very unpleasant welcomes with their branches and boughs, which we could not avoid, it being so exceeding dark. My guide, as before so now, put on harder than I, with my weary bones, could follow, so left me and the way behind him. Now returned my distressed apprehensions of the place where I was: the dolesome woods, my company next to none, going I knew not whither, and encompassed with terrifying darkness—the least of which was enough to startle a more masculine courage. Added to which the reflections, as in the afternoon of the day before, that my call[10] was very questionable, which until then I had not so prudently as I ought considered. Now, coming to the foot of a hill, I found great difficulty in ascending; but being got to the top, was there amply recompensed with the friendly appearance of the Kind Conductress of the night,[11] just then advancing above the horizontal line. The raptures which the sight of that fair planet produced in me, caused me, for the moment, to forget my present weariness and past toils, and inspired me for most of the remaining way with very diverting thoughts, some of which, with the other occurrences of the day, I reserved to note down when I should come to my stage. My thoughts on the sight of the moon were to this purpose:

Fair Cynthia,[12] *all the homage that I may*
Unto a creature, unto thee I pay.
In lonesome woods to meet so kind a guide,
To me's worth more than all the world beside.
Some joy I felt just now, when safe got o'er
Yon surly river to this rugged shore,
Deeming rough welcomes from these clownish trees
Better than lodgings with Nereidees.[13]
Yet swelling fears surprise; all dark appears—
Nothing but light can dissipate those fears.
My fainting vitals can't lend strength to say,
But softly whisper, O I wish 'twere day.
The murmur hardly warm'd the ambient[14] *air,*
E're thy bright aspect rescues from despair:
Makes the old hag her sable mantle loose,
And a bright joy does through my soul diffuse.
The boisterous trees now lend a passage free,
And pleasant prospects thou givest light to see.

9. **children in the wood:** referring to the popular story in which two children are left in the forest, where they die during the night.

10. **call:** prompting, that is, my wish to make the journey.
11. **Kind Conductress:** the moon, which lights up her path.
12. **Fair Cynthia:** the moon, personified as a goddess.
13. **Nereidees:** Nereids (nîr′ē-ĭdz), daughters of the mythological water god Nereus; sea nymphs.
14. **ambient:** encircling.

From hence we kept on, with more ease than before: the way being smooth and even, the night warm and serene, and the tall and thick trees at a distance, especially when the moon glared light through the branches, fill'd my imagination with the pleasant delusion of a sumptuous city, fill'd with famous buildings and churches, with their spiring steeples, balconies, galleries and I know not what—grandeurs which I had heard of, and which the stories of foreign countries had given me the idea of:

Here stood a lofty church—there is a steeple,
And there the grand parade—O see the people!
That famous castle there, were I but nigh,
To see the moat and bridge, and walls so high—
They're very fine! says my deluded eye.

Being thus agreeably entertained without a thought of anything but thoughts themselves,

I on a sudden was roused from these pleasing imaginations by the post's sounding his horn, which assured me he was arrived at the stage, where we were to lodge; and that music was then most musical and agreeable to me. . . .

Saturday, October the seventh. We set out early in the morning, and being something unacquainted with the way, having asked it of some we met, they told us we must ride a mile or two and turn down a lane on the right hand, and by their direction we rode on. But not yet

coming to the turning, we met a young fellow and asked him how far it was to the lane which turn'd down towards Guilford. He said we must ride a little further, and turn down by the corner of Uncle Sam's lot. My guide vented his spleen[15] at the lubber; and we soon after came into the road, and keeping still on, without anything further remarkable, about two a clock afternoon we arrived at New Haven. . . .

They are governed by the same laws as we in Boston (or little differing) throughout this whole colony of Connecticut, and much the same way of church government, and many of them good, sociable people, and I hope religious too; but a little too much independent in their principles, and, as I have been told, were formerly in their zeal very rigid in their administrations toward such as their laws made offenders, even to a harmless kiss or innocent merriment among young people. Whipping

15. **vented his spleen:** displayed his anger.

being a frequent and counted an easy punishment, about which, as other crimes, the judges were absolute in their sentences. . . .

Their diversions in this part of the country are on Lecture Days and Training Days mostly.[16] On the former there is riding from town to town. And on Training Days the youth divert themselves by shooting at the target, as they call it (but it very much resembles a pillory), where he that hits nearest the white has some yards of red ribbon presented him, which being tied to his hatband, the two ends streaming down his back, he is led away in triumph, with great applause, as the winners

16. **Lecture Days:** midweek religious lectures, held on Thursdays; **Training Days:** days set for military drills.

Colonial inn signs. The first inscription reads: "Gentlemen you are welcome sit down at your ease. Pay what you call for & drink what you please."

of the Olympic Games. They generally marry very young—the males oftener, as I am told, under twenty than above. They generally make public weddings, and have a way something singular (as they say) in some of them, *viz.* just before joining hands, the bridegroom quits the place, who is soon followed by the bridesmen, and as it were dragged back to duty—being the reverse to the former practice among us, to steal Mrs.' pride. . . .[17]

Being at a merchant's house, in comes a tall country fellow, with his alfogeos[18] full of tobacco; for they seldom lose their cud, but keep chewing and spitting as long as their eyes are open. He advanced to the middle of the room, made an awkward nod, and spitting a large deal of aromatic tincture, he gave a scrape with his shovel-like shoe, leaving a small shovel full of dirt on the floor; made a full stop, hugging his own pretty body with his hands under his arms, stood staring round him, like a cat let out of a basket. At last, like the creature Balaam rode on,[19] he opened his mouth and said: "Have you any ribbenen for hatbands to sell I pray?" The questions and answers about the pay being past, the ribbon is brought and opened. Bumpkin Simpers cries: "It's confounded gay, I vow." And beckoning to the door, in comes Joan Tawdry, dropping about fifty curtsies, and stands by him. He shows her the ribbon. *"Law you,"* says she, *"it's right Gent, do you take it, tis dreadful pretty."* Then she inquires, *"Have you any hood silk I pray?"* Which being brought and bought, "Have you any *thread silk to sew it with,"* says she, which being accommodated with they departed. They generally stand after they come in a great while speechless, and sometimes don't say a word till they are asked what they want, which I impute to the awe they stand in of the merchants, who they are constantly almost indebted to, and must take what they bring without liberty to choose for themselves. But they serve them as well, making the merchants stay long enough for their pay.

We may observe here the great necessity and benefit both of education and conversation. For these people have as large a portion of mother wit, and sometimes a larger, than those who have been brought up in cities, but for want of improvements render themselves almost ridiculous, as above. I should be glad if they would leave such follies, and am sure all that love clean houses (at least) would be glad on't too. . . .

Around December 8, Madam Knight reaches New York.

The city of New York is a pleasant, well compacted place, situated on a commodious river which is a fine harbor for shipping. The buildings brick generally, very stately and high, though not altogether like ours in Boston. The bricks in some of the houses are of diverse colors and laid in checkers, being glazed look very agreeable. The inside of them are neat to admiration, the wooden work—for only the walls are plastered—and the summers and gist[20] are planed and kept very white scoured, as so is all the partitions if made of boards. . . .

They are generally of the Church of England and have a New England gentleman for their minister, and a very fine church set out with all customary requisites. There are also a Dutch, and diverse conventicles,[21] as they call them, *viz.* Baptist, Quakers, &c. They are not strict in keeping the Sabbath as in Boston and other places where I had been, but seem to deal with great exactness as far as I see or deal with. They are sociable to one another and courteous and civil to strangers, and fare well

17. **Mrs.' pride:** Madam Knight's meaning seems to be that weddings in Boston featured the same practice—only there the bride was "dragged back to duty," to soften her pride.
18. **alfogeos** (ăl-fō'jĭ-ōs): saddlebags, but here used comically to mean cheeks.
19. **creature Balaam rode on:** referring to the donkey owned by the Biblical prophet Balaam (bā'ləm). After Balaam beat the animal three times, God inspired it to speak and to reprove Balaam (Numbers 22–24).

20. **summers and gist:** beams and joints.
21. **conventicles:** religious meetings.

Mrs. Elizabeth Freake and Baby Mary (c. 1674). Oil on canvas. Artist Unknown.

in their houses. The English go very fashionable in their dress. But the Dutch, especially the middling sort, differ from our women, in their habit go loose, wear French mouches, which are like a cap and a headband in one, leaving their ears bare, which are set out with jewels of a large size and many in number. And their fingers hooped with rings, some with large stones in them of many colors, as were their pendants in their ears, which you should see very old women wear as well as young.

Sarah Kemble Knight   **47**

They have vendues[22] very frequently and make their earnings very well by them, for they treat with good liquor liberally, and the customers drink as liberally and generally pay for't as well, by paying for that which they bid up briskly for, after the sack[23] has gone plentifully about, tho' sometimes good penny-worths are got there. Their diversions in the winter is riding sleighs about three or four miles out of town, where they have houses of entertainment at a place called the Bowery, and some go to friends' houses who handsomely treat them. Mr. Burroughs[24] carried his spouse and daughter and myself out to one Madame Downes, a gentlewoman that lived at a farmhouse, who gave us a handsome entertainment of five or six dishes and choice beer and metheglin,[25] cider, &c., all of which she said was the produce of her farm. I believe we met fifty or sixty sleighs that day. They fly with great swiftness, and some are so furious that they'll turn out of the path for none except a loaded cart. Nor do they spare for any diversion the place affords, and sociable to a degree, their tables being as free to their neighbors as to themselves.

22. **vendues** (vĕn-dōōz′, -dyōōz′): public sales or auctions.
23. **sack:** wine imported from Spain.
24. **Mr. Burroughs:** a New York merchant.
25. **metheglin** (mə-thĕg′lĭn): a drink made of honey and water.

Reading Check

1. Who was Madam Knight's guide on the journey to Connecticut?
2. Which of the hazards of travel did Madam Knight most dread?
3. What did she learn about wedding customs in New Haven?
4. What forms of entertainment did she observe in New York?

For Study and Discussion

Analyzing and Interpreting the Selection

1. Madam Knight finds many features of her trip frightening. Sometimes she relieves her fears by indulging in fantasies, "diverting thoughts." **a.** What specifically about the journey frightens her? **b.** What are some of her "diverting thoughts," especially about the moon?
2. Being a Boston schoolteacher, Madam Knight sees things as might a well-educated city person. **a.** What signs of her reading appear in her journal? **b.** How does her city upbringing affect the way she sees "Bumpkin Simpers" and "Joan Tawdry"? **c.** What does she find unusual about the behavior of people in New Haven and New York?

Close Reading

Paraphrasing a Passage

Paraphrase the following passage so that the content is clear:

They generally stand after they come in a great while speechless, and sometimes don't say a word till they are asked what they want, which I impute to the awe they stand in of the merchants, who they are constantly almost indebted to, and must take what they bring without liberty to choose for themselves. But they serve them as well, making the merchants stay long enough for their pay.

We may observe here the great necessity and benefit both of education and conversation. For these people have as large a portion of mother wit, and sometimes a larger, than those who have been brought up in cities, but for want of improvements render themselves almost ridiculous.

Descriptive Writing

Describing a Trip

Describe the comforts and discomforts of a trip you took. Or else, tell how the customs of some place you visited resembled and differed from those of the place where you live.

As William Bradford typifies the early Puritan settlers of New England, William Byrd typifies the gentleman planters of early Virginia. He was born in what is now Richmond, Virginia. His family—unlike the families of English gentlemen—achieved its status not by noble birth but through business. Byrd's father traded rum and molasses, bought and sold tobacco, and imported white servants and black slaves. He wanted William to be well educated and sent him at the age of seven to school in England. Byrd stayed in England until he was nearly thirty years old, returning only once briefly to Virginia. While abroad, he became a lawyer and, still in his early twenties, was elected to a famous association of scientists, The Royal Society.

Returning to Virginia upon his father's death, Byrd inherited a 26,000-acre estate known as Westover. He turned the estate and himself into models of Virginian aristocratic life, based on the life he had known in England. He imported fine furniture, glass, and silver, bought paintings, and amassed a library of 3,600 books, one of the largest in the colonies. Buying more land, he eventually owned a plantation of 200,000 acres. While supervising its operation, he found time to maintain the standards of a gentleman. He studied Latin and Greek, collected specimens of local animals and plants to send abroad for scientific study, and fulfilled his public obligations by serving on the politically important Governor's Council.

Virginia Historical Society, Richmond

William Byrd (c. 1740). Oil on canvas by School of Sir Godfrey Kneller.

Like other planters, Byrd also wrote—prolifically: diaries (kept in a code), travel books, scientific dispatches, poems, essays, and letters. The best known of his works is *The History of the Dividing Line* (1729), describing a surveying expedition into the wilderness to draw a boundary line between Virginia and North Carolina. The *History* combines the gentleman's active interest in society with the frontiersman's keen eye for nature. Its sharp style and racy humor make it the liveliest account in American literature of the early American frontier.

William Byrd **49**

The History of the Dividing Line

The Dismal Swamp

March 14. Before nine of the clock this morning, the provisions, bedding, and other necessaries were made up into packs for the men to carry on their shoulders into the Dismal. They were victualed for eight days at full allowance, nobody doubting but that would be abundantly sufficient to carry them through that inhospitable place; nor indeed was it possible for the poor fellows to stagger under more. As it was, their loads weighed from sixty to seventy pounds, in just proportion to the strength of those who were to bear them.

'Twould have been unconscionable[1] to have saddled them with burdens heavier than that, when they were to lug them through a filthy bog which was hardly practicable with no burden at all.

Besides this luggage at their backs, they were obliged to measure the distance, mark the

1. **unconscionable** (ŭn′kŏn′shən-ə-bəl): unreasonable.

A drawing of Byrd's property in North Carolina, from one of his journals.

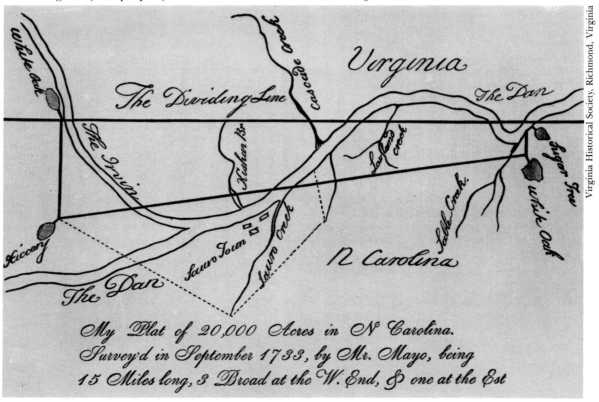

Virginia Historical Society, Richmond, Virginia

trees, and clear the way for the surveyors every step they went. It was really a pleasure to see with how much cheerfulness they undertook, and with how much spirit they went through all this drudgery. For their greater safety, the commissioners took care to furnish them with Peruvian bark,[2] rhubarb, and hipocoacanah,[3] in case they might happen, in that wet journey, to be taken with fevers or fluxes.

Although there was no need for example to inflame persons already so cheerful, yet to enter[4] the people with better grace, the author and two more of the commissioners accompanied them half a mile into the Dismal. The skirts of it were thinly planted with dwarf reeds and gall bushes but, when we got into the Dismal itself, we found the reeds grew there much taller and closer and, to mend the matter, was so interlaced with bamboo briers that there was no scuffling through them without the help of pioneers. At the same time, we found the ground moist and trembling under our feet like a quagmire, insomuch that it was an easy matter to run a ten-foot pole up to the head in it, without exerting any uncommon strength to do it.

Two of the men, whose burdens were the least cumbersome, had orders to march before with their tomahawks and clear the way, in order to make an opening for the surveyors. By their assistance we made a shift to push the line half a mile in three hours, and then reached a small piece of firm land about one hundred yards wide standing up above the rest like an island. Here the people were glad to lay down their loads and take a little refreshment, while the happy man whose lot it was to carry the jug of rum began already, like Aesop's bread-carrier,[5] to find it grow a good deal lighter.

After reposing about an hour, the commissioners recommended vigor and constancy to their fellow travelers, by whom they were answered with three cheerful huzzas in token of obedience. This ceremony was no sooner over but they took up their burdens and attended the motion of the surveyors who, though they worked with all their might, could reach but one mile farther, the same obstacles still attending them which they had met with in the morning.

However small this distance may seem to such as are used to travel at their ease, yet our poor men, who were obliged to work with an unwieldy load at their backs, had reason to think it a long way; especially in a bog where they had no firm footing, but every step made a deep impression, which was instantly filled with water. At the same time they were laboring with their hands to cut down the reeds, which were ten feet high, their legs were hampered with the briers. Besides, the weather happened to be very warm, and the tallness of the reeds kept off every friendly breeze from coming to refresh them. And, indeed, it was a little provoking to hear the wind whistling among the branches of the white cedars, which grew here and there amongst the reeds, and at the same time not have the comfort to feel the least breath of it.

In the meantime the three commissioners returned out of the Dismal the same way they went in and, having joined their brethren, proceeded that night as far as Mr. Wilson's.

This worthy person lives within sight of the Dismal, in the skirts whereof his stocks range and maintain themselves all the winter, and yet he knew as little of it as he did of *Terra Australis Incognita*.[6] He told us a Canterbury tale[7] of a North Briton whose curiosity spurred him a long way into this great desert,[8] as he called it,

2. **Peruvian bark:** quinine.
3. **hipocoacanah:** a medicinal herb now known as ipecac.
4. **enter:** start off.
5. **Aesop's bread-carrier:** According to the fable, the man who wanted the lightest burden on the journey was laughed at for choosing the bread, which was the heaviest; but by night the bread had all been distributed and he had only the empty basket to carry.

6. *Terra Australis Incognita* (tĕr′ə ô-strāl′əs ĭn-kŏg′nə-tə): unknown southern land.
7. **Canterbury tale:** here, an incredible tale. *The Canterbury Tales* are famous stories in verse by the first great English poet, Geoffrey Chaucer.
8. **desert:** here, the word refers to the swamp and means "a place uninhabited by people."

near twenty years ago, but he, having no compass, nor seeing the sun for several days together, wandered about till he was almost famished; but at last he bethought himself of[9] a secret his countrymen make use of to pilot themselves in a dark day.

He took a fat louse out of his collar and exposed it to the open day on a piece of white paper which he brought along with him for his journal. The poor insect, having no eyelids, turned himself about till he found the darkest part of the heavens, and so made the best of his way towards the north. By this direction he steered himself safe out, and gave such a frightful account of the monsters he saw and the distresses he underwent, that no mortal since has been hardy enough to go upon the like dangerous discovery.

9. **bethought himself of:** remembered.

Reading Check

1. Who were the members of the expedition into the Dismal?
2. What precautions were taken for the safety of the men?
3. According to Byrd, what was the mood of the men?
4. What obstacles made the work difficult?

For Study and Discussion

Analyzing and Interpreting the Selection
1. Because the Puritans were preoccupied with the spiritual meaning of America, they did not write much about the physical wilderness around them, as did some Southerners such as Byrd. What details does Byrd present in the fourth and seventh paragraphs to convey the dense foliage and oppressive heat of the Southern frontier?
2. Much early Southern writing is enlivened by humor. A notable example occurs at the end of the selection. Byrd calls it a "Canterbury tale," but we would call it a **tall tale.** It illustrates a type of humor common in early American writing, growing out of

distorted views of the New World or exaggerated reports about it. Retell Byrd's tall tale in your own words. Another sly bit of humor occurs at the end of the fifth paragraph. Put that also in your own words.
3. What impression do you form of Byrd's role in the expedition?
4. How does Byrd prove himself a cultured man as well as an able frontiersman?

Literary Elements

The Journal
Byrd's *History* exists in two versions. The version you have read is the one Byrd wished to have published. It was based on an earlier version that he wrote day by day during the surveying trip. Such a record of daily events is called a **journal.** The journal has been an important American literary form, especially in introspective New England. Ralph Waldo Emerson and Henry David Thoreau both kept detailed journals which, like Byrd's, became the basis of later published works.

In their original state, journals are the stuff of history. They record private impressions of events in a particular time and place, and are usually intended for the writer's eyes only. In their polished state, journals are the stuff of literature. The writer now has a reading public in mind and revises first impressions in order to create a particular effect. Read over Byrd's account of the surveyors' visit to Mr. Wilson. Then read the same episode as it appears in Byrd's original journal:

. . . we rode away to Captain Wilson's, who treated us with pork upon pork. He was a great lover of conversation, and rather than it should drop, he would repeat the same story over and over. Firebrand [one of the commissioners] chose rather to litter the floor than lie with the parson, and since he could not have the best bed he sullenly would have none at all. However, it broiled upon his stomach so much, that he swore enough in the night to bring the devil into the room had not the chaplain been there. . . . [next morning] We sent away the baggage about eight o'clock under the guard of four men. We paid off a long reckoning to Captain Wilson for our men and horses, but Firebrand forgot to pay for the washing of his linen, which saved him two shillings at least.

Between versions, Byrd's account changed drastically. The revised version presents Wilson as a "worthy person"; the original version presents him as amusingly tiresome, a man who told "the same story over and over." Byrd seems to have found Wilson a bit boring. But tact, or a fear of being accused of slander, perhaps, restrained him from presenting Wilson that way in print.

The nature of Byrd's revisions suggests that he wished to present himself and his fellow commissioners to readers in London as gentlemen. The later account describes the men as "reposing about an hour," after which they "recommended vigor and constancy to their fellow travelers." What in Byrd's original journal indicates that he privately viewed Firebrand, the commissioner, as considerably less than a gentleman?

The differences between Byrd's two versions illustrate the fact that a writer almost always composes with a reader in mind. In wishing to appear before the reader as a certain kind of person—tolerant, brave, or smart—the writer almost always censors and transforms the original experience. Thus, part of the meaning of any piece of writing is the reader.

Language and Vocabulary

Using Context to Derive Meaning

The **context** of a word refers to the words that surround it and to the situation in which it is used. The context may slightly change the meaning of a familiar word. Context clues make it possible to guess the meaning of an unfamiliar word.

Consider the first sentence of Byrd's fourth paragraph:

Although there was no need for example to inflame persons already so cheerful, yet to enter the people with better grace, the author and two more of the commissioners accompanied them half a mile into the Dismal.

Inflame, meaning "to set on fire," is probably a familiar word to you. But the context calls for a different meaning. Byrd tells us that the men are *cheerful* despite their heavy work. He changes the literal meaning of *inflame* by linking it with *cheerful.* In this context, *inflame* means not "to set on fire" but "to arouse." Byrd's sentence could be rewritten: "The men were already so cheerful, there was no need to try to lift their spirits."

In some cases, of course, context will not be a sufficient clue to meaning. In other cases, the context may be ambiguous, and you may make a wrong guess. Whenever you are unsure of the meaning of an unfamiliar word, look up the word in a dictionary. But in many cases, guessing the meaning of a word from its context will save you the trouble of looking it up and will increase the ease of your reading and your appreciation of the selection.

Use the context of the following sentences to guess the meaning of the italicized words. If you cannot arrive at the meaning, refer to the dictionary. Be able to explain how you arrived at your definition.

1. . . . we found the ground moist and trembling under our feet like a *quagmire* . . .
2. Two of the men, whose burdens were the least *cumbersome,* had orders to march before with their tomahawks and clear the way. . . .
3. At the same time they were laboring with their hands to cut down the reeds, which were ten feet high, their legs were *hampered* with the briers.
4. And, indeed, it was a little *provoking* to hear the wind whistling among the branches of the white cedars, which grew here and there amongst the reeds, and at the same time not have the comfort to feel the least breath of it.

Yale University Art Gallery, New Haven, Connecticut

Rev. Jonathan Edwards. Oil on canvas
by Joseph Badger (1708–1765).

The Puritan minister Jonathan Edwards once wrote a short treatise entitled "Of Insects." In it he recorded his observations of spiders as they sailed from tree to tree, and from their behavior he drew the conclusion that everything in God's universe exists for some purpose. The surprising fact about "Of Insects" is neither that its descriptions of insects are exact nor that its arguments are ingenious, but that Edwards wrote it when he was eleven years old.

Born in East Windsor, Connecticut, in 1703, Edwards entered Yale College at the age of thirteen. Soon he began writing philosophical works on the nature of existence and of the mind. At the age of seventeen he discovered that thunder and lightning no longer terrified him. Indeed, he now found them beautiful—one of the several signs that made him certain he had experienced grace. In his early twenties he married Sarah Pierrepont of New Haven, a woman as otherworldly and absorbed in God as he, and began preaching at one of the leading American churches, in Northampton, Massachusetts.

Edwards' power as a preacher became evident during the Great Awakening, the revival of religious fervor that swept the American colonies from about 1735 to 1742. Suddenly, people all over America began denouncing their sins and dedicating themselves anew to God. During this time Edwards wrote and preached such sermons as "Sinners in the Hands of an Angry God," which aroused his listeners to frenzy. As he depicted the furnace of eternal torturous fire awaiting sinners, members of the congregation began calling out, "What shall I do to be saved? Oh, I am going to Hell—Oh what shall I do for Christ?" One listener wrote that the "shrieks and cries were piercing and amazing"; the "great moaning and crying" forced Edwards to stop before he had finished preaching the sermon. Edwards approved of such outbursts but feared that they might sometimes arise not from sincere religious feeling but from delusion or hysteria. In fact, the Great Awakening did not last long.

Edwards' passionate conviction brought him fame but also antagonism. As happened to Edward Taylor, his insistence on grace as the essence of religious life displeased many members of his Northampton church. In 1750 the church dismissed him as minister. He moved to the raw town of Stockbridge, Massachusetts, where he preached to Indians and wrote several of his longest works, works of rigorous logic such as *Freedom of the Will* (1754) and *The Nature of True Virtue* (published in 1765). In 1757 he was elected president of Princeton University, but he died just after taking office, from the effects of a smallpox inoculation.

Edwards' writings remained popular, helping to keep Puritan ideas alive even after Puritanism had vanished. His method of reading nature as a representation of spiritual truth, for instance, survives in the attempts of Henry David Thoreau to read moral meanings in the beans and pickerel at Walden Pond. Edwards' works endured because he was a great writer, able to express in seemingly simple prose a subtle and complex vision of human life. He and Benjamin Franklin were the first of the American writers to show the Old World that the New World could produce its share of genius.

Sarah Pierrepont

According to legend, Edwards, when he was twenty years old, wrote this brief address to his future wife before he had ever seen her.

They say there is a young lady in [New Haven] who is beloved of that Great Being, who made and rules the world, and that there are certain seasons in which this Great Being, in some way or other invisible, comes to her and fills her mind with exceeding sweet delight, and that she hardly cares for anything, except to meditate on him—that she expects after a while to be received up where he is, to be raised up out of the world and caught up into heaven; being assured that he loves her too well to let her remain at a distance from him always. There she is to dwell with him, and to be ravished with his love and delight forever. Therefore, if you present all the world before her, with the richest of its treasures, she disregards it and cares not for it, and is unmindful of any pain or affliction. She has a strange sweetness in her mind, and singular purity in her affections; is most just and conscientious in all her conduct; and you could not persuade her to do anything wrong or sinful, if you would give her all the world, lest she should offend this Great Being. She is of a wonderful sweetness, calmness and universal benevolence of mind; especially after this Great God has manifested himself to her mind. She will sometimes go about from place to place, singing sweetly; and seems to be always full of joy and pleasure; and no one knows for what. She loves to be alone, walking in the fields and groves, and seems to have someone invisible always conversing with her.

FROM

Sinners in the Hands of an Angry God

. . . [T]here is nothing between you and Hell but the air; it is only the power and mere pleasure of God that holds you up.

You probably are not sensible of this; you find you are kept out of Hell, but do not see the hand of God in it, but look at other things, as the good state of your bodily constitution, your care of your own life, and the means you use for your own preservation. But indeed these things are nothing; if God should withdraw his hand, they would avail no more to keep you from falling than the thin air to hold up a person that is suspended in it.

Your wickedness makes you as it were heavy as lead, and to tend downwards with great weight and pressure towards Hell; and if God should let you go, you would immediately sink and swiftly descend and plunge into the bottomless gulf, and your healthy constitution, and your own care and prudence, and best contrivance, and all your righteousness, would have no more influence to uphold you and keep you out of Hell than a spider's web would have to stop a falling rock. . . . There are the black clouds of God's wrath now hanging directly over your heads, full of the dreadful storm, and big with thunder; and were it not for the restraining hand of God it would immediately burst forth upon you. The sovereign pleasure of God for the present stays[1] his rough wind; otherwise it would come with fury, and your destruction would come like a whirlwind, and you would be like the chaff of the summer threshing floor.

The wrath of God is like great waters that are dammed for the present; they increase more and more, and rise higher and higher, till an outlet is given; and the longer the stream is stopped, the more rapid and mighty is its course when once it is let loose. 'Tis true that judgment against your evil works has not been executed hitherto; the floods of God's vengeance have been withheld; but your guilt in the meantime is constantly increasing, and you are every day treasuring up more wrath; the waters are continually rising and waxing more and more mighty; and there is nothing but the mere pleasure of God that holds the waters back that are unwilling to be stopped, and press hard to go forward; if God should only withdraw his hand from the floodgate, it would immediately fly open, and the fiery floods of the fierceness and wrath of God would rush forth with inconceivable fury, and would come upon you with omnipotent power; and if your strength were ten thousand times greater than it is, yea, ten thousand times greater than the strength of the stoutest, sturdiest devil in Hell, it would be nothing to withstand or endure it.

The bow of God's wrath is bent, and the arrow made ready on the string, and justice bends the arrow at your heart, and strains the bow, and it is nothing but the mere pleasure of God, and that of an angry God, without any promise or obligation at all, that keeps the arrow one moment from being made drunk with your blood.

Thus are all you that never passed under a great change of heart, by the mighty power of the Spirit of God upon your souls; all that were never born again, and made new creatures, and raised from being dead in sin, to a state of new and before altogether unexperienced light and life (however you may have reformed your life in many things, and may have had religious affections, and may keep up a form of religion in your families and closets,[2] and in the house of God, and may be strict in it), you are thus in the hands of an angry God; 'tis nothing but his mere pleasure that keeps you from being this moment swallowed up in everlasting destruction.

However unconvinced you may now be of the truth of what you hear, by and by you will be fully convinced of it. Those that are gone from being in the like circumstances with you, see that it was so with them; for destruction came suddenly upon most of them, when they expected nothing of it, and while they were saying, "Peace and safety": now they see that those things on which they depended for peace and safety were nothing but thin air and empty shadows.

The God that holds you over the pit of Hell, much as one holds a spider, or some loathsome insect, over the fire, abhors you, and is dreadfully provoked; his wrath towards you burns like fire; he looks upon you as worthy of nothing else but to be cast into the fire; he is of purer eyes than to bear to have you in his sight; you are ten thousand times more abominable in his eyes than the most hateful venomous serpent is in ours. . . .

O sinner! Consider the fearful danger you are in: 'tis a great furnace of wrath, a wide and bottomless pit, full of the fire of wrath, that you are held over in the hand of that God, whose wrath is provoked and incensed as much against you as against many of the damned in Hell: you hang by a slender thread, with the flames of divine wrath flashing about it, and ready every moment to singe it, and burn it asunder; and you have no interest in any mediator, and nothing to lay hold of to save yourself, nothing to keep off the flames of wrath, nothing of your own, nothing that

---

1. **stays:** restrains.

2. **closets:** private rooms.

𝕭𝖑𝖆𝖟𝖎𝖓𝖌=𝕾𝖙𝖆𝖗𝖘
Meſſengers of GOD's Wrath:
In a few ſerious and ſolemn Meditations upon the wonderful

COMET:

Which now appears in our Horizon, *April*, 1759 : Together with a ſolemn Caⅼⅼ to Sinners, and Counⅽⅼ to Saints ; how to behave themſelves when GOD is in this wiſe ſpeaking to them from Heaven.

CANST thou by ſearching find out *God*,
 The high and Holy one,
Or the almighty Majeſty,
 Unto Perfection.
Where waſt thou, ſaith th'eternal GOD,
 To *Job*, that holy Man,
When I the Earth's Foundations laid,
 Declare now if you can.
When th'Morning Stars together ſang,
 With glorious Melody,
And all the Sons of GOD did ſhout
 With loud triumphant Joy ?
Where is the Place where Light doth dwell,
 And as for Darkneſs, where ?
If thou doſt know its vaſt Receſs,
 My Servant now declare.
The lovely Pſalmiſt, when he'd ſpread
 The great JEHOVAH's Fame,
Declares,---He numbers all the Stars,
 And calls them all by Name.
That Fire, and Miſt, and Hail, and Snow,
 Whirlwinds with one Accord,
Obey the holy juſt Command
 Of their moſt glorious Lord.
And in the Time of *Iſrael's* Straights,
 That awful Day,
The Stars in martial Order fought,
 'Gainſt wicked *Siſera*.
Theſe are among the wond'rous Works
 Of the eternal ONE,
Who alſo chearfully obey,
 When he ſpeaks, lo ! tis done,
He bids them ſtand o'er Kingdoms, Towns,
 All in a flaming Fire ;
And great Attention to his Voice,
 The Lord doth now require.
The ancient Fathers learn'd and wiſe,
 When they did ſee them burn,
Prognoſticated evil Things,
 Soon on the World would come.
Heralds of GOD his Meſſengers,
 The World to preach unto,
And learn'd and wiſe and holy Men
 Fully agree thereto.
O what amazing Changes, have

An hundred Inſtances or more
 I might have added here,
But by two faithful Witneſſes
 Great Truths eſtabliſh'd are.
In ſixteen hundred ſixty four
 Behold in lofty Sky,
A flaming Comet did appear
 Large and conſpicuouſly.
Soon after which moſt awful Sight
 A bloody War began
'Twixt *England* and the *Hollanders*
 Moſt violent did become.
An awful Plague in *England* too
 As ever had been known,
Near Seven Thouſand in one Week,
 Unto the Pit went down.
That in the Space of but one Year,
 An hundred thouſand fell,
Victims unto voracious Death,
 An awful Spectacle.
Soon after which, even the next Year,
 The *Papiſt* do conſpire,
And by their Craft and Subtilty,
 LONDON they ſet on Fire.
Behold vaſt Clouds of Smoke aſcend,
 And fill the Clouds you,
By means whereof the Moon was dark
 And Sun became like Blood.
In ſixteen Hundred ſixty five
 In our Hemiſphere,
A burning blazing Comet did
 For many Nights appear.
Which follow'd was with ſcorching Drought
 In *Britain*, and this Land,
And might have ſoon deſtroy'd us all,
 Hadn't GOD witheld his Hand.
Thus we were ſpar'd ; but O behold,
 What awful Trouble fell,
On many Places in the World
 No Tongue can fully tell.
To name but one or two dear Soul's
 Or more if you require,
In *Hungary* four hundred Towns
 Deſtroy'd by Sword and Fire.
Great Floods o'erflow'd the *Netherlands*,

A fam'd Philoſopher of old,
 Conjectur'd that before
The mighty GOD to Judgment comes
 In his majeſtick Power ;
Comets and fearful Sights more brief
 Then ever yet have been,
More frequently and commonly
 Would in the World be ſeen,
And are not we now Witneſſes,
 Let all our Fathers ſay,
If ever GOD before them paſt
 In ſuch awful Way.

IMPROVEMENT.

AND now O Earth, O Earth attend,
 The mighty Voice of GOD,
Who in his Wrath is coming down
 By Sickneſs ; Fire and Sword.
GOD calls aloud, awake, awake,
 And from your Slumber riſe,
When in the Heavens he ſets ſuch Sights
 Of Wonder and Surprize.
Adore the mighty ſovereign LORD
 And bow before him low,
Who ſends his timely Warnings forth
 Before he ſtrikes the Blow.
Prepare, O Land, prepare for what
 The LORD's about to do,
For what awful Events are nigh
 The LORD alone doth know.
Unto your Chambers enter ſtrait
 GOD's Folk, and ſhut the Door,
Till all the Storms of his fierce Wrath
 Shall all be paſt and o'er.
And O you chriſtleſs graceleſs Souls,
 Can you abide GOD's Power ?
When out of *Zion* he will ſhout
 And as a Lion roar.
When all his Wrath ſet in array
 Againſt your Souls will blaze,
O tell me Sinner, tell me where
 You'l find a ſecure Place.
If Death o'ertakes you in your Sins
 Then down to Hell you muſt,
And with the Priſoners there in Chains
 Eternally be curs'd.

Broadside from 1759.
The New-York Historical Society

you ever have done, nothing that you can do, to induce God to spare you one moment. . . .

How dreadful is the state of those that are daily and hourly in the danger of this great wrath and infinite misery! But this is the dismal case of every soul in this congregation that has not been born again, however moral and strict, sober and religious, they may otherwise be. Oh that you would consider it, whether you be young or old! There is reason to think that there are many in this congregation now hearing this discourse, that will actually be the subjects of this very misery to all eternity. We know not who they are, or in what seats they sit or what thoughts they now have: it may be they are now at ease, and hear all these things without much disturbance, and are now flattering themselves that they are not the persons, promising themselves that they shall escape. If we knew that there was one person, and but one, in the whole congregation, that was to be the subject of this misery, what an awful thing would it be to think of! If we knew who it was, what an awful sight would it be to see such a person! How might all the rest of the congregation lift up a lamentable and bitter cry over him! But alas! Instead of one, how many is it likely will remember this discourse in Hell? And it would be a wonder if some that are now present should not be in Hell in a very short time, before this year is out. And it would be no wonder if some person that now sits here in some seat of this meetinghouse in health, and quiet and secure, should be there before tomorrow morning. Those of you that finally continue in a natural condition, that shall keep out of Hell longest, will be there in a little time! Your damnation does not slumber; it will come swiftly, and in all probability very suddenly upon many of you. You have reason to wonder that you are not already in Hell. 'Tis doubtless the case of some that heretofore you have seen and known, that never deserved Hell more than you, and that heretofore appeared as likely to have been now alive as you; their case is past all hope; they are crying in extreme misery and perfect despair; but here you are in the land of the living, and in the house of God, and have an opportunity to obtain salvation. What would not those poor damned, helpless souls give for one day's opportunity such as you now enjoy!

And now you have an extraordinary opportunity, a day wherein Christ has thrown the door of mercy wide open, and stands in the door calling and crying with a loud voice to poor sinners; a day wherein many are flocking to him, and pressing into the kingdom of God. Many are daily coming from the east, west, north and south; many that were very lately in the same miserable condition that you are in, are now in a happy state, with their hearts filled with love to him that has loved them and washed them from their sins in his own blood, and rejoicing in hope of the glory of God. How awful is it to be left behind at such a day! To see so many others feasting, while you are pining and perishing! To see so many rejoicing and singing for joy of heart, while you have cause to mourn for sorrow of heart, and howl for vexation of spirit! How can you rest one moment in such a condition? . . .

Therefore let everyone that is out of Christ now awake and fly from the wrath to come. The wrath of Almighty God is now undoubtedly hanging over a great part of this congregation: let everyone fly out of Sodom.[3] "Haste and escape for your lives, look not behind you, escape to the mountain, lest you be consumed."[4]

3. **Sodom:** in the Bible, a city destroyed because of its people's sinfulness.
4. **Haste . . . consumed:** from Genesis 19:17, the angels' warning to Lot, the one upright man in Sodom.

Reading Check

1. What warning does Edwards deliver to his congregation?
2. What does Edwards consider essential for salvation?
3. According to Edwards, why isn't it enough to be moral, sober, and religious?

For Study and Discussion

Analyzing and Interpreting the Selections

Sarah Pierrepont

1. In this sketch of the woman who became his wife, Edwards describes someone under the influence of grace. What details in the address create a picture of Sarah Pierrepont as "strange" and "singular"?

2. In one form or another, Edwards repeats the word *sweet* four times. How can *sweet* be said to summarize Sarah's personality?

Sinners in the Hands of an Angry God

1. Edwards compares God's wrath to several things. **a.** Cite at least three comparisons. **b.** How do these comparisons heighten one's awareness of humanity's perilous state?

2. In this sermon, Edwards speaks of an angry God. Yet in another of his writings, Edwards speaks of God as "majesty and meekness joined together." **a.** Where in the sermon is God also shown to be merciful? **b.** What vision of hope does Edwards offer to his congregation?

Literary Elements

The Forms of Discourse: Persuasion

The discussion on page 22 points out that writing can be classified by four types of discourse: persuasion, exposition, description, and narration. Edwards' sermon is an instance of writing as persuasion, in which the writer tries to convince the audience to adopt some opinion or take some action, or do both. What actions does Edwards wish his audience to take?

To analyze a piece of persuasive writing, one should consider four elements: the speaker, the audience, the occasion, and the means of persuasion.

The speaker. Speakers or writers who seek to persuade usually try to show they are well qualified to offer an opinion. They do so by implying that they have special knowledge of the subject or are like the audience and can therefore speak for them. To some extent, Edwards' sermon must have been persuasive to his audience simply because they knew Edwards himself to be a brilliant and virtuous man. Several times in the sermon, however, Edwards also implies that he has greater knowledge of the problem of salvation than does his audience. Find three examples of this technique of persuasion in the sermon.

The audience. A speech or piece of writing is often designed to appeal to a particular audience. For example, a television commercial for a toy, meant to appeal to children, is written differently from a commercial for a detergent, meant to appeal to homemakers. In the sixth paragraph Edwards speaks to his audience intimately. What does the paragraph tell us about the people in Edwards' audience? How does he try to appeal to this particular group of people?

The occasion. Many persuasive works are written for a special occasion. The occasion itself may become an argument supporting the other arguments of the work. Edwards preached his sermon during the religious revival, the Great Awakening. Reread the next-to-last paragraph and tell how Edwards draws on the occasion of the revival to support his other arguments.

The means of persuasion. Many techniques have been developed to change people's minds. A persuasive writer or speaker may argue logically, may appeal to past traditions or to authorities on the subject, or may work on the audience's emotions. Edwards especially appeals to authority and to emotion. Several times he refers to the authority of the Bible to support his own arguments. In appealing to emotion, Edwards uses devices often found in poetry and fiction. For example, to dramatize the danger his listeners stand in by not having undergone "a great change of heart"—that is, by not having experienced grace—he fills his sermon with sharp imagery. What images of sudden danger and imminent destruction does he use in the third and fourth paragraphs? To what does Edwards compare human beings?

Analyze a modern example of persuasion, perhaps a newspaper editorial, political speech, or television commercial. Discuss the four aspects of persuasive writing: What sort of person is the speaker? To what kinds of people is the message addressed? What is the occasion? What are the means of persuasion?

Conclude your analysis with a summary of the idea or argument expressed in your example of persuasion. Then, if you like, offer an opinion in favor of or against this argument, keeping in mind the four elements of persuasive writing.

FROM

Language on the American Frontier

FREDERIC G. CASSIDY

We may now look in some detail at the elements of which the new American English was formed. When the words which the colonists had brought proved inadequate to the new environment, they responded in three chief ways: they borrowed from the Indians or from other Europeans, they gave new meanings to old words, they made new combinations. It is interesting to notice at what time the various Indian words, for example, came in. Naturally enough, the first of these were the names of animals and plants of the new world, especially those valuable for food.

Even before 1620, *moose, raccoon, opossum, terrapin, persimmon, moccasin, tomahawk,* and *totem* had entered the English language. Within the next thirty years, by the middle of the century, *muskrat, sachem, papoose, quahog, hominy, powwow, skunk, squash, squaw, wampum,* and *wigwam* had followed. Still other seventeenth-century borrowings were *hickory, manitou, woodchuck,* and *Tammany.* Eighteenth-century additions are *pecan, muskellunge, Catawba, succotash, catalpa, caucus;* and the nineteenth century saw the adoption of *chipmunk, sequoia, tamarack, mugwump, mackinaw, teepee, cayuse,* and climactically, at the very end of the century, *hooch.*

Some of these Indian words did not come directly: both *bayou* and *cisco* came through French—*bayou* in Louisiana from Choctaw *bayuk,* and *cisco* in the Great Lakes area. The name of this fish, *cisco,* is in fact an abbreviation of French *ciscoette,* itself an abbreviation of the Ojibwa *pemitewiskawet.* Thus, these Indian words have been naturalized first into French, then into English, the *-ette* suffix probably due to analogy with the common suffix that we

have also borrowed in such words as *cigarette* and *quartette,* and the first syllable of *bayou* probably recalling French *baie.* The French habit of abbreviating long Indian words for simplicity is seen not only in *ciscoette,* but also in *caribou,* which they reduced from Algonkian *buccarebou.* They also shortened Indian tribal names: *Sioux* is all that they left of *Nadouessioux,* and the *ark of Ozark* is their abbreviation of *Arkansas.*

Another thing to notice is the succession of borrowings as the moving frontier brought the whites into contact with different tribes. Early loans were mostly from Algonkian languages, a few from Iroquois; across the Mississippi, more words were taken from the Sioux; still later the languages of the Northwest and Southwest were levied upon. We have two well-known words for an Indian dwelling: *wigwam* taken before 1628 from Algonkian, and *teepee* taken before 1872 from Siouan. *Hooch* is a western word, abbreviated from Tlingit *hootsnuwu.*

Indian terms have entered strikingly into our political language. The *powwows* of the red men, with their big meetings, deliberations, oratory, and dances—aided often enough by the white men's firewater—struck a responsive chord. Not only *powwow,* but *mugwump, Tammany, sachem,* and others testify to this influence. Nor should we forget that from Indian sources have come into the language a host of American place names, some euphonious, like *Ohio* and *Missouri,* others that fall less comfortably upon the ear, like *Ogunquit, Walla Walla, Keokuk, Puyallup,* and the now proverbial *Podunk.*

In the process of naturalization, words are not only abbreviated and otherwise simplified in pronunciation, but many are frankly made over and suited to English word patterns. The notorious example of this process is *woodchuck*, which makes us think of an animal which lives in the *woods*, and *chucks*. Everybody knows, of course, *what* it chucks, though nobody is certain how much it would if it could. All this accretion of nursery lore is due entirely to the naturalization of the word by speakers of *English:* its original in Algonkian has no such implications—it is simply the name for a kind of weasel, *wejack*, mistakenly applied.

As to the words which English-speakers on the American frontier borrowed from other Europeans, the chief sources were, of course, French and Spanish, though Dutch and German have also added their bit. The far-flung French outposts and colonies in the Great Lakes and Mississippi system have furnished several geographical terms: *butte, coulee* (probably first adopted in Wisconsin), *sault (Sault Ste. Marie* is the best known), *rapids, prairie.* From the intrepid *voyageurs* and *coureurs de bois* who made first contacts with the Indians of the interior come *portage* and *cache, calumet* and *lacrosse.* But the French loans have entered at every cultural level from the most homely upward: *shivaree* and *sashay, pumpkin* and *chowder, bureau* and *depot, cent, dime,* and *picayune,* and the word that has become utterly American in atmosphere of song and story—*levee.*

The direct Spanish influence came somewhat later but has been very marked and is still continuing. Few of our state names show the influence of French—*Vermont, Louisiana, Illinois,* possibly some others; many more are Spanish—*Florida, California, Nevada, Colorado, Arizona, Montana.* From Spanish have come the topographic terms *arroyo, mesa, canyon, sierra,* and *savannah,* to say nothing of *tornado.* Spanish names for plants and animals are particularly numerous: *alfalfa, marijuana, mosquito, bonito, palomino, armadillo, alligator* are purely Spanish, but the Spaniards have also passed on to us such originally Indian words as *avo-cado, yucca, mesquite, coyote,* and now *peyote.* We have discarded the name of the fish *tunny,* which came into British use through French, and have substituted the American word *tuna,* which came to us from the Spanish—who, by the way, got it from the English to begin with!

I will not attempt to go through the whole list of Spanish loans—it is too long; but let me at least suggest the fields to which these words belong. Food and drink—*tamale, barbecue, chili con carne, cafeteria;* building—*adobe, patio, plaza, pueblo;* clothing—*chaps, poncho, sombrero,* ten *gallon* hat; ranch life—*rodeo, stampede, corral, lariat, bronco, buckaroo, mustang;* legal and penal—*hoosegow, calaboose, desperado, vigilante;* mining—*bonanza* and *placer.*

Let me touch next, rapidly, on the Dutch and German loans. The Dutch, of course, had a successful colony centrally placed in the lower Hudson valley. From this point, their influence spread into southeastern New England, up the Hudson, and into New Jersey. Overrun by superior numbers, they nevertheless left several words that are essential to American English—some of which, indeed, have gone around the world—so *Yankee, boss,* and *Santa Claus.* Others in daily use are *cookie, cole slaw, caboose, scow, snoop,* and *spook.* German loans came considerably later and mostly refer to foods—*delicatessen, frankfurter, hamburger, wiener, noodle, pretzel, sauerkraut,* and so on; but some relate to education—*kindergarten, semester, seminar;* and to various other things less uplifting—*loafer, bum, dumb* (in the sense of stupid), *pinochle,* and *spiel.* Even the exclamation *ouch* is German, and the new suffix *-fest,* used in popular combinations such as *slug-fest* in boxing, *run-fest* in baseball, and *talk-fest,* which may be found at any *coffee-clutch.*

So much for foreign elements—there is no time to mention others taken from the Africans, the Irish, the Chinese, the Jews. All were incorporated in the flowing lava of the frontier and have become an inseparable part of it. We turn next to the English words which acquired a new meaning under frontier conditions. One remarkable example is the word *lumber.* In

England it had meant, and still means, castoff material of any sort—what most Americans would call *junk*. The first task of the settlers in the new land, however, was to make clearings in the forest primeval. Trees were in the way; when cut down, they lay about everywhere. The wood from them, in fact, was so much lumber, in the old sense of the word. So it naturally acquired the new sense of *wood*, and by now *lumber* has displaced *timber* as the general term.

One other notorious example: *corn* in the old country had meant grain of any sort— wheat, barley, oats. On the American frontier, the new grain which was the most accessible and best suited to the climate, upon which the Indians depended and which they taught the white man to grow, was *maize*. The settlers began by calling it *Indian corn,* but that was immediately abbreviated to plain *corn*. From it was made *pone, hominy, suppawn, succotash.* American settlers adopted all of these—they even made it the basis of a drink. In Dr. Mitford Mathews' *Dictionary of Americanisms,* published in 1951, are listed no less than 151 words and phrases in which corn is used in its new sense—*cornbread, cornsilk, corn belt, cornbird, corn-cracker* are just a few of the commoner ones.

Then there is the third way in which the vocabulary has been increased: by forming new combinations. These too are very numerous, but a few of the more striking may be offered in approximately the order of their creation. From the seventeenth century: *log house, snowshoe, pine knot, bayberry;* from the eighteenth century: *salt lick, mountain laurel, horse-thief, minuteman, cotton gin;* and from the nineteenth century: *cocktail, gerrymander, sod fence, Indian giver, know-nothing, stern-wheeler, cowboy, mail order,* and *sideburns.*

The intimate connection of language with the frontier cannot be better demonstrated, however, than by showing the additions made in the course of a single exploration. Fortunately, the most famous one has been studied in Dr. E. H. Criswell's work entitled *Lewis and Clark: Linguistic Pioneers.* The expedition lasted some twenty-eight months, from May, 1804, till September, 1806, and went from St. Louis through the Louisiana Territory to the Pacific and back. Of the 29 regular members of the group, nine are believed to have kept journals, and seven of these journals survive. Dr. Criswell has digested these painstakingly and offers the following conclusions: The seven writers, among them, used 1,107 Americanisms of all kinds, of which 583 were unrecorded before. In addition, their use of 301 words, meanings, and combinations is the earliest on record. As to the source of the words, 143 were new adoptions, 86 were words that were going out of use in Britain, and 91 were survivals of words already obsolete in Britain but still alive in America. A large number are names of fauna and flora newly encountered, and many relate to Indians, but there are all kinds. Examples of fresh combinations are *beaver pond, council lodge, tow-cord, Indian mush, melon-bug.* Some old words that acquire new meanings are *goldfinch, apron, button, run, bear claw.* The additions to the language made by this one expedition are impressive. Yet they represent only one small record, one small insight into what was a continuous, ebullient language activity by millions of others—scouts, Indian fighters, trappers, miners, settlers—a vast part of which went *un*recorded. There can be no question that hundreds of the verbal creations that bubbled up along the hot fringe of the frontier are now irrecoverably lost.

For Study and Discussion

1a. What does Cassidy mean by "the process of naturalization"? **b.** What examples does he give of Indian words naturalized into French and into English?

2. Cassidy gives two examples of specialization (the meaning of a word changing to a narrower meaning). **a.** What are these two words? **b.** What were their original meanings and what did they change to?

The Beginnings of the American Tradition

Each of the following statements may be used as the basis of a composition about early American literature:

1. In the genuine Puritan tradition, character and morality are seen as permanent values achievable only by personal spiritual conquest, life is constantly spiritualized, and the humblest events and acts are related to a divine context.

   > Kenneth B. Murdock
   > (from "The Puritan Legacy")

   What evidence can you find in the selections you have read in this unit to support this statement? Write an essay, referring to specific passages in the works of William Bradford, Anne Bradstreet, Edward Taylor, and Jonathan Edwards.

2. What the early colonists wrote was realistic, rarely sentimental. . . . The necessity to confront daily foes in both the physical and spiritual worlds gave their writing distinctive toughness; as their outlook on life was free of gaudiness and irrelevance, so their literature was one of strength.

   > Russel B. Nye
   > (from *American Literary History 1607–1830*)

   In an essay, discuss this statement in light of the literature you have read in this unit. Be sure to consider the works of John Smith, William Bradford, and William Byrd.

3. Although differences have been noted in the literature of the Southern and New England colonies, there are also points of similarity: (1) Early American literature does not exist as an end in itself, but serves some practical purpose, whether it is a guide to virtuous living or a narrative of a boundary survey; (2) Literature reflects the writer's keen powers of observation, whether in recording the external life—the natural features of the land—or in examining the internal life; (3) Writing is plain and realistic—it makes use of everyday language and experience.

   In an essay, discuss this statement in relation to any four authors whose work you have read in this unit.

For Further Reading

For General Background

Boorstin, Daniel J., *The Americans: The Colonial Experience* (Random House, 1958)

Davis, Richard Beale, *Intellectual Life in the Colonial South, 1585–1763*, 3 vols. (University of Tennessee Press, 1978)

Heimert, Alan, and Andrew Delbanco, eds., *The Puritans in America: A Narrative Anthology* (Harvard University Press, 1985)

Miller, Perry, and Thomas H. Johnson, eds., *The Puritans* (Harper Torchbooks, 1963)

Morison, Samuel Eliot, *Builders of the Bay Colony* (Houghton Mifflin, 1964)

Nye, Russel B., *American Literary History 1607–1830* (Knopf, 1970)

Narratives of Exploration

Hodge, Frederick W., and Theodore H. Lewis, eds., *Spanish Explorers in the Southern United States: 1528–1543* (Charles Scribner's Sons, 1907, rpt. 1977)
  Contains narratives of expeditions of Cabeza de Vaca, De Soto, and Coronado.

For Background on Individual Authors

Smith

Barbour, Philip L., *The Three Worlds of Captain John Smith* (Houghton Mifflin, 1964)

Smith, Bradford, *Captain John Smith: His Life and Legend* (Lippincott, 1953)

Bradford

Fleming, Thomas J., *One Small Candle* (Norton, 1976)

Bradstreet

Stanford, Ann, *Anne Bradstreet: The Worldly Puritan* (Burt Franklin & Co., 1975)

White, Elizabeth Wade, *Anne Bradstreet: The Tenth Muse* (Oxford University Press, 1971)

Taylor

Grabo, Norman S., *Edward Taylor* (Twayne, 1961)

Keller, Karl, *The Example of Edward Taylor* (University of Massachusetts Press, 1975)

Byrd

Marambaud, Pierre L., *William Byrd of Westover 1674–1744* (University Press of Virginia, 1971)

Edwards

Winslow, Ola Elizabeth, *Jonathan Edwards 1703–1758* (1940; rpt. Collier Books, 1961)

George Washington at Verplanck's Point, New York, 1782 by John Trumbull (1756–1843). Oil on canvas.
Courtesy, The Henry Francis du Pont Winterthur Museum

THE REVOLUTIONARY PERIOD
1760–1800

Like the Puritans and the first Southern settlers, Americans who lived through the second half of the eighteenth century often wrote in order to understand and report on their lives in the New World. But they wrote in a different spirit from that of the earlier writers. A single event commanded their attention, and the America they lived in was no longer a wilderness.

The Age of Reason

Writers of this period were all conscious of belonging to what is called the Age of Reason. Whether English or American, they believed that by using reason human beings could manage themselves and their societies without depending on authorities and past traditions. Reason, they also believed, thrived on freedom—freedom of speech, freedom from arbitrary rulers, freedom to experiment, freedom especially to question existing laws and institutions. By the free use of reason, human beings could progress: social evils could be corrected, superstition and ignorance ended, and the general quality of existence improved.

The leading writers of the period concerned themselves with the state of life on earth. Unlike the Puritans, they had little interest in the hereafter or the supernatural. They tended to write on science, ethics, or government rather than on religion. Typical of the spirit of the Age of Reason are such men as Benjamin Franklin and Thomas Jefferson—Franklin by his ingenious inventions designed to make life more comfortable, Jefferson by his hatred of any restriction on human inquiry, and both men by their love of moderation and order.

Americans of the Age of Reason differed in one dramatic way, however, from their English contemporaries. They were given the chance to test their ideas about freedom and progress by creating a new society. The chance came when the thirteen colonies decided—or, as they felt, were forced—to become independent.

The American Revolution

The American Revolution was fought not only with muskets but also with thousands of pamphlets, essays, songs, poems, and speeches. As had not been true earlier, citizens of New England, of the South, and of the Middle Colonies began writing about a single, vastly important subject. In doing so they began to think of themselves not as New Yorkers or Rhode Islanders or Virginians, but as Americans.

The war of words began around 1763. The English government started a program of taxing the colonies to help pay the costs of the French and Indian War and of protecting America from other European nations in the future. Americans wrote, argued, and dem-

THE FRUITS OF ARBITRARY POWER, OR THE BLOODY MASSACRE,

Boston Massacre, or "Fruits of Arbitrary Power" by Henry Pelham (1749–1806).

onstrated against the taxes noisily enough to persuade England to
withdraw the Stamp Act of 1765. Fearing that such a retreat would
be taken for weakness, England imposed a new tax program in 1767,
the Townshend Acts. When Americans again reacted with angry
essays and speeches, and refused to buy English products as well,
the mother country sent eight hundred soldiers into Boston. On
March 5, 1770, the troops killed five persons on King Street.
After this "Boston Massacre," Britain again backed down, withdrawing both the Townshend Acts and the troops.

Introduction   **67**

1723	BENJAMIN FRANKLIN (1706–1790) arrives in Philadelphia
	FRANKLIN *Poor Richard's Almanack* (1732–1757)
1740–1745	The "Great Awakening"
1752	Franklin experiments with lightning; discovers it is electrical
1754–1763	French and Indian War
1765	Stamp Act
1767	Townshend Acts
	First American play produced, *The Prince of Parthia* (1767)
1770	Boston Massacre
	FRANKLIN begins *Autobiography* (1771)
1773	Boston Tea Party
	PHILLIS WHEATLEY (1753?–1784) *Poems on Various Subjects, Religious and Moral* (1773)
1774	First Continental Congress assembles in Philadelphia
1775–1783	Revolutionary War

Benjamin Franklin

Boston Massacre

The Declaration of Independence

Thomas Paine

Thomas Jefferson

PATRICK HENRY (1736–1799)
"Speech in the Virginia Convention" (1775)

1775 — Battle of Lexington and Concord

Second Continental Congress assembles in
Philadelphia (1775)

THOMAS PAINE (1737–1809)
Common Sense (1776);
The Crisis (1776–1783)

THOMAS JEFFERSON (1743–1826)
The Declaration of Independence (1776)

1778 — Treaty of Alliance with France

1781 — Cornwallis surrenders to Washington at Yorktown,
Virginia, ending all serious fighting on the American
continent

MICHEL-GUILLAUME JEAN DE CRÈVECOEUR
(1735–1813)
Letters from an American Farmer (1782)

1788 — Ratification of Constitution

1789 — George Washington inaugurated as first President of
the United States

First American novel published, *The Power of Sympathy*
(1789)

1800 — Washington, D.C., named capital of the United States

Peace and quiet followed, but only for three years. In 1773 Parliament set a new tax on tea. That December, some Bostonians dumped chests full of the taxed tea into their harbor—an event that became known as the Boston Tea Party. Parliament decided to punish not only the demonstrators, but the whole city. It closed Boston Harbor, reducing the city's food supply and stopping its trade. Moreover, Parliament passed acts that virtually abolished the government of Massachusetts. Enraged and frightened, other colonies aided Boston and met in Philadelphia in 1774 as a Continental Congress to decide what to do.

War had not been declared, but the American Revolution had begun. In March 1775 the young lawyer Patrick Henry announced to the Virginia Assembly: "There is no longer any room for hope. . . . we must fight! I repeat it, sir, we must fight!" Three months later British troops attacked American strongholds on Bunker Hill near Boston, killing about one hundred fifty Americans and wounding about three hundred. By the following year, Congress asked

The Horse America Throwing His Master (1779). In this cartoon King George holds a riding whip made up of hand weapons.
Library of Congress

THE HORSE AMERICA, *throwing his Master.*
Pub.^d as the Act directs, Augt 1.st 1779, by Wm White, Angel Court, Westminster.

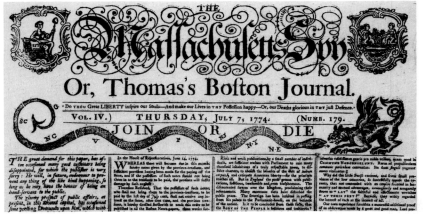

Join or Die, a popular slogan, as used in *The Massachusetts Sun, or Thomas's Boston Journal*, July 7, 1774.
Library of Congress

another young Virginia lawyer, Thomas Jefferson, to draft a document declaring to the world that the colonies were now "free and independent states."

American and British armies fought each other across America for the next seven years. The Americans at first met with defeat. A few months after the Declaration of Independence, Washington's army was pushed out of New York and across New Jersey. In this crisis an English immigrant named Tom Paine wrote a passionate essay assuring Americans that "though the flame of liberty may sometimes cease to shine, the coal can never expire." His assurance proved true in 1781, when Washington took his army to Yorktown, Virginia, and made an American victory certain by forcing the surrender of some ten thousand British troops. In 1788 a new country, the United States of America, began to exist under a democratic constitution.

The Growth of American Culture

Amid the uproar and gunfire occurred a second, very different revolution. The arts in America flourished as never before. They did so partly because by 1763 America had existed for one hundred fifty years and was ready for a richer cultural life, and partly because the Revolution itself inspired people to express their feelings and ideas, but mostly because during the Revolutionary period American cities grew swiftly and the country's population almost doubled. When the Frenchman Michel-Guillaume Jean de Crèvecoeur pictured the New World for Europeans in 1782, he told them that "an hundred year ago all was

The Death of General Wolfe (1770) by Benjamin West (1738–1820).
Oil on canvas.
National Gallery of Canada, Ottawa

wild, woody, and uncultivated." But new immigrants to America, he said, would now behold "fair cities, substantial villages, extensive fields, an immense country filled with decent houses, good roads, orchards, meadows, and bridges. . . ."

Artistic achievements that were common in Europe but new to America appeared at every stage of the Revolution. In 1767, only months before Parliament passed the Townshend Acts, actors known as The American Company gave the first professional production of an American play, *The Prince of Parthia.* A year after the Boston Massacre, a Philadelphia Quaker named Benjamin West exhibited in London a painting called *The Death of General Wolfe,* whose method of depicting a historic event influenced European art. In the same year that his townsmen dumped the hated tea, a Boston leather worker named William Billings published *The New-England Psalm-*

Singer, the first volume of American-composed music. Months before George Washington was inaugurated as President in 1789, newspapers advertised the publication of *The Power of Sympathy,* the first American novel.

The years from 1763 to 1789 added much else to American culture: the building of a string of theaters from New York to Charleston; the first native American actor and dancer; the first American museums; the first American epic poems; several painters who still rank high in the history of American art, such as John Singleton Copley, John Trumbull, Charles Willson Peale, and Gilbert Stuart; and two remarkable women—Patience Wright of New Jersey, the first American sculptor, and Phillis Wheatley of Boston, a young black slave who became a celebrated poet.

Some of these achievements have now been forgotten. But to Americans at the time, it seemed that while gaining political independence, the country had also shown artistic excellence, and that for both reasons the New World could now claim a place of dignity and importance beside the Old.

The Newark Museum

Admiral Richard Howe (c. 1770), miniature wax sculpture by Patience Wright (1725–1786).

Review

1. What did writers of this period believe could be accomplished through the free use of reason?
2. What subjects were writers of the Age of Reason concerned with?
3. What led the English government to begin a harsh program of taxing the colonies?
4. Name three individuals who helped fight the American Revolution with words rather than muskets.
5. What factors were responsible for the flourishing of American culture during the Revolutionary period?

Benjamin Franklin by James Reed Lambdin (1807–1889). Oil on canvas.

"The First American," as Benjamin Franklin has been called, was born in the capital of New England Puritanism, Boston, just as Puritanism was dying out. He left Boston at the age of seventeen, but Puritan ideals stayed with him. As Puritans hoped to be made pure by God's grace, he tried to make himself morally perfect by self-discipline. He failed to do so, but he did carry out another kind of self-transformation. By cleverness and hard work he changed himself from the poorly educated son of a candle- and soap-maker into a world-famous scientist, diplomat, philosopher, and writer.

A few paragraphs cannot describe, but only list, Franklin's many interests and accomplishments. He made his living mostly as a hard-working Philadelphia printer. But he also helped improve the city's pavements, street lighting, sanitation, fire companies, and police; ran a magazine and a newspaper; founded or helped to found a debating club, a hospital, the American Philosophical Society, the first circulating library in America, and the college that became the University of Pennsylvania; studied earthquakes, ocean currents, and wind; improved or invented the lightning rod, bifocal eyeglasses, a device for lifting books off high shelves, a rocking chair that could swat flies, a musical instrument made of moistened glass bowls called the armonica, and a stove that was sold throughout America and Europe; addressed the English House of Commons on the Stamp Act, drew an important political cartoon, and served as first Postmaster General of America; assisted in creating the Declaration of Independence and the Constitution of the United States; discovered the laws of electricity (for which

he won honorary degrees from Harvard and Yale and a gold medal from the English Royal Academy); and became perhaps the first American millionaire.

Franklin was also a brilliant writer. Following his precept that writing should be "smooth, clear, and short," he perfected the Puritan plain style. He kept a huge correspondence and wrote on everything from love to musical harmony to chess. Most popular among his earlier works were the *Poor Richard* almanacs, noted for their witty sayings. (According to one story, the Continental Congress was afraid to let him draft the Declaration of Independence because he might slip a joke into it.) During the war he wrote cutting satires on British policy such as "An Edict by the King of Prussia." In 1771 he began his *Autobiography*, describing his rise from "poverty and obscurity . . . to a state of affluence and some degree of reputation in the world. . . ." Although never completed, the *Autobiography* has been translated into a dozen languages and read by millions.

The contrast between Franklin's humble beginnings and his vast success has made him a symbol of America. And like America, he has had his critics. Some have questioned his sincerity: he praised reason, but once called it "a guide quite blind"; he wished to benefit mankind, but told a doctor that "Half the lives you save are not worth saving, as being useless, and almost all the other half ought not to be saved as being mischievous." Such inconsistencies can be viewed as a sign of Franklin's belief in self-development. He refused to be held to outmoded opinions. Viewed less favorably, his inconsistencies suggest opportunism, a willingness to please in order to get ahead. Herman Melville, the author of *Moby-Dick*, made a catalog of Franklin's roles, beginning "Printer, postmaster, almanac maker, essayist, chemist, orator. . . ." He ended with the one role Franklin ignored: Franklin "was everything," Melville said, "but a poet." Actually Franklin did write some poems, but Melville's meaning is clear: although Franklin mastered the practical side of life, he ignored the soul.

Franklin's admirers, then, have seen him as resourceful and adaptable, a proof of the opportunities for success in America. His critics have seen him as a man who spent his life getting ahead without asking where he was going. No one can deny, however, that the "First American" lived with fabulous energy—perhaps growing, perhaps not, but always changing, always new.

(Left) Benjamin Franklin's famous stove, invented in 1742.

(Right) Wooden hand press operated by Franklin when he was a journeyman printer in London, 1726.

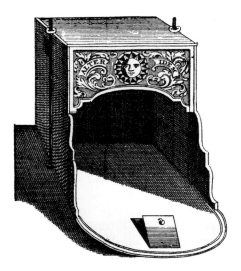

Benjamin Franklin **75**

FROM
The Autobiography

My brother had, in 1720 or '21, begun to print a newspaper. It was the second that appeared in America, and was called the *New England Courant.* The only one before it was the *Boston News-Letter.* I remember his being dissuaded by some of his friends from the undertaking, as not likely to succeed, one newspaper being, in their judgment, enough for America. At this time (1771) there are not less than five-and-twenty. He went on, however, with the undertaking, and after having worked in composing the types and printing off the sheets, I was employed to carry the papers through the streets to the customers. He had some ingenious men among his friends who amused themselves by writing little pieces for this paper, which gained it credit, and made it more in demand; and these gentlemen often visited us. Hearing their conversations, and their accounts of the approbation their papers were received with, I was excited to try my hand among them. But being still a boy, and suspecting that my brother would object to printing anything of mine in his paper if he knew it to be mine, I contrived to disguise my hand, and writing an anonymous paper, I put it in at night under the door of the printing house. It was found in the morning and communicated to his writing friends when they called in as usual. They read it, commented on it in my hearing, and I had the exquisite pleasure of finding it met with their approbation, and that, in their different guesses at the author, none were named but men of some character among us for learning and ingenuity.

I suppose now that I was rather lucky in my judges, and that perhaps they were not really so very good ones as I then esteemed them. Encouraged, however, by this, I wrote and conveyed in the same way to the press several more papers, which were equally approved, and I kept my secret till my small fund of sense for such performances was pretty well exhausted, and then I discovered it; when I began to be considered a little more by my brother's acquaintance, and in a manner that did not quite please him, as he thought, probably with reason, that it tended to make me too vain. And perhaps this might be one occasion of the differences that we frequently had about this time. Though a brother, he considered himself as my master, and me as his apprentice, and accordingly expected the same services from me as he would from another; while I thought he demeaned me too much in some he required of me, who from a brother expected more indulgence. Our disputes were often brought before our father, and I fancy I was either generally in the right, or else a better pleader, because the judgment was generally in my favor. But my brother was passionate, and had often beaten me, which I took extremely amiss; and, thinking my apprenticeship very tedious, I was continually wishing for some opportunity of shortening it, which at length offered in a manner unexpected.

One of the pieces in our newspaper, on some political point which I have now forgotten, gave offense to the Assembly. He was taken up, censured, and imprisoned for a month by the Speaker's warrant, I suppose because he

Vendors Display Wares at Third and Market Streets (1799). Hand-colored engraving by William Birch.

would not discover his author. I too was taken up and examined before the council; but, though I did not give them any satisfaction, they contented themselves with admonishing me, and dismissed me, considering me, perhaps, as an apprentice who was bound to keep his master's secrets. During my brother's confinement, which I resented a good deal, notwithstanding our private differences, I had the management of the paper; and I made bold to give our rulers some rubs in it, which my brother took very kindly, while others began to consider me in an unfavorable light, as a young genius that had a turn for libeling and satire. My brother's discharge was accompanied with an order of the House (a very odd one) *that James Franklin should no longer print the paper called the New England Courant.* There was a consultation held in our printing house among his friends what he should do in this case. Some proposed to evade the order by changing the name of the paper; but my brother seeing inconveniences in that, it was finally concluded on as a better way to let it be printed for the future under the name of *Benjamin Franklin.* And to avoid the censure of the Assembly that might fall on him as still printing it by his apprentice, the contrivance was that my old indenture should be returned to me, with a full discharge on the back of it, to

Benjamin Franklin   **77**

be shown on occasion; but to secure to him the benefit of my service, I was to sign new indentures for the remainder of the term, which were to be kept private. A very flimsy scheme it was, but however it was immediately executed, and the paper went on accordingly under my name for several months. At length, a fresh difference arising between my brother and me, I took upon me to assert my freedom, presuming that he would not venture to produce the new indentures. It was not fair in me to take this advantage, and this I therefore reckon one of the first errata[1] of my life. But the unfairness of it weighed little with me when under the impressions of resentment for the blows his passion too often urged him to bestow upon me, though he was otherwise not an ill-natured man. Perhaps I was too saucy[2] and provoking.

When he found I would leave him, he took care to prevent my getting employment in any other printing house of the town, by going round and speaking to every master, who accordingly refused to give me work. I then thought of going to New York, as the nearest place where there was a printer; and I was rather inclined to leave Boston when I reflected that I had already made myself a little obnoxious to the governing party; and, from the arbitrary proceedings of the Assembly in my brother's case, it was likely I might, if I stayed, soon bring myself into scrapes. . . .

A friend arranges for Franklin's passage on a New York sloop.

So I sold some of my books to raise a little money, was taken on board privately, and as we had a fair wind, in three days I found myself in New York, near three hundred miles from home, a boy of but seventeen, without the least recommendation to, or knowledge of, any person in the place, and with very little money in my pocket.

My inclinations for the sea were by this time worn out, or I might now have gratified them. But, having a trade, and supposing myself a pretty good workman, I offered my service to the printer in the place, old Mr. William Bradford (who had been the first printer in Pennsylvania, but removed from thence upon the quarrel of George Keith). He could give me no employment, having little to do and help enough already; but, says he, "My son at Philadelphia has lately lost his principal hand, Aquila Rose, by death; if you go thither, I believe he may employ you." Philadelphia was one hundred miles farther. I set out, however, in a boat for Amboy,[3] leaving my chest and things to follow me round by sea. In crossing the bay, we met with a squall that tore our rotten sails to pieces, prevented our getting into the kill,[4] and drove us upon Long Island. . . .

One of the passengers, a Dutchman, falls overboard, and Franklin rescues him.

When we drew near the island, we found it was at a place where there could be no landing, there being a great surf on the stony beach. So we dropped anchor and swung round towards the shore. Some people came down to the water edge and hallooed[5] to us, as we did to them. But the wind was so high, and the surf so loud, that we could not hear so as to understand each other. There were canoes on the shore, and we made signs and hallooed that they should fetch us, but they either did not understand us, or thought it impracticable. So they went away, and night coming on, we had no remedy but to wait till the wind should abate; and in the meantime the boatman and I concluded to sleep if we could, and so crowded into the scuttle[6] with the Dutchman who was still wet, and the spray, beating over the head of our boat, leaked through to us so that we were soon almost as wet as he. In this

1. **errata** (ĭ-rä′tə): errors.
2. **saucy:** here, impudent.

3. **Amboy:** a town on the New Jersey coast.
4. **kill:** creek or stream.
5. **halloed:** called.
6. **scuttle:** opening or hatchway.

manner, we lay all night with very little rest. But, the wind abating the next day, we made a shift to reach Amboy before night, having been thirty hours on the water, without victuals or any drink but a bottle of filthy rum, the water we sailed on being salt.

In the evening I found myself very feverish, and went into bed. But, having read somewhere that cold water drunk plentifully was good for a fever, I followed the prescription, sweat plentifully most of the night, my fever left me, and in the morning, crossing the ferry, I proceeded on my journey on foot, having fifty miles to Burlington, where I was told I should find boats that would carry me the rest of the way to Philadelphia.

It rained very hard all the day; I was thoroughly soaked, and by noon a good deal tired; so I stopped at a poor inn where I stayed all night, beginning now to wish I had never left home. I cut so miserable a figure, too, that I found, by the questions asked me, I was suspected to be some runaway servant, and in danger of being taken up on that suspicion. However, I proceeded the next day and got in the evening to an inn, within eight or ten miles of Burlington, kept by one Dr. Brown. . . .

At his house I lay that night, and the next morning reached Burlington, but had the mortification to find that the regular boats were gone a little before my coming and no other expected to go till Tuesday, this being Saturday; wherefore I returned to an old woman in the town of whom I had bought gingerbread to eat on the water, and asked her advice. She invited me to lodge at her house till a passage by water should offer; and being tired with my foot traveling, I accepted the invitation. She, understanding I was a printer, would have had me stay at that town and follow my business, being ignorant of the stock necessary to begin with. She was very hospitable, gave me a dinner of oxcheek with great good will, accepting only a pot of ale in return; and I thought myself fixed till Tuesday should come. However, walking in the evening by the side of the river, a boat came by, which I found was going towards Philadelphia with several people in her. They took me in, and as there was no wind, we rowed all the way; and about midnight, not having yet seen the city, some of the company were confident we must have passed it, and would row no farther; the others knew not where we were; so we put towards the shore, got into a creek, landed near an old fence, with the rails of which we made a fire, the night being cold in October, and there we remained till daylight. Then one of the company knew the place to be Cooper's Creek, a little above Philadelphia, which we saw as soon as we got out of the creek, and arrived there about eight or nine o'clock on the Sunday morning, and landed at the Market Street wharf.

I have been the more particular in this description of my journey, and shall be so of my first entry into that city, that you may in your mind compare such unlikely beginnings with the figure I have since made there. I was in my working dress, my best clothes being to come round by sea. I was dirty from my journey; my pockets were stuffed out with shirts and stockings; I knew no soul nor where to look for lodging. I was fatigued with traveling, rowing, and want of rest. I was very hungry, and my whole stock of cash consisted of a Dutch dollar and about a shilling in copper. The latter I gave the people of the boat for my passage, who at first refused it, on account of my rowing; but I insisted on their taking it, a man being sometimes more generous when he has but a little money than when he has plenty, perhaps through fear of being thought to have but little.

Then I walked up the street, gazing about, till near the markethouse I met a boy with bread. I had made many a meal on bread, and, inquiring where he got it, I went immediately to the baker's he directed me to, in Second Street, and asked for biscuit, intending such as we had in Boston; but they, it seems, were not made in Philadelphia. Then I asked for a threepenny loaf, and was told they had none such. So, not considering or knowing the difference of money, and the greater cheapness nor the names of his bread, I bade him give me threepenny worth of any sort. He gave me, accordingly, three great puffy rolls. I was surprised at the quantity, but took it, and, having no room in my pockets, walked off with a roll under each arm and eating the other. Thus I went up Market Street as far as Fourth Street, passing by the door of Mr. Read, my future wife's father; when she, standing at the door, saw me, and thought I made, as I certainly did, a most awkward, ridiculous appearance. Then I turned and went down Chestnut Street and part of Walnut Street, eating my roll all the way, and, coming round, found myself again at Market Street wharf, near the boat I came in, to which I went for a draft of the river water; and, being filled with one of my rolls, gave the other two to a woman and her child that came down the river in the boat with us, and were waiting to go farther. Thus refreshed, I walked again up the street, which by this time had many clean-dressed people in it, who were all walking the same way. I joined them, and thereby was led into the great meetinghouse of the Quakers near the market. I sat down among them, and, after looking round awhile and hearing nothing said, being very drowsy through labor and want of rest the preceding night, I fell fast asleep, and continued so till the meeting broke up, when one was kind enough to rouse me. This was, therefore, the first house I was in, or slept in, in Philadelphia.

The following selection from the Autobiography *tells what happened six or seven years later, after Franklin had established himself as a Philadelphia businessman.*

It was about this time that I conceived the bold and arduous project of arriving at moral perfection. I wished to live without committing any fault at any time; I would conquer all that either natural inclination, custom, or company might lead me into. As I knew, or thought I knew, what was right and wrong, I did not see why I might not *always* do the one and avoid the other. But I soon found I had undertaken a task of more difficulty than I had imagined. While my attention was taken up in guarding against one fault, I was often surprised by another. Habit took the advantage of inattention. Inclination was sometimes too strong for reason. I concluded, at length, that the mere speculative conviction that it was our interest to be completely virtuous was not sufficient to prevent our slipping, and that the contrary habits must be broken, and good ones acquired and established, before we can have any dependence on a steady, uniform rectitude of conduct. For this purpose I therefore contrived the following method.

In the various enumerations of the moral virtues I had met with in my reading, I found that catalog more or less numerous, as different writers included more or fewer ideas under the same name. Temperance, for example, was by some confined to eating and drinking, while by others it was extended to mean the moderating every other pleasure, appetite, inclination, or passion, bodily or mental, even to our avarice and ambition. I proposed to myself, for the sake of clearness, to use rather more names, with fewer ideas annexed to each, than a few names with more ideas; and I included under thirteen names of virtues all that at that time occurred to me as necessary or desirable, and annexed to each a short precept, which fully expressed the extent I gave to its meaning.

These names of virtues, with their precepts, were:

1. TEMPERANCE. Eat not to dullness. Drink not to elevation.
2. SILENCE. Speak not but what may benefit others or yourself. Avoid trifling conversation.
3. ORDER. Let all your things have their places. Let each part of your business have its time.
4. RESOLUTION. Resolve to perform what you ought. Perform without fail what you resolve.

5. FRUGALITY. Make no expense but to do good to others or yourself: i.e., waste nothing.

6. INDUSTRY. Lose no time. Be always employed in something useful. Cut off all unnecessary actions.

7. SINCERITY. Use no hurtful deceit. Think innocently and justly; and, if you speak, speak accordingly.

8. JUSTICE. Wrong none by doing injuries, or omitting the benefits that are your duty.

9. MODERATION. Avoid extremes. Forbear resenting injuries so much as you think they deserve.

10. CLEANLINESS. Tolerate no uncleanliness in body, clothes, or habitation.

11. TRANQUILITY. Be not disturbed at trifles, or at accidents common or unavoidable.

12. CHASTITY. Rarely use venery but for health or offspring; never to dullness, weakness, or the injury of your own or another's peace or reputation.

13. HUMILITY. Imitate Jesus and Socrates.

My intention being to acquire the *habitude* of all these virtues, I judged it would be well not to distract my attention by attempting the whole at once but to fix it on one of them at a time; and, when I should be master of that, then to proceed to another, and so on till I should have gone through the thirteen. And as the previous acquisition of some might facilitate the acquisition of certain others, I arranged them with that view as they stand above. *Temperance* first, as it tends to procure that coolness and clearness of head which is so necessary where constant vigilance was to be kept up, and guard maintained against the unremitting attraction of ancient habits and the force of perpetual temptations. This being acquired and established, *Silence* would be more easy; and my desire being to gain knowledge at the same time that I improved in virtue, and considering that in conversation it was obtained rather by the use of the ears than of the tongue, and therefore wishing to break a habit I was getting into of prattling, punning, and joking, which only made me acceptable to

trifling company, I gave *Silence* the second place. This and the next, *Order,* I expected would allow me more time for attending to my project and my studies. *Resolution,* once become habitual, would keep me firm in my endeavors to obtain all the subsequent virtues; *Frugality* and *Industry,* by freeing me from my remaining debt, and producing affluence and independence, would make more easy the practice of *Sincerity* and *Justice,* etc., etc. Conceiving then, that, agreeable to the advice of Pythagoras[7] in his Golden Verses, daily examination would be necessary, I contrived the following method for conducting that examination.

I made a little book, in which I allotted a page for each of the virtues. I ruled each page with red ink, so as to have seven columns, one for each day of the week, marking each column with a letter for the day. I crossed these columns with thirteen red lines, marking the beginning of each line with the first letter of one of the virtues, on which line and in its proper column I might mark, by a little black spot, every fault I found upon examination to have been committed respecting that virtue upon that day.

I determined to give a week's strict attention to each of the virtues successively. Thus, in the first week, my great guard was to avoid even the least offense against *Temperance,* leaving the other virtues to their ordinary chance, only marking every evening the faults of the day. Thus, if in the first week I could keep my first line, marked T, clear of spots, I supposed the habit of that virtue so much strengthened, and its opposite weakened, that I might venture extending my attention to include the next, and for the following week keep both lines clear of spots. Proceeding thus to the last, I could go through a course complete in thirteen weeks, and four courses in a year. And like him who, having a garden to weed, does not attempt to eradicate all the bad herbs at once,

---

7. **Pythagoras** (pĭ-thăg'ər-əs): a famous Greek philosopher and mathematician of the sixth century B.C.

which would exceed his reach and his strength, but works on one of the beds at a time, and, having accomplished the first, proceeds to a second; so I should have (I hoped) the encouraging pleasure of seeing on my pages the progress I made in virtue, by clearing successively my lines of their spots, till in the end, by a number of courses, I should be happy in viewing a clean book, after a thirteen weeks' daily examination. . . .

The precept of *Order* requiring that *every part of my business should have its allotted time,* one page in my little book contained the following scheme of employment for the twenty-four hours of a natural day.

The Morning Question, What good shall I do this day?	5 6 7 8	Rise, wash, and address *Powerful goodness;* contrive day's business and take the resolution of the day; prosecute[8] the present study: and breakfast.
	9 10 11	Work.
	12 1	Read, or overlook my accounts, and dine.
	2 3 4 5	Work.
	6 7 8 9	Put things in their places, supper, music, or diversion, or conversation, examination of the day.
Evening Question, What good have I done today?	10 11 12 1 2 3 4	Sleep.

8. **prosecute:** carry on.

I entered upon the execution of this plan for self-examination, and continued it with occasional intermissions for some time. I was surprised to find myself so much fuller of faults than I had imagined, but I had the satisfaction of seeing them diminish. To avoid the trouble of renewing now and then my little book, which, by scraping out the marks on the paper of old faults to make room for new ones in a new course, became full of holes, I transferred my tables and precepts to the ivory leaves of a memorandum book, on which the lines were drawn with red ink that made a durable stain, and on those lines I marked my faults with a black-lead pencil, which marks I could easily wipe out with a wet sponge. After a while I went through one course only in a year and afterward only one in several years, till at length I omitted them entirely, being employed in voyages and business abroad, with a multiplicity of affairs that interfered; but I always carried my little book with me.

My scheme of *Order* gave me the most trouble; and I found that, though it might be practicable where a man's business was such as to leave him the disposition[9] of his time, that of a journeyman printer, for instance, it was not possible to be exactly observed by a master, who must mix with the world and often receive people of business at their own hours. *Order,* too, with regard to places for things, papers, etc., I found extremely difficult to acquire. I had not been early accustomed to *Method,* and, having an exceeding good memory, I was not so sensible of the inconvenience attending want of method. This article, therefore, cost me so much painful attention, and my faults in it vexed me so much, and I made so little progress in amendment, and had such frequent relapses, that I was almost ready to give up the attempt, and content myself with a faulty character in that respect, like the man who, in buying an ax of a smith, my neighbor, desired to have the whole of its surface as bright as the edge. The smith consented to

9. **disposition:** here, management.

grind it bright for him if he would turn the wheel; he turned, while the smith pressed the broad face of the ax hard and heavily on the stone, which made the turning of it very fatiguing. The man came every now and then from the wheel to see how the work went on, and at length would take his ax as it was, without further grinding. "No," says the smith, "turn on, turn on; we shall have it bright by and by; as yet, 'tis only speckled." "Yes," says the man, "but—*I think I like a speckled ax best.*" And I believe this may have been the case with many who, having, for want of some such means as I employed, found the difficulty of obtaining good and breaking bad habits in other points of vice and virtue, have given up the struggle, and concluded that *a speckled ax was best.* For something, that pretended to be reason, was every now and then suggesting to me that such extreme nicety as I exacted of myself might be a kind of foppery[10] in morals, which, if it were known, would make me ridiculous; that a perfect character might be attended with the inconvenience of being envied and hated; and that a benevolent man should allow a few faults in himself, to keep his friends in countenance.

In truth, I found myself incorrigible with respect to *Order;* and now I am grown old, and my memory bad, I feel very sensibly the want of it. But, on the whole, though I never arrived at the perfection I had been so ambitious of obtaining, but fell far short of it, yet I was, by the endeavor, a better and a happier man than I otherwise should have been if I had not attempted it; as those who aim at perfect writing by imitating the engraved copies, though they never reach the wished-for excellence of those copies, their hand is mended by the endeavor, and is tolerable while it continues fair and legible.

10. **foppery** (fŏp′ə-rē): foolishness.

And it may be well my posterity should be informed that to this little artifice, with the blessing of God, their ancestor owed the constant felicity of his life, down to his seventy-ninth year, in which this is written. What reverses may attend the remainder is in the hand of Providence; but, if they arrive, the reflection on past happiness enjoyed ought to help his bearing them with more resignation. To *Temperance* he ascribes his long-continued health, and what is still left to him of a good constitution. To *Industry* and *Frugality,* the early easiness of his circumstances and acquisition of his fortune, with all that knowledge that enabled him to be a useful citizen, and obtained for him some degree of reputation among the learned. To *Sincerity* and *Justice,* the confidence of his country, and the honorable employs it conferred upon him. And to the joint influence of the whole mass of the virtues, even in the imperfect state he was able to acquire them, all that evenness of temper, and that cheerfulness in conversation, which makes his company still sought for, and agreeable even to his younger acquaintance. I hope, therefore, that some of my descendants may follow the example and reap the benefit.

Reading Check

1. Why did Franklin submit his articles to his brother's newspaper anonymously?
2. Why was Franklin's brother imprisoned by the Assembly?
3. What caused Franklin to continue his journey from New York to Philadelphia?
4. Which of his list of virtues gave Franklin the most trouble?
5. What is the point of the story about the speckled ax?

Second Street North from Market. Hand-colored engraving
by William Birch.
John Carter Brown Library at Brown University

For Study and Discussion

Analyzing and Interpreting the Selection

1. Those who see Franklin as a symbol of American character often cite his self-reliance and independence. **a.** How does Franklin as a young apprentice journalist embody these qualities? **b.** What episodes in his journey from Boston to Philadelphia illustrate these qualities?

2. Franklin describes the journey in detail so that the reader can compare his "unlikely beginnings" with his subsequent success. What details in the selection emphasize the difference between the older, famous Franklin and the boy who ran away from Boston?

3. The English novelist D. H. Lawrence criticized Franklin's plan for achieving moral perfection because it turned people, he said, into a "moral machine." In what ways might Franklin's plan be called mechanical?

4. Franklin admits that he failed to achieve moral perfection. What kept him from achieving it? Reread Franklin's story of the speckled ax and tell how it sums up his attitude toward his failure.

Close Reading

Paraphrasing for Clarity

Paraphrase the following passage so that the content is clear:

> I wished to live without committing any fault at any time. . . . But I soon found I had undertaken a task of more difficulty than I had imagined. While my attention was taken up in guarding against one fault, I was often surprised by another. Habit took the advantage of inattention. Inclination was sometimes too strong for reason. I concluded, at length, that the mere speculative conviction that it was our interest to be completely virtuous was not sufficient to prevent our slipping, and that the contrary habits must be broken, and good ones acquired and established, before we can have any dependence on a steady, uniform rectitude of conduct.

Literary Elements

The Autobiography: First-Person Point of View

An **autobiography** presents the writer's life as a continuous narrative, a sort of story. Because of the Puritans' emphasis on examining one's soul and the lasting American emphasis on individualism, the autobiography has been a popular and important literary form in America.

Like most autobiographers, Franklin tells his life story in the first person, writing as "I." The **first-person point of view** can give writing immediacy and intimacy. The writer speaks as the person to whom the events actually happened. The writer can also speak to the reader confidentially, person to person. The first-person point of view has some disadvantages as well. The writer cannot speak with firsthand knowledge about events he or she did not witness, even when they may be important to the story. And the writer's viewpoint colors and may distort the entire account. Franklin tends to focus on his rise in the world; someone else writing about Franklin's life might have stressed his faults.

Language and Vocabulary

Locating Definitions
Explaining Related Words

Franklin states that he found several definitions for *temperance*. What other definitions for the word does he give? Look up *temperance* in a dictionary and find definitions that Franklin does not include. Find definitions for the following words and be prepared to explain their relationship to *temperance: temperament, intemperate, temperature, tempera, distemper.*

Writing About Literature

Examining Puritan Influences

The biographical introduction states that Franklin "left Boston at the age of seventeen, but Puritan ideals stayed with him." What Puritan influences are apparent in the excerpts from Franklin's *Autobiography*? Write a short essay in which you examine the Puritan elements in Franklin's work.

Narrative and Descriptive Writing

Writing an Autobiographical Essay

Write an autobiographical essay on some important event in your life, using the first-person point of view. Strive for immediacy by describing what you saw, heard, smelled, touched, or tasted, and by addressing the reader as a friend.

Poor Richard's Almanack

Poor Richard, 1733.

AN

Almanack

For the Year of Christ

1733,

Being the First after LEAP YEAR:

And makes since the Creation   Years

By the Account of the Eastern *Greeks*	7241
By the Latin Church, when ☉ ent. ♈	6932
By the Computation of *W.W.*	5742
By the *Roman* Chronology	5682
By the *Jewish* Rabbies	5494

Wherein is contained

The Lunations, Eclipses, Judgment of the Weather, Spring Tides, Planets Motions & mutual Aspects, Sun and Moon's Rising and Setting, Length of Days, Time of High Water, Fairs, Courts, and observable Days.

Fitted to the Latitude of Forty Degrees, and a Meridian of Five Hours West from *London*, but may without sensible Error, serve all the adjacent Places, even from *Newfoundland* to *South-Carolina.*

By RICHARD SAUNDERS, Philom.

PHILADELPHIA:

Printed and sold by *B. FRANKLIN,* at the New Printing-Office near the Market.

Hunger is the best pickle.

Keep thy shop, and thy shop will keep thee.

Love your neighbor; yet don't pull down your hedge.

A slip of the foot you may soon recover, but a slip of the tongue you may never get over.

Early to bed and early to rise, makes a man healthy, wealthy, and wise.

God helps them that help themselves.

Don't throw stones at your neighbors', if your own windows are glass.

He that scatters thorns, let him not go barefoot.

Three may keep a secret if two of them are dead.

Tart words make no friends; a spoonful of honey will catch more flies than a gallon of vinegar.

Fish and visitors smell in three days.

If you would know the value of money, try to borrow some.

A small leak will sink a great ship.

He that lieth down with dogs, shall rise up with fleas.

Now that I have a sheep and cow everybody bids me good morrow.

Drive thy business; let it not drive thee.

Dost thou love life? Then do not squander time; for that's the stuff life is made of.

Title page of first edition of
Poor Richard's Almanack.

Analyzing and Interpreting the Selection

1. Poor Richard's sayings express many beliefs associated with Franklin himself. **a.** Which sayings recommend industry? **b.** Which recommend self-reliance? **c.** Which might be cited to show that Franklin understood the failings of human nature? **2.** Franklin believed that in order to succeed, a person must not only be virtuous, but also seem virtuous to the community so as to gain its trust. **a.** Which of Poor Richard's sayings connect virtue and wealth? **b.** Which suggest the importance of an honorable reputation?

Almanacs, Aphorisms, and Proverbs

Franklin's sayings appeared in the *Poor Richard* almanacs, published annually in America for twenty-five years. Each issue of *Poor Richard* sold over ten thousand copies; it was the most popular of many early American almanacs.

Usually about twenty pages long, each almanac was divided into months, and each month into a list of days. Next to each day appeared a weather prediction for the day, the times of high and low tide, and the hours of sunrise and sunset from which people could set their clocks. The almanacs also provided such useful information as the dates of large meetings and fairs, and tables of measures and distances. At the top or bottom of most pages were verses and sayings, humorous and usually moral. Almanacs continue to be published and read; probably the best-known example is *The Farmer's Almanac.*

The sayings sprinkled through the almanacs are also called **aphorisms** or **proverbs.** All three terms mean a brief statement—usually one sentence—that expresses some truth about life in terse, easily remembered form. Writers of essays often use aphorisms to emphasize a point or summarize an argument.

Franklin invented few of Poor Richard's sayings. Rather, he took older sayings and rewrote them in crisper language. Sometimes he shortened the original. For instance, he clipped the proverb "The greatest talkers are the least doers" to "Great talkers, little doers." At other times he changed an abstraction into a concrete image. He sharpened the saying "What maintains one vice costeth more than ten virtues" by changing it to "What maintains one vice would bring up two children."

Turn the following common beliefs into sayings, either by shortening them or by making them more concrete: "You can't succeed in life without working hard"; "The way people are brought up determines what sort of people they'll become"; "The gains you've already made are more valuable than future gains you merely dream about."

Writing Aphorisms

Write several aphorisms or proverbs for today. Remember that aphorisms contain some truth about life. Remember also that effective aphorisms depend on crisp language and compression. Often an interesting aphorism is created by converting an abstract idea into a concrete image.

A Printer's Epitaph (1728)

The Body of
B. Franklin,
Printer;
Like the Cover of an old Book,
Its Contents torn out,
And stript of its Lettering and Gilding,
Lies here, Food for Worms.
But the Work shall not be wholly lost:
For it will, as he believ'd, appear once more,
In a new & more perfect Edition,
Corrected and amended
By the Author.
He was born Jan. 6, 1706.
Died 17–

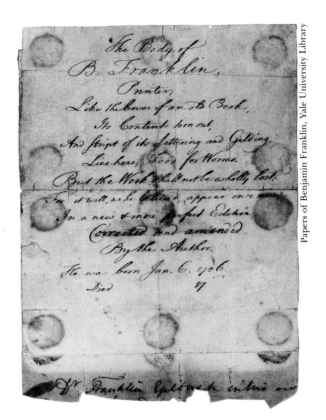

Franklin composed his own epitaph
when he was twenty-two.

For Study and Discussion

Analyzing and Interpreting the Poem

1. An **epitaph** is a short statement about death or a dead person, sometimes in verse and usually carved on a tombstone. Franklin's epitaph makes a revealing contrast beside this popular Puritan epitaph:

> *Life is uncertain, Death is sure*
> *Sin the wound and Christ the cure.*

How do the two epitaphs suggest the difference between the Puritan age into which Franklin was born, and the Age of Reason in which he matured?

2. Franklin's epitaph shows that poets are not the only writers who use **similes.** Similes are figures of speech that compare two different things, using connecting words such as *like* or *as.* (See page 333.) Although Franklin's corpse may not seem like a book, the fact that Franklin was a printer makes the comparison appropriate. Franklin finds other resemblances that convey his view of death wittily to the mind and vividly to the eye. **a.** To what does he implicitly compare the cover, contents, and lettering of the book? **b.** How do you interpret his statement that the book will appear again "In a new & more perfect Edition,/Corrected and amended/By the Author"?

Creative Writing

Writing an Epitaph

Write an epitaph on some well-known person, using an appropriate simile to suggest the essential nature of that person's life. You might begin: "Here lies [Thomas Edison, Ludwig van Beethoven, Cleopatra, Louis Armstrong, Emily Dickinson, Babe Ruth, etc.], like . . ."

The Shelburne Museum, Vermont

Patrick Henry by an unknown artist.

"I know not what course others may take; but as for me, give me liberty or give me death!" These words have made Patrick Henry famous in American history, but he may not have spoken them. Although he delivered the two best-known speeches of the Revolution, no one printed them or fully wrote them down. We can read them only as reconstructions, pieced together, years after Henry's death, from the memories and notes of people who heard them.

Patrick Henry's speeches may be half legendary, but he was a real man, born on the Virginia frontier to a cultivated family. His father taught him Latin, so that he could read the classics, training that prepared him to become one among the many noted Southern orators. As a teen-ager, he ran a store with his brother and at the age of eighteen he married and took up farming. By twenty-three, he had several children and large debts. He began to study, and then practiced, law, gaining a reputation by winning most of his cases. Not yet thirty years old, he was elected to the Virginia House of Burgesses.

The Revolution made Henry a prominent speaker. His listeners commented that he had a clear, powerful voice and that he used his tall, awkward body expressively. He delivered the first of his important speeches to the legislators of Virginia in 1765, in opposition to the Stamp Act. He closed by mentioning Julius Caesar and King Charles the First, who were assassinated and executed, respectively, for political reasons. When he warned the present English king to "profit by their example," his implied threat brought shouts of "Treason! Treason!" He replied, "If that be treason, make the most of it!" In his "liberty or death" speech ten years later, he urged armed resistance to England. This time his boldness brought more than shouts. The governor of Virginia proclaimed him an outlaw.

Henry not only survived but was himself elected governor of Virginia, serving for five one-year terms. He remained active in politics until the end of his life, although his political views grew conservative and put him at odds with some earlier friends, especially Thomas Jefferson. Still, Henry helped to write the Virginia constitution and led the movement to add a bill of rights to the Constitution of the United States.

Virginia named a county after Patrick Henry, which was later divided into a part called Patrick and a part called Henry. It seems a fitting honor for the man we must still regard as the author of the Revolution's two most fiery speeches.

Speech in the Virginia Convention

In 1775 the Virginia House of Burgesses held a revolutionary convention at which Patrick Henry introduced the resolution that "Virginia be immediately put in a posture of defense." There was strong opposition. Some of the legislators feared a popular rebellion even more than they feared England. Henry rose to deliver his most famous speech in support of his resolution.

Mr. President: No man thinks more highly than I do of the patriotism, as well as abilities, of the very worthy gentlemen who have just addressed the house. But different men often see the same subject in different lights; and, therefore, I hope it will not be thought disrespectful to those gentlemen, if, entertaining, as I do, opinions of a character very opposite to theirs, I shall speak forth my sentiments freely and without reserve. This is no time for ceremony. The question before the house is one of awful moment to this country. For my own part, I consider it as nothing less than a question of freedom or slavery. And in proportion to the magnitude of the subject ought to be the freedom of the debate. It is only in this way that we can hope to arrive at truth, and fulfill the great responsibility which we hold to God and our country. Should I keep back my opinions at such a time, through fear of giving offense, I should consider myself as guilty of treason toward my country, and of an act of disloyalty toward the Majesty of Heaven, which I revere above all earthly kings.

Mr. President, it is natural to man to indulge in the illusions of hope. We are apt to shut our eyes against a painful truth, and listen to the song of that siren till she transforms us into beasts. Is that the part of wise men, engaged in a great and arduous struggle for liberty? Are we disposed to be of the number of those who having eyes see not, and having ears hear not, the things which so nearly concern their temporal salvation? For my part, whatever anguish of spirit it may cost, I am willing to know the whole truth; to know the worst and to provide for it.

I have but one lamp by which my feet are guided, and that is the lamp of experience. I know of no way of judging of the future but by the past. And judging by the past, I wish to know what there has been in the conduct of the British ministry for the last ten years to justify those hopes with which gentlemen have been pleased to solace themselves and the house? Is it that insidious smile with which our petition has been lately received? Trust it not, sir; it will prove a snare to your feet. Suffer not yourselves to be betrayed with a kiss. Ask yourselves how this gracious reception of our petition comports with those warlike preparations which cover our waters and darken our land. Are fleets and armies necessary to a work of love and reconciliation? Have we shown ourselves so unwilling to be reconciled that force must be called in to win back our love? Let us not deceive ourselves, sir. These are the implements of war and subjugation—the last arguments to which kings resort.

I ask gentlemen, sir, what means this martial array, if its purpose be not to force us to submission? Can gentlemen assign any other possible motive for it? Has Great Britain any enemy in this quarter of the world, to call for all this accumulation of navies and armies? No, sir, she has none. They are meant for us: they

Patrick Henry Arguing "the Parson's Cause" (c. 1830). Oil painting thought to be the work of George Cooke (1793–1849). This work depicts Henry at Hanover Courthouse in 1763, when his brilliant oratory first brought him widespread recognition.

The Virginia Historical Society, Richmond

can be meant for no other. They are sent over to bind and rivet upon us those chains which the British ministry have been so long forging.

And what have we to oppose to them? Shall we try argument? Sir, we have been trying that for the last ten years. Have we anything new to offer upon the subject? Nothing. We have held the subject up in every light of which it is capable; but it has been all in vain. Shall we resort to entreaty and humble supplication? What terms shall we find which have not been already exhausted? Let us not, I beseech you, sir, deceive ourselves longer.

Sir, we have done everything that could be done to avert the storm which is now coming on. We have petitioned; we have remonstrated; we have supplicated; we have prostrated ourselves before the throne, and have implored its interposition[1] to arrest the tyrannical hands of the ministry and Parliament. Our petitions have been slighted; our remonstrances have produced additional violence and insult; our supplications have been disregarded; and we have been spurned with contempt from the foot of the throne! In vain, after these things, may we indulge the fond[2] hope of peace and reconciliation. There is no longer any room for hope. If we wish to be free, if we mean to preserve inviolate those inestimable privileges for which we have been so long contending, if we mean not basely to abandon the noble struggle in which we have been so long engaged, and which we have pledged ourselves never to abandon until the glorious object of our contest shall be obtained—we must fight! I repeat it, sir, we must fight! An appeal to arms and to the God of Hosts is all that is left us!

They tell us, sir, that we are weak—unable to cope with so formidable an adversary. But when shall we be stronger? Will it be the next week, or the next year? Will it be when we are totally disarmed, and when a British guard shall be stationed in every house? Shall we gather strength by irresolution and inaction? Shall we acquire the means of effectual resistance by lying supinely on our backs and hugging the delusive phantom of hope until our enemies shall have bound us hand and foot? Sir, we are not weak, if we make a proper use of those means which the God of nature hath placed in our power. Three millions of people, armed in the holy cause of liberty, and in such a country as that which we possess, are invincible by any force which our enemy can send against us. Besides, sir, we shall not fight our battles alone. There is a just God who presides over the destinies of nations and who will raise up friends to fight our battles for us. The battle, sir, is not to the strong alone; it is to the vigilant, the active, the brave. Besides, sir, we have no election.[3] If we were base enough to desire it, it is now too late to retire from the contest. There is no retreat but in submission and slavery! Our chains are forged! Their clanging may be heard on the plains of Boston! The war is inevitable—and let it come! I repeat it, sir, let it come!

It is in vain, sir, to extenuate the matter. Gentlemen may cry, "Peace, peace"—but there is no peace. The war is actually begun! The next gale that sweeps from the north[4] will bring to our ears the clash of resounding arms! Our brethren are already in the field! Why stand we here idle? What is it that gentlemen wish? What would they have? Is life so dear, or peace so sweet, as to be purchased at the price of chains and slavery? Forbid it, Almighty God! I know not what course others may take; but as for me, give me liberty or give me death!

3. **election:** choice.
4. **The next gale . . . north:** Some Massachusetts colonists had already shown open resistance to the British.

1. **interposition:** intervention; stepping in to help solve a problem.
2. **fond:** foolish.

Analyzing and Interpreting the Speech

1. Henry's powerful call to arms is an example of oratory as literature. Two important persuasive devices used by Henry and other orators are (1) **repetition** of key points, and (2) **rhetorical questions** (questions to which the answers are obvious). Find one use of repetition and one rhetorical question in Henry's speech.

2. Like other persuasive writers, Henry uses vivid figures of speech. Interpret the following figures of speech: the "lamp of experience" (paragraph 3); "storm" (paragraph 6); the clanging "chains" (paragraph 7).

3. Throughout the speech Henry insists that Americans who trust Britain deceive themselves. Cite several metaphors for deception and illusion that appear in the speech.

Allusion

One persuasive device Henry uses effectively is **allusion.** Allusions are references made for the sake of comparison. The writers can allude to persons, events, literary works, or almost anything—present or past, real or imaginary. Allusions do not fully describe what they refer to; they hint at it. In the second paragraph, for instance, Henry warns Americans not to listen to the "song of that siren." In Greek mythology the sirens were creatures—part woman, part bird—whose enchanting singing lured sailors to their destruction. Henry may also be alluding to the story of Circe, an enchantress who turned men into animals. The brief reference to the siren's song invites the audience to think of the entire mythical story, implying that if Americans allow themselves to be lulled by pleasant-sounding British promises, they, like the sailors, will be destroyed.

Henry's speech contains Biblical allusions, which you may need to look up in order to understand. The second paragraph speaks of "those who having eyes see not"—alluding to Ezekiel 12:2–3. Locate the passage and tell what Henry's allusion suggests.

In the third paragraph Henry warns the audience, "Suffer not yourselves to be betrayed with a kiss." Here he alludes to Luke 22:47–48, in which Judas kisses Jesus with pretended affection and loyalty. Read the passage and tell what comparison Henry draws by this allusion.

Distinguishing Meanings of Synonyms

It has been said that there are no synonyms in English. Words that seem to mean the same thing often do not. Good writers try to choose the word that conveys the exact meaning intended.

Henry describes Americans' pleas to England as "petitions" and "supplications." These words denote slightly different forms of pleading. A *petition* is a solemn, formal request, usually in writing. A *supplication* is a humble request. Henry uses several other words that denote various kinds of pleading: *entreaty, implore, remonstrate.* Using a dictionary, describe the slight differences among these words.

Using Devices of Persuasion in a Speech

Write a brief speech urging a club or group to take some course of action. In your speech, use the following persuasive devices: repetition of a key point, rhetorical questions, and at least one allusion. Read the speech to your class and see if they can identify and understand the allusion.

In the war of words to win support for the American or the English side, America's hardest blows were struck by an Englishman—Tom Paine. The early events of his stormy life perhaps taught him sympathy for underdogs. He left school at thirteen and worked unsuccessfully as a sailor, teacher, grocer, tax collector, and corset maker. He read much and managed to educate himself, but by his mid-thirties he faced imprisonment for debt. A meeting with Benjamin Franklin during one of Franklin's stays in England persuaded him to emigrate to America.

For a man of Paine's bold opinions, America in 1775 was the right place and the right time. Early that year, only weeks after arriving in Philadelphia, he published an article blasting slavery as equal to murder and asking Americans to give it up. Later the same year he wrote a forty-seven page pamphlet entitled *Common Sense*, asking the colonists to think the unthinkable: that the English king was a "Royal Brute," that the very idea of monarchy insulted human dignity, and that war must come because "the period of debate is closed." *Common Sense*, published in 1776, sold 120,000 copies in three months. Reprinted around the world, it has been called the most important pamphlet in American history.

In 1776 Paine joined the Continental Army as it retreated across New Jersey, having been driven from New York by the British. Sitting on a log and using a drum for a desk, he wrote the first of his *Crisis* papers. On Washington's orders it was read aloud at camp to the defeated troops. How it affected them we can only imagine, but its first sentence remains moving: "These are the times that try men's souls."

Paine did not profit from the huge sales of his writings and paid dearly for his outspokenness. Poverty-stricken at the end of the American Revolution,

National Gallery of Art, Washington, gift of Marian B. Maurice

Thomas Paine (1806–1807) by John Wesley Jarvis (1781–1840).

he sailed for Europe to try to sell some inventions, only to be caught up in the French Revolution. Although no friend to kings, he urged that the overthrown French king be imprisoned rather than executed. His view angered the more violent French revolutionaries, who imprisoned Paine himself. It was probably only a guard's mistake in marking his door that saved him from being beheaded.

Paine was not treated much better when he returned to America in 1802. For his support of the French Revolution and for his attacks on organized religion, he was denounced as a "lying, drunken, brutal infidel" and even denied the right to vote. The "filthy Tom Paine" died in New Rochelle, New York, but abuse followed him literally to the grave. His tombstone was desecrated, and when his coffin was later dug up and taken to England, it was denied burial. No one knows what became of the body of the man who helped create American independence by his stingingly plain words.

The Crisis, Number 1

These are the times that try men's souls. The summer soldier and the sunshine patriot will, in this crisis, shrink from the service of their country; but he that stands it *now* deserves the love and thanks of man and woman. Tyranny, like hell, is not easily conquered; yet we have this consolation with us, that the harder the conflict, the more glorious that triumph. What we obtain too cheap, we esteem too lightly: it is dearness only that gives everything its value. Heaven knows how to put a proper price upon its goods, and it would be strange indeed if so celestial an article as *freedom* should not be highly rated. Britain, with an army to enforce her tyranny, has declared that she has a right not only to *tax*, but "to *bind* us in *all cases whatsoever*"; and if being *bound in that manner* is not slavery, then is there not such a thing as slavery upon earth. Even the expression is impious, for so unlimited a power can belong only to God. . . .

I have as little superstition in me as any man living, but my secret opinion has ever been, and still is, that God Almighty will not give up a people to military destruction, or leave them unsupportedly to perish, who have so earnestly and so repeatedly sought to avoid the calamities of war, by every decent method which wisdom could invent. Neither have I so much of the infidel in me as to suppose that He has relinquished the government of the world, and given us up to the care of devils; and as I do not, I cannot see on what grounds the king of Britain can look up to heaven for help against us: a common murderer, a highwayman, or a housebreaker has as good a pretense as he. . . .

I once felt all that kind of anger which a man ought to feel against the mean[1] principles that are held by the Tories.[2] A noted one, who kept a tavern at Amboy, was standing at his door, with as pretty a child in his hand, about eight or nine years old, as I ever saw, and after speaking his mind as freely as he thought was prudent, finished with this unfatherly expression, "Well! give me peace in my day." Not a man lives on the continent, but fully believes that a separation must sometime or other finally take place, and a generous parent should have said, "If there must be trouble, let it be in my day, that my child may have peace"; and this single reflection, well applied, is sufficient to awaken every man to duty. Not a place upon earth might be so happy as America. Her situation is remote from all the wrangling world, and she has nothing to do but to trade with them. A man can distinguish himself between temper and principle, and I am as confident as I am that God governs the world, that America will never be happy till she gets clear of foreign dominion. Wars, without ceasing, will break out till that period arrives, and the continent must in the end be conqueror; for though the flame of liberty may sometimes cease to shine, the coal can never expire. . . .

The heart that feels not now is dead; the blood of his children will curse his cowardice who shrinks back at a time when a little might have saved the whole, and made *them* happy. I love the man that can smile in trouble, that can gather strength from distress, and grow brave by reflection. 'Tis the business of little minds to shrink; but he whose heart is firm, and whose conscience approves his conduct, will pursue his principles unto death. My own line of reasoning is to myself as straight and clear as a ray of light. Not all the treasures of

---

1. **mean:** here, small-minded.

2. **Tories:** those colonists who supported the British.

the world, so far as I believe, could have induced me to support an offensive war, for I think it murder; but if a thief breaks into my house, burns and destroys my property, and kills or threatens to kill me, or those that are in it, and to "bind me in all cases whatsoever" to his absolute will, am I to suffer it? What signifies it to me whether he who does it is a king or a common man; my countryman or not my countryman; whether it be done by an individual villain, or an army of them? If we reason to the root of things we shall find no difference; neither can any just cause be assigned why we should punish in the one case and pardon in the other.

For Study and Discussion

Analyzing and Interpreting the Selection

1. In the first paragraph, Paine criticizes the "summer soldier and the sunshine patriot." To what sort of people does his phrase refer?

2. Where in *The Crisis* does Paine reaffirm the Puritan belief that America is divinely guided?

3. In the third paragraph, Paine uses his own experience to argue a point. What point does he make in telling his readers about the tavernkeeper at Amboy?

4. In the last paragraph Paine uses a common persuasive device, the **argument by analogy.** In arguing by analogy, a writer compares two similar situations, implying that the outcome of one will resemble the outcome of the other. What conclusion can be drawn from Paine's analogy between the political situation in America and the case of a thief who breaks into someone's house?

Literary Elements

The Aphoristic Style

Although Paine's language is simple and blunt, he composes some sentences with extra care, achieving what is called an **aphoristic** style. These sentences are not links in the chain of argument but memorable statements in themselves: "What we obtain too cheap, we esteem too lightly"; "Tyranny, like hell, is not easily conquered." In each case Paine cuts and polishes the sentence to make it stand out.

To write in the aphoristic style involves applying to prose many devices ordinarily used in poetry. For example, the force of "These are the times that try men's souls" arises in part from the emphatic rhythm and from the slight alliteration in *t*imes-*t*ry, the*se*-times-men's-*s*ouls. The effectiveness of "What we obtain too cheap, we esteem too lightly" partly depends on the balance between the two clauses. The structure of the second part of the sentence reflects as if in a mirror the structure of the first part. Select at least one other aphoristic statement and explain what devices Paine uses to make it effective.

Close Reading

Paraphrasing a Passage

Rewrite the following passage by Paine in a good modern style. On the basis of what you have written, discuss the changes in expression that have taken place since 1776. Note particularly the italicized words and phrases.

> *I have as little superstition in me* as any man living, but my *secret* opinion has ever been, and still is, that God Almighty will not *give up a people to military destruction,* or leave them *unsupportedly* to perish, who have so earnestly and so repeatedly sought to avoid the calamities of war, by every decent method which *wisdom could invent.* Neither *have I so much of the infidel in me* as to suppose that He has relinquished the government of the world, and *given us up to the care of devils.* . . .

Writing About Literature

Comparing Two Persuasive Works

Write a composition in which you compare Paine's paper with Henry's speech as persuasive works. In your composition, consider the following questions: What differences between the two works stem from the fact that one was intended to be heard and the other to be read, as well as heard? Although Paine was not addressing a group of listeners, what evidence is there that, like Henry, he had a specific audience in mind? Is Paine's purpose, like Henry's, to persuade his audience to take specific action or to maintain a particular opinion? How does Paine's purpose influence the arguments he uses? Which author, in your opinion, presents a more logical case? Why?

Probably the most dramatic coincidence in American history occurred the day John Adams died in Massachusetts. His last words were, "Thomas Jefferson still survives." But in Virginia earlier that same day, Thomas Jefferson also died. The coincidence is remarkable not only because Adams and Jefferson were both leaders of the Revolution, nor only because they were lifelong friends. The day on which they both died happened to be the Fourth of July, 1826, the fiftieth anniversary of the Declaration of Independence.

A champion of equal rights and of intellectual and political freedom, Jefferson had the tastes and some of the privileges of an aristocrat. His father, a man of substantial property, died when Jefferson was fourteen, having provided him with a thorough classical education and leaving him some 5,000 acres of land. In 1760, Jefferson entered the College of William and Mary, where he is said to have studied fifteen hours a day. After being graduated, he followed the path taken by Patrick Henry and many other Southern statesmen: he studied law, was admitted to the bar, and, in 1768, was elected to the Virginia House of Burgesses.

The Revolution made Jefferson prominent as it did many public-minded Southerners. In 1774 he published a widely read pamphlet on American rights. It probably prompted the Continental Congress to choose him to draft a declaration explaining to a "candid world" why the colonies felt it necessary to become "free and independent states." For part of the war he acted as governor of Virginia. Jefferson wished to retire after the Revolution, but was drawn again into public affairs. A skillful diplomat, he succeeded Benjamin Franklin in 1785 as minister to France. He became Secretary of State under George Washington. In 1801, after a bitterly fought election, he became President himself. His accomplishments in office included the Louisiana Purchase, which added to the United States over 820,000 square miles of land formerly owned by France. This huge tract was later carved into thirteen states or parts of states.

Thomas Jefferson (1810–1815) by Gilbert Stuart (1755–1828). Oil on wood.

Jefferson is remembered mostly as a statesman. But like Franklin and other figures of the Age of Reason, he was extremely versatile. Intensely interested in education, he drew up the program of studies for the University of Virginia. Well-read in science, languages, and philosophy, he avidly collected books, ten thousand of which he sold to Congress as the basis for what is now the Library of Congress. A lover of the arts, he attended the theater, collected paintings, and played the violin. (His wife Martha played the piano and harpsichord.) A fine architect, he designed much of his beautiful home, Monticello, and planned the buildings and campus of the University of Virginia. Whether remembered as a statesman, or as a patron of the arts, or as an architect, or as the author of the Declaration of Independence, or as the third President, Thomas Jefferson—to quote John Adams—"still survives."

Thomas Jefferson **97**

Original draft of Declaration of Independence.

The Declaration of Independence

In his *Autobiography*, Jefferson tells how the Continental Congress appointed a committee "to prepare a declaration of independence," consisting of "J. Adams, Dr. Franklin, Roger Sherman, Robert R. Livingston, and myself." The committee asked Jefferson to draft the declaration. The final version adopted by the Congress differs somewhat from Jefferson's draft. Jefferson explains, "The parts struck out by Congress shall be distinguished by a black line drawn under them; and those inserted by them shall be placed in the margin or in a concurrent column."

A DECLARATION BY THE REPRESENTATIVES OF THE UNITED STATES OF AMERICA, IN GENERAL CONGRESS ASSEMBLED

When in the course of human events it becomes necessary for one people to dissolve the political bands which have connected them with another, and to assume among the powers of the earth the separate and equal station to which the laws of nature and of nature's God entitle them, a decent respect to the opinions of mankind requires that they should declare the causes which impel them to the separation.

We hold these truths to be sacred and undeniable: that all men are created equal; that they are endowed by their Creator with inherent and inalienable rights; that among these are life, liberty, and the pursuit of happiness; that to secure these rights, governments are instituted among men, deriving their just powers from the consent of the governed; that whenever any form of government becomes destructive of these ends, it is the right of the people to alter or to abolish it, and to institute new government, laying its foundation on such principles, and organizing its powers in such form, as to them shall seem most likely to effect their safety and happiness. Prudence, indeed, will dictate that governments long established should not be changed for light and transient causes; and accordingly all experience hath shown that mankind are more disposed to suffer while evils are sufferable than to right themselves by abolishing the forms to which they are accustomed. But when a long train of abuses and usurpations, begun at a distinguished period and pursuing invariably the same object, evinces a design to reduce them under absolute despotism, it is their right, it is their duty, to throw off such government, and to provide new guards for their future security. Such has been the patient sufferance of these colonies; and such is now the necessity

self-evident
certain

which constrains them to expunge their former systems of government. The history of the present king of Great Britain is a history of unremitting injuries and usurpations, among which appears no solitary fact to contradict the uniform tenor of the rest, but all have in direct object the establishment of an absolute tyranny over these states. To prove this, let facts be submitted to a candid world for the truth of which we pledge a faith yet unsullied by falsehood.

    alter

    repeated

    all having

He has refused his assent to laws the most wholesome and necessary for the public good.

He has forbidden his governors to pass laws of immediate and pressing importance, unless suspended in their operation till his assent should be obtained; and when so suspended, he has utterly neglected to attend to them.

He has refused to pass other laws for the accommodation of large districts of people, unless those people would relinquish the right of representation in the legislature, a right inestimable to them, and formidable to tyrants only.

He has called together legislative bodies at places unusual, uncomfortable, and distant from the depository of their public records, for the sole purpose of fatiguing them into compliance with his measures.

He has dissolved representative houses repeatedly and continually for opposing with manly firmness his invasions on the rights of the people.

He has refused for a long time after such dissolutions to cause others to be elected, whereby the legislative powers, incapable of annihilation, have returned to the people at large for their exercise, the state remaining in the meantime exposed to all the dangers of invasion from without and convulsions within.

He has endeavored to prevent the population of these states; for that purpose obstructing the laws for naturalization of foreigners, refusing to pass others to encourage their migrations hither, and raising the conditions of new appropriations of lands.

He has suffered the administration of justice totally to cease in some of these states, refusing his assent to laws for establishing judiciary powers.

    obstructed

    by

He has made our judges dependent on his will alone, for the tenure of their offices, and the amount and payment of their salaries.

He has erected a multitude of new offices by a self-assumed power and sent hither swarms of officers to harass our people and eat out their substance.

He has kept among us in times of peace standing armies and ships of war without the consent of our legislatures.

He has affected to render the military independent of, and superior to, the civil power.

He has combined with others to subject us to a jurisdiction foreign to our constitutions and unacknowledged by our laws, giving his assent to their acts of pretended legislation: for quartering large bodies of armed troops among us; for protecting them by a mock trial from punishment for any murders which they should commit on the inhabitants of these states; for cutting off our trade with all parts of the world; for imposing taxes on us without our consent; for depriving us [in many cases] of the benefits of trial by jury; for transporting us beyond seas to be tried for pretended offenses; for abolishing the free system of English laws in a neighboring province, establishing therein an arbitrary government, and enlarging its boundaries, so as to render it at once an example and fit instrument for introducing the same absolute rule into these states; for taking away our charters [colonies], abolishing our most valuable laws, and altering fundamentally the forms of our governments; for suspending our own legislatures, and declaring themselves invested with power to legislate for us in all cases whatsoever.

He has abdicated government here withdrawing his governors, and declaring us out of his allegiance and protection. [by declaring us out of his protection, and waging war against us.]

He has plundered our seas, ravaged our coasts, burnt our towns, and destroyed the lives of our people.

He is at this time transporting large armies of foreign mercenaries to complete the works of death, desolation, and tyranny already begun with circumstances of cruelty and perfidy [scarcely paralleled in the most barbarous ages, and totally] unworthy the head of a civilized nation.

He has constrained our fellow citizens taken captive on the high seas to bear arms against their country, to become the executioners of their friends and brethren, or to fall themselves by their hands.

He has [excited domestic insurrection among us, and has] endeavored to bring on the inhabitants of our frontiers the merciless Indian savages, whose known rule of warfare is an undistinguished destruction of all ages, sexes, and conditions of existence.

He has incited treasonable insurrections of our fellow citizens, with the allurements of forfeiture and confiscation of our property.

He has waged cruel war against human nature itself, violating its most sacred rights of life and liberty in the persons of a distant people who never offended him, captivating and carrying them into slavery in another hemisphere, or to incur miserable death in their transportation thither. This piratical warfare, the opprobrium[1] of infidel powers, is the warfare of the Christian king of Great Britain. Determined to keep open a market where men should be bought and sold, he has prostituted his negative[2] for suppressing every legislative attempt to prohibit or to restrain this execrable[3] commerce. And that this assemblage of horrors might want no fact of distinguished die, he is now exciting those very people to rise in arms among us, and to purchase that liberty of which he has deprived them, by murdering the people on whom he also obtruded them: thus paying off former

---

1. **opprobrium** (ə-prō′brē-əm): disgrace.   2. **negative:** here, the right of veto.
3. **execrable** (ĕk′sĭ-krə-bəl): detestable.

crimes committed against the liberties of one people with crimes which he urges them to commit against the lives of another.

In every stage of these oppressions we have petitioned for redress in the most humble terms: our repeated petitions have been answered only by repeated injuries.

A prince whose character is thus marked by every act which may define a tyrant is unfit to be the ruler of a [ ] people who mean to be free. Future ages will scarcely believe that the hardiness of one man adventured, within the short compass of twelve years only, to lay a foundation so broad and so undisguised for tyranny over a people fostered and fixed in principles of freedom.

Nor have we been wanting in attentions to our British brethren. We have warned them from time to time of attempts by their legislature to extend a jurisdiction over these our states. We have reminded them of the circumstances of our emigration and settlement here, no one of which could warrant so strange a pretension; that these were effected at the expense of our own blood and treasure, unassisted by the wealth or the strength of Great Britain; that in constituting indeed our several forms of government, we had adopted one common king, thereby laying a foundation for perpetual league and amity with them; but that submission to their parliament was no part of our constitution, nor ever in idea, if history may be credited; and we [ ] appealed to their native justice and magnanimity as well as to the ties of our common kindred to disavow these usurpations which were likely to interrupt our connection and correspondence. They too have been deaf to the voice of justice and of consanguinity,[5] and when occasions have been given them, by the regular course of their laws, of removing from their councils the disturbers of our harmony, they have, by their free election, reestablished them in power. At this very time too they are permitting their chief magistrate to send over not only soldiers of our common blood, but Scotch and foreign mercenaries to invade and destroy us. These facts have given the last stab to agonizing affection, and manly spirit bids us to renounce forever these unfeeling brethren. We must endeavor to forget our former love for them, and hold them as we hold the rest of mankind, enemies in war, in peace friends. We might have been a free and a great people together; but a communication of grandeur and of freedom it seems is below their dignity. Be it so, since they will have it. The road to happiness and to glory is open to us too. We will tread it apart from them, and acquiesce in the necessity which denounces[6] our eternal separation [ ]!

We, therefore, the Representatives of the United States of America

free

an unwarrantable/us

have
and we have conjured[4] them
by
would inevitably

We must therefore
and hold them, as we hold the rest of mankind, enemies in war, in peace friends.

---

4. **conjured:** here, appealed to, begged.   5. **consanguinity:** (kŏn′săng-gwĭn′ə-tē): relationship resulting from common ancestry; blood relationship.   6. **denounces:** here, makes known in a solemn or official manner.

The Declaration of Independence (1787–1812) by John Trumbull. Oil on canvas.

in General Congress assembled, [ ] do in the name and by authority of the good people of these states reject and renounce all allegiance and subjection to the kings of Great Britain and all others who may hereafter claim by, through, or under them; we utterly dissolve all political connection which may heretofore have subsisted between us and the people or parliament of Great Britain; and finally we do assert and declare these colonies to be free and independent states, and that as free and independent states, they have full power to levy war, conclude peace, contract alliances, establish commerce, and to do all other acts and things which independent states may of right do.

And for the support of this declaration, [ ] we mutually pledge to each other our lives, our fortunes, and our sacred honor.

appealing to the Supreme Judge of the world for the rectitude of our intentions,

colonies solemnly publish and declare that these united colonies are and of right ought to be free and independent states; that they are absolved from all allegiance to the British Crown, and that all political connection between them and the State of Great Britain is and ought to be totally dissolved;

with a firm reliance on the protection of divine providence,

For Study and Discussion

Analyzing and Interpreting the Selection

1. As members of an age of reason, Jefferson and other Revolutionary leaders wished to seem not hotheaded but reasonable. **a.** What reason is given in the first paragraph for issuing the Declaration? **b.** In the second paragraph, how do the writers try to show that their actions have not been hasty?

2a. In the second paragraph, whom do the Revolutionaries blame for America's difficulties? **b.** According to them, what was his motive? **c.** In the long bill of particulars, how do they emphasize that America's troubles came from him alone and not the people of Great Britain? **d.** Why is this an important distinction?

3. Jefferson's high reputation as a writer is based in part on the Declaration of Independence. Jefferson uses various rhetorical devices in the Declaration, including **repetition** and **parallelism** (the repetition of phrases or sentences that are similar in structure or meaning). Find passages in the Declaration that exemplify these devices.

Literary Elements

Persuasion: Beginning, Middle, and End

Although it is a unique document, the Declaration of Independence is constructed like any good argument or essay and like most good stories and poems. That is, it has a clear beginning, middle, and end. It begins by announcing the subject; the long middle section explains and illustrates the subject; the ending summarizes the subject and draws a conclusion.

So, in the first paragraph the Revolutionaries announce as their subject the need "for one people to dissolve the political bands which have connected them with another. . . ." The bulk of the Declaration explains why the "bands" must be broken, offering first general and then specific reasons. The general reasons include several "self-evident" truths—truths that need no proof because they belong to the nature of things, such as the principle that "all men are created equal." The specific reasons appear in the long list of criminal acts committed against America. The Declaration ends by restating the subject in the form of a conclusion: "these united colonies are and of right ought to be free and independent states. . . ."

Try to plan your own compositions according to the basic form of the Declaration: (a) short statement of the subject; (b) elaboration of the subject; (c) summary of the subject, with conclusions.

Language and Vocabulary

Comparing Words in Two Versions

All good writers try to say exactly what they have in mind, not something merely close to it. To say something exactly means choosing exactly the right word. In the margin of the text appear many revisions made in the Declaration before it was published. They demonstrate that Jefferson and his associates chose their words carefully. Using a dictionary, try to decide why Jefferson and the other delegates chose the following words and made the following changes. How does a "decent" respect for the opinions of mankind differ from simple "respect"? How do "inalienable rights" differ from "rights"? How does the "pursuit of happiness" differ from mere "happiness"? How do the following substitutions of words change the original meaning of the statements in which they occur: *alter* for *expunge* (second paragraph); *repeated* for *unremitting* (second paragraph); *obstructed* for *suffered* (the bill of particulars)?

Writing About Literature

Discussing Changes in the Declaration

Write a composition discussing the nature of the changes made in Jefferson's version of the Declaration. Notice that several whole paragraphs near the end were eliminated or completely rewritten. In your composition, consider which changes were made to improve style and which were made for political reasons. Try to give your composition a beginning, middle, and end.

The "J. Hector St. John" who became internationally known as the author of *Letters from an American Farmer* was born and died in France, and his real name was Michel-Guillaume Jean de Crèvecoeur (pronounced mĭ-shĕl′ gē-yōm′ zhäN də krĕv-kœr′). The difference between the two names reflects both Crèvecoeur's life and his work. He experienced and wrote about the transformation of a European into an American. In the process he learned bitterly about the distance that sometimes separated promise from reality in America.

Crèvecoeur was educated at a Jesuit school in Normandy, where he learned English. He first saw the New World at the age of nineteen when he sailed to Canada to serve in the French and Indian War as a soldier and map maker. After being wounded and hospitalized, he traveled as a surveyor in upstate New York and in Vermont, under the name "James Hector St. John." He became a citizen of New York in 1765, soon married an American woman, and settled on a 120-acre farm which he named Pine Hill.

Crèvecoeur did not stay settled long. The Revolution turned the region around his farm into a battle zone. He seems to have taken neither the loyalist nor the patriot side, perhaps because he sympathized with humble people on both sides. As a result, the Revolutionaries forced him to leave his farm, and the British imprisoned him for a month as a suspected spy. Apparently disgusted with the war, he left his wife, daughter, and two sons in America and sailed in 1780 to London, where his *Letters* were published two years later. The book remains a classic statement of the meaning of America to immigrants. Its fame led to Crèvecoeur's being appointed by the French government as a representative to New York, New Jersey, and Connecticut.

Crèvecoeur's return to America in 1783 proved grim. The war had ended, but he found his wife dead, his farm burned, and his children taken to Boston. The man who had praised America for its vast promise to Europeans retired in 1790 to Normandy, where he had been born. Poor and unknown, he lived there with his father for the last twenty-three years of his life.

Plan of a newly cleared American farm.

Library of Congress

Michel-Guillaume Jean de Crèvecoeur **105**

FROM
Letters from an American Farmer

In this great American asylum,[1] the poor of Europe have by some means met together, and in consequence of various causes; to what purpose should they ask one another what countrymen they are? Alas, two thirds of them had no country. Can a wretch who wanders about, who works and starves, whose life is a continual scene of sore affliction or pinching penury; can that man call England or any other kingdom his country? A country that had no bread for him, whose fields procured him no harvest, who met with nothing but the frowns of the rich, the severity of the laws, with jails and punishments; who owned not a single foot of the extensive surface of this planet? No! urged by a variety of motives, here they came. Everything has tended to regenerate them: new laws, a new mode of living, a new social system; here they are become men: in Europe they were as so many useless plants, wanting vegetative mold,[2] and refreshing showers; they withered, and were mowed down by want, hunger, and war; but now by the power of transplantation, like all other plants they have taken root and flourished! Formerly they were not numbered in any civil lists[3] of their country except in those of the poor; here they rank as citizens. By what invisible power has this surprising metamorphosis[4] been performed? By that of the laws and that of their industry. . . .

What then is the American, this new man? He is either an European or the descendant of an European, hence that strange mixture of blood which you will find in no other country. I could point out to you a family whose grandfather was an Englishman, whose wife was Dutch, whose son married a French woman, and whose present four sons have now four wives of different nations. *He* is an American, who, leaving behind him all his ancient prejudices and manners, receives new ones from the new mode of life he has embraced, the new government he obeys, and the new rank he holds. He becomes an American by being received in the broad lap of our great *Alma Mater.*[5] Here individuals of all nations are melted into a new race of men, whose labors and posterity will one day cause great changes in the world. Americans are the Western pilgrims, who are carrying along with them that great mass of arts, sciences, vigor, and industry which began long since in the East; they will finish the great circle.

The Americans were once scattered all over Europe; here they are incorporated into one of the finest systems of population which has ever appeared, and which will hereafter become distinct by the power of the different climates they inhabit. The American ought therefore to love this country much better than that wherein either he or his forefathers were born. Here the rewards of his industry follow with equal steps the progress of his labor; his

1. **asylum** (ə-sī′ləm): place of refuge.
2. **vegetative mold:** soil enriched with decayed vegetable matter.
3. **civil lists:** lists containing names of distinguished persons.
4. **metamorphosis** (mĕt′ə-môr′fə-sĭs): transformation.

5. ***Alma Mater*** (ăl′mə mä′tər); literally, "fostering mother," usually applied to a school or college, but here applied to America.

labor is founded on the basis of nature, *self-interest;* can it want a stronger allurement? Wives and children, who before in vain demanded of him a morsel of bread, now, fat and frolicsome, gladly help their father to clear those fields whence exuberant crops are to arise to feed and to clothe them all, without any part being claimed either by a despotic prince, a rich abbot,[6] or a mighty lord. Here religion demands but little of him: a small voluntary salary to the minister, and gratitude to God; can he refuse these? The American is a new man, who acts upon new principles; he must therefore entertain new ideas, and form new opinions. From involuntary idleness, servile dependence, penury, and useless labor, he has passed to toils of a very different nature, rewarded by ample subsistence.[7]—This is an American.

6. **abbot:** head of a monastery.
7. **subsistence:** livelihood.

For Study and Discussion

Analyzing and Interpreting the Selection
1. In the first paragraph, Crèvecoeur describes the experience of European immigrants to America. **a.** Why, in his view, are they glad to leave Europe? **b.** What happens to them when they begin living in America?
2. Crèvecoeur concludes his letter by posing a famous question: "What then is the American, this new man?" **a.** How does he answer the question—that is, what does he take to be the essential meaning of "American"? **b.** In what sense is the American a "new man"?

Literary Elements

The Literary Letter
Crèvecoeur reported his experiences in the New World in a book of imaginary letters written to an English friend, "Mr. F. B." This kind of letter, known as a **literary letter,** is an ancient form that has been used to write essays, novels, and even poems.

Crèvecoeur's letters are supposedly written by an American farmer named "James." James writes to a friend, but actually addresses an audience of anonymous readers, "eavesdroppers" on the correspondence. Through James, Crèvecoeur offers examples and arguments for his opinions, aiming to have them accepted by a larger public.

How does the second paragraph of the selection from *Letters from an American Farmer* illustrate the method of the literary letter—combining the persuasive advantages of an intimate tone with those of solid evidence and example?

Creative Writing

Composing a Literary Letter
Compose a literary letter addressed to an imaginary friend but intended for a wide audience. Contrast America today with eighteenth-century America as described by Crèvecoeur, telling which one in your opinion is preferable.

Phillis Wheatley (1773).

PHILLIS WHEATLEY
1753?–1784

Little is known about the life of the first widely applauded American poet except that she happened to be a young black slave. Her name, Phillis Wheatley, was given her by the prosperous and cultivated Wheatley family of Boston, in whose household she began to serve shortly after she was brought over from Africa at about the age of seven. The Wheatleys were involved in missionary work to convert Indians and blacks to Christianity, and they raised the young girl as a Christian. They taught her to read and write English, probably in part so that she could read the Bible—which, by one account, she learned to do fluently only sixteen months after arriving in Boston. Soon she began to read Latin classics and English poets and to write poetry herself. In 1767 a Rhode Island newspaper published one of her poems, concerning a shipwreck. She was then about thirteen years old.

In 1772 she accompanied the Wheatleys' son on a memorable voyage to England. Treated as a celebrity, she was presented with a gift copy of John Milton's *Paradise Lost* by the Lord Mayor of London. She was also befriended by an English noblewoman active in missionary work, the Countess of Huntingdon. The Countess probably helped pay for the publication of a whole volume of Wheatley's works, *Poems on Various Subjects, Religious and Moral.*

Wheatley returned home in the fall of 1773, only months before the Boston Tea Party. As the Revolutionary War drew on, she wrote several poems defending the American cause. One of them, written in October 1775, was addressed to George Washington, who had just taken command of the American armies. He wanted to publish the poem himself but feared that his patronage would be mistaken for vanity. Instead he wrote to the poet, saying he would "be happy to see a person so favored by the Muses" and inviting her to visit him at the Continental Army camp. She made the visit, but we do not know what they said to each other.

Wheatley's quick rise to fame was matched by an equally quick fall. Having been granted freedom by her master, she married John Peters, a jack-of-all-trades who seems to have worked variously as a lawyer, baker, doctor, and grocer. In 1779 a second volume of her poems was advertised, but it was never published. Impoverished and imprisoned for debt, Peters seems to have fled to North Carolina, taking with him the manuscript of his wife's poems, which was subsequently lost. Wheatley apparently took work in a rooming house. Around 1784, two of her three children died. In December of that year, she was dead herself at about the age of thirty.

Several Americans marked Phillis Wheatley's death with poems praising the life and works of a woman who had become known as an "extraordinary poetical genius." But her fame had its price. She came to look upon herself as a middle-class Bostonian. When asked to return to Africa as a missionary herself, she declined. She could not speak the language, she said, and she would be out of place: "how like a Barbarian should I look to the Natives." Another price she paid for becoming a famous poet was to be praised less for the quality of her poems than for the fact that she was young, female, and recently taken from Africa. That fact, however, continues to make her poems remarkable and worth reading today.

To His Excellency General Washington

Celestial choir! enthron'd in realms of light,
  Columbia's° scenes of glorious toils I write.
While freedom's cause her anxious breast alarms,
She flashes dreadful in refulgent° arms.
See mother earth her offspring's fate bemoan,   5
And nations gaze at scenes before unknown!
See the bright beams of heaven's revolving light
Involved in sorrows and the veil of night!
  The goddess comes, she moves divinely fair,
Olive and laurel binds her golden hair: 10
Wherever shines this native of the skies,
Unnumber'd charms and recent graces rise.
  Muse!° bow propitious while my pen relates
How pour her armies through a thousand gates,
As when Eolus° heaven's fair face deforms,   15
Enwrapp'd in tempest and a night of storms;
Astonish'd ocean feels the wild uproar,
The refluent° surges beat the sounding shore;
Or thick as leaves in Autumn's golden reign,
Such, and so many, moves the warrior's train.   20
In bright array they seek the work of war,
Where high unfurl'd the ensign° waves in air.
Shall I to Washington their praise recite?
Enough thou know'st them in the fields of fight.
Thee, first in peace and honours,—we demand   25
The grace and glory of thy martial band.
Fam'd for thy valour, for thy virtues more,
Hear every tongue thy guardian aid implore!
  One century scarce perform'd its destined round,
When Gallic° powers Columbia's fury found;   30
And so may you, whoever dares disgrace
The land of freedom's heaven-defended race!
Fix'd are the eyes of nations on the scales,
For in their hopes Columbia's arm prevails.
Anon Britannia° droops the pensive head,   35
While round increase the rising hills of dead.
Ah! cruel blindness to Columbia's state!
Lament thy thirst of boundless power too late.
  Proceed, great chief, with virtue on thy side,
Thy ev'ry action let the goddess guide.   40
A crown, a mansion, and a throne that shine,
With gold unfading, WASHINGTON! be thine.

2. **Columbia:** America personified as a woman.

4. **refulgent** (rĭ-fŭl′jənt): radiant.

13. **Muse:** one of the nine goddesses presiding over literature, the arts, and the sciences.
15. **Eolus** (ē′ə-ləs): in Greek mythology, the god of the winds.
18. **refluent** (rĕf′lōō-ənt): ebbing; flowing back.

22. **ensign** (ĕn′sən): flag.

30. **Gallic** (găl′ĭk): French. The poet is referring to the victory of the colonists in the French and Indian War.

35. **Britannia:** England.

Apotheosis of George Washington and Benjamin Franklin (c. 1785). The theme of this plate-printed cloth is American independence. Washington is shown above, guiding the chariot of America. Below, Minerva leads Franklin and Liberty toward the Temple of Fame.

For Study and Discussion

Analyzing and Interpreting the Poem

1. We have seen that American writers often regard their country as divinely guided. In what phrases or lines does Phillis Wheatley link America with heaven and the divine?

2. America in the poem is represented as a woman or goddess named Columbia. The device of treating nature, ideas, or inanimate objects as if they were human beings is called **personification. a.** What human details does Wheatley give to Columbia?

b. As she describes them, what are Columbia's (that is, America's) feelings toward England?

3. Like all colonists, Americans tended to imitate the ways of the mother country. **a.** What words in the closing lines of the poem suggest that Americans at the time viewed Washington in terms of English customs? **b.** What words in the poem suggest that Wheatley herself was trying to imitate the sophistication of English culture by writing in a learned and ornate style?

Revolutionary Songs

Not only in pamphlets and speeches did Revolutionary Americans express their feelings about taxes, armies, and oppression. They wheeled through the streets carts bearing life-sized effigies of English officials; they performed plays and skits; they made their cities glow at night with fireworks and candle-lit pictures of General Washington. And they sang—at taverns and military camps, in their homes and churches, at crowded rallies. Singing did more than spread political ideas; it spread political *feelings*. By bringing people together to join hands and voices, it instilled what John Adams called the "sensation of freedom."

Hundreds of songs on political subjects were written and sung, but three became especially popular. The earliest was the "Liberty Song" (1768) by the Pennsylvania lawyer John Dickinson. In just nine stanzas and a repeated chorus it summed up American sentiments about taxation. The first stanza depicts liberty as a woman who must be protected, an often-used image with strong unconscious appeals. The chorus calls for patient but unbending resistance to taxes imposed by England:

> *Come join hand in hand, brave Americans all,*
> *And rouse your bold hearts at fair Liberty's call;*
> *No tyrannous acts, shall suppress your just claim,*
> *Or stain with dishonor America's name.*
> > *In freedom we're born, and in freedom we'll live;*
> > *Our purses are ready,*
> > *Steady, Friends, steady,*
> *Not as* slaves, *but as* freemen *our money we'll give.*

Few people today know the "Liberty Song," but everyone knows the popular Revolutionary song originally called "The Farmer and his Son's return from a visit to the CAMP." Today we call it "Yankee Doodle." The history of "Yankee Doodle" is obscure. The tune was probably at first a British march. Most of the words, as we know them, were probably written around 1775, just after the forming of the American army. In the Revolutionary version, the speaker is a young boy visiting Washington's camp. The first of the fifteen stanzas and the chorus go:

> *FATHER and I went down to camp,*
> *Along with Captain Gooding,*
> *And there we see the men and boys*
> *As thick as hasty pudding.*
> > *Yankey doodle keep it up, yankey doodle dandy,*
> > *Mind the music and the step,*
> *And with the girls be handy.*

Illustration from broadside "The Yankey's Return from Camp."

Whatever the origins of "Yankee Doodle," its youthful, naive, and exuberant hero has become an enduring symbol of the American character.

Although "Yankee Doodle" now ranks almost as a second national anthem, it was not the most popular song of the Revolution. Credit for writing that belongs to a lame, one-eyed, sometime garbage collector who was also the first American composer—William Billings of Boston. The tune of his "Chester" recalls New England church music; the words argue stubbornly that righteousness can overcome oppression. Sung throughout America during the Revolution, "Chester" begins:

> *Let tyrants shake their iron rod,*
> *And slavery clank her galling chains;*
> *We fear them not; we trust in God—*
> *New England's God forever reigns.*

Because they could compress complicated ideas and create feelings of unity and determination, political songs became enormously popular during the Revolution. An old saying has it that whoever writes a nation's songs need not care who writes its laws.

The Revolutionary Period

In contrast to the earliest American literature, much of the writing of this period is devoted to a single overwhelming subject—the American Revolution. As stated in the unit introduction, "The American Revolution was fought not only with muskets but also with thousands of pamphlets, essays, songs, poems, and speeches." Just as the earlier generation had struggled merely to survive in a new and often hostile environment, so this generation fought desperately to uphold the colonists' right to a dignified and free life. In the process, the legendary statesmen and writers of the Revolutionary Period created an ageless body of literature that has been studied and admired the world over.

Here are two statements that have been made about this era of American letters. Write a carefully documented essay in which you discuss one of the statements in terms of the literature you have studied in this unit. Consider the lives of the authors and the history of the period in your discussion.

1. [During] the revolutionary years . . . the view spread that America was created as a refuge from tyranny with a common heritage of freedom. American poets began to develop the shared theme of the rising glory of America . . . where humanity could realize its age-old dreams of a full and rich life.

> Everett Emerson
> (from "The Cultural Context
> of the American Revolution")

2. During the Revolution books became weapons. To do their work they must reach a wider audience than most earlier American writings had. . . . This resulted in more, and in some ways better, writing. Authors were forced to experiment with language and with various literary types.

> Kenneth B. Murdock
> (from "The Colonial and
> Revolutionary Period")

For General Background

Bailyn, Bernard, *The Ideological Origins of the American Revolution* (Harvard University Press, 1967)

Emerson, Everett, ed., *American Literature 1764–1789: The Revolutionary Years* (University of Wisconsin Press, 1977)

Rankin, Hugh F., *The Theater in Colonial America* (University of North Carolina Press, 1965)

Silverman, Kenneth, *A Cultural History of the American Revolution* (T. Y. Crowell, 1976)

Tyler, Moses Coit, *The Literary History of the American Revolution 1763–1783* (1897; rpt. Frederick Ungar Publishing Co., 1957)

For Leisure Reading

Alden, John, *The American Revolution* (Harper & Row, 1954)

Bridenbaugh, Carl and Jessica, *Rebels and Gentlemen: Philadelphia in the Age of Franklin* (Greenwood, 1978)

Forbes, Esther, *Paul Revere and the World He Lived In* (Houghton Mifflin, 1962)

Franklin, Benjamin, *The Autobiography* (numerous paperback editions available)

———, "An Edict by the King of Prussia"; "The Ephemera"

Lemay, J. A. Leo, ed., *The Oldest Revolutionary: Essays on Benjamin Franklin* (University of Pennsylvania Press, 1976)

Malone, Dumas, *Jefferson the Virginian* (Little, Brown and Company, 1948)

Mason, Julian D., Jr., ed., *The Poems of Phillis Wheatley* (University of North Carolina Press, 1966)

Nye, Russel B., *The Cultural Life of the New Nation 1776–1830* (Harper & Row, 1960)

Peterson, Merrill D., ed., *Thomas Jefferson: A Profile* (Hill and Wang, 1967)

Van Doren, Carl C., *Benjamin Franklin* (Greenwood, 1973)

Zall, P. M., ed., *Ben Franklin Laughing: Anecdotes from Original Sources by and About Benjamin Franklin* (University of California Press, 1980)

FIRST HARVEST
1800–1840

Kindred Spirits (1849) by Asher B. Durand (1796–1886). Oil on canvas.

UNDER MY WINGS EVERY THING PROSPERS

A view of New Orleans from the Plantation of Marigny, November, 1803.
Oil painting by J. L. Boqueta de Woiseri.

In the decade before the American Revolution, when Crèvecoeur posed his famous question, "What then is the American, this new man?" (page 106), the answer seemed simple and optimistic. Crèvecoeur saw "in this great American asylum" a refuge for the poor and oppressed of Europe. Here the abundance of available land and the "mild laws" of British colonial rule soon transformed the homeless immigrant into a prosperous farmer. The American lived in a society free of those privileges of birth and rank that, in Europe, gave advantage to the few and held the many in subjection. Since every man could through his own industry become a self-sufficient farmer and landowner, a basic equality was assured. There would be neither poverty nor ostentatious wealth, and the economic independence of every citizen would make political tyranny impossible. Crèvecoeur looked forward to increasing political and religious harmony and the gradual elimination of all forms of oppression and prejudice. The American had been "melted," as he put it, from the many nationalities of Europe; he was "a new man," forming new opinions and acting upon new principles and ideas. The political or religious prejudice common to Europe, he observed, evaporated in the more expansive air of this vast continent, and the immigrant took on a larger identity as an American. Thus the land itself helped to create the American nationality.

Despite his interest in this new nationality, Crèvecoeur ignored the political and economic changes that were creating a new spirit of nationalism. His vision of a society of contented and self-subsistent farmers, a democratic dream of simplicity, equality, and tolerance, portrayed an America without conflict or even significant change. Yet conflict about the rights of Americans was even then sweeping the colonies, and profound change, in the form of armed rebellion, would soon drive Crèvecoeur himself temporarily from America. The spirit of nationalism developed from just those forces that he hoped America would escape: revolution and then a second war with England in 1812, rapid industrialization, and increasingly centralized economic and political systems.

If political changes were a powerful influence toward nationalism, the economic changes that followed were scarcely less so. In 1789, the year that George Washington became the first President of the United States, an English mechanic named Samuel Slater arrived in America with plans for a textile mill. Four years later, Eli Whitney perfected his cotton gin. The development of native industries, hastened by European wars that at times cut America off from foreign goods, soon created, in Crèvecoeur's words, "great manufacturers employing thousands." While cities grew with new factories, the wilderness frontier pushed outward. In 1803 President Jefferson negotiated the Louisiana Purchase from France, extending the boundaries of the United States to the Rocky Mountains. Farmers in the

Pawtucket Bridge and Falls (Slater's Mill). Watercolor and ink by unknown artist.

Rhode Island Historical Society

Pioneers Traveling Down the Ohio River in Flatboats. Colored woodcut by Felix O. C. Darley (1822–1888).

new lands clamored for roads and canals to move their produce to city markets. These improvements, along with new means of transportation (the steamboat and then the railroad), helped to bind the states together as a nation.

In political terms, the struggle for nationalism continued long after the Constitution established the nation as a fact. Despite improvements in transportation, communication between widely separated sections of the country remained difficult; when California and Oregon joined the Union, the easiest way to reach them from the East was by a 20,000-mile sea voyage around Cape Horn. Political factions, far from disappearing as Crèvecoeur had expected, became the basis of national political parties and thereby enabled citizens to express their views on national issues. But the tendency to divide into small and often extreme factions remained a danger to the life of the nation. As he left the Presidency in 1837, Andrew Jackson warned that internal divisions were the greatest present threat to America. Slavery, as it spread with the planting of cotton across the South, became the focus of the most dangerous of these divisions, a widening split between North and South. For these reasons many European observers (and some Americans) expected the United States to break up into several nations. But such observers overlooked the fact that through the years the idea of the Union of these states had become for most Americans, whatever their differences, an article of faith. Years later, when internal division reached the point of civil war, Abraham Lincoln expressed the feelings of the majority of his compatriots when he referred to the preservation of the Union as a sacred trust. "The Union," Ralph Waldo Emerson observed, "is a part of the religion of this people."

The spirit of nationalism was also reflected in a drive toward cultural independence, especially in literature. Before the Revolution, Crèvecoeur looked forward to America's carrying on the European—particularly the English—literary tradition. After independence, however, there was a call for a specifically national literature that would express the values and ideals of the new nation. Often this call was more patriotic than literary, for literature is not a product to be supplied on demand. American writers grew up with English literature as their major literary heritage, and they did not discard it. Instead, they made use of the available literary forms and adapted them to their own experience as Americans. No major writer was without significant influences from other literatures. American literature did in time become distinctive in its materials, themes, and attitudes, not by proclaiming its distinctness, but through normal cultural change. American culture matured by taking its place among the other great cultures of the world.

Classicism and Romanticism

The United States solidified as a nation during the period of major cultural change characterized by the shift from classicism to Romanticism. Although this change eventually affected every aspect of culture, including all the arts, education, philosophy, and even science, it was most immediately apparent in literature. The triumph in America of nineteenth-century Romanticism over eighteenth-century classicism was an intellectual revolution second in importance only to the political revolution that brought the nation into being.

Classicism rested first upon the belief that reason is the dominating characteristic both of nature and of human nature, and that both are governed by fixed, unchanging laws. In the popular eighteenth-century image, nature was viewed as a self-contained machine, like a watch, whose laws of operation could be rationally understood. Classicism emphasized reason over the imagination, the social over the personal, the common over the individual. In literature, classicism valued clarity, order, and balance. The imagination, though essential to literature, had to be restrained by reason and common sense.

| 1790–c. 1850 | Industrial Revolution |

1790–c. 1850 — Industrial Revolution

1793 — Eli Whitney develops the cotton gin

1800 — Library of Congress founded

Washington Irving

1803 — Louisiana Purchase adds over 820,000 square miles of land to the United States

1804–1806 — Lewis and Clark explore Louisiana Territory

William Cullen Bryant

1807 — Robert Fulton successfully demonstrates his steamboat, the *Clermont*, on the Hudson River

WASHINGTON IRVING (1783–1859)
A History of New York . . . by Diedrich Knickerbocker (1809)

1812–1814 — War of 1812 between the United States and Great Britain.

North American Review founded (1815)

WILLIAM CULLEN BRYANT (1794–1878)
"Thanatopsis" (1817)

IRVING
The Sketch Book (1819)

Thanatopsis

James Fenimore Cooper

Edgar Allan Poe

1820 Missouri Compromise

Saturday Evening Post founded (1821)

1823 Monroe Doctrine

JAMES FENIMORE COOPER (1789–1851)
The Pioneers (1823), first of the Leatherstocking Tales

1825 Erie Canal opens, connecting New York to the West

EDGAR ALLAN POE (1809–1849)
Tamerlane and Other Poems (1827)

1828 Construction begins on the Baltimore and Ohio Railroad; *Tom Thumb*, the first steam locomotive, travels at a maximum speed of 10 mph

NOAH WEBSTER
An American Dictionary of the English Language (1828)

1836 Samuel Morse invents the telegraph

POE
"The Raven" (1845)

The Architect's Dream (1840) by Thomas Cole (1801–1848). Oil on canvas.

In effect, it was literature's function to illustrate the common values of humanity and the rational laws of human existence. Classicism upheld tradition, often to the point of resisting change, because tradition seemed a reliable testing ground for those laws. The human values and literary standards that endure over long periods of time could be regarded as universally valid.

Romanticism, in contrast, placed central importance upon the emotions and upon the individual. For Romantic writers, reason, though important, was not the only or even the surest guide to truth. Instead, Romantic writers emphasized intuition, that inner perception of truth which is independent of reason. To discover the truth, Emerson would write in "The American Scholar," a man must "learn to detect and watch that gleam of light which flashes across his mind from within." "The inner world," the German philosopher Georg Wilhelm Friedrich Hegel (hā′gəl) observed, "is the content of Romantic art." The key to this inner world is the imagination, which gives expression to those intuitions that mark each person's unique being. For the Romantics, all art is the imaginative expression of the inner essence of the individual. Nothing was more characteristic of Romanticism than its defense of the potential of the individual and its claim for individual freedom. Against the classicists' emphasis upon human limitations, the Romantics stressed the human potential for social progress and spiritual growth. "Who," Emerson asked, "can set bounds to the possibilities of man?"

The Moonlit Landscape
(1819) by Washington
Allston (1779–1843).
Oil on canvas.

This expansive spirit obviously suited the needs of a new nation that was expanding physically, economically, and politically. In its early development, from about 1800 to 1830, American Romanticism was less a philosophy than a number of changing attitudes that were often closely related to a growing sense of nationalism. The Romantic emphasis upon the individual, for instance, reflected the political ideal set forth in the Declaration of Independence, that "all men are created equal." This led naturally to a new emphasis upon the dignity and worth of the common individual and to social reforms that were meant to fulfill this ideal of equality. Humanitarian reform—in everything from the abolition of slavery to improvements in education—was one mark of Romanticism.

In literature, however, Romantics were less concerned with social or political reform than with the expression of their own intuitive experience. The problem for Romantic writers was to find a means of bringing their inner world to imaginative expression in terms that could be shared with others. Although the early Romantic writers varied widely in the forms they chose, certain subjects were characteristic of Romantic attitudes:

Nature. Against the classicist view of nature as a system of rational laws, the Romantic emphasized the beauty, strangeness, and mystery of nature. The Romantic saw nature not as a machine but as organic process, constant development, and change. Nature, as William Cullen Bryant pointed out, "speaks a various language" in its many changes and so serves the imagination as an expression of our own inner changes. This emphasis upon an organic connection between the human imagination and the natural world was a view especially suited to American circumstances. American writers had grown up at the edge of a continental wilderness. The mystery and grandeur of that vast and still unknown land were part of their heritage and a powerful influence on their imaginations.

The first creators of a new American literature all showed this influence in different ways. Washington Irving found in legend and folklore a view of the natural world colored by emotion, by superstition, and by the ancient belief that supernatural beings inhabit the wild places of the earth. From these materials he wrote stories that illustrated American character types, old truths about human nature, and the dramatic possibilities of the American landscape. As a poet, Bryant became the first national spokesperson for a new "religion of nature" in which the natural world serves as an inexhaustible source of moral and spiritual lessons: nature confirms our deepest intuitions of truth. Our first major novelist, James Fenimore Cooper, turned to nature in its most primitive form on the wilderness frontier. In the character of Natty Bumppo he created our first national literary hero, a solitary figure whose values are defined by life outside society, in the wilderness. Of the early Romantic writers, only Edgar Allan Poe seemed unresponsive to this new sense of nature. But in fact Poe was the most thoroughly Romantic of them all. In his poems and stories, the external world of nature is literally a product of the imagination and, in its distortions and fantastic "unreality," reflects the narrator's emotional state. No other writer went as far as Poe in asserting the connection between the human imagination and nature, for he made the outer world entirely subservient to the inner one.

The Past. The rise of nationalism brought with it a new interest in the American past. In the work of later Romantic poets, dramatic incidents from our early history became standard literary material. But this interest grew slowly, and, among early Romantic writers, only Irving and Cooper show a direct interest in a national past. (Poe's work always plunges us into a "past," but it is a shadowy, indefinite one that is unrelated to the actualities of history.) Irving found in legend and folklore an unofficial record of American character and belief—not the great events of history but the shared memories and wisdom and fantasies of common people that were embodied in "old stories." Cooper, on the other hand, often dealt directly with great historical events: the Revolution, the border wars involving Indians, and especially the conquest of the wilderness. From the work of these writers—and many others who followed—American literature gradually developed a sense of a national past and of an emerging national character.

The Inner World of Human Nature. The emphasis that Romanticism placed upon the emotions, upon intuition, and upon the individual encouraged the exploration and the expression of the writer's most private inner being. It soon became apparent that this interior world of intense feeling is not ruled by reason, and an interest in the irrational depths of human nature became characteristic of Romantic writers. The greatest achievements in a psychological literature were reserved for such later writers as Nathaniel Hawthorne and Herman Melville, but the concern was there in the early Romantics. Bryant's best poems work inward from observations of nature to the feelings those observations evoke within himself. His greatest poem, "Thanatopsis," is a searching examination of our psychological reactions to the prospect of death. Cooper, despite his concentration on broad themes and vivid action, was deeply interested in the effects of wilderness life upon the inner life. Natty Bumppo is an appropriate Romantic hero, not just because he is a figure of heroic action, but also because he represents a "natural" view of life that is both simple and profound. But it was Poe among our early writers who carried this exploration of the inner self to its greatest depths. He created stories and poems that often resemble dreams, that set reason and normal reality aside, and that extend the irrational elements of the mind to the point of madness.

Although the writers who appeared after 1840 would surpass many of the achievements of the early Romantics, a strong beginning had been made. American writers had found in Romanticism a new way of expressing their experience as Americans. In the process they expressed the nationalistic spirit of the age and created a truly significant national literature.

Review

1. How was the American frontier extended by the Louisiana Purchase in 1803?
2. What two new forms of transportation helped to unify the nation?
3. What issue became the most divisive force during this period?
4. What major cultural and intellectual change affected the literature of this period?
5. How did the Romantic view of nature differ from the classicist view?
6. What three subjects were characteristic of early Romantic writers?
7. Which poet became spokesperson for a "religion of nature"?
8. Which writer is known for his novels about the wilderness frontier?
9. How did the work of Irving and Cooper show an interest in a national past?
10. How did Poe's stories and poems set him apart from other writers of this period?

Washington Irving by Daniel Huntington (1816–1906). Oil on canvas.

American in both subject and spirit. His relation as a writer to native American materials would remain uncertain: his two most famous stories—"Rip Van Winkle" and "The Legend of Sleepy Hollow"—are adaptations of German folk tales to American settings. He was likely to describe even the western American wilderness through comparisons with Europe.

The youngest son of a prosperous New York merchant, Irving was expected to follow his brothers into a profession or into business. In early manhood he practiced law in a casual fashion and at times worked in his family's import business. During these years his amateur literary activities demonstrated little more than a general interest in the arts and a modest capacity for social satire. His first substantial work, *A History of New York . . . by Diedrich Knickerbocker* (1809), was intended partly as a hoax: it is presented as a manuscript left behind by an eccentric historian as compensation to his landlord for back rent. Nevertheless, it reveals Irving's confusions about his purposes as a writer. *Knickerbocker* is an extravagant burlesque of American history that deflates heroic events of the past and ridicules great men (President Jefferson among them). But the book so mocks history and makes such fun of every idea or action that its final effect is to make any human activity seem not just comic but meaningless. Irving would need a firmer perspective on human values before he could develop as a writer.

He found that perspective some years later in England, where during a period after 1815 he tried unsuccessfully to save a branch of his family's business from bankruptcy. This depressing experience confirmed his dislike of business and turned him again to writing. This time he wrote as a serious professional who was determined to make his career. He found in the local customs, traditions, folklore, and legends of English life a different kind of history from the wars and conquests he had mocked in *Knickerbocker*. This past was a shared heritage of old ways, old beliefs, and old tales that could enrich life in the present by giving people a connection with the past. Excited by the literary possibilities of this material, he sought it out in England and then across Europe. The result, *The Sketch Book of Geoffrey Crayon, Gent.*, appeared in 1819. Its scenes and incidents are drawn chiefly from English life, but two stories, "Rip Van Winkle" and "The Legend of Sleepy Hollow," adapt old German folk tales to the Hudson River and Catskill Mountains of New York

It is appropriate that the first American to achieve a notable reputation as a literary artist was born in the final year of the Revolutionary War and named after George Washington. Independence made Americans more aware of the distinctive qualities of their own culture and gradually created interest in a national literature. Although Washington Irving would benefit from this interest, he did not immediately recognize or pursue it. He came somewhat late to his career as a professional writer, and he established his reputation first in England with *The Sketch Book*, a book that was more English than

Sunnyside (1850–1860) by George Inness (1825–1896). Oil on canvas.
Sunnyside was Irving's home at Tarrytown on the Hudson.

that Irving had known as a boy. He thereby gave America its share in this past. Other books followed with clocklike regularity: folk tales and legends, observations of places and customs, a biography of Columbus, two books on Old Spain. When Irving finally returned to the United States in 1832, it was to a hero's welcome as our foremost man of letters, famous both at home and abroad. Thereafter, taking time out to serve for four years as minister to Spain, he lived the life of a professional writer who could turn any subject to his use. His books included more biographies, the record of a personal tour of the West, histories of the fur trade, and a final five-volume biography of George Washington.

Irving wrote almost no fiction during the last twenty-five years of his life, and fiction does not have a large part in his work as a whole. Yet he is best remembered now for a few stories. "Rip Van Winkle" has been called the most popular story in the world, and one American actor played in a stage version of it for forty-five years! Irving's view of fiction may seem strange to us now. He did not share the belief of later Romantic writers that the creative artist must be "original." He wanted his fiction to approach the quality of legends or folk tales, which are the common possession of many people. In his role as author-narrator, Irving often seems to be operating by hearsay, and this allows him to mix realistic detail with elements of the supernatural—to let Rip Van Winkle sleep for twenty years or to introduce the devil in a Massachusetts swamp—just as folk tales do.

Washington Irving **127**

The Devil and Tom Walker

A few miles from Boston in Massachusetts, there is a deep inlet, winding several miles into the interior of the country from Charles Bay, and terminating in a thickly wooded swamp or morass. On one side of this inlet is a beautiful dark grove; on the opposite side the land rises abruptly from the water's edge into a high ridge, on which grow a few scattered oaks of great age and immense size. Under one of these gigantic trees, according to old stories, there was a great amount of treasure buried by Kidd the pirate. The inlet allowed a facility to bring the money in a boat secretly and at night to the very foot of the hill; the elevation of the place permitted a good lookout to be kept that no one was at hand; while the remarkable trees formed good landmarks by which the place might easily be found again. The old stories add, moreover, that the devil presided at the hiding of the money and took it under his guardianship; but this, it is well known, he always does with buried treasure, particularly when it has been ill-gotten. Be that as it may, Kidd never returned to recover his wealth; being shortly after seized at Boston, sent out to England, and there hanged for a pirate.

About the year 1727, just at the time that earthquakes were prevalent in New England, and shook many tall sinners down upon their knees, there lived near this place a meager, miserly fellow, of the name of Tom Walker. He had a wife as miserly as himself: they were so miserly that they even conspired to cheat each other. Whatever the woman could lay hands on she hid away; a hen could not cackle but she was on the alert to secure the new-laid egg. Her husband was continually prying about to detect her secret hoards, and many and fierce were the conflicts that took place about what ought to have been common property. They lived in a forlorn-looking house that stood alone and had an air of starvation. A few straggling savin[1] trees, emblems of sterility, grew near it; no smoke ever curled from its chimney; no traveler stopped at its door. A miserable horse, whose ribs were as articulate as the bars of a gridiron, stalked about a field, where a thin carpet of moss, scarcely covering the ragged beds of puddingstone, tantalized and balked his hunger; and sometimes he would lean his head over the fence, look piteously at the passer-by, and seem to petition deliverance from this land of famine.

The house and its inmates had altogether a bad name. Tom's wife was a tall termagant, fierce of temper, loud of tongue, and strong of arm. Her voice was often heard in wordy warfare with her husband; and his face sometimes showed signs that their conflicts were not confined to words. No one ventured, however, to interfere between them. The lonely wayfarer shrunk within himself at the horrid clamor and clapperclawing;[2] eyed the den of discord askance; and hurried on his way, rejoicing, if a bachelor, in his celibacy.

One day that Tom Walker had been to a distant part of the neighborhood, he took what he considered a shortcut homeward, through the swamp. Like most shortcuts, it was an ill-

1. **savin** (săv′ĭn): a juniper of eastern North America and Europe.
2. **clapperclawing** (klăp′ər-klô′ĭng): clawing or scratching.

Cleveland Museum of Art, Mr. and Mrs. William H. Marlatt Fund

The Devil and Tom Walker by John Quidor (1801–1881). Oil on canvas.

chosen route. The swamp was thickly grown with great gloomy pines and hemlocks, some of them ninety feet high, which made it dark at noonday, and a retreat for all the owls of the neighborhood. It was full of pits and quagmires, partly covered with weeds and mosses, where the green surface often betrayed the traveler into a gulf of black, smothering mud; there were also dark and stagnant pools, the abodes of the tadpole, the bullfrog, and the water snake; where the trunks of pines and hemlocks lay half drowned, half rotting, looking like alligators sleeping in the mire.

Tom had long been picking his way cautiously through this treacherous forest; stepping from tuft to tuft of rushes and roots, which afforded precarious footholds among deep sloughs; or pacing carefully, like a cat, along the prostrate trunks of trees; startled now and then by the sudden screaming of the bittern, or the quacking of a wild duck rising on the wing from some solitary pool. At length he arrived at a firm piece of ground, which ran out like a peninsula into the deep bosom of the swamp. It had been one of the strongholds of the Indians during their wars with the first colonists. Here they had thrown up a kind of fort, which they had looked upon as almost impregnable, and had used as a place of refuge for their squaws and children. Nothing remained of the old Indian fort but a few embankments, gradually sinking to the level of the surrounding earth, and already overgrown in part by oaks and other forest trees, the fo-

Washington Irving **129**

liage of which formed a contrast to the dark pines and hemlocks of the swamp.

It was late in the dusk of evening when Tom Walker reached the old fort, and he paused there awhile to rest himself. Anyone but he would have felt unwilling to linger in this lonely, melancholy place, for the common people had a bad opinion of it, from the stories handed down from the time of the Indian wars, when it was asserted that the savages held incantations here, and made sacrifices to the evil spirit.

Tom Walker, however, was not a man to be troubled with any fears of the kind. He reposed himself for some time on the trunk of a fallen hemlock, listening to the boding cry of the tree toad, and delving with his walking staff into a mound of black mold at his feet. As he turned up the soil unconsciously, his staff struck against something hard. He raked it out of the vegetable mold, and lo! a cloven skull, with an Indian tomahawk buried deep in it, lay before him. The rust on the weapon showed the time that had elapsed since this deathblow had been given. It was a dreary memento of the fierce struggle that had taken place in this last foothold of the Indian warriors.

"Humph!" said Tom Walker, as he gave it a kick to shake the dirt from it.

"Let that skull alone!" said a gruff voice. Tom lifted up his eyes, and beheld a great black man seated directly opposite him, on the stump of a tree. He was exceedingly surprised, having neither heard nor seen anyone approach; and he was still more perplexed on observing, as well as the gathering gloom would permit, that the stranger was neither Negro nor Indian. It is true he was dressed in a rude half-Indian garb, and had a red belt or sash swathed round his body; but his face was neither black nor copper-color, but swarthy and dingy, and begrimed with soot, as if he had been accustomed to toil among fires and forges. He had a shock of coarse black hair, that stood out from his head in all directions, and bore an ax on his shoulder.

He scowled for a moment at Tom with a pair of great red eyes.

"What are you doing on my grounds?" said the black man, with a hoarse, growling voice.

"Your grounds!" said Tom, with a sneer, "no more your grounds than mine; they belong to Deacon Peabody."

"Deacon Peabody be d——d," said the stranger, "as I flatter myself he will be, if he does not look more to his own sins and less to those of his neighbors. Look yonder, and see how Deacon Peabody is faring."

Tom looked in the direction that the stranger pointed and beheld one of the great trees, fair and flourishing without, but rotten at the core, and saw that it had been nearly hewn through, so that the first high wind was likely to blow it down. On the bark of the tree was scored the name of Deacon Peabody, an eminent man, who had waxed wealthy by driving shrewd bargains with the Indians. He now looked around, and found most of the tall trees marked with the name of some great man of the colony, and all more or less scored by the ax. The one on which he had been seated, and which had evidently just been hewn down, bore the name of Crowninshield; and he recollected a mighty rich man of that name, who made a vulgar display of wealth, which it was whispered he had acquired by buccaneering.

"He's just ready for burning!" said the black man, with a growl of triumph. "You see, I am likely to have a good stock of firewood for winter."

"But what right have you," said Tom, "to cut down Deacon Peabody's timber?"

"The right of a prior claim," said the other. "This woodland belonged to me long before one of your white-faced race put foot upon the soil."

"And pray, who are you, if I may be so bold?" said Tom.

"Oh, I go by various names. I am the wild huntsman in some countries; the black miner in others. In this neighborhood I am known by the name of the black woodsman. I am he to whom the red men consecrated this spot, and in honor of whom they now and then roasted a white man, by way of sweet-smelling sacrifice. Since the red men have been exterminated by you white savages, I amuse myself by presiding at the persecutions of Quakers and Anabaptists;[3] I am the great patron and prompter of slave dealers, and the grand master of the Salem witches."

"The upshot of all which is that, if I mistake not," said Tom, sturdily, "you are he commonly called Old Scratch."

"The same, at your service!" replied the black man, with a half-civil nod.

Such was the opening of this interview, according to the old story; though it has almost too familiar an air to be credited. One would think that to meet with such a singular personage, in this wild, lonely place, would have shaken any man's nerves; but Tom was a hard-minded fellow, not easily daunted, and he had lived so long with a termagant wife that he did not even fear the devil.

It is said that after this commencement they had a long and earnest conversation together, as Tom returned homeward. The black man told him of great sums of money buried by Kidd the pirate, under the oak trees on the high ridge, not far from the morass. All these were under his command, and protected by his power, so that none could find them but such as propitiated his favor. These he offered to place within Tom Walker's reach, having conceived an especial kindness for him; but they were to be had only on certain conditions. What these conditions were may be easily surmised, though Tom never disclosed them publicly. They must have been very hard, for he required time to think of them, and he was not a man to stick at trifles when money was in view. When they had reached the edge of the swamp, the stranger paused. "What proof have I that all you have been telling me is true?" said Tom. "There's my signature," said

the black man, pressing his finger on Tom's forehead. So saying, he turned off among the thickets of the swamp, and seemed, as Tom said, to go down, down, down, into the earth, until nothing but his head and shoulders could be seen, and so on, until he totally disappeared.

When Tom reached home, he found the black print of a finger burnt, as it were, into his forehead, which nothing could obliterate. The first news his wife had to tell him was the sudden death of Absalom Crowninshield, the rich buccaneer. It was announced in the papers with the usual flourish that "a great man had fallen in Israel."[4]

Tom recollected the tree which his black friend had just hewn down and which was ready for burning. "Let the freebooter roast," said Tom; "who cares!" He now felt convinced that all he had heard and seen was no illusion.

He was not prone to let his wife into his confidence; but as this was an uneasy secret, he willingly shared it with her. All her avarice was awakened at the mention of hidden gold, and she urged her husband to comply with the black man's terms, and secure what would make them wealthy for life. However Tom might have felt disposed to sell himself to the devil, he was determined not to do so to oblige his wife; so he flatly refused, out of the mere spirit of contradiction. Many and bitter were the quarrels they had on the subject; but the more she talked, the more resolute was Tom not to be damned to please her.

At length she determined to drive the bargain on her own account, and if she succeeded, to keep all the gain to herself. Being of the same fearless temper as her husband, she set off for the old Indian fort toward the close of a summer's day. She was many hours absent. When she came back, she was reserved and sullen in her replies. She spoke something of a black man, whom she had met about twilight, hewing at the root of a tall tree. He was sulky, however, and would not come to terms; she

3. **Quakers and Anabaptists:** The Quakers were persecuted for their pacifism and refusal to take oaths. The Anabaptists, a religious sect that began in Switzerland, were persecuted for their opposition to infant baptism.

4. **a . . . Israel:** a reference to II Samuel 3:38 in the Bible.

was to go again with a propitiatory offering, but what it was she forbore to say.

The next evening she set off for the swamp, with her apron heavily laden. Tom waited and waited for her, but in vain; midnight came, but she did not make her appearance: morning, noon, night returned, but still she did not come. Tom now grew uneasy for her safety, especially as he found she had carried off in her apron the silver teapot and spoons, and every portable article of value. Another night elapsed, another morning came; but no wife. In a word, she was never heard of more.

What was her real fate nobody knows, in consequence of so many pretending to know. It is one of those facts which have become confounded by a variety of historians. Some asserted that she lost her way among the tangled mazes of the swamp, and sank into some pit or slough; others, more uncharitable, hinted that she had eloped with the household booty and made off to some other province; while others surmised that the tempter had decoyed her into a dismal quagmire, on the top of which her hat was found lying. In confirmation of this, it was said a great black man, with an ax on his shoulder, was seen late that very evening coming out of the swamp, carrying a bundle tied in a check apron, with an air of surly triumph.

The most current and probable story, however, observes that Tom Walker grew so anxious about the fate of his wife and his property that he set out at length to seek them both at the Indian fort. During a long summer's afternoon he searched about the gloomy place, but no wife was to be seen. He called her name repeatedly, but she was nowhere to be heard. The bittern alone responded to his voice, as he flew screaming by; or the bullfrog croaked dolefully from a neighboring pool. At length, it is said, just in the brown hour of twilight, when the owls began to hoot, and the bats to flit about, his attention was attracted by the clamor of carrion crows hovering about a cypress tree. He looked up, and beheld a bundle tied in a check apron, and hanging in the branches of the tree, with a great vulture perched hard by, as if keeping watch upon it. He leaped with joy; for he recognized his wife's apron, and supposed it to contain the household valuables.

"Let us get hold of the property," said he consolingly to himself, "and we will endeavor to do without the woman."

As he scrambled up the tree, the vulture spread its wide wings, and sailed off screaming into the deep shadows of the forest. Tom seized the checked apron, but woeful sight! found nothing but a heart and liver tied up in it!

Such, according to this most authentic old story, was all that was to be found of Tom's wife. She had probably attempted to deal with the black man as she had been accustomed to deal with her husband; but though a female scold is generally considered a match for the devil, yet in this instance she appears to have had the worst of it. She must have died game, however; for it is said Tom noticed many prints of cloven feet deeply stamped about the tree, and found handfuls of hair that looked as if they had been plucked from the coarse black shock of the woodsman. Tom knew his wife's prowess by experience. He shrugged his shoulders, as he looked at the signs of a fierce clapperclawing. "Egad," said he to himself, "Old Scratch must have had a tough time of it!"

Tom consoled himself for the loss of his property with the loss of his wife, for he was a man of fortitude. He even felt something like gratitude towards the black woodsman, who, he considered, had done him a kindness. He sought, therefore, to cultivate a further acquaintance with him, but for some time without success; the old blacklegs played shy, for, whatever people may think, he is not always to be had for calling for: he knows how to play his cards when pretty sure of his game.

At length, it is said, when delay had whetted Tom's eagerness to the quick, and prepared him to agree to anything rather than not gain the promised treasure, he met the black man one evening in his usual woodsman's dress, with his ax on his shoulder, sauntering along the swamp, and humming a tune. He affected to receive Tom's advances with great indifference, made brief replies, and went on humming his tune.

By degrees, however, Tom brought him to business, and they began to haggle about the terms on which the former was to have the pirate's treasure. There was one condition which need not be mentioned, being generally understood in all cases where the devil grants favors; but there were others about which, though of less importance, he was inflexibly obstinate. He insisted that the money found through his means should be employed in his service. He proposed, therefore, that Tom should employ it in the black traffic; that is to say, that he should fit out a slave ship. This, however, Tom resolutely refused: he was bad enough in all conscience; but the devil himself could not tempt him to turn slave trader.

Finding Tom so squeamish on this point, he did not insist upon it, but proposed, instead, that he should turn usurer; the devil being extremely anxious for the increase of usurers, looking upon them as his peculiar[5] people.

To this no objections were made, for it was just to Tom's taste.

"You shall open a broker's shop in Boston next month," said the black man.

"I'll do it tomorrow, if you wish," said Tom Walker.

"You shall lend money at two percent a month."

"Egad, I'll charge four!" replied Tom Walker.

"You shall extort bonds, foreclose mortgages, drive the merchants to bankruptcy ——"

"I'll drive them to the devil," cried Tom Walker.

"You are the usurer for my money!" said blacklegs with delight. "When will you want the rhino?"[6]

5. **peculiar:** here, special or particular.
6. **rhino:** slang for "money."

"This very night."

"Done!" said the devil.

"Done!" said Tom Walker.—So they shook hands and struck a bargain.

A few days' time saw Tom Walker seated behind his desk in a countinghouse in Boston.

His reputation for a ready-moneyed man, who would lend money out for a good consideration, soon spread abroad. Everybody remembers the time of Governor Belcher,[7] when money was particularly scarce. It was a time of paper credit. The country had been deluged with government bills; the famous Land Bank[8] had been established; there had been a rage for speculating; the people had run mad with schemes for new settlements, for building cities in the wilderness; land-jobbers[9] went about with maps of grants, and townships, and El Dorados[10] lying nobody knew where, but which everybody was ready to purchase. In a word, the great speculating fever which breaks out every now and then in the country had raged to an alarming degree, and everybody was dreaming of making sudden fortunes from nothing. As usual the fever had subsided; the dream had gone off, and the imaginary fortunes with it; the patients were left in doleful plight, and the whole country resounded with the consequent cry of "hard times."

At this propitious time of public distress did Tom Walker set up as usurer in Boston. His door was soon thronged by customers. The needy and adventurous, the gambling speculator, the dreaming land-jobber, the thriftless tradesman, the merchant with cracked credit; in short, everyone driven to raise money by desperate means and desperate sacrifices hurried to Tom Walker.

Thus Tom was the universal friend of the needy and acted like a "friend in need"; that is to say, he always exacted good pay and good

7. **Belcher:** Jonathan Belcher was governor of Massachusetts and New Hampshire from 1730 to 1741.
8. **Land Bank:** a bank that loaned money secured by mortgages to the bank.
9. **land-jobbers:** people in the business of selling land.
10. **El Dorado** (ĕl də-rä′dō): a place of fabulous riches; Spanish for "the golden."

security. In proportion to the distress of the applicant was the hardness of his terms. He accumulated bonds and mortgages; gradually squeezed his customers closer and closer; and sent them at length, dry as a sponge, from his door.

In this way he made money hand over hand, became a rich and mighty man, and exalted his cocked hat upon 'Change.[11] He built himself, as usual, a vast house, out of ostentation; but left the greater part of it unfinished and unfurnished, out of parsimony. He even set up a carriage in the fullness of his vainglory, though he nearly starved the horses which drew it; and as the ungreased wheels groaned and screeched on the axletrees, you would have thought you heard the souls of the poor debtors he was squeezing.

As Tom waxed old, however, he grew thoughtful. Having secured the good things of this world, he began to feel anxious about those of the next. He thought with regret on the bargain he had made with his black friend, and set his wits to work to cheat him out of the conditions. He became, therefore, all of a sudden, a violent churchgoer. He prayed loudly and strenuously, as if heaven were to be taken by force of lungs. Indeed, one might always tell when he had sinned most during the week, by the clamor of his Sunday devotion. The quiet Christians who had been modestly and steadfastly traveling Zionward were struck with self-reproach at seeing themselves so suddenly outstripped in their career by this new-made convert. Tom was as rigid in religious as in money matters; he was a stern supervisor and censurer of his neighbors, and seemed to think every sin entered up to their account became a credit on his own side of the page. He even talked of the expediency of reviving the persecution of Quakers and Anabaptists. In a word, Tom's zeal became as notorious as his riches.

Still, in spite of all this strenuous attention

11. **'Change:** the Exchange, the place where merchants, brokers, and bankers met to do business.

to forms, Tom had a lurking dread that the devil, after all, would have his due. That he might not be taken unawares, therefore, it is said he always carried a small Bible in his coat pocket. He had also a great folio Bible on his countinghouse desk, and would frequently be found reading it when people called on business; on such occasions he would lay his green spectacles in the book, to mark the place, while he turned round to drive some usurious bargain.

Some say that Tom grew a little crackbrained in his old days, and that fancying his end approaching, he had his horse new shod, saddled and bridled, and buried with his feet uppermost; because he supposed that at the last day the world would be turned upside down; in which case he should find his horse standing ready for mounting, and he was determined at the worst to give his old friend a run for it. This, however, is probably a mere old wives' fable. If he really did take such a precaution, it was totally superfluous; at least so says the authentic old legend, which closes this story in the following manner.

One hot summer afternoon in the dog days, just as a terrible black thunder-gust was coming up, Tom sat in his countinghouse, in his white linen cap and India silk morning gown. He was on the point of foreclosing a mortgage, by which he would complete the ruin of an unlucky land speculator for whom he had professed the greatest friendship. The poor landjobber begged him to grant a few months' indulgence. Tom had grown testy and irritated, and refused another day.

"My family will be ruined and brought upon the parish," said the land-jobber.

"Charity begins at home," replied Tom; "I must take care of myself in these hard times."

"You have made so much money out of me," said the speculator.

Tom lost his patience and his piety. "The devil take me," said he, "if I have made a farthing!"

Just then there were three loud knocks at the street door. He stepped out to see who was there. A black man was holding a black horse, which neighed and stamped with impatience. "Tom, you're come for," said the black fellow, gruffly. Tom shrank back, but too late. He had left his little Bible at the bottom of his coat pocket, and his big Bible on the desk buried under the mortgage he was about to foreclose: never was sinner taken more unawares. The black man whisked him like a child into the saddle, gave the horse the lash, and away he galloped, with Tom on his back, in the midst of the thunderstorm. The clerks stuck their pens behind their ears, and stared after him from the windows. Away went Tom Walker, dashing down the streets; his white cap bobbing up and down, his morning gown fluttering in the wind, and his steed striking fire out of the pavement at every bound. When the clerks turned to look for the black man he had disappeared.

Tom Walker never returned to foreclose the mortgage. A countryman who lived on the border of the swamp reported that in the height of the thunder-gust he had heard a great clattering of hoofs and a howling along the road, and running to the window caught sight of a figure, such as I have described, on a horse that galloped like mad across the fields, over the hills, and down into the black hemlock swamp towards the old Indian fort; and that shortly after, a thunderbolt falling in that direction seemed to set the whole forest in a blaze.

The good people of Boston shook their heads and shrugged their shoulders, but had been so much accustomed to witches and goblins, and tricks of the devil in all kinds of shapes, from the first settlement of the colony, that they were not so much horror-struck as might have been expected. Trustees were appointed to take charge of Tom's effects. There was nothing, however, to administer upon. On searching his coffers all his bonds and mortgages were found reduced to cinders. In place of gold and silver his iron chest was filled with chips and shavings; two skeletons lay in his stable instead of his half-starved horses, and

the very next day his great house took fire and was burnt to the ground.

Such was the end of Tom Walker and his ill-gotten wealth. Let all griping money brokers lay this story to heart. The truth of it is not to be doubted. The very hole under the oak trees, whence he dug Kidd's money, is to be seen to this day; and the neighboring swamp and old Indian fort are often haunted in stormy nights by a figure on horseback, in morning gown and white cap, which is doubtless the troubled spirit of the usurer. In fact, the story has resolved itself into a proverb, and is the origin of that popular saying, so prevalent throughout New England, of "The Devil and Tom Walker."

Reading Check

1. Whom does Tom Walker meet at the old fort in the swamp?
2. What "signature" does Tom find when he returns home?
3. What discovery gives Tom a clue about his wife's fate?
4. What occupation does Tom take up at the suggestion of the devil?
5. After Tom disappears, what happens to his wealth?

Commentary

A folk-tale quality governs the overall meaning of Washington Irving's fiction. But the folk-tale form imposes sharp limits on character development since it usually deals with types or *stock* characters. Irving showed little interest in the personal psychology of his characters, and they have little individuality. Instead, they are types of human motivation and behavior, such as Dame Van Winkle, Rip's wife, whose constant abuse of her husband proves the point that "a tart temper never mellows with age, and a sharp tongue is the only edged tool that grows keener with constant use." The same words might describe Tom's wife in "The Devil and Tom Walker," who is likewise a *stereotype* of the tormenting wife.

Events in this story are made to seem remote in time, as if to assure us that they belong to legend and could not happen now. Irving's tone—his attitude toward his subject—is genial and mildly humorous. We may have to remind ourselves that the story is actually about a man's selling his soul to the devil. The humorous tone keeps us from taking this act seriously, and it quickly turns our attention to the question of how the devil will finally collect his part of the bargain. Even the grisly scene in which Tom finds his wife's heart and liver evokes a smile instead of a shudder, for we already know that Tom has come to the swamp more in search of his property than of his wife and that he will console himself for the loss of the one with the gratifying riddance of the other. For all its comic tone, however, this story, like all of Irving's fiction, does make a serious point about human values. To want this world's goods and power too much, at the expense of human relationships and sympathies, is indeed to make a bad bargain with the devil, whether openly as Tom does or in the privacy of one's own heart. This ancient wisdom is embodied in an old folk saying that is repeated in the story: The devil would have his due, however crafty a Tom Walker may be in keeping a Bible at hand to ward off the Evil One or in burying a saddled horse to outrun him on Judgment Day. It was Irving's talent to make fiction of such old knowledge of life and human nature.

For Study and Discussion

Analyzing and Interpreting the Story

1. One way Irving suggests that his story is really a folk tale is by shifting back and forth between events that the narrator reports on his own account and those he attributes to hearsay by such signals as "it was asserted," "it was whispered," or "according to old stories." Examine this device in the opening paragraph. **a.** For what facts does the narrator take direct responsibility? **b.** What is attributed to hearsay?

2. Irving takes little apparent trouble to characterize Tom and his wife as individuals. In the second paragraph, they are presented as "so miserly that they even conspired to cheat each other" of their common property. Yet there are some differences between them, if not in greed at least in temper. What characteristics of the wife suggest that she already belongs to the devil and that he will get her without having to bargain?

3. The place the devil frequents is always significant in fictional treatments of him. Here the swamp, with its "pits and quagmires" to trap the unwary traveler, seems a fit setting for an infernal being. Irving's devil occupies a special place within the swamp: the site of a former Indian fort. What does the history of this place tell you about the human activities that are of special interest and profit to the devil and that so "amuse" him?

4. In the literary tradition, the devil takes on many forms and disguises, since he has "business" all over the world. Here the fullest description of him occurs when Tom first meets him. **a.** What details of his physical appearance give him this "Everyman" quality? **b.** What details remind us that he is the devil in traditional terms? **c.** What details a few paragraphs later refer to his special dealings in the New World?

5. In a bargain with the devil, we are interested in the terms. We know that sooner or later the devil gets the sinner's soul, while the sinner is given something he or she desperately wants. Tom, we are told, settles for money. He has changed his condition but not, apparently, escaped his nature. What details about his mansion and the way he keeps his horses show you that, for all his wealth, he has not lost his anxiety about money?

6. Like most sophisticated New Yorkers, Irving had no admiration for Puritan Massachusetts. In his mind Massachusetts was associated with the Salem witch trials of 1692, only thirty-five years before the time of this story. Examine the paragraph on page 134 describing Tom as a "violent churchgoer." **a.** In what way is this paragraph a satirical comment on Puritans? **b.** What words and phrases in the paragraph link religion to "money matters"?

Writing About Literature

Examining Familiar Sayings

Washington Irving makes use of a number of old sayings throughout "The Devil and Tom Walker." Sometimes he gives a direct illustration of a saying like "the devil would have his due." At other times a familiar saying is given an ironic twist. Write a composition in which you examine some of these sayings. Show whether Irving is illustrating these sayings or whether he is giving them an ironic turn. Conclude with a discussion of what these sayings contribute to the story.

James Fenimore Cooper by John Wesley Jarvis (1780–1840).

Cooper's literary importance, like Herman Melville's, is largely a rediscovery of our own time. Although his novels were often immensely popular when they were published, they were read as adventure stories. As the taste for adventure fiction declined, so did his reputation, and his novels were regarded as suitable only for adolescent readers. In the 1920s, however, critics began seriously to reconsider Cooper's work and to find that his themes reached deep into the emerging American character and the social questions of his time. Today his stature as a major writer is firmly established.

Cooper, who wrote more than thirty novels, a naval history, and several volumes of social comment and travel observations, had no early intention of becoming a writer. Born the son of a prominent judge and wealthy landowner, he was raised on his family's enormous estate in what is now Cooperstown in upstate New York. He attended Yale but was expelled for lackluster performance as a student and for repeated pranks, which included bringing a donkey into a classroom. He then worked as a seaman on a merchant vessel and, in 1808, was commissioned an officer in the United States Navy. He would later draw upon his naval experiences in several sea novels. Following the death of his father, he resigned his commission, married, and settled into the life of a gentleman landowner. The pleasant legend is that he began his first novel after being challenged by his wife to write a better book than the British novel he was then reading—and loudly condemning. The result, *Precaution* (1820), was a bad imitation of the society novels popular at the time in England. But he had caught the writing fever he was never to lose. The next year he published *The Spy*, a novel about the American Revolution, a subject much more suited to his talent for depicting exciting action in a vast natural setting. It was immediately acclaimed as a fresh and original work, the first novel to make serious use of American history. Two years later, in 1823, Cooper turned to the frontier experience in *The Pioneers*. He had found his greatest theme.

The Pioneers was the first of five related novels, called the Leatherstocking Tales, that became Cooper's masterwork. They portray the life of a wilderness figure, Natty Bumppo, from adolescence to his death more than sixty years later. His life parallels America's wilderness experience. In his youth, western New York State is still wilderness. In his old age, he must walk a thousand miles to escape the sound of the settlers' axes and the smoke of their fires as they cut and burn the great forests to make farms. He spends his last years on the treeless prairies five hundred miles beyond the Mississippi River. But President Jefferson's Louisiana Purchase has recently made even this vast wilderness a part of the United States. At the moment of Natty's death, the explorers Lewis and Clark are completing their survey of a land route to the Pacific Ocean, and settlers will inevitably follow.

The meeting point of wilderness and civilization is the constantly moving frontier, and Cooper's subject is the effect of the frontier upon the American character. Westward expansion was the great social fact of the age, but its meaning for our national development was far from clear. Cooper knew that the wilderness, by freeing men from the restraints of civilized life, could bring out the worst in human nature, creating lawless violence and a senseless waste of natural resources. Each novel has its renegades and outlaws and its scenes of terrible waste to show the destructive effects of the frontier experience. But a magnificent primeval wilderness also offered America the opportunity to return to the natural moral law that is the basis of morality in human life, and to recover those natural virtues that are obscured or corrupted by society. This is the theme that Cooper explores through the character of Natty Bumppo.

That character, except for some childhood impressions of religion, is formed by the wilderness. From early youth Natty leads the life of a hunter and warrior, usually with only Indian companions. He cannot read or write. He has no family ties, no need for money or material goods, and no use for the "wasty ways" and troublesome laws of the settlements. Yet he is not an outlaw or a barbarian. From nature he has learned a deep reverence for the Creator, for the wise use of nature's gifts, and for justice and truth in dealing with others. As a hunter and warrior he must often shed blood, but he preserves an essential innocence, taking animal life only for food and human life only for self-protection and in warfare. He is proof that the inevitable cruelties and violence of America's frontier experience need not corrupt the American character. Leatherstocking is the original wilderness hero in our literature: solitary man in the presence of only nature and God. In his purity and innocence, his self-reliance and sense of justice, he reveals humanity's basic moral nature and represents Cooper's hope for the moral renewal of American society.

Natty's life does not follow a normal course in Cooper's books. He is an old man when we first meet him in *The Pioneers*, and his death occurs in *The Prairie* (1827), the third of the five novels. Having brought his hero to an appropriate end at the moment when America's last frontier was crossed, Cooper thought of his story as closed. But thirteen years later he resurrected Leatherstocking and started him on a reverse journey toward youth, and in the last of the Tales, *The Deerslayer* (1841), we see Natty at his youngest and most innocent. This strange pattern expresses an important theme for Cooper's imagination and represents a vital aspect of America's conception of itself. America began old, a society formed by the ideas and values of Europe. But under the influence of a wilderness environment America became young, the New World of the second chance and fresh beginnings. It is our most cherished myth. Through the wilderness, America could begin again and again. Natty Bumppo is the idealized wilderness hero whose life enacts that basic myth of a return to innocence and eternal youth.

Otsego Lake, New York, the setting for *The Deerslayer*. The hill in the background is Mount Wellington, known locally as the "Sleeping Lion."

The Deerslayer

This last of the five Leatherstocking Tales completes the portrayal of Natty Bumppo's life by showing his passage from adolescent hunter to full manhood as a wilderness warrior. In that process Natty must define himself in relation to both Indian and white ways of life. From his upbringing among the Delaware Indians he has learned the forest skills, physical courage, and strict code of honor that are now being tested on his first warpath against their enemies, the Hurons. But this self-definition must also test his feelings about the white civilization he is leaving behind, especially his feelings about marriage and family as the fundamental relationships of social existence.

Just hours before this scene, Natty has acted decisively on both these matters. Facing a Huron warrior in a single combat that has the ritual quality of a duel, he has for the first time taken a human life, and then received a new name from his fallen foe. "Deerslayer," the dying Huron points out, is a good name for a "boy." But the Indian way is to name a man again for his special qualities as a warrior. Henceforth, Natty will be called "Hawkeye" for his quick, keen sight in battle.

Shortly thereafter, as a mark of his new manhood and the solitary life he will lead in the wilderness, Natty rejects a basic social bond by twice refusing marriage, first to a white woman and then, in the scene that follows, to the widow of the Huron warrior he has slain. Providence, he believes, brought him to the Delawares as a child because he was meant to "live single" in the wilderness, bridging the white and Indian worlds. He will keep certain moral beliefs (Natty calls them "gifts") from his white background but will act as a Delaware "in all things touchin' Injins."

Both parts of this double heritage lead to the following chapter. Having captured Natty in warfare, the Hurons have released him on a brief parole, to carry a message to a nearby group of whites, because they know him as a warrior like themselves who will keep his promise to return to captivity. And Natty has accepted the mission because he feels responsible to people of his own race and would save those lives if he could. He is both Indian and white. Once he has fulfilled his parole by returning to the Hurons, the rules of Indian warfare allow him to escape by any means if he can.

Buckskin moccasins embroidered with
moosehair, made by Huron Indians.
Museum of the American Indian

Title page of *The Deerslayer.* Illustration by F. O. C. Darley for the 1861 edition of the book.

It was an imposing scene, into which Deerslayer now found himself advancing. All the older warriors were seated on the trunk of the fallen tree, waiting his approach with grave decorum. On the right stood the young men, armed, while the left was occupied by the women and children. In the center was an open space of considerable extent, always canopied by leaves, but from which the underbrush, dead wood, and other obstacles had been carefully removed. The more open area had probably been much used by former parties, for this was the place where the appearance of a sward was the most decided. The arches of the woods, even at high noon, cast their somber shadows on the spot, which the brilliant rays of the sun that struggled through the leaves contributed to mellow and, if such an expression can be used, to illuminate. It was probably from a similar scene that the mind of man first got its idea of the effects of Gothic tracery[1] and churchly hues; this temple of nature producing some such effect, so far as light and shadows were concerned, as the well-known offspring of human invention.

As was not unusual among the tribes and wandering bands of the aborigines, two chiefs shared in nearly equal degrees the principal and primitive authority that was wielded over these children of the forest. There were several who might claim the distinction of being chief men, but the two in question were so much superior to all the rest in influence that, when they agreed, no one disputed their mandates, and when they were divided, the band hesitated, like men who had lost their governing principle of action. It was also in conformity with practice—perhaps we might add, in conformity with nature, that one of the chiefs was indebted to his mind for his influence, whereas the other owed his distinction altogether to qualities that were physical. One was a senior, well known for eloquence in debate, wisdom in council, and prudence in measures, while his great competitor, if not his rival, was a brave, distinguished in war, notorious for ferocity, and remarkable, in the way of intellect, for nothing but the cunning and expedients of the warpath. The first was Rivenoak, who has already been introduced to the reader, while the last was called le Panthère, in the language of the Canadas, or the Panther, to resort to the vernacular of the English colonies. The appellation of the fighting chief was supposed to indicate the qualities of the warrior, agreeably to a practice of the red man's nomenclature: ferocity, cunning, and treachery being, perhaps, the distinctive features of his character. The title had been received from the French, and was prized so much the more from that circumstance, the Indian submitting profoundly to the greater intelligence of his paleface allies, in most things of this nature. How well the sobriquet[2] was merited will be seen in the sequel.

Rivenoak and the Panther sat side by side, awaiting the approach of their prisoner, as Deerslayer put his moccasined foot on the strand; nor did either move or utter a syllable until the young man had advanced into the center of the area, and proclaimed his presence with his voice. This was done firmly, though in the simple manner that marked the character of the individual.

"Here I am, Mingos,"[3] he said, in the dialect of the Delawares, a language that most present understood; "here I am, and there is the sun. One is not more true to the laws of natur' than the other has proved true to his word. I am your prisoner; do with me what you please. My business with man and 'arth is settled; nothing remains now but to meet the white man's God, accordin' to a white man's duties and gifts."

A murmur of approbation escaped even the women at this address, and for an instant there was a strong and pretty general desire to adopt into the tribe one who owned so brave a spirit. Still there were dissenters from this wish,

1. **Gothic tracery:** the lacy openwork characteristic of medieval architecture.

2. **sobriquet** (sō′brĭ-kā′, -kĕt′): nickname.
3. **Mingos:** Deerslayer's general term for any enemies of the Delawares; here, the Hurons.

James Fenimore Cooper   **141**

Three Delaware Indians (1857–1869) by George Catlin (1796–1872). Oil on cardboard.
National Gallery of Art, Washington, Paul Mellon Collection

among the principal of whom might be classed the Panther, and his sister, le Sumac, so called from the number of her children, who was the widow of le Loup Cervier,[4] now known to have fallen by the hand of the captive. Native ferocity held one in subjection, while the corroding passion of revenge prevented the other from admitting any gentler feeling at the moment. Not so with Rivenoak. This chief arose, stretched his arm before him in a gesture of courtesy, and paid his compliments with an ease and dignity that a prince might have en-

vied. As, in that band, his wisdom and eloquence were confessedly without rivals, he knew that on himself would properly fall the duty of first replying to the speech of the paleface.

"Paleface, you are honest," said the Huron orator. "My people are happy in having captured a man and not a skulking fox. We now know you; we shall treat you like a brave. If you have slain one of our warriors and helped to kill others, you have a life of your own ready to give away in return. Some of my young men thought that the blood of a paleface was too thin, that it would refuse to run under the

4. **le Loup Cervier:** French for "lynx."

Huron knife. You will show them it is not so; your heart is stout as well as your body. It is a pleasure to make such a prisoner; should my warriors say that the death of le Loup Cervier ought not be forgotten, that he cannot travel toward the land of spirits alone, and that his enemy must be sent to overtake him, they will remember that he fell by the hand of a brave, and send you after him with such signs of our friendship as shall not make him ashamed to keep your company. I have spoken; you know what I have said."

"True enough, Mingo, all true as the gospel," returned the simple-minded hunter; "you *have* spoken, and I *do* know not only what you have *said*, but, what is still more important, what you *mean*. I dare to say your warrior, the Lynx, was a stouthearted brave, and worthy of your fri'ndship and respect, but I do not feel unworthy to keep his company, without any passport from your hands. Nevertheless, here I am, ready to receive judgment from your council, if, indeed, the matter was not detarmined among you afore I got back."

"My old men would not sit in council over a paleface until they saw him among them," answered Rivenoak, looking around him a little ironically; "they said it would be like sitting in council over the winds; they go where they will and come back as they see fit, and not otherwise. There was one voice that spoke in your favor, Deerslayer, but it was alone, like the song of the wren whose mate has been struck by the hawk."

"I thank that voice whosoever it may have been, Mingo, and will say it was as true a voice, as the rest were lying voices. A furlough is as binding on a paleface, if he be honest, as it is on a redskin; and was it not so, I would never bring disgrace on the Delawares, among whom I may be said to have received my edication. But words are useless and lead to braggin' feelin's; here I am; act your will on me."

Rivenoak made a sign of acquiescence, and then a short conference was privately held among the chiefs. As soon as the latter ended, three or four young men fell back from among the armed group and disappeared. Then it was signified to the prisoner that he was at liberty to go at large on the point until a council was held concerning his fate. There was more of seeming than of real confidence, however, in this apparent liberality, inasmuch as the young men mentioned already formed a line of sentinels across the breadth of the point, inland, and escape from any other part was out of the question. Even the canoe was removed beyond this line of sentinels, to a spot where it was considered safe from any sudden attempt. These precautions did not proceed from a failure of confidence, but from the circumstance that the prisoner had now complied with all the required conditions of his parole, and it would have been considered a commendable and honorable exploit to escape from his foes. So nice, indeed, were the distinctions drawn by the savages, in cases of this nature, that they often gave their victims a chance to evade the torture, deeming it as creditable to the captors to overtake, or to outwit a fugitive, when his exertions were supposed to be quickened by the extreme jeopardy of his situation, as it was for him to get clear from so much extraordinary vigilance.

Nor was Deerslayer unconscious or forgetful of his rights and of his opportunities. Could he now have seen any probable opening for an escape, the attempt would not have been delayed a minute. But the case seemed desperate. He was aware of the line of sentinels, and felt the difficulty of breaking through it unharmed. The lake offered no advantages, as the canoe would have given his foes the greatest facilities for overtaking him; else would he have found it no difficult task to swim as far as the castle.[5] As he walked about the point, he even examined the spot as to ascertain if it offered no place of concealment, but its openness, its size, and the hundred watchful glances that were turned toward him, even while those who made them affected not

5. **castle:** short for "Muskrat Castle," an ironically named modest log house standing on piles some distance out in the lake.

to see him, prevented any such expedient from succeeding. The dread and disgrace of failure had no influence on Deerslayer, who deemed it ever a point of honor to reason and feel like a white man, rather than as an Indian, and who felt it a sort of duty to do all he could that did not involve a dereliction from principle in order to save his life. Still he hesitated about making the effort, for he also felt that he ought to see the chance of success before he committed himself.

In the meantime the business of the camp appeared to proceed in its regular train. The chiefs consulted apart, admitting no one but the Sumac to their councils; for she, the widow of the fallen warrior, had an exclusive right to be heard on such an occasion. The young men strolled about in indolent listlessness, awaiting the result with Indian impatience, while the females prepared the feast that was to celebrate the termination of the affair, whether it proved fortunate or otherwise for our hero. No one betrayed feeling, and an indifferent observer, beyond the extreme watchfulness of the sentinels, would have detected no extraordinary movement or sensation to denote the real state of things. Two or three old women put their heads together, and it appeared unfavorably to the prospect of Deerslayer, by their scowling looks and angry gestures, but a group of Indian girls were evidently animated by a different impulse, as was apparent by stolen glances that expressed pity and regret. In this condition of the camp an hour soon glided away.

Suspense is, perhaps, the feeling of all others that is most difficult to be supported. When Deerslayer landed, he fully expected in the course of a few minutes to undergo the tortures of an Indian revenge, and he was prepared to meet his fate manfully, but the delay proved far more trying than the nearer approach of suffering, and the intended victim began seriously to meditate some desperate effort at escape, as it might be from sheer anxiety to terminate the scene, when he was suddenly summoned to appear, once more, in front of his judges, who had already arranged the band in its former order in readiness to receive him.

"Killer of the Deer," commenced Rivenoak, as soon as his captive stood before him, "my aged men have listened to wise words; they are ready to speak. You are a man whose fathers came from beyond the rising sun; we are children of the setting sun; we turn our faces toward the Great Sweet Lakes when we look toward our villages. It may be a wise country and full of riches toward the morning, but it is very pleasant toward the evening. We love most to look in that direction. When we gaze at the east we feel afraid, canoe after canoe bringing more and more of your people in the track of the sun, as if their land was so full as to run over. The red men are few already; they have need of help. One of our best lodges has lately been emptied by the death of its master; it will be a long time before his son can grow big enough to sit in his place. There is his widow! She will want venison to feed her and her children, for her sons are yet like the young of the robin before they quit the nest. By your hand has this great calamity befallen her. She has two duties; one to le Loup Cervier, and one to his children. Scalp for scalp, life for life, blood for blood, is one law; to feed her young another. We know you, Killer of the Deer. You are honest; when you say a thing, it is so. You have but one tongue, and that is not forked like a snake's. Your head is never hid in the grass; all can see it. What you say, that will you do. You are just. When you have done wrong, it is your wish to do right again as soon as you can. Here is the Sumac; she is alone in her wigwam, with children crying around her for food—yonder is a rifle; it is loaded and ready to be fired. Take the gun; go forth and shoot a deer; bring the venison and lay it before the widow of le Loup Cervier; feed her children; call yourself her husband. After which, your heart will no longer be Delaware but Huron; le Sumac's ears will not hear the cries of her children; my people will count the proper number of warriors.

In declining this offer, Natty makes it clear that both his white and Indian heritages prevent such a marriage: his belief that Providence intended his life to be solitary, and his upbringing as a Delaware, which would not permit marriage to a Huron.

These words were scarcely out of the mouth of Deerslayer before a common murmur betrayed the dissatisfaction with which they had been heard. The aged women, in particular, were loud in their expressions of disgust, and the gentle Sumac herself, a woman quite old enough to be our hero's mother, was not the least pacific in her denunciations. But all the other manifestations of disappointment and discontent were thrown into the background by the fierce resentment of the Panther. This grim chief had thought it a degradation to permit his sister to become the wife of a paleface of the Yengeese[6] at all, and had only given a reluctant consent to the arrangement—one by no means unusual among the Indians, however—at the earnest solicitations of the bereaved widow; and it goaded him to the quick to find his condescension slighted, the honor he had with so much regret been persuaded to accord condemned. The animal from which he got his name does not glare on his intended prey with more frightful ferocity than his eyes gleamed on the captive, nor was his arm backward in seconding the fierce resentment that almost consumed his breast.

"Dog of the palefaces!" he exclaimed in Iroquois, "go yell among the curs of your own evil hunting grounds!"

The denunciation was accompanied by an appropriate action. Even while speaking his arm was lifted and the tomahawk hurled. Luckily the loud tones of the speaker had drawn the eye of Deerslayer toward him, else would that moment have probably closed his career. So great was the dexterity with which this dangerous weapon was thrown, and so deadly the intent, that it would have riven the skull of the prisoner, had he not stretched forth an arm and caught the handle in one of

6. **Yengeese:** Yankees.

its turns with a readiness quite as remarkable as the skill with which the missile had been hurled. The projectile force was so great, notwithstanding, that when Deerslayer's arm was arrested, his hand was raised above and behind his own head, and in the very attitude necessary to return the attack. It is not certain whether the circumstance of finding himself unexpectedly in this menacing posture and armed, tempted the young man to retaliate, or whether sudden resentment overcame his forbearance and prudence. His eye kindled, however, and a small red spot appeared on each cheek, while he cast all his energy into the effort of his arm and threw back the weapon at his assailant. The unexpectedness of this blow contributed to its success, the Panther neither raising an arm nor bending his head to avoid it. The keen little ax struck the victim in a perpendicular line with the nose, directly between the eyes, literally braining him on the spot. Sallying forward, as the serpent darts at its enemy even while receiving its own death wound, this man of powerful frame fell his length into the open area formed by the circle, quivering in death. A common rush to his relief left the captive for a single instant quite without the crowd, and willing to make one desperate effort for life, he bounded off with the activity of a deer. There was but a breathless instant, then the whole band, old and young, women and children, abandoning the lifeless body of the Panther where it lay, raised the yell of alarm and followed in pursuit.

Sudden as had been the event which induced Deerslayer to make this desperate trial of speed, his mind was not wholly unprepared for the fearful emergency. In the course of the past hour, he had pondered well on the chances of such an experiment and had shrewdly calculated all the details of success and failure. At the first leap, therefore, his body was completely under the direction of an intelligence that turned all its efforts to the best account and prevented everything like hesitation or indecision at the important instant of the start. To this alone was he indebted for the first great advantage, that of getting through the line of sentinels unharmed. The manner in which this was done, though sufficiently simple, merits a description.

Although the shores of the point were not fringed with bushes, as was the case with most of the others on the lake, it was owing altogether to the circumstance that the spot had been so much used by hunters and fishermen. This fringe commenced on what might be termed the mainland, and was as dense as usual, extending in long lines both north and south. In the latter direction, then, Deerslayer held his way, and as the sentinels were a little without the commencement of this thicket before the alarm was clearly communicated to them, the fugitive had gained its cover. To run among the bushes, however, was out of the question, and Deerslayer held his way for some forty or fifty yards in the water, which was barely knee deep, offering as great an obstacle to the speed of his pursuers as it did to his own. As soon as a favorable spot presented, he darted through the line of bushes and issued into the open woods.

Several rifles were discharged at Deerslayer while in the water, and more followed as he came out into the comparative exposure of the clear forest. But the direction of his line of flight, which partially crossed that of the fire, the haste with which the weapons had been aimed, and the general confusion that prevailed in the camp prevented any harm from being done. Bullets whistled past him, and many cut twigs from the branches at his side, but not one touched even his dress. The delay caused by these fruitless attempts was of great service to the fugitive, who had gained more than a hundred yards on even the leading men of the Hurons, ere something like concert and order had entered into the chase. To think of following with rifle in hand was out of the question, and after emptying their pieces in vague hopes of wounding their captive, the best runners of the Indians threw them aside, calling out to the women and boys to recover and load them again, as soon as possible.

Deerslayer knew too well the desperate nature of the struggle in which he was engaged to lose one of the precious moments. He also knew that his only hope was to run in a straight line, for as soon as he began to turn, or double, the greater number of his pursuers would put escape out of the question. He held his way, therefore, in a diagonal direction up the acclivity, which was neither very high nor very steep, in this part of the mountain, but which was sufficiently toilsome for one contending for life to render it painfully oppressive. There, however, he slackened his speed to recover breath, proceeding even at a quick walk, or a slow trot, along the more difficult parts of the way. The Hurons were whooping and leaping behind him; but this he disregarded, well knowing they must overcome the difficulties he had surmounted, ere they could reach the elevation to which he had attained. The summit of the first hill was not quite near him, and he saw, by the formation of the land, that a deep glen intervened before the base of a second hill could be reached. Walking deliberately to the summit, he glanced eagerly about him in every direction in quest of a cover. None offered in the ground, but a fallen tree lay near him, and desperate circumstances required desperate remedies. This tree lay in a line parallel to the glen, at the brow of the hill; to leap on it, and then to force his person as close as possible under its lower side, took but a moment. Previously to disappearing from his pursuers, however, Deerslayer stood on the height and gave a cry of triumph, as if exulting at the sight of the descent that lay before him. In the next instant he was stretched beneath the tree.

No sooner was this expedient adopted than the young man ascertained how desperate had been his own efforts by the violence of the pulsations in his frame. He could hear his heart beat, and his breathing was like the action of a bellows in quick motion. Breath was gained, however, and the heart soon ceased to throb as if about to break through its confinement. The footsteps of those who toiled up the opposite side of the acclivity were now audible, and presently voices and treads announced the arrival of the pursuers. The foremost shouted as they reached the height; then, fearful that their enemy would escape under favor of the descent, each leaped upon the fallen tree and plunged into the ravine, trusting to get a sight of the pursued, ere he reached the bottom. In this manner, Huron followed Huron, until Natty began to hope the whole had passed. Others succeeded, however, until quite forty had leaped over the tree; and then he counted them, as the surest mode of ascertaining how many could be behind. Presently all were in the bottom of the glen, quite a hundred feet below him, and some had even ascended part of the opposite hill, when it became evident an inquiry was making as to the direction he had taken. This was the critical moment, and one of nerves less steady, or of a training that had been neglected, would have seized it to rise and fly. Not so with Deerslayer. He still lay quiet, watching with jealous vigilance every movement and fast regaining his breath.

For several minutes Natty's ruse works, and he is able to reverse his course and so gain precious distance in his flight. But when he is seen again by the Hurons, he realizes that he cannot escape so many pursuers in the woods. He turns instead to the lake, running through the Huron camp itself to reach the only canoe on the shore. If he can get beyond the nearby point and out into the open lake, he will be seen and, he hopes, rescued by friends who are in a log house built on pilings well out in the lake. (The house was built that way for defense.) When he reaches the canoe it has no paddle, but he pushes off anyway, lying flat in the canoe and hoping to be carried by the breeze beyond the point and out into the lake.

Perhaps the situation of Deerslayer had not been more critical that day than it was at this moment. It certainly had not been one half as tantalizing. He lay perfectly quiet for two or three minutes, trusting to the single sense of hearing, confident that the noise in the lake would reach his ears, did anyone venture to approach by swimming. Once or twice he fancied that the element was stirred by the cautious movement of an arm, and then he perceived it was the wash of the water on the pebbles of the strand; for, in mimicry of the ocean, it is seldom that those little lakes are so totally tranquil as not to possess a slight heaving and setting on their shores. Suddenly all the voices ceased, and a deathlike stillness pervaded the spot, a quietness as profound as if all lay in the repose of inanimate life. By this time the canoe had drifted so far as to render nothing visible to Deerslayer, as he lay on his back, except the blue void of space, and a few of those brighter rays that proceed from the effulgence of the sun, marking his proximity. It was not possible to endure this uncertainty long. The young man well knew that the profound stillness foreboded evil, the savages never being so silent as when about to strike a blow, resembling the stealthy foot of the panther ere he takes his leap. He took out a knife, and was about to cut a hole through the bark in order to get a view of the shore, when he paused from a dread of being seen in the operation, which would direct the enemy where to aim their bullets. At this instant a rifle *was* fired, and the ball pierced both sides of the canoe, within eighteen inches of the spot where his head lay. This was close work, but our hero had too lately gone through that which was closer to be appalled. He lay still half a minute longer, and then he saw the summit of an oak coming slowly within his narrow horizon.

Unable to account for this change, Deerslayer could restrain his impatience no longer. Hitching his body along with the utmost caution, he got his eye at the bullethole, and fortunately commanded a very tolerable view of the point. The canoe, by one of those imperceptible impulses that so often decide the fate of men as well as the course of things, had inclined southerly, and was slowly drifting down the lake. It was lucky that Deerslayer had given it a shove sufficiently vigorous to send it past the end of the point ere it took this inclination, or it must have gone ashore again. As it was, it drifted so near it as to bring the tops of two or three trees within the range of the young man's view, as has been mentioned, and, indeed, to come in quite as close proximity with the extremity of the point as was at all safe. The distance could not much have exceeded a hundred feet, though fortunately a light current of air from the southwest began to set it slowly offshore.

Deerslayer now felt the urgent necessity of resorting to some expedient to get further from his foes and, if possible, to apprise his friends[7] of his situation. The distance rendered the last difficult, while the proximity to the point rendered the first indispensable. As was usual in such craft, a large, round, smooth stone was in each end of the canoe for the double purpose of seats and ballast; one of these was within reach of his feet. The stone he contrived to get so far between his legs as to reach it with his hands, and then he managed to roll it to the side of its fellow in the bows, where the two served to keep the trim of the light boat, while he worked his own body as far aft as possible. Before quitting the shore, and as soon as he perceived that the paddles were gone, Deerslayer had thrown a bit of dead branch into the canoe, and this was within reach of his arm. Removing the cap he wore, he put it on the end of this stick, and just let it appear over the edge of the canoe, as far as possible from his own person. This ruse was scarcely adopted before the young man had a proof how much he had underrated the intelligence of his enemies. In contempt of an artifice so shallow and commonplace, a bullet was fired directly through another part of

the canoe, which actually raised his skin. He dropped the cap, and instantly raised it immediately over his head, as a safeguard. It would seem that this second artifice was unseen, or what was more probable, the Hurons, feeling certain of recovering their captive, wished to take him alive.

Deerslayer lay passive a few minutes longer, his eye at the bullethole, however, and much did he rejoice at seeing that he was drifting gradually further and further from the shore. When he looked upward, the treetops had disappeared, but he soon found that the canoe was slowly turning, so as to prevent his getting a view of anything at his peephole but of the two extremities of the lake. He now bethought him of the stick, which was crooked, and offered some facilities for rowing, without the necessity of rising. The experiment succeeded, on trial, better even than he had hoped, though his great embarrassment was to keep the canoe straight. That his present maneuver was seen soon became apparent by the clamor on the shore, and a bullet entering the stern of the canoe, traversed its length, whistling between the arms of our hero, and passed out at the head. This satisfied the fugitive that he was getting away with tolerable speed and induced him to increase his efforts. He was making a stronger push than common when another messenger from the point broke the stick outboard and at once deprived him of his oar. As the sound of voices seemed to grow more and more distant, however, Deerslayer determined to leave all to the drift, until he believed himself beyond the reach of bullets. This was nervous work, but it was the wisest of all the expedients that offered; and the young man was encouraged to persevere in it by the circumstance that he felt his face fanned by the air, a proof that there was a little more wind.

7. **friends:** Natty's closest friend, the Delaware brave Chingachgook, and several others are waiting at Muskrat Castle.

For Study and Discussion

Analyzing and Interpreting the Selection

1. In the Leatherstocking Tales, nature often serves as a solemn, dignified setting for important human actions. How is the natural setting given religious significance as Natty first approaches the gathered Hurons?
2. Authority among the Hurons is divided between two chiefs. What different qualities of leadership are illustrated in Rivenoak and the Panther?
3. Why do the Hurons, after meeting in council, invite Natty to join their tribe and to change his "heart" from Delaware to Huron?
4. Natty, in his escape, cannot hope to simply out-run so many pursuers. **a.** What tricks show his wilderness skills? **b.** What particular trick fails to fool the Hurons?
5. You have seen that John Smith's account of the Indians in Virginia (page 16) reveals an *ambivalent* attitude. There are qualities about the Indians that he liked and others he disliked. Do you find a similar ambivalence in Cooper's presentation of the Hurons?

Writing About Literature

Discussing an Indian View of Expansion

The westward expansion of American civilization was the great social fact of Cooper's time and was looked upon as "progress" by white Americans. In a brief composition, discuss the way this expansion is viewed by the Huron chief Rivenoak in his speech to Natty (page 144).

Birchbark tray with moosehair design representing a Huron Indian shooting a deer.
Museum of the American Indian

WILLIAM CULLEN BRYANT
1794–1878

William Cullen Bryant.

William Cullen Bryant's long life has a special relation to the great changes that transformed America in the nineteenth century. At the time of his birth, the new, small nation consisted of fifteen states, nearly all of them on the Atlantic coast, and most Americans were still farmers. By the time he died, westward expansion had carried settlement across the continent. The American population, swollen by millions of new immigrants, had increased ten times over. The Union had survived the ordeal of civil war to become a vast industrialized nation of thirty-eight states.

For fifty years Bryant was deeply involved in the political issues that tested the nation's ability to adapt traditional values to a new industrial society. At the age of thirty-one, he moved from his native region of rural Massachusetts to New York City and turned his major literary efforts from poetry to journalism. As editor of the influential newspaper the New York *Evening Post,* he became a national spokesman for liberal causes both old and new—the aboliton of slavery, freedom of speech and religion, the right of workers to organize in unions, the repeal of laws that imprisoned debtors, and the election of Andrew Jackson and Abraham Lincoln. One aspect of Romanticism was its humanitarian concern for the "common man" and its hope for the democratic possibilities of American life. No Romantic poet was a more passionate warrior than Bryant in the service of those social ideals.

Bryant has been called "the father of American poetry." With the exception of Edward Taylor, who was not discovered and read until the twentieth century, he was the first American to produce a body of work that could be matched against the achievements of English poets. His poetry—much of it written before he was thirty—reveals a deep childhood influence. His father, a country doctor in Cummington, Massachusetts, was an enthusiastic amateur naturalist. As a boy, Bryant roamed the countryside and learned to be an accurate observer of nature and to reflect upon its meaning. At sixteen he first read the English Romantic poets William Wordsworth and Samuel Taylor Coleridge. He responded immediately to Wordsworth's view that nature has spiritual and moral meaning, for it was true of his own experience. He had written verses, mostly in imitation of eighteenth-century poets, throughout his boyhood. But at seventeen he wrote the first version of his most famous poem, "Thanatopsis." It was a major work in establishing the new Romantic movement in American literature.

Along with Irving's sketches and stories and Cooper's Leatherstocking novels, Bryant's most enduring poems belong to the emerging Romantic literature of the early nineteenth century. Bryant turned to nature as a reflection of the human spirit and a potential answer to humanity's most searching questions about its own nature. In his poems the natural world is at once the visible face of God, a source of moral lessons, and a means of exploring the human imagination. "Is there any one" he asked in a lecture on poetry, "for whom the works of Nature have no associations but such as relate to his animal wants?" Beyond our "animal wants," Bryant observed, nature speaks to the human imagination, that part of us that does not sleep even when we do but "is still awake and busy . . . fabricating dreams." The connections that the imagination makes between the natural world and our inner emotions are "the sources of poetry, and they are not only part of ourselves, but of the universe, and will expire only with the last of the creatures of God."

To a Waterfowl

Despite many years of scientific study since Bryant's time, we still do not understand fully how migrating birds find their way. Here, as in many of his poems, Bryant is interested in the connection between his own imagination and a mystery of nature.

Whither, midst falling dew,
While glow the heavens with the last steps of day,
Far, through their rosy depths, dost thou pursue
    Thy solitary way?

Vainly the fowler's° eye   5
Might mark thy distant flight to do thee wrong,
As, darkly seen against the crimson sky,
    Thy figure floats along.

Seek'st thou the plashy brink
Of weedy lake, or marge° of river wide,   10
Or where the rocking billows rise and sink
    On the chafed oceanside?

There is a Power whose care
Teaches thy way along that pathless coast—
The desert and illimitable air—   15
    Lone wandering, but not lost.

All day thy wings have fanned,
At that far height, the cold thin atmosphere,
Yet stoop not, weary, to the welcome land,
    Though the dark night is near.   20

And soon that toil shall end;
Soon shalt thou find a summer home, and rest,
And scream among thy fellows; reeds shall bend,
    Soon, o'er thy sheltered nest.

Thou'rt gone, the abyss of heaven   25
Hath swallowed up thy form; yet, on my heart
Deeply hath sunk the lesson thou hast given,
    And shall not soon depart.

He who, from zone to zone,
Guides through the boundless sky thy certain flight,   30
In the long way that I must tread alone,
    Will lead my steps aright.

5. **fowler:** hunter.

10. **marge:** word meaning "edge or border."

For Study and Discussion

Analyzing and Interpreting the Poem

To a Waterfowl

1. In the first stanza, the observation of the waterfowl in flight is put not as a statement but as a question. **a.** What does this question about the bird's destination suggest to you about the poet's mood or state of mind? **b.** Migrating birds usually travel in flocks and follow a leader. What different effect is conveyed by the poem's focus upon a "solitary" bird?

2. In stanza 2, the poet imagines a hunter watching the waterfowl. How does the introduction of this second human observer help to establish the poet's sympathy with the bird?

3. In stanza 6, the poet imagines the future homecoming of the bird in images of rest, fellowship, and shelter. Why is it important that the poet should imagine this homecoming for the bird before it disappears? In answering, consider the image of the bird in stanza 5.

4. Stanza 7 is a turning point in the poem, moving from observation of the bird and meditation about its flight to a statement of the meaning of this experience. Stanza 8 draws a direct parallel between the bird's flight and the poet's earthbound journey through life. How do lines 25–26 anticipate this parallel?

5. The "lesson" of this experience touches the poet's heart. **a.** What inner assurance has the poet gained? **b.** What has provided this new assurance?

Language and Vocabulary

Locating Archaic Words

"To a Waterfowl" contains a number of *archaic* words—words that are no longer in actual use. Sometimes an *archaism* is merely an old spelling of a word we still use, as *shalt* is an archaic spelling of *shall*. In other cases, an archaic word is one that has been replaced by another in ordinary usage. The word *you*, for example, long ago came into the language as a more formal version of the pronoun *thou*. *Thou* had been used to address family, close friends, and children. That distinction disappeared in the eighteenth century: *you* replaced *thou* in ordinary usage, and by Bryant's time *thou* was archaic. Such old-fashioned words, and such contractions as *o'er* for *over*, became part of a "poetic" language that was different from ordinary speech. Bryant's use of such terms reflects the great influence of eighteenth-century poetry, with its deliberate use of archaic words. Pick out the words in the poem that seem old-fashioned, and look them up in a dictionary to see if they are listed as archaic.

Thanatopsis°

To him who in the love of Nature holds
Communion with her visible forms, she speaks
A various language; for his gayer hours
She has a voice of gladness, and a smile
And eloquence of beauty, and she glides   5
Into his darker musings, with a mild
And healing sympathy, that steals away
Their sharpness ere° he is aware. When thoughts
Of the last bitter hour come like a blight
Over thy spirit, and sad images   10
Of the stern agony, and shroud, and pall,
And breathless darkness, and the narrow house,°
Make thee to shudder, and grow sick at heart—
Go forth, under the open sky, and list
To Nature's teachings, while from all around—   15
Earth and her waters, and the depths of air—
Comes a still voice—

       Yet a few days, and thee
The all-beholding sun shall see no more
In all his course; nor yet in the cold ground,
Where thy pale form was laid, with many tears,   20
Nor in the embrace of ocean, shall exist
Thy image. Earth, that nourished thee, shall claim
Thy growth, to be resolved to earth again,
And, lost each human trace, surrendering up
Thine individual being, shalt thou go   25
To mix forever with the elements,
To be a brother to the insensible rock
And to the sluggish clod, which the rude swain°
Turns with his share,° and treads upon. The oak
Shall send his roots abroad, and pierce thy mold.   30

  Yet not to thine eternal resting-place
Shalt thou retire alone, nor couldst thou wish
Couch more magnificent. Thou shalt lie down
With patriarchs of the infant world—with kings,
The powerful of the earth—the wise, the good,   35
Fair forms, and hoary seers of ages past,
All in one mighty sepulcher. The hills
Rock-ribbed and ancient as the sun, the vales

°**Thanatopsis** (thăn′ə-tŏp′sĭs): a meditation on death.   8. **ere** (âr): before.
12. **narrow house:** grave.   28. **swain** (swān): country youth.   29. **share:** plowshare.

Stretching in pensive quietness between;
The venerable woods—rivers that move   40
In majesty, and the complaining brooks
That make the meadows green; and, poured round all,
Old Ocean's gray and melancholy waste—
Are but the solemn decorations all
Of the great tomb of man. The golden sun,   45
The planets, all the infinite host of heaven,
Are shining on the sad abodes of death,
Through the still lapse of ages. All that tread
The globe are but a handful to the tribes
That slumber in its bosom.—Take the wings   50
Of morning,° pierce the Barcan° wilderness,
Or lose thyself in the continuous woods
Where rolls the Oregon,° and hears no sound,
Save his own dashings—yet the dead are there:
And millions in those solitudes, since first   55
The flight of years began, have laid them down
In their last sleep—the dead reign there alone.
So shalt thou rest, and what if thou withdraw
In silence from the living, and no friend
Take note of thy departure? All that breathe   60
Will share thy destiny. The gay will laugh
When thou art gone, the solemn brood of care
Plod on, and each one as before will chase
His favorite phantom; yet all these shall leave
Their mirth and their employments, and shall come   65
And make their bed with thee. As the long train
Of ages glide away, the sons of men,
The youth in life's green spring, and he who goes
In the full strength of years, matron, and maid,
The speechless babe, and the gray-headed man—   70
Shall one by one be gathered to thy side,
By those, who in their turn shall follow them.

   So live, that when thy summons comes to join
The innumerable caravan, which moves
To that mysterious realm, where each shall take   75
His chamber in the silent halls of death,
Thou go not, like the quarry-slave at night,
Scourged to his dungeon, but, sustained and soothed
By an unfaltering trust, approach thy grave,
Like one who wraps the drapery of his couch   80
About him, and lies down to pleasant dreams.

Imaginary Landscape: Scene from Thanatopsis (1850) by Asher Durand. Oil on canvas.

50–51. **Take . . . morning:** an allusion to Psalm 139:9.   51. **Barcan:** pertaining to Barca, a desert region on the Mediterranean coast of North Africa.   53. **Oregon:** now known as the Columbia River, between Oregon and Washington.

Commentary

Bryant's meditation on death was for generations one of the best known of all American poems, creating wide attention for Romantic attitudes toward this difficult subject. A concern with death was characteristic of the early Romantic poets for several reasons. Their interest in the ancient past and earlier civilizations made them acutely aware of the many human societies that have disappeared. The present stands upon the buried past, and from this view the earth is indeed "the great tomb of man." The Romantics also celebrated individualism and the powers of the self. Since death is the final restriction upon the self and its powers, it became an important theme in their poetry. Finally, their intense interest in nature contributed to this concern with death. Against the earlier eighteenth-century view of nature as a mechanical pattern of repetition, the Romantics emphasized the organic process of constant change in nature: Every living thing fulfills its appointed life cycle of birth, growth, decay, and death. Human life is only a part of this process. The Romantic poets were aware that the beauty they looked upon would be renewed for other eyes, but that they themselves must pass from the scene.

In Romantic poetry, the subject of death could easily lead to *sentimentalism,* an expression of feeling that is excessive for the subject and becomes an indulgence in emotion for its own sake. Certain English poets of Bryant's time so often used death to evoke the "delicious pain" of pleasurable sadness that they came to be called the "Graveyard School" of poets. On the whole, "Thanatopsis" avoids this sentimentalizing of death. It neither disguises the fact nor dwells too much upon its sadness. The opening lines of the poem (lines 1–30) acknowledge the support that nature offers for many of our needs: "a voice of gladness" to answer to our joy, a "healing sympathy" to relieve our "darker musings." But this "communion" with nature also confirms the fact that we are indeed nature's creatures and subject to its laws. For the "shudder" that comes with the thought of death, nature has only the stern lesson that all "individual being" must be surrendered to the earth that nourished it. Our last communion with nature will be as "brother to . . . the sluggish clod" and as food for the oak.

Bryant's meditation then turns, in lines 31–72, to that human attribute that sets us apart from nature and makes us fear death: our consciousness of time. Alone among the creatures of the earth, we are conscious of our own existence and dread its end. If we are to accept death without bitterness, which means truly to accept our lives, we must relate our consciousness of time to nature. Our awareness of our mortality must become a part of our existence as natural beings.

In our mortality we share our individual being with all other beings. We do not "retire alone" to the grave but lie down with ancient patriarchs and kings, the good and fair and wise of all the ages. Our awareness of time, which in the poem's first section seems to isolate us as separate beings who "grow sick at heart" at the thought of death, here unites us with all humanity. What we see, others have seen. There is no remote wilderness, no new part of the earth (lines 50–57), that has not become the home of the dead. Nor should we envy those who will remain when we are gone. The same awareness of time that ties us to the past also binds us to the future: "All that breathe / Will share thy destiny." The earth is truly our "home," in death as in life.

The movement of the poem is toward trust, and toward release from fear and bitterness. This is the note of the final section (lines 73–81). Our broader consciousness of time—relating us both to nature and to the "innumerable caravan" of humanity—makes possible an acceptance of our natural being and its natural completion in death. Then death will not be the slave's fearful "dungeon" but a change of consciousness as natural as the sleep of one who "lies down to pleasant dreams."

For Study and Discussion

Analyzing and Interpreting the Poem

1. The opening section of the poem (lines 1–30) turns quickly from the comforts of nature to thoughts of the "bitter hour" of death. What physical details of death are used to intensify the "stern agony" of such thoughts?

2. The earth in the first section seems confining and "cold" and "sluggish," the "narrow house" of one's personal grave. Although the earth is still a "tomb" in the second section, it also takes on beauty and magnitude. What details accomplish this change in lines 37–47?

3. Whereas the first section of the poem emphasizes one's "individual being" and its loss in death, the second section emphasizes one's place in the human procession as a whole. How is this idea conveyed in the vision of those who will live after one's own lifetime (lines 66–72)?

4. One way that death is made less threatening in the second and third sections of the poem is by comparing it with sleep. Compare the description of death and the image of the grave in lines 8–12 with the description of sleep in lines 78–81. What is the difference in tone between these two passages?

Blank Verse

"Thanatopsis" is not written in rhyme. It does, however, have a regular rhythm, a pattern of stressed and unstressed syllables. If the opening line is broken down into syllables

Tŏ hím whŏ ín thĕ lóve ŏf Ná tŭre hólds
1   2   3   4   5   6   7   8   9   10

we find a pattern in which one unstressed syllable (marked ˘) is followed by one stressed syllable (marked ´). English verse is based on stress, and the unit used to measure rhythm in a line of poetry is called a **foot.** A foot consists usually of two or three syllables, one of which is stressed. In the line above, each foot consists of one unstressed syllable followed by one stressed syllable (˘´). This kind of foot is called an **iamb.** Since the line has five such feet, its **meter** (the rhythmic pattern) is called **iambic pentameter.** (The prefix *penta* means "five," as in *pentagon,* a five-sided figure.) Poetry consisting of verse lines of unrhymed iambic pentameter is called **blank verse.**

Through a long literary tradition, different verse forms have proven suitable for different purposes in poetry. Blank verse, which is close to normal speech in its rhythm, has often been used in dramatic poetry, such as William Shakespeare's plays, and in poems on serious subjects, such as John Milton's *Paradise Lost.* It is appropriate on both counts to "Thanatopsis," a meditation on the subject of death, which gives the impression that the poet is directly addressing the reader. With its fixed rhythm and regular line length, blank verse is less "free" than **free verse,** in which the rhythm is irregular and the lines vary in length. But it is also more open than most types of rhymed verse. A **couplet,** for instance, completes a thought in two rhyming lines. Blank verse allows a much more extended development of a thought, sometimes through many lines. Again, this is appropriate to poetry that deals seriously with complex and profound subjects.

The danger for the poet who uses blank verse is that the regular rhythm may become monotonous and even singsong. Bryant guards against this by introducing slight variations in rhythm. Line 6, for instance, begins with a stressed syllable, and other lines make similar variations. Rhythm is also varied by the careful use of pauses within lines, called **caesuras** (sĭ-zhoor´əz). Caesuras are "sense pauses," hesitations in the rhythm that are necessary to the sense of the line. They may be created by punctuation, but they may also result from the meanings of words or the natural rhythms of language. In line 24, for instance, there is a caesura immediately after the opening unstressed *and,* which gives that word a stress it would not otherwise have. In the same line the last two syllables of *surrendering* must be slurred to put stress on the final word *up.* Through such devices, stress is varied according to meaning.

The reader of blank verse should recognize the basic rhythms of the lines but should avoid a mechanical pattern of emphasis that ignores the meaning of the words. It is useful to think of blank verse as a heightened or unusually intense form of speech in which the rhythm, carefully controlled through stress and caesura, is essential to the meaning.

1. Find three lines of "Thanatopsis" in which there is a variation of the basic rhythm, and point out the variation. Is it dependent upon stress or caesura?
2. Carefully examine line 42:

That make the meadows green; and, poured round all,

Where do the stresses fall in this line? Where are the caesuras?
3. Read aloud ten lines or so of "Thanatopsis," keeping in mind the way blank verse should properly be read. As you read, be aware of both the poem's basic iambic rhythm and its variations.

EDGAR ALLAN POE
1809–1849

Edgar Allan Poe.

No other American writer's biography has been as distorted as Edgar Allan Poe's was for many years. The "Poe myth" portrayed a life that was spectacularly immoral when in fact it was only unusually miserable and dreary—and even dull. The legend of a Poe who combined "the fiend, the brute, and the genius" began early and persisted long. On the day of Poe's funeral, a literary rival and secret enemy published an anonymous letter that praised Poe's work but abused his character. He later followed with a "Memoir" that was full of malice, lies, and outright forgeries. As unlucky in death as he had been in life, Poe became the subject of a fantasy that matched the fantasies of his stories.

The truth was more prosaic. Poe was born to traveling actors, who were then situated in Boston. The father soon abandoned the family, and Poe's mother died destitute in a Richmond, Virginia, rooming house when Poe was two years old. He was taken into the home of John Allan, a wealthy Richmond tobacco merchant, but he was never formally adopted. Mrs. Allan apparently lavished affection upon the child, but Poe's relationship with Allan himself was probably never secure. He was raised and educated as the son of aristocrats, but both he and others knew that he had no legal rights as Allan's heir. The insecurity of his position became fully clear when, at seventeen, he entered the University of Virginia with an allowance from Allan that Poe considered too small to cover necessary expenses. Within a year he had contracted substantial debts, some of them from gambling, and had to leave the university when Allan refused to pay.

The next few years of Poe's life were made up of rather pathetic attempts to establish his independence and to be reconciled with Allan. He served two years in the army and then, in a vain effort to please Allan, spent several unhappy months as a cadet at West Point. He also made periodic visits home that were meant to regain Allan's favor but that usually led to bitter quarrels. The troubled relationship finally ended after Mrs. Allan died and Allan remarried, making it clear that Poe would not be his heir. Poe did, of course, want to be Allan's heir, but he wanted acknowledgment as a "son" even more. What the failure of the relationship meant to Poe was summed up years later in a single grim sentence. "The want of parental affection," he wrote, "has been the heaviest of my trials."

Poe had first tried his literary fortunes at the age of eighteen with a thin book of poems which he expanded in two later editions, all without receiving any significant recognition. After he left West Point in 1831 with nothing further to be expected from Allan, he lived for a time in Baltimore at the home of his aunt, Mrs. Maria Clemm. He turned from poetry to fiction in the hope of making a living. He went to work for an influential magazine, the *Southern Literary Messenger,* and in 1835 he became its editor. In the same year he married his cousin, Virginia Clemm, who was then thirteen years old, and the kindly Mrs. Clemm became a devoted mother to her two "strange children." In a manner, Poe had at last been adopted.

He was an industrious and skillful editor. Under his guidance the *Messenger*'s circulation quadrupled, and his own essays soon established his reputation as a leading literary critic. Unfortunately, he was developing another reputation as well, for emotional instability and bouts of drunkenness. His drinking has been vastly exaggerated; his constitution could not tolerate alcohol and even a slight amount made him senseless. But the instability it revealed would persist throughout his life. He could work under great pressure, but continued frustration would always upset his uncertain emotional balance and send him looking for "a world elsewhere," either in drink or in illusions of future prosperity. Dissatisfied with his meager salary, he left the *Messenger* in 1837 with unrealistic plans for establishing his own magazine and so becoming financially secure. Frustration with the present and unfounded hopes for the future became the pattern. "I live continually in a reverie of the future," he wrote later. "My life has been . . . a scorn of all things present, in an earnest longing for the future." The imagination became for Poe an escape from the actual and a passage to an inner world of a different reality.

Throughout the rest of his brief life, Poe was associated, sometimes as editor, with various magazines in Philadelphia and New York. During this period, he wrote many of his best stories, along with much hack work. Despite his frantic efforts he could not escape grinding poverty ("Ligeia," one of his finest stories, sold for ten dollars!), and frustration drove him from one unrealistic project for a new magazine to another. The publication of "The Raven" in 1845 brought him a measure of fame but no increase of income. After 1842, Virginia's illness deprived him of a basic source of stability. Her death five years later from tuberculosis, at the age of twenty-four, plunged him into a confused search for emotional security with several women. In the last year of his life, he was twice engaged to be married. The second engagement was to a Richmond widow who had once been his boyhood sweetheart. Returning north from Richmond on a business trip before his intended marriage, Poe stopped off in Baltimore. His movements and his companions there have remained a mystery, but six days later he was found in torn clothing lying unconscious on a sidewalk in the rain. He died without fully regaining consciousness.

Poe's accomplishments in a short, frenzied life were substantial. He was the most important American poet before Walt Whitman. His poems, with their unreal atmosphere and musical effects, had a considerable influence on the late nineteenth-century French symbolist poets and, through them, on all modern poetry. His literary criticism was a major contribution to a developing theory of Romantic literature. He is credited, along with Nathaniel Hawthorne, with giving the short story its modern form; and the detective story has been traced back to his invention. But these honors do not really describe Poe's unique contribution to American literature. Typically, the function of the imagination in Poe's work is to separate us from the recognizable world of ordinary reality in order to explore the inner, often irrational world of the human mind. This exploration is conducted in at least two quite different ways. In the stories of detection like "The Purloined Letter" and "The Murders in the Rue Morgue," Poe's master detective Dupin controls both the outer world of events and the inner mental world, deducing the motives of others and even reconstructing the unconscious process of their thought. From seemingly incomprehensible events and motives, he remakes a world of reason before our eyes. On the other hand, in the stories of terror like "The Fall of the House of Usher" (and in poems like "The Raven"), we watch the world of reason disintegrate as the victim is swept into the strange, irrational depths of his own being. It is above all for his exploration of this dark side of our inner experience that Poe remains an important writer.

The Fall of the House of Usher

Son cœur est un luth suspendu:
Sitôt qu'on le touche il résonne.[1]
DE BÉRANGER

During the whole of a dull, dark, and soundless day in the autumn of the year, when the clouds hung oppressively low in the heavens, I had been passing alone, on horseback, through a singularly dreary tract of country, and at length found myself, as the shades of the evening drew on, within view of the melancholy House of Usher. I know not how it was—but, with the first glimpse of the building, a sense of insufferable gloom pervaded my spirit. I say insufferable; for the feeling was unrelieved by any of that half-pleasurable, because poetic, sentiment with which the mind usually receives even the sternest natural images of the desolate or terrible. I looked upon the scene before me—upon the mere house, and the simple landscape features of the domain—upon the bleak walls—upon the vacant eyelike windows—upon a few rank sedges[2]—and upon a few white trunks of decayed trees—with an utter depression of soul which I can compare to no earthly sensation more properly than to the afterdream of the reveler upon opium—the bitter lapse into everyday life—the hideous dropping off of the veil. There was an iciness, a sinking, a sickening of the heart—an unredeemed dreariness of thought which no goad-ing of the imagination could torture into aught[3] of the sublime. What was it—I paused to think—what was it that so unnerved me in the contemplation of the House of Usher? It was a mystery all insoluble; nor could I grapple with the shadowy fancies that crowded upon me as I pondered. I was forced to fall back upon the unsatisfactory conclusion that while, beyond doubt, there *are* combinations of very simple natural objects which have the power of thus affecting us, still the analysis of this power lies among considerations beyond our depth. It was possible, I reflected, that a mere different arrangement of the particulars of the scene, of the details of the picture, would be sufficient to modify, or perhaps to annihilate its capacity for sorrowful impression; and, acting upon this idea, I reined my horse to the precipitous brink of a black and lurid tarn[4] that lay in unruffled luster by the dwelling, and gazed down—but with a shudder even more thrilling than before—upon the remodeled and inverted images of the gray sedge, and the ghastly tree stems, and the vacant and eyelike windows.

Nevertheless, in this mansion of gloom, I now proposed to myself a sojourn of some weeks. Its proprietor, Roderick Usher, had been one of my boon companions in boyhood; but many years had elapsed since our last

1. *Son cœur . . . il résonne:* "His heart is a suspended lute; Whenever one touches it, it resounds." From the poem "Le Refus," by Pierre Jean de Béranger (1780–1857).
2. **sedges:** grasslike plants.
3. **aught:** anything.
4. **tarn:** small lake or pool.

House of Usher, a watercolor illustration by Arthur Rackham (1867–1939) for
Tales of Mystery and Imagination (1935).

meeting. A letter, however, had lately reached me in a distant part of the country—a letter from him—which, in its wildly importunate nature, had admitted of no other than a personal reply. The Ms.[5] gave evidence of nervous agitation. The writer spoke of acute bodily illness—of a mental disorder which oppressed him—and of an earnest desire to see me, as his best and indeed his only personal friend, with a view of attempting, by the cheerfulness of my society, some alleviation of his malady. It was the manner in which all this, and much more, was said—it was the apparent *heart* that went with his request—which allowed me no room for hesitation; and I accordingly obeyed forthwith what I still considered a very singular summons.

Although, as boys, we had been even intimate associates, yet I really knew little of my friend. His reserve had been always excessive and habitual. I was aware, however, that his very ancient family had been noted, time out of mind, for a peculiar sensibility of temperament, displaying itself, through long ages, in many works of exalted art, and manifested, of late, in repeated deeds of munificent yet unobtrusive charity, as well as in a passionate devotion to the intricacies, perhaps even more than to the orthodox and easily recognizable beauties, of musical science. I had learned, too, the very remarkable fact that the stem of the Usher race, all time-honored as it was, had put forth, at no period, any enduring branch; in other words, that the entire family lay in the direct line of descent, and had always, with very trifling and very temporary variation, so lain. It was this deficiency, I considered, while running over in thought the perfect keeping of the character of the premises with the accredited character of the people, and while speculating upon the possible influence which the one, in the long lapse of centuries, might have exercised upon the other—it was this deficiency, perhaps, of collateral[6] issue, and the consequent undeviating transmission, from sire to son, of the patrimony[7] with the name, which had, at length, so identified the two as to merge the original title of the estate in the quaint and equivocal appellation of the "House of Usher"—an appellation which seemed to include, in the minds of the peasantry who used it, both the family and the family mansion.

I have said that the sole effect of my somewhat childish experiment—that of looking down within the tarn—had been to deepen the first singular impression. There can be no doubt that the consciousness of the rapid increase of my superstition—for why should I not so term it?—served mainly to accelerate the increase itself. Such, I have long known, is the paradoxical law of all sentiments having terror as a basis. And it might have been for this reason only, that, when I again uplifted my eyes to the house itself, from its image in the pool, there grew in my mind a strange fancy—a fancy so ridiculous, indeed, that I but mention it to show the vivid force of the sensations which oppressed me. I had so worked upon my imagination as really to believe that about the whole mansion and domain there hung an atmosphere peculiar to themselves and their immediate vicinity—an atmosphere which had no affinity with the air of heaven, but which had reeked up from the decayed trees, and the gray wall, and the silent tarn—a pestilent and mystic vapor, dull, sluggish, faintly discernible, and leaden-hued.

Shaking off from my spirit what *must* have been a dream, I scanned more narrowly the real aspect of the building. Its principal feature seemed to be that of an excessive antiquity. The discoloration of ages had been great. Minute fungi overspread the whole exterior, hanging in a fine tangled web-work from the eaves. Yet all this was apart from any extraordinary dilapidation. No portion of the masonry had fallen; and there appeared to be a wild inconsistency between its still perfect ad-

5. **Ms.:** manuscript.
6. **collateral** (kə-lăt′ər-əl): descended from the same ancestors, but in a different line.

7. **patrimony** (păt′rə-mō′nē): something which is inherited.

aptation of parts, and the crumbling condition of the individual stones. In this there was much that reminded me of the specious totality of old woodwork which has rotted for long years in some neglected vault, with no disturbance from the breath of the external air. Beyond this indication of extensive decay, however, the fabric gave little token of instability. Perhaps the eye of a scrutinizing observer might have discovered a barely perceptible fissure, which, extending from the roof of the building in front, made its way down the wall in a zigzag direction, until it became lost in the sullen waters of the tarn.

Noticing these things, I rode over a short causeway to the house. A servant in waiting took my horse, and I entered the Gothic[8] archway of the hall. A valet, of stealthy step, thence conducted me, in silence, through many dark and intricate passages in my progress to the studio of his master. Much that I encountered on the way contributed, I know not how, to heighten the vague sentiments of which I have already spoken. While the objects around me—while the carvings of the ceilings, the somber tapestries of the walls, the ebon blackness of the floors, and the phantasmagoric[9] armorial trophies which rattled as I strode, were but matters to which, or to such as which, I had been accustomed from my infancy—while I hesitated not to acknowledge how familiar was all this—I still wondered to find how unfamiliar were the fancies which ordinary images were stirring up. On one of the staircases, I met the physician of the family. His countenance, I thought, wore a mingled expression of low cunning and perplexity. He accosted me with trepidation and passed on. The valet now threw open a door and ushered me into the presence of his master.

The room in which I found myself was very large and lofty. The windows were long, narrow, and pointed, and at so vast a distance from the black oaken floor as to be altogether inaccessible from within. Feeble gleams of en-

crimsoned light made their way through the trellised panes and served to render sufficiently distinct the more prominent objects around; the eye, however, struggled in vain to reach the remoter angles of the chamber, or the recesses of the vaulted and fretted[10] ceiling. Dark draperies hung upon the walls. The general furniture was profuse, comfortless, antique, and tattered. Many books and musical instruments lay scattered about, but failed to give any vitality to the scene. I felt that I breathed an atmosphere of sorrow. An air of stern, deep, and irredeemable gloom hung over and pervaded all.

Upon my entrance, Usher arose from a sofa on which he had been lying at full length, and greeted me with a vivacious warmth which had much in it, I at first thought, of an overdone cordiality—of the constrained effort of the *ennuyé*[11] man of the world. A glance, however, at his countenance convinced me of his perfect sincerity. We sat down; and for some moments, while he spoke not, I gazed upon him with a feeling half of pity, half of awe. Surely, man had never before so terribly altered, in so brief a period, as had Roderick Usher! It was with difficulty that I could bring myself to admit the identity of the wan being before me with the companion of my early boyhood. Yet the character of his face had been at all times remarkable. A cadaverousness of complexion; an eye large, liquid, and luminous beyond comparison; lips somewhat thin and very pallid, but of a surpassingly beautiful curve; a nose of a delicate Hebrew model, but with a breadth of nostril unusual in similar formations; a finely molded chin, speaking, in its want of prominence, of a want of moral energy; hair of a more than weblike softness and tenuity; these features, with an inordinate expansion above the regions of the temple, made up altogether a countenance not easily to be forgotten. And now in the mere exaggeration of the prevailing character of these features, and of the expression they were wont to convey, lay so much of

8. **Gothic:** here, dark, high, and ornate.
9. **phantasmagoric** (făn-tăz′mə-gôr′ĭk): fantastic.

10. **fretted:** carved in an ornamental pattern.
11. *ennuyé* (än′nwē-ā′): French word meaning "bored."

change that I doubted to whom I spoke. The now ghastly pallor of the skin, and the now miraculous luster of the eye, above all things startled and even awed me. The silken hair, too, had been suffered to grow all unheeded, and as, in its wild gossamer texture, it floated rather than fell about the face, I could not, even with effort, connect its Arabesque[12] expression with any idea of simple humanity.

In the manner of my friend I was at once struck with an incoherence—an inconsistency; and I soon found this to arise from a series of feeble and futile struggles to overcome an habitual trepidancy—an excessive nervous agitation. For something of this nature I had indeed been prepared, no less by his letter, than by reminiscences of certain boyish traits, and by conclusions deduced from his peculiar physical conformation and temperament. His action was alternately vivacious and sullen. His voice varied rapidly from a tremulous indecision (when the animal spirits seemed utterly in abeyance[13]) to that species of energetic concision—that abrupt, weighty, unhurried, and hollow-sounding enunciation—that leaden, self-balanced, and perfectly modulated guttural utterance, which may be observed in the lost drunkard, or the irreclaimable eater of opium, during the periods of his most intense excitement.

It was thus that he spoke of the object of my visit, of his earnest desire to see me, and of the solace he expected me to afford him. He entered, at some length, into what he conceived to be the nature of his malady. It was, he said, a constitutional and a family evil, and one for which he despaired to find a remedy—a mere nervous affection,[14] he immediately added, which would undoubtedly soon pass off. It displayed itself in a host of unnatural sensations. Some of these, as he detailed them, interested and bewildered me; although, perhaps, the terms and the general manner of the narration had their weight. He suffered much

from a morbid acuteness of the senses; the most insipid food was alone endurable; he could wear only garments of certain texture; the odors of all flowers were oppressive; his eyes were tortured by even a faint light; and there were but peculiar sounds, and these from stringed instruments, which did not inspire him with horror.

To an anomalous species of terror I found him a bounden slave. "I shall perish," said he, "I *must* perish in this deplorable folly. Thus, thus, and not otherwise, shall I be lost. I dread the events of the future, not in themselves, but in their results. I shudder at the thought of any, even the most trivial, incident, which may operate upon this intolerable agitation of soul. I have, indeed, no abhorrence of danger, except in its absolute effect—in terror. In this unnerved, in this pitiable, condition, I feel that the period will sooner or later arrive when I must abandon life and reason together, in some struggle with the grim phantasm, FEAR."

I learned, moreover, at intervals, and through broken and equivocal hints, another singular feature of his mental condition. He was enchained by certain superstitious impressions in regard to the dwelling which he tenanted, and whence, for many years, he had never ventured forth—in regard to an influence whose supposititious[15] force was conveyed in terms too shadowy here to be restated—an influence which some peculiarities in the mere form and substance of his family mansion had, by dint of long sufferance, he said, obtained over his spirit—an effect which the physique of the gray walls and turrets, and of the dim tarn into which they all looked down, had, at length, brought about upon the morale of his existence.

He admitted, however, although with hesitation, that much of the peculiar gloom which thus afflicted him could be traced to a more natural and far more palpable origin—to the severe and long-continued illness—indeed to the evidently approaching dissolution—of a

---

12. **Arabesque** (ăr'ə-běsk'): fantastic.
13. **in abeyance** (ə-bā'əns): suppressed.
14. **affection:** here, affliction.

15. **supposititious** (sə-pŏz'ə-tĭsh'əs): supposed.

Separation (1893) by Edvard Munch (1863–1944). Oil on canvas.
Munch-Museum, Oslo, Norway

tenderly beloved sister, his sole companion for long years, his last and only relative on earth. "Her decease," he said, with a bitterness which I can never forget, "would leave him (him, the hopeless and the frail) the last of the ancient race of the Ushers." While he spoke, the lady Madeline (for so was she called) passed slowly through a remote portion of the apartment, and, without having noticed my presence, dis-

appeared. I regarded her with an utter astonishment not unmingled with dread; and yet I found it impossible to account for such feelings. A sensation of stupor oppressed me as my eyes followed her retreating steps. When a door, at length, closed upon her, my glance sought instinctively and eagerly the countenance of the brother; but he had buried his face in his hands, and I could only perceive that a far more than ordinary wanness had overspread the emaciated fingers through which trickled many passionate tears.

The disease of the lady Madeline had long baffled the skill of her physicians. A settled apathy, a gradual wasting away of the person, and frequent although transient affections of a partially cataleptical[16] character were the unusual diagnosis. Hitherto she had steadily borne up against the pressure of her malady, and had not betaken herself finally to bed; but on the closing in of the evening of my arrival at the house, she succumbed (as her brother told me at night with inexpressible agitation) to the prostrating power of the destroyer; and I learned that the glimpse I had obtained of her person would thus probably be the last I should obtain—that the lady, at least while living, would be seen by me no more.

For several days ensuing, her name was unmentioned by either Usher or myself; and during this period I was busied in earnest endeavors to alleviate the melancholy of my friend. We painted and read together, or I listened, as if in a dream, to the wild improvisations of his speaking guitar. And thus, as a closer and still closer intimacy admitted me more unreservedly into the recesses of his spirit, the more bitterly did I perceive the futility of all attempt at cheering a mind from which darkness, as if an inherent positive quality, poured forth upon all objects of the moral and physical universe in one unceasing radiation of gloom.

I shall ever bear about me a memory of the many solemn hours I thus spent alone with the master of the House of Usher. Yet I should fail in any attempt to convey an idea of the exact character of the studies, or of the occupations, in which he involved me, or led me the way. An excited and highly distempered ideality[17] threw a sulfureous[18] luster over all. His long improvised dirges will ring forever in my ears. Among other things, I hold painfully in mind a certain singular perversion and amplification of the wild air of the last waltz of Von Weber.[19] From the paintings over which his elaborate fancy brooded, and which grew, touch by touch, into vaguenesses at which I shuddered the more thrillingly, because I shuddered knowing not why—from these paintings (vivid as their images now are before me) I would in vain endeavor to educe more than a small portion which should lie within the compass of merely written words. By the utter simplicity, by the nakedness of his designs, he arrested and overawed attention. If ever mortal painted an idea, that mortal was Roderick Usher. For me at least, in the circumstances then surrounding me, there arose out of the pure abstractions which the hypochondriac contrived to throw upon his canvas, an intensity of intolerable awe, no shadow of which felt I ever yet in the contemplation of the certainly glowing yet too concrete reveries of Fuseli.[20]

One of the phantasmagoric conceptions of my friend, partaking not so rigidly of the spirit of abstraction may be shadowed forth, although feebly, in words. A small picture presented the interior of an immensely long and rectangular vault or tunnel, with low walls, smooth, white, and without interruption or device. Certain accessory points of the design served well to convey the idea that this excavation lay at an exceeding depth below the surface of the earth. No outlet was observed in any portion of its vast extent, and no torch or other artificial source of light was discernible; yet a flood of intense rays rolled throughout, and bathed the whole in a ghastly and inappropriate splendor.

I have just spoken of that morbid condition of the auditory nerve which rendered all music intolerable to the sufferer, with the exception of certain effects of stringed instruments. It

---

16. **cataleptical** (kăt′l-ĕp′tĭ-kəl): in a state in which consciousness and feeling are suddenly lost and the body assumes a deathlike rigidity.
17. **distempered ideality:** feverish obsession.
18. **sulfureous** (sŭl-fyo͝or′ē-əs); greenish-yellow.

19. **Von Weber:** Carl Maria von Weber (1786–1826), a German composer.
20. **Fuseli:** Henry Fuseli (or Füssli), a Swiss painter (1742–1825) who lived in England.

was, perhaps, the narrow limits to which he thus confined himself upon the guitar which gave birth, in great measure, to the fantastic character of his performances. But the fervid facility of his impromptus could not be so accounted for. They must have been, and were, in the notes, as well as in the words of his wild fantasias (for he not unfrequently accompanied himself with rhymed verbal improvisations), the result of that intense mental collectedness and concentration to which I have previously alluded as observable only in particular moments of the highest artificial excitement. The words of one of these rhapsodies I have easily remembered. I was, perhaps, the more forcibly impressed with it, as he gave it, because, in the under or mystic current of its meaning, I fancied that I perceived, and for the first time, a full consciousness on the part of Usher, of the tottering of his lofty reason upon her throne. The verses, which were entitled "The Haunted Palace," ran very nearly, if not accurately, thus:

I

In the greenest of our valleys,
By good angels tenanted,
Once a fair and stately palace—
Radiant palace—reared its head.
In the monarch Thought's dominion—
It stood there!
Never seraph spread a pinion
Over fabric half so fair.

II

Banners yellow, glorious, golden,
On its roof did float and flow
(This—all this—was in the olden
Time long ago);
And every gentle air that dallied,
In that sweet day,
Along the ramparts plumed and pallid,
A wingèd odor went away.

III

Wanderers in that happy valley
Through two luminous windows saw

Spirits moving musically
To a lute's well-tunèd law;
Round about a throne, where sitting
(Porphyrogene!)[21]
In state his glory well befitting,
The ruler of the realm was seen.

IV

And all with pearl and ruby glowing,
Was the fair palace door,
Through which came flowing, flowing, flowing
And sparkling evermore,
A troop of Echoes whose sweet duty
Was but to sing,
In voices of surpassing beauty,
The wit and wisdom of their king.

V

But evil things, in robes of sorrow,
Assailed the monarch's high estate;
(Ah, let us mourn, for never morrow
Shall dawn upon him, desolate!)
And, round about his home, the glory
That blushed and bloomed
Is but a dim-remembered story
Of the old time entombed.

VI

And travelers now within that valley,
Through the red-litten[22] windows see
Vast forms that move fantastically
To a discordant melody;
While, like a rapid ghastly river,
Through the pale door,
A hideous throng rush out forever,
And laugh—but smile no more.

I well remembered that suggestions arising from this ballad led us into a train of thought wherein there became manifest an opinon of Usher's, which I mention not so much on account of its novelty (for other men have

---

21. **Porphyrogene** (pôr′fĭ-rō′jĕn): pertaining to royalty or "the purple." The word comes from porphyry, a dark red or purple rock.
22. **litten:** a poetic word meaning "lighted."

thought thus), as on account of the pertinacity with which he maintained it. This opinion, in its general form, was that of the sentience[23] of all vegetable things. But in his disordered fancy, the idea had assumed a more daring character, and trespassed, under certain conditions, upon the kingdom of inorganization.[24] I lack words to express the full extent, or the earnest *abandon* of his persuasion. The belief, however, was connected (as I have previously hinted) with the gray stones of the home of his forefathers. The conditions of the sentience had been here, he imagined, fulfilled in the method of collocation of these stones—in the order of their arrangement, as well as in that of the many fungi which overspread them, and of the decayed trees which stood around—above all, in the long undisturbed endurance of this arrangement, and in its reduplication in the still waters of the tarn. Its evidence—the evidence of the sentience—was to be seen, he said (and I here started as he spoke), in the gradual yet certain condensation of an atmosphere of their own about the waters and the walls. The result was discoverable, he added, in that silent yet importunate and terrible influence which for centuries had molded the destinies of his family, and which made *him* what I now saw him—what he was. Such opinions need no comment, and I will make none.

Our books—the books which, for years, had formed no small portion of the mental existence of the invalid—were, as might be supposed, in strict keeping with this character of phantasm. We pored together over such works as the Ververt et Chartreuse[25] of Gresset; the Belphegor of Machiavelli; the Heaven and Hell of Swedenborg; the Subterranean Voyage of Nicholas Klimm by Holberg; the Chiromancy of Robert Flud, of Jean D'Indaginé, and of De la Chambre; the Journey into the Blue Distance of Tieck; and the City of the Sun of Campanella. One favorite volume was a small octave edition of the Directorium Inquisitorium, by the Dominican Eymeric de Gironne; and there were passages in Pomponius Mela, about the old African Satyrs and Ægipans, over which Usher would sit dreaming for hours. His chief delight, however, was found in the perusal of an exceedingly rare and curious book in quarto Gothic—the manual of a forgotten church— the *Vigiliæ Mortuorum secundum Chorum Ecclesiæ Maguntinæ.*

I could not help thinking of the wild ritual of this work, and of its probable influence upon the hypochondriac, when, one evening, having informed me abruptly that the lady Madeline was no more, he stated his intention of preserving her corpse for a fortnight (previously to its final interment), in one of the numerous vaults within the main walls of the building. The worldly reason, however, assigned for this singular proceeding, was one which I did not feel at liberty to dispute. The brother had been led to his resolution (so he told me) by consideration of the unusual character of the malady of the deceased, of certain obtrusive and eager inquiries on the part of her medical men, and of the remote and exposed situation of the burial ground of the family. I will not deny that when I called to mind the sinister countenance of the person whom I met upon the staircase, on the day of my arrival at the house, I had no desire to oppose what I regarded as at best but a harmless, and by no means an unnatural precaution.[26]

At the request of Usher, I personally aided him in the arrangements for the temporary entombment. The body having been encoffined, we two alone bore it to its rest. The vault in which we placed it (and which had been so long unopened that our torches, half smothered in its oppressive atmosphere, gave us little opportunity for investigation) was small,

---

23. **sentience** (sĕn′chĭ-əns): consciousness.
24. **kingdom of inorganization:** the world of inanimate objects.
25. **Ververt et Chartreuse, etc.:** All of the books listed are works of mysticism or magic.

26. **I will . . . precaution:** Usher wishes to prevent his sister's body from being dissected by doctors. The person on the staircase with the "sinister countenance" is the family physician.

damp, and entirely without means of admission for light; lying, at great depth, immediately beneath that portion of the building in which was my own sleeping apartment. It had been used, apparently, in remote feudal times, for the worst purposes of a donjon-keep,[27] and, in later days, as a place of deposit for powder, or some other highly combustible substance, as a portion of its floor, and the whole interior of a long archway through which we reached it, were carefully sheathed with copper. The door, of massive iron, had been, also, similarly protected. Its immense weight caused an unusually sharp grating sound, as it moved upon its hinges.

Having deposited our mournful burden upon trestles within this region of horror, we partially turned aside the yet unscrewed lid of the coffin, and looked upon the face of the tenant. A striking similitude between the brother and sister now first arrested my attention; and Usher, divining, perhaps, my thoughts, murmured out some few words from which I learned that the deceased and himself had been twins, and that sympathies of a scarcely intelligible nature had always existed between them. Our glances, however, rested not long upon the dead—for we could not regard her unawed. The disease which had thus entombed the lady in the maturity of youth had left, as usual in all maladies of a strictly cataleptical character, the mockery of a faint blush upon the bosom and the face, and that suspiciously lingering smile upon the lip which is so terrible in death. We replaced and screwed down the lid, and, having secured the door of iron, made our way, with toil, into the scarcely less gloomy apartments of the upper portion of the house.

And now, some days of bitter grief having elapsed, an observable change came over the features of the mental disorder of my friend. His ordinary manner had vanished. His ordinary occupations were neglected or forgotten. He roamed from chamber to chamber with hurried, unequal, and objectless step. The pallor of his countenance had assumed, if possible, a more ghastly hue—but the luminousness of his eye had utterly gone out. The once occasional huskiness of his tone was heard no more; and a tremulous quaver, as if of extreme terror, habitually characterized his utterance. There were times, indeed, when I thought his unceasingly agitated mind was laboring with some oppressive secret, to divulge which he struggled for the necessary courage. At times, again, I was obliged to resolve all into the mere inexplicable vagaries[28] of madness, for I beheld him gazing upon vacancy for long hours, in an attitude of the profoundest attention, as if listening to some imaginary sound. It was no wonder that his condition terrified—that it infected me. I felt creeping upon me, by slow yet certain degrees, the wild influences of his own fantastic yet impressive superstitions.

It was, especially, upon retiring to bed late in the night of the seventh or eighth day after the placing of the lady Madeline within the donjon, that I experienced the full power of such feelings. Sleep came not near my couch—while the hours waned and waned away, I struggled to reason off the nervousness which had dominion over me. I endeavored to believe that much, if not all, of what I felt was due to the bewildering influence of the gloomy furniture of the room—of the dark and tattered draperies, which, tortured into motion by the breath of a rising tempest, swayed fitfully to and fro upon the walls, and rustled uneasily about the decorations of the bed. But my efforts were fruitless. An irrepressible tremor gradually pervaded my frame; and, at length, there sat upon my very heart an incubus[29] of utterly causeless alarm. Shaking this off with a gasp and a struggle, I uplifted myself upon the pillows, and peering earnestly within the intense darkness of the chamber, hearkened—I know not why, except that an instinctive spirit prompted me—to certain low and indefinite sounds which came, through the

27. **donjon-keep:** dungeon.

28. **vagaries** (vā′gə-rēz): whims.
29. **incubus** (ĭn′kyə-bəs): nightmare.

pauses of the storm, at long intervals, I knew not whence. Overpowered by an intense sentiment of horror, unaccountable yet unendurable, I threw on my clothes with haste (for I felt I should sleep no more during the night), and endeavored to arouse myself from the pitiable condition into which I had fallen, by pacing to and fro through the apartment.

I had taken but few turns in this manner, when a light step on an adjoining staircase arrested my attention. I presently recognized it as that of Usher. In an instant afterward he rapped, with a gentle touch, at my door, and entered, bearing a lamp. His countenance was, as usual, cadaverously wan—but, moreover, there was a species of mad hilarity in his eyes—an evidently restrained hysteria in his whole demeanor. His air appalled me—but anything was preferable to the solitude which I had so long endured, and I even welcomed his presence as a relief.

"And you have not seen it?" he said abruptly, after having stared about him for some moments in silence—"you have not then seen it?—but, stay! you shall." Thus speaking, and having carefully shaded his lamp, he hurried to one of the casements, and threw it freely open to the storm.

The impetuous fury of the entering gust nearly lifted us from our feet. It was, indeed, a tempestuous yet sternly beautiful night, and one wildly singular in its terror and its beauty. A whirlwind had apparently collected its force in our vicinity; for there were frequent and violent alterations in the direction of the wind; and the exceeding density of the clouds (which hung so low as to press upon the turrets of the house) did not prevent our perceiving the lifelike velocity with which they flew careering from all points against each other, without passing away into the distance. I say that even their exceeding density did not prevent our perceiving this—yet we had no glimpse of the moon or stars, nor was there any flashing forth of the lightning. But the under surfaces of the huge masses of agitated vapor, as well as all terrestrial objects immediately around us, were glowing in the unnatural light of a faintly luminous and distinctly visible gaseous exhalation which hung about and enshrouded the mansion.

"You must not—you shall not behold this!" said I, shuddering, to Usher, as I led him, with a gentle violence, from the window to a seat. "These appearances, which bewilder you, are merely electrical phenomena not uncommon—or it may be that they have their ghastly origin in the rank miasma[30] of the tarn. Let us close this casement; the air is chilling and dangerous to your frame. Here is one of your favorite romances. I will read, and you shall listen: and so we will pass away this terrible night together."

The antique volume which I had taken up was the *Mad Trist* of Sir Launcelot Canning;[31] but I had called it a favorite of Usher's more in sad jest than in earnest; for, in truth, there is little in its uncouth and unimaginative prolixity which could have had interest for the lofty and spiritual ideality of my friend. It was, however, the only book immediately at hand; and I indulged a vague hope that the excitement which now agitated the hypochondriac might find relief (for the history of mental disorder is full of similar anomalies) even in the extremeness of the folly which I should read. Could I have judged, indeed, by the wild overstrained air of vivacity with which he hearkened, or apparently hearkened, to the words of the tale, I might well have congratulated myself upon the success of my design.

I had arrived at that well-known portion of the story where Ethelred, the hero of the Trist, having sought in vain for peaceable admission into the dwelling of the hermit, proceeds to make good an entrance by force. Here, it will be remembered, the words of the narrative run thus:

And Ethelred, who was by nature of a doughty heart, and who was now mighty

30. **rank miasma** (mī-ăz′mə): thick, harmful atmosphere.
31. **Mad Trist of Sir Launcelot Canning:** The book and author were Poe's invention.

withal, on account of the powerfulness of the wine which he had drunken, waited no longer to hold parley with the hermit, who, in sooth, was of an obstinate and maliceful turn, but, feeling the rain upon his shoulders, and fearing the rising of the tempest, uplifted his mace outright, and, with blows, made quickly room in the plankings of the door for his gauntleted hand; and now pulling therewith sturdily, he so cracked, and ripped, and tore all asunder, that the noise of the dry and hollow-sounding wood alarumed and reverberated throughout the forest.

At the termination of this sentence, I started and, for a moment, paused; for it appeared to me (although I at once concluded that my excited fancy had deceived me)—it appeared to me that, from some very remote portion of the mansion, there came indistinctly to my ears what might have been, in its exact similarity of character, the echo (but a stifled and dull one certainly) of the very cracking and ripping sound which Sir Launcelot had so particularly described. It was, beyond doubt, the coincidence alone which had arrested my attention; for, amid the rattling of the sashes of the casements, and the ordinary, commingled noises of the still increasing storm, the sound in itself had nothing, surely, which should have interested or disturbed me. I continued the story:

But the good champion Ethelred, now entering within the door, was sore enraged and amazed to perceive no signal of the maliceful hermit; but, in the stead thereof, a dragon of a scaly and prodigious demeanor, and of a fiery tongue, which sate in guard before a palace of gold, with a floor of silver; and upon the wall there hung a shield of shining brass with this legend enwritten—

Who entereth herein, a conqueror hath bin;
Who slayeth the dragon, the shield he shall win.

And Ethelred uplifted his mace, and struck upon the head of the dragon, which fell before him, and gave up his pesty breath, with a shriek so horrid and harsh and withal so piercing, that Ethelred had fain to close his ears with his hands against the dreadful noise of it, the like whereof was never before heard.

Here again I paused abruptly, and now with a feeling of wild amazement—for there could be no doubt whatever that, in this instance, I did actually hear (although from what direction it proceeded I found it impossible to say) a low and apparently distant, but harsh, protracted, and most unusual screaming or grating sound—the exact counterpart of what my fancy had already conjured up for the dragon's unnatural shriek as described by the romancer.

Oppressed, as I certainly was, upon the occurrence of the second and most extraordinary coincidence, by a thousand conflicting sensations, in which wonder and extreme terror were predominant, I still retained sufficient presence of mind to avoid exciting, by any observation, the sensitive nervousness of my companion. I was by no means certain that he had noticed the sounds in question; although, assuredly, a strange alteration had, during the last few minutes, taken place in his demeanor. From a position fronting my own, he had gradually brought round his chair, so as to sit with his face to the door of the chamber; and thus I could but partially perceive his features, although I saw that his lips trembled as if he were murmuring inaudibly. His head had dropped upon his breast—yet I knew that he was not asleep, from the wide and rigid opening of the eye as I caught a glance of it in profile. The motion of his body, too, was at variance with this idea—for he rocked from side to side with a gentle yet constant and uniform sway. Having rapidly taken notice of all this, I resumed the narrative of Sir Launcelot, which thus proceeded:

And now, the champion, having escaped from the terrible fury of the dragon, bethinking himself of the brazen shield, and of the breaking up of the enchantment which was upon it, removed the carcass from out of the way before him, and approached valorously over the silver pavement of the castle to where the shield was upon the wall; which in sooth tarried not for his full coming, but fell down at his feet upon the silver floor, with a mighty great and terrible ringing sound.

No sooner had these syllables passed my lips, than—as if a shield of brass had indeed, at the moment, fallen heavily upon a floor of silver—I became aware of a distinct, hollow, metallic, and clangorous, yet apparently muffled, reverberation. Completely unnerved, I leaped to my feet; but the measured rocking movement of Usher was undisturbed. I rushed to the chair in which he sat. His eyes were bent fixedly before him, and throughout his whole countenance there reigned a stony rigidity. But, as I placed my hand upon his shoulder, there came a strong shudder over his whole person; a sickly smile quivered about his lips; and I saw that he spoke in a low, hurried, and gibbering murmur, as if unconscious of my presence. Bending closely over him, I at length drank in the hideous import of his words.

"Not hear it?—yes, I hear, it, and *have* heard it. Long—long—long—many minutes, many hours, many days, have I heard it—yet I dared not—oh, pity me, miserable wretch that I am!—I dared not—I *dared* not speak! *We have put her living in the tomb!* Said I not that my senses were acute? I *now* tell you that I heard her first feeble movements in the hollow coffin. I heard them—many, many days ago—yet I dared not—*I dared not speak!* And now—tonight—Ethelred—ha! ha!—the breaking of the hermit's door, and the death-cry of the dragon, and the clangor of the shield—say, rather, the rending of her coffin, and the grating of the iron hinges of her prison, and her struggles within the coppered archway of the vault! Oh whither shall I fly? Will she not be here anon?[32]

32. **anon** (ə-nŏn´): soon.

Is she not hurrying to upbraid me for my haste? Have I not heard her footstep on the stair? Do I not distinguish that heavy and horrible beating of her heart? Madman!"—here he sprang furiously to his feet, and shrieked out his syllables, as if in the effort he were giving up his soul—*"Madman! I tell you that she now stands without the door!"*

As if in the superhuman energy of his utterance there had been found the potency of a spell, the huge antique panels to which the speaker pointed threw slowly back, upon the instant, their ponderous and ebony jaws. It was the work of the rushing gust—but then without those doors there *did* stand the lofty and enshrouded figure of the lady Madeline of Usher. There was blood upon her white robes, and the evidence of some bitter struggle upon every portion of her emaciated frame. For a moment she remained trembling and reeling to and fro upon the threshold, then, with a low moaning cry, fell heavily inward upon the person of her brother, and in her violent and now final death agonies, bore him to the floor a corpse, and a victim to the terrors he had anticipated.

From that chamber, and from that mansion, I fled aghast. The storm was still abroad in all its wrath as I found myself crossing the old causeway. Suddenly there shot along the path a wild light, and I turned to see whence a gleam so unusual could have issued; for the vast house and its shadows were alone behind me. The radiance was that of the full, setting, and blood-red moon, which now shone vividly through that once barely discernible fissure, of which I have before spoken as extending from the roof of the building, in a zigzag direction, to the base. While I gazed, this fissure rapidly widened—there came a fierce breath of the whirlwind—the entire orb of the satellite burst at once upon my sight—my brain reeled as I saw the mighty walls rushing asunder—there was a long tumultuous shouting sound like the voice of a thousand waters—and the deep and dank tarn at my feet closed sullenly and silently over the fragments of the "House of Usher."

Reading Check

1. What emotion does the narrator feel when he first sees the House of Usher?
2. What trouble has Roderick Usher described in his letter to the narrator?
3. Whom does the narrator meet while being led to Usher's studio?
4. What are the symptoms of the lady Madeline's illness?
5. How does her condition change on the night the narrator arrives?
6. What strange theory does Roderick Usher have about the Usher mansion?
7. Where is the vault in which the lady Madeline's body is placed?
8. How does the narrator attempt to calm Usher during the storm?
9. What does Usher say he has done to his sister?
10. What happens to the House of Usher?

Commentary

Among Poe's tales of terror, "The Fall of the House of Usher" illustrates with special vividness his critical doctrine that unity of effect depends on unity of *tone*, the attitude a writer takes toward a subject. Every detail—from the opening description of the dank tarn and the dark rooms of the house to the unearthly storm that accompanies Madeline's emergence from the tomb—helps to convey the terror that overwhelms and finally destroys the fragile mind of Roderick Usher. But terror, even terror so extreme that it results in madness and death, is meaningless unless it illustrates a principle of human nature. It is this underlying significance that gives Poe's story its interest as a work of literature.

One approach to this significance lies in noticing the many subtle connections that the story establishes among its parts. Roderick and Madeline, we learn, are not just brother and sister but twins, and they share "sympathies of a scarcely intelligible nature" which connect his mental disintegration to her physical decline. As her mysterious illness approaches physical paralysis, his mental agitation takes the form of a "morbid acuteness of the senses" that separates his body from the physical world by making all normal sensations painful. He can stand the taste of only the blandest foods, bear the touch of only certain textures of cloth, endure only the dimmest light and the mildest sounds. Roderick and Madeline are not just twins but the mental and physical components of a single being or soul.

This being, the last inheritor of the long Usher line, is in turn intimately connected to the family house. The phrase "House of Usher" has come to designate "both the family and the family mansion." Roderick, in fact, has developed a theory that the very stones of the house have consciousness and embody the fate of the Usher family. He also makes the connection between a house and person in his poem, "The Haunted Palace," using a palace as an elaborate parallel for the human mind. The crack in the Usher mansion, at first barely visible, suggests a fundamental split or fault in this twin personality of the last of the Ushers and foretells the final ruin of both mansion and family.

The narrator's connection to the Ushers is through the past: he and Roderick were once close companions in boyhood but have been separated for many years. Thus the narrator's response to Roderick's urgent appeal is a revisiting of his own past and the person he once was, but now seen from a different perspective. In fact, in the opening paragraphs he prepares himself for this encounter by experimenting with perspective as he examines the inverted image of the house in the tarn. And as he first walks through the gloomy rooms he is aware that the old and tattered furnishings, familiar to him since "infancy," are also strange and unfamiliar, like objects seen in a dream. He has the same perspective when he first sees Roderick again and realizes how "altered" his former companion is. Nevertheless, despite his awareness of the differences that time has made in their relationship, he is more and more drawn into Roderick's fantasy world and barely escapes from it at the end. If we look closely, we see that the true focus of the story is upon the narrator's reaction to and understanding of these strange events. He makes a perilous journey into the fearful underworld of the mind and is nearly destroyed by it.

The narrator has been summoned to rescue Roderick from an illness in which the self has been given over entirely to the interior world of the imagination, blotting out all reality. Roderick has not ventured out of the House of Usher for many years.

The isolation of his life from outer reality is indicated by the separate "atmosphere"—a "pestilent and mystic vapor"—that seems to arise from the decayed trees and dank tarn. Like the house, Roderick has been untouched by "the external air," and his appearance is not just unhealthy but unearthly; the narrator cannot connect it "with any idea of simple humanity."

In this story Poe explores the workings of the human imagination but, at the same time, points out the destructive dangers of that journey. To some extent Roderick is an artist. This is one part of his Usher heritage, and through it he pursues a world of fantasy. His music is an aid to reverie. His reading, given to us in the long list of books (page 168), is devoted to extremes of the human imagination: tales of torture and mysticism, of devils and half-human creatures, of journeys into the interior of the earth and outward into a world of spirits. But, above all, it is his painting that reveals his obsession. It portrays "a vault or tunnel" deep within the earth, with no entrance or exit, brilliantly lighted but from no visible source. This is the exact image of the self-enclosed, interior world of Roderick's fantasy that shuts out all natural lights and is illuminated in "ghastly . . . splendor" only from within.

Roderick is unlike an artist, however, in having lost control of his fantasy world, so that it becomes all of reality. Madeline, his twin part, is paralyzed in the semblance of death and is buried in a vault that is also a dungeon. With this part of himself imprisoned in apparent death, there is an immediate change in Roderick: "the luminousness of his eye had utterly gone out." What is revealed, when fantasy suppresses the physical self and natural reality, is the stark terror of madness and of mental death. Madeline's actual death reunites the twin natures of their one being, claiming Roderick as well, a "victim to the terrors he had anticipated." Even to look into that underworld of the mind where fantasy becomes reality is to invite madness, and twice during the final scene Roderick calls the narrator "Madman!" But the narrator escapes, to watch the House of Usher crumble into that underworld which is its true home.

Analyzing and Interpreting the Story

1. The long opening sentence immediately establishes a **mood** for the story. **a.** What physical details—of time and place—accomplish this? **b.** What is the effect of using the word *soundless* to describe the day?

2. The description of the interior of the Usher mansion intensifies the impression of gloom and decay given by the outside. What does the fact that Roderick's studio is reached "through many dark and intricate passages" suggest about his personality or state of mind?

3. One aspect of Roderick's mental illness is his overwhelming dread of the future, not so much for what it holds in store, but for the terror it will bring, which he is sure will destroy his reason. His poem, "The Haunted Palace," expresses this fear of madness. It presents an elaborate **allegory,** a story in which characters or settings represent abstract ideas or qualities. The palace stands for a human head and mind. In the final stanza, what images suggest that the palace is now haunted by madness?

4. For all his original intention of helping Roderick, the narrator seems himself drawn more and more into Roderick's frame of mind. **a.** What evidence of this appears in the narrator's description of his feelings when he tries to sleep and then rises from bed on the night of the storm? **b.** Roderick comes to the narrator's room that night. How does the "mad hilarity in his eyes" fulfill the prophecy of his poem?

5. What hints given early in the story foreshadow the final crumbling of the House of Usher into the tarn?

Poe's Evocative Sentences

The sentences in this story are frequently long and complicated. The opening sentence is typical of Poe's style:

> During the whole of a dull, dark, and soundless day in the autumn of the year, when the clouds

hung oppressively low in the heavens, I had been passing alone, on horseback, through a singularly dreary tract of country, and at length found myself, as the shades of the evening drew on, within view of the melancholy House of Usher.

The main clause of this sentence gives its basic meaning: "I had been passing alone . . . and at length found myself . . . within view of the melancholy House of Usher." To further understand this sentence, you must relate all the modifying clauses and phrases (which give the time of the day, describe the landscape, and so on) to the main clause. To grasp all the implications of the sentence, you must be aware of phrases such as "dull, dark, and soundless day," "oppressively low," and "a singularly dreary tract of country." Finally, you should read this and several other sentences out loud to make yourself aware of their rhythm. Note the pauses that slow the sentence down and give the reader an opportunity to feel its full effect: in this sentence there are at least seven.

Choose one of Poe's long sentences to analyze. Determine the main clause in the sentence. Explain the relationship of this clause to modifying clauses and phrases. Note the use of evocative adjectives and adverbs. Read the sentence aloud to determine its rhythm. Be prepared to explain the effect that Poe achieves in the sentence.

Language and Vocabulary

Noting Connotative Meanings of Words
In "The Fall of the House of Usher," Poe builds an atmosphere of gloom from the very first sentence. Following are phrases that he uses to help create atmosphere. If you do not already know the meanings of the italicized words, look them up in the glossary or in a dictionary.

1. . . . clouds hung *oppressively* low . . .
2. . . . *precipitous* brink of a black and lurid tarn . . .
3. . . . An air of stern, deep, and *irredeemable* gloom . . .
4. . . . the *wan* being before me . . .
5. . . . A *cadaverousness* of complexion . . .
6. . . . the *luminousness* of his eye . . .

7. . . . the history of mental disorder is full of similar *anomalies* . . .

Which of the italicized words can be used *only* when writing about a gloomy or dangerous situation? Which ones could equally well be used in writing about a different situation? Find at least five other words in this story that add to the atmosphere of gloom (for example, *reeked, decayed, ghastly*). For these words, try to substitute words or phrases that communicate an opposite feeling, such as lightheartedness or joy.

Writing About Literature

Responding to a Critical Interpretation
Richard Wilbur has said that the typical Poe story is "an allegory of dream-experience: it occurs within the mind of a poet; the characters are not distinct personalities, but principles or faculties of the poet's divided nature; the steps of the action correspond to the successive states of a mind moving into sleep; and the end of the action is the end of a dream." In a short essay discuss the relevance of Wilbur's comment to "The Fall of the House of Usher."

Creative Writing

Creating a Single Emotional Effect
Write a paragraph that creates a single emotional effect. It may be fear, joy, horror, love, pity, or some other emotion that occurs to you. You may wish to describe a scene or narrate a short incident. Like Poe, choose every word and construct every sentence carefully, keeping in mind the single effect you wish to create.

The Masque° of the Red Death

The "Red Death" had long devastated the country. No pestilence had ever been so fatal, or so hideous. Blood was its Avatar[1] and its seal—the redness and the horror of blood. There were sharp pains, and sudden dizziness, and then profuse bleeding at the pores, with dissolution. The scarlet stains upon the body and especially upon the face of the victim, were the pest ban which shut him out from the aid and from the sympathy of his fellow men. And the whole seizure, progress, and termination of the disease, were the incidents of half an hour.

But the Prince Prospero was happy and dauntless and sagacious. When his dominions were half depopulated, he summoned to his presence a thousand hale and lighthearted friends from among the knights and dames of his court, and with these retired to the deep seclusion of one of his castellated[2] abbeys. This was an extensive and magnificent structure, the creation of the prince's own eccentric yet august taste. A strong and lofty wall girdled it in. This wall had gates of iron. The courtiers, having entered, brought furnaces and massy[3] hammers and welded the bolts. They resolved to leave means neither of ingress or egress to the sudden impulses of despair or of frenzy from within. The abbey was amply provisioned. With such precautions the courtiers might bid defiance to contagion. The external world could take care of itself. In the meantime it was folly to grieve, or to think. The prince had provided all the appliances of pleasure. There were buffoons, there were improvisatori,[4] there were ballet dancers, there were musicians, there was Beauty, there was wine. All these and security were within. Without was the "Red Death."

It was toward the close of the fifth or sixth month of his seclusion, and while the pestilence raged most furiously abroad, that the Prince Prospero entertained his thousand friends at a masked ball of the most unusual magnificence.

It was a voluptuous scene, that masquerade. But first let me tell of the rooms in which it was held. There were seven—an imperial suite. In many palaces, however, such suites form a long and straight vista, while the folding doors slide back nearly to the walls on either hand, so that the view of the whole extent is scarcely impeded. Here the case was very different; as might have been expected from the duke's love of the *bizarre*. The apartments were so irregularly disposed that the vision embraced but little more than one at a time. There was a sharp turn at every twenty or thirty yards, and at each turn a novel effect. To the right and left, in the middle of each wall, a tall and nar-

---

° **Masque** (măsk): a masked ball; a masquerade.
1. **Avatar** (ăv′ə-tär′): a sign of an invisible force; an embodiment or manifestation.
2. **castellated** (kăs′tə-lā′tĭd): having towers like that of a castle.
3. **massy:** here, massive.

4. **improvisatori** (ĭm′prə-vē′zə-tôr′ē): actors who make up scenes at the suggestions of onlookers.

row Gothic window looked out upon a closed corridor which pursued the windings of the suite. These windows were of stained glass whose color varied in accordance with the prevailing hue of the decorations of the chamber into which it opened. That at the eastern extremity was hung, for example, in blue—and vividly blue were its windows. The second chamber was purple in its ornaments and tapestries, and here the panes were purple. The third was green throughout, and so were the casements. The fourth was furnished and lighted with orange—the fifth with white—the sixth with violet. The seventh apartment was closely shrouded in black velvet tapestries that hung all over the ceiling and down the walls, falling in heavy folds upon a carpet of the same material and hue. But in this chamber only, the color of the windows failed to correspond with the decorations. The panes here were scarlet—a deep blood color. Now in no one of the seven apartments was there any lamp or candelabrum, amid the profusion of golden ornaments that lay scattered to and fro or depended from the roof. There was no light of any kind emanating from lamp or candle within the suite of chambers. But in the corridors that followed the suite, there stood, opposite to each window, a heavy tripod, bearing a brazier of fire that projected its rays through the tinted glass and so glaringly illumined the room. And thus were produced a multitude of gaudy and fantastic appearances. But in the western or black chamber the effect of the firelight that streamed upon the dark hangings through the blood-tinted panes was ghastly in the extreme, and produced so wild a look upon the countenances of those who entered, that there were few of the company bold enough to set foot within its precincts at all.

It was in this apartment, also, that there stood against the western wall, a gigantic clock of ebony. Its pendulum swung to and fro with a dull, heavy, monotonous clang; and when the minute hand made the circuit of the face, and the hour was to be stricken, there came from the brazen lungs of the clock a sound which was clear and loud and deep and exceedingly musical, but of so peculiar a note and emphasis that, at each lapse of an hour, the musicians of the orchestra were constrained to pause, momentarily, in their performance, to hearken to the sound; and thus the waltzers perforce ceased their evolutions; and there was a brief disconcert of the whole gay company; and, while the chimes of the clock yet rang, it was observed that the giddiest grew pale, and the more aged and sedate passed their hands over their brows as if in confused reverie or meditation. But when the echoes had fully ceased, a light laughter at once pervaded the assembly; the musicians looked at each other and smiled as if at their own nervousness and folly, and made whispering vows, each to the other, that the next chiming of the clock should produce in them no similar emotion; and then, after the lapse of sixty minutes (which embrace three thousand and six hundred seconds of the Time that flies), there came yet another chiming of the clock, and then were the same disconcert and tremulousness and meditation as before.

But, in spite of these things, it was a gay and magnificent revel. The tastes of the duke were peculiar. He had a fine eye for colors and effects. He disregarded the *decora*[5] of mere fashion. His plans were bold and fiery, and his conceptions glowed with barbaric luster. There are some who would have thought him mad. His followers felt that he was not. It was necessary to hear and see and touch him to be *sure* that he was not.

He had directed, in great part, the movable embellishments of the seven chambers, upon occasion of this great *fête;* and it was his own guiding taste which had given character to the masqueraders. Be sure they were grotesque. There were much glare and glitter and piquancy and phantasm—much of what has been since seen in *Hernani.*[6] There were arabesque figures with unsuited limbs and ap-

5. *decora* (dā-kôr′ä): Latin for "dictates."
6. *Hernani* (ĕr-nä′nē): a romantic stage tragedy of 1830 by the French author Victor Hugo (1802–1885).

pointments. There were delirious fancies such as the madman fashions. There was much of the beautiful, much of the wanton, much of the *bizarre,* something of the terrible, and not a little of that which might have excited disgust. To and fro in the seven chambers there stalked, in fact, a multitude of dreams. And these—the dreams—writhed in and about, taking hue from the rooms, and causing the wild music of the orchestra to seem as the echo of their steps. And, anon, there strikes the ebony clock which stands in the hall of the velvet. And then, for a moment, all is still, and all is silent save the voice of the clock. The dreams are stiff-frozen as they stand. But the echoes of the chime die away—they have endured but an instant—and a light, half-subdued laughter floats after them as they depart. And now again the music swells, and the dreams live, and writhe to and fro more merrily than ever, taking hue from the many-tinted windows through which stream the rays from the tripods. But to the chamber which lies most westwardly of the seven, there are now none of the maskers who venture; for the night is waning away; and there flows a ruddier light through the blood-colored panes; and the blackness of the sable drapery appalls; and to him whose foot falls upon the sable carpet, there comes from the near clock of ebony a muffled peal more solemnly emphatic than any which reaches *their* ears who indulge in the more remote gaieties of the other apartments.

But these other apartments were densely crowded, and in them beat feverishly the heart of life. And the revel went whirlingly on, until at length there commenced the sounding of midnight upon the clock. And then the music ceased, as I have told; and the evolutions of the waltzers were quieted; and there was an uneasy cessation of all things as before. But now there were twelve strokes to be sounded by the bell of the clock; and thus it happened, perhaps, that more of thought crept, with more of time, into the meditations of the thoughtful among those who reveled. And thus, too, it happened, perhaps, that before

the last echoes of the last chime had utterly sunk into silence, there were many individuals in the crowd who had found leisure to become aware of the presence of a masked figure which had arrested the attention of no single individual before. And the rumor of this new presence having spread itself whisperingly around, there arose at length from the whole company a buzz, or murmur, expressive of disapprobation and surprise—then, finally, of terror, of horror, and of disgust.

In an assembly of phantasms such as I have painted, it may well be supposed that no ordinary appearance could have excited such sensation. In truth the masquerade license of the night was nearly unlimited; but the figure in question had out-Heroded Herod,[7] and gone beyond the bounds of even the prince's indefinite decorum. There are chords in the hearts of the most reckless which cannot be touched without emotion. Even with the utterly lost, to whom life and death are equally jests, there are matters of which no jest can be made. The whole company, indeed, seemed now deeply to feel that in the costume and bearing of the stranger neither wit nor propriety existed. The figure was tall and gaunt, and shrouded from head to foot in the habiliments of the grave. The mask which concealed the visage was made so nearly to resemble the countenance of a stiffened corpse that the closest scrutiny must have had difficulty in detecting the cheat. And yet all this might have been endured, if not approved, by the mad revelers around. But the mummer[8] had gone so far as to assume the type of the Red Death. His vesture was dabbled in *blood*—and his broad brow, with all the features of the face, was besprinkled with the scarlet horror.

When the eyes of Prince Prospero fell upon this spectral image (which with a slow and sol-

7. **out-Heroded Herod:** had acted in extreme, perhaps crazed fashion. As the King of Judea, Herod sought to destroy the infant Jesus by ordering the slaughter of all children. He was depicted in later times as a raging, sometimes demented figure. Shakespeare uses the phrase in *Hamlet* (III, 2) for overacting.
8. **mummer:** masked figure.

The Masque of the Red Death (1883) by Odilon Redon (1840–1916). Charcoal on brown paper.

emn movement, as if more fully to sustain its *rôle,* stalked to and fro among the waltzers) he was seen to be convulsed, in the first moment with a strong shudder either of terror or distaste; but, in the next, his brow reddened with rage.

"Who dares?" he demanded hoarsely of the courtiers who stood near him—"who dares insult us with this blasphemous mockery? Seize him and unmask him—that we may know whom we have to hang at sunrise, from the battlements!"

It was in the eastern or blue chamber in which stood the Prince Prospero as he uttered these words. They rang throughout the seven rooms loudly and clearly—for the prince was a bold and robust man, and the music had become hushed at the waving of his hand.

It was in the blue room where stood the prince, with a group of pale courtiers by his side. At first, as he spoke, there was a slight rushing movement of this group in the direction of the intruder, who at the moment was also near at hand, and now, with deliberate and stately step, made closer approach to the speaker. But from a certain nameless awe with which the mad assumptions of the mummer had inspired the whole party, there were found none who put forth hand to seize him; so that, unimpeded, he passed within a yard of the prince's person; and, while the vast assembly, as if with one impulse, shrank from the centers of the rooms to the walls, he made his way uninterruptedly, but with the same solemn and measured step which had distinguished him from the first, through the blue chamber to the purple—through the purple to the green—through the green to the orange—through this again to the white—and even thence to the violet, ere a decided movement had been made to arrest him. It was then, however, that the Prince Prospero, maddening with rage and the shame of his own momentary cowardice, rushed hurriedly through the six chambers, while none followed him on account of a deadly terror that had seized upon all. He bore aloft a drawn dagger, and had approached, in rapid impetuosity, to within three or four feet of the retreating figure, when the latter, having attained the extremity of the velvet apartment, turned suddenly and confronted his pursuer. There was a sharp cry—and the dagger dropped gleaming upon the sable carpet, upon which, instantly afterwards, fell prostrate in death the Prince Prospero. Then, summoning the wild courage of despair, a throng of the revelers at once threw themselves into the black apartment, and, seizing the mummer, whose tall figure stood erect and motionless within the shadow of the ebony clock, gasped in unutterable horror at finding the grave cerements and corpselike mask which they handled with so violent a rudeness, untenanted by any tangible form.

And now was acknowledged the presence of the Red Death. He had come like a thief in the night.[9] And one by one dropped the revelers in the blood-bedewed halls of their revel, and died each in the despairing posture of his fall. And the life of the ebony clock went out with that of the last of the gay. And the flames of the tripods expired. And Darkness and Decay and the Red Death held illimitable dominion over all.

9. **a thief in the night:** A Biblical reference to I Thessalonians 5:2–3, signifying swift and unexpected death: "For yourselves know perfectly that the day of the Lord so cometh as a thief in the night.

"For when they shall say, Peace and safety; then sudden destruction cometh upon them, as travail upon a woman with child; and they shall not escape."

Reading Check

1. How does Prince Prospero plan to keep away the Red Death?
2. Where in the palace is the masked ball held?
3. How does the seventh apartment differ from the other chambers?
4. How do the revelers react to the sound of the ebony clock?
5. What do the revelers find when they seize the stranger in the velvet apartment?

Commentary

In his literary criticism, Poe made clear his dislike of *allegory*—narrative in which characters or objects are equated with meanings outside the narrative itself. (Refer to the *Guide to Literary Terms and Techniques* for a further definition of allegory.) He argued that allegory was by its nature an inferior literary form, expressing mere "ingenuity" rather than the creative imagination. Because it has a dual purpose, to evoke interest in both the narrative and the abstract ideas for which the narrative stands, allegory distracts the reader from the singleness of effect that Poe most valued in literature. "Under the best circumstances," he wrote, "it must always interfere with that unity of effect which, to the artist, is worth all the allegory in the world."

Yet on occasion Poe himself openly used allegory, as in "The Haunted Palace" verses that he inserted into "The Fall of the House of Usher" (see page 167), and many readers have perceived allegorical elements in "The Masque of the Red Death." The masquerade, for example, takes place in seven connected but carefully separated rooms, reminding us of the widespread significance that the number seven has had in the human past. The history of the world itself was once thought to consist of seven ages, as an individual life was supposed to have seven stages. The ancient world was said to have exactly seven wonders (among them the pyramids of Egypt and the Hanging Gardens of Babylon); and in the Middle Ages universities divided all knowledge into seven subjects or "arts." People of that time and later heard about the seven deadly sins—and the corresponding seven cardinal virtues—in sermons and saw them portrayed, often allegorically, in drama and poetry. Seven is also an important number in mysticism and in myths.

An allegorical reading of Poe's story usually takes the seven rooms to represent the ancient idea of the seven ages of man, from birth to death, through which Prospero rushes in pursuit of a figure masked as a victim of the Red Death, only to fall dead himself at last in the final black room of eternal night. It is important, as well, that the story has no characters in the usual sense, which again implies that these figures are allegorical. Only Prince Prospero speaks or even has a name, one which suggests happiness and good fortune. Human happiness seeks to wall out the threat of death, as Prospero creates a refuge from his "half-depopulated" land, and even to turn life into a dance, an uncaring pleasure party: "The external world could take care of itself. . . . it was folly to grieve, or to think." But as the Biblical reference of the final paragraph makes clear, the end of earthly life comes "like a thief in the night," and even those who seek "peace and safety . . . shall not escape." Prospero's dance of life in the midst of death has become a *danse macabre*, the dance of death portrayed in old paintings as a dancing allegorical figure of death (often a skeleton) leads a throng of people to the grave.

In contrast, a "masque" was originally a light-hearted form of entertainment at the royal courts of Italy and England, combining lavish costumes with song and dance and an allegorical plot—always with a happy outcome. At the end the players took off their masks and danced with members of the audience. Poe borrows the elements of this old form—the costumes, the dance, even the royal court—but turns his masque into a dark allegory in which the Red Death of plague gains "illimitable dominion over all" and plunges the world itself into final darkness.

An approach to "The Masque of the Red Death" through its *symbols* (for a definition of symbol see the *Guide to Literary Terms and Techniques*) emphasizes other aspects of the story and yields somewhat broader meanings. One prominent pattern of symbols governs the use of time in the story. Most obvious is the "gigantic clock of ebony" which stands in the seventh room, itself all draped in black velvet. The clock is of course a literal object, but it quickly takes on symbolic overtones: it has not only a "face," as we speak of clocks, but "lungs," from which issue chimes that are "exceedingly musical" but "so peculiar" that the orchestra and dancers are immobilized while the clock strikes, "and all is silent save the voice of the clock." The clock, then, not only measures time for the revelers but somehow controls their lives. The masked figure of the Red Death appears at the stroke of midnight, moves through the rooms to the same silent dread that accompanies the chimes, and finally stands "motionless within the shadow of the ebony clock." Time and the Red Death are therefore symbolically connected, and "the life of the ebony clock" expires with the last of the dancers.

The connection between time and the Red Death is a key to the symbolic meaning of the story. The seven brilliantly colored rooms are laid out east to west, reminding us of the course of the sun that measures our earthly time. They are lighted only from the outside, from the flames of braziers that shine through glass stained the same color as the interior of the room and all its furnishings. This is true of the first six. Only the seventh has windows of a different color, "scarlet—a deep blood color" to illuminate that westernmost black chamber with an ebony clock on its western wall, once again linking the colors red and black with time.

Strangely, infection from the Red Death manifests itself in "scarlet stains upon the body and especially upon the face of the victim" as the blood bursts through the pores. The very substance of life becomes the mark of death. It is this contagion that Prince Prospero would lock out of his sanctuary, which is also a prison, since those welded gates allow neither entrance nor egress.

Within these walls Prospero has created a world of his imagination and peopled it with masked figures that reflect "his own guiding taste." And again we have the paradox first expressed in the Red Death: as the substance of life is also the mark of its dissolution, so the imagination cannot escape its own mortality. Six brilliant rooms of pleasure lead to a seventh, which is also Prospero's creation, where few dancers venture because there the sound of time is inescapable, and light from "the blood-tinted panes" reveals the dread scarlet stains of their mortality. The dancers are so much the products of Prospero's imagination that Poe calls them "a multitude of dreams" that writhe and whirl through the brilliant rooms. But at the sound of the clock, the "dreams are stiff-frozen as they stand," in a momentary rigor mortis that anticipates the final one. In a symbolic reading of this story, death is not an outside antagonist, a foreign intruder to be repelled, but a part of ourselves. Its physical sign is the very blood of our being. Its presence in our mental life is shown by the dominance of time in our imaginations (always, for Poe, the deepest and most revealing part of the mind), where we hear the echoes of the "ebony clock" we all carry within.

For Study and Discussion

Analyzing and Interpreting the Story

1. In writing a story about pestilence or plague, Poe would have in mind such historical examples as the bubonic plague—the Black Death—of the Middle Ages and the much more recent cholera epidemics that ravaged Philadelphia in the 1790s and Baltimore in his own lifetime. But in this story, plague takes the strange form of a red death rather than a black one. What paradox is suggested by this change?

2. In the second paragraph, the brief characterization of Prince Prospero—as a "happy and dauntless and sagacious" man—seems altogether favorable. **a.** How are we to regard his seeking safety by shutting out the world? **b.** Is there anything to suggest that creating this "security" also creates a prison?

3. Much of the tale describes the seven rooms in which the masquerade is held. Unlike other royal apartments, in which the rooms open out upon each other in a straight "vista," these rooms are on a corridor of sharp turns, so that each room is a separate visual experience. **a.** Why does this detail seem important? **b.** Why is it significant that the rooms are illuminated by light shining from the corridor through the narrow gothic windows of stained glass?

4. The dancers themselves appear in their wild costumes as bizarre and grotesque and deformed and finally as nightmare figures, a "multitude of dreams" drifting to and fro in those seven rooms. What does this tell us about the refuge that Prince Prospero has created against the dying outside world?

5. At first reading, the seven rooms seem equally vivid and bizarre. But the dancers tend to avoid the seventh or farthest room. **a.** Why should this be so? **b.** What fears does that room seem to arouse?

Writing About Literature

Discussing References to Time and Color

Write a brief essay in which you discuss the references to time and to colors in "The Masque of the Red Death." In your discussion, try to explain why, when the figure masked as the Red Death is finally seized, the shroud and mask are found to be "untenanted by any tangible form."

To Helen

"To Helen" is often praised as a near-perfect statement of the Romantics' idealized love of pure beauty. Poe claimed that the mother of a school friend was the inspiration for Helen. However, the poem is not about any actual woman but about an ideal of beauty that can exist only in the imagination.

Helen, thy beauty is to me
  Like those Nicéan barks of yore,
That gently, o'er a perfumed sea,
  The weary, way-worn wanderer bore
  To his own native shore.   5

On desperate seas long wont to roam,
  Thy hyacinth° hair, thy classic face,
Thy Naiad airs have brought me home
  To the glory that was Greece,
  And the grandeur that was Rome.   10

Lo! in yon brilliant window-niche
  How statue-like I see thee stand,
The agate lamp within thy hand!
  Ah, Psyche, from the regions which
  Are Holy Land!   15

7. **hyacinth** (hī′ə-sĭnth): An adjective used in the Homeric poems to describe hair that was *hyacinthine*, usually meaning golden and wavy.

For Study and Discussion

Analyzing and Interpreting the Poem

1. The first stanza develops a simile for Helen's beauty: it is "like those Nicéan barks of yore" that bore the weary wanderer home. What is the effect of this comparison of her beauty to something from the remote past?

2. In the second stanza the wanderer comes "home" to two great ages of history and imagines the glory and grandeur of those periods. How does Helen help the speaker accomplish this feat of imagination?

3. Poe was a tireless reviser of his poems. Lines 9–10 of an earlier version of this poem read:

> *To the beauty of fair Greece,*
> *And the grandeur of old Rome.*

Which version do you prefer? Why?

4. In stanza 3, Helen is directly present, standing in a window recess in brilliant light. But it is questionable whether this vision brings her any closer as a real person. What is the effect of seeing her "statue-like" and holding an "agate lamp"? (In antiquity, lamps made of agate were associated with immortality.)

Literary Elements

Allusions

The figure of Helen is the means by which the poet's imagination creates a sense of pure beauty. The name itself may have either of two associations: with the Greek goddess of light (as the poem's Helen is last seen), or with Helen of Troy, whose incomparable beauty is celebrated in both mythology and literature. In either case it is clear that the poet's imagination locates ideal beauty in the classical past, and several words in the poem refer to that past. No convincing explanation of "Nicéan" (line 2) has been found, and it is probably an invention that is meant to contribute its musical quality to the poem and to suggest classical associations. Other words are direct references to ancient beliefs and stories. Look up "Naiad" (line 8) and "Psyche" (line 14) in your dictionary. What do these references, or **allusions,** contribute to Helen's meaning in the poem?

The Raven

Once upon a midnight dreary, while I pondered, weak and weary,
Over many a quaint and curious volume of forgotten lore—
While I nodded, nearly napping, suddenly there came a tapping,
As of someone gently rapping, rapping at my chamber door.
" 'Tis some visitor," I muttered, "tapping at my chamber door—   5
                   Only this and nothing more."

Ah, distinctly I remember it was in the bleak December;
And each separate dying ember wrought its ghost upon the floor.
Eagerly I wished the morrow—vainly I had sought to borrow
From my books surcease of sorrow—sorrow for the lost Lenore—   10
For the rare and radiant maiden whom the angels name Lenore—
                   Nameless *here* forevermore.

And the silken, sad, uncertain rustling of each purple curtain
Thrilled me—filled me with fantastic terrors never felt before;
So that now, to still the beating of my heart, I stood repeating,   15
" 'Tis some visitor entreating entrance at my chamber door—
Some late visitor entreating entrance at my chamber door—
                   This it is and nothing more."

Presently my soul grew stronger; hesitating then no longer,   20
"Sir," said I, "or Madam, truly your forgiveness I implore;
But the fact is I was napping, and so gently you came rapping,
And so faintly you came tapping, tapping at my chamber door,
That I scarce was sure I heard you"—here I opened wide the door—
                   Darkness there and nothing more.

Deep into that darkness peering, long I stood there wondering, fearing,   25
Doubting, dreaming dreams no mortal ever dared to dream before;
But the silence was unbroken, and the stillness gave no token,
And the only word there spoken was the whispered word, "Lenore!"
This I whispered, and an echo murmured back the word "Lenore!"
                   Merely this and nothing more.   30

Back into the chamber turning, all my soul within me burning,
Soon again I heard a tapping somewhat louder than before.
"Surely," said I, "surely that is something at my window lattice;
Let me see, then, what thereat is, and this mystery explore—
Let my heart be still a moment and this mystery explore—   35
                   'Tis the wind and nothing more!"

Illustrations on pages 185 and 186 by Édouard Manet (1832–1883), from a series of lithographs for Stéphane Mallarmé's French translation of "The Raven" (1875).

Open here I flung the shutter, when, with many a flirt and flutter,
In there stepped a stately Raven of the saintly days of yore;
Not the least obeisance made he; not a minute stopped or stayed he;
But, with mien of lord or lady, perched above my chamber door—   40
Perched upon a bust of Pallas° just above my chamber door—
                    Perched, and sat, and nothing more.

41. **Pallas** (păl′əs): Pallas Athena, the Greek goddess of wisdom, called Minerva by the Romans.

Then this ebony bird beguiling my sad fancy into smiling,
By the grave and stern decorum of the countenance it wore,
"Though thy crest be shorn and shaven, thou," I said, "art sure no craven,   45
Ghastly grim and ancient Raven wandering from the Nightly shore—
Tell me what thy lordly name is on the Night's Plutonian° shore!"
Quoth the Raven "Nevermore."

47. **Plutonian** (plo͞o-tō′nē-ən): referring to Pluto, who in Greek and Roman mythology was the god of the dead and the ruler of the underworld.

Much I marveled this ungainly fowl to hear discourse so plainly,
Though its answer little meaning—little relevancy bore;   50
For we cannot help agreeing that no living human being
Ever yet was blessed with seeing bird above his chamber door—
Bird or beast upon the sculptured bust above his chamber door,
                             With such name as "Nevermore."

But the Raven, sitting lonely on the placid bust, spoke only   55
That one word, as if his soul in that one word he did outpour.
Nothing farther then he uttered, not a feather then he fluttered—
Till I scarcely more than muttered "Other friends have flown before—
On the morrow *he* will leave me, as my Hopes have flown before."
                          Then the bird said "Nevermore."   60

Startled at the stillness broken by reply so aptly spoken,
"Doubtless," said I, "what it utters is its only stock and store
Caught from some unhappy master whom unmerciful Disaster
Followed fast and followed faster till his songs one burden bore—
Till the dirges of his Hope that melancholy burden bore   65
                               Of 'Never—nevermore.' "

But the Raven still beguiling all my fancy into smiling,
Straight I wheeled a cushioned seat in front of bird, and bust and door;
Then, upon the velvet sinking, I betook myself to linking
Fancy unto fancy, thinking what this ominous bird of yore—   70
What this grim, ungainly, ghastly, gaunt, and ominous bird of yore
                            Meant in croaking "Nevermore."

This I sat engaged in guessing, but no syllable expressing
To the fowl, whose fiery eyes now burned into my bosom's core;
This and more I sat divining, with my head at ease reclining   75
On the cushion's velvet lining that the lamp-light gloated o'er,
But whose velvet-violet lining with the lamp-light gloating o'er,
                             She shall press, ah, nevermore!

Then, methought, the air grew denser, perfumed from an unseen censer
Swung by Seraphim° whose foot-falls tinkled on the tufted floor.   80
"Wretch," I cried, "thy God hath lent thee—by these angels he hath sent thee
Respite—respite and nepenthe° from thy memories of Lenore!
Quaff, oh, quaff this kind nepenthe and forget this lost Lenore!"
                          Quoth the Raven "Nevermore."

---

80. **Seraphim** (sĕr'ə-fĭm): angels.   82. **nepenthe** (nĭ-pĕn'thē): a drug thought by the ancient Greeks to relieve sorrow.

"Prophet!" said I, "thing of evil!—prophet still, if bird or devil!—   85
Whether Tempter sent, or whether tempest tossed thee here ashore,
Desolate yet all undaunted, on this desert land enchanted—
On this home by Horror haunted—tell me truly, I implore—
Is there—*is* there balm in Gilead?°—tell me—tell me, I implore!"
                                        Quoth the Raven "Nevermore."   90

"Prophet!" said I, "thing of evil!—prophet still, if bird or devil!
By that Heaven that bends above us—by that God we both adore—
Tell this soul with sorrow laden if, within the distant Aidenn,°
It shall clasp a sainted maiden whom the angels name Lenore—
Clasp a rare and radiant maiden whom the angels name Lenore."   95
                                        Quoth the Raven "Nevermore."

"Be that word our sign of parting, bird or fiend!" I shrieked, upstarting—
"Get thee back into the tempest and the Night's Plutonian shore!
Leave no black plume as a token of that lie thy soul hath spoken!
Leave my loneliness unbroken—quit the bust above my door!   100
Take thy beak from out my heart, and take thy form from off my door!"
                                        Quoth the Raven "Nevermore."

And the Raven, never flitting, still is sitting, *still* is sitting
On the pallid bust of Pallas just above my chamber door;
And his eyes have all the seeming of a demon's that is dreaming,   105
And the lamp-light o'er him streaming throws his shadow on the floor;
And my soul from out that shadow that lies floating on the floor
                                        Shall be lifted—nevermore!

89. **balm in Gilead** (gĭl'ē-əd): a healing ointment made in Gilead, a region of ancient Palestine (see Jeremiah 8:22); therefore, relief from affliction.   93. **Aidenn** (ā'dən): an Arabic word meaning "Eden" or "heaven."

For Study and Discussion

Analyzing and Interpreting the Poem

1. The first stanza of "The Raven" presents a speaker who is physically exhausted and under obvious emotional strain. He reads, as we learn in the next stanza, to distract himself from sorrow, but the "quaint and curious volume of forgotten lore" implies a taste for the occult or the fantastic. How do these details relate to his later assumption that the raven is an agent of the supernatural?

2. The second stanza establishes the speaker's grief for the lost Lenore, and the third stanza sharply increases the emotional tension. **a.** Why, in lines 15–18, does he need to reassure himself by repeat-ing that the tapping is only some late-night visitor—"and nothing more"? **b.** What else does he seem to expect?

3. At first the raven makes the speaker smile (line 43). But his first speech to the raven associates the bird with Pluto, the ruler of infernal regions (lines 45–48). What does this tell us about what is truly in his mind?

4. Lines 49–78 take the speaker through a number of reactions: surprise that the bird speaks; the melancholy assumption that this companion will fly from him as "other friends" have done; a sensible explanation of how the bird may have learned its single word; and even playful amusement. Still, it becomes clear that, beneath his apparent assurance, the speaker is moving toward hysteria. **a.** What loss of control is indicated in line 74? **b.** Why is it appropriate that this stanza should end with the *speaker* now using the word *nevermore?*

5. From line 79 on the speaker seems to lose whatever emotional control he had. How is the disorder of his senses indicated in lines 79–80?

6. Since the raven repeats only a single word, the significance of *Nevermore* as an answer depends entirely on the question asked. In the dialogue of lines 81–95, how does the speaker use the bird to confirm his own worst fears?

7. After the frenzy with which he proclaims that the raven's word is a "lie" and tries to drive the bird from him, the speaker seems strangely calm in the last stanza, as if he had recovered his reason. **a.** How does the repetition of the phrase, "still is sitting" (line 103) indicate that this is not so? **b.** How does the poet make this repeated phrase sound even more ominous? **c.** Which other lines in the final stanza suggest that the speaker may never return to his senses?

Literary Elements

Devices of Sound: Alliteration, Internal Rhyme, Refrain

"The Raven" creates a hypnotic effect as it takes readers into the speaker's increasingly irrational world, where the question of what the raven means by its single repeated word seems a reasonable one. To some extent, readers must share that state of hallucination which makes the question meaningful to the speaker.

One device Poe uses to accomplish this hypnotic effect is frequent **alliteration,** the repetition of consonant sounds, usually at the beginning of words: "*n*early *n*apping," "*g*hastly *g*rim," "*f*ollowed *f*ast." A second device is **internal rhyme,** rhyme that occurs within a line. For example:

> *Nothing farther then he* uttered, *not a feather then he* fluttered

A third device is the use of a **refrain,** a phrase or line that is regularly repeated, usually at the end of a stanza. In "The Raven" the concluding line of each stanza is seven or eight syllables long, roughly half the length of the other lines, thereby drawing attention to itself. These final lines are different in content, but they all end with the word *more,* either alone or in combination. As the poem develops, this refrain accumulates ominous meaning, the variations disappear, and the last word, whether spoken by the raven or by the speaker, becomes insistently *Nevermore.*

The overall effect of these devices is to separate sounds from sense, to lull us into expecting a pattern of sounds that becomes more important than the actual meaning of the words, and thereby to persuade us that the speaker's story may actually be true. For example, line 38

In there stepped a stately Raven of the saintly days of yore

presents the bird's action (its stepping in) and its appearance (stately), both of which we can accept as fact. But the rest of the line is purely subjective. There is no reason to assume, with the speaker, that the bird has come, supernaturally, from a time long past. Nor is there reason to agree that those days were saintly. That past and its "forgotten lore" appear to be the source of the superstitions that dominate the speaker's mind and make him think of the bird as a "prophet" from the land of the dead. It is the alliteration (*stepped . . . stately . . . saintly*) that makes *saintly* seem an appropriate word. And "days of yore" has its place in the dominant rhyme-sound of the poem: *door, floor, shore, core, wore, more,* and so on. This hypnotic pattern of sounds gives the word *Nevermore* its special significance. As we are drawn into the poem in this way, we come to share the speaker's point of view, and accept his vision as reality.

Find examples of these different devices of sound in the poem. How do these devices reinforce the meaning of the lines? How do they contribute to the poem's overall hypnotic effect?

Creative Writing

Writing an Imaginary Account

In a famous essay, "The Philosophy of Composition," Poe gives an account of how he wrote "The Raven." First he decided what the effect of the poem was to be, then he chose a subject and poetic devices, and finally he worked out the form of his stanzas and the details of the narrative.

Locate the essay in a collection of Poe's works. Read it and then write an imaginary account of the composition of "To Helen" or "The Bells" (page 190). Present Poe's theory of poetry, then describe the intended effect of the poem, and, finally, tell how you (as Poe) went about creating that effect.

The Bells

"The Bells" is a famous *tour de force*, a French phrase that means "a feat of skill in carrying out a difficult task." Here the task Poe set himself was to create, in language and meter, sense through sound, until the sound becomes the sense. In most poems, the meanings of the words are of primary importance. The sounds of the words and the rhythms of the lines add musicality and emphasis. Here, however, the rhythm and repetition of sounds dominate our attention, and to appreciate "The Bells" we must read it aloud. The poem is largely a creation of moods that are suggested by the different uses we make of bells.

Illustrations on pages 191 and 194 by Edmund Dulac (1882–1953), colored lithographs for a 1912 edition of *The Bells and Other Poems,* Hodder and Stoughton, London

I

Hear the sledges with the bells—
    Silver bells!
What a world of merriment their melody foretells!
   How they tinkle, tinkle, tinkle,
    In the icy air of night!   5
  While the stars that oversprinkle
  All the heavens, seem to twinkle
   With a crystalline delight;
    Keeping time, time, time,
    In a sort of Runic° rhyme,   10
To the tintinnabulation that so musically wells
   From the bells, bells, bells, bells,
    Bells, bells, bells—
From the jingling and the tinkling of the bells.

10. **Runic** (roo′nĭk): pertaining to runes, characters in an ancient alphabet, believed to have mystical significance.

II

Hear the mellow wedding bells—   15
    Golden bells!
What a world of happiness their harmony foretells!
   Through the balmy air of night
   How they ring out their delight!—
    From the molten-golden notes,   20
    And all in tune,
   What a liquid ditty floats
To the turtle-dove that listens, while she gloats
    On the moon!
    Oh, from out the sounding cells,   25
What a gush of euphony° voluminously wells!
    How it swells!

26. **euphony** (yoo′fə-nē): pleasing sounds.

Edgar Allan Poe **191**

How it dwells
On the Future!—how it tells
Of the rapture that impels   30
To the swinging and the ringing
Of the bells, bells, bells—
Of the bells, bells, bells, bells,
Bells, bells, bells—
To the rhyming and the chiming of the bells!   35

III

Hear the loud alarum bells—
Brazen bells!
What a tale of terror, now, their turbulency tells!
In the startled ear of night
How they scream out their affright!   40
Too much horrified to speak,
They can only shriek, shriek,
Out of tune,
In a clamorous appealing to the mercy of the fire—
In a mad expostulation with the deaf and frantic fire,   45
Leaping higher, higher, higher,
With a desperate desire,
And a resolute endeavor
Now—now to sit, or never,
By the side of the pale-faced moon.   50
Oh, the bells, bells, bells!
What a tale their terror tells
Of Despair!
How they clang, and clash, and roar!
What a horror they outpour   55
On the bosom of the palpitating air!
Yet the ear, it fully knows,
By the twanging
And the clanging,
How the danger ebbs and flows;   60
Yet the ear distinctly tells,
In the jangling
And the wrangling,
How the danger sinks and swells,
By the sinking or the swelling in the anger of the bells—   65
Of the bells—
Of the bells, bells, bells, bells,
Bells, bells, bells—
In the clamor and the clangor of the bells!

IV

Hear the tolling of the bells— 70
    Iron bells!
What a world of solemn thought their monody° compels!
  In the silence of the night
  How we shiver with affright
At the melancholy menace of their tone! 75
  For every sound that floats
  From the rust within their throats
    Is a groan.
    And the people—ah, the people—
    They that dwell up in the steeple, 80
      All alone,
  And who, tolling, tolling, tolling,
    In that muffled monotone,
Feel a glory in so rolling
    On the human heart a stone— 85
They are neither man nor woman—
They are neither brute nor human—
    They are Ghouls—
  And their king it is who tolls—
  And he rolls, rolls, rolls, 90
    Rolls
    A paean° from the bells;
  And his merry bosom swells
    With the paean of the bells!
And he dances, and he yells; 95
Keeping time, time, time,
In a sort of Runic rhyme,
    To the paean of the bells—
    Of the bells—
Keeping time, time, time, 100
In a sort of Runic rhyme,
    To the throbbing of the bells—
  Of the bells, bells, bells—
  To the sobbing of the bells—
Keeping time, time, time, 105
  As he knells, knells, knells,
In a happy Runic rhyme,
    To the rolling of the bells—
  Of the bells, bells, bells—
  To the tolling of the bells— 110
Of the bells, bells, bells, bells,
    Bells, bells, bells—
To the moaning and the groaning of the bells.

72. monody (mŏn′ə-dē): a type of music carried by one voice. In ancient Greece, a monody was sung as a dirge or funeral song; thus the word suggests tragedy and sorrow.

92. paean (pē′ən): a song of joy, victory, or praise.

Analyzing and Interpreting the Poem

1. In section I, the silver bells of sleighs create such "a world of merriment" that even the stars seem to be "keeping time." How are the stars, which are of course soundless, linked to the sounds of the bells through the rhymes?

2. The golden wedding bells of section II shift the mood from the childish merriment of sleigh bells to the happiness of mature love. Here all is "harmony," and everything is "in tune." How is this harmony conveyed in such phrases as "molten-golden" and "euphony voluminously"?

3. Section III turns abruptly to the alarm bells that announce disaster. Now the harmony is gone, all is "out of tune," and the rhythm and many of the words are jagged and harsh rather than smooth. In lines 57–64, what sounds are repeated to give this sense of harsh discord?

4. The iron funeral bells of the final section again shift the mood, and the music is now a "monody." There is an interesting change within this section. After the slow lines of the beginning, which suggest a funeral march, the rhymes (beginning with line 79) become more rapid and the rhythm quickens, as in a fast dance. Who is the "king" who dances and yells in this last part of the poem?

Literary Elements

Devices of Sound: Onomatopoeia and Assonance

"The Bells" is noted for its **onomatopoeia,** the use of words whose sounds suggest their meaning, as do *buzz, clatter,* and *hiss.* Actually, Poe's poem has few words that are strictly onomatopoetic. One of them, *tintinnabulation,* which suggests the overlapping sounds of bells shaken rapidly, is an invented word. But the overall onomatopoetic effect of the poem is strong, even hypnotic. This is accomplished in part through the careful control of pace or tempo: the tinkling melody of section I; the slower, richer sounds of section II; the staccato jangle of section III; and the changing pace of the final section, which begins as a solemn dirge and ends in a frenzied dance. Especially when the poem is read aloud, these strictly controlled rhythms tend to dominate the sense of the words and to create a mood.

Other devices that contribute to the poem's musical effect are **assonance,** the repetition of vowel sounds, and **alliteration,** the repetition of consonant sounds. Often these occur together. For instance, in line 84

Feel a glory in so rolling

the *o* sound is used three times (assonance). But there is also a subtle repetition, in reversed form, of consonants: the *lor* of *glory* becomes the *rol* of *rolling* (alliteration). Most noticeable is the alliteration of *l* sounds in *Feel, glory,* and *rolling.* The poem as a whole is remarkable for using so few sounds and repeating them so effectively.

1. Give examples of onomatopoeia, assonance, and alliteration in "The Bells." Explain how these heighten the effectiveness of the lines in which they occur.

2. Show how other sound devices—rhyme, rhythm, and repetition—increase the emotional effect of the poem.

3. Compare the last lines of the four sections of the poem (lines 14, 35, 69, and 113). Describe the different effects of these lines and show how each effect depends on sound devices.

Writing About Literature

Writing a Paraphrase

Write a brief composition in which you *paraphrase,* or summarize, "The Bells," and then tell what qualities of the poem are lost in your paraphrase. (For example, is it as emotionally effective as the poem?) Can any summary of a poem convey all of the poem's qualities?

1. Asher Brown Durand, whose *Kindred Spirits* is reproduced on page 115, was a member of the Hudson River School of painters. Other artists in this group were Thomas Cole and Frederick Church. Find out what information your library has about this group of artists and whether reproductions of the landscapes they painted are available.

2. The contending principles of classicism and Romanticism were expressed in paintings as well as in literature. *The Architect's Dream* by Thomas Cole (page 122), for example, is dominated by the massive regularity of an institutional building whose classical arches and columns stretch into the distance. The tops of gothic spires at the left provide balance but are clearly subordinate to the classical forms that fill two-thirds of the picture, and the scene as a whole is carefully framed—and bounded—by draperies at a window. When the curtains are opened on the hidden world of sleep, therefore, and the dream world is revealed, it is a world restrained and controlled by the rational forms of classical architecture.

Compare this with Washington Allston's *The Moonlit Landscape* (page 123). Here all color and shadow come from moonlight. The human figures, seen in silhouette and in motion, are dwarfed by the landscape. The rectangular houses are left shadowy and indistinct in the distance, while the curved arches of the bridge serve to frame the beams of the moon. The beached boats, two with their sails still raised as if in the same momentarily arrested motion of the horse with its suspended foreleg, make curves against the moonlight. Nature, as sky, moon, and landscape, dominates the painting, and the hills stretch away to a distant and indistinct horizon.

What characteristics of these paintings make the one an expression of classical principles and the other of Romantic principles? In your library, find an encyclopedia or a history of American architecture that has photographs of two of the most famous of American houses, George Washington's Mount Vernon and Thomas Jefferson's Monticello. What classical or Romantic principles are expressed in these structures?

3. B. George Catlin first traveled the wilderness West in 1832 and soon became our most famous painter of Indian life, journeying widely to visit scattered tribes and to depict their dress and orna-ments and ceremonies in his paintings. (At least once, in Minnesota, he was the first white man known to have encountered certain tribes, and the beautiful red claystone these Indians used for their pipes is called catlinite after him.) By 1837, when he opened his Indian Gallery in New York, nearly 500 of his paintings were on display. He later took his Gallery abroad and so became a major influence on white people's understanding of American Indians.

Catlin was interested in every detail that distinguished one tribe from another. The figures shown on page 142 (the Delawares were the Indians who raised Natty Bumppo, a white orphan) were obviously chosen to represent their distinctive styles of dress. What detail of the woman's blanket might be distinctive to her tribe? What details of dress distinguish the men from one another and why might these be important?

4. Asher Durand's *Thanatopsis* (page 155), like Bryant's poem of the same title, is named for an important theme in Romantic painting and poetry, a meditation on death. How has Durand conveyed this meditative, foreboding quality through his treatment of nature in this scene?

5. Poe has been called "the father of the modern short story" because he was the first to define it as a distinct literary form. In a review of Nathaniel Hawthorne's *Twice-Told Tales* (*Graham's Magazine*, May 1842), he expressed his theory of the construction of a "tale."

A skillful literary artist has constructed a tale. If wise, he has not fashioned his thoughts to accommodate his incidents; but having conceived, with deliberate care, a certain unique or single *effect* to be wrought out, he then invents such incidents—he then combines such events as may best aid him in establishing this preconceived effect. If his very initial sentence tend not to the outbringing of this effect, then he has failed in his first step. In the whole composition there should be no word written, of which the tendency, direct or indirect, is not to the one preestablished design. And by such means, with such care and skill, a picture is at length painted which leaves in the mind of him who contemplates it with a kindred art, a sense of the fullest satisfaction.

To what degree does Poe succeed in achieving these aims in the stories you have read? Consider each of his points in your evaluation.

First Harvest

The writing of this period is a powerful contribution to an original, distinctive national literature. Whereas the early colonists often wrote to keep a record of their life in a new land and the authors of the Revolution wrote in the service of a larger political cause, Irving, Cooper, Bryant, and Poe offered works of the imagination, born of the American spirit and psyche and rooted in the American landscape. The literature of this age had as its background recent American history. Its heroes were American characters, and its setting was the United States, a new nation.

In literature, early American Romanticism took as many different forms of expression as there were writers. Yet beneath their differences these first writers of our new national literature often shared at least some of the central attitudes and ideas of the Romantic movement as a whole: a reliance upon imagination and intuition as the most important means of perception; a tendency to value individualism over all social forms or systems; a faith in nature as a revelation of truth and moral values; an interest in the past, especially in legend and myth, and in primitive forms of society and culture; and a concern with those "deeper" aspects of the human psychology that lie beyond rational awareness.

Select at least one of these aspects of American Romanticism and write an essay in which you discuss its presence in one or more of the selections in this unit. Be sure to support your generalizations with specific evidence from the literature.

For Further Reading

For Background or Commentary on Individual Authors

Irving

Brooks, Van Wyck, *The World of Washington Irving* (Dutton, 1944)

Roth, Martin, *Comedy and America: The Lost World of Washington Irving* (Assoc. Faculty Press, 1976)

Cooper

Franklin, Wayne, *The New World of James Fenimore Cooper* (University of Chicago, 1982)

Grossman, James, *James Fenimore Cooper* (Stanford University Press, 1949)

Slotkin, Richard, *Regeneration Through Violence: The Mythology of the American Frontier, 1600–1860* (Wesleyan, 1973)

Bryant

Brown, Charles H., *William Cullen Bryant* (Scribner, 1971)

Poe

Hoffman, Daniel, *Poe Poe Poe Poe Poe Poe Poe* (Avon, 1978)

Wagenknecht, Edward, *Edgar Allan Poe: The Man Behind the Legend* (1963)

For Leisure Reading

Irving's Tales

The Sketch Book
Tales of a Traveler

Cooper's Novels

The Spy
The Deerslayer
The Last of the Mohicans
The Pathfinder
The Pioneers
The Prairie

Bryant's Poems

"Inscription for the Entrance to a Wood"
"I Cannot Forget with What Fervid Devotion"
"To the Fringed Gentian"
"Robert of Lincoln"
"The Yellow Violet"
"A Winter Piece"
"A Forest Hymn"

Poe's Short Stories

"The Pit and the Pendulum"
"The Cask of Amontillado"
"The Murders in the Rue Morgue"
"A Descent into the Maelström"
"The Tell-Tale Heart"
"The Gold-Bug"
"The Purloined Letter"
"Ligeia"
"The Black Cat"
"William Wilson"

THE FLOWERING OF NEW ENGLAND
1840–1860

Detail from *Boston Common from Charles Street Mall* (1835–1840) by George Harvey (1801–1878). Watercolor.

Spectacular, unrestrained growth characterized nearly every aspect of American life from the beginning of Andrew Jackson's administration in 1829 to the onset of the Civil War in 1861. Geographical expansion swept westward with the conquest of territory in the Southwest in the Mexican War (1846–1848) and the negotiation of new borders with the British in the Northwest. The earlier trickle of fur traders into the Western wilderness became a swelling stream of agricultural emigrants searching for new land and of treasure-seekers rushing to the newly discovered gold fields of California. The nation's population, which had doubled between 1790 and 1830, doubled again before 1870. But as America was growing it was changing. A nation that had developed its basic values in a context of farms, villages, and small cities had to face the new concentrations of population and economic power created by an industrial and urban society. The old and deep American belief in individualism, with its attendant promises of liberty and equality of opportunity, had to confront the sudden fact of a mass society in which many were barred by poverty or lack of education from any possibility of self-development. Reform was as much the spirit of the age as expansion, but its aim was less the creation of a new society than the recovery of the one originally promised in the principles of the Declaration of Independence.

Thus, America was propelled by two forces: dissatisfaction with the present and optimism about the future. This optimism was based in part on the dynamic progress in science and technology. If America still lagged behind Britain and Europe in scientific research, it soon excelled in the practical application of scientific knowledge, in everything from soil and mineral surveys of wilderness lands to the invention and development of machine tools.

This new technology was directly related to the monumental tasks that faced the expanding nation. The introduction of the reaper and other agricultural machines helped to open the Western lands to farming; and new roads, canals, and railroads helped to master vast distances. The railroad, especially, became the center of the expanding economy: 10,000 miles of railroad crisscrossed the Eastern states by 1860. A new system of communications also helped to conquer distance and bind the nation together. The first telegraph line was strung between Baltimore and Washington in 1844. This technological wonder spread so rapidly that it reached California in 1861. Few could resist the contagious optimism of such progress. The poet-philosopher Ralph Waldo Emerson felt "pity for our fathers for dying before steam and galvanism [electricity] . . . and before we borrowed the might of the elements."

If the elements themselves were free, there were distinct social costs to the industrial system they served. Manufacturers were quick to recognize the efficiencies of mass-production methods and the advantages of replacing skilled workers with machinery that could

The Canal Boy (c. 1850). Wood engraving by H. & C. Koovoets, New York.
The Library of Congress

be tended by unskilled and low-paid workers, often women and children. Such methods sharply increased productivity, but they also created ugly mill towns where workers huddled in wretched shacks and endured conditions of labor that were little better than slavery. To some, the material progress that accompanied the new technology made it clear that basic American values were being left far behind. Emerson observed that "things are in the saddle and ride mankind." He warned, "The weaver becomes the web, the machinist the machine." A child whose life was blighted by ten- or twelve-hour workdays in a factory could not fulfill Jefferson's democratic ideal of citizens who were free to develop their full potential.

As Americans felt their most cherished values threatened by industrial forces, reform groups sprang up across the land. Some reform groups, seeking to establish society on an entirely new basis, created Utopian communities. Between 1820 and 1850, at least fifty-eight such communities were founded, each with its special economic theory or religious doctrine and each expecting to become a model of social perfection for the country at large. But the most effective American reformers in this period did not seek to overturn the social system or escape from it; rather they sought to adapt new industrial conditions to traditional American values.

1829–1837 Andrew Jackson administration

EMILY DICKINSON (1830–1886)

WILLIAM LLOYD GARRISON founds
The Liberator (1831)

1831 American Anti-Slavery Society founded

RALPH WALDO EMERSON (1803–1882)
Nature (1836);
"The American Scholar" (1837)

NATHANIEL HAWTHORNE (1804–1864)
Twice-Told Tales (1837)

The Dial (1840–1844)

1841–1847 Brook Farm experiment

1846–1848 Mexican War

1848 California Gold Rush

First Women's Rights Convention, held in Seneca Falls,
New York

JAMES RUSSELL LOWELL (1819–1891)
Biglow Papers, First Series;
A Fable for Critics (1848)

HAWTHORNE
The Scarlet Letter (1850)

Harper's Magazine founded (1850)

Emily Dickinson

Nathaniel Hawthorne

View of the Battleground

Henry David Thoreau

John Greenleaf Whittier

HERMAN MELVILLE (1819–1891)
Moby-Dick (1851)

HARRIET BEECHER STOWE
Uncle Tom's Cabin (1852)

1853 — New York and Chicago connected by rail

HENRY DAVID THOREAU (1817–1862)
Walden (1854)

HENRY WADSWORTH LONGFELLOW (1807–1882)
The Song of Hiawatha (1855)

1857 — Dred Scott decision

Atlantic Monthly founded (1857)

1858 — Lincoln-Douglas debates

OLIVER WENDELL HOLMES (1809–1894)
Autocrat of the Breakfast-Table (1858)

1859 — First oil well

John Brown raids Harpers Ferry

1860 — South Carolina secedes from the Union

1861 — Abraham Lincoln becomes President; the Civil War begins

JOHN GREENLEAF WHITTIER (1807–1892)
Snowbound (1866)

Girls' Evening School (1840) by unknown artist. Pencil and watercolor.
Museum of Fine Arts, Boston, M. and M. Karolik Collection

Education for all quickly became a focus of reform. Before 1800 no state had a system of public education; schools were supported privately or by churches. By 1860 every state had tax-supported public schools, in some cases extending through college. The rapid spread of education encouraged the still more rapid growth of newspapers, magazines, and other means of adult education: libraries, museums, trade and professional associations, and, most of all, the lyceum, an association of citizens who invited prominent intellectuals to give public lectures. The first lyceum was organized in a Massachusetts town in 1826. Within a few years there were three thousand lyceums, and speakers on topics of public interest were appearing even in small villages. The lyceum system had enormous impact on American society, both in providing information and in shaping public opinion. Emerson, who lectured widely on the lyceum circuit, said of his work: "Here is a pulpit that makes all other pulpits ineffectual."

Another broad area of reform was women's rights. In legal terms, women were minors and under the control of their husbands or male relatives. A woman's right to own property was subject to this control, as was her right to sign a contract or to make a will. And, of course, she could not vote. Still, the roles of women were changing. The rapid expansion of the school system meant that women had to be trained and hired as teachers, for there were not enough men available. Thereafter, it became increasingly illogical to maintain that women were intellectually capable of being teachers but not of being writers or doctors or lawyers or scientists. Although opportunities in almost every field began opening up for women, one particular role brought them much public attention. From the first, many women were deeply involved in reform movements, often taking positions of leadership. This, in turn, made them more aware of their subservient position in society at large.

By the late 1840s this awareness led to a new focus on women's special concerns, and the first women's convention rewrote the Declaration of Independence to declare that "all men *and* women are created equal." If equality was the reformers' ultimate goal, the more immediate one was to establish basic human rights for women, beginning with the franchise, the right to vote. In a ringing speech to open that convention of 1848, Elizabeth Cady Stanton separated the right to vote from the larger question of male-female equality and then reminded her audience how deeply the vote was embedded in the most cherished principles of American society—government by the consent of the governed, equality before the law, the belief, reaching back to the eighteenth century, in every person's "natural" rights to life and liberty and to hold property.

We are assembled to protest against a form of government, existing without the consent of the governed—to declare our right to be free as man is free, to be represented in the government which we are taxed to support, to have such disgraceful laws as give man the power to chastise and imprison his wife, to take the wages which she earns, the property which she inherits, and, in case of separation, the children of her love; laws which make her the mere dependent on his bounty. It is to protest against such unjust laws as these that we are assembled today, and to have them, if possible, forever erased from our statute books, deeming them a shame and a disgrace to a Christian republic in the nineteenth century. . . .

And, strange as it may seem to many, we now demand our right to vote according to the declaration of the government under which we live. . . . We have no objection to discuss the question of equality, for we feel that the weight of argument lies wholly with us, but we wish the question of equality kept distinct from the question of rights, for the proof of the one does not determine the truth of

Elizabeth Cady Stanton
(1815–1902).
National Portrait Gallery,
Smithsonian Institution

the other. All white men in this country have the same rights, however they may differ in mind, body or estate. The right is ours. The question now is, how shall we get possession of what rightfully belongs to us. . . . [T]o have drunkards, idiots, horse-racing, rum-selling rowdies, ignorant foreigners, and silly boys fully recognized, while we ourselves are thrust out from all the rights that belong to citizens, it is too grossly insulting to the dignity of woman to be longer quietly submitted to. The right is ours. Have it we must. Use it we will. The pens, the tongues, the fortunes, the indomitable wills of many women are already pledged to secure this right. The great truth, that no just government can be formed without the consent of the governed, we shall echo and re-echo in the ears of the unjust judge, until by continual coming we shall weary him. . . .

But what would woman gain by voting? Men must know the advantages of voting, for they all seem very tenacious about the right. Think you, if woman had a vote in this government, that all those laws affecting her interests would so entirely violate every principle of right and justice? Had woman a vote to give, might not the officeholders and seekers propose some change in her condition? Might not Woman's Rights become as great a question as free soil?

The Bloomer Costume (1851). Color lithograph by Nathaniel Currier. This costume was devised to reform women's dress in the mid-nineteenth century.

The feminist movement, like most of the reform movements, fell short of its goals: even the right to vote was many decades away. But it did establish some rights for women—among them the right to be educated—and it prepared the way for further reforms.

By far the stormiest and most disruptive issue in this period was slavery. Around 1830 the antislavery cause in the North broke away from the overall reform movement. Reformers devised a number of long-term schemes to return all slaves to freedom, but every approach to the problem proved ineffectual. Eventually, Northern opinion shifted in favor of the outright abolition of slavery. In his abolitionist newspaper, *The Liberator,* William Lloyd Garrison declared that there could be no compromise on this issue: "I will not retreat a single inch. . . ." Most Northerners were far more moderate than Garrison, but the abolitionist cause daily gained new supporters, including many persons of influence. Many writers became involved. The poet James Russell Lowell wrote for and edited abolitionist newspapers. Another poet, John Greenleaf Whittier, for many years devoted his life to the cause. Henry David Thoreau spoke out publicly in defense of the Kansas firebrand John Brown, even after Brown's violent struggle to free the slaves by force had carried him to armed insurrection against the government and to execution for treason. As passions rose, the issue of slavery came to overshadow all others.

This era had begun with the hope of realizing the high promise of American individualism. Many had struggled to modify the sometimes harsh conditions of an industrialized society and to preserve traditional values. But the excesses and conflicts that accompanied growing materialism moved the nation toward civil war, and the mood of hopeful reform gave way to somber foreboding.

Literature in the American Renaissance

The rush of optimism that had at first characterized American expansion and reform also characterized American literature. Explosive technological growth in publishing and the increased size of the reading audience opened new opportunities to writers. Literary achievements during this period were of such high quality that the period is sometimes referred to as the American Renaissance. Within a single generation, American literature found its place among the great national literatures of the world. From obscure Massachusetts towns like Concord, Salem, and Pittsfield, as well as from Boston and New York, came books that are still read and admired the world over. As Emerson observed, "There is a moment in the history of every nation when, proceeding out of this brute youth, the perceptive powers reach their ripeness and have not yet become microscopic: so that man, at that instant, extends across the entire scale." Launched in part by the appearance in 1836 of Emerson's *Nature,* the period from 1840 to 1860 became just such a moment of ripened powers in American literature: a time when generative ideas about God, people, nature, and society came together in a creative tension that inspired great talents. Without in any way losing its nationalistic tone, American literature achieved a universal voice that spoke for people "across the entire scale."

Transcendentalism

A major source of these generative ideas was an intellectual movement that was neither a religion nor a philosophy nor a literary theory, although it had elements of all three. Put simply, transcendentalism is the view that the basic truths of the universe lie beyond the knowledge we obtain from our senses. Through the senses, we learn the facts and laws of the physical world, and through our capacity to reason we learn to use this information, creating, for instance, science and technology. But there is another realm of knowledge that goes beyond or transcends what we hear or see or learn from books. It is through intuition that we "know" the existence of our own souls and their relation to a reality beyond the physical world. Intuition, which Emerson called the "highest power of the Soul," is a power that "never *reasons,* never proves, it simply perceives. . . ."

Transcendentalists paid the closest possible attention to this "highest power of the Soul" in a continual search for inspiration and insight. As a group, they consisted of a small number of individualists, most of them friends of Emerson who lived in or near Concord. Like the early Puritans, the transcendentalists affirmed the individual's ability to experience God firsthand. Unlike the Puritans, however, they believed that this ability was given to everyone, not just to an "elect" few. As they explored their inner spiritual life, the transcendentalists found their deepest intuitions confirmed by evidence of a similar spirit in nature. From this came the revolutionary perception that is at the heart of their writings: the spiritual unity of all forms of being, with God, humanity, and nature sharing a universal soul.

Transcendentalists took many of their ideas from the Romantic traditions that some scholars believe originated in England. Romantics generally held great faith in the goodness of the natural world and in the value of individualism. Armed with their perception of a universal soul, transcendentalist writers brought new intensity to these views of nature and self. Since nature shares with humanity in the universal soul that permeates all being, no part of the natural world could be trivial or insignificant: *all* is symbolic of spirit. Seen in this light, nature demands a new reverence from the writer and a deeper attention to all its details. It was above all Thoreau, combining

In Nature's Wonderland (1835) by Thomas Doughty (1793–1856).
Oil on canvas.
Detroit Institute of Art, Founder Society, Purchase, Bibbs-Williams Fund

transcendentalist ideas with superb talents as a naturalist, who developed this approach to nature as a symbol. *Walden,* where natural, human, and spiritual meanings are elaborately interwoven, is the supreme example of transcendentalist art.

But even for Thoreau, the study of nature was important primarily as a means to self-knowledge. Transcendentalist writers delved deep into the mysteries of human personality, especially its irrational elements. "Man is a stream whose source is hidden," Emerson wrote, and in another place he pointed to what he called "the subterranean and invisible tunnels and channels" in each of us. In their recognition

Introduction   **209**

of individual insight as a source of spiritual and intellectual richness, transcendentalist writers opened the way in American literature to a complex human psychology.

Aside from its achievements in works of literature, the general achievement of transcendentalism was to relate all individuals to both the natural world and to their own inner worlds. It increased the territory of human understanding. Even those who disagreed with the transcendentalists were often stimulated to new self-awareness by their ideas. James Russell Lowell, who was not sympathetic to transcendentalist thinking, nevertheless paid tribute to Emerson's intellectual force: "he made us conscious of the supreme and everlasting originality of whatever bit of soul might be in any of us."

The Anti-Transcendentalists

Many writers were largely unaffected by the revolutionary ferment of transcendentalist ideas. Lowell, Henry Wadsworth Longfellow, and Oliver Wendell Holmes—their lives centered upon Boston and Harvard College—had other intellectual sources for their work and held conceptions of poetry that were sharply different from Emerson's. These three authors were called the "Brahmins," after the highest caste in Hindu society. They were, in a sense, high-caste New Englanders—cultured and socially important individuals who represented good taste and distinguished achievement. Whittier found in his Quaker heritage his own tradition of spiritual inspiration, and he was little affected by the changing intellectual temper of the age. The poems of Emily Dickinson do show the effects of transcendentalist ideas, but as Dickinson's poems were not published during her lifetime, they played no part in the intellectual and literary life of the period.

Significantly, one of the most important results of transcendentalism was to stimulate the creative imaginations of those who most profoundly opposed its doctrines. Nathaniel Hawthorne and Herman Melville, the two greatest fiction writers of the American Renaissance, both recognized the revolutionary power of transcendentalist ideas. And both responded, not just by criticizing those ideas but by finding in their dissent a means of defining their own perceptions of life.

Hawthorne and Melville found both in nature and in human nature radical contradictions not accounted for in the transcendentalist philosophy that humanity was godlike and evil nonexistent. They saw life in its tragic dimension: the unbridgeable gap between human desires and human possibilities, the mixture of good and evil in even the loftiest of human motives. Soon after first reading Hawthorne's work, Melville praised the older writer for his grasp of this principle: "Certain it is that this great power of blackness in him derives its force from its appeals to the Calvinistic sense of Innate Depravity and Original Sin, from whose visitations . . . no deeply thinking mind is always and wholly free. For, in certain moods, no man can weigh this world without throwing in something, somehow like Original Sin, to strike the uneven balance."

Neither Hawthorne nor Melville believed in any literal way in those old Puritan doctrines, but they found in such traditional conceptions of a God-ordered world a convenient means of expressing their own conclusions about human nature. They found in humanity a strange mixture of will and desire, an "uneven balance" opposed to transcendentalist optimism. In exploring the human spirit, they sought a clear sense of the American actuality, what Melville called "the intense feeling of usable truth": "By usable truth, we mean the absolute condition of present things as they strike the eye of the man who fears them not."

As America approached the terrible catastrophe of civil war, the "usable truth" of the time seemed closer to the somber spirit of Hawthorne and Melville than to the first hopefulness of Emerson and Thoreau. Yet, as Melville liked to point out, nothing runs unmixed in life, and both spirits were necessary to the full maturity of American literature. It is a mark of the great bounty of this astonishing period of our literary history that it gave us both our most optimistic forecast of human possibilities and our most searching appraisal of human limits.

Review

1. Give two examples of the "spectacular" growth that characterized the thirty years preceding the Civil War.
2. What development was chiefly responsible for feelings of optimism about the future?
3. What two technological developments helped to bridge vast distances of the expanding nation?
4. In what way were workers adversely affected by the new technology?
5. What three areas of reform were prominent in this period?
6. Why is this literary period sometimes called the American Renaissance?
7. In what way is *intuition* central to transcendental belief?
8. Who were the two writers chiefly responsible for developing transcendental ideas?
9. Why were Lowell, Longfellow, and Holmes known as "Brahmins"?
10. In what way were Hawthorne and Melville anti-transcendentalists?

RALPH WALDO EMERSON
1803–1882

Ralph Waldo Emerson (c. 1870). Photograph.

"Great geniuses," Emerson once wrote, "have the shortest biographies. Their cousins can tell you nothing about them." This remark reflects Emerson's view that those who change our understanding of the world do so through the power of their ideas. Outwardly their lives may be unremarkable and leave little for cousins to remember. Their real life exists within the mind. Although it was not Emerson's intention, he might have been speaking of himself. For many who read and heard him, especially the young, his ideas were an intellectual awakening to a revolutionary sense of the world. To understand his life, we must turn not to the recollections of cousins but to his *Journals* where, from the age of sixteen, he recorded the life of his mind. Emerson is truly one of our "great geniuses" whose outer life yields a short biography.

Emerson was born in Boston, the son of a Unitarian minister whose ancestors were clergymen back to the time of the Puritans. The father's early death left Emerson's mother and her five sons in what Emerson later called "the iron hand of poverty." But in this family, a son's education justified any sacrifice, and Emerson entered Harvard at the age of fourteen. As we know from his *Journals*, the dozen years after his graduation were a time of self-doubt, indecision, serious illness, and several false starts toward a career. The last of these false starts led him to enter the ministry. Three years later, when he was twenty-nine, he resigned his pastorate, perhaps partly in reaction to the death of his wife after only a year of marriage. To some, he may have appeared to be drifting, to lack purpose, but he was seeking an inner direction, searching his mind and feelings for the inner needs that would show him his work. His resignation from the pulpit, an important step for this son of seven generations of ministers, brought this process near completion. He would still speak of religion and the spiritual life, but from outside the church. After some months in Europe, he returned to settle in the village of Concord, Massachusetts, married again, and took up the career of writing and lecturing that he would follow until his death. His first "little book," *Nature,* appeared in 1836; it was the opening statement of a new faith.

Emerson drew his ideas from many artists, philosophers, and religious thinkers, from all parts of the world, but he made those ideas his own. His intellectual accomplishment was to overturn the eighteenth-century view of nature as a machine and of God as the master mechanic. This concept of nature as a "World Machine," run by natural law, could account for much, but, in Emerson's view, it could not account for a human being's spiritual existence, the "God in us" as he put it, and the fact that we find our spiritual existence reflected in the world of nature. Beyond natural law and human reason, there must exist a higher, spiritual law that permeates all forms of life. Emerson sought to explain the experience of spirit or soul that human beings feel in themselves and see also in nature.

This effort at explanation carried his thought in directions that at first may seem contradictory. The presence of spirit in nature led him to the idea of the Over-Soul, an ultimate spiritual unity that encompasses all existence and in which each human being has an individual share. As Emerson put it, "It is one soul which animates all men." The existence of the Over-Soul explains why, at moments of spiritual intensity, we feel our individual being so strongly and at the same time feel our relationship to all being.

Emerson also maintained that the experience of spirit begins in the individual. Emerson gave great, almost overwhelming, emphasis to the self; "Trust thyself: every heart vibrates to that iron string," he wrote in "Self-Reliance." Again and again he held the self up as the basis of morality, as superior to society, and as the ultimate standard of value. In this he opened himself to misunderstanding. He was accused of valuing self above others. But Emerson made a distinction between the outer self, by which others know us, and the essential self, which is each person's share of universal being or the Over-Soul. It was his purpose, in fact, to give moral and spiritual meaning to the individualism that Americans so prized. He had only contempt for the view of individualism as narrow self-interest, which he called "selfism." He believed that individualism was a step toward the recognition of God within us, that each being represented the embodiment of spirit, and that human possibilities were limitless.

Emerson's message to the young—of his own and succeeding generations—was exhilarating. Against the mechanical nature of the materialists, he offered an organic nature that was alive and vitally connected to our own spirit. He placed us *inside* the world in a new way. Against self-interest he offered a self-trust through which the individual could participate in the greatest of all enterprises, the spiritual development of human life. In later years, the stubborn resistance of social evils and Emerson's own waning powers tempered his optimism. But he never lost his basic faith that "the soul's emphasis is always right," that the inner experiences of the human being are the true guide to reality. Later generations have often criticized Emerson for being far too optimistic about human nature and progress. But hope—about ourselves and about the world— is a fundamental condition of being alive, and American writers and thinkers have returned to Emerson again and again. No writer has been more influential in shaping American literature.

View of the Battleground (c. 1850) by unknown artist. Oil on canvas.
North Bridge battleground and the Old Manse are shown at the upper left above the monument; the town of Concord is in the background at the right.
Concord Free Public Library

Emerson Selections and Commentary

Emerson's literary work is scattered in poems, essays, lectures, and even in the journals from which these published works grew. "This Book is my Savings Bank," he said in a journal entry before his literary career had begun, and for many years he deposited there the first formulations of the thoughts that would later be developed for lectures or for publication. That evolving body of thought, more than any individual expression of it, constitutes his literary achievement.

The fundamental call to the reader in Emerson's work is to the act of experiencing the world, and the most important single word in his writings is *soul*. The meanings he associated with soul, however, go beyond the narrow dictionary definition of a spiritual self that is distinct from the body. For Emerson, the soul is related to our intellectual perceptions, to our moral natures as individuals, and perhaps most of all to our sense of ourselves as organic beings who are at this moment alive in the world. The soul is the activator of these various parts of ourselves. When the soul is aroused, we perceive and evaluate life in a new way, but most especially we *feel* our existence with a new keenness. Early in his first book, *Nature,* Emerson records an instance from his own experience: "Crossing a bare common, in snow puddles, at twilight, under a clouded sky, without having in my thoughts any occurrence of special good fortune, I have enjoyed a perfect exhilaration. I am glad to the brink of fear." Such times of supreme aliveness, of joy in one's being so intense that it touches even the fear of nonbeing, are the work of the aroused soul. They do not depend upon favorable circumstances or personal good fortune, and they are not planned or prepared for. Instead, at such moments we are surprised by joy, seized unexpectedly by a vivid sense of being that is so much richer than our ordinary lives that Emerson could compare it only to waking from sleep. We all, he wrote in an early journal entry, "want awakening. Get the soul out of bed, out into God's universe, to a perception of its beauty, and hearing of its call, and your vulgar man, your . . . selfish sensualist, awakes . . . and is conscious of force to shake the world."

That force is spirit, at once the essence of our human being and of the world's being: "The world proceeds from the same spirit as the body of man." The double action of the soul is to open to us the hidden recesses of our own natures and so vastly to expand our sense of our lives, and at the same time to teach "the perception that the world was made by a mind like ours." The vital center of Emerson's call to experience is the promise that we can *be* more fully, both in ourselves and in the world. When the soul is active, "Man is conscious of a universal soul within or behind his individual life," as he put it in one place; at such times, as he said in another, "I am not alone or unacknowledged."

If we have the potential to be changed so dramatically through the soul's powers, to find in ourselves intellectual and moral capacities and a joy of being that in ordinary circumstances we do not even suspect, the obvious question is why this transformation is so little evident in individual lives ("in a century, . . . one or two approximations to the right state of every man," Emerson estimated) or in the broad sweep of human history. For the individual, the chief obstacles to change are personal comfort and the safety of traditional beliefs: "God offers to every mind its choice between truth and repose." But for humanity as a whole Emerson required a more elaborate answer. He gave part of it in the introduction to *Nature*, where he argues that habit and tradition have become a way of living secondhand, by the truths and ideas of other times, and a barrier against the soul's insights.

> Our age is retrospective. It builds the sepulchers of the fathers. It writes biographies, histories, and criticism. The foregoing generations beheld God and nature face to face; we, through their eyes. Why should not we also enjoy an original relation to the universe? Why should not we have a poetry and philosophy of insight and not of tradition, and a religion by revelation to us, and not the history of theirs? Embosomed for a season in nature, whose floods of life stream around and through us, and invite us, by the powers they supply, to action proportioned to nature, why should we grope among the dry bones of the past, or put the living generation into masquerade out of its faded wardrobe? The sun shines today also. There is more wool and flax in the fields. There are new lands, new men, new thoughts. Let us demand our own works and laws and worship.
>
> —*Nature*

Nature itself draws us from dependence upon the past and invites us to a richer state of being. In nature we are restored to "reason and faith," freed from "all mean egotism," and opened to the soul's perception of those "currents of the Universal Being" that underlie our lives and to the wondrous beauty of a creation that reflects our own spirit.

> In the woods is perpetual youth. Within these plantations of God, a decorum and sanctity reign, a perennial festival is dressed, and the guest sees not how he should tire of them in a thousand years. In the woods, we return to reason and faith. There I feel that nothing can befall me in life—no disgrace, no calamity, (leaving me my eyes), which nature cannot repair. Standing on the bare ground—my head bathed by the blithe air and uplifted into infinite space—all mean egotism vanishes. I become a transparent eyeball. I am nothing; I see all; the currents of the Universal Being circulate through me; I am part or parcel of God. The name of the nearest

Cartoon of Emerson's "transparent eyeball" by Christopher Cranch. From *Illustration of the New Philosophy* (c. 1844).
Courtesy The Houghton Library, Harvard University

"Standing on the bare ground, — my head bathed by the blithe air, & uplifted into infinite space, — all mean egotism vanishes. I become a transparent Eyeball."   *Nature*, p. 13.

friend sounds then foreign and accidental: to be brothers, to be acquaintances, master or servant, is then a trifle and a disturbance. I am the lover of uncontained and immortal beauty. In the wilderness, I find something more dear and connate than in streets or villages. In the tranquil landscape, and especially in the distant line of the horizon, man beholds somewhat as beautiful as his own nature.

—Nature

This call for a revolution in thought and attitude is followed by a radical inquiry into subjects that have remained of interest—and often still mysterious—since Emerson's time: the meaning of physical facts in nature as an expression of an original design and, especially, their relation to a corresponding sense of design in the human mind; a new understanding of the aesthetic faculty that makes us value beauty in persons, in natural objects, and in art; the origins of language and the way they express a "radical correspondence between visible things and human thoughts"; and nature, in the form of science, as a discipline of the mind in the universal laws that underlie both nature and mind.

Throughout *Nature,* Emerson is of course implicitly calling for practical reform and renewal. "We want men and women," as he said elsewhere, "who shall renovate life and our social state. . . . " But the primary emphasis of this first book is that the great secrets of nature and of our own human nature are one, and that we have in us a capacity for being and for growth of which we have scarcely dreamed. Once we truly ask the reason and purpose of the world,

> many truths arise to us out of the recesses of consciousness. We learn that the highest is present to the soul of man; that the dread universal essence, which is not wisdom, or love, or beauty, or power, but all in one, and each entirely, is that for which all things exist, and that by which they are; that spirit creates; that behind nature, throughout nature, spirit is present; one and not compound it does not act upon us from without, that is, in space and time, but spiritually, or through ourselves: therefore, that spirit, that is, the Supreme Being, does not build up nature around us, but puts it forth through us, as the life of the tree puts forth new branches and leaves through the pores of the old. As a plant upon the earth, so a man rests upon the bosom of God; he is nourished by unfailing fountains, and draws at his need inexhaustible power. Who can set bounds to the possibilities of man?
>
> —*Nature*

In the year following *Nature,* 1837, Emerson was invited to address Harvard's Phi Beta Kappa Society, the best scholars at the college. His lecture, "The American Scholar," was a call not only to a love of ideas but to action and "the conversion of the world." The young men in his audience felt they were listening to a new Declaration of Independence, this time of *intellectual* independence. "Our day of dependence," Emerson said, "our long apprenticeship to the learning of other lands, draws to a close." Before that can be completed, however, we must adopt a new idea of the American scholar to fit the new facts of a democratic culture. Our scholar will not be the aloof "thinker" of older societies, where the class role defines the person. Instead, the American scholar will simply be "Man Thinking," the intellectual function of the individual in a culture which values the individual above all: "The main enterprise of the world . . . is the upbuilding of a man."

The most important influence in shaping the mind and character of this future scholar, stronger even than books, will be nature, "this web of God" that surrounds every life. From the first hint that nature "resembles his own spirit," the young scholar will learn "to worship the soul" and through study to discover "that nature is the opposite [the mirror image] of the soul, answering to it part for part." The ancient advice, "Know thyself," and the modern scientific precept, "Study nature," lead to the same end. "The world—this shadow of the soul, or *other me*—lies wide around. Its attractions are the keys which unlock my thoughts and make me acquainted with myself."

Armed with this insight—and the discipline that results from it—the scholar will acquire the self-trust, freedom, and bravery necessary to his high office. His duties are "to cheer, to raise, and to guide men by showing them facts amidst appearances." The central fact beneath the world's appearances is that "the one thing in the world, of value, is the active soul," which gives value both to the world and to life. Once we conceive the "boundless resources of the soul," we see a similarly unlimited potential for change in society, in humanity, even in nature.

It is a mischievous notion that we are come late into nature; that the world was finished a long time ago. As the world was plastic and fluid in the hands of God, so it is ever to so much of his attributes as we bring to it. To ignorance and sin, it is flint. They adapt themselves to it as they may; but in proportion as a man has any thing in him divine, the firmament flows before him and takes his signet and form. Not he is great who can alter matter, but he who can alter my state of mind. . . .The great man makes the great thing. . . . The unstable estimates of men crowd to him whose mind is filled with a truth, as the heaped waves of the Atlantic follow the moon.

For this self-trust, the reason is deeper than can be fathomed—darker than can be enlightened. I might not carry with me the feeling of my audience in stating my own belief. But I have already shown the ground of my hope, in adverting to the doctrine that man is one. I believe man has been wronged; he has wronged himself. He has almost lost the light that can lead him back to his prerogatives. Men are become of no account. Men in history, men in the world of today, are bugs, are spawn, and are called "the mass" and "the herd."

—*The American Scholar*

Despite this loss of individualism in the modern world, Emerson could already see hopeful signs of change in the America of his time. One was the increasing democracy in the arts, especially in literature, which was taking new interest in the lives "of the poor, the feelings of the child, the philosophy of the street, the meaning of household life. . . . It is a great stride. It is a sign—is it not?—of new vigor. . . . I ask not for the great, the remote, the romantic; what is doing in Italy or Arabia. . . . I embrace the common." Only a truly democratic culture, he knew, could foster the full development of every individual that was the ultimate promise of American society:

Harvard University with procession of alumni, 1836.
The Bettmann Archive

Another sign of our times . . . is the new importance given to the single person. Every thing that tends to insulate the individual—to surround him with barriers of natural respect, so that each man shall feel the world is his, and man shall treat with man as a sovereign state with a sovereign state—tends to true union as well as greatness. . . . The scholar is that man who must take up into himself all the ability of the time, all the contributions of the past, all the hopes of the future. He must be an university of knowledges. If there be one lesson more than another which should pierce his ear, it is, The world is nothing, the man is all; in yourself is the law of all nature, . . . in yourself slumbers the whole of Reason; it is for you to know all; it is for you to dare all. Mr. President and Gentlemen, this confidence in the unsearched might of man belongs, by all motives, by all prophecy, by all preparation, to the American Scholar. We have listened too long to the courtly muses of Europe. The spirit of the American freeman is already suspected to be timid, imitative, tame. Public and private avarice make the air we breathe thick and fat. The scholar is decent, indolent, complaisant. See already the tragic consequence. The mind of this country, taught to aim at low objects, eats upon itself. There is no work for any but the decorous and the complaisant. Young men of the fairest promise, who begin life upon our shores, inflated by

Ralph Waldo Emerson **219**

the mountain winds, shined upon by all the stars of God, find the earth below not in unison with these but are hindered from action by the disgust which the principles on which business is managed inspire, and turn drudges, or die of disgust, some of them suicides. What is the remedy? They did not yet see, and thousands of young men as hopeful now crowding to the barriers for the career do not yet see, that if the single man plant himself indomitably on his instincts, and there abide, the huge world will come round to him. Patience—patience; with the shades of all the good and great for company; and for solace the perspective of your own infinite life; and for work the study and the communication of principles, the making those instincts prevalent, the conversion of the world. . . . We will walk on our own feet; we will work with our own hands; we will speak our own minds. . . . A nation of men will for the first time exist, because each believes himself inspired by the Divine Soul which also inspires all men.

—*The American Scholar*

The next year, 1838, Emerson again carried his message to Harvard, this time to the graduating class of young ministers at the Divinity School. Soon after his lecture Emerson had reason to remind himself of the scholar's necessary self-trust and bravery. "The Divinity School Address" evoked a storm of outraged protest (Emerson referred to it, ironically, as "this storm in our washbowl") in which he was attacked for "infidelity" and even "atheism." His criticism of religious tradition and conformity was taken as an attack upon Christianity itself, but in fact Emerson was seeing in Christ the fulfillment of the human potential that the soul promised.

Jesus Christ belonged to the true race of prophets. He saw with open eye the mystery of the soul. Drawn by its severe harmony, ravished with its beauty, he lived in it, and had his being there. Alone in all history he estimated the greatness of man. One man was true to what is in you and me. He saw that God incarnates himself in man, and evermore goes forth anew to take possession of his World.

—*The Divinity School Address*

As this passage indicates, Emerson found in religion, as in nature, a *continuing* revelation of the truth that God has infused into the human soul.

We have contrasted the Church with the Soul. In the soul then let the redemption be sought. Wherever a man comes, there comes revolution. The old is for slaves. When a man comes, all books are legible, all things transparent, all religions are forms. . . . The stationariness of religion; the assumption that the age of inspiration is past, that the Bible is closed; the fear of degrading the character of Jesus by representing him as a man; indicate with sufficient clearness the falsehood of our theology. It is the office of a true teacher to show us that God is, not was; that He speaketh, not spake. The true Christianity—a faith like Christ's in the infinitude of men—is lost. None believeth in the soul of man, but only in some man or person old and departed.

—The Divinity School Address

In a journal entry a few weeks later, Emerson observed that his attackers believed that "the religion of God, the being of God, . . . [is] dependent on what we say of it, . . . the natural feeling in the mind whose religion is external. . . . The aim of a true teacher now would be to bring men back to a trust in God and destroy before their eyes these idolatrous propositions: to teach the doctrine of the perpetual revelation." A doctrine of "perpetual revelation" of course promises revolution, radical change, and it was this that the Harvard faculty heard in Emerson's address. He would be banned from speaking at Harvard for more than twenty years.

The reaction to "The Divinity School Address" is part of the background of Emerson's most famous essay, "Self-Reliance." "For nonconformity the world whips you with its displeasure," he said there, remembering the displeasure which his own nonconformity had aroused. "Self-Reliance" is a distillation of his ideas up to this point in his life, complicated thoughts boiled down into short sentences. But the essay has a harsh new edge of criticism directed against society and social institutions, which, as he now had reason to know, both resist reform and scorn the reformer. "Self-Reliance" is our most famous statement of American individualism, as it is the source of the best-known quotations from Emerson. But as these quotations remind us, Emerson now sees individualism in sharp, even deadly conflict with society. The effect of "society" is not to strengthen the individual but to breed conformity and fear:

Trust thyself: every heart vibrates to that iron string.

Society everywhere is in conspiracy against the manhood of every one of its members.

The virtue in most request is conformity.

Whoso would be a man must be a nonconformist.

A foolish consistency is the hobgoblin of little minds . . .

To be great is to be misunderstood.

We are afraid of truth, afraid of fortune, afraid of death, and afraid of each other.

Nothing is at last sacred but the integrity of your own mind.

But such criticisms of society are finally less important in "Self-Reliance" than the powers—of perception, of virtue, most of all of "the sense of being"—that are opened to the individual through the active soul.

The Philosophers' Camp (1857) by William James Stillman. Emerson is in the center, between the scientists dissecting a trout at the left and the marksmen at the right.

The magnetism which all original action exerts is explained when we inquire the reason of self-trust. Who is the Trustee? What is the aboriginal Self, on which a universal reliance may be grounded? What is the nature and power of that science-baffling star, without parallax,[1] without calculable elements, which shoots a ray of beauty even into trivial and impure actions, if the least mark of independence appear? The inquiry leads us to that source, at once the essence of genius, of virtue, and of life, which we call Spontaneity or Instinct. We denote this primary wisdom as Intuition, whilst all later teachings are tuitions. In that deep force, the last fact behind which analysis cannot go, all things find their common origin. For the sense of being which in calm hours rises, we know not how, in the soul, is not diverse from things, from space, from light, from time, from man, but one with them and proceeds obviously from the same source whence their life and being also proceed. We first share the life by which things exist and afterwards see them as appearances in nature and forget that we have shared their cause.

1. **parallax** (păr′ə-lăks′): change of position.

Here is the fountain of action and of thought. Here are the lungs of that inspiration which giveth man wisdom and which cannot be denied without impiety and atheism. We lie in the lap of immense intelligence, which makes us receivers of its truth and organs of its activity. When we discern justice, when we discern truth, we do nothing of ourselves, but allow a passage to its beams. If we ask whence this comes, if we seek to pry into the soul that causes, all philosophy is at fault. Its presence or its absence is all we can affirm. Every man discriminates between the voluntary acts of his mind and his involuntary perceptions, and knows that to his involuntary perceptions a perfect faith is due. He may err in the expression of them, but he knows that these things are so, like day and night, not to be disputed.

—*Self-Reliance*

Emerson was also coming to recognize, even as he was losing hope for social progress, how revolutionary a true individualism would be: "It is easy to see that a greater self-reliance must work a revolution in all the offices and relations of men; in their religion; in their education; in their pursuits; their modes of living. . . ."

As it turned out, this revolution was continually postponed. Society did not improve: "Our young people have thought and written much on labor and reform, and for all that . . . neither the world nor themselves have got on a step." For all the fervor of the abolitionists, including his own, slavery continued, and the country stumbled toward inevitable civil war. Emerson was deeply depressed by the Fugitive Slave Law, which required the free states to hunt down escaped slaves and send them back into slavery. But he could do nothing but express his rage in his journal: "this filthy enactment was made in the nineteenth century by people who could read and write. I will not obey it, by God." Even western expansion did not, as he had once hoped, lead to a corresponding expansion of the national mind and character. "Great country, diminutive minds," he noted in his journal. Nor did civil war itself bring evident renewal: "We hoped that in the peace, after such a war, a great expansion would follow in the mind of the country; grand views in every direction,—true freedom in politics, in religion, in social science, in thought. But the energy of the nation seems to have expended itself in the war. . . ."

Disappointed by this lack of true social progress, Emerson was thrown back upon his hopes for the individual—and the undoubted powers of the soul. He reminded himself that if life has many slack hours of discouragement, of the dead-alive feeling when the soul is inactive, still there is another, truer measurement of time: "We must be very suspicious of the deceptions of the element of time. It takes a good deal of time to eat or to sleep, or to earn a hundred dollars, and a very little time to entertain a hope and an insight which becomes the light of our life." We must "learn to look for the permanent in the mutable and fleeting," to hold to the soul's knowledge amid the distractions of the body's necessities: "I affirm the divinity of man; but . . . I know how much is my debt to bread and coffee and flannel and heated room. . . ." "Man," as he would say now, "lives by pulses," and true life is measured out not in its duration but its intensity: ". . . in seeking to find what is the heart of the day, we come to the quality of the moment. . . . It is the depth at which we live that imports. We pierce [in those deeper moments] to the eternity," and then life seems of "vast duration." He was glad to remember an old French saying, that God works in moments.

Even nature, although it remained the physical expression of universal spirit, changed for Emerson over the years and no longer seemed so simply beneficial. "The way of Providence is a little rude," he said in "Fate," a late essay. An earthquake in Italy had recently crushed "ten thousand persons" in seconds, and lesser natural catastrophes are the material of daily news. Our own "western prairie shakes with fever and ague," and nature everywhere, in a memorable phrase, has its "leapers and bloody jumpers" and the sound of "the crackle of the bones of [their] prey. . . ." This bloody preying of creature upon creature, one species "living at the expense" of others in a nature red in tooth and claw, was now for Emerson the inescapable "system" of the natural world. And, he reminded his readers, "our habits are like theirs." Humanity is in fact the most "expensive" species in this chain of eating, "however scrupulously the slaughter-house is concealed" from the dinner table.

Such thoughts were part of Emerson's growing understanding of nature in terms of evolution and of human life as a part of the natural history of the earth. Nature now meant limitation. "Nature is what you may do. There is much you may not." Human nature is what evolution has made it, a limitation upon the present powers of the soul. If, earlier, Emerson had emphasized human freedom and the potential for change, now he fully recognized the "negative power" of circumstance and of all that "hints of the terms by which our life is walled up," from the accidents of nature and the faults of our individual temperaments to the universal fact of mortality.

Emerson was not made pessimistic by these new perceptions. Nor did he lose faith in the soul's insights and powers. But his earliest optimism was tempered in these later years by a realistic assessment of all there is in both the world's nature and our human nature that stubbornly resists the soul's idealism.

In "Fate," his strongest essay of this period, life is precariously poised between the expansive freedom promised by the soul and the "fate" imposed by the natural and historical circumstances that surround every individual life. The conditions of our times and of ourselves everywhere wall us in, and a certain determinism in life cannot be denied. But a famous passage in that essay works out at length what Emerson meant by saying, "So far as a man thinks, he is free." Opposing fate is the "power" of the soul, the God within. Man, strangely, is a "stupendous antagonism," a part of "the order of nature" but not wholly, for he sees and comprehends that order and in that way transcends it. He is himself a creature, one that even physically betrays his connections with the lower animals. Yet he is not *just* creature, for he perceives his "creatureliness" as no true creature can. Within the apparently blind forces of nature, man is the conscious agent, part of "the spirit which composes and decomposes nature. . . ." As Emerson said elsewhere, "he who sees through the design, presides over it. . . ." Human freedom is a necessary component of fate.

Thus we trace Fate in matter, mind, and morals; in race . . . and in thought and character as well. It is everywhere bound or limitation. But Fate has its lord; limitation its limits—is different seen from above and from below, from within and from without. For though Fate is immense, so is Power, which is the other fact in the

Storm-Tossed Frigate (1845) by Thomas Chambers (1808–?1866).
National Gallery of Art, Washington, gift of Edgar W. and Bernice C. Garbisch

dual world, immense. If Fate follows and limits Power, Power attends and antagonizes Fate. We must respect Fate as natural history, but there is more than natural history. For who and what is this criticism that pries into the matter? Man is not order of nature, sack and sack, belly and members, link in a chain, nor any ignominious baggage; but a stupendous antagonism, a dragging together of the poles of the Universe. He betrays his relation to what is below him—thick-skulled, small-brained, fishy, quadrumanous,[2] quadruped ill-disguised, hardly escaped into biped—and has paid for the new powers by loss of some of the old ones. But the lightning which explodes and fashions planets, maker of planets and suns, is in him. On one side elemental order, sandstone and granite, rock ledges, peat bog, forest, sea and shore; and on the other part thought, the spirit which composes and decomposes nature—here they are, side by side, god and devil, mind and matter, king and conspirator, belly and spasm, riding peacefully together in the eye and brain of every man.

Nor can he blink the free will. To hazard the contradiction—freedom is necessary. If you please to plant yourself on the side of Fate, and say, Fate is all; then we say, a part of Fate is the freedom of man. Forever wells up the impulse of choosing and acting in the soul. Intellect annuls Fate. So far as a man thinks, he is free.

—*Fate*

Perhaps as much as his specific ideas it is this conviction that the human spirit always transcends its circumstances that accounts for Emerson's enormous and still continuing influence upon American literature. He is a constant reminder that the truest dimensions of our lives are the inner ones: "What is life but what a man is thinking all day?" He believed, as the artist must, that the clearest path to the inner recesses of the human spirit is through the imagination, and so he assures all artists of the worth of their endeavors. But he understood also that, for everyone, the imagination is that absolute human freedom which must be preserved within whatever fatalities of life. It should be said of him as he said of his friend and fellow writer Henry David Thoreau at Thoreau's death: "He knew the worth of the Imagination for the uplifting and consolation of human life. . . ."

To his disappointment, Emerson never became the poet whose creative imagination readily finds the forms and words that uplift and console others. Instead, his literary legacy is in the lectures and essays by which the scholar seeks "to cheer, to raise, and to guide men. . . ." Even his essays are less valued as wholes than for individual sentences and insights. Yet those sentences and ideas have hooked themselves deeply into the American consciousness. Emerson's hope that a democratic culture can truly foster the development of every

2. **quadrumanous** (kwŏ-drōō′mə-nəs): with all four feet functioning as hands.

person remains a hope still, the necessary promise of political democracy. His belief that the soul's perceptions can provide a moral principle for our existence, serve as a spur to fundamental change, and lead us to realize our full potential as individuals remains a tantalizing ideal.

Most of all, perhaps, Emerson's legacy has been his faith in the soul's powers—to invigorate and expand our sense of being alive, to "reattach the deeds of everyday to the holy and mysterious recesses of life," to make us truly at home in our momentary existence as organic beings in a world that is intimately related to us because the same spirit made both. "In some sort," Emerson observed, "the end of life is that the man should take the universe up into himself"— that is, should come to feel so completely *in* his life that the whole outer universe would seem a familiar part of his own consciousness. The world's being and his own would then seem indistinguishable. How infinite was Emerson's belief in the human spirit may be guessed from an almost casual remark in his journal: "A great deal of God in the Universe but not valuable to us until we can make it up into man." Short of that ultimate sharing of the divine consciousness, however, we must have a foundation for our identity as individual human beings who live in the world. Emerson supplies one in a reassuring sentence that could serve as the bedrock of all his work: "The soul's emphasis is always right."

Emerson's concern is always with the fundamental questions of meaning in the world and understanding in us. Nothing could be more human. The appropriate summation of his thought may therefore be a passage that speaks of a "region of destiny, of aspiration, of the unknown" in our deepest selves that cannot be "inventoried" in our outward lives; of the understandings that glimmer just beyond the reach of our minds; of the awe-inspiring "Life" of spirit that underlies our transitory individual lives. As it happens, the passage is not from a lecture or published essay. It is just Emerson, a man always interested in the thoughts that pass through his mind, speaking his mind—and heart—to himself in the privacy of his journal. He is attesting, as always, to his faith that the human being is not a completed creature but a "golden possibility" of intellectual, moral, and spiritual development. It is a faith that a democratic culture can never afford to lose.

It is the largest part of a man that is not inventoried. He has many enumerable parts: he is social, professional, political, sectarian, literary, and is this or that set and corporation. But after the most exhausting census has been made, there remains as much more which no tongue can tell. And this remainder is that which interests. This is that which the preacher and the poet and the musician speak to. This is that which the strong genius works upon; the region of destiny, of aspiration, of the unknown. Ah, they have a secret persuasion that as little as they pass for in the world, they are immensely rich in expectancy and power. Nobody has ever yet dispossessed this adhesive self to arrive at any glimpse or guess of the awful Life that lurks under it.

Far the best part, I repeat, of every mind is not that which he knows, but that which hovers in gleams, suggestions, tantalizing, unpossessed, before him. His firm recorded knowledge soon loses all interest for him. But this dancing chorus of thoughts and hopes is the quarry of his future, is his possibility, and teaches him that his man's life is of a ridiculous brevity and meanness, but that it is his first age and trial only of his young wings, that vast revolutions, migrations, and gyres on gyres in the celestial societies invite him.

—*The Journals*

For Study and Discussion

Analyzing and Interpreting the Selections

1. The first selection from *Nature* (page 215) builds toward the "new"—"new lands, new men, new thoughts." How does Emerson characterize the "old," the past?

2. In the third selection from *Nature* (page 217), Emerson argues that the spirit which created the universe also created us and is the soul in us. How should we understand the proposition that spirit "does not build up nature around us, but puts it forth through us"?

3. In the first selection from "The American Scholar" (page 218), "self-trust" is clearly the highest kind of individualism. What is contrasted with this self-trust?

4. The second selection from "The American Scholar" (page 219) develops a contrast between the scholar of the present and the American scholar of the future. **a.** What are the essential differences between them? **b.** What part does the "Divine Soul" play in all this?

5. The passage from "Self-Reliance" (page 222) sums up views that we have seen in earlier Emerson essays. **a.** If all that is taught to us by others may be called "tuitions," what kind of knowledge is classified as "intuition"? **b.** Where else in Emerson have we seen this idea?

6. The passage from "Fate" (page 225) works out a complex relationship between fate and freedom in human life. In what sense is it true for Emerson that "a part of Fate is the freedom of man"?

Writing About Literature

Considering the Importance of *Possibility* in Emerson's View of Life

In the passage from Emerson's journals (page 227), it is evident that he most values that "largest" aspect of the human being that cannot be "inventoried"—that is, cannot be classified, measured, or categorized. This "remainder" is "the region of destiny, of aspiration, of the unknown" in every person. Similarly, the most interesting part of our mental life occurs in those "gleams" or "suggestions" that flicker beyond our actual thoughts. In a brief essay, consider why this evidence of "possibility" in human beings should be so important in Emerson's view of life.

The Rhodora:

ON BEING ASKED, WHENCE IS THE FLOWER?

In May, when sea winds pierced our solitudes,
I found the fresh Rhodora in the woods,
Spreading its leafless blooms in a damp nook,
To please the desert and the sluggish brook.
The purple petals, fallen in the pool,   5
Made the black water with their beauty gay;
Here might the redbird come his plumes to cool,
And court the flower that cheapens his array.
Rhodora! if the sages ask thee why
This charm is wasted on the earth and sky,   10
Tell them, dear, that if eyes were made for seeing,
Then Beauty is its own excuse for being:
Why thou wert there, O rival of the rose!
I never thought to ask, I never knew;
But, in my simple ignorance, suppose   15
The selfsame Power that brought me there brought you.

Brahma

"Brahma" reflects Emerson's many years of studying Oriental scriptures. In the Hindu sacred writings, Brahma is the supreme soul of the universe, absolute and eternal, from which all things spring, to which all things return, and in which all contradictions are resolved. Emerson uses the concept of Brahma to assert that those matters which are most mysterious or painful, those experiences in which we find no appropriateness or sense, are nevertheless meaningful beyond our understanding.

If the red slayer think he slays,
  Or if the slain think he is slain,
They know not well the subtle ways
  I keep, and pass, and turn again.

Far or forgot to me is near;   5
  Shadow and sunlight are the same;
The vanished gods to me appear;
  And one to me are shame and fame.

They reckon ill who leave me out;
  When me they fly, I am the wings;   10
I am the doubter and the doubt,
  And I the hymn the Brahmin° sings.

The strong gods pine for my abode,
  And pine in vain the sacred Seven;°
But thou, meek lover of the good!   15
  Find me, and turn thy back on heaven.

12. **Brahmin:** here, Hindu priest.   14. **sacred Seven:** the most revered Hindu saints.

Brahma. Granite sculpture. South Indian, Tamil Nadu, Chola Dynasty, 907–1053. Brahma is shown with four faces to signify that he is all-seeing.

Engagement at the North Bridge in Concord by Amos Doolittle (1754–1832). Colored engraving.

Concord Hymn

SUNG AT THE COMPLETION OF THE BATTLE MONUMENT,
JULY 4, 1837

Emerson wrote this poem for the dedication of a monument commemorating the Minute Men, who fought the British at the battles of Lexington and Concord, April 19, 1775, and thus signaled the beginning of the Revolutionary War.

By the rude bridge that arched the flood,
   Their flag to April's breeze unfurled,
Here once the embattled farmers stood
   And fired the shot heard round the world.

The foe long since in silence slept;   5
   Alike the conqueror silent sleeps;
And Time the ruined bridge has swept
   Down the dark stream which seaward creeps.

On this green bank, by this soft stream,
   We set today a votive° stone;   10
That memory may their deed redeem,
   When, like our sires, our sons are gone.

Spirit, that made those heroes dare
   To die, and leave their children free,
Bid Time and Nature gently spare   15
   The shaft we raise to them and thee.

10. **votive:** dedicated in fulfillment of a vow.

Ralph Waldo Emerson   **231**

Analyzing and Interpreting the Poems

The Rhodora

1. The poet finds the rhodora hidden away in the woods, as if "To please the desert and the sluggish brook." How do these facts relate to the question that prefaces the poem?

2. The question of why the flower is hidden, its "charm . . . wasted on the earth and sky," seems to be put aside by the poet's saying, "I never thought to ask, I never knew." Still, there is an answer in the poem. In what way is the poet's "simple ignorance" really a profound wisdom?

Brahma

1. Emerson approaches the problems of pain and death through **paradox,** a statement that is self-contradictory yet true. In "Brahma" the basic paradox is that all time is present and all "far" is "near." The distinctions that human beings make between time and space, and even life and death, disappear in the higher, and (to us) paradoxical, reality of the Brahma. The opening stanza deals with death, but from Brahma's perspective, not ours. In what sense can death be an illusion?

2. The second and third stanzas present a series of paradoxes we can understand only by remembering that, in Brahma, all opposites are united. In the light of this, explain the paradox in line 11.

3. In the final stanza, the paradox is that those who seek Brahma directly do so "in vain." How is it that the "meek lover of the good" is able to find Brahma in this world?

Concord Hymn

1. What is meant by "the shot heard round the world"?

2a. What appeal is made in the poem's last stanza?
b. Look up *hymn* in a dictionary. Why is it a suitable word to describe this poem?

Literary Elements

Personification

Personification is a figure of speech that attributes human characteristics to something that is not a person: an object, an animal or plant, an idea. Although we are usually not conscious of it, the use of personification is common in our daily speech as well as in poetry. Certain personifications—for ex-

ample, "money talks"—have become so familiar that we do not think of them as personifications. Others, through long use, have taken on a literal meaning: the *eye* of a needle, the *foot* of a hill. Some critics have objected to the use of personification in poetry, saying that it is a misuse of language: "an angry sea," for instance, does not literally feel displeasure or belligerence. Yet personification remains a natural way of relating the world to human experience. By attributing human characteristics to nature, we suggest a deeply felt unity between ourselves and the natural world.

A specific type of personification is **apostrophe,** a figure of speech that directly addresses an absent person, an abstract quality, or something intangible. Apostrophe occurs in "The Rhodora." The poet addresses the flower as if it were a person. In what way does this strike a balance between the poet and nature and add meaning to the final line?

Perfect and Approximate Rhyme

Although **rhyme** is not essential to poetry in the way that rhythm is, it is an important element in many poems. Rhyme may be defined as the repetition of stressed sounds that are either identical or similar. Rhyme is often one of several means by which a poet creates order in a poem: words that are rhymed often seem to be "brought together" and to contribute meaning to each other.

Perfect or **exact rhyme** depends on words in which different initial consonants are followed by the same vowel sounds: *tie/lie.* If any consonants follow the vowels, they too must be identical in sound: *meet/feet* or *fix/sticks.* In Emerson's "Brahma," lines 9–12 have perfect rhymes: *out/doubt; wings/sings.*

In **approximate rhymes,** which are sometimes called **slant rhymes** or **off rhymes,** only the final consonant sounds are identical, and the vowel sounds are different: *come/tomb.* The opening lines of "The Rhodora" use an approximate rhyme: *solitudes/woods.* Here only the final consonant sounds are the same. Poets often use approximate rhymes, as they do changes in rhythm, to impart a deliberate roughness to their poems and to achieve dramatic effects. The danger of too great regularity is that a poem will take on a singsong effect, with the reader losing the sense of the words. Approximate rhyme helps to prevent this.

Find additional examples of perfect rhyme and approximate rhyme in Emerson's poems.

HENRY DAVID THOREAU
1817–1862

Henry David Thoreau (1856).
Daguerreotype by Benjamin Maxham.

During his senior year at Harvard College, some time after reading Emerson's *Nature,* Thoreau announced a lifelong theme. "The end of life," he wrote, "is education." If the words were conventional, the intent was not. Thoreau insisted upon treating his life as an experiment in self-education, sometimes in ways that scandalized his Concord neighbors, distressed the relatives who had scrimped to send him to college, and seemed to outsiders mere selfishness or egotism. When he found he could not make his living as a writer, he did not seek a career considered appropriate to a Harvard graduate. Instead, he sharply reduced his needs and earned his livelihood working at temporary jobs. By earning a year's living for six weeks' work, he left himself free for the communion with nature that was the basis of both his life and his writing.

To many, Thoreau's life style appeared idle. Even Emerson, speaking at Thoreau's funeral, lamented the lack of "ambition" that he felt had kept the younger man from a position of leadership. But Emerson was mistaken. Although Thoreau's life was socially obscure, it was extravagantly ambitious on the personal level. He had set himself to realize Emerson's most revolutionary ideas in practice, to test transcendentalist philosophy in experience. Like Emerson, Thoreau believed that nature is a reflection of an inner spiritual reality. His life was spent in the pursuit of the essentials of reality and of experiences that would bring him close to these essentials. He went to live in a hut he built at Walden Pond so that he could strip his life of inessential things. By the end of this two-year stay, he had learned that "if one advances confidently in the direction of his dreams, and endeavors to live the life which he has imagined, he will meet with a success unexpected in common hours. He will put some things behind, will pass an invisible boundary. . . ." In pursuit of his dreams—that is, of an inner reality—he was the self-reliant nonconformist that Emerson urged all people to be. "If a man does not keep pace with his companions," Thoreau wrote, "perhaps it is because he hears a different drummer. Let him step to the music which he hears, however measured or far away."

In the years after college, Thoreau served his literary apprenticeship by writing essays and poems and helping to edit the transcendentalist journal, *The Dial.* Meanwhile, he supported himself by a brief period of schoolteaching, by serving as handyman in the Emerson household, and by working in his father's small business of manufacturing pencils. While living at Walden Pond, he completed his first book, *A Week on the Concord and Merrimack Rivers* (1849), and filled his journals with the material for his masterwork, *Walden.* Unfortunately, the literary recognition he hoped for did not follow. Nor was he successful as a lecturer, a profession that gave Emerson and many other writers a source of income. Even so, Thoreau remained dedicated to his program of "education" through intimacy with na-

Henry David Thoreau **233**

ture and to the writing that would express this experience.

During his stay at Walden Pond, Thoreau had one striking clash with society. To show his disapproval of the Mexican War and slavery, he refused to pay taxes and, as a result, he spent a night in jail. Out of this incident came the essay "Civil Disobedience." It has since become famous as a statement of the individual's moral responsibility to resist immoral acts of government.

It was his life in nature, however, that was Thoreau's great theme. His knowledge of the woods and fields, of the rivers, ponds, and swamps, of every plant and animal, was astounding. "His power of observation seemed to indicate additional senses," Emerson said. "He saw as with a microscope, heard as with ear trumpet, and his memory was a photographic register of everything he saw and heard." No fact of nature seemed to escape him. "And yet," as Emerson pointed out, "none knew better than he that it is not the fact which imports, but the impression or effect of the fact on your mind. Every fact lay in glory in his mind, a type of the order and beauty of the whole."

The relation of the order and beauty of nature to the human mind and spirit is the subject of *Walden* (1854), the supreme work in transcendentalist writing. It is the record of Thoreau's life at the pond, but condensed into a single year. In *Walden*, he attributes spiritual significance to each fact of his life. He achieves this through his use of the seasons. In summer, he could live most directly in nature; his unfinished hut was little more than a roof against the rain. In autumn, Thoreau finished his house, plastering the walls and building the fireplace. This was a period of reflection, of storing up the experiences of summer for winter use as a squirrel stores nuts. In winter, Thoreau especially valued signs of life: the animals that do not hibernate, the pickerel that still swim beneath the ice of the pond. But winter was primarily the season of reading, meditation, and self-discipline, of transforming experience into wisdom. Thoreau compared spring, the time of rebirth, to the Creation, repeated each year.

This seasonal framework closely related Thoreau's inner life to nature, but he was not recommending that others follow in his footsteps. *Walden* can be read in many ways—as social criticism, as inspiration to self-reform, as brilliant observations of nature—but above all, it is a hymn to the possibilities of life. Thoreau had proved from the most direct experience that it is possible to transcend our circumstances and to feel our individual being in relation to all being, to feel the spirit in ourselves which is also the spirit of the universe. He died of tuberculosis before his forty-fifth birthday, his work largely unrecognized by the world. But few lives have known so much inner success.

Main Street, south side, Concord, Massachusetts. Nineteenth-century photograph.

FROM
Walden

FROM **Where I Lived, and What I Lived For**

When first I took up my abode in the woods, that is, began to spend my nights as well as days there, which, by accident, was on Independence day, or the Fourth of July, 1845, my house was not finished for winter, but was merely a defense against the rain, without plastering or chimney, the walls being of rough weather-stained boards, with wide chinks, which made it cool at night. The upright white hewn studs and freshly planed door and window casings gave it a clean and airy look, especially in the morning, when its timbers were saturated with dew, so that I fancied that by noon some sweet gum would exude from them. To my imagination it retained throughout the day more or less of this auroral[1] character, reminding me of a certain house on a mountain which I had visited the year before. This was an airy and unplastered cabin, fit to entertain a traveling god, and where a goddess might trail her garments. The winds which passed over my dwelling were such as sweep over the ridges of mountains, bearing the broken strains, or celestial parts only, of terrestrial music. The morning wind forever blows, the poem of creation is uninterrupted; but few are the ears that hear it. Olympus[2] is but the outside of the earth everywhere. . . .

I went to the woods because I wished to live deliberately, to front only the essential facts of life, and see if I could not learn what it had to teach, and not, when I came to die, discover that I had not lived. I did not wish to live what was not life, living is so dear; nor did I wish to practice resignation, unless it was quite necessary. I wanted to live deep and suck out all the marrow of life, to live so sturdily and Spartanlike[3] as to put to rout all that was not life, to cut a broad swath and shave close, to drive life into a corner, and reduce it to its lowest terms, and, if it proved to be mean, why then to get the whole and genuine meanness of it, and publish its meanness to the world; or if it were sublime, to know it by experience, and be able to give a true account of it in my next excursion. For most men, it appears to me, are in a strange uncertainty about it, whether it is of the devil or of God, and have *somewhat hastily* concluded that it is the chief end of man here to "glorify God and enjoy him forever."[4]

Still we live meanly, like ants; though the fable tells us that we were long ago changed into men; like pygmies we fight with cranes;[5] it is error upon error, and clout upon clout, and our best virtue has for its occasion a superfluous and evitable[6] wretchedness. Our life is frittered away by detail. An honest man has hardly need to count more than his ten fingers, or in extreme cases he may add his ten toes, and lump the rest. Simplicity, simplicity, sim-

1. **auroral** (ô-rôr′əl): Aurora was the Greek mythological goddess of the dawn.
2. **Olympus:** in Greek mythology, the mountain where the gods lived.
3. **Spartanlike:** The citizens of Sparta, an ancient Greek state, were known for their rigorous, deliberately simple lives.
4. **"glorify . . . forever":** the answer to the first question ("What is the chief end of man?") in the Westminster (Presbyterian) catechism.
5. **like . . . cranes:** In the *Iliad,* Homer tells of pygmies so small that they were threatened by flights of cranes.
6. **evitable:** avoidable.

Drawing of Walden Pond (1869) by May Alcott, sister of Louisa May Alcott.
Orchard House, Concord

plicity! I say, let your affairs be as two or three, and not a hundred or a thousand; instead of a million count half a dozen, and keep your accounts on your thumbnail. In the midst of this chopping sea of civilized life, such are the clouds and storms and quicksands and thousand-and-one items to be allowed for, that a man has to live, if he would not founder and go to the bottom and not make his port at all, by dead reckoning,[7] and he must be a great calculator indeed who succeeds. Simplify, simplify. Instead of three meals a day, if it be necessary eat but one; instead of a hundred dishes, five; and reduce other things in proportion. Our life is like a German Confederacy,[8] made up of petty states, with its boundary forever fluctuating, so that even a German cannot tell you how it is bounded at any moment. The nation itself, with all its so-called internal improvements, which, by the way, are all external and superficial, is just such an unwieldy and overgrown establishment, cluttered with furniture and tripped up by its own traps, ruined by luxury and heedless expense, by want of calculation and a worthy aim, as the million households in the land; and the only cure for it, as for them, is in a rigid economy, a stern and more than Spartan simplicity of life and elevation of purpose. It lives too fast. Men think that it is essential that the *Nation* have commerce, and export ice, and talk through a telegraph, and ride thirty miles an hour, without a doubt, whether *they* do or not; but whether we should live like baboons or like men, is a little uncertain. If we do not get out sleepers,[9] and forge rails, and devote days and nights to the work, but go to tinkering upon our *lives* to improve *them*, who will build railroads? And if railroads are not built, how shall we get to heaven in season? But if we stay at home and mind our business, who will want

railroads? We do not ride on the railroad; it rides upon us.

FROM **Sounds**

I did not read books the first summer; I hoed beans. Nay, I often did better than this. There were times when I could not afford to sacrifice the bloom of the present moment to any work, whether of the head or hands. I love a broad margin to my life. Sometimes, in a summer morning, having taken my accustomed bath, I sat in my sunny doorway from sunrise till noon, rapt in a revery, amidst the pines and hickories and sumachs, in undisturbed solitude and stillness, while the birds sang around or flitted noiseless through the house, until by the sun falling in at my west window, or the noise of some traveler's wagon on the distant highway, I was reminded of the lapse of time. I grew in those seasons like corn in the night, and they were far better than any work of the hands would have been. They were not time subtracted from my life, but so much over and above my usual allowance. I realized what the Orientals mean by contemplation and the forsaking of works. For the most part, I minded not how the hours went. The day advanced as if to light some work of mine; it was morning, and lo, now it is evening, and nothing memorable is accomplished. Instead of singing like the birds, I silently smiled at my incessant good fortune. As the sparrow had its trill, sitting on the hickory before my door, so had I my chuckle or suppressed warble which he might hear out of my nest. My days were not days of the week, bearing the stamp of any heathen deity, nor were they minced into hours and fretted by the ticking of a clock; for I lived like the Puri Indians, of whom it is said that "for yesterday, today, and tomorrow they have only one word, and they express the variety of meaning by pointing backward for yesterday, forward for tomorrow, and overhead for the passing day." This was sheer idleness to my fellow townsmen, no doubt; but if the birds and flowers had tried me by their standard, I

---

7. **dead reckoning:** a system of navigating without aid of the stars.
8. **German Confederacy:** From 1815 to 1866, Germany was a loose union of thirty-eight independent states with no king, no capital, and no common government.
9. **sleepers:** railway ties.

should not have been found wanting. A man must find his occasions in himself, it is true. The natural day is very calm, and will hardly reprove his indolence.

I had this advantage, at least, in my mode of life, over those who were obliged to look abroad for amusement, to society and the theater, that my life itself was become my amusement and never ceased to be novel.

FROM **Brute Neighbors**

One day when I went out to my woodpile, or rather my pile of stumps, I observed two large ants, the one red, the other much larger, nearly half an inch long, and black, fiercely contending with one another. Having once got hold they never let go, but struggled and wrestled and rolled on the chips incessantly. Looking farther, I was surprised to find that the chips were covered with such combatants, that it was not a *duellum*, but a *bellum*,[10] a war between two races of ants, the red always pitted against the black, and frequently two red ones to one black. The legions of these Myrmidons[11] covered all the hills and vales in my woodyard, and the ground was already strewn with the dead and dying, both red and black. It was the only battle which I have ever witnessed, the only battlefield I ever trod while the battle was raging; internecine war; the red republicans on the one hand, and the black imperialists on the other. On every side they were engaged in deadly combat, yet without any noise that I could hear, and human soldiers never fought so resolutely. I watched a couple that were fast locked in each other's embraces, in a little sunny valley amid the chips, now at noonday prepared to fight till the sun went down, or life went out. The smaller red champion had fastened himself like a vise to his adversary's front, and through all the tumblings on that field never for an instant ceased to gnaw at one of his feelers near the root, having already caused the other to go by the board; while the stronger black one dashed him from side to side, and, as I saw on looking nearer, had already divested him of several of his members. They fought with more pertinacity than bulldogs. Neither manifested the least disposition to retreat. It was evident that their battle cry was Conquer or die. In the meanwhile there came along a single red ant on the hillside of this valley, evidently full of excitement, who either had dispatched his foe, or had not yet taken part in the battle; probably the latter, for he had lost none of his limbs; whose mother had charged him to return with his shield or upon it.[12] Or perchance he was some Achilles, who had nourished his wrath apart, and had now come to avenge or rescue his Patroclus.[13] He saw this unequal combat from afar—for the blacks were nearly twice the size of the red—he drew near with rapid pace till he stood on his guard within half an inch of the combatants; then, watching his opportunity, he sprang upon the black warrior, and commenced his operations near the root of his right foreleg, leaving the foe to select among his own members; and so there were three united for life, as if a new kind of attraction had been invented which put all other locks and cements to shame. I should not have wondered by this time to find that they had their respective musical bands stationed on some eminent chip, and playing their national airs the while, to excite the slow and cheer the dying combatants. I was myself excited somewhat even as if they had been men. The more you think of it, the less the difference. And certainly there is not the fight recorded in Concord history, at least, if in the history of America, that will bear a moment's comparison with this, whether for the numbers engaged in

---

10. *duellum . . . bellum:* not a duel but a war (Latin).
11. **Myrmidons** (mûr′mə-dŏnz′-dənz): according to Greek legend, warriors from ancient Thessaly.

12. **mother . . . upon it:** a reference to the belief that Spartan mothers in ancient Greece told their sons to choose death rather than to surrender in battle.
13. **Achilles** (ə-kĭl′ēz) **. . . Patroclus** (pə-trō′kləs): In the *Iliad*, Achilles, the greatest of the Greek warriors, is spurred into battle after his friend Patroclus is killed by the Trojan prince Hector.

it, or for the patriotism and heroism displayed. For numbers and for carnage it was an Austerlitz or Dresden.[14] Concord Fight![15] Two killed on the patriots' side, and Luther Blanchard wounded! Why here every ant was a Buttrick—"Fire! for God's sake fire!"—and thousands shared the fate of Davis and Hosmer. There was not one hireling there. I have no doubt that it was a principle they fought for, as much as our ancestors, and not to avoid a threepenny tax on their tea;[16] and the results of this battle will be as important and memorable to those whom it concerns as those of the battle of Bunker Hill, at least.

I took up the chip on which the three I have particularly described were struggling, carried it into my house, and placed it under a tumbler on my windowsill, in order to see the issue. Holding a microscope to the first-mentioned red ant, I saw that, though he was assiduously gnawing at the near foreleg of his enemy, having severed his remaining feeler, his own breast was all torn away, exposing what vitals he had there to the jaws of the black warrior, whose breastplate was apparently too thick for him to pierce; and the dark carbuncles of the sufferer's eyes shone with ferocity such as war only could excite. They struggled half an hour longer under the tumbler, and when I looked again the black soldier had severed the heads of his foes from their bodies, and the still living heads were hanging on either side of him like ghastly trophies at his saddlebow, still apparently as firmly fastened as ever, and he was endeavoring with feeble struggles, being without feelers and with only the remnant of a leg, and I know not how many other wounds, to divest himself of them; which at length, after half an hour more, he accomplished. I raised the glass, and he went off over the windowsill

in that crippled state. Whether he finally survived that combat, and spent the remainder of his days in some Hotel des Invalides,[17] I do not know; but I thought that his industry would not be worth much thereafter. I never learned which party was victorious, nor the cause of the war; but I felt for the rest of that day as if I had had my feelings excited and harrowed by witnessing the struggle, the ferocity and carnage, of a human battle before my door.

FROM **The Pond in Winter**

After a still winter night I awoke with the impression that some question had been put to me, which I had been endeavoring in vain to answer in my sleep, as what—how—when—where? But there was dawning Nature, in whom all creatures live, looking in at my broad windows with serene and satisfied face, and no question on *her* lips. I awoke to an answered question, to Nature and daylight. The snow lying deep on the earth dotted with young pines, and the very slope of the hill on which my house is placed, seemed to say, Forward! Nature puts no question and answers none which we mortals ask. She has long ago taken her resolution. "O Prince, our eyes contemplate with admiration and transmit to the soul the wonderful and varied spectacle of this universe. The night veils without doubt a part of this glorious creation; but day comes to reveal to us this great work, which extends from earth even into the plains of the ether."[18]

Then to my morning work. First I take an ax and pail and go in search of water, if that be not a dream. After a cold and snowy night it needed a divining rod to find it. Every winter the liquid and trembling surface of the pond, which was so sensitive to every breath, and reflected every light and shadow, becomes solid to the depth of a foot or a foot and a

---

14. **Austerlitz** (ôs'tər-lĭts' ous'-) **. . . Dresden:** two of Napoleon's victorious battles during the Napoleonic Wars.
15. **Concord Fight:** the first major battle of the American Revolution, on April 19, 1775. The two killed were Isaac Davis and David Hosmer. Major John Buttrick was in command of the five hundred minutemen.
16. **tax on their tea:** The colonists staged the Boston Tea Party as an objection to this tax.

17. **Hotel des Invalides** (ō-těl' däz ȧn-vȧ-lēd'): a hospital in Paris for wounded veterans.
18. **ether:** a hypothetical substance once believed to occupy space; hence, space or the upper air.

Henry David Thoreau **239**

half, so that it will support the heaviest teams, and perchance the snow covers it to an equal depth, and it is not to be distinguished from any level field. Like the marmots in the surrounding hills, it closes its eyelids and becomes dormant for three months or more. Standing on the snow-covered plain, as if in a pasture amid the hills, I cut my way first through a foot of snow, and then a foot of ice, and open a window under my feet, where, kneeling to drink, I look down into the quiet parlor of the fishes, pervaded by a softened light as through a window of ground glass, with its bright sanded floor the same as in summer; there a perennial waveless serenity reigns as in the amber twilight sky, corresponding to the cool and even temperament of the inhabitants. Heaven is under our feet as well as over our heads.

Early in the morning, while all things are crisp with frost, men come with fishing reels and slender lunch, and let down their fine lines through the snowy field to take pickerel and perch; wild men, who instinctively follow other fashions and trust other authorities than their townsmen, and by their goings and comings stitch towns together in parts where else they would be ripped. They sit and eat their luncheon in stout fearnaughts[19] on the dry oak leaves on the shore, as wise in natural lore as the citizen is in artificial. They never consulted with books, and know and can tell much less than they have done. The things which they practice are said not yet to be known. Here is one fishing for pickerel with grown perch for bait. You look into his pail with wonder as into a summer pond, as if he kept summer locked up at home, or knew where she had retreated. How, pray, did he get these in midwinter? O, he got worms out of rotten logs since the ground froze, and so he caught them. His life itself passes deeper in nature than the studies of the naturalist penetrate; himself a subject for the naturalist. The latter raises the moss and bark gently with his knife in search of insects; the former lays open logs to their core with his ax, and moss and bark fly far and wide. He gets his living by barking trees. Such a man has some right to fish, and I love to see nature carried out in him. The perch swallows

19. **fearnaughts:** heavy woolen coats.

the grubworm, the pickerel swallows the perch, and the fisherman swallows the pickerel; and so all the chinks in the scale of being are filled.

Spring

Walden is melting apace. There is a canal two rods wide along the northerly and westerly sides, and wider still at the east end. A great field of ice has cracked off from the main body. I hear a song sparrow singing from the bushes on the shore—*olit, olit, olit—chip, chip, chip, che char—che wiss, wiss, wiss.* He too is helping to crack it. How handsome the great sweeping curves in the edge of the ice, answering somewhat to those of the shore, but more regular! It is unusually hard, owing to the recent severe but transient cold, and all watered or waved like a palace floor. But the wind slides eastward over its opaque surface in vain, till it reaches the living surface beyond. It is glorious to behold this ribbon of water sparkling in the sun, the bare face of the pond full of glee and youth, as if it spoke the joy of the fishes within it, and of the sands on its shore—a silvery

sheen as from the scales of a *leuciscus,*[20] as it were all one active fish. Such is the contrast between winter and spring. Walden was dead and is alive again. But this spring it broke up more steadily, as I have said.

The change from storm and winter to serene and mild weather, from dark and sluggish hours to bright and elastic ones, is a memorable crisis which all things proclaim. It is seemingly instantaneous at last. Suddenly an influx of light filled my house, though the evening was at hand, and the clouds of winter still overhung it, and the eaves were dripping with sleety rain. I looked out the window, and lo! where yesterday was cold gray ice there lay the transparent pond already calm and full of hope as in a summer evening, reflecting a summer evening sky in its bosom, though none was visible overhead, as if it had intelligence with some remote horizon. I heard a robin in the distance, the first I had heard for many a thousand years, methought, whose note I shall not forget for many a thousand more—the same sweet and powerful song as of yore. O

20. *leuciscus* (lōō-sĭs′kəs): a small, freshwater fish.

the evening robin, at the end of a New England summer day! If I could ever find the twig he sits upon! I mean *he*; I mean *the twig*. This at least is not the *Turdus migratorius*.[21] The pitch pines and shrub oaks about my house, which had so long drooped, suddenly resumed their several characters, looked brighter, greener, and more erect and alive, as if effectually cleansed and restored by the rain. I knew that it would not rain any more. You may tell by looking at any twig of the forest, aye, at your very woodpile, whether its winter is past or not. As it grew darker, I was startled by the *honking* of geese flying low over the woods, like weary travelers getting in late from southern lakes, and indulging at last in unrestrained complaint and mutual consolation. Standing at my door, I could hear the rush of their wings; when, driving toward my house, they suddenly spied my light, and with hushed clamor wheeled and settled in the pond. So I came in, and shut the door, and passed my first spring night in the woods.

In the morning I watched the geese from the door through the mist, sailing in the middle of the pond, fifty rods off, so large and tumultuous that Walden appeared like an artificial pond for their amusement. But when I stood on the shore they at once rose up with a great flapping of wings at the signal of their commander, and when they had got into rank circled about over my head, twenty-nine of them, and then steered straight to Canada, with a regular *honk* from the leader at intervals, trusting to break their fast in muddier pools. A "plump" of ducks rose at the same time and took the route to the north in the wake of their noisier cousins.

For a week I heard the circling groping clangor of some solitary goose in the foggy mornings, seeking its companion, and still peopling the woods with the sound of a larger life than they could sustain. In April the pigeons were seen again flying express in small flocks, and

in due time I heard the martins twittering over my clearing, though it had not seemed that the township contained so many that it could afford me any, and I fancied that they were peculiarly of the ancient race that dwelt in hollow trees ere white men came. In almost all climes the tortoise and the frog are among the precursors and heralds of this season, and birds fly with song and glancing plumage, and plants spring and bloom, and winds blow, to correct this slight oscillation of the poles and preserve the equilibrium of Nature.

As every season seems best to us in its turn, so the coming in of spring is like the creation of Cosmos out of Chaos and the realization of the Golden Age.[22]

FROM THE **Conclusion**

I left the woods for as good a reason as I went there. Perhaps it seemed to me that I had several more lives to live, and could not spare any more time for that one. It is remarkable how easily and insensibly we fall into a particular route, and make a beaten track for ourselves. I had not lived there a week before my feet wore a path from my door to the pondside; and though it is five or six years since I trod it, it is still quite distinct. It is true, I fear that others may have fallen into it, and so helped to keep it open. The surface of the earth is soft and impressible by the feet of men; and so with the paths which the mind travels. How worn and dusty, then, must be the highways of the world, how deep the ruts of tradition and conformity! I did not wish to take a cabin passage, but rather to go before the mast and on the deck of the world, for there I could best see the moonlight amid the mountains. I do not wish to go below now.

I learned this, at least, by my experiment;

---

21. ***Turdus migratorius*** (tûr′dŭs mī′grə-tôr′ē-əs): migratory thrush.

22. **creation . . . Golden Age:** According to Greek and Roman mythology, the creation was followed by the Golden Age, a time of perfect peace, happiness, and innocence.

that if one advances confidently in the direction of his dreams, and endeavors to live the life which he has imagined, he will meet with a success unexpected in common hours. He will put some things behind, will pass an invisible boundary; new, universal, and more liberal laws will begin to establish themselves around and within him; or the old laws be expanded, and interpreted in his favor in a more liberal sense, and he will live with the license of a higher order of beings. In proportion as he simplifies his life, the laws of the universe will appear less complex, and solitude will not be solitude, nor poverty poverty, nor weakness weakness. If you have built castles in the air, your work need not be lost; that is where they should be. Now put the foundations under them. . . .

Why should we be in such desperate haste to succeed, and in such desperate enterprises? If a man does not keep pace with his companions, perhaps it is because he hears a different drummer. Let him step to the music which he hears, however measured or far away. It is not important that he should mature as soon as an apple tree or an oak. Shall he turn his spring into summer? If the condition of things which we were made for is not yet, what were any reality which we can substitute? We will not be shipwrecked on a vain reality. Shall we with pains erect a heaven of blue glass over ourselves, though when it is done we shall be sure to gaze still at the true ethereal heaven far above, as if the former were not? . . .

However mean your life is, meet it and live it; do not shun it and call it hard names. It is not so bad as you are. It looks poorest when you are richest. The faultfinder will find faults even in paradise. Love your life, poor as it is. You may perhaps have some pleasant, thrilling, glorious hours, even in a poorhouse. The setting sun is reflected from the windows of the almshouse[23] as brightly as from the rich man's abode; the snow melts before its door as early in the spring. I do not see but a quiet

mind may live as contentedly there, and have as cheering thoughts, as in a palace. The town's poor seem to me often to live the most independent lives of any. Maybe they are simply great enough to receive without misgiving. Most think that they are above being supported by the town; but it oftener happens that they are not above supporting themselves by dishonest means, which should be more disreputable. Cultivate poverty like a garden herb, like sage. Do not trouble yourself much to get new things, whether clothes or friends. Turn the old; return to them. Things do not change; we change. Sell your clothes and keep your thoughts. God will see that you do not want society. If I were confined to a corner of a garret all my days, like a spider, the world would be just as large to me while I had my thoughts about me. The philosopher[24] said: "From an army of three divisions one can take away its general, and put it in disorder; from the man the most abject and vulgar one cannot take away his thought." Do not seek so anxiously to be developed, to subject yourself to many influences to be played on; it is all dissipation. Humility like darkness reveals the heavenly lights. The shadows of poverty and meanness gather around us, "and lo! creation widens to our view."[25] We are often reminded that if there were bestowed on us the wealth of Croesus,[26] our aims must still be the same, and our means essentially the same. Moreover, if you are restricted in your range by poverty, if you cannot buy books and newspapers, for instance, you are but confined to the most significant and vital experiences; you are compelled to deal with the material which yields the most sugar and the most starch. It is life near the bone where it is sweetest. You are defended from being a trifler. No man loses ever on a lower level by magnanimity on a higher. Superfluous wealth can buy superflui-

23. **almshouse:** poorhouse.

24. **philosopher:** Confucius.
25. **"and . . . view":** a reference to a sonnet by the poet Joseph Blanco White (1775–1841).
26. **Croesus** (krē'səs): a king in the sixth century B.C. famous for his enormous wealth.

ties only. Money is not required to buy one necessary of the soul. . . .

The life in us is like the water in the river. It may rise this year higher than man has ever known it, and flood the parched uplands; even this may be the eventful year, which will drown out all our muskrats. It was not always dry land where we dwell. I see far inland the banks which the stream anciently washed, before science began to record its freshets. Everyone has heard the story which has gone the rounds of New England, of a strong and beautiful bug which came out of the dry leaf of an old table of apple-tree wood, which had stood in a farmer's kitchen for sixty years, first in Connecticut, and afterward in Massachusetts—from an egg deposited in the living tree many years earlier still, as appeared by counting the annual layers beyond it; which was heard gnawing out for several weeks, hatched perchance by the heat of an urn. Who does not feel his faith in a resurrection and immortality strengthened by hearing of this? Who knows what beautiful and winged life, whose egg has been buried for ages under many concentric layers of woodenness in the dead dry life of society, deposited at first in the alburnum[27] of the green and living tree, which has been gradually converted into the semblance of its well-seasoned tomb—heard perchance gnawing out now for years by the astonished family of man, as they sat round the festive board—may unexpectedly come forth from amidst society's most trivial and handselled furniture, to enjoy its perfect summer life at last!

I do not say that John or Jonathan[28] will realize all this; but such is the character of that morrow which mere lapse of time can never make to dawn. The light which puts out our eyes is darkness to us. Only that day dawns to which we are awake. There is more day to dawn. The sun is but a morning star.

27. **alburnum:** the moist, soft wood underneath the bark of a tree, where water is conducted; also known as sapwood.
28. **John or Jonathan:** John Bull and Brother Jonathan, names long used to represent England and America.

Reading Check

1. What is Thoreau's solution to the clutter and complications of everyday life?
2. According to Thoreau, how did the people of Concord react to his lack of industry?
3. What was the outcome of the battle Thoreau witnessed on the wood chip?
4. Why did Thoreau admire the fishermen at Walden Pond?
5. Why did Thoreau decide to leave the woods?

For Study and Discussion

Analyzing and Interpreting the Selections

Where I Lived, and What I Lived For

1. Thoreau's method as a writer is often to move from the small fact to the larger truth. In the first sentence, he tells the reader that his unfinished house allowed the air to blow through. How does this simple fact become important in the discussion of "winds" in the last part of the paragraph?
2. The theme of the next paragraphs is the effort to "live deliberately" in order to "live deep." In what way did living in the woods enable Thoreau to improve the quality of his life?
3. The final paragraph asserts that "we live meanly, like ants." **a.** What explanation does Thoreau give for this way of life? **b.** Why does he place so much emphasis on simplicity?
4. What paradox is expressed in the final sentence of this passage? (For a discussion of **paradox,** see page 232.)

Sounds

1. This passage celebrates idleness but not merely as laziness or shirking of work. The state of "revery" which on those sunny mornings allows Thoreau to forget "the lapse of time" has its own purpose in his life. Why does he feel that these hours "were not time subtracted from my life, but so much over and above my usual allowance"?
2. Thoreau's own inner state on those days was expressed by a silent smile or an occasional chuckle. How are these expressions of himself related to the sounds he hears from nature?
3. The single word for time in the language of the

Puri Indians is contrasted to the hours that are "fretted by the ticking of the clock." Why should this discussion of time lead immediately to Thoreau's fellow townsmen in Concord and their criticism of his "idleness"?

Brute Neighbors

1. In this famous instance of Thoreau's close observation of nature, how does he make the war between armies of ants seem significant?

2. Concord, site of one of the first battles of the American Revolution, was justly proud of its place in history. **a.** What is Thoreau's purpose in comparing the war of the ants to the "Concord Fight" of the past? **b.** What is the tone of his references to the Spartans and the heroes of the Trojan War and to Napoleon's campaigns?

3. Present for the first time at a "war" or a "battle" of any kind, Thoreau declares that "I was myself excited somewhat even as if they had been men." **a.** How does he convey this excitement to his reader? **b.** Why is it important that the description shifts from the general field of battle to the three ants he separates from the others and watches through a magnifying glass?

4. At the end Thoreau observes that he "never learned which party was victorious, nor the cause of the war...." How is this statement also a comment on human warfare?

5a. How would you describe the overall tone in this passage? **b.** What particular words or incidents seem most clearly to indicate that tone?

The Pond in Winter

1. Thoreau says he "awoke to an answered question, to Nature and daylight." What makes him see that nature transcends all questions and doubts about existence?

2. At the end of the second paragraph, Thoreau says, "Heaven is under our feet as well as over our heads." What details in the paragraph support this statement?

3. The final paragraph focuses upon the fishermen who came to Walden Pond from the town. **a.** In what way are the fishermen "as wise in natural lore as the citizen is in artificial"? **b.** What evidence proves that these "wild men" have penetrated more deeply into nature than the trained naturalist?

Spring

1. This selection gives a sense of the awakening and rebirth that accompanies spring. Beginning with the

ribbon of water along the shore, the first paragraph develops an impression of movement until the "living surface" of the pond seems itself "all one active fish." What images create this impression?

2. Introduced in the second paragraph is the idea that spring is "a memorable crisis," in part because it is at once gradual and sudden. What changes in nature mark that mysterious point at which winter turns into spring?

3. The concluding sentence compares the coming of spring to "the creation of Cosmos out of Chaos and the realization of the Golden Age." What sense impressions, especially of sound and sight, prepare for this statement?

Conclusion

1. In his conclusion Thoreau again applies the lessons of his experiment to broader experiences. In the first paragraph, what general lesson about conformity is to be drawn from the path he wore between his house and the pond?

2. The example in the third paragraph of the man who "hears a different drummer" is one of the most quoted passages from *Walden*. How does this passage support the earlier criticism of conformity?

3. The powerful fifth paragraph centers upon the rebirth that is possible once we have opened ourselves to nature and to our true inner being. Within this context, what is the "moral" of the story of the beautiful bug that hatched after being buried many years in an old wooden table?

4. In some respects the final sentences of "Conclusion" sum up all of *Walden*. Thoreau reminds us that finding our "perfect summer life," as did the beautiful bug, is not merely a matter of waiting. According to Thoreau, in what way may any of us prepare to experience spiritual awakening?

Close Reading

Style and Purpose

Readers of *Walden* soon recognize that it is a book of many styles, which shift with remarkable flexibility in accordance with Thoreau's changing purposes. At bottom, always, are the facts, in Thoreau's view the necessary foundation of meaning; and sometimes the style seems merely "factual," the unadorned observation of a minor aspect of nature: "One day when I went out to my woodpile, or rather my pile of stumps, I observed two large ants, the one red, the other much larger, nearly half an inch long, and black, fiercely contending with one another." The slow, frequently interrupted pace of the sentence and the unemphatic details make the observation itself seem unimportant. But that same passage from "Brute Neighbors" (page 238) grows through metaphor, analogy, and allusion until this battle of ants has the excitement and magnitude of human warfare, from the ancient Greeks at Troy to the revolutionary Minutemen of Thoreau's native Concord: "The more you think of it, the less the difference." If anything, honor goes to the ants for the selfless instinct that drives them either to conquer or die in the attempt, and Thoreau can easily imagine that they fight for a higher principle than the "threepenny tax" that inspired the Boston Tea Party. By means of several different styles, a world so tiny it is best observed under a microscope ("the dark carbuncles of the sufferer's eyes shone with ferocity such as war only could excite") has been invested with human significance.

The opening paragraph of "The Pond in Winter" (page 239) is different both in purpose and style. In general, the winter chapters of *Walden* are a time of reflection, of taking nature up into consciousness, as summer had been a period of living outwardly, almost unconsciously, in nature. Thoreau wakes "after a still winter night" with the sense that some unanswered question had come to him in sleep, the part of our lives hidden from our consciousness, and the slow rhythm of the sentence builds toward the abrupt, staccato questions: "what—how—when—where?" But nature, "in whom all creatures live," has no such urgency, and the rhythm is slowed again, partly through alliteration, as the dawn looks in his "windows with serene and satisfied face. . . ." We are thus reminded, almost slyly, that we are the creatures, nature the creation. That gives increased force to the next short sentence: "I awoke to an answered question, to Nature and daylight." Nature puts aside the question of the night by drawing him to the dawning day; the young pines deep in snow, "the very slope of the hill . . . seemed to say, Forward!" The point is emphasized in the following short sentences: immortal nature does not ask or answer the questions of mortals. Yet nature does speak to the soul, the immortal part of us. A quotation from sacred Hindu literature, conveying, of course, the sacredness of nature, closes the paragraph. Again the rhythm slows as the sentences expand. The "wonderful and varied spectacle of this universe" passes through our eyes to the soul. Night "veils . . . a part of this glorious creation," just as a part of us is then hidden from ourselves in sleep; "but day comes to reveal to us this great work" once again and so to meet the soul's need. It is in this sense that the dawn has answered his question of the night.

Consider the style of the paragraph that follows in "The Pond in Winter." How has the introductory paragraph prepared for Thoreau's own "morning work"? Why should he wonder if water itself "be not a dream"? Are there other images of sleep in the passage? A "divining rod," usually a small forked branch, is sometimes used on land to find subsurface water in order to sink a well. How is Thoreau using it here? Is he giving the term more than its ordinary meaning—perhaps its original one?

The paragraph mixes factual observations with striking images. The hole in the ice, for example, becomes a "window" looking "down into the quiet parlor of the fishes," and the pond itself is personified so that it has "eyelids" to close like the hibernating woodchucks. What images prepare us for the striking observation of the final sentence? The two shortest sentences are the opening and closing ones. Can you see a pattern in the rhythm of the sentences in the paragraph? Why might the longest sentence come just before that final one?

Writing About Literature

Discussing Thoreau's Relevance

Write a composition in which you discuss Thoreau's relevance to our time. Consider the following points: Is Thoreau's general point of view a good one for our age? Has the growth of an industrial society made his point of view outmoded? How much of what he specifically says is important to people living today? How much is irrelevant?

Relating Thoreau's Experiences to Emerson's Ideas

In both his actions and his writings, Thoreau was much influenced by Emerson's *Nature*. Reread the excerpts from *Nature* on pages 215–217. Then show how Thoreau applied one or more of Emerson's ideas to his own experiment in living at Walden Pond. Use specific passages from *Nature* and from Thoreau's statement of purpose, "Where I Lived, and What I Lived For," to support your conclusions.

Emerson, the romantic prophet who believed in the profound possibilities of each human being, himself confessed that he had not given enough weight to one major aspect of human experience. "I could never give much reality to evil," he admitted. To Nathaniel Hawthorne, evil was very real indeed. The doctrine of original sin, so important to his Puritan ancestors, was never very far from Hawthorne's view of life. Born in Salem, Massachusetts, where, a century before, women had been hanged as witches, he wrote, "I felt it almost a destiny to make Salem my home." The first of Hawthorne's American forebears was a stern judge, well known for his persecution of the Quakers. That man's son, John Hathorne, was active in prosecuting suspected witches and committed about one hundred of them to jail. Of these men, Hawthorne wrote, "I take shame upon myself for their sakes and pray that any curse incurred by them . . . may be now and henceforth removed." In Hawthorne's view, unlike that of the Puritans, the greatest sinners were so concerned with themselves that they coldly denied their sympathy to other human beings. He saw evil as a force that leaves its mark on generation after generation, and in his stories and novels he traced the effects of its corrupting presence.

By the time of Hawthorne's birth in the seaport town of Salem, his family had long declined from its original prominence in Massachusetts affairs. His father, a ship's captain, was lost at sea when Hawthorne was only four, and the boy grew up under the somewhat gloomy influence of a grieving widow. He attended Bowdoin College in Maine, where he became friends with Henry Wadsworth Longfellow, who would later become America's foremost poet, and Franklin Pierce, who would rise in politics to become President of the United States. Hawthorne's own career showed no such promise. He was graduated in 1825 without distinction and without preparation for any of the professions usually followed by ambitious young men. He wanted, instead, to

Nathaniel Hawthorne (1840) by Charles Osgood (1809–1890). Oil on canvas.

become a writer, and he returned to his mother's house in Salem to begin his apprenticeship.

The following twelve years, from the time he was twenty-one until he was thirty-three, are often regarded as a mysterious period in Hawthorne's life. Living at home and writing for long hours every day, he devoted himself to learning his craft. Only seldom did he see friends or break his routine for a brief trip. Although such intense periods of self-discipline are common enough among serious young writers, Hawthorne's was unusual in the strictness of his seclusion and the many years that elapsed before he was ready to face the world with his work. Those "twelve dark years," as he called them, had a profound effect upon him. He felt more and more isolated from the social world. "By some witchcraft or other," he wrote Longfellow in 1837, ". . . I have been carried apart from the main current of life and find it impossible to get back again." He did, of course, "get back again," but he brought with him a lasting sense of the dangers of isolation. Much later he wrote, "This perception of an infinitely shivering solitude . . . is one of the most forlorn results of any accident, misfortune, crime or peculiarity of character, that puts an individual ajar with the world." Human isolation was a theme he explored again and again.

Hawthorne's "dark years" ended in 1837 with the publication of the first volume of *Twice-Told Tales*. Although this collection of stories sold poorly, it confirmed Hawthorne in his profession as writer. Soon thereafter he became engaged to be married and took a dull job in the Boston customhouse. In 1841, thinking that it might provide a permanent way of life after his marriage and give him greater leisure to write, he joined the transcendentalist experiment in communal living known as Brook Farm. Hawthorne found the farm work unpleasant, however, and was unimpressed with the schemes for reform. This idealistic group would not, he thought, change a wicked world into a good one. He left after seven months, married, and moved to Concord, where he lived in the Old Manse, the house where Emerson had written *Nature*.

After several years in which Hawthorne managed to support his growing family with the money from his stories, he had to accept a political job at the Salem customhouse. He lost this position when the opposing party won the next election and turned Hawthorne's friends out of office. For a year, he was able to devote himself single-mindedly to writing, and in 1850 he published his masterwork, *The Scarlet Letter*. In this story of sin and guilt among the earliest Puritans, he probed the dark side of human nature more deeply than any American before him. He was immediately recognized as a major writer. He soon produced two more novels, *The House of the Seven Gables* (1851) and *The Blithedale Romance* (1852). He also completed a fourth collection of short stories and two books for children.

Despite his new fame, Hawthorne could not make a good living at writing. In 1853 President Franklin Pierce relieved his old college friend of financial worries by appointing him the American consul at Liverpool, England. After four years in this post, Hawthorne was again displaced by a change of political administrations. Before returning home to Concord, he lived for a year in Italy. From this visit came his last published novel, *The Marble Faun* (1860). In his last years of life, he was often depressed by the mounting horrors of the Civil War, by nagging financial worries, and by fears that his talent was failing. In May of 1864, he went on a walking tour in New Hampshire to restore his health, and died in his sleep.

The day after he attended Hawthorne's funeral,

Title page of *Tanglewood Tales*.
The Bettmann Archive

Emerson wrote in his *Journals* of "the painful solitude of the man, which, I suppose, could no longer be endured and he died of it." Emerson was not speaking of Hawthorne's outward life, which was shared with family and friends, but of the deep sense of isolation Hawthorne revealed in his writings. Emerson confessed that he felt little sympathy for those dark tales, which are a profound criticism of transcendentalist optimism. As Hawthorne said of himself, he was a writer "burrowing . . . into the depths of our common nature." What he found there was an inner world in which every human being is alone "in that saddest of all prisons, his own heart. . . ." The mysteries of the human heart and the question of human evil are the true subjects of Hawthorne's art.

Dr. Heidegger's Experiment

That very singular man, old Dr. Heidegger, once invited four venerable friends to meet him in his study. There were three white-bearded gentlemen, Mr. Medbourne, Colonel Killigrew, and Mr. Gascoigne, and a withered gentlewoman, whose name was the Widow Wycherly. They were all melancholy old creatures, who had been unfortunate in life, and whose greatest misfortune it was that they were not long ago in their graves. Mr. Medbourne, in the vigor of his age, had been a prosperous merchant, but had lost his all by a frantic speculation and was now little better than a mendicant. Colonel Killigrew had wasted his best years, and his health and substance, in the pursuit of sinful pleasures, which had given birth to a brood of pains, such as the gout and divers other torments of soul and body. Mr. Gascoigne was a ruined politician, a man of evil fame, or at least had been so till time had buried him from the knowledge of the present generation and made him obscure instead of infamous. As for the Widow Wycherly, tradition tells us that she was a great beauty in her day; but, for a long while past, she had lived in deep seclusion, on account of certain scandalous stories which had prejudiced the gentry of the town against her. It is a circumstance worth mentioning that each of these three old gentlemen, Mr. Medbourne, Colonel Killigrew, and Mr. Gascoigne, were early lovers of the Widow Wycherly, and had once been on the point of cutting each other's throats for her sake. And, before proceeding further, I will merely hint that Dr. Heidegger and all his four guests were sometimes thought to be a little beside themselves—as is not unfrequently the case with old people, when worried either by present troubles or woeful recollections.

"My dear old friends," said Dr. Heidegger, motioning them to be seated, "I am desirous of your assistance in one of those little experiments with which I amuse myself here in my study."

If all stories were true, Dr. Heidegger's study must have been a very curious place. It was a dim, old-fashioned chamber, festooned with cobwebs and besprinkled with antique dust. Around the walls stood several oaken bookcases, the lower shelves of which were filled with rows of gigantic folios[1] and black-letter quartos,[2] and the upper with little parchment-covered duodecimos.[3] Over the central bookcase was a bronze bust of Hippocrates,[4] with which, according to some authorities, Dr. Heidegger was accustomed to hold consultations in all difficult cases of his practice. In the obscurest corner of the room stood a tall and narrow oaken closet, with its door ajar, within which doubtfully appeared a skeleton. Between two of the bookcases hung a looking glass, presenting its high and dusty plate within a tarnished gilt frame. Among many wonderful stories related of this mirror, it was fabled that the spirit of all the doctor's deceased patients dwelt within its verge and would stare him in the face whenever he looked thitherward. The opposite side of the chamber was ornamented with the full-length portrait of a young lady, arrayed in the faded magnificence of silk, satin, and brocade, and with a visage as faded as her dress. Above half a century ago, Dr. Heidegger had been on the point of marriage with this young lady; but being affected with some slight disorder, she had swallowed one of her lover's prescriptions and died on the bridal evening. The greatest curiosity of the study remains to be mentioned;

1. **folios:** books from twelve to twenty inches in height.
2. **quartos:** books about nine and one-half by twelve and one-half inches.
3. **duodecimos** (dōō'ō-dĕs'ə-mōz'): small volumes, about five by eight inches.
4. **Hippocrates** (hĭ-pŏk'rə-tēz'): a Greek physician (460?–370? B.C.).

it was a ponderous folio volume, bound in black leather, with massive silver clasps. There were no letters on the back, and nobody could tell the title of the book. But it was well known to be a book of magic; and once, when a chambermaid had lifted it, merely to brush away the dust, the skeleton had rattled in its closet, the picture of the young lady had stepped one foot upon the floor, and several ghastly faces had peeped forth from the mirror; while the brazen head of Hippocrates frowned and said, "Forbear!"

Such was Dr. Heidegger's study. On the summer afternoon of our tale, a small round table, as black as ebony, stood in the center of the room, sustaining a cut-glass vase of beautiful form and elaborate workmanship. The sunshine came through the window, between the heavy festoons of two faded damask curtains, and fell directly across this vase; so that a mild splendor was reflected from it on the ashen visages of the five old people who sat around. Four champagne glasses were also on the table.

"My dear old friends," repeated Dr. Heidegger, "may I reckon on your aid in performing an exceedingly curious experiment?"

Now Dr. Heidegger was a very strange old gentleman, whose eccentricity had become the nucleus for a thousand fantastic stories. Some of these fables, to my shame be it spoken, might possibly be traced back to my own veracious self; and if any passages of the present tale should startle the reader's faith, I must be content to bear the stigma of a fiction monger.

When the doctor's four guests heard him talk of his proposed experiment, they anticipated nothing more wonderful than the murder of a mouse in an air pump, or the examination of a cobweb by the microscope, or some similar nonsense, with which he was constantly in the habit of pestering his intimates. But without waiting for a reply, Dr. Heidegger hobbled across the chamber and returned with the same ponderous folio, bound in black leather, which common report affirmed to be a book of magic. Undoing the silver clasps, he

opened the volume and took from among its black-letter pages a rose, or what was once a rose, though now the green leaves and crimson petals had assumed one brownish hue, and the ancient flower seemed ready to crumble to dust in the doctor's hands.

"This rose," said Dr. Heidegger, with a sigh, "this same withered and crumbling flower, blossomed five and fifty years ago. It was given me by Sylvia Ward, whose portrait hangs yonder; and I meant to wear it in my bosom at our wedding. Five and fifty years it has been treasured between the leaves of this old volume. Now, would you deem it possible that this rose of half a century could ever bloom again?"

"Nonsense!" said the Widow Wycherly, with a peevish toss of her head. "You might as well ask whether an old woman's wrinkled face could ever bloom again."

"See!" answered Dr. Heidegger.

He uncovered the vase and threw the rose into the water which it contained. At first, it lay lightly on the surface of the fluid, appearing to imbibe none of its moisture. Soon, however, a singular change began to be visible. The crushed and dried petals stirred and assumed a deepening tinge of crimson, as if the flower were reviving from a deathlike slumber; the slender stalk and twigs of foliage became green; and there was the rose of half a century, looking as fresh as when Sylvia Ward had first given it to her lover. It was scarcely full blown; for some of its delicate red leaves curled modestly around its moist bosom, within which two or three dewdrops were sparkling.

"That is certainly a very pretty deception," said the doctor's friends; carelessly, however, for they had witnessed greater miracles at a conjurer's show; "pray how was it effected?"

"Did you never hear of the 'Fountain of Youth'?" asked Dr. Heidegger, "which Ponce de Leon,[5] the Spanish adventurer, went in search of two or three centuries ago?"

5. **Ponce de Leon:** explorer who discovered Florida (1460?–1521).

"But did Ponce de Leon ever find it?" said the Widow Wycherly.

"No," answered Dr. Heidegger, "for he never sought it in the right place. The famous Fountain of Youth, if I am rightly informed, is situated in the southern part of the Floridian peninsula, not far from Lake Macaco. Its source is overshadowed by several gigantic magnolias, which, though numberless centuries old, have been kept as fresh as violets by the virtues of this wonderful water. An acquaintance of mine, knowing my curiosity in such matters, has sent me what you see in the vase."

"Ahem!" said Colonel Killigrew, who believed not a word of the doctor's story; "and what may be the effect of this fluid on the human frame?"

"You shall judge for yourself, my dear colonel," replied Dr. Heidegger; "and all of you, my respected friends, are welcome to so much of this admirable fluid as may restore to you the bloom of youth. For my own part, having had much trouble in growing old, I am in no hurry to grow young again. With your permission, therefore, I will merely watch the progress of the experiment."

While he spoke, Dr. Heidegger had been filling the four champagne glasses with the water of the Fountain of Youth. It was apparently impregnated with an effervescent gas, for little bubbles were continually ascending from the depths of the glasses and bursting in silvery spray at the surface. As the liquor diffused a pleasant perfume, the old people doubted not that it possessed cordial and comfortable properties; and though utter skeptics as to its rejuvenescent power, they were inclined to swallow it at once. But Dr. Heidegger besought them to stay a moment.

"Before you drink, my respectable old friends," said he, "it would be well that, with the experience of a lifetime to direct you, you should draw up a few general rules for your guidance, in passing a second time through the perils of youth. Think what a sin and shame it would be if, with your peculiar ad-

vantages, you should not become patterns of virtue and wisdom to all the young people of the age!"

The doctor's four venerable friends made him no answer, except by a feeble and tremulous laugh; so very ridiculous was the idea that, knowing how closely repentance treads behind the steps of error, they should ever go astray again.

"Drink, then," said the doctor, bowing. "I rejoice that I have so well selected the subjects of my experiment."

With palsied hands, they raised the glasses to their lips. The liquor, if it really possessed such virtues as Dr. Heidegger imputed to it, could not have been bestowed on four human beings who needed it more woefully. They looked as if they had never known what youth or pleasure was, but had been the offspring of Nature's dotage, and always the gray, decrepit, sapless, miserable creatures who now sat stooping round the doctor's table, without life enough in their souls or bodies to be animated even by the prospect of growing young again. They drank off the water and replaced their glasses on the table.

Assuredly there was an almost immediate improvement in the aspect of the party, not unlike what might have been produced by a glass of generous wine, together with a sudden glow of cheerful sunshine brightening over all their visages at once. There was a healthful suffusion on their cheeks, instead of the ashen hue that had made them look so corpselike. They gazed at one another and fancied that some magic power had really begun to smooth away the deep and sad inscriptions which Father Time had been so long engraving on their brows. The Widow Wycherly adjusted her cap, for she felt almost like a woman again.

"Give us more of this wondrous water!" cried they, eagerly. "We are younger—but we are still too old! Quick—give us more!"

"Patience, patience!" quoth Dr. Heidegger, who sat watching the experiment with philosophic coolness. "You have been a long time growing old. Surely, you might be content to grow young in half an hour! But the water is at your service."

Again he filled their glasses with the liquor of youth, enough of which still remained in the vase to turn half the old people in the city to the age of their own grandchildren. While the bubbles were yet sparkling on the brim, the doctor's four guests snatched their glasses from the table and swallowed the contents at a single gulp. Was it delusion? Even while the draft was passing down their throats, it seemed to have wrought a change on their whole systems. Their eyes grew clear and bright; a dark shade deepened among their silvery locks, they sat around the table, three gentlemen of middle age, and a woman hardly beyond her buxom prime.

"My dear widow, you are charming!" cried Colonel Killigrew, whose eyes had been fixed upon her face, while the shadows of age were flitting from it like darkness from the crimson daybreak.

The fair widow knew, of old, that Colonel Killigrew's compliments were not always measured by sober truth; so she started up and ran to the mirror, still dreading that the ugly visage of an old woman would meet her gaze. Meanwhile, the three gentlemen behaved in such a manner as proved that the water of the Fountain of Youth possessed some intoxicating qualities; unless, indeed, their exhilaration of spirits were merely a lightsome dizziness caused by the sudden removal of the weight of years. Mr. Gascoigne's mind seemed to run on political topics, but whether relating to the past, present, or future could not easily be determined, since the same ideas and phrases have been in vogue these fifty years. Now he rattled forth full-throated sentences about patriotism, national glory, and the people's right; now he muttered some perilous stuff or other, in a sly and doubtful whisper, so cautiously that even his own conscience could scarcely catch the secret; and now, again, he spoke in measured accents and a deeply deferential tone, as if a royal ear were listening to his well-turned periods. Colonel Killigrew all this time

had been trolling forth a jolly bottle song and ringing his glass in symphony with the chorus, while his eyes wandered toward the buxom figure of the Widow Wycherly. On the other side of the table, Mr. Medbourne was involved in a calculation of dollars and cents, with which was strangely intermingled a project for supplying the East Indies with ice, by harnessing a team of whales to the polar icebergs.

As for the Widow Wycherly, she stood before the mirror curtsying and simpering to her own image and greeting it as the friend whom she loved better than all the world beside. She thrust her face close to the glass, to see whether some long-remembered wrinkle or crow's-foot had indeed vanished. She examined whether the snow had so entirely melted from her hair that the venerable cap could be safely thrown aside. At last, turning briskly away, she came with a sort of dancing step to the table.

"My dear old doctor," cried she, "pray favor me with another glass!"

"Certainly, my dear madam, certainly!" replied the complaisant doctor; "See! I have already filled the glasses."

There, in fact, stood the four glasses, brimful of this wonderful water, the delicate spray of which, as it effervesced from the surface, resembled the tremulous glitter of diamonds. It was now so nearly sunset that the chamber had grown duskier than ever; but a mild and moonlike splendor gleamed from within the vase, and rested alike on the four guests and on the doctor's venerable figure. He sat in a high-backed, elaborately carved oaken armchair, with a gray dignity of aspect that might have well befitted that very Father Time whose power had never been disputed save by this fortunate company. Even while quaffing the third draft of the Fountain of Youth, they were almost awed by the expression of his mysterious visage.

But the next moment, the exhilarating gush of young life shot through their veins. They were now in the happy prime of youth. Age, with its miserable train of cares and sorrows and diseases, was remembered only as the troubles of a dream, from which they had joyously awakened. The fresh gloss of the soul, so early lost, and without which the world's successive scenes had been but a gallery of faded pictures, again threw its enchantment over all their prospects. They felt like new-created beings in a new-created universe.

"We are young! We are young!" they cried exultingly.

Youth, like the extremity of age, had effaced the strongly marked characteristics of middle life and mutually assimilated them all. They were a group of merry youngsters, almost maddened with the exuberant frolicsomeness of their years. The most singular effect of their gaiety was an impulse to mock the infirmity and decrepitude of which they had so lately been the victims. They laughed loudly at their old-fashioned attire, the wide-skirted coats and flapped waistcoats of the young men, and the ancient cap and gown of the blooming girl. One limped across the floor like a gouty grandfather; one set a pair of spectacles astride of his nose and pretended to pore over the black-letter pages of the book of magic; a third seated himself in an armchair and strove to imitate the venerable dignity of Dr. Heidegger. Then all shouted mirthfully and leaped about the room. The Widow Wycherly—if so fresh a damsel could be called a widow—tripped up to the doctor's chair, with a mischievous merriment in her rosy face.

"Doctor, you dear old soul," cried she, "get up and dance with me!" And then the four young people laughed louder than ever, to think what a queer figure the poor old doctor would cut.

"Pray excuse me," answered the doctor quietly. "I am old and rheumatic, and my dancing days were over long ago. But either of these gay young gentlemen will be glad of so pretty a partner."

"Dance with me, Clara!" cried Colonel Killigrew.

"No, no, I will be her partner!" shouted Mr. Gascoigne.

"She promised me her hand, fifty years ago!" exclaimed Mr. Medbourne.

They all gathered round her. One caught both her hands in his passionate grasp—another threw his arm about her waist—the third buried his hand among the glossy curls that clustered beneath the widow's cap. Blushing, panting, struggling, chiding, laughing, her warm breath fanning each of their faces by turns, she strove to disengage herself, yet still remained in their triple embrace. Never was there a livelier picture of youthful rivalship, with bewitching beauty for the prize. Yet, by a strange deception, owing to the duskiness of the chamber and the antique dresses which they still wore, the tall mirror is said to have reflected the figures of the three old, gray, withered grandsires ridiculously contending for the skinny ugliness of a shriveled grandam.

But they were young: their burning passions proved them so. Inflamed to madness by the coquetry of the girl-widow, who neither granted nor quite withheld her favors, the three rivals began to interchange threatening glances. Still keeping hold of the fair prize, they grappled fiercely at one another's throats. As they struggled to and fro, the table was overturned, and the vase dashed into a thousand fragments. The precious Water of Youth flowed in a bright stream across the floor, moistening the wings of a butterfly, which, grown old in the decline of summer, had alighted there to die. The insect fluttered lightly through the chamber and settled on the snowy head of Dr. Heidegger.

"Come, come, gentlemen!—come, Madam Wycherly," exclaimed the doctor, "I really must protest against this riot."

They stood still and shivered; for it seemed as if gray Time were calling them back from their sunny youth, far down into the chill and darksome vale of years. They looked at old Dr. Heidegger, who sat in his carved armchair, holding the rose of half a century, which he had rescued from among the fragments of the shattered vase. At the motion of his hand, the four rioters resumed their seats; the more readily because their violent exertions had wearied them, youthful though they were.

"My poor Sylvia's rose!" ejaculated Dr. Heidegger, holding it in the light of the sunset clouds; "it appears to be fading again."

And so it was. Even while the party were looking at it, the flower continued to shrivel up, till it became as dry and fragile as when the doctor had first thrown it into the vase. He shook off the few drops of moisture which clung to its petals.

"I love it as well thus as in its dewy freshness," observed he, pressing the withered rose to his withered lips. While he spoke, the butterfly fluttered down from the doctor's snowy head and fell upon the floor.

His guests shivered again. A strange chillness, whether of the body or spirit they could not tell, was creeping gradually over them all. They gazed at one another, and fancied that each fleeting moment snatched away a charm, and left a deepening furrow where none had been before. Was it an illusion? Had the changes of a lifetime been crowded into so brief a space, and were they now four aged people, sitting with their old friend Dr. Heidegger?

"Are we grown old again, so soon?" cried they, dolefully.

In truth they had. The Water of Youth possessed merely a virtue more transient than that of wine. The delirium which it created had effervesced away. Yes! they were old again. With a shuddering impulse that showed her a woman still, the widow clasped her skinny hands before her face and wished that the coffin lid were over it, since it could be no longer beautiful.

"Yes, friends, ye are old again," said Dr. Heidegger, "and lo! the Water of Youth is all lavished on the ground. Well—I bemoan it not; for if the fountain gushed at my very doorstep, I would not stoop to bathe my lips in it—no, though its delirium were for years instead of moments. Such is the lesson ye have taught me!"

But the doctor's four friends had taught no such lesson to themselves. They resolved forth-with to make a pilgrimage to Florida, and quaff at morning, noon, and night, from the Fountain of Youth.

Reading Check

1. Whose portrait does Dr. Heidegger keep in his study?
2. What does Dr. Heidegger claim is contained in the cut-glass vase?
3. How is a rose used in Dr. Heidegger's experiment?
4. What rivalry that existed in youth is renewed after Dr. Heidegger's guests drink from the contents of the vase?
5. Why does Dr. Heidegger decline to drink any of the fluid in the vase?

For Study and Discussion

Analyzing and Interpreting the Story

1. Each of Dr. Heidegger's four guests represents the waste of something that people prize: fortune, health, power, beauty. What is Dr. Heidegger testing by giving each of these people a second chance?

2. The third paragraph describes the doctor's dusty, old-fashioned study. Among its many oddities is a tall mirror, in which it is said the doctor sees the images of his deceased patients. The mirror serves as a combined reminder of death and of the limits of his healing powers. **a.** In what way is the portrait of the young lady also a reminder of death and human limitations? **b.** What other details of the setting indicate the "experiment" will involve the supernatural?

3. Dr. Heidegger cautions his four friends about "passing a second time through the perils of youth." **a.** What is their reaction to his advice? **b.** In light of what happens, do you think their reaction is wise or foolish?

4. Despite their impatience, the old people return to youth only gradually. **a.** Which of their thoughts and actions while "growing young" indicate that they have not learned anything from their former failures? **b.** Although they act as if they were "merry youngsters," why do they remain "withered" and "shriveled" in the mirror's reflection?

5. While grappling at each other's throats for the favor of the flirtatious widow, the three men break the vase that holds the precious water. How do their actions in this scene compare with the way they spent their "first" youth?

6. At the end of the story, the four subjects are determined to seek the Fountain of Youth. What lesson has Dr. Heidegger learned from the experiment?

Literary Elements

Allegory and Symbolism

"Dr. Heidegger's Experiment" has been described as an **allegory.** An allegory is a tale in which characters or objects stand for certain abstract qualities, such as Hope, Faith, Shame, Vice. The most famous allegory in English is John Bunyan's *The Pilgrim's Progress* (1678). Here a man named Christian journeys to the Celestial City, meeting along the way characters named Hope, Worldly Wiseman, Despair, and others who are personifications of human qualities. In allegories, the complexities of human character are usually less important than the abstract qualities that the characters represent.

In "Dr. Heidegger's Experiment," the characters do not have allegorical names. For instance, Mr. Medbourne is not called "Greed." Yet his whole character seems to be summed up in the sentence that introduces him. "Mr. Medbourne, in the vigor of his age, had been a prosperous merchant, but had lost his all by a frantic speculation and was now little better than a mendicant." When he is restored to youth, he immediately resumes these old pursuits, becoming "involved in a calculation of dollars and cents." It appears that greed is the whole of his character. Each of the characters represents a particular aspect of human nature to the exclusion of other aspects.

Allegory is related to **symbolism.** Whereas an allegory stresses the abstract meaning, a symbol contains an actual *and* an abstract meaning. A common example of a symbol is a flag. It is literally a piece of cloth, but as the flag of a country, it is also associated with political and historical events, loyalty, patriotism, and many other public and private feelings. Every culture has its symbols. Literature draws upon these symbols but also creates others. Thoreau, for instance, made the act of building his house at Walden Pond a symbol of structuring his life, and he found in the seasons of the year a symbol for the stages of human existence.

Hawthorne's story uses certain objects as symbols. For example, a mirror is, in literal terms, an object in which we can see our own reflection. But, as Dr. Heidegger also sees in his own mirror the images of his deceased patients, the mirror symbolizes his past failures, those patients he could not save. This symbol is a key to the character of Heidegger, who is so aware of human limitations that he would not be young again even if he could be.

1. Examine the characters of Colonel Killigrew, Mr. Gascoigne, and the Widow Wycherly. What different allegorical meaning does each of them have?

2. Choose from Dr. Heidegger's study some object other than the mirror and describe how it functions as a symbol.

Language and Vocabulary

Explaining Words in Context

Explain the meaning of each of the following excerpts from the story, and show how each one adds to the story's supernatural aspect. Be sure you know the meaning of the italicized words.

1. . . . time had . . . made him *obscure* instead of *infamous.* (Mr. Gascoigne)

2. . . . a very strange old gentleman, whose *eccentricity* had become the *nucleus* for a thousand fantastic stories. (Dr. Heidegger)

3. . . . its *rejuvenescent* power . . . (the water)

4. . . . gray, *decrepit, sapless,* miserable creatures . . . (the four guests)

Writing About Literature

Responding to an Interpretation

Defend or attack the following statement: "Dr. Heidegger's Experiment" illustrates a passage from Ecclesiastes— "Vanity of vanities . . . vanity of vanities; all is vanity." Before you write, consider all possible meanings of the words *vanity* and *vain.* For example, a person can be called "vain," or it can be said that someone lived "in vain."

The Minister's Black Veil

A Parable

Hawthorne wrote the following footnote to the title of this story: "Another clergyman in New England, Mr. Joseph Moody, of York, Maine, who died about eighty years since, made himself remarkable by the same eccentricity that is here related to the Reverend Mr. Hooper. In his case, however, the symbol had a different import. In early life he had accidentally killed a beloved friend; and from that day till the hour of his own death, he hid his face from men."

The sexton stood in the porch of Milford meetinghouse, pulling busily at the bell rope. The old people of the village came stooping along the street. Children with bright faces tripped merrily beside their parents, or mimicked a graver gait, in the conscious dignity of their Sunday clothes. Spruce bachelors looked sidelong at the pretty maidens and fancied that the Sabbath sunshine made them prettier than on weekdays. When the throng had mostly streamed into the porch, the sexton began to toll the bell, keeping his eye on the Reverend Mr. Hooper's door. The first glimpse of the clergyman's figure was the signal for the bell to cease its summons.

"But what has good Parson Hooper got upon his face?" cried the sexton in astonishment.

All within hearing immediately turned about and beheld the semblance of Mr. Hooper, pacing slowly his meditative way towards the meetinghouse. With one accord they started, expressing more wonder than if some strange minister were coming to dust the cushions of Mr. Hooper's pulpit.

"Are you sure it is our parson?" inquired Goodman[1] Gray of the sexton.

"Of a certainty it is good Mr. Hooper," replied the sexton. "He was to have exchanged pulpits with Parson Shute, of Westbury; but Parson Shute sent to excuse himself yesterday, being to preach a funeral sermon."

1. **Goodman:** a title of address similar to "Mr."

The cause of so much amazement may appear sufficiently slight. Mr. Hooper, a gentlemanly person of about thirty, though still a bachelor, was dressed with due clerical neatness, as if a careful wife had starched his band and brushed the weekly dust from his Sunday's garb. There was but one thing remarkable in his appearance. Swathed about his forehead, and hanging down over his face, so low as to be shaken by his breath, Mr. Hooper had on a black veil. On a nearer view it seemed to consist of two folds of crepe, which entirely concealed his features, except the mouth and chin, but probably did not intercept his sight, further than to give a darkened aspect to all living and inanimate things. With this gloomy shade before him, good Mr. Hooper walked onward at a slow and quiet pace, stooping somewhat, and looking on the ground, as is customary with abstracted men, yet nodding kindly to those of his parishioners who still waited on the meetinghouse steps. But so wonder-struck were they that his greeting hardly met with a return.

"I can't really feel as if good Mr. Hooper's face was behind that piece of crepe," said the sexton.

"I don't like it," muttered an old woman, as she hobbled into the meetinghouse. "He has changed himself into something awful, only by hiding his face."

"Our parson has gone mad!" cried Goodman Gray, following him across the threshold.

A rumor of some unaccountable phenomenon had preceded Mr. Hooper into the meetinghouse and set all the congregation astir. Few could refrain from twisting their heads towards the door; many stood upright and turned directly about; while several little boys clambered upon the seats and came down again with a terrible racket. There was a general bustle, a rustling of the women's gowns and shuffling of the men's feet, greatly at variance with that hushed repose which should attend the entrance of the minister. But Mr. Hooper appeared not to notice the perturbation of his people. He entered with an almost noiseless step, bent his head mildly to the pews on each side, and bowed as he passed his oldest parishioner, a white-haired great-grandsire, who occupied an armchair in the center of the aisle. It was strange to observe how slowly this venerable man became conscious of something singular in the appearance of his pastor. He seemed not fully to partake of the prevailing wonder, till Mr. Hooper had ascended the stairs and showed himself in the pulpit, face to face with his congregation, except for the black veil. That mysterious emblem was never once withdrawn. It shook with his measured breath, as he gave out the psalm; it threw its obscurity between him and the holy page, as he read the Scriptures; and while he prayed, the veil lay heavily on his uplifted countenance. Did he seek to hide it from the dread Being whom he was addressing?

Such was the effect of this simple piece of crepe, that more than one woman of delicate nerves was forced to leave the meetinghouse. Yet perhaps the pale-faced congregation was almost as fearful a sight to the minister as his black veil to them.

Mr. Hooper had the reputation of a good preacher, but not an energetic one: he strove to win his people heavenward by mild, persuasive influences, rather than to drive them thither by the thunders of the Word. The sermon which he now delivered was marked by the same characteristics of style and manner as the general series of his pulpit oratory. But there was something, either in the sentiment

Second Church (dedicated 1806), Dorchester, Massachusetts. Engraving (c. 1889).
The Bettmann Archive

of the discourse itself, or in the imagination of the auditors, which made it greatly the most powerful effort that they had ever heard from their pastor's lips. It was tinged, rather more darkly than usual, with the gentle gloom of Mr. Hooper's temperament. The subject had reference to secret sin, and those sad mysteries which we hide from our nearest and dearest, and would fain conceal from our own consciousness, even forgetting that the Omniscient[2] can detect them. A subtle power was breathed into his words. Each member of the congregation, the most innocent girl, and the man of hardened breast, felt as if the preacher had crept upon them, behind his awful veil, and discovered their hoarded iniquity of deed or thought. Many spread their clasped hands

2. **the Omniscient:** God, in his all-knowing aspect.

on their bosoms. There was nothing terrible in what Mr. Hooper said, at least, no violence; and yet, with every tremor of his melancholy voice, the hearers quaked. An unsought pathos came hand in hand with awe. So sensible were the audience of some unwonted attribute in their minister that they longed for a breath of wind to blow aside the veil, almost believing that a stranger's visage would be discovered, though the form, gesture, and voice were those of Mr. Hooper.

At the close of the services, the people hurried out with indecorous confusion, eager to communicate their pent-up amazement, and conscious of lighter spirits the moment they lost sight of the black veil. Some gathered in little circles, huddled closely together, with their mouths all whispering in the center; some went homeward alone, wrapt in silent meditation; some talked loudly and profaned the Sabbath day with ostentatious laughter. A few shook their sagacious heads, intimating that they could penetrate the mystery; while one or two affirmed that there was no mystery at all, but only that Mr. Hooper's eyes were so weakened by the midnight lamp as to require a shade. After a brief interval, forth came good Mr. Hooper also, in the rear of his flock. Turning his veiled face from one group to another, he paid due reverence to the hoary heads, saluted the middle-aged with kind dignity as their friend and spiritual guide, greeted the young with mingled authority and love, and laid his hands on the little children's heads to bless them. Such was always his custom on the Sabbath day. Strange and bewildered looks repaid him for his courtesy. None, as on former occasions, aspired to the honor of walking by their pastor's side. Old Squire Saunders, doubtless by an accidental lapse of memory, neglected to invite Mr. Hooper to his table, where the good clergyman had been wont to bless the food almost every Sunday since his settlement. He returned, therefore, to the parsonage, and, at the moment of closing the door, was observed to look back upon the people, all of whom had their eyes fixed upon the minister. A sad smile gleamed faintly from beneath the black veil and flickered about his mouth, glimmering as he disappeared.

"How strange," said a lady, "that a simple black veil such as any woman might wear on her bonnet should become such a terrible thing on Mr. Hooper's face!"

"Something must surely be amiss with Mr. Hooper's intellects," observed her husband, the physician of the village. "But the strangest part of the affair is the effect of this vagary, even on a sober-minded man like myself. The black veil, though it covers only our pastor's face, throws its influence over his whole person and makes him ghostlike from head to foot. Do you not feel it so?"

"Truly do I," replied the lady; "and I would not be alone with him for the world. I wonder he is not afraid to be alone with himself!"

"Men sometimes are so," said her husband.

The afternoon service was attended with similar circumstances. At its conclusion, the bell tolled for the funeral of a young lady. The relatives and friends were assembled in the house, and the more distant acquaintances stood about the door, speaking of the good qualities of the deceased, when their talk was interrupted by the appearance of Mr. Hooper, still covered with his black veil. It was now an appropriate emblem. The clergyman stepped into the room where the corpse was laid and bent over the coffin, to take a last farewell of his deceased parishioner. As he stooped, the veil hung straight down from his forehead, so that, if her eyelids had not been closed forever, the dead maiden might have seen his face. Could Mr. Hooper be fearful of her glance, that he so hastily caught back the black veil? A person who watched the interview between the dead and living scrupled not to affirm that, at the instant when the clergyman's features were disclosed, the corpse had slightly shuddered, rustling the shroud and muslin cap, though the countenance retained the composure of death. A superstitious old woman was the only witness of this prodigy. From the coffin Mr. Hooper passed into the chamber of the mourners, and thence to the head of the staircase, to make the funeral prayer. It was a tender and heart-dissolving prayer, full of sorrow, yet so imbued with celestial hopes that the music of a heavenly harp, swept by the fingers of the dead, seemed faintly to be heard among the saddest accents of the minister. The people trembled, though they but darkly understood him when he prayed that they, and himself, and all of mortal race, might be ready, as he trusted this young maiden had been, for the dreadful hour that should snatch the veil from their faces. The bearers went heavily forth, and the mourners followed, saddening all the street, with the dead before them, and Mr. Hooper in his black veil behind.

"Why do you look back?" said one in the procession to his partner.

"I had a fancy," replied she, "that the minister and the maiden's spirit were walking hand in hand."

"And so had I, at the same moment," said the other.

That night, the handsomest couple in Milford village were to be joined in wedlock. Though reckoned a melancholy man, Mr. Hooper had a placid cheerfulness for such occasions, which often excited a sympathetic smile where livelier merriment would have been thrown away. There was no quality of his disposition which made him more beloved than this. The company at the wedding awaited his arrival with impatience, trusting that the strange awe, which had gathered over him throughout the day, would now be dispelled. But such was not the result. When Mr. Hooper came, the first thing that their eyes rested on was the same horrible black veil, which had added deeper gloom to the funeral, and could portend nothing but evil to the wedding. Such was its immediate effect on the guests that a cloud seemed to have rolled duskily from beneath the black crepe and dimmed the light of the candles. The bridal pair stood up before the minister. But the bride's cold fingers quivered in the tremulous hand of the bridegroom, and her deathlike paleness caused a whisper that the maiden who had been buried a few hours before was come from her grave to be married. If ever another wedding were so dismal, it was that famous one where they tolled the wedding knell.[3] After performing the ceremony, Mr. Hooper raised a glass of wine to his lips, wishing happiness to the new-married couple in a strain of mild pleasantry that ought to have brightened the features of the guests, like a cheerful gleam from the hearth. At that instant, catching a glimpse of his figure in the looking glass, the black veil involved his own spirit in the horror with which it overwhelmed all others. His frame shuddered, his lips grew white, he spilt the untasted wine upon the carpet, and rushed forth into the darkness. For the Earth, too, had on her Black Veil.

The next day, the whole village of Milford talked of little else than Parson Hooper's black veil. That, and the mystery concealed behind it, supplied a topic for discussion between acquaintances meeting in the street and good women gossiping at their open windows. It was the first item of news that the tavernkeeper told to his guests. The children babbled of it on their way to school. One imitative little imp covered his face with an old black handkerchief, thereby so affrighting his playmates that the panic seized himself, and he well-nigh lost his wits by his own waggery.[4]

It was remarkable that of all the busybodies and impertinent people in the parish, not one ventured to put the plain question to Mr. Hooper, wherefore he did this thing. Hitherto, whenever there appeared the slightest call for such interference, he had never lacked advisers, nor shown himself averse to be guided by their judgment. If he erred at all, it was by so painful a degree of self-distrust that even the mildest censure would lead him to consider an indifferent action as a crime. Yet, though so well acquainted with this amiable weakness, no individual among his parishioners chose to

3. **If . . . knell:** a reference to Hawthorne's story "The Wedding Knell."
4. **waggery:** mischievousness.

make the black veil a subject of friendly remonstrance. There was a feeling of dread, neither plainly confessed nor carefully concealed, which caused each to shift the responsibility upon another, till at length it was found expedient to send a deputation of the church, in order to deal with Mr. Hooper about the mystery before it should grow into a scandal. Never did an embassy so ill discharge its duties. The minister received them with friendly courtesy but became silent after they were seated, leaving to his visitors the whole burden of introducing their important business. The topic, it might be supposed, was obvious enough. There was the black veil swathed round Mr. Hooper's forehead, and concealing every feature above his placid mouth, on which, at times, they could perceive the glimmering of a melancholy smile. But that piece of crepe, to their imagination, seemed to hang down before his heart, the symbol of a fearful secret between him and them. Were the veil but cast aside, they might speak freely of it, but not till then. Thus they sat a considerable time, speechless, confused, and shrinking uneasily from Mr. Hooper's eye, which they felt to be fixed upon them with an invisible glance. Finally, the deputies returned abashed to their constituents, pronouncing the matter too weighty to be handled, except by a council of the churches, if, indeed, it might not require a general synod.[5]

But there was one person in the village unappalled by the awe with which the black veil had impressed all beside herself. When the deputies returned without an explanation, or even venturing to demand one, she, with the calm energy of her character, determined to chase away the strange cloud that appeared to be settling round Mr. Hooper, every moment more darkly than before. As his plighted wife, it should be her privilege to know what the black veil concealed. At the minister's first visit, therefore, she entered upon the subject with a direct simplicity, which made the task easier both for him and her. After he had seated himself, she fixed her eyes steadfastly upon the veil, but could discern nothing of the dreadful gloom that had so overawed the multitude: it was but a double fold of crepe, hanging down from his forehead to his mouth, and slightly stirring with his breath.

"No," said she aloud, and smiling, "there is nothing terrible in this piece of crepe, except that it hides a face which I am always glad to look upon. Come, good sir, let the sun shine from behind the cloud. First lay aside your black veil: then tell me why you put it on."

Mr. Hooper's smile glimmered faintly.

"There is an hour to come," said he, "when all of us shall cast aside our veils. Take it not amiss, beloved friend, if I wear this piece of crepe till then."

"Your words are a mystery, too," returned the young lady. "Take away the veil from them, at least."

"Elizabeth, I will," said he, "so far as my vow may suffer me. Know, then, this veil is a type and a symbol, and I am bound to wear it ever, both in light and darkness, in solitude and before the gaze of multitudes, and as with strangers, so with my familiar friends. No mortal eye will see it withdrawn. This dismal shade must separate me from the world: even you, Elizabeth, can never come behind it!"

"What grievous affliction hath befallen you," she earnestly inquired, "that you should thus darken your eyes forever?"

"If it be a sign of mourning," replied Mr. Hooper, "I, perhaps, like most other mortals, have sorrows dark enough to be typified by a black veil."

"But what if the world will not believe that it is the type of an innocent sorrow?" urged Elizabeth. "Beloved and respected as you are, there may be whispers that you hide your face under the consciousness of secret sin. For the sake of your holy office, do away this scandal!"

The color rose into her cheeks as she intimated the nature of the rumors that were already abroad in the village. But Mr. Hooper's mildness did not forsake him. He even smiled

5. **synod:** an ecclesiastical council.

again—that same sad smile, which always appeared like a faint glimmering of light, proceeding from the obscurity beneath the veil.

"If I hide my face for sorrow, there is cause enough," he merely replied; "and if I cover it for secret sin, what mortal might not do the same?"

And with this gentle but unconquerable obstinacy did he resist all her entreaties. At length Elizabeth sat silent. For a few moments she appeared lost in thought, considering, probably, what new methods might be tried to withdraw her lover from so dark a fantasy, which, if it had no other meaning, was perhaps a symbol of mental disease. Though of a firmer character than his own, the tears rolled down her cheeks. But in an instant, as it were, a new feeling took the place of sorrow: her eyes were fixed insensibly on the black veil when, like a sudden twilight in the air, its terrors fell around her. She arose and stood trembling before him.

"And do you feel it then, at last?" said he mournfully.

She made no reply, but covered her eyes with her hand and turned to leave the room. He rushed forward and caught her arm.

"Have patience with me, Elizabeth!" cried he, passionately. "Do not desert me, though this veil must be between us here on earth. Be mine, and hereafter there shall be no veil over my face, no darkness between our souls! It is but a mortal veil—it is not for eternity! O! you know not how lonely I am, and how frightened, to be alone behind my black veil. Do not leave me in this miserable obscurity forever!"

"Lift the veil but once, and look me in the face," said she.

"Never! It cannot be!" replied Mr. Hooper.

"Then farewell!" said Elizabeth.

She withdrew her arm from his grasp and slowly departed, pausing at the door to give one long, shuddering gaze that seemed almost to penetrate the mystery of the black veil. But, even amid his grief, Mr. Hooper smiled to think that only a material emblem had separated him from happiness, though the horrors which it shadowed forth must be drawn darkly between the fondest of lovers.

From that time no attempts were made to remove Mr. Hooper's black veil or, by a direct appeal, to discover the secret which it was supposed to hide. By persons who claimed a superiority to popular prejudice, it was reckoned merely an eccentric whim, such as often mingles with the sober actions of men otherwise rational, and tinges them all with its own semblance of insanity. But with the multitude, good Mr. Hooper was irreparably a bugbear.[6] He could not walk the street with any peace of mind, so conscious was he that the gentle and timid would turn aside to avoid him, and that others would make it a point of hardihood to throw themselves in his way. The impertinence of the latter class compelled him to give up his customary walk at sunset to the burial ground; for when he leaned pensively over the gate, there would always be faces behind the gravestones, peeping at his black veil. A fable went the rounds that the stare of the dead people drove him thence. It grieved him, to the very depth of his kind heart, to observe how the children fled from his approach, breaking up their merriest sports, while his melancholy figure was yet afar off. Their instinctive dread caused him to feel more strongly than aught else that a preternatural horror was interwoven with the threads of the black crepe. In truth, his own antipathy to the veil was known to be so great that he never willingly passed before a mirror, nor stooped to drink at a still fountain, lest, in its peaceful bosom, he should be affrighted by himself. This was what gave plausibility to the whispers that Mr. Hooper's conscience tortured him for some great crime too horrible to be entirely concealed, or otherwise than so obscurely intimated. Thus, from beneath the black veil, there rolled a cloud into the sunshine, an ambiguity of sin or sorrow, which enveloped the poor minister, so that love or sympathy could never reach him. It was said that ghost and fiend consorted with him there.

6. **bugbear:** object of dread.

With self-shudderings and outward terrors, he walked continually in its shadow, groping darkly within his own soul or gazing through a medium that saddened the whole world. Even the lawless wind, it was believed, respected his dreadful secret and never blew aside the veil. But still good Mr. Hooper sadly smiled at the pale visages of the worldly throng as he passed by.

Among all its bad influences, the black veil had the one desirable effect of making its wearer a very efficient clergyman. By the aid of his mysterious emblem—for there was no other apparent cause—he became a man of awful power over souls that were in agony for sin. His converts always regarded him with a dread peculiar to themselves, affirming, though but figuratively, that before he brought them to celestial light they had been with him behind the black veil. Its gloom, indeed, enabled him to sympathize with all dark affections. Dying sinners cried aloud for Mr. Hooper, and would not yield their breath till he appeared; though ever, as he stooped to whisper consolation, they shuddered at the veiled face so near their own. Such were the terrors of the black veil, even when Death had bared his visage! Strangers came long distances to attend service at his church, with the mere idle purpose of gazing at his figure, because it was forbidden them to behold his face. But many were made to quake ere they departed! Once, during Governor Belcher's[7] administration, Mr. Hooper was appointed to preach the election sermon.[8] Covered with his black veil, he stood before the chief magistrate, the council, and the representatives, and wrought so deep an impression that the legislative measures of that year were characterized by all the gloom and piety of our earliest ancestral sway.

In this manner Mr. Hooper spent a long life, irreproachable in outward act, yet shrouded in dismal suspicions; kind and loving, though unloved and dimly feared; a man apart from men, shunned in their health and joy, but ever summoned to their aid in mortal anguish. As years wore on, shedding their snows above his sable veil, he acquired a name throughout the New England churches, and they called him Father Hooper. Nearly all his parishioners, who were of mature age when he was settled, had been borne away by many a funeral: he had one congregation in the church, and a more crowded one in the churchyard; and having wrought so late into the evening, and done his work so well, it was now good Father Hooper's turn to rest.

Several persons were visible by the shaded candlelight, in the death chamber of the old clergyman. Natural connections he had none. But there was the decorously grave, though unmoved physician, seeking only to mitigate the last pangs of the patient whom he could not save. There were the deacons, and other eminently pious members of his church. There, also, was the Reverend Mr. Clark, of Westbury, a young and zealous divine, who had ridden in haste to pray by the bedside of the expiring minister. There was the nurse, no hired handmaiden of death, but one whose calm affection had endured thus long in secrecy, in solitude, amid the chill of age, and would not perish, even at the dying hour. Who, but Elizabeth! And there lay the hoary head of good Father Hooper upon the death pillow, with the black veil still swathed about his brow, and reaching down over his face, so that each more difficult gasp of his faint breath caused it to stir. All through life that piece of crepe had hung between him and the world: it had separated him from cheerful brotherhood and woman's love, and kept him in that saddest of all prisons, his own heart; and still it lay upon his face, as if to deepen the gloom of his darksome chamber and shade him from the sunshine of eternity.

For some time previous, his mind had been confused, wavering doubtfully between the past and the present and hovering forward, as

---

7. **Governor Belcher:** Jonathan Belcher (1682–1757), royal governor of the Massachusetts Bay Colony, 1730–1741.

8. **election sermon:** It was a great honor for a minister to be chosen to make this formal address.

it were, at intervals, into the indistinctness of the world to come. There had been feverish turns, which tossed him from side to side, and wore away what little strength he had. But in his most convulsive struggles, and in the wildest vagaries of his intellect, when no other thought retained its sober influence, he still showed an awful solicitude lest the black veil should slip aside. Even if his bewildered soul could have forgotten, there was a faithful woman at his pillow, who, with averted eyes, would have covered that aged face, which she had last beheld in the comeliness of manhood. At length the death-stricken old man lay quietly in the torpor of mental and bodily exhaustion, with an imperceptible pulse, and breath that grew fainter and fainter, except when a long, deep, and irregular inspiration seemed to prelude the flight of his spirit.

The minister of Westbury approached the bedside.

"Venerable Father Hooper," said he, "the moment of your release is at hand. Are you ready for the lifting of the veil that shuts in time from eternity?"

Father Hooper at first replied merely by a feeble motion of his head; then, apprehensive, perhaps, that his meaning might be doubtful, he exerted himself to speak.

"Yea," said he, in faint accents, "my soul hath a patient weariness until that veil be lifted."

"And is it fitting," resumed the Reverend Mr. Clark, "that a man so given to prayer, of such a blameless example, holy in deed and thought, so far as mortal judgment may pronounce; is it fitting that a father in the church should leave a shadow on his memory that may seem to blacken a life so pure? I pray you, my venerable brother, let not this thing be! Suffer us to be gladdened by your triumphant aspect as you go to your reward. Before the veil of eternity be lifted, let me cast aside this black veil from your face!"

And thus speaking, the Reverend Mr. Clark bent forward to reveal the mystery of so many years. But, exerting a sudden energy that made all the beholders stand aghast, Father Hooper snatched both his hands from beneath the bedclothes and pressed them strongly on the black veil, resolute to struggle if the minister of Westbury would contend with a dying man.

"Never!" cried the veiled clergyman. "On earth, never!"

"Dark old man!" exclaimed the affrighted minister, "with what horrible crime upon your soul are you now passing to the judgment?"

Father Hooper's breath heaved; it rattled in his throat; but, with a mighty effort, grasping forward with his hands, he caught hold of life and held it back till he should speak. He even raised himself in bed; and there he sat, shivering with the arms of death around him, while the black veil hung down, awful, at that last moment, in the gathered terrors of a lifetime. And yet the faint, sad smile, so often there, now seemed to glimmer from its obscurity and linger on Father Hooper's lips.

"Why do you tremble at me alone?" cried he, turning his veiled face round the circle of pale spectators. "Tremble also at each other! Have men avoided me, and women shown no pity, and children screamed and fled, only for my black veil? What but the mystery which it obscurely typifies has made this piece of crepe so awful? When the friend shows his inmost heart to his friend; the lover to his best beloved; when man does not vainly shrink from the eye of his Creator, loathsomely treasuring up the secret of his sin; then deem me a monster for the symbol beneath which I have lived, and die! I look around me, and, lo! on every visage a Black Veil!"

While his auditors shrank from one another, in mutual affright, Father Hooper fell back upon his pillow, a veiled corpse, with a faint smile lingering on the lips. Still veiled, they laid him in his coffin, and a veiled corpse they bore him to the grave. The grass of many years has sprung up and withered on that grave, the burial stone is moss-grown, and good Mr. Hooper's face is dust; but awful is still the thought that it moldered beneath the Black Veil!

1. What is the subject of Parson Hooper's sermon on the first Sunday he appears wearing the black veil?
2. Why does an embassy of parishioners visit Mr. Hooper?
3. Why does Elizabeth break her engagement to Mr. Hooper?
4. What influence does the veil have on Reverend Hooper's effectiveness as a clergyman?
5. At the hour of his death, what does Father Hooper claim to see on everyone's face?

Commentary

"The Minister's Black Veil" has so little plot or action that we can easily miss its subtle pattern of meanings. These meanings are developed not through what characters do but through their attitudes. Everything in the story turns upon an apparently simple act—Mr. Hooper's sudden decision to appear in a black veil—but the motivation behind this act remains obscure, perhaps even to Hooper himself. He specifies no action of which he is ashamed, and outwardly his life seems blameless. We know only how the veil affects him and how it affects others.

The first half of the story illustrates this effect upon others. We must remember that there has been no apparent change in Hooper's quietly sympathetic manner or modest behavior. The only difference is the one made by the veil in his appearance; and this change would be insignificant except for its effect. As one woman observes, "He has changed himself into something awful, only by hiding his face."

Just why this should be so is a central concern of the story. As a result of wearing the veil, Hooper becomes a man apart, isolated from love and sympathy, suspected and even feared by his congregation. Yet, strangely enough, the veil makes him a more effective minister. It gives him indefinable authority. His preaching takes on new power, and he displays a remarkable understanding of people who are troubled by sin. The veil makes Hooper a sig-

nificant figure by *separating* him from the congregation. But, as the author remarks, ". . . perhaps the pale-faced congregation was almost as fearful a sight to the minister as his black veil to them." Whatever the veil signifies, its meaning seems to involve the congregation as much as it does Hooper. As he delivers his sermon on "secret sin," its effect on the congregation is remarkable. "Each member of the congregation, the most innocent girl, and the man of hardened breast, felt as if the preacher had crept upon them, behind his awful veil, and discovered their hoarded iniquity of deed or thought." The veil is in some way connected with secret sin. It not only makes Mr. Hooper different, but it also brings out the way in which he and his congregation are similar.

Only Elizabeth, Hooper's fiancée, seems at first unawed by the veil. To her it is merely a cloth that hides the face she most delights to see. But, "like a sudden twilight in the air," Elizabeth suddenly senses the unapproachable inner isolation of the man who wears it, and its "terrors" fall upon her, too.

Hooper is shunned and even feared by others in their times of health and happiness. But, more and more, he is summoned to the beds of "dying sinners." "By the aid of his mysterious emblem . . . he became a man of awful power over souls that were in agony for sin." Perhaps without recognizing it, the people have taken him at his word and regard the man, along with his veil, as a symbol, a reminder of that dark isolation all must face in death.

It is this symbolic quality of his life and the secret sin typified by the veil that the minister again emphasizes on his deathbed. "Why do you tremble at me alone?" he cries. "Tremble also at each other! . . . What but the mystery which it obscurely typifies has made this piece of crepe so awful? . . . I look around me, and, lo! on every visage a Black Veil!" Those around him shrink from each other, enacting the very separation of which he spoke. In wearing a black veil, Hooper has perceived in everyone a hidden self of sinful deeds or wishes and has dramatized the isolation of person from person and of people from God. In his example, however, he suffers most from his lesson. He makes the dark side of people the whole truth of human existence. His own "kind and loving" nature is lost for all. His perception of an ultimate human isolation leaves him the man most isolated in what Hawthorne describes as "that saddest of all prisons, his own heart. . . ."

Analyzing and Interpreting the Story

1. The first paragraph presents the congregation before the appearance of the Reverend Mr. Hooper. **a.** What is the mood of the scene before the arrival of the minister? **b.** How does the mood change after Hooper appears in the black veil?

2. The minister officiates at both a funeral and a wedding on the day he first appears with the veil. We would expect the veil to be inappropriate to the joy of a wedding, but it seems equally disturbing at the funeral. **a.** Why might one woman imagine, during the procession to the graveyard, that the minister walks "hand in hand" with the dead girl's spirit? **b.** In what sense does he now seem "dead" to others?

3. At first Elizabeth refuses to see anything evil in the veil. Then, suddenly, "in an instant, as it were," a new emotion replaces sorrow. As she stares at the black veil, she begins to comprehend its terrible significance. **a.** What revelation does Elizabeth experience? **b.** Why is she suddenly terrified?

4. Over the years rumors are spread about the reason for the minister's actions. As there are no explicit clues toward a "crime" in the ordinary sense, in what larger sense does Hooper feel he is guilty of a crime?

5. In old age, the minister becomes known as "Father Hooper" and is honored by being asked to preach the election sermon. What evidence, however, indicates that the community's reactions to Hooper are the same as on the first day of the veil?

6. In your opinion, what is the meaning of the veil?

Literary Elements

Parable

"The Minister's Black Veil" is subtitled "A Parable." A **parable** is a short narrative that draws a moral lesson or illustrates a religious truth. It resembles an allegory (see page 255) in having an obvious moral intention. Unlike an allegory, however, a parable need not have characters or objects that stand for abstract qualities. If we consider Hawthorne's story a parable, what moral lesson can be drawn from it?

Writing About Literature

Responding to an Interpretation

Edgar Allan Poe called "The Minister's Black Veil" "a masterly composition" in which the obvious meaning conceals a deeper one that is delicately hinted at: "The moral put into the mouth of the dying minister will be supposed to convey the true import of the narrative; and that a crime of dark dye (having reference to the 'young lady' [over whose funeral Hooper presides]) has been committed, is a point which only minds congenial with that of the author will perceive."

Write a composition in which you agree or disagree with Poe's interpretation that the story is really about "a crime of dark dye." Before you write, you may find it helpful to reread the paragraphs describing the young lady's funeral. In your paper, consider the following points: Can both Poe's interpretation and the interpretation given in the Commentary be true? Does Poe's interpretation tell us more about Hawthorne or Poe?

The Notebooks and Other Writings

His notebooks show another side of Hawthorne. If his stories typically explore human isolation and the hidden mysteries of the heart, in his notebooks we more often see a shrewd and interested observer of customs and manners and of people in the outward, ordinary selves that they present to the world.

He knew the subjects of the following portraits in quite different ways. While Hawthorne lived in Concord, Thoreau was of course his fellow townsman—not well known (in his first notes about Thoreau, Hawthorne misspelled his name), certainly not a friend, but still an interesting young man. Hawthorne could see more significance in his odd life than most others did. Melville, on the other hand, Hawthorne did know as a friend, although at the time of this notebook entry they had not met for several years. This brief but perceptive characterization has become a valuable part of our understanding of Melville's mind and personality.

The portrait of Lincoln was intended for an article in the *Atlantic Monthly* called "Chiefly About War Matters," but did not appear in print until after Hawthorne's death. Hawthorne met Lincoln for only a few minutes at one of those obligatory White House ceremonies that an overworked president could not avoid even in wartime. Hawthorne saw in "Uncle Abe," as many others did, "the pattern American," the representative common man. Yet he was shrewd enough to guess that there were dimensions of Lincoln's character not revealed by this exterior and to sense that in a time of "tremendous responsibility," with its very life at stake, the nation might somehow have found the right leader.

Henry D. Thoreau

Thursday, September 1st, [1842].

Mr. Thorow dined with us yesterday. He is a singular character—a young man with much of wild original nature still remaining in him; and so far as he is sophisticated, it is in a way and method of his own. He is as ugly as sin, long-nosed, queer-mouthed, and with uncouth and somewhat rustic, although courteous manners, corresponding very well with such an exterior. But his ugliness is of an honest and agreeable fashion, and becomes him much better than beauty. He was educated, I believe, at Cambridge, and formerly kept school in this town; but for two or three years back, he has repudiated all regular modes of getting a living. . . . Mr. Thorow is a keen and delicate observer of nature—a genuine observer, which, I suspect, is almost as rare a character as even an original poet; and Nature, in return for his love, seems to adopt him as her especial child, and shows him secrets which few others are allowed to witness. He is familiar with beast, fish, fowl, and reptile, and has strange stories to tell of adventures, and friendly passages with these lower brethren of mortality. Herb and flower, likewise, wherever they grow, whether in garden or wild wood, are his familiar friends. He is also on intimate terms with the clouds, and can tell the portents of storms. It is a characteristic trait, that he has a great regard for the memory of the Indian tribes, whose wild life would have suited him so well; and strange to say, he seldom walks over a ploughed field without picking up an arrowpoint, a spearhead, or other relic of the red men—as if their spirits willed him to be the inheritor of their simple wealth.

With all this he has more than a tincture of literature—a deep and true taste for poetry, especially the elder poets, although more exclusive than is desirable, like all other Transcendentalists, so far as I am acquainted with them. He is a good writer—at least, he has written one good article, a rambling disquisition on Natural History . . .—which, he says, was chiefly made up from journals of his own observations. Methinks this article gives a very fair image of his mind and character—so true, minute, and literal in observation, yet giving the spirit as well as letter of what he sees, even as a lake reflects its wooded banks, showing every leaf, yet giving the wild beauty of the whole scene;—then there are passages in the article of cloudy and dreamy metaphysics, partly affected, and partly the natural exhalations of his intellect;—and also passages where his thoughts seem to measure and attune themselves into spontaneous verse, as they rightfully may, since there is real poetry in him. There is a basis of good sense and moral truth, too, throughout the article, which also is a reflection of his character; for he is not unwise to think and feel, however imperfect in his own mode of action. On the whole, I find him a healthy and wholesome man to know.

Herman Melville

[Southport, England] November 20th, [1856] Thursday.

A week ago last Monday, Herman Melville came to see me at the Consulate,[1] looking much as he used to do (a little paler, and perhaps a little sadder), in a rough outside coat, and with his characteristic gravity and reserve of manner. He had crossed from New York to Glasgow in a screw steamer,[2] about a fortnight before, and had since been seeing Edinburgh and other interesting places. . . . Melville has not been well, of late; he has been affected with neuralgic complaints in his head and limbs, and no doubt has suffered from too constant literary occupation, pursued without much success, latterly; and his writings, for a long while past, have indicated a morbid state of mind. So he left his place at Pittsfield, and has established his wife and family, I believe, with his father-in-law in Boston, and is thus far on his way to Constantinople. I do not wonder that he found it necessary to take an airing through the world, after so many years of toilsome pen labor and domestic life, following upon so wild and adventurous a youth as his was. . . .

He stayed with us from Tuesday till Thursday; and, on the intervening day, we took a pretty long walk together, and sat down in a hollow among the sand hills (sheltering ourselves from the high, cool wind) and smoked a cigar. Melville, as he always does, began to reason of Providence and futurity, and of everything that lies beyond human ken, and informed me that he had "pretty much made up his mind to be annihilated"; but still he does not seem to rest in that anticipation; and, I think, will never rest until he gets hold of a definite belief. It is strange how he persists—and has persisted ever since I knew him, and probably long before—in wandering to-and-fro over these deserts, as dismal and monotonous as the sand hills amid which we were sitting. He can neither believe, nor be comfortable in his unbelief; and he is too honest and courageous not to try to do one or the other. If he were a religious man, he would be one of the most truly religious and reverential; he has a very high and noble nature, and better worth immortality than most of us.

1. **Consulate:** Hawthorne was serving at this time as American Consul in England.
2. **screw steamer:** a ship driven by a screw propeller.

Abraham Lincoln (1862). Photograph by Mathew Brady (1823?–1896).

Abraham Lincoln

[March–April, 1862]

By and by there was a little stir on the staircase and in the passageway, and in lounged a tall, loose-jointed figure, of an exaggerated Yankee port[1] and demeanor, whom (as being about the homeliest man I ever saw, yet by no means repulsive or disagreeable) it was impossible not to recognize as Uncle Abe.

Unquestionably, Western man though he be, and Kentuckian by birth, President Lincoln is the essential representative of all Yankees, and the veritable specimen, physically, of what the world seems determined to regard as our characteristic qualities. It is the strangest and yet the fittest thing in the jumble of human vicissitudes, that he, out of so many millions, unlooked for, unselected by any intelligible process that could be based upon his genuine qualities, unknown to those who chose him, and unsuspected of what endowments may adapt him for his tremendous responsibility, should have found the way open for him to fling his lank personality into the chair of state,—where, I presume, it was his first impulse to throw his legs on the council table, and tell the Cabinet Ministers a story. There is no describing his lengthy awkwardness, nor the uncouthness of his movement; and yet it seemed as if I had been in the habit of seeing him daily, and had shaken hands with him a thousand times in some village street; so true was he to the aspect of the pattern American, though with a certain extravagance which, possibly, I exaggerated still further by the delighted eagerness with which I took it in. If put to guess his calling and livelihood, I should have taken him for a country schoolmaster as soon as anything else. He was dressed in a rusty black frock coat[2] and pantaloons, unbrushed, and worn so faithfully that the suit had adapted itself to the curves and angularities of his figure, and had grown to be an outer skin of the man. He had shabby slippers on his feet. His hair was black, still unmixed with gray, stiff, somewhat bushy, and had apparently been acquainted with neither brush nor comb that morning. . . . His complexion is dark and sallow, betokening, I fear, an insalubrious[3] atmosphere around the White House; he has thick black eyebrows and an impending brow; his nose is large, and the lines about his mouth are very strongly defined.

The whole physiognomy is as coarse a one as you would meet anywhere in the length and

1. **port:** here, bearing.

2. **frock coat:** an overcoat with knee-length skirts.
3. **insalubrious** (ĭn′sə-lōō′brē-əs): not wholesome.

breadth of the States; but, withal, it is redeemed, illuminated, softened, and brightened by a kindly though serious look out of his eyes, and an expression of homely sagacity, that seems weighted with rich results of village experience. A great deal of native sense; no bookish cultivation, no refinement; honest at heart, and thoroughly so, and yet, in some sort, sly—at least, endowed with a sort of tact and wisdom that are akin to craft, and would impel him, I think, to take an antagonist in flank, rather than to make a bull-run at him right in front. But, on the whole, I liked this sallow, queer, sagacious visage, with the homely human sympathies that warmed it; and, for my small share in the matter, would as lief[4] have Uncle Abe for a ruler as any man whom it would have been practicable to put in his place.

4. **lief** (lēf): willingly.

For Study and Discussion

Analyzing and Interpreting the Selections

Thoreau

1. In the first paragraph, Hawthorne describes Thoreau in somewhat contradictory terms: "ugly as sin" but in "an honest and agreeable" way that is attractive, with "uncouth" but nevertheless "courteous" manners, educated at Harvard but refusing "all regular modes of getting a living." What dominant impression of Thoreau do we take from this paragraph?

2. Nearly everyone who met him recognized Thoreau's special relationship with nature. What evidence does Hawthorne offer for this?

3. Hawthorne judged Thoreau, who at the time had published only one article, to be a "good writer." What does he see as Thoreau's strengths and weaknesses as a writer?

Melville

1. Hawthorne recognizes that Melville is not physically well. What evidence makes him feel that this condition has emotional causes?

2. The final paragraph of Hawthorne's comment is our most famous description of Melville as the eternal questioner of all things in heaven and earth. Why, despite his own opinion that those questions are "dismal and monotonous" and profitless, does Hawthorne conclude that Melville is "better worth immortality than most of us"?

Lincoln

1. The first part of Hawthorne's description emphasizes Lincoln's physical appearance ("about the homeliest man I ever saw"), but this kind of appraisal alternates with his effort to see the man within. Discuss these two strains of Hawthorne's reaction as they appear in the second paragraph.

2. Hawthorne, like the other writers of his time, missed the mark when he assumed that Lincoln had no "bookish cultivation" (see Lincoln's biography, page 366). Despite this, he finds qualities in the man that make him feel he would as soon "have Uncle Abe for a ruler as any man" at this point in our history. What are these qualities?

Herman Melville (c. 1847) by Asa Weston Twitchell (1820–1904). Oil on canvas.

"Until I was twenty-five," Melville told Hawthorne, "I had no development at all. From my twenty-fifth year I date my life. Three weeks have scarcely passed, at any time between then and now, that I have not unfolded within myself." When he sent this letter, Melville was working at top speed on his masterpiece, *Moby-Dick*. It was his intellectual development that Melville dated from his twenty-fifth year. It was then he began an arduous program of reading, and as he "swam through libraries" he found writers, especially Shakespeare, who fired his own imagination. But if his imagination was set in motion by books, the experiences it would explore had been accumulated far from libraries. When he reached that turning point in his early manhood, Melville already had an "education" that no other writer of his time could match. He had sailed the oceans and knew their "rimmed varieties of races and climes," and he had even lived briefly among cannibals. Probably no other writer of his century had so wide an acquaintance with the peoples, customs, and places of the world. Although he did not fully realize the value of this education at the time, Melville could look back through Ishmael in *Moby-Dick* and say that a whaling ship had been "my Yale College and my Harvard."

Melville was born in New York to a family that had known considerable public distinction and that, on his mother's side, was still prominent and well-to-do. But Melville's father gradually failed in business and died when the boy was twelve, leaving only debts. Thereafter the family had to exist as the dependents of relatives, a bitter circumstance for a proud boy who had been raised to expect far better things. During adolescence Melville combined clerking jobs with brief periods of schooling. At nineteen, unable to find anything better, he shipped as a seaman aboard a merchant vessel on a voyage to England. There he was horrified by the degraded life he saw in the Liverpool slums; still with no better prospects, he went to sea again in January of 1841, this time aboard the whaler *Acushnet*, bound for the

Pacific. Eighteen months later he deserted the ship at Nuku Hiva in the Marquesas Islands and stumbled upon a remote tribe of natives who in many ways lived an idyllic life—but also practiced cannibalism. For a month or two Melville was apparently both guest and captive of these people, before he was able to escape aboard a passing whaler which took him to Tahiti. He soon shipped aboard still another whaler. Some months later, in order to get passage home, he enlisted at Honolulu for service aboard a United States naval vessel. After many calls at foreign ports, he was eventually discharged at Boston at the end of 1844. He had been wandering strange lands and seas for nearly four years.

During the next years Melville wrote five novels from these experiences. The first, *Typee* (1846), is a fictionalized history of his stay at Nuku Hiva. As the first modern novel of South Seas adventure, it was an immediate success and started a fad for such narratives. Unlike Hawthorne, whose literary reputation grew gradually and was firmly established by his best work, Melville found an early fame, but one that did not permit him to grow and change. A second novel, *Omoo* (1847), based on his experience in Tahiti, was also a success. He was able to marry, settling first in New York City and then on a farm near Pittsfield, Massachusetts. There he met

Hawthorne, who lived for a year in a neighboring village, and the friendship of the older writer became an important influence on Melville's literary development. But his third novel, *Mardi* (1849), sharply disappointed his readers. *Mardi* is once again a travel narrative, but it is also an allegorical voyage of the mind. Deep by now into his program of reading and self-examination, Melville was reviewing his experience and finding new meanings in the world he once traveled so heedlessly. But an audience that had welcomed physical adventures was not receptive to mental ones, and the book sold poorly. He tried to recover financially by quickly writing a book on his first voyage and another on his navy service, but these had limited success.

By 1850, as he began writing *Moby-Dick*, Melville had reached both the height of his creative powers and a crisis point in his career. He had long outgrown his earliest work, but, as he complained to Hawthorne, readers seemed still to know him only "as a man who had lived among the cannibals." He felt himself growing ever closer to "the Art of Telling the Truth," but the declining sales of his books placed him under great financial pressure. "Dollars damn me," he told Hawthorne. "Try to get a living by the Truth—and go to the Soup Societies [charity kitchens]. . . . What I feel most moved to write, that is banned—it will not pay. Yet, altogether, write the *other* way I cannot." In *Moby-Dick* he was turning to the one part of his sailor's life that, strangely enough, he had not used for fiction—his experience aboard whaling ships. His book was to be a monument to the whaling industry, complete with masses of information. But in the course of writing it, Melville found that his adventure story had become a deep-diving exploration of the mysteries of nature and "the tragedies of human thought." Predictably, however, few readers were willing to follow him into depths where they had to swim for their lives. *Moby-Dick*, perhaps the most remarkable of all American books, was not a success. Again driven by dollars, Melville immediately wrote *Pierre* (1852), but this still darker and more difficult novel was even less popular. As if to complete his loss of reputation, a fire in a publisher's warehouse in 1853 destroyed the remaining stock of his books. For a time he tried magazine writing and produced such brilliant stories as "Bartleby the Scrivener" and "Benito Cereno," but they brought him little money ("He has lost his prestige," an editor noted coldly), and he was already looking for other work. When his last novel, *The Confidence Man*, appeared in 1857, it closed out a decade of almost unbelievable productivity.

Melville's remaining literary achievements were essentially private ones. For nearly twenty years he labored obscurely as a customs inspector in a New York dock. In this sense of failure, he avoided literary associations, and students who sought him out found him "a cloistered thinker" who seemed unwilling to discuss his books. Apparently with a need to compress and discipline his thoughts, he wrote only poetry now, and only one long work: a poetic narrative of a journey he had made years before to the Holy Land, a search for faith that ends, typically, in uncertainty. His one last great work of fiction was *Billy Budd*, written after his retirement from the customhouse but not published until long after his death. When Melville died in 1891, forty years after the publication of *Moby-Dick*, he was remembered— if at all—as the author of one or two entertaining stories of the South Seas. His rediscovery in the 1920s began with a new appreciation of *Moby-Dick* and then extended to his other works as scholars brought them to public attention. Melville's place in the foremost rank of American writers is now assured.

What modern readers find in Melville is a vividly dramatic imagination that expresses a relentlessly questioning mind. Like the transcendentalists, he sought evidence of the human spirit in the principles of nature. But against Emerson's optimistic view that one spirit animates all being, Melville had to acknowledge his own perception of division and disunity: however beautiful the sunlit surface of the ocean, sharks and other terrors still swim in its dark depths; if, as he said, the visible spheres were formed in love, the invisible ones were formed in fright. No less than the most hopeful reformer of his time did he value the heart's longing for a world of innocence and ideal justice, but he found that the world of historical actuality has little use for the heart's wishes. Above all, it was the presence of ineradicable evil in all of existence that haunted Melville's imagination. He saw this underside of reality in both nature and human nature, and it was this perception he most valued in Hawthorne's work: "It is that blackness in Hawthorne that . . . fixes and fascinates me." Yet, as Hawthorne recognized, Melville went far beyond him in exploring "the horrors of the half-known life" that lie beneath the surfaces of existence.

Papeete, Tahiti Island, South Pacific (c. 1850). Colored lithograph.
The Mariners' Museum, Newport News, Virginia

FROM

Typee

Typee is a fictionalized account of Melville's experiences in the South Seas. The narrator, an American sailor, jumps ship in the Marquesas Islands to escape from a tyrannical captain. In his flight through jungle and over mountains he becomes lost, severely injures his leg in a fall, and finally blunders into the secluded valley of the Typees, a people much feared by other islanders and known to be cannibals. There he is treated kindly but also held prisoner. For weeks he is in despair—homesick, isolated by his ignorance of the language (he has lost even his name, since the Typees cannot say it correctly), fearful for his life, so immobilized by his injury that he must be carried about like a baby.

This passage first describes his recovery in body and spirit. Thereafter he becomes a keen observer of Typee life and even a participant in its daily affairs. He also becomes Melville's spokesperson for a radically new perspective on the cultures and societies of America and Europe—on Western civilization. American writers from the beginning had drawn comparisons between the Old World and the New, and Henry James would later make the American's encounter with Europe a major literary theme of the post-Civil War period (see *Daisy Miller,* page 519). But no other writer had Melville's experience of a totally different, non-Western culture. He discovered, for example, that the Typees did not have our Western consciousness of time, of the value of memory and anticipation of the future. They had forgotten the original meaning of their gods and of the taboos that governed their daily conduct, and they appeared never to think of the future. Were they happier for that, living blissfully without apparent awareness of the passage of time and therefore without fear of inevitable death? How had they eliminated any form of competition from their social existence? Did the terrible fact of cannibalism (practiced only ritually, on enemies slain in warfare) make them the worst of barbarians, or did the innumerable cruelties and vices of our society make us the true "savages" of the world?

Melville could not, of course, pull up his own roots in Western civilization; he had to escape from the Typees and come home. But he came home a lifelong questioner, and *Typee* brought to American literature a perspective on civilized life we had not seen before.

Day after day wore on, and still there was no perceptible change in the conduct of the islanders towards me. Gradually I lost all knowledge of the regular occurrence of the days of the week, and sank insensibly into that kind of apathy which ensues after some violent outbreak of despair. My limb suddenly healed, the swelling went down, the pain subsided, and I had every reason to suppose I should soon completely recover from the affliction that had so long tormented me.

As soon as I was enabled to ramble about the valley in company with the natives, troops of whom followed me whenever I sallied out of the house, I began to experience an elasticity of mind which placed me beyond the reach of those dismal forebodings to which I had so lately been a prey. Received wherever I went with the most deferential kindness; regaled perpetually with the most delightful fruits; ministered to by dark-eyed nymphs; and enjoying besides all the services of the devoted Kory-Kory,[1] I thought that, for a sojourn among cannibals, no man could have well made a more agreeable one.

To be sure, there were limits set to my wanderings. Towards the sea my progress was barred by an express prohibition of the savages; and after having made two or three ineffectual attempts to reach it, as much to gratify my curiosity as anything else, I gave up the idea. It was in vain to think of reaching it by stealth, since the natives escorted me in numbers wherever I went, and not for one single moment that I can recall to mind was I ever permitted to be alone.

The green and precipitous elevations that stood ranged around the head of the vale where Marheyo's[2] habitation was situated, effectually precluded all hope of escape in that quarter, even if I could have stolen away from the thousand eyes of the savages.

But these reflections now seldom obtruded upon me; I gave myself up to the passing hour, and if ever disagreeable thoughts arose in my mind, I drove them away. When I looked around the verdant recess in which I was buried, and gazed up to the summits of the lofty eminence that hemmed me in, I was well disposed to think that I was in the "Happy Valley,"[3] and that beyond those heights there was nought but a world of care and anxiety.

As I extended my wanderings in the valley and grew more familiar with the habits of its inmates, I was fain to confess that, despite the disadvantages of his condition, the Polynesian savage, surrounded by all the luxurious provisions of Nature, enjoyed an infinitely happier, though certainly a less intellectual existence, than the self-complacent European. . . .

In a primitive state of society, the enjoyments of life, though few and simple, are spread over a great extent, and are unalloyed; but Civilization, for every advantage she imparts, holds a hundred evils in reserve; the

1. **Kory-Kory:** an amiable young native who has been assigned to serve and guard the narrator.

2. **Marheyo:** the head of the household where the narrator lives during his stay with the Typees.
3. **"Happy Valley":** possibly an allusion to the idyllic and isolated valley in *The History of Rasselas* by Samuel Johnson (1709–1784), an English writer.

heart burnings, the jealousies, the social rivalries, the family dissensions, and the thousand self-inflicted discomforts of refined life, which make up in units the swelling aggregate of human misery, are unknown among these unsophisticated people.

But it will be urged that these shocking unprincipled wretches are cannibals. Very true; and a rather bad trait in their character it must be allowed. But they are such only when they seek to gratify the passion of revenge upon their enemies; and I ask whether the mere eating of human flesh so very far exceeds in barbarity that custom which only a few years since was practiced in enlightened England— a convicted traitor, perhaps a man found guilty of honesty, patriotism, and suchlike heinous crime, had his head lopped off with a huge axe, his bowels dragged out and thrown into a fire; while his body, carved into four quarters,[4] was with his head exposed upon pikes, and permitted to rot and fester among the public haunts of men!

The fiendlike skill we display in the invention of all manner of death-dealing engines, the vindictiveness with which we carry on our wars, and the misery and desolation that follow in their train, are enough of themselves to distinguish the white civilized man as the most ferocious animal on the face of the earth. . . .

But it is needless to multiply the examples of civilized barbarity; they far exceed, in the amount of misery they cause, the crimes which we regard with such abhorrence in our less enlightened fellow creatures.

The term "savage" is, I conceive, often misapplied, and, indeed, when I consider the vices, cruelties, and enormities of every kind that spring up in the tainted atmosphere of a feverish civilization, I am inclined to think that so far as the relative wickedness of the parties is concerned, four or five Marquesan islanders sent to the United States as missionaries might be quite as useful as an equal number of Amer-

icans dispatched to the islands in a similar capacity. . . .

In the altered frame of mind to which I have referred, every object that presented itself to my notice in the valley struck me in a new light, and the opportunities I now enjoyed of observing the manners of its inmates, tended to strengthen my favorable impressions. One peculiarity that fixed my admiration was the perpetual hilarity reigning through the whole extent of the vale. There seemed to be no cares, griefs, troubles, or vexations in all Typee. The hours tripped along as gaily as the laughing couples down a country dance.

There were none of those thousand sources of irritation that the ingenuity of civilized man has created to mar his own felicity. There were no foreclosures of mortgages, no protested notes, no bills payable, no debts of honor in Typee; no unreasonable tailors and shoemakers, perversely bent on being paid; no duns of any description; no assault-and-battery attorneys to foment discord, backing their clients up to a quarrel, and then knocking their heads together; no poor relations, everlastingly occupying the spare bedchamber, and diminishing the elbowroom at the family table; no destitute widows, with their children starving on the cold charities of the world; no beggars; no debtors' prisons; no proud and hardhearted nabobs in Typee; or, to sum up all in one word—no Money! That "root of all evil" was not to be found in the valley.

In this secluded abode of happiness there were no cross old women, no cruel stepdames, no withered spinsters, no lovesick maidens, no sour old bachelors, no inattentive husbands, no melancholy young men, no blubbering youngsters, and no squalling brats. All was mirth, fun, and high good humor. Blue devils, hypochondria, and doleful dumps went and hid themselves among the nooks and crannies of the rocks.

Here you would see a parcel of children frolicking together the livelong day, and no quarreling, no contention among them. The same number in our own land could not have

4. **quarters:** the legal punishment known as being drawn and quartered, which was practiced well into the nineteenth century.

played together for the space of an hour without biting or scratching one another. There you might have seen a throng of young females, not filled with envyings of each others' charms, nor displaying the ridiculous affectations of gentility, nor yet moving in whalebone corsets, like so many automatons, but free, inartificially happy, and unconstrained.

There were some spots in that sunny vale where they would frequently resort to decorate themselves with garlands of flowers. To have seen them reclining beneath the shadows of one of the beautiful groves, the ground about them strewn with freshly gathered buds and blossoms, employed in weaving chaplets and necklaces, one would have thought that all the train of Flora[5] had gathered together to keep a festival in honor of their mistress.

With the young men there seemed almost always some matter of diversion or business on hand that afforded a constant variety of enjoyment. But, whether fishing, or carving canoes, or polishing their ornaments, never was there exhibited the least sign of strife or contention among them.

As for the warriors, they maintained a tranquil dignity of demeanor, journeying occasionally from house to house, where they were always sure to be received with the attention bestowed upon distinguished guests. The old men, of whom there were many in the vale, seldom stirred from their mats, where they would recline for hours and hours, smoking and talking to one another with all the garrulity of age.

But the continual happiness, which, so far as I was able to judge, appeared to prevail in the valley, sprung principally from that all-pervading sensation which Rousseau[6] has told us he at one time experienced—the mere buoyant sense of a healthful physical existence. And, indeed, in this particular, the Typees had ample reason to felicitate themselves, for sickness was almost unknown. During the whole period of my stay, I saw but one invalid among them; and on their smooth, clear skins you observed no blemish or mark of disease.

---

5. **Flora:** in Roman mythology, the goddess of flowers.
6. **Rousseau:** Jean Jacques Rousseau (roo-sō'), a French philosopher and writer (1712–1778).

Reading Check

1. How is the narrator prevented from escaping from the valley?
2. What does the narrator learn about the practice of cannibalism among the Typees?
3. Which English custom does the narrator liken in barbarism to cannibalism?
4. According to the narrator, what is the chief obstacle to happiness in his own civilization?

For Study and Discussion

Analyzing and Interpreting the Selection

1. In the opening paragraph it seems the narrator must get worse before he can get well. Why would the loss of "all knowledge of the regular occurrence of the days of the week" be first a part of his "apathy" and then a preparation for his recovery?

2. Once physically recovered, the narrator enjoys a new "elasticity of mind" and freedom from "dismal forebodings" that allows him to enjoy life again. **a.** How is this happiness related to the "buoyant sense of . . . physical existence" he attributes to Rousseau near the end? **b.** How might this new state of mind prepare him to view these natives sympathetically?

3. One key to the happiness of the Typees, the narrator believes, is the absence of money. What miseries of civilized life does he attribute to money?

4. The discussion of who is and is not a "savage" particularly struck Melville's first readers and enraged some of them. **a.** How does he extend this discussion in the matter of missionaries? **b.** How would missionaries from cannibals have been received in America and Europe? **c.** What is Melville's tone in this passage?

5. The narrator discusses several age groups in turn—children, young women, young men, warriors, old men. **a.** Is there a common basis for their general happiness? **b.** As Melville describes their life, does this seem to us a sufficient basis for happiness? What would we find missing?

Herman Melville   **275**

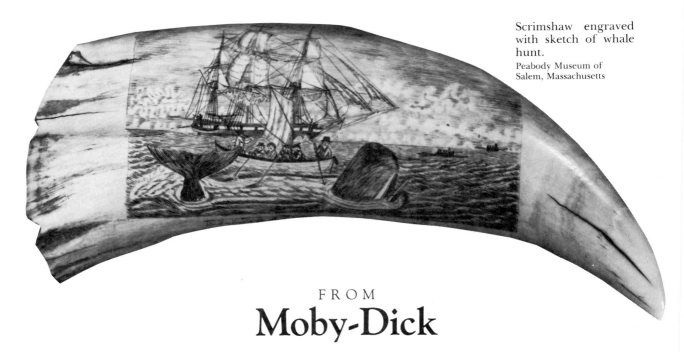

Scrimshaw engraved with sketch of whale hunt.
Peabody Museum of Salem, Massachusetts

FROM
Moby-Dick

Moby-Dick is the story of the fateful voyage of the *Pequod*, a whaling ship commanded by the compelling, mysterious figure Captain Ahab, magnificent in his strengths and weaknesses. Throughout the novel, Ahab relentlessly pursues the white whale that years before had taken off his leg and made a "poor pegging lubber" of him. Among the other interesting characters in the novel are the officers of the *Pequod:* Starbuck, the first mate; Stubb, the second mate; and Flask, the third mate. The ship's harpooners are Queequeg, "a native of Kokovoko, an island far away to the West and South"; Tashtego, an Indian from Gay Head on Martha's Vineyard; and Daggoo, an African of gigantic size and strength.

The following passage introduces the reader to Captain Ahab, who makes his first appearance some days after the *Pequod* has put to sea. The narrator of *Moby-Dick* is Ishmael, who has joined this voyage as a common sailor.

FROM Ahab

Now, it being Christmas when the ship shot from out her harbor, for a space we had biting polar weather, though all the time running away from it to the southward; and by every degree and minute of latitude which we sailed, gradually leaving that merciless winter and all its intolerable weather behind us. It was one of those less lowering, but still gray and gloomy enough mornings of the transition, when with a fair wind the ship was rushing through the water with a vindictive sort of leaping and melancholy rapidity, that as I mounted to the deck at the call of the forenoon watch, so soon as I leveled my glance towards the taffrail,[1] foreboding shivers ran over me. Reality outran apprehension; Captain Ahab stood upon his quarter-deck.[2]

1. **taffrail:** the rail around a ship's stern.
2. **quarter-deck:** a part of the upper deck usually reserved for officers.

There seemed no sign of common bodily illness about him, nor of the recovery from any. He looked like a man cut away from the stake when the fire has overrunningly wasted all the limbs without consuming them or taking away one particle from their compacted aged robustness. His whole high, broad form seemed made of solid bronze, and shaped in an unalterable mold, like Cellini's cast Perseus.[3] Threading its way out from among his gray hairs, and continuing right down one side of his tawny scorched face and neck, till it disappeared in his clothing, you saw a slender rodlike mark, lividly whitish. It resembled that perpendicular seam sometimes made in the straight, lofty trunk of a great tree when the upper lightning tearingly darts down it, and without wrenching a single twig, peels and grooves out the bark from top to bottom ere running off into the soil, leaving the tree still greenly alive, but branded. Whether that mark was born with him, or whether it was the scar left by some desperate wound, no one could certainly say. By some tacit consent, throughout the voyage little or no allusion was made to it, especially by the mates. But once Tashtego's senior, an old Gay-Head Indian among the crew, superstitiously asserted that not till he was full forty years old did Ahab become that way branded, and then it came upon him, not in the fury of any mortal fray, but in an elemental strife at sea. Yet this wild hint seemed inferentially negatived by what a gray Manxman[4] insinuated, an old sepulchral man, who, having never before sailed out of Nantucket,[5] had never ere this laid eye upon wild Ahab. Nevertheless, the old sea traditions, the immemorial credulities, popularly invested this old Manxman with preternatural powers of discernment. So that no white sailor seriously contradicted him when he said that if ever Captain Ahab should be tranquilly laid out—which might hardly come to pass, so he muttered—then, whoever should do that last office for the dead, would find a birthmark on him from crown to sole.

So powerfully did the whole grim aspect of Ahab affect me, and the livid brand which streaked it, that for the first few moments I hardly noted that not a little of this overbearing grimness was owing to the barbaric white leg upon which he partly stood. It had previously come to me that this ivory leg had at sea been fashioned from the polished bone of the sperm whale's jaw. "Aye, he was dismasted off Japan," said the old Gay-Head Indian once; "but like his dismasted craft, he shipped[6] another mast without coming home for it. He has a quiver of 'em."

I was struck with the singular posture he maintained. Upon each side of the *Pequod*'s quarter-deck, and pretty close to the mizzen shrouds, there was an auger hole, bored about half an inch or so into the plank. His bone leg steadied in that hole; one arm elevated, and holding by a shroud; Captain Ahab stood erect, looking straight out beyond the ship's ever-pitching prow. There was an infinity of firmest fortitude, a determinate, unsurrenderable willfulness, in the fixed and fearless forward dedication of that glance. Not a word he spoke; nor did his officers say aught to him; though by all their minutest gestures and expressions, they plainly showed the uneasy, if not painful, consciousness of being under a troubled master-eye. And not only that, but moody stricken Ahab stood before them with a crucifixion in his face; in all the nameless regal overbearing dignity of some mighty woe.

Ere long, from his first visit in the air, he withdrew into his cabin. But after that morning, he was every day visible to the crew; either standing in the pivot-hole, or seated upon an ivory stool he had, or heavily walking the deck.

3. **Cellini's cast Perseus:** The Italian sculptor Benvenuto Cellini (1500–1571) created a famous statue of Perseus, a hero of Greek mythology.
4. **Manxman:** a native of the Isle of Man, one of the British Isles, situated between Northern Ireland and England.
5. **Nantucket:** an island off Massachusetts and a seaport from which many whalers, including the *Pequod*, embarked.

6. **shipped:** took aboard.

As the sky grew less gloomy, indeed, began to grow a little genial, he became still less and less a recluse; as if, when the ship had sailed from home, nothing but the dead wintry bleakness of the sea had then kept him so secluded. And, by and by, it came to pass that he was almost continually in the air; but, as yet, for all that he said, or perceptibly did, on the at last sunny deck, he seemed as unnecessary there as another mast. But the *Pequod* was only making a passage now, not regularly cruising; nearly all whaling preparatives needing supervision the mates were fully competent to, so that there was little or nothing, out of himself, to employ or excite Ahab, now; and thus chase away, for that one interval, the clouds that layer upon layer were piled upon his brow, as ever all clouds choose the loftiest peaks to pile themselves upon.

Nevertheless, ere long, the warm, warbling persuasiveness of the pleasant holiday weather we came to, seemed gradually to charm him from his mood. For, as when the red-cheeked dancing girls, April and May, trip home to the wintry, misanthropic woods, even the barest, ruggedest, most thunder-cloven old oak will at least send forth some few green sprouts, to welcome such glad-hearted visitants; so Ahab did, in the end, a little respond to the playful allurings of that girlish air. More than once did he put forth the faint blossom of a look which, in any other man, would have soon flowered out in a smile.

The quarter-deck is a center of dramatic action in *Moby-Dick*. Here Ahab reveals his secret purpose, to track down and kill the great white whale. Here he binds the crew—even Starbuck, the reluctant first mate—to his relentless pursuit. The whaling voyage, which was to be an ordinary business venture, becomes instead the instrument of Ahab's vengeance.

FROM **The Quarter-Deck**

One morning shortly after breakfast, Ahab, as was his wont, ascended the cabin gangway to the deck. There most sea captains usually walk at that hour, as country gentlemen, after the same meal, take a few turns in the garden.

Soon his steady, ivory stride was heard, as to-and-fro he paced his old rounds, upon planks so familiar to his tread that they were all over dented, like geological stones, with the peculiar mark of his walk. Did you fixedly gaze, too, upon that ribbed and dented brow, there also, you would see still stranger footprints—the footprints of his one unsleeping, ever-pacing thought.

But on the occasion in question, those dents looked deeper, even as his nervous step that morning left a deeper mark. And so full of his thought was Ahab that at every uniform turn that he made, now at the mainmast and now at the binnacle,[7] you could almost see that thought turn in him as he turned, and pace in him as he paced; so completely possessing him, indeed, that it all but seemed the inward mold of every outer movement.

"D'ye mark him, Flask?" whispered Stubb; "the chick that's in him pecks the shell. 'Twill soon be out."

The hours wore on—Ahab now shut up within his cabin; anon, pacing the deck, with the same intense bigotry of purpose[8] in his aspect.

It drew near the close of day. Suddenly he came to a halt by the bulwarks, and inserting his bone leg into the auger hole there, and with one hand grasping a shroud, he ordered Starbuck to send everybody aft.

"Sir!" said the mate, astonished at an order

7. **binnacle:** the case that holds the ship's compass.
8. **bigotry** (bĭg′ə-trē) **of purpose:** almost frenzied single-mindedness; bigotry suggests exclusion of other ideas.

seldom or never given on shipboard except in some extraordinary case.

"Send everybody aft," repeated Ahab. "Mastheads there! come down!"

When the entire ship's company were assembled, and with curious and not wholly unapprehensive faces were eyeing him, for he looked not unlike the weather horizon when a storm is coming up, Ahab, after rapidly glancing over the bulwarks, and then darting his eyes among the crew, started from his standpoint, and as though not a soul were nigh him resumed his heavy turns upon the deck. With bent head and half-slouched hat he continued to pace, unmindful of the wondering whispering among the men; till Stubb cautiously whispered to Flask that Ahab must have summoned them there for the purpose of witnessing a pedestrian feat. But this did not last long. Vehemently pausing, he cried:

"What do ye do when ye see a whale, men?"

"Sing out for him!" was the impulsive rejoinder from a score of clubbed voices.

"Good!" cried Ahab, with a wild approval in his tones, observing the hearty animation into which his unexpected question had so magnetically thrown them.

"And what do ye next, men?"

"Lower away, and after him!"

"And what tune is it ye pull to, men?"

"A dead whale or a stove[9] boat!"

More and more strangely and fiercely glad and approving grew the countenance of the old man at every shout; while the mariners began to gaze curiously at each other, as if marveling how it was that they themselves became so excited at such seemingly purposeless questions.

But they were all eagerness again as Ahab, now half revolving in his pivot-hole, with one hand reaching high up a shroud, and tightly, almost convulsively grasping it, addressed them thus:

"All ye mastheaders have before now heard me give orders about a white whale. Look ye! d'ye see this Spanish ounce of gold?"— holding up a broad bright coin to the sun—"it is a sixteen-dollar piece, men. D'ye see it? Mr. Starbuck, hand me yon top maul."

While the mate was getting the hammer, Ahab, without speaking, was slowly rubbing the gold piece against the skirts of his jacket, as if to heighten its luster, and without using any words was meanwhile lowly humming to himself, producing a sound so strangely muffled and inarticulate that it seemed the mechanical humming of the wheels of his vitality in him.

Receiving the top maul from Starbuck, he advanced towards the mainmast with the hammer uplifted in one hand, exhibiting the gold with the other, and with a high raised voice exclaiming: "Whosoever of ye raises me a white-headed whale with a wrinkled brow and a crooked jaw; whosoever of ye raises me that white-headed whale, with three holes punctured in his starboard fluke—look ye, whosoever of ye raises me that same white whale, he shall have this gold ounce, my boys!"

"Huzza! huzza!" cried the seamen, as with swinging tarpaulins they hailed the act of nailing the gold to the mast.

"It's a white whale, I say," resumed Ahab, as he threw down the top maul: "a white whale. Skin your eyes for him, men; look sharp for white water; if ye see but a bubble, sing out."

All this while Tashtego, Daggoo, and Queequeg had looked on with even more intense interest and surprise than the rest, and at the mention of the wrinkled brow and crooked jaw they had started as if each was separately touched by some specific recollection.

"Captain Ahab," said Tashtego, "that white whale must be the same that some call Moby-Dick."

"Moby-Dick?" shouted Ahab. "Do ye know the white whale then, Tash?"

"Does he fantail[10] a little curious, sir, before he goes down?" said the Gayheader deliberately.

9. **stove:** with a hole broken in.

10. **fantail:** spread the tail like a fan.

"And has he a curious spout, too," said Daggoo, "very bushy, even for a parmacety,[11] and mighty quick, Captain Ahab?"

"And he have one, two, tree—oh! good many iron in him hide, too, Captain," cried Queequeg disjointedly, "all twiske-tee betwisk, like him—him—" faltering hard for a word, and screwing his hand round and round as though uncorking a bottle—"like him—him—"

"Corkscrew!" cried Ahab, "aye, Queequeg, the harpoons lie all twisted and wrenched in him; aye, Daggoo, his spout is a big one, like a whole shock of wheat, and white as a pile of our Nantucket wool after the great annual sheepshearing; aye, Tashtego, and he fantails like a split jib in a squall. Death and devils! men, it is Moby-Dick ye have seen—Moby-Dick—Moby-Dick!"

"Captain Ahab," said Starbuck, who, with Stubb and Flask, had thus far been eyeing his superior with increasing surprise, but at last seemed struck with a thought which somewhat explained all the wonder. "Captain Ahab, I have heard of Moby-Dick—but it was not Moby-Dick that took off thy leg?"

"Who told thee that?" cried Ahab; then pausing, "Aye, Starbuck; aye, my hearties all round; it was Moby-Dick that dismasted me; Moby-Dick that brought me to this dead stump I stand on now. Aye, aye," he shouted with a terrific, loud, animal sob, like that of a heart-stricken moose; "aye, aye! it was that accursed white whale that razeed me; made a poor pegging lubber[12] of me forever and a day!" Then tossing both arms, with measureless imprecations he shouted out: "Aye, aye! and I'll chase him round Good Hope, and round the Horn, and round the Norway Maelstrom, and round perdition's flames before I give him up. And this is what ye have shipped for, men! to chase that white whale on both sides of land, and over all sides of earth, till he spouts black blood and rolls fin out. What say ye, men, will ye splice hands on it, now? I think ye do look brave."

"Aye, aye!" shouted the harpooneers and seamen, running closer to the excited old man: "A sharp eye for the White Whale; a sharp lance for Moby-Dick!"

"God bless ye," he seemed to half sob and half shout, "God bless ye, men. Steward! go draw the great measure of grog. But what's this long face about, Mr. Starbuck; wilt thou not chase the white whale? art not game for Moby-Dick?"

"I am game for his crooked jaw, and for the jaws of Death too, Captain Ahab, if it fairly comes in the way of the business we follow; but I came here to hunt whales, not my commander's vengeance. How many barrels will thy vengeance yield thee even if thou gettest it, Captain Ahab? it will not fetch thee much in our Nantucket market."

"Nantucket market! Hoot! But come closer, Starbuck; thou requirest a little lower layer. If money's to be the measurer, man, and the accountants have computed their great countinghouse the globe, by girdling it with guineas, one to every three parts of an inch; then, let me tell thee that my vengeance will fetch a great premium *here!*"

"He smites his chest," whispered Stubb; "what's that for? methinks it rings most vast, but hollow."

"Vengeance on a dumb brute!" cried Starbuck, "that simply smote thee from blindest instinct! Madness! To be enraged with a dumb thing, Captain Ahab, seems blasphemous."

"Hark ye yet again—the little lower layer. All visible objects, man, are but as pasteboard masks. But in each event—in the living act, the undoubted deed—there, some unknown but still reasoning thing puts forth the moldings of its features from behind the unreasoning mask. If man will strike, strike through the mask! How can the prisoner reach outside except by thrusting through the wall? To me, the white whale is that wall, shoved near to me. Sometimes I think there's naught beyond. But

---

11. **parmacety:** dialect for *spermaceti,* the waxy substance taken from a sperm whale's head and used in making candles.
12. **lubber:** a clumsy person.

'tis enough. He tasks me; he heaps me; I see in him outrageous strength, with an inscrutable malice sinewing it. That inscrutable thing is chiefly what I hate; and be the white whale agent, or be the white whale principal, I will wreak that hate upon him. Talk not to me of blasphemy, man; I'd strike the sun if it insulted me. For could the sun do that, then could I do the other; since there is ever a sort of fair play herein, jealousy presiding over all creations. But not my master, man, is even that fair play. Who's over me? Truth hath no confines. Take off thine eye! more intolerable than fiends' glarings is a doltish stare! So, so; thou reddenest and palest, my heat has melted thee to anger-glow. But look ye, Starbuck, what is said in heat, that thing unsays itself. There are men from whom warm words are small indignity. I meant not to incense thee. Let it go. Look! see yonder Turkish cheeks of spotted tawn—living, breathing pictures painted by the sun. The pagan leopards—the unrecking and unworshiping things that live, and seek and give no reasons for the torrid life they feel! The crew, man, the crew! Are they not one and all with Ahab, in this matter of the whale? See Stubb! he laughs! See yonder Chilean! he snorts to think of it. Stand up amid the general hurricane, thy one tossed sapling cannot, Starbuck! And what is it? Reckon it. 'Tis but to help strike a fin; no wondrous feat for Starbuck. What is it more? From this one poor hunt, then, the best lance out of all Nantucket, surely he will not hang back, when every foremasthand has clutched a whetstone. Ah! constrainings seize thee; I see! the billow lifts thee! Speak, but speak!—Aye, aye! thy silence, then, *that* voices thee. (*Aside*) Something shot from my dilated nostrils, he has inhaled it in his lungs. Starbuck now is mine; cannot oppose me now without rebellion."

"God keep me!—keep us all!" murmured Starbuck, lowly.

But in his joy at the enchanted, tacit acquiescence of the mate, Ahab did not hear his foreboding invocation; nor yet the low laugh from the hold; nor yet the presaging vibrations

of the winds in the cordage; nor yet the hollow flap of the sails against the masts, as for a moment their hearts sank in. For again Starbuck's downcast eyes lighted up with the stubbornness of life; the subterranean laugh died away; the winds blew on; the sails filled out; the ship heaved and rolled as before. Ah, ye admonitions and warnings! why stay ye not when ye come? But rather are ye predictions than warnings, ye shadows! Yet not so much predictions from without as verifications of the foregoing things within. For with little external to constrain us, the innermost necessities in our being, these still drive us on.

"The measure! the measure!" cried Ahab.

Receiving the brimming pewter, and turning to the harpooneers, he ordered them to produce their weapons. Then ranging them before him near the capstan,[13] with their harpoons in their hands, while his three mates stood at his side with their lances, and the rest of the ship's company formed a circle round the group, he stood for an instant searchingly eyeing every man of his crew. But those wild eyes met his, as the bloodshot eyes of the prai-

13. **capstan:** a large cylinder that turns and around which cables are wound.

rie wolves meet the eye of their leader ere he rushes on at their head in the trail of the bison; but, alas! only to fall into the hidden snare of the Indian.

"Drink and pass!" he cried, handing the heavy charged flagon to the nearest seaman. "The crew alone now drink. Round with it, round! Short drafts—long swallows, men; 'tis hot as Satan's hoof. So, so; it goes round excellently. It spiralizes in ye; forks out at the serpent-snapping eye. Well done; almost drained. That way it went, this way it comes. Hand it me—here's a hollow! Men, ye seem the years; so brimming life is gulped and gone. Steward, refill!

"Attend now, my braves. I have mustered ye all round this capstan; and ye mates, flank me with your lances; and ye harpooneers, stand there with your irons; and ye, stout mariners, ring me in, that I may in some sort revive a noble custom of my fishermen fathers before me. O men, you will yet see that— Ha! boy, come back? bad pennies come not sooner. Hand it me. Why, now, this pewter had run brimming again, wert not thou St. Vitus' imp[14]—away, thou ague!

"Advance, ye mates! Cross your lances full before me. Well done! Let me touch the axis." So saying, with extended arm, he grasped the three level, radiating lances at their crossed center; while so doing, suddenly and nervously twitched them; meanwhile glancing intently from Starbuck to Stubb, from Stubb to Flask. It seemed as though, by some nameless, interior volition, he would fain have shocked into them the same fiery emotion accumulated within the Leyden jar[15] of his own magnetic life. The three mates quailed before his strong, sustained, and mystic aspect. Stubb and Flask looked sideways from him; the honest eye of Starbuck fell downright.

"In vain!" cried Ahab; "but, maybe, 'tis well. For did ye three but once take the full-forced shock, then mine own electric thing, *that* had perhaps expired from out me. Perchance, too, it would have dropped ye dead. Perchance ye need it not. Down lances! And now, ye mates, I do appoint ye three cupbearers to my three pagan kinsmen there—yon three most honorable gentlemen and noblemen, my valiant harpooneers. Disdain the task? What, when the great Pope washes the feet of beggars, using his tiara for ewer? Oh, my sweet cardinals! your own condescension, *that* shall bend ye to it. I do not order ye; ye will it. Cut your seizings and draw the poles, ye harpooneers!"

Silently obeying the order, the three harpooneers now stood with the detached iron part of their harpoons, some three feet long, held, barbs up, before him.

"Stab me not with that keen steel! Cant them; cant them over! know ye not the goblet end? Turn up the socket! So, so; now, ye cupbearers, advance. The irons! take them; hold them while I fill!" Forthwith, slowly going from one officer to the other, he brimmed the harpoon sockets with the fiery waters from the pewter.

"Now, three to three, ye stand. Commend the murderous chalices! Bestow them, ye who are now made parties to this indissoluble league. Ha! Starbuck! but the deed is done! Yon ratifying sun now waits to sit upon it. Drink, ye harpooneers! drink and swear, ye men that man the deathful whaleboat's bow— Death to Moby-Dick! God hunt us all if we do not hunt Moby-Dick to his death!" The long, barbed steel goblets were lifted; and to cries and maledictions[16] against the white whale, the spirits were simultaneously quaffed down with a hiss. Starbuck paled, and turned, and shivered. Once more, and finally, the replenished pewter went the rounds among the frantic crew; when, waving his free hand to them, they all dispersed; and Ahab retired within his cabin.

14. **St. Vitus' imp:** Saint Vitus is the patron saint of persons afflicted with chorea, a nervous disorder characterized by irregular, jerking movements.

15. **Leyden** (lĭd'n) **jar:** a device for storing electrical charges, consisting of a glass jar coated with tinfoil inside and outside and a metal rod connected to the inner lining and passing through the lid.

16. **maledictions:** curses.

Moby-Dick is at last sighted in the Pacific Ocean. The *Pequod*'s boats, led by Ahab himself, pursue the whale for two days, during which one boat is sunk and Ahab's ivory leg broken off. As the third day of the chase dawns, the captain and crew prepare for a final confrontation with the great whale.

Ahab makes several references in this chapter to an earlier prophecy about his death. Before the voyage began, Ahab had smuggled aboard a special crew to man his own whaleboat in hunting Moby-Dick, keeping them hidden in the hold until needed. Wild and barbaric in appearance, they are Zoroastrians in religion—that is, believers that the earth is a place of eternal warfare between absolute good and absolute evil, a belief Ahab shares. Their leader, Fedallah, is referred to as "the Parsee." (Zoroastrians are also known as Parsees.) He prophesied that he would die before Ahab, but that Ahab would see him again; that there would be two hearses at Ahab's death, the second made of American wood (the whale proves to be the first "hearse," the ship the second); and that Ahab could die only by hemp—that is, by hanging. Each part of the prophecy proves true in this chapter, although not in ways that we might expect.

The Chase—Third Day

The morning of the third day dawned fair and fresh, and once more the solitary night man at the foremasthead was relieved by crowds of the daylight lookouts, who dotted every mast and almost every spar.

"D'ye see him?" cried Ahab; but the whale was not yet in sight.

"In his infallible wake, though; but follow that wake, that's all. Helm there; steady, as thou goest, and hast been going. What a lovely day again! were it a new-made world, and made for a summerhouse to the angels, and this morning the first of its throwing open to them, a fairer day could not dawn upon that world. Here's food for thought, had Ahab time to think; but Ahab never thinks; he only feels, feels, feels; *that's* tingling enough for mortal man! to think's audacity. God only has that right and privilege. Thinking is, or ought to be, a coolness and a calmness; and our poor hearts throb, and our poor brains beat too much for that. And yet I've sometimes thought my brain was very calm—frozen calm, this old skull cracks so, like a glass in which the contents turned to ice, and shiver it. And still this hair is growing now; this moment growing, and heat must breed it; but no, it's like that sort of common grass that will grow anywhere, between the earthy clefts of Greenland ice or in Vesuvius lava. How the wild winds blow it; they whip it about me as the torn shreds of split sails lash the tossed ship they cling to. A vile wind that has no doubt blown ere this through prison corridors and cells, and wards of hospitals, and ventilated them, and now comes blowing hither as innocent as fleeces. Out upon it!—it's tainted. Were I the wind, I'd blow no more on such a wicked, miserable world. I'd crawl somewhere to a cave, and slink there. And yet 'tis a noble and heroic thing, the wind! who ever conquered it? In every fight it has the last and bitterest blow. Run tilting at it, and you but run through it. Ha! a coward wind that strikes stark naked men, but will not stand to receive a single blow. Even Ahab is a braver thing—a nobler thing than *that*. Would now the wind but had a body; but all the things that most exasperate and outrage mortal man, all these things are bodiless, but only bodiless as objects, not as agents. There's a most special, a most cunning, oh, a most malicious difference! And yet I say again, and swear it now, that there's something all glorious and gracious in the wind. These warm trade winds, at least, that in the clear heavens blow straight on, in strong and steadfast, vigorous mildness; and veer not from their mark, however the baser currents of the sea may turn and tack, and mightiest Mississippies of the land swift and swerve about, uncertain where to go at last. And by the eternal poles! these same trades that so directly blow my good ship on; these trades, or something like them—something so unchangeable, and full as strong, blow my keeled soul along! To it! Aloft there! What d'ye see?"

"Nothing, sir."

"Nothing! and noon at hand! The doubloon[17] goes a-begging! See the sun! Aye, aye, it must be so. I've oversailed him. How, got the start? Aye, he's chasing *me* now; not I, *him*—that's bad; I might have known it, too. Fool! the lines—the harpoons he's towing. Aye, aye, I have run him by last night. About! about! Come down, all of ye but the regular lookouts! Man the braces!"

Steering as she had done, the wind had been somewhat on the *Pequod*'s quarter, so that now being pointed in the reverse direction, the braced ship sailed hard upon the breeze as she rechurned the cream in her own white wake.

"Against the wind he now steers for the open jaw," murmured Starbuck to himself, as he coiled the new-hauled main brace upon the rail. "God keep us, but already my bones feel damp within me, and from the inside wet my flesh. I misdoubt[18] me that I disobey my God in obeying him!"

"Stand by to sway me up!" cried Ahab, advancing to the hempen basket.[19] "We should meet him soon."

"Aye, aye, sir," and straightway Starbuck did Ahab's bidding, and once more Ahab swung on high.

17. **doubloon:** the gold coin Ahab had offered to the first man to spot the whale.
18. **misdoubt:** suspect.
19. **hempen basket:** Eager to be in a position to sight Moby-Dick, Ahab had earlier constructed a rope basket in which he could be lifted to the top of the mainmast by means of an improvised pulley device.

A whole hour now passed; gold-beaten out to ages. Time itself now held long breaths with keen suspense. But at last, some three points off the weather bow, Ahab descried the spout again, and instantly from the three mastheads three shrieks went up as if the tongues of fire had voiced it.

"Forehead to forehead I meet thee, this third time, Moby-Dick! On deck there!—brace sharper up; crowd her into the wind's eye. He's too far off to lower yet, Mr. Starbuck. The sails shake! Stand over that helmsman with a top maul! So, so; he travels fast, and I must down. But let me have one more good round look aloft here at the sea; there's time for that. An old, old sight, and yet somehow so young; aye, and not changed a wink since I first saw it, a boy, from the sand hills of Nantucket! The same!—the same!—the same to Noah as to me. There's a soft shower to leeward. Such lovely leewardings! They must lead somewhere—to something else than common land, more palmy than the palms. Leeward! the white whale goes that way; look to windward, then; the better if the bitterer quarter. But, goodbye, goodbye, old masthead! What's this?—green? aye, tiny mosses in these warped cracks. No such green weather stains on Ahab's head! There's the difference now between man's old age and matter's. But aye, old mast, we both grow old together; sound in our hulls, though, are we not, my ship? Aye, minus a leg, that's all. By heaven, this dead wood has the better of my live flesh every way. I can't compare with it; and I've known some ships made of dead trees outlast the lives of men made of the most vital stuff of vital fathers. What's that he said? he should still go before me, my pilot; and yet to be seen again? But where? Will I have eyes at the bottom of the sea, supposing I descend those endless stairs? and all night I've been sailing from him, wherever he did sink to. Aye, aye, like many more thou told'st direful truth as touching thyself, O Parsee; but, Ahab, there thy shot fell short. Goodbye, masthead—keep a good eye upon the whale, the while I'm gone. We'll talk tomorrow, nay, tonight, when the white whale lies down there, tied by head and tail."

He gave the word; and still gazing round him, was steadily lowered through the cloven blue air to the deck.

In due time the boats were lowered; but as standing in his shallop's stern, Ahab just hovered upon the point of the descent, he waved to the mate—who held one of the tackle ropes on deck—and bade him pause.

"Starbuck!"

"Sir?"

"For the third time my soul's ship starts upon this voyage, Starbuck."

"Aye, sir, thou wilt have it so."

"Some ships sail from their ports, and ever afterwards are missing, Starbuck!"

"Truth, sir: saddest truth."

"Some men die at ebb tide; some at low water; some at the full of the flood—and I feel now like a billow that's all one crested comb, Starbuck. I am old—shake hands with me, man."

Their hands met; their eyes fastened, Starbuck's tears the glue.

"Oh, my Captain, my Captain!—noble heart—go not—go not!—see, it's a brave man that weeps; how great the agony of the persuasion then!"

"Lower away!" cried Ahab, tossing the mate's arm from him. "Stand by the crew!"

In an instant the boat was pulling round close under the stern.

"The sharks! the sharks!" cried a voice from the low cabin window there; "O master, my master, come back!"

But Ahab heard nothing; for his own voice was high-lifted then; and the boat leaped on.

Yet the voice spake true; for scarce had he pushed from the ship when numbers of sharks, seemingly rising from out the dark waters beneath the hull, maliciously snapped at the blades of the oars every time they dipped in the water, and in this way accompanied the boat with their bites. It is a thing not uncommonly happening to the whale-boats in those swarming seas, the sharks at times apparently following them in the same prescient[20] way that vultures hover over the banners of the marching regiments in the East. But these were the first sharks that had been observed by the *Pequod* since the White Whale had been first descried; and whether it was that Ahab's crew were all such tiger-yellow barbarians, and therefore their flesh more musky to the senses of the sharks—a matter sometimes well known to affect them—however it was, they seemed to follow that one boat without molesting the others.

"Heart of wrought steel!" murmured Starbuck gazing over the side, and following with his eyes the receding boat—"canst thou yet ring boldly to that sight?—lowering thy keel among ravening sharks, and followed by them, open-mouthed to the chase; and this the critical third day?—For when three days flow together in one continuous intense pursuit, be sure the first is the morning, the second the noon, and the third the evening and the end of that thing—be that end what it may. Oh! my God! what is this that shoots through me, and leaves me so deadly calm, yet expectant—fixed at the top of a shudder! Future things swim before me, as in empty outlines and skeletons; all the past is somehow grown dim. Mary, girl, thou fadest in pale glories behind me; boy! I seem to see but thy eyes grown wondrous blue.[21] Strangest problems of life seem clearing; but clouds sweep between— Is my journey's end coming? My legs feel faint, like his who has footed it all day. Feel thy heart—beats it yet? Stir thyself, Starbuck!—stave it off—move, move! speak aloud!—Masthead there! See ye my boy's hand on the hill?—Crazed—aloft there!—keep thy keenest eye upon the boats—mark well the whale!—Ho! again!—drive off that hawk! see! he pecks—he tears the vane"—pointing to the red flag flying at the main-truck—"Ha, he soars away with it!—Where's the old man now? see'st thou that sight, O Ahab—shudder, shudder!"

20. **prescient** (prē'shē-ənt): knowing beforehand.
21. **Mary . . . blue:** Starbuck is addressing his wife and son, whom he last saw in Nantucket.

Herman Melville **285**

Wood engraving of "Mocha Dick," a whale renowned among sailors who greeted each other by asking "Any news of Mocha Dick?"

The boats had not gone very far when by a signal from the mastheads—a downward pointed arm, Ahab knew that the whale had sounded; but intending to be near him at the next rising, he held on his way a little sideways from the vessel, the becharmed crew maintaining the profoundest silence as the head-beat waves hammered and hammered against the opposing bow.

"Drive, drive in your nails, O ye waves! to their uttermost heads drive them in! ye but strike a thing without a lid; and no coffin and no hearse can be mine—and hemp only can kill me! Ha! ha!"

Suddenly the waters around them slowly swelled in broad circles; then quickly upheaved, as if sideways sliding from a submerged berg of ice, swiftly rising to the surface. A low rumbling sound was heard; a subterraneous hum; and then all held their breaths; as bedraggled with trailing ropes and harpoons and lances, a vast form shot lengthwise, but obliquely from the sea. Shrouded in a thin drooping veil of mist, it hovered for a moment in the rainbowed air, and then fell swamping back into the deep. Crushed thirty feet upwards, the waters flashed for an instant like heaps of fountains, then brokenly sank in a shower of flakes, leaving the circling surface creamed like new milk round the marble trunk of the whale.

"Give way!" cried Ahab to the oarsmen, and the boats darted forward to the attack; but maddened by yesterday's fresh irons that corroded in him, Moby-Dick seemed combinedly possessed by all the angels that fell from heaven. The wide tiers of welded tendons overspreading his broad white forehead, beneath the transparent skin, looked knitted together; as head on, he came churning his tail among the boats, and once more flailed them apart, spilling out the irons and lances from the two mates' boats, and dashing in one side of the upper part of their bows, but leaving Ahab's almost without a scar.

While Daggoo and Queequeg were stopping the strained planks, and as the whale swimming out from them turned, and showed one entire flank as he shot by them again, at that moment a quick cry went up. Lashed round and round to the fish's back, pinioned in the turns upon turns in which, during the past night, the whale had reeled the involutions of the lines around him, the half-torn body of the Parsee was seen; his sable raiment frayed to shreds; his distended eyes turned full upon old Ahab.

The harpoon dropped from his hand.

"Befooled, befooled!"—drawing in a long lean breath—"Aye, Parsee! I see thee again —Aye, and thou goest before; and this, *this* then is the hearse that thou didst promise. But I hold thee to the last letter of thy word. Where is the second hearse? Away, mates, to the ship! those boats are useless now; repair them if ye can in time, and return to me; if not, Ahab is enough to die— Down, men! the first thing that but offers to jump from this boat I stand in, that thing I harpoon. Ye are not other men, but my arms and my legs; and so obey me.— Where's the whale? gone down again?"

But he looked too nigh the boat; for as if bent upon escaping with the corpse he bore, and as if the particular place of the last encounter had been but a stage in his leeward voyage, Moby-Dick was now again steadily swimming forward; and had almost passed the ship—which thus far had been sailing in the contrary direction to him, though for the present her headway had been stopped. He seemed swimming with his utmost velocity, and now only intent upon pursuing his own straight path in the sea.

"Oh! Ahab," cried Starbuck, "not too late is it, even now, the third day, to desist. See! Moby-Dick seeks thee not. It is thou, thou, that madly seekest him!"

Setting sail to the rising wind, the lonely boat was swiftly impelled to leeward, by both oars and canvas. And at last when Ahab was sliding by the vessel, so near as plainly to distinguish Starbuck's face as he leaned over the rail, he hailed him to turn the vessel about, and follow him, not too swiftly, at a judicious interval.

Herman Melville **287**

Glancing upwards he saw Tashtego, Quee-queg, and Daggoo, eagerly mounting to the three mastheads; while the oarsmen were rocking in the two staved boats which had just been hoisted to the side, and were busily at work in repairing them. One after the other, through the portholes, as he sped, he also caught flying glimpses of Stubb and Flask, busying themselves on deck among bundles of new irons and lances. As he saw all this, as he heard the hammers in the broken boats, far other hammers seemed driving a nail into his heart. But he rallied. And now marking that the vane or flag was gone from the mainmast-head, he shouted to Tashtego, who had just gained that perch, to descend again for an-other flag, and a hammer and nails, and so nail it to the mast.

Whether fagged by the three days' running chase, and the resistance to his swimming in the knotted hamper he bore; or whether it was some latent deceitfulness and malice in him: whichever was true, the White Whale's way now began to abate, as it seemed, from the boat so rapidly nearing him once more; though indeed the whale's last start had not been so long a one as before. And still as Ahab glided over the waves the unpitying sharks ac-companied him; and so pertinaciously stuck to the boat, and so continually bit at the plying oars that the blades became jagged and crunched, and left small splinters in the sea at almost every dip.

"Heed them not! those teeth but give new rowlocks to your oars. Pull on! 'tis the better rest, the sharks' jaw, than the yielding water."

"But at every bite, sir, the thin blades grow smaller and smaller!"

"They will last long enough! pull on!—But who can tell"—he muttered—"whether these sharks swim to feast on the whale or on Ahab? But pull on! Aye, all alive, now—we near him. The helm! take the helm! let me pass"—and so saying, two of the oarsmen helped him for-ward to the bows of the still flying boat.

At length as the craft was cast to one side, and ran ranging along with the White Whale's flank, he seemed strangely oblivious of its ad-vance—as the whale sometimes will—and Ahab was fairly within the smoky mountain mist which, thrown off from the whale's spout, curled round his great Monadnock[22] hump; he was even thus close to him; when, with body arched back, and both arms lengthwise high-lifted to the poise, he darted his fierce iron and his far fiercer curse into the hated whale. As both steel and curse sank to the socket, as if sucked into a morass, Moby-Dick sidewise writhed; spasmodically rolled his nigh flank against the bow; and, without staving a hole in it, so suddenly canted the boat over that had it not been for the elevated part of the gunwale to which he then clung, Ahab would once more have been tossed into the sea. As it was, three of the oarsmen—who foreknew not the precise instant of the dart, and were therefore unpre-pared for its effects—these were flung out; but so fell that in an instant two of them clutched the gunwale again, and rising to its level on a combing wave, hurled themselves bodily inboard again; the third man helplessly dropping astern, but still afloat and swim-ming.

Almost simultaneously, with a mighty voli-tion of ungraduated, instantaneous swiftness, the White Whale darted through the weltering sea. But when Ahab cried out to the steersman to take new turns with the line, and hold it so; and commanded the crew to turn round on their seats, and tow the boat up to the mark; the moment the treacherous line felt that dou-ble strain and tug, it snapped in the empty air!

"What breaks in me? Some sinew cracks!— 'tis whole again; oars! oars! Burst in upon him!"

Hearing the tremendous rush of the sea-crashing boat, the whale wheeled round to present his blank forehead at bay; but in that evolution, catching sight of the nearing black hull of the ship; seemingly seeing in it the source of all his persecutions; bethinking it—it may be—a larger and nobler foe; of a sud-

22. **Monadnock:** a mountain in New Hampshire.

den, he bore down upon its advancing prow, smiting his jaws amid fiery showers of foam.

Ahab staggered; his hand smote his forehead. "I grow blind; hands! stretch out before me that I may yet grope my way. Is't night?"

"The whale! The ship!" cried the cringing oarsmen.

"Oars! oars! Slope downwards to thy depths, O sea, that ere it be forever too late, Ahab may slide this last, last time upon his mark! I see: the ship! the ship! Dash on, my men! will ye not save my ship?"

But as the oarsmen violently forced their boat through the sledgehammering seas, the before whale-smitten bow ends of two planks burst through, and in an instant almost, the temporarily disabled boat lay nearly level with the waves, its half-wading, splashing crew trying hard to stop the gap and bale out the pouring water.

Meantime, for that one beholding instant, Tashtego's masthead hammer remained suspended in his hand; and the red flag, half wrapping him as with a plaid, then streamed itself straight out from him, as his own forward-flowing heart; while Starbuck and Stubb, standing upon the bowsprit beneath, caught sight of the down-coming monster just as soon as he.

"The whale, the whale! Up helm, up helm! Oh, all ye sweet powers of air, now hug me close! Let not Starbuck die, if die he must, in a woman's fainting fit. Up helm, I say—ye fools, the jaw! the jaw! Is this the end of all my bursting prayers? all my lifelong fidelities? Oh, Ahab, Ahab, lo, thy work. Steady! helmsman, steady. Nay, nay! Up helm again! He turns to meet us! Oh, his unappeasable brow drives on towards one, whose duty tells him he cannot depart. My God, stand by me now!"

"Stand not by me, but stand under me, whoever you are that will now help Stubb; for Stubb, too, sticks here. I grin at thee, thou grinning whale! Who ever helped Stubb, or kept Stubb awake, but Stubb's own unwinking eye? And now poor Stubb goes to bed upon a mattress that is all too soft; would it were stuffed with brushwood! I grin at thee, thou grinning whale! Look ye, sun, moon, and stars! I call ye assassins of as good a fellow as ever spouted up his ghost. For all that, I would yet ring glasses with thee, would ye but hand the cup! Oh, oh! oh, oh! thou grinning whale, but there'll be plenty of gulping soon! Why fly ye not, O Ahab! For me, off shoes and jackets to it; let Stubb die in his drawers! A most moldy and oversalted death, though—cherries! cherries! cherries! Oh, Flask, for one red cherry ere we die!"

"Cherries? I only wish that we were where they grow. Oh, Stubb, I hope my poor mother's drawn my part-pay ere this; if not, few coppers will now come to her, for the voyage is up."

From the ship's bows, nearly all the seamen now hung inactive; hammers, bits of plank, lances, and harpoons, mechanically retained in their hands, just as they had darted from their various employments; all their enchanted eyes intent upon the whale, which, from side to side strangely vibrating his predestinating head, sent a broad band of over-spreading semicircular foam before him as he rushed. Retribution, swift vengeance, eternal malice were in his whole aspect, and spite of all that mortal man could do, the solid white buttress of his forehead smote the ship's starboard bow till men and timbers reeled. Some fell flat upon their faces. Like dislodged trucks, the heads of the harpooneers aloft shook on their bull-like necks. Through the breach, they heard the waters pour, as mountain torrents down a flume.

"The ship! The hearse!—the second hearse!" cried Ahab from the boat; "its wood could only be American!"

Diving beneath the settling ship, the whale ran quivering along its keel; but turning underwater, swiftly shot to the surface again, far off the other bow, but within a few yards of Ahab's boat, where, for a time, he lay quiescent.

"I turn my body from the sun. What ho, Tashtego! let me hear thy hammer. Oh! ye three unsurrendered spires of mine; thou un-cracked keel; and only god-bullied hull; thou firm deck, and haughty helm, and pole-pointed prow—death-glorious ship! must ye then perish, and without me? Am I cut off from the last fond pride of meanest ship-wrecked captains? Oh, lonely death on lonely life! Oh, now I feel my topmost greatness lies in my topmost grief. Ho, ho! from all your furthest bounds, pour ye now in, ye bold bil-lows of my whole foregone life, and top this one piled comber of my death! Towards thee I roll, thou all-destroying but unconquering whale; to the last I grapple with thee; from hell's heart I stab at thee; for hate's sake I spit my last breath at thee. Sink all coffins and all hearses to one common pool! and since neither can be mine, let me then tow to pieces, while still chasing thee, though tied to thee, thou damned whale! *Thus,* I give up the spear!"

The harpoon was darted; the stricken whale flew forward; with igniting velocity the line ran through the groove—ran foul. Ahab stooped to clear it; he did clear it; but the flying turn caught him round the neck, and voicelessly as Turkish mutes bowstring their victim, he was shot out of the boat, ere the crew knew he was gone. Next instant, the heavy eye splice in the rope's final end flew out of the stark-empty tub, knocked down an oarsman, and smiting the sea, disappeared in its depths.

For an instant, the tranced boat's crew stood still; then turned. "The ship? Great God, where is the ship?" Soon they through dim, bewildering mediums saw her sidelong fading phantom, as in the gaseous fata morgana,[23] only the uppermost masts out of water; while fixed by infatuation, or fidelity, or fate, to their once lofty perches, the pagan harpooneers still maintained their sinking lookouts on the sea. And now, concentric circles seized the lone boat itself, and all its crew, and each floating oar, and every lance pole, and spinning, ani-mate and inanimate, all round and round in

23. **fata morgana:** a mirage seen at sea.

one vortex, carried the smallest chip of the *Pequod* out of sight.

But as the last whelmings intermixingly poured themselves over the sunken head of the Indian at the mainmast, leaving a few inches of the erect spar yet visible, together with long streaming yards of the flag, which calmly undulated, with ironical coincidings, over the destroying billows they almost touched—at that instant, a red arm and a ham-mer hovered backwardly uplifted in the open air, in the act of nailing the flag faster and yet faster to the subsiding spar. A sky hawk that tauntingly had followed the maintruck down-wards from its natural home among the stars, pecking at the flag, and incommoding Tash-tego there; this bird now chanced to intercept its broad fluttering wing between the hammer and the wood; and simultaneously feeling that ethereal thrill, the submerged savage beneath, in his deathgasp, kept his hammer frozen there; and so the bird of heaven, with archan-gelic shrieks, and his imperial beak thrust up-wards, and his whole captive form folded in the flag of Ahab, went down with his ship, which, like Satan, would not sink to hell till she had dragged a living part of heaven along with her, and helmeted herself with it.

Now small fowls flew screaming over the yet yawning gulf; a sullen white surf beat against its steep sides; then all collapsed, and the great shroud of the sea rolled on as it rolled five thousand years ago.

Reading Check

1. What are Ahab's two distinguishing phys-ical features?
2. What reward does Ahab promise to the first seaman to sight Moby-Dick?
3. What is Starbuck's objection to the pur-suit of the white whale?
4. How does Ahab die?
5. What happens to the *Pequod*?

Commentary

Moby-Dick is at once an adventure story, a profound study of human character, and an informative report on the little-known occupation of whaling. It has also been called an American epic, since it creates from native legends a tale of heroic action on a grand scale. As he wrote, Melville had at hand technical books providing information on whales and the whaling industry. But the basic incidents of his story came from materials familiar to every sailor on a whaleship: the history of the ship *Essex,* which was sunk by a sperm whale in the Pacific; and the legend of a giant white whale, known as Mocha Dick, that so often escaped capture that it became the subject of many superstitions and was blamed for the loss of several ships and many mysterious deaths at sea.

But these matters are the barest nucleus of Melville's book. Into it he poured all he knew of life and his deepest feelings about those half-glimpsed meanings—of the vast universe and of our own inner worlds—that elude our knowledge. His fictional ship, the *Pequod,* is the ship of humanity, bearing in its crew representatives of the world's races and cultures. In Ishmael, the book's narrator, Melville created a participant-observer whose broad sympathies and remarkably flexible mind allow him to incorporate in himself the varied viewpoints of this strange crew. He responds to their common experience at every level, from factual observation to poetic meditation. Ishmael's reflections on the action are the intellectual center of the novel. But the dramatic center of the novel is unquestionably Captain Ahab, one of the most compelling characters in literature. The forces that drive Ahab on his doomed voyage are one key to the book's many meanings.

On an earlier voyage, Ahab lost a leg to the jaws of the giant white whale, Moby-Dick. In seeking vengeance upon a dumb brute that attacked and maimed him out of blind instinct, he may seem merely mad, as Starbuck would like to believe. But Ahab's madness is of a deeper sort. In the attack of the white whale, he has felt the pain and shock by which human beings must recognize their own mortality. He has brooded upon this experience until Moby-Dick—seemingly invulnerable and immortal—has become the symbol of all that is inscrutable and malicious in the universe, all that defies our will, resists our understanding, and frustrates our desire for ideal justice. Ahab means to strike through the "pasteboard masks" of nature to reach the inner reality. "All visible objects," he tells Starbuck, ". . . are but as pasteboard masks. But in each event . . . there, some unknown but still reasoning thing puts forth the moldings of its features from behind the unreasoning mask. If man will strike, strike through the mask!" Ahab, we discover, is "transcendental mad": he asks no less than absolute truth, the ultimate meaning of this existence in which we are subject to the accidents of fate and the hidden purposes of God. Like the transcendentalists, Ahab seeks the spiritual reality behind ex-

Cross-section of a whaling ship.
The Bettmann Archive

Herman Melville **291**

perience, but what he finds turns the transcendentalist vision upside down: not a benevolent universe that answers humanity's spiritual needs but one that is inscrutable and actively hostile. His soul seared by the experience that mutilated his body, Ahab is a defiant rebel against all human limitations. He will sacrifice life itself in his search for truth: "Truth hath no confines," he declares.

Still, Ahab must not be dismissed as merely evil. In his struggle against all those things that limit human life, there is the heroic grandeur of humanity's long effort to know the meaning of existence. He is noble and religious as well as sacrilegious—"a grand, ungodly, godlike man." Nor is his "madness" his alone. Others recognize in him the authority of the man who has suffered. As we see in "The Quarter-Deck" chapter, the whole crew is swept up in his need to strike back at the blows of life, to have revenge upon all that baffles us or speaks to us of ultimate death.

But it is Ishmael, not Ahab, who realizes the meaning of this fateful voyage. It is through Ishmael's vision that we see that Ahab's quest for absolute truth must result in suicide, the sacrifice of the ship of humanity. Life, Ishmael discovers, is always a voyage into uncharted waters. It offers no certainties but only the ever-changing meanings of human experience. In Ishmael's vision, we must live within the limitations of our understanding, come to terms with our mortality, and welcome brotherhood with all fellow mortals. The ultimate mysteries of existence symbolized by the white whale still elude us. Ahab believes he sees in Moby-Dick a principle of absolute evil, but Ishmael observes early in the novel that the great whale has no face, no expression: people read only their own meanings into that blank whiteness.

Melville saw deep dangers in the transcendentalist desire to establish meanings for God, humanity, and nature, and especially in the desire to transcend human limits. Seekers of absolutes deceive themselves. We live in a neutral universe that has "meaning" only in our human perceptions, and historical actualities are our only guides to truth. Melville knew that, to many, his book would be unorthodox, even shocking. But he also knew that in exploring the profundities of mortal existence on this ocean-ringed earth, he had served the cause of truth. Having finished *Moby-Dick*, he wrote to Hawthorne: "I have written a wicked book, and feel spotless as the lamb."

For Study and Discussion

Analyzing and Interpreting the Selections

Ahab

1. Ishmael takes his impression of Ahab's character from details of appearance and manner. We sense Ahab's feelings and personality only by inference—what the details suggest to us of his nature. In the second paragraph, in a series of striking images, Ahab appears a man cut away from the fire or forged from bronze or seamed by lightning like a great tree. What do these "fiery" images suggest about Ahab's character?

2. The ship's officers make no allusion to the livid scar that seems to run over Ahab's entire body. But there is much talk of this scar among the superstitious crew. What is the effect of making Ahab the subject of superstitious stories?

3. Ishmael is so struck by Ahab's overall appearance that it is not until the third paragraph that he notices the most obvious thing—the ivory leg made from a sperm whale's jaw. How does this "barbaric" white leg contribute to the "overbearing grimness" of the captain's appearance?

4. As the ship sails south, Ahab's mood seems to improve with the improving weather. What comparison in the last paragraph indicates that Ahab has other aspects to his nature besides the grim hardness we see first?

The Quarter-Deck

1. In an extraordinary break from custom, Ahab suddenly orders the entire crew to the quarter-deck. **a.** What is the underlying purpose of his "seemingly purposeless questions"? **b.** In what specific ways does the crew respond?

2. In the long speech beginning "Hark ye yet again" (page 280), it is clear that Ahab pursues Moby-Dick out of his rage at the human condition, and that retaliation for his personal injury has become a minor concern. Study this speech. In what sense does he see each human being as a "prisoner" and the white whale as a "wall" that hides a further reality?

3. It is in this speech, also, that Ahab triumphs over Starbuck, a brave and thoughtful man who sees Ahab's vengeance as madness. Why do you think Starbuck yields to Ahab's obsession?

4. The ritual that Ahab contrives, in which the mates (the final killers of a whale) serve as cupbearers to the harpooneers (those who strike the first blow), is meant to bind the crew to Ahab's will and to his oath of vengeance: "Death to Moby-Dick!" What details in the description of the ritual show the ritual and oath to be expressions of Ahab's madness?

The Chase—Third Day

1. Ahab is so obsessed with destroying Moby-Dick that all nature seems an antagonist. In his first long speech, Ahab taunts the wind as a "coward" that strikes but will not stand and fight. "Would now the wind but had a body; but all the things that most exasperate and outrage mortal man, all these things are bodiless. . . ." In "The Quarter-Deck" chapter, Ahab speaks of striking or fighting another mortal enemy—the "pasteboard masks" (page 280). What does Ahab hope to achieve by battling nature's mysteries?

2. Ahab notices bits of green moss growing in the tiny cracks of the mast. What is suggested in his observation that the old mast bears evidence of new life but that his own old head does not?

3. As Ahab's whaleboat pulls away from the ship, a sea hawk tears the captain's flag from the mast. What omen do you find in this incident?

4. When Moby-Dick rises from the depths, Ahab sees the Parsee once more. His body is lashed to the whale's back, and his distended eyes stare at Ahab. Despite this warning of death, what holds Ahab to his purpose?

5. Ahab madly defies the whale to the end. He pays for his revenge with his own life and the lives of his entire crew except Ishmael. As the *Pequod* sinks, a hawk is imprisoned against the mast, and this "bird of heaven" is carried down into "the great shroud of the sea." What does this symbolize about Ahab's mad quest?

Literary Elements

Moby-Dick As Symbol

A symbol usually has several meanings. (For a discussion of symbols, see page 255.) Melville's white whale is often regarded as the most complex symbol in American literature. Among other things, Moby-Dick symbolizes "the ungraspable phantoms of life." As Melville liked to point out, more than three-fifths of the earth's surface is ocean, an alien environment that hides in its depths a different and mostly unknown creation. As a foreign, untamed part of nature, the ocean represented to Melville the unseen regions of human nature, those "innermost necessities of our being" that are beyond our grasp. In being a part of the ocean's mysteries, the great whale is a symbol of all that is deep-diving in ourselves. "I love all men who dive [in thought]," Melville wrote. "Any fish can swim near the surface, but it takes a great whale to go down stairs five miles or more. . . ."

In his gigantic size, in his apparent intelligence, and above all, in his strange whiteness, Moby-Dick is a special symbol of "thought-diving." White suggests purity and innocence, but it is also the pallor of illness and death and the color of ghosts. To a sailor, the white fog, in which one can easily lose all sense of direction, is a mortal danger. There is, Ishmael affirms, a stabbing fear in this whiteness: "Is it that by its indefiniteness it shadows forth the heartless immensities of the universe, and thus stabs us from behind with the thought of annihilation, when beholding the white depths of the milky way?" Against the vastness of the universe (the endless snows of a polar landscape is another example), we are struck by the thought of our own mortality.

Each sailor aboard the *Pequod* attaches his own meaning to Moby-Dick. But Ahab gives himself over completely to his personal vision, abandoning all the securities by which human beings must live. Ishmael can sympathize with Ahab's motives but must warn against his example. It is human to explore the strange seas of experience in search of meaning, but it is suicide to abandon all safe harbors in the pursuit of a final truth: ". . . as this appalling ocean surrounds the verdant land, so in the soul of man there lies one insular Tahiti, full of peace and joy, but encompassed by all the horrors of the half-known life. God keep thee! Push not off from that isle, thou canst never return!"

Writing About Literature

Analyzing Ahab as Symbol

In certain respects, Captain Ahab is also a symbol. Reread the paragraphs on page 277 that describe his physical appearance and bearing. Keep in mind Ahab's relationship to the white whale, his past and present actions, and his fate. Then, in an essay, tell what you think Ahab symbolizes. Be sure to support your statements with specific references to the selection.

Drawing of battle of Shiloh on April 6, 1862, by B. H. Lovie. The circles indicate positions of Confederate batteries.

Shiloh: A Requiem

The Civil War battle of Shiloh was fought near the Shiloh Baptist Church in Tennessee in April 1862. The battle was marked by the heavy loss of life on both the Union and Confederate sides. Melville called the following poem a *requiem*. A requiem is a musical composition or poem lamenting the dead.

Skimming lightly, wheeling still,
  The swallows fly low
Over the field in clouded days,
  The forest-field of Shiloh—
Over the field where April rain   5
Solaced the parched ones stretched in pain
Through the pause of night
That followed the Sunday fight
  Around the church of Shiloh—
The church so lone, the log-built one,   10

That echoed to many a parting groan
  And natural prayer
  Of dying foemen mingled there—
Foemen at morn, but friends at eve—
  Fame or country least their care: 15
(What like a bullet can undeceive!)
  But now they lie low,
While over them the swallows skim,
  And all is hushed at Shiloh.

The Maldive Shark

About the Shark, phlegmatical one,
Pale sot of the Maldive sea,°
The sleek little pilot fish,° azure and slim,
How alert in attendance be.
From his saw-pit of mouth, from his charnel° of maw   5
They have nothing of harm to dread,
But liquidly glide on his ghastly flank
Or before his Gorgonian° head;
Or lurk in the port of serrated teeth
In white triple tiers of glittering gates,   10
And there find a haven when peril's abroad,
An asylum in jaws of the Fates!
They are friends; and friendly they guide him to prey,
Yet never partake of the treat—
Eyes and brains to the dotard lethargic and dull,   15
Pale ravener of horrible meat.

2. **Maldive sea:** a part of the Indian Ocean. 3. **pilot fish:** small fish often found accompanying a shark. 5. **charnel:** cemetery or house where corpses are kept. 8. **Gorgonian:** The Gorgons, monsters of Greek mythology, were three sisters who had snakes for hair and whose appearance was so horrible that the sight of them turned human beings to stone.

For Study and Discussion

Analyzing and Interpreting the Poems

Shiloh: A Requiem

1. What is the tone of the poem? Is it simply one of sorrow for the dead as implied by its subtitle or does it suggest other feelings?

2. Among the ironies of the poem is the fact that the battle was fought at a church and on a Sunday. But the strongest irony is the fact that these young men who were foes in the morning of that day were "friends at eve." **a.** In what way does death turn bitter enemies into "friends"? **b.** In what way does death clear up illusions about war and its causes?

The Maldive Shark

1. The opening four lines contrast the dull, sluggish ("phlegmatical") shark with the sleek, beautiful pilot fish that attend him. In the light of what we learn about the function of the pilot fish, what irony do you find in their "alert" attendance?

2. What details of the shark's appearance convey the deadly nature of a predator?

3. The seemingly harmless pilot fish actually guide the shark to his prey. In pointing out this behavior, what does Melville imply about nature?

Writing About Literature

Discussing Attitudes Toward Nature

In a brief composition, discuss the attitude toward nature expressed in "The Maldive Shark." Is it optimistic or pessimistic? In your opinion, how does this attitude compare with Captain Ahab's view of the world?

HENRY WADSWORTH LONGFELLOW
1807–1882

No other American poet, not even Robert Frost, has matched Henry Wadsworth Longfellow's popularity at the height of his career. During his lifetime his poetry was admired throughout Europe and translated into twenty-four languages. In America he was the poet who was everywhere read and everywhere quoted. His seventy-fifth birthday was observed in schoolrooms throughout the country. After his death, a bust of Longfellow was placed in the Poet's Corner of Westminster Abbey, which contains the tombs or monuments of such famous English poets as Chaucer, Shakespeare, and Milton. Longfellow was the first American poet to be so honored.

With a sure sense of his audience, Longfellow himself supplied the word that has since been used to describe his place in literary history. He confidently asked of his readers

At your warm fireside, when the lamps are lighted,
To have my place reserved among the rest. . . .

He is known now as the foremost of the Fireside Poets, a group that includes James Russell Lowell, Oliver Wendell Holmes, and John Greenleaf Whittier. As the term suggests, the Fireside Poets wrote for a family audience, usually on subjects of general appeal: nature, home and family, religious and moral lessons, and patriotism.

Longfellow was born the son of a lawyer in Portland, Maine, and was educated at nearby Bowdoin College, where Nathaniel Hawthorne was his classmate. His father warned him that America was not yet wealthy enough "to afford encouragement to merely literary men," and he would have to combine his writing with another profession. He considered the ministry and the law but, finally, accepted the opportunity to become Bowdoin's first professor of modern languages. In preparation for his duties, he lived and traveled for several years in Europe, studying languages and absorbing impressions of

Henry Wadsworth Longfellow (1869).
Engraving.

the "Old World." Thereafter, first at Bowdoin and then at Harvard, he combined the teaching of languages with his career as a poet. With each new book, his reputation grew until, in his late forties, he could support himself by his writing. In 1854, after eighteen years at Harvard, he resigned his professorship to devote himself for the rest of his life to his poems.

Not a man engaged by the public issues of his time, Longfellow chose general subjects for his poetry. For Longfellow, poetry was less a special vision than an expression of the common knowledge and feelings of all who share in a culture. He believed his task was to create in memorable form a common heritage for Americans and in the process to create an audience for poetry. Through his poems, which were remarkably varied in form and meter, Longfellow shared with thousands of Americans the recreated past of "Paul Revere's Ride," the Plymouth Colony legend of *The Courtship of Miles Standish*, the Indian myths of *The Song of Hiawatha*, and a tragic episode of Canadian-American history in *Evange-* *line*. Walt Whitman wrote that Longfellow "strikes a splendid average, and does not sing exceptional passions, or humanity's jagged escapades. . . . On the contrary, his songs soothe and heal." America, Whitman concluded, "may be reverently thankful" for such a poet.

A Psalm of Life

WHAT THE HEART OF THE YOUNG MAN
SAID TO THE PSALMIST°

Tell me not, in mournful numbers,°
   Life is but an empty dream!
For the soul is dead that slumbers,
   And things are not what they seem.

Life is real—life is earnest—   5
   And the grave is not its goal:
Dust thou art, to dust returnest,°
   Was not spoken of the soul.

Not enjoyment, and not sorrow,
   Is our destined end or way;   10
But to *act,* that each tomorrow
   Find us farther than today.

Art is long, and time is fleeting,
   And our hearts, though stout and brave,
Still, like muffled drums, are beating   15
   Funeral marches to the grave.

In the world's broad field of battle,
   In the bivouac of Life,
Be not like dumb, driven cattle!
   Be a hero in the strife!   20

Trust no Future, howe'er pleasant!
   Let the dead Past bury its dead!
Act—act in the glorious Present!
   Heart within, and God o'erhead!

Lives of great men all remind us   25
   We can make *our* lives sublime,
And, departing, leave behind us
   Footsteps on the sands of time.

Footsteps, that, perhaps another,
   Sailing o'er life's solemn main,   30
A forlorn and shipwrecked brother,
   Seeing, shall take heart again.

Let us then be up and doing,
   With a heart for any fate;
Still achieving, still pursuing,   35
   Learn to labor and to wait.

° **Psalmist:** the unspecified psalmist referred to has been thought to be either David of Psalm 103 or the writer of Ecclesiastes 3:20. 1. **numbers:** meters, rhythm. 7. **to dust returnest:** "For dust thou art, and unto dust shalt thou return" (Genesis 3:19).

Nature

As a fond mother, when the day is o'er,
   Leads by the hand her little child to bed,
   Half willing, half reluctant to be led,
   And leave his broken playthings on the floor,
Still gazing at them through the open door,   5
   Nor wholly reassured and comforted
   By promises of others in their stead,
   Which, though more splendid, may not please him more;
So Nature deals with us, and takes away
   Our playthings one by one, and by the hand   10
   Leads us to rest so gently, that we go
Scarce knowing if we wish to go or stay,
   Being too full of sleep to understand
   How far the unknown transcends the what we know.

The Arrow and the Song

I shot an arrow into the air,
It fell to earth, I knew not where;
For, so swiftly it flew, the sight
Could not follow it in its flight.

I breathed a song into the air,   5
It fell to earth, I knew not where;
For who has sight so keen and strong,
That it can follow the flight of song?

Long, long afterward, in an oak
I found the arrow, still unbroke;   10
And the song, from beginning to end,
I found again in the heart of a friend.

Evangeline

A Tale of Acadie

Evangeline is a long narrative in verse. The first part of the poem tells the story of an idyllic French village in eighteenth-century Nova Scotia, which the French called Acadie. When the British conquer the French colonies in the New World, the Acadians are driven into exile, and two betrothed lovers, Evangeline Bellefontaine and Gabriel Lajeunesse, are separated. The second part of the poem tells of Evangeline's long, devoted search for Gabriel, first down the Mississippi River to Louisiana, where the Acadians came to be called Cajuns, the ancestors of the people still known by that name; and then through the western, northern, and eastern parts of what are now the United States. She finds Gabriel at last just as he is dying.

Evangeline's devotion, her humility, and her deep religious trust in God make it clear that this is a spiritual journey. Although a romantic story of separated lovers is the basis of action in the poem, Longfellow's real interest is in depicting the steadfast courage of a remarkable woman and in describing the enormously varied and unfamiliar landscapes through which she pursues her search. Two well-known passages from the poem are included here.

Longfellow chose an unusual meter for this poem, unrhymed hexameter, a line consisting of six feet. Although it was a standard verse form in classic Greek and Latin poetry (no doubt the source of Longfellow's fondness for it), hexameter is not easily adapted to English, and *Evangeline* is the most notable example of it in the language. It is obviously a slow measure (the English poet Alexander Pope complained that hexameter "like a wounded snake, drags its slow length along"), as is evident in a scansion of the first two lines:

This is the | forest pri | meval. The | murmuring | pines and the | hemlocks,
Bearded with | moss, and in | garments | green, indis | tinct in the | twilight.

This slow movement and long line nevertheless seem suited to the meditative and often melancholy tone of the poem.

The Land of Evangeline (1874) by Joseph Rusling Meeker (1827–1889). Oil on canvas.
St. Louis Art Museum, Purchase: Funds given by Mrs. W. P. Edgerton, by exchange

Prelude

This is the forest primeval. The murmuring pines and the hemlocks,
Bearded with moss, and in garments green, indistinct in the twilight,
Stand like Druids of eld,° with voices sad and prophetic,
Stand like harpers hoar,° with beards that rest on their bosoms.
Loud from its rocky caverns, the deep-voiced neighboring ocean   5
Speaks, and in accents disconsolate answers the wail of the forest.

   This is the forest primeval; but where are the hearts that beneath it
Leaped like the roe,° when he hears in the woodland the voice of the huntsman?
Where is the thatch-roofed village, the home of Acadian farmers—

3. **Druids of eld:** members of a pre-Christian religious order of priests in ancient Europe.   4. **harpers hoar:** minstrels who are gray with age.   8. **roe:** deer.

Men whose lives glided on like rivers that water the woodlands, 10
Darkened by shadows of earth, but reflecting an image of heaven?
Waste are those pleasant farms, and the farmers forever departed!
Scattered like dust and leaves, when the mighty blasts of October
Seize them, and whirl them aloft, and sprinkle them far o'er the ocean.
Naught but tradition remains of the beautiful village of Grand-Pré.° 15

Ye who believe in affection that hopes, and endures, and is patient,
Ye who believe in the beauty and strength of woman's devotion,
List to the mournful tradition still sung by the pines of the forest;
List to a Tale of Love in Acadie, home of the happy.

FROM **Part Two**

Far in the West there lies a desert land, where the mountains 20
Lift, through perpetual snows, their lofty and luminous summits.
Down from their jagged, deep ravines, where the gorge, like a gateway,
Opens a passage rude to the wheels of the emigrant's wagon,°
Westward the Oregon flows and the Walleway and Owyhee.
Eastward, with devious course, among the Wind River Mountains, 25
Through the Sweetwater Valley precipitate leaps the Nebraska;
And to the south, from Fontaine-qui-bout and the Spanish Sierras,
Fretted with sands and rocks, and swept by the wind of the desert,
Numberless torrents, with ceaseless sound, descend to the ocean,
Like the great chords of a harp, in loud and solemn vibrations. 30
Spreading between these streams are the wondrous, beautiful prairies;
Billowy bays of grass ever rolling in shadow and sunshine,
Bright with luxuriant clusters of roses and purple amorphas.
Over them wandered the buffalo herds, and the elk and the roebuck;
Over them wandered the wolves, and herds of riderless horses; 35
Fires that blast and blight, and winds that are weary with travel;
Over them wander the scattered tribes of Ishmael's children,°
Staining the desert with blood; and above their terrible war-trails
Circles and sails aloft, on pinions majestic, the vulture,
Like the implacable soul of a chieftain slaughtered in battle, 40
By invisible stairs ascending and scaling the heavens.
Here and there rise smokes from the camps of these savage marauders;
Here and there rise groves from the margins of swift-running rivers;
And the grim, taciturn bear, the anchorite monk° of the desert,
Climbs down their dark ravines to dig for roots by the brookside, 45
And over all is the sky, the clear and crystalline heaven,
Like the protecting hand of God and inverted above them.

15. **Grand-Pré** (grăn′ prā): the home of Evangeline and Gabriel.   23. **emigrant's wagon:** *Evangeline* was published in 1847, at the height of the westward migration of farmers to Oregon and California.   37. **Ishmael's children:** a reference to the then popular notion that the Indians of the western plains were descended from the original ten scattered tribes of ancient Israel.   44. **anchorite monk:** The solitary bear is compared to a religious hermit.

The Tide Rises, the Tide Falls

The tide rises, the tide falls,
The twilight darkens, the curlew° calls;
Along the sea sands damp and brown
The traveler hastens toward the town,
   And the tide rises, the tide falls.   5

Darkness settles on roofs and walls,
But the sea, the sea in the darkness calls;
The little waves, with their soft white hands,
Efface the footprints in the sands,
   And the tide rises, the tide falls.   10

The morning breaks; the steeds in their stalls
Stamp and neigh as the hostler calls;
The day returns, but nevermore
Returns the traveler to the shore,
   And the tide rises, the tide falls.   15

2. **curlew:** a shore bird whose call is associated with evening.

Time and Tide (c. 1873). Oil painting by Alfred Thompson Bricher. Dallas Museum of Art, Foundation for the Arts Collection, gift of Mr. and Mrs. Frederick Mayer

Analyzing and Interpreting the Poems

A Psalm of Life

1. In its opening stanza the poem rejects the "mournful" rhythms of language that bear a sad or melancholy message. The lines of this poem are short and are frequently interrupted ("Life is real—life is earnest—"). How does this active, energetic rhythm relate to the meaning of the poem?

2. Overall, the poem is a call to action and to an attitude of vigorous courage in facing life. What are the obstacles that this attitude must apparently overcome?

3. Consider the view of time set forth in lines 21–24. **a.** How does this relate to the philosophy of action in the poem? **b.** Why is calling life "a bivouac" (line 18) appropriate in this context?

4. The poem speaks both of the immortality of the soul (lines 7–8) and the lasting effect of individual achievements (lines 25–28). "Footprints in the sands

of time" has long been the most famous line in the poem. Does it seem to have two different implications?

Nature

1. This poem is based on an **analogy,** that is, a comparison between things that are in some respects similar. **a.** To what is the process of dying compared? **b.** In what sense is a person of any age like a "little child" in leaving life behind?

2. Our occupations in this world are spoken of as "playthings." In what sense do they become "broken"?

3. Although the poem is about death, it does not present death as terrifying. According to the poem, how is the pain of death softened by Nature?

The Arrow and the Song

1. This short poem concerns the long-term effects of actions and words. How are they connected in the opening couplets of the first two stanzas?

2. What lesson should be drawn from the analogy that is made between the arrow and the song in the last stanza?

Evangeline

1. In the opening stanza the images and sounds of primeval nature convey an impression of sadness and melancholy. What words contribute to this?

2. The second stanza makes equally melancholy references to an abandoned village, farms going to waste, and a vanished population. **a.** According to lines 11 and 12, what was life like there for the Acadians? **b.** Why is it appropriate that the disappearance of this life and these people is put in terms of a natural event, the winds of October blowing away the leaves of summer?

3. The third stanza, without naming her, introduces Evangeline. **a.** How is the "mournful tradition" of her story related to nature? **b.** How does that make a transition from the earlier stanzas?

4. The lines from Part Two portray many aspects of nature, both attractive and unattractive. What dominant impression do we take of this wild land?

5. A seemingly strange comparison is made between the vulture that circles above the "terrible war-trails" of the Indians and the soul of a chief "slaughtered in battle." What is the basis of this comparison?

6. The final image of the sky, "Like the protecting hand of God," is clearly reassuring. Can it be related to earlier religious references in the stanza?

The Tide Rises, the Tide Falls

1. In this poem, the analogy between the sea and human life is developed mostly through details of atmosphere and setting. What details of setting in the first stanza suggest that this "traveler" is nearing death?

2. Explain the significance of lines 8–9, in which the breaking waves are pictured as white hands that wipe out the traveler's footprints.

3. The refrain, "And the tide rises, the tide falls," occurs three times. What is the effect of this repetition?

4. What do the signs of awakening life in the final stanza indicate about Longfellow's attitude toward death?

5. Longfellow used the image of footprints in sand forty years earlier in "A Psalm of Life" (page 297). How is the image in that poem given a different meaning?

Literary Elements

The Sonnet

"Nature" is a sonnet. A **sonnet** is a poem of fourteen lines, usually written in iambic pentameter, that follows a specific pattern of rhymes. The sonnet is one of the most challenging of all poetic forms, and has attracted poets over the centuries. The sonnet has proved durable because it is at once large enough to permit full development of an idea and yet strict enough in its form to impose order and intensity upon the treatment of that idea.

The two principal kinds of sonnets are known as the **Petrarchan,** or **Italian, sonnet** and the **Shakespearean,** or **English, sonnet.** These two kinds of sonnets are distinguished by their different rhyme schemes. The English sonnet is composed of three **quatrains** (groups of four lines) and a final **couplet** (two rhymed lines). In the rhyme scheme of the English sonnet, the first line of each quatrain rhymes with the third, the second line with the fourth. The rhyme scheme of the three quatrains and the final couplet is therefore represented this way: *abab cdcd efef gg.* There is a close relationship between the sonnet's rhyme scheme and the development of the poet's idea. Usually, each quatrain is a variation on the basic theme, and the final couplet draws a conclusion about it.

The Italian sonnet, which is the form Longfellow always used, has a different rhyme scheme. It has

two divisions: the first eight lines are the **octave,** and the final six lines are the **sestet.** The octave usually employs only two rhyme sounds in a very strict pattern, rhyming *abba abba.* The sestet permits some variation, as we can see in "Nature."

As in an English sonnet, the structure and rhyme scheme of an Italian sonnet are closely related to the idea. The division into octave and sestet usually dictates that the sonnet's idea be divided into two parts. In some Italian sonnets, for example, the octave states a general proposition, and the sestet makes a specific application of the idea. In other Italian sonnets, the octave establishes one part of a comparison and the sestet completes it. In yet others, the octave poses a question or problem, and the sestet resolves it.

1. Write out the rhyme scheme of "Nature," using the letters *a, b,* and so on.

2. Explain how the sestet of "Nature" establishes the second part of the comparison that is explored in the poem.

Writing About Literature

Comparing an Aspect of Two Poems

Bryant's "Thanatopsis" (page 153), a meditation on death, and Longfellow's "A Psalm of Life" grow out of different moods and express different philosophies. Yet they nevertheless have certain resemblances. Write an essay in which you compare the treatment of time in the two poems.

JOHN GREENLEAF WHITTIER
1807–1892

John Greenleaf Whittier (1881). Photograph.

John Greenleaf Whittier's background, unlike that of the other Fireside Poets, included no cultural or educational advantages. Whittier represented a very different New England tradition. He was born in a log house on a small farm that an ancestor had cleared from the Massachusetts wilderness in 1688. A feeling for rural family life, for the seasons and the land, for frugal ways and simple pleasures was deeply ingrained in Whittier, and it is the theme of his greatest poem, *Snowbound.*

Whittier received only a sketchy education in the local schools, but he found a lifelong intellectual influence and moral direction in his family's Quaker religion. By emphasizing the individual's intuition or "inner light" as the guide to spiritual truth, Quakerism makes study and self-expression a moral duty. From early childhood, Whittier's imagination was nourished by the Bible and the mysticism of religious writings. He was equally influenced by the social principles of his faith. Pacifists by conviction, Quakers emphasize the place of conscience in all social actions. It is appropriate that the most important moral and social cause of Whittier's life should have been the abolition of slavery.

While still in his teens and working as a shoemaker's apprentice, Whittier began sending poems to newspapers. Soon he was drawn into a number of reform movements, devoting his principal energies to the antislavery cause. His meager income came from his work as a journalist for small antislavery newspapers. He became active in politics and served a term in the Massachusetts legislature. Once he was stoned and shot at as an "agitator" in New Hampshire. Tall, commanding, dressed in Quaker black, he was a notable speaker at abolitionist rallies. For these meetings and for newspapers, he wrote literally hundreds of political poems, most of them quickly forgotten. The long struggle had its costs for Whittier's career and for his conscience. He once called himself "a fighting Quaker" and added, sadly, that he was "sometimes more fighter than Quaker." A man who abhorred violence, he had hoped in vain that the violence of slavery could end without the violence of war. When the Civil War came and the abolition of slavery was achieved at long last, Whittier withdrew from public affairs to devote himself to his work.

Even in his busiest years of political activity, Whittier produced a thin trickle of poems that were more literary than political. By 1857, when he was fifty, his reputation among fellow writers was high enough so that he was asked to be one of the founders of a new literary magazine, *The Atlantic Monthly.* He had long lamented the fact that poets paid little attention to rural New England, to "the poetry of human life and simple nature, of the hearth and farm field." He was in effect describing the subject matter of his own best poems: the local customs and regional legends of rural people, the tightknit quality of family farm life, the historical narratives that passed from generation to generation in small villages. The publication of *Snowbound* in 1866 brought him national fame and, at last, modest prosperity. His seventieth birthday in 1877 was celebrated at a gathering of notable literary figures of three generations, from Bryant through Mark Twain; accounts of the event appeared in the press across the land. Despite this late recognition, Whittier remained modest and retiring, devoted always to the "plain speech" of his Quaker heritage. He was a faithful recorder of the simple rural life he knew best, a life that was fast disappearing.

F R O M
Snowbound

A Winter Idyll°

Snowbound, Whittier's masterpiece, is a narrative poem of 759 lines. A farm
family and their guests are isolated by a snowstorm until teamsters break
through the snow and once again connect the farm to the outside world.
These snowbound people gradually become representatives of human experience in many times and places: the elders tell stories of witches and
Indians and wilderness life; the schoolteacher contributes legends of Greece
and Rome; and a woman guest describes remote lands she has known.
Through it all runs a deep theme of affection and faith, of people bound
together in a warmth no winter cold can chill. Cut off from the larger world,
they prove the enduring worth of the human community.
    The opening section of the poem, below, describes the coming of the storm
and the activities of the first days.

The sun that brief December day
Rose cheerless over hills of gray,
And, darkly circled, gave at noon
A sadder light than waning moon.
Slow tracing down the thickening sky   5
Its mute and ominous prophecy,
A portent seeming less than threat,
It sank from sight before it set.
A chill no coat, however stout,
Of homespun stuff could quite shut out,   10
A hard, dull bitterness of cold,
That checked, mid-vein, the circling race
Of lifeblood in the sharpened face,
The coming of the snowstorm told.
The wind blew east; we heard the roar   15
Of Ocean on his wintry shore,
And felt the strong pulse throbbing there
Beat with low rhythm our inland air.

Meanwhile we did our nightly chores—
Brought in the wood from out of doors,   20
Littered the stalls, and from the mows
Raked down the herd's-grass for the
    cows:
Heard the horse whinnying for his corn;

And, sharply clashing horn on horn,
Impatient down the stanchion° rows   25
The cattle shake their walnut bows;
While, peering from his early perch
Upon the scaffold's pole of birch,
The cock his crested helmet bent
And down his querulous challenge sent.   30

Unwarmed by any sunset light
The gray day darkened into night,
A night made hoary with the swarm
And whirl-dance of the blinding storm,
As zigzag, wavering to and fro   35
Crossed and recrossed the wingèd snow:
And ere the early bedtime came
The white drift piled the window frame,
And through the glass the clothesline
    posts
Looked in like tall and sheeted ghosts.   40

So all night long the storm roared on:
The morning broke without a sun;
In tiny spherule° traced with lines
Of Nature's geometric signs,

° **Idyll** (īd'l): a literary work describing a simple, pleasant
pastoral scene.

25. **stanchion** (stăn'chən): a device put around a cow's
neck to keep it in its stall.   43. **spherule** (sfîr'ōol): a little
sphere.

In starry flake, and pellicle° 45
All day the hoary meteor fell;
And, when the second morning shone,
We looked upon a world unknown,
On nothing we could call our own.
Around the glistening wonder bent 50
The blue walls of the firmament,
No cloud above, no earth below—
A universe of sky and snow!
The old familiar sights of ours
Took marvelous shapes; strange domes
      and towers 55
Rose up where sty or corncrib stood,
Or garden wall, or belt of wood;
A smooth white mound of brush-pile
      showed,
A fenceless drift what once was road;
The bridle post an old man sat 60
With loose-flung coat and high cocked
      hat;
The wellcurb had a Chinese roof;°
And even the long sweep,° high aloof,
In its slant splendor, seemed to tell
Of Pisa's leaning miracle.° 65

A prompt, decisive man, no breath
Our father wasted: "Boys, a path!"
Well pleased (for when did farmer boy
Count such a summons less than joy?)
Our buskins° on our feet we drew; 70
With mittened hands, and caps drawn
      low,
To guard our necks and ears from snow,
We cut the solid whiteness through.
And, where the drift was deepest, made
A tunnel walled and overlaid 75
With dazzling crystal: we had read
Of rare Aladdin's° wondrous cave,
And to our own his name we gave,

With many a wish the luck were ours
To test his lamp's supernal powers. 80
We reached the barn with merry din,
And roused the prisoned brutes within.
The old horse thrust his long head out,
And grave with wonder gazed about;
The cock his lusty greeting said, 85
And forth his speckled harem led;
The oxen lashed their tails, and hooked,
And mild reproach of hunger looked;
The hornèd patriarch of the sheep,
Like Egypt's Amun° roused from sleep, 90
Shook his sage head with gesture mute,
And emphasized with stamp of foot.

All day the gusty north wind bore
The loosening drift its breath before;
Low circling round its southern zone, 95
The sun through dazzling snow-mist
      shone.
No church bell lent its Christian tone
To the savage air, no social smoke
Curled over the woods of snow-hung
      oak.
A solitude made more intense 100
By dreary-voicèd elements,
The shrieking of the mindless wind,
The moaning tree boughs swaying blind,
And on the glass the unmeaning beat
Of ghostly fingertips of sleet. 105
Beyond the circle of our hearth
No welcome sound of toil or mirth
Unbound the spell, and testified
Of human life and thought outside.
We minded that the sharpest ear 110
The buried brooklet could not hear,
The music of whose liquid lip
Had been to us companionship,
And, in our lonely life, had grown
To have an almost human tone. 115

As night drew on, and, from the crest
Of wooded knolls that ridged the west,
The sun, a snow-blown traveler, sank

45. **pellicle** (pĕl'ĭ-kəl): a thin film. 62. **wellcurb . . .
roof:** When asked how this could be, Whittier explained
that a board had been placed across the curb to hold the
bucket and that this gave the roof effect. 63. **sweep:** a
pole with a bucket at one end, used to get water from a
well. 65. **Pisa's . . . miracle:** a famous slanting tower in
Pisa, Italy. 70. **buskins:** high, laced boots. 77. **Aladdin:**
the youth in the *Arabian Nights* who discovered great treasure in a cave through the power of a magical lamp.

90. **Egypt's Amun:** an Egyptian god frequently represented with a ram's head; usually spelled Amon or Am-
mon.

Winter Scene in New Haven, Connecticut (1858) by George Henry Durrie
(1820–1863). Oil on canvas.
National Musem of American Art, Smithsonian Institution

From sight beneath the smothering bank,
We piled, with care, our nightly stack   120
Of wood against the chimney back—
The oaken log, green, huge, and thick,
And on its top the stout backstick;
The knotty forestick laid apart,
And filled between with curious art   125
The ragged brush; then, hovering near,
We watched the first red blaze appear,
Heard the sharp crackle, caught the
     gleam
On whitewashed wall and sagging beam,

Until the old rude-furnished room   130
Burst, flowerlike, into rosy bloom;
While radiant with a mimic flame
Outside the sparkling drift became,
And through the bare-boughed lilac tree
Our own warm heart seemed blazing
     free.   135
The crane and pendent trammels°
     showed,

136. **crane . . . trammels:** Trammels are adjustable pot-
hooks that are hung on a swinging arm (crane) attached
to the hearth.

The Turks' heads° on the andirons
    glowed;
While childish fancy, prompt to tell
The meaning of the miracle,
Whispered the old rhyme: *"Under the tree,*   140
When fire outdoors burns merrily,
There the witches are making tea."

The moon above the eastern wood
Shone at its full; the hill range stood
Transfigured in the silver flood,   145
Its blown snows flashing cold and keen,
Dead white, save where some sharp
    ravine
Took shadow, or the somber green
Of hemlocks turned to pitchy black
Against the whiteness at their back.   150
For such a world and such a night
Most fitting that unwarming light,
Which only seemed where'er it fell
To make the coldness visible.

Shut in from all the world without,   155
We sat the clean-winged hearth° about,
Content to let the north wind roar
In baffled rage at pane and door,
While the red logs before us beat
The frost-line back with tropic heat;   160
And ever, when a louder blast
Shook beam and rafter as it passed,
The merrier up its roaring draft
The great throat of the chimney
    laughed,
The house dog on his paws outspread   165
Laid to the fire his drowsy head,
The cat's dark silhouette on the wall
A couchant° tiger's seemed to fall;
And, for the winter fireside meet,
Between the andirons' straddling feet,   170
The mug of cider simmered slow,
The apples sputtered in a row,
And, close at hand, the basket stood
With nuts from brown October's wood.

137. **Turks' heads:** The design of the top of the andiron
resembled a turban. 156. **clean-winged hearth:** A turkey
wing was used for a hearth broom. 168. **couchant**
(kou′chənt): lying down.

Analyzing and Interpreting the Poem
1. Lines 1–18 describe the signs of the oncoming
storm, principally in visual images (the sun sinking
in a "thickening sky") or in impressions of feeling
("A hard, dull bitterness of cold"). **a.** What sounds
convey the approach of the storm? **b.** How does
the description of "nightly chores" in lines 19–30
contrast with the description of setting in the opening section?
2. What details in lines 50–80 show that, to a boy's
imagination, the world is not merely changed but
made wonderful by the great snowfall?
3. Lines 93–115 emphasize the absence of any signs
of human life: no sound of church bells, no smoke
from chimneys. What sounds of the weather contribute to this sense of solitude?
4a. What details in the remainder of the selection
give a sense of comfort and security? **b.** How does
the "unwarming" moonlight emphasize the sense of
warmth inside the house?

Literary Elements

Imagery
One important way that writers convey meaning is
through **images,** words or phrases that evoke the
sensations of sight, hearing, touch, smell, or taste.
Although most images are visual, others convey sensations without presenting anything to the eye. For
example, line 11, "A hard, dull bitterness of cold,"
combines two words of touch (*hard, dull*) and one
of taste (*bitterness*) to convey the feeling of cold. As
this line also suggests, images often reflect the writer's personal response to an experience. Whittier
might have used the more usual word *piercing* for
this cold that cuts through the stoutest coat. Instead,
he chose to convey the numbing quality of extreme
cold. Although a reader may never have had an
experience that resembles the one a writer depicts,
both writer and reader share a capacity for physical
sensations. Through their use of imagery, writers
can establish a common ground between a personal
experience and the experience of any reader.

1. Find six images in this excerpt from *Snowbound*.
Tell why each one is effective.
2. Find two evocative images in a prose work by
each of the following writers: Washington Irving,
Edgar Allan Poe, Henry David Thoreau.

John Greenleaf Whittier   **309**

OLIVER WENDELL HOLMES
1809–1894

Oliver Wendell Holmes. Engraving.

It would be hard to imagine the profession of literature in New England in the nineteenth century without the witty, energetic presence of Dr. Holmes. No one could more accurately represent one side of the New England tradition than this descendant of Anne Bradstreet, who had a gentleman traveler's easy familiarity with the great capitals of Europe but remained cheerfully convinced that "the Boston State House is the hub of the solar system." A man of immense vitality and wide-ranging interests, he was a natural leader in the cultural life of his beloved city. He helped organize the Saturday Club, a group of writers and scientists (he himself was both) whose monthly meetings for informal conversations were long remembered for their intellectual brilliance; and he was one of the founders of *The Atlantic Monthly,* a magazine that gave New England writers, including Holmes, a national audience. Characteristically, it was also Holmes who first called his own class of Boston aristocrats the "Brahmins," after the high priests of the Hindu religion. The name was half-humorous, and he was quick to add that this group was a "harmless, inoffensive, untitled aristocracy." But the remark was nevertheless revealing. Holmes felt both a certain reverence for the cultural aristocracy to which he belonged and a need to poke gentle fun at it. A mixture of traditional aristocratic social values and a democratic comic spirit was at the core of the man.

Holmes was born in Cambridge, in a house that had figured in battles of the American Revolution, to a minister's family that represented the best of traditional New England culture. He graduated from Harvard, briefly studied law, which bored him, and turned to medicine. Because France was then a leader in medical research, he took several years of his training in Paris, returning to complete his medical degree at Harvard in 1836. It is a measure of his enormous energy that in that same year he established a medical practice, published a long scientific study of fever, published his first volume of poems, won a major prize for science, and wrote a long poem (it took more than an hour to read aloud) for his class reunion at Harvard!

It was as a professor of medicine for many years at Harvard that Holmes made his reputation in science. He was a brilliant teacher and an enthusiastic spokesman for progress in medicine. He was the champion of faith in Science, a word he capitalized to indicate its importance. This faith tempered his conservative social views. For instance, he made fun of many aspects of the feminist struggle for political equality, but he also advocated the admission of women to medical schools, a radical idea at that time. In sober essays and witty poems, and especially in what he called his "medicated" novels, Holmes also used his faith in science to attack the Puritan religious views of his forefathers. To deal with immorality and crime, he believed, we must replace the idea of "sin" with a scientific understanding of psychological disturbance and inherited behavior traits. Modern science, which he regarded as "the true successor" to earlier religions, gave Holmes his cheerful confidence in human progress.

If his "medicated" novels were too much like philosophical arguments to be successful as novels, Holmes invented a more genial form in the "conversations" that were collected in *The Autocrat of the Breakfast-Table* (1858) and then in three further volumes. For these sketches he created several residents of a boardinghouse who talk, often wittily and sometimes wisely, of all the things that interested Holmes, from horse racing, prizefighting, and rattlesnakes to ancient warfare and mythology. This loose form permitted him to shift from the serious to the comic, to insert poems, jokes, and stories, to parade his great store of knowledge, and above all to express his delight in the play of ideas and personalities that makes good conversation.

Although he wrote in many forms, Holmes is best remembered for his poems. With the notable exception of "The Chambered Nautilus," his best poetry is light verse. If his emotions were stirred, he could write passionately: "Old Ironsides" was written to save the battleship *Constitution* from being scrapped. More often, poetry was for Holmes an exercise of wit and wordplay, a pleasure much like conversation. He had a modest estimate of his own talent, saying that his verse compared to major poetry as a tinkling instrument to the sound of a full band. Nevertheless, he observed, "I hold it to be a gift of a certain value to give that slight passing spasm of pleasure which a few ringing couplets often cause. . . ." Generations of readers have agreed that Holmes gives that pleasure.

Old Ironsides

In a battle in the War of 1812, the American frigate *Constitution* routed the British *Guerrière* and suffered so little damage that it became known as "Old Ironsides." However, in 1830, the ship, lying untended in a Boston navy yard, was called unseaworthy, and plans were made for its demolition.

Holmes wrote the following poem as a protest against the destruction of the ship. First published in the Boston *Daily Advertiser,* it was copied in newspapers and scattered on broadsides all over the country. Such indignation was aroused that the ship was preserved as a national memorial. Holmes was then twenty-one, and the poem made him famous virtually overnight.

Ay, tear her tattered ensign down!
  Long has it waved on high,
And many an eye has danced to see
  That banner in the sky;
Beneath it rung the battle shout,   5
  And burst the cannon's roar—
The meteor of the ocean air
  Shall sweep the clouds no more.

Her deck, once red with heroes' blood,
  Where knelt the vanquished foe,   10
When winds were hurrying o'er the
    flood,
  And waves were white below,
No more shall feel the victor's tread,
  Or know the conquered knee—
The harpies° of the shore shall pluck   15
  The eagle of the sea!

Oh, better that her shattered hulk
  Should sink beneath the wave;
Her thunders shook the mighty deep,
  And there should be her grave;   20
Nail to the mast her holy flag,
  Set every threadbare sail,
And give her to the god of storms,
  The lightning and the gale!

15. **harpies:** In Greek mythology, a Harpy was a grotesque winged monster with the head of a woman and the legs and talons of a bird. Here, the word refers to greedy, grasping people.

The Chambered Nautilus

The pearly nautilus is a snaillike sea creature of the South Pacific and Indian oceans. As it grows, the nautilus creates from its own secretions each year a new chamber of shell to house its expanding body. The name *nautilus*, meaning "sailor," grew out of the old belief that the little creature could sail by raising a membrane. No doubt the nautilus first interested the scientist in Holmes, but it touched the poet in him even more.

This is the ship of pearl, which, poets feign,
    Sails the unshadowed main—
    The venturous bark that flings
On the sweet summer wind its purpled wings
In gulfs enchanted, where the Siren° sings,   5
    And coral reefs lie bare,
Where the cold sea-maids rise to sun their streaming hair.

Its webs of living gauze no more unfurl;
    Wrecked is the ship of pearl!
    And every chambered cell,   10
Where its dim dreaming life was wont to dwell,
As the frail tenant shaped his growing shell,
    Before thee lies revealed—
Its irised ceiling rent, its sunless crypt unsealed!

Year after year beheld the silent toil   15
    That spread his lustrous coil;
    Still, as the spiral grew,
He left the past year's dwelling for the new,
Stole with soft step its shining archway through,
    Built up its idle door,   20
Stretched in his last-found home, and knew the old no more.

Thanks for the heavenly message brought by thee,
    Child of the wandering sea,
    Cast from her lap, forlorn!
From thy dead lips a clearer note is born   25
Than ever Triton° blew from wreathèd horn!
    While on mine ears it rings,
Through the deep caves of thought I hear a voice that sings:

5. **Siren:** In classical mythology, the sirens were sea nymphs who lured mariners to their deaths by singing enchanting songs. 26. **Triton** (trī′tən): an ancient sea god whose lower half resembled that of a fish. He is usually represented as blowing a trumpet made of a seashell.

Shell, 1927. Photograph by Edward Weston. © 1981 Arizona Board of Regents, Center for Creative Photography.

Build thee more stately mansions, O my soul,
    As the swift seasons roll!
      Leave thy low-vaulted past!   30
Let each new temple, nobler than the last,
Shut thee from heaven with a dome more vast,
    Till thou at length art free,
Leaving thine outgrown shell by life's unresting sea!   35

Oliver Wendell Holmes   **313**

Detail from *Constitution in Boston Harbor* (c. 1848) by Fitz Hugh Lane (1804–1866).

Literary Elements

Stanza Forms

A **stanza** is a unit of poetry longer than a line. ("The Chambered Nautilus" has five stanzas.) It is a means of arranging lines of poetry in a pattern, usually according to rhyme and meter. The stanza in poetry serves the same basic function as the paragraph in prose: that is, it organizes thoughts or ideas in units. But a stanza usually employs certain elements of language—repetition of sounds, stress patterns—in a way that is not typical of prose. These elements give unity to a stanza and create its pattern.

A poem's stanza form is usually related to the thought being expressed. For instance, in "The Chambered Nautilus," Oliver Wendell Holmes invented a complex stanza form that reflects the gravity and nobility of the poem's ideas. The seven-line stanzas are rhymed *aabbbcc*, a pattern that suggests formality and strict control. The first, fourth, and fifth lines of each stanza are iambic pentameter; the second, third, and sixth lines are iambic trimeter. The longer final line of each stanza adds one more element to the pattern. It is a line of six feet, iambic hexameter; its longer length, slowing the rhythm, gives an impression of solemn finality that is appropriate to this poem.

Describe the stanza form of the following poems in terms of rhyme scheme, meter, and line length.

"To a Waterfowl," page 151
"To Helen," page 183
"There's a Certain Slant of Light," page 328

For Study and Discussion

Analyzing and Interpreting the Poems

Old Ironsides

1. What words and images in the poem connect "Old Ironsides" with something larger and more awesome than an ordinary battleship?
2. Who might the "harpies of the shore" be?
3. Instead of scrapping the ship, what alternative does Holmes propose?

The Chambered Nautilus

1. Stanzas 3–5 of this poem move from close observation of the chambered shell to a comparison between the life of the nautilus and the progress of the human soul. How does the speaker interpret the shell's "heavenly message"?
2. How do the details and images in stanza 3 prepare the reader for the concluding comparison?

Writing About Literature

Comparing Poems

Compare "To a Waterfowl" and "The Chambered Nautilus." Show how both poems make use of comparisons.

Creative Writing

Developing an Analogy

Write an essay or a poem in which you make an observation of an animal, a plant, or some other object of nature. Then draw an analogy between the object and some aspect of human life, just as Holmes compares the chambered nautilus to the human soul.

James Russell Lowell (1857). Photograph.

Lowell's career was so varied that it might stand as a summary of the accomplishments of the Fireside Poets. He was Oliver Wendell Holmes's nearest rival in wit and cleverness, and Longfellow's in the ability to write in many verse forms. Like Whittier, Lowell was active in politics and worked as a journalist in the abolitionist movement. If as a sophisticated Harvard graduate he could not identify as closely with country life as Whittier did, he nevertheless invented in Hosea Biglow a rural New Englander whose vivid local dialect and salty opinions became widely known. Lowell was not only among the founders of *The Atlantic Monthly,* but served as its first editor, and later became a coeditor of the still more distinguished *North American Review.* Fame came quickly to this most versatile—and perhaps most gifted—of the Fireside Poets.

Like Holmes, who was his Cambridge neighbor, Lowell was the son of a minister and the descendant of a prominent family. After graduating from Harvard Law School he spent an unhappy year practicing law before publishing his first book of poems. With that, he turned gratefully to a career as a writer. Strongly influenced by the humanitarian views of his fiancée, Maria White, he was soon contributing regularly to antislavery journals, and after their marriage in 1844, he lived for a time in Philadelphia and wrote editorials for the abolitionist periodical *Pennsylvania Freeman.* Meanwhile, he carried forward the literary part of his work in essays and a constant output of poems. With his career firmly launched, he returned to Cambridge to live, and quickly made evident his widely varied interests and remarkable productivity. In a single year, 1848, when he was twenty-nine, he issued his collected poems in two volumes, published a long poetic narrative of medieval knighthood, gathered his popular dialect verse in book form as the first series of *Biglow Papers,* and wrote an important work of literary criticism, *A Fable for Critics.*

Lowell's new fame was soon overshadowed by personal tragedy in the deaths of three of his chil-

dren and then, in 1853, of his wife. The loss of his beloved Maria, as he observed long afterward, changed not just his personal life but his career. Her influence had provided a discipline for his scattered energies that he was seldom to feel again. His early achievements show an exceptional promise that was never fulfilled. The first *Biglow Papers* were a literary triumph. They were written as a protest against the Mexican War. But these verses transcend that political purpose. Lowell carried the tradition of Down East humor a major step forward through the satirical use of Yankee dialect and the creation of a memorable literary character in the shrewd, homespun poet Hosea Biglow. The later sections of the *Papers* are inferior to the first, and a second series is remembered now only for such nonpolitical portraits of country life as "The Courtin'."

There were many honors and accomplishments in Lowell's long career: his professorship, his editorial positions, diplomatic service as American minister to both Spain and England, honorary degrees from major universities. No literary man wrote more thoughtfully about the Civil War than Lowell did in essays on the meaning of the Union and the causes of rebellion. In his "Commemoration Ode" at the end of the war, he was among the first of our writers to recognize the greatness of Abraham Lincoln. Still, Lowell's work lacked coherence and development, making his literary career a minor one. He himself recognized this failure, observing in old age that his life had been "mainly wasted" and that he had "thrown away more than most men ever had." As he later estimated, his poetry contained "good bits"—isolated achievements—rather than a clear line of major works.

The Courtin'

God makes sech nights, all white an' still
    Fur'z you can look or listen,
Moonshine an' snow on field an' hill,
    All silence, an' all glisten.

Zekle crep' up quite unbeknown   5
    An' peeked in thru' the winder,
An' there sot Huldy all alone,
    'ith no one nigh to hender.°

A fireplace filled the room's one side
    With half a cord o' wood in—   10
There warn't no stoves (tell comfort died)
    To bake ye to a puddin'.

The wa'nut logs shot sparkles out
    Towards the pootiest,° bless her,
An' leetle flames danced all about   15
    The chiny on the dresser.

Agin the chimbley crook-necks° hung,
    An' in amongst 'em rusted
The ole queen's-arm° thet gran'ther Young
    Fetched back f'om Concord busted.   20

The very room, coz she was in,
    Seemed warm f'om floor to ceilin',
An' she looked full ez rosy agin
    Ez the apples she was peelin'.

'Twas kin' o' kingdom-come to look   25
    On sech a blessed cretur,
A dogrose° blushin' to a brook
    Ain't modester nor sweeter.

He was six foot o' man, A-1,
    Clear grit an' human natur'.   30
None couldn't quicker pitch a ton
    Nor dror a furrer straighter.

He'd sparked it with full twenty gals,
    Hed squired 'em, danced 'em, druv
      'em,
Fust this one, an' then thet, by spells—   35
    All is, he couldn't love 'em.

But long o' her his veins 'ould run
    All crinkly like curled maple,
The side she breshed felt full o' sun
    Ez a south slope in Ap'il.   40

She thought no v'ice hed sech a swing
    Ez hisn in the choir;
My! when he made Ole Hunderd° ring,
    She *knowed* the Lord was nigher.

An' she'd blush scarlit, right in prayer,   45
    When her new meetin'-bonnet
Felt somehow thru' its crown a pair
    O' blue eyes sot upun it.

Thet night, I tell ye, she looked *some!*
    She seemed to 've gut a new soul,   50
For she felt sartin-sure he'd come,
    Down to her very shoe-sole.

She heered a foot, an' knowed it tu,
    A-raspin' on the scraper—
All ways to once her feelin's flew   55
    Like sparks in burnt-up paper.

He kin' o' l'itered on the mat,
    Some doubtfle o' the sekle,°
His heart kep' goin' pity-pat,
    But hern went pity Zekle.   60

An' yit she gin her cheer a jerk
    Ez though she wished him furder,
An' on her apples kep' to work,
    Parin' away like murder.

---

8. **hender:** hinder. 14. **pootiest:** prettiest. 17. **crook-necks:** gourds. 19. **queen's-arm:** a musket used in the Revolution. 27. **dogrose:** a plant with pink flowers.

43. **Ole Hunderd:** the melody to which Psalm 100 was sung. 58. **sekle:** sequel.

"You want to see my Pa, I s'pose?" 65
  "Wal . . . no . . . I come dasignin' "—
"To see my Ma? She's sprinklin' clo'es
  Agin to-morrer's i'nin'."

To say why gals acts so or so,
  Or don't, 'ould be persumin'; 70
Mebby to mean *yes* an' say *no*
  Comes nateral to women.

He stood a spell on one foot fust,
  Then stood a spell on t'other,
An' on which one he felt the wust 75
  He couldn't ha' told ye nuther.

Says he, "I'd better call agin."
  Says she, "Think likely, Mister."
Thet last word pricked him like a pin,
  An'. . . Wal, he up an' kist her. 80

When Ma bimeby upon 'em slips,
  Huldy sot pale ez ashes,
All kin' o' smily roun' the lips
  An' teary roun' the lashes.

For she was jes' the quiet kind 85
  Whose naturs never vary,
Like streams that keep a summer mind
  Snowhid in Jenooary.

The blood clost roun' her heart felt glued
  Too tight for all expressin', 90
Tell mother see how metters stood,
  An' gin 'em both her blessin'.

Then her red come back like the tide
  Down to the Bay o' Fundy,°
An' all I know is they was cried° 95
  In meetin' come nex' Sunday.

94. **Bay o' Fundy:** an inlet of the Atlantic Ocean in Canada, known for its swift tidal currents. 95. **they was cried:** The banns (the announcement of their approaching marriage) were read in church.

Analyzing and Interpreting the Poem
1. In this poem of country life, human appearances and feelings are compared to nature. **a.** To what are Zekle's feelings compared in lines 37–40? **b.** What comparison is made in lines 85–88?
2. What in your opinion is Lowell's attitude toward the characters in the poem? Does he make them broadly comical, or does he treat them realistically and sympathetically? Give reasons for your answer.
3. The dialect of the poem consists of regional pronunciations ("ez" for "as," "heered" for "heard," and so on) as well as many expressions that seem unique to these New England country people. **a.** Pick out three expressions that distinguish this rural speech from standard speech. **b.** In what ways does the dialect add to or detract from the effectiveness of the poem?

Spelling Dialect Words
A writer using dialect must find spellings that adequately convey the special pronunciations of a particular region. However, spellings must not be made too difficult for the reader to understand. The writer must try to find spellings that show how people actually speak, not how they are supposed to speak.

Find ten words in "The Courtin' " that are spelled to show dialect pronunciations. Draw three columns on your paper. In the first column, write the words as Lowell spells them. In the second column, give the standard spelling. In the third column, spell the words to show how you or a friend pronounce them. Listen carefully before writing. Do not write "hundred" when you actually say "hunert."

James Russell Lowell **317**

Meter and Scansion

The basic unit of meter in poetry is the *foot*. A foot is made up of one stressed syllable and, usually, one or more unstressed syllables. The most common foot in English verse is the *iamb,* which consists of one unstressed syllable followed by a stressed syllable. The kind of meter used in a line of poetry is combined with the number of units, or feet, to give the line its name. Since there are five iambs per line in Longfellow's "Nature," the lines are called *iambic pentameter:*

And leave | his bro | ken play | things on | the floor

Since, in an iambic foot, an unstressed syllable is followed by one that is stressed, the movement of the foot is toward the stress. Therefore, iambic meter is known as *rising* meter; it rises toward the stress. The three other meters common to English poetry are also based on the placement of stress within the foot.

Trochaic meter. The foot called the *trochee* is the reverse of the iamb. A trochee consists of a stressed syllable followed by an unstressed syllable. Since the movement of trochaic meter is away from the stress, it is known as *falling* meter. Poe's "The Raven" is written in trochaic meter:

Once up | on a | midnight | dreary, | while I | pondered, | weak and | weary

Anapestic meter. The *anapest,* like the iamb, rises toward a final stress. But an anapest consists of three syllables, two unstressed syllables followed by a stressed syllable. Often anapestic meter produces a sense of rapid movement, as in this line from the song "The Man on the Flying Trapeze":

Oh, he flies | through the air | with the great | est of ease

Or it may convey a tripping rhythm, as in this line from Lowell's satirical poem *A Fable for Critics:*

That he talks | of things some | times as if | they were dead

Dactylic meter. The *dactyl,* which also has three syllables, is the reverse of the anapest. In a dactyl, a stressed syllable is followed by two unstressed syllables. Dactylic meter is usually used in jingles and light verse, but it has been used successfully in serious poetry, such as Longfellow's narrative poem *Evangeline:*

This is the | forest pri | meval. The | murmuring | pines and the | hemlocks

Scansion. The rhythm of a line of poetry is usually described in terms of its meter and its length. The analysis of the rhythm in a poem is called scansion. In scanning a line of poetry, we divide it into feet. We indicate the stressed and unstressed syllables to determine the kind of poetic foot the line employs and the number of feet it contains. From this analysis we can give the line its metrical name. In addition to *pentameter,* the terms describing the number of feet in a line are *monometer* (one foot), *dimeter* (two feet), *trimeter* (three feet), *tetrameter* (four feet), and *hexameter* (six feet).

In a poem that is entirely regular in meter, scansion is simple. For instance, in the opening stanza of Whittier's *Snowbound,* the regularity of the meter is quickly apparent, and scansion indicates that the lines are iambic tetrameter. In some poems, however, several meters may be mixed. For example, in this single line from Longfellow's "The Tide Rises, the Tide Falls,"

Darkness | settles | on roofs | and walls

two trochees are followed by two iambs. Such changes of rhythm within a line allow a poet to create particular effects through stress— here the falling stress for settling darkness.

Describe the meter of the following lines of poetry, noting any variations in the meter.

"To a Waterfowl," line 4 (page 151)
"The Bells," line 14 (page 190)
"Brahma," line 6 (page 230)
"The Tide Rises, the Tide Falls," lines 11–12 (page 302)
"The Courtin'," lines 11–12 (page 316)

EMILY DICKINSON
1830–1886

Emily Dickinson. Drawing after a daguerreotype.

In 1862, Thomas Wentworth Higginson, an influential literary figure, received four poems from a shy young woman who wanted to know if they were "alive." They were intense works, obviously the product of a highly individual talent. Later, in a letter to Higginson, their author described herself as "small, like the wren" with hair "bold, like the chestnut burr" and "eyes, like the sherry in the glass, that the guest leaves." She lived with her family in Amherst, Massachusetts, and saw few people. Although Higginson carried on a lengthy correspon-

dence with Emily Dickinson, he met her only twice and described her as "remote" and "unique." Her personality, almost as intense and highly charged as her poetry, made him uncomfortably tired. He wrote, "I was never with anyone who drained my nerve power so much. Without touching her, she drew from me. I am glad not to live near her." While she lived, only seven of her nearly eighteen hundred poems were published, all anonymously and some against her wishes. Although several of her friends urged her to publish, she seemed reluctant to thrust herself and her work before the public. Four years after her death Higginson and Mabel Loomis Todd, a neighbor of Emily's, assembled a first selection of her poetry, which she had called "my letter to the world." Gradually more of her work was published, until in 1955 a complete edition of her poems was brought out. Today it is obvious that Emily Dickinson is a poet of major stature and that the poems discovered after her death, tied neatly together in little blue packets, are a legacy beyond price.

Emily Dickinson rarely left Amherst, a small college town that preserved the sober church-centered ways of an older Puritan New England. Her father was a lawyer, a formidable man who dominated his family and who achieved some prominence in politics and was treasurer of Amherst College for forty years. Growing up in Amherst, she was much like other girls her age. Her letters to her friends and her brother, away at school, are full of wit and high spirits. But as she grew older, she became more reluctant to be drawn away from home, even for an hour at a time.

As far as is known, there were few important outward events in Emily Dickinson's life. The year 1862 seems to have been a turning point. In that year she wrote more poems than in any other, roughly a poem a day. In that year also, Charles Wadsworth, a Presbyterian minister and the man Emily loved, departed for San Francisco. Apparently she saw Wadsworth, an older man, only three or four times. Although he was kind to her, he did not return her love. It was about the time of his departure that she took to dressing entirely in white. During the last ten years of her life, she refused to leave her house and garden or to meet any strangers. In 1884 her health broke down, and two years later she died.

That Emily Dickinson lived an intense inner life her poetry leaves no doubt. In a letter to Higginson,

Dickinson House in Amherst, Massachusetts. Lithograph by John Bachelder (c. 1855).

she described her standards for judging poetry. "If I read a book and it makes my whole body so cold no fire can ever warm me, I know *that* is poetry. If I feel physically as if the top of my head were taken off, I know *that* is poetry. These are the only ways I know it. Is there any other way?" Many of her own poems seem to call for as deep a response. They are both traditional and unusual. Their great subject, the connection between the happenings of everyday life and the world of the spirit, relates them to the works of older New England writers. Their rhythms are based upon the rhythms of church hymns. But Emily Dickinson's mode of expression—concise, informal, often abrupt—is so personal that it seems to belong not to a particular tradition or period of time but especially and only to herself.

This Is My Letter to the World

This is my letter to the World
That never wrote to Me—
The simple News that Nature told—
With tender Majesty

Her Message is committed
To Hands I cannot see—
For love of Her—Sweet—countrymen—
Judge tenderly—of Me

Emily Dickinson   **321**

The first editors of Dickinson's poems were distressed by their unconventional punctuation, meter, and rhyme, and by certain words that seemed odd or ill-chosen. Consequently, these editors decided to change the poems to conform to conventional standards. Below are two versions of a Dickinson poem. The first appears as she originally wrote it, and the second reflects her editors' changes.

I Never Saw a Moor

I never saw a Moor—
I never saw the Sea—
Yet know I how the Heather looks
And what a Billow be.

I never spoke with God
Nor visited in Heaven—
Yet certain am I of the spot
As if the Checks° were given—

I never saw a moor,
   I never saw the sea;
Yet know I how the heather looks,
   And what a wave must be.

I never spoke with God,
   Nor visited in heaven;
Yet certain am I of the spot
   As if the chart were given.

8. **Checks:** the colored railway checks that conductors give to passengers when they collect their tickets. The check's color reminds the conductor that the passenger has paid a fare to a specific destination.

Exultation Is the Going

Exultation is the going
Of an inland soul to sea,
Past the houses—past the headlands—
Into deep Eternity—

Bred as we, among the mountains,
Can the sailor understand
The divine intoxication
Of the first league out from land?

Approaching Storm, Beach near Newport (c. 1860) by Martin Johnson Heade (1819–1904). Oil on canvas.
Museum of Fine Arts, Boston, M. and M. Karolik Collection

I Taste a Liquor Never Brewed

I taste a liquor never brewed—
From Tankards scooped in Pearl—
Not all the Vats upon the Rhine
Yield such an Alcohol!

Inebriate of Air—am I—   5
And Debauchee of Dew—
Reeling—thro endless summer days—
From inns of Molten Blue—

When "Landlords" turn the drunken Bee
Out of the Foxglove's door—   10
When Butterflies—renounce their "drams"—
I shall but drink the more!

Till Seraphs swing their snowy Hats—
And Saints—to windows run—
To see the little Tippler   15
Leaning against the—Sun—

Some Keep the Sabbath Going to Church

Some keep the Sabbath going to Church—
I keep it, staying at Home—
With a Bobolink for a Chorister—
And an Orchard, for a Dome—

Some keep the Sabbath in Surplice— 5
I just wear my Wings—
And instead of tolling the Bell, for Church,
Our little Sexton—sings.

God preaches, a noted Clergyman—
And the sermon is never long, 10
So instead of getting to Heaven, at last—
I'm going, all along.

"Faith" Is a Fine Invention

"Faith" is a fine invention
When Gentlemen can *see*—
But *Microscopes* are prudent
In an Emergency.

"Hope" Is the Thing with Feathers

"Hope" is the thing with feathers—
That perches in the soul—
And sings the tune without the words—
And never stops—at all—

And sweetest—in the Gale—is heard— 5
And sore must be the storm—
That could abash the little Bird
That kept so many warm—

I've heard it in the chillest land—
And on the strangest Sea— 10
Yet, never, in Extremity,
It asked a crumb—of Me.

Passion Flowers and Humming-birds (1865) by Martin Johnson Heade.

Success Is Counted Sweetest

Success is counted sweetest
By those who ne'er succeed.
To comprehend a nectar
Requires sorest need.

Not one of all the purple Host   5
Who took the Flag today
Can tell the definition
So clear of Victory

As he defeated—dying—
On whose forbidden ear   10
The distant strains of triumph
Burst agonized and clear!

The Soul Selects
Her Own Society

The Soul selects her own Society—
Then—shuts the Door—
To her divine Majority—
Present no more—

Unmoved—she notes the Chariots—paus-
    ing—   5
At her low Gate—
Unmoved—an Emperor be kneeling
Upon her Mat—

I've known her—from an ample nation—
Choose One—   10
Then—close the Valves of her attention—
Like Stone—

Interior with a Seated Woman (1908) by Vilhelm
Hammershøi (1864–1916). Oil on canvas.
Aarhus Kunstmuseum

I Took My Power
in My Hand

I took my Power in my Hand—
And went against the World—
'Twas not so much as David—had—
But I—was twice as bold—

I aimed my Pebble—but Myself
Was all the one that fell—
Was it Goliath—was too large—
Or was myself—too small?

Much Madness
Is Divinest Sense

Much Madness is divinest Sense—
To a discerning Eye—
Much Sense—the starkest Madness—
'Tis the Majority
In this, as All, prevail—
Assent—and you are sane—
Demur—you're straightway dangerous—
And handled with a Chain—

It Sifts
from Leaden Sieves

It sifts from Leaden Sieves—
It powders all the Wood.
It fills with Alabaster° Wool
The Wrinkles of the Road—

It makes an Even Face   5
Of Mountain, and of Plain—
Unbroken Forehead from the East
Unto the East again—

It reaches to the Fence—
It wraps it Rail by Rail   10
Till it is lost in Fleeces—
It deals Celestial Vail°

To Stump, and Stack—and Stem—
A Summer's empty Room—
Acres of Joints, where Harvests were,   15
Recordless, but for them—

It Ruffles Wrists of Posts
As Ankles of a Queen—
Then stills it's° Artisans°—like Ghosts—
Denying they have been—   20

3. **Alabaster:** a form of gypsum, white and translucent.
12. **Vail:** veil. 19. **it's:** an early form of the possessive
its. **Artisans:** craftsmen.

A Narrow Fellow
in the Grass

A narrow Fellow in the Grass
Occasionally rides—
You may have met Him—did you not
His notice sudden is—

The Grass divides as with a Comb—   5
A spotted shaft is seen—
And then it closes at your feet
And opens further on—

He likes a Boggy Acre
A Floor° too cool for Corn—   10
Yet when a Boy, and Barefoot—
I more than once at Noon
Have passed, I thought, a Whip lash
Unbraiding in the Sun
When stooping to secure it   15
It wrinkled, and was gone—

Several of Nature's People
I know, and they know me—
I feel for them a transport
Of cordiality—   20

But never met this Fellow
Attended, or alone
Without a tighter breathing
And Zero at the Bone—

10. **A Floor:** here, the soil or ground.

Apparently
with No Surprise

Apparently with no surprise
To any happy Flower
The Frost beheads it at its play—
In accidental power—
The blonde Assassin passes on—
The Sun proceeds unmoved
To measure off another Day
For an Approving God.

Emily Dickinson   **327**

There Came a Wind like a Bugle

There came a Wind like a Bugle—
It quivered through the Grass
And a Green Chill upon the Heat
So ominous did pass
We barred the Windows and the Doors   5
As from an Emerald° Ghost—
The Doom's° electric Moccasin
That very instant passed—
On a strange Mob of panting Trees
And Fences fled away   10
And Rivers where the Houses ran
Those looked that lived—that Day—
The Bell within the steeple wild
The flying tidings told—
How much can come   15
And much can go,
And yet abide the World!

6. **Emerald:** green.   7. **Doom's:** literally, the Day of
Judgment, which in an earlier New England was often
described as a cataclysmic storm.

There's a Certain Slant of Light

There's a certain Slant of light,
Winter Afternoons—
That oppresses, like the Heft
Of Cathedral Tunes—

Heavenly Hurt, it gives us—   5
We can find no scar,
But internal difference,
Where the Meanings, are—

None may teach it—Any—
'Tis the Seal Despair—   10
An imperial affliction
Sent us of the Air—

When it comes, the Landscape listens—
Shadows—hold their breath—
When it goes, 'tis like the Distance   15
On the look of Death—

My Life Closed Twice Before Its Close

My life closed twice before its close;
It yet remains to see
If Immortality unveil
A third event to me,

So huge, so hopeless to conceive
As these that twice befel.
Parting is all we know of heaven,
And all we need of hell.

Mourning Picture (1980) by Edwin Romanzo Elmer (1850–1923). Oil on canvas.

Smith College Museum of Art, Northampton, Massachusetts, Purchased 1953

Because I Could Not Stop for Death

Because I could not stop for Death—
He kindly stopped for me—
The Carriage held but just Ourselves—
And Immortality.

We slowly drove—He knew no haste   5
And I had put away
My labor and my leisure too,
For His Civility—

We passed the School, where Children
    strove
At Recess—in the Ring—   10
We passed the Fields of Gazing Grain—
We passed the Setting Sun—

Or rather—He passed Us—
The Dews drew quivering and chill—
For only Gossamer, my Gown—   15
My Tippet°—only Tulle—

We paused before a House that seemed
A Swelling of the Ground—
The Roof was scarcely visible—
The Cornice—in the Ground—   20

Since then—'tis Centuries—and yet
Feels shorter than the Day
I first surmised the Horses' Heads
Were toward Eternity—

16. **Tippet:** a garment resembling a scarf, worn over the shoulders and hanging down in front.

The Bustle in a House

The Bustle in a House
The Morning after Death
Is solemnest of industries
Enacted upon Earth—

The Sweeping up the Heart
And putting Love away
We shall not want to use again
Until Eternity.

Emily Dickinson   **329**

Commentary

Emily Dickinson's intense concern with consciousness and her uncertainties about her religious belief led her to write many poems that explore death as the end of consciousness. Although the world after death is known to us only through faith, the restless imagination must probe even this world. "Because I Could Not Stop for Death" is one of her more romantic examinations of this world, but it bears many of the general features of her poetry.

Characteristically, she treats this somber subject with a light tone. Death is not a terrifying figure but a civil, courteous gentleman or suitor. Because we do not willingly stop our lives for death, we must be taken. In keeping with the poem's tone, the taking here is presented as a "kindly" inducement to ride in a carriage. And since immortality makes a third passenger, there seems little threat in the experience. The journey itself, in the second and third stanzas, is a leisurely review of familiar scenes. Death knows "no haste," and the poet has "put away" all her concerns of work and leisure. This is a reminder that death is the end of human time and energy, but the tone is mild, even reassuring. The scenes that are passed on the journey are equally pleasant—schoolchildren at recess (representing the poet's own childhood), the fields of grain (perhaps her ripening or adulthood). Only the setting sun suggests the inevitable end of a person's mortal time.

The fourth stanza introduces a darker tone. The journey had seemed destined to pass the sun (which measures human time) and thereby to transcend mortality. Instead, the journey is passed *by* the sun, leaving the poet to the dark earth and ill-clad for the sudden chill of the gathering dew. Her gown is only gossamer, her scarf only tulle. The carriage is, after all, a hearse, and its destination is not some heaven beyond the sun but only the cemetery.

In the fifth stanza, the carriage reaches the grave. It is described as a house, a word that has comforting connotations. However, the roof is so low as to be "scarcely visible," and the repetition of the word *ground* reminds us that this is a final house within the earth.

If the early stanzas take a romantic view of the end of life, with death as an attractive suitor, the final stanza completes an ironic reversal of this view. It is "Centuries," now, since the poet's death. But in God's "Eternity," centuries feel shorter than a single day in life. The contrast is between our human time and God's timelessness. Left behind by the sun that marks off our days, consciousness is oblivious to the passage of time. Even if consciousness is immortal, meaningful existence requires the "Day" of human measurement and evidences of life, such as children and fields of grain. Ironically, immortality becomes a meaningless gift. Consciousness, our awareness of existence, cannot feel itself without the world that gave it being.

For Study and Discussion

Analyzing and Interpreting the Poems

This Is My Letter to the World

1. Dickinson loved both writing and receiving letters. "A letter," she wrote to a friend, "always feels to me like immortality because it is the mind alone" that one encounters, without the physical presence of the person. How might this sense of immortality be related to her speaking of her poetry as "my letter to the World"?

2. If the message of her poetry is "the simple News that Nature told," it is a message "committed / To Hands I cannot see." How does this develop the idea about a letter and the world in lines 1–2?

3. At the end the poet asks that she be judged "tenderly" by her readers. How is this related to the "tender Majesty" of line 4?

I Never Saw a Moor

1. The first stanza deals with something that is "known" without having been seen—as we might "know" what a desert or a jungle looks like from pictures or descriptions. In what way is the knowledge presented in the second stanza different from that of the first stanza?

2. The editors' substitution of the word *chart* (meaning "map") for Dickinson's word *Checks* changes the poet's meaning. Dickinson is writing not just of having a map of heaven, but of having the same assurance of her destination that railway passengers have after the conductor has given them their checks. Examine the two versions of the poem. **a.** What emphasis is gained in the original by the use of the dash and by the unusual capitalization of words? **b.** What is the effect of substituting *wave* for *Billow*?

Exultation Is the Going

1. Why is the sea a fitting metaphor for eternity?

2. "Exultation" is described as both a physical journey in space and an inner journey of the soul into eternity. Once the soul has left all land behind, there is the feeling of "divine intoxication." To what earthly experience is this "intoxication" compared?

I Taste a Liquor Never Brewed

1. Dickinson again presents a feeling of transcendence in terms of intoxication. **a.** What words and images refer to drinking or drunkenness? **b.** What things intoxicate the poet in stanza 2?

2. The third stanza compares the poet to bees and butterflies, which have their own kind of joyous intoxication. **a.** Who is the "Landlord" of bees and butterflies? **b.** How would the poet react to even the most extreme disapproval of her intoxication?

3. What religious references in the final stanza suggest that the intoxicating communion with nature is also a reaching toward divinity?

Some Keep the Sabbath Going to Church

1. The first two lines establish the situation of the poem: while others "keep the Sabbath" in the traditional way by "going to Church," the poet does so by "staying at Home." In lines 3–4, what aspects of a church are transferred to nature?

2. The second stanza states that "Some" (the ministers) wear special robes for church, but the poet just wears her "Wings." **a.** What does *Wings* stand for? **b.** What do you think Dickinson means by the final two lines of the poem?

3. Dickinson presents the serious matter of her religious worship in a playful, informal way. What examples do you find of her light tone?

"Faith" Is a Fine Invention

1. What words might you use instead of *faith* and *microscopes*?

2. What does it mean to *see*?

"Hope" Is the Thing with Feathers

1. What effect does Dickinson achieve by making hope a "little Bird" that "perches in the soul"?

2. Hardship is presented in the poem in physical terms—as storms, extreme cold, and strange seas. In what sense can it be said that, within ourselves, hope "sings the tune without the words"?

3. Hope exists without our being aware of it. We simply draw on hope when we need to. How do the last two lines support this idea?

Success Is Counted Sweetest

1. According to this poem, who most values success? Why?

2. This poem uses words in unexpected ways for emphasis. **a.** What is the meaning of *comprehend* as it is used in line 3? **b.** In what sense is the ear of the defeated man "forbidden" in line 10? **c.** Why might the sounds of triumph bring agony to the defeated man?

The Soul Selects Her Own Society

1. The relations to others that the soul chooses are clearly different from—and more exclusive than—the social relations we have with friends and acquaintances. How does Dickinson play upon this exclusiveness in the "divine Majority" of line 3?

2a. In the second stanza, what is the soul being compared to as it remains "Unmoved" by the attention of those in "Chariots" or even by a kneeling "Emperor"? **b.** For this purpose, is it appropriate that the soul is feminine throughout the poem?

3. The final exclusiveness of the soul in making human ties is indicated in the third stanza in her choosing a single person from an "ample nation": "Then—close the Valves of her attention—/ Like Stone." **a.** What comparison is made for the soul here? **b.** Does the phrase "Like Stone" suggest how others will see this exclusiveness?

I Took My Power in My Hand

1. The context for this poem appears in the references to David and Goliath. If the poet can be envisioned as David, taking her "Pebble" in her hand as her "Power," in what sense are we to see the world as Goliath?

2a. Does the second stanza indicate that this is a poem of the poet's defeat? How should we understand that it was not the stone "but Myself / Was all the one that fell?" **b.** Does the assertion that she "was twice as bold" as David influence the way we are to see her apparent defeat?

Much Madness Is Divinest Sense

1. Like Emerson's "Brahma" (page 230), this poem is based on a paradox. **a.** How does the first line invert our usual understanding of madness and sense? **b.** Explain how this paradox can be true.

2. By the end of the poem, majority opinion has become a tyranny over the individual. What earlier phrases prepare us for the startling final line?

It Sifts from Leaden Sieves

1. The opening "It" is repeated a number of times but never named. At what point do we know that the subject of the poem is a snowstorm?

2. In the first stanza the snow "sifts" from a leaden

sky as flour does from a sieve; it "powders" the trees and fills the "Wrinkles" of the roads. **a.** How do these images relate to Dickinson's image of the landscape as a "Face" in the second stanza? **b.** Why, in lines 7 and 8, do we see only "Unbroken Forehead" as the snow continues?
3. Lines 12–16 describe the disappearance, under a "Celestial Vail," of evidence of the summer's work—stump of tree, haystack, stem of harvested crop, the "Joints" of farmland fields. How, in this context, should we interpret line 14, "A Summer's empty Room"?
4. Once the snow's work of transformation is over, it "stills" its flakes (its "Artisans"), which disappear "like Ghosts—/Denying they have been." In an earlier version of the poem, thinking of white feathers, Dickinson wrote "like Swans." What is the effect of the change to "Ghosts"?

Apparently with No Surprise
1. These eight short lines about the ordinary fact of a killing frost make their impact through unexpected turns of language and attitude: we do not usually think of a flower as being happy or playing or of the white frost as a "blonde Assassin." **a.** What is the effect of the poem's saying that death comes to the flower "Apparently with no surprise"? **b.** Is this related to the fact that the frost's destructiveness is an "accidental power"?
2. How does this almost playful language become a play upon words in line 6, "The Sun proceeds unmoved"?
3. Readers often feel that the poem turns serious in the final two lines—or reveals a seriousness that was there all along. **a.** How should we relate the "Approving God" at the end to the rest of the poem? **b.** Is there an implied criticism of nature's indifference in the poem?

A Narrow Fellow in the Grass
1. Like "It Sifts from Leaden Sieves," this is a poem that does not announce its subject openly. **a.** At what point do we know that the poem is about snakes? **b.** When we look back on it, does the first line suggest an old saying about deceptive persons?
2. The "sudden" "notice" that a snake gives of its presence is extended in the second stanza as the grass opens and closes. **a.** What is suggested in speaking of the grass dividing "as with a Comb"? **b.** What other images in the poem relate the snake to one's person?
3. Part of the fear inspired by snakes (aside from

the poisonous species) comes from their being cold-blooded creatures. **a.** How is that characteristic developed in the third stanza? **b.** Is it important that the snake should resemble an ordinary object as it uncoils in the noontime sun?
4. The poet feels a cordial relationship with many of nature's creatures but has never met this "Fellow" without a shortened breath and a sharp inner feeling. "And Zero at the Bone—" is not a usual expression to describe a feeling, yet it is an effective and memorable phrase. What feeling does it convey?

There Came a Wind like a Bugle
1. This description of the coming and passing of a storm is most impressive in its highly original imagery, beginning with the opening line. In what way might we think of the storm's wind as "like a Bugle"?
2. In lines 2 and 3 the wind quivers (like a giant snake?) through the grass, bringing "a Green Chill" upon the summer heat. What makes it appropriate, in describing a storm, that "Green Chill" combines the senses of vision and touch?
3. The ordinary response to a storm, shutting up the house, has an "ominous" quality here: it is as if "we" were barring doors and windows against an "Emerald Ghost." **a.** What effect does Dickinson achieve with this image and with the following one of the storm's passing as "Doom's electric Moccasin"? **b.** How does that latter image convey both the lightning-charged atmosphere and the storm's stealth?
4. As the storm quickly passes, its rush is conveyed by its effects upon the landscape. What is happening as we see "a strange Mob of panting Trees"?
5. In Dickinson's time, church bells tolled not just for services but to announce deaths and other disasters. Here, however, they are rung by the storm itself. What is being announced in those "flying tidings" of the last three lines?

There's a Certain Slant of Light
1. Dickinson compares a certain winter light to solemn religious music. In what way might such music be oppressive or make us feel "Heavenly Hurt"?
2. The subject of the second and third stanzas is the inner self, "where the Meanings, are." When we are touched by despair, in what sense, according to Dickinson, is that "An imperial affliction / Sent us of the Air"?
3. In the presence of this stabbing despair, the world seems to stop (lines 13–14). Why, after it

passes, is this same despair "like the Distance / On the look of Death"?

My Life Closed Twice Before Its Close
1. The specific events that twice "closed" the poet's life are not mentioned. What suggests that they were a kind of death?
2. The final two lines indicate that the events had to do with "parting." The suffering caused by parting or separation is "all we need of hell." In what way is parting also "all we know of heaven"?

The Bustle in a House
Dickinson describes the activity after a death as the "Bustle in a House." What do the phrases "Sweeping up" and "putting Love away" convey about what truly happens during a time of grief?

Literary Elements

Simile and Metaphor
Two important figures of speech are **simile** and **metaphor.** A simile makes an explicit comparison between things that are basically different but can be thought of as alike in some respect. When the Scottish poet Robert Burns writes, "O My Luve's like a red, red rose, / That's newly sprung in June," the connecting link between his love and the rose is beauty and freshness. Such comparisons are signaled by a word such as *like* or *as*. In a metaphor, the comparison is implied rather than stated, and no signal word is used. For example, Dickinson writes, " 'Hope' is the thing with feathers." Hope is not said to be *like* a bird but *is* a bird. The rest of the poem explores this metaphor.

Simile and metaphor illustrate the mind's great capacity for imagination. Connecting separate parts of experience by analogy or comparison enables us to relate the world to our inner needs. In personalizing what goes on around us, simile and metaphor figure prominently in the language of poetry—and of prose that approaches poetry in intensity. "Poetry," Robert Frost observed, "provides the one permissible way of saying one thing and meaning another." While this statement is a playful exaggeration, it does point to the fact that poetry relates ideas to their emotional meanings. In this way, as Frost also observed, all poetry is metaphor. It uses language not just for its literal meanings but also for its full range of connotations.

1. Reread "The Soul Selects Her Own Society." The final two lines contain a simile. To what is the closing of "the Valves" compared? What idea does this simile suggest?
2. The "Valves" of line 11 clearly make the soul a metaphor in the poem. What earlier details also give the soul a metaphorical character?
3. Select another metaphor that you consider especially striking from a poem by Emily Dickinson. Explain how this metaphor connects separate experiences and thus relates the outer world to inner needs.

Writing About Literature

Responding to an Interpretation
Express your agreement or disagreement with the following statement about Emily Dickinson by Van Wyck Brooks. Use details from her poems to support your opinions.

> Miss Dickinson lived in a world of paradox, for while her eye was microscopic, her imagination dwelt with mysteries and grandeurs. Ribbons and immortality were mingled in her mind, which passed from one to the other with the speed of lightning. . . .

Comparing an Aspect of Two Poems
Compare the treatment of death in Dickinson's "Because I Could Not Stop for Death" with that in Bryant's "Thanatopsis" (page 153). Consider the following points: Which poem is for you more moving? Which poem is more sensible in its attitude toward death?

Extending Your Study

1. The grandeur of the natural setting in Thomas Doughty's *In Nature's Wonderland,* page 209, dwarfing the solitary human figure, suggests that this is nature seen from the Romantic point of view. How does the use of light in the painting contribute to this effect?

2. *The Philosophers' Camp* by William James Stillman, page 222, portrays an activity that Emerson very much enjoyed, a camping trip of the Adirondack Club. These companionable intellectuals liked to get out to the woods and lakes to hunt and fish but most of all to talk and reflect in a natural setting. Nevertheless, in Stillman's painting, Emerson, who stands at the center next to the largest tree, is clearly set apart from the two groups formed by the others. Is there evidence in the selections from Emerson's writings to suggest why Stillman might have portrayed him this way?

3. May Alcott's drawing, on page 236, of Thoreau's cabin at Walden Pond places it, fancifully, high on a hill and nearly hidden in the trees. The actual cabin was drawn much more realistically by Thoreau's sister Sophie in a sketch that appeared on the title page of *Walden* and is reproduced on page 235. Compare the drawings. What different impressions do we take from the two versions of the cabin?

4. *The Harbor of Papeete,* in Tahiti (page 272), illustrates a South Seas island as Melville would have seen it. The realistic scene, when we consider what it represents historically, is also highly symbolic.

Ships of Western nations that are competing for dominance in the area lie at anchor in a quiet harbor. A few days before Melville first saw Papeete, a French admiral, trying to drive out British influence there, declared Tahiti a French protectorate and forced the native queen to flee. An island's harbor, therefore, was its gateway to the great outside world from which change, for good or ill, was sure to come. This was how Melville used the harbor and ocean in *Typee*—either as an escape route to a greater world or a menacing threat of intrusion into an idyllic island life, depending on the narrator's mood. Ringing the harbor in this picture is a thin belt of Western-style buildings, the scattered outposts of nations half a world away. Behind that is the thick forest canopy where, deep in the interior, native life is still hidden away from Western eyes.

Read over the passage from *Typee* once more and then consider it in the light of this print. As Melville looks at life among the Typees and contrasts it with life in Western civilization, he is deep in the interior of the island and observing a native society then unknown to Americans and Europeans. What kinds of changes would he expect to come from Western intrusion into Typee life?

5. The drawing by Henry Lovie of the Battle of Shiloh, page 294, takes up the scene at a different time from Melville's "Shiloh: A Requiem." Can the poem and the drawing nevertheless be related to each other as responses to an event? Could Lovie's drawing have portrayed an empty scene, after the men and horses and flags and cannons were gone, and captured the same mood as Melville does in his poem?

6. Joseph Meeker's *The Land of Evangeline,* page 300, is meant to illustrate both the physical setting and something of the mood of Longfellow's poem. Compare the picture with the passage from *Evangeline.* What details has the painter chosen to emphasize? Is there anything in the painting that seems to express the mood or emotional atmosphere of the poem?

7. Edward Weston's famous photograph, *Shell, 1927,* page 313, gives us a vivid image of the spiral structure of this strange creature of the sea. What part of Holmes's poem, "The Chambered Nautilus," seems most precisely related to this structure? The nautilus is a "Child of the wandering sea," and the poem often reminds us of that. How does the poem establish a relationship between the "unresting sea" as the nautilus knows it and "life" as we know it in human terms?

8. In the nineteenth century, it was customary for many people to mourn their dead in public ways— in their fashion of dress, in certain rituals, in the activities that were allowed or forbidden during the mourning period. In Edwin Elmer's *Mourning Picture,* pages 328–329, what details suggest that people tried to create an entire atmosphere of mourning at a time of loss?

The Flowering of New England

1. The rich and bountiful literature of this era constitutes a "renaissance" in American letters, during which radically opposed ideas and viewpoints found lasting artistic expression. The literature of this time offers both optimistic and pessimistic views of human spirit and potential. The former view is summed up in the term *transcendentalism,* whose chief representatives were Emerson and Thoreau. The latter view, found in the works of Hawthorne and Melville, is expressed in part in the following statement:

> Melville shares with Hawthorne an interest in the darker side of human nature and destiny, and like Hawthorne he is fascinated by the involutions of human psychology, by the ultimate alienation that may be the human lot . . . and by the distortions of the ego. . . .
>
> Richard Chase
> (from *Major Writers of America*)

Write an essay discussing this statement in light of the selections by Hawthorne and Melville that you have read. Be sure to point out specific passages in the course of your discussion.

2. The nineteenth-century French critic Charles Sainte-Beuve once defined *classic* authors in the following way:

> A true classic . . . is an author who has enriched the human mind, increased its treasure and caused it to advance a step; who has discovered some moral and not equivocal truth, or revealed some eternal passion in that heart where all seemed known and discovered; who has expressed his thought, observations, or invention, in no matter what form, only provided it be broad and great, refined and sensible, sane and beautiful in itself; who has spoken to all in his own peculiar style, a style . . . new and old, easily contemporary with all time.

In an essay, discuss the above statement in relation to two authors whose work you have studied in this unit. Remember to back up any conclusions you make with specific references to the selections.

For assistance in developing your essays, see the section called *Writing About Literature* at the back of this textbook.

For Further Reading

For General Background

Brooks, Van Wyck, *The Flowering of New England, 1815–1865* (Dutton, 1936)

Lewis, R. W. B., *The American Adam: Innocence, Tragedy, and Tradition in the Nineteenth Century* (University of Chicago Press, 1955)

Matthiessen, F. O., *American Renaissance: Art and Expression in the Age of Emerson and Whitman* (Oxford University Press, 1941, 1968)

Smith, Henry Nash, *Virgin Land* (Harvard University Press, 1950, 1970)

For Background on Individual Authors

Emerson

Allen, Gay Wilson, *Waldo Emerson* (Viking, 1981)

Bishop, Jonathan, *Emerson on the Soul* (AMS Press, 1964)

Porte, Joel, *Representative Man: Ralph Waldo Emerson in His Time* (Oxford, 1979)

Whicher, Stephen, *Freedom and Fate* (University of Pennsylvania, 1953)

Thoreau

Harding, Walter, *The Days of Henry Thoreau: A Biography* (Princeton, 1965)

Howarth, William, *The Book of Concord* (Viking, 1982)

Paul, Sherman, ed., *Thoreau: A Collection of Critical Essays* (Prentice-Hall, 1962)

Wagenknecht, Edward, *Henry David Thoreau, What Manner of Man* (University of Massachusetts, 1981)

Hawthorne

Kaul, A. ed., *Hawthorne: A Collection of Critical Essays* (Prentice-Hall, 1966)

Mellows, James R., *Nathaniel Hawthorne in His Time* (Houghton Mifflin, 1980)

Turner, Arlin, *Nathaniel Hawthorne, an Introduction and Interpretation* (Barnes & Noble, 1961)

Melville

Chase, Richard, *Herman Melville: A Critical Study* (Hafner Publishing Co., 1949, 1971)

Howard, Leon, *Herman Melville* (University of Minnesota Press, 1961)

Leyda, Jay, *The Melville Log*, 2 vols. (Gordian, 1951, 1969)

Longfellow

Arvin, Newton, *Longfellow: His Life and Work* (Little, Brown, 1963)

Whittier

Wagenknecht, Edward, *John Greenleaf Whittier, A Portrait in Paradox* (Oxford University Press, 1967)

Holmes

Hoyt, Edwin, *The Improper Bostonian, Dr. Oliver Wendell Holmes* (Morrow, 1979)

Lowell

Duberman, Martin B., *James Russell Lowell* (Houghton Mifflin, 1966)

Howard, Leon, *Victorian Knight-Errant* (Greenwood, 1971)

Dickinson

Anderson, Charles Roberts, *Emily Dickinson's Poetry* (Holt, Rinehart and Winston, 1960)

Sewall, Richard B., *The Life of Emily Dickinson* (Farrar, Straus and Giroux, 1974)

For Leisure Reading and Extra Projects

Emerson

Essays "Circles," "Experience," "Thoreau"

Poems "Uriel," "Threnody," "The Snow-Storm," "Hamatreya"

Thoreau's Works

Walden, "Civil Disobedience," "A Plea for Captain Brown"

Hawthorne's Tales and Novels

"My Kinsman, Major Molineux," "Rappaccini's Daughter," "The Maypole of Merry Mount," "The Ambitious Guest," "The Birthmark," "Young Goodman Brown," "Ethan Brand," *The Scarlet Letter, The House of the Seven Gables, The Blithedale Romance*

Melville's Novels and Stories

Moby-Dick, Billy Budd, Typee, Piazza Tales

Longfellow's Poems

The Song of Hiawatha, Evangeline, The Courtship of Miles Standish, "My Lost Youth"

Whittier's Poems

"Ichabod," "The Barefoot Boy," "Skipper Ireson's Ride," "The Eternal Goodness," "The Friend's Burial," "Maud Muller," "Abraham Davenport"

Holmes's Poetry and Prose

"The Ballad of the Oysterman," "The Last Leaf," "The Deacon's Masterpiece," *The Autocrat of the Breakfast-Table*

Lowell's Works

"The Vision of Sir Launfal," "To the Dandelion," Introduction to *The Biglow Papers, Second Series, A Fable for Critics*

Dickinson's Poems

"The Heart Asks Pleasure First," "I Years Had Been from Home," "The Brain Is Wider Than the Sky," "I Asked No Other Thing," "A Bird Came Down the Walk"

A HOUSE DIVIDED AND RESTORED
1860–1890

A Midnight Ride on the Mississippi (1890). Currier and Ives lithograph showing a race between the *Natchez* and the *Eclipse*.

Library of Congress

*Evening Gun, Fort
Sumter* by Conrad Wise
Chapman (1842–1910).
Oil on canvas.

Word over all, beautiful as the sky,
Beautiful that war and all its deeds of carnage must in time be
utterly lost,
That the hands of the sisters Death and Night incessantly softly
wash again, and ever again, this soiled world;
For my enemy is dead, a man divine as myself is dead. . . .
Walt Whitman, "Reconciliation"

Only slowly, after the outbreak of civil war in 1861, did most Americans realize the extent of the national tragedy. Those, in both North and South, who had believed that the war would end quickly, perhaps with a single decisive battle, had to face instead the mounting horrors of four long years of struggle. Walt Whitman described the terrible uncertainties and increasing sorrow of those years as the nation's life hung in the balance: "that many-threaded drama, with its sudden and strange surprises, its confounding of prophecies, its moments of despair, the dread of foreign interference, the interminable campaigns, the bloody battles, the mighty and cumbrous and green armies . . . —with, over the whole land, the last three years of the struggle, an unending, universal mourning-wail of women, parents, orphans. . . ." To Whitman, whose poem "When Lilacs Last in the Dooryard Bloom'd" is the finest of all the tributes to the fallen president, the assassination of Abraham Lincoln at the war's end seemed the last act in a dreadful drama of sacrifice. Still, as Whitman also knew, this tragic war had performed the positive functions of tragedy as well: the flaw of sectional differences based on slavery had at last been faced and eradicated, and through pain had come new self-knowledge and strength. The nation would not again feel the supreme confidence in human potential that had been the faith of the transcendentalists, but it had a firmer sense of human limitations.

Even in peace, the spirit of brotherhood Whitman spoke for did not come easily to a nation still dominated by the passions of war. The South, devastated by war and then subjected by the federal government to shortsighted and sometimes vindictive policies of reconstruction, was slow to recover and to take its place in the growing national prosperity. In the North the situation was far different. Almost without pause the great industrial system that had produced the materials of war was turned to the production of civilian goods. In many respects the postwar decades simply continued trends already established before the war. Samuel Morse's telegraph was followed now by Alexander Graham Bell's telephone, patented in 1876. The railroad, the foundation of commerce since the 1840s, spanned the continent at last in 1869. It was still the age of steam and steel, but electricity and oil were increasingly important. With the development of alternating current, urban centers would begin to have electric lights in the 1880s; but even in rural areas the old whale-oil lamps, for which Melville had once hunted the mighty sperm whale in the far Pacific, were replaced by kerosene lighting. As the economy expanded, immigration from abroad resumed, and once again, between 1870 and 1890, the nation's population doubled, with cities growing fastest of all. Although food production soared with the help

The Battery, the Bay and Harbor of New York (c. 1855) by Samuel Waugh. Watercolor on canvas.
Museum of the City of New York

of new machinery and improved farming methods, America was less and less the predominantly agricultural nation that Jefferson and Crèvecoeur had envisioned.

In one respect the postwar era was different from the 1850s: the voices of reform, if not entirely silenced, were far less evident. So intent was the nation upon the expansion of commerce and industry that all other values seemed to be set aside. Vast new fortunes were being accumulated as never before in America. This unrestrained exploitation of both natural and human resources, justified always in the name of "progress," has led historians to call the 1870s the Great Barbecue or the Age of the Robber Barons. But the most durable name for the period was supplied by Mark Twain in the title of his first novel, *The Gilded Age*. By "gilded" Twain meant to contrast the cheap cynicism and gaudy materialism of this time with the wisdom and humane values associated with the golden age of antiquity. Under whatever name, however, this unlovely period stored up massive social problems for the future in the widening gulf between the rich and the poor and in the corrupting influence of wealth upon American politics. The 1880s and 1890s would see the rise of protective associations of debt-ridden farmers and unions of exploited industrial workers. Reform had a new face in this harsher age: it was less a matter of stirring the American conscience than of developing a base of political and economic power. It was difficult in the postwar period to find evidence of the high idealism that had been so strong a force in earlier reform movements.

Literature: From Romanticism to Realism

Literature in this period also turned from human potentialities and aspirations to the actualities of existence in America. By 1865, the New England Renaissance had run its course. Thoreau and Hawthorne were dead; Emerson was old; and Melville, except for some occasional poetry, was silent. Longfellow and Whittier were still immensely popular, but their eyes were turned mostly toward the past. Only Walt Whitman provided a connection between the romantic idealism of the 1850s and the changed realities of the postwar period. In its first edition of 1855, his *Leaves of Grass* shocked its few readers, but in time his free verse would revolutionize modern poetry. Whitman's vision drew upon traditional American individualism, upon the intuitive faith developed by Emerson and the transcendentalists, and upon his own deep belief in democracy and trust in the common people. Whitman both celebrated and criticized the postwar age, recognizing in the expansive energies of the time a valuable expression of American nationalism but deploring the materialism that often seemed to corrupt democratic values.

Local Color and Regionalism

In contrast to Whitman, who asserted that the poet must "absorb" every aspect of America and express a nationalistic spirit that all Americans could share, the writers whose careers began after the war were often identified with a particular place or region. Several factors contributed to the growth of the "local-color" movement in literature. The war itself had pitted sectional interests against a belief in national sovereignty, emphasizing the great regional differences in American society. But the war also eased the political tensions arising from those sectional differences, by reuniting the states into a single Union. Once the threat of physical division had passed, Americans could again take an interest in the sheer diversity of their vast land. During the war, Nevada had been granted statehood, and Americans had poured into other territories in the Far West. To Easterners, such remote parts of their country were less familiar than Europe, which they knew through books. But it was not just the remote West that was strange to most Americans. Through the years, every region of the country had developed distinctive speech patterns and dialects, local customs and folkways, and recognizable character types that ranged from the Western miner to the New England farmer. By emphasizing these distinctive and "colorful" regional traits, writers of the local-color movement helped to familiarize Americans with their own nation.

Behind the popularity of local-color writing was a shift, throughout the Western world, from Romanticism to *realism* in literature. Originating in France and coming later to the United States through British writers, realism placed less emphasis on the imagination and more on observed fact. In this it reflected the new importance of science and the new method of viewing every aspect of life scientifically, including human behavior. The novelist Henry James spoke of realism as "a powerful impulse to mirror the unmitigated realities of life"—that is, to reflect reality without softening or idealizing its features. The foremost American exponent of realism, William Dean Howells, defined it "as nothing more and nothing less than the truthful treatment of material," meaning that the writer's primary responsibility was to be an accurate observer and reporter of the life around him. Realism reflected the general shift of concern in this period from human potentialities to human actualities, from ideas to facts, from personal vision to observed social behavior.

The local-color movement formed an important transition between Romanticism and realism. In its close attention to the dialect, customs, and character types of a particular region, local-color writing showed the kind of objective observation of social facts that is typical of realism. But in its treatment of human emotion and motivation, local-color fiction was often sentimental. Bret Harte's stories of life in the California mining camps, which took America by storm in the late

Detail from *Washing Gold, Calaveras, California* (1853). Gouache. Artist unknown.

1860s, are an example. Harte had an excellent eye for the details of Western scenery and dress and manners and a good ear for the dialects of the mining camps. His gentlemen gamblers and rough-spoken miners were a bold addition to the range of characters in American literature. As social types they implied the raw realities of life in temporary and semilawless communities where the only object was to get rich before the gold ran out. But Harte's realism extended only to the surfaces of this material. His need to romanticize his characters for the purpose of drawing an idealistic moral led him to treat them as stereotypes and to ignore the deeper realities of his subject in favor of its "colorful" aspects.

In the South, regional literary interests were powerfully influenced by the war. The South Carolina poet Henry Timrod, who had been little more than an amateur versifier, found in the tragedy of war a subject that brought new force and maturity to his work, making him the foremost poet of the Confederacy. After the war his most important successor, Sidney Lanier, went far beyond Timrod in moving regional concerns into the mainstream of American poetry. Lanier devoted himself to experiments in poetic form and looked forward to a new *national* culture in which the arts would provide a new sense of community.

A long-prominent literary form of the South that had used local-color materials was the humorous story or sketch. Southwestern humor concentrated on the backwoods and the frontier and often exploited the crudity and violence of that life. Its chief narrative elements were fistfights and shooting matches, practical jokes, spectacular hunts for wild animals, deceptive horse trades in which the "hero" outcheated his rival, and the antisocial activities of rogues and semioutlaws. Despite its attention to local manners and dialect, Southwestern humor produced little of permanent literary value. It depended too greatly upon exaggeration to make its point, and its violence was too seldom redeemed by wit. It was boisterous, bawdy, and sometimes disgusting, but it was only occasionally funny. As tastes changed, the South developed a more typical local-color literature in the dialect stories and animal fables of Joel Chandler Harris and the carefully wrought stories of local manners and customs of George Washington Cable and Kate Chopin.

Nevertheless, Southwestern humor created a storehouse of folklore and tall tales for later writers. Mark Twain's work had deep roots in this material. The sketch that brought him his first fame, "The Notorious Jumping Frog of Calaveras County" (page 391), adapts standard elements of Southwestern humor to a California setting. It is a tall tale recounted by an uneducated, meandering narrator who doesn't so much wander from the point of his stories as fail to see that they have one. In the familiar way of Southwestern humor, the sketch makes comic use of animals and centers upon a bet or contest that is won by a trick. Yet in Twain's hands these old materials were already taking on a new literary significance as elements that could be transformed into true comedy through the artful development of language and character. Simon Wheeler's monologue in the frog sketch would lead in Twain's work toward such later narratives as "Baker's Bluejay Yarn" (page 398), where the humor is not in the incident itself but in the rich comic resources of spoken language as the expression of Baker's character. Much later, in the 1930s and 1940s, the South would enjoy a remarkable period of literary achievement known as the Southern Renaissance. Once again the old material of Southwestern humor would reappear, now as an influence on the imaginations of such writers as Erskine Caldwell, Eudora Welty, Robert Penn Warren, Flannery O'Connor, and above all William Faulkner, the South's greatest writer. In this way, Southwestern humor contributed its frontier spirit to the local-color movement and became an important part of the South's literary tradition.

ROBERT E. LEE (1807–1870)

CHIEF JOSEPH (1840?–1904)

FREDERICK DOUGLASS (1817?–1895)
My Bondage and My Freedom (1855)

WALT WHITMAN (1819–1892)
Leaves of Grass (1855)

The Battery (c. 1855)

1861–1865 Civil War

1862 Emancipation Proclamation

ABRAHAM LINCOLN (1809–1865)
"The Gettysburg Address" (1863)

Chief Joseph

1865 President Lincoln assassinated

HENRY TIMROD (1828–1867)
"Ode on the Confederate Dead" (1866)

1867 United States purchases Alaska

LOUISA MAY ALCOTT (1832–1888)
Little Women (1868)

Henry Timrod

1869 — First transcontinental railroad completed

BRET HARTE (1836–1902)
"The Outcasts of Poker Flat" (1869)

1876 — Alexander Graham Bell invents the telephone

MARK TWAIN (1835–1910)
Tom Sawyer (1876)

Mark Twain

1879 — Thomas Alva Edison perfects the incandescent electric light

SIDNEY LANIER (1842–1881)
The Science of English Verse (1880)

TWAIN
Life on the Mississippi (1883)

TWAIN
Huckleberry Finn (1884)

1886 — American Federation of Labor founded

Ambrose Bierce

AMBROSE BIERCE (1842–1914?)
"An Occurrence at Owl Creek Bridge" (1891)

Harriet Beecher Stowe.
National Archives

Sarah Orne Jewett.
The Bettmann Archive

In New England local-color writing also owed something to the regional tradition of American humor, for it often expressed the wry, "common sense" spirit that had earlier characterized the Down East sketches of Seba Smith. The best of the New England local-color writers were women. Long before the war Harriet Beecher Stowe was famous for *Uncle Tom's Cabin* (1852), the most influential of the antislavery novels that aroused Northern feelings against slavery. (When she and President Lincoln were introduced in 1862, he supposedly called her "the little lady who wrote the book that made this big war!") But the fame of that novel has obscured Stowe's later accomplishments in the local-color fiction of Massachusetts, especially the nostalgic character studies of *Oldtown Folks,* in which she felt she had best captured the spirit of an earlier New England. That spirit has a darker cast in the work of Mary E. Wilkins Freeman, whose ironic stories are small but vivid illustrations of the restrictions of village life and especially of the social repression of women. Irony is an important note in the writing of still another woman, Sarah Orne Jewett, whose sketches of life on the coast of Maine represent the fullest development of local-color fiction in New England. Her meticulously crafted stories, although they reflect a lifelong immersion in the manners, speech, and customs of her native region, transcend local concerns to illuminate universal issues of human life. Her sharply etched characters have the same psychological precision that we find in Edwin Arlington Robinson's portraits of Richard Cory and Miniver Cheevy (page 497). From the seemingly narrow materials of her native Down East region, Jewett created local character types who are true to human nature in any region.

Of all the sections of the country in which local-color writing flourished, none created so much interest as the Far West. Americans had been fascinated with their western frontier for more than two centuries, but the Far West, especially California, created a new kind of excitement. California had been settled in a rush—the Gold Rush of 1849, which drew people from all over the world. (A British cartoon pictured British citizens setting off for California in rowboats!) San Francisco, a sleepy village of eight hundred people in 1848, became in a few years a financial capital rivaling New York. As gold began to run out in California, prospectors struck a still richer bonanza— the Comstock Lode just across the line in Nevada. But it was not just the mineral wealth of this newest frontier that dazzled the nation. As word of its scenery, climate, and agriculture drifted back, the Golden State seemed to be the fabulous part of America. (Like other travelers of the time, Mark Twain brought back specimens of California minerals and fruits to show fascinated Easterners.) Under such circumstances, interest in local-color fiction of the Far West was bound to be high. San Francisco, an intellectual and cultural capital as well as a financial one, soon had its "Literary Frontier" of writers, most of them journalists who also wrote fiction and poetry. The best produc-

Stockton, 1856 by
**Alburtus D. O.
Browere (1814–1887).**
Oil on canvas.
The Fine Arts Museums of
San Francisco, Museum
purchase

tions of this group were the short stories of Bret Harte and Ambrose
Bierce.

Mark Twain did most to bring the Western spirit into the mainstream of American literature. Twain was influenced by several regional literary traditions from both the South and West, and perhaps
mostly by the oral tradition of American humorists and storytellers.
He raised these regional materials to national significance in books
that have a permanent place in American literature and are now read
throughout the world. One part of this achievement was his creation
of a *vernacular* style—that is, a style based on the patterns and rhythms
of language as Americans actually spoke it. This was also the aim of
the local colorists and, after them, the realists. In a sense, Twain,
with his knowledge of many dialects and his nearly flawless ear for
the intonations of speech, only did best what others attempted, creating from these local variations a remarkably flexible language that
spoke eloquently to Americans of every class and region.

In Twain's work, however, the vernacular extends beyond style to
character and narrative perspective, defining a system of values opposed to conventional social attitudes and stereotypes. Twain realized
the most important potential of vernacular humor and developed it
into a deft instrument of social criticism and a means of establishing
character. *Adventures of Huckleberry Finn,* Twain's masterpiece, is a
triumphant fusion of vernacular humor and local-color writing. The
vernacular perspective exposes the prejudices and injustices of a
hypocritical society. The social types of the novel are carefully drawn
in terms of regional characteristics and with meticulous attention to

dialect, an influence of the local-color movement. But perhaps the greatest triumph of the novel is its embodiment of the vernacular perspective in its central characters. In a white orphan boy and a runaway slave we have vernacular characters whose shrewd common sense and basic humanity cut through the hypocrisies of society to define human values outside social conventions. The vernacular language of the narrative is equally capable of creating broad satire and of evoking the most sensitive moods and feelings.

The Gilded Age that followed the Civil War did not match the earlier American Renaissance in literary abundance. The greatest poet of the postwar age, Walt Whitman, drew his intellectual and spiritual energies from the expansive optimism of an earlier time, especially from the transcendentalist vision of human beings' spiritual potential. The bitter realities of war and the selfish materialism that follow it gave later writers a more limited sense of human possibilities. As a literary theory, realism tended to restrict the imagination, to value fact over idea. The movement toward regional interests, while valuable in emphasizing the special qualities of life in a particular area, nevertheless threatened to make literature *merely* regional rather than national. It was partly in reaction to this provincial character of contemporary literature that Henry James, the greatest American realistic novelist of the postwar period, chose the broadest possible theme for his work: the contrasts that could be drawn between America and Europe. Yet in Mark Twain's best work, the regional traditions of American literature—local color and vernacular humor— became a national expression that carried America's voice to the world. Once again the language of American literature was revitalized, and the local became the universal.

Review

1. What developments of the postwar decades contributed to the growth of national prosperity?
2. Why did Twain call the 1870s the "Gilded Age"?
3. How were the reform movements of this period different from earlier movements?
4. How does Whitman represent a bridge between the romantic idealism of the past and the realities of the postwar period?
5. How did local-color writing reflect a shift from Romanticism to realism?
6. What literary types were created in the local-color fiction of Bret Harte?
7. What literary form was prominent in Southwestern humor?
8. Name three New England local-color writers.
9. What does the term *vernacular style* mean?
10. What traditions did Twain unify in his writing?

WALT WHITMAN
1819–1892

The appearance in 1855 of a thin book of poems called *Leaves of Grass* marks a major turning point in American literature. As Emerson's *Nature* in 1836 had introduced a new philosophy, so Walt Whitman's book announced a new poetry. It was once believed that Whitman burst upon the literary scene without training or preparation, a roughneck genius whose only inspiration was nature. It is true enough that there is nothing in his earlier journalism or few moralistic stories to predict the emergence of the poet of 1855. But the record of Whitman's reading and the book reviews he wrote for newspapers show that he read widely in both contemporary literature and the ancient classics, and he acknowledged the special influence of Emerson. By the late 1840s he was consciously preparing himself for a career as a poet. He was, as he said later, "simmering," and Emerson's ideas brought him to a "boil." And it was Emerson who in "The Poet" defined the role of the poet in a democracy as the representative man who in speaking for himself speaks for us all. This was the role Whitman was eager to assume, and he assumed it in the opening lines of his first poem:

> *I celebrate myself,*
> *And what I assume you shall assume . . .*

For the unprepared reader the poems that followed this declaration could scarcely have been more startling, either in form or content. Whitman discarded traditional metrical patterns in favor of free verse, a technical liberation that matched Emerson's declaration of America's intellectual independence. His poems seemed equally free in content. In the Preface he argued that poetry must embrace every aspect of life, and in his poems he wrote without apology on subjects that had previously been excluded from poetry as ugly or shameful. The language of this poetry was vivid and exciting, and also bewildering in its rapid shifts from vast abstractions to intimate personal revelations.

Walt Whitman (c. 1866). Photograph by Mathew B. Brady (1823?–1896).

Most disturbing of all, perhaps, was the voice of the poet heard in these poems. It was brash and confident, a democratic voice that would speak of all things without "hindrance." With Emerson, Whitman believed that oratory was the most democratic of the arts: the form in which individuals speak out freely and directly to an audience. He not only inserted his own personality into his poems but insisted on its presence.

Whitman was born the son of a Long Island farmer who also built houses in Brooklyn. Both places were home to Whitman and would figure strongly in his poetry. The boy's formal schooling ended when he was eleven, and he soon thereafter began working in a printing office. This led him into journalism as a reporter and then as an editor. He was successful as a journalist and eventually became editor of the Brooklyn *Eagle*, an important newspaper. He resigned from this position in 1848 because his stand against slavery was too strong for the paper's owners. For a time he worked on a paper in New Orleans, and the journey there gave him a lasting sense of the vastness of America and the variety of its people.

He withdrew from journalism in 1850 to work part time as a carpenter with his father while writing the twelve poems for the first edition of *Leaves of Grass*. A second and much expanded edition appeared in 1856, and others followed as Whitman added new poems, dropped others, and rearranged his poems to reflect his changing perceptions of his work. Although he wrote a number of prose works, *Leaves of Grass* became his lifelong occupation as he added the poems that recorded his most essential experiences. Notable among the sources of new poems were his experiences caring for wounded soldiers during the war as a volunteer in Washington hospitals, and his reaction to the assassination of President Lincoln. For Whitman, the highest ideals of American democracy were embodied in Lincoln, a wise and compassionate man of the common people who rose to moral leadership of his nation. Whitman's poem "When Lilacs Last in the Dooryard Bloom'd" is a masterwork, the finest of the many poems on Lincoln.

In 1873 Whitman suffered a severe stroke and lived thereafter as a semi-invalid. Emerson had greeted him in 1855 "at the beginning of a great career"; in his last years he was honored by many admirers as America's greatest poet. But he knew, as he said near the end, that his work had not gained the acceptance he had hoped for as an expression of the nation's democratic faith: "My volume is a candidate for the future," he wrote.

Put in abstract terms, Whitman's philosophy in many ways resembles Emerson's. He too believed that the physical world is the embodiment of spirit, and that the human soul urgently seeks connection with this spiritual reality. Indicating this connection is the poet's job. People expect the poet, Whitman wrote, "to indicate the path between reality and their own souls." Emerson would have said as much. But in Whitman the emphasis is different, as any reader is immediately aware. His poetry celebrates the "divine condition" of being alive with an intensity that seems to unite all forms of life—human, animal, natural—without discrimination. "It's as if

Leaves
of
Grass.

—··—

Brooklyn, New York:
1855.

Title page of *Leaves of Grass* (1855).
The Bettmann Archive

the beasts spoke," Thoreau observed in admiration. In the life of the senses, Whitman emphasized not just the eyes, as Emerson did, but all the senses, especially touch. In social terms, no aspect of life and no person was beyond the poet's sympathies, and few readers were yet ready for such total social democracy. At the same time, Whitman was the insistent poet of the self and of the self's expansion through absorption of the world until it seems to contain "all." Although he was speaking as the *representative* poet, he seemed to many a mere egotist. It is easier to see now that, for Whitman, the spiritual development of the self that he tried to enact in his poems was the fulfillment of the promise of democracy for every individual.

FROM
Song of Myself

1

I celebrate myself, and sing myself,
And what I assume you shall assume,
For every atom belonging to me as good belongs to you.

I loaf and invite my soul,
I lean and loaf at my ease observing a spear of summer grass.   5

My tongue, every atom of my blood, formed from this soil, this air,
Born here of parents born here from parents the same, and
    their parents the same,
I, now thirty-seven years old in perfect health begin,
Hoping to cease not till death.

Creeds and schools in abeyance,   10
Retiring back a while sufficed at what they are, but never
    forgotten,°
I harbor for good or bad, I permit to speak at every hazard,
Nature without check with original energy.

21

I am the poet of the Body and I am the poet of the Soul,
The pleasures of heaven are with me and the pains of hell are
    with me,   15
The first I graft and increase upon myself, the latter I translate
    into a new tongue.

I am the poet of the woman the same as the man,
And I say it is as great to be a woman as to be a man,
And I say there is nothing greater than the mother of men.

I chant the chant of dilation° or pride,   20
We have had ducking and deprecating° about enough,
I show that size is only development.

Have you outstripped the rest? are you the President?
It is a trifle, they will more than arrive there every one, and
    still pass on.

I am he that walks with the tender and growing night,   25
I call to the earth and sea half-held by the night.

10–11. **Creeds . . . forgotten:** Certain creeds and schools of thought for a while
sufficed, but are now retiring to the back of the poet's mind. 20. **dilation:** here,
expansion. 21. **deprecating** (dĕp′rĭ-kāt′ĭng): disapproving.

31

I believe a leaf of grass is no less than the journey-work of the
  stars,
And the pismire° is equally perfect, and a grain of sand, and
  the egg of the wren,
And the tree toad is a chef-d'œuvre° for the highest,
And the running blackberry° would adorn the parlors of
  heaven,   30
And the narrowest hinge in my hand puts to scorn all
  machinery,
And the cow crunching with depress'd head surpasses any
  statue,
And a mouse is miracle enough to stagger sextillions of infi-
  dels°. . . .

52

The spotted hawk swoops by and accuses me, he complains of
  my gab and my loitering.

I too am not a bit tamed, I too am untranslatable,   35
I sound my barbaric yawp over the roofs of the world.

The last scud of day holds back for me,
It flings my likeness after the rest and true as any on the
  shadow'd wilds,
It coaxes me to the vapor and the dusk.

I depart as air, I shake my white locks at the runaway sun,   40
I effuse° my flesh in eddies, and drift it in lacy jags.

I bequeath myself to the dirt to grow from the grass I love,
If you want me again look for me under your boot-soles.

You will hardly know who I am or what I mean,
But I shall be good health to you nevertheless,   45
And filter and fiber your blood.

Failing to fetch me at first keep encouraged,
Missing me one place search another,
I stop somewhere waiting for you.

Walt Whitman with butter-
fly photographed at Ocean
Grove, New Jersey, in 1883.
The Bettmann Archive

28. **pismire** (pĭs′mīr′): ant.   29. **chef-d'œuvre** (shĕ-də′vr): masterpiece.
30. **running blackberry:** The blackberry sends out runners in the ground.
33. **infidels:** nonbelievers.   41. **effuse:** pour out.

For Study and Discussion

Analyzing and Interpreting the Poem

1. The opening section of *Song of Myself* celebrates the poet's individuality or self. How do these lines make it clear that this self is also representative and universal, sharing its being with all others?

2. In *Nature*, Emerson said that the present generation should enjoy an original relationship with the universe, treating life as a still-untried experiment and seeing nature with fresh sight rather than through the eyes of those who lived before us. How do lines 10–13 reflect this theme?

3. In section 21, the poet erases the usual distinctions that we make in life—like that between the body and the soul—by resolving all parts into the whole of the poet's being and his poem. "The pleasures of heaven," he tells us, "I graft and increase upon myself. . . ." How does he deal with the miseries of life—"the pains of hell"?

4. Having praised men and women equally, the poet chants of the pride that all should share in their common humanity. What does the poet think of pride based upon size or accomplishments or high office?

5. Lines 25–26 portray the poet as a companion of the earth and sea. How does this image reinforce the theme of the poet as an all-inclusive presence?

6. In section 31, what examples does the poet give of common things that are really equal to more awesome things?

7. Section 52, the final section of the poem, sums up many themes. One is the return of the self to nature. **a.** What images describe the diffusion of the self into nature? **b.** What images does the poet use to suggest that his message and spirit will remain after he is gone?

8. Walt Whitman was particularly aware of the wonders of the five senses. Find examples in these selections of his enjoyment of each of the senses.

Literary Elements

Free Verse

As an appropriate form for his liberating view of life and for a poetry that would allow every aspect of life to speak without restraint, Whitman chose **free verse.** Such verse is "free" in the sense that it lacks regular meter and line length. But this places even greater emphasis upon rhythm, just as powerful speech does. Whitman tried to approximate the natural cadences of speech in his poetry, carefully varying the length of his lines according to his intended emphasis. In section 52, for example, the first long line is really two sentences joined. The emphatic elements of the last phrase are the short slang word *gab* and then the long word *loitering*, which must be pronounced slowly if it is to be heard clearly.

Many poets have scorned this form (Robert Frost compared it to playing tennis without a net), but it is in fact a very ancient form (the Psalms of the Bible are written in free verse). As Whitman shows, it can be very effective. If this form ignores some elements of poetic structure, it gives greater importance to others, notably repetition and parallel construction. Examine the last three lines of section 52. What examples of parallelism can you find in these lines? What examples of the repetition of words and phrases can you find in these excerpts from *Song of Myself*?

Language and Vocabulary

Discussing Whitman's Diction

Whitman's vocabulary is usually vigorous and often startling. Many of his unusual words surprise by their very simplicity. These are not long and learned words but sturdy, homely words that reflect his interest in life's simple pursuits. One example is the italicized word in the following line: "And the narrowest *hinge* in my hand puts to scorn all machinery" (line 31).

Referring to other examples from *Song of Myself*, discuss Whitman's diction. In your discussion, consider the following questions:

1. In what way are homely words appropriate to the subject matter of *Song of Myself*?

2. To what extent does Whitman's choice of words reflect his personality?

3. Do you think the poem is improved by an occasional surprising word or phrase? If so, in what way?

One's-Self I Sing

One's-self I sing, a simple separate person,
Yet utter the word Democratic, the word En-Masse.

Of physiology from top to toe I sing,
Not physiognomy alone nor brain alone is worthy for the
    Muse, I say the Form complete is worthier far,
The Female equally with the Male I sing.

Of Life immense in passion, pulse, and power,
Cheerful, for freest action form'd under the laws divine,
The Modern Man I sing.

I Hear America Singing

I hear America singing, the varied carols I hear,
Those of mechanics, each one singing his as it should be blithe
    and strong,
The carpenter singing his as he measures his plank or beam,
The mason singing his as he makes ready for work, or leaves
    off work,
The boatman singing what belongs to him in his boat, the
    deckhand singing on the steamboat deck,   5
The shoemaker singing as he sits on his bench, the hatter
    singing as he stands,
The woodcutter's song, the plowboy's on his way in the morn-
    ing, or at noon intermission or at sundown,
The delicious singing of the mother, of the young wife at work,
    or of the girl sewing or washing,
Each singing what belongs to him or her and to none else,
The day what belongs to the day—at night the party of young
    fellows, robust, friendly,   10
Singing with open mouths their strong melodious songs.

The Jolly Flatboatmen in Port
(1857) by George Caleb
Bingham (1811–1879).
Oil on canvas.
St. Louis Museum of Art

When I Heard the Learn'd Astronomer

When I heard the learn'd astronomer,
When the proofs, the figures, were ranged in columns before
  me,
When I was shown the charts and diagrams, to add, divide, and
  measure them,
When I sitting heard the astronomer where he lectured with
  much applause in the lecture room,
How soon unaccountable I became tired and sick,
Till rising and gliding out I wander'd off by myself,
In the mystical moist night air, and from time to time,
Look'd up in perfect silence at the stars.

A Noiseless Patient Spider

A noiseless patient spider,
I mark'd where on a little promontory it stood isolated,
Mark'd how to explore the vacant vast surrounding,
It launch'd forth filament, filament, filament, out of itself,
Ever unreeling them, ever tirelessly speeding them.   5

And you O my soul where you stand,
Surrounded, detached, in measureless oceans of space,
Ceaselessly musing, venturing, throwing, seeking the spheres
    to connect them,
Till the bridge you will need be form'd, till the ductile anchor
    hold,
Till the gossamer thread you fling catch somewhere, O my soul.   10

For Study and Discussion

Analyzing and Interpreting the Poems

One's-Self I Sing
This brief poem takes up familiar themes in Whitman's work. How are the ideas expressed here similar to those in section 21 of *Song of Myself*?

I Hear America Singing
1. One of the strongest themes in Whitman's poetry is the celebration of work, because work is the universal lot of ordinary people, and because a nation is bound together as much by its crafts as by its political institutions and laws. The first line speaks of the "varied carols" of the nation's work songs. How does the phrase "varied carols" suggest variety within an overall harmony?
2. How are the songs of the young men at the end of the poem different from those that come before?

When I Heard the Learn'd Astronomer
1. This poem turns upon a comparison of two types of knowledge: the learned astronomer's kind—his proofs, figures, and diagrams—and another kind, which the poet feels in "the mystical moist night air." What kind of knowledge does the poet find by looking "in perfect silence at the stars"?
2. How is the theme of this poem related to section 31 of *Song of Myself*?

A Noiseless Patient Spider
1. What analogy does the poet draw between the spider and his own soul?
2. Emphasis is placed on the isolation of the spider and of the human soul. How does this image of a separate self seeking connection with the universe reflect Whitman's vision of life?

Beat! Beat! Drums!

The occasion of this poem was the defeat of the Northern forces at the first battle of Bull Run. Until then Whitman believed, like most Northerners, that the war would be over quickly. Now it was clear that it would be a long struggle, that the North would have to be completely mobilized, and that the war spirit would dominate every aspect of life.

Beat! beat! drums!—blow! bugles! blow!
Through the windows—through doors—burst like a ruthless
    force,
Into the solemn church, and scatter the congregation,
Into the school where the scholar is studying;
Leave not the bridegroom quiet—no happiness must he have
    now with his bride,   5
Nor the peaceful farmer any peace, plowing his field or gath-
    ering his grain,
So fierce you whirr and pound you drums—so shrill you bugles
    blow.

Beat! beat! drums!—blow! bugles! blow!
Over the traffic of cities—over the rumble of wheels in the
    streets;
Are beds prepared for sleepers at night in the houses? no
    sleepers must sleep in those beds,   10
No bargainers' bargains by day—no brokers or speculators—
    would they continue?
Would the talkers be talking? would the singer attempt to sing?
Would the lawyer rise in the court to state his case before the
    judge?
Then rattle quicker, heavier drums—you bugles wilder blow.

Beat! beat! drums!—blow! bugles! blow!   15
Make no parley—stop for no expostulation,
Mind not the timid—mind not the weeper or prayer,
Mind not the old man beseeching the young man,
Let not the child's voice be heard, nor the mother's entreaties,
Make even the trestles to shake the dead where they lie awaiting
    the hearses,   20
So strong you thump O terrible drums—so loud you bugles
    blow.

Field dressing station
during Battle of
Chancellorsville.
Drawing by Edwin Forbes,
dated May 2, 1863.

A March in the Ranks Hard-Prest, and the Road Unknown

A march in the ranks hard-prest, and the road unknown,
A route through a heavy wood with muffled steps in the darkness,
Our army foil'd with loss severe, and the sullen remnant retreating,
Till after midnight glimmer upon us the lights of a dim-lighted
building,
We come to an open space in the woods, and halt by the dim-
lighted building,   5
'Tis a large old church at the crossing roads, now an impromptu
hospital,
Entering but for a minute I see a sight beyond all the pictures
and poems ever made,
Shadows of deepest, deepest black, just lit by moving candles
and lamps,
And by one great pitchy torch stationary with wild red flame
and clouds of smoke,

By these, crowds, groups of forms vaguely I see on the floor,
    some in the pews laid down,   10
At my feet more distinctly a soldier, a mere lad, in danger of
    bleeding to death, (he is shot in the abdomen,)
I stanch the blood temporarily, (the youngster's face is white as
    a lily,)
Then before I depart I sweep my eyes o'er the scene fain to
    absorb it all,
Faces, varieties, postures beyond description, most in obscurity,
    some of them dead,
Surgeons operating, attendants holding lights, the smell of
    ether, the odor of blood,   15
The crowd, O the crowd of the bloody forms, the yard outside
    also fill'd,
Some on the bare ground, some on planks or stretchers, some
    in the death-spasm sweating,
An occasional scream or cry, the doctor's shouted orders or
    calls,
The glisten of the little steel instruments catching the glint of
    the torches,
These I resume as I chant, I see again the forms, I smell the
    odor,   20
Then hear outside the orders given, *Fall in, my men, fall in;*
But first I bend to the dying lad, his eyes open, a half-smile
    gives he me,
Then the eyes close, calmly close, and I speed forth to the
    darkness,
Resuming, marching, ever in darkness marching, on in the
    ranks,
The unknown road still marching.   25

Reconciliation

Word over all, beautiful as the sky,
Beautiful that war and all its deeds of carnage must in time be
    utterly lost,
That the hands of the sisters Death and Night incessantly softly
    wash again, and ever again, this soil'd world;
For my enemy is dead, a man divine as myself is dead,
I look where he lies white-faced and still in the coffin—I draw
    near,
Bend down and touch lightly with my lips the white face in the
    coffin.

For Study and Discussion

Analyzing and Interpreting the Poems

Beat! Beat! Drums!

1. Whitman discarded the usual metrical patterns of poetry and experimented with the natural rhythms of language. What effect is gained by joining the first line, with its short, harsh, punctuated words, to the longer, slower lines that follow? (Note that the rest of the stanza is actually one long sentence.)

2. What images does Whitman use to show how the sounds of war drown out all other sounds and disrupt normal human activities?

3. In what way is it ironic that the trestles that hold the coffins of the dead are shaken by the sounds of the drums and bugles?

A March in the Ranks Hard-Prest, and the Road Unknown

1. In this, one of the most anguished of Whitman's Civil War poems, the opening lines carefully set a scene: a hard-pressed "sullen remnant" of a defeated army marches in retreat through woods at night over an unknown road. When the soldiers stop at a crossroad and the poet steps inside the old church now serving as a temporary hospital, he sees "a sight beyond all the pictures and poems ever made. . . ." What picture does he create for us by bringing it piece by piece out of the darkness?

2. What is the effect of the shifts in color from "shadows of deepest, deepest black" through the first dim light, then the "wild red flame" of the torch, and finally to an individual soldier's face "white as a lily"?

3. Before leaving, the poet tries to fix every part of this scene—its sights, sounds, smells—forever in his mind. What evidence do we have that he succeeds?

4. Look carefully at the last two lines, lines 24 and 25. The troops are again "marching," a word used three times in these two lines, and again in darkness on an unknown road. **a.** How have the darkness and the unknown destination taken on a new meaning because of the scene at the church? **b.** How should we interpret the final line?

Reconciliation

1. This poem turns upon a word, its title. In what sense can "reconciliation" be a "word over all," covering the earth like a beautiful sky?

2. The image of death and night as sisters who "softly wash again, and ever again, this soil'd world" is striking. What reconciliation is being suggested here?

3. The final act of the poem is the touch of the poet's lips to the face of his enemy as he lies in the coffin. What reconciliation is being enacted in this kiss of the dead?

Writing About Literature

Discussing the Progression of a Theme

"Beat! Beat! Drums!," "A March in the Ranks Hard-Prest, and the Road Unknown," and "Reconciliation" take up the war at three points: the onset of the war and the changes it will bring, a powerful scene from the war itself, and the war's end, when the enemy lies dead. Discuss this progression in a brief composition, paying particular attention to the changes of mood through the three poems.

Summarizing Whitman's Vision

Write a brief essay in which you summarize Whitman's vision of the universe—the relationship of human beings to each other, to nature, and to themselves.

Expressing an Opinion

In his Preface to the 1855 edition of *Leaves of Grass*, Whitman describes the kind of poet America needs. Here is an excerpt from that description:

> The American poets are to enclose old and new for America is the race of races. . . . [The poet's] spirit responds to his country's spirit . . . he incarnates its geography and natural life and rivers and lakes. . . . To him enter the essences of the real things and past and present events. . . .

Write a composition in which you agree or disagree with Whitman's requirements for an American poet. Base your opinion on your own reading of poetry and support your statements with specific references to poems you consider great. In your discussion, consider how well Whitman fits his own description of the American poet.

Spirituals

Negro spirituals were an important expression of slave life in the South. Although they may have been inspired originally by the religious revivals that slaves attended with their masters, spirituals became a form of poetry for black people, reflecting their language, music, and special concerns. One such concern was the hope for spiritual salvation, a powerful emotion for people who lived their earthly lives in bondage. However, many spirituals had a double meaning. If they embodied a deep yearning for final happiness in heaven, they also expressed a more immediate desire for earthly freedom. Some were known as "signal" songs and were used to convey messages that overseers would not understand. The spiritual "Steal Away," for instance, speaks of stealing away to Jesus, but the song apparently was also used to tell fellow slaves to "steal away" to secret meetings where escapes were planned. "Follow the Drinking Gourd" told runaway slaves to follow the Big Dipper in the night sky, because it pointed to the North Star and so indicated the way to freedom.

The religious leaders of the Old Testament were prominent in Negro spirituals. Moses was especially popular because he had led the Israelites out of slavery in Egypt. "Go Down, Moses" speaks of this ancient deliverance from bondage, at the same time clearly referring to black slavery. For some the song had a still more immediate meaning. A remarkable woman, Harriet Tubman, herself an escaped slave, was famous for returning to the South many times to lead other slaves to freedom. She was known as "Moses," and the song expressed the hope that she would again go "way down in Egypt land" and deliver slaves to freedom. Similarly, "Swing Low, Sweet Chariot" is about being carried home to heaven by a band of angels, but to slaves "home" also meant freedom. Born of terrible oppression, Negro spirituals became a powerful religious poetry of hope, both for the release of the soul in heaven and for freedom on earth.

Go Down, Moses

Go down, Moses,
Way down in Egypt land
Tell old Pharaoh
To let my people go.

When Israel was in Egypt land   5
Let my people go
Oppressed so hard they could not stand
Let my people go.

Go down, Moses,
Way down in Egypt land   10
Tell old Pharaoh
"Let my people go."

"Thus saith the Lord," bold Moses said,
"Let my people go;
If not I'll smite your first-born dead   15
Let my people go."

Go down, Moses,
Way down in Egypt land,
Tell old Pharaoh,
"Let my people go!"   20

Swing Low, Sweet Chariot

Swing low, sweet chariot,
Coming for to carry me home,
Swing low, sweet chariot,
Coming for to carry me home.

I looked over Jordan and what did I see   5
Coming for to carry me home,
A band of angels, coming after me,
Coming for to carry me home.

If you get there before I do,
Coming for to carry me home,   10
Tell all my friends I'm coming too,
Coming for to carry me home.

Swing low, sweet chariot,
Coming for to carry me home,
Swing low, sweet chariot,   15
Coming for to carry me home.

For Study and Discussion

Analyzing and Interpreting the Poems

1. Spirituals made extensive use of religious metaphors to express the all-absorbing desire for freedom. In "Go Down, Moses," for example, ancient "Egypt land" is a metaphor for the South. **a.** What might be the metaphorical meaning of the Egyptian Pharaoh? **b.** Of the Israelites whom Moses called "my people"?

2. In "Swing Low, Sweet Chariot," what is the metaphorical meaning of the chariot that will bear the singer to heaven?

3. The river Jordan formed a boundary to ancient Israel, the promised land toward which Moses led his people. What would be its likely meaning in this spiritual?

Writing About Literature

Comparing Versions of a Spiritual

Both spirituals you have just read exist in other versions. You might find some of these variant versions in books on black literature or American music. Write a short essay comparing another version of one of these spirituals to the version given here. What changes do you find? How do the changes affect the song's meaning? You might discover that another version has an additional stanza or two. How do these stanzas reinforce the meaning of the spiritual?

Discussing Religious Allusions

If you prefer, locate a different spiritual, and briefly discuss its religious allusions. Check any unfamiliar references in a dictionary or encyclopedia.

FREDERICK DOUGLASS
1817?–1895

Frederick Douglass (c. 1844). Attributed to Elisha Hammond (1779–1882). Oil on canvas.

In the American pattern of self-development, Frederick Douglass rose from low beginnings to a position of leadership through hard work and the exercise of his native talents. In his case, this struggle was not just against poverty and limited opportunities but against the chains of slavery and enforced ignorance. He was born a slave in Maryland and was separated from his mother while still an infant. He could not even be sure of his exact age, since no record was kept of his birth. After spending his childhood and youth in bondage, he celebrated his entrance into manhood by escaping from slavery, and later settling with his wife in Massachusetts. As a slave he had been denied any formal education. Nevertheless, in an extraordinary act that testifies to the power of the human spirit, he had taught himself to read and write. And like other remarkable self-made individuals—from Benjamin Franklin in the eighteenth century to Richard Wright in the twentieth—he used his literacy as a passport to a wider world. Douglass was "self-created" even to the extent of naming himself, "Douglass" being the name he took after his flight from slavery, to avoid pursuit.

In 1841, three years after his escape to the North, Douglass spoke at an abolitionist meeting in Massachusetts. His natural eloquence was quickly recognized by the leaders of the movement and led to his employment as a lecturer for the abolitionist cause. Despite the obvious danger for a black man who advertised himself as an escaped slave, he continued this work for years. From 1845 to 1847 he lectured abroad, and his power as a speaker did much to influence British opinion in favor of the abolition of slavery in America. The British, in fact, raised money by public subscription to pay for his legal freedom.

Back in America, Douglass worked for the "Underground Railroad," the secret organization of abolitionist sympathizers who provided food, shelter, and transportation for slaves escaping to the North.

He continued to lecture, and published a newspaper, the *North Star.* Named for the star that guided slaves in flight, it soon became the most influential of the black newspapers. During the war Douglass used this influence to raise black troops for the Union armies. In his later years he held several government positions, including a diplomatic post as American Consul General to Haiti.

Although he became involved in other areas of reform, and lectured, for instance, in support of women's rights, Douglass understandably concentrated his energies on the social betterment of black people. Since his own life was so dramatic an example of what education could do even for a man raised in slavery, he made education his most insistent theme. Winning legal emancipation from slavery was only the first step. Thereafter, to educate the black was, he said, "to invest him with a power that shall open to him the treasures of freedom." Like his reform themes, the best of Douglass' writing came directly from his own life, especially his early experiences. Narratives of fugitive slaves were a popular form of literature (in part because they were exciting adventure narratives), and at least sixty were published in the years before the war. None was more powerful than Douglass' autobiography, *My Bondage and My Freedom* (1855). In a plain style that was as American as his life, he gave eloquent expression to the human spirit that even slavery could not crush.

Frederick Douglass **363**

My Bondage and My Freedom

"Make a noise," "make a noise," and "bear a hand," are the words usually addressed to the slaves when there is silence amongst them. This may account for the almost constant singing heard in the Southern states. There was, generally, more or less singing among the teamsters, as it was one means of letting the overseer know where they were, and that they were moving on with the work. But, on allowance day, those who visited the great house farm were peculiarly excited and noisy. While on their way, they would make the dense old woods, for miles around, reverberate with their wild notes. These were not always merry because they were wild. On the contrary, they were mostly of a plaintive cast, and told a tale of grief and sorrow. In the most boisterous outbursts of rapturous sentiment, there was ever a tinge of deep melancholy. I have never heard any songs like those anywhere since I left slavery, except when in Ireland. There I heard the same *wailing notes,* and was much affected by them. It was during the famine of 1845–1846. In all the songs of the slaves, there was ever some expression in praise of the great house farm; something which would flatter the pride of the owner, and, possibly, draw a favorable glance from him.

> *"I am going away to the great house farm,*
>   *O yea! O yea! O yea!*
> *My old master is a good old master,*
>   *O yea! O yea! O yea!"*

This they would sing, with other words of their own improvising—jargon to others, but full of meaning to themselves. I have sometimes thought that the mere hearing of these songs would do more to impress truly spiritual-minded men and women with the soul-crushing and death-dealing character of slavery than the reading of whole volumes of its mere physical cruelties. They speak to the heart and to the soul of the thoughtful. I cannot better express my sense of them now than ten years ago, when, in sketching my life, I thus spoke of this feature of my plantation experience:

"I did not, when a slave, understand the deep meanings of those rude and apparently incoherent songs. I was myself within the circle, so that I neither saw nor heard as those without might see and hear. They told a tale which was then altogether beyond my feeble comprehension; they were tones, loud, long and deep, breathing the prayer and complaint of souls boiling over with the bitterest anguish. Every tone was a testimony against slavery, and a prayer to God for deliverance from chains. The hearing of those wild notes always depressed my spirits, and filled my heart with ineffable sadness. The mere recurrence, even now, afflicts my spirit, and while I am writing these lines, my tears are falling. To those songs I trace my first glimmering conceptions of the dehumanizing character of slavery. I can never get rid of that conception. Those songs still follow me, to deepen my hatred of slavery, and quicken my sympathies for my brethren in bonds. If any one wishes to be impressed with a sense of the soul-killing power of slavery, let him go to Colonel Lloyd's plantation, and, on allowance day, place himself in the deep pine woods, and there let him, in silence, thoughtfully analyze the sounds that shall pass through the chambers of his soul, and if he is not thus impressed, it will only be because 'there is no flesh in his obdurate heart.'"

A Ride for Liberty—The Fugitive Slaves (c. 1862) by Eastman Johnson (1824–1906). Oil on board.

For Study and Discussion

Analyzing and Interpreting the Selection

1. Frederick Douglass suggests that slave songs began as a response to the overseer's command to "make a noise." What reasons might an overseer have for making this command?

2. When he heard those songs in his boyhood, Douglass did not understand their true meaning. How might his understanding have increased after his experience in Ireland during the famine of 1845–1846?

3. The final paragraph, quoted from an earlier version of his autobiography, gives Douglass' final understanding of those songs. **a.** What characteristics of the songs does he emphasize? **b.** Which of these characteristics can be found in the two spirituals "Go Down, Moses" and "Swing Low, Sweet Chariot" (page 362)?

Writing About Literature

Reporting on Another Autobiographical Passage

Select another passage from Douglass' autobiography, and report on it in a brief essay. What experiences does Douglass describe? What insight does he gain? What do you learn about his character?

ABRAHAM LINCOLN
1809–1865

Abraham Lincoln. This photograph was taken on April 10, 1865, four days before his assassination.

No American President has so touched the imagination of his people as Lincoln. From his birth to nearly illiterate parents in a Kentucky log cabin to his tragic death at the hand of an assassin, his life has become an expression of our nation's life. In a sparse autobiography written shortly before he was nominated for the presidency, Lincoln characteristically treated his life as altogether unremarkable. He stressed the brief and scanty nature of his formal education in backwoods Indiana schools. He reached manhood able to "read, write, and cipher to the rule of three, but that was all." He related with equal matter-of-factness his family's drift westward to Illinois and his own movement from farm work to a store clerk's job and then to service in the Illinois legislature and the study of law. After a term in Congress, he returned to private life and "practiced law more assiduously than ever before. . . . I was losing interest in politics when the repeal of the Missouri Compromise aroused me again. What I have done since then is pretty well known."

What is omitted from Lincoln's bare-bones sketch is all that seems to have given his life its unerring direction and to have united his destiny with the nation's. As a close friend later observed, "He had passed through all the grades of society when he reached the presidency, and he had found common sense a sure reliance and he put it into practice. . . . Lincoln was a great common man." The genius of a common man who is also a great man may lie in his ability to recognize the truest aspirations of his people, to perceive the issues they must confront together, and to provide leadership toward the future. It was so with Lincoln.

It was, as he wrote, the repeal of the Missouri Compromise that revived his interest in politics. The Compromise (1820) had admitted Maine to the Union as a free state in exchange for the admission of Missouri as a slave state. As new territories were admitted to the Union, it allowed the government to maintain a precarious balance between slave and free states. The repeal of the Compromise in 1854, permitting the admission of new states without regard to their status as slave or free, threatened to destroy that balance. Lincoln made this threat apparent to the people in his famous "House Divided" speech of 1858, when he noted that the slavery controversy was intensifying: "In my opinion it will not cease until a crisis shall have been reached and passed. 'A house divided against itself cannot stand.' I believe this government cannot endure permanently half slave and half free." Lincoln made the preservation of the Union—"the world's best hope," he called it—the guiding principle of his life. His perception of the nation's crisis carried him to the White House and, reluctantly, into civil war. The nation's division would be healed and the Union preserved, but only after a terrible crisis had "been reached and passed."

So dominant were politics and war in Lincoln's life that few of his contemporaries noticed his power as a writer. William Cullen Bryant, James Russell Lowell, and Walt Whitman—writers themselves—made no mention of his masterly prose style in their tributes to his genius. Yet Lincoln, like Jefferson, was a President whose writings have a permanent place in American literature. An avid reader all his life, he carefully studied the best books that came his way, committing to memory many passages from the Bible and Shakespeare, reading these and other works aloud in order to hear the rhythms of the sentences, and copying out passages that expressed ideas with special vividness. He taught himself logic and grammar with painstaking care. From this study came a prose style that was precise and controlled, balanced and logical. Its rhythms often raise colloquial language to poetry and convey the meditative and even mystical quality of Lincoln's mind. We feel in the compression of this style the presence of a man whose thought was grounded in his being and who was determined to mean his words. In a wartime message to Congress, Lincoln wrote: "In times like the present, men should utter nothing for which they would not willingly be responsible through time and in eternity." His greatest speeches, which now are read throughout the world, hold to this high standard.

The Gettysburg Address

Edward Everett, a distinguished orator, preceded Lincoln in the ceremony at the Gettysburg battlefield on November 19, 1863; he spoke for two hours. Lincoln had told a reporter that his own address would be "short, short, short," and, in fact, it lasted hardly five minutes. These ten sentences have been called "one of the great American poems."

Four score and seven years ago our fathers brought forth on this continent a new nation, conceived in liberty, and dedicated to the proposition that all men are created equal.

Now we are engaged in a great civil war, testing whether that nation, or any nation so conceived and so dedicated, can long endure. We are met on a great battlefield of that war. We have come to dedicate a portion of that field as a final resting place for those who here gave their lives that that nation might live. It is altogether fitting and proper that we should do this.

But, in a larger sense, we cannot dedicate—we cannot consecrate—we cannot hallow—this ground. The brave men, living and dead, who struggled here, have consecrated it far above our poor power to add or detract. The world will little note nor long remember what we say here, but it can never forget what they did here. It is for us the living, rather, to be dedicated here to the unfinished work which they who fought here have thus far so nobly advanced. It is rather for us to be here dedicated to the great task remaining before us—that from these honored dead we take increased devotion to that cause for which they gave the last full measure of devotion—that we here highly resolve that these dead shall not have died in vain—that this nation, under God, shall have a new birth of freedom—and that government of the people, by the people, for the people, shall not perish from the earth.

Analyzing and Interpreting the Speech

1. This seemingly simple speech is very carefully structured. For instance, it begins with the past, turns to the present, and then looks toward the future. How does the sentence beginning "The world will little note . . ." draw past, present, and future together?

2. Another progression in the speech moves from the birth of the nation to its temporary death and then to its rebirth. In the third paragraph, how does Lincoln envision the nation's rebirth?

3. Lincoln suggests that his words will soon be forgotten, but the soldiers' actions will live on. What must the living do to truly honor the dead?

Oratory as Literature

The growth of democracy encouraged general participation in government decisions and greatly increased the power of public opinion. This gave new importance to the ancient art of **oratory,** or public speaking. Ralph Waldo Emerson and Walt Whitman believed that oratory was the great democratic art: individuals spoke their hearts to fellow citizens and asked to be judged by their words. Political leaders were known by their major speeches, which were regularly reprinted in newspapers across the country.

Lincoln's speeches depart from the fashion of the time, which favored a more florid and ornate style. He customarily avoided elaborate figures of speech and kept his diction simple. We have no doubt of the deep feeling behind his words, but the passion is conveyed through restrained rhythm and repetition rather than through deliberately dramatic expressions. The appeal to the emotions is thus carefully controlled. For these reasons, in addition to their important historical content, Lincoln's speeches are still valued as literature.

1. Cite examples of repetition in "The Gettysburg Address." What effect does the repetition have?

2. The word *dedicated* is introduced in the first sentence. Follow Lincoln's use of this word and its present-tense form *dedicate* through the speech. In what different ways is this word used?

Gettysburg, Pennsylvania, on the day of Lincoln's Address. Photograph from Brady Collection.
Library of Congress

Robert E. Lee. Photograph by Mathew Brady, taken a few days after surrender at Appomattox.

ROBERT E. LEE
1807–1870

When civil war broke out in 1861, Robert E. Lee was offered the command of the Federal Army. His reputation as a brilliant staff officer had been established years before in the war with Mexico. He rose rapidly from captain to lieutenant colonel, and his commanding general gave much of the credit for the American victory at Veracruz to Lee's "skill, valor, and undaunted energy." Thereafter he served as superintendent of the United States Military Academy at West Point and as a cavalry officer on the frontier. He commanded the troops that put down John Brown's raid on the federal arsenal at Harpers Ferry, Virginia. Experienced in command duty in the field, and known to possess one of the best military minds of his time, Lee could look forward to the highest honors of his profession. In offering him the command of the federal forces, Lincoln was acknowledging his exceptional abilities.

Lee found that he had to refuse Lincoln's offer, stating, "though opposed to secession and deprecating war, I could take no part in an invasion of the Southern States." With great regret, he resigned his commission in the United States Army, "a service," as he wrote, "to which I have devoted the best years of my life, and all the ability I possessed." In that sad letter of resignation, he added: "Save in defense of my native state, I never again desire to draw my sword."

Lee's roots in Virginia ran deep. His own family was one of the most esteemed in Virginia, and his wife was the great-granddaughter of Martha Washington. The secession of his native state meant that he indeed had to draw his sword, first as commander of Virginia's forces and eventually as general in chief of all the Confederate armies. His extraordinary military talents served the South in campaigns that have since been studied in textbooks as brilliant examples of strategy. One of his biographers has written that Lee's greatness consisted of the ability "to look calmly beyond the dangers and perils of his immediate front to the situation in the whole theater of war, that power, in short, which takes Lee out of the ranks of the good ordinary and places him in the select band of the supreme generals."

Lee was not only a great but a greatly loved military leader. On two occasions before his troops began a charge, they shouted, "Lee to the rear," seized the reins of his horse, and forced him to a place of safety. On the sad day when he rode back from Appomattox after surrendering to Grant, soldiers crowded around him and cheered him. Lee's general spirit shines forth in his letters and in such documents as his "Farewell to the Army of Northern Virginia." In peace he advised his beloved South to create a new and better life within the Union. In his later years, he served as president of Washington College, which was later renamed Washington and Lee in his honor.

Letter to His Son

January 23, 1861

I received Everett's *Life of Washington*[1] which you sent me, and enjoyed its perusal. How his spirit would be grieved could he see the wreck of his mighty labors! I will not, however, permit myself to believe, until all ground of hope is gone, that the fruit of his noble deeds will be destroyed, and that his precious advice and virtuous example will so soon be forgotten by his countrymen. As far as I can judge by the papers, we are between a state of anarchy and civil war. May God avert both of these evils from us! I fear that mankind will not for years be sufficiently Christianized to bear the absence of restraint and force. I see that four states[2] have declared themselves out of the Union; four more will apparently follow their example. Then, if the border states are brought into the gulf of revolution, one half of the country will be arrayed against the other. I must try and be patient and await the end, for I can do nothing to hasten or retard it.

The South, in my opinion, has been aggrieved by the acts of the North, as you say. I feel the aggression and am willing to take every proper step for redress. It is the principle I contend for, not individual or private benefit. As an American citizen, I take great pride in my country, her prosperity and institutions, and would defend any state if her rights were invaded. But I can anticipate no greater calamity for the country than a dissolution of the Union. It would be an accumulation of all the evils we complain of, and I am willing to sacrifice everything but honor for its preservation. I hope, therefore, that all constitutional means will be exhausted before there is a resort to force. Secession is nothing but revolution. The framers of our Constitution never exhausted so much labor, wisdom and forbearance in its formation, and surrounded it with so many guards and securities, if it was intended to be broken by every member of the Confederacy at will. It was intended for "perpetual union," so expressed in the preamble, and for the establishment of a government, not a compact, which can only be dissolved by revolution or the consent of all the people in convention assembled. It is idle to talk of secession. Anarchy would have been established, and not a government, by Washington, Hamilton, Jefferson, Madison, and the other patriots of the Revolution. . . . Still, a Union that can only be maintained by swords and bayonets, and in which strife and civil war are to take the place of brotherly love and kindness, has no charm for me. I shall mourn for my country and for the welfare and progress of mankind. If the Union is dissolved, and the government disrupted, I shall return to my native state and share the miseries of my people; and, save in defense, will draw my sword on none.

---

1. **Everett's *Life of Washington*:** Edward Everett (1794–1865), noted American scholar and orator who spoke at Gettysburg before Lincoln delivered his famous address.
2. **four states:** South Carolina, Mississippi, Florida, and Alabama.

For Study and Discussion

Analyzing and Interpreting the Selection
1. While feeling that the South has been wronged by the North, Lee equates secession with revolution. **a.** What are his reasons for this belief?   **b.** Lee's feeling for the sanctity of the Union is nearly as strong as Lincoln's. Yet how is his attitude different?
2. Although the letter is to his son, the great issues Lee addresses make it more than a personal communication. What gives it a universal quality?

Writing About Literature

Comparing Lincoln and Lee as Writers
Compare Lincoln and Lee as writers with specific reference to the selections.

Detail from *Green River* (Wyoming) by Thomas Moran (1837–1926). Oil on canvas. The large rock formation in the rear is Castle Butte.
Museum of Western Art, Denver

Voices of Native Americans

Long before Europeans came to North America as conquerors or settlers, American Indians had developed a rich oral literature that was passed from generation to generation, the young memorizing in their turn the treasured legends, myths, tales, and poetry they learned from their elders. Because it was not a written literature, this cultural heritage depended for its continuation upon the established customs and relationships of stable tribal societies. From the seventeenth century on, in a relentless progression across the continent, these Indian communities were disrupted and finally destroyed by the constant incursions of expanding white settlement. By the time of the American Revolution, Thomas Jefferson was deploring the fact that Indian tribal cultures and languages were being lost forever because no one troubled to study and record them. It would be at least another century before such study became systematic and widespread. The literature that remains to us from the first Native Americans is a small fraction of the original.

Yet that fraction is both marvelously abundant and diverse. Indian cultures developed within individual tribes or in small language groups, with the result that many tribes contributed their distinctive tales, poems, and myths to the present-day collections of Indian literatures. Still, within that great diversity some common themes do emerge.

As we might expect, a deep sense of relation to nature is everywhere apparent in Native American literature. The natural world may be the scene of adventures and exploits in Indian tales, even the place for pranks and jokes, but the underlying spirit is always a reverence for nature. So close are the human and natural worlds that the beasts may speak in human language or themselves possess a spirit that resembles the human soul. Nature is an unbroken continuity of creatures, a seamless robe that enfolds all life. A song of the Tewa tribe (page 373) therefore asks nature to weave "a garment of brightness" for our human lives so that we, too, may "walk fittingly" in a world of singing birds and green grass. In the same spirit of reverence, a ritual prayer of the Zuni tribe (page 373) is used to "present" or introduce a new baby, a few days after birth, to the rising sun and the sacred natural world.

A profound relation to nature is also apparent in the stories of the original creation of the world that are characteristic of Native American literatures. In "The Blackfeet Genesis" (page 374), for example, it is significant that not only people but the birds and animals as well could understand the words of the Creator when the earth was first made. Such stories explain existence—how the various parts of nature and the different species of animals, including humans, came to be, even the presence of death in the world—and always with a sense that all living things are related.

As we might also expect in cultures that were passed on through the spoken word, a talent for oratory was highly valued in Indian communities and was an important element of leadership. From even the earliest contacts between Europeans and Native Americans, a few speeches of great chiefs have been preserved. Captain John Smith, for example, published his version of a speech by the Algonquian chief Powhatan, the father of Pocahontas. In later years, unfortunately, the speeches of great chiefs all too often record Indian defeats as they were driven from their homelands. Yet the eloquence of Black Hawk's farewell (page 376) and Chief Joseph's speech of surrender (page 378) is an indication of the high place that oratory holds in the Native American literary heritage.

The Tewa (tā′wə, tē′wə) and the Zuni (zōō′nyē, sōō′nē) Indians are pueblo tribes of the American Southwest.

Song of the Sky Loom
(Tewa)

O our Mother the Earth, O our Father
   the Sky,
Your children are we, and with tired
   backs
We bring you the gifts you love.
Then weave for us a garment of bright-
   ness;
May the warp be the white light of morn-
   ing,   5
May the weft be the red light of evening,
May the fringes be the falling rain,
May the border be the standing rainbow.
Thus weave for us a garment of bright-
   ness,
That we may walk fittingly where birds
   sing,   10
That we may walk fittingly where grass
   is green,
O our Mother the Earth, O our Father
   the Sky.

Prayer Spoken While Presenting an Infant to the Sun
(Zuni)

Now this is the day.
Our child,
Into the daylight
You will go out standing.
Preparing for your day,   5
We have passed our days.
When all your days were at an end,
When eight days were past,
Our sun father
Went in to sit down at his sacred place.   10

And our night fathers,
Having come out standing to their sacred
   place,
Passed a blessed night.
Now this day,
Our fathers, Dawn priests,   15
Have come out standing to their sacred
   place,
Our sun father,
Having come out standing to his sacred
   place,
Our child, it is your day,
This day,   20
The flesh of the white corn, prayer meal,
To our sun father
This prayer meal we offer.

May your road be fulfulled.
Reaching to the road of your sun father,   25
When your road is fulfilled,
In your thoughts may we live,
May we be the ones whom your thoughts
   will embrace,
For this, on this day
To our sun father,   30
We offer prayer meal.
To this end:
May you help us all to finish our roads.

For Study and Discussion

Analyzing and Interpreting the Poems

Song of the Sky Loom
1. The sky is imagined as a loom in this poem. What elements are to compose the garment the sky is to weave for us?
2. The poem is enclosed by the references to "our Mother the Earth . . . our Father the Sky." How does this conception of human beings as "children" of the natural world reflect the mood of the poem?

Prayer Spoken While Presenting an Infant
1. In addition to "presenting" a child to the rising sun for the first time, this poem symbolically enacts the passing of life from one generation to the next. How is this shown in the poem?
2. The poem is a prayer. How does the language reflect this religious function?

The Blackfeet Genesis

The Blackfeet were Indians of the Western plains, the country of the antelope and buffalo and, in the mountains, bighorn sheep.

All animals of the Plains at one time heard and knew him, and all birds of the air heard and knew him. All things that he had made understood him when he spoke to them—the birds, the animals, and the people.

Old Man was traveling about, south of here, making the people. He came from the south, traveling north, making animals and birds as he passed along. He made the mountains, prairies, timber, and brush first. So he went along, traveling northward, making things as he went, putting rivers here and there, and falls on them, putting red paints here and there in the ground—fixing up the world as we see it today. He made the Milk River [the Teton] and crossed it, and, being tired, went up on a little hill and lay down to rest. As he lay on his back, stretched out on the ground, with arms extended, he marked himself out with stones—the shape of his body, head, legs, arms, and everything. There you can see those rocks today. After he had rested, he went on northward, and stumbled over a knoll and fell down on his knees. Then he said, "You are a bad thing to be stumbling against"; so he raised up two large buttes there, and named them the Knees, and they are called so to this day. He went on farther north, and with some of the rocks he carried with him he built the Sweet Grass Hills.

Old Man covered the plains with grass for the animals to feed on. He marked off a piece of ground, and in it he made to grow all kinds of roots and berries—camas, wild carrots, wild turnips, sweetroot, bitterroot, sarvis berries, bull berries, cherries, plums, and rosebuds. He put trees in the ground. He put all kinds of animals on the ground. When he made the bighorn with its big head and horns, he made

it out on the prairie. It did not seem to travel easily on the prairie; it was awkward and could not go fast. So he took it by one of its horns, and led it up into the mountains, and turned it loose; and it skipped about among the rocks and went up fearful places with ease. So he said, "This is the place that suits you; this is what you are fitted for, the rocks, and the mountains." While he was in the mountains, he made the antelope out of dirt, and turned it loose, to see how it would go. It ran so fast that it fell over some rocks and hurt itself. He saw that this would not do, and took the antelope down on the prairie, and turned it loose; and it ran away fast and gracefully, and he said, "This is what you are suited to."

One day Old Man determined that he would make a woman and a child; so he formed them both—the woman and the child, her son—of clay. After he had molded the clay in human shape, he said to the clay, "You must be people," and then he covered it up and left it, and went away. The next morning he went to the place and took the covering off, and saw that the clay shapes had changed a little. The second morning there was still more change, and the third still more. The fourth morning he went to the place, took the covering off, looked at the images, and told them to rise and walk; and they did so. They walked down to the river with their Maker, and then he told them that his name was Na'pi [Old Man].

As they were standing by the river, the woman said to him, "How is it? will we always live, will there be no end to it?" He said: "I have never thought of that. We will have to decide it. I will take this buffalo chip and throw it in the river. If it floats, when people die, in four days they will become alive again; they

Rocky Mountain Sheep (1845) by John Jay Audubon (1785–1851). Colored lithograph.
Amon Carter Museum, Fort Worth, Texas

will die for only four days. But if it sinks, there will be an end to them." He threw the chip into the river, and it floated. The woman turned and picked up a stone, and said: "No, I will throw this stone in the river; if it floats we will always live, if it sinks people must die, that they may always be sorry for each other." The woman threw the stone into the water, and it sank. "There," said Old Man, "you have chosen. There will be an end to them."

It was not many nights after that the woman's child died, and she cried a great deal for it. She said to Old Man: "Let us change this. The law that you first made, let that be a law." He said: "Not so. What is made law must be law. We will undo nothing that we have done. The child is dead, but it cannot be changed. People will have to die."

For Study and Discussion

Analyzing and Interpreting the Selection

1. Why does the legend emphasize the fact that, at the time of the creation, the birds and animals could understand the language of the creator ("Old Man")?

2. In part, this story of the creation explains the local landscape: the rocks on a hill that appear to outline a human body, the isolated hills (buttes) that are called the Knees. How is the appropriateness of each animal to its native habitat explained?

3. Once people have been created, there is the question of eternal life. "How is it?" the woman asks. "Will we always live, will there be no end to it?" **a.** How is the presence of death explained by the story? **b.** Why was the woman not content with the first outcome of the creator's experiment on this question?

Voices of Native Americans **375**

FROM
Black Hawk's Farewell

A chief of the Sauk Indians, Black Hawk gave his name to the war in which defeat led to the removal of the Sauk and Fox tribes from the upper Mississippi Valley. Abraham Lincoln, then a store clerk in an Illinois village, served in Black Hawk's War but did not see action. This speech is Black Hawk's surrender.

Black Hawk (1832) by George Catlin (1796–1872). Oil on canvas.
National Museum of American Art, Smithsonian Institution

You have taken me prisoner with all my warriors. I am much grieved, for I expected, if I did not defeat you, to hold out much longer, and give you more trouble before I surrendered. I tried hard to bring you into ambush, but your last general understands Indian fighting. The first one was not so wise. When I saw that I could not beat you by Indian fighting, I determined to rush on you, and fight you face to face. I fought hard. But your guns were well aimed. The bullets flew like birds in the air, and whizzed by our ears like the wind through the trees in winter. My warriors fell around me; it began to look dismal. I saw my evil day at hand. The sun rose dim on us in the morning, and at night it sank in a dark cloud, and looked like a ball of fire. That was the last sun that shone on Black Hawk. His heart is dead, and no longer beats quick in his bosom. He is now a prisoner to the white men; they will do with him as they wish. But he can stand torture, and is not afraid of death. He is no coward. Black Hawk is an Indian.

He has done nothing for which an Indian ought to be ashamed. He has fought for his countrymen, the squaws and papooses, against white men, who came, year after year, to cheat them and take away their lands. You know the cause of our making war. It is known to all white men. They ought to be ashamed of it. The white men despise the Indians, and drive them from their homes. But the Indians are not deceitful. The white men speak bad of the Indian, and look at him spitefully. But the Indian does not tell lies; Indians do not steal.

An Indian who is as bad as the white men, could not live in our nation; he would be put to death, and eaten up by the wolves. The white men are bad schoolmasters; they carry false looks and deal in false actions; they smile in the face of the poor Indian to cheat him. . . .

We looked up to the Great Spirit. We went to our great father.[1] We were encouraged. His great council gave us fair words and big promises; but we got no satisfaction. Things were growing worse. There were no deer in the forest. The opossum and beaver were fled; the springs were drying up, and our squaws and papooses without victuals to keep them from starving; we called a great council and built a large fire. The spirit of our fathers arose and spoke to us to avenge our wrongs or die. We all spoke before the council fire. It was warm and pleasant. We set up the war whoop, and dug up the tomahawk; our knives were ready, and the heart of Black Hawk swelled high in his bosom when he led his warriors to battle. He is satisfied. He will go to the world of spirits contented. He has done his duty. His father will meet him there, and commend him.

Black Hawk is a true Indian, and disdains to cry like a woman. He feels for his wife, his children and friends. But he does not care for himself. He cares for his nation and the Indians. They will suffer. He laments their fate. . . .

Farewell, my nation! Black Hawk tried to save you, and avenge your wrongs. He drank the blood of some of the whites. He has been taken prisoner, and his plans are stopped. He can do no more. He is near his end. His sun is setting, and he will rise no more. Farewell to Black Hawk.

For Study and Discussion

Analyzing and Interpreting the Selection

1. In the first paragraph, Black Hawk pictures battle in images of nature—bullets flying like birds and sounding like wind in bare trees. What signs did nature give on the "evil day" of his defeat?

2. Although defeated, Black Hawk is still a proud man and chief. What are the sources of his pride?

---

1. **great father:** the President of the United States, Andrew Jackson.

Chief Joseph of the Nez Percé represents the final stage of the Indians' struggle against white domination. The son of a chief who had been converted to Christianity by white missionaries, he was educated in a mission school and became chief in his turn in 1871. Some years later he was ordered to comply with a "treaty" he considered illegitimate and to remove his people from their vast homeland in the American Northwest. Instead, he led his warriors against troops of the United States Army. Although he was a brilliant tactician and managed to protect the women and children of his tribe while conducting a long retreat, this was a war he could not win. His eloquent speech of surrender in 1877 is an example of the power of Indian oratory. Two years later, Chief Joseph's views of Indian life and beliefs were published in a magazine for a white audience, a notable exception to the usual American practice of seeing Indians entirely from the point of view of whites.

Chief Joseph (1903). Photograph by Edward Sheriff Curtis (1868–1952).

The Surrender Speech of Chief Joseph

I am tired of fighting. Our chiefs are killed. Looking Glass is dead. Toohulhulsote is dead. The old men are all dead. It is the young men who say no and yes. He who led the young men is dead. It is cold and we have no blankets. The little children are freezing to death. My people, some of them, have run away to the hills and have no blankets, no food. No one knows where they are—perhaps they are freezing to death. I want to have time to look for my children and see how many of them I can find. Maybe I shall find them among the dead. Hear me, my chiefs, I am tired. My heart is sad and sick. From where the sun now stands I will fight no more forever.

Hear me, my chiefs! I am tired; my heart is sick and sad.

An Indian's Views of Indian Affairs

My friends, I have been asked to show you my heart. I am glad to have a chance to do so. I want the white people to understand my people. Some of you think an Indian is like a wild animal. This is a great mistake. I will tell you all about our people, and then you can judge whether an Indian is a man or not. I believe much trouble and blood would be saved if we opened our hearts more. I will tell you in my way how the Indian sees things. The white man has more words to tell you how they look to him, but it does not require many words to speak the truth. What I have to say will come from my heart, and I will speak with a straight tongue. Ah-cum-kin-i-ma-me-hut (the Great Spirit) is looking at me, and will hear me.

My name is In-mut-too-yah-lat-lat (Thunder traveling over the Mountains). I am chief of the Wal-lam-wat-kin band of Chute-pa-lu, or Nez Percés (nose-pierced Indians). I was born in eastern Oregon, thirty-eight winters ago. My father was chief before me. When a young man, he was called Joseph by Mr. Spaulding, a missionary. He died a few years ago. He left a good name on earth. He advised me well for my people.

Our fathers gave us many laws, which they had learned from their fathers. These laws were good. They told us to treat all men as they treated us; that we should never be the first to break a bargain; that it was a disgrace to tell a lie; that we should speak only the truth; that it was a shame for one man to take from another his wife or [to take] his property without paying for it. We were taught to believe that the Great Spirit sees and hears everything, and that he never forgets; that hereafter he will give every man a spirit-home according to his deserts: if he has been a good man, he will have a good home; if he has been a bad man, he will have a bad home. This I believe, and all my people believe the same.

For Study and Discussion

Analyzing and Interpreting the Selections

1. His surrender speech shows Chief Joseph's concern for the defenseless women and children of his people. What evidence do we see of the breakdown of the usual authority of tribal life?

2. In "An Indian's Views of Indian Affairs," what conception of the Indian held by white people is Chief Joseph trying to correct?

3. Chief Joseph emphasizes the importance of "laws" in Indian culture. The source of these laws is a belief in God, the "Great Spirit." How are these laws passed on in Indian life?

HENRY TIMROD
1828–1867

Henry Timrod by Poindexter Page Carter. Oil on canvas.

In a cruel irony of history, the war that devastated Timrod's beloved homeland also inspired his best poems. His verse written before the war was thin and conventional, fainty echoing William Wordsworth and other English Romantics. But the tragedy of the Civil War, touching his deepest emotions, gave him a firm sense of his identity as a Southern poet and gave his poems a new force and authority.

The magnitude of the South's anguish, dwarfing any merely personal expression, demanded the classical restraint and control which are characteristic of his best poems.

Henry Timrod was born in Charleston, South Carolina, the son of a bookbinder. Although the family was poor, he was sent to one of Charleston's finest schools and then to the University of Georgia. His intention was to become a professor. Less than two years later, however, he was forced to withdraw, already a victim of the ill health and inadequate finances that would thwart his plans throughout his short life. Instead of assuming a professorship, he was reduced to tutoring the children of wealthy plantation owners in order to make a meager living. Meanwhile, he began to study law in preparation for a different career. His literary interests brought him naturally into association with other young Charleston writers, and he contributed poems to various newspapers and magazines.

When war came, Timrod enlisted in the Confederate Army. Again illness forced him to change his plans, and he was mustered out in less than a year. Still eager to serve the Confederate cause, he became a war correspondent, and the privations and hardships of this work were scarcely less than those a soldier endured. His journalism led him in 1864 to a brief appointment as the editor of a newspaper in Columbia, South Carolina. Once again his plans were abruptly changed, this time not by illness but by General Sherman's Union army, which invaded and captured Columbia. Depleted in spirit and financially destitute, he was rapidly failing in his long struggle with tuberculosis. He died two years later, not yet forty years old.

All of Timrod's important poems were written during or immediately after the war. His themes are uniformly patriotic and often tinged with the somber melancholy that perhaps expressed his sense of impending defeat. Even a poem written to celebrate the coming of spring, in the terrible year 1863, speaks of a "nameless pathos in the air / Which dwells with all things fair." However his talent might have developed in another situation, the tragic circumstances of his time forced him into a narrow concern with the Confederate cause, leaving no room for the expression of larger themes or broader sympathies. He therefore remains a minor poet. He has often been called the "Laureate of the Confederacy," a title that both praises his achievement and acknowledges its limits.

Confederate graveyard at Magnolia Cemetery, Charleston, South Carolina.

Ode on the Confederate Dead

SUNG AT THE OCCASION OF DECORATING THE GRAVES AT MAGNOLIA CEMETERY,
CHARLESTON, S.C., 1867

Sleep sweetly in your humble graves,
  Sleep, martyrs of a fallen cause;
Though yet no marble column craves
  The pilgrim here to pause.

In seeds of laurel in the earth   5
  The blossom of your fame is blown,
And somewhere, waiting for its birth,
  The shaft is in the stone!°

Meanwhile, behalf the tardy years
  Which keep in trust your storied tombs,   10
Behold! your sisters bring their tears,
  And these memorial blooms.

Small tributes! but your shades will smile
  More proudly on these wreaths today,
Than when some cannon-molded pile   15
  Shall overlook this bay.

    Stoop, angels, hither from the skies!
      There is no holier spot of ground
    Than where defeated valor lies,
      By mourning beauty crowned!   20

8. **shaft . . . stone:** a reference to King Arthur, who became King of England by pulling the sword Excalibur
from the stone in which it was embedded.

For Study and Discussion

Analyzing and Interpreting the Poem

1. In this ceremony the living pay honor to their fallen soldiers. Which lines in the poem indicate that this simple tribute is more appropriate than the monuments that will later be placed here?

2. What words and phrases convey a religious feeling?

3. Emily Dickinson, a contemporary of Timrod's, once wrote, "After great pain, a formal feeling comes," a reference to the human need for ceremony or form in commemorating loss. Timrod's poem, written for a public ceremony to commemorate loss, is both precisely regular in its meter and rhyme scheme and formal in its language. **a.** What is the effect of the poet's addressing the dead directly, as if they were a living audience? **b.** Does the formality of the poem help us to accept this convention?

Literary Elements

The Ode

Timrod calls his poem an **ode.** Originally, in Greek and Roman literature, odes were songs that were sung in honor of gods or heroes. Often the chorus danced in a formal pattern of movement while singing the ode. An ode was a public form of poetry, celebrating a subject of public interest and involving the performance of a group of people. In later periods of history, especially during the nineteenth century, the ode was often used for more personal subjects and no longer involved a public performance. John Keats's "Ode on a Grecian Urn" is a famous example. Certain characteristics of the ode have remained unchanged. It is still defined as a serious poem on a dignified theme, and its formal and even lofty language conveys the speaker's admiration for the subject.

Timrod's "Ode on the Confederate Dead" is traditional in several respects. It does not celebrate a single hero, but treats all the fallen Confederate soldiers as heroes, "martyrs of a fallen cause." The language of the poem is formal and conveys a sense of solemnity through its use of religious expressions. The poem is also a public work. It was written specifically for the occasion of decorating the graves and was meant to be sung as part of the ceremony. It is not difficult to imagine that the placing of the wreaths upon the graves had the ritual character of a formal dance. Finally, the poet clearly feels profound admiration for his subject, finding in the "defeated valor" of the dead soldiers and in the mourning of their sisters subjects as worthy of praise as a famous victory. His sense of the significance of this ceremony is indicated by his calling upon the angels to witness it.

1. In addition to the poem's religious language, certain words and expressions suggest its traditional character. The word *laurel* in line 5 refers to the laurel shrub but also has a special meaning in relation to heroes. Look up this word in a dictionary to find this second meaning.

2. The word *shades* in line 13 also has a traditional meaning. How is this word used here?

Writing About Literature

Discussing Mood in Two Works

Lincoln's "Gettysburg Address" was written in the midst of the Civil War to commemorate the soldiers who had fallen in a great battle. Timrod's "Ode on the Confederate Dead" was written after the war was over, to honor the "defeated valor" of the soldiers who now lay in the Charleston cemetery. Write a brief essay in which you discuss the difference of mood in these two works. How does it show itself in the writer's choice of words? What comparison can be drawn between the rhythm of Lincoln's sentences and the rhythm of the lines in Timrod's poem?

Sidney Lanier. Engraving by H. B. Hall's Sons, New York.

SIDNEY LANIER
1842–1881

After Henry Timrod, Sidney Lanier was the first important poet to emerge from the South. Although the two men shared many elements of their common regional background, they had sharply different outlooks. Timrod's best poems are directly related to the Civil War and express his mourning for the South's defeat. Lanier was also deeply affected by the war, but it left him with a lasting horror of warfare and little sympathy for lost causes. He wanted the South to end its dependence on "King Cotton," which tied the region to the textile mills of the industrialized North, in favor of a simpler agriculture. But what he really looked forward to was a "highly civilized state of society" in which the arts, especially music, would provide the basis for a new sense of community. As a step in this direction, he developed a theory that united the rhythms of poetry with the "natural" rhythms of music, for him the greatest of the arts. He wrote poems that were as progressive and experimental as Timrod's were traditional.

Born a lawyer's son in Macon, Georgia, Lanier early developed a love of music, teaching himself to play the flute so well that he later played professionally. At fourteen he entered Oglethorpe University, and after graduation he stayed on for a time as a tutor. Poetry and music were his strongest interests, but no career suggested itself, and his father favored the more practical profession of law. Lanier's immediate plan was to go to Germany, presumably to study music. But the war prevented this and postponed all career decisions. Lanier enlisted at the age of nineteen and served for nearly four years. He was captured by Union forces and spent the last months of the war in a Federal prison. There he contracted the tuberculosis that brought him to an early death.

After the war Lanier worked as a clerk, taught school, studied law in his father's office, and practiced briefly in Atlanta. But he disliked law, and he could find little hope for his ideal of culture in a South desolated by war. Without "an atmosphere of art," he wrote a friend, he found life "a mere drought and famine." In the hope of finding greater cultural activity, he moved to Baltimore. There he played flute in a symphony orchestra and gradually established a modest reputation as a poet. To supplement his small income, he lectured on literature at Johns Hopkins University and adapted literary classics for young readers. However, this left little time for writing poetry, and ill health frequently interrupted his work. Without time to write, he complained, he was "crushing back poem after poem—I have several volumes of poems in the form of memoranda on the backs of envelopes . . . and the like! . . . If I could write nothing but poetry for the next two years! . . ." Unfortunately, two years were all the time left to him when he wrote that letter. He died at thirty-nine, with most of his creative projects unfinished.

His last years were nevertheless his most fruitful. Lanier had long sought to base the metrics of poetry on the measures of music. He had studied earlier forms of the English language, and his research led

to a book, *The Science of English Verse* (1880). His
"science" tried to prove too much, however, and
erected a theory that would not work in practice.
Nevertheless, his musical conception of verse gradually gave his poetry a new fluidity, which contrasted with the stiff and awkward movement of his
early poems. He wrote a highly praised choral composition, a cantata, to be sung at the ceremonies
marking the nation's centennial in Philadelphia in
1876. In one of his most acclaimed poems, "The
Symphony," musical instruments "speak" words. He
planned a still larger musical-poetic composition to
celebrate the great salt marshes of his native Georgia in a sequence of *Hymns to the Marshes,* although
only a few parts were completed at his death. Most
of all, however, his attempt to relate music and poetry shows itself in the cadence of the language in
the late poems, the rhythmic flow of the sounds and
words. "Song of the Chattahoochee," for example,
should not be thought of as a song to be set to
music. Yet the poem gives "voice" to the river, as
Poe does to bells in "The Bells," in ways that remind
us of the structure and flow of music.

Song of the Chattahoochee°

Out of the hills of Habersham,°
Down the valleys of Hall°
I hurry amain° to reach the plain,
Run the rapid and leap the fall,
Split at the rock and together again,   5
Accept my bed, or° narrow or wide,
And flee from folly° on every side
With a lover's pain to attain the plain
    Far from the hills of Habersham,
    Far from the valleys of Hall.   10

° **Chattahoochee** (chăt′ə-hōō′chē). 1-2. **Habersham . . .
Hall:** two counties in Georgia through which the Chattahoochee flows. 3. **amain:** at full speed or force. 6. **or:**
either. 7. **folly:** here, diversions or distractions.

All down the hills of Habersham,
All through the valleys of Hall,
The rushes cried *Abide, abide,*
The willful waterweeds held me thrall,°
The laving° laurel turned my tide,   15
The ferns and the fondling grass said *Stay,*
The dewberry dipped for to work delay,
And the little reeds sighed *Abide, abide,*
    Here in the hills of Habersham,
    Here in the valleys of Hall.   20

High o'er the hills of Habersham,
Veiling the valleys of Hall,
The hickory told me manifold°
Fair tales of shade, the poplar tall
Wrought me her shadowy self to hold,   25
The chestnut, the oak, the walnut, the pine,
Overleaning, with flickering meaning and sign,
Said, *Pass not, so cold, these manifold*
    Deep shades of the hills of Habersham,
    These glades in the valleys of Hall.   30

And oft in the hills of Habersham,
And oft in the valleys of Hall,
The white quartz shone, and the smooth
        brook-stone
Did bar me of passage with friendly brawl,
And many a luminous jewel lone   35
—Crystals clear or a-cloud with mist,
Ruby, garnet and amethyst—
Made lures with the lights of streaming stone
    In the clefts of the hills of Habersham,
    In the beds of the valleys of Hall.   40

But oh, not the hills of Habersham,
And oh, not the valleys of Hall
Avail:° I am fain for to water the plain.
Downward the voices of Duty call—
Downward, to toil and be mixed with
        the main;   45
The dry fields burn, and the mills are to turn,
And a myriad flowers mortally yearn,
And the lordly main from beyond the plain
    Calls o'er the hills of Habersham,
    Calls through the valleys of Hall.   50

14. **thrall:** in servitude. 15. **laving:** washing, bathing.
23. **manifold:** of many kinds, varied. 43. **Avail:** are of
use or have force.

Sidney Lanier **385**

For Study and Discussion

Analyzing and Interpreting the Poem

1. The flow of the river is of course a descent.
a. What words in the first stanza convey this downward movement? **b.** What words suggest the speed of the river in this first stage of its flow?

2. In the second stanza other voices are added—in the italicized words—to the river's voice. How are the words of the rushes, grass, and reeds related to the actions of the waterweeds, laurel, and dewberry?

3. The brief message of the plants in the second stanza grows into the "fair tales" of the trees in stanza three. Consider their plea to "*Pass not, so cold*" in line 28. Does this refer just to the coolness of shaded waters or to another kind of coldness?

4. It seems unlikely that the streambed stones of the fourth stanza are actually gemstones—ruby, garnet, amethyst. Explain how "the lights of streaming stone" within the water's flow could appear as "many a luminous jewel" at the bottom of the river.

5. In the final stanza the Chattahoochee descends to the plain and to "Duty" and "toil"—the work it must do before returning to the sea. **a.** What change of mood and movement—from the headlong, tumbling rush of the early stanzas—do we find here? **b.** How is it conveyed in the language?

Literary Elements

Refrain, Internal Rhyme, Alliteration

The subject of "Song of the Chattahoochee" is the river's movement from its origin in "the hills of Habersham" and "the valleys of Hall" through its descent to the coastal plain and its disappearance into the sea. But this journey is of course also a return, a cycle. Each stanza opens and closes with a slightly varying **refrain** to indicate this cycle: in the river's end is its beginning.

The six lines enclosed within the refrain in each stanza also have a strict pattern. They must always indicate movement: hurried, tumbling movement in the first stanza as the river plunges out of the hills and through the valleys, then a slowing movement as the flow is physically impeded by water plants, held back by the appeal of the trees and their cool shade, and lured by "the lights of streaming stone" in its own riverbed as it moves inevitably toward "the voices of Duty" and the work it must perform before being mixed with the sea again.

Within the regular rhyme scheme of each stanza (*abcbcddcab*), the third, fifth, and eighth lines rhyme. But in addition, the third and eighth lines usually have the same **internal rhyme**—that is, a correspondence of sounds within as well as at the end of the lines:

> *I hurry* amain *to reach the* plain
> *With a lover's* pain *to attain the* plain

Internal rhymes intensify our sense of the harmony Lanier so values in nature. So does another poetic device, **alliteration**—the repetition of the same initial sound in two or several words in a line: "*H*ere in the *h*ills of *H*abersham." But alliteration has a further purpose in this poem. "Run the rapid" and "flee from folly" in the first stanza speed the movement, in keeping with the rapid flow of the river at that point. But in the second stanza "willful waterweeds" and "laving laurel" are hard to pronounce together and actually slow our reading of those lines, again in keeping with the reduced speed of the river as plants impede its movement.

How alliteration can affect our reading, perhaps all unconsciously, may be illustrated by line 38: "Made lures with the lights of streaming stone." The line begins slowly—we cannot say "lures with" rapidly—and gathers speed with "streaming stone." But "lights of streaming stone" also embodies an important idea in an arresting phrase. It is of course the water that actually *streams* over the stones. But reflections from the river bottom make the stones themselves appear to move, "streaming" along with the river. Lanier's purpose in "Song of the Chattahoochee" is to convey the "music" of a river's fluid cycle, and refrain, internal rhyme, and alliteration all have their place in that.

Analyze the use of internal rhyme and alliteration in the second stanza. Tell how these poetic devices contribute to the meaning of the passage.

Writing About Literature

Discussing the Poet's Choice of Words

Briefly discuss Lanier's choice of words in the final stanza. Does the linking of *downward* to *duty* and *toil* have a depressing effect? What of the use of the word *mortally*? The striking number of *l* and *s* words in the earlier stanzas convey fluid movement. Are there fewer of them here? Does the final refrain have a different effect from the earlier ones?

MARK TWAIN (SAMUEL LANGHORNE CLEMENS) 1835–1910

In 1866, at the age of thirty-one, Mark Twain left San Francisco for the East. A cartoon shows him riding high in the air astride an oversized frog as it makes a gigantic leap across the country. Two years earlier he had heard a tall tale in a mining camp and had written it up as the story "The Notorious Jumping Frog of Calaveras County." Published first in New York, it was reprinted in newspapers throughout the country, becoming a celebrated example of Western humor. Now, as the cartoon indicated, Twain was leaping toward fame, with the frog as his magic carpet. Forty-one years later, when he visited England for the last time to receive an honorary degree from Oxford University, he was the most famous American alive, cheered by crowds and honored by the Queen. He was recognized almost anywhere in the world, and he was delighted to be known as "the most conspicuous person on the planet."

Twain knew there was something fabulous in his career, and in his books he made his own life his greatest fable. His life touched nearly every phase of the nation's life through three-quarters of a century, giving his personal experience a continental breadth. This was what his friend William Dean Howells, the novelist, meant when he called Twain "the Lincoln of our literature": the national character and experience had again found voice in a representative man.

He was born Samuel Langhorne Clemens in the tiny hamlet of Florida, Missouri. The family soon moved to the more promising town of Hannibal. Later, in his books, Twain made his boyhood in Hannibal on the banks of the Mississippi River a national possession, the myth of everyone's childhood. Often in his writings he called Hannibal "St. Petersburg" (meaning "Heaven") to convey the enchantment of childhood in a setting of a wide river, great forests, a mysterious cave, and a suitably scary haunted house.

Mark Twain (c. 1903). Photograph.
The Bettmann Archive

Twain's father died a bankrupt and disappointed man when Twain was eleven. Despite exceptional intelligence and personal integrity, he had invested his energies and dwindling funds in enterprises that always failed. To the boy, his father's life became a lasting lesson in missed opportunities and bad timing: his father had every requirement for success except the ability to grasp opportunity at the right moment. Both in his books and in his life, Mark Twain would show an obsessive concern with timing as the key to success. For his first thirty years, much of his life was an aimless drifting, often with gnawing fears of failure. But during those years, without realizing it, he stored up just the experiences he needed as a writer. In his creative work he learned to trust his inner sense of timing, often putting a manuscript aside for years as he waited for the "tank" of inspiration to fill up again. On the lecture platform he was a master of timing—the exact pause of suspense, the precise delivery of a joke—and he boasted that he changed his tempo for every performance, to suit the mood of his audience. As he looked back on his life, timing became his conception of destiny. He liked to say that he had known the girl he would marry at the instant of first seeing her photograph. Even his premature birth seemed to make him destiny's special child, since it brought him into the world when Halley's comet appeared spectacularly in the night sky. He would claim that Mark Twain and Halley's comet were nature's "unaccountable freaks" and would "go out together" as they had come in. He died, as he had predicted, when Halley's comet again became visible, in the spring of 1910.

Timing could convert even hardship to opportunity. Forced by his father's death to leave school, Twain was apprenticed to a printer. This trade, although he disliked it, allowed him to move about frequently during his restless adolescence—to St. Louis, New York, Philadelphia, Cincinnati—and gave him a useful education. As it had been for Benjamin Franklin and Walt Whitman, the print shop was for Twain the poor boy's college. He picked up a wide range of information by setting it into type, and in handling "acres" of literary material he learned to distinguish good writing from bad. At twenty-one, still restless, he again apprenticed himself, this time as a steamboat pilot on the Mississippi. Nothing could have been more fortunate for him. This work had glamour and power to suit his young imagination (on the river, the pilot's word was law even to the captain), but it also required absolute discipline, great skill, and an astounding memory. Since the safety of many lives depended upon the pilot, it demanded the highest responsibility. For Twain's bright but undisciplined mind and still immature character, this was valuable training. In learning every snag, bend, and channel of 1,200 miles of river, he learned to respect knowledge and skill and for the first time really used his mind. Twain may have taken his pen name from the cry of the steamboat leadsmen, "by the mark,

twain," which meant that the water was a safe depth of two fathoms. After four years the Civil War closed the river, and the steamboat would thereafter give way to the railroad and the tugboat. But by then Twain already had what he needed: an awareness of his own ability, a powerful memory, and a wide acquaintance with human nature. When he found a well-drawn character in a book, he said later, he took a "personal interest in him, for the reason that I have known him before—met him on the river."

After two weeks in a Missouri militia unit in which, as he said, he learned nothing about fighting but a great deal about retreating, Twain put the Civil War behind him and went west to Nevada. For the next five years he seemed again to drift—into silver mining and wild speculations in mining claims, into newspaper jobs in Nevada and San Francisco and a bleak winter of futile prospecting in worn-out California gold fields, into writing travel letters from Hawaii and delivering his first lectures. He dreamed of great riches, went broke, and changed his projects constantly. Yet somehow in this apparent aimlessness he was serving another apprenticeship, this time as a writer. He had become "Mark Twain" and had written sketches that showed the beginnings of his vernacular style. He had a direction at last. He wrote to his brother that he felt "a 'call' to literature, of a low order—*i.e.*, humorous. It is nothing to be proud of, but it is my strongest suit. . . ." From then on he would be "seriously scribbling to excite the *laughter* of God's creatures."

His timing was perfect. Lecture audiences were developing a taste for native humor which would open the way for Twain as a public entertainer. In 1867, when the first luxury cruise ship left New York for Europe and the Holy Land, Twain was aboard, having persuaded a California paper to pay his way as an observer. His travel letters became a new kind of travel book—humorous, brash, and irreverent—that caught the spirit of an America eager to measure itself against the cultures of the Old World. *The Innocents Abroad* (1869) was an instant best seller. He was soon convinced that he could succeed as a writer without the drudgery of daily journalism. He moved to Hartford, Connecticut, where, as a sign of permanence (and of his new prosperity), he built a huge, ornate house that a local paper described as one of the "oddest" buildings ever designed as a dwelling. If Mark Twain was at last settling down as a respectable member

Mark Twain's home in Hartford, Connecticut (c. 1874–1885).
Mark Twain Memorial, Hartford

of polite Eastern society, it was with a Western disregard for convention and with a strong sense of his own past: in part, his great, gaudy house resembled an enormous steamboat.

As a writer Twain turned to this past as the deepest source of his creative imagination. With his usual good luck in timing he found that his past enclosed a vanished America that readers were delighted to remember. He began with his most recent past in *Roughing It* (1872), recalling an exuberant West of mining booms and desperadoes, stagecoaches, and the pony express. Soon he moved directly into fiction and more deeply into memory, to Hannibal and his boyhood. *The Adventures of Tom Sawyer* (1876) is, as he called it, a "hymn to boyhood," fulfilling boyhood's deepest wishes for fame, heroism, treasure, and adulation, and commemorating an earlier frontier America. *Life on the Mississippi* (1883) re-creates the vanished age of the steamboat on the great river. But it was in *Adventures of Huckleberry Finn* (1885) that Twain's genius reached its highest powers. Here the fantasy childhood of *Tom Sawyer* is tempered by the harsh realities of a slaveholding society that were also part of Twain's boyhood. In the characters of a white orphan and a runaway slave, *Huckleberry Finn* conducts a profound examination of the prewar South: its religion and traditions, the grandeur of the river seen against the violence and cruelty of the towns along its banks, the deep human desire for freedom struggling against the destructive power of slavery. In this masterpiece, American humor and the vernacular style achieved their greatest triumph and became powerful instruments for analyzing human nature and criticizing society.

Never again would Twain achieve just this balance between pessimism and optimism or so rounded a view of life. Such later works as *A Connecticut Yankee in King Arthur's Court, Pudd'nhead Wilson,* "The Man That Corrupted Hadleyburg," and *The Mysterious Stranger* were increasingly harsh attacks upon the injustices of society and the folly of mankind. His earlier work had been sustained by the frontier spirit, especially by its faith in human progress. As he felt his own spirit and the spirit of the nation's youth slip away in a more complex age, Twain had to face his growing disillusion both with the idea of progress and with human nature itself. His humor, once an instrument of healthy criticism, became a bitter condemnation of the illusions and self-deceptions of "the damned human race." His loss of faith in democratic progress turned his attention inward, revealing the deep complexities of his own personality. "The change is in *me*," he told Howells. "Everyone is a moon and has a dark side which he never shows to anybody," he wrote. In writings that he did not publish during his lifetime, he explored the dark corners of his own nature. Even timing took on a new, grim meaning in this period. It no longer meant the capacity to master circumstances but the domination of life by fate.

Yet readers were right in feeling that Twain's late cynicism was only the transparent mask of his earlier hopefulness and that his basic love of life and people was still there. Even in his disillusionment he embodied his age, for with the closing of the Western frontiers in the 1890s, all America sensed that its national youth had come to an end. More than any other writer, Twain had made the spirit of that youth a part of the national consciousness—and of the world's consciousness of America. Through his work the borders of American literature expanded to include the Mississippi Valley and the Great West. In his best books, the colloquial speech of those regions achieved the rhythms and expressiveness of a natural poetry and thereby revitalized the literary language. Above all he raised American humor to an art and through it showed Americans their own humanity. Humor, Twain knew, begins in human imperfections, and at its best it reconciles people to an imperfect world. "There is no humor in heaven," he wrote.

Many later writers have paid tribute to Twain's genius, but William Faulkner spoke not just for writers but all Americans when he said that "all of us . . . are his heirs."

Cartoon by W. J. Welch
(c. 1869), used on a
poster advertising a
lecture by Twain.
The Bettmann Archive

The Notorious Jumping Frog
of Calaveras° County

In compliance with the request of a friend of mine, who wrote me from the East, I called on good-natured, garrulous old Simon Wheeler, and inquired after my friend's friend, Leonidas W. Smiley, as requested to do, and I hereunto append the result. I have a lurking suspicion that *Leonidas W.* Smiley is a myth; that my friend never knew such a personage; and that he only conjectured that if I asked old Wheeler about him, it would remind him of his infamous *Jim* Smiley, and he would go to work and bore me to death with some exasperating reminiscence of him as long and as tedious as it should be useless to me. If that was the design, it succeeded.

I found Simon Wheeler dozing comfortably by the barroom stove of the dilapidated tavern

° **Calaveras:** "Pronounced Cal-e-*va*-ras" (Twain's note), a county in California.

in the decayed mining camp of Angel's,[1] and I noticed that he was fat and baldheaded, and had an expression of winning gentleness and simplicity upon his tranquil countenance. He roused up, and gave me good day. I told him that a friend of mine had commissioned me to make some inquiries about a cherished companion of his boyhood named *Leonidas W.* Smiley—Rev. *Leonidas W.* Smiley, a young minister of the gospel, who he had heard was at one time a resident of Angel's Camp. I added that if Mr. Wheeler could tell me anything about this Rev. Leonidas W. Smiley, I would feel under many obligations to him.

Simon Wheeler backed me into a corner and blockaded me there with his chair, and then sat down and reeled off the monotonous narrative which follows this paragraph. He never smiled, he never frowned, he never changed his voice from the gentle-flowing key to which he tuned his initial sentence, he never betrayed the slightest suspicion of enthusiasm; but all through the interminable narrative there ran a vein of impressive earnestness and sincerity, which showed me plainly that, so far from his imagining that there was anything ridiculous or funny about his story, he regarded it as a really important matter, and admired its two heroes as men of transcendent genius in *finesse*.[2] I let him go on in his own way, and never interrupted him once.

"Rev. Leonidas W. H'm, Reverend Le—well, there was a feller here once by the name of *Jim* Smiley, in the winter of '49—or maybe it was the spring of '50—I don't recollect exactly, somehow, though what makes me think it was one or the other is because I remember the big flume[3] warn't finished when he first come to the camp; but anyway, he was the curiousest man about always betting on anything that turned up you ever see, if he could get anybody to bet on the other side; and if he couldn't he'd change sides. Any way that suited the other man would suit *him*—any way just so's he got a bet, *he* was satisfied. But still he was lucky, uncommon lucky; he most always come out winner. He was always ready and laying for a chance; there couldn't be no solit'ry thing mentioned but that feller'd offer to bet on it, and take ary side you please, as I was just telling you. If there was a horse race, you'd find him flush or you'd find him busted at the end of it; if there was a dogfight, he'd bet on it; if there was a catfight, he'd bet on it; if there was a chickenfight, he'd bet on it; why, if there was two birds setting on a fence, he would bet you which one would fly first; or if there was a camp meeting, he would be there reg'lar to bet on Parson Walker, which he judged to be the best exhorter[4] about here, and so he was too, and a good man. If he even see a straddlebug[5] start to go anywheres, he would bet you how long it would take him to get to—to wherever he was going to, and if you took him up, he would foller that straddlebug to Mexico but what he would find out where he was bound for and how long he was on the road. Lots of the boys here has seen that Smiley, and can tell you about him. Why, it never made no difference to *him*—he'd bet on *any* thing—the dangdest feller. Parson Walker's wife laid very sick once, for a good while, and it seemed as if they warn't going to save her; but one morning he come in, and Smiley up and asked him how she was, and he said she was considerable better—thank the Lord for his inf'nite mercy—and coming on so smart that with the blessing of Prov'dence she'd get well yet; and Smiley, before he thought, says, 'Well, I'll resk two-and-a-half[6] she don't anyway.'

"Thish-yer Smiley had a mare—the boys called her the fifteen-minute nag, but that was only in fun, you know, because of course she was faster than that—and he used to win money on that horse, for all she was so slow and always had the asthma, or the distemper,

---

1. **Angel's:** Angel's Camp, a gold mining settlement.
2. *finesse* (fĭ-nĕs'): skill; cleverness.
3. **flume** (floom): an inclined trough, usually made of wood, to carry a flow of water.

4. **exhorter** (ĕg-zôrt'ər): here, preacher.
5. **straddlebug:** beetle.
6. **resk two-and-a-half:** risk a bet of $2.50.

or the consumption,[7] or something of that kind. They used to give her two or three hundred yards' start, and then pass her under way; but always at the fag end[8] of the race she'd get excited and desperate-like, and come cavorting and straddling up, and scattering her legs around limber, sometimes in the air, and sometimes out to one side among the fences, and kicking up m-o-r-e dust and raising m-o-r-e racket with her coughing and sneezing and blowing her nose—and *always* fetch up at the stand just about a neck ahead, as near as you could cipher it down.[9]

"And he had a little small bull pup, that to look at him you'd think he warn't worth a cent but to set around and look ornery[10] and lay for a chance to steal something. But as soon as money was up on him he was a different dog; his underjaw'd begin to stick out like the fo'castle[11] of a steamboat, and his teeth would uncover and shine like the furnaces. And a dog might tackle him and bullyrag him, and bite him, and throw him over his shoulder two or three times, and Andrew Jackson—which was the name of the pup—Andrew Jackson would never let on but what *he* was satisfied, and hadn't expected nothing else—and the bets being doubled and doubled on the other side all the time, till the money was all up; and then all of a sudden he would grab that other dog jest by the j'int of his hind leg and freeze to it—not chaw, you understand, but only just grip and hang on till they throwed up the sponge, if it was a year. Smiley always come out winner on that pup, till he harnessed[12] a dog once that didn't have no hind legs, because they'd been sawed off in a circular saw,[13] and when the thing had gone along far enough, and the money was all up, and he come to make a snatch for his pet holt, he see in a minute how he'd been imposed on, and how the other dog had him in the door, so to speak, and he 'peared surprised, and then he looked sorter discouraged-like, and didn't try no more to win the fight, and so he got shucked out bad. He give Smiley a look, as much as to say his heart was broke, and it was *his* fault, for putting up a dog that hadn't no hind legs for him to take holt of, which was his main dependence in a fight, and then he limped off a piece and laid down and died. It was a good pup, was that Andrew Jackson, and would have made a name for hisself if he'd lived, for the stuff was in him and he had genius—I know it, because he hadn't no opportunities to speak of, and it don't stand to reason that a dog could make such a fight as he could under them circumstances if he hadn't no talent. It always makes me feel sorry when I think of that last fight of his'n, and the way it turned out.

"Well, thish-yer Smiley had rat tarriers,[14] and chicken cocks, and tomcats and all them kind of things, till you couldn't rest, and you couldn't fetch nothing for him to bet on but he'd match you. He ketched a frog one day, and took him home, and said he cal'lated[15] to educate him; and so he never done nothing for three months but set in his backyard and learn that frog to jump. And you bet he *did* learn him, too. He'd give him a little punch behind, and the next minute you'd see that frog whirling in the air like a doughnut—see him turn one summerset, or maybe a couple, if he got a good start, and come down flat-footed and all right, like a cat. He got him up so in the matter of ketching flies, and kep' him in practice so constant, that he'd nail a fly every time as fur as he could see him. Smiley said all a frog wanted was education, and he could do 'most anything—and I believe him. Why, I've seen him set Dan'l Webster[16] down here on this floor—Dan'l Webster was the name of the

7. **consumption:** tuberculosis.
8. **fag end:** last part.
9. **cipher it down:** calculate it.
10. **ornery** (ôr'nə-rē): ugly; of mean disposition.
11. **fo'castle** (fōk'səl, fŏr'kăs'əl): a raised structure near the front, or bow, of a steamboat.
12. **harnessed:** here, took on in a fight.
13. **in a circular saw:** in a sawmill accident.
14. **rat tarriers:** rat terriers, dogs used for catching rats.
15. **cal'lated:** calculated; planned.
16. **Dan'l Webster:** Daniel Webster, congressman, U.S. senator, statesman, and the most famous orator of his time. See Benét's story "The Devil and Daniel Webster," page 641.

frog—and sing out, 'Flies, Dan'l, flies!' and quicker'n you could wink he'd spring straight up and snake a fly off'n the counter there, and flop down on the floor ag'in as solid as a gob of mud, and fall to scratching the side of his head with his hind foot as indifferent as if he hadn't no idea he'd been doin' any more'n any frog might do. You never see a frog so modest and straightfor'ard as he was, for all he was so gifted. And when it come to fair and square jumping on a dead level, he could get over more ground at one straddle[17] than any animal of his breed you ever see. Jumping on a dead level was his strong suit, you understand; and when it come to that, Smiley would ante up money on him as long as he had a red.[18] Smiley was monstrous proud of his frog, and well he might be, for fellers that had traveled and been everywheres all said he laid over any frog that ever *they* see.

"Well, Smiley kep' the beast in a little lattice box, and he used to fetch him downtown sometimes and lay for a bet. One day a feller—a stranger in the camp, he was—come acrost him with his box, and says:

"'What might it be that you've got in the box?'

"And Smiley says, sorter indifferent-like, 'It might be a parrot, or it might be a canary, maybe, but it ain't—it's only just a frog.'

"And the feller took it, and looked at it careful, and turned it round this way and that, and says, 'H'm—so 'tis. Well, what's *he* good for?'

"'Well,' Smiley says, easy and careless, 'he's good enough for *one* thing, I should judge—he can outjump any frog in Calaveras County.'

"The feller took the box again, and took another long, particular look, and give it back to Smiley, and says, very deliberate, 'Well,' he says, 'I don't see no p'ints[19] about that frog that's any better'n any other frog.'

"'Maybe you don't,' Smiley says. 'Maybe you understand frogs and maybe you don't understand 'em; maybe you've had experience, and

maybe you ain't only a amature,[20] as it were. Anyways, I've got *my* opinion, and I'll resk forty dollars that he can outjump any frog in Calaveras County.'

"And the feller studied a minute, and then says, kinder sad-like, 'Well, I'm only a stranger here, and I ain't got no frog; but if I had a frog, I'd bet you.'

"And then Smiley says, 'That's all right—that's all right—if you'll hold my box a minute, I'll go and get you a frog.' And so the feller took the box, and put up his forty dollars along with Smiley's, and set down to wait.

"So he set there a good while thinking and thinking to himself, and then he got the frog out and prized his mouth open and took a teaspoon and filled him full of quail shot[21]—filled him pretty near up to his chin—and set him on the floor. Smiley he went to the swamp and slopped around in the mud for a long time, and finally he ketched a frog, and fetched him in, and give him to this feller, and says:

"'Now, if you're ready, set him alongside of Dan'l, with his forepaws just even with Dan'l's, and I'll give the word.' Then he says, 'One—two—three—*git!*' and him and the feller touched up the frogs from behind, and the new frog hopped off lively, but Dan'l give a heave, and hysted up his shoulders—so—like a Frenchman, but it warn't no use—he couldn't budge; he was planted as solid as a church, and he couldn't no more stir than if he was anchored out. Smiley was a good deal surprised, and he was disgusted too, but he didn't have no idea what the matter was, of course.

"The feller took the money and started away; and when he was going out at the door, he sorter jerked his thumb over his shoulder—so—at Dan'l, and says again, very deliberate, 'Well,' he says, '*I* don't see no p'ints about that frog that's any better'n any other frog.'

"Smiley he stood scratching his head and looking down at Dan'l a long time, and at last

---

17. **straddle:** jump.
18. **a red:** a red cent or copper penny.
19. **p'ints:** points, distinctive characteristics or qualities.

20. **amature:** amateur.
21. **quail shot:** small lead pellets used in shotgun shells.

he says, 'I do wonder what in the nation[22] that frog throw'd off for—I wonder if there ain't something the matter with him—he 'pears to look mighty baggy, somehow.' And he ketched Dan'l by the nap of the neck, and hefted him, and says, 'Why blame my cats if he don't weigh five pound!' and turned him upside down and he belched out a double handful of shot. And then he see how it was, and he was the maddest man—he set the frog down and took out after that feller, but he never ketched him. And——"

[Here Simon Wheeler heard his name called from the front yard, and got up to see what was wanted.] And turning to me as he moved

away, he said: "Just set where you are, stranger, and rest easy—I ain't going to be gone a second."

But, by your leave, I did not think that a continuation of the history of the enterprising vagabond *Jim* Smiley would be likely to afford me much information concerning the Rev. *Leonidas W.* Smiley, and so I started away.

At the door I met the sociable Wheeler returning, and he buttonholed me and recommenced:

"Well, thish-yer Smiley had a yaller one-eyed cow that didn't have no tail, only just a short stump like a bannanner, and——"

However, lacking both time and inclination, I did not wait to hear about the afflicted cow, but took my leave.

22. **nation:** damnation.

Mark Twain   **395**

Commentary

Mark Twain found his voice as a writer for the first time in "The Notorious Jumping Frog of Calaveras County." In earlier sketches he had often wavered uncertainly between the language of a polite, educated commentator and a rough, slangy backwoodsman who was actually the key figure of the narrative. As a typical sketch shifted confusingly between these voices, it lost unity of tone and effect. Later, as in "Baker's Bluejay Yarn," the language of the backwoodsman becomes the expression of his character and so creates a unified effect; and in *Adventures of Huckleberry Finn*, Twain immersed his own voice in Huck's to create one of the most flexible narrative voices in literature.

But Twain was still far from these future strategies at the time of the frog sketch. Here he partly solves the problem of voice by creating a frame for the narrative. An introductory narrator, unmistakably "Eastern" in background and correct, even stilted, in his language, explains the circumstances of the narrative that is to follow, assures us that he himself found it boring and "useless," introduces the uncouth Westerner who will tell the story, and then steps aside: "I let him go on in his own way and never interrupted him once." The first narrator reappears only at the end, to close the story by reminding us of his personal disdain for this "history of the enterprising vagabond *Jim* Smiley" as he takes his leave.

The story is therefore Simon Wheeler's to tell, and his voice is the vernacular—the common speech of an uneducated Western miner. In the tradition of oral humor, his narrative mispronounces many words and is frequently ungrammatical. But it is also expressive of his personality, a style that creates at least the outline of a character. We are informed by the introductory narrator that Wheeler tells his story with "impressive earnestness and simplicity" and no hint of humor. But in the story itself this simplicity and unconsciousness are conveyed in Wheeler's own language and are essential to its humor. We laugh because he does *not* see anything comic in the history of the bull pup Andrew Jackson, who "would have made a name for hisself if he'd lived," or in his describing the frog Dan'l Webster as "so modest and straightfor'ard . . . , for all he was so gifted." Twain was already learning that when oral humor is translated to the printed page, the teller is as important as the tale. It is Wheeler's voice which creates the story.

"The Notorious Jumping Frog" shows its origin in oral humor in other ways as well. As a story that must seem to be told rather than written, it proceeds erratically, with many apparently irrelevant details, by a process of association in the speaker's mind. Jim Smiley was "the dangdest feller" for wanting to bet on *everything*—even the likelihood that Parson Walker's wife might not recover from her illness—and for taking "ary side you please" in any bet, and all his exploits are of equal interest to Simon Wheeler. So we hear at length about Smiley's involvement with other animals and even insects before we reach the frog episode. Nor is that incident really a climax of what has gone before. In Wheeler's mind, the story has no logical conclusion. If the introductory narrator had not fled, he would have had to hear next about Smiley's "yaller one-eyed cow that didn't have no tail, only just a short stump like a bannanner. . . ."

In its oral form, as Twain heard it in the mining camps, the humor of the story would have been the trick by which the stranger won the bet. When he announces that Dan'l Webster "can outjump any frog in Calaveras County," Jim Smiley is "making his play" in the style of the Old West—daring any challenge. But Dan'l Webster is highly trained, a sure winner in a fair contest. The "fun" would be in seeing Smiley outsmarted by an unimpressed stranger who doesn't "see no p'ints about that frog that's any better'n any other frog."

But in Twain's written version the humor is in the style—Simon Wheeler's language and point of view. His enthusiastic simplicity invests Jim Smiley's affairs with absurd (and therefore comic) significance: "Smiley said all a frog wanted was education, and he could do 'most anything—and I believe him." This earnestness includes the grotesque without noticing it, as when he reports Andrew Jackson's last fight, with "a dog . . . that didn't have no hind legs, because they'd been sawed off in a circular saw. . . ." Wheeler's vernacular can be vividly descriptive when recounting how Smiley's horse would get "excited and desperate-like" near the end of a race, or how Andrew Jackson would become "a different dog" when all the bets were made: then "his underjaw'd begin to stick out like the fo'castle of a steamboat, and his teeth would uncover and shine like the furnaces." The vernacular extends to pathos (often, for Twain, an essential element of humor) when Wheeler recalls how Andrew Jackson died of a broken heart and wounded pride: "It always makes me feel sorry when I think of that last fight of his'n, and the way it turned out."

In working up this sketch for publication, Twain learned a good deal about transferring oral humor into written narrative. Perhaps the one remaining false note is the introductory narrator, who makes himself too bored, aloof, and finicky to be a credible reporter of Simon Wheeler's story. Twain would have to come to trust the vernacular more fully to convey its own message. But his developing conviction that character is the true source of humor, his continuing discovery of the rich resources of language in the vernacular, even the connection he would so frequently make between the vernacular perspective and the fascinating world of animal behavior—these are already evident in the sketch of the notorious frog.

For Study and Discussion

Analyzing and Interpreting the Selection

1. Simon Wheeler's long first sentence tells us something about how his mind works in telling a story. Look carefully at the part of the sentence before the first semicolon. What is the effect, for the story that follows, of these shifts and backtrackings and the slow pace of the opening?

2. Part of Wheeler's purpose at first is to convince his listener that Jim Smiley really was "the dangdest feller" for betting on anything at all. Is there a progression from the first mention of a horse race, which, of course, is something many people bet on, through the further examples of that opening paragraph?

3. The story of Andrew Jackson has some inherently unfunny elements: dogfights in general and especially the idea of a fight with a crippled dog, and Andrew Jackson's sad death. How does Wheeler's way of telling the story turn this unpromising material to humorous account?

4. Our sense of what is humorous often depends upon **incongruity,** the joining of things that seem inappropriate to each other and therefore ridiculous, as in naming a frog for a famous statesman or in offering to bet Parson Walker that his wife won't recover from her illness. Choose an element from the story—a scene, a character (human or animal), or even a sentence—that you regard as successful humor. Does it depend upon something incongruous?

5. The actual jumping contest occupies barely a paragraph of the story. **a.** Is this appropriate, or has Twain failed to develop the climax of his story properly? **b.** In either case, how does your answer explain the way the story ends?

Baker's Bluejay Yarn

Twain's reminiscence about a California miner who understands the conversation of animals occurs, somewhat strangely, in a travel book about Europe. But it was often Twain's way during his many travels (he made more than forty sea voyages during his life) to be homesick for old scenes and stories from his youth and early manhood. Here, while walking in a German forest, he is reminded by the caws of ravens of the idea that animals talk to each other and, by association, of a man who claimed he could understand them. Jim Baker resembles Simon Wheeler of "The Notorious Jumping Frog" in being simple-hearted and kindly. But by now Twain had learned to develop the possibilities of vernacular language for the revelation of character. This sketch has no frame, merely a paragraph of introduction. And Baker is far more the creator of his story than Wheeler had been. Not only is Baker the sole interpreter of all he reports; since only he understands animal talk, the story grows out of his character. He has studied animals so closely because they are his only neighbors, and it is his Sunday-morning loneliness and "thinking of the home away yonder in the states, that I hadn't heard from in thirteen years" that leads to his diversion with bluejays. Turning his native vernacular to dramatic and even poetic effect, Jim Baker becomes the artist who creates a new imaginative reality from the old materials of the tall tale and oral humor.

Animals talk to each other, of course. There can be no question about that; but I suppose there are very few people who can understand them. I never knew but one man who could. I knew he could, however, because he told me so himself. He was a middle-aged, simple-hearted miner who lived in a lonely corner of California, among the woods and mountains, a good many years, and had studied the ways of his only neighbors, the beasts and birds, until he believed he could accurately translate any remark which they made. This was Jim Baker. According to Jim Baker, some animals have only a limited education, and use only very simple words, and scarcely ever a comparison or a flowery figure; whereas, certain other animals have a large vocabulary, a fine command of language and a ready and fluent delivery; consequently these latter talk a great deal; they like it; they are conscious of their talent, and they enjoy "showing off." Baker said, that after long and careful observation, he had come to the conclusion that the bluejays were the best talkers he had found among birds and beasts. Said he:

"There's more *to* a bluejay than any other creature. He has got more moods, and more different kinds of feelings than other creatures; and, mind you, whatever a bluejay feels, he can put into language. And no mere commonplace language, either, but rattling, out-and-out book-talk—and bristling with metaphor, too—just bristling! And as for command of language—why *you* never see a bluejay get stuck for a word. No man ever did. They just boil out of him! And another thing: I've noticed a good deal, and there's no bird, or cow, or anything that uses as good grammar as a bluejay. You may say a cat uses good grammar. Well, a cat does—but you let a cat get excited once; you let a cat get to pulling fur with another cat on a shed, nights, and you'll hear grammar that will give you the lockjaw. Ignorant people think it's the *noise* which fighting cats make that is so aggravating, but it ain't so; it's the sickening grammar they use. Now I've never heard a jay use bad grammar but very seldom; and when they do, they are as ashamed as a human; they shut right down and leave.

"You may call a jay a bird. Well, so he is, in a measure—because he's got feathers on him, and don't belong to no church, perhaps; but otherwise he is just as much a human as you be. And I'll tell you why. A jay's gifts, and instincts, and feelings, and interests, cover the whole ground. A jay hasn't got any more principle than a Congressman. A jay will lie, a jay will steal, a jay will deceive, a jay will betray; and four times out of five, a jay will go back on his solemnest promise. The sacredness of an obligation is a thing which you can't cram into no bluejay's head. Now, on top of all this, there's another thing; a jay can out-swear any gentleman in the mines. You think a cat can swear. Well, a cat can; but you give a bluejay a subject that calls for his reserve powers, and where is your cat? Don't talk to *me*—I know too much about this thing. And there's yet another thing; in the one little particular of scolding—just good, clean, out-and-out scolding—a bluejay can lay over anything, human or divine. Yes, sir, a jay is everything that a man is. A jay can cry, a jay can laugh, a jay can feel shame, a jay can reason and plan and discuss, a jay likes gossip and scandal, a jay has got a sense of humor, a jay knows when he is an ass just as well as you do—maybe better. If a jay ain't human, he better take in his sign, that's all. Now I'm going to tell you a perfectly true fact about some bluejays.

"When I first begun to understand jay language correctly, there was a little incident happened here. Seven years ago, the last man in this region but me moved away. There stands his house—been empty ever since; a log house, with a plank roof—just one big room, and no more; no ceiling—nothing between the rafters and the floor. Well, one Sunday morning I was sitting out here in front of my cabin, with my cat, taking the sun, and looking at the blue hills, and listening to the leaves rustling so lonely in the trees, and thinking of the home away yonder in the states, that I hadn't heard from in thirteen years, when a bluejay lit on that house, with an acorn in his mouth, and says, 'Hello, I reckon I've struck something.' When he spoke, the acorn dropped out of his mouth and rolled down the roof, of course, but he didn't care; his mind was all on the thing he had struck. It was a knothole in the roof. He cocked his head to one side, shut one eye and put the other one to the hole, like a 'possum looking down a jug; then he glanced up with his bright eyes, gave a wink or two with his wings—which signifies gratification, you understand—and says, 'It looks like a hole, it's located like a hole,—blamed if I don't believe it *is* a hole!'

"Then he cocked his head down and took another look; he glances up perfectly joyful, this time; winks his wings and his tail both, and says, 'Oh, no, this ain't no fat thing, I reckon! If I ain't in luck!—why it's a perfectly elegant hole!' So he flew down and got that acorn, and fetched it up and dropped it in, and was just tilting his head back, with the heavenliest smile on his face, when all of a sudden he was paralyzed into a listening attitude and that smile faded gradually out of his countenance like breath off'n a razor, and the queerest look of surprise took its place. Then he says, 'Why, I didn't hear it fall!' He cocked his eye at the hole again, and took a long look; raised up and shook his head; stepped around to the other side of the hole and took another look from that side; shook his head again. He studied a while, then he just went into the *details*— walked round and round the hole and spied into it from every point of the compass. No use. Now he took a thinking attitude on the comb of the roof and scratched the back of his head with his right foot a minute, and finally says, 'Well, it's too many for *me*, that's certain; must be a mighty long hole; however, I ain't got no time to fool around here, I got to 'tend to business; I reckon it's all right—chance it, anyway.'

"So he flew off and fetched another acorn and dropped it in, and tried to flirt his eye to the hole quick enough to see what become of it, but he was too late. He held his eye there as much as a minute; then he raised up and sighed, 'Confound it, I don't seem to understand this thing, no way; however, I'll tackle her again.' He fetched another acorn, and done his level best to see what become of it, but he couldn't. He says, 'Well, *I* never struck no such a hole as this before; I'm of the opinion it's a totally new kind of hole.' Then he begun to get mad. He held in for a spell, walking up and down the comb of the roof and shaking his head and muttering to himself; but his feelings got the upper hand of him, presently, and he broke loose and cussed himself black in the face. I never see a bird take on so about a little thing. When he got through he walks to the hole and looks in again for half a minute; then he says, 'Well, you're a long hole, and a deep hole, and a mighty singular hole altogether—but I've started in to fill you, and I'm d——d if I *don't* fill you, if it takes a hundred years!'

"And with that, away he went. You never see a bird work so since you was born. He laid into his work . . . and the way he hove acorns into that hole for about two hours and a half was one of the most exciting and astonishing spectacles I ever struck. He never stopped to take a look anymore—he just hove 'em in and went for more. Well, at last he could hardly flop his wings, he was so tuckered out. He comes a-drooping down, once more, sweating like an ice-pitcher, drops his acorn in and says, '*Now* I guess I've got the bulge on you by this time!' So he bent down for a look. If you'll believe me, when his head come up again he was just pale with rage. He says, 'I've shoveled acorns enough in there to keep the family thirty years, and if I can see a sign of one of 'em I wish I may land in a museum with a belly full of sawdust in two minutes!'

"He just had strength enough to crawl up on to the comb and lean his back agin the chimbly, and then he collected his impressions and begun to free his mind. I see in a second that what I had mistook for profanity in the mines was only just the rudiments, as you may say.

"Another jay was going by, and heard him doing his devotions, and stops to inquire what was up. The sufferer told him the whole circumstance, and says, 'Now yonder's the hole, and if you don't believe me, go and look for yourself.' So this fellow went and looked, and comes back and says, 'How many did you say you put in there?' 'Not any less than two tons,' says the sufferer. The other jay went and looked again. He couldn't seem to make it out, so he raised a yell, and three more jays come. They all examined the hole, they all made the sufferer tell it over again, then they all discussed it, and got off as many leather-headed opinions about it as an average crowd of humans could have done.

"They called in more jays; then more and more, till pretty soon this whole region 'peared to have a blue flush about it. There must have been five thousand of them; and such another jawing and disputing and ripping and cussing, you never heard. Every jay in the whole lot put his eye to the hole and delivered a more chuckleheaded opinion about the mystery than the jay that went there before him. They examined the house all over, too. The door was standing half open, and at last one old jay happened to go and light on it and look in. Of course, that knocked the mystery galley-west in a second. There lay the acorns, scattered all over the floor. He flopped his wings and raised a whoop. 'Come here!' he says, 'Come here, everybody; hang'd if this fool hasn't been trying to fill up a house with acorns!' They all came a-swooping down like a blue cloud, and as each fellow lit on the door and took a glance, the whole absurdity of the contract that that first jay had tackled hit him home and he fell over backwards suffocating with laughter, and the next jay took his place and done the same.

"Well, sir, they roosted around here on the housetop and the trees for an hour, and guffawed over that thing like human beings. It ain't any use to tell me a bluejay hasn't got a sense of humor, because I know better. And memory, too. They brought jays here from all over the United States to look down that hole, every summer for three years. Other birds, too. And they could all see the point, except an owl that come from Nova Scotia to visit the Yo Semite, and he took this thing in on his way back. He said he couldn't see anything funny in it. But then he was a good deal disappointed about Yo Semite, too."

For Study and Discussion

Analyzing and Interpreting the Selection

1. From long familiarity with animal talk, Baker has decided that bluejays have the best command of language—"and no mere commonplace language, either, but rattling, out-and-out book-talk—and bristling with metaphor, too—just bristling!" Why is it that jays, among all animals, have the greatest need for self-expression?

2. One trick of Baker's monologue is to assert something that no one could deny ("*You* never see a bluejay get stuck for a word. No man ever did.") and then, in the same tone of reasonable confidence, to grant his listener a point that no one would think of making: "You may say a cat uses good grammar. Well, a cat does. . . ." How does this technique of drawing his listener into his argument contribute to its comic effect?

3. From the earliest stories of childhood on we are familiar with the literary practice of humanizing animals by giving them speech and human characteristics. Read carefully through the third paragraph, beginning, "You may call a jay a bird." **a.** What character traits does Baker use to prove that a jay, except that "he's got feathers on him, and don't belong to no church, perhaps, . . . is just as much a human as you be"? **b.** What is being satirized in this "proof" of a jay's humanity?

4. Twain's growing mastery of the vernacular for literary use shows itself in the range of Jim Baker's speech, which moves effortlessly from slang to metaphor and simile, as when he reports that the first bluejay "gave a wink or two with his wings" or that "all of a sudden he was paralyzed into a listening attitude and that smile faded gradually out of his countenance like breath off'n a razor [the razor meant here is an old-fashioned straight-edge razor with a broad, shiny blade that would cloud with moisture]. . . ." Look carefully at the description of the gathering of thousands of jays. What aspects of this passage show the poetic power of Baker's language?

5. A major point of Baker's yarn is presumably to prove not only that jays talk but that they are essentially "human" in their behavior as well. What responses of theirs to the first jay's story are used as proof?

6. Along with memory, a sense of humor seems to be essential to being either a jay or a human being, and most other birds who saw the knothole got the point as well. Why does the story end with the owl from Nova Scotia who "took this thing in on his way back" from a visit to Yosemite and "couldn't see anything funny in it"?

FROM

Adventures of
Huckleberry Finn

This famous passage occurs just after Huck, the narrator of the novel, has witnessed the final murders that complete an old feud between two Kentucky families and has once again escaped to a raft on the Mississippi River with his friend, the runaway slave Jim. The peace and safety of the river are therefore in sharp contrast in Huck's mind to the violence and terrible cruelty he has just seen on land, as this sunrise is in contrast to the darkness that closed out the feud. The passage shows Huck's deep responsiveness to nature and Twain's triumphant use of the vernacular for subtle and complex literary effects.

Two or three days and nights went by; I reckon I might say they swum by, they slid along so quiet and smooth and lovely. Here is the way we put in the time. It was a monstrous big river down there—sometimes a mile and a half wide; we run nights, and laid up and hid daytimes; soon as night was most gone, we stopped navigating and tied up—nearly always in the dead water under a towhead,[1] and then cut young cottonwoods and willows and hid the raft with them. Then we set out the lines. Next we slid into the river and had a swim, so as to freshen up and cool off; then we set down on the sandy bottom where the water was about knee deep, and watched the daylight come. Not a sound, anywheres—perfectly still—just like the whole world was asleep, only sometimes the bullfrogs a-cluttering, maybe. The first thing to see, looking away over the water, was a kind of dull line—that was the woods on t'other side—you couldn't make nothing else out; then a pale place in the sky; then more paleness, spreading around; then the river softened up, away off, and warn't black any more, but gray; you could see little dark spots drifting along, ever so far away—

trading scows, and such things; and long black streaks—rafts; sometimes you could hear a sweep[2] screaking; or jumbled up voices, it was so still, and sounds come so far; and by-and-by you could see a streak on the water which you know by the look of the streak that there's a snag there in a swift current which breaks on it and makes that streak look that way; and you see the mist curl up off of the water, and the east reddens up, and the river, and you make out a log cabin in the edge of the woods, away on the bank on t'other side of the river, being a woodyard, likely, and piled by them cheats so you can throw a dog through it anywheres;[3] then the nice breeze springs up, and comes fanning you from over there, so cool and fresh, and sweet to smell, on account of the woods and the flowers, but sometimes not that way, because they've left dead fish laying around, gars,[4] and such, and they do get pretty rank; and next you've got the full day, and everything smiling in the sun, and the songbirds just going it!

2. **sweep:** a long oar.
3. **anywheres:** A woodyard's customers were often cheated because piles of wood were sold by total volume, including gaps.
4. **gars:** freshwater fish with long bodies, hard scales, beaklike snouts, and sharp teeth.

1. **towhead:** sand bar, a ridge of sand formed in a river or near a shore by the force of currents.

Frontispiece of *Adventures of Huckleberry Finn.*
Sketch by E. W. Kemble (1884).

Close Reading

Understanding Twain's Vernacular Style

To be effective as literature, the vernacular must seem to be speech—a personal voice—even when it is not speaking in dialogue. For a writer, it is a problem of finding the right tone, idiom, and rhythm, because each of these characteristics is the mark of an individual personality. The result, if it is successful, is subtly different from written language. For example, as Huck watches the light come to the river he observes that "by-and-by you could see a streak on the water which you know by the look of the streak that there's a snag there in a swift current which breaks on it and makes that streak look that way. . . ." Written language would convey the same information far more efficiently: "A snag in the swift current made a streak on the water." But the leisurely pace, the slightly awkward and ungrammatical backing and filling ("which you

know by the look of the streak that there's a snag there"), even the hesitations and minor repetitions—these are the style of Huck's personality and the rhythms of his speech, *his* way of conveying his experience. Huck is only one of many such speakers that Twain invented, but he is our most brilliant creation in the vernacular.

In this passage, Huck seeks first to describe the routine movement of time on the river ("Here is the way we put in the time.") and then to slow time down to a typical morning, and then still further to a single dawn. The overall movement of time is governed by the motion of the raft (the "heavenliest" motion on earth, Twain once observed), and the metaphor and rhythm of the opening sentence convey this: "Two or three days and nights went by; I reckon I might say they swum by, they slid along so quiet and smooth and lovely." The routine actions of every morning are ordered by time signals—"then . . . and then . . . next. . . ." This brings Huck to the point of the passage, the time of sitting in the water, facing east, and watching "the daylight come" to a world asleep.

Consider the style of what follows, from the sentence beginning, "Not a sound, anywheres. . . ." After that sentence, the rest of the passage is a single, extraordinarily long sentence. What is the effect of this rhythm that never comes to a complete stop as Huck's "voice" flows on? How are the necessary pauses of speech and the shifts from one detail to another indicated? How is the passage of time shown as daylight increases? What part do sounds play in this waking up of the world? Two items seem to intrude upon the spell of innocence and beauty created by the passage: the woodpiles cunningly constructed to cheat the steamboats that bought them, and the smell of dead trash fish that people have discarded. Do these reminders of unpleasant facts break the mood of the piece or instead strengthen it by making it more realistic? How are the developing sights and sounds completed in "the full day" at the end? What aspects of Huck's character might we infer from this passage?

Life on the Mississippi

Life on the Mississippi is in part a humorous chronicle of Twain's cub pilot days on the Mississippi River. Eager for travel and adventure, the author takes passage on an old steamboat, the *Paul Jones,* which journeys from Cincinnati to New Orleans and, in the following excerpt, heads back up the river to St. Louis. Determined to "learn" the mighty Mississippi, he persuades Mr. Bixby, the pilot of the *Paul Jones,* to teach him the stretch of the river between New Orleans and St. Louis.

The Belle Creole at New Orleans (c. 1845–1849). Oil on canvas.

FROM **A Cub Pilot's Experience**

The boat backed out from New Orleans at four in the afternoon, and it was "our watch" until eight. Mr. Bixby, my chief, "straightened her up," plowed her along past the sterns of the other boats that lay at the levee, and then said, "Here, take her; shave those steamships as close as you'd peel an apple." I took the wheel and my heart went down into my boots; for it seemed to me that we were about to scrape the side off every ship in the line, we were so close. I held my breath and began to claw the boat away from the danger, and I had my own opin-

ion of the pilot who had known no better than to get us into such peril, but I was too wise to express it. In half a minute I had a wide margin of safety intervening between the *Paul Jones* and the ships, and within ten seconds more I was set aside in disgrace and Mr. Bixby was going into danger again and flaying me alive with abuse of my cowardice. I was stung but I was obliged to admire the easy confidence with which my chief loafed from side to side of his wheel and trimmed the ships so closely that disaster seemed ceaselessly imminent. When he had cooled a little he told me that the easy water was close ashore and the current outside, and therefore we must hug the bank upstream, to get the benefit of the former, and stay well out downstream, to take advantage of the latter. In my own mind I resolved to be a downstream pilot and leave the upstreaming to people dead to prudence.

Now and then Mr. Bixby called my attention to certain things. Said he, "This is Six-Mile Point." I assented. It was pleasant enough information but I could not see the bearing of it. I was not conscious that it was a matter of any interest to me. Another time he said, "This is Nine-Mile Point." Later he said, "This is Twelve-Mile Point." They were all about level with the water's edge; they all looked about alike to me; they were monotonously unpicturesque. I hoped Mr. Bixby would change the subject. But no, he would crowd up around a point, hugging the shore with affection, and then say: "The slack water ends here, abreast this bunch of China trees; now we cross over." So he crossed over. He gave me the wheel once or twice but I had no luck. I either came near chipping off the edge of a sugar plantation, or I yawed[1] too far from shore and so dropped back into disgrace again and got abused.

The watch was ended at last, and we took supper and went to bed. At midnight the glare of a lantern shone in my eyes, and the night watchman said:

"Come, turn out!"

---

1. **yawed:** turned unintentionally from the proper course.

And then he left. I could not understand this extraordinary procedure; so I presently gave up trying to and dozed off to sleep. Pretty soon the watchman was back again, and this time he was gruff. I was annoyed. I said:

"What do you want to come bothering around here in the middle of the night for? Now, as like as not, I'll not get to sleep again tonight."

The watchman said:

"Well, if this ain't good, I'm blessed."

The "off-watch" was just turning in and I heard some brutal laughter from them, and such remarks as "Hello, watchman! ain't the new cub turned out yet? He's delicate, likely. Give him some sugar in a rag and send for the chambermaid to sing 'Rock-a-bye Baby,' to him."

About this time Mr. Bixby appeared on the scene. Something like a minute later I was climbing the pilothouse steps with some of my clothes on and the rest in my arms. Mr. Bixby was close behind, commenting. Here was something fresh—this thing of getting up in the middle of the night to go to work. It was a detail in piloting that had never occurred to me at all. I knew that boats ran all night but somehow I had never happened to reflect that somebody had to get up out of a warm bed to run them. I began to fear that piloting was not quite so romantic as I had imagined it was; there was something very real and work-like about this new phase of it.

It was a rather dingy night, although a fair number of stars were out. The big mate was at the wheel and he had the old tub pointed at a star and was holding her straight up the middle of the river. The shores on either hand were not much more than half a mile apart, but they seemed wonderfully far away and ever so vague and indistinct. The mate said:

"We've got to land at Jones's plantation, sir."

The vengeful spirit in me exulted. I said to myself, "I wish you joy of your job, Mr. Bixby; you'll have a good time finding Mr. Jones's plantation such a night as this, and I hope you never *will* find it as long as you live."

Mr. Bixby said to the mate:

"Upper end of the plantation, or the lower?"

"Upper."

"I can't do it. The stumps there are out of water at this stage. It's no great distance to the lower and you'll have to get along with that."

"All right, sir. If Jones don't like it, he'll have to lump it, I reckon."

And then the mate left. My exultation began to cool and my wonder to come up. Here was a man who not only proposed to find this plantation on such a night but to find either end of it you preferred. I dreadfully wanted to ask a question, but I was carrying about as many short answers as my cargo room would admit of, so I held my peace. All I desired to ask Mr. Bixby was the simple question whether he was ass enough to really imagine he was going to find that plantation on a night when all plantations were exactly alike and all of the same color. But I held in. I used to have fine inspirations of prudence in those days.

Mr. Bixby made for the shore and soon was scraping it, just the same as if it had been daylight. And not only that but singing: "Father in heaven, the day is declining," etc. It seemed to me that I had put my life in the keeping of a peculiarly reckless outcast. Presently he turned on me and said:

"What's the name of the first point above New Orleans?"

I was gratified to be able to answer promptly, and I did. I said I didn't know.

"Don't *know?*"

This manner jolted me. I was down at the foot again, in a moment. But I had to say just what I had said before.

"Well, you're a smart one!" said Mr. Bixby. What's the name of the *next* point?"

Once more I didn't know.

"Well, this beats anything. Tell me the name of *any* point or place I told you."

I studied awhile and decided that I couldn't.

"Look here! What do you start out from, above Twelve-Mile Point, to cross over?"

"I—I—don't know."

"You—you—don't know?" mimicking my

drawling manner of speech. "What *do* you know?"

"I—I—nothing for certain."

"By the great Caesar's ghost, I believe you! You're the stupidest dunderhead I ever saw or ever heard of, so help me Moses! The idea of *you* being a pilot—*you!* Why, you don't know enough to pilot a cow down a lane."

Oh, but his wrath was up! He was a nervous man, and he shuffled from one side of his wheel to the other as if the floor was hot. He would boil awhile to himself and then overflow and scald me again.

"Look here! What do you suppose I told you the names of those points for?"

I tremblingly considered a moment and then the devil of temptation provoked me to say:

"Well to—to—be entertaining, I thought."

This was a red rag to the bull. He raged and stormed so (he was crossing the river at the time) that I judged it made him blind, because he ran over the steering oar of a trading scow.[2] Of course the traders sent up a volley of redhot profanity. Never was a man so grateful as Mr. Bixby was, because he was brimful and here were subjects who could *talk back.* He threw open a window, thrust his head out, and such an irruption followed as I never had heard before. The fainter and farther away the scowmen's curses drifted, the higher Mr. Bixby lifted his voice and the weightier his adjectives grew. When he closed the window he was empty. You could have drawn a seine[3] through his system and not caught curses enough to disturb your mother with. Presently he said to me in the gentlest way:

"My boy, you must get a little memorandum book, and every time I tell you a thing, put it down right away. There's only one way to be a pilot and that is to get this entire river by heart. You have to know it just like ABC. . . ."

By the time we had gone seven or eight hundred miles up the river, I had learned to be a tolerably plucky upstream steersman, in daylight, and before we reached St. Louis I had made a trifle of progress in night work, but only a trifle. I had a notebook that fairly bristled with the names of towns, "points," bars, islands, bends, reaches, etc., but the information was to be found only in the notebook—none of it was in my head. It made my heart ache to think I had only got half of the river set down, for as our watch was four hours off and four hours on, day and night, there was a long four-hour gap in my book for every time I had slept since the voyage began.

My chief was presently hired to go on a big New Orleans boat and I packed my satchel and went with him. She was a grand affair. When I stood in her pilothouse I was so far above the water that I seemed perched on a mountain, and her decks stretched so far away, fore and aft, below me, that I wondered how I could ever have considered the little *Paul Jones* a large craft. There were other differences too. The *Paul Jones*'s pilothouse was a cheap, dingy, battered rattletrap, cramped for room, but here was a sumptuous glass temple: room enough to have a dance in, showy red and gold window curtains, an imposing sofa, leather cushions and a back to the high bench where visiting pilots sit to spin yarns and "look at the river," bright, fanciful "cuspidors"[4] instead of a broad wooden box filled with sawdust, nice new oilcloth on the floor, a hospitable big stove for winter, a wheel as high as my head costly with inlaid work, a wire tiller rope, bright brass knobs for the bells, and a tidy, white-aproned, black "texas tender,"[5] to bring up tarts and ices and coffee during midwatch, day and night. Now this was "something like," and so I began to take heart once more to believe that piloting was a romantic sort of occupation after all. The moment we were under way I began to prowl about the great steamer and fill myself with joy. She was as clean and as dainty as a drawing room; when I looked down her long, gilded

---

2. **scow:** a large, square-ended, flat-bottomed boat.
3. **seine** (sān): a large fishing net.

4. **cuspidors:** spittoons.
5. **texas tender:** The "texas" referred to the officers' quarters on a Mississippi steamboat. It was so designated because it was the largest cabin on board the steamboat.

Pilothouse of a Mississippi steamboat. Drawing from *The Great South* (1875) by Edward W. King.

saloon, it was like gazing through a splendid tunnel; she had an oil picture, by some gifted sign painter, on every stateroom door; she glittered with no end of prism-fringed chandeliers; the clerk's office was elegant, the bar was marvelous, and the barkeeper had been barbered and upholstered at incredible cost. The boiler-deck (i.e., the second story of the boat, so to speak) was as spacious as a church, it seemed to me, so with the forecastle, and there was no pitiful handful of deckhands, firemen, and roustabouts down there but a whole battalion of men. The fires were fiercely glaring from a long row of furnaces and over them were eight huge boilers! This was unutterable pomp. The mighty engines—but enough of this. I had never felt so fine before. And when I found that the regiment of natty servants respectfully "sir'd" me, my satisfaction was complete.

A Daring Deed

When I returned to the pilothouse St. Louis was gone and I was lost. Here was a piece of river which was all down in my book but I could make neither head nor tail of it: you understand, it was turned around. I had seen it when coming upstream but I had never faced about to see how it looked when it was behind me. My heart broke again, for it was plain that I had got to learn this troublesome river *both ways*.

The pilothouse was full of pilots, going down to "look at the river." What is called the "upper river" (the two hundred miles between St. Louis and Cairo, where the Ohio comes in) was low, and the Mississippi changes its channel so constantly that the pilots used to always find it necessary to run down to Cairo to take a fresh look when their boats were to lie in port a week, that is, when the water was at a low stage. A deal of this "looking at the river" was done by poor fellows who seldom had a berth and whose only hope of getting one lay in their being always freshly posted and therefore ready to drop into the shoes of some reputable pilot for a single trip, on account of such pilot's sudden illness or some other necessity. And a good many of them constantly ran up and down inspecting the river, not because they ever really hoped to get a berth but because (they being guests of the boat) it was cheaper to "look at the river" than stay ashore and pay board. In time these fellows grew dainty in their tastes and only infested boats that had an established reputation for setting good tables. All visiting pilots were useful, for they were always ready and willing, winter or summer, night or day, to go out in the yawl[6] and help buoy the channel or assist the boat's pilots in any way they could. They were likewise welcomed because all pilots are tireless talkers when gathered together, and as they talk only about the river they are always understood and are always interesting. Your true pilot cares nothing about anything on earth but the river, and his pride in his occupation surpasses the pride of kings.

We had a fine company of these river inspectors along this trip. There were eight or ten, and there was abundance of room for them in our great pilothouse. Two or three of them wore polished silk hats, elaborate shirt-fronts, diamond breastpins, kid gloves, and patent-leather boots. They were choice in their English, and bore themselves with a dignity proper to men of solid means and prodigious reputation as pilots. The others were more or less loosely clad, and wore upon their heads tall felt cones that were suggestive of the days of the Commonwealth.[7]

I was a cipher[8] in this august company and felt subdued, not to say torpid. I was not even

of sufficient consequence to assist at the wheel when it was necessary to put the tiller hard down in a hurry; the guest that stood nearest did that when occasion required—and this was pretty much all the time, because of the crookedness of the channel and the scant water. I stood in a corner, and the talk I listened to took the hope all out of me. One visitor said to another:

"Jim, how did you run Plum Point, coming up?"

"It was in the night there, and I ran it the way one of the boys on the *Diana* told me; started out about fifty yards above the woodpile on the false point and held on the cabin under Plum Point till I raised the reef—quarter less twain[9]—then straightened up for the middle bar till I got well abreast the old one-limbed cottonwood in the bend, then got my stern on the cottonwood and head on the low place above the point, and came through a-booming—nine and a half."

"Pretty square crossing, ain't it?"

"Yes, but the upper bar's working down fast."

Another pilot spoke up and said:

"I had better water than that and ran it lower down; started out from the false point—mark twain—raised the second reef abreast the big snag in the bend and had quarter less twain."

One of the gorgeous ones remarked:

"I don't want to find fault with your leadsmen but that's a good deal of water for Plum Point, it seems to me."

There was an approving nod all around as this quiet snub dropped on the boaster and "settled" him. And so they went on talk-talk-talking. Meantime, the thing that was running in my mind was, "Now, if my ears hear aright, I have not only to get the names of all the towns and islands and bends, and so on by heart, but I must even get up a warm personal acquaintanceship with every old snag and one-limbed cottonwood and obscure woodpile that

6. **yawl:** the ship's small boat.
7. **Commonwealth:** the English government under Oliver and Richard Cromwell, from 1649 to 1660.
8. **cipher:** here, someone of no value or importance.

9. **twain:** two fathoms or twelve feet. A "quarter less twain" is a quarter of a fathom (1½ feet) less than twain, or 10½ feet.

ornaments the banks of this river for twelve hundred miles; and more than that, I must actually know where these things are in the dark, unless these guests are gifted with eyes that can pierce through two miles of solid blackness. I wish the piloting business was in Jericho and I had never thought of it."

At dusk Mr. Bixby tapped the big bell three times (the signal to land) and the captain emerged from his drawing room in the forward end of the "texas," and looked up inquiringly. Mr. Bixby said:

"We will lay up here all night, captain."

"Very well, sir."

That was all. The boat came to shore and was tied up for the night. It seemed to me a fine thing that the pilot could do as he pleased, without asking so grand a captain's permission. I took my supper and went immediately to bed, discouraged by my day's observations and experiences. My late voyage's notebooking was but a confusion of meaningless names. It had tangled me all up in a knot every time I had looked at it in the daytime. I now hoped for respite in sleep, but no, it reveled all through my head till sunrise again, a frantic and tireless nightmare.

Next morning I felt pretty rusty and low-spirited. We went booming along, taking a good many chances, for we were anxious to "get out of the river" (as getting out to Cairo was called) before night should overtake us. But Mr. Bixby's partner, the other pilot, presently grounded the boat and we lost so much time getting her off that it was plain the darkness would overtake us a good long way above the mouth. This was a great misfortune, especially to certain of our visiting pilots, whose boats would have to wait for their return, no matter how long that might be. It sobered the pilothouse talk a good deal. Coming upstream, pilots did not mind low water or any kind of darkness; nothing stopped them but fog. But downstream work was different; a boat was too nearly helpless with a stiff current pushing behind her, so it was not customary to run downstream at night in low water.

There seemed to be one small hope, however: if we could get through the intricate and dangerous Hat Island crossing before night, we could venture the rest, for we would have plainer sailing and better water. But it would be insanity to attempt Hat Island at night. So there was a deal of looking at watches all the rest of the day and a constant ciphering upon the speed we were making; Hat Island was the eternal subject; sometimes hope was high and sometimes we were delayed in a bad crossing and down it went again. For hours all hands lay under the burden of this suppressed excitement; it was even communicated to me and I got to feeling so solicitous[10] about Hat Island, and under such an awful pressure of responsibility, that I wished I might have five minutes on shore to draw a good, full, relieving breath and start over again. We were standing no regular watches. Each of our pilots ran such portions of the river as he had run when coming upstream, because of his greater familiarity with it, but both remained in the pilothouse constantly.

An hour before sunset Mr. Bixby took the wheel and Mr. W. stepped aside. For the next thirty minutes every man held his watch in his hand and was restless, silent, and uneasy. At last somebody said, with a doomful sigh:

"Well, yonder's Hat Island—and we can't make it."

All the watches closed with a snap, everybody sighed and muttered something about its being "too bad, too bad—ah, if we could only have got here half an hour sooner!" and the place was thick with the atmosphere of disappointment. Some started to go out but loitered, hearing no bell tap to land. The sun dipped behind the horizon, the boat went on. Inquiring looks passed from one guest to another, and one who had his hand on the doorknob and had turned it, waited, then presently took away his hand and let the knob turn back again. We bore steadily down the bend. More looks were exchanged and nods of surprised

___

10. **solicitous:** here, troubled or apprehensive.

admiration—but no words. Insensibly the men drew together behind Mr. Bixby, as the sky darkened and one or two dim stars came out. The dead silence and sense of waiting became oppressive. Mr. Bixby pulled the cord and two deep, mellow notes from the big bell floated off on the night. Then a pause, and one more note was struck. The watchman's voice followed from the hurricane deck:

"Labboard[11] lead, there! Stabboard lead!"

The cries of the leadsmen began to rise out of the distance and were gruffly repeated by the word-passers on the hurricane deck.

"M-a-r-k three! M-a-r-k three! Quarter-less-three! Half twain! Quarter twain! M-a-r-k twain! Quarter-less——"

Mr. Bixby pulled two bell ropes and was answered by faint jinglings far below in the engine room, and our speed slackened. The steam began to whistle through the gauge cocks. The cries of the leadsmen went on—and it is a weird sound, always, in the night. Every pilot in the lot was watching now, with fixed eyes, and talking under his breath. Nobody was calm and easy but Mr. Bixby. He would put his wheel down and stand on a spoke, and as the steamer swung into her (to me) utterly invisible marks—for we seemed to be in the midst of a wide and gloomy sea—he would meet and fasten her there. Out of the murmur of half-audible talk one caught a coherent sentence now and then—such as:

"There; she's over the first reef all right!"

After a pause, another subdued voice:

"Her stern's coming down just *exactly* right, by *George!* Now she's in the marks; over she goes!"

Somebody else muttered:

"Oh, it was done beautiful—*beautiful!*"

Now the engines were stopped altogether and we drifted with the current. Not that I could see the boat drift, for I could not, the stars being all gone by this time. This drifting was the dismalest work; it held one's heart still.

Presently I discovered a blacker gloom than that which surrounded us. It was the head of the island. We were closing right down upon it. We entered its deeper shadow, and so imminent seemed the peril that I was likely to suffocate, and I had the strongest impulse to do *something,* anything, to save the vessel. But still Mr. Bixby stood by his wheel, silent, intent as a cat, and all the pilots stood shoulder to shoulder at his back.

"She'll not make it!" somebody whispered.

The water grew shoaler[12] and shoaler by the leadsman's cries, till it was down to:

"Eight-and-a-half! E-i-g-h-t feet! E-i-g-h-t feet! Seven-and——"

Mr. Bixby said warningly through his speaking tube to the engineer:

"Stand by, now!"

"Aye, aye, sir!"

"Seven-and-a-half! Seven feet! *Six*-and——"

We touched bottom! Instantly Mr. Bixby set a lot of bells ringing, shouted through the tube, "*Now,* let her have it—every ounce you've got!" then to his partner, "Put her hard down! snatch her! snatch her!" The boat rasped and ground her way through the sand, hung upon the apex of disaster a single tremendous instant, and then over she went! And such a shout as went up at Mr. Bixby's back never loosened the roof of a pilothouse before!

There was no more trouble after that. Mr. Bixby was a hero that night, and it was some little time, too, before his exploit ceased to be talked about by river men.

Fully to realize the marvelous precision required in laying the great steamer in her marks in that murky waste of water, one should know that not only must she pick her intricate way through snags and blind reefs, and then shave the head of the island so closely as to brush the overhanging foliage with her stern, but at one place she must pass almost within arm's reach of a sunken and invisible wreck that would snatch the hull timbers from under her if she should strike it—and destroy a quarter

---

11. **Labboard:** a dialect pronunciation of *larboard,* meaning the left side of a ship when one faces front. *Stabboard* is dialect for *starboard,* the right side of the ship.

12. **shoaler:** shallower.

of a million dollars' worth of steamboat and cargo in five minutes, and maybe a hundred and fifty human lives into the bargain.

The last remark I heard that night was a compliment to Mr. Bixby, uttered in soliloquy and with unction[13] by one of our guests. He said:

"By the Shadow of Death, but he's a lightning pilot!"

13. **unction:** fervor.

Reading Check

1. According to Bixby, why is it necessary to stay close to shore while going upstream?
2. Why does Bixby tell Twain to get a memorandum book?
3. Why is Twain lost when the boat leaves St. Louis?
4. Who are the visiting pilots that Twain meets?
5. Why is the Hat Island crossing treacherous?

For Study and Discussion

Analyzing and Interpreting the Selection

1. For the sake of dramatic contrast, Twain presents himself as young and ignorant of the river, thereby emphasizing the experience and skill that a pilot must acquire. In the early paragraphs, what evidence do we have of this cub pilot's romantic illusions about the pilot's job?
2. During the first night watch, Mr. Bixby's questions again allow Twain to present himself as a simpleton. This scene also shows the irreverent humor for which Twain is famous. What in Twain's answers demonstrates this aspect of his character?
3. By the time the boat reaches St. Louis, Twain has acquired some skill in steering upstream in daylight and has a notebook full of information. However, it makes his "heart ache" to realize that during his off watches he has missed half the river. What other enormous gap in his knowledge has he not yet thought of?
4. When Mr. Bixby is hired by a splendid New Orleans boat, Twain's faith in the romance of pi-

loting is restored by all the pomp and glitter. But then he is disappointed as he listens to the visiting pilots who go along to "look at the river." Why does he find their talk discouraging?
5. On the upriver journey from New Orleans, Mr. Bixby appears to be a nervous, short-tempered man. **a.** What different aspects of his character emerge in the dramatic episode of the Hat Island crossing? **b.** How does Twain indicate his own admiration for his "chief"?

Literary Elements

Twain's Comic Technique

Twain's comic technique involves a combination of exaggeration and humorous metaphor. How is this technique shown in the following passages?

[Mr. Bixby] would boil awhile to himself and then overflow and scald me again. (page 407)

You could have drawn a seine through his system and not caught curses enough to disturb your mother with. (page 407)

Find other humorous passages in the selection and explain why they are effective.

Writing About Literature

Discussing Characterization Through Speech

A notable part of Twain's talent is his ability to develop character through speech and to move easily among various dialects and standard English. (In a note to *Adventures of Huckleberry Finn* he boasted that the book had seven distinct dialects, all based upon "personal familiarity with these several forms of speech.") Write a brief essay on one of the following topics:

1. Compare Simon Wheeler of "The Notorious Jumping Frog" and Jim Baker of "Baker's Bluejay Yarn" as narrators. Can you find differences in their use of language or way of speaking? Are these differences related to their characters?
2. The narrator of the passage from *Life on the Mississippi* speaks standard English. How does Twain nevertheless make him an individual with individual characteristics within this conventional language? Does the difference between the narrator as he was then, at the time of the events, and as he is now, at the time of telling his story, play a part in this?

BRET HARTE
1836–1902

Bret Harte (c. 1870). Photograph by Napoleon Sarony.

At the beginning of 1871, as Mark Twain had done four years earlier, Bret Harte left San Francisco for the East. When he went East, Twain was at the beginning of his literary career; beyond Nevada and California, his slender fame rested upon a single story. Harte, on the other hand, held the most important literary position in the West as editor of California's best magazine, the *Overland Monthly*. In less than three years, the eight stories he wrote for the *Overland* had made the magazine known throughout America and even in England and had catapulted Harte to spectacular fame. In his images of life in the early California mining camps and in the character types he drew of the "Forty-Niners" (miners of the gold rush days), America found an enchanting picture of a still-remote West. Harte went East not, as Twain had, as an untried writer aspiring to a career, but as a conquering hero. He had an unprecedented contract from the *Atlantic Monthly* for any twelve items he wished to contribute during the next year, at a salary few American writers could command. Harte was then thirty-four. Few recognized that his stories, for all their apparent novelty, were already repeating fixed formulas. No one could have known that his literary career had already passed its peak.

Although Harte achieved fame as a regional Western writer, his basic attitudes were more Eastern than Western. He was born Francis Brett Harte in Albany, New York, to a family that had known considerable social standing but had now fallen upon hard times and would soon experience still greater insecurity after the early death of Harte's father. Harte went West in 1854. During the next years, with no evident sense of direction, he worked as a schoolteacher, tutor, expressman, and clerk, and briefly tried prospecting.

Soon Harte found his way into journalism, first as a typesetter and then as a writer. He had long written sentimental verses that showed no more promise than any other amateur poet's. Journalism pruned and sharpened his style and made him a professional writer. Most of his early writing was in the form of sketches, literary essays, and satiric articles critical of California manners and mores. Then, in 1868, he became the editor of the new *Overland*, and the second issue carried "The Luck of Roaring Camp," the first of the half-dozen stories on which Harte's reputation still rests. By now the early gold rush days were far enough in the past—nearly twenty years—so that they were subject to romantic idealization. In his picture of that past, Harte captured an appealing mixture of mild humor, colorful character types who spoke an equally colorful language, and situations in which simple virtues finally triumphed over apparent immoralities. The gentleman gambler willing to risk all on the turn of a card, the innocent young schoolteacher from New England, the miner whose rough manner conceals an essential innocence—the staples of Western movies and television plays—were Harte's inventions.

Once he left San Francisco, his career quickly took a downward turn. By 1878 Harte was glad to be saved from mounting debts by an appointment to a consular post in Germany, and he lived the rest of his life abroad. He continued to write and to market his stories, but by now all the vitality was gone and only the formulas remained. Nevertheless, in his best stories Bret Harte left his mark on American literature. A lasting image of the West was more his creation than any other writer's.

The Outcasts of Poker Flat

As Mr. John Oakhurst, gambler, stepped into the main street of Poker Flat on the morning of the twenty-third of November, 1850, he was conscious of a change in its moral atmosphere since the preceding night. Two or three men, conversing earnestly together, ceased as he approached and exchanged significant glances. There was a Sabbath lull in the air, which, in a settlement unused to Sabbath influences, looked ominous.

Mr. Oakhurst's calm, handsome face betrayed small concern in these indications. Whether he was conscious of any predisposing cause was another question. "I reckon they're after somebody," he reflected; "likely it's me." He returned to his pocket the handkerchief with which he had been whipping away the red dust of Poker Flat from his neat boots, and quietly discharged his mind of any further conjecture.

In point of fact, Poker Flat was "after somebody." It had lately suffered the loss of several thousand dollars, two valuable horses, and a prominent citizen. It was experiencing a spasm of virtuous reaction, quite as lawless and ungovernable as any of the acts that had provoked it. A secret committee had determined to rid the town of all improper persons. This was done permanently in regard to two men who were then hanging from the boughs of a sycamore in the gulch, and temporarily in the banishment of certain other objectionable characters. I regret to say that some of these were ladies. It is but due to the sex, however, to state that their impropriety was professional, and it was only in such easily established standards of evil that Poker Flat ventured to sit in judgment.

Mr. Oakhurst was right in supposing that he was included in this category. A few of the committee had urged hanging him as a possible example and a sure method of reimbursing themselves from his pockets of the sums he had won from them. "It's agin justice," said Jim Wheeler, "to let this yer young man from Roaring Camp—an entire stranger—carry away our money." But a crude sentiment of equity residing in the breasts of those who had been fortunate enough to win from Mr. Oakhurst overruled this narrower local prejudice.

Mr. Oakhurst received his sentence with philosophic calmness, none the less coolly that he was aware of the hesitation of his judges. He was too much of a gambler not to accept fate. With him life was at best an uncertain game, and he recognized the usual percentage in favor of the dealer.

A body of armed men accompanied the deported wickedness of Poker Flat to the outskirts of the settlement. Besides Mr. Oakhurst, who was known to be a coolly desperate man, and for whose intimidation the armed escort was intended, the expatriated party consisted of a young woman familiarly known as "The Duchess"; another who had won the title of "Mother Shipton";[1] and "Uncle Billy," a suspected sluice robber[2] and confirmed drunkard. The cavalcade provoked no comments from the spectators, nor was any word uttered by the escort. Only when the gulch which marked the uttermost limit of Poker Flat was reached, the leader spoke briefly and to the point. The exiles were forbidden to return at the peril of their lives.

As the escort disappeared, their pent-up feelings found vent in a few hysterical tears

---

1. **"Mother Shipton":** The original Mother Shipton was supposed to have been a notorious English witch.
2. **sluice robber:** Miners separated gold ore from other material by running water over it through channels called *sluices.* Sluice robbing was considered a particularly cowardly way of stealing gold.

from the Duchess, some bad language from Mother Shipton, and a Parthian[3] volley of expletives from Uncle Billy. The philosophic Oakhurst alone remained silent. He listened calmly to Mother Shipton's desire to cut somebody's heart out, to the repeated statements of the Duchess that she would die in the road, and to the alarming oaths that seemed to be bumped out of Uncle Billy as he rode forward. With the easy good humor characteristic of his class, he insisted upon exchanging his own riding horse, "Five-Spot," for the sorry mule which the Duchess rode. But even this act did not draw the party into any closer sympathy. The young woman adjusted her somewhat draggled plumes with a feeble, faded coquetry; Mother Shipton eyed the possessor of Five-Spot with malevolence, and Uncle Billy included the whole party in one sweeping anathema.

The road to Sandy Bar—a camp that, not having as yet experienced the regenerating influences of Poker Flat, consequently seemed to offer some invitation to the emigrants—lay over a steep mountain range. It was distant a day's severe travel. In that advanced season the party soon passed out of the moist, temperate regions of the foothills into the dry, cold, bracing air of the Sierras. The trail was narrow and difficult. At noon the Duchess, rolling out of her saddle upon the ground, delcared her intention of going no farther, and the party halted.

The spot was singularly wild and impressive. A wooded amphitheater, surrounded on three sides by precipitous cliffs of naked granite, sloped gently toward the crest of another precipice that overlooked the valley. It was, undoubtedly, the most suitable spot for a camp, had camping been advisable. But Mr. Oakhurst knew that scarcely half the journey to Sandy Bar was accomplished, and the party were not equipped or provisioned for delay. This fact he pointed out to his companions

curtly, with a philosophic commentary on the folly of "throwing up their hand before the game was played out." But they were furnished with liquor, which in this emergency stood them in place of food, fuel, rest, and prescience. In spite of his remonstrances, it was not long before they were more or less under its influence. Uncle Billy passed rapidly from a bellicose state into one of stupor, the Duchess became maudlin, and Mother Shipton snored. Mr. Oakhurst alone remained erect, leaning against a rock, calmly surveying them.

Mr. Oakhurst did not drink. It interfered with a profession which required coolness, impassiveness, and presence of mind, and, in his own language, he "couldn't afford it." As he gazed at his recumbent fellow exiles, the loneliness begotten of his pariah trade, his habits of life, his very vices, for the first time, seriously oppressed him. He bestirred himself in dusting his black clothes, washing his hands and face, and other acts characteristic of his studiously neat habits, and for a moment forgot his annoyance. The thought of deserting his weaker and more pitiable companions never perhaps occurred to him. Yet he could not help feeling the want of that excitement which, singularly enough, was most conducive to that calm equanimity for which he was notorious. He looked at the gloomy walls that rose a thousand feet sheer above the circling pines around him, at the sky ominously clouded, at the valley below, already deepening into shadow; and, doing so, suddenly he heard his own name called.

A horseman slowly ascended the trail. In the fresh, open face of the newcomer Mr. Oakhurst recognized Tom Simson, otherwise known as "The Innocent," of Sandy Bar. He had met him some months before over a "little game" and had, with perfect equanimity, won the entire fortune—amounting to some forty dollars—of that guileless youth. After the game was finished, Mr. Oakhurst drew the youthful speculator behind the door and thus addressed him: "Tommy, you're a good little man, but you can't gamble worth a cent. Don't

3. **Parthian:** The Parthians were an ancient people who, when retreating during a battle, were supposed to have turned around to shoot their arrows at the enemy.

try it over again." He then handed him his money back, pushed him gently from the room, and so made a devoted slave of Tom Simson.

There was a remembrance of this in his boyish and enthusiastic greeting of Mr. Oakhurst. He had started, he said, to go to Poker Flat to seek his fortune. "Alone?" No, not exactly alone; in fact (a giggle), he had run away with Piney Woods. Didn't Mr. Oakhurst remember Piney? She that used to wait on the table at the Temperance House? They had been engaged a long time, but old Jake Woods had objected, and so they had run away, and were going to Poker Flat to be married, and here they were. And they were tired out, and how lucky it was they had found a place to camp, and company. All this the Innocent delivered rapidly, while Piney, a stout, comely damsel of fifteen, emerged from behind the pine tree, where she had been blushing unseen, and rode to the side of her lover.

Mr. Oakhurst seldom troubled himself with sentiment, still less with propriety; but he had a vague idea that the situation was not fortunate. He retained, however, his presence of mind sufficiently to kick Uncle Billy, who was about to say something, and Uncle Billy was sober enough to recognize in Mr. Oakhurst's kick a superior power that would not bear trifling. He then endeavored to dissuade Tom Simson from delaying further, but in vain. He even pointed out the fact that there was no provision, nor means of making a camp. But, unluckily, the Innocent met this objection by assuring the party that he was provided with an extra mule loaded with provisions, and by the discovery of a rude attempt at a log house near the trail. "Piney can stay with Mrs. Oakhurst," said the Innocent, pointing to the Duchess, "and I can shift for myself."

Nothing but Mr. Oakhurst's admonishing foot saved Uncle Billy from bursting into a roar of laughter. As it was, he felt compelled to retire up the canyon until he could recover his gravity. There he confided the joke to the tall pine trees, with many slaps of his leg, con-

Pass in the Sierra Nevada of California.
Lithograph.

tortions of his face, and the usual profanity. But when he returned to the party, he found them seated by a fire—for the air had grown strangely chill and the sky overcast—in apparently amicable conversation. Piney was actually talking in an impulsive girlish fashion to the Duchess, who was listening with an interest and animation she had not shown for many days. The Innocent was holding forth, apparently with equal effect, to Mr. Oakhurst and Mother Shipton, who was actually relaxing into amiability. "Is this yer a d——d picnic?" said Uncle Billy, with inward scorn, as he surveyed the sylvan group, the glancing firelight, and

the tethered animals in the foreground. Suddenly an idea mingled with the alcoholic fumes that disturbed his brain. It was apparently of a jocular nature, for he felt impelled to slap his leg again and cram his fist into his mouth.

As the shadows crept slowly up the mountain, a slight breeze rocked the tops of the pine trees and moaned through their long and gloomy aisles. The ruined cabin, patched and covered with pine boughs, was set apart for the ladies. As the lovers parted, they unaffectedly exchanged a kiss, so honest and sincere that it might have been heard above the swaying pines. The frail Duchess and the malevolent Mother Shipton were probably too stunned to remark upon this last evidence of simplicity, and so turned without a word to the

hut. The fire was replenished, the men lay down before the door, and in a few minutes were asleep.

Mr. Oakhurst was a light sleeper. Toward morning he awoke benumbed and cold. As he stirred the dying fire, the wind, which was now blowing strongly, brought to his cheek that which caused the blood to leave it—snow!

He started to his feet with the intention of awakening the sleepers, for there was no time to lose. But, turning to where Uncle Billy had been lying, he found him gone. A suspicion leaped to his brain, and a curse to his lips. He ran to the spot where the mules had been tethered—they were no longer there. The tracks were already rapidly disappearing in the snow.

The momentary excitement brought Mr. Oakhurst back to the fire with his usual calm. He did not waken the sleepers. The Innocent slumbered peacefully, with a smile on his good-humored, freckled face; the virgin Piney slept beside her frailer sisters as sweetly as though attended by celestial guardians; and Mr. Oakhurst, drawing his blanket over his shoulders, stroked his mustaches and waited for the dawn. It came slowly in a whirling mist of snowflakes that dazzled and confused the eye. What could be seen of the landscape appeared magically changed. He looked over the valley and summed up the present and future in two words, "Snowed in!"

A careful inventory of the provisions, which, fortunately for the party, had been stored within the hut, and so escaped the felonious fingers of Uncle Billy, disclosed the fact that with care and prudence, they might last ten days longer. "That is," said Mr. Oakhurst *sotte voce*[4] to the Innocent, "if you're willing to board us. If you ain't—and perhaps you'd better not—you can wait till Uncle Billy gets back with provisions." For some occult reason, Mr. Oakhurst could not bring himself to disclose Uncle Billy's rascality, and so offered the hypothesis that he had wandered from the camp

4. *sotto voce* (sŏt′ō vō′chē): in an undertone.

and had accidentally stampeded the animals. He dropped a warning to the Duchess and Mother Shipton, who of course knew the facts of their associate's defection. "They'll find out the truth about us *all* when they find out anything," he added significantly, "and there's no good frightening them now."

Tom Simson not only put all his worldly store at the disposal of Mr. Oakhurst, but seemed to enjoy the prospect of their enforced seclusion. "We'll have a good camp for a week, and then the snow'll melt, and we'll all go back together." The cheerful gaiety of the young man and Mr. Oakhurst's calm infected the others. The Innocent, with the aid of pine boughs, extemporized a thatch for the roofless cabin, and the Duchess directed Piney in the rearrangement of the interior with a taste and tact that opened the blue eyes of that provincial maiden to their fullest extent. "I reckon now you're used to fine things at Poker Flat," said Piney. The Duchess turned away sharply to conceal something that reddened her cheeks through their professional tint, and Mother Shipton requested Piney not to "chatter." But when Mr. Oakhurst returned from a weary search for the trail, he heard the sound of happy laughter echoed from the rocks. He stopped in some alarm, and his thoughts first naturally reverted to the whiskey, which he had prudently cached. "And yet it don't somehow sound like whiskey," said the gambler. It was not until he caught sight of the blazing fire through the still blinding storm, and the group around it, that he settled to the conviction that it was "square fun."

Whether Mr. Oakhurst had cached his cards with the whiskey as something debarred the free access of the community, I cannot say. It was certain that, in Mother Shipton's words, he "didn't say 'cards' once" during the evening. Haply the time was beguiled by an accordion, produced somewhat ostentatiously by Tom Simson from his pack. Notwithstanding some difficulties attending the manipulation of this instrument, Piney Woods managed to pluck several reluctant melodies from its keys, to an accompaniment by the Innocent on a pair of bone castanets. But the crowning festivity of the evening was reached in a rude camp-meeting hymn, which the lovers, joining hands, sang with great earnestness and vociferation. I fear that a certain defiant tone and Covenanters'[5] swing to its chorus, rather than any devotional quality, caused it speedily to infect the others, who at last joined in the refrain:

"I'm proud to live in the service of the Lord,
And I'm bound to die in His army."

The pines rocked, the storm eddied and whirled above the miserable group, and the flames of their altar leaped heavenward, as if in token of the vow.

At midnight the storm abated, the rolling clouds parted, and the stars glittered keenly above the sleeping camp. Mr. Oakhurst, whose professional habits had enabled him to live on the smallest possible amount of sleep, in dividing the watch with Tom Simson, somehow managed to take upon himself the greater part of that duty. He excused himself to the Innocent by saying that he had "often been a week without sleep." "Doing what?" asked Tom. "Poker!" replied Oakhurst sententiously. "When a man gets a streak of luck, he don't get tired. The luck gives in first. Luck," continued the gambler reflectively, "is a mighty queer thing. All you know about it for certain is that it's bound to change. And it's finding out when it's going to change that makes you. We've had a streak of bad luck since we left Poker Flat— you come along, and slap, you get into it, too. If you can hold your cards right along, you're all right. For," added the gambler, with cheerful irrelevance,

"I'm proud to live in the service of the Lord,
And I'm bound to die in His army."

The third day came, and the sun, looking through the white-curtained valley, saw the

5. **Covenanters:** in seventeenth-century Scotland, adherents of the Presbyterian Covenant to resist the rule of the Anglican churches.

outcasts dividing their slowly decreasing store of provisions for the morning meal. It was one of the peculiarities of that mountain climate that its rays diffused a kindly warmth over the wintry landscape, as if in regretful commiseration of the past. But it revealed drift on drift of snow piled high around the hut—a hopeless, uncharted, trackless sea of white lying below the rocky shores to which the castaways still clung. Through the marvelously clear air the smoke of the pastoral village of Poker Flat rose miles away. Mother Shipton saw it and, from a remote pinnacle of her rocky fastness, hurled in that direction a final malediction. It was her last vituperative attempt and, perhaps for that reason, was invested with a certain degree of sublimity. It did her good, she privately informed the Duchess. "Just you go out there and cuss, and see." She then set herself to the task of amusing "the child," as she and the Duchess were pleased to call Piney. Piney was no chicken, but it was a soothing and original theory of the pair thus to account for the fact that she didn't swear and wasn't improper.

When night crept up again through the gorges, the reedy notes of the accordion rose and fell in fitful spasms and long-drawn gasps by the flickering campfire. But music failed to fill entirely the aching void left by insufficient food, and a new diversion was proposed by Piney—storytelling. Neither Mr. Oakhurst nor his female companions caring to relate their personal experiences, this plan would have failed too, but for the Innocent. Some months before he had chanced upon a stray copy of Mr. Pope's[6] ingenious translation of the *Iliad*. He now proposed to narrate the principal incidents of that poem—having thoroughly mastered the argument and fairly forgotten the words—in the current vernacular of Sandy Bar. And so, for the rest of that night, the Homeric demigods again walked the earth. Trojan bully and wily Greek wrestled in the winds, and the great pines in the canyon

seemed to bow to the wrath of the son of Peleus.[7] Mr. Oakhurst listened with great satisfaction. Most especially was he interested in the fate of "Ashheels," as the Innocent persisted in denominating the "swift-footed Achilles."

So with small food and much of Homer and the accordion, a week passed over the heads of the outcasts. The sun again forsook them, and again from leaden skies the snowflakes were sifted over the land. Day by day closer around them drew the snowy circle, until at last they looked from their prison over drifted walls of dazzling white that towered twenty feet above their heads. It become more and more difficult to replenish their fires, even from the fallen trees beside them, now half hidden in the drifts. And yet no one complained. The lovers turned from the dreary prospect and looked into each other's eyes, and were happy. Mr. Oakhurst settled himself coolly to the losing game before him. The Duchess, more cheerful than she had been, assumed the care of Piney. Only Mother Shipton—once the strongest of the party—seemed to sicken and fade. At midnight on the tenth day, she called Oakhurst to her side. "I'm going," she said, in a voice of querulous weakness, "but don't say anything about it. Don't waken the kids. Take the bundle from under my head, and open it." Mr. Oakhurst did so. It contained Mother Shipton's rations for the last week, untouched. "Give 'em to the child," she said, pointing to the sleeping Piney. "You've starved yourself," said the gambler. "That's what they call it," said the woman querulously, as she lay down again and, turning her face to the wall, passed quietly away.

The accordion and the bones were put aside that day, and Homer was forgotten. When the body of Mother Shipton had been committed to the snow, Mr. Oakhurst took the Innocent aside and showed him a pair of snowshoes, which he had fashioned from the old packsad-

---

6. **Mr. Pope:** Alexander Pope (1688–1744), an English poet.

7. **son of Peleus** (pēl′yo͞os): Achilles (ə-kĭl′ēz), a character in Homer's *Iliad*.

dle. "There's one chance in a hundred to save her yet," he said, pointing to Piney; "but it's there," he added, pointing toward Poker Flat. "If you can reach there in two days, she's safe." "And you?" asked Tom Simson. "I'll stay here," was the curt reply.

The lovers parted with a long embrace. "You are not going, too?" said the Duchess, as she saw Mr. Oakhurst apparently waiting to accompany him. "As far as the canyon," he replied. He turned suddenly and kissed the Duchess, leaving her pallid face aflame and her trembling limbs rigid with amazement.

Night came, but not Mr. Oakhurst. It brought the storm again and the whirling snow. Then the Duchess, feeding the fire, found someone had quietly piled beside the hut enough fuel to last a few days longer. The tears rose to her eyes, but she hid them from Piney.

The women slept but little. In the morning, looking into each other's faces, they read their fate. Neither spoke, but Piney, accepting the position of the stronger, drew near and placed her arm around the Duchess' waist. They kept this attitude for the rest of the day. That night the storm reached its greatest fury and, rending asunder the protecting vines, invaded the very hut.

Toward morning they found themselves unable to feed the fire, which gradually died away. As the embers slowly blackened, the Duchess crept closer to Piney and broke the silence of many hours: "Piney, can you pray?" "No, dear," said Piney simply. The Duchess, without knowing exactly why, felt relieved and putting her head upon Piney's shoulder, spoke no more. And so reclining, the younger and purer pillowing the head of her soiled sister upon her virgin breast, they fell asleep.

The wind lulled as if it feared to waken them. Feathery drifts of snow, shaken from the long pine boughs, flew like white-winged birds and settled about them as they slept. The moon through the rifted clouds looked down upon what had been the camp. But all human stain, all trace of earthly travail, was hidden beneath the spotless mantle mercifully flung from above.

They slept all that day and the next, nor did they waken when voices and footsteps broke the silence of the camp. And when pitying fingers brushed the snow from their wan faces, you could scarcely have told from the equal peace that dwelt upon them which was she that had sinned. Even the law of Poker Flat recognized this and turned away, leaving them still locked in each other's arms.

But at the head of the gulch, on one of the largest pine trees, they found the deuce of clubs pinned to the bark with a bowie knife. It bore the following, written in pencil in a firm hand:

> BENEATH THIS TREE
> LIES THE BODY
> OF
> JOHN OAKHURST,
> WHO STRUCK A STREAK OF BAD LUCK
> ON THE 23RD OF NOVEMBER, 1850,
> AND
> HANDED IN HIS CHECKS
> ON THE 7TH DECEMBER, 1850.

And pulseless and cold, with a Derringer[8] by his side and a bullet in his heart, though still calm as in life, beneath the snow lay he who was at once the strongest and yet the weakest of the outcasts of Poker Flat.

8. **Derringer:** a small pistol.

Reading Check

1. Where do the exiles head when they are turned out of Poker Flat?
2. Why do the riders stop halfway through the journey?
3. How did Oakhurst make a friend of Tom Simson?
4. What sacrifice does Mother Shipton make?
5. How does Oakhurst try to save the lives of Tom Simson and Piney Woods?

For Study and Discussion

Analyzing and Interpreting the Story

1a. What do you learn about the moral code of the Old West from this story? **b.** Why did the citizens suddenly decide to clean up Poker Flat? **c.** Why did they banish Oakhurst instead of hanging him?

2. It is part of Oakhurst's business, as a gambler, to be aware of what other people have on their minds, as in a poker game. How is this awareness shown in the first two paragraphs?

3. The social outcasts in this story presumably represent the worst elements of frontier society. Three of them, however, undergo a moral reformation through which we discover their true virtue. Even before he steals the mules and deserts the others, what indications do we have that Uncle Billy is unlike the others and will not reform?

4. Tom Simson and his fiancée, Piney Woods, are an innocent contrast to the outcasts of Poker Flat. Why do Mother Shipton and the Duchess take such pains to keep Piney ignorant of the truth?

5. It is typical of Harte to introduce a classical literary reference in a Western setting—here the storytelling from Homer's *Iliad*. What parallels are drawn between Homer's poem and the situation of the outcasts?

6. "Snowed in" high in the Sierras, these people, who would have nothing in common in ordinary life, become a mutually supportive human community. In many ways Oakhurst is the strongest member of this community. How do you interpret the final observation that he is the "weakest" of these outcasts as well?

7. Despite the story's essential seriousness, there are a number of humorous touches. Give examples of these. Which examples can be called "regional humor"—that is, humor depending on the characteristics of a particular region?

Language and Vocabulary

Defining Words

Bret Harte's characterization depends in part on the use of precise adjectives and nouns. Define the following italicized words and tell how they deepen your understanding of the characters.

1. . . . [Oakhurst's] professon which required coolness, *impassiveness*, and presence of mind . . . (page 415)

2. . . . that calm *equanimity* for which [Oakhurst] was notorious. (page 415)

3. . . . that *guileless* youth [Tom]. (page 415)

4. . . . the *malevolent* Mother Shipton . . . (page 417)

5. . . . [Uncle Billy's] *felonious* fingers . . . (page 417)

Writing About Literature

Analyzing Characterization

In your opinion, are the characters in this story realistically drawn? Are their actions "in character," or well-motivated? Write a composition in which you discuss the following incidents: Oakhurst returning to Tom Simson the money he lost in gambling; Uncle Billy's desertion; Mother Shipton giving Oakhurst the bundle of food; the Duchess asking Piney if she can pray and feeling relieved at her answer.

AMBROSE BIERCE
1842–1914?

In 1913, at the age of seventy, still ramrod-straight and looking like a soldier, Ambrose Bierce walked across the Texas border into Mexico—and never returned. Perhaps he did not intend to return. With a journalist's credentials that allowed him to join the forces of the Mexican revolutionary Pancho Villa as an "observer," Bierce was again going to a civil war. He not only recognized the danger but welcomed it. "If you hear of my being stood up against a Mexican stone wall and shot to rags," he wrote his niece, "please know that I think that a pretty good way to depart this life. It beats old age, disease, or falling down the cellar stairs." But no one heard anything: he simply disappeared without a trace, to become the subject of many legends. Some people believed that the man they had known as "Bitter Bierce" committed suicide, because that seemed a logical consequence of his pessimistic attitude toward life. But it is equally possible that he died in the war itself.

Bierce was born in Ohio, the youngest child in a large and impoverished family, and grew up on an unsuccessful farm in Indiana. There he developed a lasting dislike of farm life. Despite his poverty, the elder Bierce had brought books along in his own migration from New England, and these gave the boy a taste for the classics of English literature and literary ambitions of his own. Through the help of an uncle, he left the farm for a year at a military academy in Kentucky. When the Civil War broke out soon thereafter, Bierce immediately enlisted in the Union army. He proved to be an exceptional soldier. He rose from private to major, fought in many of the war's major battles, and was cited more than a dozen times for acts of extraordinary bravery. Late in the war he suffered a severe wound in which, as he put it, his head was "broken like a walnut," but he returned to the front after a summer's convalescence.

After the war Bierce accompanied his commander on a military survey of the Western territories. When the expedition reached San Francisco,

Ambrose Bierce (1896). Sketch by F. S. Campbell.

he left the army and began a successful career as a journalist. Soon he was prominent among the writers of California's "Literary Frontier." A mixture of crude satire and personal attacks on public figures was then popular in the city's newspapers, and Bierce's cynical commentary as "The Town Crier" made him the foremost of these local satirists. A book of definitions, which he titled *The Devil's Dictionary* (1906), perhaps best expresses Bierce's cynical outlook. Some definitions are amusing (a *bore* is "a person who talks when you wish him to listen"), and many are cynical (*meekness* is an "uncommon patience in planning a revenge that is worthwhile").

In some basic way Bierce's war experience determined his view of life. He was deeply affected by the waste and futility of war, and nothing so enraged him as the sentimental glorification of battle by those who had not fought. Bierce found in the violence and death of war some shocking, inescapable truth about life. His best short stories, though written over many years, all come back to the war and to the ironies of violent death: the accidents by which one is spared and another taken, the defenses people erect to convince themselves that their own lives are sacred and their destinies are of their own choosing. Bierce explored his obsessive view of life brilliantly in short stories that have a military precision and sparseness, without a wasted word. Like the planter in the story that follows, life in Bierce's fiction is suspended over thin air, and it has the intensity of the planter's plunge to doom.

An Occurrence at Owl Creek Bridge

I

A man stood upon a railroad bridge in northern Alabama, looking down into the swift water twenty feet below. The man's hands were behind his back, the wrists bound with a cord. A rope loosely encircled his neck. It was attached to a stout cross timber above his head, and the slack fell to the level of his knees. Some loose boards laid upon the sleepers[1] supporting the metals of the railway supplied a footing for him and his executioners—two private soldiers of the Federal army, directed by a sergeant who in civil life may have been a deputy sheriff. At a short remove upon the same temporary platform was an officer in the uniform of his rank, armed. He was a captain. A sentinel at each end of the bridge stood with his rifle in the position known as "support," that is to say, vertical in front of the left shoulder, the hammer resting on the forearm thrown straight across the chest—a formal and unnatural position, enforcing an erect carriage of the body. It did not appear to be the duty of these two men to know what was occurring at the center of the bridge; they merely blockaded the two ends of the foot plank which traversed it.

Beyond one of the sentinels, nobody was in sight; the railroad ran straight away into a forest for a hundred yards, then, curving, was lost to view. Doubtless there was an outpost farther along. The other bank of the stream was open ground—a gentle acclivity topped with a stockade of vertical tree trunks, loopholed for rifles, with a single embrasure through which protruded the muzzle of a brass cannon commanding the bridge. Midway of the slope between bridge and fort were the spectators—a single company of infantry in line, at "parade rest," the butts of the rifles on the ground, the barrels inclining slightly backward against the right shoulder, the hands crossed upon the stock. A lieutenant stood at the right of the line, the point of his sword upon the ground, his left hand resting upon his right. Excepting the group of four at the center of the bridge, not a man moved. The company faced the bridge, staring stonily, motionless. The sentinels, facing the banks of the stream, might have been statues to adorn the bridge. The captain stood with folded arms, silent, observing the work of his subordinates, but making no sign. Death is a dignitary who when he comes announced is to be received with formal manifestations of respect, even by those most familiar with him. In the code of military etiquette, silence and fixity are forms of deference.

The man who was engaged in being hanged was apparently about thirty-five years of age. He was a civilian, if one might judge from his habit, which was that of a planter. His features were good—a straight nose, firm mouth, broad forehead, from which his long, dark hair was combed straight back, falling behind his ears to the collar of his well-fitting frock coat. He wore a mustache and pointed beard, but no whiskers; his eyes were large and dark gray, and had a kindly expression which one would hardly have expected in one whose neck was in the hemp. Evidently this was no vulgar assassin. The liberal military code makes provision for hanging many kinds of persons, and gentlemen are not excluded.

The preparations being complete, the two

---

1. **sleepers:** railroad ties supporting a track.

private soldiers stepped aside and each drew away the plank upon which he had been standing. The sergeant turned to the captain, saluted, and placed himself immediately behind that officer, who in turn moved apart one pace. These movements left the condemned man and the sergeant standing on the two ends of the same plank, which spanned three of the crossties of the bridge. The end upon which the civilian stood almost, but not quite, reached a fourth. This plank had been held in place by the weight of the captain; it was now held by that of the sergeant. At a signal from the former, the latter would step aside, the plank would tilt, and the condemned man go between two ties. The arrangement commended itself to his judgment as simple and effective. His face had not been covered nor his eyes bandaged. He looked a moment at his "unsteadfast footing," then let his gaze wander to the swirling water of the stream racing madly beneath his feet. A piece of dancing driftwood caught his attention and his eyes followed it down the current. How slowly it appeared to move! What a sluggish stream!

He closed his eyes in order to fix his last thoughts upon his wife and children. The water, touched to gold by the early sun, the brooding mists under the banks at some distance down the stream, the fort, the soldiers, the piece of drift—all had distracted him. And now he became conscious of a new disturbance. Striking through the thought of his dear ones was a sound which he could neither ignore nor understand, a sharp, distinct, metallic percussion like the stroke of a blacksmith's hammer upon the anvil; it had the same ringing quality. He wondered what it was, and whether immeasurably distant or nearby—it seemed both. Its recurrence was regular, but as slow as the tolling of a death knell. He awaited each stroke with impatience and—he knew not why—apprehension. The intervals of silence grew progressively longer; the delays became maddening. With their greater infrequency the sounds increased in strength and sharpness. They hurt his ear like

Olivier Plantation (1861) by Adrien Persac. Watercolor and collage.
Louisiana State Museum, New Orleans

the thrust of a knife; he feared he would shriek. What he heard was the ticking of his watch.

He unclosed his eyes and saw again the water below him. "If I could free my hands," he thought, "I might throw off the noose and spring into the stream. By diving I could evade the bullets and, swimming vigorously, reach the bank, take to the woods, and get away

home. My home, thank God, is as yet outside their lines; my wife and little ones are still beyond the invader's farthest advance."

As these thoughts, which have here to be set down in words, were flashed into the doomed man's brain rather than evolved from it, the captain nodded to the sergeant. The sergeant stepped aside.

II

Peyton Farquhar was a well-to-do planter of an old and highly respected Alabama family. Being a slave owner and like other slave own- ers a politician, he was naturally an original secessionist and ardently devoted to the Southern cause. Circumstances of an imperious nature, which it is unnecessary to relate here, had prevented him from taking service with the gallant army which had fought the disastrous campaigns ending with the fall of Corinth, and he chafed under the inglorious restraint, longing for the release of his energies, the larger life of the soldier, the opportunity for distinction. That opportunity, he felt, would come, as it comes to all in wartime. Meanwhile he did what he could. No service was too humble for him to perform in aid of the South, no adventure too perilous for him to undertake if consistent with the character of a civilian who was at heart a soldier, and who in good faith and without too much qualification assented to at least a part of the frankly villainous dictum that all is fair in love and war.

One evening while Farquhar and his wife were sitting on a rustic bench near the entrance to his grounds, a gray-clad soldier rode up to the gate and asked for a drink of water. Mrs. Farquhar was only too happy to serve him with her own white hands. While she was fetching the water her husband approached the dusty horseman and inquired eagerly for news from the front.

"The Yanks are repairing the railroads," said the man, "and are getting ready for another advance. They have reached the Owl Creek bridge, put it in order, and built a stockade on the north bank. The commandant has issued an order, which is posted everywhere, declaring that any civilian caught interfering with the railroad, its bridges, tunnels, or trains will be summarily hanged. I saw the order."

"How far is it to the Owl Creek bridge?" Farquhar asked.

"About thirty miles."

"Is there no force on this side the creek?"

"Only a picket post[2] half a mile out, on the railroad, and a single sentinel at this end of the bridge."

"Suppose a man—a civilian and student of hanging—should elude the picket post and perhaps get the better of the sentinel," said Farquhar, smiling, "what could he accomplish?"

The soldier reflected. "I was there a month ago," he replied. "I observed that the flood of last winter had lodged a great quantity of driftwood against the wooden pier at this end of the bridge. It is now dry and would burn like tow."[3]

The lady had now brought the water, which the soldier drank. He thanked her ceremoni-

ously, bowed to her husband, and rode away. An hour later, after nightfall, he repassed the plantation, going northward in the direction from which he had come. He was a Federal scout.

III

As Peyton Farquhar fell straight downward through the bridge he lost consciousness and was as one already dead. From this state he was awakened—ages later, it seemed to him—by the pain of a sharp pressure upon his throat, followed by a sense of suffocation. Keen, poignant agonies seemed to shoot from his neck downward through every fiber of his body and limbs. These pains appeared to flash along well-defined lines of ramification and to beat with an inconceivably rapid periodicity. They seemed like streams of pulsating fire heating him to an intolerable temperature. As to his head, he was conscious of nothing but a feeling of fullness—of congestion. These sensations were unaccompanied by thought. The intellectual part of his nature was already effaced; he had power only to feel, and feeling was torment. He was conscious of motion. Encompassed in a luminous cloud, of which he was now merely the fiery heart, without material substance, he swung through unthinkable arcs of oscillation, like a vast pendulum. Then all at once, with terrible suddenness, the light about him shot upward with the noise of a loud plash; a frightful roaring was in his ears, and all was cold and dark. The power of thought was restored; he knew that the rope had broken and he had fallen into the stream. There was no additional strangulation; the noose about his neck was already suffocating him and kept the water from his lungs. To die of hanging at the bottom of a river!—the idea seemed to him ludicrous. He opened his eyes in the darkness and saw above him a gleam of light, but how distant, how inaccessible! He was still sinking, for the light became fainter and fainter until it was a mere glimmer. Then it began to grow and brighten, and he knew that

2. **picket post:** an outpost of soldiers sent ahead to warn of a surprise attack.
3. **tow:** coarse fibers of hemp or flax.

he was rising toward the surface—knew it with reluctance, for he was now very comfortable. "To be hanged and drowned," he thought, "that is not so bad; but I do not wish to be shot. No; I will not be shot; that is not fair."

He was not conscious of an effort, but a sharp pain in his wrist apprised him that he was trying to free his hands. He gave the struggle his attention, as an idler might observe the feat of a juggler, without interest in the outcome. What splendid effort!—what magnificent, what superhuman strength! Ah, that was a fine endeavor! Bravo! The cord fell away; his arms parted and floated upward, the hands dimly seen on each side in the growing light. He watched them with a new interest as first one and then the other pounced upon the noose at his neck. They tore it away and thrust it fiercely aside, its undulations resembling those of a water snake. "Put it back, put it back!" He thought he shouted these words to his hands, for the undoing of the noose had been succeeded by the direst pang that he had yet experienced. His neck ached horribly; his brain was on fire; his heart, which had been fluttering faintly, gave a great leap, trying to force itself out at his mouth. His whole body was racked and wrenched with an insupportable anguish! But his disobedient hands gave no heed to the command. They beat the water vigorously with quick, downward strokes, forcing him to the surface. He felt his head emerge; his eyes were blinded by the sunlight; his chest expanded convulsively, and with a supreme and crowning agony his lungs engulfed a great draft of air, which instantly he expelled in a shriek!

He was now in full possession of his physical senses. They were, indeed, preternaturally keen and alert. Something in the awful disturbances of his organic system had so exalted and refined them that they made record of things never before perceived. He felt the ripples upon his face and heard their separate sounds as they struck. He looked at the forest on the bank of the stream, saw the individual trees, the leaves and the veining of each leaf—

saw the very insects upon them: the locusts, the brilliant-bodied flies, the gray spiders stretching their webs from twig to twig. He noted the prismatic colors in all the dewdrops upon a million blades of grass. The humming of the gnats that danced above the eddies of the stream, the beating of the dragonflies' wings, the strokes of the water spiders' legs, like oars which had lifted their boat—all these made audible music. A fish slid along beneath his eyes and he heard the rush of its body parting the water.

He had come to the surface facing down the stream; in a moment the visible world seemed to wheel slowly round, himself the pivotal point, and he saw the bridge, the fort, the soldiers upon the bridge, the captain, the sergeant, the two privates, his executioners. They were in silhouette against the blue sky. They shouted and gesticulated, pointing at him. The captain had drawn his pistol, but did not fire; the others were unarmed. Their movements were grotesque and horrible, their forms gigantic.

Suddenly he heard a sharp report and something struck the water smartly within a few inches of his head, spattering his face with spray. He heard a second report, and saw one of the sentinels with his rifle at his shoulder, a light cloud of blue smoke rising from the muzzle. The man in the water saw the eye of the man on the bridge gazing into his own through the sights of the rifle. He observed that it was a gray eye and remembered having read that gray eyes were keenest, and that all famous marksmen had them. Nevertheless, this one had missed.

A counterswirl had caught Farquhar and turned him half round; he was again looking into the forest on the bank opposite the fort. The sound of a clear, high voice in a monotonous singsong now rang out behind him and came across the water with a distinctness that pierced and subdued all other sounds, even the beating of the ripples in his ears. Although no soldier, he had frequented camps enough to know the dread significance of that deliberate, drawling, aspirated chant; the lieutenant onshore was taking a part in the morning's work. How coldly and pitilessly—with what an even, calm intonation, presaging and enforcing tranquillity in the men—with what accurately measured intervals fell those cruel words:

"Attention, company! . . . Shoulder arms! . . . Ready! . . . Aim! . . . Fire!"

Farquhar dived—dived as deeply as he could. The water roared in his ears like the voice of Niagara, yet he heard the dulled thunder of the volley and, rising again toward the surface, met shining bits of metal, singularly flattened, oscillating slowly downward. Some of them touched him on the face and hands, then fell away, continuing their descent. One lodged between his collar and neck; it was uncomfortably warm and he snatched it out.

As he rose to the surface, gasping for breath, he saw that he had been a long time underwater; he was perceptibly farther downstream—nearer to safety. The soldiers had almost finished reloading; the metal ramrods flashed all at once in the sunshine as they were drawn from the barrels, turned in the air, and thrust into their sockets. The two sentinels fired again, independently and ineffectually.

The hunted man saw all this over his shoulder; he was now swimming vigorously with the current. His brain was as energetic as his arms and legs; he thought with the rapidity of lightning.

"The officer," he reasoned, "will not make that martinet's[4] error a second time. It is as easy to dodge a volley as a single shot. He has probably already given the command to fire at will. God help me, I cannot dodge them all!"

An appalling plash within two yards of him was followed by a loud, rushing sound, *diminuendo*,[5] which seemed to travel back through the air to the fort and died in an explosion which stirred the very river to its deeps! A rising sheet of water, which curved over him, fell down upon him, blinded him, strangled him! The cannon had taken a hand in the game. As he shook his head free from the commotion of the smitten water, he heard the deflected shot humming through the air ahead, and in an instant it was cracking and smashing the branches in the forest beyond.

"They will not do that again," he thought; "the next time they will use a charge of grape.[6] I must keep my eye upon the gun; the smoke will apprise me—the report arrives too late; it lags behind the missile. That is a good gun."

Suddenly he felt himself whirled round and round—spinning like a top. The water, the banks, the forests, the now distant bridge, fort, and men—all were commingled and blurred. Objects were represented by their colors only; circular horizontal streaks of color—that was all he saw. He had been caught in a vortex and was being whirled on with a velocity of advance and gyration which made him giddy and sick. In a few moments he was flung upon the gravel at the foot of the left bank of the stream—the southern bank—and behind a projecting point which concealed him from his enemies. The sudden arrest of his motion, the abrasion of one of his hands on the gravel, restored him, and he wept with delight. He dug his fingers into the sand, threw it over himself in handfuls, and audibly blessed it. It looked like diamonds, rubies, emeralds; he could think of nothing beautiful which it did not resemble. The trees upon the bank were giant garden plants; he noted a definite order in their arrangement, inhaled the fragrance of their blooms. A strange, roseate light shone through the spaces among their trunks and the wind made in their branches the music of aeolian harps.[7] He had no wish to perfect his escape—was content to remain in that enchanting spot until retaken.

A whiz and rattle of grapeshot among the

----

4. **martinet:** a very strict military officer who puts discipline and regulations above common sense.
5. *diminuendo* (dĭ-mĭn′yoo-ĕn′dō): a musical term indicating a gradual reduction in loudness.

6. **grape:** grapeshot, a cluster of small iron balls designed to disperse in the air when shot from a gun or cannon.
7. **aeolian** (ē-ō′lē-ən) **harps:** harps that produce music by the movement of the wind across the strings.

branches high above his head roused him from his dream. The baffled cannoneer had fired him a random farewell. He sprang to his feet, rushed up the sloping bank, and plunged into the forest.

All that day he traveled, laying his course by the rounding sun. The forest seemed interminable; nowhere did he discover a break in it, not even a woodman's road. He had not known that he lived in so wild a region. There was something uncanny in the revelation.

By nightfall he was fatigued, footsore, famishing. The thought of his wife and children urged him on. At last he found a road which led him in what he knew to be the right direction. It was as wide and straight as a city street, yet it seemed untraveled. No fields bordered it, no dwelling anywhere. Not so much as the barking of a dog suggested human habitation. The black bodies of the trees formed a straight wall on both sides, terminating on the horizon in a point, like a diagram in a lesson in perspective. Overhead, as he looked up through this rift in the wood, shone great golden stars looking unfamiliar and grouped in strange constellations. He was sure they were arranged in some order which had a secret and malign significance. The wood on either side was full of singular noises, among which—once, twice, and again—he distinctly heard whispers in an unknown tongue.

His neck was in pain and lifting his hand to it he found it horribly swollen. He knew that it had a circle of black where the rope had bruised it. His eyes felt congested; he could no longer close them. His tongue was swollen with thirst; he relieved its fever by thrusting it forward from between his teeth into the cold air. How softly the turf had carpeted the untraveled avenue—he could no longer feel the roadway beneath his feet!

Doubtless, despite his suffering, he had fallen asleep while walking, for now he sees another scene—perhaps he has merely recovered from a delirium. He stands at the gate of his own home. All is as he left it, and all bright and beautiful in the morning sunshine. He must have traveled the entire night. As he pushes open the gate and passes up the wide white walk, he sees a flutter of female garments; his wife, looking fresh and cool and sweet, steps down from the veranda to meet him. At the bottom of the steps she stands waiting, with a smile of ineffable joy, an attitude of matchless grace and dignity. Ah, how beautiful she is! He springs forward with extended arms. As he is about to clasp her, he feels a stunning blow upon the back of his neck; a blinding white light blazes all about him with a sound like the shock of a cannon—then all is darkness and silence!

Peyton Farquhar was dead; his body, with a broken neck, swung gently from side to side beneath the timbers of the Owl Creek bridge.

Reading Check

1. Peyton Farquhar is a civilian. Why is he sentenced to hang?
2. While preparations are being completed for his execution, what sound distracts Farquhar from thoughts of his family?
3. At the last moment Farquhar thinks of a desperate escape plan. What is it?
4. How was Farquhar trapped by the Federal scout who visited his plantation?
5. What is the last scene Farquhar imagines before he dies?

Union Soldier.

Confederate Soldier.

For Study and Discussion

Analyzing and Interpreting the Story

1. The opening paragraphs present first a close-up view of the condemned man and then, gradually, a larger picture that includes a sergeant and his helpers, a captain, two sentries, a railroad and a fort, and a company of infantry—all fixed and motionless, like a painting or photograph. How does this rigid, quiet scene create suspense?

2. The third paragraph gives a detailed physical description of the planter, even to the "kindly expression" of his eyes. Why do you suppose it is important that we not think of him as a "vulgar assassin"?

3. The rest of Part I depicts the planter's distorted perceptions, particularly of movement and time. At this moment before death, he sees a slowed-down world: we know that the stream beneath him is "racing madly," but he sees it as "sluggish." How is his reaction to the ticking of his watch also distorted?

4. Part II of the story characterizes Peyton Farquhar as a civilian who had longed for "the larger life of the soldier, the opportunity for distinction."

In light of subsequent events, what is ironic about Farquhar's longings?

5. Part III concentrates on Farquhar's perceptions. What details from this final scene suggest that the events take place in his mind?

6. The story's last sentence is abrupt and surprising. What comment on life and death do you think this sentence makes?

Writing About Literature

Analyzing Character Psychology

Ambrose Bierce is often regarded as one of the first *modern* American writers, in part because of his concern with character psychology. "An Occurrence at Owl Creek Bridge" deals primarily with a man's state of mind only seconds before he dies. Write an essay in which you discuss critically the following questions: How convincing are the descriptions of Peyton Farquhar's thoughts and sensations? Which details in Part III of the story seem to you especially plausible? Why is the last scene that Peyton Farquhar imagines appropriate from a psychological standpoint? (Consider what you learn about him in Part II.)

FROM
Life on the Mississippi
MARK TWAIN

In the early part of the nineteenth century, American English began to develop a flavor of its own, very different from its parent, British English. As new frontiers opened and a new age of nationalism dawned, the language became more expansive. Not only was the vocabulary becoming distinctly American, but so were the rhythms of speech and modes of expression. It was fast becoming a language of tall talk, which, according to H. L. Mencken, "ran to grotesque metaphors and farfetched exaggerations and out of [which] came a great many Americanisms that still flourish." Here is an example of a boasting contest from Mark Twain's *Life on the Mississippi*.

"Whoo-oop! I 'm the old original iron-jawed, brass-mounted, copper-bellied corpse-maker from the wilds of Arkansaw!—Look at me! I'm the man they call Sudden Death and General Desolation! Sired by a hurricane, dam'd[1] by an earthquake, half-brother to the cholera, nearly related to the smallpox on the mother's side! Look at me! I take nineteen alligators and a bar'l of whiskey for breakfast when I 'm in robust health, and a bushel of rattlesnakes and a dead body when I 'm ailing! I split the everlasting rocks with my glance, and I squench the thunder when I speak! Whoo-oop! Stand back and give me room according to my strength! Blood 's my natural drink, and the wails of the dying is music to my ear! Cast your eye on me, gentlemen!—and lay low and hold your breath, for I 'm bout to turn myself loose! . . ."

"Whoo-oop! Bow your neck and spread, for the kingdom of sorrow 's a-coming! Hold me down to the earth, for I feel my powers a-working! whoo-oop! I'm a child of sin, *don't* let me get a start! Smoked glass, here, for all! Don't attempt to look at me with the naked eye, gentlemen! When I 'm playful I use the meridians of longitude and parallels of latitude for a seine, and drag the Atlantic Ocean for

whales! I scratch my head with the lightning and purr myself to sleep with the thunder! When I 'm cold, I bile the Gulf of Mexico and bathe in it; when I 'm hot I fan myself with an equinoctial storm;[2] when I 'm thirsty I reach up and suck a cloud dry like a sponge; when I range the earth hungry, famine follows in my tracks! Whoo-oop! Bow your neck and spread! I put my hand on the sun's face and make it night in the earth; I bite a piece out of the moon and hurry the seasons; I shake myself and crumble the mountains! Contemplate me through leather—*don't* use the naked eye! I 'm the man with a petrified heart and biler-iron bowels! The massacre of isolated communities is the pastime of my idle moments, the destruction of nationalities the serious business of my life! The boundless vastness of the great American desert is my enclosed property, and I bury my dead on my own premises!" He jumped up and cracked his heels together three times before he lit (they cheered him again), and as he come down he shouted out: "Whoo-oop! bow your neck and spread, for the pet child of calamity's a-coming!"

1. **dam'd:** from the word *dam,* meaning "mother."

2. **equinoctial** (ē′kwə-nŏk′shəl, ĕk′wə-) **storm:** a violent storm that occurs about the time of an equinox, when day and night are of equal length.

For Study and Discussion

1. One example of what Mencken calls "grotesque metaphors" is "When I'm playful I use the meridians of longitude and parallels of latitude for a seine, and drag the Atlantic Ocean for whales!" **a.** Explain this metaphor in your own words. **b.** Find other examples of farfetched exaggeration in the excerpt.

2. Phonetic spellings, which represent sounds as they are actually spoken, often give linguists clues to earlier pronunciations of words. What evidence in the Twain selection tells you how *boil* and *boiler* were pronounced around 1850?

3. Here is another nineteenth-century brag to compare with Twain's:

> I'm that same David Crockett, fresh from the backwoods, half horse, half alligator, a little touched with the snapping turtle; can wade the Mississippi, leap the Ohio, ride upon a streak of lightning, and slip without a scratch down a honey locust [a tree with thorny branches]; can whip my weight in wildcats—and if any gentleman pleases, for a ten-dollar bill, he may throw in a panther— hug a bear too close for comfort, and eat any man opposed to Jackson.

a. Point out similarities and differences. **b.** What do both selections reveal about frontier values?

Extending Your Study

1. Despite many regulations to discourage the practice, steamboats often raced on the Mississippi and other rivers. Fast boats (and "lightning pilots") were much admired and were therefore constantly challenged by ambitious rivals. The *Eclipse*, pictured racing the *Natchez* in the lithograph on page 337, was widely known for its speed, and the *Natchez* participated in the most famous Mississippi race of all, from New Orleans to St. Louis, with the *Robert Lee*. From your library, get a copy of Mark Twain's *Life on the Mississippi* and read Chapter XVI, "Racing Days." What details does Twain use to convey the excitement of steamboat racing during the "flush times" on the Mississippi? If being on a fast boat was exciting, being on a slow one was boring. What exaggerations convey how slow the *John J. Roe* was? Why does Twain believe that being on a slow boat is more "dangerous" than being on a fast one?

2. The Civil War began with the attack on Fort Sumter in South Carolina, which gave the fort a special significance as the first battleground of the war. What mood about the war is conveyed by Conrad Wise Chapman's painting of Fort Sumter on page 338? What does picturing the fort at evening contribute to this mood?

3. Flatboats of the type shown in George Caleb Bingham's painting on page 355 were invented in Pennsylvania about a century earlier and were used to transport freight down major rivers and as floating shelters for pioneer families who were moving westward. Since they could travel only downriver, the cumbersome flatboats were dismantled and sold for their timber when they reached their destination. Like other pioneers, flatboatmen had their own folklore and heroes, most notably the legendary Mike Fink, who was credited with taking a flatboat over the falls of the Ohio River. Look up Mike Fink's biography in an American folklore source. Then write a paragraph explaining how frontier skills are celebrated in the story of his life.

4. The dress and adornments of American Indians differed from tribe to tribe. In George Catlin's painting of Chief Black Hawk, page 376, and Edward Curtis' photograph of Chief Joseph, page 378, what features of their costumes might have served as tribal identifications?

5. The poster, on page 391, for a lecture in Brooklyn by Mark Twain in 1869, could take for granted the fame of his story of a jumping frog and so did not need to mention it; the writer and the frog were already associated in the public mind. Still, the poster presents some interesting problems of interpretation. Did the unknown artist mean to portray Twain as a humorist? If so, what aspects of the illustration contribute to this? What is the effect of portraying Twain with an outsize head, diminutive body, and tiny cap? Is Twain clearly in charge of his "steed" in this picture, or do we feel that the frog has command of the rider?

A House Divided and Restored

1. In an essay, examine the impact of the Civil War on the writers of this period. What different perspectives on the war do you discern among these authors? In your discussion, consider the work of at least two of the following writers: Abraham Lincoln, Robert E. Lee, Walt Whitman, Henry Timrod, and Ambrose Bierce.

2. As the following statements suggest, both Walt Whitman and Mark Twain offered something new to American letters:

> [In *Song of Myself* the poet expresses] an enormous brilliant egotism. . . . The idea of perfect freedom, of the "eligibility" of the self to everything else—the nation, the cosmos, all other selves—this is the valuable illusion created by Whitman's first great poem.
>
> Richard Chase
> (from *Walt Whitman Reconsidered*)

> [Twain's] principal service to the American language . . . lay within the recognized limits of literary prose. Within those limits he was a radical innovator, a prime mover who changed the medium by incorporating in it the syntax, the idioms, and especially the vocabulary of the common life.
>
> Bernard DeVoto
> (from the Introduction to
> *The Portable Mark Twain*)

In an essay, discuss either of these statements in light of the selections by Whitman or Twain you have read in this unit. Be sure to refer to particular passages in the selections.

3. This period is notable for the rise of the local-color movement in literature. As stated on page 341, the local-color movement "formed an important transition between Romanticism and realism. In its close attention to the dialect, customs, and character types of a particular region, local-color writing showed the kind of objective observation of social facts that is typical of realism. But in its treatment of human emotion and motivation, local-color fiction was often sentimental." In what ways do the selections in this unit blend realism and Romanticism? In an essay, discuss the work of two of the following authors: Mark Twain, Bret Harte, Ambrose Bierce.

For Further Reading

For Background on Individual Authors

Whitman

Allan, Gay W., *The Solitary Singer: A Critical Biography of Walt Whitman* (New York University, 1967)

_____, *The New Walt Whitman Handbook* (New York University, 1975)

Kaplan, Justin, *Walt Whitman: A Life* (S&S, 1980)

Pierce, R., ed., *Whitman: A Collection of Critical Essays* (Prentice-Hall, 1962)

Zweig, Paul, *Walt Whitman: The Making of the Poet* (Basic, 1984)

Lincoln

Basler, R., ed., *Abraham Lincoln, His Speeches and Writings* (World Publishing, 1946)

Oates, Stephen, *Abraham Lincoln: The Man Behind the Myths* (Harper & Row, 1984)

Sandburg, Carl, *Abraham Lincoln: The Prairie Years*, 2 vols. (Harcourt Brace Jovanovich, 1926)

_____, *Abraham Lincoln: The War Years*, 4 vols. (Harcourt Brace Jovanovich, 1939)

_____, *Abraham Lincoln: The Prairie Years and the War Years* (Paperbound, Harvest, 1983)

Vidal, Gore, *Lincoln* (Random House, 1984)

Lee

Brooks, William E., *Lee of Virginia: A Biography* (Greenwood, 1975)

Timrod

Parks, Ed Winfield, *Henry Timrod* (Twayne, 1964)

Lanier

De Bellis, Jack, *Sidney Lanier* (Twayne, 1972)

Native Americans

Astrov, Margaret, ed., *The Winged Serpent: American Indian Prose and Poetry* (John Day, 1946)

Hamilton, Charles, ed., *Cry of the Thunderbird: The American Indian's Own Story* (University of Oklahoma, 1950)

Rosenteil, A., *Red and White: Indian Views of the White Man* (Universe Books, 1983)

Sanders, Thomas E. and Walter W. Peek, *Literature of the American Indian* (Macmillan, 1973)

Venderwerth, W. C., *Indian Oratory: A Collection of Famous Speeches* (University of Oklahoma, 1971)

Twain

Budd, Louis J., *Our Mark Twain: The Making of a Public Personality* (University of Pennsylvania, 1983)

Cox, James M., *Mark Twain: The Fate of Humor* (Princeton, 1966)

Hill, Hamlin, *Mark Twain, God's Fool* (Harper & Row, 1973)

Howells, William Dean, *My Mark Twain: Reminiscences and Criticisms* (1910; rpt. Louisiana State University, 1967)

Kaplan, Justin, *Mr. Clemens and Mark Twain* (S&S, 1966)

Smith, Henry N., *Mark Twain: The Development of a Writer* (Harvard, 1962)

Wecter, Dixon, *Sam Clemens of Hannibal* (Houghton Mifflin, 1952)

Harte

Duckett, Margaret, *Mark Twain and Bret Harte* (University of Oklahoma, 1964)

O'Connor, Richard, *Bret Harte* (Little, Brown, 1966)

Stewart, George R., *Bret Harte: Argonaut and Exile* (1931; rpt. AMS Press)

Bierce

Davidson, Cathy N., ed., *Critical Essays on Ambrose Bierce* (Twayne, 1982)

Fatout, Paul, *Ambrose Bierce, the Devil's Lexicographer* (University of Oklahoma Press, 1951)

Genander, M., *Ambrose Bierce* (G. K. Hall, 1971)

For Leisure Reading

Whitman's Poems

"Out of the Cradle Endlessly Rocking," "There Was a Child Went Forth," "When Lilacs Last in the Dooryard Bloom'd," "Passage to India," "Crossing Brooklyn Ferry"

Whitman's Prose

Democratic Vistas, A Backward Glance, Specimen Days

Timrod's Poems

"A Cry to Arms," "The Unknown Dead"

Lanier's Poems

"The Marshes of Glynn," "The Waving of the Corn"

Twain's Prose Works

The Innocents Abroad, Roughing It, The Adventures of Tom Sawyer, A Connecticut Yankee in King Arthur's Court, "The Man That Corrupted Hadleyburg," *The Mysterious Stranger*

Harte's Stories

"The Luck of Roaring Camp," "Tennessee's Partner"

Bierce's Prose Works

"Chickamauga," *The Devil's Dictionary*

REALISM AND NATURALISM
1890–1914

The Bridge, Blackwell's Island (1909) by George Bellows (1882–1925).
Oil on canvas. Bellows, who was fascinated by the construction in
New York, painted this canvas after the bridge was completed.
Toledo Museum of Art, gift of Edward Drummond Libbey

The first Land Run in the Oklahoma Territory took place on April 22, 1889.
Here settlers are shown registering at Orlando.
The Bettmann Archive

An Age of New Forces

In part, life in the United States from 1890 to 1914 was still shaped by forces already in place at the end of the Civil War in 1865. The process of industrialization, first accelerated by the war, continued to transform America ever further away from the simple agricultural economy that Jefferson had praised as the surest base for democracy. Cities, swollen by millions of immigrants to provide labor for new factories and mills, marked the advance of industrialism as they doubled and redoubled in size. The frontier, for nearly three centuries a central fact of American life, was considered closed after the census of 1890. A continental nation was now officially settled. Even the symbols by which Americans knew themselves were changing. When the country celebrated the hundredth anniversary of Jefferson's Declaration of Independence, at the Philadelphia Centennial Exposition of 1876, the Agricultural Building was less interesting to most visitors than Machinery Hall. There, raised on a platform to make it the center of all eyes, a gigantic steam engine moved its enormous pistons to supply power, through a wilderness of cogs and shafts beneath the floor, to 8000 lesser machines, down to a simple candy mixer. An example of centralized power that exerted its force through far-flung tentacles, it seemed a fitting image of the age.

But every such image was quickly surpassed. A still more impressive national celebration, the World's Columbian Exposition in Chicago in 1893 (it was meant to commemorate the four-hundredth anniversary of Columbus' voyage but opened late) not only had more powerful steam engines but an Electricity Building with twelve great dynamos to light and run the huge fair. The historian Henry Adams, a grandson and great-grandson of presidents and immersed from childhood in American political history, felt in the presence of those dynamos the religious awe that is "the natural expression of men before silent and infinite force" and began the study of a new kind of history, of "the economies or developments of force." The dynamo, transmitting an invisible force, seemed "a symbol of infinity" for our age, just as religious symbols had been in earlier times. Yet the historian could not keep pace with technological and scientific change. At still another exposition, in Paris in 1900, Adams learned of the new importance of X-rays, which until then "had played no part whatever in man's consciousness," and heard hints of still more mysterious forces in the atom. With these new forces, he felt, human history had strayed not just into a New World, as in the development of America, but a new universe: "In these seven years [between Chicago in 1893 and Paris in 1900] man had translated himself into a new universe which had no common scale of measurement with the old."

The Electricity Building, World's Columbian Exposition of 1893 by Childe Hassam (1859–1935). Watercolor.
Chicago Historical Society

HENRY JAMES (1843–1916)
Daisy Miller (1878)

WILLIAM DEAN HOWELLS (1837–1920)
The Rise of Silas Lapham (1885)

1893 Chicago World's Fair; first gasoline-powered automobile

STEPHEN CRANE (1871–1900)
Maggie, A Girl of the Streets (1893)

CRANE
The Red Badge of Courage (1895)

The Electricity Building

1895 Motion-picture projector developed

1896 Gold discovered in the Klondike

PAUL LAURENCE DUNBAR (1872–1906)
Lyrics of Lowly Life (1896)

CRANE
"The Open Boat" (1897)

Stephen Crane

1898 Spanish-American War

THEODORE DREISER (1871–1945)
Sister Carrie (1900)

1901 First transatlantic radio communication

JAMES
The Ambassadors (1903)

Paul Laurence Dunbar

1903	Wright brothers make first airplane flight

JACK LONDON (1876–1916)
The Call of the Wild (1903)

LONDON
The Sea-Wolf (1904)

WILLA CATHER (1873–1947)
"The Sculptor's Funeral" (1905)

UPTON SINCLAIR (1878–1968)
The Jungle (1906)

1911	First transcontinental airplane flight

1914	World War I begins

EDGAR LEE MASTERS (1869–1950)
Spoon River Anthology (1915)

Jack London

1917	United States enters World War I

CATHER
My Ántonia (1918)

1918	World War I ends

EDWIN ARLINGTON ROBINSON (1869–1935)
Collected Poems (1922)

Willa Cather

For most Americans, untroubled by Adams' dread of an unknown future, technological change simply meant progress, making the extraordinary soon seem ordinary. The completion of the first transcontinental railroad in 1869 had been celebrated as an historic event; by 1885 there were four transcontinental railroads. The telephone was a novelty at the Philadelphia Exposition of 1876, but by 1900 more than a million were in use in America, linking remote regions through long distance lines. Taking advantage of this new web of communication and transportation, manufacturers could produce standardized goods for a national market. Even American time was standardized as, for the sake of the railroads and business efficiency, dozens of local time zones were reduced to just four across the continent.

Yet the new forces that bound Americans together also, paradoxically, threatened to once again divide them—this time less on sectional than on class lines. An economy integrated by national systems

Hester Street (1905) by George Benjamin Luks (1867–1933). Oil on canvas.

of transportation and distribution was also subject to centralized control. Control of the railroads, of utilities, of the oil, steel, and meat-packing industries, even at times of basic food crops, passed into a few hands, concentrating wealth and power in a way never seen before in the United States. Meanwhile, enormous ghettos of an impoverished underclass mushroomed in city slums amidst municipal corruption. New economic forces had created both unprecedented national prosperity and wider divisions between rich and poor, capital and labor, creditors and debt-ridden farmers, native-born Americans and immigrants who struggled for the same jobs.

Once again, as in the 1830s and 1840s, the relationship between the economic transformation of America and the country's moral condition was in question. And once again reform was in order. The old American yearning for civic virtue and social justice, affronted at every hand by the exploitation and political corruption that flowed from excessive economic power, would create new social forces—national labor movements and unions, farmers' "alliances," "populist" political parties, antitrust laws to prohibit monopolies, regulatory commissions for railroads and utilities and some entire industries—to restore a balance in American society. But reform no longer meant moral persuasion as in the time of the abolitionists. Now, using the new forces of the age, it meant exposure in the public press, government investigations (sometimes of Congress itself), new laws and regulations to control seemingly lawless businesses and industries. Lincoln Steffens' *The Shame of the Cities,* exposing a pattern of corruption in city after city that made partners of criminals and respected businessmen, had a national impact because it was published in a nationally distributed magazine. Jacob Riis, who studied "the

Lincoln Steffens.

Brown Brothers

Jacob Riis (rēs).

National Portrait Gallery, Smithsonian Institution

foul core of New York's slums" for twenty years, made brilliant use of photographs in *How the Other Half Lives* to show human misery that was beyond the reach of words. Photography had become an important force in modern communications. One by one the great new industries were dragged into the glare of public exposure as reformers taught Americans the force of some unfamiliar words: "monopoly," "tycoon," "robber baron," "malefactor of great wealth," and worst of all, "plutocracy"—a ruling class based solely upon wealth. The reformers themselves came to be known by a word new to most Americans; they were the "muckrakers"—those whose unpleasant task it was to rake over the corruption in American society and so expose it to the light.

As the United States became the world's most industrialized nation, it also became, almost unknowingly, a world power. That new status was confirmed in 1898 when a dispute with Spain over Spanish policy in Cuba, then a Spanish possession, grew into the Spanish-American War. Entering with a strange lightheartedness upon a "splendid little war," America in ten brief weeks captured an empire which Spain had acquired over centuries. Part of that empire was in the Far East, and it was a mark of a changed America that its new territories were mostly won by the far-ranging force of the United States Navy, now a modern "steel navy" and an instrument of international power.

If the war itself was exhilarating (there had never been a Fourth of July celebration like the one of 1898, fed by news of one victory after another), the aftermath was sobering. America, itself a former colony, was now an imperialist nation struggling in the Philippines to put down an insurrection by Filipinos who wanted independence and self-government. American reformers, including some of the most respected voices in the land, had still another cause. The newspaper satirist Finley Peter Dunne, speaking through the vernacular of his "Mr. Dooley," observed that " 'tis not more thin two months since [we] larned whether [the Philippines] were islands or canned goods," and already we think we can govern them. Mark Twain, enraged that in the Philippines we were betraying cherished American freedoms, thundered that the stars and stripes should be replaced by the skull and crossbones flag flown by pirates.

It was not without strain that America dealt with the new internal and external forces that accompanied the nation into the twentieth century. Still, the overall mood of the time was positive. Slowly, the most obvious evils of the age (the abuses of child labor, for example, or the worst discriminations against women) gave way to new laws, to education, even to the long-range growth of prosperity—twice the rate of population growth through most of this period. By 1900 violent labor strife had somewhat subsided, and the buccaneers of great fortunes were showing new signs of social responsibility by endowing libraries and universities and medical research. United States foreign policy retreated from its imperialistic excesses and took

Lithograph showing the destruction of the U.S. battleship *Maine* in the harbor of Havana, Cuba, February 15, 1898. This incident raised the cry, "Remember the Maine!"

The Granger Collection

a popular turn when terms were negotiated for America to build the Panama Canal. Most Americans could see progress in society and improving opportunities for their children. From a later vantage point, this would seem an exceptionally happy and confident time, which was cut off abruptly by 1914 and the terrible realities of modern world war. The nation had nevertheless changed profoundly in this brief period. After 1890, America no longer had an internal frontier, a moving line on the map that separated the known and settled from an unknown future; now it was a settled country defined like any other by external borders. By 1914, those borders, in the form of territories and possessions, included islands in the Caribbean and the far Pacific. Although many Americans were not yet ready to acknowledge the fact, the United States was now an international power with worldwide interests, its fate inescapably tied to the fate of a world at war.

Portrait of Professor Henry A. Rowland by Thomas Eakins (1844–1916). Oil on canvas. Shown in the painting are the precision instruments used by Rowland, who was a brilliant physicist.

Literature in an Age of Science

Although they were less evident in everyday life than technological change, new scientific ideas—and a new scientific "attitude"—were no less a force in America in this period. Impressed by constant progress in technology, Americans were ready to believe that the discipline of science could be applied to every aspect of life, from politics and war and the national economy to society and personality and even philosophy and religion. Inevitably, literature was affected by this attitude and became increasingly intermingled with sociology, psychology, "scientific" philosophies, and various economic and social reforms.

Edward Bellamy.
The Bettmann Archive

One result was the sudden popularity of Utopian novels depicting a perfect future society achieved through science. In the most famous of these, Edward Bellamy's *Looking Backward,* citizens of Boston in the year 2000 enjoy the material abundance produced by advanced technology and live happily in a scientifically planned society which has eliminated conflict, competition, inequality, and crime. (Bellamy Clubs, whose members hoped to use the book as a plan of action, quickly sprang up in several cities.) Even William Dean Howells, our foremost spokesman for realism in literature, wrote a Utopian novel in the 1890s. In a variation on the theme, *A Connecticut Yankee in King Arthur's Court,* Mark Twain placed a contemporary American in sixth-century England, where he reinvents modern technology and seeks to replace superstition and ignorance with "the magic of science" and to create a perfect democratic society—nineteenth-century America, that is, without its flaws. Unfortunately, those flaws—both in society and in the Yankee—are beyond the reach of science, and the story turns at the end into an anti-Utopian novel as the Yankee uses modern technology for the last time, to destroy his creation.

But the deepest impact of science upon literature in this period came not from technology and visions of new societies but from radical changes in the natural sciences and their effect upon many areas of thought. The dominant event in this intellectual revolution was the publication in 1859 of Charles Darwin's *The Origin of Species,* which, with *The Descent of Man* in 1871, proposed that the biological species, including mankind, were not fixed at some moment of creation but have evolved over an immense span of time from earlier species. Darwin's views, powerfully reinforced by related discoveries in botany and geology and growing fossil evidence of extinct species, evoked many different responses. For some, evolutionary science was an attack upon the Biblical account of creation and therefore upon religion. For others, it was encouraging evidence that humanity was not just changing but improving, growing toward some undefined perfection.

Evolution made a special impact on the new "social sciences." Some sociologists argued that the evolutionary principle of natural selection, by which the "fittest" of a species adapt to changing conditions and survive, applies equally to human social systems: society, too, was meant to be a struggle "red in tooth and claw" for survival, with dominance going to the "strong." But other social scientists found evolution a powerful support for reform. As one of them observed, "the law of natural selection applies to all the moral history of mankind, as well as the physical. Evil must die ultimately as the weaker element, in the struggle with good."

In literature the response to evolution was no less mixed. The new science influenced not only the general philosophy of life in this period but also the writer's special concern with human character. For most writers, character was now less "free," less self-determined, than

(Left) Hamlin Garland; (top right) Frank Norris; (bottom right) Upton Sinclair.

before; heredity and environment, given new scientific importance by the theory of evolution, became the "determinants" of character, defining its possibilities. At the same time, evolution provided writers with new metaphors, new ways of seeing the social environment in relation to nature.

By 1890, the titles of literary works often indicate that their authors were viewing life primarily in terms of struggle and drawing upon predatory aspects of nature for ways to describe social forces. In his most famous story, Hamlin Garland depicted the plight of the Midwestern farmer in the clutches of the capitalist landowner as being "Under the Lion's Paw." Frank Norris, portraying the process by which California wheat ranchers were being strangled to economic death by the steel tentacles of all-powerful, monopolistic railroads, called his novel *The Octopus.* The brutal oppression of immigrant workers in the Chicago meatpacking industry led Upton Sinclair to write *The Jungle:* for this underclass of victims, life in the most technologically advanced society in the world was as much a primitive struggle for survival as it is for animals in wildest nature. Even writers who did not take this extreme view of society as a predatory state of nature drew readily upon comparisons between the biological evolution of humanity and the present state of American social development. "Our civilization," Theodore Dreiser observed in *Sister Carrie*

(1900), "is still in a middle stage, scarcely beast, in that it is no longer wholly guided by instinct; scarcely human, in that it is not yet wholly guided by reason."

From Realism to Naturalism

One response to the "blind forces" (Dreiser's phrase) that evolutionary science seemed to point to in existence came in the shift from realism to naturalism. By 1890, realism already seemed inadequate to many writers, especially the young. Howells' definition of realism as "nothing more and nothing less than the truthful treatment of material" was little more than a call to accurate observation. It did not indicate how the writer was to penetrate the surface of life—or of human character—to see the principles operating within. Personal experience seemed too limited a ground from which to view those enormous forces that, according to science, govern existence. "My experience," the psychologist William James pointed out, "is what I agree to attend to"—a narrow selection from the millions of possible human experiences at any moment of time. In an age of science, some writers not only welcomed the insights of science but sought to apply them in their own record of experience.

The views of the French novelist Émile Zola were an important influence upon this new scientific attitude in literature. He proposed that the writer must approach human character and society in the same spirit of "scientific investigation" that "the chemist and the physicist" bring to their study of the physical world. For Zola, the "laws" of individual and social development were as fixed as those of a science: "Determinism governs everything." The two principal forces in this all-controlling determinism were, once again, heredity and environment. The writer must study the inherited traits of individual character and the social condition of the time. Together, these elements determine the course of any action, the outcome of any life. Free will or self-determination is mostly an illusion, although chance is granted a role in human affairs. Still, even the effects of chance are obliterated in the inevitable course determined by the interaction of inherited character traits and the social environment.

"Naturalism" remains one of the most troubled and misused words in literary criticism, but to the extent that they subscribed to these supposedly scientific views of life, writers of this period can be called naturalists, although no American writer was consistently and solely naturalistic. Zola's rules for fiction were at once too restrictive and too demanding. In America, at least, in a relatively classless and restlessly mobile society, little could be known of long family histories that would illustrate the heredity of an individual. At the same time, the social environment, although it could be better studied than heredity, proved too complex and rapidly changing to reveal its "laws" in a scientific formulation.

Frank Norris, an avowed follower of Zola's ideas, wrote novels about the opposing forces of economics and nature but could not maintain the objectivity necessary to the "scientific investigation" of his material; and instead of scientific "laws," the novels end with conventional morals saying that good will prevail over evil. Norris tried to deal with heredity (most spectacularly in the case of a young man whose inherited insanity carries him back to a prehuman stage of development as a beast, a wolf), but these efforts are far less impressive than his novelist's sense of character and action. Jack London could achieve a kind of scientific objectivity in "To Build a Fire" (page 483) as he portrayed an anonymous human being in a struggle for his life with hostile nature. But London's novels, which are more explicitly naturalistic, overdramatize the instinctual and the primitive in life at the expense of human significance. Stephen Crane,

Baxter Street Court (22 Baxter Street). Photograph by Jacob Riis (1849–1914).

whose first book, *Maggie, a Girl of the Streets,* is perhaps our best study of the deterministic effects of slum life upon human character, was less naturalistic in his later and more complex work. In "The Open Boat" (page 452), for example, nature is "flatly indifferent" to human fate, but the center of the story is the human community and mutual concern that develop among the survivors—far different from the naturalistic view of social systems. Theodore Dreiser, whose novels do more than any others to link the current state of social development to biological evolution, was regularly carried beyond naturalistic views by his strong sense of the great mysteries in human existence.

The literary achievements of naturalism are therefore mixed. No doubt its emphasis upon underlying principles in human experience was a useful corrective to a superficial understanding of literary realism. Its appeal to the methods of science was also important in a time when writers needed a means of grasping strange new views of nature, society, and human nature. But Henry James, whose novels in the period from 1890 to 1914 make him the dominant literary figure of the time, was largely untouched by naturalism, even though he was closely familiar with French literary theory and fully aware of the limitations of individual experience that his brother William had pointed out. Product of an earlier age, James continued the realistic tradition of his time, steadily deepening his imaginative grasp of experience and of human psychology. As a literary legacy, naturalism has exerted a powerful influence upon twentieth-century literature. That legacy has nevertheless been tempered by a view that James argued in his criticism and affirmed in his fiction: reality in literature is the product of the writer's individual perceptions rather than of any theory of the world.

Review

1. What date marked the official close of the American frontier?
2. Why was the steam engine considered a fitting image of the age?
3. What were two technological changes that bound Americans more closely together in the last decade of the nineteenth century?
4. How were Americans divided by the new economic forces?
5. Who were the muckrakers?
6. Explain the relationship between the Utopian novel and new scientific ideas of the age.
7. What was the most significant impact of science upon literature?
8. According to the naturalists, what two forces governed the individual life?
9. Name some American writers often classified as naturalists.
10. How is the work of Henry James different from that of the naturalists?

STEPHEN CRANE
1871–1900

Stephen Crane. Photograph.
The Bettmann Archive

The drama and intensity of Crane's brief life make it resemble his best stories. This resemblance is appropriate in a writer who often used life to test literature, proving the truth of his intuitions by the actualities of experience. When he wrote in *The Red Badge of Courage* of a Civil War battle fought before he was born, Crane had to depend upon impressions drawn from Mathew Brady's superb photographs of the war and from the stories of veterans. Years later, when he witnessed battle firsthand as a war correspondent in Greece, he was relieved to discover that his novel was "all right." Crane had a

journalist's need to see for himself, to ground his writing in observed fact. This zest for experience inevitably drew him to the most violent of human activities, including wars and revolutions. As a correspondent he was reckless of his personal safety, as if his observations must be tested against the threat of death. Yet what finally counted was less the facts than his impressions: they were the true experience. In factual circumstances the Greco-Turkish War did not resemble the American Civil War of *The Red Badge.* But what Crane was able to test there was the accuracy of his imagination, the impressions he had recorded in his novel of how battle would look, sound, and above all *feel* to him.

Crane, the youngest of fourteen children of a Methodist minister, lived in several New Jersey towns during his childhood. The economic circumstances of this large family were restricted, and they became more so after the early death of the father. Crane's earliest ambition was to be a soldier, and for a time he attended a military academy. He also gained apprentice experience in journalism by serving as a cub reporter for a news agency operated by an older brother. By the time he reached college age he had a new ambition—to become a professional baseball player. Beyond baseball he had little interest in college, however, and after a term each at Lafayette College and Syracuse University, he seemed glad to leave.

Crane's first full-time job was as a reporter for a New York newspaper. He lost this by writing an article about a labor demonstration that harshly criticized middle-class attitudes toward the poor. Thereafter he existed precariously as a free-lance writer, contributing whatever items he could to newspapers. But he was also gathering valuable material. In college he had written the first draft of a story about slum life. Now he learned firsthand how the world looked to those who lived that life in the saloons and police stations and Bowery flophouses of New York. Rewritten, *Maggie, A Girl of the Streets* (1893) was the first naturalistic American novel, an unflinching exposure of urban squalor. Such material—so different from the sentimentalized portraits in Bret Harte's stories—was too shocking for the publishers, and Crane had to issue his book (under a pseudonym) on borrowed money. But it brought him recognition from such writers as Hamlin Garland and William Dean Howells, and his career was launched. Two years later, in 1895, he published *The Red Badge of Courage* and was immediately hailed as an original genius who, Howells said, had sprung "fully armed" into literature.

Fame brought journalistic assignments as a correspondent, allowing Crane to travel for that on-the-spot experience he required. Travels in the West and in Mexico (where he was nearly killed) furnished material for several later stories. Having joined an ill-advised expedition to supply arms to Cuban revolutionaries, he was shipwrecked off the Florida coast and spent a day and night at sea in a tiny dinghy. This experience became the basis of "The Open Boat," one of his finest stories. After this he reported the Greco-Turkish War and then settled for a time in England, where Henry James and Joseph Conrad were among his literary friends and where Crane, despite great financial pressure, wrote some of his best stories. But too much war and exposure had taken their toll. He was already gravely ill with tuberculosis, and he died before his twenty-ninth birthday.

Crane's fiction does not show that complex development of character we expect in novels. His strength, instead, is in reporting honestly the emotions aroused by extreme stress, often in characters who do not have names. "I understand," he once wrote, "that a man is born into the world with his own pair of eyes, and he is not at all responsible for his vision—he is merely responsible for his personal honesty. To keep close to this personal honesty is my supreme ambition." Crane's own vision showed him a world that is without higher purpose, a neutral universe in which human life is meaningful only to each individual. That perception is always behind Crane's work, waiting to shock those who, like the correspondent in "The Open Boat," wish that nature cared for our welfare as we care for it ourselves, wish at least for justice if not for mercy. But, to Crane, life is not just. Crane shared with other naturalistic writers an awareness of the scientific ideas of his time, especially of the influence of the environment in determining destiny. But he was more interested, after all, in those persistent illu-

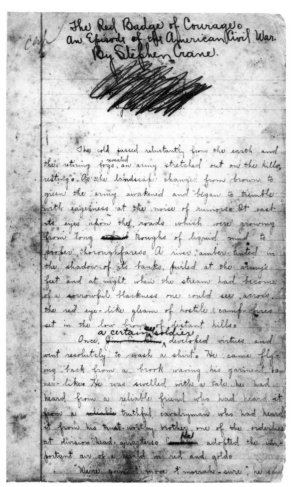

Manuscript page of *The Red Badge of Courage.*
University of Virginia Library

sions by which human beings assert their subjective desires for meaning in a meaningless universe. If those illusions are often pathetic, they are also essential to human dignity, and Crane's best stories explore them brilliantly.

The Open Boat

A Tale Intended to Be After the Fact: Being the Experience of Four Men from the Sunk Steamer Commodore.

Northeaster (1895) by Winslow Homer (1836–1910). Oil on canvas.
Metropolitan Museum of Art, gift of George A. Hearn

I

None of them knew the color of the sky. Their eyes glanced level, and were fastened upon the waves that swept toward them. These waves were of the hue of slate, save for the tops, which were of foaming white, and all of the men knew the colors of the sea. The horizon narrowed and widened, and dipped and rose, and at all times its edge was jagged with waves that seemed thrust up in points like rocks.

Many a man ought to have a bathtub larger than the boat which here rode upon the sea. These waves were most wrongfully and barbarously abrupt and tall, and each froth top was a problem in small-boat navigation.

The cook squatted in the bottom, and looked with both eyes at the six inches of gunwale which separated him from the ocean. His sleeves were rolled over his fat forearms, and the two flaps of his unbuttoned vest dangled as he bent to bail out the boat. Often he said, "Gawd! that was a narrow clip." As he remarked it he invariably gazed eastward over the broken sea.

The oiler, steering with one of the two oars in the boat, sometimes raised himself suddenly to keep clear of water that swirled in over the stern. It was a thin little oar, and it seemed often ready to snap.

The correspondent, pulling at the other oar, watched the waves and wondered why he was there.

The injured captain, lying in the bow, was at this time buried in that profound dejection and indifference which comes, temporarily at least, to even the bravest and most enduring when, willy-nilly, the firm fails, the army loses, the ship goes down. The mind of the master of a vessel is rooted deep in the timbers of her, though he command for a day or a decade; and this captain had on him the stern impression of a scene in the grays of dawn of seven turned faces, and later a stump of a topmast with a white ball on it, that slashed to and fro at the waves, went low and lower, and down. Thereafter there was something strange in his voice. Although steady, it was deep with mourning, and of a quality beyond oration or tears.

"Keep 'er a little more south, Billie," said he.

"A little more south, sir," said the oiler in the stern.

A seat in this boat was not unlike a seat upon a bucking bronco, and, by the same token, a bronco is not much smaller. The craft pranced and reared and plunged like an animal. As each wave came, and she rose for it, she seemed like a horse making at a fence outrageously high. The manner of her scramble over these walls of water is a mystic thing, and, moreover, at the top of them were ordinarily these problems in white water, the foam racing down from the summit of each wave, requiring a new leap, and a leap from the air. Then, after scornfully bumping a crest, she would slide and race and splash down a long incline, and arrive bobbing and nodding in front of the next menace.

A singular disadvantage of the sea lies in the fact that, after successfully surmounting one wave, you discover that there is another behind it, just as important and just as nervously anxious to do something effective in the way of swamping boats. In a ten-foot dinghy one can get an idea of the resources of the sea in the line of waves that is not probable to the average experience, which is never at sea in a dinghy. As each slaty wall of water approached, it shut all else from the view of the men in the boat, and it was not difficult to imagine that this particular wave was the final outburst of the ocean, the last effort of the grim water. There was a terrible grace in the move of the waves, and they came in silence, save for the snarling of the crests.

In the wan light the faces of the men must have been gray. Their eyes must have glinted in strange ways as they gazed steadily astern. Viewed from a balcony, the whole thing would, doubtless, have been weirdly picturesque. But the men in the boat had no time to see it, and if they had had leisure, there were other things to occupy their minds. The sun swung steadily up the sky, and they knew it was broad day because the color of the sea changed from slate to emerald green streaked with amber lights, and the foam was like tumbling snow. The process of the breaking day was unknown to them. They were aware only of this effect upon the color of the waves that rolled toward them.

In disjointed sentences the cook and the correspondent argued as to the difference between a lifesaving station and a house of ref-

uge. The cook had said: "There's a house of refuge just north of the Mosquito Inlet Light, and as soon as they see us they'll come off in their boat and pick us up."

"As soon as who see us?" said the correspondent.

"The crew," said the cook.

"Houses of refuge don't have crews," said the correspondent. "As I understand them, they are only places where clothes and grub are stored for the benefit of shipwrecked people. They don't carry crews."

"Oh, yes, they do," said the cook.

"No, they don't," said the correspondent.

"Well, we're not there yet, anyhow," said the oiler in the stern.

"Well," said the cook, "perhaps it's not a house of refuge that I'm thinking of as being near Mosquito Inlet Light; perhaps it's a lifesaving station."

"We're not there yet," said the oiler in the stern.

II

As the boat bounced from the top of each wave the wind tore through the hair of the hatless men, and as the craft plopped her stern down again the spray slashed past them. The crest of each of these waves was a hill, from the top of which the men surveyed for a moment a broad, tumultuous expanse, shining and wind-riven. It was probably splendid, it was probably glorious, this play of the free sea, wild with lights of emerald and white and amber.

"Bully good thing it's an onshore wind," said the cook. "If not, where would we be? Wouldn't have a show."

"That's right," said the correspondent.

The busy oiler nodded his assent.

Then the captain, in the bow, chuckled in a way that expressed humor, contempt, tragedy, all in one. "Do you think we've got much of a show now, boys?" said he.

Whereupon the three were silent, save for a trifle of hemming and hawing. To express any particular optimism at this time they felt to be childish and stupid, but they all doubtless possessed this sense of the situation in their minds. A young man thinks doggedly at such times. On the other hand, the ethics of their condition was decidedly against any open suggestion of hopelessness. So they were silent.

"Oh, well," said the captain, soothing his children, "we'll get ashore all right."

But there was that in his tone which made them think; so the oiler quoth, "Yes! if this wind holds."

The cook was bailing. "Yes! if we don't catch hell in the surf."

Canton-flannel[1] gulls flew near and far. Sometimes they sat down on the sea, near patches of brown seaweed that rolled over the waves with a movement like carpets on a line in a gale. The birds sat comfortably in groups, and they were envied by some in the dinghy, for the wrath of the sea was no more to them than it was to a covey of prairie chickens a thousand miles inland. Often they came very close and stared at the men with black, bead-like eyes. At these times they were uncanny and sinister in their unblinking scrutiny, and the men hooted angrily at them, telling them to be gone. One came, and evidently decided to alight on the top of the captain's head. The bird flew parallel to the boat, and did not circle, but made short sidelong jumps in the air in chicken fashion. His black eyes were wistfully fixed upon the captain's head. "Ugly brute," said the oiler to the bird. "You look as if you were made with a jackknife." The cook and the correspondent swore darkly at the creature. The captain naturally wished to knock it away with the end of the heavy painter,[2] but he did not dare do it, because anything resembling an emphatic gesture would have capsized this freighted boat; and so, with his open hand, the captain gently and carefully waved the gull away. After it had been discouraged from the pursuit the captain breathed easier on account of his hair, and others breathed easier because the bird struck their minds at this time as being somehow gruesome and ominous.

In the meantime the oiler and the correspondent rowed; and also they rowed. They sat together in the same seat, and each rowed an oar. Then the oiler took both oars; then the correspondent took both oars; then the oiler; then the correspondent. They rowed and they rowed. The very ticklish part of the business was when the time came for the reclining one in the stern to take his turn at the oars. By the very last star of truth, it is easier to steal eggs from under a hen than it was to change seats in the dinghy. First the man in the stern slid his hand along the thwart and moved with care, as if he were of Sèvres.[3] Then the man in the rowing seat slid his hand along the other thwart. It was all done with the most extraordinary care. As the two sidled past each other, the whole party kept watchful eyes on the coming wave, and the captain cried: "Look out, now! Steady, there!"

The brown mats of seaweed that appeared from time to time were like islands, bits of earth. They were traveling, apparently, neither one way nor the other. They were, to all intents, stationary. They informed the men in the boat that it was making progress slowly toward the land.

The captain, rearing cautiously in the bow after the dinghy soared on a great swell, said that he had seen the lighthouse at Mosquito Inlet. Presently the cook remarked that he had seen it. The correspondent was at the oars then, and for some reason he too wished to look at the lighthouse; but his back was toward the far shore, and the waves were important, and for some time he could not seize an opportunity to turn his head. But at last there came a wave more gentle than the others, and when at the crest of it he swiftly scoured the western horizon.

"See it?" said the captain.

---

1. **canton-flannel:** cotton flannel.
2. **painter:** the bow or rope of a boat.

3. **Sèvres** (sĕvrə): the famous center of porcelain and ceramics in France.

"No," said the correspondent, slowly; "I didn't see anything."

"Look again," said the captain. He pointed. "It's exactly in that direction."

At the top of another wave the correspondent did as he was bid, and this time his eyes chanced on a small, still thing on the edge of the swaying horizon. It was precisely like the point of a pin. It took an anxious eye to find a lighthouse so tiny.

"Think we'll make it, Captain?"

"If this wind holds and the boat don't swamp, we can't do much else," said the captain.

The little boat, lifted by each towering sea and splashed viciously by the crests, made progress that in the absence of seaweed was not apparent to those in her. She seemed just a wee thing wallowing miraculously, top up, at the mercy of five oceans. Occasionally a great spread of water, like white flames, swarmed into her.

"Bail her, cook," said the captain, serenely.

"All right, Captain," said the cheerful cook.

III

It would be difficult to describe the subtle brotherhood of men that was here established on the seas. No one said that it was so. No one mentioned it. But it dwelt in the boat, and each man felt it warm him. They were a captain, an oiler, a cook, and a correspondent, and they were friends—friends in a more curiously ironbound degree than may be common. The hurt captain, lying against the water jar in the bow, spoke always in a low voice and calmly; but he could never command a more ready and swiftly obedient crew than the motley three of the dinghy. It was more than a mere recognition of what was best for the common safety. There was surely in it a quality that was personal and heartfelt. And after this devotion to the commander of the boat, there was this comradeship, that the correspondent, for instance, who had been taught to be cynical of

men, knew even at the time was the best experience of his life. But no one said it was so. No one mentioned it.

"I wish we had a sail," remarked the captain. "We might try my overcoat on the end of an oar, and give you two boys a chance to rest." So the cook and the correspondent held the mast and spread wide the overcoat; the oiler steered; and the little boat made good way with her new rig. Sometimes the oiler had to scull sharply to keep a sea from breaking into the boat, but otherwise sailing was a success.

Meanwhile the lighthouse had been growing slowly larger. It had now almost assumed color, and appeared like a little gray shadow on the sky. The man at the oars could not be prevented from turning his head rather often to try for a glimpse of this little gray shadow.

At last, from the top of each wave, the men in the tossing boat could see land. Even as the lighthouse was an upright shadow on the sky, this land seemed but a long black shadow on the sea. It certainly was thinner than paper. "We must be about opposite New Smyrna,"[4] said the cook, who had coasted this shore often in schooners. "Captain, by the way, I believe they abandoned that lifesaving station there about a year ago."

"Did they?" said the captain.

The wind slowly died away. The cook and the correspondent were not now obliged to slave in order to hold high the oar; but the waves continued their old impetuous swooping at the dinghy, and the little craft, no longer under way, struggled woundily over them. The oiler or the correspondent took the oars again.

Shipwrecks are apropos of nothing. If men could only train for them and have them occur when the men had reached pink condition, there would be less drowning at sea. Of the four in the dinghy none had slept any time worth mentioning for two days and two nights previous to embarking in the dinghy, and in the excitement of clambering about the deck

4. **New Smyrna:** New Smyrna Beach, an Atlantic coast city of Florida, about fifteen miles south of Daytona Beach.

of a foundering ship they had also forgotten to eat heartily.

For these reasons, and for others, neither the oiler nor the correspondent was fond of rowing at this time. The correspondent wondered ingenuously how in the name of all that was sane could there be people who thought it amusing to row a boat. It was not an amusement; it was a diabolical punishment, and even a genius of mental aberrations could never conclude that it was anything but a horror to the muscles and a crime against the back. He mentioned to the boat in general how the amusement of rowing struck him, and the weary-faced oiler smiled in full sympathy. Previously to the foundering, by the way, the oiler had worked double watch in the engine room of the ship.

"Take her easy now, boys," said the captain. "Don't spend yourselves. If we have to run a surf you'll need all your strength, because we'll sure have to swim for it. Take your time."

Slowly the land arose from the sea. From a black line it became a line of black and a line of white—trees and sand. Finally the captain said that he could make out a house on the shore. "That's the house of refuge, sure," said the cook. "They'll see us before long, and come out after us."

The distant lighthouse reared high. "The keeper ought to be able to make us out now, if he's looking through a glass," said the captain. "He'll notify the lifesaving people."

"None of those other boats could have got ashore to give word of the wreck," said the oiler, in a low voice, "else the lifeboat would be out hunting us."

Slowly and beautifully the land loomed out of the sea. The wind came again. It had veered from the northeast to the southeast. Finally a new sound struck the ears of the men in the boat. It was the low thunder of the surf on the shore. "We'll never be able to make the lighthouse now," said the captain. "Swing her head a little more north, Billie."

"A little more north, sir," said the oiler.

Whereupon the little boat turned her nose once more down the wind, and all but the oarsman watched the shore grow. Under the influence of this expansion, doubt and direful apprehension were leaving the minds of the men. The management of the boat was still most absorbing, but it could not prevent a quiet cheerfulness. In an hour, perhaps, they would be ashore.

Their backbones had become thoroughly used to balancing in the boat, and they now rode this wild colt of a dinghy like circus men. The correspondent thought that he had been drenched to the skin, but happening to feel in the top pocket of his coat, he found therein eight cigars. Four of them were soaked with sea water; four were perfectly scatheless. After a search, somebody produced three dry matches; and thereupon the four waifs rode in their little boat and, with an assurance of an impending rescue shining in their eyes, puffed at the big cigars, and judged well and ill of all men. Everybody took a drink of water.

IV

"Cook," remarked the captain, "there don't seem to be any signs of life about your house of refuge."

"No," replied the cook. "Funny they don't see us!"

A broad stretch of lowly coast lay before the eyes of the men. It was of low dunes topped with dark vegetation. The roar of the surf was plain, and sometimes they could see the white lip of a wave as it spun up the beach. A tiny house was blocked out black upon the sky. Southward, the slim lighthouse lifted its little gray length.

Tide, wind, and waves were swinging the dinghy northward. "Funny they don't see us," said the men.

The surf's roar was here dulled, but its tone was nevertheless thunderous and mighty. As the boat swam over the great rollers the men sat listening to this roar. "We'll swamp sure," said everybody.

It is fair to say here that there was not a lifesaving station within twenty miles in either direction; but the men did not know this fact, and in consequence they made dark and opprobrious[5] remarks concerning the eyesight of the nation's lifesavers. Four scowling men sat in the dinghy, and surpassed records in the invention of epithets.

"Funny they don't see us."

The lightheartedness of a former time had completely faded. To their sharpened minds it was easy to conjure pictures of all kinds of incompetency and blindness and, indeed, cowardice. There was the shore of the populous land, and it was bitter and bitter to them that from it came no sign.

"Well," said the captain, ultimately, "I suppose we'll have to make a try for ourselves. If we stay out here too long, we'll none of us have strength left to swim after the boat swamps."

And so the oiler, who was at the oars, turned the boat straight for the shore. There was a sudden tightening of muscles. There was some thinking.

"If we don't all get ashore," said the captain—"if we don't all get ashore, I suppose you fellows know where to send news of my finish?"

They then briefly exchanged some addresses and admonitions. As for the reflections of the men, there was a great deal of rage in them. Perchance they might be formulated thus: "If I am going to be drowned—if I am going to be drowned—if I am going to be drowned, why, in the name of the seven mad gods[6] who rule the sea, was I allowed to come thus far and contemplate sand and trees? Was I brought here merely to have my nose dragged away as I was about to nibble the sacred cheese of life? It is preposterous! If this old ninny-woman, Fate, cannot do better than this, she should be deprived of the management of men's fortunes. She is an old hen who knows not her intention. If she has decided to drown me, why did she not do it in the beginning, and save me all this trouble? The whole affair is absurd.—But no; she cannot mean to drown me. She dare not drown me. She cannot drown me. Not after all this work!" Afterward the man might have had an impulse to shake his fist at the clouds. "Just you drown me, now, and then hear what I call you!"

The billows that came at this time were more formidable. They seemed always just about to break and roll over the little boat in a turmoil of foam. There was a preparatory and long growl in the speech of them. No mind unused to the sea would have concluded that the dinghy could ascend these sheer heights in time. The shore was still afar. The oiler was a wily surfman. "Boys," he said swiftly, "she won't live three minutes more, and we're too far out to swim. Shall I take her to sea again, Captain?"

"Yes; go ahead!" said the captain.

This oiler, by a series of quick miracles and fast and steady oarsmanship, turned the boat in the middle of the surf and took her safely to sea again.

There was a considerable silence as the boat bumped over the furrowed sea to deeper water. Then somebody in gloom spoke: "Well, anyhow, they must have seen us from the shore by now."

The gulls went in slanting flight up the wind toward the gray, desolate east. A squall, marked by dingy clouds, and clouds brick-red, like smoke from a burning building, appeared from the southeast.

"What do you think of those lifesaving people? Ain't they peaches?"

"Funny they haven't seen us."

"Maybe they think we're out here for sport! Maybe they think we're fishin'. Maybe they think we're fools."

It was a long afternoon. A changed tide tried to force them southward, but wind and wave said northward. Far ahead, where coastline, sea, and sky formed their mighty angle, there were little dots which seemed to indicate a city on the shore.

5. **opprobrious** (ə-prō′brē-əs): contemptuously scornful.
6. **seven mad gods:** a reference to the gods of ancient Greece; here, implying fate.

"St. Augustine?"[7]

The captain shook his head. "Too near Mosquito Inlet."

And the oiler rowed, and then the correspondent rowed; then the oiler rowed. It was a weary business. The human back can become the seat of more aches and pains than are registered in books for the composite anatomy of a regiment. It is a limited area, but it can become the theater of innumerable muscular conflicts, tangles, wrenches, knots, and other comforts.

"Did you ever like to row, Billie?" asked the correspondent.

"No," said the oiler; "hang it!"

When one exchanged the rowing seat for a place in the bottom of the boat, he suffered a bodily depression that caused him to be careless of everything save an obligation to wiggle one finger. There was cold sea water swashing to and fro in the boat, and he lay in it. His head, pillowed on a thwart, was within an inch of the swirl of a wave-crest, and sometimes a particularly obstreperous sea came inboard and drenched him once more. But these matters did not annoy him. It is almost certain that if the boat had capsized he would have tumbled comfortably out upon the ocean as if he felt sure that it was a great, soft mattress.

"Look! There's a man on the shore!"

"Where?"

"There! See 'im? See 'im?"

"Yes, sure! He's walking along."

"Now he's stopped. Look! He's facing us!"

"He's waving at us!"

"So he is! By thunder!"

"Ah, now we're all right! Now we're all right! There'll be a boat out here for us in half an hour."

"He's going on. He's running. He's going up to that house there."

The remote beach seemed lower than the sea, and it required a searching glance to discern the little black figure. The captain saw a floating stick, and they rowed to it. A bath towel was by some weird chance in the boat, and tying this on the stick, the captain waved it. The oarsman did not dare turn his head, so he was obliged to ask questions.

"What's he doing now?"

"He's standing still again. He's looking, I think.—There he goes again—toward the house.—Now he's stopped again."

"Is he waving at us?"

"No, not now; he was, though."

"Look! There comes another man!"

"He's running."

"Look at him go, would you!"

"Why, he's on a bicycle. Now he's met the other man. They're both waving at us. Look!"

"There comes something up the beach."

"What the devil is that thing?"

"Why, it looks like a boat."

"Why, certainly, it's a boat."

"No; it's on wheels."

"Yes, so it is. Well, that must be the lifeboat. They drag them along shore on a wagon."

"That's the lifeboat, sure."

"No, by——, it's—it's an omnibus."

"I tell you it's a lifeboat."

"It is not! It's an omnibus. I can see it plain. See? One of these big hotel omnibuses."

"By thunder, you're right. It's an omnibus, sure as fate. What do you suppose they are doing with an omnibus? Maybe they are going around collecting the life crew, hey?"

"That's it, likely. Look! There's a fellow waving a little black flag. He's standing on the steps of the omnibus. There come those other two fellows. Now they're all talking together. Look at the fellow with the flag. Maybe he ain't waving it!"

"That ain't a flag, is it? That's his coat. Why, certainly, that's his coat."

"So it is; it's his coat. He's taken it off and is waving it around his head. But would you look at him swing it!"

"Oh, say, there isn't any lifesaving station there. That's just a winter-resort hotel omnibus that has brought over some of the boarders to see us drown."

---

7. **St. Augustine:** a city sixty-five miles north of New Smyrna Beach, on Florida's northeastern Atlantic coast.

"What's that idiot with the coat mean? What's he signaling, anyhow?"

"It looks as if he were trying to tell us to go north. There must be a lifesaving station up there."

"No; he thinks we're fishing. Just giving us a merry hand. See? Ah, there, Willie!"

"Well, I wish I could make something out of those signals. What do you suppose he means?"

"He don't mean anything; he's just playing."

"Well, if he'd just signal us to try the surf again, or to go to sea and wait, or go north, or go south, there would be some reason in it. But look at him! He just stands there and keeps his coat revolving like a wheel. The ass!"

"There come more people."

"Now there's quite a mob. Look! Isn't that a boat?"

"Where? Oh, I see where you mean. No, that's no boat."

"That fellow is still waving his coat."

"He must think we like to see him do that. Why don't he quit it? It don't mean anything."

"I don't know. I think he is trying to make us go north. It must be that there's a lifesaving station there somewhere."

"Say, he ain't tired yet. Look at 'im wave!"

"Wonder how long he can keep that up. He's been revolving his coat ever since he caught sight of us. He's an idiot. Why aren't they getting men to bring a boat out? A fishing boat—one of those big yawls—could come out here all right. Why don't he do something?"

"Oh, it's all right now."

"They'll have a boat out here for us in less than no time, now that they've seen us."

A faint yellow tone came into the sky over the low land. The shadows on the sea slowly deepened. The wind bore coldness with it, and the men began to shiver.

"Holy smoke!" said one, allowing his voice to express his impious mood, "if we keep on monkeying out here! If we've got to flounder out here all night!"

"Oh, we'll never have to stay here all night! Don't you worry. They've seen us now, and it won't be long before they'll come chasing out after us."

The shore grew dusky. The man waving a coat blended gradually into this gloom, and it swallowed in the same manner the omnibus and the group of people. The spray, when it dashed uproariously over the side, made the voyagers shrink and swear like men who were being branded.

"I'd like to catch the chump who waved the coat. I feel like socking him one, just for luck."

"Why? What did he do?"

"Oh, nothing, but then he seemed so cheerful."

In the meantime the oiler rowed, and then the correspondent rowed, and then the oiler rowed. Gray-faced and bowed forward, they mechanically, turn by turn, plied the leaden oars. The form of the lighthouse had vanished from the southern horizon, but finally a pale star appeared, just lifting from the sea. The streaked saffron in the west passed before the all-merging darkness, and the sea to the east was black. The land had vanished, and was expressed only by the low and drear thunder of the surf.

"If I am going to be drowned—if I am going to be drowned—if I am going to be drowned, why, in the name of the seven mad gods who rule the sea, was I allowed to come thus far and contemplate sand and trees? Was I brought here merely to have my nose dragged away as I was about to nibble the sacred cheese of life?"

The patient captain, drooped over the water jar, was sometimes obliged to speak to the oarsman.

"Keep her head up! Keep her head up!"

"Keep her head up, sir." The voices were weary and low.

This was surely a quiet evening. All save the oarsman lay heavily and listlessly in the boat's bottom. As for him, his eyes were just capable of noting the tall black waves that swept forward in a most sinister silence, save for an occasional subdued growl of a crest.

The cook's head was on a thwart, and he

looked without interest at the water under his nose. He was deep in other scenes. Finally he spoke. "Billie," he murmured dreamfully, "what kind of pie do you like best?"

V

"Pie!" said the oiler and the correspondent, agitatedly. "Don't talk about those things, blast you!"

"Well," said the cook, "I was just thinking about ham sandwiches, and——"

A night on the sea in an open boat is a long night. As darkness settled finally, the shine of the light, lifting from the sea in the south, changed to full gold. On the northern horizon a new light appeared, a small bluish gleam on the edge of the waters. These two lights were the furniture of the world. Otherwise there was nothing but waves.

Two men huddled in the stern, and distances were so magnificent in the dinghy that the rower was enabled to keep his feet partly warm by thrusting them under his companions. Their legs indeed extended far under the rowing seat until they touched the feet of the captain forward. Sometimes, despite the efforts of the tired oarsman, a wave came piling into the boat, an icy wave of the night, and the chilling water soaked them anew. They would twist their bodies for a moment and groan, and sleep the dead sleep once more, while the water in the boat gurgled about them as the craft rocked.

The plan of the oiler and the correspondent was for one to row until he lost the ability, and then arouse the other from his sea-water couch in the bottom of the boat.

The oiler plied the oars until his head drooped forward and the overpowering sleep blinded him; and he rowed yet afterward. Then he touched a man in the bottom of the boat, and called his name. "Will you spell me for a little while?" he said meekly.

"Sure, Billie," said the correspondent, awaking and dragging himself to a sitting position. They exchanged places carefully, and the oiler, cuddling down in the sea water at the cook's side, seemed to go to sleep instantly.

The particular violence of the sea had ceased. The waves came without snarling. The obligation of the man at the oars was to keep the boat headed so that the tilt of the rollers would not capsize her, and to preserve her from filling when the crests rushed past. The black waves were silent and hard to be seen in the darkness. Often one was almost upon the boat before the oarsman was aware.

In a low voice the correspondent addressed the captain. He was not sure that the captain was awake, although this iron man seemed to be always awake. "Captain, shall I keep her making for that light north, sir?"

The same steady voice answered him. "Yes. Keep it about two points off the port bow."

The cook had tied a life belt around himself in order to get even the warmth which this clumsy cork contrivance could donate, and he seemed almost stovelike when a rower, whose teeth invariably chattered wildly as soon as he ceased his labor, dropped down to sleep.

The correspondent, as he rowed, looked down at the two men sleeping underfoot. The cook's arm was around the oiler's shoulders, and, with their fragmentary clothing and haggard faces, they were the babes of the sea—a grotesque rendering of the old babes in the wood.

Later he must have grown stupid at his work, for suddenly there was a growling of water, and a crest came with a roar and a swash into the boat, and it was a wonder that it did not set the cook afloat in his life belt. The cook continued to sleep, but the oiler sat up, blinking his eyes and shaking, with the new cold.

"Oh, I'm awful sorry, Billie," said the correspondent, contritely.

"That's all right, old boy," said the oiler, and lay down again and was asleep.

Presently it seemed that even the captain dozed, and the correspondent thought that he was the one man afloat on all the oceans. The wind had a voice as it came over the waves, and it was sadder than the end.

There was a long, loud swishing astern of the boat, and a gleaming trail of phosphorescence, like blue flame, was furrowed on the black waters. It might have been made by a monstrous knife.

Then there came a stillness, while the correspondent breathed with the open mouth and looked at the sea.

Suddenly there was another swish and another long flash of bluish light, and this time it was alongside the boat, and might almost have been reached with an oar. The correspondent saw an enormous fin speed like a shadow through the water, hurling the crystalline spray and leaving the long glowing trail.

The correspondent looked over his shoulder at the captain. His face was hidden, and he seemed to be asleep. He looked at the babes of the sea. They certainly were asleep. So, being bereft of sympathy, he leaned a little way to one side and swore softly into the sea.

But the thing did not then leave the vicinity of the boat. Ahead or astern, on one side or the other, at intervals long or short, fled the long sparkling streak, and there was to be heard the *whiroo* of the dark fin. The speed and power of the thing was greatly to be admired. It cut the water like a gigantic and keen projectile.

The presence of this biding thing did not affect the man with the same horror that it would if he had been a picnicker. He simply looked at the sea dully and swore in an undertone.

Nevertheless, it is true that he did not wish to be alone with the thing. He wished one of his companions to awake by chance and keep him company with it. But the captain hung motionless over the water jar, and the oiler and the cook in the bottom of the boat were plunged in slumber.

VI

"If I am going to be drowned—if I am going to be drowned—if I am going to be drowned, why, in the name of the seven mad gods who rule the sea, was I allowed to come thus far and contemplate sand and trees?"

During this dismal night, it may be remarked that a man would conclude that it was really the intention of the seven mad gods to drown him, despite the abominable injustice of it. For it was certainly an abominable injustice to drown a man who had worked so hard, so hard. The man felt it would be a crime most unnatural. Other people had drowned at sea since galleys swarmed with painted sails, but still——

When it occurs to a man that nature does not regard him as important, and that she feels she would not maim the universe by disposing of him, he at first wishes to throw bricks at the temple, and he hates deeply the fact that there are no bricks and no temples. Any visible expression of nature would surely be pelleted with his jeers.

Then, if there be no tangible thing to hoot, he feels, perhaps, the desire to confront a personification and indulge in pleas, bowed to one knee, and with hands supplicant, saying, "Yes, but I love myself."

A high cold star on a winter's night is the word he feels that she says to him. Thereafter he knows the pathos of his situation.

The men in the dinghy had not discussed these matters, but each had, no doubt, reflected upon them in silence and according to his mind. There was seldom any expression upon their faces save the general one of complete weariness. Speech was devoted to the business of the boat.

To chime the notes of his emotion, a verse mysteriously entered the correspondent's head. He had even forgotten that he had forgotten this verse, but it suddenly was in his mind.

A soldier of the Legion[8] lay dying in Algiers;
There was lack of woman's nursing, there
    was dearth of woman's tears;
But a comrade stood beside him, and he
    took that comrade's hand,

8. **Legion:** the French Foreign Legion.

*And he said, "I never more shall see my
own, my native land."*

In his childhood the correspondent had
been made acquainted with the fact that a soldier of the Legion lay dying in Algiers, but he
had never regarded it as important. Myriads
of his schoolfellows had informed him of the
soldier's plight, but the dinning had naturally
ended by making him perfectly indifferent. He
had never considered it his affair that a soldier
of the Legion lay dying in Algiers, nor had it
appeared to him as a matter for sorrow. It was
less to him than the breaking of a pencil's
point.

Now, however, it quaintly came to him as a
human, living thing. It was no longer merely
a picture of a few throes in the breast of a
poet, meanwhile drinking tea and warming his
feet at the grate; it was an actuality—stern,
mournful, and fine.

The correspondent plainly saw the soldier.
He lay on the sand with his feet out straight
and still. While his pale left hand was upon his
chest in an attempt to thwart the going of his
life, the blood came between his fingers. In the
far Algerian distance, a city of low square
forms was set against a sky that was faint with
the last sunset hues. The correspondent,
plying the oars and dreaming of the slow and
slower movements of the lips of the soldier,
was moved by a profound and perfectly im-
personal comprehension. He was sorry for the
soldier of the Legion who lay dying in Algiers.

The thing which had followed the boat and
waited had evidently grown bored at the delay.
There was no longer to be heard the slash of
the cutwater, and there was no longer the
flame of the long trail. The light in the north
still glimmered, but it was apparently no
nearer to the boat. Sometimes the boom of the
surf rang in the correspondent's ears, and he
turned the craft seaward then and rowed
harder. Southward, someone had evidently
built a watch fire on the beach. It was too low
and too far to be seen, but it made a shimmering, roseate reflection upon the bluff in

back of it, and this could be discerned from
the boat. The wind came stronger, and sometimes a wave suddenly raged out like a mountain cat, and there was to be seen the sheen
and sparkle of a broken crest.

The captain, in the bow, moved on his water
jar and sat erect. "Pretty long night," he observed to the correspondent. He looked at the
shore. "Those lifesaving people take their
time."

"Did you see that shark playing around?"

"Yes, I saw him. He was a big fellow, all
right."

"Wish I had known you were awake."

Later the correspondent spoke into the bottom of the boat.

"Billie!" There was a slow and gradual dis-
entanglement. "Billie, will you spell me?"

"Sure," said the oiler.

As soon as the correspondent touched the
cold, comfortable sea water in the bottom of
the boat and had huddled close to the cook's
life belt he was deep in sleep, despite the fact
that his teeth played all the popular airs. This
sleep was so good to him that it was but a
moment before he heard a voice call his name
in a tone that demonstrated the last stages of
exhaustion. "Will you spell me?"

"Sure, Billie."

The light in the north had mysteriously vanished, but the correspondent took his course
from the wide-awake captain.

Later in the night they took the boat farther
out to sea, and the captain directed the cook
to take one oar at the stern and keep the boat
facing the seas. He was to call out if he should
hear the thunder of the surf. This plan enabled the oiler and the correspondent to get
respite together. "We'll give those boys a
chance to get into shape again," said the captain. They curled down and, after a few pre-
liminary chatterings and trembles, slept once
more the dead sleep. Neither knew they had
bequeathed to the cook the company of another shark, or perhaps the same shark.

As the boat caroused on the waves, spray
occasionally bumped over the side and gave

them a fresh soaking, but this had no power to break their repose. The ominous slash of the wind and the water affected them as it would have affected mummies.

"Boys," said the cook, with the notes of every reluctance in his voice, "she's drifted in pretty close. I guess one of you had better take her to sea again." The correspondent, aroused, heard the crash of the toppled crests.

As he was rowing, the captain gave him some whiskey and water, and this steadied the chills out of him. "If I ever get ashore and anybody shows me even a photograph of an oar——"

At last there was a short conversation.

"Billie!—Billie, will you spell me?"

"Sure," said the oiler.

VII

When the correspondent again opened his eyes, the sea and the sky were each of the gray hue of the dawning. Later, carmine and gold was painted upon the waters. The morning appeared finally, in its splendor, with a sky of pure blue, and the sunlight flamed on the tips of the waves.

On the distant dunes were set many little black cottages, and a tall white windmill reared above them. No man, nor dog, nor bicycle appeared on the beach. The cottages might have formed a deserted village.

The voyagers scanned the shore. A conference was held in the boat. "Well," said the captain, "if no help is coming, we might better try a run through the surf right away. If we stay out here much longer we will be too weak to do anything for ourselves at all." The others silently acquiesced in this reasoning. The boat was headed for the beach. The correspondent wondered if none ever ascended the tall wind tower, and if then they never looked seaward. This tower was a giant, standing with its back to the plight of the ants. It represented in a degree, to the correspondent, the serenity of nature amid the struggles of the individual—nature in the wind, and nature in the vision of men. She did not seem cruel to him then, nor

beneficent, nor treacherous, nor wise. But she was indifferent, flatly indifferent. It is, perhaps, plausible that a man in this situation, impressed with the unconcern of the universe, should see the innumerable flaws of his life and have them taste wickedly in his mind and wish for another chance. A distinction between right and wrong seems absurdly clear to him, then, in this new ignorance of the grave-edge, and he understands that if he were given another opportunity he would mend his conduct and his words, and be better and brighter during an introduction or at a tea.

"Now, boys," said the captain, "she is going to swamp sure. All we can do is to work her in as far as possible, and then when she swamps, pile out and scramble for the beach. Keep cool now, and don't jump until she swamps sure."

The oiler took the oars. Over his shoulders he scanned the surf. "Captain," he said, "I think I'd better bring her about, and keep her head-on to the seas, and back her in."

"All right, Billie," said the captain. "Back her in." The oiler swung the boat then, and, seated in the stern, the cook and the correspondent were obliged to look over their shoulders to contemplate the lonely and indifferent shore.

The monstrous inshore rollers heaved the boat high until the men were again enabled to see the white sheets of water scudding up the slanted beach. "We won't get in very close," said the captain. Each time a man could wrest his attention from the rollers, he turned his glance toward the shore, and in the expression of the eyes during this contemplation there was a singular quality. The correspondent, observing the others, knew that they were not afraid, but the full meaning of their glances was shrouded.

As for himself, he was too tired to grapple fundamentally with the fact. He tried to coerce his mind into thinking of it, but the mind was dominated at this time by the muscles, and the muscles said they did not care. It merely occurred to him that if he should drown it would be a shame.

There were no hurried words, no pallor, no

plain agitation. The men simply looked at the shore. "Now, remember to get well clear of the boat when you jump," said the captain.

Seaward the crest of a roller suddenly fell with a thunderous crash, and the long white comber came roaring down upon the boat.

"Steady now," said the captain. The men were silent. They turned their eyes from the shore to the comber and waited. The boat slid up the incline, leaped at the furious top, bounced over it, and swung down the long back of the wave. Some water had been shipped, and the cook bailed it out.

But the next crest crashed also. The tumbling, boiling flood of white water caught the boat and whirled it almost perpendicular. Water swarmed in from all sides. The correspondent had his hands on the gunwale at this time, and when the water entered at that place he swiftly withdrew his fingers, as if he objected to wetting them.

The little boat, drunken with this weight of water, reeled and snuggled deeper into the sea.

"Bail her out, cook! Bail her out!" said the captain.

"All right, Captain," said the cook.

"Now, boys, the next one will do for us sure," said the oiler. "Mind to jump clear of the boat."

The third wave moved forward, huge, furious, implacable. It fairly swallowed the dinghy, and almost simultaneously the men tumbled into the sea. A piece of life belt had lain in the bottom of the boat, and as the correspondent went overboard, he held this to his chest with his left hand.

The January water was icy, and he reflected immediately that it was colder than he had expected to find it off the coast of Florida. This appeared to his dazed mind as a fact important enough to be noted at the time. The coldness of the water was sad; it was tragic. This fact was somehow mixed and confused with his opinion of his own situation so that it seemed almost a proper reason for tears. The water was cold.

When he came to the surface he was conscious of little but the noisy water. Afterward he saw his companions in the sea. The oiler was ahead in the race. He was swimming strongly and rapidly. Off to the correspondent's left, the cook's great white and corked back bulged out of the water; and in the rear the captain was hanging with his one good hand to the keel of the overturned dinghy.

There is a certain immovable quality to a shore, and the correspondent wondered at it amid the confusion of the sea.

It seemed also very attractive; but the correspondent knew that it was a long journey, and he paddled leisurely. The piece of life preserver lay under him, and sometimes he whirled down the incline of a wave as if he were on a hand-sled.

But finally he arrived at a place in the sea where travel was beset with difficulty. He did not pause swimming to inquire what manner of current had caught him, but there his progress ceased. The shore was set before him like a bit of scenery on a stage, and he looked at it, and understood with his eyes each detail of it.

As the cook passed, much farther to the left, the captain was calling to him, "Turn over on your back, cook! Turn over on your back and use the oar."

"All right, sir." The cook turned on his back, and, paddling with an oar, went ahead as if he were a canoe.

Presently the boat also passed to the left of the correspondent, with the captain clinging with one hand to the keel. He would have appeared like a man raising himself to look over a board fence if it were not for the extraordinary gymnastics of the boat. The correspondent marveled that the captain could still hold to it.

They passed on nearer to shore—the oiler, the cook, the captain—and following them went the water jar, bouncing gaily over the seas.

The correspondent remained in the grip of this strange new enemy, a current. The shore, with its white slope of sand and its green bluff, topped with little silent cottages, was spread like a picture before him. It was very near to him then, but he was impressed as one who, in a gallery, looks at a scene from Brittany or Algiers.

He thought: "I am going to drown? Can it be possible? Can it be possible? Can it be possible?" Perhaps an individual must consider his own death to be the final phenomenon of nature.

But later a wave perhaps whirled him out of this small deadly current, for he found suddenly that he could again make progress toward the shore. Later still he was aware that the captain, clinging with one hand to the keel of the dinghy, had his face turned away from the shore and toward him, and was calling his name. "Come to the boat! Come to the boat!"

In his struggle to reach the captain and the boat, he reflected that when one gets properly wearied drowning must really be a comfortable arrangement—a cessation of hostilities accompanied by a large degree of relief; and he was glad of it, for the main thing in his mind for some moments had been horror of the temporary agony; he did not wish to be hurt.

Presently he saw a man running along the shore. He was undressing with most remarkable speed. Coat, trousers, shirt, everything flew magically off him.

"Come to the boat!" called the captain.

"All right, Captain!" As the correspondent paddled, he saw the captain let himself down to bottom and leave the boat. Then the correspondent performed his one little marvel of the voyage. A large wave caught him and flung him with ease and supreme speed completely over the boat and far beyond it. It struck him even then as an event in gymnastics and a true miracle of the sea. An overturned boat in the surf is not a plaything to a swimming man.

The correspondent arrived in water that reached only to his waist, but his condition did not enable him to stand for more than a moment. Each wave knocked him into a heap, and the undertow pulled at him.

Then he saw the man who had been running and undressing, and undressing and running, come bounding into the water. He dragged ashore the cook, and then waded toward the captain; but the captain waved him away and sent him to the correspondent. He was naked—naked as a tree in winter; but a halo was about his head, and he shone like a saint. He gave a strong pull, and a long drag, and a bully heave at the correspondent's hand. The correspondent, schooled in the minor formulae, said, "Thanks, old man." But suddenly the man cried, "What's that?" He pointed a swift finger. The correspondent said, "Go."

In the shallows, face downward, lay the oiler. His forehead touched sand that was periodically, between each wave, clear of the sea.

The correspondent did not know all that transpired afterward. When he achieved safe ground he fell, striking the sand with each particular part of his body. It was as if he had dropped from a roof, but the thud was grateful to him.

It seems that instantly the beach was populated with men with blankets, clothes, and flasks, and women with coffeepots and all the remedies sacred to their minds. The welcome of the land to the men from the sea was warm and generous; but a still and dripping shape was carried slowly up the beach, and the land's welcome for it could only be the different and sinister hospitality of the grave.

When it came night, the white waves paced to and fro in the moonlight, and the wind brought the sound of the great sea's voice to the men on the shore, and they felt that they could then be interpreters.

Reading Check

1. Identify the four men in the dinghy.
2. Only one of the men is identified by name. Who it is?
3. What is the first place the men try to reach?
4. What do the men use for a sail?
5. How much time do the men spend in the dinghy before reaching land?

Analyzing and Interpreting the Story

1a. What impression of the waves and the sea do you get from the first paragraphs of Parts I and II? **b.** How does the author use the point of view of these paragraphs to suggest that the four men have formed a "subtle brotherhood . . . on the seas"?

2a. What is it in the presence of the gulls that makes the men angry and violent? **b.** How does their inability to repulse the gulls reinforce their predicament?

3a. In Part IV, what, besides the wind, tide, and waves, prevents the men from attempting to reach the shore? **b.** How does the mood of optimism and lightheartedness at the end of Part III change in Part IV?

4. In an angry soliloquy, the narrator sums up the men's rage toward Fate and "the seven mad gods who rule the sea." What does the metaphor of nibbling on "the sacred cheese of life" imply about their situation as individuals against the sea?

5. Like the ominous presence of the gulls, the shark's dark fin cutting through the icy water implies a force that is much stronger than, and somewhat mocking toward, the four men. **a.** What great force does the shark represent? **b.** What is the one thing that would make the correspondent feel less frightened in the presence of this force?

6a. What is the correspondent's view of nature in Part VII? **b.** In what way does the wind-tower, "standing with its back to the plight of the ants," represent not only nature, but the struggle against nature that the four men endure? **c.** Considering the abilities of each man throughout the ordeal at sea, why is the oiler's drowning in the surf bitterly ironic? **d.** How does the oiler's fate illustrate the correspondent's view of nature?

Analyzing Crane's Perspective

Crane's naturalistic view of life in "The Open Boat" is conveyed partly through his very careful use of perspective, beginning with the first sentence: "None of them knew the color of the sky." The reality the four men see always depends upon their general condition as a shipwrecked group and their special circumstances as individuals. It is the captain, for instance, who holds in his mind's eye that despairing vision of the ship sinking beneath the waves. If nature, as the correspondent finally thinks, is "indifferent, flatly indifferent," then the meanings the men see in their experience, whether it is the "sinister" actions of the suddenly "ugly" gulls or the apparently murderous intentions of the shark or the hostile "snarls" of the waves or even the incomprehensible antics of the arm-waving man on shore—all such interpretations of experience depend upon the perspective of the viewer.

In a brief essay, apply this idea to the final paragraph of the story. Now, when these survivors hear "the great sea's voice," in the night, what makes them its "interpreters" and what meaning would they now hear in it?

War Is Kind

Stephen Crane was a poet as well as a novelist and short-story writer. One critic described his poetry as "Whitman condensed and Dickinson expanded." Like Whitman he seldom used rhyme and generally avoided conventional rhythms and words that anyone could possibly label "poetic." Like Dickinson he crafted short lines condensed in meaning. And, like both earlier poets, Crane was ahead of his time: his poems, unorthodox and difficult, foreshadow the complex symbolism and free verse used by American poets in the twentieth century.

Do not weep, maiden, for war is kind.
Because your lover threw wild hands toward the sky
And the affrighted steed ran on alone,
Do not weep.
War is kind.   5

    Hoarse, booming drums of the regiment,
    Little souls who thirst for fight,
    These men were born to drill and die.
    The unexplained glory flies above them,
    Great is the battle-god, great, and his kingdom—   10
    A field where a thousand corpses lie.

Do not weep, babe, for war is kind.
Because your father tumbled in the yellow trenches,
Raged at his breast, gulped and died,
Do not weep.   15
War is kind.

    Swift blazing flag of the regiment,
    Eagle with crest of red and gold,
    These men were born to drill and die.
    Point for them the virtue of slaughter,   20
    Make plain to them the excellence of killing
    And a field where a thousand corpses lie.

Mother whose heart hung humble as a button
On the bright splendid shroud of your son,
Do not weep.   25
War is kind.

The Scream of Shrapnel at San Juan Hill, Cuba (1898) by Frederic Remington (1861–1909). Oil on canvas.

For Study and Discussion

Analyzing and Interpreting the Poem

1. In stanzas 1, 3, and 5 of "War Is Kind," the speaker addresses the lovers, children, and mothers of soldiers killed in war. How is the image of war presented in stanzas 2 and 4 different from the image of war presented in the rest of the poem?

2. In what way is the refrain, "War is kind," severely ironic?

Writing About Literature

Comparing Poetic Styles

Crane's free verse is quite different from Walt Whitman's. (For a discussion of Whitman's free verse, see page 353.) Read aloud a passage from Whitman's "Song of Myself" and the poem by Crane, and consider the following questions: In terms of line length and rhythm, how does Crane's free verse differ from Whitman's? Which poet is more freely emotional? Which poet is more indirect and ironic? How are the differences in line length and rhythm appropriate to the emotions that the two poets express?

The Bettmann Archive

WILLA CATHER
1873–1947

Willa Cather was born in the hills of western Virginia. When she was ten, her family moved to a farm on the vast plains of Nebraska. There she found the materials for many of her novels: the land, open to the sky, rolling without interruption throughout the varying seasons to the distant horizons; the people—Slavic, Scandinavian, German, and old American stock—living in sod-roofed dugouts and bare farmhouses and trying to preserve old moral and cultural values in an age of materialism. A critic has written of the importance of this period of her life: "Her enduring values were the values of this society, but they were not merely pioneer and agrarian values. There was a touch of Europe in Nebraska everywhere during her girlhood, and much of her distinctive literary culture was to be drawn from it."

Willa Cather borrowed books in French and German from her neighbors and was taught Greek and Latin by a storekeeper called "Uncle Billy" Ducker. She attended the University of Nebraska, where she supported herself by doing newspaper work, and after her graduation in 1895, she got a job with the Pittsburgh *Daily Leader.* Later she became a high school teacher of English. In the years following college, her stories began to appear in national magazines, and in 1905 she published a collection of short stories, *The Troll Garden,* which included "The Sculptor's Funeral." In 1906, she went to New York where she worked as managing editor of *McClure's Magazine.* Then, at thirty-nine, she resigned in order to give her full energy to writing a series of novels shaped by her idyllic memories of her prairie childhood, notably *O Pioneers!, The Song of the Lark,* and *My Ántonia.* Not all her memories of life on the prairie were happy ones, however, as such stories as "The Sculptor's Funeral" and "A Wagner Matinée" attest. Even in her happiest novels, a dark note intruded, in Alfred Kazin's words, an awareness of "thousands of farm women suffering alone in their kitchens, living in a strange world amidst familiar scenes, wearing their lives out with endless chores

Willa Cather.

and fears." In such novels as *A Lost Lady* and *The Professor's House,* she traces the dilemma of individuals who move in societies too small for their aspirations.

In her late novels—*Death Comes for the Archbishop* and *Shadows on the Rock*—she turned her attention to the older Catholic cultures of the Southwest and of French colonial Quebec. All her novels are marked by an awareness of sounds and colors, of landscape, and of the changing seasons. The characters that drew her greatest sympathy were artists, priests, and women of moral sensitivity—people who stand for spiritual values in a world overly concerned with getting ahead and accumulating money.

The story that follows is a stark example of realistic writing. As realistic art often does, it offers an unappealing and critical view of certain elements of human nature. The story is built around two essential conflicts. It contrasts the bleak existence of a remote, late-frontier town with that of a broader, more cultured world, and it dramatizes the gap that separates the perceptive and sensitive person from the crass and dull. Cather takes sides in these conflicts: her choice of details, and the accumulated power of those details, particularly in many of the descriptive passages, clearly indicate where her sympathies lie. The author makes a judgment about certain characters in "The Sculptor's Funeral," and she wants the reader to share this judgment.

The Sculptor's Funeral

A group of the townspeople stood on the station siding of a little Kansas town, awaiting the coming of the night train, which was already twenty minutes overdue. The snow had fallen thick over everything; in the pale starlight the line of bluffs across the wide, white meadows south of the town made soft, smoke-colored curves against the clear sky. The men on the siding stood first on one foot and then on the other, their hands thrust deep into their trousers pockets, their overcoats open, their shoulders screwed up with the cold; and they glanced from time to time toward the southeast, where the railroad track wound along the river shore. They conversed in low tones and moved about restlessly, seeming uncertain as to what was expected of them. There was but one of the company who looked as if he knew exactly why he was there, and he kept conspicuously apart, walking to the far end of the platform, returning to the station door, then pacing up the track again, his chin sunk in the high collar of his overcoat, his burly shoulders drooping forward, his gait heavy and dogged. Presently he was approached by a tall, spare, grizzled man clad in a faded Grand Army[1] suit, who shuffled out from the group and advanced with a certain deference, craning his neck forward until his back made the angle of a jackknife three-quarters open.

"I reckon she's a-goin' to be pretty late agin tonight, Jim," he remarked in a squeaky falsetto. "S'pose it's the snow?"

"I don't know," responded the other man with a shade of annoyance, speaking from out an astonishing cataract of red beard that grew fiercely and thickly in all directions.

The spare man shifted the quill toothpick he was chewing to the other side of his mouth.

"It ain't likely that anybody from the East will come with the corpse, I s'pose," he went on reflectively.

"I don't know," responded the other, more curtly than before.

"It's too bad he didn't belong to some lodge or other. I like an order funeral myself. They seem more appropriate for people of some reputation," the spare man continued, with an ingratiating concession in his shrill voice, as he carefully placed his toothpick in his vest pocket. He always carried the flag at the G.A.R. funerals in town.

The heavy man turned on his heel, without replying, and walked up the siding. The spare man rejoined the uneasy group. "Jim's ez full ez a tick, ez ushel," he commented commiseratingly.

Just then a distant whistle sounded, and there was a shuffling of feet on the platform. A number of lanky boys, of all ages, appeared as suddenly and slimily as eels wakened by the crack of thunder; some came from the waiting room, where they had been warming themselves by the red stove, or half asleep on the slat benches; others uncoiled themselves from baggage trucks or slid out of express wagons. Two clambered down from the driver's seat of a hearse that stood backed up against the siding. They straightened their stooping shoulders and lifted their heads, and a flash of momentary animation kindled their dull eyes at that cold, vibrant scream, the worldwide call for men. It stirred them like the note of a trumpet; just as it had often stirred the man who was coming home tonight, in his boyhood.

The night express shot, red as a rocket, from out the eastward marshlands and wound along the river shore under the long lines of shivering poplars that sentineled the meadows, the escaping steam hanging in gray masses against the pale sky and blotting out the Milky Way.

1. **Grand Army:** the Grand Army of the Republic (or G.A.R.), an organization of veterans of the Civil War.

In a moment the red glare from the headlight streamed up the snow-covered track before the siding and glittered on the wet, black rails. The burly man with the disheveled red beard walked swiftly up the platform toward the approaching train, uncovering his head as he went. The group of men behind him hesitated, glanced questioningly at one another, and awkwardly followed his example. The train stopped, and the crowd shuffled up to the express car just as the door was thrown open, the man in the G.A.R. suit thrusting his head forward with curiosity. The express messenger appeared in the doorway, accompanied by a young man in a long ulster[2] and traveling cap.

"Are Mr. Merrick's friends here?" inquired the young man.

The group on the platform swayed uneasily. Philip Phelps, the banker, responded with dignity: "We have come to take charge of the body. Mr. Merrick's father is very feeble and can't be about."

"Send the agent out here," growled the express messenger, "and tell the operator to lend a hand."

The coffin was got out of its rough box and down on the snowy platform. The townspeople drew back enough to make room for it and then formed a close semicircle about it, looking curiously at the palm leaf[3] which lay across the black cover. No one said anything. The baggage man stood by his truck, waiting to get at the trunks. The engine panted heavily, and the fireman dodged in and out among the wheels with his yellow torch and long oilcan, snapping the spindle boxes. The young Bostonian, one of the dead sculptor's pupils, who had come with the body, looked about him helplessly. He turned to the banker, the only one of that black, uneasy, stoop-shouldered group who

2. **ulster:** overcoat.
3. **palm leaf:** a symbol of achievement.

The Sculptor's Studio (c. 1872–1873) by John J. Hammer (1842–1906). Oil on canvas.

seemed enough of an individual to be addressed.

"None of Mr. Merrick's brothers are here?" he asked uncertainly.

The man with the red beard for the first time stepped up and joined the others. "No, they have not come yet; the family is scattered. The body will be taken directly to the house." He stooped and took hold of one of the handles of the coffin.

"Take the long hill road up, Thompson; it will be easier on the horses," called the livery man as the undertaker snapped the door of the hearse and prepared to mount to the driver's seat.

Laird, the red-bearded lawyer, turned again to the stranger: "We didn't know whether there would be anyone with him or not," he explained. "It's a long walk, so you'd better go up in the hack." He pointed to a single battered conveyance, but the young man replied stiffly: "Thank you, but I think I will go up with the hearse. If you don't object," turning to the undertaker, "I'll ride with you."

They clambered up over the wheels and drove off in the starlight up the long, white hill toward the town. The lamps in the still village were shining from under the low, snow-burdened roofs; and beyond, on every side, the plains reached out into emptiness, peaceful and wide as the soft sky itself, and wrapped in a tangible, white silence.

When the hearse backed up to a wooden sidewalk before a naked, weather-beaten frame house, the same composite, ill-defined group that had stood upon the station siding was huddled about the gate. The front yard was an icy swamp, and a couple of warped planks, extending from the sidewalk to the door, made a sort of rickety footbridge. The gate hung on one hinge, and was opened wide with difficulty. Steavens, the young stranger, noticed that something black was tied to the knob of the front door.

The grating sound made by the casket, as it was drawn from the hearse, was answered by a scream from the house; the front door was wrenched open, and a tall, corpulent woman rushed out bareheaded into the snow and flung herself upon the coffin, shrieking: "My boy, my boy! And this is how you've come home to me!"

As Steavens turned away and closed his eyes with a shudder of unutterable repulsion, another woman, also tall, but flat and angular, dressed entirely in black, darted out of the house and caught Mrs. Merrick by the shoulders, crying sharply: "Come, come, Mother; you musn't go on like this!" Her tone changed to one of obsequious solemnity as she turned to the banker: "The parlor is ready, Mr. Phelps."

The bearers carried the coffin along the narrow boards, while the undertaker ran ahead with the coffin-rests. They bore it into a large, unheated room that smelled of dampness and disuse and furniture polish, and set it down under a hanging lamp ornamented with jingling glass prisms and before a "Rogers group"[4] of John Alden and Priscilla, wreathed with smilax.[5] Henry Steavens stared about him with the sickening conviction that there had been a mistake and that he had somehow arrived at the wrong destination. He looked at the clover-green Brussels,[6] the fat plush upholstery, among the hand-painted china plaques and panels and vases, for some mark of identification—for something that might once conceivably have belonged to Harvey Merrick. It was not until he recognized his friend in the crayon portrait of a little boy in kilts and curls, hanging above the piano, that he felt willing to let any of these people approach the coffin.

"Take the lid off, Mr. Thompson; let me see my boy's face," wailed the elder woman between her sobs. This time Steavens looked fearfully, almost beseechingly, into her face,

Courtesy John Rogers, New Canaan, Connecticut

Painted plaster statuette by John Rogers (1829–1904).

red and swollen under its masses of strong, black, shiny hair. He flushed, dropped his eyes, and then, almost incredulously, looked again. There was a kind of power about her face—a kind of brutal handsomeness, even; but it was scarred and furrowed by violence, and so colored and coarsened by fiercer passions that grief seemed never to have laid a gentle finger there. The long nose was distended and knobbed at the end, and there were deep lines on either side of it; her heavy, black brows almost met across her forehead, her teeth were large and square, and set far apart—teeth that could tear. She filled the room; the men were obliterated, seemed tossed about like twigs in an angry water, and even Steavens felt himself being drawn into the whirlpool.

The daughter—the tall, rawboned woman in

4. **"Rogers group":** Plaster reproductions of statuette groups by John Rogers, often with historical or sentimental themes, were common in late nineteenth-century American homes.
5. **smilax:** a delicate twining plant with green leaves.
6. **Brussels:** a patterned carpet.

crepe, with a mourning comb in her hair which curiously lengthened her long face, sat stiffly upon the sofa, her hands, conspicuous for their large knuckles, folded in her lap, her mouth and eyes drawn down, solemnly awaiting the opening of the coffin. Near the door stood a mulatto woman, evidently a servant in the house, with a timid bearing and an emaciated face pitifully sad and gentle. She was weeping silently, the corner of her calico apron lifted to her eyes, occasionally suppressing a long, quivering sob. Steavens walked over and stood beside her.

Feeble steps were heard on the stairs, and an old man, tall and frail, odorous of pipe smoke, with shaggy, unkempt gray hair and a dingy beard, tobacco-stained about the mouth, entered uncertainly. He went slowly up to the coffin and stood rolling a blue cotton handkerchief between his hands, seeming so pained and embarrassed by his wife's orgy of grief that he had no consciousness of anything else.

"There, there, Annie, dear, don't take on so," he quavered timidly, putting out a shaking hand and awkwardly patting her elbow. She turned and sank upon his shoulder with such violence that he tottered a little. He did not even glance toward the coffin, but continued to look at her with a dull, frightened, appealing expression, as a spaniel looks at the whip. His sunken cheeks slowly reddened and burned with miserable shame. When his wife rushed from the room, her daughter strode after her with set lips. The servant stole up to the coffin, bent over it for a moment, and then slipped away to the kitchen, leaving Steavens, the lawyer, and the father to themselves. The old man stood looking down at his dead son's face. The sculptor's splendid head seemed even more noble in its rigid stillness than in life. The dark hair had crept down upon the wide forehead; the face seemed strangely long, but in it there was not that repose we expect to find in the faces of the dead. The brows were so drawn that there were two deep lines above the beaked nose, and the chin was thrust forward defiantly. It was as though the strain of life had been so sharp and bitter that death could not at once relax the tension and smooth the countenance into perfect peace—as though he were still guarding something precious, which might even yet be wrested from him.

The old man's lips were working under his stained beard. He turned to the lawyer with timid deference: "Phelps and the rest are comin' back to set up with Harve, ain't they?" he asked. "Thankee, Jim, thankee." He brushed the hair back gently from his son's forehead. "He was a good boy, Jim; always a good boy. He was ez gentle ez a child and the kindest of 'em all—only we didn't none of us ever onderstand him." The tears trickled slowly down his beard and dropped upon the sculptor's coat.

"Martin, Martin! Oh, Martin! come here," his wife wailed from the top of the stairs. The old man started timorously: "Yes, Annie, I'm coming." He turned away, hesitated, stood for a moment in miserable indecision; then reached back and patted the dead man's hair softly, and stumbled from the room.

"Poor old man, I didn't think he had any tears left. Seems as if his eyes would have gone dry long ago. At his age nothing cuts very deep," remarked the lawyer.

Something in his tone made Steavens glance up. While the mother had been in the room, the young man had scarcely seen anyone else; but now, from the moment he first glanced into Jim Laird's florid face and bloodshot eyes, he knew that he had found what he had been heartsick at not finding before—the feeling, the understanding, that must exist in someone, even here.

The man was red as his beard, with features swollen and blurred by dissipation, and a hot, blazing blue eye. His face was strained—that of a man who is controlling himself with difficulty—and he kept plucking at his beard with a sort of fierce resentment. Steavens, sitting by the window, watched him turn down the glaring lamp, still its jangling pendants with an angry gesture, and then stand with his hands locked behind him, staring down into the master's face. He could not help wondering what link there had been between the porcelain vessel and so sooty a lump of potter's clay.

From the kitchen an uproar was sounding; when the dining-room door opened, the import of it was clear. The mother was abusing the maid for having forgotten to make the dressing for the chicken salad which had been prepared for the watchers. Steavens had never heard anything in the least like it; it was injured, emotional, dramatic abuse, unique and masterly in its excruciating cruelty, as violent and unrestrained as had been her grief of twenty minutes before. With a shudder of disgust the lawyer went into the dining room and closed the door into the kitchen.

"Poor Roxy's getting it now," he remarked when he came back. "The Merricks took her out of the poorhouse years ago; and if her loyalty would let her, I guess the poor old thing could tell tales that would curdle your blood. She's the mulatto woman who was standing in here a while ago, with her apron to her eyes. The old woman is a fury; there never was anybody like her. She made Harvey's life a hell for him when he lived at home; he was so sick ashamed of it. I never could see how he kept himself sweet."

"He was wonderful," said Steavens slowly, "wonderful; but until tonight I have never known how wonderful."

"That is the eternal wonder of it, anyway; that it can come even from such a dung heap as this," the lawyer cried, with a sweeping gesture which seemed to indicate much more than the four walls within which they stood.

"I think I'll see whether I can get a little air. The room is so close I am beginning to feel rather faint," murmured Steavens, struggling with one of the windows. The sash was stuck, however, and would not yield, so he sat down dejectedly and began pulling at his collar. The lawyer came over, loosened the sash with one blow of his red fist, and sent the window up a few inches. Steavens thanked him, but the nausea which had been gradually climbing into his throat for the last half-hour left him with but

one desire—a desperate feeling that he must get away from this place with what was left of Harvey Merrick. Oh, he comprehended well enough now the quiet bitterness of the smile that he had seen so often on his master's lips!

Once when Merrick returned from a visit home, he brought with him a singularly feeling and suggestive bas-relief[7] of a thin, faded old woman, sitting and sewing something pinned to her knee; while a full-lipped, full-blooded little urchin, his trousers held up by a single gallows,[8] stood beside her, impatiently twitching her gown to call her attention to a butterfly he had caught. Steavens, impressed by the tender and delicate modeling of the thin, tired face, had asked him if it were his mother. He remembered the dull flush that had burned up in the sculptor's face.

The lawyer was sitting in a rocking chair beside the coffin, his head thrown back and his eyes closed. Steavens looked at him earnestly, puzzled at the line of the chin, and wondering why a man should conceal a feature of such distinction under that disfiguring shock of beard. Suddenly, as though he felt the young sculptor's keen glance, Jim Laird opened his eyes.

"Was he always a good deal of an oyster?"[9] he asked abruptly. "He was terribly shy as a boy."

"Yes, he was an oyster, since you put it so," rejoined Steavens. "Although he could be very fond of people, he always gave one the impression of being detached. He disliked violent emotion; he was reflective, and rather distrustful of himself—except, of course, as regarded his work. He was sure enough there. He distrusted men pretty thoroughly and women even more, yet somehow without believing ill of them. He was determined, indeed, to believe the best; but he seemed afraid to investigate."

7. **bas-relief** (bä′rĭ-lēf′): a type of sculpture in which the figures are a part of the background and project only slightly from it; a coin is an example of one type of relief.
8. **gallows** (găl′əs): suspender (colloquial).
9. **oyster:** a shy, quiet person (slang).

"A burnt dog dreads the fire," said the lawyer grimly, and closed his eyes.

Steavens went on and on, reconstructing that whole miserable boyhood. All this raw, biting ugliness had been the portion of the man whose mind was to become an exhaustless gallery of beautiful impressions—so sensitive that the mere shadow of a poplar leaf flickering against a sunny wall would be etched and held there forever. Surely, if ever a man had the magic word in his fingertips, it was Merrick. Whatever he touched, he revealed its holiest secret; liberated it from enchantment and restored it to its pristine loveliness. Upon whatever he had come in contact with, he had left a beautiful record of the experience—a sort of ethereal signature; a scent, a sound, a color that was his own.

Steavens understood now the real tragedy of his master's life; neither love nor wine, as many had conjectured; but a blow which had fallen earlier and cut deeper than anything else could have done—a shame not his, and yet so unescapably his, to hide in his heart from his very boyhood. And without—the frontier warfare; the yearning of a boy, cast ashore upon a desert of newness and ugliness and sordidness, for all that is chastened and old, and noble with traditions.

At eleven o'clock the tall, flat woman in black announced that the watchers were arriving, and asked them to "step into the dining room." As Steavens rose, the lawyer said dryly: "You go on—it'll be a good experience for you. I'm not equal to that crowd tonight; I've had twenty years of them."

As Steavens closed the door after him he glanced back at the lawyer, sitting by the coffin in the dim light, with his chin resting on his hand.

The same misty group that had stood before the door of the express car shuffled into the dining room. In the light of the kerosene lamp they separated and became individuals. The minister, a pale, feeble-looking man with white hair and blond chin-whiskers, took his seat beside a small table, and placed his Bible upon it. The Grand Army man sat down behind the stove and tilted his chair back comfortably against the wall, fishing his quill toothpick from his waistcoat pocket. The two bankers, Phelps and Elder, sat off in a corner behind the dinner table, where they could finish their discussion of the new usury law[10] and its effect on chattel[11] security loans. The real-estate agent, an old man with a smiling, hypocritical face, soon joined them. The coal and lumber dealer and the cattle shipper sat on opposite sides of the hard coal-burner, their feet on the nickelwork. Steavens took a book from his pocket and began to read. The talk around him ranged through various topics of local interest while the house was quieting down. When it was clear that the members of the family were in bed, the Grand Army man hitched his shoulders and, untangling his long legs, caught his heels on the rounds of his chair.

"S'pose there'll be a will, Phelps?" he queried in his weak falsetto.

The banker laughed disagreeably, and began trimming his nails with a pearl-handled pocketknife.

"There'll scarcely be any need for one, will there?" he queried in his turn.

The restless Grand Army man shifted his position again, getting his knees still nearer his chin. "Why, the ole man says Harve's done right well lately," he chirped.

The other banker spoke up. "I reckon he means by that Harve ain't asked him to mortgage any more farms lately, so as he could go on with his education."

"Seems like my mind don't reach back to a time when Harve wasn't bein' edycated," tittered the Grand Army man.

There was a general chuckle. The minister took out his handkerchief and blew his nose sonorously. Banker Phelps closed his knife

10. **usury** (yōō′zhə-rē) **law:** a law regulating the amount of interest that can be charged on a loan. In modern usage the term *usury* means an excessive rate of interest.
11. **chattel** (chăt′l): any item of personal property except real estate.

with a snap. "It's too bad the old man's sons didn't turn out better," he remarked with reflective authority. "They never hung together. He spent money enough on Harve to stock a dozen cattle farms, and he might as well have poured it into Sand Creek. If Harve had stayed at home and helped nurse what little they had, and gone into stock on the old man's bottom farm, they might all have been well fixed. But the old man had to trust everything to tenants and was cheated right and left."

"Harve never could have handled stock none," interposed the cattleman. "He hadn't it in him to be sharp. Do you remember when he bought Sander's mules for eight-year-olds, when everybody in town knew that Sander's father-in-law gave 'em to his wife for a wedding present eighteen years before, an' they was full-grown mules then?"

The company laughed discreetly, and the Grand Army man rubbed his knees with a spasm of childish delight.

"Harve never was much account for anything practical, and he shore was never fond of work," began the coal and lumber dealer. "I mind the last time he was home; the day he left, when the old man was out to the barn helpin' his hand hitch up to take Harve to the train, and Cal Moots was patchin' up the fence; Harve, he come out on the step and sings out, in his ladylike voice: 'Cal Moots, Cal Moots! please come cord my trunk.'"

"That's Harve for you," approved the Grand Army man. "I kin hear him howlin' yet, when he was a big feller in long pants and his mother used to whale him with a rawhide in the barn for lettin' the cows git foundered in the cornfield when he was drivin' 'em home from pasture. He killed a cow of mine that-a-way onct— a pure Jersey and the best milker I had, an' the ole man had to put up for her. Harve, he was watchin' the sun set acrost the marshes when the anamile got away."

"Where the old man made his mistake was in sending the boy East to school," said Phelps, stroking his goatee and speaking in a deliberate, judicial tone. "There was where he got his head full of nonsense. What Harve needed, of all people, was a course in some first-class Kansas City business college."

The letters were swimming before Steavens' eyes. Was it possible that these men did not understand, that the palm on the coffin meant nothing to them? The very name of their town would have remained forever buried in the postal guide had it not been now and again mentioned in the world in connection with Harvey Merrick's. He remembered what his master had said to him on the day of his death, after the congestion of both lungs had shut off any probability of recovery, and the sculptor had asked his pupil to send his body home. "It's not a pleasant place to be lying while the world is moving and doing and bettering," he had said with a feeble smile, "but it rather seems as though we ought to go back to the place we came from, in the end. The townspeople will come in for a look at me; and after they have had their say, I shan't have much to fear from the judgment of God!"

The cattleman took up the comment. "Forty's young for a Merrick to cash in; they usually hang on pretty well. Probably he helped it along with whiskey."

"His mother's people were not long-lived, and Harvey never had a robust constitution," said the minister mildly. He would have liked to say more. He had been the boy's Sunday-school teacher, and had been fond of him; but he felt that he was not in a position to speak. His own sons had turned out badly, and it was not a year since one of them had made his last trip home in the express car, shot in a gambling house in the Black Hills.

"Nevertheless, there is no disputin' that Harve frequently looked upon the wine when it was red, also variegated, and it shore made an oncommon fool of him," moralized the cattleman.

Just then the door leading into the parlor rattled loudly, and everyone stared involuntarily, looking relieved when only Jim Laird came out. The Grand Army man ducked his head when he saw the spark in his blue, bloodshot eye. They were all afraid of Jim; he was a drunkard, but he could twist the law to suit his client's needs as no other man in all western Kansas could do, and there were many who tried. The lawyer closed the door behind him, leaned back against it and folded his arms, cocking his head a little to one side. When he assumed this attitude in the courtroom, ears were always pricked up, as it usually foretold a flood of withering sarcasm.

"I've been with you gentlemen before," he began in a dry, even tone, "when you've sat by the coffins of boys born and raised in this town; and, if I remember rightly, you were never any too well satisfied when you checked them up. What's the matter anyhow? Why is it that reputable young men are as scarce as millionaires in Sand City? It might almost seem to a stranger that there was some way something the matter with your progressive town. Why did Ruben Sayer, the brightest young lawyer you ever turned out, after he had come home from the university as straight as a die, take to drinking and forge a check and shoot himself? Why did Bill Merrit's son die of the shakes in a saloon in Omaha? Why was Mr. Thomas' son, here, shot in a gambling house? Why did young Adams burn his mill to beat the insurance companies, and go to the pen?"

The lawyer paused and unfolded his arms, laying one clenched fist quietly on the table. "I'll tell you why. Because you drummed nothing but money and knavery into their ears from the time they wore knickerbockers; because you carped away at them as you've been carping here tonight, holding our friends Phelps and Elder up to them for their models, as our grandfathers held up George Washington and John Adams. But the boys were young, and raw at the business you put them to, and how could they match coppers with such artists as Phelps and Elder? You wanted them to be successful rascals; they were only unsuccessful ones—that's all the difference. There was only one boy ever raised in this borderland between ruffianism and civilization who didn't come to grief, and you hated

Harvey Merrick more for winning out than you hated all the other boys who got under the wheels. Lord, Lord, how you did hate him! Phelps, here, is fond of saying that he could buy and sell us out any time he's a mind to; but we knew Harve wouldn't have given a tinker's dam for his bank and all his cattle farms put together; and a lack of appreciation, that way, goes hard with Phelps.

"Old Nimrod thinks Harve drank too much; and this from such as Nimrod and me!

"Brother Elder says Harve was too free with the old man's money—fell short in filial consideration, maybe. Well, we can all remember the very tone in which Brother Elder swore his own father was a liar, in the county court; and we all know that the old man came out of that partnership with his son as bare as a sheared lamb. But maybe I'm getting personal, and I'd better be driving ahead at what I want to say."

The lawyer paused a moment, squared his heavy shoulders, and went on: "Harvey Merrick and I went to school together, back East. We were dead in earnest, and we wanted you all to be proud of us someday. We meant to be great men. Even I, and I haven't lost my sense of humor, gentlemen, I meant to be a great man. I came back here to practice, and I found you didn't in the least want me to be a great man. You wanted me to be a shrewd lawyer—oh, yes! Our veteran here wanted me to get him an increase of pension, because he had dyspepsia; Phelps wanted a new county survey that would put the widow Wilson's little bottom farm inside his south line; Elder wanted to lend money at five percent a month, and get it collected; and Stark here wanted to wheedle old women up in Vermont into investing their annuities in real-estate mortgages that are not worth the paper they are written on. Oh, you needed me hard enough, and you'll go on needing me!

"Well, I came back here and became the damned shyster you wanted me to be. You pretend to have some sort of respect for me; and yet you'll stand up and throw mud at

Harvey Merrick, whose soul you couldn't dirty and whose hands you couldn't tie. Oh, you're a discriminating lot of Christians! There have been times when the sight of Harvey's name in some Eastern paper has made me hang my head like a whipped dog; and, again, times when I liked to think of him off there in the world, away from all this hog wallow, climbing the big, clean upgrade he'd set for himself.

"And we? Now that we've fought and lied and sweated and stolen, and hated as only the disappointed strugglers in a bitter, dead little Western town know how to do, what have we got to show for it? Harvey Merrick wouldn't have given one sunset over your marshes for all you've got put together, and you know it. It's not for me to say why, in the inscrutable wisdom of God, a genius should ever have been called from this place of hatred and bitter waters; but I want this Boston man to know that the drivel he's been hearing here tonight is the only tribute any truly great man could have from such a lot of sick, side-tracked, burnt-dog, land-poor sharks as the here-present financiers of Sand City—upon which town may God have mercy!"

The lawyer thrust out his hand to Steavens as he passed him, caught up his overcoat in the hall, and had left the house before the Grand Army man had time to lift his ducked head and crane his long neck about at his fellows.

Next day Jim Laird was drunk and unable to attend the funeral services. Steavens called twice at his office, but was compelled to start East without seeing him. He had a presentiment that he would hear from him again, and left his address on the lawyer's table; but if Laird found it, he never acknowledged it. The thing in him that Harvey Merrick had loved must have gone underground with Harvey Merrick's coffin; for it never spoke again, and Jim got the cold he died of driving across the Colorado mountains to defend one of Phelps's sons, who had got into trouble out there by cutting government timber.

Reading Check

1. Who has accompanied Merrick's coffin to Sand City?
2. Which of the townspeople has remained Harvey Merrick's staunchest defender?
3. Which of the family members seems most genuinely grief-stricken?
4. Why do the townspeople feel that Harvey Merrick was not a success?
5. According to Jim Laird, why have the young men of the town turned out so badly?

For Study and Discussion

Analyzing and Interpreting the Story

1a. What important character is introduced in the first paragraph of the story? **b.** How is his importance stressed?

2a. Does the author's treatment of the characters who appear at the beginning of the story strike you as sympathetic or unsympathetic? **b.** What seems to be the author's attitude toward the boys waiting at the train station? **c.** What words and images does she use to describe them?

3. After the train arrives, the story is told primarily through the point of view of Henry Steavens. **a.** How does the use of this point of view influence your attitude toward the other characters? **b.** Give three examples of Steavens' reactions and tell how they influence your own reactions.

4a. What impression is given of Harvey Merrick's sister, mother, and father? **b.** What details of appearance help give this impression? **c.** In what way do the actions of these characters support the impression?

5. What does Jim Laird's remark, "A burnt dog dreads the fire," imply about Harvey Merrick's early years?

6a. How do the remarks of the two bankers, the Grand Army man, the cattle dealer, and the coal and lumber dealer help characterize the town? **b.** How do they help you understand Harvey Merrick?

7. How does Jim Laird influence your feelings about Harvey Merrick and the town?

8. The story concludes with a detail about Jim Laird's death. How does the detail reinforce what we know about Jim and about the townspeople?

9. One theme in this story is the struggle of the sensitive individual against a hostile environment. Considering what you learn about Harvey Merrick in the course of the story, why do you think he was able to triumph over his environment?

Writing About Literature

Analyzing Laird's Character

In this story, the lawyer, Jim Laird, is the most important character, serving as a bridge between the western Kansas village and the greater world represented by Boston and "back East." He is the only one who has known and understood the dead sculptor, Harvey Merrick, and these townspeople who now sit at the sculptor's wake. Laird is also the most complicated character in the story. He is an idealist who respects intelligence, appreciates creative genius, and honors a high moral standard but at the same time is a failed idealist who has become a "shyster" lawyer and learned to "twist the law to suit his client's needs as no other man in all western Kansas could do."

Write an essay in which you consider the two sides of Laird's character as Cather's means for making the central point of the story, the exposure of a "bitter, dead little Western town. . . ." How should we understand Laird's behavior on the day of the funeral? Why does the story end as it does?

Descriptive Writing

Using Suggestive Details

The description of the Merricks' living room tells a great deal about the inhabitants (and about a former inhabitant—Harvey Merrick). Reread this description. Then write a short description of a house or a room that suggests through its details the kind of person or persons who live there.

JACK LONDON
1876–1916

The circumstances of London's life were so improbable that any account of them must read like fiction, and in fact he wrote his autobiography in the form of a novel. Born in San Francisco, he was the child of an astrologer father and a mother who, as a "medium," talked to the spirits of the dead. He grew up mostly uncared for and virtually without schooling in the harsh poverty of the slums, surviving by his wits and physical strength. At the age when most children are in school, he knew brutal factory labor and the seamiest side of big-city life. By the time he was eighteen he had been an illegal "oyster pirate" in San Francisco, had shipped on a sealing voyage to Japan, had marched with an "army" of unemployed men across half the country to publicize their cause, had "ridden the rods" as a hobo and been jailed as a vagrant, and had become a formidable drunkard and all-around tough.

But there was another and more purposeful side to London's life. Sometime in his youth he became an avid reader (up to nineteen hours a day, he claimed) with a voracious appetite for learning. His personal circumstances had made him acutely sensitive to social injustice. Despite his lack of formal education (usually reported as one semester of high school), he entered the University of California by means of examinations. He was dissatisfied with college life, and he left in his first year to follow the latest gold rush to the Yukon. Nevertheless, London's erratic intelligence continued to develop. He did not bring back gold from the Klondike, but he returned with impressions and ideas that would soon become his literary material as, barely into his twenties, he began to write fiction.

Two important influences converged in London's thinking at this point. Life in the frozen Yukon had shown him nature in its harshest form, as the enemy of human survival. At the same time he had seen men struggle harshly with each other, without the usual restraints of laws and civilized communities, for the wealth that symbolized power and dominance. London seized upon the idea of the "prim-

Jack London. Photographed writing aboard ship.

itive" in human nature and of life itself as a struggle for survival and dominance—first against nature and then against other people—in which the strong endure and the weak perish.

Once London's enormous popularity was launched by such early novels as *The Call of the Wild* (1903) and *The Sea-Wolf* (1904), he wrote at an incredible pace, producing some fifty volumes in the last sixteen years of his life. This work earned him more than a million dollars and paid for a life style that included a yacht and a rich man's ranch, but it brought him little satisfaction. His life deteriorated through unhappy marriages and struggles with alcoholism, and ended at forty, apparently in the suicide he had predicted for himself years before in his autobiographical novel, *Martin Eden* (1909).

Overall, the reputation of London's novels has declined sharply since his death. They are criticized for their sensationalism, melodrama, and simplistic views of life, even as their raw power is still recognized. His books of personal reporting—on such matters as hobo life on the road or his experiences in the slums of London—have fared better and are valued as social history. But most of all it is London's short stories that seem destined to last. He was a master of the brief episode in which the individual struggles with the elemental forces of nature. This most basic of all stories—the struggle for life against the threat of death—drew upon London's considerable gifts for description and the creation of suspense.

To Build a Fire

Day had broken cold and gray, exceedingly cold and gray, when the man turned aside from the main Yukon[1] trail and climbed the high earth-bank, where a dim and little-traveled trail led eastward through the fat spruce timberland. It was a steep bank, and he paused for breath at the top, excusing the act to himself by looking at his watch. It was nine o'clock. There was no sun nor hint of sun, though there was not a cloud in the sky. It was a clear day, and yet there seemed an intangible pall over the face of things, a subtle gloom that made the day dark, and that was due to the absence of the sun. This fact did not worry the man. He was used to the lack of sun. It had been days since he had seen the sun, and he knew that a few more days must pass before that cheerful orb, due south, would just peep above the skyline and dip immediately from view.

The man flung a look back along the way he had come. The Yukon lay a mile wide and hidden under three feet of ice. On top of this ice were as many feet of snow. It was all pure white, rolling in gentle undulations where the ice jams of the freeze-up had formed. North and south, as far as his eye could see, it was unbroken white, save for a dark hairline that curved and twisted from around the spruce-covered island to the south, and that curved and twisted away into the north, where it disappeared behind another spruce-covered island. This dark hairline was the trail—the main trail—that led south five hundred miles to the Chilcoot Pass, Dyea,[2] and salt water; and that led north seventy miles to Dawson, and still on to the north a thousand miles to Nulato, and finally to St. Michael, on Bering Sea, a thousand miles and half a thousand more.

But all this—the mysterious, far-reaching hairline trail, the absence of sun from the sky, the tremendous cold, and the strangeness and weirdness of it all—made no impression on the man. It was not because he was long used to it. He was a newcomer in the land, a *chechaquo*,[3] and this was his first winter. The trouble with him was that he was without imagination. He was quick and alert in the things of life, but only in the things, and not in the significances. Fifty degrees below zero meant eighty-odd degrees of frost. Such fact impressed him as being cold and uncomfortable, and that was all. It did not lead him to meditate upon his frailty as a creature of temperature, and upon man's frailty in general, able only to live within certain narrow limits of heat and cold; and from there on it did not lead him to the conjectural[4] field of immortality and man's place in the universe. Fifty degrees below zero stood for a bite of frost that hurt and that must be guarded against by the use of mittens, earflaps, warm moccasins, and thick socks. Fifty degrees below zero was to him just precisely fifty degrees below zero. That there should be anything more to it than that was a thought that never entered his head.

As he turned to go on, he spat speculatively. There was a sharp explosive crackle that startled him. He spat again. And again, in the air, before it could fall to the snow, the spittle crackled. He knew that at fifty below spittle crackled on the snow, but this spittle had crackled in the air. Undoubtedly it was colder than

1. **Yukon** (yo͞o′kŏn): a territory in northwestern Canada, east of Alaska.
2. **Dyea** (dī′ā): a former village in southeastern Alaska. During the gold rush of 1896, Dyea was the supply center and starting point of the trail over the Chilcoot Pass to the northern mining fields and towns such as Dawson and Nulato.
3. *chechaquo* (chē-chä′kwō): in Alaska and the Yukon, a newcomer or tenderfoot.
4. **conjectural** (kən-jĕk′chər-əl): based on guesswork. To conjecture is to come to conclusions based on partial or merely probable evidence.

Trapper in the Wilderness by Sydney Laurence (1865–1940). Oil on canvas.
The Shelburne Museum, Vermont, gift of Mr. and Mrs. William N. Beach

fifty below—how much colder he did not know. But the temperature did not matter. He was bound for the old claim on the left fork of Henderson Creek, where the boys were already. They had come over across the divide from the Indian Creek country, while he had come the roundabout way to take a look at the possibilities of getting out logs in the spring from the islands in the Yukon. He would be in to camp by six o'clock; a bit after dark, it was true, but the boys would be there, a fire would be going, and a hot supper would be ready. As for lunch, he pressed his hand against the protruding bundle under his jacket. It was also under his shirt, wrapped up in a handkerchief and lying against the naked skin. It was the only way to keep the biscuits from freezing. He smiled agreeably to himself as he thought of those biscuits, each cut open and sopped in bacon grease, and each enclosing a generous slice of fried bacon.

He plunged in among the big spruce trees.

The trail was faint. A foot of snow had fallen since the last sled had passed over, and he was glad he was without a sled, traveling light. In fact, he carried nothing but the lunch wrapped in the handkerchief. He was surprised, however, at the cold. It certainly was cold, he concluded, as he rubbed his numb nose and cheekbones with his mittened hand. He was a warm-whiskered man, but the hair on his face did not protect the high cheekbones and the eager nose that thrust itself aggressively into the frosty air.

At the man's heels trotted a dog, a big native husky, the proper wolf dog, gray-coated and without any visible or temperamental difference from its brother, the wild wolf. The animal was depressed by the tremendous cold. It knew that it was no time for traveling. Its instinct told it a truer tale than was told to the man by the man's judgment. In reality, it was not merely colder than fifty below zero; it was colder than sixty below, than seventy below. It was seventy-five below zero. Since the freezing point is thirty-two above zero, it meant that one hundred and seven degrees of frost obtained. The dog did not know anything about thermometers. Possibly in its brain there was no sharp consciousness of a condition of very cold such as was in the man's brain. But the brute had its instinct. It experienced a vague but menacing apprehension that subdued it and made it slink along at the man's heels, and that made it question eagerly every unwonted[5] movement of the man as if expecting him to go into camp or to seek shelter somewhere and build a fire. The dog had learned fire, and it wanted fire, or else to burrow under the snow and cuddle its warmth away from the air.

The frozen moisture of its breathing had settled on its fur in a fine powder of frost, and especially were its jowls, muzzle, and eyelashes whitened by its crystaled breath. The man's red beard and mustache were likewise frosted, but more solidly, the deposit taking the form of ice and increasing with every warm, moist breath he exhaled. Also, the man was chewing tobacco, and the muzzle of ice held his lips so rigidly that he was unable to clear his chin when he expelled the juice. The result was that a crystal beard of the color and solidity of amber was increasing its length on his chin. If he fell down it would shatter itself, like glass, into brittle fragments. But he did not mind the appendage. It was the penalty all tobacco chewers paid in that country, and he had been out before in two cold snaps. They had not been so cold as this, he knew, but by the spirit thermometer[6] at Sixty Mile he knew they had been registered at fifty below and at fifty-five.

He held on through the level stretch of woods for several miles, crossed a wide flat, and dropped down a bank to the frozen bed of a small stream. This was Henderson Creek, and he knew he was ten miles from the forks. He looked at his watch. It was ten o'clock. He was making four miles an hour, and he calculated that he would arrive at the forks at half past twelve. He had decided to celebrate that event by eating his lunch there.

The dog dropped in again at his heels, with a tail drooping discouragement, as the man swung along the creek bed. The furrow of the old sled trail was plainly visible, but a dozen inches of snow covered the marks of the last runners. In a month no man had come up or down that silent creek. The man held steadily on. He was not much given to thinking, and just then particularly he had nothing to think about save that he would eat lunch at the forks and that at six o'clock he would be in camp with the boys. There was nobody to talk to; and, had there been, speech would have been impossible because of the ice muzzle on his mouth. So he continued monotonously to chew tobacco and to increase the length of his amber beard.

Once in a while the thought reiterated itself that it was very cold and that he had never experienced such cold. As he walked along he

5. **unwonted:** unfamiliar.

6. **spirit thermometer:** an alcohol thermometer used in extreme cold.

rubbed his cheekbones and nose with the back of his mittened hand. He did this automatically, now and again changing hands. But, rub as he would, the instant he stopped his cheekbones went numb, and the following instant the end of his nose went numb. He was sure to frost his cheeks; he knew that, and experienced a pang of regret that he had not devised a nose strap of the sort Bud wore in cold snaps. Such a strap passed across the cheeks, as well, and saved them. But it didn't matter much, after all. What were frosted cheeks? A bit painful, that was all; they were never serious.

Empty as the man's mind was of thoughts, he was keenly observant, and he noticed the changes in the creek, the curves and bends and timber jams, and always he sharply noted where he placed his feet. Once, coming around a bend, he shied abruptly, like a startled horse, curved away from the place where he had been walking, and retreated several paces back along the trail. The creek he knew was frozen clear to the bottom—no creek could contain water in that arctic winter—but he knew also that there were springs that bubbled out from the hillsides and ran along under the snow and on top of the ice of the creek. He knew that the coldest snaps never froze these springs, and he knew likewise their danger. They were traps. They hid pools of water under the snow that might be three inches deep, or three feet. Sometimes a skin of ice half an inch thick covered them, and in turn was covered by the snow. Sometimes there were alternate layers of water and ice skin, so that when one broke through he kept on breaking through for a while, sometimes wetting himself to the waist.

That was why he had shied in such panic. He had felt the give under his feet and heard the crackle of a snow-hidden ice skin. And to get his feet wet in such a temperature meant trouble and danger. At the very least it meant delay, for he would be forced to stop and build a fire, and under its protection to bare his feet while he dried his socks and moccasins. He stood and studied the creek bed and its banks, and decided that the flow of water came from the right. He reflected awhile, rubbing his nose and cheeks, then skirted to the left, stepping gingerly and testing the footing for each step. Once clear of the danger, he took a fresh chew of tobacco and swung along at his four-mile gait.

In the course of the next two hours he came upon several similar traps. Usually the snow above the hidden pools had a sunken, candied appearance that advertised the danger. Once again, however, he had a close call; and once, suspecting danger, he compelled the dog to go on in front. The dog did not want to go. It hung back until the man shoved it forward, and then it went quickly across the white, unbroken surface. Suddenly it broke through, floundered to one side, and got away to firmer footing. It had wet its forefeet and legs, and almost immediately the water that clung to it turned to ice. It made quick efforts to lick the ice off its legs, then dropped down in the snow and began to bite out the ice that had formed between the toes. This was a matter of instinct. To permit the ice to remain would mean sore feet. It did not know this. It merely obeyed the mysterious prompting that arose from the deep crypts of its being. But the man knew, having achieved a judgment on the subject, and he removed the mitten from his right hand and helped tear out the ice particles. He did not expose his fingers more than a minute, and was astonished at the swift numbness that smote[7] them. It certainly was cold. He pulled on the mitten hastily, and beat the hand savagely across his chest.

At twelve o'clock the day was at its brightest. Yet the sun was too far south on its winter journey to clear the horizon. The bulge of the earth intervened between it and Henderson Creek, where the man walked under a clear sky at noon and cast no shadow. At half past twelve, to the minute, he arrived at the forks of the creek. He was pleased at the speed he had made. If he kept it up, he would certainly

7. **smote:** past tense of the verb *smite*, which means to strike powerfully and suddenly.

be with the boys by six. He unbuttoned his jacket and shirt and drew forth his lunch. The action consumed no more than a quarter of a minute, yet in that brief moment the numbness laid hold of the exposed fingers. He did not put the mitten on, but, instead, struck the fingers a dozen sharp smashes against his leg. Then he sat down on a snow-covered log to eat. The sting that followed upon the striking of his fingers against his leg ceased so quickly that he was startled. He had had no chance to take a bit of biscuit. He struck the fingers repeatedly and returned them to the mitten, baring the other hand for the purpose of eating. He tried to take a mouthful, but the ice muzzle prevented. He had forgotten to build a fire and thaw out. He chuckled at his foolishness, and as he chuckled he noted the numbness creeping into the exposed fingers. Also, he noted that the stinging which had first come to his toes when he sat down was already passing away. He wondered whether the toes were warm or numb. He moved them inside the moccasins and decided that they were numb.

He pulled the mitten on hurriedly and stood up. He was a bit frightened. He stamped up and down until the stinging returned into the feet. It certainly was cold, was his thought. That man from Sulphur Creek had spoken the truth when telling how cold it sometimes got in the country. And he had laughed at him at the time! That showed one must not be too sure of things. There was no mistake about it, it *was* cold. He strode up and down, stamping his feet and threshing his arms, until reassured by the returning warmth. Then he got out matches and proceeded to make a fire. From the undergrowth, where high water of the previous spring had lodged a supply of seasoned twigs, he got his firewood. Working carefully from a small beginning, he soon had a roaring fire, over which he thawed the ice from his face and in the protection of which he ate his biscuits. For the moment the cold of space was outwitted. The dog took satisfaction in the fire, stretching out close enough for warmth and far enough away to escape being singed.

When the man had finished, he filled his pipe and took his comfortable time over a smoke. Then he pulled on his mittens, settled the earflaps of his cap firmly about his ears, and took the creek trail up the left fork. The dog was disappointed and yearned back toward the fire. This man did not know cold. Possibly all the generations of his ancestry had been ignorant of cold, of real cold, of cold one hundred and seven degrees below freezing point. But the dog knew; all its ancestry knew, and it had inherited the knowledge. And it knew that it was not good to walk abroad in such fearful cold. It was the time to lie snug in a hole in the snow and wait for a curtain of cloud to be drawn across the face of outer space, whence this cold came. On the other hand, there was no keen intimacy between the dog and the man. The one was the toil slave of the other, and the only caresses it had ever received were the caresses of the whiplash and of harsh and menacing throat sounds that threatened the whiplash. So the dog made no effort to communicate its apprehension to the man. It was not concerned in the welfare of the man; it was for its own sake that it yearned back toward the fire. But the man whistled, and spoke to it with the sound of whiplashes, and the dog swung in at the man's heels and followed after.

The man took a chew of tobacco and proceeded to start a new amber beard. Also, his moist breath quickly powdered with white his mustache, eyebrows, and lashes. There did not seem to be so many springs on the left fork of the Henderson, and for half an hour the man saw no signs of any. And then it happened. At a place where there were no signs, where the soft, unbroken snow seemed to advertise solidity beneath, the man broke through. It was not deep. He wet himself halfway to the knees before he floundered out to the firm crust.

He was angry, and cursed his luck aloud. He had hoped to get into camp with the boys at six o'clock, and this would delay him an hour, for he would have to build a fire and dry out his footgear. This was imperative at that low temperature—he knew that much; and he turned aside to the bank, which he climbed. On top, tangled in the underbrush about the trunks of several small spruce trees, was a high-water deposit of dry firewood—sticks and twigs, principally, but also larger portions of seasoned branches and fine, dry, last year's grasses. He threw down several large pieces on top of the snow. This served for a foundation and prevented the young flame from drowning itself in the snow it otherwise would melt. The flame he got by touching a match to a small shred of birch bark that he took from his pocket. This burned even more readily than paper. Placing it on the foundation, he fed the young flame with wisps of dry grass and with the tiniest dry twigs.

He worked slowly and carefully, keenly aware of his danger. Gradually, as the flame grew stronger, he increased the size of the twigs with which he fed it. He squatted in the snow, pulling the twigs out from their entanglement in the brush and feeding directly to the flame. He knew there must be no failure. When it is seventy-five below zero, a man must not fail in his first attempt to build a fire—that is, if his feet are wet. If his feet are dry, and he fails, he can run along the trail for half a mile and restore his circulation. But the circulation of wet and freezing feet cannot be restored by running when it is seventy-five below. No matter how fast he runs, the wet feet will freeze the harder.

All this the man knew. The old-timer on Sulphur Creek had told him about it the previous fall, and now he was appreciating the advice. Already all sensation had gone out of his feet. To build the fire he had been forced to remove his mittens, and the fingers had quickly gone numb. His pace of four miles an hour had kept his heart pumping blood to the surface of his body and to all the extremities. But the instant he stopped, the action of the pump eased down. The cold of space smote the unprotected tip of the planet, and he, being on that unprotected tip, received the full force of the blow. The blood of his body re-

coiled before it. The blood was alive, like the dog, and like the dog it wanted to hide away and cover itself up from the fearful cold. So long as he walked four miles an hour, he pumped that blood, willy-nilly, to the surface; but now it ebbed away and sank down into the recesses of his body. The extremities were the first to feel its absence. His wet feet froze the faster, and his exposed fingers numbed the faster, though they had not yet begun to freeze. Nose and cheeks were already freezing, while the skin of all his body chilled as it lost its blood.

But he was safe. Toes and nose and cheeks would be only touched by the frost, for the fire was beginning to burn with strength. He was feeding it with twigs the size of his finger. In another minute he would be able to feed it with branches the size of his wrist, and then he could remove his wet footgear, and, while it dried, he could keep his naked feet warm by the fire, rubbing them at first, of course, with snow. The fire was a success. He was safe. He remembered the advice of the old-timer on Sulphur Creek, and smiled. The old-timer had been very serious in laying down the law that no man must travel alone in the Klondike after fifty below. Well, here he was; he had had the accident; he was alone; and he had saved himself. Those old-timers were rather womanish, some of them, he thought. All a man had to do was to keep his head, and he was all right. Any man who was a man could travel alone. But it was surprising, the rapidity with which his cheeks and nose were freezing. And he had not thought his fingers could go lifeless in so short a time. Lifeless they were, for he could scarcely make them move together to grip a twig, and they seemed remote from his body and from him. When he touched a twig, he had to look and see whether or not he had hold of it. The wires were pretty well down between him and finger ends.

All of which counted for little. There was the fire, snapping and crackling and promising life with every dancing flame. He started to untie his moccasins. They were coated with ice;

Seldovia, Alaska, February 12, 1912 by Sydney Laurence. Oil on canvas board.
Anchorage Historical and Fine Arts Museum, gift of Mr. and Mrs. Robert O. Kinsey

the thick German socks were like sheaths of iron halfway to the knees; and the moccasin strings were like rods of steel all twisted and knotted as by some conflagration.[8] For a moment he tugged with his numb fingers, then, realizing the folly of it, he drew his sheath knife.

But before he could cut the strings, it happened. It was his own fault or, rather, his mistake. He should not have built the fire under the spruce tree. He should have built it in the open. But it had been easier to pull the twigs from the brush and drop them directly on the fire. Now the tree under which he had done this carried a weight of snow on its boughs. No wind had blown for weeks, and each bough was fully freighted. Each time he had pulled a twig he had communicated a slight agitation to the tree—an imperceptible agitation, so far as he was concerned, but an agitation sufficient to bring about the disaster. High up in the tree one bough capsized its load of snow. This fell on the boughs beneath, capsizing them. This

8. **conflagration** (kŏn′flə-grā′shən): a large, destructive fire.

process continued, spreading out and involving the whole tree. It grew like an avalanche, and it descended without warning upon the man and the fire, and the fire was blotted out! Where it had burned was a mantle of fresh and disordered snow.

The man was shocked. It was as though he had just heard his own sentence of death. For a moment he sat and stared at the spot where the fire had been. Then he grew very calm. Perhaps the old-timer on Sulphur Creek was right. If he had only had a trail mate he would have been in no danger now. The trail mate could have built the fire. Well, it was up to him to build the fire over again, and this second time there must be no failure. Even if he succeeded, he would most likely lose some toes. His feet must be badly frozen by now, and there would be some time before the second fire was ready.

Such were his thoughts, but he did not sit and think them. He was busy all the time they were passing through his mind. He made a new foundation for a fire, this time in the open, where no treacherous tree could blot it out. Next he gathered dry grasses and tiny twigs from the high-water flotsam. He could not bring his fingers together to pull them out, but he was able to gather them by the handful. In this way he got many rotten twigs and bits of green moss that were undesirable, but it was the best he could do. He worked methodically, even collecting an armful of the larger branches to be used later when the fire gathered strength. And all the while the dog sat and watched him, a certain yearning wistfulness in its eyes, for it looked upon him as the fire provider, and the fire was slow in coming.

When all was ready, the man reached in his pocket for a second piece of birch bark. He knew the bark was there, and, though he could not feel it with his fingers, he could hear its crisp rustling as he fumbled for it. Try as he would, he could not clutch hold of it. And all the time, in his consciousness, was the knowledge that each instant his feet were freezing. This thought tended to put him in a panic, but

he fought against it and kept calm. He pulled on his mittens with his teeth, and threshed his arms back and forth, beating his hands with all his might against his sides. He did this sitting down, and he stood up to do it; and all the while the dog sat in the snow, its wolf brush of a tail curled around warmly over its forefeet, its sharp wolf ears pricked forward intently as it watched the man. And the man, as he beat and threshed with his arms and hands, felt a great surge of envy as he regarded the creature that was warm and secure in its natural covering.

After a time he was aware of the first faraway signals of sensation in his beaten fingers. The faint tingling grew stronger till it evolved into a stinging ache that was excruciating, but which the man hailed with satisfaction. He stripped the mitten from his right hand and fetched forth the birch bark. The exposed fingers were quickly going numb again. Next he brought out his bunch of sulphur matches. But the tremendous cold had already driven the life out of his fingers. In his effort to separate one match from the others, the whole bunch fell in the snow. He tried to pick it out of the snow, but failed. The dead fingers could neither touch nor clutch. He was very careful. He drove the thought of his freezing feet, and nose, and cheeks, out of his mind, devoting his whole soul to the matches. He watched, using the sense of vision in place of that of touch, and when he saw his fingers on each side of the bunch, he closed them—that is, he willed to close them, for the wires were down, and the fingers did not obey. He pulled the mitten on his right hand, and beat it fiercely against his knee. Then, with both mittened hands, he scooped the bunch of matches, along with much snow, into his lap. Yet he was no better off.

After some manipulation he managed to get the bunch between the heels of his mittened hands. In this fashion he carried it to his mouth. The ice crackled and snapped when by a violent effort he opened his mouth. He drew the lower jaw in, curled the upper lip out of the way, and scraped the bunch with his upper teeth in order to separate a match. He succeeded in getting one, which he dropped on his lap. He was no better off. He could not pick it up. Then he devised a way. He picked it up in his teeth and scratched it on his legs. Twenty times he scratched before he succeeded in lighting it. As it flamed he held it with his teeth to the birch bark. But the burning brimstone went up his nostrils and into his lungs, causing him to cough spasmodically. The match fell into the snow and went out.

The old-timer on Sulphur Creek was right, he thought in the moment of controlled despair that ensued: after fifty below, a man should travel with a partner. He beat his hands, but failed in exciting any sensation. Suddenly he bared both hands, removing the mittens with his teeth. He caught the whole bunch between the heels of his hands. His arm muscles not being frozen enabled him to press the hand heels tightly against the matches. Then he scratched the bunch along his leg. It flared into flame, seventy sulphur matches at once! There was no wind to blow them out. He kept his head to one side to escape the strangling fumes, and held the blazing bunch to the birch bark. As he so held it, he became aware of sensation in his hand. His flesh was burning. He could smell it. Deep down below the surface he could feel it. The sensation developed into pain that grew acute. And still he endured it, holding the flame of the matches clumsily to the bark that would not light readily because his own burning hands were in the way, absorbing most of the flame.

At last, when he could endure no more, he jerked his hands apart. The blazing matches fell sizzling into the snow, but the birch bark was alight. He began laying dry grasses and the tiniest twigs on the flame. He could not pick and choose, for he had to lift the fuel between the heels of his hands. Small pieces of rotten wood and green moss clung to the twigs, and he bit them off as well as he could with his teeth. He cherished the flame carefully and awkwardly. It meant life, and it must not perish. The withdrawal of blood from the surface of his body now made him begin to shiver, and he grew more awkward. A large piece of green moss fell squarely on the little fire. He tried to poke it out with his fingers, but his shivering frame made him poke too far, and he disrupted the nucleus of the little fire, the burning grasses and tiny twigs separating and scattering. He tried to poke them together again, but in spite of the tenseness of the effort, his shivering got away with him, and the twigs were hopelessly scattered. Each twig gushed a puff of smoke and went out. The fire provider had failed. As he looked apathetically about him, his eyes chanced on the dog, sitting across the ruins of the fire from him, in the snow, making restless, hunching movements, slightly lifting one forefoot and then the other, shifting its weight back and forth on them with wistful eagerness.

The sight of the dog put a wild idea into his head. He remembered the tale of the man, caught in a blizzard, who killed a steer and crawled inside the carcass, and so was saved. He would kill the dog, and bury his hands in the warm body until the numbness went out of them. Then he could build another fire. He spoke to the dog, calling it to him; but in his voice was a strange note of fear that frightened the animal, who had never known the man to speak in such way before. Something was the matter, and its suspicious nature sensed danger—it knew not what danger, but somewhere, somehow, in its brain arose an apprehension of the man. It flattened its ears down at the sound of the man's voice, and its restless, hunching movements and the liftings and shiftings of its forefeet became more pronounced; but it would not come to the man. He got on his hands and knees and crawled toward the dog. This unusual posture again excited suspicion, and the animal sidled mincingly away.

The man sat up in the snow for a moment and struggled for calmness. Then he pulled on his mittens, by means of his teeth, and got upon his feet. He glanced down at first in order to assure himself that he was really standing up, for the absence of sensation in his feet left him unrelated to the earth. His erect position in itself started to drive the webs of suspicion from the dog's mind; and when he spoke peremptorily,[9] with the sound of whiplashes in his voice, the dog rendered its customary allegiance and came to him. As it came within reaching distance, the man lost his control. His arms flashed out to the dog, and he experienced genuine surprise when he discovered that his hands could not clutch, that there was neither bend nor feeling in the fingers. He had forgotten for the moment that they were frozen and that they were freezing more and more. All this happened quickly, and before the animal could get away, he encircled its body with his arms. He sat down in the snow, and in this fashion held the dog, while it snarled and whined and struggled.

But it was all he could do, hold its body encircled in his arms and sit there. He realized that he could not kill the dog. There was no way to do it. With his helpless hands he could neither draw nor hold his sheath knife nor throttle the animal. He released it, and it plunged wildly away, with tail between its legs, and still snarling. It halted forty feet away and surveyed him curiously, with ears sharply pricked forward.

The man looked down at his hands in order to locate them, and found them hanging on the ends of his arms. It struck him as curious that one should have to use his eyes in order to find out where his hands were. He began threshing his arms back and forth, beating the mittened hands against his sides. He did this for five minutes, violently, and his heart pumped enough blood up to the surface to put a stop to his shivering. But no sensation was roused in the hands. He had an impression that they hung like weights on the ends of his arms, but when he tried to run the impression down, he could not find it.

A certain fear of death, dull and oppressive, came to him. This fear quickly became poignant as he realized that it was no longer a mere matter of freezing his fingers and toes, or of losing his hands and feet, but that it was a matter of life and death with the chances against him. This threw him into a panic, and he turned and ran up the creek bed along the old, dim trail. The dog joined in behind and kept up with him. He ran blindly, without intention, in fear such as he had never known in his life. Slowly, as he plowed and floundered through the snow, he began to see things again—the banks of the creek, the old timber jams, the leafless aspens, and the sky. The running made him feel better. He did not shiver. Maybe, if he ran on, his feet would thaw out; and, anyway, if he ran far enough, he would reach camp and the boys. Without doubt he would lose some fingers and toes and some of his face; but the boys would take care of him, and save the rest of him when he got there. And at the same time there was another thought in his mind that said he would never get to the camp and the boys; that it was too many miles away, that the freezing had too great a start on him, and that he would soon be stiff and dead. This thought he kept in the background and refused to consider. Sometimes it pushed itself forward and demanded to be heard, but he thrust it back and strove to think of other things.

It struck him as curious that he could run at all on feet so frozen that he could not feel them when they struck the earth and took the weight of his body. He seemed to himself to skim along above the surface, and to have no connection with the earth. Somewhere he had once seen a winged Mercury,[10] and he wondered if Mercury felt as he felt when skimming over the earth.

His theory of running until he reached camp and the boys had one flaw in it: he lacked the endurance. Several times he stumbled, and finally he tottered, crumpled up, and fell. When

9. **peremptorily** (pə-rĕmp′tə-rə-lē): commandingly.

10. **Mercury:** in Roman mythology, the messenger of the gods; he is usually depicted as having winged feet.

he tried to rise, he failed. He must sit and rest, he decided, and next time he would merely walk and keep on going. As he sat and regained his breath, he noted that he was feeling quite warm and comfortable. He was not shivering, and it even seemed that a warm glow had come to his chest and trunk. And yet, when he touched his nose or cheeks, there was no sensation. Running would not thaw them out. Nor would it thaw out his hands and feet. Then the thought came to him that the frozen portions of his body must be extending. He tried to keep this thought down, to forget it, to think of something else; he was aware of the panicky feeling that it caused, and he was afraid of the panic. But the thought asserted itself, and persisted, until it produced a vision of his body totally frozen. This was too much, and he made another wild run along the trail. Once he slowed down to a walk, but the thought of the freezing extending itself made him run again.

And all the time the dog ran with him, at his heels. When he fell down a second time, it curled its tail over its forefeet and sat in front of him, facing him, curiously eager and intent. The warmth and security of the animal angered him, and he cursed it till it flattened down its ears appeasingly. This time the shivering came more quickly upon the man. He was losing in his battle with the frost. It was creeping into his body from all sides. The thought of it drove him on, but he ran no more than a hundred feet, when he staggered and pitched headlong. It was his last panic. When he had recovered his breath and control, he sat up and entertained in his mind the conception of meeting death with dignity. However, the conception did not come to him in such terms. His idea of it was that he had been making a fool of himself, running around like a chicken with its head off—such was the simile that occurred to him. Well, he was bound to freeze anyway, and he might as well take it decently. With this new-found peace of mind came the first glimmerings of drowsiness. A good idea, he thought, to sleep off to death. It was like taking an anesthetic. Freezing was not so bad as people thought. There were lots worse ways to die.

He pictured the boys finding his body next day. Suddenly he found himself with them, coming along the trail and looking for himself. And, still with them, he came around a turn in the trail and found himself lying in the snow. He did not belong with himself any more, for even then he was out of himself, standing with the boys and looking at himself in the snow. It certainly was cold, was his thought. When he got back to the States he could tell the folks what real cold was. He drifted on from this to a vision of the old-timer on Sulphur Creek. He could see him quite clearly, warm and comfortable, and smoking a pipe.

"You were right, old hoss; you were right," the man mumbled to the old-timer of Sulphur Creek.

Then the man drowsed off into what seemed to him the most comfortable and satisfying sleep he had ever known. The dog sat facing him and waiting. The brief day drew to a close in a long, slow twilight. There were no signs of a fire to be made, and, besides, never in the dog's experience had it known a man to sit like that in the snow and make no fire. As the twilight drew on, its eager yearning for the fire mastered it, and with a great lifting and shifting of forefeet, it whined softly, then flattened its ears down in anticipation of being chidden[11] by the man. But the man remained silent. Later the dog whined loudly. And still later it crept close to the man and caught the scent of death. This made the animal bristle and back away. A little longer it delayed, howling under the stars that leaped and danced and shone brightly in the cold sky. Then it turned and trotted up the trail in the direction of the camp it knew, where were the other food providers and fire providers.

11. **chidden** (chĭd′n): scolded.

Reading Check

1. Where is the man in the story heading?
2. Why does he try to avoid the springs?
3. What advice had the old-timer on Sulphur Creek given him about travel in the Klondike?
4. Why does the second fire go out?
5. Why is the man unable to build a third fire?

For Study and Discussion

Analyzing and Interpreting the Story

1a. Where in the story does the man first become aware of the danger of the cold?   **b.** How does this awareness affect his later actions?   **c.** If he had realized the danger earlier and more fully, what might he have done differently?

2. In introducing the man, London describes him as being "quick and alert," but "without imagination." How does this lack of imagination mislead him?

3. The dog's equivalent of human imagination is evidently its instinct. How does the dog's instinct enable it to escape the man's fate?

4a. What does the story suggest about the kind of individual who is most likely to survive challenges and trials?   **b.** What does London feel is more important—physical strength or an awareness of the possible consequences of one's actions?

5a. What does the story suggest about humanity's place in nature?   **b.** What purpose do you think the author might have had in not giving his character a name?

Language and Vocabulary

Analyzing Devices of Repetition

The repetition of words can be one of a writer's most effective devices. In "To Build a Fire," Jack London uses simple words over and over again for a single dominant effect. Find two passages in the story that convey a dominant impression. What is the impression? What repeated words or phrases create each impression?

Writing About Literature

Discussing a Character's Fate

In "To Build a Fire," the man is hindered by his lack of imagination and his carelessness. On the other hand, he is also a victim of simple bad luck. Which do you think is the primary cause of his demise? Write a short essay expressing your opinion. Select details from the story to support your position.

Explaining Methods of Building Mood

A dominant mood of this story is that of grim hopelessness. In a short essay explain some of the ways in which London builds up this mood. For example, how does he use setting to create a sense of overwhelming isolation? Do not limit your discussion to the device of repetition.

EDWIN ARLINGTON ROBINSON
1869–1935

Edwin Arlington Robinson (1933) by Richard Hood (1910–   ). Drypoint.

Edwin Arlington Robinson grew up in Gardiner, Maine, a town on the Kennebec River that became the Tilbury Town of his poetry. Robinson's father had been a prosperous timber merchant, but after his death, his family suddenly found itself poor. Two promising older brothers died young, and their mother's death was preceded by a long and painful illness. Robinson's poems grew out of his response to his family and his region, a land of suddenly diminished opportunities, of large old-fashioned houses, and of lonely dreamers who had once been prosperous and happy.

After two years at Harvard, Robinson was forced to leave college because of his family's dwindling fortunes. He found his way to New York City, the "town down the river," where he lived in Greenwich Village, a quarter that has been the home of many artists and writers. In those years he was so poor that he often could pack all his possessions into one suitcase. He was a slight, shy man with little talent for practical affairs, but with great sympathy for those who were dispossessed, lonely, and troubled.

When Robinson began publishing his poetry in the 1890s, there were few good American poets and almost no audience for him. He had to pay for the printing of his first two books, *The Torrent and the Night Before* and *The Children of the Night*. Friends secretly subsidized the publication of *Captain Craig*, his third book, and former President Theodore Roosevelt used his influence to effect the publication of a fourth, *The Town Down the River*. When Robinson's poetry was discovered by Roosevelt, the poet was working underground inspecting loads of construction materials in an uncompleted subway. Roosevelt secured Robinson a clerkship in the New York Custom House, an action that recalls an earlier use of political patronage on Nathaniel Hawthorne's behalf. From now on, Robinson's worst financial difficulties were over. After 1911 he customarily spent his summers at the MacDowell Colony for artists in New Hampshire, and in the last years of

his life, his books earned enough money to support him. He received the Pulitzer Prize for poetry three times, in 1922, 1925, and 1928, and in the 1920s he was generally regarded as the greatest living American poet.

During the modern American poetic revival that began in the second decade of the century, Robinson was hailed as the foremost figure of the "New Poetry," but he had little in common with other figures of the revival such as Carl Sandburg and Amy Lowell. He had begun writing poetry long before most of them, and the forms he worked in were traditional, not experimental. Many of his poems are sonnets, and a great many are written in tight stanza forms. The poems most popular in his own lifetime were his long narratives about the court of King Arthur: *Merlin, Lancelot,* and *Tristram.* He was a master of the dramatic monologue, a form perfected earlier by the English poet Robert Browning. Robert Frost summed up Robinson's achievement by writing that his old friend had "stayed content with the old way to be new."

Robinson's poems about Richard Cory and the other inhabitants of Tilbury Town are bitter poems, but their biting quality is leavened by a restrained style and a wry appreciation of life's ironies. In a memoir published shortly after Robinson's death, Robert Frost wrote that Robinson's "outer seriousness" was balanced by an "inner humor," and he spoke of Robinson's "happy skill. His theme was unhappiness itself, but his skill was as happy as it was playful."

Man (1946) by Ben Shahn (1898–1969). Tempera on composition board.
Collection, The Museum of Modern Art, New York, gift of Mr. and Mrs. E. Powis Jones

Richard Cory

Whenever Richard Cory went down town,
We people on the pavement looked at him:
He was a gentleman from sole to crown,
Clean favored, and imperially slim.

And he was always quietly arrayed,   5
And he was always human when he talked;
But still he fluttered pulses when he said,
"Good-morning," and he glittered when he walked.

And he was rich—yes, richer than a king—
And admirably schooled in every grace: 10
In fine, we thought that he was everything
To make us wish that we were in his place.

So on we worked, and waited for the light,
And went without the meat, and cursed the bread;
And Richard Cory, one calm summer night,   15
Went home and put a bullet through his head.

Miniver Cheevy

Miniver Cheevy, child of scorn,
    Grew lean while he assailed the seasons;
He wept that he was ever born,
    And he had reasons.

Miniver loved the days of old   5
    When swords were bright and steeds were prancing;
The vision of a warrior bold
    Would set him dancing.

Miniver sighed for what was not,
    And dreamed, and rested from his labors;   10
He dreamed of Thebes° and Camelot,°
    And Priam's° neighbors.

Miniver mourned the ripe renown
    That made so many a name so fragrant;
He mourned Romance, now on the town,°   15
    And Art, a vagrant.

11. **Thebes** (thēbz): a famous city of ancient Greece. **Camelot:** the legendary town where King Arthur and the Knights of the Round Table resided. 12. **Priam** (prī'əm): king of Troy during the Trojan War. 15. **on the town:** on public relief or welfare.

Miniver loved the Medici,°
    Albeit° he had never seen one;
He would have sinned incessantly
    Could he have been one.   20

Miniver cursed the commonplace
    And eyed a khaki suit with loathing;
He missed the medieval grace
    Of iron clothing.

Miniver scorned the gold he sought,   25
    But sore annoyed was he without it;
Miniver thought, and thought, and thought,
    And thought about it.

Miniver Cheevy, born too late,
    Scratched his head and kept on thinking;   30
Miniver coughed, and called it fate,
    And kept on drinking.

17. **Medici** (mĕ′dē-chē): the leading family of Florence, Italy, during the fifteenth and sixteenth centuries.   18. **Albeit** (ôl-bē′ĭt): although.

Mr. Flood's Party

Old Eben Flood, climbing alone one night
Over the hill between the town below
And the forsaken upland hermitage
That held as much as he should ever know
On earth again of home, paused wearily.   5
The road was his with not a native near;
And Eben, having leisure, said aloud,
For no man else in Tilbury Town to hear:

"Well, Mr. Flood, we have the harvest moon
Again, and we may not have many more;   10
The bird is on the wing, the poet° says,
And you and I have said it here before.
Drink to the bird." He raised up to the light
The jug that he had gone so far to fill,
And answered huskily: "Well, Mr. Flood,   15
Since you propose it, I believe I will."

11. **poet:** Edward Fitzgerald in his translation of *The Rubáiyát of Omar Khayyám.*

Alone, as if enduring to the end
A valiant armor of scarred hopes outworn,
He stood there in the middle of the road
Like Roland's ghost° winding a silent horn.   20
Below him, in the town among the trees,
Where friends of other days had honored him,
A phantom salutation of the dead
Rang thinly till old Eben's eyes were dim.

Then, as a mother lays her sleeping child   25
Down tenderly, fearing it may awake,
He set the jug down slowly at his feet
With trembling care, knowing that most things break;
And only when assured that on firm earth
It stood, as the uncertain lives of men   30
Assuredly did not, he paced away,
And with his hand extended paused again:

"Well, Mr. Flood, we have not met like this
In a long time; and many a change has come
To both of us, I fear, since last it was   35
We had a drop together. Welcome home!"
Convivially returning with himself,
Again he raised the jug up to the light;
And with an acquiescent quaver said:
"Well, Mr. Flood, if you insist, I might.   40

"Only a very little, Mr. Flood—
For auld lang syne.° No more, sir; that will do."
So, for the time, apparently it did,
And Eben evidently thought so too;
For soon amid the silver loneliness   45
Of night he lifted up his voice and sang,
Secure, with only two moons listening,
Until the whole harmonious landscape rang—

"For auld lang syne." The weary throat gave out,
The last word wavered, and the song was done.   50
He raised again the jug regretfully
And shook his head, and was again alone.
There was not much that was ahead of him,
And there was nothing in the town below—
Where strangers would have shut the many doors   55
That many friends had opened long ago.

20. **Roland's ghost:** Roland was a legendary hero who, in leading the forces of Charlemagne against the Saracens at Roncevalles, blew his horn for help before he died. 42. **auld lang syne:** old times.

Analyzing and Interpreting the Poems

Richard Cory

1a. What is meant by the statement, "he glittered when he walked"? **b.** What is meant in lines 13–14? **c.** How do these lines emphasize the difference between Cory and the other townspeople?

2. Why do you think Robinson used the pronoun *we* rather than the pronoun *I*? That is, why does he describe the reaction of a group of people to Richard Cory rather than the reaction of one sensitive individual? (To answer this question, you may find it helpful to reread the poem, substituting *I* wherever *we* occurs.)

3a. What was your reaction to the last line of the poem? **b.** Do you think, judging from the details that precede this line, that your reaction was the one Robinson was building toward? Explain.

Miniver Cheevy

1. Why is miniver, the white fur trimming used on people's garments in the Middle Ages, an appropriate name for the character in this poem?

2a. Explain how lines 23–24 reveal the poet's attitude toward Miniver Cheevy. **b.** How do other lines reflect the poet's attitude toward Cheevy? **c.** How does the ending of the poem affect your attitude toward Cheevy?

Mr. Flood's Party

1. What does the first stanza tell you about Mr. Flood's circumstances?

2a. How is the precise place where Mr. Flood stops important to the poem? **b.** How do the first and last stanzas emphasize this importance?

3a. Why do you think Mr. Flood is compared to Roland, a heroic figure of the Middle Ages? **b.** Why are this simile and the line "A valiant armor of scarred hopes outworn" appropriate to Mr. Flood? **c.** How do they make of him something more than a drunken, lonely old man?

4a. How are **pathos** (the arousal of pity and sympathy) and humor blended in this poem? **b.** What effect does this blend of serious and comic elements have on you as you read the poem?

Considering Differences Between a Poem and a Story

Robinson shares a number of qualities with good modern short-story writers, particularly the ability to create interesting situations and striking characters. In a brief composition, consider the differences between the short narrative or dramatic poem and the short story. What would a poem such as "Richard Cory" lose if it were adapted as a story? What would it gain?

EDGAR LEE MASTERS
1869–1950

Edgar Lee Masters was born in Kansas but grew up in southern Illinois, the same country where, forty years earlier, Lincoln had been a storekeeper, lawyer, and aspiring politician. In Masters' boyhood, the Middle West was not greatly changed from what it had been in the days of the pioneers. As a boy Masters knew Lincoln's old law partner, William Herndon. Later he recalled his grandfather's tales of wolf hunts in Tennessee, prairie schooners, and camp meetings held in the forest. After a brief stay at Knox College, Masters studied law in his father's law office in Lewistown, Illinois. He wrote many poems in traditional forms, imitating Edgar Allan Poe, John Keats, and Percy Bysshe Shelley. As a young man with literary ambitions, he found small-town life oppressive. In his autobiography he wrote, "I feel that no poet in English or American history had a harder life than mine was in the beginning at Lewistown among a people whose flesh and vibrations were better calculated to poison, to pervert, and even to kill a sensitive nature." When he was twenty-three, he moved to Chicago where he became the partner of a leading criminal lawyer and built up a large law practice. In his spare time, he wrote poems, plays, essays, but none of his work attracted much attention.

In 1914 William Marion Reedy, an editor friend of Masters, gave him a copy of *Epigrams from the Greek Anthology.* The *Greek Anthology* is a collection of short Greek poems, many of them epitaphs that, in a few pointed lines, sum up the span of an individual's life. These poems gave Masters the idea of writing their Middle Western counterparts, uncovering the lives he had known in the small towns of southern Illinois. Instead of the traditional forms and meters he had used in his previous poetry, Masters chose to write his epitaphs in free verse, a form enjoying a revival in the work of Carl Sandburg and other contributors to the Chicago magazine *Poetry.* The epitaphs for the citizens of Spoon River are varied. A few of the inhabitants of the

Edgar Lee Masters.
Photographed July 9, 1946.

graveyard on the hill had lived full lives and were content, but far more were the bitter, frustrated victims of spiritual isolation. When *Spoon River Anthology* appeared, it was enthusiastically praised by some reviewers, bitterly attacked by others, and soon became a best seller. In drawing attention to the private tragedies of small Middle Western towns, it prepared the way for fiction writers such as Sinclair Lewis and Sherwood Anderson. Today *Spoon River Anthology* is regarded as an American classic. While the *Anthology* contains many fine individual poems, its full force is revealed only after it is read in its entirety.

In 1920 Masters was able to give up the practice of law and devote himself entirely to literature. He wrote books of poetry, novels, biographies, and his autobiography, *Across Spoon River,* at the pace of about a book a year. None of his other books was nearly as successful as his *Anthology* or is as highly regarded. Yet, because of this single achievement, his place as an American poet and chronicler of the small town is secure.

George Gray

I have studied many times
The marble which was chiseled for me—
A boat with a furled sail at rest in a harbor.
In truth it pictures not my destination
But my life.   5
For love was offered me and I shrank from its disillusionment;
Sorrow knocked at my door, but I was afraid;
Ambition called to me, but I dreaded the chances.
Yet all the while I hungered for meaning in my life.
And now I know that we must lift the sail   10
And catch the winds of destiny
Wherever they drive the boat.
To put meaning in one's life may end in madness,
But life without meaning is the torture
Of restlessness and vague desire—   15
It is a boat longing for the sea and yet afraid.

Lucinda Matlock

I went to the dances at Chandlerville,
And played snap-out° at Winchester.
One time we changed partners,
Driving home in the moonlight of middle June,
And then I found Davis.   5
We were married and lived together for seventy years,
Enjoying, working, raising the twelve children,
Eight of whom we lost
Ere I had reached the age of sixty.
I spun, I wove, I kept the house, I nursed the sick,   10
I made the garden, and for holiday
Rambled over the fields where sang the larks,

2. **snap-out:** a game also known as "snap-the-whip" or "crack-the-whip," in which the leader of a long line of players makes a sudden turn and those on the end are flung off by centrifugal force. The game is often played on ice skates.

And by Spoon River gathering many a shell,
And many a flower and medicinal weed—
Shouting to the wooded hills, singing to the green valleys.   15
At ninety-six I had lived enough, that is all,
And passed to a sweet repose.
What is this I hear of sorrow and weariness,
Anger, discontent and drooping hopes?
Degenerate sons and daughters,   20
Life is too strong for you—
It takes life to love Life.

Mother Combing Her Child's Hair (c. 1901) by Mary Cassatt (1845–1926).
Pastel and gouache on tan paper.

Dancing on the Barn Floor (1831) by William Sidney Mount (1807–1868).
Oil on canvas.
The Museums at Stony Brook, gift of Mr. and Mrs. Ward Melville

Fiddler Jones

The earth keeps some vibration going
There in your heart, and that is you.
And if the people find you can fiddle,
Why, fiddle you must, for all your life.
What do you see, a harvest of clover?   5
Or a meadow to walk through to the river?
The wind's in the corn; you rub your hands
For beeves° hereafter ready for market;
Or else you hear the rustle of skirts
Like little girls when dancing at Little Grove.   10
To Cooney Potter a pillar of dust
Or whirling leaves meant ruinous drouth;°
They looked to me like Red-Head Sammy
Stepping it off, to "Toor-a-Loor."
How could I till my forty acres   15
Not to speak of getting more,
With a medley of horns, bassoons and piccolos
Stirred in my brain by crows and robins
And the creak of a windmill—only these?
And I never started to plow in my life   20
That someone did not stop in the road
And take me away to a dance or picnic.
I ended up with forty acres;
I ended up with a broken fiddle—
And a broken laugh, and a thousand memories,   25
And not a single regret.

8. **beeves:** plural of beef.   12. **drouth:** drought.

For Study and Discussion

Analyzing and Interpreting the Poems

1a. How does the sculpture on George Gray's grave—a boat at rest in a harbor—symbolize his life? **b.** Why is madness preferable to a life without meaning? **c.** What is George Gray's attitude toward life now?
2. How would you characterize Lucinda Matlock's life? Was it ordinary or unusual? Happy or unhappy?
3a. Who are the "sons and daughters" Lucinda addresses at the end of the poem? **b.** Why does she call them "degenerate"? **c.** Contrast their attitude toward life with her own.

4a. How is Fiddler Jones different from the other farmers in the community? **b.** He gives several examples of the way different people may view the same thing. What distinguishes his view of life?
5. Why do you think Fiddler Jones has "not a single regret"?

PAUL LAURENCE DUNBAR
1872–1906

Paul Laurence Dunbar.
Culver Pictures

During his brief life, Paul Laurence Dunbar became the first black writer to attain national prominence and the first to support himself wholly by his writing. Dunbar was born in Dayton, Ohio, the son of former slaves (his father had escaped to Canada via the Underground Railroad). Though poor and unschooled, they were ambitious for their son and predicted greatness for him. The only black student in his high school class, Dunbar was the president of the literary society, editor of the school newspaper, and class poet.

After graduation, he took a job as an elevator operator and composed poems in his spare time. His high school teacher remembered him, however, and during a meeting in Dayton of the Western Association of Writers, asked him to prepare an address of welcome. Dunbar delivered a poem. Impressed with the twenty-year-old Dunbar, the members of the association showed some of his poems to the famous writer James Whitcomb Riley, who responded with an encouraging letter of congratulation. Within a year, using money he had earned as an elevator operator, Dunbar published his first volume of poetry, *Oak and Ivy* (1893).

A second collection, *Majors and Minors,* appeared the following year and received a laudatory review from the most influential literary critic of the day, William Dean Howells, who called Dunbar the first poet to "feel the Negro life aesthetically and express it lyrically." The publication of *Lyrics of Lowly Life* (1896), with an introduction by Howells, made Dunbar a famous and popular poet.

To Dunbar's great disappointment and frustration, however, what critics and the public most admired were his sentimental, supposedly authentic plantation lyrics written in black dialect. Dunbar strove to write first and foremost as a poet of the English language, expressing universal values and feelings. Thus, many of his poems, including the two that follow, are written in an elegant, formal style. He said in a letter that his ambition was to "be able to interpret my own people through song and story, and to prove to the many that after all we are more human than African."

In his later years, Dunbar was a much respected literary figure. He gave popular platform readings in America and England. In spite of the tuberculosis that hindered him and eventually cut short his life, Dunbar continued to write at a prodigious rate, producing in the last ten years of his life four novels, four books of short stories, and three more volumes of verse.

Douglass

Ah, Douglass, we have fall'n on evil days,
   Such days as thou, not even thou didst know,
   When thee, the eyes of that harsh long ago
Saw, salient,° at the cross of devious ways,
And all the country heard thee with amaze.　　　　　　　5
   Not ended then, the passionate ebb and flow,
   The awful tide that battled to and fro;
We ride amid a tempest of dispraise.

Now, when the waves of swift dissension swarm,
   And Honor, the strong pilot, lieth stark,°　　　　　10
Oh, for thy voice high-sounding o'er the storm,
   For thy strong arm to guide the shivering bark,°
The blast-defying power of thy form,
   To give us comfort through the lonely dark.

4. **salient** (sā′lē-ənt): prominent.　10. **stark:** stiff, as a corpse.　12. **bark:** boat.

Frederick Douglass. An excerpt from Douglass' autobiography, *My Bondage and My Freedom,* appears on page 364.

Life's Tragedy

It may be misery not to sing at all
  And to go silent through the brimming day.
It may be sorrow never to be loved,
  But deeper griefs than these beset the way.

To have come near to sing the perfect song   5
  And only by a half-tone lost the key,
There is the potent sorrow, there the grief,
  The pale, sad staring of life's tragedy.

To have just missed the perfect love,
  Not the hot passion of untempered youth,   10
But that which lays aside its vanity
  And gives thee, for thy trusting worship, truth—

This, this it is to be accursed indeed;
  For if we mortals love, or if we sing,
We count our joys not by the things we have,   15
  But by what kept us from the perfect thing.

For Study and Discussion

Analyzing and Interpreting the Poems
Douglass
1. How does the poet use the metaphor of a boat caught in a storm, and in need of a pilot, to praise the strength of Frederick Douglass, the famous black abolitionist?
2. To what does "the awful tide that battled to and fro" refer?

Life's Tragedy
1a. According to this poem, what is life's tragedy? **b.** What image does the poet use in line 8 to describe this tragedy?
2. In stanza 3, how does the poet distinguish perfect love from imperfect love?
3. The poet asserts that part of life's tragedy lies in our inability to remain content with "the things we have"—we measure ourselves not by what we have attained, but by what we have not attained. Do you agree or disagree with the poet's view?

Writing About Literature

Analyzing Dunbar's Use of Sonnet Form
Write a composition in which you analyze Paul Laurence Dunbar's use of the sonnet form in the poem "Douglass." Remember that there are two basic sonnet forms, the **Shakespearean** and the **Petrarchan.** Which form does Dunbar use? What is the poem's rhyme scheme? How does the poet organize his ideas? How does he vary meter for emphasis?

The American Novel

> . . . The novel can't be compared to the epic, or to the monuments of poetic drama. But it is the best we can do just now. It is a sort of latter-day lean-to, a hovel in which the spirit takes shelter. A novel is balanced between a few true impressions and the multitude of false ones that make up most of what we call life. It tells us that for every human being there is a diversity of existences, that the single existence is itself an illusion in part, that these many existences signify something, tend to something, fulfill something; it promises us meaning, harmony, and even justice. . . .
>
> —Saul Bellow, *The Nobel Lecture*

A novel can be defined as a prose narrative that is longer than a short story. Some novels are very long, some barely longer than a long short story. But all novels are more complex, more ambitious undertakings than stories. Often a novel introduces many more characters than a short story, and many novels give a much more detailed picture of the society in which the characters move. A novel also enables the writer to make a more powerful statement about the world or the universe than does a short story. While a short story generally reveals a writer's artistry—the mastery of form and detail—a novel reveals, in addition, the size of the writer's vision and ability to deal with complex situations. Many of the short-story writers represented in this book are also fine novelists. In the following pages, we will consider what they and other writers have done to develop the American novel.

The Beginnings of the Novel in America

In the last decade of the eighteenth century, two novels appeared that indicated several important directions that the American novel would take. One, *Modern Chivalry,* was by a Pennsylvania politician and judge, Hugh Henry Brackenridge. Modeled on Cervantes' *Don Quixote*, Brackenridge's novel tells of the travels through Pennsylvania of Captain John Farrago and his servant, Teague O'Regan. A journey through some part of this country was to be an important element in later novels that exposed and commented upon a particular segment of American life. The scrapes Teague gets into and from which he is rescued by Farrago give the author many opportunities to comment on society, especially on the problems facing the new American democracy. At one point Brackenridge cautions, "The demagogue is the first destroyer of the Constitution by deceiving the people. . . . He is an aristocrat and seeks after more power than is just. He will never rest short of despotic rule."

Charles Brockden Brown
(1806). Engraving.

Several years later, a very different kind of novel appeared. Charles Brockden Brown's *Wieland* was influenced by English novels like Horace Walpole's *The Castle of Otranto*. These novels, involving mysterious plots, melodramatic characters, and elements of suspense and horror, are known as *Gothic* novels, and Brown is generally regarded as the first "American Gothic" novelist. *Wieland* is about the tragic experiments of a ventriloquist who persuades others that they are hearing mysterious voices. One literary historian has commented that "*Wieland* derives its strength not merely from the exploitation of sensation, but from the blending of the Gothic method with philosophical, psychological, and moral implications to create a powerful, even if unbalanced, book." Using grotesque characters and situations to explore moral problems is a characteristic of many later American novels, from Nathaniel Hawthorne's *The House of the Seven Gables* to William Faulkner's *Light in August*.

The Great Early Novelists

Though Brackenridge and Brown produced works that are considered significant by literary historians, their novels are rarely read today. Many years passed before America produced a truly important novelist, one whose novels were admired by Americans and Europeans alike and who, because he created one of the great characters of literature, is still read today. In 1823 James Fenimore Cooper's *The Pioneers*, the first of five *Leatherstocking Tales* dealing with the frontiersman Natty

Bumppo, was published. In depicting Bumppo, the "natural man" who serves as a bond between the innocent ways of the forest and the complex ways of society, Cooper created one of the central character types of American literature.

Five years after *The Pioneers*, Nathaniel Hawthorne's first novel, *Fanshawe*, appeared. The author regarded this work as a failure, and it is rarely read today. Many years later—in 1850—Hawthorne produced one of the masterpieces of American literature, *The Scarlet Letter*. Unlike Cooper's novels of adventure, *The Scarlet Letter* is a compact, intricately worked-out story of how the lives of four people are affected by one sin. *The Scarlet Letter* is as notable for its artistry as for its psychological and moral depth. It showed later novelists— among them, Henry James and Willa Cather—what American writers could accomplish when they set out to write not only serious, morally complex novels but also carefully shaped works of art in which hardly one word, one detail is wasted.

Hawthorne's friend Herman Melville produced a very different novel. *Moby-Dick* is a large, sprawling work. No one would call it perfectly constructed, but many readers prize it above all other American novels for its tumultuous grapplings with the meaning of life and for its profoundly posed questions about human beings and their place in the universe. *Moby-Dick,* as an exploration of the technique and form of the novel, probably has had little influence on subsequent novelists. It is a unique work of genius. But its example has encouraged modern novelists to wrestle with the same questions that troubled Melville, perhaps in the hope that such profound issues would inspire in them an eloquence comparable to his.

Postwar Novelists

Mark Twain, the greatest American prose writer in the decade after the Civil War, did not publish his masterpiece, *Adventures of Huckleberry Finn*, until 1884. During his lifetime, Twain was known primarily as a humorist and a lecturer, a beloved public figure. Today his reputation rests on a small part of his work, notably *The Adventures of Tom Sawyer, Life on the Mississippi, Roughing It*, and above all, *Huckleberry Finn*. Ernest Hemingway wrote, "All modern American literature comes from one book by Mark Twain called *Huckleberry Finn.*" It was the example of this novel that influenced writers such as Hemingway and Sherwood Anderson to develop a simple, flexible style based on common speech rhythms. And the story of the relationship between Huck the boy and Jim the runaway slave is one of the most moving and profound stories told by an American.

As realism came to dominate American writing, novelists turned more and more to close observation of the world they knew. William

William Dean Howells.

Theodore Dreiser.

Ellen Glasgow.

Dean Howells, influential as a magazine editor and critic, was also one of the foremost novelists of the period. Novels such as *The Rise of Silas Lapham* display minute observation of specific sections of society and of the interaction between different social levels. Henry James, who lived much of his life in England and wrote as much about the English as about Americans, spent his artistic life striving to make the novel a more sensitive, subtle, and complex instrument for exploring the life around him. In his early novels, including *Daisy Miller, Washington Square,* and *The American,* and in later, large works, such as *The Wings of the Dove, The Ambassadors,* and *The Golden Bowl,* he probed not only social complexities but the mysteries of the individual personality.

Stephen Crane's *The Red Badge of Courage* is an outstanding example of the realistic novel. Although Crane lived to complete other novels and some fine short stories, his early death is one of the tragedies of American literature. Another important realistic writer is Frank Norris, whose novel *The Octopus* deals with the bitter commercial war between wheat farmers and the railroads, and whose *McTeague* carefully traces the degenerating effects of greed on one man. Regarded by some critics as a giant among realistic writers, Theodore Dreiser wrote long, detailed novels, among them *Sister Carrie* and *An American Tragedy.*

Three women practiced the art of the realistic novel in a more restrained, subtle manner than either Dreiser or Norris. Willa Cather wrote of Nebraska farmers and of men and women trapped by the limitations that society placed on them. Among the best of her finely crafted novels are *O Pioneers!, My Ántonia, The Professor's House,* and *Death Comes for the Archbishop.* Ellen Glasgow, a member of a distin-

Edith Wharton.

Sinclair Lewis.

Pearl Buck.

guished Virginia family, wrote about the contrast between the old and new South in works such as *Barren Ground* and *Vein of Iron*. Edith Wharton, a New Yorker and a friend of Henry James, wrote about the wealthy "aristocracy" of American cities in *The House of Mirth* and *The Age of Innocence*. *Ethan Frome*, set in isolated New England farm country, is perhaps her best-known book, although her least typical.

The Modern American Novel

There have been a number of outstanding American novelists since World War I. Three of the most important—Ernest Hemingway, F. Scott Fitzgerald, and William Faulkner—are discussed in the biographical introductions to their stories. Another important postwar novelist, Sinclair Lewis, caricatured some of the crudities of postwar life in *Main Street* and *Babbitt*. In *Arrowsmith* and *Dodsworth* he gave two American types, the scientist and the businessman, more sympathetic treatment. John Dos Passos, in *Manhattan Transfer* and in his trilogy of novels called *U.S.A.*, used experimental techniques to capture the movement of a city and of the entire country. Thornton Wilder wrote several distinguished novels including one—*The Bridge of San Luis Rey*—that won him a Pulitzer Prize. Pearl Buck, winner of a Nobel Prize, wrote *The Good Earth*, a remarkable study of a Chinese family. John Steinbeck, who received a Pulitzer Prize for *The Grapes of Wrath*, was also awarded a Nobel Prize. Thomas Wolfe's novels have been praised for their poetry and vitality and have been criticized for their

Norman Mailer.

Joseph Heller.

Joyce Carol Oates.

shapelessness. His first, and probably his best, novel is *Look Homeward, Angel.*

Some more recent novelists who have produced important works are Eudora Welty (*Delta Wedding, The Optimist's Daughter*); Ralph Ellison (*Invisible Man*); Saul Bellow (*Henderson the Rain King, Herzog*); J. D. Salinger (*The Catcher in the Rye*); Norman Mailer (*The Armies of the Night*); Joseph Heller (*Catch-22, Something Happened*); John Updike (*Rabbit, Run, Rabbit Redux*); Joyce Carol Oates (*Them, Wonderland*); and Alice Walker (*The Color Purple*). All these writers continue to build on the base that Hawthorne, Melville, Twain, and James created. All continue to make the American novel a vital, changing form. It is difficult to predict what directions the novel will take in the future. But it is almost certain that American novelists will continue to create exciting, challenging works—unsettling in their commentaries on society, moving in their examinations of the individual personality, exhilarating in their explorations of the novel as an artistic form.

Henry James might well have said, as Thoreau did of himself, that he was born in the nick of time, at the moment when the development of ideas or social circumstances exactly suited the direction that his life would take. Thoreau meant that he reached his maturity just when transcendentalist ideas made possible a new relationship with nature. For James, the conjunction of ideas and circumstances was more complex. His career would not only reflect the general attitudes of the new realistic movement in American writing after the Civil War; it would also represent a new dedication to art for its own sake, a new critical appreciation of the novel as a literary form, and above all a new international view of society and culture. For all of these later concerns, James's upbringing seems to have been a direct preparation.

He was born in New York City, the second son of well-to-do parents who during the next years moved their growing family restlessly from place to place both here and abroad. James was taken to England as a baby of six months, and his earliest conscious memory was a view of a street in Paris. His eccentric father had no fixed occupation. Instead, he had intense interests, especially in theology, philosophy, and education, and wrote often on those subjects. The father was determined, in reaction against the rigid schooling he himself had endured, that his children should be educated in the most liberal way and in several languages. James was therefore irregularly taught, sometimes in schools, more often by tutors, in England, France, Switzerland, and Germany as well as the United States. Whenever the family momentarily settled, however, it was a house of books and of enthusiastic interest in ideas, art, music, and the theater, the last having a special fascination for James from earliest childhood. A favorite memory was of himself at twelve with his brother William, then fourteen, the two of them wearing tall hats and black gloves as they strolled the streets of Paris on their way to the theater or a museum.

Henry James (1913) by John Singer Sargent (1856–1925). Oil on canvas.

James would later recognize the immense gaps left by his erratic education. He could not, for instance, "face . . . at the blackboard the simplest geometric challenge," and he was equally weak in other standard school subjects. But the greatest fault of his father's educational scheme was that it did not direct the sons toward any profession: "What we were to do instead was just to *be* something, something unconnected with specific doing"; and the growing boy was increasingly dissatisfied with this vague future. In late adolescence he briefly tried painting, before deciding that he had only a mediocre talent. At nineteen, in search of some practical course, he spent a meaningless year at Harvard Law School, ignoring his studies and feeling himself an outsider, an observer, as he had always been at home in the midst of his large and loving but tempestuous family.

Within this aimless drifting, the two poles that drew him were art and Europe. By the age of twenty-one, he was settled in his own mind that his art would be writing fiction, and he developed this commitment though a career of fifty years. The

Garden room of Lamb House, Sussex, England, which James used as a study.

decision itself cleared many inner doubts. He could see now that his habitual role of observer and his endless "dawdling" were not a passive standing aside from life but the artist's way of acting upon experience with the "grasping imagination" necessary to seize its meaning. In place of uncertainty he now had work. What is impressive in his earliest fiction is less its quality than the steadiness of his production, his determination, in this family that so discouraged professionalism, to live by his pen as a professional writer. It is significant also that from the first he was writing reviews and critical articles as well as fiction. He would not only be an artist highly conscious of his own craft but a critic who would lead readers to a greater appreciation of what he called, in a famous essay, "The Art of Fiction."

James's new career as an artist, in turn, directed him inevitably toward Europe, which was for him both the means to personal independence and the test of his art. In a long visit to Rome in his mid-twenties, he felt himself finally taking full command of his life. "At last—for the first time—I live!" he wrote to William, with understandable exaggeration. In this place where history so overshadowed the present, he could foresee his future, a productive life as an artist whose work would be judged not just in American terms but on the world scene, where, he believed, all true art belonged. He would soon come to know European writers whose work he had been reading, he would become something of an expert on recent French writers, and in the future he would have his own high place in international literature. He would return to America, but only temporarily. By 1875 he was settled in Paris, and then, changing his mind, he moved the next year to London. Except for one long visit late in his life, he would never live in America again.

Europe was essential to James in another way, as a source of material for his fiction at a time when both Europe and America were newly ready for such fiction. Once the Civil War was over and the Union secure, Americans had a new sense of their national identity. They took a new interest in their own diversity, the regional differences that were formerly so politically divisive, in the form of local-color fiction. At the same time they looked outward in a new way to see America as a part of the international scene and to measure themselves against Europe. Just two years after the war, a paddle-wheel steamer left New York with the passengers who would begin the new age of mass tourism. Mark Twain, till then a minor local colorist, was aboard both to see the sights and to observe his fellow sightseers as they experienced the Old World. His book about the trip, *Innocents Abroad*, would take this confrontation of cultures as lightly as possible, as humor and horseplay, but its instant popularity was early evidence of America's readiness for the international novel as James would write it.

James was not interested in mass tourism, but he was intensely interested in the drama that ensues when individuals encounter foreign cultures in ways that test their resources as persons and thereby reveal the characteristics of their societies. The result could range from a light comedy of manners to profound psychological and moral questions about human nature. In his fiction, James was a psychologist and a moralist, even a "historian of fine consciences," as a fellow writer, Joseph Conrad, called him. But for James our moral and psychological qualities as human beings were products of our social existence, expressed in our social acts. He agreed fully with the widely held premise of the new literary realism, that our social existence both defines and fulfills us as human beings. It is a view directly opposed to the transcendentalist belief of forty years earlier, that society is an encumbrance, even an antagonist, for the true individual.

It followed that literature, especially the novel, was for James directly related to the quality and complexity of our social existence. As he observed in a study of Hawthorne, "it takes a great deal of history to produce a little literature, . . . a complex social machinery to set a writer in motion." He had come, he knew, just at the right moment to his "international subject" of Americans in Europe and Europeans in America. For his native country, as he said, the Civil War made "a great deal of history. . . . It introduced into the national consciousness a certain sense of proportion and relation, of the world being a more complicated place than it had hitherto seemed. . . ." With that, America—and Europe in its relation to America—was ready for a new kind of literature. Even before his career was fairly begun, he had a sense of his major theme. In his early twenties he wrote to a friend: "We are Americans born. . . . I look upon it as a great blessing; and I think to be an American is an excellent preparation for culture. . . . We can deal freely with forms of civilization not our own, can pick and choose and assimilate. . . . We must of course have something of our own—something distinctive . . .—and I take it we shall find it in our moral consciousness. . . ."

From this perception—and its many extensions—came the long list of James's novels and stories, *Daisy Miller* (1878) being among the first. James's long career would have several phases and, of course, other interests. But the international theme, first and last, expressed his conviction that human beings are most interesting in their capacity for social and cultural development—which is also moral development—and that this is best portrayed in the meeting of European and American cultures. Daisy is herself a lightweight traveler in the long procession of the American "pilgrims" to Europe and seems scarcely aware of the cultural and social differences she is experiencing. Three years later, in Isabel Archer of *The Portrait of a Lady*, James showed a more complex young American woman discovering herself in Europe, and Isabel in her turn would be followed by the still more complex figures of James's late novels: *The Wings of the Dove* (1902), *The Ambassadors* (1903), and *The Golden Bowl* (1904). Nevertheless, Daisy's story has a grace of its own and indicates what James meant in saying that being an American is a "complex fate."

Once he had settled into his career, James's life was uneventful; the drama was all in his books. He was immensely sociable, exchanged innumerable visits and letters with a wide circle of friends, remained close to his family, and traveled often. But he lived and worked alone, his life dedicated to what he called the "sacred rage" of his art. His early popularity dropped sharply with the novels of his middle period, which were openly documents of social criticism, and did not fully recover with his late works. His deepest disappointment was probably his lack of success in writing for the stage, which had fascinated him since childhood. Strangely enough, a number of his works have in recent years been successfully produced as plays, movies, and television shows. He was deeply distressed by World War I, which meant the end of the Europe he had known. To express his commitment to his beloved and now embattled England, he became a British subject in the second year of the war, the year before he died.

Daisy Miller:
A Study

Part I

At the little town of Vevey,[1] in Switzerland, there is a particularly comfortable hotel. There are, indeed, many hotels; for the entertainment of tourists is the business of the place, which, as many travelers will remember, is seated upon the edge of a remarkably blue lake—a lake that it behooves every tourist to visit. The shore of the lake presents an unbroken array of establishments of this order, of every category, from the "grand hotel" of the newest fashion, with a chalk-white front, a hundred balconies, and a dozen flags flying from its roof, to the little Swiss *pension*[2] of an elder day, with its name inscribed in German-looking lettering upon a pink or yellow wall, and an awkward summerhouse in the angle of the garden. One of the hotels at Vevey, however, is famous, even classical, being distinguished from many of its upstart neighbors by an air both of luxury and of maturity. In this region, in the month of June, American travelers are extremely numerous; it may be said, indeed, that Vevey assumes at this period some of the characteristics of an American watering place. There are sights and sounds which evoke a vision, an echo, of Newport and Saratoga.[3] There is a flitting hither and thither of "stylish" young girls, a rustling of muslin

1. **Vevey** (və-vā′): a resort town on Lake Geneva.
2. *pension* (päN-syôN′): a residential hotel.
3. **Newport . . . Saratoga:** Newport, Rhode Island, and Saratoga Springs, New York, were fashionable resorts in the nineteenth century.

The Harbor at L'Orient (1869) by Berthe Morisot (1841–1895). Oil on canvas.
National Gallery of Art, Washington, Ailsa Mellon Bruce Collection

flounces, a rattle of dance music in the morning hours, a sound of high-pitched voices at all times. You receive an impression of these things at the excellent inn of the "Trois Couronnes,"[4] and are transported in fancy to the Ocean House or to Congress Hall.[5] But at the "Trois Couronnes," it must be added, there are other features that are much at variance with these suggestions: neat German waiters, who look like secretaries of legation; Russian princesses sitting in the garden; little Polish boys walking about, held by the hand, with their governors; a view of the sunny crest of the Dent du Midi[6] and the picturesque towers of the Castle of Chillon.[7]

I hardly know whether it was the analogies or the differences that were uppermost in the mind of a young American, who, two or three years ago, sat in the garden of the "Trois Couronnes," looking about him rather idly at some of the graceful objects I have mentioned. It was a beautiful summer morning, and in whatever fashion the young American looked at things, they must have seemed to him charming. He had come from Geneva the day before, by the little steamer, to see his aunt, who was staying at the hotel—Geneva having been for a long time his place of residence. But his aunt had a headache—his aunt had almost always a headache—and now she was shut up in her room, smelling camphor, so that he was at liberty to wander about. He was some seven-and-twenty years of age; when his friends spoke of him, they usually said that he was at Geneva, "studying." When his enemies spoke of him they said—but, after all, he had no enemies; he was an extremely amiable fellow and universally liked. What I should say is, simply, that when certain persons spoke of him they affirmed that the reason of his spending so much time at Geneva was that he was extremely devoted to a lady who lived there—a foreign lady—a person older than himself. Very few Americans—indeed I think none—had ever seen this lady, about whom there were some singular stories. But Winterbourne had an old attachment for the little metropolis of Calvinism;[8] he had been put to school there as a boy, and he had afterward gone to college there—circumstances which had led to his forming a great many youthful friendships. Many of these he had kept, and they were a source of great satisfaction to him.

After knocking at his aunt's door and learning that she was indisposed, he had taken a walk about the town, and then he had come in to his breakfast. He had now finished his breakfast; but he was drinking a small cup of coffee, which had been served to him on a little table in the garden by one of the waiters who looked like an attaché.[9] At last he finished his coffee and lit a cigarette. Presently a small boy came walking along the path—an urchin of nine or ten. The child, who was diminutive for his years, had an aged expression of countenance, a pale complexion, and sharp little features. He was dressed in knickerbockers, with red stockings, which displayed his poor little spindleshanks; he also wore a brilliant red cravat. He carried in his hand a long alpenstock,[10] the sharp point of which he thrust into everything that he approached—the flower beds, the garden benches, the trains of the ladies' dresses. In front of Winterbourne he paused, looking at him with a pair of bright, penetrating little eyes.

"Will you give me a lump of sugar?" he asked in a sharp, hard little voice—a voice immature and yet, somehow, not young.

Winterbourne glanced at the small table

---

4. **"Trois Couronnes"** (trwȧ ko͞o′rôn): French for "Three Crowns."
5. **Ocean House . . . Congress Hall:** hotels at Newport and Saratoga.
6. **Dent du Midi** (däⁿ′ dü mē′dē′): the highest peak in a group of Swiss mountains called the Dents du Midi.
7. **Castle of Chillon** (shē′yoⁿ): a thirteenth-century castle on Lake Geneva, used as the setting of Lord Byron's poem "The Prisoner of Chillon" (1816).

8. **metropolis of Calvinism:** Through the influence of John Calvin (1509–1564), Geneva became the intellectual center of Protestantism in the sixteenth century.
9. **attaché** (ăt′ə-shā′, ă-tă′shā′): a minor diplomatic employee.
10. **alpenstock** (ăl′pən-stŏk′): a pole or staff with a metal point, used in mountain climbing.

near him, on which his coffee service rested, and saw that several morsels of sugar remained. "Yes, you may take one," he answered; "but I don't think sugar is good for little boys."

This little boy stepped forward and carefully selected three of the coveted fragments, two of which he buried in the pocket of his knickerbockers, depositing the other as promptly in another place. He poked his alpenstock, lance-fashion, into Winterbourne's bench and tried to crack the lump of sugar with his teeth.

"Oh, blazes; it's har-r-d!" he exclaimed, pronouncing the adjective in a peculiar manner.

Winterbourne had immediately perceived that he might have the honor of claiming him as a fellow countryman. "Take care you don't hurt your teeth," he said paternally.

"I haven't got any teeth to hurt. They have all come out. I have only got seven teeth. My mother counted them last night, and one came out right afterward. She said she'd slap me if any more came out. I can't help it. It's this old Europe. It's the climate that makes them come out. In America they didn't come out. It's these hotels."

Winterbourne was much amused. "If you eat three lumps of sugar, your mother will certainly slap you," he said.

"She's got to give me some candy, then," rejoined his young interlocutor. "I can't get any candy here—any American candy. American candy's the best candy."

"And are American little boys the best little boys?" asked Winterbourne.

"I don't know. I'm an American boy," said the child.

"I see you are one of the best!" laughed Winterbourne.

"Are you an American man?" pursued this vivacious infant. And then, on Winterbourne's affirmative reply—"American men are the best," he declared.

His companion thanked him for the compliment; and the child, who had now got astride of his alpenstock, stood looking about him, while he attacked a second lump of sugar. Winterbourne wondered if he himself had been like this in his infancy, for he had been brought to Europe at about this age.

"Here comes my sister!" cried the child in a moment. "She's an American girl."

Winterbourne looked along the path and saw a beautiful young lady advancing. "American girls are the best girls," he said cheerfully to his young companion.

"My sister ain't the best!" the child declared. "She's always blowing at me."

"I imagine that is your fault, not hers," said Winterbourne. The young lady meanwhile had drawn near. She was dressed in white muslin, with a hundred frills and flounces, and knots of pale-colored ribbon. She was bareheaded; but she balanced in her hand a large parasol, with a deep border of embroidery; and she was strikingly, admirably pretty. "How pretty they are!" thought Winterbourne, straightening himself in his seat, as if he were prepared to rise.

The young lady paused in front of his bench, near the parapet of the garden, which overlooked the lake. The little boy had now converted his alpenstock into a vaulting pole, by the aid of which he was springing about in the gravel and kicking it up not a little.

"Randolph," said the young lady, "what *are* you doing?"

"I'm going up the Alps," replied Randolph. "This is the way!" And he gave another little jump, scattering the pebbles about Winterbourne's ears.

"That's the way they come down," said Winterbourne.

"He's an American man!" cried Randolph, in his little hard voice.

The young lady gave no heed to this announcement, but looked straight at her brother. "Well, I guess you had better be quiet," she simply observed.

It seemed to Winterbourne that he had been in a manner presented. He got up and stepped slowly toward the young girl, throwing away his cigarette. "This little boy and I have made acquaintance," he said, with great civility. In Geneva, as he had been perfectly aware, a

Courtesy of Paramount Pictures Corporation

young man was not at liberty to speak to a young unmarried lady except under certain rarely occurring conditions; but here at Vevey, what conditions could be better than these?— a pretty American girl coming and standing in front of you in a garden. This pretty American girl, however, on hearing Winterbourne's observation, simply glanced at him; she then turned her head and looked over the parapet at the lake and the opposite mountains. He wondered whether he had gone too far; but he decided that he must advance farther rather than retreat. While he was thinking of something else to say, the young lady turned to the little boy again.

"I should like to know where you got that pole," she said.

"I bought it!" responded Randolph.

"You don't mean to say you're going to take it to Italy."

"Yes, I am going to take it to Italy!" the child declared.

The young girl glanced over the front of her dress and smoothed out a knot or two of ribbon. Then she rested her eyes upon the prospect again. "Well, I guess you had better leave it somewhere," she said after a moment.

"Are you going to Italy?" Winterbourne inquired in a tone of great respect.

The young lady glanced at him again. "Yes,

sir," she replied. And she said nothing more.

"Are you—a—going over the Simplon?"[11] Winterbourne pursued, a little embarrassed.

"I don't know," she said. "I suppose it's some mountain. Randolph, what mountain are we going over?"

"Going where?" the child demanded.

"To Italy," Winterbourne explained.

"I don't know," said Randolph. "I don't want to go to Italy. I want to go to America."

"Oh, Italy is a beautiful place!" rejoined the young man.

"Can you get candy there?" Randolph loudly inquired.

"I hope not," said his sister. "I guess you have had enough candy, and mother thinks so too."

"I haven't had any for ever so long—for a hundred weeks!" cried the boy, still jumping about.

The young lady inspected her flounces and smoothed her ribbons again; and Winterbourne presently risked an observation upon the beauty of the view. He was ceasing to be embarrassed, for he had begun to perceive that she was not in the least embarrassed herself. There had not been the slightest alteration in her charming complexion; she was evidently neither offended nor fluttered. If she looked another way when he spoke to her, and seemed not particularly to hear him, this was simply her habit, her manner. Yet, as he talked a little more and pointed out some of the objects of interest in the view, with which she appeared quite unacquainted, she gradually gave him more of the benefit of her glance; and then he saw that this glance was perfectly direct and unshrinking. It was not, however, what would have been called an immodest glance, for the young girl's eyes were singularly honest and fresh. They were wonderfully pretty eyes; and, indeed, Winterbourne had not seen for a long time anything prettier than his fair countrywoman's various features—her complexion, her nose, her ears, her teeth. He had a great relish for feminine beauty; he was addicted to observing and analyzing it; and as regards this young lady's face he made several observations. It was not at all insipid, but it was not exactly expressive; and though it was eminently delicate Winterbourne mentally accused it—very forgivingly—of a want of finish. He thought it very possible that Master Randolph's sister was a coquette;[12] he was sure she had a spirit of her own; but in her bright, sweet, superficial little visage there was no mockery, no irony. Before long it became obvious that she was much disposed toward conversation. She told him that they were going to Rome for the winter—she and her mother and Randolph. She asked him if he was a "real American"; she shouldn't have taken him for one; he seemed more like a German—this was said after a little hesitation, especially when he spoke. Winterbourne, laughing, answered that he had met Germans who spoke like Americans; but that he had not, so far as he remembered, met an American who spoke like a German. Then he asked if she should not be more comfortable in sitting upon the bench which he had just quitted. She answered that she liked standing up and walking about; but she presently sat down. She told him she was from New York State—"if you know where that is." Winterbourne learned more about her by catching hold of her small, slippery brother and making him stand a few minutes by his side.

"Tell me your name, my boy," he said.

"Randolph C. Miller," said the boy sharply. "And I'll tell you her name"; and he leveled his alpenstock at his sister.

"You had better wait till you are asked!" said this young lady calmly.

"I should like very much to know your name," said Winterbourne.

"Her name is Daisy Miller!" cried the child. "But that isn't her real name; that isn't her name on her cards."

"It's a pity you haven't got one of my cards!" said Miss Miller.

11. **Simplon** (săN-plōN'): a pass through the Alps between Switzerland and Italy.

12. **coquette** (kō-kĕt'): a flirtatious woman.

"Her real name is Annie P. Miller," the boy went on.

"Ask him *his* name," said his sister, indicating Winterbourne.

But on this point Randolph seemed perfectly indifferent; he continued to supply information with regard to his own family. "My father's name is Ezra B. Miller," he announced. "My father ain't in Europe; my father's in a better place than Europe."

Winterbourne imagined for a moment that this was the manner in which the child had been taught to intimate that Mr. Miller had been removed to the sphere of celestial rewards. But Randolph immediately added, "My father's in Schenectady. He's got a big business. My father's rich, you bet."

"Well!" ejaculated Miss Miller, lowering her parasol and looking at the embroidered border. Winterbourne presently released the child, who departed, dragging his alpenstock along the path. "He doesn't like Europe," said the young girl. "He wants to go back."

"To Schenectady, you mean?"

"Yes; he wants to go right home. He hasn't got any boys here. There is one boy here, but he always goes round with a teacher; they won't let him play."

"And your brother hasn't any teacher?" Winterbourne inquired.

"Mother thought of getting him one, to travel round with us. There was a lady told her of a very good teacher; an American lady—perhaps you know her—Mrs. Sanders. I think she came from Boston. She told her of this teacher, and we thought of getting him to travel round with us. But Randolph said he didn't want a teacher traveling round with us. He said he wouldn't have lessons when he was in the cars.[13] And we *are* in the cars about half the time. There was an English lady we met in the cars—I think her name was Miss Featherstone; perhaps you know her. She wanted to know why I didn't give Randolph lessons—give him 'instruction,' she called it. I guess he could

give me more instruction than I could give him. He's very smart."

"Yes," said Winterbourne; "he seems very smart."

"Mother's going to get a teacher for him as soon as we get to Italy. Can you get good teachers in Italy?"

"Very good, I should think," said Winterbourne.

"Or else she's going to find some school. He ought to learn some more. He's only nine. He's going to college." And in this way Miss Miller continued to converse upon the affairs of her family and upon other topics. She sat there with her extremely pretty hands, ornamented with very brilliant rings, folded in her lap, and with her pretty eyes now resting upon those of Winterbourne, now wandering over the garden, the people who passed by, and the beautiful view. She talked to Winterbourne as if she had known him a long time. He found it very pleasant. It was many years since he had heard a young girl talk so much. It might have been said of this unknown young lady, who had come and sat down beside him upon a bench, that she chattered. She was very quiet; she sat in a charming tranquil attitude, but her lips and her eyes were constantly moving. She had a soft, slender, agreeable voice, and her tone was decidedly sociable. She gave Winterbourne a history of her movements and intentions, and those of her mother and brother, in Europe and enumerated, in particular, the various hotels at which they had stopped. "That English lady, in the cars," she said—"Miss Featherstone—asked me if we didn't all live in hotels in America. I told her I had never been in so many hotels in my life as since I came to Europe. I have never seen so many—it's nothing but hotels." But Miss Miller did not make this remark with a querulous accent; she appeared to be in the best humor with everything. She declared that the hotels were very good, when once you got used to their ways, and that Europe was perfectly sweet. She was not disappointed—not a bit. Perhaps it was because she had heard so much about it be-

---

13. **the cars:** railway passenger cars.

fore. She had ever so many intimate friends that had been there ever so many times. And then she had had ever so many dresses and things from Paris. Whenever she put on a Paris dress she felt as if she were in Europe.

"It was kind of a wishing cap," said Winterbourne.

"Yes," said Miss Miller, without examining this analogy; "it always made me wish I was here. But I needn't have done that for dresses. I am sure they send all the pretty ones to America; you see the most frightful things here. The only thing I don't like," she proceeded, "is the society. There isn't any society; or, if there is, I don't know where it keeps itself. Do you? I suppose there is some society somewhere, but I haven't seen anything of it. I'm very fond of society, and I have always had a great deal of it. I don't mean only in Schenectady, but in New York. I used to go to New York every winter. In New York I had lots of society. Last winter I had seventeen dinners given me; and three of them were by gentlemen," added Daisy Miller. "I have more friends in New York than in Schenectady—more gentleman friends; and more young lady friends too," she resumed in a moment. She paused again for an instant; she was looking at Winterbourne with all her prettiness in her lively eyes and in her light, slightly monotonous smile. "I have always had," she said, "a great deal of gentlemen's society."

Poor Winterbourne was amused, perplexed, and decidedly charmed. He had never yet heard a young girl express herself in just this fashion; never, at least, save in cases where to say such things seemed a kind of demonstrative evidence of a certain laxity of deportment. And yet was he to accuse Miss Daisy Miller of actual or potential *inconduite*,[14] as they said at Geneva? He felt that he had lived at Geneva so long that he had lost a good deal; he had become dishabituated to[15] the American tone.

Never, indeed, since he had grown old enough to appreciate things, had he encountered a young American girl of so pronounced a type as this. Certainly she was very charming, but how deucedly sociable! Was she simply a pretty girl from New York State—were they all like that, the pretty girls who had a good deal of gentlemen's society? Or was she also a designing, an audacious, an unscrupulous young person? Winterbourne had lost his instinct in this matter, and his reason could not help him. Miss Daisy Miller looked extremely innocent. Some people had told him that, after all, American girls were exceedingly innocent; and others had told him that, after all, they were not. He was inclined to think Miss Daisy Miller was a flirt—a pretty American flirt. He had never, as yet, had any relations with young ladies of this category. He had known, here in Europe, two or three women—persons older than Miss Daisy Miller, and provided, for respectability's sake, with husbands—who were great coquettes—dangerous, terrible women, with whom one's relations were liable to take a serious turn. But this young girl was not a coquette in that sense; she was very unsophisticated; she was only a pretty American flirt. Winterbourne was almost grateful for having found the formula that applied to Miss Daisy Miller. He leaned back in his seat; he remarked to himself that she had the most charming nose he had ever seen; he wondered what were the regular conditions and limitations of one's intercourse with a pretty American flirt. It presently became apparent that he was on the way to learn.

"Have you been to that old castle?" asked the young girl, pointing with her parasol to the far-gleaming walls of the Château de Chillon.

"Yes, formerly, more than once," said Winterbourne. "You too, I suppose, have seen it?"

"No; we haven't been there. I want to go there dreadfully. Of course I mean to go there. I wouldn't go away from here without having seen that old castle."

"It's a very pretty excursion," said Winter-

---

14. *inconduite* (aN-koN'dwēt): French for "misconduct."
15. **dishabituated** (dīs'hə-bĭch'ōō-āt'əd) **to:** unaccustomed to.

Castle of Chillon in Vaud, Switzerland, at the east end of Lake Geneva.
Clyde Marsh/Bruce Coleman

bourne, "and very easy to make. You can drive, you know, or you can go by the little steamer."

"You can go in the cars," said Miss Miller.

"Yes; you can go in the cars," Winterbourne assented.

"Our courier[16] says they take you right up to the castle," the young girl continued. "We were going last week; but my mother gave out. She suffers dreadfully from dyspepsia.[17] She said she couldn't go. Randolph wouldn't go

either; he says he doesn't think much of old castles. But I guess we'll go this week, if we can get Randolph."

"Your brother is not interested in ancient monuments?" Winterbourne inquired, smiling.

"He says he doesn't care much about old castles. He's only nine. He wants to stay at the hotel. Mother's afraid to leave him alone, and the courier won't stay with him; so we haven't been to many places. But it will be too bad if we don't go up there." And Miss Miller pointed again at the Château de Chillon.

"I should think it might be arranged," said

16. **courier:** a servant hired to make arrangements and to accompany travelers.
17. **dyspepsia** (dĭs-pĕp′shə, -sē-ə): indigestion.

Winterbourne. "Couldn't you get someone to stay—for the afternoon—with Randolph?"

Miss Miller looked at him a moment; and then very placidly, "I wish *you* would stay with him!" she said.

Winterbourne hesitated a moment. "I should much rather go to Chillon with you."

"With me?" asked the young girl with the same placidity.

She didn't rise, blushing, as a young girl at Geneva would have done; and yet Winterbourne, conscious that he had been very bold, thought it possible she was offended. "With your mother," he answered very respectfully.

But it seemed that both his audacity and his respect were lost upon Miss Daisy Miller. "I guess my mother won't go after all," she said. "She don't like to ride round in the afternoon. But did you really mean what you said just now; that you would like to go up there?"

"Most earnestly," Winterbourne declared.

"Then we may arrange it. If mother will stay with Randolph, I guess Eugenio will."

"Eugenio?" the young man inquired.

"Eugenio's our courier. He doesn't like to stay with Randolph; he's the most fastidious man I ever saw. But he's a splendid courier. I guess he'll stay at home with Randolph if mother does, and then we can go to the castle."

Winterbourne reflected for an instant as lucidly as possible—"we" could only mean Miss Daisy Miller and himself. This program seemed almost too agreeable for credence; he felt as if he ought to kiss the young lady's hand. Possibly he would have done so—and quite spoiled the project; but at this moment another person—presumably Eugenio—appeared. A tall, handsome man, with superb whiskers, wearing a velvet morning coat and a brilliant watch chain, approached Miss Miller, looking sharply at her companion. "Oh, Eugenio!" said Miss Miller with the friendliest accent.

Eugenio had looked at Winterbourne from head to foot; he now bowed gravely to the young lady. "I have the honor to inform mademoiselle that luncheon is upon the table."

Miss Miller slowly rose. "See here, Eugenio," she said. "I'm going to that old castle, anyway."

"To the Château de Chillon, mademoiselle?" the courier inquired. "Mademoiselle has made arrangements?" he added, in a tone which struck Winterbourne as very impertinent.

Eugenio's tone apparently threw, even to Miss Miller's own apprehension, a slightly ironical light upon the young girl's situation. She turned to Winterbourne, blushing a little—a very little. "You won't back out?" she said.

"I shall not be happy till we go!" he protested.

"And you are staying in this hotel?" she went on. "And you are really an American?"

The courier stood looking at Winterbourne offensively. The young man, at least, thought his manner of looking an offense to Miss Miller; it conveyed an imputation that she "picked up" acquaintances. "I shall have the honor of presenting to you a person who will tell you all about me," he said, smiling and referring to his aunt.

"Oh, well, we'll go someday," said Miss Miller. And she gave him a smile and turned away. She put up her parasol and walked back to the inn beside Eugenio. Winterbourne stood looking after her; and as she moved away, drawing her muslin furbelows over the gravel, said to himself that she had the *tournure*[18] of a princess.

He had, however, engaged to do more than proved feasible in promising to present his aunt, Mrs. Costello, to Miss Daisy Miller. As soon as the former lady had got better of her headache he waited upon her in her apartment; and, after the proper inquiries in regard to her health, he asked her if she had observed, in the hotel, an American family—a mamma, a daughter, and a little boy.

"And a courier?" said Mrs. Costello. "Oh, yes, I have observed them. Seen them—heard them—and kept out of their way." Mrs. Costello was a widow with a fortune; a person of much distinction, who frequently intimated

---

18. *tournure* (tŏŏr′nyər): French for "carriage; poise."

that, if she were not so dreadfully liable to sick headaches, she would probably have left a deeper impress upon her time. She had a long pale face, a high nose, and a great deal of very striking white hair, which she wore in large puffs and *rouleaux*[19] over the top of her head. She had two sons married in New York and another who was now in Europe. This young man was amusing himself at Homburg,[20] and, though he was on his travels, was rarely perceived to visit any particular city at the moment selected by his mother for her own appearance there. Her nephew, who had come up to Vevey expressly to see her, was therefore more attentive than those who, as she said, were nearer to her. He had imbibed at Geneva the idea that one must always be attentive to one's aunt. Mrs. Costello had not seen him for many years, and she was greatly pleased with him, manifesting her approbation by initiating him into many of the secrets of that social sway which, as she gave him to understand, she exerted in the American capital. She admitted that she was very exclusive; but, if he were acquainted with New York, he would see that one had to be. And her picture of the minutely hierarchical constitution of the society of that city, which she presented to him in many different lights, was, to Winterbourne's imagination, almost oppressively striking.

He immediately perceived from her tone that Miss Daisy Miller's place in the social scale was low. "I am afraid you don't approve of them," he said.

"They are very common," Mrs. Costello declared. "They are the sort of Americans that one does one's duty by not—not accepting."

"Ah, you don't accept them?" said the young man.

"I can't, my dear Frederick. I would if I could, but I can't."

"The young girl is very pretty," said Winterbourne in a moment.

"Of course she's pretty. But she is very common."

"I see what you mean, of course," said Winterbourne after another pause.

"She has that charming look that they all have," his aunt resumed. "I can't think where they pick it up; and she dresses in perfection—no, you don't know how well she dresses. I can't think where they get their taste."

"But, my dear aunt, she is not, after all, a Comanche savage."

"She is a young lady," said Mrs. Costello, "who has an intimacy with her mamma's courier."

"An intimacy with the courier?" the young man demanded.

"Oh, the mother is just as bad! They treat the courier like a familiar friend—like a gentleman. I shouldn't wonder if he dines with them. Very likely they have never seen a man with such good manners, such fine clothes, so like a gentleman. He probably corresponds to the young lady's idea of a count. He sits with them in the garden, in the evening. I think he smokes."

Winterbourne listened with interest to these disclosures; they helped him to make up his mind about Miss Daisy. Evidently she was rather wild. "Well," he said, "I am not a courier, and yet she was very charming to me."

"You had better have said at first," said Mrs. Costello with dignity, "that you had made her acquaintance."

"We simply met in the garden, and we talked a bit."

"*Tout bonnement!*[21] And pray what did you say?"

"I said I should take the liberty of introducing her to my admirable aunt."

"I am much obliged to you."

"It was to guarantee my respectability," said Winterbourne.

"And pray who is to guarantee hers?"

"Ah, you are cruel!" said the young man.

---

19. *rouleaux* (rōō-lōz′): French for "rolls; coils."
20. **Homburg** (hŏm′bûrg′): Bad Homburg, a German resort.

21. *"Tout bonnement!"* (tōō bôn′mäN): French for "Indeed! Is that so!"

"She's a very nice young girl."

"You don't say that as if you believed it," Mrs. Costello observed.

"She is completely uncultivated," Winterbourne went on. "But she is wonderfully pretty, and, in short, she is very nice. To prove that I believe it, I am going to take her to the Château de Chillon."

"You two are going off there together? I should say it proved just the contrary. How long had you known her, may I ask, when this interesting project was formed? You haven't been twenty-four hours in the house."

"I had known her half an hour!" said Winterbourne, smiling.

"Dear me!" cried Mrs. Costello. "What a dreadful girl!"

Her nephew was silent for some moments. "You really think, then," he began earnestly, and with a desire for trustworthy information, "you really think that—" But he paused again.

"Think what, sir?" said his aunt.

"That she is the sort of young lady who expects a man—sooner or later—to carry her off?"

"I haven't the least idea what such young ladies expect a man to do. But I really think that you had better not meddle with little American girls that are uncultivated, as you call them. You have lived too long out of the country. You will be sure to make some great mistake. You are too innocent."

"My dear aunt, I am not so innocent," said Winterbourne, smiling and curling his mustache.

"You are too guilty, then!"

Winterbourne continued to curl his mustache meditatively. "You won't let the poor girl know you then?" he asked at last.

"Is it literally true that she is going to the Château de Chillon with you?"

"I think that she fully intends it."

"Then, my dear Frederick," said Mrs. Costello, "I must decline the honor of her acquaintance. I am an old woman, but I am not too old—thank Heaven—to be shocked!"

"But don't they all do these things—the young girls in America?" Winterbourne inquired.

Mrs. Costello stared a moment. "I should like to see my granddaughters do them!" she declared grimly.

This seemed to throw some light upon the matter, for Winterbourne remembered to have heard that his pretty cousins in New York were "tremendous flirts." If, therefore, Miss Daisy Miller exceeded the liberal margin allowed to these young ladies, it was probable that anything might be expected of her. Winterbourne was impatient to see her again, and he was vexed with himself that, by instinct, he should not appreciate her justly.

Though he was impatient to see her, he hardly knew what he should say to her about his aunt's refusal to become acquainted with her; but he discovered, promptly enough, that with Miss Daisy Miller there was no great need of walking on tiptoe. He found her that evening in the garden, wandering about in the warm starlight, like an indolent sylph,[22] and swinging to and fro the largest fan he had ever beheld. It was ten o'clock. He had dined with his aunt, had been sitting with her since dinner, and had just taken leave of her till the morrow. Miss Daisy Miller seemed very glad to see him; she declared it was the longest evening she had ever passed.

"Have you been all alone?" he asked.

"I have been walking round with mother. But mother gets tired walking round," she answered.

"Has she gone to bed?"

"No; she doesn't like to go to bed," said the young girl. "She doesn't sleep—not three hours. She says she doesn't know how she lives. She's dreadfully nervous. I guess she sleeps more than she thinks. She's gone somewhere after Randolph; she wants to try to get him to go to bed. He doesn't like to go to bed."

"Let us hope she will persuade him," observed Winterbourne.

"She will talk to him all she can; but he

22. **sylph** (sĭlf): a slender, graceful girl.

doesn't like her to talk to him," said Miss Daisy, opening her fan. "She's going to try to get Eugenio to talk to him. But he isn't afraid of Eugenio. Eugenio's a splendid courier, but he can't make much impression on Randolph! I don't believe he'll go to bed before eleven." It appeared that Randolph's vigil was in fact triumphantly prolonged, for Winterbourne strolled about with the young girl for some time without meeting her mother. "I have been looking round for that lady you want to introduce me to," his companion resumed. "She's your aunt." Then, on Winterbourne's admitting the fact and expressing some curiosity as to how she had learned it, she said she had heard all about Mrs. Costello from the chambermaid. She was very quiet and very *comme il faut*,[23] she wore white puffs; she spoke to no one, and she never dined at the table d'hôte.[24] Every two days she had a headache. "I think that's a lovely description, headache and all!" said Miss Daisy, chattering along in her thin, gay voice. "I want to know her ever so much. I know just what *your* aunt would be; I know I should like her. She would be very exclusive. I like a lady to be exclusive; I'm dying to be exclusive myself. Well, we *are* exclusive, mother and I. We don't speak to everyone— or they don't speak to us. I suppose it's about the same thing. Anyway, I shall be ever so glad to know your aunt."

Winterbourne was embarrassed. "She would be most happy," he said; "but I am afraid those headaches will interfere."

The young girl looked at him through the dusk. "But I suppose she doesn't have a headache every day," she said sympathetically.

Winterbourne was silent a moment. "She tells me she does," he answered at last—not knowing what to say.

Miss Daisy Miller stopped and stood looking at him. Her prettiness was still visible in the darkness; she was opening and closing her enormous fan. "She doesn't want to know me!"

she said suddenly. "Why don't you say so? You needn't be afraid. I'm not afraid!" And she gave a little laugh.

Winterbourne fancied there was a tremor in her voice; he was touched, shocked, mortified by it. "My dear young lady," he protested, "she knows no one. It's her wretched health."

The young girl walked on a few steps, laughing still. "You needn't be afraid," she repeated. "Why should she want to know me?" Then she paused again; she was close to the parapet of the garden, and in front of her was the starlit lake. There was a vague sheen upon its surface, and in the distance were dimly-seen mountain forms. Daisy Miller looked out upon the mysterious prospect, and then she gave another little laugh. "Gracious! she *is* exclusive!" she said. Winterbourne wondered whether she was seriously wounded, and for a moment almost wished that her sense of injury might be such as to make it becoming in him to attempt to reassure and comfort her. He had a pleasant sense that she would be very approachable for consolatory purposes. He felt then, for the instant, quite ready to sacrifice his aunt conversationally; to admit that she was a proud, rude woman and to declare that they needn't mind her. But before he had time to commit himself to this perilous mixture of gallantry and impiety, the young lady, resuming her walk, gave an exclamation in quite another tone. "Well; here's mother! I guess she hasn't got Randolph to go to bed." The figure of a lady appeared, at a distance, very indistinct in the darkness, and advancing with a slow and wavering movement. Suddenly it seemed to pause.

"Are you sure it is your mother? Can you distinguish her in this thick dusk?" Winterbourne asked.

"Well!" cried Miss Daisy Miller with a laugh, "I guess I know my own mother. And when she has got on my shawl, too! She is always wearing my things."

The lady in question, ceasing to advance, hovered vaguely about the spot at which she had checked her steps.

23. **comme il faut** (kô-mēl-fō′): French for "proper, well mannered."
24. **table d'hôte** (tä′bəl-dōt′): the public dining table.

"I am afraid your mother doesn't see you," said Winterbourne. "Or perhaps," he added—thinking, with Miss Miller, the joke permissible—"perhaps she feels guilty about your shawl."

"Oh, it's a fearful old thing!" the young girl replied serenely. "I told her she could wear it. She won't come here, because she sees you."

"Ah, then," said Winterbourne, "I had better leave you."

"Oh, no; come on!" urged Miss Daisy Miller.

"I'm afraid your mother doesn't approve of my walking with you."

Miss Miller gave him a serious glance. "It isn't for me; it's for you—that is, it's for *her*. Well; I don't know who it's for! But mother doesn't like any of my gentlemen friends. She's right down timid. She always makes a fuss if I introduce a gentleman. But I *do* introduce them—almost always. If I didn't introduce my gentlemen friends to mother," the young girl added in her little soft, flat monotone, "I shouldn't think I was natural."

"To introduce me," said Winterbourne, "you must know my name." And he proceeded to pronounce it.

"Oh, dear; I can't say all that!" said his companion with a laugh. But by this time they had come up to Mrs. Miller, who, as they drew near, walked to the parapet of the garden and leaned upon it, looking intently at the lake and turning her back to them. "Mother!" said the young girl in a tone of decision. Upon this the elder lady turned round. "Mr. Winterbourne," said Miss Daisy Miller, introducing the young man very frankly and prettily. "Common" she was, as Mrs. Costello had pronounced her; yet it was a wonder to Winterbourne that, with her commonness, she had a singularly delicate grace.

Her mother was a small, spare, light person, with a wandering eye, a very exiguous[25] nose, and a large forehead decorated with a certain amount of thin, much-frizzled hair. Like her daughter, Mrs. Miller was dressed with extreme elegance; she had enormous diamonds in her ears. So far as Winterbourne could observe, she gave him no greeting—she certainly was not looking at him. Daisy was near her, pulling her shawl straight. "What are you doing, poking round here?" this young lady inquired; but by no means with that harshness of accent which her choice of words may imply.

"I don't know," said her mother, turning toward the lake again.

"I shouldn't think you'd want that shawl!" Daisy exclaimed.

"Well—I do!" her mother answered with a little laugh.

"Did you get Randolph to go to bed?" asked the young girl.

"No; I couldn't induce him," said Mrs. Miller very gently. "He wants to talk to the waiter. He likes to talk to that waiter."

"I was telling Mr. Winterbourne," the young girl went on; and to the young man's ear her tone might have indicated that she had been uttering his name all her life.

"Oh, yes!" said Winterbourne; "I have the pleasure of knowing your son."

Randolph's mamma was silent; she turned her attention to the lake. But at last she spoke. "Well, I don't see how he lives!"

"Anyhow, it isn't so bad as it was at Dover,"[26] said Daisy Miller.

"And what occurred at Dover?" Winterbourne asked.

"He wouldn't go to bed at all. I guess he sat up all night—in the public parlor. He wasn't in bed at twelve o'clock: I know that."

"It was half-past twelve," declared Mrs. Miller with mild emphasis.

"Does he sleep much during the day?" Winterbourne demanded.

"I guess he doesn't sleep much," Daisy rejoined.

"I wish he would!" said her mother. "It seems as if he couldn't."

25. **exiguous** (ĕg-zĭg′yo͞o-əs, ĭg-, ĕk-sĭg′-, ĭk-): meager, small.

26. **Dover:** seaport in southeast England on the English Channel and an embarkation point for France.

"I think he's real tiresome," Daisy pursued.

Then, for some moments, there was silence. "Well, Daisy Miller," said the elder lady presently, "I shouldn't think you'd want to talk against your own brother!"

"Well, he *is* tiresome, mother," said Daisy, quite without the asperity of a retort.

"He's only nine," urged Mrs. Miller.

"Well, he wouldn't go to that castle," said the young girl. "I'm going there with Mr. Winterbourne."

To this announcement, very placidly made, Daisy's mamma offered no response. Winterbourne took for granted that she deeply disapproved of the projected excursion; but he said to himself that she was a simple, easily managed person and that a few deferential protestations would take the edge from her displeasure. "Yes," he began, "your daughter has kindly allowed me the honor of being her guide."

Mrs. Miller's wandering eyes attached themselves, with a sort of appealing air, to Daisy, who, however, strolled a few steps farther, gently humming to herself. "I presume you will go in the cars," said her mother.

"Yes; or in the boat," said Winterbourne.

"Well, of course, I don't know," Mrs. Miller rejoined. "I have never been to that castle."

"It is a pity you shouldn't go," said Winterbourne, beginning to feel reassured as to her opposition. And yet he was quite prepared to find that, as a matter of course, she meant to accompany her daughter.

"We've been thinking ever so much about going," she pursued; "but it seems as if we couldn't. Of course Daisy—she wants to go round. But there's a lady here—I don't know her name—she says she shouldn't think we'd want to go to see castles *here;* she should think we'd want to wait till we got to Italy. It seems as if there would be so many there," continued Mrs. Miller with an air of increasing confidence. "Of course, we only want to see the principal ones. We visited several in England," she presently added.

"Ah, yes! in England there are beautiful cas-

tles," said Winterbourne. "But Chillon, here, is very well worth seeing."

"Well, if Daisy feels up to it—"said Mrs. Miller, in a tone impregnated with a sense of the magnitude of the enterprise. "It seems as if there was nothing she wouldn't undertake."

"Oh, I think she'll enjoy it!" Winterbourne declared. And he desired more and more to make it a certainty that he was to have the privilege of a tête-à-tête[27] with the young lady, who was still strolling along in front of them, softly vocalizing. "You are not disposed, madam," he inquired, "to undertake it yourself?"

Daisy's mother looked at him an instant askance and then walked forward in silence. Then—"I guess she had better go alone," she said simply. Winterbourne observed to himself that this was a very different type of maternity from that of the vigilant matrons who massed themselves in the forefront of social intercourse in the dark old city[28] at the other end of the lake. But his meditations were interrupted by hearing his name very distinctly pronounced by Mrs. Miller's unprotected daughter.

"Mr. Winterbourne!" murmured Daisy.

"Mademoiselle!" said the young man.

"Don't you want to take me out in a boat?"

"At present?" he asked.

"Of course!" said Daisy.

"Well, Annie Miller!" exclaimed her mother.

"I beg you, madam, to let her go," said Winterbourne ardently; for he had never yet enjoyed the sensation of guiding through the summer starlight a skiff freighted with a fresh and beautiful young girl.

"I shouldn't think she'd want to," said her mother. "I should think she'd rather go indoors."

"I'm sure Mr. Winterbourne wants to take me," Daisy declared. "He's so awfully devoted!"

"I will row you over to Chillon, in the starlight."

27. **tête-à-tête** (tāt′ə-tāt′): a private conversation.
28. **dark old city:** Geneva.

"I don't believe it!" said Daisy.

"Well!" ejaculated the elder lady again.

"You haven't spoken to me for half an hour," her daughter went on.

"I have been having some very pleasant conversation with your mother," said Winterbourne.

"Well; I want you to take me out in a boat!" Daisy repeated. They had all stopped, and she had turned round and was looking at Winterbourne. Her face wore a charming smile, her pretty eyes were gleaming, she was swinging her great fan about. No; it's impossible to be prettier than that, thought Winterbourne.

"There are half a dozen boats moored at that landing place," he said, pointing to certain steps which descended from the garden to the lake. "If you will do me the honor to accept my arm, we will go and select one of them."

Daisy stood there smiling; she threw back her head and gave a little, light laugh. "I like a gentleman to be formal!" she declared.

"I assure you it's a formal offer."

"I was bound I would make you say something," Daisy went on.

"You see it's not very difficult," said Winterbourne. "But I am afraid you are chaffing me."

"I think not, sir," remarked Mrs. Miller very gently.

"Do, then, let me give you a row," he said to the young girl.

"It's quite lovely, the way you say that!" cried Daisy.

"It will be still more lovely to do it."

"Yes, it would be lovely!" said Daisy. But she made no movement to accompany him; she only stood there laughing.

"I should think you had better find out what time it is," interposed her mother.

"It is eleven o'clock, madam," said a voice with a foreign accent out of the neighboring darkness; and Winterbourne, turning, perceived the florid personage who was in attendance upon the two ladies. He had apparently just approached.

"Oh, Eugenio," said Daisy, "I am going out in a boat!"

Eugenio bowed. "At eleven o'clock, mademoiselle?"

"I am going with Mr. Winterbourne. This very minute."

"Do tell her she can't," said Mrs. Miller to the courier.

"I think you had better not go out in a boat, mademoiselle," Eugenio declared.

Winterbourne wished to Heaven this pretty girl were not so familiar with her courier; but he said nothing.

"I suppose you don't think it's proper!" Daisy exclaimed. "Eugenio doesn't think anything's proper."

"I am at your service," said Winterbourne.

"Does mademoiselle propose to go alone?" asked Eugenio of Mrs. Miller.

"Oh, no; with this gentleman!" answered Daisy's mamma.

The courier looked for a moment at Winterbourne—the latter thought he was smiling—and then, solemnly, with a bow, "As mademoiselle pleases!" he said.

"Oh, I hoped you would make a fuss!" said Daisy. "I don't care to go now."

"I myself shall make a fuss if you don't go," said Winterbourne.

"That's all I want—a little fuss!" And the young girl began to laugh again.

"Mr. Randolph has gone to bed!" the courier announced frigidly.

"Oh, Daisy; now we can go!" said Mrs. Miller.

Daisy turned away from Winterbourne, looking at him, smiling, and fanning herself. "Good night," she said; "I hope you are disappointed, or disgusted, or something!"

He looked at her, taking the hand she offered him. "I am puzzled," he answered.

"Well; I hope it won't keep you awake!" she said very smartly; and, under the escort of the privileged Eugenio, the two ladies passed toward the house.

Winterbourne stood looking after them; he was indeed puzzled. He lingered beside the lake for a quarter of an hour, turning over the mystery of the young girl's sudden familiarities and caprices. But the only very definite conclusion he came to was that he should enjoy deucedly "going off" with her somewhere.

Two days afterward he went off with her to the Castle of Chillon. He waited for her in the large hall of the hotel, where the couriers, the servants, the foreign tourists were lounging about and staring. It was not the place he should have chosen, but she had appointed it. She came tripping downstairs, buttoning her long gloves, squeezing her folded parasol against her pretty figure, dressed in the perfection of a soberly elegant traveling costume. Winterbourne was a man of imagination and, as our ancestors used to say, sensibility;[29] as he looked at her dress and, on the great staircase, her little rapid, confiding step, he felt as if there were something romantic going forward. He could have believed he was going to elope with her. He passed out with her among all the idle people that were assembled there; they were all looking at her very hard; she had begun to chatter as soon as she joined him. Winterbourne's preference had been that they should be conveyed to Chillon in a carriage; but she expressed a lively wish to go in the little steamer; she declared that she had a passion for steamboats. There was always such a lovely breeze upon the water, and you saw such lots of people. The sail was not long, but Winterbourne's companion found time to say a great many things. To the young man himself their little excursion was so much of an escapade—an adventure—that, even allowing for her habitual sense of freedom, he had some expectation of seeing her regard it in the same way. But it must be confessed that, in this particular, he was disappointed. Daisy Miller was extremely animated, she was in charming spirits; but she was apparently not at all excited; she was not fluttered; she avoided neither his eyes nor those of anyone else; she blushed neither when she looked at him nor when she felt that people were looking at her. People continued to look at her a great deal, and Win-

terbourne took much satisfaction in his pretty companion's distinguished air. He had been a little afraid that she would talk loud, laugh overmuch, and even, perhaps, desire to move about the boat a good deal. But he quite forgot his fears; he sat smiling, with his eyes upon her face, while, without moving from her place, she delivered herself of a great number of original reflections. It was the most charming garrulity he had ever heard. He had assented to the idea that she was "common"; but was she so, after all, or was he simply getting used to her commonness? Her conversation was chiefly of what metaphysicians term the objective cast; but every now and then it took a subjective turn.

"What on *earth* are you so grave about?" she suddenly demanded, fixing her agreeable eyes upon Winterbourne's.

"Am I grave?" he asked. "I had an idea I was grinning from ear to ear."

"You look as if you were taking me to a funeral. If that's a grin, your ears are very near together."

"Should you like me to dance a hornpipe on the deck?"

"Pray do, and I'll carry round your hat. It will pay the expenses of our journey."

"I never was better pleased in my life," murmured Winterbourne.

She looked at him a moment and then burst into a little laugh. "I like to make you say those things! You're a queer mixture!"

In the castle, after they had landed, the subjective element decidedly prevailed. Daisy tripped about the vaulted chambers, rustled her skirts in the corkscrew staircases, flirted back with a pretty little cry and a shudder from the edge of the *oubliettes*,[30] and turned a singularly well-shaped ear to everything that Winterbourne told her about the place. But he saw that she cared very little for feudal antiquities and that the dusky traditions of Chillon made but a slight impression upon her. They

29. **sensibility:** sensitivity.

30. **oubliettes** ($\overline{oo}$'blē-ĕts'): dungeon cells made as pits, with openings only at the top. The Fench word literally means "places where one is forgotten."

had the good fortune to have been able to walk about without other companionship than that of the custodian; and Winterbourne arranged with this functionary that they should not be hurried—that they should linger and pause wherever they chose. The custodian interpreted the bargain generously—Winterbourne, on his side, had been generous—and ended by leaving them quite to themselves. Miss Miller's observations were not remarkable for logical consistency; for anything she wanted to say she was sure to find a pretext. She found a great many pretexts in the rugged embrasures of Chillon for asking Winterbourne sudden questions about himself—his family, his previous history, his tastes, his habits, his intentions—and for supplying information upon corresponding points in her own personality. Of her own tastes, habits, and intentions Miss Miller was prepared to give the most definite, and indeed the most favorable, account.

"Well; I hope you know enough!" she said to her companion after he had told her the history of the unhappy Bonivard.[31] "I never saw a man that knew so much!" The history of Bonivard had evidently, as they say, gone into one ear and out of the other. But Daisy went on to say that she wished Winterbourne would travel with them and "go round" with them; they might know something, in that case. "Don't you want to come and teach Randolph?" she asked. Winterbourne said that nothing could possibly please him so much; but that he had unfortunately other occupations. "Other occupations? I don't believe it!" said Miss Daisy. "What do you mean? You are not in business." The young man admitted that he was not in business; but he had engagements which, even within a day or two, would force him to go back to Geneva. "Oh, bother!" she said; "I don't believe it!" and she began to talk about something else. But a few moments later, when he was pointing out to her the

pretty design of an antique fireplace, she broke out irrelevantly, "You don't mean to say you are going back to Geneva?"

"It is a melancholy fact that I shall have to return to Geneva tomorrow."

"Well, Mr. Winterbourne," said Daisy; "I think you're horrid!"

"Oh, don't say such dreadful things!" said Winterbourne—"just at the last!"

"The last!" cried the young girl; "I call it the first. I have half a mind to leave you here and go straight back to the hotel alone." And for the next ten minutes she did nothing but call him horrid. Poor Winterbourne was fairly bewildered; no young lady had as yet done him the honor to be so agitated by the announcement of his movements. His companion, after this, ceased to pay any attention to the curiosities of Chillon or the beauties of the lake; she opened fire upon the mysterious charmer in Geneva whom she appeared to have instantly taken it for granted that he was hurrying back to see. How did Miss Daisy Miller know that there was a charmer in Geneva? Winterbourne, who denied the existence of such a person, was quite unable to discover; and he was divided between amazement at the rapidity of her induction and amusement at the frankness of her persiflage.[32] She seemed to him, in all this, an extraordinary mixture of innocence and crudity. "Does she never allow you more than three days at a time?" asked Daisy, ironically. "Doesn't she give you a vacation in summer? There's no one so hard worked but they can get leave to go off somewhere at this season. I suppose, if you stay another day, she'll come after you in the boat. Do wait over till Friday, and I will go down to the landing to see her arrive!" Winterbourne began to think he had been wrong to feel disappointed in the temper in which the young lady had embarked. If he had missed the personal accent, the personal accent was now making its appearance. It sounded very distinctly, at last, in her telling him she would stop "teas-

31. **Bonivard:** François de Bonivard (1496?–1570), a Swiss patriot imprisoned at Chillon and the hero of Byron's poem "The Prisoner of Chillon."

32. **persiflage** (pûr´sə-fläzh´): light, frivolous talk.

ing" him if he would promise her solemnly to come down to Rome in the winter.

"That's not a difficult promise to make," said Winterbourne. "My aunt has taken an apartment in Rome for the winter and has already asked me to come and see her."

"I don't want you to come for your aunt," said Daisy; "I want you to come for me." And this was the only allusion that the young man was ever to hear her make to his invidious kinswoman. He declared that, at any rate, he would certainly come. After this Daisy stopped teasing. Winterbourne took a carriage, and they drove back to Vevey in the dusk; the young girl was very quiet.

In the evening Winterbourne mentioned to Mrs. Costello that he had spent the afternoon at Chillon with Miss Daisy Miller.

"The Americans—of the courier?" asked this lady.

"Ah, happily," said Winterbourne, "the courier stayed at home."

"She went with you all alone?"

"All alone."

Mrs. Costello sniffed a little at her smelling bottle. "And that," she exclaimed, "is the young person whom you wanted me to know!"

Reading Check

1. How does Winterbourne become acquainted with Randolph Miller?
2. What does Daisy admit to missing in Europe?
3. How is Winterbourne related to Mrs. Costello?
4. Why does Mrs. Costello disapprove of the Miller family?
5. Where do the Millers plan to go when they leave Switzerland?

For Study and Discussion

Analyzing and Interpreting the Novel

1. The novel opens with a description of the resort town of Vevey on Lake Geneva and comes to focus on one of the many hotels, the "Trois Couronnes." What details in this description seem important for the story that follows?

2. The first of the Miller family that Winterbourne meets is Randolph, who requests a lump of sugar (and then takes three). Aside from his providing an introduction of sorts to Daisy, how should we describe Randolph's function in the book?

3. One part of Winterbourne's interest in Daisy is that he finds her so puzzling and unpredictable because of what he comes to think of as her "mysterious manners." What manners of hers seem to him unpredictable or mysterious in their exchanges that first morning and again that evening?

4. One of the first things we learn about Daisy is that that is not her name. The name on her calling cards is Annie P. Miller. **a.** What does her changing her name suggest about her? **b.** Is there any significance in her having chosen "Daisy"?

5. Winterbourne's interest in Daisy is in obvious conflict with his aunt's disdain for the entire family and their courier. Mrs. Costello's refusal to be introduced to Daisy is undoubtedly the young girl's first such experience. What does her way of dealing with it reveal about her character?

6. The most extended event of Part I is the visit to the Castle of Chillon. Winterbourne's estimate of Daisy keeps changing every few minutes, but after he announces that he must return to Geneva the next day she calls him "horrid" and attacks him with what he thinks of as "an extraordinary mixture of innocence and crudity." What keys to Daisy's character do we see in this?

Part II

Winterbourne, who had returned to Geneva the day after his excursion to Chillon, went to Rome toward the end of January. His aunt had been established there for several weeks, and he had received a couple of letters from her. "Those people you were so devoted to last summer at Vevey have turned up here, courier and all," she wrote. "They seem to have made several acquaintances, but the courier continues to be the most intime.[1] The young lady, however, is also very intimate with some third-rate Italians, with whom she rackets about in a way that makes much talk. Bring me that pretty novel of Cherbuliez's[2]—*Paule Méré*—and don't come later than the twenty-third."

In the natural course of events, Winterbourne, on arriving in Rome, would presently have ascertained Mrs. Miller's address at the American banker's and have gone to pay his compliments to Miss Daisy. "After what happened at Vevey I think I may certainly call upon them," he said to Mrs. Costello.

"If, after what happens—at Vevey and everywhere—you desire to keep up the acquaintance, you are very welcome. Of course a man may know everyone. Men are welcome to the privilege!"

"Pray what is it that happens—here, for instance?" Winterbourne demanded.

"The girl goes about alone with her foreigners. As to what happens further, you must apply elsewhere for information. She has picked up half a dozen of the regular Roman fortune hunters, and she takes them about to people's houses. When she comes to a party she brings with her a gentleman with a good deal of manner and a wonderful mustache."

"And where is the mother?"

"I haven't the least idea. They are very dreadful people."

Winterbourne meditated a moment. "They are very ignorant—very innocent only. Depend upon it they are not bad."

"They are hopelessly vulgar," said Mrs. Costello. "Whether or no being hopelessly vulgar is being 'bad' is a question for the metaphysicians. They are bad enough to dislike, at any rate; and for this short life that is quite enough."

The news that Daisy Miller was surrounded by half a dozen wonderful mustaches checked Winterbourne's impulse to go straightway to see her. He had perhaps not definitely flattered himself that he had made an ineffaceable impression upon her heart, but he was annoyed at hearing of a state of affairs so little in harmony with an image that had lately flitted in and out of his own meditations; the image of a very pretty girl looking out of an old Roman window and asking herself urgently when Mr. Winterbourne would arrive. If, however, he determined to wait a little before reminding Miss Miller of his claims to her consideration, he went very soon to call upon two or three other friends. One of these friends was an American lady who had spent several winters at Geneva, where she had placed her children at school. She was a very accomplished woman, and she lived in the Via Gregoriana.[3] Winterbourne found her in a little crimson drawing room, on a third floor; the room was filled with southern sunshine. He had not been there ten minutes when the servant came in, announcing "Madame Mila!" This announcement was presently followed by the entrance of little Randolph Miller, who stopped in the middle of the room and stood staring at Winterbourne. An instant later his pretty sister crossed the threshold; and then, after a considerable interval, Mrs. Miller slowly advanced.

"I know you!" said Randolph.

"I'm sure you know a great many things," exclaimed Winterbourne, taking him by the hand. "How is your education coming on?"

Daisy was exchanging greetings very prettily

---

1. **intime** (äN-tēm′): French for "intimate."
2. **Cherbuliez:** Charles Victor Cherbuliez (1829–1899), a minor French novelist.

3. **Via Gregoriana:** a fashionable street in Rome.

with her hostess; but when she heard Winterbourne's voice she quickly turned her head. "Well, I declare!" she said.

"I told you I should come, you know," Winterbourne rejoined, smiling.

"Well—I didn't believe it," said Miss Daisy.

"I am much obliged to you," laughed the young man.

"You might have come to see me!" said Daisy.

"I arrived only yesterday."

"I don't believe that!" the young girl declared.

Winterbourne turned with a protesting smile to her mother; but this lady evaded his glance and, seating herself, fixed her eyes upon her son. "We've got a bigger place than this," said Randolph. "It's all gold on the walls."

Mrs. Miller turned uneasily in her chair. "I told you if I were to bring you, you would say something!" she murmured.

"I told *you!*" Randolph exclaimed. "I tell *you,* sir!" he added jocosely, giving Winterbourne a thump on the knee. "It *is* bigger, too!"

Daisy had entered upon a lively conversation with her hostess; Winterbourne judged it becoming to address a few words to her mother. "I hope you have been well since we parted at Vevey," he said.

Mrs. Miller now certainly looked at him—at his chin. "Not very well, sir," she answered.

"She's got the dyspepsia," said Randolph. "I've got it too. Father's got it. I've got it most!"

This announcement, instead of embarrass-

ing Mrs. Miller, seemed to relieve her. "I suffer from the liver," she said. "I think it's this climate; it's less bracing than Schenectady, especially in the winter season. I don't know whether you know we reside at Schenectady. I was saying to Daisy that I certainly hadn't found anyone like Dr. Davis, and I didn't believe I should. Oh, at Schenectady, he stands first; they think everything of him. He has so much to do, and yet there was nothing he wouldn't do for me. He said he never saw anything like my dyspepsia, but he was bound to cure it. I'm sure there was nothing he wouldn't try. He was just going to try something new when we came off. Mr. Miller wanted Daisy to see Europe for herself. But I wrote to Mr. Miller that it seems as if I couldn't get on without Dr. Davis. At Schenectady he stands at the very top; and there's a great deal of sickness there, too. It affects my sleep."

Winterbourne had a good deal of pathological gossip with Dr. Davis's patient, during which Daisy chattered unremittingly to her own companion. The young man asked Mrs. Miller how she was pleased with Rome. "Well, I must say I am disappointed," she answered. "We had heard so much about it; I suppose we had heard too much. But we couldn't help that. We had been led to expect something different."

"Ah, wait a little, and you will become very fond of it," said Winterbourne.

"I hate it worse and worse every day!" cried Randolph.

"You are like the infant Hannibal,"[4] said Winterbourne.

"No, I ain't!" Randolph declared, at a venture.

"You are not much like an infant," said his mother. "But we have seen places," she resumed, "that I should put a long way before Rome." And in reply to Winterbourne's interrogation, "There's Zürich,"[5] she concluded; "I

think Zürich is lovely; and we hadn't heard half so much about it."

"The best place we've seen is the City of Richmond!" said Randolph.

"He means the ship," his mother explained. "We crossed in that ship. Randolph had a good time on the *City of Richmond.*"

"It's the best place I've seen," the child repeated. "Only it was turned the wrong way."

"Well, we've got to turn the right way sometime," said Mrs. Miller with a little laugh. Winterbourne expressed the hope that her daughter at least found some gratification in Rome, and she declared that Daisy was quite carried away. "It's on account of the society—the society's splendid. She goes round everywhere; she has made a great number of acquaintances. Of course she goes round more than I do. I must say they have been very sociable; they have taken her right in. And then she knows a great many gentlemen. Oh, she thinks there's nothing like Rome. Of course, it's a great deal pleasanter for a young lady if she knows plenty of gentlemen."

By this time Daisy had turned her attention again to Winterbourne. "I've been telling Mrs. Walker how mean you were!" the young girl announced.

"And what is the evidence you have offered?" asked Winterbourne, rather annoyed at Miss Miller's want of appreciation of the zeal of an admirer who on his way down to Rome had stopped neither at Bologna nor at Florence,[6] simply because of a certain sentimental impatience. He remembered that a cynical compatriot had once told him that American women—the pretty ones, and this gave a largeness to the axiom—were at once the most exacting in the world and the least endowed with a sense of indebtedness.

"Why, you were awfully mean at Vevey," said Daisy. "You wouldn't do anything. You wouldn't stay there when I asked you."

"My dearest young lady," cried Winter-

---

4. **Hannibal** (hăn′ə-bəl): Carthaginian general (247–183? B.C.), who was sworn as an infant to eternal hatred of Rome.
5. **Zürich** (zoͮor′ĭk): a city in northern Switzerland.

6. **Bologna** (bŏ-lō′nyä) . . . **Florence:** cities noted as art centers.

bourne with eloquence, "have I come all the way to Rome to encounter your reproaches?"

"Just hear him say that!" said Daisy to her hostess, giving a twist to a bow on this lady's dress. "Did you ever hear anything so quaint?"

"So quaint, my dear?" murmured Mrs. Walker in the tone of a partisan of Winterbourne.

"Well, I don't know," said Daisy, fingering Mrs. Walker's ribbons. "Mrs. Walker, I want to tell you something."

"Mother-r," interposed Randolph, with his rough ends to his words, "I tell you you've got to go. Eugenio'll raise—something!"

"I'm not afraid of Eugenio," said Daisy with a toss of her head. "Look here, Mrs. Walker," she went on, "you know I'm coming to your party."

"I am delighted to hear it."

"I've got a lovely dress."

"I am very sure of that."

"But I want to ask a favor—permission to bring a friend."

"I shall be happy to see any of your friends," said Mrs. Walker, turning with a smile to Mrs. Miller.

"Oh, they are not my friends," answered Daisy's mamma, smiling shyly in her own fashion. "I never spoke to them!"

"It's an intimate friend of mine—Mr. Giovanelli," said Daisy without a tremor in her clear little voice or a shadow on her brilliant little face.

Mrs. Walker was silent a moment; she gave a rapid glance at Winterbourne. "I shall be glad to see Mr. Giovanelli," she then said.

"He's an Italian," Daisy pursued with the prettiest serenity. "He's a great friend of mine—he's the handsomest man in the world—except Mr. Winterbourne! He knows plenty of Italians, but he wants to know some Americans. He thinks ever so much of Americans. He's tremendously clever. He's perfectly lovely!"

It was settled that this brilliant personage should be brought to Mrs. Walker's party, and then Mrs. Miller prepared to take her leave.

"I guess we'll go back to the hotel," she said.

"You may go back to the hotel, mother, but I'm going to take a walk," said Daisy.

"She's going to walk with Mr. Giovanelli," Randolph proclaimed.

"I am going to the Pincio,"[7] said Daisy, smiling.

"Alone, my dear—at this hour?" Mrs. Walker asked. The afternoon was drawing to a close—it was the hour for the throng of carriages and of contemplative pedestrians. "I don't think it's safe, my dear," said Mrs. Walker.

"Neither do I," subjoined Mrs. Miller. "You'll get the fever[8] as sure as you live. Remember what Dr. Davis told you!"

"Give her some medicine before she goes," said Randolph.

The company had risen to its feet; Daisy, still showing her pretty teeth, bent over and kissed her hostess. "Mrs. Walker, you are too perfect," she said. "I'm not going alone; I am going to meet a friend."

"Your friend won't keep you from getting the fever," Mrs. Miller observed.

"Is it Mr. Giovanelli?" asked the hostess.

Winterbourne was watching the young girl; at this question his attention quickened. She stood there smiling and smoothing her bonnet ribbons; she glanced at Winterbourne. Then, while she glanced and smiled, she answered with a shade of hesitation, "Mr. Giovanelli—the beautiful Giovanelli."

"My dear young friend," said Mrs. Walker, taking her hand, pleadingly, "don't walk off to the Pincio at this hour to meet a beautiful Italian."

"Well, he speaks English," said Mrs. Miller.

"Gracious me!" Daisy exclaimed, "I don't want to do anything improper. There's an easy way to settle it." She continued to glance at Winterbourne. "The Pincio is only a hundred yards distant, and if Mr. Winterbourne were as polite as he pretends he would offer to walk with me!"

7. **Pincio** (pĭn′chō): one of the hills of Rome, with a view of the city.
8. **the fever:** Roman fever, a form of malaria.

Winterbourne's politeness hastened to affirm itself, and the young girl gave him gracious leave to accompany her. They passed downstairs before her mother, and at the door Winterbourne perceived Mrs. Miller's carriage drawn up, with the ornamental courier whose acquaintance he had made at Vevey seated within. "Goodbye, Eugenio!" cried Daisy, "I'm going to take a walk." The distance from the Via Gregoriana to the beautiful garden at the other end of the Pincian Hill is, in fact, rapidly traversed. As the day was splendid, however, and the concourse of vehicles, walkers, and loungers numerous, the young Americans found their progress much delayed. This fact was highly agreeable to Winterbourne, in spite of his consciousness of his singular situation. The slow-moving, idly gazing Roman crowd bestowed much attention upon the extremely pretty young foreign lady who was passing through it upon his arm; and he wondered what on earth had been in Daisy's mind when she proposed to expose herself, unattended, to its appreciation. His own mission, to her sense, apparently, was to consign her to the hands of Mr. Giovanelli; but Winterbourne, at once annoyed and gratified, resolved that he would do no such thing.

"Why haven't you been to see me?" asked Daisy. "You can't get out of that."

"I have had the honor of telling you that I have only just stepped out of the train."

"You must have stayed in the train a good while after it stopped!" cried the young girl with her little laugh. "I suppose you were asleep. You have had time to go to see Mrs. Walker."

"I knew Mrs. Walker—" Winterbourne began to explain.

"I knew where you knew her. You knew her at Geneva. She told me so. Well, you knew me at Vevey. That's just as good. So you ought to have come." She asked him no other question than this; she began to prattle about her own affairs. "We've got splendid rooms at the hotel; Eugenio says they're the best rooms in Rome. We are going to stay all winter—if we don't die of the fever; and I guess we'll stay then. It's a great deal nicer than I thought; I thought it would be fearfully quiet; I was sure it would be awfully poky. I was sure we should be going round all the time with one of those dreadful old men that explain about the pictures and things. But we only had about a week of that, and now I'm enjoying myself. I know ever so many people, and they are all so charming. The society's extremely select. There are all kinds—English, and Germans, and Italians. I think I like the English best. I like their style of conversation. But there are some lovely Americans. I never saw anything so hospitable. There's something or other every day. There's not much dancing; but I must say I never thought dancing was everything. I was always fond of conversation. I guess I shall have plenty at Mrs. Walker's—her rooms are so small." When they had passed the gate of the Pincian Gardens, Miss Miller began to wonder where Mr. Giovanelli might be. "We had better go straight to that place in front," she said, "where you look at the view."

"I certainly shall not help you to find him," Winterbourne declared.

"Then I shall find him without you," said Miss Daisy.

"You certainly won't leave me!" cried Winterbourne.

She burst into her little laugh. "Are you afraid you'll get lost—or run over? But there's Giovanelli, leaning against that tree. He's staring at the women in the carriages: did you ever see anything so cool?"

Winterbourne perceived at some distance a little man standing with folded arms, nursing his cane. He had a handsome face, an artfully poised hat, a glass in one eye, and a nosegay in his buttonhole. Winterbourne looked at him a moment and then said, "Do you mean to speak to that man?"

"Do I mean to speak to him? Why, you don't suppose I mean to communicate by signs?"

"Pray understand, then," said Winterbourne, "that I intend to remain with you."

Daisy stopped and looked at him without a

sign of troubled consciousness in her face; with nothing but the presence of her charming eyes and her happy dimples. "Well, she's a cool one!" thought the young man.

"I don't like the way you say that," said Daisy. "It's too imperious."

"I beg your pardon if I say it wrong. The main point is to give you an idea of my meaning."

The young girl looked at him more gravely, but with eyes that were prettier than ever. "I have never allowed a gentleman to dictate to me or to interfere with anything I do."

"I think you have made a mistake," said Winterbourne. "You should sometimes listen to a gentleman—the right one."

Daisy began to laugh again. "I do nothing but listen to gentlemen!" she exclaimed. "Tell me if Mr. Giovanelli is the right one?"

The gentleman with the nosegay in his bosom had now perceived our two friends, and was approaching the young girl with obsequious rapidity. He bowed to Winterbourne as well as to the latter's companion; he had a brilliant smile, an intelligent eye; Winterbourne thought him not a bad-looking fellow. But he nevertheless said to Daisy, "No, he's not the right one."

Daisy evidently had a natural talent for performing introductions; she mentioned the name of each of her companions to the other. She strolled along with one of them on each side of her; Mr. Giovanelli, who spoke English very cleverly—Winterbourne afterward learned that he had practiced the idiom upon a great many American heiresses—addressed her a great deal of very polite nonsense; he was extremely urbane, and the young American, who said nothing, reflected upon that profundity of Italian cleverness which enables people to appear more gracious in proportion as they are more acutely disappointed. Giovanelli, of course, had counted upon something more intimate; he had not bargained for a party of three. But he kept his temper in a manner which suggested farstretching intentions. Winterbourne flattered himself that he

had taken his measure. "He is not a gentleman," said the young American; "he is only a clever imitation of one. He is a musicmaster, or a penny-a-liner,[9] or a third-rate artist. Damn his good looks!" Mr. Giovanelli had certainly a very pretty face; but Winterbourne felt a superior indignation at his own lovely fellow countrywoman's not knowing the difference between a spurious gentleman and a real one. Giovanelli chattered and jested and made himself wonderfully agreeable. It was true that if he was an imitation the imitation was brilliant. "Nevertheless," Winterbourne said to himself, "a nice girl ought to know!" And then he came back to the question whether this was in fact a nice girl. Would a nice girl—even allowing for her being a little American flirt—make a rendezvous with a presumably low-lived foreigner? The rendezvous in this case, indeed, had been in broad daylight and in the most crowded corner of Rome; but was it not impossible to regard the choice of these circumstances as a proof of extreme cynicism? Singular though it may seem, Winterbourne was vexed that the young girl, in joining her *amoroso*,[10] should not appear more impatient of his own company, and he was vexed because of his inclination. It was impossible to regard her as a perfectly well-conducted young lady; she was wanting in a certain indispensable delicacy. It would therefore simplify matters greatly to be able to treat her as the object of one of those sentiments which are called by romancers "lawless passions." That she should seem to wish to get rid of him would help him to think more lightly of her, and to be able to think more lightly of her would make her much less perplexing. But Daisy, on this occasion, continued to present herself as an inscrutable combination of audacity and innocence.

She had been walking some quarter of an hour, attended by her two cavaliers and responding in a tone of very childish gaiety, as

9. **penny-a-liner:** a hack writer who is paid a penny a line.
10. *amoroso* (ăm′ô-rō′sō): Italian for "suitor."

it seemed to Winterbourne, to the pretty speeches of Mr. Giovanelli, when a carriage that had detached itself from the revolving train drew up beside the path. At the same moment Winterbourne perceived that his friend Mrs. Walker—the lady whose house he had lately left—was seated in the vehicle and was beckoning to him. Leaving Miss Miller's side, he hastened to obey her summons. Mrs. Walker was flushed; she wore an excited air. "It is really too dreadful," she said. "That girl must not do this sort of thing. She must not walk here with you two men. Fifty people have noticed her."

Winterbourne raised his eyebrows. "I think it's a pity to make too much fuss about it."

"It's a pity to let the girl ruin herself!"

"She is very innocent," said Winterbourne.

"She's very crazy!" cried Mrs. Walker. "Did you ever see anything so imbecile as her mother? After you had all left me, just now, I could not sit still for thinking of it. It seemed too pitiful not even to attempt to save her. I ordered the carriage and put on my bonnet and came here as quickly as possible. Thank heaven, I have found you!"

"What do you propose to do with us?" asked Winterbourne, smiling.

"To ask her to get in, to drive her about here for half an hour, so that the world may see she is not running absolutely wild, and then to take her safely home."

Henry James **543**

"I don't think it's a very happy thought," said Winterbourne; "but you can try."

Mrs. Walker tried. The young man went in pursuit of Miss Miller, who had simply nodded and smiled at his interlocutor[11] in the carriage and had gone her way with her companion. Daisy, on learning that Mrs. Walker wished to speak to her, retraced her steps with a perfect good grace and with Mr. Giovanelli at her side. She declared that she was delighted to have a chance to present this gentleman to Mrs. Walker. She immediately achieved the introduction and declared that she had never in her life seen anything so lovely as Mrs. Walker's carriage rug.

"I am glad you admire it," said this lady, smiling sweetly. "Will you get in and let me put it over you?"

"Oh, no, thank you," said Daisy. "I shall admire it much more as I see you driving round with it."

"Do get in and drive with me," said Mrs. Walker.

"That would be charming, but it's so enchanting just as I am!" and Daisy gave a brilliant glance at the gentlemen on either side of her.

"It may be enchanting, dear child, but it is not the custom here," urged Mrs. Walker, leaning forward in her victoria[12] with her hands devoutly clasped.

"Well, it ought to be, then!" said Daisy. "If I didn't walk I should expire."

"You should walk with your mother, dear," cried the lady from Geneva, losing patience.

"With my mother, dear!" exclaimed the young girl. Winterbourne saw that she scented interference. "My mother never walked ten steps in her life. And then, you know," she added with a laugh, "I am more than five years old."

"You are old enough to be more reasonable. You are old enough, dear Miss Miller, to be talked about."

11. **interlocutor** (ĭn′tər-lŏk′yə-tər): questioner.
12. **victoria:** a horse-drawn carriage for two passengers, with a raised seat in front for the driver.

Daisy looked at Mrs. Walker, smiling intensely. "Talked about? What do you mean?"

"Come into my carriage and I will tell you."

Daisy turned her quickened glance again from one of the gentlemen beside her to the other. Mr. Giovanelli was bowing to and fro, rubbing down his gloves and laughing very agreeably; Winterbourne thought it a most unpleasant scene. "I don't think I want to know what you mean," said Daisy presently. "I don't think I should like it."

Winterbourne wished that Mrs. Walker would tuck in her carriage rug and drive away; but this lady did not enjoy being defied, as she afterward told him. "Should you prefer being thought a very reckless girl?" she demanded.

"Gracious!" exclaimed Daisy. She looked again at Mr. Giovanelli; then she turned to Winterbourne. There was a little pink flush in her cheek; she was tremendously pretty. "Does Mr. Winterbourne think," she asked slowly, smiling, throwing back her head and glancing at him from head to foot, "that—to save my reputation—I ought to get into the carriage?"

Winterbourne colored; for an instant he hesitated greatly. It seemed so strange to hear her speak that way of her "reputation." But he himself, in fact, must speak in accordance with gallantry. The finest gallantry, here, was simply to tell her the truth; and the truth, for Winterbourne, as the few indications I have been able to give have made him known to the reader, was that Daisy Miller should take Mrs. Walker's advice. He looked at her exquisite prettiness; and then he said very gently, "I think you should get into the carriage."

Daisy gave a violent laugh. "I never heard anything so stiff! If this is improper, Mrs. Walker," she pursued, "then I am all improper, and you must give me up. Goodbye; I hope you'll have a lovely ride!" and, with Mr. Giovanelli, who made a triumphantly obsequious salute, she turned away.

Mrs. Walker sat looking after her, and there were tears in Mrs. Walker's eyes. "Get in here, sir," she said to Winterbourne, indicating the place beside her. The young man answered that he felt bound to accompany Miss Miller; whereupon Mrs. Walker declared that if he refused her this favor she would never speak to him again. She was evidently in earnest. Winterbourne overtook Daisy and her companion and, offering the young girl his hand, told her that Mrs. Walker had made an imperious claim upon his society. He expected that in answer she would say something rather free, something to commit herself still further to that "recklessness" from which Mrs. Walker had so charitably endeavored to dissuade her. But she only shook his hand, hardly looking at him; while Mr. Giovanelli bade him farewell with a too emphatic flourish of the hat.

Winterbourne was not in the best possible humor as he took his seat in Mrs. Walker's victoria. "That was not clever of you," he said candidly, while the vehicle mingled again with the throng of carriages.

"In such a case," his companion answered, "I don't wish to be clever, I wish to be *earnest!*"

"Well, your earnestness has only offended her and put her off."

"It has happened very well," said Mrs. Walker. "If she is so perfectly determined to compromise herself, the sooner one knows it the better; one can act accordingly."

"I suspect she meant no harm," Winterbourne rejoined.

"So I thought a month ago. But she has been going too far."

"What has she been doing?"

"Everything that is not done here. Flirting with any man she could pick up; sitting in corners with mysterious Italians; dancing all the evening with the same partners; receiving visits at eleven o'clock at night. Her mother goes away when visitors come."

"But her brother," said Winterbourne, laughing, "sits up till midnight."

"He must be edified by what he sees. I'm told that at their hotel everyone is talking about her and that a smile goes round among all the servants when a gentleman comes and asks for Miss Miller."

"The servants be hanged!" said Winterbourne angrily. "The poor girl's only fault," he presently added, "is that she is very uncultivated."

"She is naturally indelicate," Mrs. Walker declared. "Take that example this morning. How long had you known her at Vevey?"

"A couple of days."

"Fancy, then, her making it a personal matter that you should have left the place!"

Winterbourne was silent for some moments; then he said, "I suspect, Mrs. Walker, that you and I have lived too long at Geneva!" And he added a request that she should inform him with what particular design she had made him enter her carriage.

"I wished to beg you to cease your relations with Miss Miller—not to flirt with her—to give her no further opportunity to expose herself—to let her alone, in short."

"I'm afraid I can't do that," said Winterbourne. "I like her extremely."

"All the more reason that you shouldn't help her to make a scandal."

"There shall be nothing scandalous in my attentions to her."

"There certainly will be in the way she takes them. But I have said what I had on my conscience," Mrs. Walker pursued. "If you wish to rejoin the young lady I will put you down. Here, by the way, you have a chance."

The carriage was traversing that part of the Pincian Garden that overhangs the wall of Rome and overlooks the beautiful Villa Borghese.[13] It is bordered by a large parapet, near which there are several seats. One of the seats, at a distance, was occupied by a gentleman and a lady, towards whom Mrs. Walker gave a toss of her head. At the same moment these persons rose and walked toward the parapet. Winterbourne had asked the coachman to stop; he now descended from the carriage. His companion looked at him a moment in silence; then, while he raised his hat, she drove majestically away. Winterbourne stood there;

13. **Villa Borghese** (vĭl′ə bōr-gā′zā): Once the summer palace of the Borghese family; at this time, the palace was an art museum and the grounds a public park.

he had turned his eyes toward Daisy and her cavalier. They evidently saw no one; they were too deeply occupied with each other. When they reached the low garden wall they stood a moment looking off at the great flat-topped pine clusters of the Villa Borghese; then Giovanelli seated himself familiarly upon the broad ledge of the wall. The western sun in the opposite sky sent out a brilliant shaft through a couple of cloud bars, whereupon Daisy's companion took her parasol out of her hands and opened it. She came a little nearer and he held the parasol over her; then, still holding it, he let it rest upon her shoulder, so that both of their heads were hidden from Winterbourne. This young man lingered a moment; then he began to walk. But he walked—not towards the couple with the parasol—towards the residence of his aunt, Mrs. Costello.

He flattered himself on the following day that there was no smiling among the servants when he, at least, asked for Mrs. Miller at her hotel. This lady and her daughter, however, were not at home; and on the next day after, repeating his visit, Winterbourne again had the misfortune not to find them. Mrs. Walker's party took place on the evening of the third day, and, in spite of the frigidity of his last interview with the hostess, Winterbourne was among the guests. Mrs. Walker was one of those American ladies who, while residing abroad, make a point, in their own phrase, of studying European society; and she had on this occasion collected several specimens of her diversely born fellow mortals to serve, as it were, as textbooks. When Winterbourne arrived, Daisy Miller was not there, but in a few moments he saw her mother come in alone, very shyly and ruefully. Mrs. Miller's hair above her exposed-looking temples was more frizzled than ever. As she approached Mrs. Walker, Winterbourne also drew near.

"You see I've come all alone," said poor Mrs. Miller. "I'm so frightened; I don't know what to do; it's the first time I've ever been to a party alone—especially in this country. I wanted to bring Randolph or Eugenio, or someone, but Daisy just pushed me off by myself. I ain't used to going round alone."

"And does not your daughter intend to favor us with her society?" demanded Mrs. Walker, impressively.

"Well, Daisy's all dressed," said Mrs. Miller with that accent of the dispassionate, if not of the philosophic, historian with which she always recorded the current incidents of her daughter's career. "She got dressed on purpose before dinner. But she's got a friend of hers there; that gentleman—the Italian—that she wanted to bring. They've got going at the piano; it seems as if they couldn't leave off. Mr. Giovanelli sings splendidly. But I guess they'll come before very long," concluded Mrs. Miller hopefully.

"I'm sorry she should come—in that way," said Mrs. Walker.

"Well, I told her that there was no use in her getting dressed before dinner if she was going to wait three hours," responded Daisy's mamma. "I didn't see the use of her putting on such a dress as that to sit round with Mr. Giovanelli."

"This is most horrible!" said Mrs. Walker, turning away and addressing herself to Winterbourne. "*Elle s'affiche.*[14] It's her revenge for my having ventured to remonstrate with her. When she comes I shall not speak to her."

Daisy came after eleven o'clock, but she was not, on such an occasion, a young lady to wait to be spoken to. She rustled forward in radiant loveliness, smiling and chattering, carrying a large bouquet and attended by Mr. Giovanelli. Everyone stopped talking and turned and looked at her. She came straight to Mrs. Walker. "I'm afraid you thought I never was coming, so I sent mother off to tell you. I wanted to make Mr. Giovanelli practice some things before he came; you know he sings beautifully, and I want you to ask him to sing. This is Mr. Giovanelli; you know I introduced him to you; he's got the most lovely voice and

14. *Elle s'affiche* (ĕl sä-fēsh′): French for "She's making a spectacle of herself."

Courtesy of Paramount Pictures Corporation

he knows the most charming set of songs. I made him go over them this evening, on purpose; we had the greatest time at the hotel." Of all this Daisy delivered herself with the sweetest, brightest audibleness, looking now at her hostess and now round the room, while she gave a series of little pats, round her shoulders, to the edges of her dress. "Is there anyone I know?" she asked.

"I think everyone knows you!" said Mrs. Walker pregnantly, and she gave a very cursory greeting to Mr. Giovanelli. This gentleman bore himself gallantly. He smiled and bowed and showed his white teeth; he curled his mustaches and rolled his eyes, and performed all the proper functions of a handsome Italian at an evening party. He sang, very prettily, half a dozen songs, though Mrs. Walker afterward declared that she had been quite unable to find out who asked him. It was apparently not Daisy who had given him his orders. Daisy sat at a distance from the piano, and though she had publicly, as it were, professed a high admiration for his singing, talked, not inaudibly, while it was going on.

"It's a pity these rooms are so small; we can't dance," she said to Winterbourne as if she had seen him five minutes before.

"I am not sorry we can't dance," Winterbourne answered; "I don't dance."

"Of course you don't dance; you're too stiff," said Miss Daisy. "I hope you enjoyed your drive with Mrs. Walker."

"No, I didn't enjoy it; I preferred walking with you."

"We paired off, that was much better," said

Henry James   **547**

Daisy. "But did you ever hear anything so cool as Mrs. Walker's wanting me to get into her carriage and drop poor Mr. Giovanelli, and under the pretext that it was proper? People have different ideas! It would have been most unkind; he had been talking about that walk for ten days."

"He should not have talked about it at all," said Winterbourne; "he would never have proposed to a young lady of this country to walk about the streets with him."

"About the streets?" cried Daisy, with her pretty stare. "Where then would he have proposed to her to walk? The Pincio is not the streets, either; and I, thank goodness, am not a young lady of this country. The young ladies of this country have a dreadfully poky time of it, so far as I can learn; I don't see why I should change my habits for *them*."

"I am afraid your habits are those of a flirt," said Winterbourne gravely.

"Of course they are," she cried, giving him her little smiling stare again. "I'm a fearful, frightful flirt! Did you ever hear of a nice girl that was not? But I suppose you will tell me now that I am not a nice girl."

"You're a very nice girl, but I wish you would flirt with me and me only," said Winterbourne.

"Ah! thank you—thank you very much; you are the last man I should think of flirting with. As I have had the pleasure of informing you, you are too stiff."

"You say that too often," said Winterbourne.

Daisy gave a delighted laugh. "If I could have the sweet hope of making you angry, I should say it again."

"Don't do that; when I am angry I'm stiffer than ever. But if you won't flirt with me, do cease at least to flirt with your friend at the piano; they don't understand that sort of thing here."

"I thought they understood nothing else!" exclaimed Daisy.

"Not in young unmarried women."

"It seems to me much more proper in young unmarried women than in old married ones," Daisy declared.

"Well," said Winterbourne, "when you deal with natives you must go by the custom of the place. Flirting is a purely American custom; it doesn't exist here. So when you show yourself in public with Mr. Giovanelli and without your mother—"

"Gracious! poor mother!" interposed Daisy.

"Though you may be flirting, Mr. Giovanelli is not; he means something else."

"He isn't preaching, at any rate," said Daisy with vivacity. "And if you want very much to know, we are neither of us flirting; we are too good friends for that; we are very intimate friends."

"Ah!" rejoined Winterbourne, "if you are in love with each other it is another affair."

She had allowed him up to this point to talk so frankly that he had no expectation of shocking her by this ejaculation; but she immediately got up, blushing visibly and leaving him to exclaim mentally that little American flirts were the queerest creatures in the world. "Mr. Giovanelli, at least," she said, giving her interlocutor a single glance, "never says such very disagreeable things to me."

Winterbourne was bewildered; he stood staring. Mr. Giovanelli had finished singing; he left the piano and came over to Daisy. "Won't you come into the other room and have some tea?" he asked, bending before her with his ornamental smile.

Daisy turned to Winterbourne, beginning to smile again. He was still more perplexed, for this inconsequent smile made nothing clear, though it seemed to prove, indeed, that she had a sweetness and softness that reverted instinctively to the pardon of offenses. "It has never occurred to Mr. Winterbourne to offer me any tea," she said with her little tormenting manner.

"I have offered advice," Winterbourne rejoined.

"I prefer weak tea!" cried Daisy, and she went off with the brilliant Giovanelli. She sat with him in the adjoining room, in the embrasure of the window, for the rest of the evening. There was an interesting performance at the piano, but neither of these young people gave heed to it. When Daisy came to take leave of Mrs. Walker, this lady conscientiously repaired the weakness of which she had been guilty at the moment of the young girl's arrival. She turned her back straight upon Miss Miller and left her to depart with what grace she might. Winterbourne was standing near the door; he saw it all. Daisy turned very pale and looked at her mother, but Mrs. Miller was humbly unconscious of any violation of the usual social forms. She appeared, indeed, to have felt an incongruous impulse to draw attention to her own striking observance of them. "Good night, Mrs. Walker," she said; "we've had a beautiful evening. You see if I let Daisy come to parties without me, I don't want her to go away without me." Daisy turned away, looking with a pale, grave face at the circle near the door; Winterbourne saw that, for the first moment, she was too much shocked and puzzled even for indignation. He on his side was greatly touched.

"That was very cruel," he said to Mrs. Walker.

"She never enters my drawing room again," replied his hostess.

Since Winterbourne was not to meet her in Mrs. Walker's drawing room, he went as often as possible to Mrs. Miller's hotel. The ladies were rarely at home, but when he found them the devoted Giovanelli was always present. Very often the brilliant little Roman was in the drawing room with Daisy alone, Mrs. Miller being apparently constantly of the opinion that discretion is the better part of surveillance. Winterbourne noted, at first with surprise, that Daisy on these occasions was never embarrassed or annoyed by his own entrance; but he very presently began to feel that she had no more surprises for him; the unexpected in her behavior was the only thing to expect. She showed no displeasure at her tête-à-tête with Giovanelli being interrupted; she could chatter as freshly and freely with two gentlemen as with one; there was always, in her conversation, the same odd mixture of audacity and

puerility. Winterbourne remarked to himself that if she was seriously interested in Giovanelli, it was very singular that she should not take more trouble to preserve the sanctity of their interviews; and he liked her the more for her innocent-looking indifference and her apparently inexhaustible good humor. He could hardly have said why, but she seemed to him a girl who would never be jealous. At the risk of exciting a somewhat derisive smile on the reader's part, I may affirm that with regard to the women who had hitherto interested him, it very often seemed to Winterbourne among the possibilities that, given certain contingencies, he should be afraid—literally afraid—of these ladies; he had a pleasant sense that he should never be afraid of Daisy Miller. It must be added that this sentiment was not altogether flattering to Daisy; it was part of his conviction, or rather of his apprehension, that she would prove a very light young person.

But she was evidently very much interested in Giovanelli. She looked at him whenever he spoke; she was perpetually telling him to do this and to do that; she was constantly "chaffing" and abusing him. She appeared completely to have forgotten that Winterbourne had said anything to displease her at Mrs. Walker's little party. One Sunday afternoon, having gone to St. Peter's[15] with his aunt, Winterbourne perceived Daisy strolling about the great church in company with the inevitable Giovanelli. Presently he pointed out the young girl and her cavalier to Mrs. Costello. This lady looked at them a moment through her eyeglass, and then she said, "That's what makes you so pensive in these days, eh?"

"I had not the least idea I was pensive," said the young man.

"You are very much preoccupied; you are thinking of something."

"And what is it," he asked, "that you accuse me of thinking of?"

"Of that young lady's—Miss Baker's, Miss Chandler's—what's her name? Miss Miller's in-

15. **St. Peter's:** St. Peter's Cathedral, the principal church of Rome.

trigue with that little barber's block."[16]

"Do you call it an intrigue," Winterbourne asked—"an affair that goes on with such peculiar publicity?"

"That's their folly," said Mrs. Costello, "it's not their merit."

"No," rejoined Winterbourne with something of that pensiveness to which his aunt had alluded. "I don't believe that there is anything to be called an intrigue."

"I have heard a dozen people speak of it; they say she is quite carried away by him."

"They are certainly very intimate," said Winterbourne.

Mrs. Costello inspected the young couple again with her optical instrument. "He is very handsome. One easily sees how it is. She thinks him the most elegant man in the world, the finest gentleman. She has never seen anything like him; he is better even than the courier. It was the courier probably who introduced him, and if he succeeds in marrying the young lady, the courier will come in for a magnificent commission."

"I don't believe she thinks of marrying him," said Winterbourne, "and I don't believe he hopes to marry her."

"You may be very sure she thinks of nothing. She goes on from day to day, from hour to hour, as they did in the Golden Age.[17] I can imagine nothing more vulgar. And at the same time," added Mrs. Costello, "depend upon it that she may tell you any moment that she is 'engaged.'"

"I think that is more than Giovanelli expects," said Winterbourne.

"Who is Giovanelli?"

"The little Italian. I have asked questions about him and learned something. He is apparently a perfectly respectable little man. I believe he is in a small way a *cavaliere avvocato*.[18] But he doesn't move in what are called the first circles. I think it is really not absolutely impossible that the courier introduced him. He is evidently immensely charmed with Miss Miller. If she thinks him the finest gentleman in the world, he, on his side, has never found himself in personal contact with such splendor, such opulence, such expensiveness, as this young lady's. And then she must seem to him wonderfully pretty and interesting. I rather doubt that he dreams of marrying her. That must appear to him too impossible a piece of luck. He has nothing but his handsome face to offer, and there is a substantial Mr. Miller in that mysterious land of dollars. Giovanelli knows that he hasn't a title to offer. If he were only a count or a *marchese!*[19] He must wonder at his luck at the way they have taken him up."

"He accounts for it by his handsome face and thinks Miss Miller a young lady *qui se passe ses fantaisies!*"[20] said Mrs. Costello.

"It is very true," Winterbourne pursued, "that Daisy and her mamma have not yet risen to that stage of—what shall I call it?—of culture, at which the idea of catching a count or a *marchese* begins. I believe that they are intellectually incapable of that conception."

"Ah! but the *avvocato* can't believe it," said Mrs. Costello.

Of the observation excited by Daisy's "intrigue," Winterbourne gathered that day at St. Peter's sufficient evidence. A dozen of the American colonists in Rome came to talk with Mrs. Costello, who sat on a little portable stool at the base of one of the great pilasters.[21] The vesper service was going forward in splendid chants and organ tones in the adjacent choir, and meanwhile, between Mrs. Costello and her friends, there was a great deal said about poor little Miss Miller's going really "too far." Winterbourne was not pleased with what he heard; but when, coming out upon the great steps of the church, he saw Daisy, who had emerged

16. **barber's block:** an overdressed dandy or fop.
17. **Golden Age:** here, a mythical period of total innocence.
18. *cavaliere avvocato* (kä′və-lyâ′rä av′ō-kä′tō): Italian for "gentleman lawyer."

19. *marchese* (mär-kā′sä): marquis, a rank of nobility next below a duke.
20. *"qui . . . fantaisies!"*: French for "who gives in to her whims!"
21. **pilasters** (pĭ-lăs′tərz): shallow projections from a wall, usually imitating the form of columns.

before him, get into an open cab with her accomplice and roll away through the cynical streets of Rome, he could not deny to himself that she was going very far indeed. He felt very sorry for her—not exactly that he believed that she had completely lost her head, but because it was painful to hear so much that was pretty, and undefended, and natural assigned to a vulgar place among the categories of disorder. He made an attempt after this to give a hint to Mrs. Miller. He met one day in the Corso[22] a friend—a tourist like himself—who had just come out of the Doria Palace,[23] where he had been walking through the beautiful gallery. His friend talked for a moment about the superb portrait of Innocent X, by Velásquez,[24] which hangs in one of the cabinets of the palace, and then said, "And in the same cabinet, by the way, I had the pleasure of contemplating a picture of a different kind—that pretty American girl whom you pointed out to me last week." In answer to Winterbourne's inquiries, his friend narrated that the pretty American girl—prettier than ever—was seated with a companion in the secluded nook in which the great papal portrait was enshrined.

"Who was her companion?" asked Winterbourne.

"A little Italian with a bouquet in this buttonhole. The girl is delightfully pretty, but I thought I understood from you the other day that she was a young lady *du meilleur monde*."[25]

"So she is!" answered Winterbourne; and having assured himself that his informant had seen Daisy and her companion but five minutes before, he jumped into a cab and went to call on Mrs. Miller. She was at home; but she apologized to him for receiving him in Daisy's absence.

"She's gone out somewhere with Mr. Giovanelli," said Mrs. Miller. "She's always going round with Mr. Giovanelli."

"I have noticed that they are very intimate," Winterbourne observed.

"Oh! it seems as if they couldn't live without each other!" said Mrs. Miller. "Well, he's a real gentleman anyhow. I keep telling Daisy she's engaged!"

"And what does Daisy say?"

"Oh, she says she isn't engaged. But she might as well be!" this impartial parent resumed. "She goes on as if she was. But I've made Mr. Giovanelli promise to tell me, if *she* doesn't. I should want to write to Mr. Miller about it—shouldn't you?"

Winterbourne replied that he certainly should; and the state of mind of Daisy's mamma struck him as so unprecedented in the annals of parental vigilance that he gave up as utterly irrelevant the attempt to place her upon her guard.

After this Daisy was never at home, and Winterbourne ceased to meet her at the houses of their common acquaintance, because, as he perceived, these shrewd people had quite made up their minds that she was going too far. They ceased to invite her, and they intimated that they desired to express to observant Europeans the great truth that, though Miss Daisy Miller was a young American lady, her behavior was not representative—was regarded by her compatriots as abnormal. Winterbourne wondered how she felt about all the cold shoulders that were turned toward her, and sometimes it annoyed him to suspect that she did not feel at all. He said to himself that she was too light and childish, too uncultivated and unreasoning, too provincial, to have reflected upon her ostracism or even to have perceived it. Then at other moments he believed that she carried about in her elegant and irresponsible little organism a defiant, passionate, perfectly observant consciousness of the impression she produced. He asked himself whether Daisy's defiance came from the consciousness of innocence or from her being,

22. **Corso:** a Roman street.
23. **Doria Palace:** a Roman baroque palace open to tourists as an art gallery.
24. **Velásquez:** Diego Rodriquez de Silva y Velásques (və-läs′kĭs, -käs, və-läs′-; *Spanish* vā-läth′käth), a Spanish painter (1599–1660), whose portrait of Pope Innocent X hangs in the Doria Gallery.
25. *"du meilleur monde"* (dü mä′yûr mōnd): French for "of the better society."

essentially, a young person of the reckless class. It must be admitted that holding oneself to a belief in Daisy's "innocence" came to seem to Winterbourne more and more a matter of fine-spun gallantry. As I have already had occasion to relate, he was angry at finding himself reduced to chopping logic[26] about this young lady; he was vexed at his want of instinctive certitude as to how far her eccentricities were generic, national, and how far they were personal. From either view of them he had somehow missed her, and now it was too late. She was "carried away" by Mr. Giovanelli.

A few days after his brief interview with her mother, he encountered her in that beautiful abode of flowering desolation known as the Palace of the Caesars.[27] The early Roman spring had filled the air with bloom and perfume, and the rugged surface of the Palatine was muffled with tender verdure. Daisy was strolling along the top of one of those great mounds of ruin that are embanked with mossy marble and paved with monumental inscriptions. It seemed to him that Rome had never been so lovely as just then. He stood looking off at the enchanting harmony of line and color that remotely encircles the city, inhaling the softly humid odors and feeling the freshness of the year and the antiquity of the place reaffirm themselves in mysterious interfusion. It seemed to him also that Daisy had never looked so pretty; but this had been an observation of his whenever he met her. Giovanelli was at her side, and Giovanelli, too, wore an aspect of even unwonted brilliancy.

"Well," said Daisy, "I should think you would be lonesome!"

"Lonesome?" asked Winterbourne.

"You are always going round by yourself. Can't you get anyone to walk with you?"

"I am not so fortunate," said Winterbourne, "as your companion."

26. **chopping logic:** making weak distinctions in order to excuse her behavior.
27. **Palace of the Caesars:** ruins of palaces erected by the Caesars on the Palatine (păl'ə-tīn') Hill, the chief of Rome's seven hills.

Giovanelli, from the first, had treated Winterbourne with distinguished politeness; he listened with a deferential air to his remarks; he laughed punctiliously at his pleasantries; he seemed disposed to testify to his belief that Winterbourne was a superior young man. He carried himself in no degree like a jealous wooer; he had obviously a great deal of tact; he had no objection to your expecting a little humility of him. It even seemed to Winterbourne at times that Giovanelli would find a certain mental relief in being able to have a private understanding with him—to say to him, as an intelligent man, that, bless you, *he* knew how extraordinary was this young lady and didn't flatter himself with delusive—or at least *too* delusive—hopes of matrimony and dollars. On this occasion he strolled away from his companion to pluck a sprig of almond blossom, which he carefully arranged in his buttonhole.

"I know why you say that," said Daisy, watching Giovanelli. "Because you think I go round too much with *him!*" And she nodded at her attendant.

"Everyone thinks so—if you care to know," said Winterbourne.

"Of course I care to know!" Daisy exclaimed seriously. "But I don't believe it. They are only pretending to be shocked. They don't really care a straw what I do. Besides, I don't go round so much."

"I think you will find they do care. They will show it—disagreeably."

Daisy looked at him a moment. "How—disagreeably?"

"Haven't you noticed anything?" Winterbourne asked.

"I have noticed you. But I noticed you were as stiff as an umbrella the first time I saw you."

"You will find I am not so stiff as several others," said Winterbourne, smiling.

"How shall I find it?"

"By going to see the others."

"What will they do to me?"

"They will give you the cold shoulder. Do you know what that means?"

Daisy was looking at him intently; she began to color. "Do you mean as Mrs. Walker did the other night?"

"Exactly!" said Winterbourne.

She looked away at Giovanelli, who was decorating himself with his almond blossom. Then looking back at Winterbourne, "I shouldn't think you would let people be so unkind!" she said.

"How can I help it?" he asked.

"I should think you would say something."

"I do say something;" and he paused a moment. "I say that your mother tells me that she believes you are engaged."

"Well, she does," said Daisy very simply.

Winterbourne began to laugh. "And does Randolph believe it?" he asked.

"I guess Randolph doesn't believe anything," said Daisy. Randolph's skepticism excited Winterbourne to further hilarity, and he observed that Giovanelli was coming back to them. Daisy, observing it too, addressed herself again to her countryman. "Since you have mentioned it," she said, "I *am* engaged." . . . Winterbourne looked at her; he had stopped laughing. "You don't believe it!" she added.

He was silent a moment; and then, "Yes, I believe it!" he said.

"Oh, no, you don't," she answered. "Well, then—I am not!"

The young girl and her cicerone[28] were on their way to the gate of the enclosure, so that Winterbourne, who had but lately entered, presently took leave of them. A week afterward he went to dine at a beautiful villa on the Caelian Hill[29] and, on arriving, dismissed his hired vehicle. The evening was charming, and he promised himself the satisfaction of walking home beneath the Arch of Constantine[30] and past the vaguely lighted monuments of the Forum.[31] There was a waning moon in the sky, and her radiance was not brilliant, but she was veiled in a thin cloud-curtain which seemed to diffuse and equalize it. When, on his return from the villa (it was eleven o'clock), Winterbourne approached the dusky circle of the Colosseum,[32] it recurred to him, as a lover of the picturesque, that the interior in the pale moonshine would be well worth a glance. He turned aside and walked to one of the empty arches, near which, as he observed, an open carriage—one of the little Roman street cabs—was stationed. Then he passed in, among the cavernous shadows of the great structure, and emerged upon the clear and silent arena. The place had never seemed to him more impressive. One half of the gigantic circus[33] was in deep shade; the other was sleeping in the luminous dusk. As he stood there, he began to murmur Byron's famous lines out of *Manfred;*[34] but before he had finished his quotation he remembered that if nocturnal meditations in the Colosseum are recommended by the poets, they are deprecated by the doctors. The historic atmosphere was there, certainly; but the historic atmosphere, scientifically considered, was no better than a villainous miasma.[35] Winterbourne walked to the middle of the arena to take a more general glance, intending thereafter to make a hasty retreat. The great cross in the center was covered with shadow; it was only as he drew near it that he made it out distinctly. Then he saw that two persons were stationed upon the low steps which formed its base. One of these was a woman, seated; her companion was standing in front of her.

Presently the sound of the woman's voice came to him distinctly in the warm night air. "Well, he looks at us as one of the old lions or tigers may have looked at the Christian mar-

28. **cicerone** (sĭs′ə-rō′nē): guide.
29. **Caelian** (sē′lē-ən) **Hill:** one of the seven hills.
30. **Arch of Constantine:** an arch built to commemorate a Roman military victory in the year 312.
31. **Forum:** the marketplace and center of business and judicial affairs in ancient Rome.
32. **Colosseum** (kŏl′ə-sē′əm): the ancient Roman arena where the early Christians suffered martyrdom.
33. **circus:** here, circle.
34. *Manfred:* Lord Byron's verse drama of 1817. The famous lines are from Act III, Scene 4: "I do remember me, that in my youth, / When I was wandering—upon such a night—/I stood within the Coliseum's wall, / Midst the chief relics of almighty Rome."
35. **miasma** (mī-ăz′mə, mē-): dangerous or infectious influence.

554 REALISM AND NATURALISM

tyrs!"[36] These were the words he heard in the familiar accent of Miss Daisy Miller.

"Let us hope he is not very hungry," responded the ingenious Giovanelli. "He will have to take me first; you will serve for dessert!"

Winterbourne stopped with a sort of horror; and, it must be added, with a sort of relief. It was as if a sudden illumination had been flashed upon the ambiguity of Daisy's behavior and the riddle had become easy to read. She was a young lady whom a gentleman need no longer be at pains to respect. He stood there looking at her—looking at her companion, and not reflecting that though he saw them vaguely, he himself must have been more brightly visible. He felt angry with himself that he had bothered so much about the right way of regarding Miss Daisy Miller. Then, as he was going to advance again, he checked himself; not from the fear that he was doing her injustice, but from a sense of the danger of appearing unbecomingly exhilarated by this sudden revulsion from cautious criticism. He turned away toward the entrance of the place; but as he did so he heard Daisy speak again.

"Why, it was Mr. Winterbourne! He saw me—and he cuts[37] me!"

What a clever little reprobate she was, and how smartly she played at injured innocence! But he wouldn't cut her. Winterbourne came forward again and went toward the great cross. Daisy had got up; Giovanelli lifted his hat. Winterbourne had now begun to think simply of the craziness, from a sanitary point of view,

36. **lions . . . martyrs:** The early Christians who refused to renounce their faith were thrown to hungry beasts of prey.
37. **cuts me:** refuses to speak to me.

The Colosseum at Rome by Moonlight
by F. L. Bridell (1830–1863).
Oil on canvas.
Southampton Art Gallery and Museums, England

of a delicate young girl lounging away the evening in this nest of malaria. What if she *were* a clever little reprobate? that was no reason for her dying of the *perniciosa*.[38] "How long have you been here?" he asked almost brutally.

Daisy, lovely in the flattering moonlight, looked at him a moment. Then—"All the evening," she answered gently. . . . "I never saw anything so pretty."

"I am afraid," said Winterbourne, "that you will not think Roman fever very pretty. This is the way people catch it. I wonder," he added, turning to Giovanelli, "that you, a native Roman, should countenance such a terrible indiscretion."

"Ah," said the handsome native, "for myself, I am not afraid."

"Neither am I—for you! I am speaking for this young lady."

Giovanelli lifted his well-shaped eyebrows and showed his brilliant teeth. But he took Winterbourne's rebuke with docility. "I told the Signorina[39] it was a grave indiscretion; but when was the Signorina ever prudent?"

"I never was sick, and I don't mean to be!" the Signorina declared. "I don't look like much, but I'm healthy! I was bound to see the Colosseum by moonlight; I shouldn't have wanted to go home without that; and we have had the most beautiful time, haven't we, Mr. Giovanelli? If there has been any danger, Eugenio can give me some pills. He has got some splendid pills."

"I should advise you," said Winterbourne, "to drive home as fast as possible and take one!"

"What you say is very wise," Giovanelli rejoined. "I will go and make sure the carriage is at hand." And he went forward rapidly.

Daisy followed with Winterbourne. He kept looking at her; she seemed not in the least embarrassed. Winterbourne said nothing; Daisy chattered about the beauty of the place. "Well, I *have* seen the Colosseum by moon-

light!" she exclaimed. "That's one good thing." Then, noticing Winterbourne's silence, she asked him why he didn't speak. He made no answer; he only began to laugh. They passed under one of the dark archways; Giovanelli was in front with the carriage. Here Daisy stopped a moment looking at the young American. "*Did* you believe I was engaged the other day?" she asked.

"It doesn't matter what I believed the other day," said Winterbourne, still laughing.

"Well, what do you believe now?"

"I believe that it makes very little difference whether you are engaged or not!"

He felt the young girl's pretty eyes fixed upon him through the thick gloom of the archway; she was apparently going to answer. But Giovanelli hurried her forward. "Quick, quick," he said; "if we get in by midnight we are quite safe."

Daisy took her seat in the carriage, and the fortunate Italian placed himself beside her. "Don't forget Eugenio's pills!" said Winterbourne, as he lifted his hat.

"I don't care," said Daisy in a little strange tone, "whether I have Roman fever or not!" Upon this the cabdriver cracked his whip, and they rolled away over the desultory patches of the antique pavement.

Winterbourne—to do him justice, as it were—mentioned to no one that he had encountered Miss Miller, at midnight, in the Colosseum with a gentleman; but nevertheless, a couple of days later, the fact of her having been there under these circumstances was known to every member of the little American circle and commented accordingly. Winterbourne reflected that they had of course known it at the hotel and that, after Daisy's return, there had been an exchange of remarks between the porter and the cabdriver. But the young man was conscious at the same moment that it had ceased to be a matter of serious regret to him that the little American flirt should be "talked about" by low-minded menials. These people, a day or two later, had serious information to give: the little American

---

38. ***perniciosa*** (pâr-nē'sē-ō'sə): Italian for "malaria."
39. **Signorina** (sēn'yō-rē'nə): Italian title for a girl or unmarried woman.

flirt was alarmingly ill. Winterbourne, when the rumor came to him, immediately went to the hotel for more news. He found that two or three charitable friends had preceded him and that they were being entertained in Mrs. Miller's salon by Randolph.

"It's going round at night," said Randolph—"that's what made her sick. She's always going round at night. I shouldn't think she'd want to—it's so plaguey dark. You can't see anything here at night, except when there's a moon. In America there's always a moon!" Mrs. Miller was invisible; she was now, at least, giving her daughter the advantage of her society. It was evident that Daisy was dangerously ill.

Winterbourne went often to ask for news of her, and once he saw Mrs. Miller, who, though deeply alarmed, was—rather to his surprise—perfectly composed and, as it appeared, a most efficient and judicious nurse. She talked a good deal about Dr. Davis, but Winterbourne paid her the compliment of saying to himself that she was not, after all, such a monstrous goose. "Daisy spoke of you the other day," she said to him. "Half the time she doesn't know what she's saying, but that time I think she did. She gave me a message; she told me to tell you. She told me to tell you that she never was engaged to that handsome Italian. I am sure I am very glad; Mr. Giovanelli hasn't been near us since she was taken ill. I thought he was so much of a gentleman; but I don't call that very polite! A lady told me that he was afraid I was angry with him for taking Daisy round at night. Well, so I am; but I suppose he knows I'm a lady. I would scorn to scold him. Anyway, she says she's not engaged. I don't know why she wanted you to know; but she said to me three times—'Mind you tell Mr. Winterbourne.' And then she told me to ask if you remembered the time you went to that castle in Switzerland. But I said I wouldn't give any such messages as that. Only, if she is not engaged, I'm sure I'm glad to know it."

But, as Winterbourne had said, it mattered very little. A week after this the poor girl died; it had been a terrible case of the fever. Daisy's grave was in the little Protestant cemetery, in an angle of the wall of imperial Rome, beneath the cypresses and thick spring flowers. Winterbourne stood there beside it, with a number of other mourners, a number larger than the scandal excited by the young lady's career would have led you to expect. Near him stood Giovanelli, who came nearer still before Winterbourne turned away. Giovanelli was very pale; on this occasion he had no flower in his buttonhole; he seemed to wish to say something. At last he said, "She was the most beautiful young lady I ever saw, and the most amiable." And then he added in a moment, "And she was the most innocent."

Winterbourne looked at him and presently repeated his words, "And the most innocent?"

"The most innocent!"

Winterbourne felt sore and angry. "Why the devil," he asked, "did you take her to that fatal place?"

Mr. Giovanelli's urbanity was apparently imperturbable. He looked on the ground a moment, and then he said, "For myself, I had no fear; and she wanted to go."

"That was no reason!" Winterbourne declared.

The subtle Roman again dropped his eyes. "If she had lived, I should have got nothing. She would never have married me, I am sure."

"She would never have married you?"

"For a moment I hoped so. But no. I am sure."

Winterbourne listened to him; he stood staring at the raw protuberance among the April daisies. When he turned away again, Mr. Giovanelli, with his light slow step, had retired.

Winterbourne almost immediately left Rome; but the following summer he again met his aunt, Mrs. Costello, at Vevey. Mrs. Costello was fond of Vevey. In the interval Winterbourne had often thought of Daisy Miller and her mystifying manners. One day he spoke of her to his aunt—said it was on his conscience that he had done her injustice.

"I am sure I don't know," said Mrs. Costello. "How did your injustice affect her?"

"She sent me a message before her death which I didn't understand at the time. But I have understood it since. She would have appreciated one's esteem."

"Is that a modest way," asked Mrs. Costello, "of saying that she would have reciprocated one's affection?"

Winterbourne offered no answer to this question; but he presently said, "You were right in that remark that you made last summer. I was booked to make a mistake. I have lived too long in foreign parts."

Nevertheless, he went back to live at Geneva, whence there continue to come the most contradictory accounts of his motives of sojourn: a report that he is "studying" hard—an intimation that he is much interested in a very clever foreign lady.

Reading Check

1. Why does Daisy ask Winterbourne to accompany her to the Pincio?
2. At what point does Winterbourne lose all respect for Daisy?
3. What message does Daisy leave for Winterbourne during her illness?
4. What is the cause of Daisy's death?
5. What does Giovanelli reveal to Winterbourne at Daisy's grave?

For Study and Discussion

Analyzing and Interpreting the Novel

1. Mrs. Costello's judgment of the Millers closed Part I, and it opens Part II. **a.** What has confirmed her judgment—especially of Daisy—in the meantime? **b.** To her view that they are "very dreadful people," Winterbourne replies that "They are very ignorant—very innocent only." What is the distinction between these two judgments?

2. Rome is a much more "serious" place than Vevey, and Daisy's actions have more consequences there. The first such action that we see is Daisy's walk on the Pincio with Giovanelli and her refusal to get into Mrs. Walker's carriage. What makes this a serious act of defiance?

3. Although he is a minor character, Giovanelli is very carefully drawn. He apparently believes for a time that he might capture this rich American girl (he has practiced on other American heiresses) and later knows that he will not, but he never changes his manner and cannot be flustered or upset. **a.** How does this show itself in the way he treats Winterbourne? **b.** What characteristic gesture of Giovanelli's is related to the idea that he might pick a "daisy"?

4. Once Daisy has been turned away by Mrs. Walker and the other Americans, Winterbourne sees her only in the company of Giovanelli. But he is still puzzled by how they act together, and he rejects his aunt's view that there is an "intrigue" between them. What puzzles him about their behavior?

5. Winterbourne's next-to-last interview with Daisy, before the midnight meeting at the fatal Colosseum, is at the ruins of the Palace of the Caesars. He tells her that "everyone" believes she is behaving recklessly "—if you care to know." "Of course I care to know!" she replies. "But I don't believe it. They are only pretending to be shocked. They don't really care a straw what I do." What explanation of her behavior should we see in that exchange?

6. At Daisy's gravesite Winterbourne asks Giovanelli, who is very pale now and for once without a flower in his buttonhole, why he took Daisy to that "fatal place." How should we interpret Giovanelli's answer?

Commentary

Daisy Miller quickly became James's best-known work, and it continued to overshadow his later novels for many years. He had offered it first to an American editor, who rejected it without comment but told others he regarded Daisy as "an outrage on American girlhood." Published in England, the book proved so popular that "pirated" editions (in the absence of an international copyright law) immediately appeared in America and sold widely—without, of course, earning a penny for James.

But popularity did not necessarily mean approval. Daisy was discussed, sometimes by people who had not read the book, as if she were an actual person and a representative of American society. Writers on etiquette were appealed to as experts: Was Daisy an immoral girl or merely an ignorant one? Were her manners—and her language, which was just as questionable—truly "vulgar"? Did young American girls in Europe actually go about unchaperoned with foreign men? Meanwhile, British reviewers sniffed snobbishly that English girls were not at all like Daisy or implied, somewhat enviously, that American girls enjoyed more freedom than others and probably had a better time.

These disputes were mostly off the point of James's novel, but they did recognize that Daisy's character represented important changes in American society. The Millers, as Randolph proclaims, are "rich," but they are clearly people of "new money"—that is, of a fortune made in the post-Civil War years, in the prosperity built upon the industrial base that the war itself had created. A generation earlier in America, a wealthy family at just this stage of social development would have been rare. Even a few years earlier such a family would have been less likely to send the mother and children (the father, significantly, remains at home in Schenectady tending to his "big business") on a tour of Europe. Touring Europe had suddenly come to stand for some undefined but valuable social and cultural experience to people who suddenly had the means to do so. Naive as travelers and utterly ignorant of Europe, they are uncertain about what they should see and are intimidated even by the casual remarks of chance acquaintances: "there's a lady here," Mrs. Miller replies when she is asked to visit the castle of Chillon, "—I don't know her name—she says she shouldn't think we'd want to go to see castles *here;* she should think we'd want to wait till we got to Italy." But these travelers are still more uncertain about what they are to "get" from looking at castles and ruins and works of art—how they are to be changed by this experience. "Can you get good teachers in Italy?" Daisy asks Winterbourne. It is a question that echoes through the novel as we realize that if Europe is to be a good "teacher," there must also be willing learners.

For different reasons Randolph and Mrs. Miller will learn nothing from Europe. With his "aged expression of countenance" and his "sharp, hard little voice" that is at once "immature" and yet "not young," Randolph is a spoiled child who won't mind, won't go to bed, eats too many sweets, and won't have "lessons." At the same time he is a miniature of the adult he will become: the cynical materialist who measures all things by an "American" standard of size and conspicuousness—"American candy's

the best candy"—"American men are the best"—"We've got a bigger place than this. . . . It's all gold on the walls." As Daisy says, Randolph has nothing to learn. "I guess he could give me more instruction than I could give him."

The pathetic and bewildered Mrs. Miller cannot learn from Europe either. She is a traditional mother in untraditional circumstances whose children are clearly beyond her and out of her control. "I don't see how he lives!" she says of Randolph's refusal to go to bed, and she responds to his addiction to sweets by threatening to slap him if any more teeth fall out. As for Daisy, "It seems as if there was nothing she wouldn't undertake," Mrs. Miller says timidly. She avoids if possible even being introduced to Daisy's young gentlemen, yet must rely on Giovanelli to inform her if he and Daisy become engaged. Mrs. Miller's own response to Europe is restricted to her indigestion and her inability to find here an equivalent of her revered Dr. Davis at home, who took her liver so seriously. It is significant that she becomes a dignified and effectual person only in the traditional role of a mother caring for a sick child. Seeing her in the crisis of Daisy's illness transformed into "a most efficient and judicious nurse," Winterbourne realizes that she is not such a "monstrous goose" after all, only a woman who has been far out of her depth in Europe.

It is of course in Daisy that we feel the greatest potential for learning from Europe, and the question of why her encounter with the Old World is so destructive is at the center of the novel. Daisy is a fresh and beautiful young girl, but she is also—insistently—an *American* girl, and this somehow betrays her in Europe.

What Daisy seems most to lack is that sense of "relation" that James said must come to America as a consequence of the Civil War, a sense of "proportion" that relates the individual to society and that society to the greater world. "I'm very fond of society," Daisy says. But her only way of relating to society is by personal triumph. "Last winter I had seventeen dinners given me; and three of them were by gentlemen," she tells Winterbourne. Without "proportion" she must always take the world personally. One result is a perfection of personal appearance. As the haughty Mrs. Costello acknowledges, Daisy dresses in "perfection."

Yet a meaningful encounter with Europe demands more than exquisite taste in clothes. Daisy knows nothing of Europe except that her prettiest dresses come from Paris, not even the pass through the Alps they will take to Italy. Her way of telling Winterbourne where she has traveled is to mention the hotels. When he tries to tell her about Chillon, she isn't interested in "feudal antiquities." Instead, their tour of the castle is for her an occasion for asking him many personal questions "and for supplying information upon corresponding points in her own personality." Even in Rome's Colosseum, perhaps the place in all the world where the weight of the past most humbles the observer, on the bloody ground where gladiators fought to the death for the entertainment of crowds and religious martyrs were thrown to ravening beasts—even there, Daisy can feel the past only by making it personal to herself. "Well," she says mockingly for Winterbourne's hearing, "he looks at us as one of the old lions or tigers may have looked at the Christian martyrs."

Unable to feel related to the world in any fulfilling way, Daisy must make the world feel her, the force of her personality. And that, beneath her personal beauty and amiability, becomes the self-destructive principle of her character. She needs to *make* people say things, if only to be resisted. If no one will make a "fuss" about her going out in a rowboat with a gentleman at midnight, then she doesn't want to go. "Oh, I hoped you would make a fuss!" Now her refusal has the same purpose as her earlier acceptance. "I hope you are disappointed, or disgusted, or something!" she says to Winterbourne. Even her flirting, as he comes to understand only later, is not an invitation to advances but a way of being "personal," of evoking response.

All this is one thing in Vevey, which in summer is so like an American resort. It is quite another in Rome, at the heart of "Europe." There her rudeness and recklessness have a new import. Daisy will not, as the old saying has it, do in Rome as the Romans do. "The young ladies of this country have a dreadfully poky time of it . . . ; I don't see why I should change my habits for *them*." But she also defies American ideas of "custom," of what "is done here," as Mrs. Walker puts it. James merely sketches this part of Daisy's story, but it is clear that after her exclusion from Mrs. Walker's house Daisy is quickly "dropped" by the other Americans in Rome, until the only "society" open to her is the companionship of the fortune-hunting Giovanelli. By the time of the scene at the Colosseum, Daisy seems already, beneath her bravado, to feel "lost": "I don't care," she cries, "whether I have Roman fever or not!"

In the cemetery Winterbourne hears again, from Giovanelli, the word he himself has used for Daisy, although he won't fully understand its meaning until many months after her death. Daisy was "innocent" in much more than the physical sense. Self-named and largely self-created (her family can neither guide nor understand her), she is "innocent" of that "relation" to the world that, for James, is necessary for our social and moral development. It was her encounter with Europe that exposed this lack in her culture and so destroyed her. Still, Daisy was not without her own portion of that "moral consciousness" that James believed was to be America's distinctive contribution to an international culture. Three times from her deathbed she asked her mother to be sure to tell Winterbourne that she was not engaged. For all her wildness, she was not so deluded as to imagine that the "beautiful" little Giovanelli was a real suitor, a prospective husband; nor, for all her defiance, was she beyond caring that Winterbourne might think she had so thrown herself away. As he says months later to his proud old aunt, who understands this no more than she has understood anything else about Daisy, "She would have appreciated one's esteem."

Writing About Literature

Analyzing Point of View

Although Frederick Winterbourne is not actually the narrator of the novel, he serves a narrator's function because we always see Daisy through his point of view and in his reactions to her. Write an essay in which you examine the basis of Winterbourne's judgments of her and the points at which they change. Try also to account for his final remark about Daisy to his aunt. In what way had his long residence in Europe prepared—or "booked"—him to make a mistake?

FROM

The Origins and Development of the English Language

THOMAS PYLES and JOHN ALGEO

According to the authors, "English is unmistakably one language, with two major national dialects: British and American." There are national differences in vocabulary, in pronunciation, and in idiom. In this excerpt, the writers focus on the matter of spelling.

Noah Webster (1758–1843), who is referred to below as "a sort of linguistic guru," was an American educator. He is remembered for *An American Dictionary of the English Language*, published in 1828, and for his efforts to reform spelling.

Somewhat exotic to American eyes, though by no means unfamiliar to those of the educated, are *cheque* (for drawing money from a bank), *cyder, cypher, gaol, kerb* (of a street), *pyjamas, syren,* and *tyre* (around a wheel). But *check, cider, cipher, jail, curb, pajamas, siren,* and *tire* are also current in England in varying degrees.

Noah Webster, whom many regard as a sort of linguistic guru, was responsible for excising the *u* from a group of words spelled in his day prevailingly in *-our: armour, behaviour, colour, favour, flavour, harbour, labour, neighbour,* and the like. The resultant American *-or* spellings are today far more obnoxious to the English than the alternative forms with *-our* are to Americans, who, in addition to reading a great many books printed in England, are quite accustomed to seeing *glamour* and *saviour* in books printed in their own country. All such words were current in earlier British English without the *u,* though most Britishers today are probably unaware of the fact; Webster was making no radical change in English spelling habits. Furthermore, the English had themselves struck the *u* from a great many words earlier spelled *-our,* alternating with *-or: author, doctor, emperor, error, governor, horror, mirror,* and *senator,* among others.

Webster is also responsible for the American practice of using *-er* instead of the British *-re* in a number of words—for instance, *calibre, centre, litre, manouevre, metre* (of poetry or of the unit of length in the metric system), *sepulchre,* and *theatre.* The last of these spellings has nowadays probably a wider currency in American English than has *theater;* it is regarded by many of its users as en elegant (because British) spelling and by others as an affectation. Except for *litre,* which did not come into English until the nineteenth century, all these words occur in earlier British English with *-er.*

The fact that *c* before *e* indicates [s] must have irritated Webster. At one time he wanted to have *acre* spelled *aker,* but he was still left with *lucre* and *mediocre,* in the case of which he seems to have given up fighting the good fight. There was also *ogre,* about which little could be done; *oger* would have suggested [ojər].

The American use of *-se* in *defense, offense,* and *pretense,* in which the English usually have *-ce,* is also attributable to the precept and practice of Webster, though he did not recommend *fense* for *fence,* which is simply an aphetic[1] form

1. **aphetic** (ə-fĕt'ĭk): referring to the loss of a short unstressed vowel at the beginning of a word.

of *defense* (or *defence*). Spellings with *-se* have occurred in earlier British English for all these words, including *fence*. *Suspense* is now usually so spelled in British English.

Webster proposed dropping final *k* in such words as *almanack, musick, physick, publick,* and *traffick,* bringing about a change that has occurred in British English as well, though not because old Noah recommended it. His proposed *burdoc, cassoc,* and *hassoc* now regularly end in *k,* whereas *havock,* in which he neglected to drop the *k,* is everywhere spelled without it.

Though he was not the first to recommend doing so, Webster is doubtless to be credited with the American spelling practice of not doubling final *l* when adding a suffix except in words stressed on their final syllables—for example, *gróvel, groveled, groveler, groveling,* but *propél, propelled, propeller, propelling, propellant.* Modern British spelling usually doubles *l* before a suffix regardless of the position of the stress, as in *grovelled, groveller,* and so forth.

The British use of *ae* and *oe* (or *æ* and *œ*) looks strange to Americans in *anaemic, gynaecology, haemorrhage, paediatrician,* and in *diarrhoeia, homoeopathy, manoeuvre,* and *oesophagus,* but not in *aesthetic, archaeology,* and *encyclopaedia,* which are fairly common in American usage. Some words earlier written with one or the other of these digraphs[2] long ago underwent simplification—for example, *phaenomenon, oeconomy,* and *poenology.* Others are in the process of simplification: *hemorrhage, hemorrhoids,* and *medieval* are frequent British variants of the forms with *ae,* but *haematic, haemoglobin, haemophilia,* and *haemostatic* seem not to have lost the *a* as yet.

Most British writers use *-ise* for the verbal suffix written *-ize* in America in such words as *baptize, organize,* and *sympathize.* However, the *Times* of London, the *OED,* H. C. Wyld's *Universal Dictionary* (1932), the various editions of Daniel Jones's *English Pronouncing Dictionary,* and a number of other publications of considerable intellectual prestige prefer the spelling with *z,* which, in the words of the *OED,* is "at once etymological and phonetic." (The suffix is ultimately from Greek *-izein.*) The *ct* of *connection* and *inflection* is due to the influence of *connect* and *inflect.* The etymologically sounder spellings *connexion* and *inflexion,* reflecting their sources in Latin *connexiōn(em)* and *inflexiōn(em),* are used by most writers, or at any rate by most printers, in England.

Spelling reform has been a recurring preoccupation of would-be language engineers on both sides of the Atlantic. Webster, who loved tinkering with all aspects of language, had contemplated far flashier spelling reforms than those he succeeded in getting adopted. For instance, he advocated lopping off the final *e* of *-ine, -ite,* and *-ive* in final syllables (thus *medicin, definit, fugitiv*), using *oo* for *ou* in *group* and *soup,* writing *tung* for *tongue,* and deleting the *a* in *bread, feather,* and the like; but in time he abandoned these unsuccessful, albeit sensible, spellings. The financier Andrew Carnegie and President Theodore Roosevelt both supported a reformed spelling in the early years of this century, including such simplifications as *catalog* for *catalogue, claspt* for *clasped, gage* for *gauge, program* for *programme,* and *thoro* for *thorough.* Some of these spellings they advocated have been generally adopted, some are still used as variants, but many are rarely used now.

For Study and Discussion

1. What examples can you add to the eight groups of words cited by the authors?

2. Bernard Shaw was interested in phonetic spelling and introduced a number of simplifications into his own plays. Read *Pygmalion* or one of the other plays and report on Shaw's spelling innovations.

---

2. **digraph** (dī′grăf): a pair of letters often run together (like *ae*) to represent a sound.

Realism and Naturalism

1. Consider the following statements by two great French writers about realism and naturalism in American literature:

> The realist, if he is an artist, will seek not to give us a banal photograph of life but a vision of it that is fuller, sharper, more convincing than reality itself.
>
> Guy de Maupassant

> [The naturalists] consider that man cannot be separated from his surroundings, that he is completed by his clothes, his house, his city, and his country; and hence we shall not note a single phenomenon of his brain or heart without looking for the causes or the consequences in his surroundings.
>
> Émile Zola

What evidence can you find in the selections by Stephen Crane, Willa Cather, and Jack London to support either or both of these statements? Compose an essay, referring to specific passages in the selections.

2. The following statements refer to the poems of Edwin Arlington Robinson:

> These hard little poems are specimens of human experience in a world in which agony is real and happiness but a wish.

> [One] theme recurs endlessly, the tragedy of each human being . . .

> Each life, if it moves upward, mounts a "darkening hill."
>
> Stanley T. Williams
>
> (from *Literary History of the United States*)

Discuss these statements in light of the poems by Robinson you have read in this unit. Be sure to refer to specific passages in the poems. If you like, discuss the degree to which the statements also apply to the work of Edgar Lee Masters.

For Further Reading

For Background on Individual Authors

Crane

Berryman, John, *Stephen Crane* (Octagon, 1975)
Cady, Edwin H., *Stephen Crane* (G. K. Hall, 1980)
Hoffman, Daniel G., *The Poetry of Stephen Crane* (Columbia University Press, 1957)
Katz, Joseph, ed., *The Complete Poems of Stephen Crane* (Cornell University Press, 1972)
Nagel, James, *Stephen Crane and Literary Impressionism* (Pennsylvania State University Press, 1980)
Stallman, R. W., *Stephen Crane* (Braziller, 1968)

Cather

Bennett, Mildred R., *The World of Willa Cather* (University of Nebraska Press, 1961)
Brown, E. K., and Leon Edel, *Willa Cather: A Critical Biography* (Knopf, 1953)
Daiches, David, *Willa Cather: A Critical Introduction* (Greenwood, 1971)
Gerber, Philip, *Willa Cather* (G. K. Hall, 1975)
Schroeter, James, ed., *Willa Cather and Her Critics* (Cornell University Press, 1967)

London

Hedrick, Joan D., *Solitary Comrade: Jack London and His Work* (University of North Carolina Press, 1982)
Labor, Earle, *Jack London* (Twayne, 1974)

Robinson

Coxe, Louis O., *Edwin Arlington Robinson* (University of Minnesota Press, 1962)
Murphy, Francis, ed., *Edwin Arlington Robinson: A Collection of Critical Essays* (1970)

For Students' Leisure Reading

Crane's works

The Red Badge of Courage
"The Blue Hotel"
"The Bride Comes to Yellow Sky"
"An Episode of War"
"The Upturned Face"

Cather's works

Death Comes for the Archbishop
My Ántonia
O Pioneers!
"Paul's Case"
"Neighbour Rosicky"

London's works

The Call of the Wild
The Sea-Wolf
White Fang
Martin Eden
"Love of Life"
"The Mexican"

Robinson's poems

"Luke Havergal"
"The House on the Hill"
"Cliff Klingenhagen"
"Eros Turannos"
"George Crabbe"
"For a Dead Lady"
"The Mill"

Masters' poems from *Spoon River Anthology*

"Hod Putt"
"Serepta Mason"
"Constance Hately"
"Barney Hainsfeather"
"Clarence Fawcett"
"Seth Compton"
"Flossie Canabis"
"Petit, the Poet"
"Hortense Robbins"
"Albert Schirding"
"Jonas Keene"
"Anne Rutledge"

Dunbar's poems

"Dawn"
"Compensation"
"The Debt"
"Sympathy"
"Life"
"My Sort o' Man"
"A Song"

James's works

The Turn of the Screw
Washington Square
"Four Meetings"
"The Real Thing"

Watch, 1925 by Gerald Murphy (1888–1964). Oil on canvas.
Dallas Museum of Art, gift of the artist

Street Scene, Autumn (1974–1977) by Sidney Goodman (1936–   ).
Oil on canvas.

Virginia Museum of Fine Arts, Richmond, gift of Sydney and Frances Lewis

Extension and Disenchantment

During this century the United States has attained a position of world leadership in material wealth and industrial and technological accomplishment. The most powerful nation on earth, it has achieved the greatness for which it has always seemed destined. However, it has also inherited its share of problems attendant on world leadership. Two world wars (1914–1918 and 1939–1945) shook and altered the world. Although the United States emerged victorious from these struggles, it had, in the interim, experienced a massive, crippling depression (1930–1941). The war in Korea in the 1950s, the Vietnam War in the 1960s and 1970s, and the continuing Cold War since 1946 contributed to a heightening of international tension and domestic unrest. Increased industrialization quickened the pace of life, and a host of new social, economic, and psychological problems arose. One of the most significant of these was an awareness of the growing fragmentation of society. Individuals felt isolated, no longer bound to each other by traditional standards of conduct or by the structure of society. They felt swallowed up by vast forces over which they had little or no control. The emphasis on large corporations, mass production, and mechanization widened the gulf between workers and employers. Americans grew disenchanted with the nation's political life. Various "liberation movements" of women and minorities became increasingly felt. Many people felt they could no longer respect their leaders and that there was no close fundamental connection between themselves and their government. As a consequence of this fragmentation, people had a sense of wandering in a void as bits and pieces of a society that was no longer whole.

Twentieth-century American literature—a literature of many perspectives—reflects these complex and diverse developments. Contemporary American writers express the separateness of the self and the modern sense of isolation and alienation. But they also do more—they struggle to find a common ground in which we all recognize a shared humanity.

The Great War and a New Consciousness

Americans were in a self-confident mood as the twentieth century began. The nation was growing rapidly (the population would increase from 76,000,000 in 1900 to 103,500,000 in 1918) and emerging as a world power. We had reason to feel proud, in 1914, of our accomplishment in building the Panama Canal. Another step in the development of American power was Henry Ford's introduction in 1913 of the assembly line at the Detroit factories of the Ford Motor Company. With workers engaged at individual tasks, productivity increased at Ford.

City Interior, 1936 by Charles Sheeler (1883–1965). Oil on composition board. Worcester Art Museum

This resulted in greater output, which in turn led to increased profits and imitation of assembly-line methods by other industrial companies. In 1914 Ford cut the working day from nine to eight hours and established a minimum wage of five dollars a day for employees over twenty-one. The labor problems that had persisted in the nation through the last decades of the nineteenth century appeared to be abating. When America entered World War I in 1917, three years after it had begun, idealistic young Americans marched off to the European front singing "Over There," a popular song which proclaimed that "The Yanks are coming"—to make the world "safe for democracy," as President Woodrow Wilson put it when he formally declared war on Germany.

Although the European democracies emerged intact as well as victorious, World War I irreparably changed the world. The most immediate consequences of the war were terrible devastation and waste. Weapons had been introduced whose capacities for carnage were shocking: tanks, submarines, and poison gas were used for the

Poster (1915) by Henry Reuterdahl (1871–1925).
Courtesy of Society of Illustrators, Museum of American Illustration, New York

United States soldiers in the trenches during World War I.
National Archives

first time. More than eight million people perished, many in hand-to-hand combat. Europe was paralyzed after four years of brutal conflict, and entire national economies were crushed.

The United States emerged from the Great War as the world's leading economic and military power. But as our soldiers returned from Europe, they brought home a disillusionment with the old order that was to replace America's characteristic optimism. American writers such as T. S. Eliot, Ernest Hemingway, F. Scott Fitzgerald, John Dos Passos, and Ezra Pound, who had in varying ways been affected by the war, were bereft of idealism. Instead, they had an overriding feeling of inevitable doom and a view of the world as violent, vulgar, and spiritually empty. The writers of the postwar period agreed with Gertrude Stein that they were "all a lost generation," confronted with futility and the loss of idealism and searching desperately for a new source of hope.

EZRA POUND (1885–1972)
Personae (1909)

EDNA ST. VINCENT MILLAY (1892–1950)
"Renascence" (1912)

Imagist movement begins; *Poetry: A Magazine of Verse* founded (1912)

ROBERT FROST (1874–1963)
A Boy's Will (1913)

1914–1918 World War I

FROST
North of Boston (1914)

CARL SANDBURG (1878–1967)
Chicago Poems (1916)

T. S. ELIOT (1888–1965)
Prufrock and Other Observations (1917)

SHERWOOD ANDERSON (1876–1941)
Winesburg, Ohio (1919)

1920 League of Nations founded; Nineteenth Amendment to the Constitution—women's suffrage; first commercial radio broadcast

EUGENE O'NEILL (1888–1953)
Beyond the Horizon (1920)

SINCLAIR LEWIS (1885–1951)
Main Street (1920)

ELIOT
The Waste Land (1922)

E. E. CUMMINGS (1894–1962)
The Enormous Room (1922)

WALLACE STEVENS (1879–1955)
Harmonium (1923)

F. SCOTT FITZGERALD (1896–1940)
The Great Gatsby (1925)

ERNEST HEMINGWAY (1899–1961)
The Sun Also Rises (1926)

1927 Lindbergh makes first nonstop solo flight from New York to Paris

The Jazz Singer, first "talking" motion picture

American soldiers in the trenches during World War I

Edna St. Vincent Millay

Ernest Hemingway

John Steinbeck

William Carlos Williams

1929 Stock Market crash begins the Great Depression

WILLIAM FAULKNER (1897–1962)
The Sound and the Fury (1929)

HEMINGWAY
A Farewell to Arms (1929)

THOMAS WOLFE (1900–1938)
Look Homeward, Angel (1929)

SINCLAIR LEWIS receives Nobel Prize (1930)

PEARL BUCK (1892–1973)
The Good Earth (1931)

EUGENE O'NEILL receives Nobel Prize (1936)

JOHN DOS PASSOS (1896–1970)
Trilogy *U.S.A.* completed (1936)

THORNTON WILDER (1897–1975)
Our Town (1938)

PEARL BUCK receives Nobel Prize (1938)

1939 First commercial television

JOHN STEINBECK (1902–1968)
The Grapes of Wrath (1939)

1939–1945 World War II

RICHARD WRIGHT (1908–1960)
Native Son (1940)

1945 First atomic bomb dropped

United Nations founded

WILLIAM CARLOS WILLIAMS (1883–1963)
Paterson (1946)

T. S. ELIOT receives Nobel Prize (1948)

ARTHUR MILLER (1915–   )
Death of a Salesman (1949)

1950–1953 Korean War

WILLIAM FAULKNER receives 1949 Nobel Prize
(1950)

J. D. SALINGER (1919–   )
The Catcher in the Rye (1951)

1952 — First hydrogen bomb tested

MARIANNE MOORE (1887–1972)
Collected Poems (1952)

RALPH ELLISON (1914–   )
Invisible Man (1952)

JAMES BALDWIN (1924–1987)
Go Tell It on the Mountain (1953)

1954 — Supreme Court rules segregation in the public schools unconstitutional

ERNEST HEMINGWAY receives Nobel Prize (1954)

O'NEILL
Long Day's Journey into Night (1956)

1958 — First American satellite in orbit

ROBERT LOWELL (1917–1977)
Life Studies (1959)

1961 — First manned spaceflight

JOSEPH HELLER (1923–   )
Catch-22 (1961)

1962 — American troops sent to South Vietnam

EDWARD ALBEE (1928–   )
Who's Afraid of Virginia Woolf? (1962)

JOHN STEINBECK receives Nobel Prize (1962)

KATHERINE ANNE PORTER (1890–1980)
Ship of Fools (1962)

1963 — President John F. Kennedy assassinated

Nuclear test ban treaty with U.S.S.R. and Great Britain

1964 — Civil Rights Act

SAUL BELLOW (1915–   )
Herzog (1964)

Marianne Moore

James Baldwin

Centennial of Statue of Liberty

Bernard Malamud

John Updike

1966 National Organization for Women (NOW) founded

BERNARD MALAMUD (1914–1986)
The Fixer (1966)

1968 Vietnam peace talks begin in Paris

Martin Luther King, Jr., assassinated

Robert Kennedy assassinated

NORMAN MAILER (1923–   )
The Armies of the Night (1968)

1969 American astronauts land on the moon

VLADIMIR NABOKOV (1899–1977)
Ada (1969)

ELIZABETH BISHOP (1911–1979)
The Complete Poems (1970)

JOHN UPDIKE (1932–   )
Rabbit Redux (1971)

EUDORA WELTY (1909–   )
The Optimist's Daughter (1972)

FLANNERY O'CONNOR (1925–1964)
The Complete Stories (1972)

1972 Watergate Affair

1973 Vietnam cease-fire

1974 President Richard Nixon resigns

1976 Nation celebrates Bicentennial

SAUL BELLOW receives Nobel Prize (1976)

1978 Equal Rights Amendment (ERA) passed by Congress
and delivered to states for ratification

ISAAC BASHEVIS SINGER (1904–   )
receives Nobel Prize (1978)

1986 Centennial of Statue of Liberty

1987 Nation celebrates Bicentennial of Constitution

Literary Modernism

Like the Civil War before it, World War I ushered in a dark, rich period of anger and experimentation in American literature. The term *modernism* is given to the international movement that developed in the postwar period. Writers felt that it was necessary to break with the past. Pound urged his colleagues to "make it new" and almost all writers agreed that new ways of seeing demanded new ways of saying. Literary modernism, as exemplified in American literature by such writers as Pound, Eliot, Cummings, Hemingway, and Fitzgerald, combined the subject matter of political and social dissent with experimental forms and language.

Demands for "new ways of saying" led to unconventional literary appearances—no punctuation, no capital letters, endless sentences, obscure phrasing often difficult to understand. A prominent example of modernism in American literature is T. S. Eliot's poem *The Waste Land*. In this long poem Eliot's pessimistic conclusion, that World War I was dramatic evidence of the collapse of Western civilization, is presented in a style that is difficult and highly allusive.

Faulkner's novels offer another example of the modernist method. In the fiction of his predecessors, a single narrative voice was used to tell the story. In *As I Lay Dying* Faulkner dispensed with this device. Instead he has fifteen characters tell his story, alternating the novel's point of view among them. In this way the reader hears many sides of a story and comes to recognize how important individual perception is in shaping reality.

Photograph of a dust storm in Cimarron County, Oklahoma, 1936.
Arthur Rothstein
Library of Congress

Bread line during the Great Depression.
The Bettmann Archive

Distrust of the old, conventional ways of perceiving society also led to new kinds of literary subject matter: race, class, sex, revolution, economics, the lives and perspectives of the disillusioned, the outcast, the dispossessed, the maverick, the minority ethnic. Edith Wharton (*The House of Mirth, The Custom of the Country*) and then F. Scott Fitzgerald (*The Great Gatsby, Tender Is the Night*) showed how alluring but how destructively false were the values and appearances of the privileged few at the top of society; Sinclair Lewis (*Main Street, Babbitt*) criticized what he saw as hypocrisy in the lives and values of the established middle class; Theodore Dreiser (*Sister Carrie, An American Tragedy*) showed how precarious were the lives of working-class people; John Steinbeck (*The Grapes of Wrath*) glorified the lives and values of the oppressed outcasts at the economic bottom of American society; and Ernest Hemingway (*In Our Time, A Farewell to Arms*) and John Dos Passos (*Three Soldiers, U.S.A.*) cast into doubt the assumptions of martial glory and patriotism.

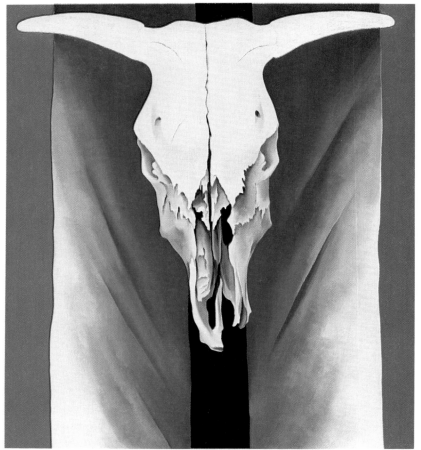

Cow's Skull: Red, White, and Blue (1931) by Georgia O'Keeffe (1887–1986). Oil on canvas.

Metropolitan Museum of Art, Alfred Stieglitz Collection

Literary Traditionalism

While no writer in the postwar period escaped the influence of new ideas and new techniques, many writers continued to work in the mainstream of traditional American literature, often combining modernist techniques with characteristic American themes. Regionalism, which developed after the Civil War, continued to be an important element in the work of such writers as Robert Frost, Ellen Glasgow, Katherine Anne Porter, and William Faulkner. Many writers continued to find realism a suitable vehicle for the novel. Theodore Dreiser's greatest novel, *An American Tragedy,* appeared in 1925, right at the height of the modernist upheaval. Still, it is undeniable that the modernist impulse to "make it new" dominated postwar American literature.

Emphasis on the Self in Literature

One of the essential characteristics of modern literature is that it attempts to find common ground in a world no longer unified in belief. In the Middle Ages, most people in Europe essentially shared one common view of God, the cosmos, and human beings. One church mediated that common view, and society had basically the same shape and organization throughout the Continent. Much literature was significantly theological in outlook and orientation, for to dramatize the theology was to express what most Europeans knew and believed about all existence. But as the European medieval world broke down and our modern world emerged from it, many different ideas about God, nature, and human beings sprang up. As shared old beliefs began to crumble under the impact of scientific discovery, less and less was there a single, central perspective common to all, satisfactorily expressing the meaning of all human experience. Consequently, as the reality of a unified external world disappeared and private, internal reality became more important, modern literature began to emphasize the individual perception. Under the guiding genius of Americans like Henry James and Europeans like James Joyce, modern literature began to emphasize sensibility and human consciousness as central subjects in themselves.

James Joyce, Paris (1928). Silver gelatin print.
Berenice Abbott / Commerce Graphics Ltd., Inc.

Twentieth-century theories of psychology reflected and strengthened the increasing emphasis on the inner self. Furthermore, the American ideology of economic individualism intensified the modernist emphasis upon the separate person. Contemporary American literature tries to find in the self, in the intricacies of the individual, the identity of the society. It is fair to say that in exploring the possibilities and meanings of the self, contemporary American literature explores the possibilities and meanings of America.

Pluralism in Literature

Contemporary American literature no longer reflects a predominantly male point of view, as the poetry of Denise Levertov, Anne Sexton, Adrienne Rich, and Sylvia Plath makes clear. The South is by no means merely an appendage in our national culture, for the brilliant and internationally acclaimed work of William Faulkner, Eudora Welty, and Flannery O'Connor, among many others, has made "Southern regionalism" a universal in modern literature. Black writers, beginning to emerge after the Civil War, made a great step forward with the Harlem Renaissance, and, with Richard Wright, Langston Hughes, Zora Neale Hurston, James Baldwin, Ralph Ellison, and Alice Walker, took their place among the American giants of contemporary literature. Gwendolyn Brooks combines both the black's and the woman's American point of view. So too, other minorities, like Jews, became outstanding after World War II in the creation of contemporary American literature. Norman Mailer, Bernard Malamud, Isaac Bashevis Singer, and Saul Bellow are but a few of the names that bring ethnic minority experience into the forefront of contemporary American literature. And, at this moment, like blacks, Jews, Irish, Poles, Germans, Italians, Scandinavians, American Indians, Asian Americans, and so many, many others, Hispanic Americans—Américo Paredes, Rolando Hinojosa, Richard Rodriguez, to name a few—are becoming another feature in the American literary landscape.

The different minority groups that have moved to the forefront in American literature in recent decades have enriched our culture by redefining what it means to be an American. Thus, the minority black brings us not only the alienated sense of what black life is like in America but also brings us a sense of our oneness beneath the differences. (At the end of Ralph Ellison's acclaimed novel, *Invisible Man,* the nameless black hero, speaking from his underground hideaway beneath a New York City flaming with race war, asks, "Who knows but that, on the lower frequencies, I speak for you?") Thus, the mother holding her daughter at her breast, as in Anne Sexton's "The Fortress," speaks of life's uncertainties and a woman's nurturing

Studs Terkel, Toni Morrison, and Donald Barthelme shown at the American Writers' Congress held in New York City in 1981.
© Nancy Crampton

realism in a world made lastingly recognizable to anyone, male or female. ("I promise you love. Time will not take that away.") And thus, in what is perhaps one of the best statements of the proposition, the minority Jew, Augie March, says at the end of Nobel Prizewinner Saul Bellow's novel *The Adventures of Augie March,* "Why, I am a sort of Columbus of those near-at-hand. . . . I may well be a flop at this line of endeavor. Columbus too thought he was a flop, probably, when they sent him back in chains. Which didn't prove there was no America."

Consciousness of Experience

In many cases, this pluralism—the existence of many distinctive groups in contemporary literature—attempts to express the separateness of the self and the modern sense of isolation and alienation. But that is hardly the whole story. Like all moderns everywhere, contemporary American writers attempt to find a common ground in which we all recognize a shared humanity. Our contemporary writers are concerned with sharp consciousness of experience—of the exact detail—as the sign of what makes us human. Whether the image is used for hope or disillusion, satire or sympathy, the evocative precision of imagery in the poetry of Marianne Moore, Elizabeth Bishop, or Randall Jarrell, to name but a few, or in the prose of Ernest Hemingway and John Updike, to name but a very few more, is inextricably a part of the very intentions and ideas and *humanness* of their work. Our contemporary writers are saying at least one thing in common: in a world that seems to fall apart, if one sees clearly, truly, and precisely—if one becomes conscious of human consciousness—one begins to put the world back together into meaning we can share.

A Literature of Many Perspectives

Contemporary American literature is a literature of many perspectives. The modern search for new perspectives is the real purpose of contemporary literature's bewildering welter of brilliant imagery and experimental forms. The images in this literature are the meanings of our times and therefore illuminate our most inner and our most public lives. The vigor of contemporary American literature, much of it born in disaffection and an uneasy sense of the disintegration of the nation's most cherished ideals, is itself a sign of the democracy's strength. The pluralism—in ethnicity, in sex, in class, in political allegiances—is an announcement of the ongoing energy of the American culture; the insistence on divergent or even unique perspectives is an announcement of the ongoing force of American freedom; and the nostalgic recognition of limitation and loss (as in F. Scott Fitzgerald's fiction or Robert Penn Warren's poetry) as well as of fortitude and endurance (as in the fiction of William Faulkner and Eudora Welty) is a sign of America's coming of age. Our contemporary writers are producing what Ralph Waldo Emerson called for more than a century ago: a diverse and truly national literature.

Review

1. What factors have contributed to the growing fragmentation of American society?
2. What does the term "lost generation" refer to?
3. In the absence of a unified view of external reality, what has the modern writer turned to?
4. Give some examples of pluralism in contemporary American literature.

MODERN FICTION

Over the centuries fiction has developed into several forms, including the novel, the novella, and the short story. Among the forms of fiction, the short story is perhaps the one to which American writers have made the most significant contributions. Washington Irving fashioned entertaining and imaginative tales out of old German folk materials. Nathaniel Hawthorne constructed grim allegories that delved deeply into the mysteries of the human psyche. Edgar Allan Poe, more than anyone, furthered the craft of the short story by insisting that the short story is a distinct form with special rules of composition: a short story must have "a certain unique or single *effect.*" Around the turn of the century, Henry James pursued his ideal of the "art of fiction" in creating many masterly short stories which were always unified, organic compositions, and which remain exemplars of the art.

As the United States approached the twentieth century, however, some writers felt that the short story was in danger of becoming an empty form. A fresh style seemed necessary to express the complexities and uncertainties of modern life. Sherwood Anderson, the most impressive of the early experimentalists, argued against "wrapping life up into neat little packages," and began to create stories with an "open form," in which plot development was less important than the expression of mood and character. The modern American short story can be said to begin with Anderson's "open form," which influenced several important later writers.

The post-World War I generation of prose writers—Anderson, Hemingway, Fitzgerald, Faulkner—continued to create, with varying success, after the decade of the 1920s. New voices began to emerge with new themes: John Steinbeck, for example, chronicled with honesty and sympathy the plight of migrant laborers during the Great Depression. A number of Southern writers since Faulkner have attained prominent stature: Katherine Anne Porter, Jesse Stuart, Eudora Welty, and Caroline Gordon, to name a few, have consistently produced works of polished craft. Richard Wright was the first of a brilliant line of black writers that includes James Baldwin, Ralph Ellison, and, recently, Toni Morrison, Alice Walker, William Melvin Kelley, and James Alan McPherson. Since World War II, Vladimir Nabokov, Norman Mailer, Saul Bellow, and Isaac Bashevis Singer have been among our most distinguished prose stylists. Other notable contemporary fiction writers include Bernard Malamud, John Updike, J. D. Salinger, Joseph Heller, Thomas Pynchon, Donald Barthelme, William Gaddis, and Joyce Carol Oates.

The following selections, drawn from some of the best of our prose writers, represent the stylistic diversity and enduring quality of modern American fiction.

Sherwood Anderson (1933).
The Granger Collection

Winesburg, Ohio, Anderson's best-known work, has a short introduction explaining what his characters have in common: they are all "grotesques." Grotesques, according to Anderson, seize on one "truth," an idea or an ambition, and allow it to become an obsession. In their single-minded passion for an overriding idea, they lead lonely, possessed lives, cut off from those who pursue other "truths," or have a more balanced view of life. Anderson managed to make his grotesques into symbols of the American village. Other writers saw the village or small town as a snug, secure community bound together by common traditions and attitudes. Anderson saw it as an unhappy place full of isolated, despairing souls leading hidden lives. He was one of the first modern writers to deal with a significant American figure: the human being whose life is tragically warped by his or her dreams and ambitions.

Sherwood Anderson's father was a harness maker who was slowly put out of work as his craft became obsolete. The Andersons had seven children, and Sherwood, the third, was obliged to help support the rest. Leaving school after a year of high school, he was known around Clyde, Ohio, where he grew up, as "Jobby" because of the variety of odd jobs he held. He led a grueling life before going to Chicago at the age of twenty-four to work in an advertising agency. Eventually he moved to Elyria, Ohio, and began his own business, but it went badly, and one day, sick of responsibilities and growing debts, he fled.

After a time he returned to Chicago and took a job writing advertisements. He met Chicago intellectuals and writers, among them Theodore Dreiser and Carl Sandburg, who encouraged him to write. His early novels, *Windy McPherson's Son* and *Marching Men,* were hailed as the appearance of an original talent. Meanwhile he was sifting his experiences in small Ohio towns. Edgar Lee Masters' *Spoon River Anthology* (page 502) suggested to him the possibility of writing a prose equivalent of this work, a collection of short stories about people living in the same town and tied together by one character, George Willard, a young reporter who appears in most of the stories. When *Winesburg, Ohio* appeared in 1919, it established Anderson as an important writer. This book, with its effective use of simple language and its glimpses beneath the surfaces of isolated lives, showed the way to younger people who wanted to write simply and truthfully about the life they knew. Anderson became a literary celebrity sought out by aspiring writers, including Ernest Hemingway and William Faulkner, whose careers he aided. He wrote a number of fine short stories, collected in *The Triumph of the Egg, Horses and Men,* and *Death in the Woods, and Other Stories,* and several novels that met with varying success. He spent the last years of his life in Virginia, as a farmer and newspaper editor.

Sophistication

It was early evening of a day in the late fall and the Winesburg County Fair had brought crowds of country people to town. The day had been clear and the night came on warm and pleasant. On the Trunion Pike, where the road after it left town stretched away between berry fields now covered with dry brown leaves, the dust from passing wagons arose in clouds. Children, curled into little balls, slept on the straw scattered on wagon beds. Their hair was full of dust and their fingers black and sticky. The dust rolled away over the fields and the departing sun set it ablaze with colors.

In the main street of Winesburg crowds filled the stores and the sidewalks. Night came on, horses whinnied, the clerks in the stores ran madly about, children became lost and cried lustily, an American town worked terribly at the task of amusing itself.

Pushing his way through the crowds in Main Street, young George Willard concealed himself in the stairway leading to Doctor Reefy's office and looked at the people. With feverish eyes he watched the faces drifting past under the store lights. Thoughts kept coming into his head and he did not want to think. He stamped impatiently on the wooden steps and looked sharply about. "Well, is she going to stay with him all day? Have I done all this waiting for nothing?" he muttered.

George Willard, the Ohio village boy, was fast growing into manhood and new thoughts had been coming into his mind. All that day, amid the jam of people at the Fair, he had gone about feeling lonely. He was about to leave Winesburg to go away to some city where he hoped to get work on a city newspaper and he felt grown-up. The mood that had taken possession of him was a thing known to men and unknown to boys. He felt old and a little tired. Memories awoke in him. To his mind his new sense of maturity set him apart, made

of him a half-tragic figure. He wanted someone to understand the feeling that had taken possession of him after his mother's death.

There is a time in the life of every boy when he for the first time takes the backward view of life. Perhaps that is the moment when he crosses the line into manhood. The boy is walking through the street of his town. He is thinking of the future and of the figure he will cut in the world. Ambitions and regrets awake within him. Suddenly something happens; he stops under a tree and waits as for a voice calling his name. Ghosts of old things creep into his consciousness; the voices outside of himself whisper a message concerning the limitations of life. From being quite sure of himself and his future he becomes not at all sure. If he be an imaginative boy a door is torn open and for the first time he looks out upon the world, seeing, as though they marched in procession before him, the countless figures of men who before his time have come out of nothingness into the world, lived their lives and again disappeared into nothingness. The sadness of sophistication has come to the boy. With a little gasp he sees himself as merely a leaf blown by the wind through the streets of his village. He knows that in spite of all the stout talk of his fellows he must live and die in uncertainty, a thing blown by the winds, a thing destined like corn to wilt in the sun. He shivers and looks eagerly about. The eighteen years he has lived seem but a moment, a breathing space in the long march of humanity. Already he hears death calling. With all his heart he wants to come close to some other human, touch someone with his hands, be touched by the hand of another. If he prefers that the other be a woman, that is because he believes that a woman will be gentle, that she will understand. He wants, most of all, understanding.

Old Tavern at Hammondsville, Ohio (1926–1928) by Charles Burchfield
(1893–1967). Watercolor.
Addison Gallery of American Art, Phillips Academy, Andover, Massachusetts

When the moment of sophistication came to George Willard his mind turned to Helen White, the Winesburg banker's daughter. Always he had been conscious of the girl growing into womanhood as he grew into manhood. Once on a summer night when he was eighteen, he had walked with her on a country road and in her presence had given way to an impulse to boast, to make himself appear big and significant in her eyes. Now he wanted to see her for another purpose. He wanted to tell her of the new impulses that had come to him. He had tried to make her think of him as a man when he knew nothing of manhood and now he wanted to be with her and to try to make her feel the change he believed had taken place in his nature.

As for Helen White, she also had come to a period of change. What George felt, she in her young woman's way felt also. She was no longer a girl and hungered to reach into the grace and beauty of womanhood. She had come home from Cleveland, where she was attending college, to spend a day at the Fair. She also had begun to have memories. During the day she sat in the grandstand with a young man, one of the instructors from the college, who was a guest of her mother's. The young man was of a pedantic turn of mind and she felt at once he would not do for her purpose.

At the Fair she was glad to be seen in his company as he was well dressed and a stranger. She knew that the fact of his presence would create an impression. During the day she was happy, but when night came on she began to grow restless. She wanted to drive the instructor away, to get out of his presence. While they sat together in the grandstand and while the eyes of former schoolmates were upon them, she paid so much attention to her escort that he grew interested. "A scholar needs money. I should marry a woman with money," he mused.

Helen White was thinking of George Willard even as he wandered gloomily through the crowds thinking of her. She remembered the summer evening when they had walked together and wanted to walk with him again. She thought that the months she had spent in the city, the going to theaters and the seeing of great crowds wandering in lighted thoroughfares, had changed her profoundly. She wanted him to feel and be conscious of the change in her nature.

The summer evening together that had left its mark on the memory of both the young man and the woman had, when looked at quite sensibly, been rather stupidly spent. They had walked out of town along a country road. Then they had stopped by a fence near a field of young corn and George had taken off his coat and let it hang on his arm. "Well, I've stayed here in Winesburg—yes—I've not yet gone away but I'm growing up," he had said. "I've been reading books and I've been thinking. I'm going to try to amount to something in life.

"Well," he explained, "that isn't the point. Perhaps I'd better quit talking."

The confused boy put his hand on the girl's arm. His voice trembled. The two started to walk back along the road toward town. In his desperation George boasted, "I'm going to be a big man, the biggest that ever lived here in Winesburg," he declared. "I want you to do something, I don't know what. Perhaps it is none of my business. I want you to try to be different from other women. You see the point. It's none of my business, I tell you. I want you to be a beautiful woman. You see what I want."

The boy's voice failed and in silence the two came back into town and went along the street to Helen White's house. At the gate he tried to say something impressive. Speeches he had thought out came into his head, but they seemed utterly pointless. "I thought—I used to think—I had in my mind you would marry Seth Richmond. Now I know you won't," was all he could find to say as she went through the gate and toward the door of her house.

On the warm fall evening as he stood in the stairway and looked at the crowd drifting through Main Street, George thought of the talk beside the field of young corn and was ashamed of the figure he had made of himself. In the street the people surged up and down like cattle confined in a pen. Buggies and wagons almost filled the narrow thoroughfare. A band played and small boys raced along the sidewalk, diving between the legs of men. Young men with shining red faces walked awkwardly about with girls on their arms. In a room above one of the stores, where a dance was to be held, the fiddlers tuned their instruments. The broken sounds floated down through an open window and out across the murmur of voices and the loud blare of the horns of the band. The medley of songs got on young Willard's nerves. Everywhere, on all sides, the sense of crowding, moving life closed in about him. He wanted to run away by himself and think. "If she wants to stay with that fellow she may. Why should I care? What difference does it make to me?" he growled and went along Main Street and through Hern's Grocery into a side street.

George felt so utterly lonely and dejected that he wanted to weep but pride made him walk rapidly along, swinging his arms. He came to Wesley Moyer's livery barn and stopped in the shadows to listen to a group of men who talked of a race Wesley's stallion, Tony Tip, had won at the Fair during the afternoon. A crowd had gathered in front of the barn and before the crowd walked Wesley, prancing up and down and boasting. He held a whip in his hand and kept tapping the ground. Little puffs of dust arose in the lamplight. "Quit your talking," Wesley exclaimed. "I wasn't afraid, I knew I had 'em beat all the time. I wasn't afraid."

Ordinarily George Willard would have been intensely interested in the boasting of Moyer, the horseman. Now it made him angry. He turned and hurried away along the street. "Old windbag," he sputtered. "Why does he want to be bragging? Why don't he shut up?"

George went into a vacant lot, and as he hurried along, fell over a pile of rubbish. A nail protruding from an empty barrel tore his trousers. He sat down on the ground and swore. With a pin he mended the torn place and then arose and went on. "I'll go to Helen White's house, that's what I'll do. I'll walk right in. I'll say that I want to see her. I'll walk right in and sit down, that's what I'll do," he declared, climbing over a fence and beginning to run.

On the veranda of Banker White's house Helen was restless and distraught. The instructor sat between the mother and daughter. His talk wearied the girl. Although he had also been raised in an Ohio town, the instructor began to put on the airs of the city. He wanted to appear cosmopolitan. "I like the chance you have given me to study the background out of which most of our girls come," he declared. "It was good of you, Mrs. White, to have me down for the day." He turned to Helen and laughed. "Your life is still bound up with the life of this town?" he asked. "There are people here in whom you are interested?" To the girl his voice sounded pompous and heavy.

Helen arose and went into the house. At the door leading to a garden at the back she stopped and stood listening. Her mother began to talk. "There is no one here fit to associate with a girl of Helen's breeding," she said.

Helen ran down a flight of stairs at the back of the house and into the garden. In the darkness she stopped and stood trembling. It seemed to her that the world was full of meaningless people saying words. Afire with eagerness she ran through the garden gate and, turning a corner by the banker's barn, went into a little side street. "George! Where are you, George?" she cried, filled with nervous excitement. She stopped running, and leaned against a tree to laugh hysterically. Along the dark little street came George Willard, still saying words. "I'm going to walk right into her house. I'll go right in and sit down," he declared as he came up to her. He stopped and stared stupidly. "Come on," he said and took hold of her hand. With hanging heads they walked away along the street under the trees. Dry leaves rustled underfoot. Now that he had found her George wondered what he had better do and say.

At the upper end of the Fair Ground, in Winesburg, there is a half-decayed old grandstand. It has never been painted and the boards are all warped out of shape. The Fair Ground stands on top of a low hill rising out of the valley of Wine Creek and from the grandstand one can see at night, over a cornfield, the lights of the town reflected against the sky.

George and Helen climbed the hill to the Fair Ground, coming by the path past Waterworks Pond. The feeling of loneliness and isolation that had come to the young man in the crowded streets of his town was both broken and intensified by the presence of Helen. What he felt was reflected in her.

In youth there are always two forces fighting in people. The warm unthinking little animal struggles against the thing that reflects and remembers, and the older, the more sophisticated thing had possession of George Willard. Sensing his mood, Helen walked beside him filled with respect. When they got to the grandstand they climbed up under the roof and sat down on one of the long benchlike seats.

Country fair.

There is something memorable in the experience to be had by going into a fairground that stands at the edge of a Middle Western town on a night after the annual fair has been held. The sensation is one never to be forgotten. On all sides are ghosts, not of the dead, but of living people. Here, during the day just passed, have come the people pouring in from the town and the country around. Farmers with their wives and children and all the people from the hundreds of little frame houses have gathered within these board walls. Young girls have laughed and men with beards have talked of the affairs of their lives. The place has been filled to overflowing with life. It has itched and squirmed with life and now it is night and the life has all gone away. The si-

lence is almost terrifying. One conceals oneself standing silently beside the trunk of a tree and what there is of a reflective tendency in his nature is intensified. One shudders at the thought of the meaninglessness of life while at the same instant, and if the people of the town are his people, one lives life so intensely that tears come into the eyes.

In the darkness under the roof of the grand-stand, George Willard sat beside Helen White and felt very keenly his own insignificance in the scheme of existence. Now that he had come out of town where the presence of the people stirring about, busy with a multitude of affairs, had been so irritating, the irritation was all gone. The presence of Helen renewed and refreshed him. It was as though her woman's hand was assisting him to make some minute readjustment of the machinery of his life. He began to think of the people in the town where he had always lived with something like reverence. He had reverence for Helen. He wanted to love and to be loved by her, but he did not want at the moment to be confused by her womanhood. In the darkness he took hold of her hand and when she crept close put a hand on her shoulder. A wind began to blow and he shivered. With all his strength he tried to hold and to understand the mood that had come upon him. In that high place in the darkness the two oddly sensitive human atoms held each other tightly and waited. In the mind of each was the same thought. "I have come to this lonely place and here is this other," was the substance of the thing felt.

In Winesburg the crowded day had run itself out into the long night of the late fall. Farm horses jogged away along lonely country roads pulling their portion of weary people. Clerks began to bring samples of goods in off the sidewalks and lock the doors of stores. In the Opera House a crowd had gathered to see a show and further down Main Street the fiddlers, their instruments tuned, sweated and worked to keep the feet of youth flying over a dance floor.

In the darkness in the grandstand Helen White and George Willard remained silent. Now and then the spell that held them was broken and they turned and tried in the dim light to see into each other's eyes. They kissed but that impulse did not last. At the upper end of the Fair Ground a half-dozen men worked over horses that had raced during the afternoon. The men had built a fire and were heating kettles of water. Only their legs could be seen as they passed back and forth in the light. When the wind blew, the little flames of the fire danced crazily about.

George and Helen arose and walked away into the darkness. They went along a path past a field of corn that had not yet been cut. The wind whispered among the dry corn blades. For a moment during the walk back into town the spell that held them was broken. When they had come to the crest of Waterworks Hill they stopped by a tree and George again put his hands on the girl's shoulders. She embraced him eagerly and then again they drew quickly back from that impulse. They stopped kissing and stood a little apart. Mutual respect grew big in them. They were both embarrassed and to relieve their embarrassment dropped into the animalism of youth. They laughed and began to pull and haul at each other. In some way chastened and purified by the mood they had been in, they became, not man and woman, not boy and girl, but excited little animals.

It was so they went down the hill. In the darkness they played like two splendid young things in a young world. Once, running swiftly forward, Helen tripped George and he fell. He squirmed and shouted. Shaking with laughter, he rolled down the hill. Helen ran after him. For just a moment she stopped in the darkness. There is no way of knowing what woman's thoughts went through her mind but, when the bottom of the hill was reached and she came up to the boy, she took his arm and walked beside him in dignified silence. For some reason they could not have explained they had both got from their silent evening together the thing needed. Man or boy, woman or girl, they had for a moment taken hold of the thing that makes the mature life of men and women in the modern world possible.

Reading Check

1. Why is George Willard leaving Winesburg?
2. What has brought Helen home from college?
3. Who is the stranger visiting at Helen's home?
4. Where do George and Helen go after they find each other?

Commentary

A *symbol* is an event, a character, or an object that stands for something else, usually an idea. In modern fiction, symbolic meanings are often attached to realistic characters or details that are significant in themselves.

The main action of "Sophistication" is set in the fall, but much of the story is concerned with the remembrance of a walk George and Helen had taken in the spring. The passage of time and the movement toward maturity are symbolized by the progression of the seasons, from the time of planting and first growth to the time of harvest.

Along with references to seasonal change, the symbol of growing corn appears several times to suggest the development taking place in George and Helen. At one point (page 583), George fears that he may be "destined like corn to wilt in the sun." Before that time, he wants to experience the growth through which the corn itself has passed. During their springtime walk, George and Helen had stopped by a field of young corn along a country road. Later, George remembers their talk beside this field of young corn and is ashamed of his own youth and immaturity.

In the fall, they take another walk, this time in the Winesburg Fair Ground. Now, over a fully grown cornfield, they can see the lights of the whole town reflected against the sky. With greater maturity, George now possesses a broader and firmer vision. Like the corn, George and Helen have come to the fullest growth of their relationship. Something else now lies ahead of them. Anderson thus reminds us by references to the passing seasons and the growing corn that human experience, like many other things in life, follows natural lines of development.

For Study and Discussion

Analyzing and Interpreting the Story

1. "Sophistication" is a story of two people caught between adolescence and maturity. George and Helen strain toward a new awareness of life while they are still bound to the familiar life of Winesburg. What reasons are given in the fourth paragraph for George's "new sense of maturity"?

2. The fifth paragraph describes the moment of sophistication, when a person first takes "the backward view of life." Anderson uses the image of a passing procession to suggest George's vision of the passing of time. What image does the author use to suggest the feelings of helplessness and uncertainty that accompany sophistication?

3. The author describes youth as a struggle between two forces: "the warm unthinking little animal" and "the thing that reflects and remembers" (page 586). **a.** Find a few instances in the story of the struggle between these two forces. **b.** What do you think Anderson means by this conflict?

4. At the end of the story, what do George and Helen gain from their silent evening together that "makes the mature life of men and women in the modern world possible"?

Literary Elements

Plot: Internal and External Conflict

Any work of literature that tells a story—be it a novel, short story, play, or narrative poem—has a **plot;** that is, a pattern growing out of the events of the work and out of the order in which they are told. A plot can be regarded as a kind of skeleton that the writer fills out by using well-drawn, convincing **characters,** a vivid **setting,** an effective **point of view,** and a distinctive **style.** These other elements—character, setting, point of view, and style—determine to some extent the impression a work of fiction makes on the reader, but the basic shape of the work depends on its skeleton or plot.

Most plots involve **conflict,** which may be external or internal. A plot concerned primarily with external conflict may pit a character against other characters or against an environment. A plot concerned primarily with internal conflict may depict a character's struggle with his or her own weaknesses or show how conflicting desires or ambitions pull the character in opposite directions.

What are the conflicts in "Sophistication"? Are they primarily external or internal? Explain your answer with references to passages in the text.

Writing About Literature

Showing How Theme Is Developed

An important theme in Anderson's writing is an individual's realization that isolation and loneliness are typical of the human condition. Show how this idea is developed in "Sophistication."

KATHERINE ANNE PORTER
1890–1980

Katherine Anne Porter.
The Bettmann Archive

Katherine Anne Porter was born in Indian Creek, Texas. Her family was a large one with deep roots in the South, particularly in southern Texas and Louisiana. One of her ancestors was Daniel Boone. On the various occasions—births, christenings, con-firmations, marriages, deaths—on which her family met, family stories were told and retold. A sense of the family as a community, with its own outlook and traditions and a solid residue of love that one can draw on and return to, pervades many of her stories. Such families, it once was clear, had histories that went far into the past and would go as far into the future. Yet, after World War I, these proud, solid families seemed to belong to an old order that was slowly passing. Some of Porter's stories re-create the old order, while others deal with the crises of individuals who must cope with the disappearance of order. A number of her stories have heroes or heroines who find themselves in places far from home—in Mexico or Europe—with a sense of being cast adrift, unable to see a pattern beneath events or seeing it all too clearly and despising it.

Porter published nothing until she was over thirty. She wrote that she learned her art in isolation, thus prolonging her development but saving her from "discipleship, personal influences, and membership in groups." To support herself, she performed a number of workaday writing tasks such as reviewing books and rewriting manuscripts, and she once described these years as "a sorry living. . . . Without the help of devoted friends I should have perished many times over." In 1930 the publication of *Flowering Judas*, a collection of short stories, gained her a small devoted readership. Her next major book, *Pale Horse, Pale Rider*, was not published until 1939. By this time she was recognized as an important writer, and serious readers awaited her first novel, scheduled to appear in 1942. It did not appear until many years later.

In 1944 *The Leaning Tower*, a collection of seven short stories and a novella, added to her high reputation. Porter continued to support herself with a variety of jobs, and occasionally went to Hollywood to write for the motion pictures. In 1962 her long-awaited novel, *Ship of Fools*, was published. It was a great popular success and finally gained its author a wide audience. In 1966 she won the National Book Award and the Pulitzer Prize for her *Collected Short Stories. The Collected Essays and Occasional Writings of Katherine Anne Porter* appeared in 1970.

590 MODERN FICTION

Portrait of My Mother (1921) by Malcolm Parcell (1896–   ). Oil on canvas.
The Butler Institute of American Art, Youngstown, Ohio, purchased 1923

The Jilting of Granny Weatherall

She flicked her wrist neatly out of Doctor Harry's pudgy careful fingers and pulled the sheet up to her chin. The brat ought to be in knee breeches. Doctoring around the country with spectacles on his nose! "Get along now, take your schoolbooks and go. There's nothing wrong with me."

Doctor Harry spread a warm paw like a cushion on her forehead where the forked green vein danced and made her eyelids twitch. "Now, now, be a good girl, and we'll have you up in no time."

"That's no way to speak to a woman nearly eighty years old just because she's down. I'd have you respect your elders, young man."

"Well, Missy, excuse me." Doctor Harry patted her cheek. "But I've got to warn you, haven't I? You're a marvel, but you must be careful or you're going to be good and sorry."

"Don't tell me what I'm going to be. I'm on my feet now, morally speaking. It's Cornelia. I had to go to bed to get rid of her."

Her bones felt loose, and floated around in her skin, and Doctor Harry floated like a balloon around the foot of the bed. He floated and pulled down his waistcoat and swung his glasses on a cord. "Well, stay where you are, it certainly can't hurt you."

"Get along and doctor your sick," said Granny Weatherall. "Leave a well woman alone. I'll call for you when I want you. . . . Where were you forty years ago when I pulled through milk leg[1] and double pneumonia? You weren't even born. Don't let Cornelia lead you on," she shouted, because Doctor Harry appeared to float up to the ceiling and out. "I pay my own bills, and I don't throw my money away on nonsense!"

She meant to wave goodbye, but it was too much trouble. Her eyes closed of themselves, it was like a dark curtain drawn around the bed. The pillow rose and floated under her, pleasant as a hammock in a light wind. She listened to the leaves rustling outside the window. No, somebody was swishing newspapers: no, Cornelia and Doctor Harry were whispering together. She leaped broad awake, thinking they whispered in her ear.

"She was never like this, *never* like this!" "Well, what can we expect?" "Yes, eighty years old. . . ."

Well, and what if she was? She still had ears. It was like Cornelia to whisper around doors. She always kept things secret in such a public way. She was always being tactful and kind. Cornelia was dutiful; that was the trouble with her. Dutiful and good. "So good and dutiful," said Granny, "that I'd like to spank her." She saw herself spanking Cornelia and making a fine job of it.

1. **milk leg:** a painful swelling of the leg, usually caused by infection during childbirth.

"What'd you say, Mother?"

Granny felt her face tying up in hard knots. "Can't a body think, I'd like to know?"

"I thought you might want something."

"I do. I want a lot of things. First off, go away and don't whisper."

She lay and drowsed, hoping in her sleep that the children would keep out and let her rest a minute. It had been a long day. Not that she was tired. It was always pleasant to snatch a minute now and then. There was always so much to be done, let me see: tomorrow.

Tomorrow was far away and there was nothing to trouble about. Things were finished somehow when the time came; thank God there was always a little margin over for peace: then a person could spread out the plan of life and tuck in the edges orderly. It was good to have everything clean and folded away, with the hair brushes and tonic bottles sitting straight on the white embroidered linen: the day started without fuss and the pantry shelves laid out with rows of jelly glasses and brown jugs and white stone-china jars with blue whirligigs and words painted on them: coffee, tea, sugar, ginger, cinnamon, allspice: and the bronze clock with the lion on top nicely dusted off. The dust that lion could collect in twenty-four hours! The box in the attic with all those letters tied up, well, she'd have to go through that tomorrow. All those letters—George's letters and John's letters and her letters to them both—lying around for the children to find afterwards made her uneasy. Yes, that would be tomorrow's business. No use to let them know how silly she had been once.

While she was rummaging around she found death in her mind and it felt clammy and unfamiliar. She had spent so much time preparing for death there was no need for bringing it up again. Let it take care of itself now. When she was sixty she had felt very old, finished, and went around making farewell trips to see her children and grandchildren, with a secret in her mind: This is the very last of your mother, children! Then she made her will and came down with a long fever. That was all just a notion like a lot of other things, but it was lucky too, for she had once for all got over the idea of dying for a long time. Now she couldn't be worried. She hoped she had better sense now. Her father had lived to be one hundred and two years old and had drunk a noggin of strong hot toddy on his last birthday. He told the reporters it was his daily habit, and he owed his long life to that. He had made quite a scandal and was very pleased about it. She believed she'd just plague Cornelia a little.

"Cornelia! Cornelia!" No footsteps, but a sudden hand on her cheek. "Bless you, where have you been?"

"Here, Mother."

"Well, Cornelia, I want a noggin of hot toddy."

"Are you cold, darling?"

"I'm chilly, Cornelia. Lying in bed stops the circulation. I must have told you that a thousand times."

Well, she could just hear Cornelia telling her husband that Mother was getting a little childish and they'd have to humor her. The thing that most annoyed her was that Cornelia thought she was deaf, dumb, and blind. Little hasty glances and tiny gestures tossed around her and over her head saying, "Don't cross her, let her have her way, she's eighty years old," and she sitting there as if she lived in a thin glass cage. Sometimes Granny almost made up her mind to pack up and move back to her own house where nobody could remind her every minute that she was old. Wait, wait, Cornelia, till your own children whisper behind your back!

In her day she had kept a better house and had got more work done. She wasn't too old yet for Lydia to be driving eighty miles for advice when one of the children jumped the track, and Jimmy still dropped in and talked things over: "Now, Mammy, you've a good business head, I want to know what you think of this? . . ." Old. Cornelia couldn't change the furniture around without asking. Little things, little things! They had been so sweet when they were little. Granny wished the old days were

back again with the children young and everything to be done over. It had been a hard pull, but not too much for her. When she thought of all the food she had cooked, and all the clothes she had cut and sewed, and all the gardens she had made—well, the children showed it. There they were, made out of her, and they couldn't get away from that. Sometimes she wanted to see John again and point to them and say, Well, I didn't do so badly, did I? But that would have to wait. That was for tomorrow. She used to think of him as a man, but now all the children were older than their father, and he would be a child beside her if she saw him now. It seemed strange and there was something wrong in the idea. Why, he couldn't possibly recognize her. She had fenced in a hundred acres once, digging the post holes herself and clamping the wires with just a Negro boy to help. That changed a woman. John would be looking for a young woman with the peaked Spanish comb in her hair and the painted fan. Digging post holes changed a woman. Riding country roads in the winter when women had their babies was another thing: sitting up nights with sick horses and sick Negroes and sick children and hardly ever losing one. John, I hardly ever lost one of them! John would see that in a minute, that would be something he could understand, she wouldn't have to explain anything!

It made her feel like rolling up her sleeves and putting the whole place to rights again. No matter if Cornelia was determined to be everywhere at once, there were a great many things left undone on this place. She would start tomorrow and do them. It was good to be strong enough for everything, even if all you made melted and changed and slipped under your hands, so that by the time you finished you almost forgot what you were working for. What was it I set out to do? she asked herself intently, but she could not remember. A fog rose over the valley, she saw it marching across the creek swallowing the trees and moving up the hill like an army of ghosts. Soon it would be at the near edge of the or-

chard, and then it was time to go in and light the lamps. Come in, children, don't stay out in the night air.

Lighting the lamps had been beautiful. The children huddled up to her and breathed like little calves waiting at the bars in the twilight. Their eyes followed the match and watched the flame rise and settle in a blue curve, then they moved away from her. The lamp was lit, they didn't have to be scared and hang on to Mother any more. Never, never, never more. God, for all my life I thank Thee. Without Thee, my God, I could never have done it. Hail, Mary, full of grace.

I want you to pick all the fruit this year and see that nothing is wasted. There's always someone who can use it. Don't let good things rot for want of using. You waste life when you waste good food. Don't let things get lost. It's bitter to lose things. Now, don't let me get to thinking, not when I am tired and taking a little nap before supper. . . .

The pillow rose about her shoulders and pressed against her heart and the memory was being squeezed out of it: oh, push down the pillow, somebody: it would smother her if she tried to hold it. Such a fresh breeze blowing and such a green day with no threats in it. But he had not come, just the same. What does a woman do when she has put on the white veil and set out the white cake for a man and he doesn't come? She tried to remember. No, I swear he never harmed me but in that. He never harmed me but in that . . . and what if he did? There was the day, the day, but a whirl of dark smoke rose and covered it, crept up and over into the bright field where everything was planted so carefully in orderly rows. That was hell, she knew hell when she saw it. For sixty years she had prayed against remembering him and against losing her soul in the deep pit of hell, and now the two things were min-

Young Mother Sewing (1900)
by Mary Cassatt (1844–1926).
Oil on canvas.

gled in one and the thought of him was a smoky cloud from hell that moved and crept in her head when she had just got rid of Doctor Harry and was trying to rest a minute. Wounded vanity, Ellen, said a sharp voice in the top of her mind. Don't let your wounded vanity get the upper hand of you. Plenty of girls get jilted. You were jilted, weren't you? Then stand up to it. Her eyelids wavered and let in streams of blue-gray light like tissue paper over her eyes. She must get up and pull the shades down or she'd never sleep. She was in bed again and the shades were not down. How could that happen? Better turn over, hide from the light, sleeping in the light gave you nightmares. "Mother, how do you feel now?" and a stinging wetness on her forehead. But I don't like having my face washed in cold water!

Hapsy? George? Lydia? Jimmy? No, Cornelia, and her features were swollen and full of little puddles. "They're coming, darling, they'll all be here soon." Go wash your face, child, you look funny.

Instead of obeying, Cornelia knelt down and put her head on the pillow. She seemed to be talking but there was no sound. "Well, are you tongue-tied? Whose birthday is it? Are you going to give a party?"

Cornelia's mouth moved urgently in strange shapes. "Don't do that, you bother me, daughter."

"Oh, no, Mother. Oh, no. . . ."

Nonsense. It was strange about children. They disputed your every word. "No what, Cornelia?"

"Here's Doctor Harry."

"I won't see that boy again. He just left five minutes ago."

"That was this morning, Mother. It's night now. Here's the nurse."

"This is Doctor Harry, Mrs. Weatherall. I never saw you look so young and happy!"

"Ah, I'll never be young again—but I'd be happy if they'd let me lie in peace and get rested."

She thought she spoke up loudly, but no one answered. A warm weight on her forehead, a warm bracelet on her wrist, and a breeze went on whispering, trying to tell her something. A shuffle of leaves in the everlasting hand of God. He blew on them and they danced and rattled. "Mother, don't mind, we're going to give you a little hypodermic." "Look here, daughter, how do ants get in this bed? I saw sugar ants yesterday." Did you send for Hapsy too?

It was Hapsy she really wanted. She had to go a long way back through a great many rooms to find Hapsy standing with a baby on her arm. She seemed to herself to be Hapsy also, and the baby on Hapsy's arm was Hapsy and himself and herself, all at once, and there was no surprise in the meeting. Then Hapsy melted from within and turned flimsy as gray gauze and the baby was a gauzy shadow, and Hapsy came up close and said, "I thought you'd never come," and looked at her very searchingly and said, "You haven't changed a bit!" They leaned forward to kiss, when Cornelia began whispering from a long way off, "Oh, is there anything you want to tell me? Is there anything I can do for you?"

Yes, she had changed her mind after sixty years and she would like to see George. I want you to find George. Find him and be sure to tell him I forgot him. I want him to know I had my husband just the same and my children and my house like any other woman. A good house too and a good husband that I loved and fine children out of him. Better than I hoped for even. Tell him I was given back everything he took away and more. Oh, no, oh, no, there was something else besides the house and the man and the children. Oh, surely they were not all? What was it? Something not given back. . . . Her breath crowded down under her ribs and grew into a monstrous frightening shape with cutting edges; it bored up into her head, and the agony was unbelievable: Yes, John, get the doctor now, no more talk, my time has come.

When this one was born it should be the last. The last. It should have been born first, for it was the one she had truly wanted. Everything came in good time. Nothing left out, left over. She was strong, in three days she would be as well as ever. Better. A woman needed milk in her to have her full health.

"Mother, do you hear me?"

"I've been telling you——"

"Mother, Father Connolly's here."

"I went to Holy Communion only last week. Tell him I'm not so sinful as all that."

"Father just wants to speak to you."

He could speak as much as he pleased. It was like him to drop in and inquire about her soul as if it were a teething baby, and then stay on for a cup of tea and a round of cards and gossip. He always had a funny story of some sort, usually about an Irishman who made his little mistakes and confessed them, and the point lay in some absurd thing he would blurt out in the confessional showing his struggles between native piety and original sin. Granny felt easy about her soul. Cornelia, where are your manners? Give Father Connolly a chair. She had her secret comfortable understanding with a few favorite saints who cleared a straight road to God for her. All as surely signed and sealed as the papers for the new Forty Acres. Forever . . . heirs and assigns forever. Since the day the wedding cake was not cut, but thrown out and wasted. The whole bottom dropped out of the world, and there she was blind and sweating with nothing under feet and the walls falling away. His hand had caught her under the breast, she had not fallen, there was the freshly polished floor with the green rug on it, just as before. He had cursed like a sailor's parrot and said, "I'll kill him for you." Don't lay a hand on him, for my sake leave something to God. "Now, Ellen, you must believe what I tell you. . . ."

So there was nothing, nothing to worry about any more, except sometimes in the night one of the children screamed in a nightmare, and they both hustled out shaking and hunting for the matches and calling, "There, wait a minute, here we are!" John, get the doctor now, Hapsy's time has come. But there was Hapsy standing by the bed in a white cap.

"Cornelia, tell Hapsy to take off her cap. I can't see her plain."

Her eyes opened very wide and the room stood out like a picture she had seen somewhere. Dark colors with the shadows rising towards the ceiling in long angles. The tall black dresser gleamed with nothing on it but John's picture, enlarged from a little one, with John's eyes very black when they should have been blue. You never saw him, so how do you know how he looked? But the man insisted the copy was perfect, it was very rich and handsome. For a picture, yes, but it's not my husband. The table by the bed had a linen cover and a candle and a crucifix. The light was blue from Cornelia's silk lampshades. No sort of light at all, just frippery. You had to live forty years with kerosene lamps to appreciate honest electricity. She felt very strong and she saw Doctor Harry with a rosy nimbus around him.

"You look like a saint, Doctor Harry, and I vow that's as near as you'll ever come to it."

"She's saying something."

"I heard you, Cornelia. What's all this carrying-on?"

"Father Connolly's saying——"

Cornelia's voice staggered and bumped like a cart in a bad road. It rounded corners and turned back again and arrived nowhere. Granny stepped up in the cart very lightly and reached for the reins, but a man sat beside her and she knew him by his hands, driving the cart. She did not look in his face, for she knew without seeing, but looked instead down the road where the trees leaned over and bowed to each other and a thousand birds were singing a Mass. She felt like singing too, but she put her hand in the bosom of her dress and pulled out a rosary, and Father Connolly murmured Latin in a very solemn voice and tickled her feet.[2] Will you stop that nonsense? I'm a married woman. What if he did run away and leave me to face the priest by myself? I found another a whole world better. I wouldn't have

exchanged my husband for anybody except Saint Michael[3] himself, and you may tell him that for me with a thank-you in the bargain.

Light flashed on her closed eyelids, and a deep roaring shook her. Cornelia, is that lightning? I hear thunder. There's going to be a storm. Close all the windows. Call the children in. . . . "Mother, here we are, all of us." "Is that you, Hapsy?" "Oh, no, I'm Lydia. We drove as fast as we could." Their faces drifted above her, drifted away. The rosary fell out of her hands and Lydia put it back. Jimmy tried to help, their hands fumbled together, and Granny closed two fingers around Jimmy's thumb. Beads wouldn't do, it must be something alive. She was so amazed her thoughts ran round and round. So, my dear Lord, this is my death and I wasn't even thinking about it. My children have come to see me die. But I can't, it's not time. Oh, I always hated surprises. I wanted to give Cornelia the amethyst set—Cornelia, you're to have the amethyst set, but Hapsy's to wear it when she wants, and, Doctor Harry, do shut up. Nobody sent for you. Oh, my dear Lord, do wait a minute. I meant to do something about the Forty Acres, Jimmy doesn't need it and Lydia will later on, with that worthless husband of hers. I meant to finish the altar cloth and send six bottles of wine to Sister Borgia for her dyspepsia. I want to send six bottles of wine to Sister Borgia, Father Connolly, now don't let me forget.

Cornelia's voice made short turns and tilted over and crashed. "Oh, Mother, oh, Mother, oh, Mother. . . ."

"I'm not going, Cornelia. I'm taken by surprise. I can't go."

You'll see Hapsy again. What about her? "I thought you'd never come." Granny made a long journey outward, looking for Hapsy. What if I don't find her? What then? Her heart sank down and down, there was no bottom to death, she couldn't come to the end of it. The blue light from Cornelia's lampshade drew

---

2. **tickled her feet:** Father Connolly is administering the last rites of the Roman Catholic Church.

3. **Saint Michael:** the great prince of all the angels. In paintings he is portrayed as a handsome young man.

into a tiny point in the center of her brain, it flickered and winked like an eye, quietly it fluttered and dwindled. Granny lay curled down within herself, amazed and watchful, staring at the point of light that was herself; her body was now only a deeper mass of shadow in an endless darkness and this darkness would curl around the light and swallow it up. God, give a sign!

For the second time there was no sign. Again no bridegroom and the priest in the house. She could not remember any other sorrow because this grief wiped them all away. Oh, no, there's nothing more cruel than this—I'll never forgive it. She stretched herself with a deep breath and blew out the light.

Reading Check

1. In whose house has Granny been living?
2. Why does Granny think of the box of letters in the attic?
3. Which of her memories is most painful to her?
4. Why is she concerned about the Forty Acres?

Analyzing and Interpreting the Story

1a. What connotations does the name "Weatherall" have in the context of the story? **b.** How is it a suitable name for the main character, Granny? **c.** Cite examples to show that life has not been "too much for her."

2a. Identify the following characters and tell whether they are related primarily to Granny's "present" or to her "past": Cornelia, John, Doctor Harry, George, Father Connolly. **b.** What roles do these characters play in Granny's life and her thoughts? **c.** What is the significance of Granny's seeing Hapsy again? **d.** Where is Hapsy?

3. "She had spent so much time preparing for death there was no need for bringing it up again." Explain how, in light of the end of the story, this sentence is not true.

4a. Why is the jilting so important to Granny? **b.** How is the jilting related to the last paragraph of the story?

5. In the story figurative language is often used to convey Granny's state of mind. For example, to Granny "Doctor Harry floated like a balloon around the foot of the bed." Find three other examples of figurative language used to convey a state of mind.

Literary Elements

Plot: Order of Events and Stream of Consciousness

A writer may tell a story in strict chronological order or may order the events in some other way, perhaps by using **flashback.** In "The Jilting of Granny Weatherall," the order of events may at first seem confusing. There is a constant shifting from the present to the past. What happens in the story's present—Granny's dealings with Cornelia, Doctor Harry, and Father Connolly—is told in chronological order. Past events are told in the order in which Granny thinks of them. Such an order is called **stream of consciousness,** the flow of thoughts and feelings within a character. This order at first seems confusing, a jumble of feelings, associations, and memories. Its ultimate effect, however, is to bring readers as close to a character as the written word makes possible. As readers follow Granny's confused, fading memories, they come to understand

and sympathize with her in a way that could be achieved by no other means.

Make two charts showing the events in the story. In the first chart show the events as they would be presented if the story were told in straight chronological order. (Begin with Granny as a young girl, and end with Granny on her deathbed.) In the second chart show the events in the order in which they are presented in the story. (Begin with Granny being examined by Doctor Harry and end with Granny blowing out the light.) Explain why the author presented the events of the story in the order that they appear on the second chart. For example, why are readers told about Cornelia before they are told about John?

Language and Vocabulary

Analyzing Shifts in Tense

Indicating shifts from Granny's present to her past might have been difficult if the English language did not provide a means of indicating subtle distinctions in tense. This story, like almost all stories, is told in the past tense, which is used to describe events happening "now." When Granny begins to remember events in her past, the tense shifts to past perfect, a shift signaled by the use of the helping verb *had*. While a passage dealing with Granny's past may begin in the past perfect tense, however, this tense is not used throughout the passage. Instead, the passage usually reverts to the past tense for two reasons: (1) to show that Granny is now living mentally in the past, and (2) to avoid the awkward sentences that usually result from the frequent use of past perfect verbs.

Analyze the following paragraph to show how shifts in tense indicate shifts in time. Show also how tense is used to indicate that certain sentences represent Granny Weatherall's thoughts, as if her thoughts were being directly quoted.

> Lighting the lamps had been beautiful. The children huddled up to her and breathed like little calves waiting at the bars in the twilight. Their eyes followed the match and watched the flame rise and settle in a blue curve, then they moved away from her. The lamp was lit, they didn't have to be scared and hang on to Mother any more. Never, never, never more. God, for all my life I thank Thee.

Creative Writing

Using Stream-of-Consciousness Technique

Describe a real or imagined experience, using the stream-of-consciousness technique. Keep in mind that stream of consciousness attempts to depict the free movement of thoughts and feelings as they occur. Be sure the experience you describe is a brief one: you might describe what thoughts arise just before you fall asleep or what happens between the moment you notice a person approaching you and the moment that person passes by.

James Thurber photographed against a background of his own cartoons during his appearance on the *Today Show* in 1956.

JAMES THURBER
1894–1961

James Thurber grew up in Columbus, Ohio, and attended Ohio State University. He worked as a newspaper reporter in Columbus, Paris, and New York. During the middle 1920s, he began to contribute humorous sketches to *The New Yorker,* and in 1927 he began to work for that magazine, first as an editor and then as a writer. For the rest of his life, he was to be associated with *The New Yorker,* contributing stories, essays, and cartoons. Together with other *New Yorker* writers—notably Robert Benchley, E. B. White, Frank Sullivan, S. J. Perelman, and Ogden Nash—he created a rich tradition of modern American humor.

Like many humorists, Thurber returned again and again to favorite themes. His concerns are suggested by the titles of several of his books—*My Life and Hard Times, My World—and Welcome to It, The Beast in Me and Other Animals,* and *Men, Women, and Dogs*—and by a sequence of cartoons called "The War Between Men and Women." In Thurberland the men are often sad, bewildered, and inept; the women fierce and determined; and their dogs indifferent to men and women alike, and immersed in a fantasy world of their own. Thurber was a dedicated craftsman who rewrote as many as twenty-five times the works that embody his sad, funny point of view. Some of his short stories are regarded as little masterpieces of humor: among them, "The Secret Life of Walter Mitty," "You Could Look It Up," and "The Catbird Seat." He also wrote several fine serious stories, including "A Friend to Alexander," "One Is a Wanderer," and "The Whippoorwill." In addition, he collaborated with his old college friend Elliot Nugent on a comedy, *The Male Animal,* that had two successful runs on Broadway and was adapted as a film.

Many readers have recognized that under Thurber's humor, there is a vein of melancholy that throws the humor in relief and gives it a sharper edge. The poet T. S. Eliot called Thurber's work "a form of humor which is also a way of saying something serious." During the last years of his life, Thurber became completely blind, and his humor was more heavily tinged with melancholy than ever. But near the end of his life, he made an eloquent statement of "The Case for Comedy," calling on writers to inspire a new respect for "the innate stature and dignity of comedy. . . . It is high time that we came of age and realized that, like Emily Dickinson's hope, humor is a feathered thing that perches in the soul."

The Catbird Seat

Mr. Martin bought the pack of Camels on Monday night in the most crowded cigar store on Broadway. It was theater time and seven or eight men were buying cigarettes. The clerk didn't even glance at Mr. Martin, who put the pack in his overcoat pocket and went out. If any of the staff at F & S had seen him buy the cigarettes, they would have been astonished, for it was generally known that Mr. Martin did not smoke, and never had. No one saw him.

It was just a week to the day since Mr. Martin had decided to rub out Mrs. Ulgine Barrows.

The term "rub out" pleased him because it suggested nothing more than the correction of an error—in this case an error of Mr. Fitweiler. Mr. Martin had spent each night of the past week working out his plan and examining it. As he walked home now he went over it again. For the hundredth time he resented the element of imprecision, the margin of guesswork that entered into the business. The project as he had worked it out was casual and bold, the risks were considerable. Something might go wrong anywhere along the line. And therein lay the cunning of his scheme. No one would ever see in it the cautious, painstaking hand of Erwin Martin, head of the filing department at F & S, of whom Mr. Fitweiler had once said, "Man is fallible but Martin isn't." No one would see his hand, that is, unless it were caught in the act.

Sitting in his apartment, drinking a glass of milk, Mr. Martin reviewed his case against Mrs. Ulgine Barrows, as he had every night for seven nights. He began at the beginning. Her quacking voice and braying laugh had first profaned the halls of F & S on March 7, 1941 (Mr. Martin had a head for dates). Old Roberts, the personnel chief, had introduced her as the newly appointed special adviser to the president of the firm, Mr. Fitweiler. The woman had appalled Mr. Martin instantly, but he hadn't shown it. He had given her his dry hand, a look of studious concentration, and a faint smile. "Well," she had said, looking at the papers on his desk, "are you lifting the oxcart out of the ditch?" As Mr. Martin recalled that moment, over his milk, he squirmed slightly. He must keep his mind on her crimes as a special adviser, not on her peccadilloes[1] as a personality. This he found difficult to do, in spite of entering an objection and sustaining it. The faults of the woman as a woman kept chattering on in his mind like an unruly witness. She had, for almost two years now, baited him. In the halls, in the elevator, even in his own office, into which she romped now and then like a circus horse, she was constantly shouting these silly questions at him. "Are you lifting the oxcart out of the ditch? Are you tearing up the pea patch? Are you hollering down the rain barrel? Are you scraping around the bottom of the pickle barrel? Are you sitting in the catbird seat?"

It was Joey Hart, one of Mr. Martin's two assistants, who had explained what the gibberish meant. "She must be a Dodger[2] fan," he had said. "Red Barber announces the Dodger games over the radio and he uses those expressions—picked 'em up down South." Joey had gone on to explain one or two. "Tearing up the pea patch" meant going on a rampage; "sitting in the catbird seat" meant sitting pretty, like a batter with three balls and no strikes on him. Mr. Martin dismissed all this with an effort. It had been annoying, it had driven him near to distraction, but he was too solid a man to be moved to murder by anything so childish. It was fortunate, he reflected as he passed on to the important charges against Mrs. Barrows, that he had stood up under it so well. He had maintained always an outward appearance of polite tolerance. "Why, I even believe you like the woman," Miss Paird, his other assistant, had once said to him. He had simply smiled.

A gavel rapped in Mr. Martin's mind and the case proper was resumed. Mrs. Ulgine Barrows stood charged with willful, blatant, and persistent attempts to destroy the efficiency and system of F & S. It was competent, material, and relevant to review her advent and rise to power. Mr. Martin had got the story from Miss Paird, who seemed always able to find things out. According to her, Mrs. Barrows had met Mr. Fitweiler at a party, where she had rescued him from the embraces of a powerfully built drunken man who had mistaken the president of F & S for a famous retired Middle Western football coach. She had led him to a sofa and somehow worked upon him a monstrous magic. The aging gentleman had jumped to the conclusion there and then that this was a woman of singular attainments, equipped to bring out the best in him and in the firm. A week later he had introduced her into F & S as his special adviser. On that day confusion got its foot in the door. After Miss Tyson, Mr. Brundage, and Mr. Bartlett had been fired and Mr. Munson had taken his hat and stalked out, mailing in his resignation later, old Roberts had been emboldened to speak to Mr. Fitweiler. He mentioned that Mr. Munson's department had been "a little disrupted" and hadn't they perhaps better re-

---

1. **peccadilloes** (pĕk′ə-dĭl′ōz): minor faults.
2. **Dodger:** At the time of the story, the Dodgers played in Brooklyn, New York. Years later the baseball team moved to Los Angeles.

sume the old system there? Mr. Fitweiler had said certainly not. He had the greatest faith in Mrs. Barrow's ideas. "They require a little seasoning, a little seasoning, is all," he had added. Mr. Roberts had given it up. Mr. Martin reviewed in detail all the changes wrought by Mrs. Barrows. She had begun chipping at the cornices of the firm's edifice and now she was swinging at the foundation stones with a pickax.

Mr. Martin came now, in his summing up, to the afternoon of Monday, November 2, 1942—just one week ago. On that day, at 3 P.M., Mrs. Barrows had bounced into his office. "Boo!" she had yelled. "Are you scraping around the bottom of the pickle barrel?" Mr. Martin had looked at her from under his green eyeshade, saying nothing. She had begun to wander about the office, taking it in with her great, popping eyes. "Do you really need *all* these filing cabinets?" she had demanded suddenly. Mr. Martin's heart had jumped. "Each of these files," he had said, keeping his voice even, "plays an indispensable part in the system of F & S." She had brayed at him, "Well, don't tear up the pea patch!" and gone to the door. From there she had bawled, "But you sure have got a lot of fine scrap in here!" Mr. Martin could no longer doubt that the finger was on his beloved department. Her pickax was on the upswing, poised for the first blow. It had not come yet; he had received no blue memo from the enchanted Mr. Fitweiler bearing nonsensical instructions deriving from the obscene woman. But there was no doubt in Mr. Martin's mind that one would be forthcoming. He must act quickly. Already a precious week had gone by. Mr. Martin stood up in his living room, still holding his milk glass. "Gentlemen of the jury," he said to himself, "I demand the death penalty for this horrible person."

The next day Mr. Martin followed his routine, as usual. He polished his glasses more often and once sharpened an already sharp pencil, but not even Miss Paird noticed. Only once did

he catch sight of his victim; she swept past him in the hall with a patronizing "Hi!" At five thirty he walked home, as usual, and had a glass of milk, as usual. He had never drunk anything stronger in his life—unless you could count ginger ale. The late Sam Schlosser, the S of F & S, had praised Mr. Martin at a staff meeting several years before for his temperate habits. "Our most efficient worker neither drinks nor smokes," he had said. "The results speak for themselves." Mr. Fitweiler had sat by, nodding approval.

Mr. Martin was still thinking about that red-letter day as he walked over to the Schrafft's on Fifth Avenue near Forty-sixth Street. He got there, as he always did, at eight o'clock. He finished his dinner and the financial page of the *Sun* at a quarter to nine, as he always did. It was his custom after dinner to take a walk. This time he walked down Fifth Avenue at a casual pace. His gloved hands felt moist and warm, his forehead cold. He transferred the Camels from his overcoat to a jacket pocket. He wondered, as he did so, if they did not represent an unnecessary note of strain. Mrs. Barrows smoked only Luckies. It was his idea to puff a few puffs on a Camel (after the rubbing-out), stub it out in the ashtray holding her lipstick-stained Luckies, and thus drag a small red herring across the trail. Perhaps it was not a good idea. It would take time. He might even choke, too loudly.

Mr. Martin had never seen the house on West Twelfth Street where Mrs. Barrows lived, but he had a clear enough picture of it. Fortunately, she had bragged to everybody about her ducky first-floor apartment in the perfectly darling three-story red-brick. There would be no doorman or other attendants; just the tenants of the second and third floors. As he walked along, Mr. Martin realized that he would get there before nine thirty. He had considered walking north on Fifth Avenue from Schrafft's to a point from which it would take him until ten o'clock to reach the house. At that hour people were less likely to be coming in or going out. But the procedure would have made an awkward loop in the straight thread of his casualness, and he had abandoned it. It was impossible to figure when people would be entering or leaving the house, anyway. There was a great risk at any hour. If he ran into anybody, he would simply have to place the rubbing-out of Ulgine Barrows in the inactive file forever. The same thing would hold true if there were someone in her apartment. In that case he would just say that he had been passing by, recognized her charming house and thought to drop in.

It was eighteen minutes after nine when Mr. Martin turned into Twelfth Street. A man passed him, and a man and a woman talking. There was no one within fifty paces when he came to the house, halfway down the block. He was up the steps and in the small vestibule in no time, pressing the bell under the card that said "Mrs. Ulgine Barrows." When the clicking in the lock started, he jumped forward against the door. He got inside fast, closing the door behind him. A bulb in a lantern hung from the hall ceiling on a chain seemed to give a monstrously bright light. There was nobody on the stair, which went up ahead of him along the left wall. A door opened down the hall in the wall on the right. He went toward it swiftly, on tiptoe.

"Well, for heaven's sake, look who's here!" bawled Mrs. Barrows, and her braying laugh rang out like the report of a shotgun. He rushed past her like a football tackle, bumping her. "Hey, quit shoving!" she said, closing the door behind them. They were in her living room, which seemed to Mr. Martin to be lighted by a hundred lamps. "What's after you?" she said. "You're as jumpy as a goat." He found he was unable to speak. His heart was wheezing in his throat. "I—yes," he finally brought out. She was jabbering and laughing as she started to help him off with his coat. "No, no," he said. "I'll put it here." He took it off and put it on a chair near the door. "Your hat and gloves, too," she said. "You're in a lady's house." He put his hat on top of the coat. Mrs. Barrows seemed larger than he had thought. He kept his gloves on. "I was passing by," he said. "I recognized—is there anybody here?" She laughed louder than ever. "No," she said, "we're all alone. You're as white as a sheet, you funny man. Whatever *has* come over you? I'll mix you a toddy." She started toward a door across the room. "Scotch-and-soda be all right? But say, you don't drink do you?" She turned and gave him her amused look. Mr. Martin pulled himself together. "Scotch-and-soda will be all right," he heard himself say. He could hear her laughing in the kitchen.

Mr. Martin looked quickly around the living room for the weapon. He had counted on finding one there. There were andirons and a poker and something in a corner that looked like an Indian club. None of them would do. It couldn't be that way. He began to pace around. He came to a desk. On it lay a metal paper knife with an ornate handle. Would it be sharp enough? He reached for it and knocked over a small brass jar. Stamps spilled out of it and it fell to the floor with a clatter. "Hey," Mrs. Barrows yelled from the kitchen, "are you tearing up the pea patch?" Mr. Martin gave a strange laugh. Picking up the knife, he tried its point against his left wrist. It was blunt. It wouldn't do.

When Mrs. Barrows reappeared, carrying two highballs, Mr. Martin, standing there with his gloves on, became acutely conscious of the fantasy he had wrought. Cigarettes in his pocket, a drink prepared for him—it was all too grossly improbable. It was more than that; it was impossible. Somewhere in the back of his mind a vague idea stirred, sprouted. "For heaven's sake, take off those gloves," said Mrs. Barrows. "I always wear them in the house," said Mr. Martin. The idea began to bloom, strange and wonderful. She put the glasses on a coffee table in front of a sofa and sat on the sofa. "Come over here, you odd little man," she said. Mr. Martin went over and sat beside her. It was difficult getting a cigarette out of the pack of Camels, but he managed it. She held a

match for him, laughing. "Well," she said, handing him his drink, "this is perfectly marvelous. You with a drink and a cigarette."

Mr. Martin puffed, not too awkwardly, and took a gulp of the highball. "I drink and smoke all the time," he said. He clinked his glass against hers. "Here's nuts to that old windbag, Fitweiler," he said, and gulped again. The stuff tasted awful, but he made no grimace. "Really, Mr. Martin," she said, her voice and posture changing, "you are insulting our employer." Mrs. Barrows was now all special adviser to the president. "I am preparing a bomb," said Mr. Martin, "which will blow the old goat higher than hell." He had only had a little of the drink, which was not strong. It couldn't be that. "Do you take dope or something?" Mrs. Barrows asked coldly. "Heroin," said Mr. Martin. "I'll be coked to the gills when I bump that old buzzard off." "Mr. Martin!" she shouted, getting to her feet. "That will be all of that. You

must go at once." Mr. Martin took another swallow of his drink. He tapped his cigarette out in the ashtray and put the pack of Camels on the coffee table. Then he got up. She stood glaring at him. He walked over and put on his hat and coat. "Not a word about this," he said, and laid an index finger against his lips. All Mrs. Barrows could bring out was "Really!" Mr. Martin put his hand on the doorknob. "I'm sitting in the catbird seat," he said. He stuck his tongue out at her and left. Nobody saw him go.

Mr. Martin got to his apartment, walking, well before eleven. No one saw him go in. He had two glasses of milk after brushing his teeth, and he felt elated. It wasn't tipsiness, because he hadn't been tipsy. Anyway, the walk had worn off all effects of the whiskey. He got in bed and read a magazine for a while. He was asleep before midnight.

Mr. Martin got to the office at eight thirty the next morning, as usual. At a quarter to nine, Ulgine Barrows, who had never before arrived at work before ten, swept into his office. "I'm reporting to Mr. Fitweiler now!" she shouted. "If he turns you over to the police, it's no more than you deserve!" Mr. Martin gave her a look of shocked surprise. "I beg your pardon?" he said. Mrs. Barrows snorted and bounced out of the room, leaving Miss Paird and Joey Hart staring after her. "What's the matter with that old devil now?" asked Miss Paird. "I have no idea," said Mr. Martin, resuming his work. The other two looked at him and then at each other. Miss Paird got up and went out. She walked slowly past the closed door of Mr. Fitweiler's office. Mrs. Barrows was yelling inside, but she was not braying. Miss Paird could not hear what the woman was saying. She went back to her desk.

Forty-five minutes later, Mrs. Barrows left the president's office and went into her own, shutting the door. It wasn't until half an hour later that Mr. Fitweiler sent for Mr. Martin. The head of the filing department, neat, quiet, attentive, stood in front of the old man's desk.

Mr. Fitweiler was pale and nervous. He took his glasses off and twiddled them. He made a small, bruffing sound in his throat. "Martin," he said, "you have been with us more than twenty years." "Twenty-two, sir," said Mr. Martin. "In that time," pursued the president, "your work and your—uh—manner have been exemplary." "I trust so, sir," said Mr. Martin. "I have understood, Martin," said Mr. Fitweiler, "that you have never taken a drink or smoked." "That is correct, sir," said Mr. Martin. "Ah, yes." Mr. Fitweiler polished his glasses. "You may describe what you did after leaving the office yesterday, Martin," he said. Mr. Martin allowed less than a second for his bewildered pause. "Certainly, sir," he said. "I walked home. Then I went to Schrafft's for dinner. Afterward I walked home again. I went to bed early, sir, and read a magazine for a while. I was asleep before eleven." "Ah, yes," said Mr. Fitweiler again. He was silent for a moment, searching for the proper words to say to the head of the filing department. "Mrs. Barrows," he said finally, "Mrs. Barrows has worked hard, Martin, very hard. It grieves me to report that she has suffered a severe breakdown. It has taken the form of a persecution complex accompanied by distressing hallucinations." "I am very sorry, sir," said Mr. Martin. "Mrs. Barrows is under the delusion," continued Mr. Fitweiler, "that you visited her last evening and behaved yourself in an—uh—unseemly manner." He raised his hand to silence Mr. Martin's little pained outcry. "It is the nature of these psychological diseases," Mr. Fitweiler said, "to fix upon the least likely and most innocent party as the—uh—source of persecution. These matters are not for the lay mind to grasp, Martin. I've just had my psychiatrist, Dr. Fitch, on the phone. He would not, of course, commit himself, but he made enough generalizations to substantiate my suspicions. I suggested to Mrs. Barrows when she had completed her—uh—story to me this morning, that she visit Dr. Fitch, for I suspected a condition at once. She flew, I regret to say, into a rage, and demanded—uh—requested that I call you on the carpet. You may not know, Martin, but Mrs. Barrows had planned a reorganization of your department—subject to my approval, of course, subject to my approval. This brought you, rather than anyone else, to her mind—but again that is a phenomenon for Dr. Fitch and not for us. So, Martin, I am afraid Mrs. Barrows' usefulness here is at an end." "I am dreadfully sorry, sir," said Mr. Martin.

It was at this point that the door to the office blew open with the suddenness of a gas-main explosion and Mrs. Barrows catapulted through it. "Is the little rat denying it?" she screamed. "He can't get away with that!" Mr. Martin got up and moved discreetly to a point beside Mr. Fitweiler's chair. "You drank and smoked at my apartment," she bawled at Mr. Martin, "and you know it! You called Mr. Fitweiler an old windbag and said you were going to blow him up when you got coked to the gills on your heroin!" She stopped yelling to catch her breath and a new glint came into her popping eyes. "If you weren't such a drab, ordinary little man," she said, "I'd think you'd planned it all. Sticking your tongue out, saying you were sitting in the catbird seat, because you thought no one would believe me when I told it! It's really too perfect!" She brayed loudly and hysterically, and the fury was on her again. She glared at Mr. Fitweiler. "Can't you see how he has tricked us, you old fool? Can't you see his little game?" But Mr. Fitweiler had been surreptitiously pressing all the buttons under the top of his desk and employees of F & S began pouring into the room. "Stockton," said Mr. Fitweiler, "you and Fishbein will take Mrs. Barrows to her home. Mrs. Powell, you will go with them." Stockton, who had played a little football in high school, blocked Mrs. Barrows as she made for Mr. Martin. It took him and Fishbein together to force her out of the door into the hall, crowded with stenographers and office boys. She was still screaming imprecations at Mr. Martin, tangled and contradictory imprecations. The hubbub finally died out down the corridor.

"I regret that this has happened," said Mr. Fitweiler. "I shall ask you to dismiss it from your mind, Martin." "Yes, sir," said Mr. Martin, anticipating his chief's "That will be all" by moving to the door. "I will dismiss it." He went out and shut the door, and his step was light and quick in the hall. When he entered his department he had slowed down to his customary gait, and he walked quietly across the room to the W20 file, wearing a look of studious concentration.

Reading Check

1. Why does Mr. Martin suspect that his department is about to be disrupted?
2. How does he plan to use the pack of cigarettes?
3. At what point does he form his second plan for getting rid of Mrs. Barrows?
4. Why is his plan perfect?

For Study and Discussion

Analyzing and Interpreting the Story

Much humor depends on **incongruity,** the joining of opposites to create a situation that is totally unexpected. A man strolling along a beach wearing a top hat and tuxedo and playing a flute is an example of incongruity. The incongruities in "The Catbird Seat," though often underplayed, are important to the story's humor.

1. Why, in light of Mr. Martin's character, does his intention to do away with Mrs. Barrows seem humorous?

2. Consider Mr. Martin's behavior when he first arrives at Mrs. Barrows' apartment. **a.** How is it incongruous with what you would expect of a cold-blooded murderer? **b.** Why is this part of the story funny rather than chilling? **c.** Do you have any serious fears that Mr. Martin will actually go through with the murder?

3. What is incongruous about Mr. Martin's boasts to Mrs. Barrows?

4a. How does the humor of the final scene—in Mr. Fitweiler's office—depend on the incongruity of reversed expectations? **b.** Does the ending satisfy you? Why or why not?

5. One way a writer can reinforce the sense of incongruity in a story is by exaggerating situations and characters. The element of surprise (the clash between the expected and the unexpected), which is essential to most humor, is thereby strengthened. **a.** What are Mrs. Ulgine Barrows' primary characteristics? **b.** In what ways is she an exaggerated character type? **c.** How does her unusual name add to this exaggeration?

Literary Elements

Flat and Round Characters

The characters in a short story may be either flat or round, depending on the fullness of their development. A **round character** is complex and is seen from many angles. Granny, in "The Jilting of Granny Weatherall" (page 591), is a round character. A **flat character,** on the other hand, is one-sided and possesses no more than one or two traits. The characters in "The Catbird Seat"—Mr. Martin, Mrs. Barrows, and Mr. Fitweiler—are flat characters.

A special kind of flat character is the **stock** or **stereotyped character**—the figure who appears so often in literature that his or her nature is instantly familiar. In what ways is Mrs. Barrows a stereotype? How are Mr. Martin and Mr. Fitweiler also stereotypes?

Writing About Literature

Analyzing Plot Structure

Identify the central conflict in "The Catbird Seat." How is this conflict developed? How is it resolved? Write an essay analyzing the plot structure of the story.

F. SCOTT FITZGERALD
1896–1940

To some readers, F. Scott Fitzgerald's life is a kind of parable—the story of a writer who dreams of becoming rich and famous, succeeds, and is then destroyed by his dream; who realizes his gifts early and burns out early. This vision of Fitzgerald is too simple to encompass the complicated, divided man he actually was, and it does little justice to his best writing. Yet it touches on the reasons why he fascinates those who read him. In his stories and novels Fitzgerald managed to include all the hectic charm of the 1920s, that period of "flaming youth" and wild parties, of postwar disillusion with ideals and of obsession with sensations, of defiance of convention and aspiration for personal fulfillment. The titles of his short-story collections, *Flappers and Philosophers*, *Tales of the Jazz Age*, and *All the Sad Young Men*, recall the flavor of that era even for readers who never lived through it. More than any other writer, Fitzgerald responded to the spirit of that time and made literature of it. When the stock market crash of 1929 put an end to this period, he recorded the aftermath—the morning after the wild party.

Francis Scott Key Fitzgerald was born in St. Paul, Minnesota, to a family with social pretensions but not enough money to live up to them. Even as a boy he was noted for his charm and good looks and traveled in the best circles, but he was aware of the gap between himself and the rich. The glamour of the rich became an important fact in his life. In "The Rich Boy" he wrote, "They possess and enjoy early, and it does something to them . . . in a way that, unless you were born rich, it is very difficult to understand." In his writing the rich and the "liberated" were to become symbols of the death of the "old America" in the dawn of an age of moral irresponsibility and mindless selfishness. From the very beginning of his career, Fitzgerald would write a poignant moral history of the country.

In 1913 Fitzgerald entered Princeton University, where he failed in his principal ambition of making the football team. Nevertheless, he was a very pop-

F. Scott Fitzgerald.
The Bettmann Archive

ular undergraduate and gained early fame as a writer for the student drama society. In 1917, after the United States entered World War I, he accepted a commission in the army but did not serve overseas. In 1918, at an officers' dance in Alabama, he met and fell in love with Zelda Sayre, a Montgomery belle. Discharged from the army, he came to New York to try to earn enough money to persuade Zelda to marry him. All he could find was a job at an advertising agency at a miserable salary. After three months he returned to St. Paul to rewrite a novel he had completed in the army. *This Side of Paradise* was published in 1920 and was an enormous success. Fitzgerald, only twenty-four years old, became an important literary figure, the voice of the young men and women of the "jazz age." His short stories were published in popular magazines; he turned them out quickly for large sums of money. Once again living in New York, he was able to persuade Zelda to come North to marry him.

The Fitzgeralds were a dazzling couple. They lived on Long Island, in Rome and Paris, and on the Riviera. They gave and attended spectacular parties. They drove, drank, and spent recklessly. Through it all Fitzgerald managed to find the time to write story after story, some of them among his best and some damaged by a relentless need for productivity. Although he later commented, "I had been only a mediocre caretaker of most of the things left in my hands, even of my talent," he did make a serious attempt to live up to his gifts. An increasingly divided view of the rich pervaded his work. He was still fascinated by them, but more and more he came to distrust them and his own ambition to be one of them. This ambivalence toward the rich pervades *The Great Gatsby* (1925), a novel some critics consider one of the best written in the twentieth century.

In 1930 Zelda Fitzgerald suffered a nervous breakdown, and from then on she spent most of her time in sanitariums. Fitzgerald was obliged to find money to pay her bills; in addition, he had run up considerable debts. He worked feverishly at his writing, trying to put his life in order and to earn more than he owed. But in the world of the Depression, the concerns of the twenties seemed dated and naive. In 1935 *Tender Is the Night,* a novel that many admirers of Fitzgerald's work regard as his finest novel, was published; it sold few copies. To earn money he went to Hollywood, where he was treated as a dim figure from the past and given hack writing jobs. He has described his state of mind during these years in several disturbing, memorable essays. In 1940 he died of a heart attack. That Fitzgerald continued growing as a writer to the very end is attested to by his final, unfinished novel, *The Last Tycoon.*

F. Scott Fitzgerald with his wife, Zelda, and their daughter, Frances (Scottie).
Culver Pictures

Winter Dreams

I

Some of the caddies were poor as sin and lived in one-room houses with a neurasthenic[1] cow in the front yard, but Dexter Green's father owned the second best grocery store in Black Bear—the best one was "The Hub," patronized by the wealthy people from Sherry Island—and Dexter caddied only for pocket money.

In the fall when the days became crisp and gray, and the long Minnesota winter shut down like the white lid of a box, Dexter's skis moved over the snow that hid the fairways of the golf course. At these times the country gave him a feeling of profound melancholy—it offended him that the links should lie in enforced fallowness, haunted by ragged sparrows for the long season. It was dreary, too, that on the tees where the gay colors fluttered in summer there were now only the desolate sandboxes knee-deep in crusted ice. When he crossed the hills the wind blew cold as misery, and if the sun was out he tramped with his eyes squinted up against the hard dimensionless glare.

In April the winter ceased abruptly. The snow ran down into Black Bear Lake scarcely tarrying for the early golfers to brave the season with red and black balls. Without elation, without an interval of moist glory, the cold was gone.

Dexter knew that there was something dismal about this Northern spring, just as he knew there was something gorgeous about the fall. Fall made him clinch his hands and tremble and repeat idiotic sentences to himself, and make brisk abrupt gestures of command to imaginary audiences and armies. October

1. **neurasthenic** (nōor′əs-thĕn′ĭk): having to do with neurosis, but here meaning weak, tired, irritable.

filled him with hope which November raised to a sort of ecstatic triumph, and in this mood the fleeting brilliant impressions of the summer at Sherry Island were ready grist to his mill. He became a golf champion and defeated Mr. T. A. Hedrick in a marvelous match played a hundred times over the fairways of his imagination, a match each detail of which he changed about untiringly—sometimes he won with almost laughable ease, sometimes he came up magnificently from behind. Again, stepping from a Pierce-Arrow automobile, like Mr. Mortimer Jones, he strolled frigidly into the lounge of the Sherry Island Golf Club—or perhaps, surrounded by an admiring crowd, he gave an exhibition of fancy diving from the springboard of the club raft. . . . Among those who watched him in open-mouthed wonder was Mr. Mortimer Jones.

And one day it came to pass that Mr. Jones—himself and not his ghost—came up to Dexter with tears in his eyes and said that Dexter was the —— ——best caddy in the club, and wouldn't he decide not to quit if Mr. Jones made it worth his while, because every other —— ——caddy in the club lost one ball a hole for him—regularly——

"No, sir," said Dexter decisively, "I don't want to caddy any more." Then, after a pause: "I'm too old."

"You're not more than fourteen. Why the devil did you decide just this morning that you wanted to quit? You promised that next week you'd go over to the state tournament with me."

"I decided I was too old."

Dexter handed in his "A Class" badge, collected what money was due him from the caddy master, and walked home to Black Bear Village.

"The best—— ——caddy I ever saw,"

Cover of *Hotel Management* (March 1925) by Edward Hopper (1882–1967).

shouted Mr. Mortimer Jones over a drink that afternoon. "Never lost a ball! Willing! Intelligent! Quiet! Honest! Grateful!"

The little girl who had done this was eleven—beautifully ugly as little girls are apt to be who are destined after a few years to be inexpressibly lovely and bring no end of mis-

ery to a great number of men. The spark, however, was perceptible. There was a general ungodliness in the way her lips twisted down at the corners when she smiled, and in the—Heaven help us!—in the almost passionate quality of her eyes. Vitality is born early in such women. It was utterly in evidence now,

F. Scott Fitzgerald **611**

shining through her thin frame in a sort of glow.

She had come eagerly out on to the course at nine o'clock with a white linen nurse and five small new golf clubs in a white canvas bag which the nurse was carrying. When Dexter first saw her she was standing by the caddy house, rather ill at ease and trying to conceal the fact by engaging her nurse in an obviously unnatural conversation graced by startling and irrelevant grimaces from herself.

"Well, it's certainly a nice day, Hilda," Dexter heard her say. She drew down the corners of her mouth, smiled, and glanced furtively around, her eyes in transit falling for an instant on Dexter.

Then to the nurse: "Well, I guess there aren't many people out here this morning, are there?"

The smile again—radiant, blatantly artificial—convincing.

"I don't know what we're supposed to do now," said the nurse, looking nowhere in particular.

"Oh, that's all right. I'll fix it up."

Dexter stood perfectly still, his mouth slightly ajar. He knew that if he moved forward a step his stare would be in her line of vision— if he moved backward he would lose his full view of her face. For a moment he had not realized how young she was. Now he remembered having seen her several times the year before—in bloomers.

Suddenly, involuntarily, he laughed, a short abrupt laugh—then, startled by himself, he turned and began to walk quickly away.

"Boy!"

Dexter stopped.

"Boy——"

Beyond question he was addressed. Not only that, but he was treated to that absurd smile, that preposterous smile—the memory of which at least a dozen men were to carry into middle age.

"Boy, do you know where the golf teacher is?"

"He's giving a lesson."

"Well, do you know where the caddy master is?"

"He isn't here yet this morning."

"Oh." For a moment this baffled her. She stood alternately on her right and left foot.

"We'd like to get a caddy," said the nurse.

"Mrs. Mortimer Jones sent us out to play golf, and we don't know how without we get a caddy."

Here she was stopped by an ominous glance from Miss Jones, followed immediately by the smile.

"There aren't any caddies here except me," said Dexter to the nurse, "and I got to stay here in charge until the caddy master gets here."

"Oh."

Miss Jones and her retinue now withdrew, and at a proper distance from Dexter became involved in a heated conversation, which was concluded by Miss Jones taking one of the clubs and hitting it on the ground with violence. For further emphasis she raised it again and was about to bring it down smartly upon the nurse's bosom, when the nurse seized the club and twisted it from her hands.

"You little mean old *thing*!" cried Miss Jones wildly.

Another argument ensued. Realizing that the elements of the comedy were implied in the scene, Dexter several times began to laugh, but each time restrained the laugh before it reached audibility. He could not resist the monstrous conviction that the little girl was justified in beating the nurse.

The situation was resolved by the fortuitous appearance of the caddy master, who was appealed to immediately by the nurse.

"Miss Jones is to have a little caddy, and this one says he can't go."

"Mr. McKenna said I was to wait here till you came," said Dexter quickly.

"Well, he's here now." Miss Jones smiled cheerfully at the caddy master. Then she dropped her bag and set off at a haughty mince toward the first tee.

"Well?" The caddy master turned to Dexter.

"What you standing there like a dummy for? Go pick up the young lady's clubs."

"I don't think I'll go out today," said Dexter.

"You don't——"

"I think I'll quit."

The enormity of his decision frightened him. He was a favorite caddy, and the thirty dollars a month he earned through the summer were not to be made elsewhere around the lake. But he had received a strong emotional shock, and his perturbation required a violent and immediate outlet.

It is not so simple as that, either. As so frequently would be the case in the future, Dexter was unconsciously dictated to by his winter dreams.

II

Now, of course, the quality and the seasonabilitiy of these winter dreams varied, but the stuff of them remained. They persuaded Dexter several years later to pass up a business course at the state university—his father, prospering now, would have paid his way—for the precarious advantage of attending an older and more famous university in the East, where he was bothered by his scanty funds. But do not get the impression, because his winter dreams happened to be concerned at first with musings on the rich, that there was anything merely snobbish in the boy. He wanted not association with glittering things and glittering people—he wanted the glittering things themselves. Often he reached out for the best without knowing why he wanted it—and sometimes he ran up against the mysterious denials and prohibitions in which life indulges. It is with one of those denials and not with his career as a whole that this story deals.

He made money. It was rather amazing. After college he went to the city from which Black Bear Lake draws its wealthy patrons. When he was only twenty-three and had been there not quite two years, there were already people who liked to say: "Now *there's* a boy——" All about him rich men's sons were peddling bonds precariously, or investing patrimonies[2] precariously, or plodding through the two dozen volumes of the "George Washington Commercial Course," but Dexter borrowed a thousand dollars on his college degree and his confident mouth, and bought a partnership in a laundry.

It was a small laundry when he went into it, but Dexter made a specialty of learning how the English washed fine woolen golf stockings without shrinking them, and within a year he was catering to the trade that wore knickerbockers. Men were insisting that their Shetland hose and sweaters go to his laundry, just as they had insisted on a caddy who could find golf balls. A little later he was doing their wives' lingerie as well—and running five branches in different parts of the city. Before he was twenty-seven he owned the largest string of laundries in his section of the country. It was then that he sold out and went to New York. But the part of his story that concerns us goes back to the days when he was making his first big success.

When he was twenty-three Mr. Hart—one of the gray-haired men who like to say "Now there's a boy"—gave him a guest card to the Sherry Island Golf Club for a weekend. So he signed his name one day on the register, and that afternoon played golf in a foursome with Mr. Hart and Mr. Sandwood and Mr. T. A. Hedrick. He did not consider it necessary to remark that he had once carried Mr. Hart's bag over this same links, and that he knew every trap and gully with his eyes shut—but he found himself glancing at the four caddies who trailed them, trying to catch a gleam or gesture that would remind him of himself, that would lessen the gap which lay between his present and his past.

It was a curious day, slashed abruptly with fleeting, familiar impressions. One minute he had the sense of being a trespasser—in the next he was impressed by the tremendous superiority he felt toward Mr. T. A. Hedrick, who

2. **patrimonies** (păt′rə-mō′nēz): inheritances.

was a bore and not even a good golfer any more.

Then, because of a ball Mr. Hart lost near the fifteenth green, an enormous thing happened. While they were searching the stiff grasses of the rough there was a clear call of "Fore!" from behind a hill in their rear. And as they all turned abruptly from their search a bright new ball sliced abruptly over the hill and caught Mr. T. A. Hedrick in the abdomen.

"By Gad!" cried Mr. T. A. Hedrick, "they ought to put some of these crazy women off the course. It's getting to be outrageous."

A head and a voice came up together over the hill: "Do you mind if we go through?"

"You hit me in the stomach!" declared Mr. Hedrick wildly.

"Did I?" The girl approached the group of men. "I'm sorry. I yelled 'Fore!'"

Her glance fell casually on each of the men—then scanned the fairway for her ball.

"Did I bounce into the rough?"

It was impossible to determine whether this question was ingenuous or malicious. In a moment, however, she left no doubt, for as her partner came up over the hill she called cheerfully: "Here I am! I'd have gone on the green except that I hit something."

As she took her stance for a short mashie shot, Dexter looked at her closely. She wore a blue gingham dress, rimmed at throat and shoulders with a white edging that accentuated her tan. The quality of exaggeration, of thinness, which had made her passionate eyes and down-turning mouth absurd at eleven, was gone now. She was arrestingly beautiful. The color in her cheeks was centered like the color in a picture—it was not a "high" color, but a sort of fluctuating and feverish warmth, so shaded that it seemed at any moment it would recede and disappear. This color and the mobility of her mouth gave a continual impression of flux, of intense life, of passionate vitality—balanced only partially by the sad luxury of her eyes.

She swung her mashie impatiently and without interest, pitching the ball into a sandpit on the other side of the green. With a quick, insincere smile and a careless "Thank you!" she went on after it.

"That Judy Jones!" remarked Mr. Hedrick on the next tee, as they waited—some moments—for her to play on ahead. "All she needs is to be turned up and spanked for six months and then to be married off to an old-fashioned cavalry captain."

"My, she's good-looking!" said Mr. Sandwood, who was just over thirty.

"Good-looking!" cried Mr. Hedrick contemptuously, "she always looks as if she wanted to be kissed! Turning those big cow-eyes on every calf in town!"

It was doubtful if Mr. Hedrick intended a reference to the maternal instinct.

"She'd play pretty good golf if she'd try," said Mr. Sandwood.

"She has no form," said Mr. Hedrick solemnly.

"She has a nice figure," said Mr. Sandwood.

"Better thank the Lord she doesn't drive a swifter ball," said Mr. Hart, winking at Dexter.

Later in the afternoon the sun went down with a riotous swirl of gold and varying blues and scarlets, and left the dry, rustling night of Western summer. Dexter watched from the veranda of the Golf Club, watched the even overlap of the waters in the little wind, silver molasses under the harvest moon. Then the moon held a finger to her lips and the lake became a clear pool, pale and quiet. Dexter put on his bathing suit and swam out to the farthest raft, where he stretched dripping on the wet canvas of the springboard.

There was a fish jumping and a star shining and the lights around the lake were gleaming. Over on a dark peninsula a piano was playing the songs of last summer and of summers before that—songs from *Chin-Chin* and *The Count of Luxemburg* and *The Chocolate Soldier*[3]—and because the sound of a piano over a stretch of water had always seemed beautiful to Dexter he lay perfectly quiet and listened.

---

3. ***Chin-Chin . . . Soldier:*** popular operettas of the time.

The tune the piano was playing at that moment had been gay and new five years before when Dexter was a sophomore at college. They had played it at a prom once when he could not afford the luxury of proms, and he had stood outside the gymnasium and listened. The sound of the tune precipitated in him a sort of ecstasy and it was with that ecstasy he viewed what happened to him now. It was a mood of intense appreciation, a sense that, for once, he was magnificently attuned to life and that everything about him was radiating a brightness and a glamour he might never know again.

A low, pale oblong detached itself suddenly from the darkness of the Island, spitting forth the reverberate sound of a racing motorboat. Two white streamers of cleft water rolled themselves out behind it and almost immediately the boat was beside him, drowning out the hot tinkle of the piano in the drone of its spray. Dexter raising himself on his arms was aware of a figure standing at the wheel, of two dark eyes regarding him over the lengthening space of water—then the boat had gone by and was sweeping in an immense and purposeless circle of spray round and round in the middle of the lake. With equal eccentricity one of the circles flattened out and headed back toward the raft.

"Who's that?" she called, shutting off her motor. She was so near now that Dexter could see her bathing suit, which consisted apparently of pink rompers.

The nose of the boat bumped the raft, and as the latter tilted rakishly he was precipitated toward her. With different degrees of interest they recognized each other.

"Aren't you one of those men we played through this afternoon?" she demanded.

He was.

"Well, do you know how to drive a motorboat? Because if you do I wish you'd drive this one so I can ride on the surfboard behind. My name is Judy Jones"—she favored him with an absurd smirk—rather, what tried to be a smirk, for, twist her mouth as she might, it was not grotesque, it was merely beautiful—"and I live

in a house over there on the Island, and in that house there is a man waiting for me. When he drove up at the door I drove out of the dock because he says I'm his ideal."

There was a fish jumping and a star shining and the lights around the lake were gleaming. Dexter sat beside Judy Jones and she explained how her boat was driven. Then she was in the water, swimming to the floating surfboard with a sinuous crawl. Watching her was without effort to the eye, watching a branch waving or a seagull flying. Her arms, burned to butternut, moved sinuously among the dull platinum ripples, elbow appearing first, casting the forearm back with a cadence of falling water, then reaching out and down, stabbing a path ahead.

They moved out into the lake; turning, Dexter saw that she was kneeling on the low rear of the now uptilted surfboard.

"Go faster," she called, "fast as it'll go."

Obediently he jammed the lever forward and the white spray mounted at the bow. When he looked around again the girl was standing up on the rushing board, her arms spread wide, her eyes lifted toward the moon.

"It's awful cold," she shouted. "What's your name?"

He told her.

"Well, why don't you come to dinner tomorrow night?" His heart turned over like the flywheel of the boat, and, for the second time, her casual whim gave a new direction to his life.

III

Next evening while he waited for her to come downstairs, Dexter peopled the soft deep summer room and the sunporch that opened from it with the men who had already loved Judy Jones. He knew the sort of men they were—the men who when he first went to college had entered from the great prep schools with graceful clothes and the deep tan of healthy summers. He had seen that, in one sense, he was better than these men. He was newer and stronger. Yet in acknowledging to himself that he wished his children to be like them he was admitting that he was but the rough, strong stuff from which they eternally sprang.

When the time had come for him to wear good clothes, he had known who were the best tailors in America, and the best tailors in America had made him the suit he wore this evening. He had acquired that particular reserve peculiar to his university, that set it off from other universities. He recognized the value to him of such a mannerism and he had adopted it; he knew that to be careless in dress and manner required more confidence than to be careful. But carelessness was for his children. His mother's name had been Krimelich. She was a Bohemian of the peasant class and she had talked broken English to the end of her days. Her son must keep the set patterns.

At a little after seven Judy Jones came downstairs. She wore a blue silk afternoon dress, and he was disappointed at first that she had not put on something more elaborate. This feeling was accentuated when, after a brief greeting, she went to the door of a butler's pantry and pushing it open called: "You can serve dinner, Martha." He had rather expected that a butler would announce dinner, that there would be a cocktail. Then he put these thoughts behind him as they sat down side by side on a lounge and looked at each other.

"Father and Mother won't be here," she said thoughtfully.

He remembered the last time he had seen her father, and he was glad the parents were not to be here tonight—they might wonder who he was. He had been born in Keeble, a Minnesota village fifty miles farther north, and he always gave Keeble as his home instead of Black Bear Village. Country towns were well enough to come from if they weren't inconveniently in sight and used as footstools by fashionable lakes.

They talked of his university, which she had visited frequently during the past two years, and of the nearby city which supplied Sherry Island with its patrons, and whither Dexter would return next day to his prospering laundries.

During dinner she slipped into a moody depression which gave Dexter a feeling of uneasiness. Whatever petulance she uttered in her throaty voice worried him. Whatever she smiled at—at him, at a chicken liver, at nothing—it disturbed him that her smile could have no root in mirth, or even in amusement. When the scarlet corners of her lips curved down, it was less a smile than an invitation to a kiss.

Then, after dinner, she led him out on the dark sun porch and deliberately changed the atmosphere.

"Do you mind if I weep a little?" she said.

"I'm afraid I'm boring you," he responded quickly.

"You're not. I like you. But I've just had a terrible afternoon. There was a man I cared about, and this afternoon he told me out of a clear sky that he was poor as a church mouse. He'd never even hinted it before. Does this sound horribly mundane?"

"Perhaps he was afraid to tell you."

"Suppose he was," she answered. "He didn't start right. You see, if I'd thought of him as poor—well, I've been mad about loads of poor men, and fully intended to marry them all. But in this case, I hadn't thought of him that way, and my interest in him wasn't strong enough to survive the shock. As if a girl calmly informed her fiancé that she was a widow. He might not object to widows, but——"

"Let's start right," she interrupted herself suddenly. "Who are you, anyhow?"

For a moment Dexter hesitated. Then: "I'm nobody," he announced. "My career is largely a matter of futures."

"Are you poor?"

"No," he said frankly, "I'm probably making more money than any man my age in the Northwest. I know that's an obnoxious remark, but you advised me to start right."

There was a pause. Then she smiled and the corners of her mouth drooped and an almost imperceptible sway brought her closer to him, looking up into his eyes. A lump rose in Dexter's throat, and he waited breathless for the experiment, facing the unpredictable compound that would form mysteriously from the elements of their lips. Then he saw—she communicated her excitement to him, lavishly, deeply, with kisses that were not a promise but a fulfillment. They aroused in him not hunger demanding renewal but surfeit that would demand more surfeit . . . kisses that were like charity, creating want by holding back nothing at all.

It did not take him many hours to decide that he had wanted Judy Jones ever since he was a proud, desirous little boy.

IV

It began like that—and continued, with varying shades of intensity, on such a note right up to the denouement.[4] Dexter surrendered a part of himself to the most direct and unprincipled personality with which he had ever come in contact. Whatever Judy wanted, she went after with the full pressure of her charm. There was no divergence of method, no jockeying for position or premeditation of effects—there was a very little mental side to any of her affairs. She simply made men conscious to the highest degree of her physical loveliness. Dexter had no desire to change her. Her deficiencies were knit up with a passionate energy that transcended and justified them.

When, as Judy's head lay against his shoulder that first night, she whispered, "I don't know what's the matter with me. Last night I thought I was in love with a man and tonight I think I'm in love with you——," it seemed to him a beautiful and romantic thing to say. It was the exquisite excitability that for the moment he controlled and owned. But a week later he was compelled to view this same quality in a different light. She took him in her roadster to a picnic supper, and after supper she disappeared, likewise in her roadster, with

4. **denouement** (dā-nōō-mäN'): outcome.

another man. Dexter became enormously upset and was scarcely able to be decently civil to the other people present. When she assured him that she had not kissed the other man, he knew she was lying—yet he was glad that she had taken the trouble to lie to him.

He was, as he found before the summer ended, one of a varying dozen, who circulated about her. Each of them had at one time been favored above all others—about half of them still basked in the solace of occasional sentimental revivals. Whenever one showed signs of dropping out through long neglect, she granted him a brief honeyed hour, which encouraged him to tag along for a year or so longer. Judy made these forays upon the helpless and defeated without malice, indeed half unconscious that there was anything mischievous in what she did.

When a new man came to town everyone dropped out—dates were automatically canceled.

The helpless part of trying to do anything about it was that she did it all herself. She was not a girl who could be "won" in the kinetic sense—she was proof against cleverness, she was proof against charm; if any of these assailed her too strongly she would immediately resolve the affair to a physical basis, and under the magic of her physical splendor the strong as well as the brilliant played her game and not their own. She was entertained only by the gratification of her desires and by the direct exercise of her own charm. Perhaps from so much youthful love, so many youthful lovers, she had come, in self-defense, to nourish herself wholly from within.

Succeeding Dexter's first exhilaration came restlessness and dissatisfaction. The helpless ecstasy of losing himself in her was opiate rather than tonic. It was fortunate for his work during the winter that those moments of ecstasy came infrequently. Early in their acquaintance it had seemed for a while that there was a deep and spontaneous mutual attraction—that first August, for example—three days of long evenings on her dusky veranda, of strange wan kisses through the late afternoon, in shadowy alcoves or behind the protecting trellises of the garden arbors, of mornings when she was fresh as a dream and almost shy at meeting him in the clarity of the rising day. There was all the ecstasy of an engagement about it, sharpened by his realization that there was no engagement. It was during those three days that, for the first time, he had asked her to marry him. She said "maybe someday," she said "kiss me," she said "I'd like to marry you," she said "I love you"—she said—nothing.

The three days were interrupted by the arrival of a New York man who visited at her house for half September. To Dexter's agony, rumor engaged them. The man was the son of the president of a great trust company. But at the end of the month it was reported that Judy was yawning. At a dance one night she sat all evening in a motorboat with a local beau, while the New Yorker searched the club for her frantically. She told the local beau that she was bored with her visitor, and two days later he left. She was seen with him at the station, and it was reported that he looked very mournful indeed.

On this note the summer ended. Dexter was twenty-four, and he found himself increasingly in a position to do as he wished. He joined two clubs in the city and lived at one of them. Though he was by no means an integral part of the stag lines at these clubs, he managed to be on hand at dances where Judy Jones was likely to appear. He could have gone out socially as much as he liked—he was an eligible young man, now, and popular with downtown fathers. His confessed devotion to Judy Jones had rather solidified his position. But he had no social aspirations and rather despised the dancing men who were always on tap for the Thursday or Saturday parties and who filled in at dinners with the younger married set. Already he was playing with the idea of going East to New York. He wanted to take Judy Jones with him. No disillusion as to the world in which she had grown up could cure his illusion as to her desirability.

Remember that—for only in the light of it can what he did for her be understood.

Eighteen months after he first met Judy Jones he became engaged to another girl. Her name was Irene Scheerer, and her father was one of the men who had always believed in Dexter. Irene was light-haired and sweet and honorable, and a little stout, and she had two suitors whom she pleasantly relinquished when Dexter formally asked her to marry him.

Summer, fall, winter, spring, another summer, another fall—so much he had given of his active life to the incorrigible lips of Judy Jones. She had treated him with interest, with encouragement, with malice, with indifference, with contempt. She had inflicted on him the innumerable little slights and indignities possible in such a case—as if in revenge for having ever cared for him at all. She had beckoned him and yawned at him and beckoned him again and he had responded often with bitterness and narrowed eyes. She had brought him ecstatic happiness and intolerable agony of spirit. She had caused him untold inconvenience and not a little trouble. She had insulted him, and she had ridden over him, and she had played his interest in her against his interest in his work—for fun. She had done everything to him except to criticize him—this she had not done—it seemed to him only because it might have sullied the utter indifference she manifested and sincerely felt toward him.

When autumn had come and gone again, it occurred to him that he could not have Judy Jones. He had to beat this into his mind but he convinced himself at last. He lay awake at night for a while and argued it over. He told himself the trouble and the pain she had caused him, he enumerated her glaring deficiencies as a wife. Then he said to himself that he loved her, and after a while he fell asleep. For a week, lest he imagine her husky voice over the telephone or her eyes opposite him at lunch, he worked hard and late, and at night he went to his office and plotted out his years.

At the end of a week he went to a dance and

cut in on her once. For almost the first time since they had met he did not ask her to sit out with him or tell her that she was lovely. It hurt him that she did not miss these things—that was all. He was not jealous when he saw that there was a new man tonight. He had been hardened against jealousy long before.

He stayed late at the dance. He sat for an hour with Irene Scheerer and talked about books and about music. He knew very little about either. But he was beginning to be master of his own time now, and he had a rather priggish notion that he—the young and already fabulously successful Dexter Green—should know more about such things.

That was in October, when he was twenty-five. In January, Dexter and Irene became engaged. It was to be announced in June, and they were to be married three months later.

The Minnesota winter prolonged itself interminably, and it was almost May when the winds came soft and the snow ran down into Black Bear Lake at last. For the first time in over a year Dexter was enjoying a certain tranquillity of spirit. Judy Jones had been in Florida, and afterward in Hot Springs, and somewhere she had been engaged, and somewhere she had broken it off. At first, when Dexter had definitely given her up, it had made him sad that people still linked them together and asked for news of her, but when he began to be placed at dinner next to Irene Scheerer people didn't ask him about her any more—they told him about her. He ceased to be an authority on her.

May at last. Dexter walked the streets at night when the dampness was damp as rain, wondering that so soon, with so little done, so much of ecstasy had gone from him. May one year back had been marked by Judy's poignant, unforgivable, yet forgiven turbulence—it had been one of those rare times when he fancied she had grown to care for him. That old penny's worth of happiness he had spent for this bushel of content. He knew that Irene would be no more than a curtain spread behind him, a hand moving among gleaming

teacups, a voice calling to children . . . fire and loveliness were gone, the magic of nights and the wonder of the varying hours and seasons . . . slender lips, down-turning, dropping to his lips and bearing him up into a heaven of eyes. . . . The thing was deep in him. He was too strong and alive for it to die lightly.

In the middle of May when the weather balanced for a few days on the thin bridge that led to deep summer he turned in one night at Irene's house. Their engagement was to be announced in a week now—no one would be surprised at it. And tonight they would sit together on the lounge at the University Club and look on for an hour at the dancers. It gave him a sense of solidity to go with her—she was so sturdily popular, so intensely "great."

He mounted the steps of the brownstone house and stepped inside.

"Irene," he called.

Mrs. Scheerer came out of the living room to meet him.

"Dexter," she said, "Irene's gone upstairs with a splitting headache. She wanted to go with you, but I made her go to bed."

"Nothing serious, I——"

"Oh, no. She's going to play golf with you in the morning. You can spare her for just one night, can't you, Dexter?"

Her smile was kind. She and Dexter liked each other. In the living room he talked for a moment before he said goodnight.

Returning to the University Club, where he had rooms, he stood in the doorway for a moment and watched the dancers. He leaned against the doorpost, nodded at a man or two—yawned.

"Hello, darling."

The familiar voice at his elbow startled him. Judy Jones had left a man and crossed the room to him—Judy Jones, a slender enameled doll in cloth of gold: gold in a band at her head, gold in two slipper points at her dress's hem. The fragile glow of her face seemed to blossom as she smiled at him. A breeze of warmth and light blew through the room. His hands in the pockets of his dinner jacket tight-

Cover of *Hotel Management* (September 1925) by Edward Hopper.

ened spasmodically. He was filled with a sudden excitement.

"When did you get back?" he asked casually.

"Come here and I'll tell you about it."

She turned and he followed her. She had been away—he could have wept at the wonder of her return. She had passed through enchanted streets, doing things that were like provocative music. All mysterious happenings, all fresh and quickening hopes, had gone away with her, come back with her now.

She turned in the doorway.

"Have you a car here? If you haven't, I have."

"I have a coupé."

In then, with a rustle of golden cloth. He slammed the door. Into so many cars she had stepped—like this—like that—her back against the leather, so—her elbow resting on the door —waiting. She would have been soiled long since had there been anything to soil her—except herself—but this was her own self outpouring.

With an effort he forced himself to start the car and back into the street. This was nothing, he must remember. She had done this before, and he had put her behind him, as he would have crossed a bad account from his books.

He drove slowly downtown and, affecting abstraction, traversed the deserted streets of the business section, people here and there where a movie was giving out its crowd or where consumptive or pugilistic youth lounged in front of pool halls. The clink of glasses and the slap of hands on the bars issued from saloons, cloisters of glazed glass and dirty yellow light.

She was watching him closely and the silence was embarrassing, yet in this crisis he could find no casual word with which to profane the hour. At a convenient turning he began to zigzag back toward the University Club.

"Have you missed me?" she asked suddenly.

"Everybody missed you."

He wondered if she knew of Irene Scheerer. She had been back only a day—her absence had been almost contemporaneous with his engagement.

"What a remark!" Judy laughed sadly—without sadness. She looked at him searchingly. He became absorbed in the dashboard.

"You're handsomer than you used to be," she said thoughtfully. "Dexter, you have the most rememberable eyes."

He could have laughed at this, but he did not laugh. It was the sort of thing that was said to sophomores. Yet it stabbed at him.

"I'm awfully tired of everything, darling." She called everyone darling, endowing the endearment with careless, individual camaraderie.[5] "I wish you'd marry me."

The directness of this confused him. He should have told her now that he was going to marry another girl, but he could not tell her.

5. **camaraderie** (kä′mə-rä′də-rē): warm feeling.

He could as easily have sworn that he had never loved her.

"I think we'd get along," she continued, on the same note, "unless probably you've forgotten me and fallen in love with another girl."

Her confidence was obviously enormous. She had said, in effect, that she found such a thing impossible to believe, that if it were true he had merely committed a childish indiscretion—and probably to show off. She would forgive him, because it was not a matter of any moment but rather something to be brushed aside lightly.

"Of course you could never love anybody but me," she continued, "I like the way you love me. Oh, Dexter, have you forgotten last year?"

"No, I haven't forgotten."

"Neither have I!"

Was she sincerely moved—or was she carried along by the wave of her own acting?

"I wish we could be like that again," she said, and he forced himself to answer.

"I don't think we can."

"I suppose not. . . . I hear you're giving Irene Scheerer a violent rush."

There was not the faintest emphasis on the name, yet Dexter was suddenly ashamed.

"Oh, take me home," cried Judy suddenly; "I don't want to go back to that idiotic dance—with those children."

Then, as he turned up the street that led to the residence district, Judy began to cry quietly to herself. He had never seen her cry before.

The dark street lightened; the dwellings of the rich loomed up around them; he stopped the coupé in front of the great white bulk of the Mortimer Joneses' house, somnolent, gorgeous, drenched with the splendor of the damp moonlight. Its solidity startled him. The strong walls, the steel of the girders, the breadth and beam and pomp of it were there only to bring out the contrast with the young beauty beside him. It was sturdy to accentuate her slightness—as if to show what a breeze could be generated by a butterfly's wing.

He sat perfectly quiet, his nerves in wild

clamor, afraid that if he moved he would find her irresistibly in his arms. Two tears had rolled down her wet face and trembled on her upper lip.

"I'm more beautiful than anybody else," she said brokenly, "why can't I be happy?" Her moist eyes tore at his stability—her mouth turned slowly downward with an exquisite sadness: "I'd like to marry you if you'll have me, Dexter. I suppose you think I'm not worth having, but I'll be so beautiful for you, Dexter."

A million phrases of anger, pride, passion, hatred, tenderness fought on his lips. Then a perfect wave of emotion washed over him, carrying off with it a sediment of wisdom, of convention, of doubt, of honor. This was his girl who was speaking, his own, his beautiful, his pride.

"Won't you come in?" He heard her draw in her breath sharply.

Waiting.

"All right," his voice was trembling, "I'll come in."

V

It was strange that neither when it was over nor a long time afterward did he regret that night. Looking at it from the perspective of ten years, the fact that Judy's flare for him endured just one month seemed of little importance. Nor did it matter that by his yielding he subjected himself to a deeper agony in the end and gave serious hurt to Irene Scheerer and to Irene's parents, who had befriended him. There was nothing sufficiently pictorial about Irene's grief to stamp itself on his mind.

Dexter was at bottom hard-minded. The attitude of the city on his action was of no importance to him, not because he was going to leave the city, but because any outside attitude on the situation seemed superficial. He was completely indifferent to popular opinion. Nor, when he had seen that it was no use, that he did not possess in himself the power to move fundamentally or to hold Judy Jones,

did he bear any malice toward her. He loved her, and he would love her until the day he was too old for loving—but he could not have her. So he tasted the deep pain that is reserved only for the strong, just as he had tasted for a little while the deep happiness.

Even the ultimate falsity of the grounds upon which Judy terminated the engagement, that she did not want to "take him away" from Irene—Judy who had wanted nothing else—did not revolt him. He was beyond any revulsion or any amusement.

He went East in February with the intention of selling out his laundries and settling in New York—but the war came to America in March and changed his plans. He returned to the West, handed over the management of the business to his partner, and went into the first officers' training camp in late April. He was one of those young thousands who greeted the war with a certain amount of relief, welcoming the liberation from webs of tangled emotion.

VI

This story is not his biography, remember, although things creep into it which have nothing to do with those dreams he had when he was young. We are almost done with them and with him now. There is only one more incident to be related here, and it happens seven years farther on.

It took place in New York, where he had done well—so well that there were no barriers too high for him. He was thirty-two years old, and, except for one flying trip immediately after the war, he had not been West in seven years. A man named Devlin from Detroit came into his office to see him in a business way, and then and there this incident occurred, and closed out, so to speak, this particular side of his life.

"So you're from the Middle West," said the man Devlin with careless curiosity. "That's funny—I thought men like you were probably born and raised on Wall Street. You know—

New York, Lower Manhattan (1921) by Stefan Hirsch (1899–1964). Oil on canvas.
The Phillips Collection, Washington, D.C.

wife of one of my best friends in Detroit came from your city. I was an usher at the wedding."

Dexter waited with no apprehension of what was coming.

"Judy Simms," said Devlin with no particular interest; "Judy Jones she was once."

"Yes, I knew her." A dull impatience spread over him. He had heard, of course, that she was married—perhaps deliberately he had heard no more.

"Awfully nice girl," brooded Devlin meaninglessly, "I'm sort of sorry for her."

"Why?" Something in Dexter was alert, receptive, at once.

"Oh, Lud Simms has gone to pieces in a way. I don't mean he ill-uses her, but he drinks and runs around——"

"Doesn't she run around?"

"No. Stays at home with her kids."

"Oh."

F. Scott Fitzgerald   **623**

"She's a little too old for him," said Devlin.

"Too old!" cried Dexter. "Why, man, she's only twenty-seven."

He was possessed with a wild notion of rushing out into the streets and taking a train to Detroit. He rose to his feet spasmodically.

"I guess you're busy," Devlin apologized quickly. "I didn't realize——"

"No, I'm not busy," said Dexter, steadying his voice. "I'm not busy at all. Not busy at all. Did you say she was—twenty-seven? No, I said she was twenty-seven."

"Yes, you did," agreed Devlin dryly.

"Go on, then. Go on."

"What do you mean?"

"About Judy Jones."

Devlin looked at him helplessly.

"Well, that's—I told you all there is to it. He treats her like the devil. Oh, they're not going to get divorced or anything. When he's particularly outrageous she forgives him. In fact, I'm inclined to think she loves him. She was a pretty girl when she first came to Detroit."

A pretty girl! The phrase struck Dexter as ludicrous.

"Isn't she—a pretty girl, any more?"

"Oh, she's all right."

"Look here," said Dexter, sitting down suddenly. "I don't understand. You say she was a 'pretty girl' and now you say she's 'all right.' I don't understand what you mean—Judy Jones wasn't a pretty girl, at all. She was a great beauty. Why, I knew her, I knew her. She was ——"

Devlin laughed pleasantly.

"I'm not trying to start a row," he said. "I think Judy's a nice girl and I like her. I can't understand how a man like Lud Simms could fall madly in love with her, but he did." Then he added: "Most of the women like her."

Dexter looked closely at Devlin, thinking wildly that there must be a reason for this, some insensitivity in the man or some private malice.

"Lots of women fade just like *that*," Devlin snapped his fingers. "You must have seen it happen. Perhaps I've forgotten how pretty she was at her wedding. I've seen her so much since then, you see. She has nice eyes."

A sort of dullness settled down upon Dexter. For the first time in his life he felt like getting very drunk. He knew that he was laughing loudly at something Devlin had said, but he did not know what it was or why it was funny. When, in a few minutes, Devlin went he lay down on his lounge and looked out the window at the New York skyline into which the sun was sinking in dull lovely shades of pink and gold.

He had thought that having nothing else to lose he was invulnerable at last—but he knew that he had just lost something more, as surely as if he had married Judy Jones and seen her fade away before his eyes.

The dream was gone. Something had been taken from him. In a sort of panic he pushed the palms of his hands into his eyes and tried to bring up a picture of the waters lapping on Sherry Island and the moonlit veranda, and gingham on the golf links and the dry sun and the gold color of her neck's soft down. And her mouth damp to his kisses and her eyes plaintive with melancholy and her freshness like new fine linen in the morning. Why, these things were no longer in the world! They had existed and they existed no longer.

For the first time in years the tears were streaming down his face. But they were for himself now. He did not care about mouth and eyes and moving hands. He wanted to care, and he could not care. For he had gone away and he could never go back any more. The gates were closed, the sun was gone down, and there was no beauty but the gray beauty of steel that withstands all time. Even the grief he could have borne was left behind in the country of illusion, of youth, of the richness of life, where his winter dreams had flourished.

"Long ago," he said, "long ago, there was something in me, but now that thing is gone. Now that thing is gone, that thing is gone. I cannot cry. I cannot care. That thing will come back no more."

For Study and Discussion

Analyzing and Interpreting the Story

1a. How does being called "boy" help Dexter decide to quit caddying? **b.** Why does Dexter choose "an older and more famous university in the East" over the state university?

2. In the beginning of Part II, we are told that the story deals with "the mysterious denials and prohibitions in which life indulges," and with one of Dexter's denials in particular. **a.** In what way is Judy a "mysterious denial" in Dexter's life? **b.** To what extent is he denied Judy by circumstances, and to what extent does he himself deny Judy?

3. At the end of Part II, Dexter and Judy meet on the lake at sunset. **a.** How do they act toward each other? **b.** In what way is the entire setting—the sunset, the gentle lapping of water ("silver molasses under the harvest moon"), the piano music—appropriate for this meeting between Dexter and Judy?

4. In Judy's "direct and unprincipled personality," her charm, and her loveliness, Dexter finds an ideal of beauty. The narrator suggests that almost nothing "could cure his illusion as to her desirability," and in fact Dexter cherishes his ideal long after he realizes he will never possess it. **a.** How do Dexter's actions show his single-minded devotion to his ideal? **b.** Even after he has lost Judy forever, why does he not resent her or regret his experience?

5. At the end of the story, Dexter's illusion is finally and irreparably broken. **a.** How does he try to recall the dream? **b.** What are Dexter's winter dreams? **c.** Why are they *winter* dreams?

6. The episode with Mr. Devlin in Part VI reintro- duces geographical identities. **a.** Why does Fitzgerald make the final disillusionment a matter that cuts across regions? **b.** How are Dexter's dreams *national*? **c.** How are the values of Dexter's dreams related to what is often referred to as the "American Dream"?

Literary Elements

Character

A story's effectiveness often depends on how well the characters are presented. Even if the plot is well constructed, readers may not become emotionally involved in the story unless they can respond to its characters. Generally a writer develops a character in one or more of the following ways: (1) through the character's actions; (2) through the character's thoughts and speeches; (3) through a physical de- scription of the character; (4) through the opinions of other characters; (5) through a direct statement about the character. Which of these methods does Fitzgerald use to describe Dexter and Judy? Do you find these two characters realistically drawn? In an- swering, be sure to make specific references to the story.

Language and Vocabulary

Analyzing Style

Fitzgerald is noted for his *evocative* style, his use of words and phrases to suggest moods, hopes, dreams. For example, when Dexter first encounters the grown-up Judy, he is impressed by the "color and mobility of her mouth . . . balanced only par- tially by the sad luxury of her eyes." The phrase "sad luxury" startles at first but proves to be exactly right. It suggests the double nature of Dexter's in- fatuation with Judy, the promise he sees in her of a rich, full life as well as an undertone of emotional turbulence. Find at least three other evocative words or phrases in the story and explain how they convey Dexter's moods, hopes, and dreams.

Writing About Literature

Analyzing Character

In a brief essay, analyze the character of Judy Jones. Take into consideration the various methods of characterization described above. Include details from the story in your analysis.

WILLIAM FAULKNER
1897–1962

William Faulkner once said in an interview that in writing his novel *Sartoris* he became aware of his true subject: "I discovered that my little postage stamp of native soil was worth writing about and that I would never live long enough to exhaust it. . . . It opened up a gold mine of people, as I created a cosmos of my own." The fictional cosmos Faulkner created is Yoknapatawpha County, and it does have a reality of its own. Most students of Faulkner know, for example, that it is in northern Mississippi, that it consists of 2,400 square miles and some 15,000 persons, and that the county seat is Jefferson. More important, Faulkner has charged what happens there with a significance that only literature can infuse. Slowly, with the appearance of each novel and story, he filled in the history of the county. This is also the history of a society, the decisions it faces, the directions in which it is drawn, and its effort to maintain its traditions and code of honor.

William Faulkner was born in New Albany, Mississippi. After the fifth grade, Faulkner attended school only occasionally, but he read a good deal—especially French and modern English poetry—and took several courses at the University of Mississippi, in Oxford. During World War I he went to Canada and joined the Royal Flying Corps, in which he was made a lieutenant. After the Armistice he returned to Oxford and entered the university, where he attended classes on and off for two years.

In December 1924 Faulkner went to New Orleans, where he wrote his first novel, *Soldier's Pay*. He met Sherwood Anderson, who agreed to recommend it to a publisher. In 1925 Faulkner returned to Oxford, Mississippi. He moved into an old house that he renovated himself, and lived there most of the rest of his life.

Once back home, Faulkner began to write the novels and short stories that many critics regard as among the most important by an American writer of the twentieth century. His first notable work, *The Sound and the Fury*, appeared in 1929. The opening portion is told through Benjy, an idiot who lacks all sense of time and constantly jumbles together the past and the present. Only in the final section does Faulkner show the balanced, lucid style he uses when he feels it is appropriate to his subject. Many of Faulkner's works make similar demands on the reader, but these demands are rarely unreasonable. The involved syntax, the sudden shifts in time and subject matter, and the frequent use of symbols reflect the dark, confused emotions of his characters and the growing disorder that surrounds them. Only a few of the characters manage to escape disorder by following simple, natural occupations—farming and hunting—and by respecting the life-giving soil, the wilderness, and all living things. Other important works include *As I Lay Dying, The Hamlet, Light in August, Absalom, Absalom!,* and *Go Down, Moses*.

In the thirties and early forties, Faulkner was regarded primarily as an eccentric writer who might possibly occupy a minor place in American literature. By 1945 his novels were nearly out of print. Only gradually was he recognized as a major writer. Critics such as Robert Penn Warren and Malcolm Cowley wrote essays that penetrated his surface oddities to discover his underlying greatness: an intense concern with issues not simply peculiar to the South but involving all humanity. The violent and insane consequences of race and money in Faulkner's South become in his fiction a history of the entire United States, which, in turn, is a history of the fallen human race. The Fall in Faulkner is defined as the bartering away of humanity's identity as a natural species observing humility and "courage, and honor, and pride . . . and pity, and love of justice and of liberty" in the harsh and prehistoric conditions of the hunt for "town" identities based artificially on race, money, and respectability. Faulkner's greatness is also evident in a tremendous variety of stories and situations, ranging from earthy comedy to deep tragedy; and in an enormous power of expression. Before his death Faulkner was regarded by many as the greatest living American novelist. He was awarded the Nobel Prize in 1949.

William Faulkner (1947).
© Henri Cartier-Bresson / Magnum Photos

The Bear

He was ten. But it had already begun, long before that day when at last he wrote his age in two figures and he saw for the first time the camp where his father and Major de Spain and old General Compson and the others spent two weeks each November and two weeks again each June. He had already inherited then, without ever having seen it, the tremendous bear with one trap-ruined foot which, in an area almost a hundred miles deep, had earned itself a name, a definite designation like a living man.

He had listened to it for years: the long legend of corncribs rifled, of shotes and grown

pigs and even calves carried bodily into the woods and devoured, of traps and deadfalls overthrown and dogs mangled and slain, and shotgun and even rifle charges delivered at point-blank range and with no more effect than so many peas blown through a tube by a boy—a corridor of wreckage and destruction beginning back before he was born, through which sped, not fast, but rather with the ruthless and irresistible deliberation of a locomotive, the shaggy tremendous shape.

It ran in his knowledge before he ever saw it. It looked and towered in his dreams before he even saw the unaxed woods where it left its crooked print, shaggy, huge, red-eyed, not malevolent but just big—too big for the dogs which tried to bay it, for the horses which tried to ride it down, for the men and the bullets they fired into it, too big for the very country which was its constricting scope. He seemed to see it entire with a child's complete divination before he ever laid eyes on either—the doomed wilderness whose edges were being constantly and punily gnawed at by men with axes and plows who feared it because it was wilderness, men myriad and nameless even to one another in the land where the old bear had earned a name, through which ran not even a mortal animal but an anachronism,[1] indomitable[2] and invincible, out of an old dead time, a phantom, epitome and apotheosis[3] of the old wild life at which the puny humans swarmed and hacked in a fury of abhorrence and fear, like pygmies about the ankles of a drowsing elephant: the old bear solitary, indomitable and alone, widowered, childless, and absolved of mortality—old Priam[4] reft of his old wife and having outlived all his sons.

Until he was ten, each November he would watch the wagon containing the dogs and the bedding and food and guns and his father and Tennie's Jim, the Negro, and Sam Fathers, the Indian, son of a slave woman and a Chickasaw chief, depart on the road to town, to Jefferson, where Major de Spain and the others would join them. To the boy, at seven, eight, and nine, they were not going into the Big Bottom

On the Trail (1892) by Winslow Homer (1836–1910). Watercolor.
National Gallery of Art, Washington, gift of Ruth K. Henschel, in memory of her husband, Charles R. Henschel

1. **anachronism** (ə-năk′rə-nĭz′əm): something that is out of its proper time.
2. **indomitable** (ĭn-dŏm′ə-tə-bəl): unconquerable.
3. **apotheosis** (ə-pŏth′ē-ō′sĭs): glorification.
4. **Priam** (prī′əm): king of Troy during the Trojan War, who saw his wife and sons killed when the Greeks invaded Troy.

to hunt bear and deer, but to keep yearly rendezvous with the bear which they did not even intend to kill. Two weeks later they would return, with no trophy, no head and skin. He had not expected it. He had not even been afraid it would be in the wagon. He believed that even after he was ten and his father would let him go too, for those two weeks in November, he would merely make another one, along with his father and Major de Spain and General Compson and the others, the dogs which feared to bay at it and the rifles and shotguns which failed even to bleed it, in the yearly pageant of the old bear's furious immortality.

Then he heard the dogs. It was in the second week of his first time in the camp. He stood with Sam Fathers against a big oak beside the faint crossing where they had stood each dawn for nine days now, hearing the dogs. He had heard them once before, one morning last week—a murmur, sourceless, echoing through the wet woods, swelling presently into separate voices which he could recognize and call by name. He had raised and cocked his gun as Sam told him and stood motionless again while the uproar, the invisible course, swept up and past and faded; it seemed to him that he could actually see the deer, the buck, blond, smoke-colored, elongated with speed, fleeing, vanishing, the woods, the gray solitude, still ringing even when the cries of the dogs had died away.

"Now let the hammers down," Sam said.

"You knew they were not coming here too," he said.

"Yes," Sam said. "I want you to learn how to do when you didn't shoot. It's after the chance for the bear or the deer has done already come and gone that men and dogs get killed."

"Anyway," he said, "it was just a deer."

Then on the tenth morning he heard the dogs again. And he readied the too-long, too-heavy gun as Sam had taught him, before Sam even spoke. But this time it was no deer, no ringing chorus of dogs running strong on a free scent, but a moiling[5] yapping an octave too high, with something more than indecision and even abjectness in it, not even moving very fast, taking a long time to pass completely out of hearing, leaving then somewhere in the air that echo, thin, slightly hysterical, abject, almost grieving, with no sense of a fleeing, unseen, smoke-colored, grass-eating shape ahead of it, and Sam, who had taught him first of all to cock the gun and take position where he could see everywhere and then never move again, had himself moved up beside him; he could hear Sam breathing at his shoulder, and he could see the arched curve of the old man's inhaling nostrils.

"Hah," Sam said. "Not even running. Walking."

"Old Ben!" the boy said. "But up here!" he cried. "Way up here!"

"He do it every year," Sam said. "Once. Maybe to see who in camp this time, if he can shoot or not. Whether we got the dog yet that can bay and hold him. He'll take them to the river, then he'll send them back home. We may as well go back too; see how they look when they come back to camp."

When they reached the camp the hounds were already there, ten of them crouching back under the kitchen, the boy and Sam squatting to peer back into the obscurity where they had huddled, quiet, the eyes luminous, glowing at them and vanishing, and no sound, only that effluvium[6] of something more than dog, stronger than dog and not just animal, just beast, because still there had been nothing in front of that abject and almost painful yapping save the solitude, the wilderness, so that when the eleventh hound came in at noon and with all the others watching—even Old Uncle Ash, who called himself first a cook—Sam daubed the tattered ear and the raked shoulder with turpentine and axle grease, to the boy, it was still no living creature, but the wilderness which, leaning for the moment down, had patted lightly once the hound's temerity.

5. **moiling:** confused.

6. **effluvium** (ĭ-flōō′vē-əm): here, a real or imagined odor; an aura.

"Just like a man," Sam said. "Just like folks. Put off as long as she could having to be brave, knowing all the time that sooner or later she would have to be brave to keep on living with herself, and knowing all the time beforehand what was going to happen to her when she done it."

That afternoon, himself on the one-eyed wagon mule which did not mind the smell of blood nor, as they told him, of bear, and with Sam on the other one, they rode for more than three hours through the rapid, shortening winter day. They followed no path, no trail even that he could see; almost at once they were in a country which he had never seen before. Then he knew why Sam had made him ride the mule which would not spook. The sound one stopped short and tried to whirl and bolt even as Sam got down, blowing its breath, jerking and wrenching at the rein, while Sam held it, coaxing it forward with his voice, since he could not risk tying it, drawing it forward while the boy got down from the marred one.

Then, standing beside Sam in the gloom of the dying afternoon, he looked down at the rotted overturned log, gutted and scored with claw marks and, in the wet earth beside it, the print of the enormous warped two-toed foot. He knew now what he had smelled when he peered under the kitchen where the dogs huddled. He realized for the first time that the bear which had run in his listening and loomed in his dreams since before he could remember to the contrary, and which, therefore, must have existed in the listening and dreams of his father and Major de Spain and even old General Compson, too, before they began to remember in their turn, was a mortal animal, and that if they had departed for the camp each November without any actual hope of bringing its trophy back, it was not because it could not be slain, but because so far they had had no actual hope to.

"Tomorrow," he said.

"We'll try tomorrow," Sam said. "We ain't got the dog yet."

"We've got eleven. They ran him this morning."

"It won't need but one," Sam said. "He ain't here. Maybe he ain't nowhere. The only other way will be for him to run by accident over somebody that has a gun."

"That wouldn't be me," the boy said. "It will be Walter or Major or——"

"It might," Sam said. "You watch close in the morning. Because he's smart. That's how come he has lived this long. If he gets hemmed up and has to pick out somebody to run over, he will pick out you."

"How?" the boy said. "How will he know ——" He ceased. "You mean he already knows me, that I ain't never been here before, ain't had time to find out yet whether I——" He ceased again, looking at Sam, the old man whose face revealed nothing until it smiled. He said humbly, not even amazed, "It was me he was watching. I don't reckon he did need to come but once."

The next morning they left the camp three hours before daylight. They rode this time because it was too far to walk, even the dogs in the wagon; again the first gray light found him in a place which he had never seen before, where Sam had placed him and told him to stay and then departed. With the gun which was too big for him, which did not even belong to him, but to Major de Spain, and which he had fired only once—at a stump on the first day, to learn the recoil and how to reload it— he stood against a gum tree beside a little bayou whose black still water crept without movement out of a canebrake[7] and crossed a small clearing and into cane again, where, invisible, a bird—the big woodpecker called Lord-to-God by Negroes—clattered at a dead limb.

It was a stand like any other, dissimilar only in incidentals to the one where he had stood each morning for ten days; a territory new to him, yet no less familiar than that other one

7. **canebrake** (kān′brāk′): a densely overgrown area of cane plants.

which, after almost two weeks, he had come to believe he knew a little—the same solitude, the same loneliness through which human beings had merely passed without altering it, leaving no mark, no scar, which looked exactly as it must have looked when the first ancestor of Sam Fathers' Chickasaw predecessors crept into it and looked about, club or stone ax or bone arrow drawn and poised; different only because, squatting at the edge of the kitchen, he smelled the hounds huddled and cringing beneath it and saw the raked ear and shoulder of the one who, Sam said, had had to be brave once in order to live with herself, and saw yesterday in the earth beside the gutted log the print of the living foot.

He heard no dogs at all. He never did hear them. He only heard the drumming of the woodpecker stop short off and knew that the bear was looking at him. He never saw it. He did not know whether it was in front of him or behind him. He did not move, holding the useless gun, which he had not even had warning to cock and which even now he did not cock, tasting in his saliva that taint as of brass which he knew now because he had smelled it when he peered under the kitchen at the huddled dogs.

Then it was gone. As abruptly as it had ceased, the woodpecker's dry, monotonous clatter set up again, and after a while he even believed he could hear the dogs—a murmur, scarce a sound even, which he had probably been hearing for some time before he even remarked it, drifting into hearing and then out again, dying away. They came nowhere near him. If it was a bear they ran, it was another bear. It was Sam himself who came out of the cane and crossed the bayou, followed by the injured bitch of yesterday. She was almost at heel, like a bird dog, making no sound. She came and crouched against his leg, trembling, staring off into the cane.

"I didn't see him," he said. "I didn't, Sam!"

"I know it," Sam said. "He done the looking. You didn't hear him neither, did you?"

"No," the boy said. "I——"

"He's smart," Sam said. "Too smart." He looked down at the hound, trembling faintly and steadily against the boy's knee. From the raked shoulder a few drops of fresh blood oozed and clung. "Too big. We ain't got the dog yet. But maybe someday. Maybe not next time. But someday."

So I must see him, he thought. *I must look at him.* Otherwise, it seemed to him that it would go on like this forever, as it had gone on with his father and Major de Spain, who was older than his father, and even with old General Compson, who had been old enough to be a brigade commander in 1865. Otherwise, it would go on so forever, next time and next time, after and after and after. It seemed to him that he could never see the two of them, himself and the bear, shadowy in the limbo[8] from which time emerged, becoming time; the old bear absolved of mortality and himself partaking, sharing, a little of it, enough of it. And he knew now what he had smelled in the huddled dogs and tasted in his saliva. He recognized fear. *So I will have to see him,* he thought, without dread or even hope. *I will have to look at him.*

It was in June of the next year. He was eleven. They were in camp again, celebrating Major de Spain's and General Compson's birthdays. Although the one had been born in September and the other in the depth of winter and in another decade, they had met for two weeks to fish and shoot squirrels and turkeys and run coons and wildcats with the dogs at night. That is, he and Boon Hoggenbeck and the Negroes fished and shot squirrels and ran the coons and cats, because the proved hunters, not only Major de Spain and old General Compson, who spent those two weeks sitting in a rocking chair before a tremendous iron pot of Brunswick stew, stirring and tasting, with old Ash to quarrel with about how he was making it and Tennie's Jim to pour whiskey from the demijohn into the tin dipper from which he drank it, but even the boy's

8. **limbo:** a state or condition of oblivion.

father and Walter Ewell, who were still young enough, scorned such, other than shooting the wild gobblers with pistols for wagers on their marksmanship.

Or, that is, his father and the others believed he was hunting squirrels. Until the third day, he thought that Sam Fathers believed that too. Each morning he would leave the camp right after breakfast. He had his own gun now, a Christmas present. He went back to the tree beside the bayou where he had stood that morning. Using the compass which old General Compson had given him, he ranged from that point; he was teaching himself to be a better-than-fair woodsman without knowing he was doing it. On the second day he even found the gutted log where he had first seen the crooked print. It was almost completely crumbled now, healing with unbelievable speed, a passionate and almost visible relinquishment,[9] back into the earth from which the tree had grown.

He ranged the summer woods now, green with gloom; if anything, actually dimmer than in November's gray dissolution, where, even at noon, the sun fell only in intermittent dappling upon the earth, which never completely dried out and which crawled with snakes—moccasins and water snakes and rattlers, themselves the color of the dappling gloom, so that he would not always see them until they moved, returning later and later, first day, second day, passing in the twilight of the third evening the little log pen enclosing the log stable where Sam was putting up the horses for the night.

"You ain't looked right yet," Sam said.

He stopped. For a moment he didn't answer. Then he said peacefully, in a peaceful rushing burst as when a boy's miniature dam in a little brook gives way, "All right. But how? I went to the bayou. I even found that log again. I——"

"I reckon that was all right. Likely he's been watching you. You never saw his foot?"

9. **relinquishment:** a surrender; leaving behind something that was professed or practiced.

"I," the boy said—"I didn't—I never thought——"

"It's the gun," Sam said. He stood beside the fence motionless—the old man, the Indian, in the battered faded overalls and the five-cent straw hat which in the Negro's race had been the badge of his enslavement and was now the regalia of his freedom. The camp—the clearing, the house, the barn and its tiny lot with which Major de Spain in his turn had scratched punily and evanescently at the wilderness— faded in the dusk, back into the immemorial darkness of the woods. *The gun,* the boy thought. *The gun.*

"Be scared," Sam said. "You can't help that. But don't be afraid. Ain't nothing in the woods to hurt you unless you corner it, or it smells that you are afraid. A bear or a deer, too, has got to be scared of a coward the same as a brave man has got to be."

The gun, the boy thought.

"You will have to choose," Sam said.

He left the camp before daylight, long before Uncle Ash would wake in his quilts on the kitchen floor and start the fire for breakfast. He had only the compass and a stick for snakes. He could go almost a mile before he would begin to need the compass. He sat on a log, the invisible compass in his invisible hand, while the secret night sounds, fallen still at his movements, scurried again and then ceased for good, and the owls ceased and gave over to the waking of day birds, and he could see the compass. Then he went fast yet still quietly; he was becoming better and better as a woodsman, still without having yet realized it.

He jumped a doe and a fawn at sunrise, walked them out of the bed, close enough to see them—the crash of undergrowth, the white scut, the fawn scudding behind her faster than he had believed it could run. He was hunting right, upwind, as Sam had taught him; not that it mattered now. He had left the gun; of his own will and relinquishment he had accepted not a gambit, not a choice, but a condition in which not only the bear's heretofore inviolable anonymity but all the old rules and balances of hunter and hunted had been abrogated.[10] He would not even be afraid, not even in the moment when the fear would take him completely—blood, skin, bowels, bones, memory from the long time before it became his memory—all save that thin, clear, immortal lucidity which alone differed him from this bear and from all the other bear and deer he would ever kill in the humility and pride of his skill and endurance, to which Sam had spoken when he leaned in the twilight on the lot fence yesterday.

By noon he was far beyond the little bayou, farther into the new and alien country than he had ever been. He was traveling now not only by the old, heavy, biscuit-thick silver watch which had belonged to his grandfather. When he stopped at last, it was for the first time since he had risen from the log at dawn when he could see the compass. It was far enough. He had left the camp nine hours ago; nine hours from now, dark would have already been an hour old. But he didn't think that. He thought, *All right. Yes. But what?* and stood for a moment, alien and small in the green and topless solitude, answering his own question before it had formed and ceased. It was the watch, the compass, the stick—the three lifeless mechanicals with which for nine hours he had fended the wilderness off; he hung the watch and compass carefully on a bush and leaned the stick beside them and relinquished completely to it.

He had not been going very fast for the last two or three hours. He went no faster now, since distance would not matter even if he could have gone fast. And he was trying to keep a bearing on the tree where he had left the compass, trying to complete a circle which would bring him back to it or at least intersect itself, since direction would not matter now either. But the tree was not there, and he did as Sam had schooled him—made the next circle in the opposite direction, so that the two patterns would bisect somewhere, but crossing no print of his own feet, finding the tree at last, but in the wrong place—no bush, no compass, no watch—and the tree not even the tree, because there was a down log beside it and he did what Sam Fathers had told him was the next thing and the last.

As he sat down on the log he saw the crooked print—the warped, tremendous, two-toed indentation which, even as he watched it, filled with water. As he looked up, the wilderness coalesced, solidified—the glade, the tree he sought, the bush, the watch and the compass glinting where a ray of sunshine touched them. Then he saw the bear. It did not emerge, appear; it was just there, immobile, solid, fixed in the hot dappling of the green and windless noon, not as big as he had dreamed it, but as big as he had expected it, bigger, dimensionless, against the dappled obscurity, looking at him where he sat quietly on the log and looked back at it.

Then it moved. It made no sound. It did not hurry. It crossed the glade, walking for an instant into the full glare of the sun; when it reached the other side it stopped again and looked back at him across one shoulder while his quiet breathing inhaled and exhaled three times.

Then it was gone. It didn't walk into the woods, the undergrowth. It faded, sank back into the wilderness as he had watched a fish, a huge old bass, sink and vanish into the dark depths of its pool without even any movement of its fins.

He thought, *It will be next fall.* But it was not next fall, nor the next nor the next. He was fourteen then. He had killed his buck, and Sam Fathers had marked his face with the hot blood, and in the next year he killed a bear. But even before that accolade he had become as competent in the woods as many grown men with the same experience; by his fourteenth year he was a better woodsman than most grown men with more. There was no territory within thirty miles of the camp that he did not know—bayou, ridge, brake, landmark, tree

10. **abrogated** (ăb′rō-gāt′əd): canceled.

and path. He could have led anyone to any point in it without deviation, and brought them out again. He knew the game trails that even Sam Fathers did not know; in his thirteenth year he found a buck's bedding place, and unbeknown to his father he borrowed Walter Ewell's rifle and lay in wait at dawn and killed the buck when it walked back to the bed, as Sam had told him how the old Chickasaw fathers did.

But not the old bear, although by now he knew its footprints better than he did his own, and not only the crooked one. He could see any one of the three sound ones and distinguish it from any other, and not only by its size. There were other bears within these thirty miles which left tracks almost as large, but this was more than that. If Sam Fathers had been his mentor and the back-yard rabbits and squirrels at home his kindergarten, then the wilderness the old bear ran was his college, the old male bear itself so long unwifed and childless as to have become its own ungendered progenitor,[11] was his alma mater. But he never saw it.

He could find the crooked print now almost whenever he liked, fifteen or ten or five miles, or sometimes nearer the camp than that. Twice while on stand during the three years he heard the dogs strike its trail by accident; on the second time they jumped it seemingly, the voices high, abject, almost human in hysteria, as on that first morning two years ago. But not the bear itself. He would remember that noon three years ago, the glade, himself and the bear fixed during that moment in the windless and dappled blaze, and it would seem to him that it had never happened, that he had dreamed that too. But it had happened. They had looked at each other, they had emerged from the wilderness old as earth, synchronized to the instant by something more than the blood that moved the flesh and bones which

bore them, and touched, pledged something, affirmed something more lasting than the frail web of bones and flesh which any accident could obliterate.

Then he saw it again. Because of the very fact that he thought of nothing else, he had forgotten to look for it. He was still hunting with Walter Ewell's rifle. He saw it cross the end of a long blow-down, a corridor where a tornado had swept, rushing through rather than over the tangle of trunks and branches as a locomotive would have, faster than he had ever believed it could move, almost as fast as a deer even, because a deer would have spent most of that time in the air, faster than he could bring the rifle sights up with it. And now he knew what had been wrong during all the three years. He sat on a log, shaking and trembling as if he had never seen the woods before nor anything that ran them, wondering with incredulous amazement how he could have forgotten the very thing which Sam Fathers had told him and which the bear itself had

11. **ungendered progenitor:** its own parent, without evidence of any other creature, male or female, having given birth to it.

proved the next day and had now returned after three years to reaffirm.

And now he knew what Sam Fathers had meant about the right dog, a dog in which size would mean less than nothing. So when he returned alone in April—school was out then, so that the sons of farmers could help with the land's planting, and at last his father had granted him permission, on his promise to be back in four days—he had the dog. It was his own, a mongrel of the sort called by Negroes a fyce, a ratter, itself not much bigger than a rat and possessing that bravery which had long since stopped being courage and had become foolhardiness.

It did not take four days. Alone again, he found the trail on the first morning. It was not a stalk; it was an ambush. He timed the meeting almost as if it were an appointment with a human being. Himself holding the fyce muffled in a feed sack and Sam Fathers with two of the hounds on a piece of plowing rope, they lay down wind of the trail at dawn of the second morning. They were so close that the bear turned without even running, as if in surprised amazement at the shrill and frantic uproar of the released fyce, turning at bay against the trunk of a tree, on its hind feet; it seemed to the boy that it would never stop rising, taller and taller, and even the two hounds seemed to take a desperate and despairing courage from the fyce, following it as it went in.

Then he realized that the fyce was actually not going to stop. He flung, threw the gun away, and ran; when he overtook and grasped the frantically pin-wheeling little dog, it seemed to him that he was directly under the bear.

He could smell it, strong and hot and rank. Sprawling, he looked up to where it loomed and towered over him like a cloudburst and colored like a thunderclap, quite familiar, peacefully and even lucidly familiar, until he remembered: This was the way he had used to dream about it. Then it was gone. He didn't see it go. He knelt, holding the frantic fyce with both hands, hearing the abashed wailing of the hounds drawing farther and farther away, until Sam came up. He carried the gun. He laid it down quietly beside the boy and stood looking down at him.

"You've done seed him twice now with a gun in your hands," he said. "This time you couldn't have missed him."

The boy rose. He still held the fyce. Even in his arms and clear of the ground, it yapped frantically, straining and surging after the fading uproar of the two hounds like a tangle of wire springs. He was panting a little, but he was neither shaking nor trembling now.

"Neither could you!" he said. "You had the gun! Neither could you!"

"And you didn't shoot," his father said. "How close were you?"

"I don't know, sir," he said. "There was a big wood tick inside his right hind leg. I saw that. But I didn't have the gun then."

"But you didn't shoot when you had the gun," his father said. "Why?"

But he didn't answer, and his father didn't wait for him to, rising and crossing the room, across the pelt of the bear which the boy had killed two years ago and the larger one which his father had killed before he was born, to the bookcase beneath the mounted head of the boy's first buck. It was the room which his father called the office, from which all the plantation business was transacted; in it for the fourteen years of his life he had heard the best of all talking. Major de Spain would be there and sometimes old General Compson, and Walter Ewell and Boon Hoggenback and Sam Fathers and Tennie's Jim, too, were hunters, knew the woods and what ran them.

He would hear it, not talking himself but listening—the wilderness, the big woods, bigger and older than any recorded document of white man fatuous enough to believe he had bought any fragment of it or Indian ruthless enough to pretend that any fragment of it had been his to convey. It was of the men, not white nor black nor red, but men, hunters with the will and hardihood to endure and the humility and skill to survive, and the dogs and the bear and deer juxtaposed and reliefed against it, ordered and compelled by and within the wilderness in the ancient and unremitting contest by the ancient and immitigable rules which voided all regrets and brooked no quarter, the voices quiet and weighty and deliberate for retrospection and recollection and exact remembering, while he squatted in the blazing firelight as Tennie's Jim squatted, who stirred only to put more wood on the fire and to pass the bottle from one glass to another. Because the bottle was always present, so that after a while it seemed to him that those fierce instants of heart and brain and courage and wiliness and speed were concentrated and distilled into that brown liquor which not women, not boys and children, but only hunters drank, drinking not of the blood they had spilled but some condensation of the wild immortal spirit, drinking it moderately, humbly even, not with the pagan's base hope of acquiring the virtues of cunning and strength and speed, but in salute to them.

His father returned with the book and sat down again and opened it. "Listen," he said. He read the five stanzas aloud, his voice quiet and deliberate in the room where there was no fire now because it was already spring. Then he looked up. The boy watched him. "All right," his father said. "Listen." He read again, but only the second stanza this time, to the end of it, the last two lines, and closed the book and put it on the table beside him. "She cannot fade, though thou hast not thy bliss, forever wilt thou love, and she be fair,"[12] he said.

"He's talking about a girl," the boy said.

"He had to talk about something," his father said. Then he said, "He was talking about truth. Truth doesn't change. Truth is one thing. It covers all things which touch the heart—honor and pride and pity and justice and courage and love. Do you see now?"

He didn't know. Somehow it was simpler than that. There was an old bear, fierce and ruthless, not merely just to stay alive, but with the fierce pride of liberty and freedom, proud enough of the liberty and freedom to see it threatened without fear or even alarm; nay, who at times even seemed deliberately to put that freedom and liberty in jeopardy in order to savor them, to remind his old strong bones and flesh to keep supple and quick to defend and preserve them. There was an old man, son of a Negro slave and an Indian king, inheritor on the one side of the long chronicle of a people who had learned humility through suffering, and pride through the endurance which survived the suffering and injustice, and on the other side, the chronicle of a people even longer in the land than the first, yet who no longer existed in the land at all save in the solitary brotherhood of an old Negro's alien blood and the wild and invincible spirit of an old bear. There was a boy who wished to learn humility and pride in order to become skillful and worthy in the woods, who suddenly found himself becoming so skillful so rapidly that he feared he would never become worthy because he had not learned humility and pride, although he had tried to, until one day and as suddenly he discovered that an old man who could not have defined either had led him, as though by the hand, to that point where an old bear and a little mongrel of a dog showed him that, by possessing one thing other, he would possess them both.

And a little dog, nameless and mongrel and many-fathered, grown, yet weighing less than six pounds, saying as if to itself, "I can't be dangerous, because there's nothing much smaller than I am; I can't be fierce, because they would call it just a noise; I can't be humble, because I'm already too close to the ground to genuflect;[13] I can't be proud, because I wouldn't be near enough to it for anyone to know who was casting the shadow, and I don't even know that I'm not going to

12. **"She . . . fair"**: from John Keats's "Ode on a Grecian Urn."

13. **genuflect** (gĕn′yə-flĕkt′): kneel as in worship.

heaven, because they have already decided that I don't possess an immortal soul. So all I can be is brave. But it's all right. I can be that, even if they still call it just noise."

That was all. It was simple, much simpler than somebody talking in a book about youth and a girl he would never need to grieve over, because he could never approach any nearer her and would never have to get any farther away. He had heard about a bear, and finally got big enough to trail it, and he trailed it four years and at last met it with a gun in his hands and he didn't shoot. Because a little dog—But he could have shot long before the little dog covered the twenty yards to where the bear waited, and Sam Fathers could have shot at any time during that interminable minute while Old Ben stood on his hind feet over them. He stopped. His father was watching him gravely across the spring-rife twilight of the room; when he spoke, his words were as quiet as the twilight, too, not loud, because they did not need to be because they would last. "Courage, and honor, and pride," his father said, "and pity, and love of justice and of liberty. They all touch the heart, and what the heart holds to becomes truth, as far as we know the truth. Do you see now?

Sam, and Old Ben, and Nip, he thought. And himself too. He had been all right too. His father had said so. "Yes, sir," he said.

Reading Check

1. What is the purpose of the trip into the Big Bottom each November?
2. From whom does the boy learn how to hunt?
3. What is unusual about the print left by the old bear?
4. What happens when the boy finally tracks down the bear and has it within shooting range?

Commentary

"The Bear" may be read simply as a realistic story about hunting. A boy living in rural Mississippi in the 1880s is fascinated by the stories he hears about a huge bear haunting the still-abundant wilderness of his region, and he makes himself into a master woodsman in order to track down the bear. If you read alertly, however, you soon sense that Faulkner has a deeper purpose. In the course of cultivating the necessary skills, the boy also gains an insight into the larger nature of hunting, the wilderness, and the bear itself. Faulkner is telling us about humanity's need for communion with the wilderness as represented by the great forest and the legendary bear, and about the nobility of character that is to be achieved through this communion.

The meaning of this story is more easily grasped if you consider the clue in the two-line quotation from Keats's "Ode on a Grecian Urn," which the boy's father reads aloud in the last paragraphs of the story. The speaker in the poem regards a pastoral scene depicted on an urn. The scene is a happy one of singing, piping, dancing, and particularly of a youth chasing a fair maiden. He will never reach her for their positions on the vase will never change.

> *Bold Lover, never, never canst thou kiss,*
> *Though winning near the goal—yet, do not*
> *grieve;*
> *She cannot fade, though thou hast not thy bliss,*
> *Forever wilt thou love, and she be fair!*
> . . . .
> *"Beauty is truth, truth beauty"—that is all*
> *Ye know on earth, and all ye need to know.*

The beauty of the moment is fixed; in its permanence it becomes the truth. Faulkner tells us that the men do "not even intend to kill" the bear. In their simple wisdom they understand the "truth" of their annual pilgrimages to the woods and the "beauty" in the chase itself. So long as the object of the chase is not caught and wantonly destroyed, its "truth" and "beauty" will endure.

As a symbol of the wilderness, the bear is pictured as something extraordinary, larger than life, "a phantom," "absolved of mortality," endowed with "inviolable anonymity," and "dimensionless, against the dappled obscurity." The wilderness itself possesses "the same solitude, the same loneliness through which human beings had merely passed without altering it, leaving no mark, no scar. . . ." Against this pristine wilderness human beings and their civilization are destructive, polluting forces: "the puny humans swarmed and hacked in a fury of abhorrence and fear. . . ."

As the boy grows older, becoming truly "skillful and worthy in the woods," he acquires a respect and a reverence for the awesome wilderness and the mysterious bear. At the end of the story, he begins to comprehend what the men have long known, that the bear stands for something greater and more important than itself, that it symbolizes the beauty, freedom, and purity of the wilderness. At last he tracks down the bear. He stands close enough to shoot it easily—but he is unable to. The boy's contact with the wilderness and the bear has thus given him more than the ability to hunt. As yet he is only dimly aware of what he has gained, but his father understands: " 'Courage, and honor, and pride,' his father said, 'and pity, and love of justice and of liberty. They all touch the heart, and what the heart holds to becomes truth, as far as we know the truth.' "

For Study and Discussion

Analyzing and Interpreting the Story

1. The boy hunts the bear three times, when he is ten, eleven, and fourteen years old. The first hunt divides into several actions, as a kind of prelude to the other hunts. **a.** What does Sam teach the boy before the first hunt? **b.** How does Sam know the bear is near?

2. As the boy sees the hound return with a tattered ear and raked shoulder, he imagines a cause far more universal than a bear: " . . . it was still no living creature, but the wilderness which, leaning for the moment down, had patted lightly once the hound's temerity." Interpret this sentence.

3. During the second hunt, the boy seems to be on the track of something more than animals. Although the others think he is "hunting squirrels," what is he unconsciously teaching himself?

4. Sam tells the boy that he will have to "choose." **a.** Between what two alternatives must the boy choose? **b.** In what sense can a coward be more dangerous than a brave person?

5. As the boy advances farther into the woods, he realizes that he must abandon not only his gun but also his watch, compass, and stick. What does his abandonment of these things suggest is the real point of his hunting the bear?

6a. By the time the boy is fourteen, what qualifies him as a competent woodsman? **b.** What action marks his initiation as a true hunter?

7. After the first hunt Sam says, "We ain't got the dog yet." **a.** What kind of dog is needed for the hunt? **b.** How does this dog's nature relate to the choice that the boy has had to make?

8. What has the boy finally acquired from his experiences in the wilderness that is more important than his skill as a woodsman?

Literary Elements

Theme

Theme may be defined as the *idea behind a story*, the unspoken comment growing out of every sentence, every detail, every character, every event. In some stories, the theme is closely related to moments of revelation. Often, in the best stories, the theme is difficult to state. It is as complex as the story itself. However, making a rough statement of the theme will usually help a reader to understand a story; and finding and interpreting significant passages is a good method of arriving at the theme.

Locate several significant passages in "The Bear" and use them to arrive at a statement of the story's theme.

Writing About Literature

Evaluating Faulkner's Use of Universal Truths

In his Nobel Prize Acceptance Speech, William Faulkner states that a writer must leave "no room in his workshop for anything but the old verities and truths of the heart, the old universal truths lacking which any story is ephemeral and doomed— love and honor and pity and pride and compassion and sacrifice." In an essay, evaluate how well Faulkner himself has written about these "old universal truths" in "The Bear." Support your evaluation with quotations from the story.

Stephen Vincent Benét was born in Bethlehem, Pennsylvania, the son of an army colonel, whose father and grandfather were also army officers. Benét's father was a cultivated man who loved poetry and encouraged his sons to write. Two other Benét children, William Rose and Laura, also became well-known writers. Stephen himself published his first novel of poetry, *Five Men and Pompey,* when he was only seventeen and his second collection, *Young Adventure,* three years later, after he had graduated from Yale. William Rose Benét once wrote of his younger brother that "poetry was from the first a bright valor in his blood." In 1921 Stephen married Rosemary Carr, a writer with whom he later collaborated on *A Book for Americans.*

During the early part of his career, Benét depended for a living on the several novels he published and on the stories he wrote for popular magazines. Dissatisfied with these works, he longed for the leisure to write a long narrative poem based on his father's collection of old military records. A Guggenheim fellowship enabled him to begin this work in 1926. The result, *John Brown's Body,* became a best seller, won a Pulitzer Prize in 1929, and is acknowledged as a minor American classic. In the 1930s Benét wrote a number of stories that make American dialects into a kind of poetry. One of the best of these is "Johnny Pye and the Fool-killer." *Western Star,* his uncompleted narrative poem about the colonization of America, was published after his death in 1943.

Stephen Vincent Benét.
The Bettmann Archive

Benét's best works are those that re-create traditions and events that helped form this nation and its people, and that explore what it means to be an American. His most famous work, "The Devil and Daniel Webster," was recognized from the time of its publication as a classic blending of history and folklore into a legend that transcends a particular time and place. This short story has been made into a one-act play, a motion picture, an opera, and a television play. It seems likely that "The Devil and Daniel Webster" will remain a part of the American tradition, like the tales that grew up about Davy Crockett and Mike Fink and transformed them from historical persons into legendary figures.

The Devil and Daniel Webster

It's a story they tell in the border country, where Massachusetts joins Vermont and New Hampshire.

Yes, Dan'l Webster's dead—or, at least, they buried him. But every time there's a thunderstorm around Marshfield,[1] they say you can hear his rolling voice in the hollows of the sky. And they say that if you go to his grave and speak loud and clear, "Dan'l Webster—Dan'l Webster!" the ground'll begin to shiver and the trees begin to shake. And after a while you'll hear a deep voice saying, "Neighbor, how stands the Union?" Then you better answer the Union stands as she stood, rock-bottomed and copper-sheathed, one and indivisible, or he's liable to rear right out of the ground. At least, that's what I was told when I was a youngster.

You see, for a while, he was the biggest man in the country. He never got to be President, but he was the biggest man. There were thousands that trusted in him right next to God Almighty and they told stories about him that were like the stories of patriarchs and such. They said when he stood up to speak, stars and stripes came right out in the sky, and once he spoke against a river and made it sink into the ground. They said when he walked the woods with his fishing rod, Killall, the trout would jump out of the streams right into his pockets, for they knew it was no using putting up a fight against him; and, when he argued a case, he could turn on the harps of the blessed and the shaking of the earth underground. That was the kind of man he was, and his big farm up at Marshfield was suitable to him. The chickens he raised were all white meat down through the drumsticks, the cows were tended like children, and the big ram he

called Goliath[2] had horns with a curl like a morning-glory vine and could butt through an iron door. But Dan'l wasn't one of your gentlemen farmers; he knew all the way of the land, and he'd be up by candlelight to see that the chores got done. A man with a mouth like a mastiff, a brow like a mountain and eyes like burning anthracite—that was Dan'l Webster in his prime. And the biggest case he argued never got written down in the books, for he argued it against the devil, nip and tuck and no holds barred. And this is the way I used to hear it told.

There was a man named Jabez Stone, lived at Cross Corners, New Hampshire. He wasn't a bad man to start with, but he was an unlucky man. If he planted corn, he got borers;[3] if he planted potatoes, he got blight.[4] He had good enough land, but it didn't prosper him; he had a decent wife and children, but the more children he had, the less there was to feed them. If stones cropped up in his neighbor's field, boulders boiled up in his; if he had a horse with spavins,[5] he'd trade it for one with the staggers[6] and give something extra. There's some folks bound to be like that, apparently. But one day Jabez Stone got sick of the whole business.

He'd been plowing that morning and he'd just broke the plowshare on a rock that he could have sworn hadn't been there yesterday. And, as he stood looking at the plowshare, the off horse began to cough—that ropy kind of cough that means sickness and horse doctors.

---

1. **Marshfield:** a small town southeast of Boston, where Webster had a farm.

2. **Goliath** (gə-lī′əth): a famous giant in the Bible (I Samuel, 17) who was slain by the young David.
3. **borer:** a corn-destroying insect.
4. **blight:** a plant disease.
5. **spavins** (spăv′ənz): a disease of the leg bone that causes a horse to limp.
6. **staggers:** a disease that causes a horse to lose coordination, reel, or fall down.

There were two children down with the measles, his wife was ailing, and he had a whitlow[7] on his thumb. It was about the last straw for Jabez Stone. "I vow," he said, and he looked around him kind of desperate—"I vow it's enough to make a man want to sell his soul to the devil! And I would, too, for two cents!"

Then he felt a kind of queerness come over him at having said what he'd said; though, naturally, being a New Hampshireman, he wouldn't take it back. But, all the same, when it got to be evening and, as far as he could see, no notice had been taken, he felt relieved in his mind, for he was a religious man. But notice is always taken, sooner or later, just like the Good Book says. And, sure enough, next day, about suppertime, a soft-spoken, dark-dressed stranger drove up in a handsome buggy and asked for Jabez Stone.

Well, Jabez told his family it was a lawyer, come to see him about a legacy. But he knew who it was. He didn't like the looks of the stranger, nor the way he smiled with his teeth. They were white teeth, and plentiful—some say they were filed to a point, but I wouldn't vouch for that. And he didn't like it when the dog took one look at the stranger and ran away howling, with his tail between his legs. But having passed his word, more or less, he stuck to it, and they went out behind the barn and made their bargain. Jabez Stone had to prick his finger to sign, and the stranger lent him a silver pin. The wound healed clean, but it left a little white scar.

After that, all of a sudden, things began to pick up and prosper for Jabez Stone. His cows got fat and his horses sleek, his crops were the envy of the neighborhood, and lightning might strike all over the valley, but it wouldn't strike his barn. Pretty soon, he was one of the prosperous people of the county; they asked him to stand for selectman,[8] and he stood for it; there began to be talk of running him for

state senate. All in all, you might say the Stone family was as happy and contented as cats in a dairy. And so they were, except for Jabez Stone.

The stranger came up through the lower field, switching his boots with a cane—they were handsome black boots, but Jabez Stone never liked the look of them, particularly the toes. And after he'd passed the time of day, he said, "Well, Mr. Stone, you're a hummer! It's a very pretty property you've got here, Mr. Stone."

"Well, some might favor it and others might not," said Jabez Stone, for he was a New Hampshireman.

"Oh, no need to decry your industry!" said the stranger, very easy, showing his teeth in a smile. "After all, we know what's been done, and it's been according to contract and specifications. So when—ahem—the mortgage falls due next year, you shouldn't have any regrets."

"Speaking of that mortgage, mister," said Jabez Stone, and he looked around for help to the earth and sky, "I'm beginning to have one or two doubts about it."

"Doubts?" said the stranger, not quite so pleasantly.

"Why, yes," said Jabez Stone. "This being the USA and me always having been a religious man." He cleared his throat and got bolder. "Yes, sir," he said, "I'm beginning to have considerable doubts as to that mortgage holding in court."

"There's courts and courts," said the stranger, clicking his teeth. "Still, we might as well have a look at the original document." And he hauled out a big black pocketbook, full of papers. "Sherwin, Slater, Stevens, Stone," he muttered. "I, Jabez Stone, for a term of seven years——Oh, it's quite in order, I think."

But Jabez Stone wasn't listening, for he saw something else flutter out of the black pocketbook. It was something that looked like a moth, but it wasn't a moth. And as Jabez Stone stared at it, it seemed to speak to him in a small sort of piping voice, terrible small and thin, but terrible human. "Neighbor Stone!" it

7. **whitlow:** an inflamed sore.
8. **selectman:** one of a board of officers chosen annually in some New England towns to manage public and municipal affairs.

squeaked. "Neighbor Stone! Help me! For heaven's sake, help me!"

But before Jabez Stone could stir hand or foot, the stranger whipped out a big bandanna handkerchief, caught the creature in it, just like a butterfly, and started tying up the ends of the bandanna.

"Sorry for the interruption," he said. "As I was saying——"

But Jabez Stone was shaking all over like a scared horse.

"That's Miser Stevens' voice!" he said, in a croak. "And you've got him in your handkerchief!"

The stranger looked a little embarrassed.

"Yes, I really should have transferred him to the collecting box," he said with a simper, "but there were some rather unusual specimens there and I didn't want them crowded. Well, well, these little contretemps[9] will occur."

"I don't know what you mean by contertan," said Jabez Stone, "but that was Miser Stevens' voice! And he ain't dead! You can't tell me he is! He was just as spry and mean as a woodchuck, Tuesday!"

"In the midst of life——"[10] said the stranger, kind of pious. "Listen!" Then a bell began to toll in the valley and Jabez Stone listened, with the sweat running down his face. For he knew it was tolled for Miser Stevens and that he was dead.

"These long-standing accounts," said the stranger with a sigh; "one really hates to close them. But business is business."

He still had the bandanna in his hand, and Jabez Stone felt sick as he saw the cloth struggle and flutter.

"Are they all as small as that?" he asked hoarsely.

"Small?" said the stranger. "Oh, I see what you mean. Why, they vary." He measured Jabez Stone with his eyes, and his teeth showed. "Don't worry, Mr. Stone," he said. "You'll go with a very good grade. I wouldn't trust you outside the collecting box. Now, a man like Dan'l Webster, of course—well, we'd have to build a special box for him, and even at that, I imagine the wingspread would astonish you. But, in your case, as I was saying——"

"Put that handkerchief away!" said Jabez Stone, and he began to beg and to pray. But the best he could get at the end was a three years' extension, with conditions.

But till you make a bargain like that, you've got no idea of how fast four years can run. By the last months of those years, Jabez Stone's known all over the state and there's talk of running him for governor—and it's dust and ashes in his mouth. For every day, when he gets up, he thinks, "There's one more night gone," and every night when he lies down, he thinks of the black pocketbook and the soul of Miser Stevens, and it makes him sick at heart. Till, finally, he can't bear it any longer, and, in the last days of the last year, he hitches up his horse and drives off to seek Dan'l Webster. For Dan'l was born in New Hampshire, only a few miles from Cross Corners, and it's well known that he has a particular soft spot for old neighbors.

It was early in the morning when he got to Marshfield, but Dan'l was up already, talking Latin to the farmhands and wrestling with the ram, Goliath, and trying out a new trotter and working up speeches to make against John C. Calhoun.[11] But when he heard a New Hampshireman had come to see him, he dropped everything else he was doing, for that was Dan'l's way. He gave Jabez Stone a breakfast that five men couldn't eat, went into the living history of every man and woman in Cross Corners, and finally asked him how he could serve him.

Jabez Stone allowed that it was a kind of mortgage case.

---

9. **contretemps** (kŏn′trə-tän′): an embarrassing situation. Note Stone's pronunciation of the word in the next paragraph.
10. **In . . . life:** The remainder of this quotation is "we are in death." This is part of the burial service in *The Book of Common Prayer.*

11. **John C. Calhoun:** the great orator for the South, as Webster was for the North.

"Well, I haven't pleaded a mortgage case in a long time, and I don't generally plead now, except before the Supreme Court," said Dan'l, "but if I can, I'll help you."

"Then I've got hope for the first time in ten years," said Jabez Stone, and told him the details.

Dan'l walked up and down as he listened, hands behind his back, now and then asking a question, now and then plunging his eyes at the floor, as if they'd bore through it like gimlets.[12] When Jabez Stone had finished, Dan'l puffed out his cheeks and blew. Then he turned to Jabez Stone and a smile broke over his face like the sunrise over Monadnock.[13]

"You've certainly given yourself the devil's own row to hoe, Neighbor Stone," he said, "but I'll take your case."

"You'll take it?" said Jabez Stone, hardly daring to believe.

"Yes," said Dan'l Webster. "I've got about seventy-five other things to do and the Missouri Compromise[14] to straighten out, but I'll take your case. For if two New Hampshiremen aren't a match for the devil, we might as well give the country back to the Indians."

Then he shook Jabez Stone by the hand and said, "Did you come down here in a hurry?"

"Well, I admit I made time," said Jabez Stone.

"You'll go back faster," said Dan'l Webster, and he told 'em to hitch up Constitution and Constellation to the carriage. They were matched grays with one white forefoot, and they stepped like greased lightning.

Well, I won't describe how excited and pleased the whole Stone family was to have the great Dan'l Webster for a guest, when they finally got there. Jabez Stone had lost his hat on the way, blown off when they overtook a wind, but he didn't take much account of that.

12. **gimlets:** small tools for drilling.
13. **Monadnock** (mə-năd′nŏk′): the highest mountain in southern New Hampshire.
14. **Missouri Compromise:** an act passed by Congress in 1820 in an attempt to settle the dispute about slavery in the newly formed Western states.

But after supper he sent the family off to bed, for he had most particular business with Mr. Webster. Mrs. Stone wanted them to sit in the front parlor, but Dan'l Webster knew front parlors and said he preferred the kitchen. So it was there they sat, waiting for the stranger, with a jug on the table between them and a bright fire on the hearth—the stranger being scheduled to show up on the stroke of midnight, according to specifications.

Well, most men wouldn't have asked for better company than Dan'l Webster and a jug. But with every tick of the clock Jabez Stone got sadder and sadder. His eyes roved round, and though he sampled the jug you could see he couldn't taste it. Finally, on the stroke of 11:30 he reached over and grabbed Dan'l Webster by the arm.

"Mr. Webster, Mr. Webster!" he said, and his voice was shaking with fear and a desperate courage. "For heaven's sake, Mr. Webster, harness your horses and get away from this place while you can!"

"You've brought me a long way, neighbor, to tell me you don't like my company," said Dan'l Webster, quite peaceable, pulling at the jug.

"Miserable wretch that I am!" groaned Jabez Stone. "I've brought you a devilish way, and now I see my folly. Let him take me if he wills. I don't hanker after it, I must say, but I can stand it. But you're the Union's stay and New Hampshire's pride! He mustn't get you, Mr. Webster! He mustn't get you!"

Dan'l Webster looked at the distracted man, all gray and shaking in the firelight, and laid a hand on his shoulder.

"I'm obliged to you, Neighbor Stone," he said gently. "It's kindly thought of. But there's a jug on the table and a case in hand. And I never left a jug or a case half finished in my life."

And just at that moment there was a sharp rap on the door.

"Ah," said Dan'l Webster, very coolly, "I thought your clock was a trifle slow, Neighbor Stone." He stepped to the door and opened it.

"Come in!" he said.

The stranger came in—very dark and tall he looked in the firelight. He was carrying a box under his arm—a black, japanned[15] box with little air holes in the lid. At the sight of the box, Jabez Stone gave a low cry and shrank into a corner of the room.

"Mr. Webster, I presume," said the stranger, very polite, but with his eyes glowing like a fox's deep in the woods.

"Attorney of record for Jabez Stone," said Dan'l Webster, but his eyes were glowing too. "Might I ask your name?"

"I've gone by a good many," said the stranger carelessly. "Perhaps Scratch will do for the evening. I'm often called that in these regions."

Then he sat down at the table and poured himself a drink from the jug. The liquor was cold in the jug, but it came steaming into the glass.

"And now," said the stranger, smiling and showing his teeth, "I shall call upon you, as a law-abiding citizen, to assist me in taking possession of my property."

Well, with that the argument began—and it went hot and heavy. At first, Jabez Stone had a flicker of hope, but when he saw Dan'l Webster being forced back at point after point, he just scrunched in his corner, with his eyes on that japanned box. For there wasn't any doubt as to the deed or the signature—that was the worst of it. Dan'l Webster twisted and turned and thumped his fist on the table, but he couldn't get away from that. He offered to compromise the case; the stranger wouldn't hear of it. He pointed out the property had increased in value, and state senators ought to be worth more; the stranger stuck to the letter of the law. He was a great lawyer, Dan'l Webster, but we know who's the King of Lawyers, as the Good Book tells us, and it seemed as if, for the first time, Dan'l Webster had met his match.

Finally, the stranger yawned a little. "Your spirited efforts on behalf of your client do you

credit, Mr. Webster," he said, "but if you have no more arguments to adduce, I'm rather pressed for time"—and Jabez Stone shuddered.

Dan'l Webster's brow looked dark as a thundercloud.

"Pressed or not, you shall not have this man!" he thundered. "Mr. Stone is an American citizen, and no American citizen may be forced into the service of a foreign prince. We fought England for that in '12[16] and we'll fight all hell for it again!"

"Foreign?" said the stranger. "And who calls me a foreigner?"

"Well, I never yet heard of the dev—of your claiming American citizenship," said Dan'l Webster with surprise.

"And who with better right?" said the stranger, with one of his terrible smiles. "When the first wrong was done to the first Indian, I was there. When the first slaver put out for the Congo, I stood on her deck. Am I not in your books and stories and beliefs, from the first settlements on? Am I not spoken of, still, in every church in New England? 'Tis true the North claims me for a Southerner and the South for a Northerner, but I am neither. I am merely an honest American like yourself—and of the best descent—for, to tell the truth, Mr. Webster, though I don't like to boast of it, my name is older in this country than yours."

"Aha!" said Dan'l Webster, with the veins standing out in his forehead. "Then I stand on the Constitution! I demand a trial for my client!"

"The case is hardly one for an ordinary court," said the stranger, his eyes flickering. "And, indeed, the lateness of the hour——"

"Let it be any court you choose, so it is an American judge and an American jury!" said Dan'l Webster in his pride. "Let it be the quick[17] or the dead; I'll abide the issue!"

"You have said it," said the stranger, and

16. **'12:** the War of 1812. A major cause of the war was the impressment of American seamen into the British navy.

17. **quick:** living.

15. **japanned:** lacquered.

pointed his finger at the door. And with that, and all of a sudden, there was a rushing of wind outside and a noise of footsteps. They came, clear and distinct, through the night. And yet, they were not like the footsteps of living men.

"In God's name, who comes by so late?" cried Jabez Stone, in an ague of fear.

"The jury Mr. Webster demands," said the stranger, sipping at his boiling glass. "You must pardon the rough appearance of one or two; they will have come a long way."

And with that the fire burned blue and the door blew open and twelve men entered, one by one.

If Jabez Stone had been sick with terror before, he was blind with terror now. For there was Walter Butler, the Loyalist, who spread fire and horror through the Mohawk Valley in the times of the Revolution; and there was Simon Girty, the renegade, who saw white men burned at the stake and whooped with the Indians to see them burn. His eyes were green, like a catamount's, and the stains on his hunting shirt did not come from the blood of the deer. King Philip[18] was there, wild and proud as he had been in life, with the great gash in his head that gave him his death wound, and cruel Governor Dale,[19] who broke men on the wheel. There was Morton of Merry Mount, who so vexed the Plymouth Colony, with his flushed, loose, handsome face and his hate of the godly. There was Teach, the bloody pirate, with his black beard curling on his breast. The Reverend John Smeet, with his strangler's hands and his Geneva gown,[20] walked as daintily as he had to the gallows. The red print of the rope was still around his neck, but he carried a perfumed handkerchief in one hand. One and all, they came into the room with the fires of hell still upon them, and the stranger

18. **King Philip:** an Indian chief who organized an uprising against the white settlers in 1675 and was killed the following year.
19. **Governor Dale:** Sir Thomas Dale, English Deputy Governor of Virginia, 1611–1616, whose severe laws caused the colonists to call these the "years of slavery."
20. **Geneva gown:** minister's robe.

named their names and their deeds as they came, till the tale of twelve was told. Yet the stranger had told the truth—they had all played a part in America.

"Are you satisfied with the jury, Mr. Webster?" said the stranger mockingly, when they had taken their places.

The sweat stood upon Dan'l Webster's brow, but his voice was clear.

"Quite satisfied," he said. "Though I miss General Arnold from the company."

"Benedict Arnold is engaged upon other business," said the stranger, with a glower. "Ah, you asked for a justice, I believe."

He pointed his finger once more, and a tall man, soberly clad in Puritan garb, with the burning gaze of the fanatic, stalked into the room and took his judge's place.

"Justice Hathorne is a jurist of experience," said the stranger. "He presided at certain witch trials once held in Salem. There were others who repented of the business later, but not he."

"Repent of such notable wonders and undertakings?" said the stern old justice. "Nay, hang them—hang them all!" And he muttered to himself in a way that struck ice into the soul of Jabez Stone.

Then the trial began, and, as you might expect, it didn't look anyways good for the defense. And Jabez Stone didn't make much of a witness in his own behalf. He took one look at Simon Girty and screeched, and they had to put him back in his corner in a kind of swoon.

It didn't halt the trial, though; the trial went on, as trials do. Dan'l Webster had faced some hard juries and hanging judges in his time, but this was the hardest he'd ever faced, and he knew it. They sat there with a kind of glitter in their eyes, and the stranger's smooth voice went on and on. Every time he'd raise an objection, it'd be "Objection sustained," but whenever Dan'l objected, it'd be "Objection denied." Well, you couldn't expect fair play from a fellow like this Mr. Scratch.

It got to Dan'l in the end, and he began to heat, like iron in the forge. When he got up to speak he was going to flay that stranger with every trick known to the law, and the judge and jury too. He didn't care if it was contempt of court or what would happen to him for it. He didn't care any more what happened to Jabez Stone. He just got madder and madder, thinking of what he'd say. And yet, curiously enough, the more he thought about it, the less he was able to arrange his speech in his mind.

Till, finally, it was time for him to get up on his feet, and he did so, all ready to bust out with lightnings and denunciations. But before he started he looked over the judge and jury for a moment, such being his custom. And he noticed the glitter in their eyes was twice as strong as before, and they all leaned forward. Like hounds just before they get the fox, they looked, and the blue mist of evil in the room thickened as he watched them. Then he saw what he'd been about to do, and he wiped his forehead, as a man might who's just escaped falling into a pit in the dark.

For it was him they'd come for, not only Jabez Stone. He read it in the glitter of their eyes and in the way the stranger hid his mouth with one hand. And if he fought them with their own weapons, he'd fall into their power; he knew that, though he couldn't have told you how. It was his own anger and horror that burned in their eyes; and he'd have to wipe that out or the case was lost. He stood there for a moment, his black eyes burning like anthracite. And then he began to speak.

He started off in a low voice, though you could hear every word. They say he could call on the harps of the blessed when he chose. And this was just as simple and easy as a man could talk. But he didn't start out by condemning or reviling. He was talking about the things that make a country a country, and a man a man.

And he began with the simple things that everybody's known and felt—the freshness of a fine morning when you're young, and the taste of food when you're hungry, and the new day that's every day when you're a child. He took them up and he turned them in his hands. They were good things for any man. But with-

out freedom, they sickened. And when he talked of those enslaved, and the sorrows of slavery, his voice got like a big bell. He talked of the early days of America and the men who had made those days. It wasn't a spread-eagle speech, but he made you see it. He admitted all the wrong that had ever been done. But he showed how, out of the wrong and the right, the suffering and the starvations, something new had come. And everybody had played a part in it, even the traitors.

Then he turned to Jabez Stone and showed him as he was—an ordinary man who'd had hard luck and wanted to change it. And, because he'd wanted to change it, now he was going to be punished for all eternity. And yet there was good in Jabez Stone, and he showed that good. He was hard and mean, in some ways, but he was a man. There was sadness in being a man, but it was a proud thing too. And he showed what the pride of it was till you couldn't help feeling it. Yes, even in hell, if a man was a man, you'd know it. And he wasn't pleading for any one person any more, though his voice rang like an organ. He was telling the story and the failures and the endless journey of mankind. They got tricked and trapped and bamboozled, but it was a great journey. And no demon that was ever foaled could know the inwardness of it—it took a man to do that.

The fire began to die on the hearth and the wind before morning to blow. The light was getting gray in the room when Dan'l Webster finished. And his words came back at the end to New Hampshire ground, and the one spot of land that each man loves and clings to. He painted a picture of that, and to each one of that jury he spoke of things long forgotten. For his voice could search the heart, and that was his gift and his strength. And to one, his voice was like the forest and its secrecy, and to another like the sea and the storms of the sea; and one heard the cry of his lost nation in it, and another saw a little harmless scene he hadn't remembered for years. But each saw something. And when Dan'l Webster finished he didn't know whether or not he'd saved Jabez Stone. But he knew he'd done a miracle. For the glitter was gone from the eyes of the judge and jury, and, for the moment, they were men again, and knew they were men.

"The defense rests," said Dan'l Webster, and stood there like a mountain. His ears were still ringing with his speech, and he didn't hear anything else till he heard Judge Hathorne say, "The jury will retire to consider its verdict."

Walter Butler rose in his place and his face had a dark, gay pride on it.

"The jury has considered its verdict," he said, and looked the stranger full in the eye. "We find for the defendant, Jabez Stone."

With that, the smile left the stranger's face, but Walter Butler did not flinch.

"Perhaps 'tis not strictly in accordance with the evidence," he said, "but even the damned may salute the eloquence of Mr. Webster."

With that, the long crow of a rooster split the gray morning sky, and judge and jury were gone from the room like a puff of smoke and as if they had never been there. The stranger turned to Dan'l Webster, smiling wryly.

"Major Butler was always a bold man," he said. "I had not thought him quite so bold. Nevertheless, my congratulations, as between two gentlemen."

"I'll have that paper first, if you please," said Dan'l Webster, and he took it and tore it into four pieces. It was queerly warm to the touch. "And now," he said, "I'll have you!" and his hand came down like a bear trap on the stranger's arm. For he knew that once you bested anybody like Mr. Scratch in fair fight, his power on you was gone. And he could see that Mr. Scratch knew it too.

The stranger twisted and wriggled, but he couldn't get out of that grip. "Come, come, Mr. Webster," he said, smiling palely. "This sort of thing is ridic—ouch!—is ridiculous. If you're worried about the costs of the case, naturally, I'd be glad to pay——"

"And so you shall!" said Dan'l Webster, shaking him till his teeth rattled. "For you'll sit right down at that table and draw up a document, promising never to bother Jabez Stone nor his heirs or assigns[21] nor any other New Hampshireman till doomsday! For any hades we want to raise in this state, we can raise ourselves, without assistance from strangers."

"Ouch!" said the stranger. "Ouch! Well, they never did run very big to the barrel, but—ouch!—I agree!"

So he sat down and drew up the document. But Dan'l Webster kept his hand on his coat collar all the time.

"And, now, may I go?" said the stranger, quite humble, when Dan'l'd seen the document was in proper and legal form.

"Go?" said Dan'l, giving him another shake. "I'm still trying to figure out what I'll do with you. For you've settled the costs of the case, but you haven't settled with me. I think I'll take you back to Marshfield," he said, kind of reflective. "I've got a ram there named Goliath that can butt through an iron door. I'd kind of like to turn you loose in his field and see what he'd do."

Well, with that the stranger began to beg and to plead. And he begged and he pled so humble that finally Dan'l, who was naturally kindhearted, agreed to let him go. The stranger seemed terrible grateful for that and said, just to show they were friends, he'd tell Dan'ls fortune before leaving. So Dan'l agreed to that, though he didn't take much stock in fortunetellers ordinarily. But, naturally, the stranger was a little different.

Well, he pried and he peered at the lines in Dan'l's hands. And he told him one thing and another that was quite remarkable. But they were all in the past.

"Yes, all that's true, and it happened," said Dan'l Webster. "But what's to come in the future?"

The stranger grinned, kind of happily, and shook his head.

"The future's not as you think it," he said. "It's dark. You have a great ambition, Mr. Webster."

"I have," said Dan'l firmly, for everybody

---

21. **assigns:** persons who inherit money or property.

knew he wanted to be President.

"It seems almost within your grasp," said the stranger, "but you will not attain it. Lesser men will be made President and you will be passed over."

"And, if I am, I'll still be Daniel Webster," said Dan'l. "Say on."

"You have two strong sons," said the stranger, shaking his head. "You look to found a line. But each will die in war and neither reach greatness."

"Live or die, they are still my sons," said Dan'l Webster. "Say on."

"You have made great speeches," said the stranger. "You will make more."

"Ah," said Dan'l Webster.

"But the last great speech you make will turn many of your own against you," said the stranger. "They will call you Ichabod;[22] they will call you by other names. Even in New England, some will say you have turned your coat and sold your country, and their voices will be loud against you till you die."

"So it is an honest speech, it does not matter what men say," said Dan'l Webster. Then he looked at the stranger and their glances locked.

"One question," he said. "I have fought for the Union all my life. Will I see that fight won against those who would tear it apart?"

"Not while you live," said the stranger, grimly, "but it will be won. And after you are dead, there are thousands who will fight for your cause, because of words that you spoke."

"Why, then, you long-barreled, slab-sided, lantern-jawed, fortunetelling note shaver!" said Dan'l Webster, with a great roar of laughter, "be off with you to your own place before I put my mark on you! For, by the thirteen original colonies, I'd go to the Pit itself to save the Union!"

And with that he drew back his foot for a kick that would have stunned a horse. It was only the tip of his shoe that caught the stranger, but he went flying out of the door with his collecting box under his arm.

"And now," said Dan'l Webster, seeing Jabez Stone beginning to rouse from his swoon, "let's see what's left in the jug, for it's dry work talking all night. I hope there's pie for breakfast, Neighbor Stone."

But they say that whenever the devil comes near Marshfield, even now, he gives it a wide berth. And he hasn't been seen in the state of New Hampshire from that day to this. I'm not talking about Massachusetts or Vermont.

---

22. **Ichabod** (ĭk′ə-bŏd): the title of Whittier's poem criticizing Webster's speech of March 7, 1850, in which Webster denounced the abolitionists. Because of his speech many Northerners considered Webster a traitor. Ichabod is a Hebrew name meaning "where is the glory?" or "the glory is departed."

Reading Check

1. According to the narrator, why was Webster's biggest case never recorded?
2. What does Old Scratch keep in his collecting box?
3. What is the length of Jabez Stone's contract with the devil?
4. Who is referred to as the King of Lawyers?
5. What are the conditions Webster sets for the trial?

For Study and Discussion

Analyzing and Interpreting the Story

1. What kind of story do the first three paragraphs prepare you for? Explain.

2a. In what ways can the three main characters—Jabez Stone, Daniel Webster, and Mr. Scratch—be called typical New England men? **b.** What do you learn about New Englanders from this story?

3a. What statements does the devil make about American policies of the past? **b.** How are these statements ironic and critical? **c.** How does the contract between Stone and the devil make the case go against Webster at first?

4. Why does Webster change the tone and content of his speech to the jury when he sees that something is wrong with his approach?

5. Would you describe the tone of this story as serious or humorous? Or can you think of a better description?

6. What American traditions are celebrated in this story?

Language and Vocabulary

Examining the Role of Dialect

The New England setting is established in this story partly by an occasional use of New England dialect. For example, Daniel Webster is referred to as "Dan'l" and it is said of him that he may "rear right out of the ground." Find other examples of dialect in the story, and tell how they add to the story's atmosphere.

Writing About Literature

Discussing Elements of the Tall Tale

One of the earliest forms of American humor was the **tall tale.** The stock elements of the tall tale included soaring exaggerations, vivid settings, the use of dialect, and a hero with superhuman abilities. In an essay, discuss "The Devil and Daniel Webster" in terms of the tall-tale tradition of American humor. What elements does the story share with the tall tale?

Comparing Humor in Two Stories

Write an essay in which you compare this story with a selection by Mark Twain (pages 391–401) or "The Catbird Seat" by James Thurber (page 601). How is the humor in these selections similar to the humor in Benét's story? What do the selections by Twain and Thurber have in common with the tall tale?

Daniel Webster (1844). Detail of lithographed silhouette by E. C. and E. B. Kellogg Lithography Co.
National Portrait Gallery, Smithsonian Institution

Ernest Hemingway.
© Robert Capa / Magnum Photos

Ernest Hemingway is probably the most widely imitated American writer of the twentieth century. Few writers of our time have escaped a confrontation with him and the acceptance or rejection of his influence. The art of fiction has gained new life from techniques he perfected—a deceptively simple, rhythmic prose that is admirably suited to depicting moments of action and the rapid, terse dialogue that reflects the nature of Hemingway's characters quietly standing up to the pain of life. Hemingway has made two major contributions other than technique to American literature. The first of these is a vision of life both as a kind of perpetual battlefield where everyone is eventually wounded and as a game with almost formal moves. The second is the "Hemingway hero," a man for whom it is a point of honor to suffer with grace and dignity, and who, though sensing that defeat is inevitable, plays the game well.

Ernest Hemingway was born in Oak Park, Illinois, a suburb of Chicago. His father was a doctor who loved the out-of-doors and took his son on hunting and fishing trips in northern Michigan. At Oak Park High School he was an athlete, but he also worked on the school newspaper and published stories in the literary magazine. In 1917, when he graduated, the United States had already entered World War I. Hemingway wanted to enlist and fight in Europe, but was rejected because of eye damage he had received as a high school boxer. Instead he got a job as a cub reporter on the Kansas City *Star*. In 1918 he joined a Red Cross ambulance corps and was sent to the Italian front. He was severely wounded by an artillery shell and for three months lay convalescing in a hospital in Milan. He then returned to Illinois. Thereafter, his thoughts circled about the significance of his wound, and he also came to discover the many ways a man can be wounded in peacetime as well as on a battlefront.

For the next year or so he made his living at newspaper work. He became a friend of Sherwood Anderson and, with the older man's encourage-ment, kept trying to write poems and short stories. He spent his spare time in gymnasiums, boxing and watching boxers, fascinated by this sport where men are tested through pain and danger. Later he discovered bullfighting and wrote *Death in the Afternoon,* a book exploring the significance of the duel between human being and animal.

In 1921 he got a job as a roving correspondent with the Toronto *Star* and left for Europe. There, chiefly in Paris, he met other young Americans of his generation who had left the United States in the belief that they would find personal and artistic fulfillment in an older civilization. As a reporter, Hemingway traveled through Europe and the Near East, finding material that would later serve him as a writer of fiction. In Paris, he fell under the influence of Gertrude Stein, who had outraged many readers with her experiments in language. (Her line "A rose is a rose is a rose" is still held up as the ultimate absurdity of experimental writing.) Miss Stein sought to gain her effects by use of simple language, rhythm, and repetition. Hemingway worked hard under her tutelage, bringing stories to her for criticism and making changes as she suggested. Later he rebelled against her, but he never denied that she had helped his art.

Hemingway's earliest two books were privately

published in Paris. *In Our Time*, a collection of short stories published in 1925, was his first book to reach a general audience. The perceptive critic Edmund Wilson saw in these early books the debut of a gifted young writer, but it took the publication of *The Sun Also Rises* (1926) to give Hemingway a wide audience. This novel, about a group of English and American expatriates hunting for sensations that would allow them to forget the pain attending life, gave everyone a new phrase to describe those who had lived through World War I and who had become disillusioned with the war's ideals: "the lost generation." In his next novel, *A Farewell to Arms*, Hemingway wrote about the war itself and a romance growing out of it. His description of the retreat from Caporetto is a famous episode in the novel. All the while, he was writing brilliant short stories that later were collected in *Men Without Women* and *Winner Take Nothing*.

With each book Hemingway's personal fame grew. He was regarded as the original hero of his stories, a big tough man hunting in Africa, deep-sea fishing, and following the bullfight. As a hero who lived dangerously and gracefully, he became the embodiment of the attitudes made popular by his writing. In the thirties he covered the Spanish Civil War as a foreign correspondent. Out of this experience came his most popular novel, *For Whom the Bell Tolls*. The title of this book is taken from John Donne's famous meditation: "Any man's death diminishes me, because I am involved in mankind, and therefore never send to know for whom the bell tolls; it tolls for thee." Both the novel and its title reflect Hemingway's growing commitment to larger issues. Instead of concentrating on the ordeals of personal existence, Hemingway and his hero, Robert Jordan, are "involved with mankind," concerned not only with individual fate but with the lot of humanity. In *The Old Man and the Sea*, the last notable work published during his lifetime, Hemingway returned to his old theme, the testing of the individual, but, in the old man's calm acceptance of his fate, gave it a new dignity. In 1954 he was awarded the Nobel Prize for literature.

In 1961, after a period of mounting depression and illness, he died of a self-inflicted gunshot wound. *A Moveable Feast*, his posthumously published memoir of his early days in Paris, is regarded by some readers as one of his best works. Since his death, it seems clearer than ever that Hemingway's best work has the concise intensity of fine poetry and that his artistic quest for the fewest and best words was similar to that of many poets. In his book about hunting big game, *The Green Hills of Africa*, he described this quest: "There is a fourth and fifth dimension that can be gotten. . . . It is much more difficult than poetry. It is a prose that has never been written. But it can be written, without tricks and without cheating. With nothing that will go bad afterwards."

Hemingway and Sylvia Beach (next to him) in front of her Paris bookstore, Shakespeare and Company, in 1928. This bookshop was a favorite meeting place for American and English writers in the 1920s.

In Another Country

In the fall the war[1] was always there, but we did not go to it any more. It was cold in the fall in Milan and the dark came very early. Then the electric lights came on, and it was pleasant along the streets looking in the windows. There was much game hanging outside the shops, and the snow powdered in the fur of the foxes and the wind blew their tails. The deer hung stiff and heavy and empty, and small birds blew in the wind and the wind turned their feathers. It was a cold fall and the wind came down from the mountains.

We were all at the hospital every afternoon, and there were different ways of walking across the town through the dusk to the hospital. Two of the ways were alongside canals, but they were long. Always, though, you crossed a bridge across a canal to enter the hospital. There was a choice of three bridges. On one of them a woman sold roasted chestnuts. It was warm, standing in front of her charcoal fire, and the chestnuts were warm afterward in your pocket. The hospital was very old and very beautiful, and you entered through a gate and walked across a courtyard and out a gate on the other side. There were usually funerals starting from the courtyard. Beyond the old hospital were the new brick pavilions, and there we met every afternoon and were all very polite and interested in what was the matter, and sat in the machines that were to make so much difference.

The doctor came up to the machine where I was sitting and said: "What did you like best to do before the war? Did you practice a sport?"

I said: "Yes, football."

"Good," he said. "You will be able to play football again better than ever."

My knee did not bend and the leg dropped straight from the knee to the ankle without a calf, and the machine was to bend the knee and make it move as in riding a tricycle. But it did not bend yet, and instead the machine lurched when it came to the bending part. The doctor said: "That will all pass. You are a fortunate young man. You will play football again like a champion."

In the next machine was a major who had a little hand like a baby's. He winked at me when the doctor examined his hand, which was between two leather straps that bounced up and down and flapped the stiff fingers, and said: "And will I too play football, captain-doctor?" He had been a very great fencer, and before the war the greatest fencer in Italy.

The doctor went to his office in a back room and brought a photograph which showed a hand that had been withered almost as small as the major's, before it had taken a machine course, and after was a little larger. The major held the photograph with his good hand and looked at it very carefully. "A wound?" he asked.

"An industrial accident," the doctor said.

"Very interesting, very interesting," the major said, and handed it back to the doctor.

"You have confidence?"

"No," said the major.

There were three boys who came each day who were about the same age I was. They were all three from Milan, and one of them was to be a lawyer, and one was to be a painter, and one had intended to be a soldier, and after we finished with the machines, sometimes we walked back together to the Café Cova, which was next door to the Scala.[2] We walked the short way through the communist quarter because we were four together. The people hated us because we were officers, and from a wine-

---

1. **the war:** World War I (1914–1918).

2. **Scala:** La Scala, Milan's opera house.

Hemingway recuperating in Milan in 1918.
John F. Kennedy Library

shop some one called out, "A basso gli uffici-ali!"[3] as we passed. Another boy who walked with us sometimes and made us five wore a black silk handkerchief across his face because he had no nose then and his face was to be rebuilt. He had gone out to the front from the military academy and been wounded within an hour after he had gone into the front line for the first time. They rebuilt his face, but he came from a very old family and they could never get the nose exactly right. He went to South America and worked in a bank. But this was a long time ago, and then we did not any

of us know how it was going to be afterward. We only knew then that there was always the war, but that we were not going to it any more.

We all had the same medals, except the boy with the black silk bandage across his face, and he had not been at the front long enough to get any medals. The tall boy with a very pale face who was to be a lawyer had been a lieu-tenant of Arditi[4] and had three medals of the sort we each had only one of. He had lived a very long time with death and was a little de-tached. We were all a little detached, and there was nothing that held us together except that

3. **"A basso gli ufficiali!"** (ä bä′sō lyē o͞o′fē-chä′lē): Italian for "Down with officers!"

4. **Arditi** (är-dē′tē): shock troops or commandos. Hem-ingway served with them.

we met every afternoon at the hospital. Although, as we walked to the Cova through the tough part of town, walking in the dark, with light and singing coming out of the wine-shops, and sometimes having to walk into the street when the men and women would crowd together on the sidewalk so that we would have had to jostle them to get by, we felt held together by there being something that had happened that they, the people who disliked us, did not understand.

We ourselves all understood the Cova, where it was rich and warm and not too brightly lighted, and noisy and smoky at certain hours, and there were always girls at the tables and the illustrated papers on a rack on the wall. The girls at the Cova were very patriotic, and I found that the most patriotic people in Italy were the café girls—and I believe they are still patriotic.

The boys at first were very polite about my medals and asked me what I had done to get them. I showed them the papers, which were written in very beautiful language and full of *fratellanza* and *abnegazione*,[5] but which really said, with the adjectives removed, that I had been given the medals because I was an American. After that their manner changed a little toward me, although I was their friend against outsiders. I was a friend, but I was never really one of them after they had read the citations, because it had been different with them and they had done very different things to get their medals. I had been wounded, it was true; but we all knew that being wounded, after all, was really an accident. I was never ashamed of the ribbons, though, and sometimes, after the cocktail hour, I would imagine myself having done all the things they had done to get their medals; but walking home at night through the empty streets with the cold wind and all the shops closed, trying to keep near the street lights, I knew that I would never have done such things, and I was very much afraid to die,

and often lay in bed at night by myself, afraid to die and wondering how I would be when I went back to the front again.

The three with the medals were like hunting-hawks; and I was not a hawk, although I might seem a hawk to those who had never hunted; they, the three, knew better and so we drifted apart. But I stayed good friends with the boy who had been wounded his first day at the front, because he would never know now how he would have turned out; so he could never be accepted either, and I liked him because I thought perhaps he would not have turned out to be a hawk either.

The major, who had been the great fencer, did not believe in bravery, and spent much time while we sat in the machines correcting my grammar. He had complimented me on how I spoke Italian, and we talked together very easily. One day I had said that Italian seemed such an easy language to me that I could not take a great interest in it; everything was so easy to say. "Ah, yes," the major said. "Why, then, do you not take up the use of grammar?" So we took up the use of grammar, and soon Italian was such a difficult language that I was afraid to talk to him until I had the grammar straight in my mind.

The major came very regularly to the hospital. I do not think he ever missed a day, although I am sure he did not believe in the machines. There was a time when none of us believed in the machines, and one day the major said it was all nonsense. The machines were new then and it was we who were to prove them. It was an idiotic idea, he said, "a theory, like another." I had not learned my grammar, and he said I was a stupid impossible disgrace, and he was a fool to have bothered with me. He was a small man and he sat straight up in his chair with his right hand thrust into the machine and looked straight ahead at the wall while the straps thumped up and down with his fingers in them.

"What will you do when the war is over if it is over?" he asked me. "Speak grammatically!"

"I will go to the States."

5. *fratellanza* (frä′täl-än′zä) and *abnegazione* (äb′nā-gä′tzyō′nĕ): brotherhood and self-denial.

"Are you married?"

"No, but I hope to be."

"The more of a fool you are," he said. He seemed very angry. "A man must not marry."

"Why, Signor Maggiore?"[6]

"Don't call me 'Signor Maggiore.' "

"Why must not a man marry?"

"He cannot marry. He cannot marry," he said angrily. "If he is to lose everything, he should not place himself in a position to lose that. He should not place himself in a position to lose. He should find things he cannot lose."

He spoke very angrily and bitterly, and looked straight ahead while he talked.

"But why should he necessarily lose it?"

"He'll lose it," the major said. He was looking at the wall. Then he looked down at the machine and jerked his little hand out from between the straps and slapped it hard against his thigh. "He'll lose it," he almost shouted. "Don't argue with me!" Then he called to the attendant who ran the machines. "Come and turn this damned thing off."

He went back into the other room for the light treatment and the massage. Then I heard him ask the doctor if he might use his telephone and he shut the door. When he came back into the room, I was sitting in another machine. He was wearing his cape and had his cap on, and he came directly toward my machine and put his arm on my shoulder.

"I am so sorry," he said, and patted me on the shoulder with his good hand. "I would not be rude. My wife has just died. You must forgive me."

"Oh—"I said, feeling sick for him. "I am *so* sorry."

He stood there biting his lower lip. "It is very difficult," he said. "I cannot resign myself."

6. **Signor Maggiore** (sēn-yôr′, -yōr′ mä-jô′rĕ): a respectful title meaning "Mr. Major."

He looked straight past me and out through the window. Then he began to cry. "I am utterly unable to resign myself," he said and choked. And then crying, his head up looking at nothing, carrying himself straight and soldierly, with tears on both his cheeks and biting his lips, he walked past the machines and out the door.

The doctor told me that the major's wife, who was very young and whom he had not married until he was definitely invalided out of the war, had died of pneumonia. She had been sick only a few days. No one expected her to die. The major did not come to the hospital for three days. Then he came at the usual hour, wearing a black band on the sleeve of his uniform. When he came back, there were large framed photographs around the wall, of all sorts of wounds before and after they had been cured by the machines. In front of the machine the major used were three photographs of hands like his that were completely restored. I do not know where the doctor got them. I always understood we were the first to use the machines. The photographs did not make much difference to the major because he only looked out of the window.

Reading Check

1. Why does the narrator go to the hospital every afternoon?
2. What injury has the major suffered?
3. How does the doctor attempt to gain the major's confidence?
4. What causes the narrator's three Italian friends to change their manner toward him?
5. What happens to make the major so bitter about the subject of marriage?

On the surface "In Another Country" tells a simple story. A young man, the story's unnamed narrator, has been wounded during the war in Europe, and every afternoon he goes to a hospital in Milan for treatment on a machine. In the hospital he meets several other wounded soldiers and learns many things: he meets three young and friendly Italian officers who, like him, have been wounded. With these boys the narrator walks through the streets of Milan, and finds that they all are hated by the people "because we were officers." Besides discovering such powerful antiwar sentiment among the Italian people, the narrator discovers that the "hawks" lose respect for him when they find out that he received medals only because he is an American. A wound, being accidental, is incidental.

This point is driven home to the narrator through his meeting with a fourth young man who, during his first hour at the front, has suffered a terrible wound to his nose and will have to have his face rebuilt. From this young man's horrible misfortune the narrator learns about the total arbitrariness of war: imagine a young man, full of promise, having his face shattered during his first hour at the front while other soldiers can fight on and on, for indefinite periods of time, without suffering any injuries. Moreover, imagine suffering so terribly in a war in which your fellow citizens hate you.

Finally, the narrator meets a major who has also suffered a debilitating injury, to his hand—and who becomes by the end of the story the most significant of the young man's acquaintances. The narrator's relationship with the major develops into that of mentor, or tutor, and student. This is clearest, of course, when the major is teaching Italian grammar to the narrator. But it is also noticeable when the major is scolding the young man for wanting to marry or telling about his own wife's death. At these moments the major is doing no less than teaching his young friend about how to live.

Hemingway's characteristic concerns about appropriate personal conduct and stoicism in the face of a senseless universe are addressed in this mentor-student relationship. We see the major, devastated both by a terrible wound and the loss of his wife, conducting himself stoically and with dignity. When the doctor talks about the severity of his injury, for example, the major responds realistically. He doesn't look for false hope. The doctor shows the major pictures of a withered hand after physical therapy has resulted in minor improvement and asks, "You have confidence?" The major responds simply, "No." In the hard, senseless, and sometimes violent world that Hemingway depicts in his fiction, a world in which a boy can be injured irreparably during his very first hour at the front, life often deals you a bad hand (literally, in this story). The heroic response for Hemingway is the major's: to maintain a gruff exterior and do the best you can.

"In Another Country" is well regarded because it successfully conveys certain of Hemingway's characteristic themes. The story also provides a good example of both Hemingway's style and his modernist credo. Unlike nineteenth-century fiction, with its strict attention to a story's beginning, middle, and end, Hemingway's story starts arbitrarily, right in the middle of the action. In addition to taking this modernist literary position, Hemingway conveys a modernist attitude toward the postwar world. Machines, which can heal wounds and offer so much hope for the future, cause the almost unspeakable horrors of the war. Machines, in other words, represent the postwar world: in their ability to both injure and heal, they possess no morality.

Hemingway's style is perhaps the most imitated prose style in twentieth-century American writing. Conjunctions such as "and" and "but" are used over and over again to connect sentences and thereby tighten the story. There is a minimum of description but considerable dialogue, and when characters speak they do so in a clipped, almost abbreviated manner. There is a reliance on the most readily available word to convey meaning, and an absolute dearth of adjectives. What Hemingway achieves with this spare, almost hypnotic style is an immediacy that is striking and is an effective vehicle for a scaled down, deceptively simple story of individual fortitude.

Analyzing and Interpreting the Story

1. Reread the opening paragraph of the story. Why do you think Hemingway begins his story with a description of fall?

2. The narrator says of one of his companions, "He had lived a very long time with death and was a little detached. We were all a little detached. . . ."
a. How does Hemingway show this detachment?
b. Is the major also detached?

3a. How do the young men spend their time?
b. In what way have they been changed by the war?

4. At the opening of the story the narrator says, "In the fall the war was always there, but we did not go to it any more." Midway through the story he repeats this idea: "We only knew then that there was always the war, but that we were not going to it any more." **a.** What is the effect of this repetition? **b.** Why does Hemingway choose such simple words?

5. We are told that the major "did not believe in bravery." **a.** How is this attitude different from that of the "hawks"? **b.** How is the narrator different from his companions?

6. Toward the end of the story the major tells the narrator about his wife's death. **a.** What do you think is the purpose of this incident? **b.** Does it reveal another side to the major's character?

7. The men who have been wounded in the war seem to have suffered more than physical injury. In what other ways have they been wounded?

8. What significance is there to the title of the story?

9. Do you think the narrator is any different at the end of the story than he is at its beginning? Give reasons to support your answer.

Analyzing Style

Hemingway once told an interviewer, "I always try to write on the principle of the iceberg. There is seven-eighths of it under water for every part that shows." How well does this description fit "In Another Country"? Choose a passage of prose and analyze its style. Take into consideration the kinds of words used, the structure and length of sentences, the extent to which Hemingway relies on dialogue and description rather than explicit interpretation, and journalistic techniques. Tell what is accomplished by his spare and severe style.

JOHN STEINBECK
1902–1968

John Steinbeck.
© Erich Hartmann / Magnum Photos

When John Steinbeck was awarded the Nobel Prize for literature in 1962, the Swedish Literary Academy cited the author's "great feeling for nature, for the tilled soil, the wasteland, the mountains and the ocean coasts . . . in the midst of, and beyond, the world of human beings." The Academy also noted "a strain of grim humor which to some extent redeems his often cruel . . . motif" and a sympathy for "the oppressed, the misfits, the distressed." Much of Steinbeck's work is marked by a conflict between his feeling for nature and his sympathy for human beings. Steinbeck sees human beings as subject to all the biological forces that drive all the rest of nature. Those forces are involved in a purposive, evolutionary development of life. To be natural, rather than respectable, is, in the world of Steinbeck's fiction, to be in phase with the controlling primal force of the universe. With the detachment of a scientist, Steinbeck can view his characters as living on a purely animal level, moved by forces they can hardly understand or control. But at times there flickers in his work a vision of individuals striving toward wisdom and, even under the cruelest circumstances, retaining a measure of dignity.

Steinbeck was born in Salinas, California, the son of a county treasurer and a schoolteacher. Much of his early work is concerned with the prosperous ranches of the Salinas Valley and with the wild Monterey coast where he lived for a time. After graduating from high school, he attended Stanford University and devoted special attention to the study of marine biology. He worked at many jobs. Until the publication of *Tortilla Flat* in 1935, his writing earned him little money. In 1937 he published a best-selling novel, *Of Mice and Men,* which was made into a successful Broadway play and a motion picture. Moved by the plight of the "Okies"—Oklahoma farmers who, unable to make a living from their land, migrated to California to seek jobs as fruit pickers—he wrote *The Grapes of Wrath,* a sensational best seller which was awarded the Pulitzer Prize and made Steinbeck one of the most widely known writers of our time. A shy man, he escaped from his public by leading a marine biology expedition to the Galápagos Islands. Later, with E. F. Ricketts, another member of the party, he described the expedition in *The Sea of Cortez.*

A number of Steinbeck's later works have locales other than California. *The Moon Is Down* deals with the Nazi occupation of a Scandinavian village; *The Pearl* tells of the tragedy of a Mexican family; and *The Winter of Our Discontent* is concerned with the moral choices confronting a citizen of a New England town. *East of Eden,* a long, ambitious novel published in 1952, has been praised for its originality and called Steinbeck's finest novel. One of Steinbeck's most popular books is *Travels with Charley,* an account of the author's tour of America with his dog Charley.

Magic Mountain by John O'Shea (1881–1956). Oil on canvas.

Flight

About fifteen miles below Monterey, on the wild coast, the Torres family had their farm, a few sloping acres above a cliff that dropped to the brown reefs and to the hissing white waters of the ocean. Behind the farm the stone mountains stood up against the sky. The farm buildings huddled like the clinging aphids[1] on the mountain skirts, crouched low to the ground as though the wind might blow them into the sea. The little shack, the rattling, rotting barn were gray-bitten with sea salt, beaten by the damp wind until they had taken on the color of the granite hills. Two horses, a red cow and a red calf, half a dozen pigs and a flock of lean, multicolored chickens stocked the place. A little corn was raised on the sterile

1. **aphids** (ā′fĭdz): small insects that live on plants and suck their juices.

slope, and it grew short and thick under the wind, and all the cobs formed on the landward sides of the stalks.

Mama Torres, a lean, dry woman with ancient eyes, had ruled the farm for ten years, ever since her husband tripped over a stone in the field one day and fell full length on a rattlesnake. When one is bitten on the chest there is not much that can be done.

Mama Torres had three children, two undersized black ones of twelve and fourteen, Emilio[2] and Rosy, whom Mama kept fishing on the rocks below the farm when the sea was kind and when the truant officer was in some distant part of Monterey County. And there was Pepé,[3] the tall smiling son of nineteen, a gentle, affectionate boy, but very lazy. Pepé had a tall head, pointed at the top, and from its peak coarse black hair grew down like a thatch all around. Over his smiling little eyes Mama cut a straight bang so he could see. Pepé had sharp Indian cheekbones and an eagle nose, but his mouth was as sweet and shapely as a girl's mouth, and his chin was fragile and chiseled. He was loose and gangling, all legs and feet and wrists, and he was very lazy. Mama thought him fine and brave, but she never told him so. She said, "Some lazy cow must have got into thy father's family, else how could I have a son like thee." And she said, "When I carried thee, a sneaking lazy coyote came out of the brush and looked at me one day. That must have made thee so."

Pepé smiled sheepishly and stabbed at the ground with his knife to keep the blade sharp and free from rust. It was his inheritance, that knife, his father's knife. The long heavy blade folded back into the black handle. There was a button on the handle. When Pepé pressed the button, the blade leaped out ready for use. The knife was with Pepé always, for it had been his father's knife.

One sunny morning when the sea below the cliff was glinting and blue and the white surf creamed on the reef, when even the stone mountains looked kindly, Mama Torres called out the door of the shack, "Pepé, I have a labor for thee."

There was no answer. Mama listened. From behind the barn she heard a burst of laughter. She lifted her full long skirt and walked in the direction of the noise.

Pepé was sitting on the ground with his back against a box. His white teeth glistened. On either side of him stood the two black ones, tense and expectant. Fifteen feet away a redwood post was set in the ground. Pepé's right hand lay limply in his lap, and in the palm the big black knife rested. The blade was closed back into the handle. Pepé looked smiling at the sky.

Suddenly Emilio cried, "Ya!"

Pepé's wrist flicked like the head of a snake. The blade seemed to fly open in midair, and with a thump the point dug into the redwood post, and the black handle quivered. The three burst into excited laughter. Rosy ran to the post and pulled out the knife and brought it back to Pepé. He closed the blade and settled the knife carefully in his listless palm again. He grinned self-consciously at the sky.

"Ya!"

The heavy knife lanced out and sunk into the post again. Mama moved forward like a ship and scattered the play.

"All day you do foolish things with the knife, like a toy baby," she stormed. "Get up on thy huge feet that eat up shoes. Get up!" She took him by one loose shoulder and hoisted at him. Pepé grinned sheepishly and came halfheartedly to his feet. "Look!" Mama cried. "Big lazy, you must catch the horse and put on him thy father's saddle. You must ride to Monterey. The medicine bottle is empty. There is no salt. Go thou now, Peanut! Catch the horse."

A revolution took place in the relaxed figure of Pepé. "To Monterey, me? Alone? Sí, Mama."

She scowled at him. "Do not think, big sheep, that you will buy candy. No, I will give you only enough for the medicine and the salt."

2. **Emilio** (ä-mēl′yō).
3. **Pepé** (pā-pā′).

Pepé smiled. "Mama, you will put the hatband on the hat?"

She relented then. "Yes, Pepé. You may wear the hatband."

His voice grew insinuating. "And the green handkerchief, Mama?"

"Yes, if you go quickly and return with no trouble, the silk green handkerchief will go. If you make sure to take off the handkerchief when you eat so no spot may fall on it."

"*Sí*, Mama. I will be careful. I am a man."

"Thou? A man? Thou art a peanut."

He went to the rickety barn and brought out a rope, and he walked agilely enough up the hill to catch the horse.

When he was ready and mounted before the door, mounted on his father's saddle that was so old that the oaken frame showed through torn leather in many places, then Mama brought out the round black hat with the tooled leather band, and she reached up and knotted the green silk handkerchief about his neck. Pepé's blue denim coat was much darker than his jeans, for it had been washed much less often.

Mama handed up the big medicine bottle and the silver coins. "That for the medicine," she said, "and that for the salt. That for a candle to burn for the papa. That for *dulces*[4] for the little ones. Our friend Mrs. Rodriguez[5] will give you dinner and maybe a bed for the night. When you go to the church, say only ten paternosters[6] and only twenty-five Ave Marias.[7] Oh! I know, big coyote. You would sit there flapping your mouth over Aves all day while you looked at the candles and the holy pictures. That is not good devotion to stare at the pretty things."

The black hat, covering the high pointed head and black thatched hair of Pepé, gave him dignity and age. He sat the rangy horse well. Mama thought how handsome he was, dark and lean and tall. "I would not send thee now alone, thou little one, except for the medicine," she said softly. "It is not good to have no medicine, for who knows when the toothache will come, or the sadness of the stomach. These things are."

"*Adiós*, Mama," Pepé cried. "I will come back soon. You may send me often alone. I am a man."

"Thou art a foolish chicken."

He straightened his shoulders, flipped the reins against the horse's shoulder, and rode away. He turned once and saw that they still watched him. Emilio and Rosy and Mama. Pepé grinned with pride and gladness and lifted the tough buckskin horse to a trot.

When he had dropped out of sight over a little dip in the road, Mama turned to the black ones, but she spoke to herself. "He is nearly a man now," she said. "It will be a nice thing to have a man in the house again." Her eyes sharpened on the children. "Go to the rocks now. The tide is going out. There will be abalones[8] to be found." She put the iron hooks into their hands and saw them down the steep trail to the reefs. She brought the smooth stone metate[9] to the doorway and sat grinding her corn to flour and looking occasionally at the road over which Pepé had gone. The noonday came and then the afternoon, when the little ones beat the abalones on a rock to make them tender and Mama patted the tortillas[10] to make them thin. They ate dinner as the red sun was plunging down toward the ocean. They sat on the doorsteps and watched a big white moon come over the mountaintops.

Mama said, "He is now at the house of our friend Mrs. Rodriguez. She will give him nice things to eat and maybe a present."

Emilio said, "Someday I, too, will ride to Monterey for medicine. Did Pepé come to be a man today?"

Mama said wisely, "A boy gets to be a man

---

4. ***dulces*** (do͞ol′sās): sweets.
5. **Rodriguez** (rŏ-drē′gās′).
6. **ten paternosters:** ten repetitions of the Lord's Prayer.
7. **Ave Marias:** prayers to the Virgin Mary, beginning "Hail Mary."

8. **abalones** (ăb′ə-lō′nēz): large shellfish.
9. **metate** (mä-tä′tä′): a stone used in the southwestern United States for grinding cereal seeds.
10. **tortillas** (tôr-tē′yəs): flat Mexican bread.

when a man is needed. Remember this thing. I have known boys forty years old because there was no need for a man."

Soon afterward they retired, Mama in her big oak bed on one side of the room, Emilio and Rosy in their boxes full of straw and sheepskins on the other side of the room.

The moon went over the sky and the surf roared on the rocks. The roosters crowed the first call. The surf subsided to a whispering surge against the reef. The moon dropped toward the sea. The roosters crowed again.

The moon was near down to the water when Pepé rode on a winded horse to his home flat. His dog bounced out and circled the horse, yelping with pleasure. Pepé slid off the saddle to the ground. The weathered little shack was silver in the moonlight and the square shadow of it was black to the north and east. Against the east the piling mountains were misty with light; their tops melted into the sky.

Pepé walked wearily up the three steps and into the house. It was dark inside. There was a rustle in the corner.

Mama cried out from her bed. "Who comes? Pepé, is it thou?"

"*Sí*, Mama."

"Did you get the medicine?"

"*Sí*, Mama."

"Well, go to sleep, then. I thought you would be sleeping at the house of Mrs. Rodriguez." Pepé stood silently in the dark room. "Why do you stand there, Pepé? Did you drink wine?"

"*Sí*, Mama."

"Well, go to bed then and sleep out the wine."

His voice was tired and patient, but very firm. "Light the candle, Mama. I must go away into the mountains."

"What is this, Pepé? You are crazy." Mama struck a sulfur match and held the little blue burr until the flame spread up the stick. She set light to the candle on the floor beside her bed. "Now, Pepé, what is this you say?" She looked anxiously into his face.

He was changed. The fragile quality seemed to have gone from his chin. His mouth was less full than it had been, the lines of the lips were straighter, but in his eyes the greatest change had taken place. There was no laughter in them any more, nor any bashfulness. They were sharp and bright and purposeful.

He told her in a tired monotone, told her everything just as it had happened. A few people came into the kitchen of Mrs. Rodriguez. There was wine to drink. Pepé drank wine. The little quarrel—the man started toward Pepé and then the knife—it went almost by itself. It flew, it darted before Pepé knew it. As he talked, Mama's face grew stern, and it seemed to grow more lean. Pepé finished. "I am a man now, Mama. The man said names to me I could not allow."

Mama nodded. "Yes, thou art a man, my poor little Pepé. Thou art a man. I have seen it coming on thee. I have watched you throwing the knife into the post, and I have been afraid." For a moment her face had softened, but now it grew stern again. "Come! We must get you ready. Go. Awaken Emilio and Rosy. Go quickly."

Pepé stepped over to the corner where his brother and sister slept among the sheepskins. He leaned down and shook them gently. "Come, Rosy! Come, Emilio! The Mama says you must arise."

The little black ones sat up and rubbed their eyes in the candlelight. Mama was out of bed now, her long black skirt over her nightgown. "Emilio," she cried. "Go up and catch the other horse for Pepé. Quickly, now! Quickly." Emilio put his legs in his overalls and stumbled sleepily out the door.

"You heard no one behind you on the road?" Mama demanded.

"No, Mama. I listened carefully. No one was on the road."

Mama darted like a bird about the room. From a nail on the wall she took a canvas water bag and threw it on the floor. She stripped a blanket from her bed and rolled it into a tight tube and tied the ends with string. From a box beside the stove she lifted a flour sack half full of black stringy jerky. "Your father's black coat, Pepé. Here, put it on."

Pepé stood in the middle of the floor watching her activity. She reached behind the door and brought out the rifle, a long 38–56, worn shiny the whole length of the barrel. Pepé took it from her and held it in the crook of his elbow. Mama brought a little leather bag and counted the cartridges into his hand. "Only ten left," she warned. "You must not waste them."

Emilio put his head in the door. " *'Qui 'st 'l caballo,*[11] Mama."

"Put on the saddle from the other horse. Tie on the blanket. Here, tie the jerky to the saddle horn."

Still Pepé stood silently watching his mother's frantic activity. His chin looked hard, and his sweet mouth was drawn and thin. His little eyes followed Mama about the room almost suspiciously.

Rosy asked softly, "Where goes Pepé?"

Mama's eyes were fierce. "Pepé goes on a journey. Pepé is a man now. He has a man's thing to do."

Pepé straightened his shoulders. His mouth changed until he looked very much like Mama.

At last the preparation was finished. The loaded horse stood outside the door. The water bag dripped a line of moisture down the bay shoulder.

The moonlight was being thinned by the dawn, and the big white moon was near down to the sea. The family stood by the shack. Mama confronted Pepé. "Look, my son! Do not stop until it is dark again. Do not sleep even though you are tired. Take care of the horse in order that he may not stop of weariness. Remember to be careful with the bullets—there are only ten. Do not fill thy stomach with jerky or it will make thee sick. Eat a little jerky and fill thy stomach with grass. When thou comest to the high mountains, if thou seest any of the dark watching men, go not near to them nor try to speak to them. And

11. *'Qui 'st'l caballo* (kēst'l kä-bä'yō): Here is the horse (colloquial Spanish).

forget not thy prayers." She put her lean hands on Pepé's shoulders, stood on her toes and kissed him formally on both cheeks, and Pepé kissed her on both cheeks. Then he went to Emilio and Rosy and kissed both of their cheeks.

Pepé turned back to Mama. He seemed to look for a little softness, a little weakness in her. His eyes were searching, but Mama's face remained fierce. "Go now," she said. "Do not wait to be caught like a chicken."

Pepé pulled himself into the saddle. "I am a man," he said.

It was the first dawn when he rode up the hill toward the little canyon which let a trail into the mountains. Moonlight and daylight fought with each other, and the two warring qualities made it difficult to see. Before Pepé had gone a hundred yards, the outlines of his figure were misty; and long before he entered the canyon, he had become a gray, indefinite shadow.

Mama stood stiffly in front of her doorstep, and on either side of her stood Emilio and Rosy. They cast furtive glances at Mama now and then.

When the gray shape of Pepé melted into the hillside and disappeared, Mama relaxed. She began the high, whining keen[12] of the death wail. "Our beautiful—our brave," she cried. "Our protector, our son is gone." Emilio and Rosy moaned beside her. "Our beautiful—our brave, he is gone." It was the formal wail. It rose to a high piercing whine and subsided to a moan. Mama raised it three times and then she turned and went into the house and shut the door.

Emilio and Rosy stood wondering in the dawn. They heard Mama whimpering in the house. They went out to sit on the cliff above the ocean. They touched shoulders. "When did Pepé come to be a man?" Emilio asked.

"Last night," said Rosy. "Last night in Monterey." The ocean clouds turned red with the sun that was behind the mountains."

12. **keen:** a lamentation, or dirge, for the dead.

"We will have no breakfast," said Emilio. "Mama will not want to cook." Rosy did not answer him. "Where is Pepé gone?" he asked.

Rosy looked around at him. She drew her knowledge from the quiet air. "He has gone on a journey. He will never come back."

"Is he dead? Do you think he is dead?"

Rosy looked back at the ocean again. A little steamer, drawing a line of smoke, sat on the edge of the horizon. "He is not dead," Rosy explained. "Not yet."

Pepé rested the big rifle across the saddle in front of him. He let the horse walk up the hill and he didn't look back. The stony slope took on a coat of short brush so that Pepé found the entrance to a trail and entered it.

When he came to the canyon opening, he swung once in his saddle and looked back, but the houses were swallowed in the misty light. Pepé jerked forward again. The high shoulder of the canyon closed in on him. His horse stretched out its neck and sighed and settled to the trail.

It was a well-worn path, dark soft leaf-mold earth strewn with broken pieces of sandstone. The trail rounded the shoulder of the canyon and dropped steeply into the bed of the stream. In the shallows the water ran smoothly, glinting in the first morning sun. Small round stones on the bottom were as brown as rust with sun moss. In the sand along the edges of the stream the tall, rich wild mint grew, while in the water itself the cress,[13] old and tough, had gone to heavy seed.

The path went into the stream and emerged on the other side. The horse sloshed into the water and stopped. Pepé dropped his bridle and let the beast drink of the running water.

Soon the canyon sides became steep and the first giant sentinel redwoods guarded the trail, great round red trunks bearing foliage as green and lacy as ferns. Once Pepé was among the trees, the sun was lost. A perfumed and purple light lay in the pale green of the un-

derbrush. Gooseberry bushes and blackberries and tall ferns lined the stream, and overhead the branches of the redwoods met and cut off the sky.

Pepé drank from the water bag, and he reached into the flour sack and brought out a black string of jerky. His white teeth gnawed at the string until the tough meat parted. He chewed slowly and drank occasionally from the water bag. His little eyes were slumberous and tired, but the muscles of his face were hardset. The earth of the trail was black now. It gave up a hollow sound under the walking hoofbeats.

The stream fell more sharply. Little waterfalls splashed on the stones. Five-fingered ferns hung over the water and dropped spray from their fingertips. Pepé rode half over his saddle, dangling one leg loosely. He picked a bay leaf from a tree beside the way and put it into his mouth for a moment to flavor the dry jerky. He held the gun loosely across the pommel.

Suddenly he squared in his saddle, swung the horse from the trail and kicked it hurriedly up behind a big redwood tree. He pulled up the reins tight against the bit to keep the horse from whinnying. His face was intent and his nostrils quivered a little.

A hollow pounding came down the trail, and a horseman rode by, a fat man with red cheeks and a white stubble beard. His horse put down his head and blubbered at the trail when it came to the place where Pepé had turned off. "Hold up!" said the man, and he pulled up his horse's head.

When the last sound of the hoofs died away, Pepé came back into the trail again. He did not relax in the saddle any more. He lifted the big rifle and swung the lever to throw a shell into the chamber, and then he let down the hammer to half cock.

The trail grew very steep. Now the redwood trees were smaller and their tops were dead, bitten dead where the wind reached them. The horse plodded on; the sun went slowly overhead and started down toward the afternoon.

13. **cress** (or **watercress**): an edible white-flowered plant that grows in clear running water.

Mammoth Cove, Carmel Highlands by William Ritschel (1864–1949). Oil on canvas.

Where the stream came out of a side canyon, the trail left it. Pepé dismounted and watered his horse and filled up his water bag. As soon as the trail had parted from the stream, the trees were gone and only the thick brittle sage and manzanita[14] and the chaparral[15] edged the trail. And the soft black earth was gone, too, leaving only the light tan broken rock for the trail bed. Lizards scampered away into the brush as the horse rattled over the little stones.

Pepé turned in his saddle and looked back. He was in the open now: he could be seen from a distance. As he ascended the trail the country grew more rough and terrible and dry. The way wound about the bases of great square rocks. Little gray rabbits skittered in the brush. A bird made a monotonous high creaking. Eastward the bare rock mountain-tops were pale and powder-dry under the dropping sun. The horse plodded up and up the trail toward the little v in the ridge which was the pass.

Pepé looked suspiciously back every minute or so, and his eyes sought the tops of the ridges ahead. Once, on a white barren spur, he saw a black figure for a moment; but he looked quickly away, for it was one of the dark watch-

14. **manzanita** (măn′zə-nē′tə): shrubs.
15. **chaparral** (shăp′ə-răl′): a thicket of shrubs, thorny bushes, or dwarf trees.

John Steinbeck   **667**

ers. No one knew who the watchers were, nor where they lived, but it was better to ignore them and never to show interest in them. They did not bother one who stayed on the trail and minded his own business.

The air was parched and full of light dust blown by the breeze from the eroding mountains. Pepé drank sparingly from his bag and corked it tightly and hung it on the horn again. The trail moved up the dry shale hillside, avoiding rocks, dropping under clefts, climbing in and out of old water scars. When he arrived at the little pass he stopped and looked back for a long time. No dark watchers were to be seen now. The trail behind was empty. Only the high tops of the redwoods indicated where the stream flowed.

Pepé rode on through the pass. His little eyes were nearly closed with weariness, but his face was stern, relentless, and manly. The high mountain wind coasted sighing through the pass and whistled on the edges of the big blocks of broken granite. In the air, a red-tailed hawk sailed over close to the ridge and screamed angrily. Pepé went slowly through the broken jagged pass and looked down on the other side.

The trail dropped quickly, staggering among broken rock. At the bottom of the slope there was a dark crease, thick with brush, and on the other side of the crease a little flat, in which a grove of oak trees grew. A scar of green grass cut across the flat. And behind the flat another mountain rose, desolate with dead rocks and starving little black bushes. Pepé drank from the bag again, for the air was so dry that it encrusted his nostrils and burned his lips. He put the horse down the trail. The hoofs slipped and struggled on the steep way, starting little stones that rolled off into the brush. The sun was gone behind the westward mountain now, but still it glowed brilliantly on the oaks and on the grassy flat. The rocks and the hillsides still sent up waves of the heat they had gathered from the day's sun.

Pepé looked up to the top of the next dry withered ridge. He saw a dark form against the sky, a man's figure standing on top of a rock, and he glanced away quickly not to appear curious. When a moment later he looked up again, the figure was gone.

Downward the trail was quickly covered. Sometimes the horse floundered for footing, sometimes set his feet and slid a little way. They came at last to the bottom where the dark chaparral was higher than Pepé's head. He held up his rifle on one side and his arm on the other to shield his face from the sharp brittle fingers of the brush.

Up and out of the crease he rode, and up a little cliff. The grassy flat was before him, and the round comfortable oaks. For a moment he studied the trail down which he had come, but there was no movement and no sound from it. Finally he rode out over the flat, to the green streak, and at the upper end of the damp he found a little spring welling out of the earth and dropping into a dug basin before it seeped out over the flat.

Pepé filled his bag first, and then he let the thirsty horse drink out of the pool. He led the horse to the clump of oaks, and in the middle of the grove, fairly protected from sight on all sides, he took off the saddle and the bridle and laid them on the ground. The horse stretched his jaws sideways and yawned. Pepé knotted the lead rope about the horse's neck and tied him to a sapling among the oaks, where he could graze in a fairly large circle.

When the horse was gnawing hungrily at the dry grass, Pepé went to the saddle and took a black string of jerky from the sack and strolled to an oak tree on the edge of the grove, from under which he could watch the trail. He sat down in the crisp dry oak leaves and automatically felt for his big black knife to cut the jerky, but he had no knife. He leaned back on his elbow and gnawed at the tough strong meat. His face was blank, but it was a man's face.

The bright evening light washed the eastern ridge, but the valley was darkening. Doves flew down from the hills to the spring, and the quail came running out of the brush and joined them, calling clearly to one another.

Out of the corner of his eye Pepé saw a shadow grow out of the bushy crease. He turned his head slowly. A big spotted wildcat was creeping toward the spring, belly to the ground, moving like thought.

Pepé cocked his rifle and edged the muzzle slowly around. Then he looked apprehensively up the trail and dropped the hammer again. From the ground beside him he picked an oak twig and threw it toward the spring. The quail flew up with a roar and the doves whistled away. The big cat stood up; for a long moment he looked at Pepé with cold yellow eyes, and then fearlessly walked back into the gulch.

The dusk gathered quickly in the deep valley. Pepé muttered his prayers, put his head down on his arm and went instantly to sleep.

The moon came up and filled the valley with cold blue light, and the wind swept rustling down from the peaks. The owls worked up and down the slopes looking for rabbits. Down in the brush of the gulch a coyote gabbled. The oak trees whispered softly in the night breeze.

Pepé started up, listening. His horse had whinnied. The moon was just slipping behind the western ridge, leaving the valley in darkness behind it. Pepé sat tensely gripping his rifle. From far up the trail he heard an answering whinny and the crash of shod hoofs on the broken rock. He jumped to his feet, ran to his horse and led it under the trees. He threw on the saddle and cinched it tight for the steep trail, caught the unwilling head and forced the bit into the mouth. He felt the saddle to make sure the water bag and the sack of jerky were there. Then he mounted and turned up the hill.

It was velvet-dark. The horse found the entrance to the trail where it left the flat, and started up, stumbling and slipping on the rocks. Pepé's hand rose up to his head. His hat was gone. He had left it under the oak tree.

The horse had struggled far up the trail when the first change of dawn came into the air, a steel grayness as light mixed thoroughly with dark. Gradually the sharp snaggled edge of the ridge stood out above them, rotten granite tortured and eaten by the winds of time. Pepé had dropped his reins on the horn, leaving direction to the horse. The brush grabbed at his legs in the dark until one knee of his jeans was ripped.

Gradually the light flowed down over the ridge. The starved brush and rocks stood out in the half-light, strange and lonely in high perspective. Then there came warmth into the light. Pepé drew up and looked back, but he could see nothing in the darker valley below. The sky turned blue over the coming sun. In the waste of the mountainside, the poor dry brush grew only three feet high. Here and there, big outcroppings of unrotted granite stood up like moldering houses. Pepé relaxed a little. He drank from his water bag and bit off a piece of jerky. A single eagle flew over, high in the light.

Without warning Pepé's horse screamed and fell on its side. He was almost down before the rifle crash echoed up from the valley. From a hole behind the struggling shoulder, a stream of bright crimson blood pumped and stopped and pumped and stopped. The hoofs threshed on the ground. Pepé lay half stunned beside the horse. He looked slowly down the hill. A piece of sage clipped off beside his head and another crash echoed up from side to side of the canyon. Pepé flung himself frantically behind a bush.

He crawled up the hill on his knees and one hand. His right hand held the rifle up off the ground and pushed it ahead of him. He moved with the instinctive care of an animal. Rapidly he wormed his way toward one of the big outcroppings of granite on the hill above him. Where the brush was high he doubled up and ran; but where the cover was slight he wriggled forward on his stomach, pushing the rifle ahead of him. In the last little distance there was no cover at all. Pepé poised and then he darted across the space and flashed around the corner of the rock.

He leaned panting against the stone. When his breath came easier he moved along behind the big rock until he came to a narrow split that offered a thin section of vision down the hill. Pepé lay on his stomach and pushed the rifle barrel through the slit and waited.

The sun reddened the western ridges now. Already the buzzards were settling down toward the place where the horse lay. A small brown bird scratched in the dead sage leaves directly in front of the rifle muzzle. The coasting eagle flew back toward the rising sun.

Pepé saw a little movement in the brush far below. His grip tightened on the gun. A little brown doe stepped daintily out on the trail and crossed it and disappeared into the brush again. For a long time Pepé waited. Far below he could see the little flat and the oak trees and the slash of green. Suddenly his eyes flashed back at the trail again. A quarter of a mile down there had been a quick movement in the chaparral. The rifle swung over. The front sight nestled in the v of the rear sight. Pepé studied for a moment and then raised the rear sight a notch. The little movement in the brush came again. The sight settled on it. Pepé squeezed the trigger. The explosion crashed down the mountain and up the other side, and came rattling back. The whole side of the slope grew still. No more movement. And then a white streak cut into the granite of the slit and a bullet whined away and a crash sounded up from below. Pepé felt a sharp pain in his right hand. A sliver of granite was sticking out from between his first and second knuckles and the point protruded from his palm. Carefully he pulled out the sliver of stone. The wound bled evenly and gently. No vein or artery was cut.

Pepé looked into a little dusty cave in the rock and gathered a handful of spider web, and he pressed the mass into the cut, plastering the soft web into the blood. The flow stopped almost at once.

The rifle was on the ground. Pepé picked it up, levered a new shell into the chamber. And then he slid into the brush on his stomach. Far to the right he crawled, and then up the hill, moving slowly and carefully, crawling to cover and resting and then crawling again.

In the mountains the sun is high in its arc before it penetrates the gorges. The hot face looked over the hill and brought instant heat with it. The white light beat on the rocks and reflected from them and rose up quivering from the earth again, and the rocks and bushes seemed to quiver behind the air.

Pepé crawled in the general direction of the ridge peak, zigzagging for cover. The deep cut between his knuckles began to throb. He crawled close to a rattlesnake before he saw it, and when it raised its dry head and made a soft beginning whir, he backed up and took another way. The quick gray lizards flashed in front of him, raising a tiny line of dust. He found another mass of spider web and pressed it against his throbbing hand.

Pepé was pushing the rifle with his left hand now. Little drops of sweat ran to the ends of his coarse black hair and rolled down his cheeks. His lips and tongue were growing thick and heavy. His lips writhed to draw saliva into his mouth. His little dark eyes were uneasy and suspicious. Once when a gray lizard paused in front of him on the parched ground and turned its head sideways, he crushed it flat with a stone.

When the sun slid past noon he had not gone a mile. He crawled exhaustedly a last hundred yards to a patch of high sharp manzanita, crawled desperately, and when the patch was reached he wriggled in among the tough gnarly trunks and dropped his head on his left arm. There was little shade in the meager brush, but there was cover and safety. Pepé went to sleep as he lay and the sun beat on his back. A few little birds hopped close to him and peered and hopped away. Pepé squirmed in his sleep and he raised and dropped his wounded hand again and again.

The sun went down behind the peaks and the cool evening came, and then the dark. A coyote yelled from the hillside. Pepé started awake and looked about with misty eyes. His hand was swollen and heavy; a little thread of pain ran up the inside of his arm and settled in a pocket in his armpit. He peered about and then stood up, for the mountains were black and the moon had not yet risen. Pepé stood up in the dark. The coat of his father pressed on his arm. His tongue was swollen until it nearly filled his mouth. He wriggled out of the coat and dropped it in the brush, and then he struggled up the hill, falling over rocks and tearing his way through the brush. The rifle knocked against stones as he went. Little dry avalanches of gravel and shattered stone went whispering down the hill behind him.

After a while the old moon came up and showed the jagged ridgetop ahead of him. By moonlight Pepé traveled more easily. He bent forward so that his throbbing arm hung away from his body. The journey uphill was made in dashes and rests, a frantic rush up a few yards and then a rest. The wind coasted down the slope, rattling the dry stems of the bushes.

The moon was at meridian when Pepé came at last to the sharp backbone of the ridgetop. On the last hundred yards of the rise no soil had clung under the wearing winds. The way was on solid rock. He clambered to the top and looked down on the other side. There was a draw like the last below him, misty with moonlight, brushed with dry struggling sage and chaparral. On the other side the hill rose up sharply and at the top the jagged rotten teeth of the mountain showed against the sky. At the bottom of the cut the brush was thick and dark.

Pepé stumbled down the hill. His throat was almost closed with thirst. At first he tried to run, but immediately he fell and rolled. After that he went more carefully. The moon was just disappearing behind the mountains when he came to the bottom. He crawled into the heavy brush, feeling with his fingers for water. There was no water in the bed of the stream, only damp earth. Pepé laid his gun down and scooped up a handful of mud and put it in his mouth, and then he spluttered and scraped the earth from his tongue with his finger, for the mud drew at his mouth like a poultice. He dug a hole in the stream bed with his fingers, dug a little basin to catch water; but before it was very deep his head fell forward on the damp ground and he slept.

The dawn came and the heat of the day fell on the earth, and still Pepé slept. Late in the afternoon his head jerked up. He looked slowly around. His eyes were slits of weariness. Twenty feet away in the heavy brush a big tawny mountain lion stood looking at him. Its long thick tail waved gracefully; its ears were erect with interest, not laid back dangerously. The lion squatted down on its stomach and watched him.

Pepé looked at the hole he had dug in the earth. A half-inch of muddy water had collected in the bottom. He tore the sleeve from his hurt arm, with his teeth ripped out a little square, soaked it in the water and put it in his mouth. Over and over he filled the cloth and sucked it.

Still the lion sat and watched him. The evening came down but there was no movement on the hills. No birds visited the dry bottom of the cut. Pepé looked occasionally at the lion. The eyes of the yellow beast drooped as though he were about to sleep. He yawned and his long thin red tongue curled out. Suddenly his head jerked around and his nostrils quivered. His big tail lashed. He stood up and slunk like a tawny shadow into the thick brush.

A moment later Pepé heard the sound, the faint far crash of horses' hoofs on gravel. And he heard something else, a high whining yelp of a dog.

Pepé took his rifle in his left hand and he glided into the brush almost as quietly as the lion had. In the darkening evening he crouched up the hill toward the next ridge. Only when the dark came did he stand up. His energy was short. Once it was dark he fell over the rocks and slipped to his knees on the steep slope, but he moved on and on up the hill, climbing and scrambling over the broken hillside.

When he was far up toward the top, he lay

down and slept for a little while. The withered moon, shining on his face, awakened him. He stood up and moved up the hill. Fifty yards away he stopped and turned back, for he had forgotten his rifle. He walked heavily down and poked about in the brush, but he could not find his gun. At last he lay down to rest. The pocket of pain in his armpit had grown more sharp. His arm seemed to swell out and fall with every heartbeat. There was no position lying down where the heavy arm did not press against his armpit.

With the effort of a hurt beast, Pepé got up and moved again toward the top of the ridge. He held his swollen arm away from his body with his left hand. Up the steep hill he dragged himself, a few steps and a rest, and a few more steps. At last he was nearing the top. The moon showed the uneven sharp back of it against the sky.

Pepé's brain spun in a big spiral up and away from him. He slumped to the ground and lay still. The rock ridgetop was only a hundred feet above him.

The moon moved over the sky. Pepé half turned on his back. His tongue tried to make words, but only a thick hissing came from between his lips.

When the dawn came, Pepé pulled himself up. His eyes were sane again. He drew his great puffed arm in front of him and looked at the angry wound. The black line ran up from his wrist to his armpit. Automatically he reached in his pocket for the big black knife, but it was not there. His eyes searched the ground. He picked up a sharp blade of stone and scraped at the wound, sawed at the proud flesh and then squeezed the green juice out in big drops. Instantly he threw back his head and whined like a dog. His whole right side shuddered at the pain, but the pain cleared his head.

In the gray light he struggled up the last slope to the ridge and crawled over and lay down behind a line of rocks. Below him lay a deep canyon exactly like the last, waterless and desolate. There was no flat, no oak trees, not even heavy brush in the bottom of it. And on the other side a sharp ridge stood up, thinly brushed with starving sage, littered with broken granite. Strewn over the hill there were giant outcroppings, and on the top the granite teeth stood out against the sky.

The new day was light now. The flame of the sun came over the ridge and fell on Pepé where he lay on the ground. His coarse black hair was littered with twigs and bits of spider web. His eyes had retreated back into his head. Between his lips the tip of his black tongue showed.

He sat up and dragged his great arm into his lap and nursed it, rocking his body and moaning in his throat. He threw back his head and looked up into the pale sky. A big black bird circled nearly out of sight, and far to the left another was sailing near.

He lifted his head to listen, for a familiar sound had come to him from the valley he had climbed out of; it was the crying yelp of hounds, excited and feverish, on a trail.

Pepé bowed his head quickly. He tried to speak rapid words but only a thick hiss came from his lips. He drew a shaky cross on his breast with his left hand. It was a long struggle to get to his feet. He crawled slowly and mechanically to the top of a big rock on the ridge peak. Once there, he arose slowly, swaying to his feet, and stood erect. Far below he could see the dark brush where he had slept. He braced his feet and stood there, black against the morning sky.

There came a ripping sound at his feet. A piece of stone flew up and a bullet droned off into the next gorge. The hollow crash echoed up from below. Pepé looked down for a moment and then pulled himself straight again.

His body jarred back. His left hand fluttered helplessly toward his breast. The second crash sounded from below. Pepé swung forward and toppled from the rock. His body struck and rolled over and over, starting a little avalanche. And when at last he stopped against a bush, the avalanche slid slowly down and covered up his head.

Reading Check

1. Why does Mama Torres send Pepé to Monterey?
2. Which of his father's possessions has Pepé inherited?
3. Why must Pepé flee into the mountains?
4. How is Pepé injured during his flight?
5. How does Pepé prepare himself for his death?

For Study and Discussion

Analyzing and Interpreting the Story

1a. Describe three impressions that you get of the Torres family life from the first few paragraphs. Support each impression with details from the story. **b.** What admirable qualities do you find in Mama Torres?

2. At the beginning of the story, Pepé is described as "fragile" and "lazy." **a.** How are his appearance and behavior different when he returns from Monterey? **b.** How does Pepé's behavior during his flight support his mother's ideas of what changes a boy into a man?

3a. Is the story more, or less, interesting because you never see the pursuers or know anything about them? **b.** What is the first indication of real danger? **c.** How does Pepé's gradual shedding of his father's possessions (knife, hat, etc.) parallel the increasing hopelessness of his situation?

4a. How does Pepé's flight resemble that of an animal? **b.** What does he do during his flight to retain his dignity as a human being? **c.** Does the ending of the story satisfy you? Why or why not?

Literary Elements

Setting

Setting—the specific time and place—is rarely the most important element of a story, but it almost always influences the story's events, either directly or indirectly. A story must have an appropriate setting. For example, it is unlikely for a tender love story to take place in a butcher shop, or a duel to the death in the reading room of a library. Setting also plays a part in determining the characters of a story. Just as we are all products of our environ-

ment, so good authors show how their characters are shaped by their environment. In some stories, setting is particularly important in building atmosphere or in expressing the author's view of the world. A harsh setting, for example, may reflect the author's view that the world is harsh, and the events in the story will reflect the same point of view.

1. How are Mama Torres and Pepé shaped by their environment?

2. What kind of story does the description of the setting in the first paragraph lead you to expect?

3. Describe the changing nature of the country through which Pepé rides. How are these changes related to his chances of escape?

4. Do the various details of setting in this story confirm or contradict the description of Steinbeck's point of view in the first paragraph of the biographical introduction (page 660)? Explain.

Language and Vocabulary

Finding Origins of Words

English is perhaps the most composite of languages. Its vocabulary includes words borrowed or derived from almost every language in the world. For example, so common an English word as *sugar* comes from the ancient Indic language Sanskrit; the words *samurai* and *kimono* come from Japanese.

Look up the following words from "Flight" in a dictionary and trace their origin. In each case, was the word taken directly from another language, or were there other developments? How close is each word's present meaning to its original meaning?

abalone	canyon	coyote	pommel
avalanche	chaparral	lizard	

Descriptive Writing

Describing a Setting

Write a description of a setting that might serve as the opening paragraph of a short story. Explain the kind of story you would write, and tell why your setting would be appropriate.

Isaac Bashevis Singer, the world's foremost living Yiddish writer, was born in Radzymin, Poland. When he was four, his family moved to Warsaw, the nation's capital, where he received his formal education. Singer lived for a time in Bilgoray, a Jewish village, or *shtetl*, where, he says, "the traditions of hundreds of years ago still lived"—traditions which, in one setting or another, show up in most of his fictions. Later he returned to Warsaw to live with his brother, the writer I. J. Singer. He worked as a proofreader and editor for several literary magazines and also began to publish book reviews and stories.

In 1935 Singer moved to New York and continued his journalistic work, publishing articles, reviews, and fiction in the Yiddish newspaper the *Jewish Daily Forward*. Singer has been an American citizen since 1943, and he now lives in Manhattan's Upper West Side.

Singer was awarded the 1978 Nobel Prize for literature. He continues to write his stories, novellas, novels, and plays in Yiddish and then supervises their translation into English. Among his best-known works are *The Family Moskat* (1950), the first of his books to be translated into English; *Gimpel the Fool* (1957), a collection of short stories, the title story of which was first translated by Saul Bellow; *The Spinoza of Market Street* (1961); *A Crown of Feathers* (1973), from which the story "Lost" is taken; and the novel *Shosha* (1978). In 1981 his *Collected Stories* won the Pulitzer Prize.

Singer has long been fascinated by his people's past, particularly by their vanished way of life. Many critics have noted his preoccupation with Old World

Isaac Bashevis Singer.
© Nancy Crampton

features that are extinct or disappearing: the Polish *shtetls*, such as Bilgoray and Kreshev, and Yiddish, itself a vanishing language. Along with this interest, there is in Singer's writing a profound sympathy for the mystical and unseen sphere of life. As a child Singer accepted the conventional orthodox religious teaching of his parents and simultaneously absorbed stories about demons, imps, haunted houses, and possessions. Many of Singer's works, including the story that follows, express a dualistic view of the world that accommodates both rational and irrational elements.

Lost

When I was counseling readers for the Yiddish newspaper where I worked, all kinds of people used to bring their problems to me: betrayed husbands and wives; relatives with quarrels from the old country; immigrants who had come to America many years before and wanted to apply for citizenship but did not know the dates of their arrivals or the names of their ships. In most of the cases, my help consisted in listening and offering words of comfort. Sometimes I gave them the address of the HIAS[1] or of an organization that provided legal assistance. Usually, these advice seekers came in the middle of the week—almost never on Friday. During the years I held this job, I learned that even Jews who worked on Saturday looked upon Friday as a day of preparation for the holy Sabbath. Whether this was a matter of tradition or of atavism[2] is of no consequence here.

But one particular man came to me on Friday, late in the day, when I was ready to go home. He appeared to be in his seventies. His back was stooped. He had a white goatee and bags under his eyes. He wore a long black coat, and I thought he must be a new arrival to America. But the moment he sat down at my desk he said, "Do you see me? I began to read your paper more than sixty years ago on the first day I came to this country."

I asked him where he came from, and he mentioned a town in Poland. He told me that he had studied in a yeshiva[3] and had tried to pass examinations to enter the university. Here in America he became a teacher in a Talmud Torah,[4] and later, with training, a dental technician. Of course, he was retired now.

He said, "I know your job is to give advice, but I did not come to ask that of you. What advice can you give to a man of eighty-three? I have everything I require, and when I die there is a cemetery plot that my landsleit[5] have prepared for me. I came to you because I thought that what happened to me might interest you. You often write about the mysterious powers. You believe in demons, imps—what have you. I am not going to argue with you about their existence. Neither you have seen them nor I. Even if demons do exist, they are not in New York. What would a demon do in New York? He would get run over by a car or tangle himself in a subway and never find his way out. Demons need a synagogue, a ritual bathhouse, a poorhouse, a garret with torn prayer books—all the paraphernalia you describe in your stories. Still, hidden powers that no one can explain exist everywhere. I am not speaking just about theories. I have had an experience with them. The Yiddish newspapers wrote about it, and the English ones too. But how long do they write about anything? Here in America, if the Heavens would part and the angel Gabriel were to fly down with his six fiery wings and take a walk on Broadway, they would not write about it for more than a day or two. If you are in a rush to go light candles and bless the incoming of the Sabbath, I will come back some other time," he said, smiling and winking. "Though with a man my age one cannot be too sure."

"I am in no rush," I said. "Please sit down and tell me."

"Where shall I begin? I will begin where it all started—on the boat. I did not come here the way the other greenhorns did, a pauper. My father was wealthy. I was his oldest son. He wanted me to become a rabbi, but in those

1. **HIAS:** The Hebrew Immigrant Aid Society.
2. **atavism** (ăt′ə-vĭz′əm): the reemergence of a trait found in remote ancestors.
3. **yeshiva** (yə-shē′və): here, a school for the training of orthodox rabbis.
4. **Talmud Torah** (täl′mo͞od′tôr′ə): a school for the study of the Torah, the body of Jewish religious law.

5. *landsleit* (länts′līt): compatriots; people of one's own country.

times the Enlightenment had slowly spread from Lithuania to Poland. I secretly read Sokolov's[6] *Morning Star,* and the new ideas enticed me. When I was about to be drafted into military service, my father wanted me to maim myself: cut off a finger, or—forgive the expression—rupture myself. But I was a healthy boy—tall and strong—and I told my father plainly that I would not make myself a cripple. 'So what do you intend to do?' he asked me. 'Serve the czar and eat army rations?' And I replied, 'I will go to America.'

"In those times, to have a son in America was considered a blight on the family—like having a convert or a suicide. But I insisted, and my parents had to consent. My father gave me five hundred rubles for travel expenses, which was a fortune in those days. Most immigrants came to America penniless. They traveled below deck. I traveled second class on a German ship. I discarded my long caftan before I left Europe. I brought a copy of *Do You Speak English?* with me. In comparison with other immigrants, I journeyed like a count.

"There was a special table in the dining room for those who ate kosher food. I sat there. There were only five or six of us. There were a German rabbi and a rich merchant also from Germany. Right across from me sat a girl who was traveling alone as I was. She came from Kovno. She was about my age: I was bashful, but when a boy and a girl sit together for seventeen days, they are bound to get acquainted. She had finished Gymnasium,[7] and a Jewish girl who studied at a Gymnasium was such a rarity that I regarded her as a princess. She behaved like one, too. She kept aloof and seldom spoke. She was blond, slim, and quite tall for a girl. She dressed elegantly and spoke both Russian and German. After a few days we began to greet one another and even took a walk on the deck together. She told me that although she did not believe in the dietary laws, she had given her grandfather a holy promise to eat kosher food. I learned that she was an orphan. Her father had been a rich lumber merchant, and her grandfather owned a number of houses in Kovno. I asked her why she was going to America. In the beginning, she avoided answering; then she confided to me that she was on her way to her fiancé—a student who had become active in the revolutionary movement and had to escape from the police. The fiancé lived in New York and was supposed to be studying there in a university."

"What was her name?" I asked.

"Anna Davidovna Barzel. One morning she came to breakfast late, and the moment I saw her I knew that something terrible had happened to her. She was as white as the wall. She did not eat the food she was served. The others at the table also noticed that she was miserable and questioned her, but her answer was inaudible. That is how she was—exceedingly proud. After breakfast, I saw her standing at the railing, and she leaned over so far I feared what she might be going to do. With some hesitation, I approached her and asked, 'Anna Davidovna, what do you see there below?' She started and almost fell. At first, she looked annoyed because I had interrupted her, and I was afraid that she might be angry. Then she grew calm. She had undergone a drastic change—she seemed emaciated, sick, and dejected. Somehow I gained courage, and I said, 'Anna Davidovna, I beseech you by all that is holy to tell me what has happened. Perhaps I could help you.'

" 'No, you can't help me,' she said.

"In time she told me the following story. Before she left Kovno, her grandfather had given her one thousand rubles. She had changed the rubles for dollars in a bank, and she carried them in a little pouch around her

---

6. **Sokolov** (sô′kô-lôv): Nahum Sokolov (or Sokolow), Jewish writer and Zionist leader (1861–1936).
7. **Gymnasium** (gĭm-nä′zē-ōōm′): in certain European countries, a preparatory secondary school.

The Steerage (1907). Gravure photograph by Alfred Stieglitz (1864–1946).

Hallmark Photographic Collection, Hallmark Cards, Inc., Kansas City, Missouri

neck, along with a small notebook with her fiancé's address in it. He had an unusual name—Vladimir Machtei. The night before, when she undressed, she found that both the money and the notebook had vanished from the pouch. Instead, she found the stub of a ship's ticket there and other trivial papers that had been in a valise. She had a cabin to herself, not wanting to share one. She remembered for sure that the previous morning when she had dressed she had the bank notes and the notebook in the pouch. She was also positive that she had not taken the ticket stub and other papers from the valise. What for? A ticket stub had no value.

"In our thoughts we are all a little cynical, and it occurred to me that perhaps she was playing around with some young man and that he might have stolen her possessions. I suggested this idea lightly, and Anna turned even paler than she was already. 'You are rude and I don't want to have anything more to do with you,' she said, and turned her back on me. I felt ashamed. Actually, there was not one young man in the second class with whom she could have become intimate. I never saw her talk to anyone. She did not have a deck chair. Wherever she went, she carried a book with her. She was a reticent *barishnia*[8] of a type that no longer exists.

"From that day till the end of the trip, Anna did not speak a word to me. When I greeted her, she did not answer. I went so far as to ask the waiter to take her a note in which I apologized for my discourtesy. The waiter told me that when she saw my name she tore the note to pieces. I have forgotten to tell you my name. In the old country, they called me Shmuel Opalovsky. Here, I am Sam Opal. After the waiter told me about the note, I maneuvered it so that I would come to the table when she had finished eating. I also stayed away from meals. I was fearful of the disdain she showed me.

"We finally arrived in the land of 'the streets paved with gold.' As a rule, immigrants were taken to Ellis Island,[9] but when I showed the money I had brought with me, I was allowed to enter without delay. I was about to leave the ship, when I saw Anna. She was crying. She tried to speak to the immigration officers in Russian and then in German, but they did not understand her. I asked her what had happened, and when she saw me her eyes showed relief. It seemed that Vladimir Machtei had not come to meet her. Whether she was in despair because they wanted to take her to Ellis Island or because she had no money and no place to go, I don't remember. She was in distress, and this was my chance to correct my stupidity. I helped her get through customs, hired a carriage—there were no cars in those days—and I took her to a hotel on Avenue C. We began at once to search for Vladimir Machtei, but we never found him. As far as we could learn, no person with such a name existed in the United States.

"I must confess to you that at the time these things were happening, I suspected she had invented everything—the fiancé, the money, and the address book. But later I convinced myself that it was all true. She showed me Vladimir Machtei's letters, although she had thrown away the envelopes. She told me that he came from Poltava. Anna wrote to his aunt there, and the aunt answered that she hadn't heard from her nephew for a long time and did not have his address. My dear friend, I know that you are a busy man, so I will give you the bare facts. We got married. I have a daughter by her, grandchildren, and great-grandchildren. The baby was born two years after we married.

"But the story that I want to tell you begins only now. I lived with Anna for six years. In this period I became persuaded that I was the husband of a person not of this world. First of all, she was the most silent creature I have ever

---

8. *barishnia* (bär'ĭsh-nē'ə): a Russian term of address meaning "a young unmarried woman"; comparable to the English word *Miss*.

9. **Ellis Island:** an island in Upper New York Bay; from 1892 to 1943, a United States examination center for immigrants.

met. She did not even say yes or no—she merely nodded her head. She became talkative only when she lost something, and this happened so often that even now when I speak about it I shudder. Years later, I discussed it with psychiatrists and they presented me with all kinds of theories: Freud, Shmeud; complex, shmomplex. The fact is that things literally disappeared before her eyes and sometimes before mine. I would bring her a book from the library—a Russian book, for she never learned English. Suddenly it would vanish. I brought her a diamond ring and shortly there was no ring. I gave her household money, and I myself saw how she put the ten dollars into her purse. A half hour later, the money was gone. Each time she lost something, she became hysterical. She literally turned over everything in the house. She went so far as to rip open the mattress. I am by nature a social person, but as long as I stayed with her I remained practically in isolation. I almost never brought anyone into the house. She refused to speak Yiddish, or perhaps she really couldn't speak it. There was no lack of young people who spoke Russian, but the few times I invited some of them into the house, she ignored them. We lived in a state of crisis and constant turmoil because Anna was forever losing things. She would say to me, 'A demon follows me—a fiend.'

"I had read many books of the Enlightened ones and I was far from believing in demons, imps, sprites—the whole lot. I was born a rationalist. After all that has happened to me, I still can't believe in the supernatural. Let's not fool ourselves. Planes fly, trains move, and if you press the right button you can hear Caruso. No demon has ever stopped a plane or a train. But living with Anna made me so jittery that I would wake up in the middle of the night to make sure that my watch, my money, and my first papers[10] had not dissolved. We

were not compatible in other respects as well. A silent love is perhaps possible among animals, but to me, love involves conversation. She was pregnant for nine months and I don't recall her speaking about it once. The nurse in the clinic where she gave birth told me that she never so much as let out a groan. I had hoped that having a baby would change her character, but no. She did everything a mother should do, all in silence. My daughter began to prattle when she was a year old. At two and a half, she asked her mother innumerable questions. Anna just shrugged. I was still a teacher in the Talmud Torah, and the moment I came home I would devote myself to the child, trying to answer her questions and playing with her. I must tell you that in her own way Anna loved the child. When toys were lost—it happened often, too often—Anna became frantic. The baby herself also seemed frightened. One day I brought her a teddy bear. Almost at once the bear disappeared. Our apartment was small, and there was really no place where it could have got to. I was afraid that the child had inherited her mother's dismal fate. Thank God, she is a normal woman.

"I remember the scene with the teddy bear as if it had happened yesterday. I had gone into the kitchen to make tea—Anna was not much of a housewife and I had to prepare things myself. I heard the baby screaming. I went back to the living room, and Anna stood there, white. 'The teddy bear is gone,' she said. 'The fiend tore it from her little hands.' I felt furious and I yelled, 'You're a liar! You threw it out the window.' She said, 'Look out and see.' I did, and of course the teddy bear was not there. We lived in a decent neighborhood. Things could lie outside for days and nobody would touch them. 'You threw it into the garbage!' I yelled. 'Go and look in the garbage,' she said. I took the house apart, but there was no trace of the teddy bear. Even today, I say to myself that Anna must have hidden it somewhere—but where and for what reason? Anna seldom cried. This time tears streamed down

10. **first papers:** a document signifying an immigrant's intention to become a United States citizen. After seven years' residence in the United States, the immigrant would receive citizenship, or second, papers.

her cheeks. In all the years, I never spoke about these things—people would have considered me mad. Even after what I am about to tell you occurred, I never told the whole story to anyone. Some time ago you discussed in an article the case of a farmer who vanished before the very eyes of his wife and children. Do you remember that article?"

"Yes, I remember. I read about it in a magazine and a number of other publications."

"What was the name of the farmer? When did it happen?" Sam Opal asked me, with the glint of a reader who prides himself that he remembers what was written better than the writer himself.

"Really, I've forgotten."

"I knew that you wouldn't remember, but I do. The farmer's name was David Lang, and the farm was a few miles from Gallatin, Tennessee. I even remember the date—September 1890."

"You have a remarkable memory."

"I remember it because it interested me immensely. I decided then that you were the person who would not consider me insane. I even tried to investigate the case myself, and I wrote to the mayor of Gallatin. I never got an answer. I want you to know that precisely the same thing happened with my wife," Sam Opal said. "She vanished in broad daylight here in Manhattan. I wasn't there, because I had left her standing at the window of a shoe store and gone home. But I might just as well have been—it wouldn't have made any difference. She never returned to the house. They wrote about her disappearance in your newspaper, and in others as well. The New York police should have a record of it—they have records of thousands of missing persons. For them, this is an everyday occurrence. Their explanation is always simple: ran away, was kidnapped. Lately, they also use the word 'amnesia.' None of these answers fits the case. Could you treat me to a glass of water?"

I went to the faucet and brought the man a paper cup filled with water. All the journalists had left, even the reporters who worked in the city room. Friday they closed the press a little earlier than other days of the week. Sam Opal drank half the contents of the cup and asked, "Do you have any details about David Lang's case?"

"No, but I have read about it in a number of occult anthologies."

"How do the psychologists interpret an occurrence like this?"

"Psychologists pay no heed to such matters. What cannot be explained is considered unscientific."

"It happened in 1898, in June," Sam Opal went on. "Our girl was already more than three years old. I've forgotten to mention an important point. Anna was always afraid that she might lose Natasha—that was our little girl's name. You must understand that I did not choose this name. Anna was in her own way a Russian patriot, although we had no cause to be in love with czarist Russia. Yes, she always dreaded that the child might disappear. I feared it myself. If it can happen to a teddy bear, why not to a child? Anna almost never left Natasha alone, and when it was absolutely necessary to go somewhere, she took her along.

"That day it was cool and rainy. Anna decided that she had to buy shoes. We were going to a hotel in the Catskill Mountains and she needed a pair of summer shoes. We had a neighbor who had a daughter of fifteen. This girl loved our little Natasha. Her name was Dorothy. Anna had complete confidence in Dorothy, and she left Natasha with her. Because of Anna's lack of English, I accompanied her. She would never enter a store without buying something, so as not to disappoint the merchant. But when it comes to footwear one cannot be too considerate. I was supposed to see to it that she didn't buy shoes that would be too tight or a pair that the salesman wanted to get rid of. We lived on Second Avenue and Eighteenth Street, which was then considered uptown, and many wealthy people had moved into this neighborhood. By this time I had become a dental technician. It was a new profession in America, and it paid well. There were many shoe stores on the avenue and we window-shopped, passing from one to the other. After a while I tired of the whole business. I had a laboratory in my apartment and I wanted to return to my work. Anna had already bought socks and panties for the baby, and she gave them to me, saying, 'If I don't find the shoes I want, perhaps I will try Fifth Avenue.'

"Those were her last words to me. That was the last time I saw her. Many hours later, I informed the police. It was evening. The Irish policeman considered the whole affair a joke and he advised me to wait until later that night, or until the next morning. About one o'clock I returned to the station, and the policeman on the night shift suggested that my wife was probably visiting her boyfriend. Just the same, he wrote down everything and told me to come the next day if she had not returned. I went back for days and weeks. Anna had disappeared like a stone in the water. People came up with the theories you would expect. Perhaps she had a clandestine lover. Perhaps she had found her lost fiancé, Vladimir Machtei, and the old love had rekindled. Perhaps she had decided to return to Russia and throw a bomb at the czar. From the police I had learned that not only men ran away in America but women as well. But none of the cases about which I heard compared to mine. Anna had no lovers. The baby was dear to her. If Vladimir Machtei wanted to know Anna's whereabouts, he could have written to her grandparents. In all the years we had been in America, he never showed a sign of life. Deep inside me, I knew the tragic and unbelievable truth: that Anna was by nature or fate—call it as you like—a person born to lose and to be lost. She lost her money, her possessions, her fiancé. She might have lost the child, too, if she had not lost herself. I say 'deep in me' because my reason would never accept anything so irrational. What does it mean? How can a thing become nothing? The Pyramids have stood in place for six thousand years, and unless there is an unusual earthquake, they may last for another six thousand—or sixty thousand. In the British Museum and here in the Metropolitan, you find mummies and artifacts that have endured for many centuries. If matter can turn to nothing, all of nature is a nightmare. This is what my logic dictates to me. In the case of that farmer in Tennessee, some believed that the earth had opened its mouth and swallowed him the way it is described in the Bible of Korah and his congregation. But if the earth had opened that day on Second or Fifth Avenue, it would have swallowed more than just Anna."

"So you believe that a demon or demons took her?" I asked.

"No, I don't believe this, either."

For a long time we sat in silence, then I asked, "Did you remarry?"

"No, I could have got a divorce easily, but I remained alone all these years. I mean, I did not marry."

"Why not? Were you so much in love with Anna?"

"This was not the reason. The most faithful men and women remarry after the death of their spouse, but what had happened to me kept me back. I hoped that I would live long enough for the riddle to be solved, but I am at the end of my road and I have found no answer. A person who has witnessed what I did can no longer make plans, build a house, attach himself to people. Spiritually, I became lost myself."

"It's quite possible that she still lives somewhere," I said.

"Where? A woman in her eighties. Yes, it is possible. Somehow, I had hoped that you could give me an explanation. I would be satisfied even with a theory, but it would have to make sense."

"In Genesis it is mentioned that Enoch 'was not; for God took him.' "

"Do you believe in this?" he asked.

"I don't know what to believe in."

"Well, I won't take up any more of your

time. But I wonder what a scientist would say if I were to press this story upon him? He would have to find some solution."

"He might say that your wife was a pathological liar, or possibly insane."

"But where is she?"

"In the Hudson, in the sea, back in Russia, or perhaps even here with Vladimir Machtei."

Sam Opal rose from his chair and I rose with him. For a minute we stared at one another and neither of us spoke. Then I said, "Since I am not a scientist I will give you my own unscientific theory."

"What is it?"

"Vladimir Machtei was the demon who stole Anna's money on the ship, took away little Natasha's teddy bear, and later kidnapped Anna. She was engaged to a demon to begin with."

"Why would the demon pick on her?"

"They are said to be attracted to the shy and the beautiful."

"But he had an aunt in Poltava."

"A demon's aunt is also a demon."

Reading Check

1. Why does Sam Opal come to see the narrator?
2. Why did he leave Europe?
3. What was Anna's reason for coming to America?
4. What did she lose during the voyage?
5. According to the narrator, what happened to Anna?

For Study and Discussion

Analyzing and Interpreting the Story

1. At the center of this story is an insoluble mystery: the nature and cause of Anna's disappearance. **a.** Is a rational explanation for what happens possible? **b.** Is an irrational explanation equally possible? **c.** How is the conflict between a rational and an irrational view of the world developed in the story?

2. From the moment Sam Opal meets Anna aboard the German ship, he misunderstands and misjudges her, and is unable to communicate with her. How are Anna and Sam different in character?

3. Although this story appears to be a simple ghost tale, it contains profound implications. Sam says, "If matter can turn to nothing, all of nature is a nightmare. This is what my logic dictates to me" (page 681). Explain Sam's dilemma.

4. Sam declares at the end of the story, "Spiritually, I became lost myself." **a.** In what sense has Sam become "lost"? **b.** What kind of loss might Anna's apparently inexplicable disappearance symbolize? (Keep in mind that Anna and Sam are immigrants.)

5. Sam gives his age as eighty-three. Why has he waited so long to reveal his story?

6. The story becomes somewhat more frightening when we realize that the mystery occurred some time ago, that Sam is nearing the end of his life, and that with him the truth of the whole perplexing cycle of events will vanish forever as if it had never taken place. Bearing these facts in mind, what further ramifications does the story's title assume?

Writing About Literature

Evaluating a Critical Statement

Early in the story, Sam Opal says that "hidden powers that no one can explain exist everywhere." The poet and critic Kenneth Rexroth observes that in the writing of Isaac Bashevis Singer "life itself is haunted. . . . We all live in the shadowy frivolous world of a spiritualistic seance. . . . The point is that somewhere at the heart of reality something is running down." Write an essay in which you evaluate Rexroth's statement of Singer's view of the world. Be sure to support your conclusions with specific references to the story "Lost."

In 1954 Jesse Stuart was made poet laureate of his home state of Kentucky, about which he wrote a long series of novels, poems, and stories. He was born in a one-room log cabin in W-Hollow, Greenup County. Although his father was a poor farmer and education was scarce in his region, Stuart was able to attend the small mountain institute of Lincoln Memorial University, from which he graduated in 1929. He went on to Vanderbilt University where, for a year, he did graduate work under the poet Donald Davidson. Through the encouragement and influence of Davidson, who knew he had discovered an original talent, Stuart completed his first book of poems, *Harvest of Youth* (1930). He left Vanderbilt without a degree and returned to his native region to teach school. In small and often primitive classrooms, he discovered a passion for teaching that was to color his life and his writing.

In 1934 he published a second book, *Man with a Bull-Tongued Plow*, a collection of 703 sonnets reflecting the beauty of his life in the Kentucky mountains. This book was a success, and Stuart was emboldened to plunge more deeply into writing. In 1936 there followed his first book of short stories, *Head O' W-Hollow* and, in 1940, his first novel, *Trees of Heaven*. His interest in the novel persisted, and he attracted wide attention with *Taps for Private Tussie* (1943), *Foretaste of Glory* (1946), and several other works. One of his most popular books, *The Thread That Runs So True* (1949), is an autobiographical account of his experiences as a teacher in Kentucky and Ohio.

Jesse Stuart (1961).
The Courier-Journal and *Louisville Times*

Stuart's great appeal lies in the humor and sympathy with which he depicts mountain people. In collections of poems, such as *Kentucky Is My Land* (1952), and of short stories, such as *Plowshare in Heaven* (1958), he continued to celebrate his home region. His later works include a book of stories, *Come, Gentle Spring* (1969), and a novel, *The Land Beyond the River* (1973). Stuart confessed his opinion that, among American poets, Walt Whitman, Stephen Vincent Benét, and Edgar Lee Masters would be the most highly regarded a hundred years hence, and in such an opinion he clearly asserted his faith in a literature of and for the people.

Another April

"Now, Pap, you won't get cold," Mom said as she put a heavy wool cap over his head.

"Huh, what did ye say?" Grandpa asked, holding his big hand cupped over his ear to catch the sound.

"Wait until I get your gloves," Mom said, hollering real loud in Grandpa's ear. Mom had forgotten about his gloves until he raised his big bare hand above his ear to catch the sound of Mom's voice.

"Don't get 'em," Grandpa said, "I won't ketch cold."

Mom didn't pay any attention to what Grandpa said. She went on to get the gloves anyway. Grandpa turned toward me. He saw that I was looking at him.

"Yer Ma's a-puttin' enough clothes on me to kill a man," Grandpa said, then he laughed a coarse laugh like March wind among the pine tops at his own words. I started laughing at them, not at Grandpa's words. He thought I was laughing at them and we both laughed together. It pleased Grandpa to think that I had laughed with him over something funny that he had said. But I was laughing at the way he was dressed. He looked like a picture of Santa Claus. But Grandpa's cheeks were not cherry-red like Santa Claus's cheeks. They were covered with white thin beard—and above his eyes were long white eyebrows almost as white as percoon petals[1] and very much longer.

Grandpa was wearing a heavy wool suit that hung loosely about his big body but fitted him tightly round the waist where he was as big and as round as a flour barrel. His pant legs were as big 'round his pipestem legs as emptied meal sacks. And his big shoes, with his heavy wool socks dropping down over their tops, looked like sled runners. Grandpa wore a heavy wool shirt and over his wool shirt he wore a heavy

1. **percoon petals:** the white petals of a tree blossom native to Kentucky.

wool sweater and then his coat over the top of all this. Over his coat he wore a heavy overcoat and about his neck he wore a wool scarf.

The way Mom had dressed Grandpa you'd think there was a heavy snow on the ground but there wasn't. April was here instead and the sun was shining on the green hills where the wild plums and the wild crab apples were in bloom enough to make you think there were big snowdrifts sprinkled over the green hills. When I looked at Grandpa and then looked out the window at the sunshine and the green grass I laughed more. Grandpa laughed with me.

"I'm a-goin' to see my old friend," Grandpa said just as Mom came down the stairs with his gloves.

"Who is he, Grandpa?" I asked, but Grandpa just looked at my mouth working. He didn't know what I was saying. And he hated to ask me the second time.

Mom put the big wool gloves on Grandpa's hands. He stood there just like I had to do years ago, and let Mom put his gloves on. If Mom didn't get his fingers back in the glove-fingers exactly right Grandpa quarreled at Mom. And when Mom fixed his fingers exactly right in his gloves the way he wanted them Grandpa was pleased.

"I'll be a-goin' to see 'im," Grandpa said to Mom. "I know he'll still be there."

Mom opened our front door for Grandpa and he stepped out slowly, supporting himself with his big cane in one hand. With the other hand he held to the door facing. Mom let him out of the house just like she used to let me out in the spring. And when Grandpa left the house I wanted to go with him, but Mom wouldn't let me go. I wondered if he would get away from the house—get out of Mom's sight—and pull off his shoes and go barefooted and wade the creeks like I used to do when Mom let me out. Since Mom wouldn't let me go with Grandpa, I watched him as he walked slowly down the path in front of our house. Mom stood there watching Grandpa too. I think she was afraid that he would fall. But Mom was fooled; Grandpa toddled along the path better than my baby brother could.

"He used to be a powerful man," Mom said more to herself than she did to me. "He was a timber cutter. No man could cut more timber than my father; no man in the timber woods could sink an ax deeper into a log than my father. And no man could lift the end of a bigger saw log[2] than Pap could."

"Who is Grandpa goin' to see, Mom?" I asked.

"He's not goin' to see anybody," Mom said.

"I heard 'im say that he was goin' to see an old friend," I told her.

"Oh, he was just a-talkin'," Mom said.

I watched Grandpa stop under the pine tree in our front yard. He set his cane against the pine-tree trunk, pulled off his gloves and put them in his pocket. Then Grandpa stooped over slowly, as slowly as the wind bends down a sapling, and picked up a pine cone in his big soft fingers. Grandpa stood fondling the pine cone in his hand. Then, one by one, he pulled the little chips from the pine cone—tearing it to pieces like he was hunting for something in it—and after he had torn it to pieces he threw the pine-cone stem on the ground. Then he pulled pine needles from a low-hanging pine bough and he felt of each pine needle between his fingers. He played with them a long time before he started down the path.

"What's Grandpa doin'?" I asked Mom.

But Mom didn't answer me.

"How long has Grandpa been with us?" I asked Mom.

"Before you's born," she said. "Pap has been with us eleven years. He was eighty when he quit cuttin' timber and farmin'; now he's ninety-one."

I had heard her say that when she was a girl he'd walk out on the snow and ice barefooted

and carry wood in the house and put it on the fire. He had shoes but he wouldn't bother to put them on. And I heard her say that he would cut timber on the coldest days without socks on his feet but with his feet stuck down in cold brogan shoes and he worked stripped above the waist so his arms would have freedom when he swung his double-bitted ax. I had heard her tell how he'd sweat and how the sweat in his beard would be icicles by the time he got home from work on the cold winter days. Now Mom wouldn't let him get out of the house for she wanted him to live a long time.

As I watched Grandpa go down the path toward the hog pen he stopped to examine every little thing along his path. Once he waved his cane at a butterfly as it zigzagged over his head, its polka-dot wings fanning the blue April air. Grandpa would stand when a puff of wind came along, and hold his face against the wind and let the wind play with his white whiskers. I thought maybe his face was hot under his beard and he was letting the wind cool his face. When he reached the hog pen he called the hogs down to the fence. They came running and grunting to Grandpa just like when they were talking to him. I knew that Grandpa couldn't hear them trying to talk to him but he could see their mouths working and he knew they were trying to say something. He leaned his cane against the hog pen, reached over the fence, and patted the hogs' heads. Grandpa didn't miss patting one of our seven hogs.

As he toddled up the little path alongside the hog pen he stopped under a blooming dogwood. He pulled a white blossom from a bough that swayed over the path above his head, and he leaned his big bundled body against the dogwood while he tore each petal from the blossom and examined it carefully. There wasn't anything his dim blue eyes missed. He stopped under a redbud tree before he reached the garden to break a tiny spray of redbud blossoms. He took each blossom from the spray and examined it carefully.

2. **saw log:** a log large enough to be sawed into lumber.

Early Spring (1936–1937) by Hobson Pittman (1899–1972). Oil on canvas.
Metropolitan Museum of Art, George A. Hearn Fund

"Gee, it's funny to watch Grandpa," I said to Mom, then I laughed.

"Poor Pap," Mom said, "he's seen a lot of Aprils come and go. He's seen more Aprils than he will ever see again."

I don't think Grandpa missed a thing on the little circle he took before he reached the house. He played with a bumblebee that was bending a windflower blossom that grew near our corncrib beside a big bluff. But Grandpa didn't try to catch the bumblebee in his big bare hand. I wondered if he would and if the bumblebee would sting him, and if he would holler. Grandpa even pulled a butterfly cocoon from a blackberry brier that grew beside his path. I saw him try to tear it into shreds but he couldn't. There wasn't any butterfly in it, for I'd seen it before. I wondered if the butterfly with the polka-dot wings, that Grandpa waved his cane at when he first left the house, had come from this cocoon. I laughed when Grandpa couldn't tear the cocoon apart.

"I'll bet I can tear that cocoon apart for Grandpa if you'd let me go help him," I said to Mom.

"You leave your grandpa alone," Mom said. "Let 'im enjoy April."

Then I knew that this was the first time Mom had let Grandpa out of the house all winter. I knew that Grandpa loved the sunshine and the fresh April air that blew from the redbud and dogwood blossoms. He loved the bumblebees, the hogs, the pine cones, and pine needles. Grandpa didn't miss a thing along his walk. And every day from now on until just before frost Grandpa would take this little walk. He'd stop along and look at everything as he had done summers before. But each year he didn't take as long a walk as he had taken the year before. Now this spring he didn't go down to the lower end of the hog pen as he had done last year. And when I could first remember Grandpa going on his walks he used to go out of sight. He's go all over the farm. And he'd come to the house and take me on his knee and tell me about all that he had seen. Now Grandpa wasn't getting out of sight. I could see him from the window along all of his walk.

Grandpa didn't come back into the house at the front door. He tottled around back of the house toward the smokehouse and I ran through the living room to the dining room so I could look out at the window and watch him.

"Where's Grandpa goin'?" I asked Mom.

"Now never mind," Mom said. "Leave your grandpa alone. Don't go out there and disturb him."

"I won't bother 'im, Mom," I said. "I just want to watch 'im."

"All right," Mom said.

But Mom wanted to be sure that I didn't bother him so she followed me into the dining room. Maybe she wanted to see what Grandpa was going to do. She stood by the window and we watched Grandpa as he walked down beside our smokehouse where a tall sassafras tree's thin leaves fluttered in the blue April wind. Above the smokehouse and tall sassafras was a blue April sky—so high you couldn't see the sky-roof. It was just blue space and little white clouds floated upon this blue.

When Grandpa reached the smokehouse he leaned his cane against the sassafras tree. He let himself down slowly to his knees as he looked carefully at the ground. Grandpa was looking at something and I wondered what it was. I just didn't think or I would have known.

"There you are, my good old friend," Grandpa said.

"Who is his friend, Mom?" I asked.

Mom didn't say anything. Then I saw.

"He's playin' with that old terrapin,[3] Mom," I said.

"I know he is," Mom said.

"The terrapin doesn't mind if Grandpa strokes his head with his hand," I said.

"I know it," Mom said.

"But the old terrapin won't let me do it," I said. "Why does he let Grandpa?"

"The terrapin knows your grandpa."

"He ought to know me," I said. "But when I try to stroke his head with my hand, he closes up in his shell."

Mom didn't say anything. She stood by the window watching Grandpa and listening to Grandpa talk to the terrapin.

"My old friend, how do you like the sunshine?" Grandpa asked the terrapin.

The terrapin turned his fleshless face to one side like a hen does when she looks at you in the sunlight. He was trying to talk to Grandpa; maybe the terrapin could understand what Grandpa was saying.

"Old fellow, it's been a hard winter," Grandpa said. "How have you fared under the smokehouse floor?"

---

3. **terrapin:** a fresh-water turtle.

"Does the terrapin know what Grandpa is sayin'?" I asked Mom.

"I don't know," she said.

"I'm awfully glad to see you, old fellow," Grandpa said.

He didn't offer to bite Grandpa's big soft hand as he stroked his head.

"Looks like the terrapin would bite Grandpa," I said.

"That terrapin has spent the winters under that smokehouse for fifteen years," Mom said. "Pap has been acquainted with him for eleven years. He's been talkin' to that terrapin every spring."

"How does Grandpa know the terrapin is old?" I asked Mom.

"It's got *1847* cut on its shell," Mom said. "We know he's ninety-five years old. He's older than that. We don't know how old he was when that date was cut on his back."

"Who cut *1847* on his back, Mom?"

"I don't know, child," she said, "but I'd say whoever cut that date on his back has long been under the ground."

Then I wondered how a terrapin could get that old and what kind of a looking person he was who cut the date on the terrapin's back. I wondered where it happened—if it happened near where our house stood. I wondered who lived here on this land then, what kind of a house they lived in, and if they had a sassafras with tiny thin April leaves on its top growing in their yard, and if the person that cut the date on the terrapin's back was buried at Plum Grove, if he had farmed these hills where we lived today and cut timber like Grandpa had— and if he had seen the Aprils pass like Grandpa had seen them and if he enjoyed them like Grandpa was enjoying this April. I wondered if he had looked at the dogwood blossoms, the redbud blossoms, and talked to this same terrapin.

"Are you well, old fellow?" Grandpa asked the terrapin.

The terrapin just looked at Grandpa.

"I'm well as common for a man of my age," Grandpa said.

"Did the terrapin ask Grandpa if he was well?" I asked Mom.

"I don't know," Mom said. "I can't talk to a terrapin."

"But Grandpa can."

"Yes."

"Wait until tomatoes get ripe and we'll go to the garden together," Grandpa said.

"Does a terrapin eat tomatoes?" I asked Mom.

"Yes, that terrapin has been eatin' tomatoes from our garden for fifteen years," Mom said.

"When Mick was tossin' the terrapins out of the tomato patch, he picked up this one and found the date cut on his back. He put him back in the patch and told him to help himself. He lives from our garden every year. We don't bother him and don't allow anybody else to bother him. He spends his winters under our smokehouse floor buried in the dry ground."

"Gee, Grandpa looks like the terrapin," I said.

Mom didn't say anything; tears came to her eyes. She wiped them from her eyes with the corner of her apron.

"I'll be back to see you," Grandpa said. "I'm a-gettin' a little chilly; I'll be gettin' back to the house."

The terrapin twisted his wrinkled neck without moving his big body, poking his head deeper into the April wind as Grandpa pulled his bundled body up by holding to the sassafras-tree trunk.

"Goodbye, old friend!"

The terrapin poked his head deeper into the wind, holding one eye on Grandpa, for I could see his eye shining in the sinking sunlight.

Grandpa got his cane that was leaned against the sassafras-tree trunk and hobbled slowly toward the house. The terrapin looked at him with first one eye and then the other.

Reading Check

1. Who is the "old friend" the child's grand-father is going to see?
2. What kind of work did Grandpa do when he was younger?
3. Why does Grandpa remove his gloves?
4. Where does his walk take him?
5. What is the last place he stops at before returning to the house?

For Study and Discussion

Analyzing and Interpreting the Story

1. The child likens his heavily clothed grandfather to "a picture of Santa Claus." Yet in what ways is the grandfather also like a child?

2a. What do you learn about the grandfather's younger days, when he "used to be a powerful man"?
b. How does this information affect your impression of the grandfather?

3. How does the grandfather experience the newly arrived spring in all its rich detail?

4a. Aside from their age, how are the grandfather and the terrapin alike? b. What are the child's feelings toward his grandfather when he learns the terrapin's true age?

5. The arrival of spring marks both the passing of an old year and the beginning of a new one. Although the grandfather clearly ages with each successive April, in what sense does he also experience a renewal?

6. As the child watches his grandfather, his feelings of curiosity and amusement gradually give way to a sense of wonder. Why is spring an appropriate season for feelings of wonder?

Writing About Literature

Considering Similarities in Stories

Consider essential similarities of theme, character, or situation that you find among "Another April," "The Jilting of Granny Weatherall," by Katherine Anne Porter (page 591), and "A Worn Path," by Eudora Welty (page 691). What sympathetic comprehension of age is created in the stories by Stuart, Porter, and Welty?

Descriptive Writing

Describing a Place

Compose a short, detailed description of a place that was, or is, an important part of your life. Like Jesse Stuart, choose your words and details carefully to show your attitude toward the place. If you wish, recall sensory experiences that are associated with the place, using words that convey the exact quality of these experiences.

Reprinted from *Images of the Southern Writer.* Photograph by Mark Morrow © 1985 The University of Georgia Press

Eudora Welty.

EUDORA WELTY
1909–

Eudora Welty, like her fellow Mississippian William Faulkner, has a vivid sense of detail. Her characters move against a rich background of pine-clad hills, red clay farms, cotton fields, ramshackle houses with rusting Chevrolets in the dooryard, and little towns drowsing in the sun. The people in her world are united by a common core of shared beliefs and attitudes, and everyone has a strong sense of position in the social scheme. Welty's quiet gaze misses nothing. The ludicrous and pathetic are noted down as impartially as the brave. Compassion and tolerance pervade her work. Her best stories are often like poems and spring out of the same lyrical impulse to praise or wonder at the world. Sinclair Lewis once said of her, "Her writing is as clear . . . as the Gettysburg Address."

Eudora Welty was born in Jackson, Mississippi. She was raised in comfortable circumstances, went to school and college in Mississippi, and then transferred to the University of Wisconsin. After graduation, she went to New York where she entered Columbia University to study advertising. Unable to find a steady job in New York in the middle of the Depression, she returned to Jackson in 1931 where she spent the next nine years in a variety of jobs. During these years she began to take pictures of Mississippi subjects and wrote of them as well. Both on film and in her stories, she tried always to catch the same fugitive thing, the mysterious atmosphere of place and the meanings half divulged by the expressions and gestures of people she met. In 1936 her first published story appeared in a small magazine, and since then her reputation has climbed steadily. Her short stories and novels have won her international recognition, and her own country has awarded her many honors.

Welty's short stories have been collected in *A Curtain of Green* (1941), *The Wide Net and Other Stories* (1943), *The Golden Apples* (1949), *The Bride of the Innisfallen and Other Stories* (1955), and *The Collected Stories of Eudora Welty* (1980). Her longer works of fiction include *Delta Wedding* (1946), *The Ponder Heart* (1954), and *Losing Battles* (1970), her longest

and most ambitious work. It is a rich and ruefully comic story concerning the events of a single day as a large rural family comes together to celebrate the grandmother's birthday. She was awarded the Pulitzer Prize in 1973 for her novel, *The Optimist's Daughter*. In 1971 Eudora Welty put together a remarkable book of photographs of Mississippi life called *One Time, One Place: Mississippi in the Depression: A Snapshot Album*. In 1978 a collection of her essays and reviews, *The Eye of the Story*, was published. *One Writer's Beginnings*, an autobiographical account of her early years, appeared in 1984.

Welty received the 1941 O'Henry Award for "A Worn Path," the story that is reprinted here.

A Worn Path

It was December—a bright frozen day in the early morning. Far out in the country there was an old Negro woman with her head tied in a red rag, coming along a path through the pinewoods. Her name was Phoenix Jackson. She was very old and small and walked slowly in the dark pine shadows, moving a little from side to side in her steps, with the balanced heaviness and lightness of a pendulum in a grandfather clock. She carried a thin, small cane made from an umbrella, and with this she kept tapping the frozen earth in front of her. This made a grave and persistent noise in the still air, that seemed meditative like the chirping of a solitary little bird.

She wore a dark striped dress reaching down to her shoe tops, and an equally long apron of bleached sugar sacks, with a full pocket: all neat and tidy, but every time she took a step she might have fallen over her shoelaces, which dragged from her unlaced shoes. She looked straight ahead. Her eyes were blue with age. Her skin had a pattern all its own of numberless branching wrinkles and as though a whole little tree stood in the middle of her

forehead, but a golden color ran underneath, and the two knobs of her cheeks were illumined by a yellow burning under the dark. Under the red rag her hair came down on her neck in the frailest of ringlets, still black, and with an odor like copper.

Now and then there was a quivering in the thicket. Old Phoenix said, "Out of my way, all you foxes, owls, beetles, jack rabbits, coons and wild animals! . . . Keep out from under these feet, little bobwhites. . . . Keep the big wild hogs out of my path. Don't let none of those come running my direction. I got a long way." Under her small black-freckled hand her cane, limber as a buggy whip, would switch at the brush as if to rouse up any hiding things.

On she went. The woods were deep and still. The sun made the pine needles almost too bright to look at, up where the wind rocked. The cones dropped as light as feathers. Down in the hollow was the mourning dove—it was not too late for him.

The path ran up a hill. "Seem like there is chains about my feet, time I get this far," she said, in the voice of argument old people keep

Ex-Slave with Long Memory (1937).
Photograph by Dorothea Lange (1895–1965).
Dorothea Lange, Collection The Oakland Museum

to use with themselves. "Something always take a hold of me on this hill—pleads I should stay."

After she got to the top she turned and gave a full, severe look behind her where she had come. "Up through pines," she said at length. "Now down through oaks."

Her eyes opened their widest, and she started down gently. But before she got to the bottom of the hill a bush caught her dress.

Her fingers were busy and intent, but her skirts were full and long, so that before she could pull them free in one place they were caught in another. It was not possible to allow the dress to tear. "I in the thorny bush," she said. "Thorns, you doing your appointed work. Never want to let folks pass, no sir. Old eyes thought you was a pretty little *green* bush."

Finally, trembling all over, she stood free, and after a moment dared to stoop for her cane.

"Sun so high!" she cried, leaning back and looking, while the thick tears went over her eyes. "The time getting all gone here."

At the foot of this hill was a place where a log was laid across the creek.

"Now comes the trial," said Phoenix.

Putting her right foot out, she mounted the log and shut her eyes. Lifting her skirt, leveling her cane fiercely before her, like a festival figure in some parade, she began to march across. Then she opened her eyes and she was safe on the other side.

"I wasn't as old as I thought," she said.

But she sat down to rest. She spread her skirts on the bank around her and folded her hands over her knees. Up above her was a tree in a pearly cloud of mistletoe. She did not dare to close her eyes, and when a little boy brought her a plate with a slice of marble cake on it she spoke to him. "That would be acceptable," she said. But when she went to take it there was just her own hand in the air.

So she left that tree, and had to go through a barbed-wire fence. There she had to creep and crawl, spreading her knees and stretching her fingers like a baby trying to climb the steps. But she talked loudly to herself: she could not let her dress be torn now, so late in the day, and she could not pay for having her arm or her leg sawed off if she got caught fast where she was.

At last she was safe through the fence and risen up out in the clearing. Big dead trees, like black men with one arm, were standing in the purple stalks of the withered cotton field. There sat a buzzard.

"Who you watching?"

In the furrow she made her way along.

"Glad this not the season for bulls," she said,

looking sideways, "and the good Lord made his snakes to curl up and sleep in the winter. A pleasure I don't see no two-headed snake coming around that tree, where it come once. It took a while to get by him, back in the summer."

She passed through the old cotton and went into a field of dead corn. It whispered and shook and was taller than her head. "Through the maze now," she said, for there was no path.

Then there was something tall, black, and skinny there, moving before her.

At first she took it for a man. It could have been a man dancing in the field. But she stood still and listened, and it did not make a sound. It was as silent as a ghost.

"Ghost," she said sharply, "who be you the ghost of? For I have heard of nary death close by."

But there was no answer—only the ragged dancing in the wind.

She shut her eyes, reached out her hand, and touched a sleeve. She found a coat and inside that an emptiness, cold as ice.

"You scarecrow," she said. Her face lighted. "I ought to be shut up for good," she said with laughter. "My senses is gone. I too old. I the oldest people I ever know. Dance, old scarecrow," she said, "while I dancing with you."

She kicked her foot over the furrow, and with mouth drawn down, shook her head once or twice in a little strutting way. Some husks blew down and whirled in streamers about her skirts.

Then she went on, parting her way from side to side with the cane, through the whispering field. At last she came to the end, to a wagon track where the silver grass blew between the red ruts. The quail were walking around like pullets, seeming all dainty and unseen.

"Walk pretty," she said. "This the easy place. This the easy going."

She followed the track, swaying through the quiet bare fields, through the little strings of trees silver in their dead leaves, past cabins silver from weather, with the doors and win-dows boarded shut, all like old women under a spell sitting there. "I walking in their sleep," she said, nodding her head vigorously.

In a ravine she went where a spring was silently flowing through a hollow log. Old Phoenix bent and drank. "Sweet gum makes the water sweet," she said, and drank more. "Nobody know who made this well, for it was here when I was born."

The track crossed a swampy part where the moss hung as white as lace from every limb. "Sleep on, alligators, and blow your bubbles." Then the track went into the road.

Deep, deep the road went down between the high green-colored banks. Overhead the live oaks met, and it was as dark as a cave.

A black dog with a lolling tongue came up out of the weeds by the ditch. She was meditating, and not ready, and when he came at her she only hit him a little with her cane. Over she went in the ditch, like a little puff of milkweed.

Down there, her senses drifted away. A dream visited her, and she reached her hand up, but nothing reached down and gave her a pull. So she lay there and presently went to talking. "Old woman," she said to herself, "that black dog come up out of the weeds to stall you off, and now there he sitting on his fine tail, smiling at you."

A white man finally came along and found her—a hunter, a young man, with his dog on a chain.

"Well, Granny!" he laughed. "What are you doing there?"

"Lying on my back like a June bug waiting to be turned over, mister," she said, reaching up her hand.

He lifted her up, gave her a swing in the air, and set her down. "Anything broken, Granny?"

"No sir, them old dead weeds is springy enough," said Phoenix, when she had got her breath. "I thank you for your trouble."

"Where do you live, Granny?" he asked, while the two dogs were growling at each other.

"Away back yonder, sir, behind the ridge. You can't even see it from here."

"On your way home?"

"No sir, I going to town."

"Why, that's too far! That's as far as I walk when I come out myself, and I get something for my trouble." He patted the stuffed bag he carried, and there hung down a little closed claw. It was one of the bobwhites, with its beak hooked bitterly to show it was dead. "Now you go on home, Granny!"

"I bound to go to town, mister," said Phoenix. "The time come around."

He gave another laugh, filling the whole landscape. "I know you old people! Wouldn't miss going to town to see Santa Claus!"

But something held old Phoenix very still. The deep lines in her face went into a fierce and different radiation. Without warning, she had seen with her own eyes a flashing nickel fall out of the man's pocket onto the ground.

"How old are you, Granny?" he was saying.

"There is no telling, mister," she said, "no telling."

Then she gave a little cry and clapped her hands and said, "Git on away from here, dog! Look! Look at that dog!" She laughed as if in admiration. "He ain't scared of nobody. He a big black dog." She whispered, "Sic him!"

"Watch me get rid of that cur," said the man. "Sic him, Pete! Sic him!"

Phoenix heard the dogs fighting, and heard the man running and throwing sticks. She even heard a gunshot. But she was slowly bending forward by that time, further and further forward, the lids stretched down over her eyes, as if she were doing this in her sleep. Her chin was lowered almost to her knees. The yellow palm of her hand came out from the fold of her apron. Her fingers slid down and along the ground under the piece of money with the grace and care they would have in lifting an egg from under a setting hen. Then she slowly straightened up, she stood erect, and the nickel was in her apron pocket. A bird flew by. Her lips moved. "God watching me the whole time. I come to stealing."

The man came back, and his own dog panted about them. "Well, I scared him off that time," he said, and then he laughed and lifted his gun and pointed it at Phoenix.

She stood straight and faced him.

"Doesn't the gun scare you?" he said, still pointing it.

"No, sir, I seen plenty go off closer by, in my day, and for less than what I done," she said, holding utterly still.

He smiled, and shouldered the gun. "Well, Granny," he said, "you must be a hundred years old, and scared of nothing. I'd give you a dime if I had any money with me. But you take my advice and stay home, and nothing will happen to you."

"I bound to go on my way, mister," said Phoenix. She inclined her head in the red rag. Then they went in different directions, but she could hear the gun shooting again and again over the hill.

She walked on. The shadows hung from the oak trees to the road like curtains. Then she smelled woodsmoke, and smelled the river, and she saw a steeple and the cabins on their steep steps. Dozens of little black children whirled around her. There ahead was Natchez shining. Bells were ringing. She walked on.

In the paved city it was Christmastime. There were red and green electric lights strung and crisscrossed everywhere, and all turned on in the daytime. Old Phoenix would have been lost if she had not distrusted her eyesight and depended on her feet to know where to take her.

She paused quietly on the sidewalk where people were passing by. A lady came along in the crowd, carrying an armful of red-, green- and silver-wrapped presents; she gave off perfume like the red roses in hot summer, and Phoenix stopped her.

"Please, missy, will you lace up my shoe?" She held up her foot.

"What do you want, Grandma?"

"See my shoe," said Phoenix. "Do all right for out in the country, but wouldn't look right to go in a big building."

"Stand still then, Grandma," said the lady. She put her packages down on the sidewalk beside her and laced and tied both shoes tightly.

"Can't lace 'em with a cane," said Phoenix. "Thank you, missy. I doesn't mind asking a nice lady to tie up my shoe, when I gets out on the street."

Moving slowly and from side to side, she went into the big building, and into a tower of steps, where she walked up and around and around until her feet knew to stop.

She entered a door, and there she saw nailed up on the wall the document that had been stamped with the gold seal and framed in the gold frame, which matched the dream that was hung up in her head.

"Here I be," she said. There was a fixed and ceremonial stiffness over her body.

"A charity case, I suppose," said an attendant who sat at the desk before her.

But Phoenix only looked above her head. There was sweat on her face; the wrinkles in her skin shone like a bright net.

"Speak up, Grandma," the woman said. "What's your name? We must have your history, you know. Have you been here before? What seems to be the trouble with you?"

Old Phoenix only gave a twitch to her face as if a fly were bothering her.

"Are you deaf?" cried the attendant.

But then the nurse came in.

"Oh, that's just old Aunt Phoenix," she said. "She doesn't come for herself—she has a little grandson. She makes these trips just as regular as clockwork. She lives away back off the Old Natchez Trace."[1] She bent down. "Well, Aunt Phoenix, why don't you just take a seat? We won't keep you standing after your long trip." She pointed.

The old woman sat down, bolt upright in the chair.

"Now, how is the boy?" asked the nurse.

Old Phoenix did not speak.

"I said, how is the boy?"

But Phoenix only waited and stared straight ahead, her face very solemn and withdrawn into rigidity.

"Is his throat any better?" asked the nurse. "Aunt Phoenix, don't you hear me? Is your grandson's throat any better since the last time you came for medicine?"

With her hands on her knees, the old woman waited, silent, erect and motionless, just as if she were in armor.

"You mustn't take up our time this way, Aunt Phoenix," the nurse said. "Tell us quickly about

1. **Natchez Trace:** a road of the early nineteenth century going from Natchez, Mississippi, to Nashville, Tennessee.

your grandson, and get it over. He isn't dead, is he?"

At last there came a flicker and then a flame of comprehension across her face, and she spoke.

"My grandson. It was my memory had left me. There I sat and forgot why I made my long trip."

"Forgot?" The nurse frowned. "After you came so far?"

Then Phoenix was like an old woman begging a dignified forgiveness for waking up frightened in the night. "I never did go to school, I was too old at the Surrender,"[2] she said in a soft voice. "I'm an old woman without an education. It was my memory fail me. My little grandson, he is just the same, and I forgot it in the coming."

"Throat never heals, does it?" said the nurse, speaking in a loud, sure voice to old Phoenix. By now she had a card with something written on it, a little list. "Yes. Swallowed lye. When was it?—January—two, three years ago——"

Phoenix spoke unasked now. "No, missy, he not dead, he just the same. Every little while his throat begin to close up again, and he not able to swallow. He not get his breath. He not able to help himself. So the time come around, and I go on another trip for the soothing medicine."

"All right. The doctor said as long as you came to get it, you could have it," said the nurse. "But it's an obstinate case."

"My little grandson, he sit up there in the house all wrapped up, waiting by himself," Phoenix went on. "We is the only two left in the world. He suffer and it don't seem to put him back at all. He got a sweet look. He going to last. He wear a little patch quilt and peep out holding his mouth open like a little bird. I remembers so plain now. I not going to forget him again, no, the whole enduring time. I could tell him from all the others in creation."

"All right." The nurse was trying to hush her now. She brought her a bottle of medicine. "Charity," she said, making a check mark in a book.

Old Phoenix held the bottle close to her eyes, and then carefully put it into her pocket.

"I thank you," she said.

"It's Christmastime, Grandma," said the attendant. "Could I give you a few pennies out of my purse?"

"Five pennies is a nickel," said Phoenix stiffly.

"Here's a nickel," said the attendant.

Phoenix rose carefully and held out her hand. She received the nickel and then fished the other nickel out of her pocket and laid it beside the new one. She stared at her palm closely, with her head on one side.

Then she gave a tap with her cane on the floor.

"This is what come to me to do," she said. "I going to the store and buy my child a little windmill they sells, made out of paper. He going to find it hard to believe there such a thing in the world. I'll march myself back where he waiting, holding it straight up in this hand."

She lifted her free hand, gave a little nod, turned around, and walked out of the doctor's office. Then her slow step began on the stairs, going down.

---

2. **the Surrender:** Robert E. Lee surrendered to Ulysses S. Grant at the Appomattox Court House in Virginia on April 9, 1865, thus ending the Civil War.

Reading Check

1. Where and when does the story take place?
2. What does Phoenix consider "the trial" in her journey?
3. What does she mistake for a man?
4. What is Phoenix's purpose in going to the city?
5. Why doesn't she answer the nurse's questions?

The Point of the Story

EUDORA WELTY

A story writer is more than happy to be read by students; the fact that these serious readers think and feel something in response to his work he finds life-giving. At the same time he may not always be able to reply to their specific questions in kind. I wondered if it might clarify something, for both the questioners and myself, if I set down a general reply to the question that comes to me most often in the mail, from both students and their teachers, after some classroom discussion. The unrivaled favorite is this: "Is Phoenix Jackson's grandson really *dead?*" It refers to a short story I wrote years ago called "A Worn Path," which tells of a day's journey an old woman makes on foot from deep in the country into town and into a doctor's office on behalf of her little grandson; he is at home, periodically ill, and periodically she comes for his medicine; they give it to her as usual, she receives it and starts the journey back.

I had not meant to mystify readers by withholding any fact; it is not a writer's business to tease. The story is told through Phoenix's mind as she undertakes her errand. As the author at one with the character as I tell it, I must assume that the boy is alive. As the reader, you are free to think as you like, of course: the story invites you to believe that no matter what happens, Phoenix for as long as she is able to walk and can hold to her purpose will make her journey. The *possibility* that she would keep on even if he were dead is there in her devotion and its single-minded, single-track errand. Certainly the *artistic* truth, which should be good enough for the fact, lies in Phoenix's own answer to that question. When the nurse asks, "He isn't dead, is he?" she speaks for herself: "He still the same. He going to last."

The grandchild is the incentive. But it is the journey, the going of the errand, that is the story, and the question is not whether the grandchild is in reality alive or dead. It doesn't affect the outcome of the story or its meaning from start to finish. But it is not the question itself that has struck me as much as the idea, almost without exception implied in the asking, that for Phoenix's grandson to be dead would somehow make the story "better."

It's *all right,* I want to say to the students who write to me, for things to be what they appear to be, and for words to mean what they say. It's all right, too, for words and appearances to mean more than one thing—ambiguity is a fact of life. A fiction writer's responsibility covers not only what he presents as the facts of a given story but what he chooses to stir up as their implications; in the end, the implications, too, become facts, in the larger, fictional sense. But it is not all right, not in good faith, for things not to mean what they say.

The grandson's plight was real and it made the truth of the story, which is the story of an errand of love carried out. If the child no longer lived, the truth would persist in the "wornness" of the path. But his being dead can't increase the truth of the story, can't affect it one way or the other. I think I signal this, because the end of the story has been reached before old Phoenix gets home again: she simply starts back. To the question "Is the grandson really dead?" I could reply that it doesn't make any difference. I could also say that I did not make him up in order to let him play a trick on Phoenix. But my best answer would be: "Phoenix is alive."

The origin of a story is sometimes a trustworthy clue to the author—or can provide him with the clue—to its key image; maybe in this case it will do the same for the reader. One day I saw a solitary old woman like Phoenix. She was walking; I saw her, at middle distance, in a winter country landscape, and watched her slowly make her way across my line of vision. That sight of her made me write the story. I invented an errand for her, but that only seemed a living part of the figure she was herself: what errand other than for someone else could be making her go? And her going was the first thing, her persisting in the landscape was the real thing, and the first and the real were what I wanted and worked to keep. I brought her up close enough, by imagination, to describe her face, make her present to the eyes, but the full-length figure moving across the winter fields was the indelible one and the image to keep, and the perspective extending into the vanishing distance the true one to hold in mind.

I invented for my character, as I wrote, some passing adventures—some dreams and harassments and a small triumph or two, some jolts to her pride, some flights of fancy to console her, one or two encounters to scare her, a moment that gave her cause to feel ashamed, a moment to dance and preen—for it had to be a journey, and all these things belonged to that, parts of life's uncertainty.

A narrative line is in its deeper sense, of course, the tracing out of a meaning, and the real continuity of a story lies in this probing forward. The real dramatic force of a story depends on the strength of the emotion that has set it going. The emotional value is the measure of the reach of the story. What gives any such content to "A Worn Path" is not its circumstances, but its subject, the deep-grained habit of love.

What I hoped would come clear was that in the whole surround of this story, the world it threads through, the only certain thing at all is the worn path. The habit of love cuts through confusion and stumbles or contrives its way out of difficulty, it remembers the way even when it forgets, for a dumbfounded moment, its reason for being. The path is the thing that matters.

Her victory—old Phoenix's—is when she sees the diploma in the doctor's office, when she finds "nailed up on the wall the document that had been stamped with the gold seal and framed in the gold frame, which matched the dream that was hung up in her head." The return with the medicine is just a matter of retracing her own footsteps. It is the part of the journey, and of the story, that can now go without saying.

In the matter of function, old Phoenix's way might even do as a sort of parallel to your way of work if you are a writer of stories. The way to get there is the all-important, all-absorbing problem, and this problem is your reason for undertaking the story. Your own guide, too, is your sureness about your subject, about what this subject is. Like Phoenix, you work all your life to find your way, through all the obstructions and the false appearances and the upsets you may have brought on yourself, to reach a meaning—using inventions of your imagination, perhaps helped out by your dreams and bits of good luck. And finally too, like Phoenix, you have to assume that what you are working in aid of is life, not death.

But you would make the trip anyway—wouldn't you?—just on hope.

For Study and Discussion

Analyzing and Interpreting the Story

1. The phoenix, a mythical bird, proved to be indestructible by rising from its own ashes after consuming itself in flames. **a.** Point out two or three incidents in which Phoenix Jackson triumphs over circumstances that threaten her. **b.** How does Phoenix herself prove to be indestructible?

2. When Phoenix gets the second nickel from the attendant, she goes to buy a paper windmill for her grandson. How does her method of acquiring the nickels contribute emotional force to an important theme—her tireless love for her grandson?

3a. In what sense does Phoenix literally travel a worn path? **b.** How does the phrase refer more generally to her love for her grandson?

Writing About Literature

Supporting an Opinion

Eudora Welty says of her story: "it is the journey, the going of the errand, that is the story, and the question is not whether the grandchild is in reality alive or dead. It doesn't affect the outcome of the story or its meaning from start to finish."

Do you agree? Would the story be more satisfying if you knew for sure whether the child is alive or dead? Write an essay presenting your position.

Descriptive Writing

Describing an Action

Through precise observations of Phoenix's actions Eudora Welty captures what is unusual about Phoenix. For example, she describes Phoenix crossing a log: "Lifting her skirt, leveling her cane fiercely before her, like a festival figure in some parade, she began to march across." This sentence, with its suggestive details, not only describes an action, but also portrays two essential aspects of Phoenix's character: her dignity and her inner strength.

Write a brief description of an action performed by some person you have observed or by a character you invent. Select words and details that characterize the person performing the action.

BERNARD MALAMUD
1914–1986

Bernard Malamud.
© Nancy Crampton

Bernard Malamud (măl′ə-məd) was born in Brooklyn, New York, where his father was a grocer. Malamud once wrote of his early years, "My father . . . made a marginal living. . . . During my childhood, we all followed the fortunes of the store, moving from one neighborhood to another, wherever things seemed to be better. They were good for short periods but were very bad in the Depression." After high school, Malamud entered the City College of New York. Although he wrote a few short stories in college, his serious career as a writer did not begin until after graduation. He taught night school for a number of years and wrote during the day. He later stated, "The rise of totalitarianism, the Second World War, and the situation of the Jews in Europe helped me come to what I wanted to say as a writer."

In 1952 Malamud's first novel, *The Natural,* was published. Through the world of American baseball, it renews themes of ancient myth. The hero, a famous batter, repeats virtually all the legendary feats of the game, including knocking the cover off the ball. He is made into something like a mythical hero who must achieve great deeds and suffer great trials. From baseball Malamud moved to the world of Jewish culture, often as it figures in American society. He portrayed the experiences and feelings of Jewish people as representative of what is true for all humanity. "I try to see the Jew as a universal man," Malamud said. "The Jewish drama is a symbol of the fight for existence in the highest possible human terms."

Malamud's novels and short stories deal with the world of workers and small shopkeepers, as well as of professors and artists and people in business. Through his writing runs a thread of concern with people's desire to achieve a new, better life and with the problem of learning how hard such a change can be. Perhaps the worst trap his characters fall into is believing that there is a shortcut to success through deceiving themselves or others. Malamud's point of view had been described by some critics as tragic, by others as comic. He himself seemed to feel that in either case it is the hard realities of personal existence that are in fact central and important to everyone.

In addition to *The Natural,* Malamud produced several volumes of short stories and six other novels: *The Assistant* (1957), *A New Life* (1961), *The Fixer* (1966), *The Tenants* (1971), *Dubin's Lives* (1979), and *God's Grace* (1982). *The Assistant* was inspired in part by one of Malamud's best stories, "The First Seven Years." Malamud twice received a National Book Award for fiction: in 1959 for his short-story collection *The Magic Barrel;* and in 1967 for *The Fixer,* which also received a Pulitzer Prize.

The First Seven Years

Feld, the shoemaker, was annoyed that his helper, Sobel, was so insensitive to his reverie that he wouldn't for a minute cease his fanatic pounding at the other bench. He gave him a look, but Sobel's bald head was bent over the last[1] as he worked and he didn't notice. The shoemaker shrugged and continued to peer through the partly frosted window at the near-sighted haze of falling February snow. Neither the shifting white blur outside, nor the sudden deep remembrance of the snowy Polish village where he had wasted his youth could turn his thoughts from Max the college boy, (a constant visitor in the mind since early that morning when Feld saw him trudging through the snowdrifts on his way to school) whom he so much respected because of the sacrifices he had made throughout the years—in winter or direst heat—to further his education. An old wish returned to haunt the shoemaker: that he had had a son instead of a daughter, but this blew away in the snow for Feld, if anything, was a practical man. Yet he could not help but contrast the diligence of the boy, who was a peddler's son, with Miriam's unconcern for an education. True, she was always with a book in her hand, yet when the opportunity arose for a college education, she had said no she would rather find a job. He had begged her to go, pointing out how many fathers could not afford to send their children to college, but she said she wanted to be independent. As for education, what was it, she asked, but books, which Sobel, who diligently read the classics, would as usual advise her on. Her answer greatly grieved her father.

A figure emerged from the snow and the door opened. At the counter the man with-drew from a wet paper bag a pair of battered shoes for repair. Who he was the shoemaker for a moment had no idea, then his heart trembled as he realized, before he had thoroughly discerned the face, that Max himself was standing there, embarrassedly explaining what he wanted done to his old shoes. Though Feld listened eagerly, he couldn't hear a word, for the opportunity that had burst upon him was deafening.

He couldn't exactly recall when the thought had occurred to him, because it was clear he had more than once considered suggesting to the boy that he go out with Miriam. But he had not dared speak, for if Max said no, how would he face him again? Or suppose Miriam, who harped so often on independence, blew up in anger and shouted at him for his meddling? Still, the chance was too good to let by: all it meant was an introduction. They might long ago have become friends had they happened to meet somewhere, therefore was it not his duty—an obligation—to bring them together, nothing more, a harmless connivance to replace an accidental encounter in the subway, let's say, or a mutual friend's introduction in the street? Just let him once see and talk to her and he would for sure be interested. As for Miriam, what possible harm for a working girl in an office, who met only loud-mouthed salesmen and illiterate shipping clerks, to make the acquaintance of a fine scholarly boy? Maybe he would awaken in her a desire to go to college; if not—the shoemaker's mind at last came to grips with the truth—let her marry an educated man and live a better life.

When Max finished describing what he wanted done with his shoes, Feld marked them, both with enormous holes in the soles which he pretended not to notice, with large white-chalk x's, and the rubber heels, thinned

1. **last:** a block or form shaped like a human foot, used in repairing shoes.

to the nails, he marked with o's, though it troubled him he might have mixed up the letters. Max inquired the price, and the shoemaker cleared his throat and asked the boy, above Sobel's insistent hammering, would he please step through the side door there into the hall. Though surprised, Max did as the shoemaker requested, and Feld went in after him. For a minute they were both silent, because Sobel had stopped banging, and it seemed they understood neither was to say anything until the noise began again. When it did, loudly, the shoemaker quickly told Max why he had asked to talk to him.

"Ever since you went to high school," he said, in the dimly lit hallway, "I watched you in the morning go to the subway to school, and I said always to myself, this is a fine boy that he wants so much an education."

"Thanks," Max said, nervously alert. He was tall and grotesquely thin, with sharply cut features, particularly a beaklike nose. He was wearing a loose, long slushy overcoat that hung down to his ankles, looking like a rug draped over his bony shoulders, and a soggy, old brown hat, as battered as the shoes he had brought in.

"I am a business man," the shoemaker abruptly said to conceal his embarrassment, "so I will explain you right away why I talk to you. I have a girl, my daughter Miriam—she is nineteen—a very nice girl and also so pretty that everybody looks on her when she passes by in the street. She is smart, always with a book, and I thought to myself that a boy like you, an educated boy—I thought maybe you will be interested sometime to meet a girl like this." He laughed a bit when he had finished and was tempted to say more but had the good sense not to.

Max stared down like a hawk. For an uncomfortable second he was silent, then he asked, "Did you say nineteen?"

"Yes."

"Would it be all right to inquire if you have a picture of her?"

"Just a minute." The shoemaker went into the store and hastily returned with a snapshot that Max held up to the light.

"She's all right," he said.

Feld waited.

"And is she sensible—not the flighty kind?"

"She is very sensible."

After another short pause, Max said it was okay with him if he met her.

"Here is my telephone," said the shoemaker, hurriedly handing him a slip of paper. "Call her up. She comes home from work six o'clock."

Max folded the paper and tucked it away into his worn leather wallet.

"About the shoes," he said. "How much did you say they will cost me?"

"Don't worry about the price."

"I just like to have an idea."

"A dollar—dollar fifty. A dollar fifty," the shoemaker said.

At once he felt bad, for he usually charged two twenty-five for this kind of job. Either he should have asked the regular price or done the work for nothing.

Later, as he entered the store, he was startled by a violent clanging and looked up to see Sobel pounding with all his might upon the naked last. It broke, the iron striking the floor and jumping with a thump against the wall, but before the enraged shoemaker could cry out, the assistant had torn his hat and coat from the hook and rushed out into the snow.

So Feld, who had looked forward to anticipating how it would go with his daughter and Max, instead had a great worry on his mind. Without his temperamental helper he was a lost man, especially since it was years now that he had carried the store alone. The shoemaker had for an age suffered from a heart condition that threatened collapse if he dared exert himself. Five years ago, after an attack, it had appeared as though he would have either to sacrifice his business upon the auction block and live on a pittance thereafter, or put himself at the mercy of some unscrupulous employee

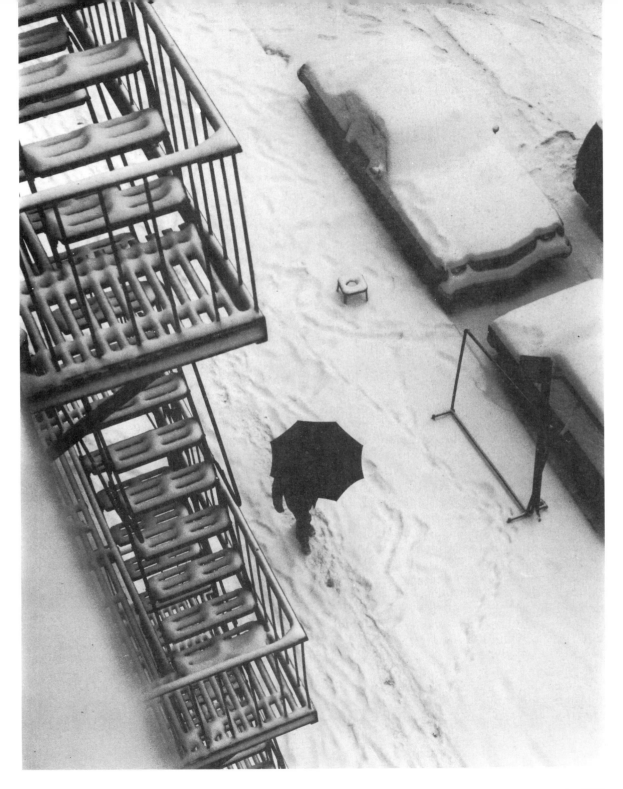

who would in the end probably ruin him. But just at the moment of his darkest despair, this Polish refugee, Sobel, appeared one night from the street and begged for work. He was a stocky man, poorly dressed, with a bald head that had once been blond, a severely plain face and soft blue eyes prone to tears over the sad books he read, a young man but old—no one would have guessed thirty. Though he confessed he knew nothing of shoemaking, he said he was apt and would work for a very little if Feld taught him the trade. Thinking that with, after all, a landsman,[2] he would have less to fear than from a complete stranger, Feld took him on and within six weeks the refugee rebuilt as good a shoe as he, and not long thereafter expertly ran the business for the thoroughly relieved shoemaker.

Feld could trust him with anything and did, frequently going home after an hour or two at the store, leaving all the money in the till, knowing Sobel would guard every cent of it. The amazing thing was that he demanded so little. His wants were few; in money he wasn't interested—in nothing but books, it seemed—which he one by one lent to Miriam, together with his profuse, queer written comments, manufactured during his lonely rooming house evenings, thick pads of commentary which the shoemaker peered at and twitched his shoulders over as his daughter, from her fourteenth year, read page by sanctified page, as if the word of God were inscribed on them. To protect Sobel, Feld himself had to see that he received more than he asked for. Yet his conscience bothered him for not insisting that the assistant accept a better wage than he was getting, though Feld had honestly told him he could earn a handsome salary if he worked elsewhere, or maybe opened a place of his own. But the assistant answered somewhat ungraciously, that he was not interested in going elsewhere, and though Feld frequently asked himself what keeps him here? why does he stay? he finally answered it that the man, no

doubt because of his terrible experiences as a refugee, was afraid of the world.

After the incident with the broken last, angered by Sobel's behavior, the shoemaker decided to let him stew for a week in the rooming house, although his own strength was taxed dangerously and the business suffered. However, after several sharp nagging warnings from both his wife and daughter, he went finally in search of Sobel, as he had once before, quite recently, when over some fancied slight—Feld had merely asked him not to give Miriam so many books to read because her eyes were strained and red—the assistant had left the place in a huff, an incident which, as usual, came to nothing for he had returned after the shoemaker had talked to him, and taken his seat at the bench. But this time, after Feld had plodded through the snow to Sobel's house—he had thought of sending Miriam but the idea became repugnant to him—the burly landlady at the door informed him in a nasal voice that Sobel was not at home, and though Feld knew this was a nasty lie, for where had the refugee to go? still for some reason he was not completely sure of—it may have been the cold and his fatigue—he decided not to insist on seeing him. Instead he went home and hired a new helper.

Having settled the matter, though not entirely to his satisfaction, for he had much more to do than before, and so, for example, could no longer lie late in bed mornings because he had to get up to open the store for the new assistant, a speechless, dark man with an irritating rasp as he worked, whom he would not trust with the key as he had Sobel. Furthermore, this one, though able to do a fair repair job, knew nothing of grades of leather or prices, so Feld had to make his own purchases; and every night at closing time it was necessary to count the money in the till, and lock up. However, he was not dissatisfied, for he lived much in his thoughts of Max and Miriam. The college boy had called her, and they arranged a meeting for this coming Friday night. The shoemaker would personally have preferred

2. **landsman** (länts′mən): a compatriot.

Saturday, which he felt would make it a date of the first magnitude, but he learned Friday was Miriam's choice, so he said nothing. The day of the week did not matter. What mattered was the aftermath. Would they like each other and want to be friends? He sighed at all the time that would have to go by before he knew for sure. Often he was tempted to talk to Miriam about the boy, to ask whether she thought she would like his type—he had told her only that he considered Max a nice boy and had suggested he call her—but the one time he tried she snapped at him—justly—how should she know?

At last Friday came. Feld was not feeling particularly well so he stayed in bed, and Mrs. Feld thought it better to remain in the bedroom with him when Max called. Miriam received the boy, and her parents could hear their voices, his throaty one, as they talked. Just before leaving, Miriam brought Max to the bedroom door and he stood there a minute, a tall, slightly hunched figure wearing a thick, droopy suit, and apparently at ease as he greeted the shoemaker and his wife, which was surely a good sign. And Miriam, although she had worked all day, looked fresh and pretty. She was a large-framed girl with a well-shaped body, and she had a fine open face and soft hair. They made, Feld thought, a first-class couple.

Miriam returned after 11:30. Her mother was already asleep, but the shoemaker got out of bed and after locating his bathrobe went into the kitchen, where Miriam, to his surprise, sat at the table, reading.

"So where did you go?" Feld asked pleasantly.

"For a walk," she said, not looking up.

"I advised him," Feld said, clearing his throat, "he shouldn't spend so much money."

"I didn't care."

The shoemaker boiled up some water for tea and sat down at the table with a cupful and a thick slice of lemon.

"So how," he sighed after a sip, "did you enjoy?"

"It was all right."

He was silent. She must have sensed his disappointment, for she added, "You can't really tell much the first time."

"You will see him again?"

Turning a page, she said that Max had asked for another date.

"For when?"

"Saturday."

"So what did you say?"

"What did I say?" she asked, delaying for a moment—"I said yes."

Afterwards she inquired about Sobel, and Feld, without exactly knowing why, said the assistant had got another job. Miriam said nothing more and began to read. The shoemaker's conscience did not trouble him; he was satisfied with the Saturday date.

During the week, by placing here and there a deft question, he managed to get from Miriam some information about Max. It surprised him to learn that the boy was not studying to be either a doctor or lawyer but was taking a business course leading to a degree in accountancy. Feld was a little disappointed because he thought of accountants as bookkeepers and would have preferred "a higher profession." However, it was not long before he had investigated the subject and discovered that Certified Public Accountants were highly respected people, so he was thoroughly content as Saturday approached. But because Saturday was a busy day, he was much in the store and therefore did not see Max when he came to call for Miriam. From his wife he learned there had been nothing especially revealing about their meeting. Max had rung the bell and Miriam had got her coat and left with him—nothing more. Feld did not probe, for his wife was not particularly observant. Instead, he waited up for Miriam with a newspaper on his lap, which he scarcely looked at so lost was he in thinking of the future. He awoke to find her in the room with him, tiredly removing her hat. Greeting her, he was suddenly inexplicably afraid to ask anything about the evening. But since she volunteered nothing he was at last

A shoemaker's shop, New York, 1943.
Marjorie Collins, Library of Congress

forced to inquire how she had enjoyed herself. Miriam began something noncommittal but apparently changed her mind, for she said after a minute, "I was bored."

When Feld had sufficiently recovered from his anguished disappointment to ask why, she answered without hesitation, "Because he's nothing more than a materialist."

"What means this word?"

"He has no soul. He's only interested in things."

He considered her statement for a long time but then asked, "Will you see him again?"

"He didn't ask."

"Suppose he will ask you?"

"I won't see him."

He did not argue; however, as the days went by he hoped increasingly she would change her mind. He wished the boy would telephone, because he was sure there was more to him than Miriam, with her inexperienced eye, could discern. But Max didn't call. As a matter of fact he took a different route to school, no longer passing the shoemaker's store, and Feld was deeply hurt.

Then one afternoon Max came in and asked for his shoes. The shoemaker took them down from the shelf where he had placed them, apart from the other pairs. He had done the work himself and the soles and heels were well built and firm. The shoes had been highly polished and somehow looked better than new. Max's Adam's apple went up once when he saw them, and his eyes had little lights in them.

"How much?" he asked, without directly looking at the shoemaker.

"Like I told you before," Feld answered sadly. "One dollar fifty cents."

Max handed him two crumpled bills and received in return a newly minted silver half dollar.

He left. Miriam had not been mentioned. That night the shoemaker discovered that his new assistant had been all the while stealing from him, and he suffered a heart attack.

Though the attack was very mild, he lay in bed for three weeks. Miriam spoke of going for Sobel, but sick as he was Feld rose in wrath against the idea. Yet in his heart he knew there was no other way, and the first weary day back in the shop thoroughly convinced him, so that night after supper he dragged himself to Sobel's rooming house.

He toiled up the stairs, though he knew it was bad for him, and at the top knocked at the door. Sobel opened it and the shoemaker entered. The room was a small, poor one, with a single window facing the street. It contained a narrow cot, a low table and several stacks of books piled haphazardly around on the floor along the wall, which made him think how queer Sobel was, to be uneducated and read so much. He had once asked him, Sobel, why you read so much? and the assistant could not answer him. Did you ever study in a college someplace? he had asked, but Sobel shook his head. He read, he said, to know. But to know what, the shoemaker demanded, and to know, why? Sobel never explained, which proved he read much because he was queer.

Feld sat down to recover his breath. The assistant was resting on his bed with his heavy back to the wall. His shirt and trousers were clean, and his stubby fingers, away from the shoemaker's bench, were strangely pallid. His face was thin and pale, as if he had been shut in this room since the day he had bolted from the store.

"So when you will come back to work?" Feld asked him.

To his surprise, Sobel burst out, "Never."

Jumping up, he strode over to the window that looked out upon the miserable street.

"Why should I come back?" he cried.

"I will raise your wages."

"Who cares for your wages!"

The shoemaker, knowing he didn't care, was at a loss what else to say.

"What do you want from me, Sobel?"

"Nothing."

"I always treated you like you was my son."

Sobel vehemently denied it. "So why you look for strange boys in the street they should go out with Miriam? Why you don't think of me?"

The shoemaker's hands and feet turned freezing cold. His voice became so hoarse he couldn't speak. At last he cleared his throat and croaked, "So what has my daughter got to do with a shoemaker thirty-five years old who works for me?"

"Why do you think I worked so long for you?" Sobel cried out. "For the stingy wages I sacrificed five years of my life so you could have to eat and drink and where to sleep?"

"Then for what?" shouted the shoemaker.

"For Miriam," he blurted—"for her."

The shoemaker, after a time, managed to say, "I pay wages in cash, Sobel," and lapsed into silence. Though he was seething with excitement his mind was coldly clear, and he had to admit to himself he had sensed all along

that Sobel felt his way. He had never so much as thought it consciously, but he had felt it and was afraid.

"Miriam knows?" he muttered hoarsely.

"She knows."

"You told her?"

"No."

"Then how does she know?"

"How does she know?" Sobel said. "Because she knows. She knows who I am and what is in my heart."

Feld had a sudden insight. In some devious way, with his books and commentary, Sobel had given Miriam to understand that he loved her. The shoemaker felt a terrible anger at him for his deceit.

"Sobel, you are crazy," he said bitterly. "She will never marry a man so old and ugly like you."

Sobel turned black with rage. He cursed the shoemaker, but then, though he trembled to hold it in, his eyes filled with tears and he broke into deep sobs. With his back to Feld, he stood at the window, fists clenched, and his shoulders shook with choked sobbing.

Watching him, the shoemaker's anger diminished. His teeth were on edge with pity for the man, and his eyes grew moist. How strange and sad that a refugee, a grown man, bald and old with his miseries, who had by the skin of his teeth escaped Hitler's incinerators,[3] should fall in love, when he had got to America, with a girl less than half his age. Day after day, for five years he had sat at his bench, cutting and hammering away, waiting for the girl to become a woman, unable to ease his heart with speech, knowing no protest but desperation.

"Ugly I didn't mean," he said half aloud.

Then he realized that what he had called ugly was not Sobel but Miriam's life if she married him. He felt for his daughter a strange and gripping sorrow, as if she were already Sobel's bride, the wife, after all, of a

---

3. **Hitler's incinerators:** During World War II, millions of Jews in Europe were murdered by the Nazis. Ovens were used to get rid of the victims' bodies.

shoemaker, and had in her life no more than her mother had had. And all his dreams for her—why he had slaved and destroyed his heart with anxiety and labor—all these dreams of a better life were dead.

The room was quiet. Sobel was standing by the window reading, and it was curious that when he read he looked young.

"She is only nineteen," Feld said brokenly. "This is too young yet to get married. Don't ask her for two years more, till she is twenty-one, then you can talk to her."

Sobel didn't answer. Feld rose and left. He went slowly down the stairs but once outside, though it was an icy night the crisp falling snow whitened the street, he walked with a stronger stride.

But the next morning, when the shoemaker arrived, heavy-hearted, to open the store, he saw he needn't have come, for his assistant was already seated at the last, pounding leather for his love.

Reading Check

1. Why does Miriam decline an offer of a college education?
2. What does Max ask Feld about Miriam before he agrees to call her?
3. Feld believes Sobel is interested in only one thing. What is it?
4. Why does Feld hire a new assistant?
5. Why does Feld go to Sobel's rooming house a second time?

For Study and Discussion

Analyzing and Interpreting the Story

1. Feld wants a "better life" for his daughter Miriam. How does he expect that Max, the college boy, will help her to it?
2a. What action of Sobel's first suggests to the reader that Sobel is in love with Miriam? **b.** Why does Feld ignore this possibility?
3. Miriam says that she does not like Max because he is a materialist (page 706). What is the implica-

tion of Feld's not understanding what she means?
4. When Sobel accuses Feld of hardheartedness in not recognizing his love, Feld replies, "I pay wages in cash." **a.** What attitude toward Sobel does this indicate? **b.** How does it help explain why Feld never thought of Sobel as a suitor for his daughter?
5a. What has Sobel done to indicate to Miriam that despite his limitations, he too is interested in a better life? **b.** What has he done to emphasize his sincerity?
6. Feld asks himself why he should have "destroyed his heart with anxiety and labor" for the future (page 708). In this respect, what does he share with Sobel?
7a. Why does Feld relent in his attitude toward Sobel? **b.** How has his understanding of life changed? **c.** Is his decision for Miriam's future that of a strictly practical man? Explain.

Literary Elements

Plot: Revelation

In many modern stories the action does not move so much toward a resolution of the plot as toward a moment of **revelation.** At the story's end, some insight is gained into a character or into that character's relationship with other characters or into the writer's view of the world. Sometimes not only the reader but also the character is afforded a moment of revelation.

In "The First Seven Years," Feld is blind to Sobel's love for Miriam. When Sobel confronts him with the truth, what Feld learns makes him reevaluate his own pattern of life and his hopes for his daughter. His moment of revelation, the story suggests, will make him a changed person.

What new understanding of himself does Feld come to at the end of the story? Why do you think he returns home from Sobel's rooming house with a "stronger stride"?

Writing About Literature

Analyzing Plot and Theme

Write an essay in which you discuss your view of the situation presented in "The First Seven Years." Why are Feld's actions in the beginning understandable, given the circumstances? Do you find Sobel to be a sympathetic character? What do you think is the theme of the story?

Flannery O'Connor.

Flannery O'Connor was born in Savannah, Georgia, but she grew up chiefly in the small town of Milledgeville, in the region of Georgia that was to form the chief background of her writing. She was educated at the Georgia State College for Women and at the State University of Iowa, where she studied under the poet Paul Engle. After graduation, she turned directly to writing as a career.

Much of her writing is noted for its sudden violent acts and for its wry, often grotesque humor. Her work has been compared to the work of other Southern writers, notably William Faulkner, Carson McCullers, and Eudora Welty. Her faith has colored much of her work. She herself commented that her writing not only captured what was important in the life around her but also reflected a strong commitment to her personal beliefs. She was a careful and hardworking craftsman. "I rewrite, edit, throw away," she once said. "It's slow and searching."

During her brief life, Flannery O'Connor completed two novels and two volumes of short stories. Her novels—*Wise Blood* (1952) and *The Violent Bear It Away* (1960)—portray characters who strongly resist efforts to awaken religious feelings within them but who are finally driven in complex and unsuspected ways to assert the power of a divine grace. In both novels and stories, she has depicted persons and scenes characteristic of her region. At the same time she has revealed a concern with depths of human feeling and behavior that range from the bleak and tragic to the richly comic.

The Complete Stories, published posthumously in 1971, won the National Book Award. *The Habit of Being,* selected letters edited by Sally Fitzgerald, appeared in 1979.

The Life You Save May Be Your Own

The old woman and her daughter were sitting on their porch when Mr. Shiftlet came up their road for the first time. The old woman slid to the edge of her chair and leaned forward, shading her eyes from the piercing sunset with her hand. The daughter could not see far in front of her and continued to play with her fingers. Although the old woman lived in this desolate spot with only her daughter and she had never seen Mr. Shiftlet before, she could tell, even from a distance, that he was a tramp and no one to be afraid of. His left coat sleeve was folded up to show there was only half an arm in it and his gaunt figure listed slightly to the side as if the breeze were pushing him. He had on a black town suit and a brown felt hat that was turned up in the front and down in the back and he carried a tin toolbox by a handle. He came on, at an amble, up her road, his face turned toward the sun which appeared to be balancing itself on the peak of a small mountain.

The old woman didn't change her position until he was almost into her yard; then she rose with one hand fisted on her hip. The daughter, a large girl in a short blue organdy dress, saw him all at once and jumped up and began to stamp and point and make excited speechless sounds.

Mr. Shiftlet stopped just inside the yard and set his box on the ground and tipped his hat at her as if she were not in the least afflicted; then he turned toward the old woman and swung the hat all the way off. He had long black slick hair that hung flat from a part in the middle to beyond the tips of his ears on either side. His face descended in forehead for more than half its length and ended suddenly with his features just balanced over a jutting steel-trap jaw. He seemed to be a young man but he had a look of composed dissatisfaction as if he understood life thoroughly.

"Good evening," the old woman said. She was about the size of a cedar fence post and she had a man's gray hat pulled down low over her head.

The tramp stood looking at her and didn't answer. He turned his back and faced the sunset. He swung both his whole and his short arm up slowly so that they indicated an expanse of sky and his figure formed a crooked cross. The old woman watched him with her arms folded across her chest as if she were the owner of the sun, and the daughter watched, her head thrust forward and her fat helpless hands hanging at the wrists. She had long pink-gold hair and eyes as blue as a peacock's neck.

He held the pose for almost fifty seconds and then he picked up his box and came on to the porch and dropped down on the bottom step. "Lady," he said in a firm nasal voice, "I'd give a fortune to live where I could see me a sun do that every evening."

"Does it every evening," the old woman said and sat back down. The daughter sat down too and watched him with a cautious sly look as if he were a bird that had come up very close. He leaned to one side, rooting in his pants pocket, and in a second he brought out a package of chewing gum and offered her a piece. She took it and unpeeled it and began to chew without taking her eyes off him. He offered the old woman a piece but she only raised her upper lip to indicate she had no teeth.

Mr. Shiftlet's pale sharp glance had already passed over everything in the yard—the pump near the corner of the house and the big fig

Lilacs (1924–1927) by Charles Burchfield. Oil on board.
Delaware Art Museum, bequest of John Saxon

tree that three or four chickens were preparing to roost in—and had moved to a shed where he saw the square rusted back of an automobile. "You ladies drive?" he asked.

"That car ain't run in fifteen year," the old woman said. "The day my husband died, it quit running."

"Nothing is like it used to be, lady," he said. "The world is almost rotten."

"That's right," the old woman said. "You from around here?"

"Name Tom T. Shiftlet," he murmured, looking at the tires.

"I'm pleased to meet you," the old woman said. "Name Lucynell Crater and daughter Lucynell Crater. What you doing around here, Mr. Shiftlet?"

He judged the car to be about a 1928 or '29 Ford. "Lady," he said, and turned and gave her his full attention, "lemme tell you something. There's one of these doctors in Atlanta that's taken a knife and cut the human heart— the human heart," he repeated, leaning forward, "out of a man's chest and held it in his hand," and he held his hand out, palm up, as if it were slightly weighted with the human heart, "and studied it like it was a day-old chicken, and lady," he said, allowing a long significant pause in which his head slid forward and his clay-colored eyes brightened, "he don't know no more about it than you or me."

"That's right," the old woman said.

"Why, if he was to take that knife and cut into every corner of it, he still wouldn't know no more than you or me. What you want to bet?"

"Nothing," the old woman said wisely. "Where you come from, Mr. Shiftlet?"

He didn't answer. He reached into his pocket and brought out a sack of tobacco and a package of cigarette papers and rolled himself a cigarette, expertly with one hand, and attached it in a hanging position to his upper lip. Then he took a box of wooden matches from his pocket and struck one on his shoe. He held the burning match as if he were studying the mystery of flame while it traveled dangerously toward his skin. The daughter began to make loud noises and to point to his hand and shake her finger at him, but when the flame was just before touching him, he leaned down with his hand cupped over it as if he were going to set fire to his nose and lit the cigarette.

He flipped away the dead match and blew a stream of gray into the evening. A sly look came over his face. "Lady," he said, "nowadays, people'll do anything anyways. I can tell you my name is Tom T. Shiftlet and I come from Tarwater, Tennessee, but you never have seen me before: how you know I ain't lying? How you know my name ain't Aaron Sparks, lady, and I come from Singleberry, Georgia, or how you know it's not George Speeds and I come from Lucy, Alabama, or how you know I ain't Thompson Bright from Toolafalls, Mississippi?"

"I don't know nothing about you," the old woman muttered, irked.

"Lady," he said, "people don't care how they lie. Maybe the best I can tell you is, I'm a man; but listen lady," he said and paused and made his tone more ominous still, "what is a man?"

The old woman began to gum a seed. "What you carry in that tin box, Mr. Shiftlet?" she asked.

"Tools," he said, put back. "I'm a carpenter."

"Well, if you come out here to work, I'll be able to feed you and give you a place to sleep but I can't pay. I'll tell you that before you begin," she said.

There was no answer at once and no particular expression on his face. He leaned back against the two-by-four that helped support the porch roof. "Lady," he said slowly, "there's some men that some things mean more to them than money." The old woman rocked without comment and the daughter watched the trigger that moved up and down in his neck. He told the old woman then that all most people were interested in was money, but he asked what a man was made for. He asked her if a man was made for money, or what. He asked her what she thought she was made for but she didn't answer, she only sat rocking and wondered if a one-armed man could put a new roof on her garden house. He asked a lot of questions that she didn't answer. He told her that he was twenty-eight years old and had lived a varied life. He had been a gospel singer, a foreman on the railroad, an assistant in an undertaking parlor, and he come over the radio for three months with Uncle Roy and his Red Creek Wranglers. He said he had fought and bled in the Arm Service of his country and visited every foreign land and that everywhere he had seen people that didn't care if they did a thing one way or another. He said he hadn't been raised thataway.

A fat yellow moon appeared in the branches of the fig tree as if it were going to roost there with the chickens. He said that a man had to escape to the country to see the world whole and that he wished he lived in a desolate place like this where he could see the sun go down every evening like God made it to do.

"Are you married or are you single?" the old woman asked.

There was a long silence. "Lady," he asked finally, "where would you find you an innocent woman today? I wouldn't have any of this trash I could just pick up."

The daughter was leaning very far down, hanging her head almost between her knees watching him through a triangular door she had made in her overturned hair; and she suddenly fell in a heap on the floor and began to whimper. Mr. Shiftlet straightened her out and helped her get back in the chair.

"Is she your baby girl?" he asked.

"My only," the old woman said "and she's the sweetest girl in the world. I would give her up for nothing on earth. She's smart too. She can sweep the floor, cook, wash, feed the chickens, and hoe. I wouldn't give her up for a casket of jewels."

"No," he said kindly, "don't ever let any man take her away from you."

"Any man come after her," the old woman said, " 'll have to stay around the place."

Mr. Shiftlet's eye in the darkness was focused on a part of the automobile bumper that glittered in the distance. "Lady," he said, jerking his short arm up as if he could point with it to her house and yard and pump, "there ain't a broken thing on this plantation that I couldn't fix for you, one-arm jackleg or not. I'm a man," he said with a sullen dignity, "even if I ain't a whole one. I got," he said, tapping his knuckles on the floor to emphasize the immensity of what he was going to say, "a moral intelligence!" and his face pierced out of the darkness into a shaft of doorlight and he stared at her as if he were astonished himself at this impossible truth.

The old woman was not impressed with the phrase. "I told you you could hang around and work for food," she said, "if you don't mind sleeping in that car yonder."

"Why listen, lady," he said with a grin of delight, "the monks of old slept in their coffins!"

"They wasn't as advanced as we are," the old woman said.

The next morning he began on the roof of the garden house while Lucynell, the daughter, sat on a rock and watched him work. He had not been around a week before the change he had made in the place was apparent. He had patched the front and back steps, built a new hog pen, restored a fence, and taught Lucynell, who was completely deaf and had never said a word in her life, to say the word "bird." The big rosy-faced girl followed him everywhere, saying "Burrttddt ddbirrrttdt," and clapping her hands. The old woman watched from a distance, secretly pleased. She was ravenous for a son-in-law.

Mr. Shiftlet slept on the hard narrow back seat of the car with his feet out the side window. He had his razor and a can of water on a crate that served him as a bedside table and he put up a piece of mirror against the back glass and kept his coat neatly on a hanger that he hung over one of the windows.

In the evenings he sat on the steps and talked while the old woman and Lucynell rocked violently in their chairs on either side of him. The old woman's three mountains were black against the dark blue sky and were visited off and on by various planets and by the moon after it had left the chickens. Mr. Shiftlet pointed out that the reason he had improved this plantation was because he had taken a personal interest in it. He said he was even going to make the automobile run.

He had raised the hood and studied the mechanism and he said he could tell that the car had been built in the days when cars were really built. You take now, he said, one man puts in one bolt and another man puts in another bolt and another man puts in another bolt so that it's a man for a bolt. That's why you have to pay so much for a car: you're paying all those men. Now if you didn't have to pay but one man, you could get you a cheaper car and one that had had a personal interest taken in it, and it would be a better car. The old woman agreed with him that this was so.

Mr. Shiftlet said that the trouble with the world was that nobody cared, or stopped and took any trouble. He said he never would have been able to teach Lucynell to say a word if he hadn't cared and stopped long enough.

"Teach her to say something else," the old woman said.

"What you want her to say next?" Mr. Shiftlet asked.

The old woman's smile was broad and toothless and suggestive. "Teach her to say 'sugarpie,' " she said.

Mr. Shiftlet already knew what was on her mind.

The next day he began to tinker with the automobile and that evening he told her that if she would buy a fan belt, he would be able to make the car run.

The old woman said she would give him the money. "You see that girl yonder?" she asked, pointing to Lucynell who was sitting on the floor a foot away, watching him, her eyes blue even in the dark. "If it was ever a man wanted to take her away, I would say, 'No man on earth is going to take that sweet girl of mine away from me!' but if he was to say, 'Lady, I don't want to take her away, I want her right here,' I would say, 'Mister, I don't blame you none. I wouldn't pass up a chance to live in a permanent place and get the sweetest girl in the world myself. You ain't no fool,' I would say."

"How old is she?" Mr. Shiftlet asked casually.

"Fifteen, sixteen," the old woman said. The girl was nearly thirty but because of her innocence it was impossible to guess.

"It would be a good idea to paint it too," Mr. Shiftlet remarked. "You don't want it to rust out."

"We'll see about that later," the old woman said.

The next day he walked into town and returned with the parts he needed and a can of gasoline. Late in the afternoon, terrible noises issued from the shed and the old woman rushed out of the house, thinking Lucynell was somewhere having a fit. Lucynell was sitting on a chicken crate, stamping her feet and screaming, "Burrddttt! bddurrddtttt!" but her fuss was drowned out by the car. With a volley of blasts it emerged from the shed, moving in a fierce and stately way. Mr. Shiftlet was in the driver's seat, sitting very erect. He had an expression of serious modesty on his face as if he had just raised the dead.

That night, rocking on the porch, the old woman began her business, at once. "You want you an innocent woman, don't you?" she asked sympathetically. "You don't want none of this trash."

"No'm, I don't," Mr. Shiftlet said.

"One that can't talk," she continued, "can't sass you back or use foul language. That's the kind for you to have. Right there," and she pointed to Lucynell sitting cross-legged in her chair, holding both feet in her hands.

"That's right," he admitted. "She wouldn't give me any trouble."

"Saturday," the old woman said, "you and her and me can drive into town and get married."

Mr. Shiftlet eased his position on the steps.

"I can't get married right now," he said. "Everything you want to do takes money and I ain't got any."

"What you need with money?" she asked.

"It takes money," he said. "Some people'll do anything anyhow these days, but the way I think, I wouldn't marry no woman that I couldn't take on a trip like she was somebody. I mean take her to a hotel and treat her. I wouldn't marry the Duchesser Windsor," he said firmly, "unless I could take her to a hotel and giver something good to eat.

"I was raised thataway and there ain't a thing I can do about it. My old mother taught me how to do."

"Lucynell don't even know what a hotel is," the old woman muttered. "Listen here, Mr. Shiftlet," she said, sliding forward in her chair, "you'd be getting a permanent house and a deep well and the most innocent girl in the world. You don't need no money. Lemme tell you something: there ain't any place in the world for a poor disabled friendless drifting man."

The ugly words settled in Mr. Shiftlet's head like a group of buzzards in the top of a tree.

He didn't answer at once. He rolled himself a cigarette and lit it and then he said in an even voice, "Lady, a man is divided into two parts, body and spirit."

The old woman clamped her gums together.

"A body and a spirit," he repeated. "The body, lady, is like a house: it don't go anywhere; but the spirit, lady, is like a automobile: always on the move, always . . .'"

"Listen, Mr. Shiftlet," she said, "my well never goes dry and my house is always warm in the winter and there's no mortgage on a thing about this place. You can go to the courthouse and see for yourself. And yonder under that shed is a fine automobile." She laid the bait carefully. "You can have it painted by Saturday. I'll pay for the paint."

In the darkness, Mr. Shiftlet's smile stretched like a weary snake waking up by a fire. After a second he recalled himself and said, "I'm only saying a man's spirit means more to him than anything else. I would have to take my wife off for the weekend without no regards at all for cost. I got to follow where my spirit says to go."

"I'll give you fifteen dollars for a weekend trip," the old woman said in a crabbed voice. "That's the best I can do."

"That wouldn't hardly pay for more than the gas and the hotel," he said. "It wouldn't feed her."

"Seventeen-fifty," the old woman said. "That's all I got so it isn't any use you trying to milk me. You can take a lunch."

Mr. Shiftlet was deeply hurt by the word "milk." He didn't doubt that she had more money sewed up in her mattress but he had already told her he was not interested in her money. "I'll make that do," he said and rose and walked off without treating with her further.

On Saturday the three of them drove into town in the car that the paint had barely dried on and Mr. Shiftlet and Lucynell were married in the Ordinary's office while the old woman witnessed. As they came out of the courthouse, Mr. Shiftlet began twisting his neck in his collar. He looked morose and bitter as if he had been insulted while someone held him. "That didn't satisfy me none," he said. "That was just something a woman in an office did, nothing but paper work and blood tests. What do they know about my blood? If they was to take my heart and cut it out," he said, "they wouldn't know a thing about me. It didn't satisfy me at all."

"It satisfied the law," the old woman said sharply.

"The law," Mr. Shiftlet said and spit. "It's the law that don't satisfy me."

He had painted the car dark green with a yellow band around it just under the windows. The three of them climbed in the front seat and the old woman said, "Don't Lucynell look pretty? Looks like a baby doll." Lucynell was dressed up in a white dress that her mother had uprooted from a trunk and there was a Panama hat on her head with a bunch of red wooden cherries on the brim. Every now and then her placid expression was changed by a sly isolated little thought like a shoot of green in the desert. "You got a prize!" the old woman said.

Mr. Shiftlet didn't even look at her.

They drove back to the house to let the old woman off and pick up the lunch. When they were ready to leave, she stood staring in the window of the car, with her fingers clenched around the glass. Tears began to seep sideways out of her eyes and run along the dirty creases in her face. "I ain't ever been parted with her for two days before," she said.

Mr. Shiftlet started the motor.

"And I wouldn't let no man have her but you because I seen you would do right. Good-bye, Sugarbaby," she said, clutching at the sleeve of the white dress. Lucynell looked straight at her and didn't seem to see her there at all. Mr. Shiftlet eased the car forward so that she had to move her hands.

The early afternoon was clear and open and surrounded by pale blue sky. Although the car would go only thirty miles an hour, Mr. Shiftlet imagined a terrific climb and dip and swerve that went entirely to his head so that he forgot his morning bitterness. He had always wanted an automobile but he had never been able to afford one before. He drove very fast because he wanted to make Mobile by nightfall.

Occasionally he stopped his thoughts long enough to look at Lucynell in the seat beside him. She had eaten the lunch as soon as they were out of the yard and now she was pulling the cherries off the hat one by one and throwing them out the window. He became depressed in spite of the car. He had driven about a hundred miles when he decided that she must be hungry again and at the next small town they came to, he stopped in front of an aluminum-painted eating place called The Hot Spot and took her in and ordered her a plate of ham and grits. The ride had made her sleepy and as soon as she got up on the stool, she rested her head on the counter and shut her eyes. There was no one in The Hot Spot but Mr. Shiftlet and the boy behind the counter, a pale youth with a greasy rag hung over his shoulder. Before he could dish up the food, she was snoring gently.

"Give it to her when she wakes up," Mr. Shiftlet said. "I'll pay for it now."

The boy bent over her and stared at the long pink-gold hair and the half-shut sleeping eyes. Then he looked up and stared at Mr. Shiftlet. "She looks like an angel of Gawd," he murmured.

"Hitchhiker," Mr. Shiftlet explained. "I can't wait. I got to make Tuscaloosa."

The boy bent over again and very carefully touched his finger to a strand of the golden hair and Mr. Shiftlet left.

He was more depressed than ever as he drove on by himself. The late afternoon had grown hot and sultry and the country had flattened out. Deep in the sky a storm was preparing very slowly and without thunder as if it meant to drain every drop of air from the earth before it broke. There were times when Mr. Shiftlet preferred not to be alone. He felt too that a man with a car had a responsibility to others and he kept his eye out for a hitch-hiker. Occasionally he saw a sign that warned: "Drive carefully. The life you save may be your own."

The narrow road dropped off on either side into dry fields and here and there a shack or a filling station stood in a clearing. The sun began to set directly in front of the automobile. It was a reddening ball that through his windshield was slightly flat on the bottom and top. He saw a boy in overalls and a gray hat standing on the edge of the road and he slowed the car down and stopped in front of him. The boy didn't have his hand raised to thumb the ride, he was only standing there, but he had a small cardboard suitcase and his hat was set on his head in a way to indicate that he had left somewhere for good. "Son," Mr. Shiftlet said, "I see you want a ride."

The boy didn't say he did or didn't but he opened the door of the car and got in, and Mr. Shiftlet started driving again. The child held the suitcase on his lap and folded his arms on top of it. He turned his head and looked out the window away from Mr. Shiftlet. Mr. Shiftlet felt oppressed. "Son," he said after a minute, "I got the best old mother in the world so I reckon you only got the second best."

The boy gave him a quick glance and then turned his face back out the window.

"It's nothing so sweet," Mr. Shiftlet continued, "as a boy's mother. She taught him his first prayers at her knee, she give him love when no other would, she told him what was right and what wasn't, and she seen that he done the right thing. Son," he said, "I never rued a day in my life like the one I rued when I left that old mother of mine."

The boy shifted in his seat but he didn't look at Mr. Shiftlet. He unfolded his arms and put one hand on the door handle.

"My mother was a angel of Gawd," Mr. Shiftlet said in a very strained voice. "He took her from heaven and giver to me and I left her." His eyes were instantly clouded over with a mist of tears. The car was barely moving.

The boy turned angrily in the seat. "You go to the devil!" he cried. "My old woman is a fleabag and yours is a stinking polecat!" and with that he flung the door open and jumped out with his suitcase into the ditch.

Mr. Shiftlet was so shocked that for about a hundred feet he drove along slowly with the door still open. A cloud, the exact color of the boy's hat and shaped like a turnip, had descended over the sun, and another, worse looking, crouched behind the car. Mr. Shiftlet felt that the rottenness of the world was about to engulf him. He raised his arm and let it fall again to his breast. "Oh Lord!" he prayed. "Break forth and wash the slime from this earth!"

The turnip continued slowly to descend. After a few minutes there was a guffawing peal of thunder from behind and fantastic raindrops, like tin-can tops, crashed over the rear of Mr. Shiftlet's car. Very quickly he stepped on the gas and with his stump sticking out the window he raced the galloping shower into Mobile.

Reading Check

1. What does Shiftlet say is his trade?
2. What object on the Crater "plantation" most interests him?
3. What arrangements are made for the weekend wedding trip?
4. Where does Shiftlet abandon Lucynell?
5. Why does he pick up a hitchhiker?

Commentary

As a devout Christian Flannery O'Connor centered her fictions, through symbol, character, and event, on the concepts of the Fall, the Redemption, and the Final Judgment. Consequently, her characters often talk about the soul, God, salvation, and sin; but because she views the world as a grotesque place of sin, her characters are usually grotesque and their pious talk is hypocritical or misplaced.

Tom T. Shiftlet solemnly scorns money and invokes the soul, the human spirit, and ethical behavior taught by his mother, but all the while he plans to swindle Mrs. Lucynell Crater and her retarded daughter out of their possessions. Wherever he goes he carries his tools. He fixes up the "plantation" and he repairs the car, but he does so only to take advantage of the people he meets. His name suggests shiftlessness. When he points out that his name is uncertain, that it could be anything, he thinks he is making a little homily about how deceptive *other* people are; but he unwittingly reveals the truth about himself. In O'Connor's fiction, people without a sense of belonging anywhere (Shiftlet is a drifter), whose only purpose is the shrewd use of others as a means of survival, are people without real selves. They are damned.

The two boys who appear toward the end of the story suggest the opposing realities beneath the surface of pious talk. The hitchhiking runaway punctures Shiftlet's sentimentalities about mothers. Ironically, Shiftlet is trying to do good, to get the boy to return home. But people without a spiritual center cannot do good, O'Connor insists; they can only mouth pieties. "You go to the devil!" cries the hitchhiker, quite appropriately. "My old woman is a fleabag and yours is a stinking polecat!" He cuts through Shiftlet's talk with the realities of a world given over to misery and "the devil," as it is in most of O'Connor's fiction. It is a world where a swindler talks about his mother as "a angel of Gawd," having just trampled all over Mrs. Crater's tearful, maternal love for her idiot daughter. Conversely, the other boy, the waiter in the cafe, sees another reality: he sees divinity even in the idiot—"She looks like an angel of Gawd." Even in this world of the devil (the cafe is "The Hot Spot"), there are glimpses of love, awe, and redemption. The boys tell opposite truths, and both truths are denied by the sanctimonious "morality" of the man whose only real concerns are his own survival and money.

And yet, even the Tom T. Shiftlets of the world are not content with merely material identity, as Shiftlet makes clear when he emerges from the marriage ceremony unhappy at being "nothing but paper work and blood tests. . . . It didn't satisfy me at all." But without a real moral, spiritual center, such O'Connor characters are doomed, never to be redeemed from the most limited identity, against which they chafe. The threatening heavens (the tornado-shaped "turnip" cloud in the storm from "deep in the sky") "guffaw" at such a human as they chase him to his destination. In moral terms, Shiftlet does not know what "careful driving" is. In spiritual terms he does not "save" his life. In religious terms O'Connor leaves no doubt about his destination.

For Study and Discussion

Analyzing and Interpreting the Story

1. Although Flannery O'Connor employs realistic diction and settings, she constantly works symbolic overtones into her writing. For instance, Tom T. Shiftlet obviously yearns to get his hands on Mrs. Crater's car. What do you think O'Connor had in mind when she chose the possible other names Mr. Shiftlet could have had: Sparks, Speeds, and Bright—as well as Shiftlet itself?

2. The comic diction invites the reader to laugh when the narrative tells us that Shiftlet "said he had fought and bled in the Arm Service of his country," and when Shiftlet says, "I wouldn't marry the Duchesser Windsor . . . unless I could take her to a hotel and giver something good to eat." **a.** What is it in the diction and the event that makes each of these passages funny? **b.** What does the comic tone at these moments do to the seriousness and sincerity of Shiftlet's assertions? **c.** How does the comic tone create irony?

3a. What are we told by Mrs. Crater's continual insistence that she wouldn't let any man take her daughter away from her? **b.** What is really on her mind? **c.** Now look at the scene in which Mrs. Crater takes leave of Lucynell. How does that modify your sense of Mrs. Crater?

4. When Mrs. Crater tells Shiftlet that he can have the car painted, "in the darkness, Mr. Shiftlet's smile stretched like a weary snake waking up by a fire." **a.** Why this image? What is suggested by "darkness," "snake," "fire," and the fact that the "snake" is "waking up"? **b.** How does the image

relate to the story as a whole? **c.** On the other hand, if Shiftlet is getting what he wanted, why does he feel depressed and angry after the wedding? Is he aware of himself as part of what he sees as "the rottenness of the world"?

5. If you are in tune with the tone of the story, you become aware that there is almost no moment in which the narrative is not funny. **a.** What do you think are the funniest moments of narration? **b.** Are there any that are not also grotesque?

Writing About Literature

Examining the Relation of Irony to Theme

Irony is the literary device whereby your expectations are reversed, whereby what is going on or being said on the surface of the narrative is undercut and reversed by implications beneath the surface.

Ironically Mrs. Crater talks about never parting with her daughter although she is "ravenous" for a son-in-law. Ironically she wants a son-in-law for security but gets one who robs her. Ironically Shiftlet complains about the "rotten" world, but is himself the primary example of its rot. Ironically Shiftlet, who complains about the difficulty of finding an innocent woman, does not want the innocent woman he gets. Ironically Lucynell's innocence is not virtue but idiocy. Irony creates one of the themes of the story: the only possible human innocence on this corrupted earth is mindlessness. But O'Connor never says this in so many words. She creates ironies by supplying specific details and then lets them speak for themselves, so that the reader has a sense that "there is more than meets the eye" going on in the story.

Examine the use of irony in any of these stories: "The Catbird Seat" (page 601), "Winter Dreams" (page 610), "In Another Country" (page 653), "Flight" (page 661). What is the relation of irony to the underlying meaning of the story?

John Updike grew up in the small Pennsylvania town of Shillington, near Reading. He graduated from Harvard in 1954, then spent a year in England studying art. After his return to the United States, he worked on the staff of *The New Yorker,* where many of his short stories have appeared.

In 1958 Updike published a collection of poems, *The Carpentered Hen and Other Tame Animals,* followed the next year by a book of stories, *The Same Door,* and his first novel, *The Poorhouse Fair.* He has published several other novels, including *Rabbit, Run* (1960) and its sequel, *Rabbit Redux* (1971), about a high school basketball star whose later life is all downhill; *The Centaur,* which won a National Book Award in 1963; *Of the Farm* (1965); his best seller *Couples* (1968); and *The Coup* (1978). He has also published further collections of poems and several volumes of short stories. In 1964 he brought together *The Olinger Stories,* based on life in the small town he knew as a boy. *Hugging the Shore,* a collection of essays and criticism, appeared in 1983.

Updike's fiction touches upon some basic issues of life in our time: faith and disbelief, and the uprooting and uncertainty of human relationships. Updike has said that a writer should capture the "complexity and ambiguity of life," and his stories, especially, show his skill at revealing what he terms "the essential strangeness I feel in the mundane." His work has often been pessimistic in outlook; its strength lies in the sharp insight he brings to the frustrations he so often depicts.

John Updike.
© Nancy Crampton

In the following story, Jay, a boy of eager wit, youthful independence, and cool self-assurance, makes his first trip to the great city of New York. There be begins to learn that life is not as clear, or *lucid,* as he had assumed. The true relationships among Jay, his father, and his Uncle Quin are understood only by the one with the lucid eye.

The Lucid Eye in Silver Town

The first time I visited New York City, I was thirteen and went with my father. I went to meet my Uncle Quin and to buy a book about Vermeer.[1] The Vermeer book was my idea, and my mother's; meeting Uncle Quin was my father's. A generation ago, my uncle had vanished in the direction of Chicago and become, apparently, rich; in the last week he had come east on business and I had graduated from the eighth grade with perfect marks. My father claimed that I and his brother were the smartest people he had ever met—"go-getters," he called us, with perhaps more irony than at the time I gave him credit for—and in his visionary way he suddenly, irresistibly felt that now was the time for us to meet. New York in those days was seven dollars away; we measured everything, distance and time, in money then. World War II was almost over but we were still living in the Depression.[2] My father and I set off with the return tickets and a five-dollar bill in his pocket. The five dollars was for the book.

My mother, on the railway platform, suddenly exclaimed, "I *hate* the Augusts." This surprised me, because we were all Augusts—I was an August, my father was an August, Uncle Quincy was an August, and she, I had thought, was an August.

My father gazed serenely over her head and said, "You have every reason to. I wouldn't blame you if you took a gun and shot us all. Except for Quin and your son. They're the only ones of us ever had any get up and git." Nothing was more infuriating about my father than his way of agreeing.

Uncle Quin didn't meet us at Pennsylvania Station. If my father was disappointed, he didn't reveal it to me. It was after one o'clock and all we had for lunch were two candy bars. By walking what seemed to me a very long way on pavements only a little broader than those of my home town, and not so clean, we reached the hotel, which seemed to sprout somehow from Grand Central Station. The lobby smelled of perfume. After the clerk had phoned Quincy August that a man who said he was his brother was at the desk, an elevator took us to the twentieth floor. Inside the room sat three men, each in a gray or blue suit with freshly pressed pants and garters peeping from under the cuffs when they crossed their legs. The men were not quite interchangeable. One had a caterpillar-shaped moustache, one had tangled blond eyebrows like my father's, and the third had a drink in his hand—the others had drinks, too, but were not gripping them so tightly.

"Gentlemen, I'd like you to meet my brother Marty and his young son," Uncle Quin said.

"The kid's name is Jay," my father added, shaking hands with each of the two men, staring them in the eye. I imitated my father, and the moustached man, not expecting my firm handshake and stare, said, "Why, hello there, Jay!"

"Marty, would you and the boy like to freshen up? The facilities are through the door and to the left."

"Thank you, Quin. I believe we will. Excuse me, gentlemen."

"Certainly."

"Certainly."

My father and I went into the bedroom of the suite. The furniture was square and new and all the same shade of maroon. On the bed was an opened suitcase, also new. The clean, expensive smells of leather and lotion were

---

1. **Vermeer** (vər-mâr′, -mîr′): Jan Vermeer (1632–1675), Dutch painter.
2. **Depression:** the Great Depression, which had started with the Stock Market Crash in 1929.

Nightview of New York City (1932).
Gelatin silver photograph.
Berenice Abbott / Commerce Graphics Ltd., Inc.

beautiful to me. Uncle Quin's underwear looked silk and was full of fleurs-de-lis.[3] When I was through in the lavatory, I made for the living room, to rejoin Uncle Quin and his friends.

"Hold it," my father said. "Let's wait in here."

"Won't that look rude?"

"No. It's what Quin wants."

"Now Daddy, don't be ridiculous. He'll think we've died in here."

"No he won't, not my brother. He's working some deal. He doesn't want to be bothered. I know how my brother works: he got us in here so we'd stay in here."

"*Really*, Pop. You're such a schemer." But I did not want to go in there without him. I looked around the room for something to read. There was nothing, not even a newspaper, except a shiny little pamphlet about the hotel itself. I wondered when we would get a chance to look for the Vermeer book. I wondered what the men in the next room were talking about. I wondered why Uncle Quin was so short, when my father was so tall. By leaning out of the window, I could see taxicabs maneuvering like windup toys.

My father came and stood beside me. "Don't lean out too far."

I edged out inches farther and took a big bite of the high, cold air, spiced by the distant street noises. "Look at the green cab cut in front of the yellow," I said. "Should they be making U-turns on that street?"

"In New York it's OK. Survival of the fittest is the only law here."

"Isn't that the Chrysler Building?"

"Yes, isn't it graceful though? It always reminds me of the queen of the chessboard."

"What's the one beside it?"

"I don't know. Some big gravestone. The one deep in back, from this window, is the Woolworth Building. For years it was the tallest building in the world."

As, side by side at the window, we talked, I

---

3. **fleur-de-lis** (flûr′də-lē′): French for "lily flower." The design, showing a three-petaled flower, was once the emblem of the French kings.

was surprised that my father could answer so many of my questions. As a young man, before I was born, he had traveled, looking for work; this was not *his* first trip to New York. Excited by my new respect, I longed to say something to remold that calm, beaten face.

"Do you really think he meant for us to stay out here?" I asked.

"Quin is a go-getter," he said, gazing over my head. "I admire him. Anything he wanted, from little on up, he went after it. Slam. Bang. His thinking is miles ahead of mine—just like your mother's. You can feel them pull out ahead of you." He moved his hands, palms down, like two taxis, the left quickly pulling ahead of the right. "You're the same way."

"Sure, sure." My impatience was not merely embarrassment at being praised; I was irritated that he considered Uncle Quin as smart as myself. At that point in my life I was sure that only stupid people took an interest in money.

When Uncle Quin finally entered the bedroom, he said, "Martin, I hoped you and the boy would come out and join us."

"Hell, I didn't want to butt in. You and those men were talking business."

"Lucas and Roebuck and I? Now, Marty, it was nothing that my own brother couldn't hear. Just a minor matter of adjustment. Both these men are fine men. Very important in their own fields. I'm disappointed that you couldn't see more of them. Believe me, I hadn't meant for you to hide in here. Now what kind of drink would you like?"

"I don't care. I drink very little any more."

"Scotch-and-water, Marty?"

"Swell."

"And the boy? What about some ginger ale, young man? Or would you like milk?"

"The ginger ale," I said.

"There was a day, you know, when your father could drink any two men under the table."

As I remember it, a waiter brought the drinks to the room, and while we were drinking them I asked if we were going to spend all afternoon in this room. Uncle Quin didn't seem to hear, but five minutes later he suggested that the boy might like to take a look around the city—Gotham, he called it. Baghdad-on-the-Subway.[4] My father said that that would be a once-in-a-lifetime treat for the kid. He always called me "the kid" when I was sick or had lost at something or was angry—when he felt sorry for me, in short. The three of us went down in the elevator and took a taxi ride down Broadway, or up Broadway—I wasn't sure. "This is what they call the Great White Way," Uncle Quin said several times. Once he apologized, "In daytime it's just another street." The trip didn't seem so much designed for sightseeing as for getting Uncle Quin to the Pickernut Club, a little restaurant set in a block of similar canopied places. I remember we stepped down into it and it was dark inside. A piano was playing *There's a Small Hotel*.

"He shouldn't do that," Uncle Quin said. Then he waved to the man behind the piano. "How are you, Freddie? How are the kids?"

"Fine, Mr. August, fine," Freddie said, bobbing his head and smiling and not missing a note.

"That's Quin's song," my father said to me as we wriggled our way into a dark curved seat at a round table.

I didn't say anything, but Uncle Quin, overhearing some disapproval in my silence, said, "Freddie's a first-rate man. He has a boy going to Colgate[5] this autumn."

I asked, "Is that really your song?"

Uncle Quin grinned and put his warm broad hand on my shoulder; I hated, at that age, being touched. "I let them think it is," he said, oddly purring. "To me, songs are like young girls. They're all pretty."

A waiter in a red coat scurried up. "Mr. August! Back from the West? How are you, Mr. August?"

"Getting by, Jerome, getting by. Jerome, I'd like you to meet my kid brother, Martin."

"How do you do, Mr. Martin. Are you paying New York a visit? Or do you live here?"

My father quickly shook hands with Jerome, somewhat to Jerome's surprise. "I'm just up for the afternoon, thank you. I live in a hick town in Pennsylvania you never heard of."

"I see, sir. A quick visit."

"This is the first time in six years that I've had a chance to see my brother."

"Yes, we've seen very little of him these past years. He's a man we can never see too much of, isn't that right?"

Uncle Quin interrupted. "This is my nephew Jay."

"How do you like the big city, Jay?"

"Fine." I didn't duplicate my father's mistake of offering to shake hands.

"Why, Jerome," Uncle Quin said. "My brother and I would like to have a Scotch-on-the-rocks. The boy would like a ginger ale."

"No, wait," I said. "What kinds of ice cream do you have?"

"Vanilla and chocolate, sir."

I hesitated. I could scarcely believe it, when the cheap drugstore at home had fifteen flavors.

"I'm afraid it's not a very big selection," Jerome said.

"I guess vanilla."

"Yes, sir. One plate of vanilla."

When my ice cream came it was a golf ball in a flat silver dish; it kept spinning away as I dug at it with my spoon. Uncle Quin watched me and asked, "Is there anything especially you'd like to do?"

"The kid'd like to get into a bookstore," my father said.

"A bookstore. What sort of book, Jay?"

I said, "I'd like to look for a good book of Vermeer."

"Vermeer," Uncle Quin pronounced slowly, relishing the r's, pretending to give the matter thought. "Dutch School."

"He's Dutch, yes."

"For my own money, Jay, the French are the

4. **Baghdad-on-the-subway:** the name given to New York City by the short-story writer O. Henry (William Sidney Porter).
5. **Colgate:** Colgate University in Hamilton, New York.

John Updike **723**

people to beat. We have four Degas[6] ballet dancers in our living room in Chicago, and I could sit and look at one of them for hours. I think it's wonderful, the feeling for balance the man had."

"Yeah, but don't Degas' paintings always remind you of colored drawings? For actually *looking* at things in terms of paint, for the lucid eye, I think Vermeer makes Degas look sick."

Uncle Quin said nothing, and my father,

after an anxious glance across the table, said, "That's the way he and his mother talk all the time. It's beyond me. I can't understand a thing they say."

"Your mother is encouraging you to be a painter, is she, Jay?" Uncle Quin's smile was very wide and his cheeks were pushed out as if each held a candy.

"Sure, I suppose she is."

"Your mother is a very wonderful woman, Jay," Uncle Quin said.

It was such an embarrassing remark, and so much depended upon your definition of "wonderful," that I dug at my ice cream, and my

6. **Degas** (də-gä′): Edgar Degas (1834–1917), a French sculptor and impressionist painter, best known for his scenes of ballet dancers, working girls, and cabaret performers.

The Young Woman with a Water Jug (c. 1664–1665) by Jan Vermeer (1632–1675). Oil on canvas.

Metropolitan Museum of Art, gift of Henry G. Marquand, 1889

father asked Uncle Quin about his own wife, Tessie. When we left, Uncle Quin signed the check with his name and the name of some company. It was close to five o'clock.

My uncle didn't know much about the location of bookstores in New York—his last fifteen years had been spent in Chicago—but he thought that if we went to Forty-second Street and Sixth Avenue we should find something. The cab driver let us out beside a park that acted as kind of a backyard for the Public Library. It looked so inviting, so agreeably dusty, with the pigeons and the men nodding on the benches and the office girls in their taut summer dresses, that without thinking, I led the two men into it. Shimmering buildings arrowed upward and glinted through the treetops. This was New York, I felt: the silver town. Towers of ambition rose, crystalline, within me. "If you stand here," my father said, "you can see the Empire State." I went and stood beneath my father's arm and followed with my eyes the direction of it. Something sharp and hard fell into my right eye. I ducked my head and blinked; it was painful.

"What's the trouble?" Uncle Quin's voice asked.

My father said, "The poor kid's got something into his eye. He has the worst luck that way of anybody I ever knew."

The thing seemed to have life. It bit. "Ow," I said, angry enough to cry.

"If we can get him out of the wind," my father's voice said, "maybe I can see it."

"No, now, Marty, use your head. Never fool with the eyes or ears. The hotel is within two blocks. Can you walk two blocks, Jay?"

"I'm blind, not lame," I snapped.

"He has a ready wit," Uncle Quin said.

Between the two men, shielding my eye with a hand, I walked to the hotel. From time to time, one of them would take my other hand, or put one of theirs on my shoulder, but I would walk faster, and the hands would drop away. I hoped our entrance into the hotel lobby would not be too conspicuous; I took my hand from my eye and walked erect, defying the impulse to stoop. Except for the one lid being shut and possibly my face being red, I imagined I looked passably suave. However, my guardians lost no time betraying me. Not only did they walk at my heels, as if I might topple any instant, but my father told one old bum sitting in the lobby, "Poor kid got something in his eye," and Uncle Quin, passing the desk, called, "Send up a doctor to Twenty-eleven."

"You shouldn't have done that, Quin," my father said in the elevator. "I can get it out, now that he's out of the wind. This is happening all the time. The kid's eyes are too far front."

"Never fool with the eyes, Martin. They are your most precious tool in life."

"It'll work out," I said, though I didn't believe it would. It felt like a steel chip, deeply embedded.

Up in the room, Uncle Quin made me lie down on the bed. My father, a clean handkerchief wadded in his hand so that one corner stuck out, approached me, but it hurt so much to open the eye that I repulsed him. "Don't torment me," I said, twisting my face away. "What good does it do? The doctor'll be up."

Regretfully my father put the handkerchief back into his pocket.

The doctor was a soft-handed man with little to say to anybody; he wasn't pretending to be the family doctor. He rolled my lower eyelid on a thin stick, jabbed with a Q-tip, and showed me, on the end of the Q-tip, an eyelash. He dropped three drops of yellow fluid into the eye to remove any chance of infection. The fluid stung, and I shut my eyes, leaning back into the pillow, glad it was over. When I opened them, my father was passing a bill into the doctor's hand. The doctor thanked him, winked at me, and left. Uncle Quin came out of the bathroom.

"Well, young man, how are you feeling now?" he asked.

"Fine."

"It was just an eyelash," my father said.

"*Just* an eyelash! Well I know how an eyelash

can feel like a razor blade in there. But, now that the young invalid is recovered, we can think of dinner."

"No, I really appreciate your kindness, Quin, but we must be getting back to the sticks. I have an eight-o'clock meeting I should be at."

"I'm extremely sorry to hear that. What sort of meeting, Marty?"

"A church council."

"So you're still doing church work. Well, God bless you for it."

"Grace wanted me to ask you if you couldn't possibly come over some day. We'll put you up overnight. It would be a real treat for her to see you again."

Uncle Quin reached up and put his arm around his younger brother's shoulders. "Martin, I'd like that better than anything in the world. But I am solid with appointments, and I must head west this Thursday. They don't let me have a minute's repose. Nothing would please my heart better than to share a quiet day with you and Grace in your home. Please give her my love, and tell her what a wonderful boy she is raising. The two of you are raising."

My father promised, "I'll do that." And, after a little more fuss, we left.

"The child better?" the old man in the lobby called to us on the way out.

"It was just an eyelash, thank you, sir," my father said.

When we got outside, I wondered if there were any bookstores still open.

"We have no money."

"None at all?"

"The doctor charged five dollars. That's how much it costs in New York to get something in your eye."

"I didn't do it on purpose. Do you think I pulled out the eyelash and stuck it in there myself? I didn't tell you to call the doctor."

"I know that."

"Couldn't we just go into a bookstore and look a minute?"

"We haven't time, Jay."

But when we reached Pennsylvania Station, it was over thirty minutes until the next train left. As we sat on a bench, my father smiled reminiscently. "Boy, he's smart, isn't he? His thinking is sixty light-years ahead of mine."

"Whose?"

"My brother. Notice the way he hid in the bathroom until the doctor was gone? That's how to make money. The rich man collects dollar bills like the stamp collector collects stamps. I knew he'd do it. I knew it when he told the clerk to send up a doctor that I'd have to pay for it."

"Well, why *should* he pay for it? *You* were the person to pay for it."

"That's right. Why should he?" My father settled back, his eyes forward, his hands crossed and limp in his lap. The skin beneath his chin was loose; his temples seemed concave. The liquor was probably disagreeing with him. "That's why he's where he is now, and that's why I am where I am."

The seed of my anger seemed to be a desire to recall him to himself, to scold him out of being old and tired. "Well, why'd you bring along only five dollars? You might have known something would happen."

"You're right, Jay. I should have brought more."

"Look. Right over there is an open bookstore. Now if you had brought *ten* dollars——"

"Is it open? I don't think so. They just left the lights in the window on."

"What if it isn't? What does it matter to us? Anyway, what kind of art book can you get for five dollars? Color plates cost money. How much do you think a decent book of Vermeer costs? It'd be cheap at fifteen dollars, even secondhand, with the pages all crummy and full of spilled coffee." I kept on, shrilly flailing the passive and infuriating figure of my father, until we left the city. Once we were on the homeward train, my tantrum ended; it had been a kind of ritual, for both of us, and he had endured my screams complacently, nodding assent, like a midwife assisting at the birth of family pride. Years passed before I needed to go to New York again.

For Study and Discussion

Analyzing and Interpreting the Story

1. John Updike's story is concerned with complex emotional relationships and with a "lucid eye," an eye that presumably sees these relationships clearly. **a.** In the first paragraph, what details suggest that Jay feels he sees things clearly? **b.** What details suggest that his father is motivated by emotional impulse?

2. Jay seems to have mixed feelings about success. **a.** What does he admire about his uncle's luggage? **b.** Why does he resent the comparisons between his success and that of his uncle?

3. Cite two details from the scene in the hotel bedroom that indicate the boy's mixed feelings about his father.

4. The scene in the Pickernut Club lets us know what kind of success Uncle Quin has achieved. **a.** How does his relationship with the waiter contrast with that of Jay's father? **b.** What does the difference between the two suggest about the father's success or lack of it?

5. Uncle Quin has taken Jay and his father in hand to show them New York. **a.** How is this intent borne out by his advising Jay on what painting to like? **b.** What detail in Jay's answer indicates that he feels he has superior knowledge of painting?

6. The central episode of the story concerns Jay's getting something in his eye and consequently not being able to buy the Vermeer book. This episode is related to the earlier discussion of Degas and of Vermeer's "lucid eye." **a.** In what way does the boy identify himself with Vermeer? **b.** What does this identification suggest about the boy's self-image?

7. Updike suggests that Jay may be prematurely proud of his sharpness of vision when the boy is partially blinded by getting something in his eye. Which character do you think has the "lucid eye"?

Point of View

Updike's story is written in the **first-person point of view,** the same point of view used in autobiographies, memoirs, and journals. The narrator, Jay, is the person to whom the events happened; consequently, this point of view has the advantage of immediacy, of telling the story from firsthand knowledge. However, the reader is also aware that Jay's viewpoint may not be accurate in all respects. He is telling the story as an adult, long after the events occurred; his memories may not be reliable. Furthermore, his viewpoint is limited to what he could see and what he thought.

Updike might have chosen to tell his story in the third person, from the point of view of another character, say, Uncle Quin or Jay's father. He might have chosen an omniscient narrator who could reveal what everybody was thinking and feeling. Why do you think he chose to have Jay tell the story? What might this point of view have to do with the title of the story?

Style

Consider Updike's use of adjectives in the following sentences:

> Shimmering buildings arrowed upward and glinted through the treetops. This was New York, I felt: the silver town. Towers of ambition rose, crystalline, within me.

The adjectives *shimmering, silver,* and *crystalline* convey the brilliant, dazzling effect that the great city has upon the boy Jay. Find another passage in the story that illustrates Updike's use of colorful adjectives, and, in a short paragraph, explain how the adjectives contribute to the overall impression of the passage.

Analyzing Credibility

Jay's trip to New York City takes place when he is thirteen, just between childhood and manhood. How does Updike make Jay a believable character? Where in the story does he behave like a child, and where does he show a dawning maturity?

John Updike   **727**

ALICE WALKER
1944–

Alice Walker.

Alice Walker's purpose as a writer is the key to the triumphant survival of her fictional heroines, a victory that transcends the violence visited upon her characters by their times, their societies, and their families. Walker uses the word "womanist" to refer to the liberation of black women, and that concept is the motivation for her writing. Her most famous book, the novel *The Color Purple* (1982), is a complete example of her central "womanist" concern, as, in a smaller and more lighthearted way, is "Everyday Use."

Essentially, Walker's thematic center is this: women have been the world's "mules"—property of men, black as well as white, who "own" them. The struggle for black equality cannot be meaningful and complete, in Walker's view, until black women are free and equal within and as a result of that struggle. Walker was born to sharecroppers in Eatonton, Georgia: her beginnings were rooted deeply in a condition in which humiliation, pain, and death had been commonplace in black experience throughout American history. For Walker, the plight of the doubly oppressed black women (debased by sexism as well as racism) becomes an intense example of the double standards forced upon women everywhere. Therefore, the triumph of the black woman stands for the freedom and equality of women of all colors in all societies and lands.

Motivated by her childhood background, by her education at Spelman College and Sarah Lawrence College (B.A., 1965), by her voter-registration work in Georgia, and by her Head Start work in Mississippi, Walker writes fiction in which, in her phrase, "the historical subconscious" is never asleep. One of her trademarks is her constant merger of the surrounding society with the unfolding of the inner, individual self in her tales and poems. Her work almost always presents black women as the central characters, and usually, as in "Everyday Use," they are women whose necessities have made them able to do anything, including so-called "man's work."

The pressing realities of their lives, beneath the stereotypes and assumptions imposed by racism and sexism, reveal the actual equality, self-sufficiency, astonishing survival-strength, and life-force of women.

Walker has written several volumes of poetry, short stories, and essays, as well as novels. She has written and edited the work of Langston Hughes and Zora Neale Hurston as well as that of "womanist" writers. She has won many honors, among which are the Rosenthal Award of the American Academy of Arts and Letters (1974) for her short stories, *In Love and Trouble* (1973); the Lillian Smith Award of the Southern Regional Council (1973) for her poems *Revolutionary Petunias* (1973); a Guggenheim Fellowship (1977–78); a Pulitzer Prize and an American Book Award (1983) for *The Color Purple.*

Although Walker has been criticized by some black writers because she explores sexist cruelties in black families and satirizes the superficially modish aspects of "new blackness" (as she does humorously in "Everyday Use"), she has been applauded by most commentators, black as well as white. Walker emphasizes the realities of black American life beneath ideological fashionableness, and she continues to hammer at sexism and racism as her major themes.

Everyday Use

for your grandmama

I will wait for her in the yard that Maggie and I made so clean and wavy yesterday afternoon. A yard like this is more comfortable than most people know. It is not just a yard. It is like an extended living room. When the hard clay is swept clean as a floor and the fine sand around the edges lined with tiny, irregular grooves, anyone can come and sit and look up into the elm tree and wait for the breezes that never come inside the house.

Maggie will be nervous until after her sister goes: she will stand hopelessly in corners, homely and ashamed of the burn scars down her arms and legs, eying her sister with a mixture of envy and awe. She thinks her sister has held life always in the palm of one hand, that "no" is a word the world never learned to say to her.

You've no doubt seen those TV shows where the child who has "made it" is confronted, as a surprise, by her own mother and father, tottering in weakly from backstage. (A pleasant surprise, of course: What would they do if parent and child came on the show only to curse out and insult each other?) On TV mother and child embrace and smile into each other's faces. Sometimes the mother and father weep, the child wraps them in her arms and leans across the table to tell how she would not have made it without their help. I have seen these programs.

Sometimes I dream a dream in which Dee and I are suddenly brought together on a TV program of this sort. Out of a dark and soft-seated limousine I am ushered into a bright room filled with many people. There I meet a smiling, gray, sporty man like Johnny Carson who shakes my hand and tells me what a fine girl I have. Then we are on the stage and Dee is embracing me with tears in her eyes. She

pins on my dress a large orchid, even though she has told me once that she thinks orchids are tacky flowers.

In real life I am a large, big-boned woman with rough, man-working hands. In the winter I wear flannel nightgowns to bed and overalls during the day. I can kill and clean a hog as mercilessly as a man. My fat keeps me hot in zero weather. I can work outside all day, breaking ice to get water for washing; I can eat pork liver cooked over the open fire minutes after it comes steaming from the hog. One winter I knocked a bull calf straight in the brain between the eyes with a sledgehammer and had the meat hung up to chill before nightfall. But of course all this does not show on television. I am the way my daughter would want me to be: a hundred pounds lighter, my skin like an uncooked barley pancake. My hair glistens in the hot bright lights. Johnny Carson has much to do to keep up with my quick and witty tongue.

But that is a mistake. I know even before I wake up. Who ever knew a Johnson with a quick tongue? Who can even imagine me looking a strange white man in the eye? It seems to me I have talked to them always with one foot raised in flight, with my head turned in whichever way is farthest from them. Dee, though. She would always look anyone in the eye. Hesitation was no part of her nature.

"How do I look, Mama?" Maggie says, showing just enough of her thin body enveloped in pink skirt and red blouse for me to know she's there, almost hidden by the door.

"Come out into the yard," I say.

Have you ever seen a lame animal, perhaps a dog run over by some careless person rich enough to own a car, sidle up to someone who is ignorant enough to be kind to him? That is the way my Maggie walks. She has been like this, chin on chest, eyes on ground, feet in shuffle, ever since the fire that burned the other house to the ground.

Dee is lighter than Maggie, with nicer hair and a fuller figure. She's a woman now, though sometimes I forget. How long ago was it that the other house burned? Ten, twelve years? Sometimes I can still hear the flames and feel Maggie's arms sticking to me, her hair smoking and her dress falling off her in little black papery flakes. Her eyes seemed stretched open, blazed open by the flames reflected in them. And Dee. I see her standing off under the sweet gum tree she used to dig gum out of; a look of concentration on her face as she watched the last dingy gray board of the house fall in toward the red-hot brick chimney. Why don't you do a dance around the ashes? I'd wanted to ask her. She had hated the house that much.

I used to think she hated Maggie, too. But that was before we raised the money, the church and me, to send her to Augusta to school. She used to read to us without pity; forcing words, lies, other folks' habits, whole lives upon us two, sitting trapped and ignorant underneath her voice. She washed us in a river of make-believe, burned us with a lot of knowledge we didn't necessarily need to know. Pressed us to her with the serious way she read, to shove us away at just the moment, like dimwits, we seemed about to understand.

Dee wanted nice things. A yellow organdy dress to wear to her graduation from high school; black pumps to match a green suit she'd made from an old suit somebody gave me. She was determined to stare down any disaster in her efforts. Her eyelids would not flicker for minutes at a time. Often I fought off the temptation to shake her. At sixteen she had a style of her own: and knew what style was.

I never had an education myself. After second grade the school was closed down. Don't ask me why: in 1927 colored asked fewer questions than they do now. Sometimes Maggie reads to me. She stumbles along good-naturedly but can't see well. She knows she is not bright. Like good looks and money, quickness passed her by. She will marry John Thomas (who has mossy teeth in an earnest face) and then I'll be free to sit here and I guess just sing church songs to myself. Although I never was a good singer. Never could carry a tune. I was always better at a man's job. I used to love to milk till I was hooked in the side in '49. Cows are soothing and slow and don't bother you, unless you try to milk them the wrong way.

I have deliberately turned my back on the house. It is three rooms, just like the one that burned, except the roof is tin; they don't make shingle roofs anymore. There are no real windows, just some holes cut in the sides, like the portholes in a ship, but not round and not square, with rawhide holding the shutters up on the outside. This house is in a pasture, too, like the other one. No doubt when Dee sees it she will want to tear it down. She wrote me once that no matter where we "choose" to live, she will manage to come see us. But she will never bring her friends. Maggie and I thought about this and Maggie asked me, "Mama, when did Dee ever *have* any friends?"

She had a few. Furtive boys in pink shirts hanging about on washday after school. Nervous girls who never laughed. Impressed with her they worshiped the well-turned phrase, the cute shape, the scalding humor that erupted like bubbles in lye. She read to them.

When she was courting Jimmy T she didn't have much time to pay to us, but turned all her faultfinding power on him. He *flew* to marry a cheap city girl from a family of ignorant flashy people. She hardly had time to recompose herself.

When she comes I will meet—but there they are!

Maggie attempts to make a dash for the house, in her shuffling way, but I stay her with my hand. "Come back here," I say. And she stops and tries to dig a well in the sand with her toe.

It is hard to see them clearly through the strong sun. But even the first glimpse of leg out of the car tells me it is Dee. Her feet were always neat-looking, as if God himself had shaped them with a certain style. From the other side of the car comes a short, stocky man. Hair is all over his head a foot long and hanging from his chin like a kinky mule tail. I hear Maggie suck in her breath. "Uhnnnh," is what it sounds like. Like when you see the wriggling end of a snake just in front of your foot on the road. "Uhnnnh."

Dee next. A dress down to the ground, in this hot weather. A dress so loud it hurts my eyes. There are yellows and oranges enough to throw back the light of the sun. I feel my whole face warming from the heat waves it throws out. Earrings gold, too, and hanging down to her shoulders. Bracelets dangling and making noises when she moves her arm up to shake the folds of the dress out of her armpits. The dress is loose and flows, and as she walks closer, I like it. I hear Maggie go "Uhnnnh" again. It is her sister's hair. It stands straight up like the wool on a sheep. It is black as night and around the edges are two long pigtails that rope about like small lizards disappearing behind her ears.

"Wa-su-zo-Tean-o!" she says, coming on in that gliding way the dress makes her move. The short stocky fellow with the hair to his navel is all grinning and he follows up with "Asalamalakim,[1] my mother and sister!" He moves to hug Maggie but she falls back, right up against the back of my chair. I feel her trembling there and when I look up I see the perspiration falling off her chin.

"Don't get up," says Dee. Since I am stout it takes something of a push. You can see me trying to move a second or two before I make it. She turns, showing white heels through her sandals, and goes back to the car. Out she

peeks next with a Polaroid. She stoops down quickly and lines up picture after picture of me sitting there in front of the house with Maggie cowering behind me. She never takes a shot without making sure the house is included. When a cow comes nibbling around the edge of the yard she snaps it and me and Maggie *and* the house. Then she puts the Polaroid in the back seat of the car, and comes up and kisses me on the forehead.

Meanwhile Asalamalakim is going through motions with Maggie's hand. Maggie's hand is as limp as a fish, and probably as cold, despite the sweat, and she keeps trying to pull it back. It looks like Asalamalakim wants to shake hands but wants to do it fancy. Or maybe he don't know how people shake hands. Anyhow, he soon gives up on Maggie.

"Well," I say. "Dee."

"No, Mama," she says. "Not 'Dee,' Wangero Leewanika Kemanjo!"

"What happened to 'Dee'?" I wanted to know.

"She's dead," Wangero said. "I couldn't bear it any longer, being named after the people who oppress me."

"You know as well as me you was named after your aunt Dicie," I said. Dicie is my sister. She named Dee. We called her "Big Dee" after Dee was born.

"But who was *she* named after?" asked Wangero.

"I guess after Grandma Dee," I said.

"And who was she named after?" asked Wangero.

"Her mother," I said, and saw Wangero was getting tired. "That's about as far back as I can trace it," I said. Though, in fact, I probably could have carried it back beyond the Civil War through the branches.

"Well," said Asalamalakim, "there you are."

"Uhnnnh," I heard Maggie say.

"There I was not," I said, "before 'Dicie' cropped up in our family, so why should I try to trace it that far back?"

He just stood there grinning, looking down on me like somebody inspecting a Model A

---

1. **Asalamalakim:** *Salaam aleikhim* (sə-läm′ ä-lä-kōōm′), an African greeting meaning "Peace be with you."

car. Every once in a while he and Wangero sent eye signals over my head.

"How do you pronounce this name?" I asked.

"You don't have to call me by it if you don't want to," said Wangero.

"Why shouldn't I?" I asked. "If that's what you want us to call you, we'll call you."

"I know it might sound awkward at first," said Wangero.

"I'll get used to it," I said. "Ream it out again."

Well, soon we got the name out of the way. Asalamalakim had a name twice as long and three times as hard. After I tripped over it two or three times he told me to just call him Hakim-a-barber. I wanted to ask him was he a barber, but I didn't really think he was, so I didn't ask.

"You must belong to those beef-cattle peoples down the road," I said. They said "Asalamalakim" when they met you, too, but they didn't shake hands. Always too busy: feeding the cattle, fixing the fences, putting up salt-lick shelters, throwing down hay. When the white folks poisoned some of the herd the men stayed up all night with rifles in their hands. I walked a mile and a half just to see the sight.

Hakim-a-barber said, "I accept some of their doctrines, but farming and raising cattle is not my style." (They didn't tell me, and I didn't ask, whether Wangero (Dee) had really gone and married him.)

We sat down to eat and right away he said he didn't eat collards and pork was unclean. Wangero, though, went on through the chitlins and corn bread, the greens and everything else. She talked a blue streak over the sweet potatoes. Everything delighted her. Even the fact that we still used the benches her daddy made for the table when we couldn't afford to buy chairs.

"Oh, Mama!" she cried. Then turned to Hakim-a-barber. "I never knew how lovely these benches are. You can feel the rump prints," she said, running her hands underneath her and along the bench. Then she gave a sigh and her hand closed over Grandma Dee's butter dish. "That's it!" she said. "I knew there was something I wanted to ask you if I could have." She jumped up from the table and went over in the corner where the churn stood, the milk in it clabber[2] by now. She looked at the churn and looked at it.

"This churn top is what I need," she said. "Didn't Uncle Buddy whittle it out of a tree you all used to have?"

"Yes," I said.

"Uh huh," she said happily. "And I want the dasher, too."

"Uncle Buddy whittle that, too?" asked the barber.

Dee (Wangero) looked up at me.

"Aunt Dee's first husband whittled the dash," said Maggie so low you almost couldn't hear her. "His name was Henry, but they called him Stash."

"Maggie's brain is like an elephant's," Wangero said, laughing. "I can use the churn top as a centerpiece for the alcove table," she said, sliding a plate over the churn, "and I'll think of something artistic to do with the dasher."[3]

When she finished wrapping the dasher the handle stuck out. I took it for a moment in my hands. You didn't even have to look close to see where hands pushing the dasher up and down to make butter had left a kind of sink in the wood. In fact, there were a lot of small sinks; you could see where thumbs and fingers had sunk into the wood. It was beautiful light yellow wood, from a tree that grew in the yard where Big Dee and Stash had lived.

After dinner Dee (Wangero) went to the trunk at the foot of my bed and started rifling through it. Maggie hung back in the kichen over the dishpan. Out came Wangero with two quilts. They had been pieced by Grandma Dee and then Big Dee and me had hung them on the quilt frames on the front porch and quilted them. One was in the Lone Star pattern. The other was Walk Around the Mountain. In both

2. **clabber:** curdled.
3. **dasher:** the plunger of a churn.

Lone Star quilt.

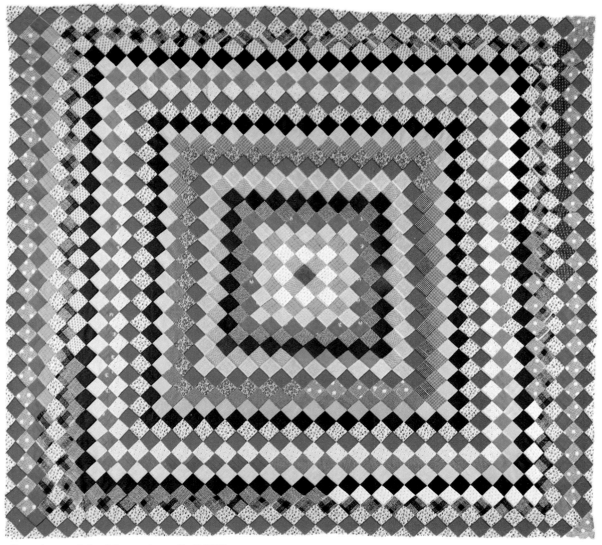

Step Around the Mountain quilt (1930).

of them were scraps of dresses Grandma Dee had worn fifty and more years ago. Bits and pieces of Grandpa Jarrell's Paisley shirts. And one teeny faded blue piece, about the size of a penny matchbox, that was from Great Grandpa Ezra's uniform that he wore in the Civil War.

"Mama," Wangero said sweet as a bird. "Can I have these old quilts?"

I heard something fall in the kitchen, and a minute later the kitchen door slammed.

"Why don't you take one or two of the others?" I asked. "These old things was just done by me and Big Dee from some tops your grandma pieced before she died."

"No," said Wangero. "I don't want those. They are stitched around the borders by machine."

"That'll make them last better," I said.

"That's not the point," said Wangero. "These

are all pieces of dresses Grandma used to wear. She did all this stitching by hand. Imagine!" She held the quilts securely in her arms, stroking them.

"Some of the pieces, like those lavender ones, come from old clothes her mother handed down to her," I said, moving up to touch the quilts. Dee (Wangero) moved back just enough so that I couldn't reach the quilts. They already belonged to her.

"Imagine!" she breathed again, clutching them closely to her bosom.

"The truth is," I said, "I promised to give them quilts to Maggie, for when she marries John Thomas."

She gasped like a bee had stung her.

"Maggie can't appreciate these quilts!" she said. "She'd probably be backward enough to put them to everyday use."

"I reckon she would," I said. "God knows I been saving 'em for long enough with nobody using 'em. I hope she will!" I didn't want to bring up how I had offered Dee (Wangero) a quilt when she went away to college. Then she had told me they were old-fashioned, out of style.

"But they're *priceless!*" she was saying now, furiously; for she has a temper. "Maggie would put them on the bed and in five years they'd be in rags. Less than that!"

"She can always make some more," I said. "Maggie knows how to quilt."

Dee (Wangero) looked at me with hatred. "You just will not understand. The point is these quilts, *these* quilts!"

"Well," I said, stumped. "What would *you* do with them?"

"Hang them," she said. As if that was the only thing you *could* do with quilts.

Maggie by now was standing in the door. I could almost hear the sound her feet made as they scraped over each other.

"She can have them, Mama," she said, like somebody used to never winning anything, or having anything reserved for her. "I can 'member Grandma Dee without the quilts."

I looked at her hard. She had filled her bottom lip with checkerberry snuff and it gave her face a kind of dopey, hangdog look. It was Grandma Dee and Big Dee who taught her how to quilt herself. She stood there with her scarred hands hidden in the folds of her skirt. She looked at her sister with something like fear but she wasn't mad at her. This was Maggie's portion. This was the way she knew God to work.

When I looked at her like that something hit me in the top of my head and ran down to the soles of my feet. Just like when I'm in church and the spirit of God touches me and I get happy and shout. I did something I never had done before: hugged Maggie to me, then dragged her on into the room, snatched the quilts out of Miss Wangero's hands and dumped them into Maggie's lap. Maggie just sat there on my bed with her mouth open.

"Take one or two of the others," I said to Dee.

But she turned without a word and went out to Hakim-a-barber.

"You just don't understand," she said, as Maggie and I came out to the car.

"What don't I understand?" I wanted to know.

"Your heritage," she said. And then she turned to Maggie, kissed her, and said, "You ought to try to make something of yourself, too, Maggie. It's really a new day for us. But from the way you and Mama still live you'd never know it."

She put on some sunglasses that hid everything above the tip of her nose and her chin.

Maggie smiled; maybe at the sunglasses. But a real smile, not scared. After we watched the car dust settle I asked Maggie to bring me a dip of snuff. And then the two of us sat there just enjoying, until it was time to go in the house and go to bed.

Reading Check

1. What caused Maggie's lameness?
2. What does Dee (Wangero) intend to do with the top of the butter churn?
3. Why does Dee want the old quilts?
4. What does she intend to do with them?
5. What is the purpose her mother has in mind for the quilts?

Commentary

The idea of the story is simple, but its implications are subtle and complex. All that happens is that a daughter (Dee) returns to the old homestead and its rural black poverty in the South. She has long since left behind the realities of the homestead and her family. She is urbanized, modernized, "liberated," and up-to-the-minute in her race-consciousness, as revealed by her African greeting and her new African name. Her companion belongs to one of the new, black Islamic identities, as his greeting makes clear. The old, black world of sharecropper poverty and all its realities is light-years behind them; yet, immersed in those realities the mother and Maggie remain behind to cope with the actualities of their lives. The objects of everyday labor, the "everyday use" of the things of their lives have become, in Dee's eyes, "quaint" and "priceless."

For Dee (Wangero), the old butter churn is a campy art object—the worn grooves in the handle are one matter in her hands and quite another in the hands of her mother. The old quilts, to the city daughter, have become fashionable objects of show, museum pieces. Her selfishness and condescension reveal how blind she is to the everyday necessities of her family's lives and labors. She no longer sees them as real people; rather she sees only something picturesque, the "folk," to be patronized in their ignorance.

But the mother and Maggie have to *live* in their shack, which to "Wangero" is a quaint object for photographs. The new home is merely a duplicate of the one that burned down, and like Maggie's body, the lives of the supposedly ignorant and backward folk are scarred by the pains and poverty of their existence.

By implication the story widens out to a broader question: who is more human and more real and who truly feels love—the self-conscious imitator of fashionable movements and slogans or the ordinary people who are left with the ongoing, dull, "everyday" work of the world? And, typical of Walker, it is those who remain buried in the realities of experience rather than those who race into ideological fashion who exhibit the strength of endurance.

Walker tells her story in a comic mode. The mother and Maggie are ignorant of fashionable ways. Wangero and her companion are ignorant of the basic realities of the life in which Maggie and the mother remain. Each pair—Maggie and the mother on the one hand, Wangero and her companion on the other—fails to understand what the other pair takes for granted. The humor arises from the discrepancies between their perceptions of things. Yet, although the misunderstandings are funny, Walker manages to maintain a serious undercurrent in which we are never left in doubt about our sympathy with and allegiance to Maggie and the mother as the ones whose understanding is in accord with the essential actualities of life.

For Study and Discussion

Analyzing and Interpreting the Story

Walker develops her story through a series of symbols and incidents, all of which work together to reveal character, for this story is, in essence, a character study.

1a. What do you learn about Maggie at the opening of the story? **b.** What does the terrible accident signify about Maggie's life? **c.** Conversely, what are you told about Dee when you learn that she just stood and watched the shack (which she hated) burn down while her mother was carrying the burning Maggie from the fire?

2. Consider the dream of the television program at the beginning of the story. Note that the mother tells the reader what she is "in real life" while she is describing the dream. How does this episode prepare you for the conflict between Dee and her family?

3. Look carefully at the scene describing Dee's arrival. **a.** What are you told by Dee's greeting (would her mother and sister understand an African language)? **b.** What are you told by the greeting of Dee's companion? **c.** What effect is achieved by the fact that the mother does not understand the greeting and thinks that the man's name is "Asalamalakim"?

4a. What are you told about Dee by the kinds of pictures she takes? **b.** What are you told about Dee's sense of family when, after she has taken her pictures, she then kisses her mother as she does? **c.** What does the discussion of names tell you about Dee's sense of her family and forebears as actual history, living people?

5a. What are the essential differences between Dee's life and Maggie's life? **b.** What are the essential differences between their characters? **c.** Why does Walker draw such intense differences—what sympathies and dislikes is she creating in the reader, and why? **d.** Maggie does not know how to give "Asalamalakim" a "black" handshake. How does that fact contribute to her characterization?

6. The mother, not Dee, is the real center of the story. **a.** Which of them is really capable of love? How do you know? **b.** Why does the mother snatch the quilts from Dee's hands and put them in Maggie's lap? **c.** The mother constantly tells us, explicitly and implicitly, that she is uneducated and unsophisticated. How well does she understand her daughters? **d.** How well does she understand the story she tells?

Writing About Literature

Comparing Characters

Eudora Welty, a white woman, and Alice Walker, a black woman, both have written stories about elderly black women. Are there differences in the essential reality or believability of the characters? Does Phoenix, in "A Worn Path" (page 691) seem any more or less real than the mother in "Everyday Use"? Support your argument with examples from the text and explain what conclusions you draw from the evidence.

Creative Writing

Writing a Character Sketch

Alice Walker presents her characters by providing hard facts about their manner, their dress, their speech, their actions, and some information about their lives. Write a brief sketch in which you present a characer. Do not directly evaluate your character. Let the facts lead your reader to conclusions about whether the character is sympathetic or unsympathetic, selfish or kind, greedy or generous, foolish or wise.

MODERN POETRY

Modern poetry has often been described as experimental. If we keep in mind that *experimental* refers to the bold search for new forms of poetic expression, we shall begin to understand what much modern poetry is about.

Among American poets, Walt Whitman and Emily Dickinson stand at the forefront of modern poetry. Whitman presented what was essentially a new world view, the transcendentalist view introduced into America primarily by Ralph Waldo Emerson. In *Leaves of Grass* (1855), he took the entire universe for his subject, relating the most dissimilar things to each other and to himself. The vast span of Whitman's subject matter—including the parts and functions of all physical nature, in which he saw the presence of God—shattered the bounds of conventional poetry, as did his revolutionary style. For Whitman abandoned the standard line lengths, rhymes, and stanza forms of traditional poetry to write a far freer and more colloquial verse. Dickinson's subjects were, in a sense, smaller—household items, natural objects found in her back yard, and ordinary daily activities—but her vision was no less grand than Whitman's. If Whitman found infinity in the large, Dickinson found it in the small. Her style, as radical in its own way as Whitman's, was based on traditional forms; her favorite stanza form was the quatrain, and many of her short, abrupt lines were grouped in couplets.

In addition to these native sources, modern American poetry owes a debt to the *symbolist* movement, a late nineteenth-century French movement that had a profound influence on poets writing in English. Symbolism is based on the assumption that all external objects are "symbols" of a deeper, truer reality. Things that seem altogether unrelated are connected by surprising, secret links. The symbolist poet tends to avoid any direct statement of meaning and instead attempts to evoke meaning by establishing a mood and focusing on highly suggestive symbols.

Modern poetry embraces a great variety of styles. In the early years of the twentieth century, the "New Poetry" movement was championed by a brilliant young American expatriate named Ezra Pound. In 1912 Pound established the *Imagist* school, whose members included William Carlos Williams, H. D., and Amy Lowell. Using Imagism as a platform, Pound vigorously urged all modern poets to "make it new." Following his lead, many poets began experimenting with form. Some of them—Williams and E. E. Cummings are notable examples—introduced typographical innovations, making a poem's appearance on the page as important as its sound and the meaning of its words. Poets began experimenting with the order of their ideas, sometimes relying more on free association than on logical sequence.

Many modern poems move quickly and unexpectedly from idea to idea, producing the sense of dislocation that some poets think is characteristic of modern life.

While some poets were attempting to create new forms, others, such as Robert Frost and Edna St. Vincent Millay, were electing to rework traditional forms. Part of Frost's great artistry lay in his ability to render blank verse in a deceptively fluid, almost conversational way. Millay was attracted to the sonnet, and she created some of the loveliest modern examples of this form.

Modern poetry is also characterized by certain pervasive themes. In one of his poems, W. H. Auden referred to the modern age as "the age of anxiety." A feeling of anxiety about the world runs through much modern poetry. Extensive industrialization, rapid technological advance, new perceptions about human nature and the universe, and the general disillusionment produced by world war have contributed to changing the shape and tempo of modern life— seemingly for the worse. Many modern poets have reacted to these changes in a number of ways: some have written poems of protest; others have expressed the desire to escape from the modern world. Still others have responded to the challenge of modern life by affirming such universal values as beauty and love.

Modern poets have been preoccupied with the nature and possibilities of human relationships, and the complex emotional and psychological elements that bear on them. In "The Love Song of J. Alfred Prufrock," T. S. Eliot wrote about a man who is afraid to love; and in later poems Eliot wrote about a barren world which only the existence of God could infuse with meaning. Ezra Pound depicted a world in which pervasive greed corrupts the possibility of fruitful human relationships. Wallace Stevens devoted a long career to constructing a kind of poetic imagination that could renew and reorder all human values. William Carlos Williams related the subject of human relationships to the simplest, most direct, and most dependable perceptions he could discover. Robert Lowell wrote directly about the intricacies and stresses of his own life. Even Robert Frost, in many ways a more conservative poet than the others, was concerned with uncertain relationships among men and women, and with the imponderable world in which they live.

Modern poetry is difficult to summarize, and few conclusions can be drawn about it. In this unit you will have an opportunity to study the work of many of the poets who have helped define and shape modern poetry, and you may want to form some conclusions of your own.

ROBERT FROST
1874–1963

© Rollie McKenna

Robert Frost.

Robert Frost is regarded as a poet of New England, even though he was born in San Francisco. He was named Robert Lee in honor of the Southern general. Frost was eleven years old when his father died and his mother took her children east, settling eventually in Lawrence, Massachusetts. Frost attended Lawrence High School and was one of the two valedictorians of his class. The other was Elinor White, whom he later married. Frost studied briefly at Dartmouth College but left after less than two months. He then spent his time assisting his mother, who was a schoolteacher, and later he worked in a mill.

During the 1890s he began writing poems and sending them out for publication, but very few were accepted. His grandfather made it possible for him to attend Harvard University, but after nearly two years he left. He later wrote, "Harvard had taken me away from the question of whether I could write or not." By this time, he was in his middle twenties and about to become a father. At this crucial point in Frost's life, Elinor appealed to his grandfather to buy them a farm in West Derry, New Hampshire. The grandfather, knowing that Frost's principal concern was poetry, asked, "Shall I give you a year? Will you settle down if I give you a year to try this out?" Frost replied, "Give me twenty." As it turned out, he spent ten long years on the "thirty acres, rather run down and poor, but with orchard, fields, pasture, woodland, and spring." He arranged his schedule to accommodate his poetry, milking his cows at midnight so that he could write poems in the late evening hours.

In 1912 Frost sold his farm. An unknown poet at the age of thirty-eight, he sailed to England with his family to seek the recognition he had failed to find in America. Gradually he came to know a number of English and American poets, including Ezra Pound, and was able to arrange for the publication of his first collection, *A Boy's Will.* His second book, *North of Boston,* published when he was forty, was widely acclaimed, and when he returned to America in 1915, he found himself an established poet.

For his subjects Frost often turned to the small farms of New England, the woods and mountains of that region, and its sturdy and self-reliant inhabitants. Frost once said that a poem should "begin in delight and end in wisdom." Readers of his work find that what begins as a description of a tuft of flowers, a bird, or the woods in a snowstorm often ends with a profound insight into life. His collections of poems appeared at rather long intervals. He wrote slowly and with great care. He sought to capture the sound of common speech in his poems—what he called "the sound of sense." But at the same time, Frost lifted common speech to a rare and penetrating eloquence.

In his old age, Frost was honored beyond all living poets since the days of Longfellow and Whittier. He won the Pulitzer Prize four times. In 1947 Oxford and Cambridge universities gave him honorary degrees. The United States Senate passed resolutions to commemorate his seventy-fifth and eighty-fifth birthdays. Frost was chosen to participate in the inauguration of President John Fitzgerald Kennedy in January, 1961. His magnificent readings brought the actual sound of his poetry to a broad audience. In an age when poetry had, on the whole, become the concern of a relatively few enthusiasts, Frost was a genuinely popular figure, regarded by the nation as one of its wise old men.

The Road Not Taken

Two roads diverged in a yellow wood,
And sorry I could not travel both
And be one traveler, long I stood
And looked down one as far as I could
To where it bent in the undergrowth;   5

Then took the other, as just as fair,
And having perhaps the better claim,
Because it was grassy and wanted wear;
Though as for that, the passing there
Had worn them really about the same,   10

And both that morning equally lay
In leaves no step had trodden black.
Oh, I kept the first for another day!
Yet knowing how way leads on to way,
I doubted if I should ever come back.   15

I shall be telling this with a sigh
Somewhere ages and ages hence:
Two roads diverged in a wood, and I—
I took the one less traveled by,
And that has made all the difference.   20

Robert Frost   **741**

Fire and Ice

Some say the world will end in fire,
Some say in ice.
From what I've tasted of desire
I hold with those who favor fire.
But if it had to perish twice,
I think I know enough of hate
To say that for destruction ice
Is also great
And would suffice.

Stopping by Woods on a Snowy Evening

Whose woods these are I think I know.
His house is in the village, though;
He will not see me stopping here
To watch his woods fill up with snow.

My little horse must think it queer   5
To stop without a farmhouse near
Between the woods and frozen lake
The darkest evening of the year.

He gives his harness bells a shake
To ask if there is some mistake.   10
The only other sound's the sweep
Of easy wind and downy flake.

The woods are lovely, dark, and deep,
But I have promises to keep,
And miles to go before I sleep,   15
And miles to go before I sleep.

Commentary

The critic Laurence Perrine has written this analysis of "Stopping by Woods on a Snowy Evening":

There is more than meets the eye in this lyric, perhaps the most famous and certainly one of the most controversial of Frost's poems. On the surface it is an unadorned narrative of a simple incident. Some readers stop there and they are rewarded with a memorable experience. Other readers find more, much more beneath the surface.

Large meanings are packed into this small poem. Think a moment about the symbols Frost uses. What does the owner of the woods mentioned in the poem stand for? Probably for the village and village life at the very least and, more likely, for the social responsibilities of civilized life as opposed to the loneliness of the woods. The little horse, too, is a symbol, representing a kind of life that does not understand why a man should stop by a patch of woods to watch the snow come down. In contrast to the world of civilization symbolized by the owner, the little horse stands for the animal or brute world. The woods, the cold, the dark, the frozen lake, and the falling snow constitute a third symbol—the powerful attraction of all this lovely dark-and-deep, which may sensibly be interpreted as the attraction of beauty. Beauty is certainly one aspect of the scene and, therefore, one meaning of the symbol. But this explanation does not exhaust its meaning. Another interpretation is that the man feels an invitation from these woods to final surrender and rest. Some readers go even further and say that the attraction of the woods represents a wish, however momentary, to die.

Several things in the poem suggest that the man is on some kind of journey, but Frost never tells us specifically what business the man is on. He may have intended to suggest any journey in life and, thereby, to leave the meaning on the broadest level. Attracted by the woods partway on his journey, the man has paused—perhaps to work out a mental conflict. He has "promises to keep" at the end of his journey. One part of this sensitive, thinking man would like to give up the conflict and surrender. But another part is aware of social responsibilities. The thought of the "lovely, dark, and deep" lingers, but the man's final decision is to cast off the mood and continue his journey. He has promises to keep and miles to go before he sleeps.

For Study and Discussion

Analyzing and Interpreting the Poems

The Road Not Taken

Explain why you agree or disagree with the following statement by Laurence Perrine: "We must interpret [the speaker's] choice of a road as a symbol for any choice in life between alternatives that appear almost equally attractive but will result through the years in a large difference in the kind of experience one knows."

Fire and Ice

1a. In which lines of the poem does the speaker suggest that he has known destructive impulses? **b.** Why does the speaker find "fire" and "ice" appropriate ways for the world to end?

2a. How much importance would ordinarily be attached to a subject introduced by the phrase, "Some say . . ."? **b.** How do these words contrast with the actual importance of the subject? **c.** Frost wrote of Edwin Arlington Robinson's poems that they balanced outer seriousness with inner humor. Is there a similar balance in "Fire and Ice"? Explain.

Stopping by Woods on a Snowy Evening

1. How do you interpret the speaker's attraction to the woods?

2a. Why should a man worried about "promises to keep" care if the owner sees him stopping in the woods? **b.** What is the significance of *ownership* at the opening of the poem?

3a. What do the last three lines suggest about everyone's life? **b.** Why do you think Frost ended the poem with the repetition of a line? **c.** What is the effect of the repetition?

4. The rhyme scheme plays a role in the poem's progression. How does the rhyme scheme connect the stanzas of the poem?

After Apple-Picking

My long two-pointed ladder's sticking through a tree
Toward heaven still,
And there's a barrel that I didn't fill
Beside it, and there may be two or three
Apples I didn't pick upon some bough.   5
But I am done with apple-picking now.
Essence of winter sleep is on the night,
The scent of apples: I am drowsing off.
I cannot rub the strangeness from my sight
I got from looking through a pane of glass   10
I skimmed this morning from the drinking trough
And held against the world of hoary° grass.
It melted, and I let it fall and break.
But I was well
Upon my way to sleep before it fell,   15
And I could tell
What form my dreaming was about to take.
Magnified apples appear and disappear,
Stem end and blossom end,
And every fleck of russet showing clear.   20
My instep arch not only keeps the ache,
It keeps the pressure of a ladder-round.
I feel the ladder sway as the boughs bend.
And I keep hearing from the cellar bin
The rumbling sound   25
Of load on load of apples coming in.
For I have had too much
Of apple-picking: I am overtired
Of the great harvest I myself desired.
There were ten thousand thousand fruit to touch,   30
Cherish in hand, lift down, and not let fall.
For all
That struck the earth,
No matter if not bruised or spiked with stubble,
Went surely to the cider-apple heap   35
As of no worth.
One can see what will trouble
This sleep of mine, whatever sleep it is.
Were he not gone,
The woodchuck could say whether it's like his   40
Long sleep, as I describe its coming on,
Or just some human sleep.

12. **hoary** (hôr′ē): old; frosted.

Mending Wall

Something there is that doesn't love a wall,
That sends the frozen-ground-swell under it
And spills the upper boulders in the sun,
And makes gaps even two can pass abreast.
The work of hunters is another thing: 5
I have come after them and made repair
Where they have left not one stone on a stone,
But they would have the rabbit out of hiding,
To please the yelping dogs. The gaps I mean,
No one has seen them made or heard them made,   10
But at spring mending-time we find them there.
I let my neighbor know beyond the hill;
And on a day we meet to walk the line
And set the wall between us once again.
We keep the wall between us as we go.   15
To each the boulders that have fallen to each.
And some are loaves and some so nearly balls
We have to use a spell to make them balance:
"Stay where you are until our backs are turned!"

We wear our fingers rough with handling them.   20
Oh, just another kind of outdoor game,
One on a side. It comes to little more:
There where it is we do not need the wall:
He is all pine and I am apple orchard.
My apple trees will never get across   25
And eat the cones under his pines, I tell him.
He only says, "Good fences make good neighbors."
Spring is the mischief in me, and I wonder
If I could put a notion in his head:
"*Why* do they make good neighbors? Isn't it   30
Where there are cows? But here there are no cows.
Before I built a wall I'd ask to know
What I was walling in or walling out,
And to whom I was like to give offense.
Something there is that doesn't love a wall,   35
That wants it down." I could say "Elves" to him,
But it's not elves exactly, and I'd rather
He said it for himself. I see him there,
Bringing a stone grasped firmly by the top
In each hand, like an old-stone savage armed.   40
He moves in darkness as it seems to me,
Not of woods only and the shade of trees.
He will not go behind his father's saying,
And he likes having thought of it so well
He says again, "Good fences make good neighbors."   45

For Study and Discussion

Analyzing and Interpreting the Poems

After Apple-Picking

1. Robert Frost uses the subject of apple picking as a metaphor for human ambition. In this context, what is suggested by the speaker's statement that he is "overtired" of the great harvest he wanted?
2a. Describe in your own words the image in lines 9–12. **b.** Why do you think the world would look strange to the speaker? **c.** How does the image of "magnified apples" in lines 18–20 suggest that his desire for a great harvest was a distorted vision?
3. The speaker observes that "essence of winter sleep is on the night." What distinction between nature's rest and people's rest is suggested by the reference to the woodchuck's hibernation?
4a. From what state of mind does the speaker need rest? **b.** What has caused this state of mind?

Mending Wall

1a. Characterize the speaker of this poem. **b.** How does his personality come out in the first line?
2a. To what might "whom" in line 34 refer? **b.** Might it have more than one possible reference? Explain.
3. Notice that the first line is repeated in line 35. What is the purpose of this repetition?
4a. What is the difference in attitude between the speaker and his neighbor? **b.** Why does it seem to the speaker that his neighbor "moves in darkness"? **c.** What is the significance of the fact that the neighbor's favorite saying, "Good fences make good neighbors," was spoken by his father?

The Death of the Hired Man

Mary sat musing on the lamp-flame at the table,
Waiting for Warren. When she heard his step,
She ran on tiptoe down the darkened passage
To meet him in the doorway with the news
And put him on his guard. "Silas is back." 5
She pushed him outward with her through the door
And shut it after her. "Be kind," she said.
She took the market things from Warren's arms
And set them on the porch, then drew him down
To sit beside her on the wooden steps. 10

"When was I ever anything but kind to him?
But I'll not have the fellow back," he said.
"I told him so last haying, didn't I?
If he left then, I said, that ended it.
What good is he? Who else will harbor him 15
At his age for the little he can do?
What help he is there's no depending on.
Off he goes always when I need him most.
He thinks he ought to earn a little pay,
Enough at least to buy tobacco with, 20
So he won't have to beg and be beholden.
'All right,' I say, 'I can't afford to pay
Any fixed wages, though I wish I could.'
'Someone else can.' 'Then someone else will have to.'
I shouldn't mind his bettering himself 25
If that was what it was. You can be certain,
When he begins like that, there's someone at him
Trying to coax him off with pocket money—
In haying time, when any help is scarce.
In winter he comes back to us. I'm done." 30

"Sh! not so loud: he'll hear you," Mary said.

"I want him to: he'll have to soon or late."

"He's worn out. He's asleep beside the stove.
When I came up from Rowe's I found him here,
Huddled against the barn door fast asleep, 35
A miserable sight, and frightening, too—
You needn't smile—I didn't recognize him—
I wasn't looking for him—and he's changed.
Wait till you see."

"Where did you say he'd been?"

"He didn't say. I dragged him to the house,   40
And gave him tea and tried to make him smoke.
I tried to make him talk about his travels.
Nothing would do: he just kept nodding off."

"What did he say? Did he say anything?"

"But little."

        "Anything? Mary, confess   45
He said he'd come to ditch the meadow for me."

"Warren!"

        "But did he? I just want to know."

"Of course he did. What would you have him say?
Surely you wouldn't grudge the poor old man
Some humble way to save his self-respect.   50
He added, if you really care to know,
He meant to clear the upper pasture, too.
That sounds like something you have heard before?
Warren, I wish you could have heard the way
He jumbled everything. I stopped to look   55
Two or three times—he made me feel so queer—
To see if he was talking in his sleep.
He ran on Harold Wilson—you remember—
The boy you had in haying four years since.
He's finished school, and teaching in his college.   60
Silas declares you'll have to get him back.
He says they two will make a team for work:
Between them they will lay this farm as smooth!
The way he mixed that in with other things.
He thinks young Wilson a likely lad, though daft   65
On education—you know how they fought
All through July under the blazing sun,
Silas up on the cart to build the load,
Harold along beside to pitch it on."

"Yes, I took care to keep well out of earshot."   70

"Well, those days trouble Silas like a dream.
You wouldn't think they would. How such things linger!
Harold's young college-boy's assurance piqued him.
After so many years he still keeps finding
Good arguments he sees he might have used.   75

I sympathize. I know just how it feels
To think of the right thing to say too late.
Harold's associated in his mind with Latin.
He asked me what I thought of Harold's saying
He studied Latin, like the violin,   80
Because he liked it—that an argument!
He said he couldn't make the boy believe
He could find water with a hazel prong—
Which showed how much good school had ever done him.
He wanted to go over that. But most of all   85
He thinks if he could have another chance
To teach him how to build a load of hay—"

"I know, that's Silas' one accomplishment.
He bundles every forkful in its place,
And tags and numbers it for future reference,   90
So he can find and easily dislodge it
In the unloading. Silas does that well.
He takes it out in bunches like big birds' nests.
You never see him standing on the hay
He's trying to lift, straining to lift himself."   95

"He thinks if he could teach him that, he'd be
Some good perhaps to someone in the world.
He hates to see a boy the fool of books.
Poor Silas, so concerned for other folk,
And nothing to look backward to with pride,   100
And nothing to look forward to with hope,
So now and never any different."

Part of a moon was falling down the west,
Dragging the whole sky with it to the hills.
Its light poured softly in her lap. She saw it   105
And spread her apron to it. She put out her hand
Among the harplike morning-glory strings,
Taut with the dew from garden bed to eaves,
As if she played unheard some tenderness
That wrought on him beside her in the night.   110
"Warren," she said, "he has come home to die:
You needn't be afraid he'll leave you this time."

"Home," he mocked gently.

                    "Yes, what else but home?
It all depends on what you mean by home.
Of course he's nothing to us, any more   115
Than was the hound that came a stranger to us
Out of the woods, worn out upon the trail."

"Home is the place where, when you have to go there,
They have to take you in."

                     "I should have called it
Something you somehow haven't to deserve."   120

Warren leaned out and took a step or two,
Picked up a little stick, and brought it back
And broke it in his hand and tossed it by.
"Silas has better claim on us you think
Than on his brother? Thirteen little miles   125
As the road winds would bring him to his door.
Silas has walked that far no doubt today.
Why doesn't he go there? His brother's rich,
A somebody—director in the bank."

"He never told us that."

                  "We know it, though."   130

"I think his brother ought to help, of course.
I'll see to that if there is need. He ought of right
To take him in, and might be willing to—
He may be better than appearances.
But have some pity on Silas. Do you think   135
If he had any pride in claiming kin
Or anything he looked for from his brother,
He'd keep so still about him all this time?"

"I wonder what's between them."

                     "I can tell you.
Silas is what he is—we wouldn't mind him—   140
But just the kind that kinsfolk can't abide.
He never did a thing so very bad.
He don't know why he isn't quite as good
As anybody. Worthless though he is,
He won't be made ashamed to please his brother."   145

"*I* can't think Si ever hurt anyone."

"No, but he hurt my heart the way he lay
And rolled his old head on that sharp-edged chair-back.
He wouldn't let me put him on the lounge.
You must go in and see what you can do.   150
I made the bed up for him there tonight.
You'll be surprised at him—how much he's broken.
His working days are done; I'm sure of it."

"I'd not be in a hurry to say that."

"I haven't been. Go, look, see for yourself.   155
But, Warren, please remember how it is:
He's come to help you ditch the meadow.
He has a plan. You mustn't laugh at him.
He may not speak of it, and then he may.
I'll sit and see if that small sailing cloud   160
Will hit or miss the moon."

                    It hit the moon.
Then there were three there, making a dim row,
The moon, the little silver cloud, and she.

Warren returned—too soon, it seemed to her—
Slipped to her side, caught up her hand and waited.   165

"Warren?" she questioned.

                    "Dead," was all he answered.

For Study and Discussion

Analyzing and Interpreting the Poem

1. "The Death of the Hired Man" is a **narrative** poem; that is, it tells a story. At the same time, it depends so much on dialogue that in many passages it resembles a play. The first ten lines establish the situation for the conversation that follows. **a.** Describe the situation in your own words. **b.** What do you learn about Mary and Warren?
2. The hired man, Silas, does not appear in the poem except through the dialogue of Warren and Mary. **a.** Why has he left Warren? **b.** What reason does he give for returning? **c.** Why might he be unwilling to go to his brother for help?
3. Lines 100–101 summarize Silas' situation. **a.** Why, in light of this, does Silas take such pride in his ability to make up a load of hay and find water with a hazel prong? **b.** Why do you think Silas keeps thinking of arguments he "might have used" with Harold, the college boy?
4. Lines 103–110 interrupt the story with a passage of description. **a.** What action of Mary's is described? **b.** What does it suggest about her character? **c.** In lines 160–165, the moon appears again in a descriptive passage. What does this image suggest about Mary?
5a. What two definitions of "home" are given in the poem? **b.** How do these definitions establish a conflict between the two speakers?

Literary Elements

Blank Verse

Frost has written that in English "there are virtually but two meters, strict iambic and loose iambic." Capable himself of drawing a remarkable range of effects from iambic meter, he stated, "The possibilities for tune from the dramatic tones of meaning struck across the rigidity of a limited meter are endless."

Frost's poetry is remarkable for capturing the sound of the speaking voice. In "The Death of the Hired Man," the normal, natural patterns of spoken English are incorporated into the formal patterns of **blank verse,** unrhymed iambic pentameter. Find examples of what might be considered "strict iambic" and "loose iambic" meter.

Writing About Literature

Examining Frost's Pessimism

Some critics have pointed out that there is a dark, pessimistic side to Frost's poetry that is overlooked by those who see Frost simply as a gentle poet of nature and rural life. Examine the claim that a dark side—an understanding of pain, loneliness, doubt, and tragedy—is also characteristic of his poetry. Make specific references to poems and lines to support your general statements.

CARL SANDBURG
1878–1967

Carl Sandburg.

Carl Sandburg, the son of Swedish immigrants, was born and raised in Galesburg, Illinois. Because his family was poor, he left school early to go to work. He had to continue his education as best he could. When the Spanish-American War broke out in 1898, he volunteered for service. During the eight months he was in the army, he wrote accounts of the fighting and of army life for his hometown newspaper. Upon his return home, he entered Lombard College in Galesburg. Shortly before graduation he suddenly left school to travel around the country and work at various jobs. After a time, he became an organizer and speaker for the Lyceum lecture circuit, addressing audiences on Walt Whitman and on the aspirations of American life. An interest in politics led him to become secretary to the mayor of Milwaukee.

Later Sandburg moved to Chicago and became a reporter for the Chicago *Daily News.* He resided in that city for some fifteen years, and his early poems are associated with its bustling life. In 1916 Sandburg's first book, *Chicago Poems,* was published. He was praised as one of the most energetic and original new poets of the time. Other collections followed rapidly.

Besides his reputation as a poet, Sandburg is well known as a biographer of Abraham Lincoln. For thirty years he collected material about Lincoln, until the Lincoln room in his house could hold no more and the overflow had to be stored in a barn. He typed the two volumes of *Abraham Lincoln: The War Years* in his attic. During the final years of his work on Lincoln, he supported himself by going on tours, reciting poetry, and singing folk songs. In the late 1930s, he was considered one of America's leading folk singers, and his anthology, *The American Songbag,* is an important collection of folk songs.

Carl Sandburg's seventy-fifth birthday was proclaimed "Carl Sandburg Day" by the governor of Illinois, and on that occasion Sandburg was presented with a decoration by the king of Sweden. On the hundred and fiftieth anniversary of Lincoln's birthday, Sandburg addressed a joint session of Congress. During the last years of his life, he lived on a farm in North Carolina where he wrote poetry and an autobiography called *Always the Young Strangers.*

Chicago

Five steam locomotives
outbound from Chicago
at dusk (c. 1940).
National Archives

Hog Butcher for the World,
Tool Maker, Stacker of Wheat,
Player with Railroads and the Nation's Freight Handler;
Stormy, husky, brawling,
City of the Big Shoulders: 5

They tell me you are wicked and I believe them, for I have
    seen your painted women under the gas lamps luring the
    farm boys.
And they tell me you are crooked and I answer: Yes, it is true
    I have seen the gunman kill and go free to kill again.
And they tell me you are brutal and my reply is: On the faces
    of women and children I have seen the marks of wanton
    hunger.

Carl Sandburg   **753**

And having answered so I turn once more to those who sneer
    at this my city, and I give them back the sneer and say to
    them:
Come and show me another city with lifted head singing so
    proud to be alive and coarse and strong and cunning.   10
Flinging magnetic curses amid the toil of piling job on job, here
    is a tall bold slugger set vivid against the little soft cities;
Fierce as a dog with tongue lapping for action, cunning as a
    savage pitted against the wilderness,
        Bareheaded,
        Shoveling,
        Wrecking,   15
        Planning,
        Building, breaking, rebuilding,
Under the smoke, dust all over his mouth, laughing with white
    teeth,
Under the terrible burden of destiny laughing as a young man
    laughs,
Laughing even as an ignorant fighter laughs who has never lost
    a battle,   20
Bragging and laughing that under his wrist is the pulse, and
    under his ribs the heart of the people,
            Laughing!
Laughing the stormy, husky, brawling laughter of Youth, half-
    naked, sweating, proud to be Hog Butcher, Tool Maker,
    Stacker of Wheat, Player with Railroads and Freight
    Handler to the Nation.

Prayers of Steel

Lay me on an anvil, O God.
Beat me and hammer me into a crowbar.
Let me pry loose old walls.
Let me lift and loosen old foundations.

Lay me on an anvil, O God.
Beat me and hammer me into a steel spike.
Drive me into the girders that hold a skyscraper together.
Take red-hot rivets and fasten me into the central girders.
Let me be the great nail holding a skyscraper through blue
    nights into white stars.

Construction Steel Workers
(1924) by Reginald Marsh
(1898–1954). Oil on canvas.
Hirschl & Adler Galleries, Inc.,
New York

Imagism

The Imagist movement began in 1912 with the efforts of Ezra Pound, an American poet who had settled in London. (See page 765 for a biography of Pound.) He gave the movement its name and defined its chief principles: (1) direct concentration on the "image"—the thing itself; (2) use of the language of common speech, and always the precise word; (3) creation of new rhythms; and (4) complete freedom in the choice of subject. Pound defined the image as "an intellectual and emotional complex presented in an instant of time." Two aspects of this definition are important: poets must seek "complex" thoughts and feelings; and they must compress such complexity into a single moment.

Other Imagists included two of Pound's friends from his student days at the University of Pennsylvania, William Carlos Williams (see page 762) and Hilda Doolittle, better known by her initials, H. D. H. D. (1886–1961) was born in Bethlehem, Pennsylvania, and educated at Bryn Mawr College. In 1911 she went to England, where she met Pound. H. D. translated Greek poetry and drama, and the themes and forms of her own poems reflect her interest in the classics.

When the Massachusetts poet Amy Lowell (1874–1925) read a poem by H. D., she became interested in the Imagist principles. Lowell belonged to a family of considerable wealth and achievement. She was a descendant of the poet James Russell Lowell; one of her brothers was a president of Harvard University and another a notable astronomer. She herself won the Pulitzer Prize in 1926 for her collection of poems *What's O'Clock*. A woman of great energy and determination, she decided when she was twenty-six that poetry was her "natural mode of expression." She journeyed to London to meet the Imagists and, with her executive skill, soon became leader of the movement. Pound thought her style sentimental, not "hard and clear" enough. He severed his connection with the Imagists and, in a famous joke, declared that his ideas had been converted from Imagism to "Amygism."

Another American poet who joined the group was John Gould Fletcher (1886–1950). Fletcher was born in Little Rock, Arkansas, and studied at Harvard. Feeling a misfit at Harvard, he dropped out four months before graduation. He published several collections of traditional poems before he discovered Imagism and came under the influence of Amy Lowell. He joined with Lowell, H. D., and several English poets to appear in a new yearly anthology, *Some Imagist Poets* (1915–1917).

Imagism was the first innovative movement in modern American poetry. In its emphasis on new rhythms, exact images, and language that is "hard and clear," it influenced and continues to influence modern poets.

In a Station of the Metro°
EZRA POUND

The apparition of these faces in the crowd;
Petals on a wet, black bough.

°**Metro**: the Paris subway.

Fan-Piece,
for Her Imperial Lord
EZRA POUND

O fan of white silk,
    clear as frost on the grass-blade,
You also are laid aside.

The Red Wheelbarrow
WILLIAM CARLOS WILLIAMS

so much depends
upon

a red wheel
barrow

glazed with rain
water

beside the white
chickens.

Heat
H. D.

O wind, rend open the heat,
cut apart the heat,
rend it to tatters.

Fruit cannot drop
through this thick air—   5
fruit cannot fall into heat
that presses up and blunts
the points of pears
and rounds the grapes.

Cut the heat—   10
plow through it,
turning it on either side
of your path.

Wind and Silver
AMY LOWELL

Greatly shining,
The Autumn moon floats in the thin sky;
And the fish-ponds shake their backs and flash their
    dragon scales
As she passes over them.

The Skaters
JOHN GOULD FLETCHER

Black swallows swooping or gliding
In a flurry of entangled loops and curves;
The skaters skim over the frozen river.
And the grinding click of their skates as they impinge
    upon the surface,
Is like the brushing together of thin wing-tips of
    silver.

Analyzing and Interpreting the Poems

1. In his poem "In a Station of the Metro," Pound directly juxtaposes two images to suggest faces glimpsed quickly on a dark subway platform. **a.** To what does he compare the faces? **b.** What does the comparison imply about the fragility of human beings? **c.** What is suggested by the image of a *wet* bough?

2a. In "Fan-Piece, for Her Imperial Lord," what does the title suggest about the identity of the speaker? **b.** In Japan, fans are sometimes used in elaborate ways to act out feelings aroused by personal situations. What do you think has been put aside besides the fan itself? **c.** How does the image in line 2 contribute to the feeling of transience in the poem?

3. In "The Red Wheelbarrow," Williams declares his deepest poetic belief, that poetry most effectively stirs the mind and feelings through images of concrete, familiar things. **a.** What do you think depends on the wheelbarrow, rain, and chickens? **b.** How are the words and lines arranged in each stanza of "The Red Wheelbarrow"? **c.** How are the images in the last three stanzas given special emphasis by this stanza form?

4a. In the first stanza of "Heat," what does the speaker ask of the wind? **b.** What images in the second and third stanzas suggest the solidity and force of the heat?

5. In "Wind and Silver," the reader's attention is led first to the moon in the sky and then to the reflection of its light in the fish ponds. **a.** How is the moon characterized? **b.** How is the appearance of its reflected light characterized? **c.** What causes the contrast between these two glimpses of the moonlight? (Consider the poem's title in your answer.)

6a. What two images are juxtaposed in the first three lines of "The Skaters"? **b.** How are the two images alike? **c.** To what is the sound of the skates compared? **d.** In what ways is the simile appropriate?

Oriental Verse Forms

Both Ezra Pound and Amy Lowell were interested in certain Oriental verse forms. Among these were two Japanese forms: the **haiku** (sometimes written **hokku**) and the **tanka.** The haiku is written in three lines of five, seven, and five syllables. The tanka consists of five lines with the following arrangement of syllables: five, seven, five, seven, and seven. These forms differ from much English poetry in their lack of movement or progression. Attention is fixed on an unchanging image in an instant of time, and that image is intended to evoke an emotion or an insight by its own power. None of the poems in this section corresponds exactly to either the haiku or the tanka, but many of them are meant to function in a similar manner. Pick one of the Imagist poems you have read and show to what degree it focuses on an unchanging image. What kind of feeling does the image suggest? Does it give rise to any insight into the nature of the poem's subject? If so, what is the insight?

Wallace Stevens.
© Rollie McKenna

Along with Frost, Pound, Eliot, and Williams, Wallace Stevens is one of the major poets of the first half of the twentieth century. However, Stevens was never closely associated with any of these poets, and, in fact, remained independent of any literary circle. He was born in Reading, Pennsylvania, and he attended Harvard as a special student for three years. Although he wrote poetry during his undergraduate days, he was convinced of the importance of living actively in the nonliterary world. After college he worked briefly as a newspaper reporter in New York, then attended law school and began to practice law. After a short time, he joined the legal department of the Hartford Accident and Indemnity Company, an insurance company of which he became a vice-president in 1934. His first collection of poems, *Harmonium*, was not published until 1923, when he was forty-four. Today *Harmonium* is regarded as one of the most important books of poetry of the twentieth century. Stevens' *Collected Poems* was awarded the Pulitzer Prize in 1955.

When Stevens first read his poems in public, he was heard to remark, "I wonder what the boys at the office would think of this." Although he never presented himself as a writer to his business associates, he did not consider poetry a mere hobby. He was a serious, dedicated poet. He felt that the business of poetry is "to help people live their lives." He meant that, in modern times, when many people seem to have lost their beliefs, it is the task of the poet to provide ways of looking at the world that stimulate and recharge the human imagination. Stevens thought of poetry as a way of letting the imagination organize reality, giving shape and meaning to one's surroundings. The poet, he wrote, "has immensely to do with giving life whatever savor it possesses. He has to do with whatever the imagination and the senses have made of the world."

In one poem Stevens wrote, "The greatest poverty is not to live in a physical world." But the power of imagination exists to illuminate and transform the physical world through the ways it is seen. Many of his poems attempt to make the reader aware of the physical world in new and subtle ways. His poems fluctuate between what he called "the mundane," or the ordinary, and the uncommon and elusive. For him, the process of poetry lay in the effort to join these two realms. Thus Stevens constantly points out the uncommon beauty of ordinary things, such as blackbirds, jars, and pears. In his long poem *The Comedian as the Letter C*, he portrays an imaginary poet who seeks inspiration in strange lands and extreme situations, only to discover that he must face the reality of the commonplace if he is to find meaningful eloquence.

In his poems Stevens often attempts to dazzle the reader's senses. His early poetry especially is marked by an exotic vocabulary, tropical luxuriance of color, and an opulence of sound. Some of his poems have striking titles, such as "Le Monocle de Mon Oncle," "Anecdote of the Prince of Peacocks," and "The Emperor of Ice Cream." Later his verse became more direct, essentially a poetry of statement. But throughout, Stevens remained true to his great subject, the role of the imagination in "pressing back against the pressure of reality" and helping us to live our lives.

Anecdote of the Jar

I placed a jar in Tennessee,
And round it was, upon a hill.
It made the slovenly wilderness
Surround that hill.

The wilderness rose up to it,   5
And sprawled around, no longer wild.
The jar was round upon the ground
And tall and of a port in air.

It took dominion everywhere.
The jar was gray and bare.   10
It did not give of bird or bush,
Like nothing else in Tennessee.

Disillusionment of Ten O'Clock

The houses are haunted
By white nightgowns.
None are green,
Or purple with green rings,
Or green with yellow rings,   5
Or yellow with blue rings,
None of them are strange,
With socks of lace
And beaded ceintures.°
People are not going   10
To dream of baboons and periwinkles.°
Only, here and there, an old sailor,
Drunk and asleep in his boots,
Catches tigers
In red weather.   15

9. **ceintures** (sĕnt′yərz): belts or girdles.   11. **periwinkles:** saltwater snails whose cone-shaped shells are
marked with dark spiral bands.

Analyzing and Interpreting the Poems

Anecdote of the Jar
1. Look up the meaning of the word *anecdote* in a dictionary. Is the title of this poem appropriate? Explain.
2. This poem has been interpreted in different ways: Some critics see the jar as a symbol of art or the human imagination, both giving order to chaotic nature. Others find the jar symbolic of human interference and tampering with nature. Find evidence in the poem to support either of these interpretations or your own interpretation.

Disillusionment of Ten O'Clock
1a. What contrast is the poet making between the white nightgowns and the bright, colored ones?
b. In what sense are the houses "haunted"?
2. The poet suggests that the people in these houses have plain, uninteresting dreams. How is the sailor different from these people?
3a. How can this poem be interpreted as a protest against a dull, unimaginative way of life?   **b.** In what way is this a poem about disillusionment?

WILLIAM CARLOS WILLIAMS
1883–1963

William Carlos Williams.
© Eve Arnold / Magnum Photos

William Carlos Williams, one of the most influential poets of the twentieth century, lived most of his life in his hometown of Rutherford, New Jersey, where he was by profession a pediatrician. Williams virtually began his poetic career with his friendship with Ezra Pound, whom he met when they were both students at the University of Pennsylvania. Though as poets he and Pound later diverged, they remained friends all their lives. When Pound settled in England, he maintained contact with Williams, who soon became part of the initial wave of the Imagist movement. In 1909 Williams published his first book of poems. It revealed a new style, and his work from then on was devoted to the development and expansion of this style.

Williams opposed Pound, and particularly T. S. Eliot, in their frequent use of allusions to history, art, religion, and foreign languages. Instead, Williams advocated what he called "the local," a grounding of poetry in the present and in the immediate realities of individual life and its surroundings. He coined the famous slogan for his poems, "No ideas but in things," by which he meant that poets should try to see the world through eyes unspoiled by traditional and irrelevant literary associations. Williams consciously developed the Whitmanian tradition in his attitudes toward subject matter. He made a point of writing about commonplace subjects. Perhaps his most famous work is the brief poem "The Red Wheelbarrow" (page 758). He also wrote about a crowd at a ball game, the common flowers in his garden or in the fields, his favorite bird (the sparrow), incidents from his medical practice, and such random sights as animals at a zoo, schoolgirls walking down a street, and a piece of paper blowing down a road. Williams argued that if modern poetry could not make use of such common experience, it would have little relevance to most people's lives. Williams strove to make his words correspond to the immediacy and uniqueness of simple things. He hoped to revitalize the language of ordinary American speech by using it in his poetry. He believed that local language, like local subjects, lay at the source of all art.

In 1946 he published the first book of *Paterson*, his major long poem. *Paterson* deals with the city of Paterson, New Jersey, near which Williams lived. He chose Paterson for his subject precisely because it was a kind of ordinary manufacturing town that had become common in America. In the poem, the poet-protagonist wanders about the city, perceiving its present, remembering its past, and meditating on his own life in it, until he is able to experience and understand all aspects of the city and, in a sense, to become the city.

In 1963 Williams was awarded the Pulitzer Prize for one of his last collections of verse, *Pictures from Breughel and Other Poems*. Since World War II, his influence on younger writers has matched and even somewhat surpassed the influence of Pound and Eliot earlier in the century. Many poets who have begun to write in the last few decades have followed the example of Williams in seeking to rejuvenate the language of poetry and to invent forms in which to express a fresh vision of reality.

Peasant Dance by Peter Brueghel the Elder (c. 1525–1569). Oil on panel.
Kunsthistorisches Museum, Vienna, Courtesy Art Resource

The Dance

In Breughel's° great picture, The Kermess,
the dancers go round, they go round and
around, the squeal and the blare and the
tweedle of bagpipes, a bugle and fiddles
tipping their bellies (round as the thick-
sided glasses whose wash they impound)
their hips and their bellies off balance
to turn them. Kicking and rolling about
the Fair Grounds, swinging their butts, those
shanks must be sound to bear up under such
rollicking measures, prance as they dance
In Breughel's great picture, The Kermess.

1. **Breughel** (broe′gəl): the Flemish painter Pieter Bruegel
(or Brueghel) the Elder (1525?–1569). His name is sometimes spelled Breughel, as Williams spells it.

William Carlos Williams **763**

Poem

As the cat
climbed over
the top of

the jamcloset
first the right
forefoot

carefully
then the hind
stepped down

into the pit of
the empty
flowerpot

Scat (1986) by Janet Fish (1938–   ). Oil on canvas.
Courtesy Robert Miller Gallery, New York

For Study and Discussion

Analyzing and Interpreting the Poem

1. Williams' poems usually follow a kind of **organic** rhythm. With organic rhythm, the poem is shaped to reflect the movement of thought, speech, or action in the poem. Using organic rhythm, Williams is apt to put greater stress than usual on each separate line, whether the line is composed of one word or several words. Each line should be read as a unit separated slightly from the line above and the line below. Read "Poem" aloud, pausing slightly at the end of each line and pausing a bit longer at the end of each stanza. How do these pauses suggest the cat's movements?

2. How do the pauses add to the humorous effect of the final stanza?

Literary Elements

Rhythm in "The Dance"

Although "The Dance" is printed as free verse, Williams departs from his customary practice to include a somewhat irregular but noticeable amount of **dactylic** rhythm. A **dactyl** is a metrical unit consisting of a stressed syllable followed by two unstressed syllables. We hear this rhythm in such words as *mérrĭmĕnt* and *dúbĭoŭs*. Williams groups his dactyls in irregular clusters of words and occasionally breaks the rhythm with extra syllables. You may notice that dactylic rhythm is the same as waltz rhythm. By using the dactyl but breaking the beat occasionally, Williams sets up a rhythm that suggests both the fixed steps and the irregular hops and lurches of the peasant dance.

1. Mark off the dactylic beat in Williams' first three lines by indicating the stressed and unstressed syllables. Mark the stressed syllables (') and the unstressed (˘). Do you find an extra syllable at the beginning or end of the first three lines? Where else in the first three lines is the dactylic rhythm irregular?

2. Indicate the word groups that form the clusters of dactyls. Look for points in the poem where one set of dactyls breaks off to be followed by a new set.

It has been said of Ezra Pound that it was he more than anyone else who made poets write *modern* poetry, editors publish it, and readers read it. To Pound, the elaborate, ornate language typical of English poetry in his day seemed artificial, and he urged poets to avoid it. His slogan was "make it new." Among his ideas that changed the course of poetry were: the "direct treatment" of the subject, the immediate and most exact presentation of what the poet had to say; the creation of new rhythms and forms appropriate to modern subjects and expressive of modern feelings; and the central importance of the image. (See *Imagism*, page 757.)

The impact of Pound's thinking on twentieth-century writing was immense. He influenced a change of style in the verse of the eminent Irish poet W. B. Yeats. He encouraged T. S. Eliot to write in the ways he advocated, and he edited Eliot's most famous poem, *The Waste Land*. His ideas are reflected in the poetry of William Carlos Williams and the fiction of Ernest Hemingway. Pound tirelessly supported the writers he liked, including Eliot, James Joyce, and Robert Frost, and on many occasions he gave money and even lodging to writers in need.

Pound's own poetry is complex and often difficult to understand. His early work drew from half a dozen different cultures, including Chinese and Provençal French, as he sought poetic models for the sensitivity and compression he admired. His early long poems include *Homage to Sextus Propertius* and *Hugh Selwyn Mauberley*. After 1920 Pound's efforts were concentrated on a gigantic work, *The Cantos*, which occupied him for the rest of his life. This poem, more than eight hundred pages long, draws into itself a bewildering mixture of history, political and economic theory, art criticism, philosophy, personal confession, and allusions to foreign languages and literatures.

Pound was born in Hailey, Idaho, and raised in

Ezra Pound.
The Bettmann Archive

Philadelphia. He studied at the University of Pennsylvania and at Hamilton College, from which he received a Ph.B. in 1905. After a year of graduate study at the University of Pennsylvania, during which he met William Carlos Williams and Hilda Doolittle (H. D.), and brief further residence in Philadelphia, he proceeded to Europe, where he was to live, first in England, then France, then Italy, for much of the remainder of his life. During World War II his career was blighted by his outspoken support of Mussolini and Italian fascism. He was indicted for treason in 1943 and arrested the following year by the American army in Italy. In 1945 he was flown to Washington, D.C., where, for some years, he was confined without trial in St. Elizabeth's Hospital for the criminally insane. As a result largely of support from the American literary community, Pound was released in 1958, and he returned to Italy to live out the rest of his days.

The River-Merchant's Wife: a Letter

LI T'AI PO

While my hair was still cut straight across my forehead°
Played I about the front gate, pulling flowers.
You came by on bamboo stilts, playing horse,
You walked about my seat, playing with blue plums.
And we went on living in the village of Chokan: 5
Two small people, without dislike or suspicion.

At fourteen I married My Lord you.
I never laughed, being bashful.
Lowering my head, I looked at the wall.
Called to, a thousand times, I never looked back.   10

At fifteen I stopped scowling,
I desired my dust to be mingled with yours
Forever and forever and forever.
Why should I climb the lookout?

At sixteen you departed,   15
You went into far Ku-to-yen, by the river of swirling eddies,
And you have been gone five months.
The monkeys make sorrowful noise overhead.

You dragged your feet when you went out.
By the gate now, the moss is grown, the different mosses,   20
Too deep to clear them away!
The leaves fall early this autumn, in wind.
The paired butterflies are already yellow with August
Over the grass in the West garden;
They hurt me. I grow older.   25
If you are coming down through the narrows of the river Kiang,
Please let me know beforehand,
And I will come out to meet you
        As far as Cho-fu-Sa.

1. **hair . . . forehead:** This was the prescribed, traditional haircut for little girls.

Wang Hsi-chi Watching Geese by Ch'ien Hsuan (c. 1235–1300). Handscroll, ink, color, and gold on paper.
Metropolitan Museum of Art, gift of the Dillon Fund, 1973

For Study and Discussion

Analyzing and Interpreting the Poem

1. Pound's poem is adapted from a Chinese poem by Li T'ai Po. The speaker is the wife of a river merchant, a trader whose business takes him away from home for long periods, in this case down the Kiang River. **a.** What stage of her life and her husband's does she refer to in the first section of the poem? **b.** What details make this reference clear?

2. According to Chinese custom, marriages were arranged without consideration for the young people's feelings. **a.** What images suggest the speaker's bashfulness and unhappiness at the time of the marriage? **b.** What change in her feelings is described in stanza 3?

3a. Find an image that suggests the husband was not anxious to leave home. **b.** Why should the sight of butterflies be painful to the wife?

4a. What emotions are suggested by the statement, "I grow older"? **b.** How does her offer to come and meet him suggest the importance of formality in their relationship?

Literary Elements

The Dramatic Lyric

Lyric is a general term referring to any poem that expresses personal emotions or thoughts. At one time, the term **lyric** had a narrower meaning, and principally referred to poems meant to be set to music and sung, such as the songs in William Shakespeare's plays. Such lyrics made much use of rhyme and regular rhythms and had precise stanza forms. Until the twentieth century most lyric poems in English used rhyme and stanza forms. Some modern American poets, such as Edna St. Vincent Millay (page 786), have continued to write lyrics in traditional forms. But other modern poets have departed from tradition, using sounds and rhythms in highly individual ways to convey emotion.

"The River-Merchant's Wife: a Letter" is what Pound called a **dramatic lyric.** Its personal feelings are attributed to an imagined character rather than to the poet. The manner in which the wife expresses her feelings is appropriate to the kind of person she is and the kind of society in which she lives. For example, the wife concludes her letter by quietly stating that she will come out to meet her husband. What other lines in the poem indicate that she understates her true feelings? How is understatement appropriate to her shy character and to the formality typical of her society?

Throughout his career Robinson Jeffers was fascinated by nature in its harsher forms: wild horses, rocky coasts, and predatory birds, such as the hawk. He once wrote that he was not interested in finding new methods or subjects for poetry but wished "only to reclaim old freedom." In his poetry Jeffers returned to a basic interpretation of human life somewhat in the severe fashion of a Biblical prophet, though with different conclusions. For him the supreme powers in the world are the natural processes, which are indifferent to human wishes and aims. For the most part he sees human beings as creatures out of harmony with the basic forces of cosmic nature.

Jeffers was born in Pittsburgh, Pennsylvania. He studied at boarding schools in Switzerland and Germany and mastered the French, Italian, and German languages. He returned to the United States in 1903 and extended his education to forestry, medicine, and law. Around 1914, Jeffers received a modest inheritance, which enabled him to settle in the village of Carmel on the California coast. There he had a stone house built; later he built Hawk Tower next to it with his own hands. Now in relative isolation, and inspired by the wild birds and rocky coast, Jeffers began to write in earnest.

Jeffers is known principally for his long narrative

Robinson Jeffers.
Photograph by Edward Weston (1886–1958).
© 1981 Arizona Board of Regents, Center for Creative Photography, Courtesy Richard A. Gleeson Library, University of San Francisco

poems, including *Tamar* (1924), *Roan Stallion* (1925), and *The Woman at Point Sur* (1927), which depict extreme situations and tragic events against the grandeur of the Big Sur country. Jeffers also adapted several plays from Greek tragedy. The most famous of these was his adaptation of Euripides' *Medea,* which had a successful run on Broadway.

Summer Holiday

When the sun shouts and people abound
One thinks there were the ages of stone and the age of bronze
And the iron age; iron the unstable metal;
Steel made of iron, unstable as his mother; the towered-up
    cities
Will be stains of rust on mounds of plaster.   5
Roots will not pierce the heaps for a time, kind rains will cure
    them,
Then nothing will remain of the iron age
And all these people but a thigh-bone or so, a poem
Stuck in the world's thought, splinters of glass
In the rubbish dumps, a concrete dam far off in the
    mountain . . .   10

Johnny Bird (1959) by John
Chamberlain (1927–   ).
Enameled steel.
Virginia Museum of Fine Arts,
Richmond, Sydney and Frances
Lewis Collection

Robinson Jeffers   **769**

Evening Ebb

The ocean has not been so quiet for a long while; five night-
    herons
Fly shorelong voiceless in the hush of the air
Over the calm of an ebb that almost mirrors their wings.
The sun has gone down, and the water has gone down
From the weed-clad rock, but the distant cloud-wall rises. The
    ebb whispers.   5
Great cloud-shadows float in the opal water.
Through rifts in the screen of the world pale gold gleams, and
    the evening
Star suddenly glides like a flying torch.
As if we had not been meant to see her; rehearsing behind
The screen of the world for another audience.   10

For Study and Discussion

Analyzing and Interpreting the Poems

Summer Holiday

1. Classical mythology tells of the existence of four ages. The earliest and the best was a golden age. Then, with declining virtue came the ages of silver, bronze, and iron. **a.** What realistic basis is there for referring to our own time as an age of iron and steel? **b.** According to Jeffers, what quality in these metals makes them a good emblem for a perishing era? **c.** How does Jeffers' view of steel contrast with Carl Sandburg's view of steel in "Prayers of Steel" (page 754)?

2. Considering the kinds of relics that have survived from previous historical ages, how realistic is Jeffers' list of survivals from our time?

3. How does the reference to earlier ages suggest that the decline of our age is inevitable?

Evening Ebb

1. The first eight lines of the poem picture an evening on the seashore as one of special beauty and repose. **a.** What movement of the sea does Jeffers refer to in line 3? **b.** What sight does the sea "mirror"?

2. The evening star, the earliest star to appear in the evening, suddenly becomes visible. **a.** What is the "screen of the world" through which the evening star gleams? **b.** What does the "screen" imply about human knowledge and its limitations?

3a. What phrase in line 10 suggests that there is much in the universe apart from humanity? **b.** What does Jeffers imply about the importance of humankind in the universe?

Marianne Moore once said that her writing could be called poetry only because there was no other name for it. Indeed her poems appear to be extremely compressed essays that happen to be printed in jagged lines on the page. Her subjects were varied: animals, laborers, artists, and the craft of poetry. From her general reading came quotations that she found striking or insightful. She included these in her poems, scrupulously enclosed in quotation marks, and sometimes identified in footnotes. Of this practice, she wrote, " 'Why the many quotation marks?' I am asked. . . . When a thing has been said so well that it could not be said better, why paraphrase it? Hence my writing is, if not a cabinet of fossils, a kind of collection of flies in amber." Close observation and concentration on detail are the methods of her poetry. Artists, she held, were successful when their work was "lit with piercing glances into the life of things."

Marianne Moore grew up in Kirkwood, Missouri, near St. Louis. After graduating from Bryn Mawr College in 1909, she taught commercial subjects at the Indian School in Carlisle, Pennsylvania. Later she became a librarian in New York City. During the 1920s she was editor of *The Dial*, an important literary magazine of the period. She lived quietly all her life, mostly in Brooklyn, New York. She spent a lot of time at the Bronx Zoo, fascinated by the animals. Her admiration of the Brooklyn Dodgers—before the team moved to Los Angeles—was widely known. It was a pleasure to watch ballplayers in action, she said, because of their deft and workmanlike ability.

Her first book of poems was published in London in 1921 by a group of friends associated with the Imagist movement. From that time on her poetry has been read with interest by succeeding generations of poets and readers. In 1952 she was awarded the Pulitzer Prize for her *Collected Poems*. She wrote that she did not write poetry "for money *or* fame. To earn a living is needful, but it can be done in routine ways. One writes because one has a burning desire to objectify what it is indispensable to one's happiness to express. . . ."

Marianne Moore tossing out the first ball to open the 1968 baseball season at the Yankee Stadium.

Poetry

I, too, dislike it: there are things that are important beyond all this fiddle.
  Reading it, however, with a perfect contempt for it, one discovers in
  it, after all, a place for the genuine.
     Hands that can grasp, eyes
      that can dilate, hair that can rise   5
        if it must, these things are important not because a

high-sounding interpretation can be put upon them but because they are
  useful. When they become so derivative as to become unintelligible,
  the same thing may be said for all of us, that we
     do not admire what   10
      we cannot understand: the bat
        holding on upside down or in quest of something to

eat, elephants pushing, a wild horse taking a roll, a tireless wolf under
  a tree, the immovable critic twitching his skin like a horse that feels a flea, the baseball fan, the statistician—   15
     nor is it valid
        to discriminate against "business documents and

schoolbooks"; all these phenomena are important. One must make a distinction
  however: when dragged into prominence by half poets, the result is not poetry,
  nor till the poets among us can be   20
     "literalists° of
      the imagination"—above
        insolence and triviality and can present

for inspection, "imaginary gardens with real toads in them," shall we have
  it. In the meantime, if you demand on the one hand   25
  the raw material of poetry in
     all its rawness and
      that which is on the other hand
        genuine, you are interested in poetry.

21. **literalists:** people who insist on the exact meanings of words.

Marianne Moore at the Bronx Zoo (1953).

For Study and Discussion

Analyzing and Interpreting the Poem

1. Marianne Moore may surprise us by saying that she dislikes poetry. **a.** What is implied by her declaration that it is "fiddle"? **b.** How is poetry related to "high-sounding interpretation"? **c.** When is poetry most unlikable?

2. In lines 4–5, the poet describes physical reactions to excitement. In what way do these reactions indicate "the genuine" in poetry?

3. Moore says that poets should be "literalists of the

imagination." One meaning of the word *literal* is "true to fact." **a.** How close to the literal are the things listed in lines 11–15? **b.** How might an interest in these things lead to an interest in poetry?

4a. What aspects of poetry are suggested by the phrase "real toads"? **b.** What does Moore think true poetry should be?

5. Marianne Moore has been called a master of the "light rhyme," rhyme that is not obvious but that enhances the poem's musical effect. **a.** What two light rhymes do you find in stanza one? **b.** Find other light rhymes in the poem.

© Rollie McKenna

T. S. Eliot (1950).

T. S. Eliot's literary career is remarkable in two ways. First, there is no poet of the twentieth century for whom critical esteem has been greater. Second, the influence he has exerted, as a poet and a critic, on other writers is without parallel in our time. Some critics have suggested that as far as poetry is concerned, the early twentieth century might well be called "the Age of Eliot."

Thomas Stearns Eliot was born in St. Louis, Missouri, to a family of New England stock. His grandfather had settled in St. Louis and founded the first Unitarian church there. He was also the principal founder of George Washington University and of Smith Academy, where Eliot himself received his secondary schooling. From 1906 to 1910, Eliot studied at Harvard, where he published poems in the literary magazine, *The Harvard Advocate*. He took a master's degree in philosophy in 1910, and also in that year completed his first important poem, "The Love Song of J. Alfred Prufrock." After a year at the Sorbonne in Paris, Eliot returned to Harvard and continued to study philosophy and linguistics while educating himself in French poetry and Sanskrit. In 1914 he was a graduate student at the University of Marburg in Germany. When World War I broke out, he left Germany and settled in England, where he met another young American poet, Ezra Pound. Pound recognized Eliot's great talent and energetically recommended "Prufrock" to Harriet Monroe, the editor of the American magazine *Poetry,* where Eliot's work first appeared for the general public.

Eliot did not publish a large number of poems. His first small book, *Prufrock and Other Observations,* appeared in 1917, and it established the tone for all his early poetry. It focused upon the frustration and despair of an urbane, sophisticated life. Though others had dealt with the presumed glamour of the modern city, Eliot pictured city life as a scene of deep doubt and anxiety. His most famous poem, *The Waste Land,* appeared in 1922. It is a highly complex, puzzling poem about which commentaries are still being written. It depicts modern civilization as a spiritual void, empty of faith and meaningful love, and paralyzed by anxiety and boredom. Most of *The Waste Land* was written by early 1921, but Eliot was unable to bring it into final form. With Pound's brilliant assistance, however, he condensed the various drafts and fragments of the poem into the work we know today. In the boldness of its ideas and the richness and power of its style, *The Waste Land* has had an enormous impact on later writers and on the general reader. The very term *waste land* has become familiar in everyday language.

In 1927 Eliot gave up his American citizenship to become a British subject. In the following year he announced his loyalty to the Church of England, a commitment directly reflected in the strong religious concerns of his later writing. Two of his most important late poems are *Ash Wednesday* (1930) and *Four Quartets* (1943). Both of these long poems explore religious themes, suggesting Eliot's conviction that the kind of spiritual desolation pictured in *The Waste Land* required deep, orthodox religious belief for its healing.

Early in his London years Eliot had also begun to publish essays that grew into one of the outstanding bodies of literary criticism in this century. In 1935 the first of a distinguished series of his plays was produced. His dramatic works, especially *Murder in the Cathedral* and a later play, *The Cocktail Party,* were performed often in this country and abroad. In 1948 Eliot was awarded the Nobel Prize for literature.

The Love Song of J. Alfred Prufrock

S'io credessi che mia risposta fosse
a persona che mai tornasse al mondo,
questa fiamma staria senza più scosse.
Ma per ciò che giammai di questo fondo
non tornò vivo alcun, s'i'odo il vero,
senza tema d'infamia ti rispondo.°

Let us go then, you and I,
When the evening is spread out against the sky
Like a patient etherized upon a table;
Let us go, through certain half-deserted streets,
The muttering retreats   5
Of restless nights in one-night cheap hotels
And sawdust restaurants with oyster-shells:
Streets that follow like a tedious argument
Of insidious° intent
To lead you to an overwhelming question . . .   10
Oh, do not ask, "What is it?"
Let us go and make our visit.

In the room the women come and go
Talking of Michelangelo.

The yellow fog that rubs its back upon the window-panes,   15
The yellow smoke that rubs its muzzle on the window-panes,
Licked its tongue into the corners of the evening,
Lingered upon the pools that stand in drains,
Let fall upon its back the soot that falls from chimneys,
Slipped by the terrace, made a sudden leap,   20
And seeing that it was a soft October night,
Curled once about the house, and fell asleep.

° ***S'io credessi . . . ti rispondo:*** The epigraph is from Dante's *Inferno.* One of the damned, asked to tell his tale, replies: "If I believed my answer were being given to someone who could ever return to the world, this flame (his voice) would shake no more. But since no one has ever returned alive from this depth, if what I hear is true, I will answer you without fear of disgrace." **9. insidious** (ĭn-sĭd′ē-əs): secretly treacherous.

And indeed there will be time
For the yellow smoke that slides along the street
Rubbing its back upon the window-panes;   25
There will be time, there will be time
To prepare a face to meet the faces that you meet;
There will be time to murder and create,
And time for all the works and days of hands
That lift and drop a question on your plate;   30
Time for you and time for me,
And time yet for a hundred indecisions,
And for a hundred visions and revisions,
Before the taking of a toast and tea.

In the room the women come and go   35
Talking of Michelangelo.

And indeed there will be time
To wonder, "Do I dare?" and, "Do I dare?"
Time to turn back and descend the stair,
With a bald spot in the middle of my hair—   40
(They will say: "How his hair is growing thin!")
My morning coat, my collar mounting firmly to the chin,
My necktie rich and modest, but asserted by a simple pin—
(They will say: "But how his arms and legs are thin!")
Do I dare   45
Disturb the universe?
In a minute there is time
For decisions and revisions which a minute will reverse.

For I have known them all already, known them all—
Have known the evenings, mornings, afternoons,   50
I have measured out my life with coffee spoons;
I know the voices dying with a dying fall
Beneath the music from a farther room.
   So how should I presume?

And I have known the eyes already, known them all—   55
The eyes that fix you in a formulated phrase,
And when I am formulated, sprawling on a pin,
When I am pinned and wriggling on the wall,
Then how should I begin
To spit out all the butt-ends of my days and ways?   60
   And how should I presume?

And I have known the arms already, known them all—
Arms that are braceleted and white and bare
(But in the lamplight, downed with light brown hair!)

A Friendly Call (1895) by William Merritt Chase (1849–1916). Oil on canvas.

Is it perfume from a dress   65
That makes me so digress?
Arms that lie along a table, or wrap about a shawl.
    And should I then presume?
    And how should I begin?

     .   .   .   .   .

Shall I say, I have gone at dusk through narrow streets   70
And watched the smoke that rises from the pipes
Of lonely men in shirt-sleeves, leaning out of windows? . . .

I should have been a pair of ragged claws
Scuttling across the floors of silent seas.

.   .   .   .   .

And the afternoon, the evening, sleeps so peacefully!   75
Smoothed by long fingers,
Asleep . . . tired . . . or it malingers,°
Stretched on the floor, here beside you and me.
Should I, after tea and cakes and ices,
Have the strength to force the moment to its crisis?   80
But though I have wept and fasted, wept and prayed,
Though I have seen my head (grown slightly bald) brought in
    upon a platter,°
I am no prophet—and here's no great matter;
I have seen the moment of my greatness flicker,
And I have seen the eternal Footman° hold my coat, and
    snicker.   85
And in short, I was afraid.

And would it have been worth it, after all,
After the cups, the marmalade, the tea,
Among the porcelain, among some talk of you and me,
Would it have been worth while,   90
To have bitten off the matter with a smile,
To have squeezed the universe into a ball
To roll it towards some overwhelming question,
To say: "I am Lazarus,° come from the dead,
Come back to tell you all, I shall tell you all"—   95
If one, settling a pillow by her head,
    Should say: "That is not what I meant at all.
    That is not it, at all."

And would it have been worth it, after all,
Would it have been worth while,   100
After the sunsets and the dooryards and the sprinkled streets,
After the novels, after the teacups, after the skirts that trail
    along the floor—
And this, and so much more?—
It is impossible to say just what I mean!
But as if a magic lantern° threw the nerves in patterns on a
    screen: 105

---

77. **malingers:** pretends to be ill.   82. **upon a platter:** a reference to the prophet
John the Baptist, whose head was presented on a platter to Salome as a reward for
her dancing. (See Matthew 14:1–12.)   85. **the eternal Footman:** Death, that is, the
one who is always waiting.   94. **Lazarus** (lăz′ər-əs): In John 11, Christ raises Lazarus
from the dead.   105. **magic lantern:** an early device for projecting images on a screen.

Would it have been worth while
If one, settling a pillow or throwing off a shawl,
And turning toward the window, should say:
  "That is not it at all,
  That is not what I meant, at all."   110

     ·   ·   ·   ·   ·

No! I am not Prince Hamlet, nor was meant to be;
Am an attendant lord, one that will do
To swell a progress,° start a scene or two,
Advise the prince; no doubt, an easy tool,
Deferential, glad to be of use,   115
Politic, cautious, and meticulous;
Full of high sentence,° but a bit obtuse;
At times, indeed, almost ridiculous—
Almost, at times, the Fool.

I grow old . . . I grow old . . .   120
I shall wear the bottoms of my trousers rolled.

Shall I part my hair behind? Do I dare to eat a peach?
I shall wear white flannel trousers, and walk upon the beach.
I have heard the mermaids singing, each to each.

I do not think that they will sing to me.   125

I have seen them riding seaward on the waves
Combing the white hair of the waves blown back
When the wind blows the water white and black.

We have lingered in the chambers of the sea
By sea-girls wreathed with seaweed red and brown   130
Till human voices wake us, and we drown.

---

113. **To swell a progress:** to increase the number of people in a parade or a scene
from a play. 117. **Full of high sentence:** speaking in a very ornate manner, often
giving advice. The allusion is to Polonius, the pompous Lord Chamberlain in Shakespeare's *Hamlet*.

Commentary

"The Love Song of J. Alfred Prufrock" depicts the consciousness of a single character, a timid, middle-aged man. Prufrock is talking or thinking to himself. The epigraph, a dramatic speech taken from Dante's *Inferno*, provides a key to Prufrock's nature. Like Dante's character, Prufrock is in a "hell," in his case the hell of his own feelings. For the first forty-eight lines of the poem, he contemplates the aimless pattern of his divided and solitary self. He is a lover, yet he is unable to bring himself to declare his love. He is both the "you and I" of line 1, pacing the city's grimy streets on his lonely walk. He observes the foggy evening settling down on him. Growing more and more hesitant, he postpones the moment of his decision. Should a middle-aged man even think of making a proposal of love? "Do I dare / Disturb the universe?" he asks. In lines 49–110, Prufrock wrestles with his desire and his doubt. And, in lines 87–110, he imagines how foolish he would feel if he were to make his proposal only to discover that the woman had never thought of him as a possible lover; he imagines her brisk cruel response: "That is not what I meant, at all."

Finally, in lines 111–131, Prufrock decides that he lacks the will to make his declaration. "I am not Prince Hamlet," he says; he will not, like Shakespeare's character, attempt to shake off his doubts and "force the moment to its crisis." He feels more like the aging, foolish Polonius, another character in *Hamlet*. He is able only to dream of romance. Thus, in the youthful fashion of the time (around 1910), he will have his trousers trimmed with cuffs at the bottom. He will "walk upon the beach," though he probably will not venture near the water. He has had a romantic vision of mermaids singing an enchanting song, but he assumes that they will not sing to him. Prufrock is paralyzed, unable to act upon his impulses and desires. He will continue to live in a world of romantic daydreams—"the chambers of the sea"—until he is awakened by the "human voices" of real life in which he "drowns."

For Study and Discussion

Analyzing and Interpreting the Poem

1. Throughout the poem, Prufrock seems to be on his way to a tea, a late afternoon party. **a.** What words in the opening line suggest that he is attempting to gather himself together, to unify his fragmented personality? **b.** What images in lines 1–12 indicate his low spirits? **c.** In line 3, Prufrock compares the evening to a "patient etherized upon a table." In what way might the world of the poem be described as anesthetized?

2. Prufrock says that one reason for his doubt is his awareness that he is growing old and that he really does not want to face any new situations. In lines 49–69 he groups together some of the things he says he has "known." **a.** How does the statement that he has known "evenings, mornings, afternoons" suggest that his life is full of sameness? **b.** What feelings about the other guests at the party are suggested by the description of their voices "dying with a dying fall"? **c.** What feelings about them are implied by Prufrock's saying that their eyes "fix" him "in a formulated phrase"?

3. Prufrock alludes to several literary and historical figures. Michelangelo was a vigorous artist, famous for such heroic tasks as painting the immense ceiling of the Sistine Chapel in Rome and sculpting the great statues of Moses and David. Why is it significant that women at the party talk about this kind of man?

4. In Shakespeare's play, Hamlet is faced with the problem of having to avenge the murder of his father, an act about which he has many doubts and fears. In the end he does take action, but only at the cost of his own life. **a.** What aspect of Hamlet is Prufrock thinking of when he says, "I am not Prince Hamlet"? **b.** What does the statement suggest about his ability to act?

5. In line 10 Prufrock says that he is moving toward "an overwhelming question." **a.** What is the question Prufrock actually wants to ask? **b.** Prufrock thinks that if he were to ask his question he would be like the Biblical figure Lazarus, whom Jesus raised from the dead. From what sort of "death" would he be raised?

6. After considering all possibilities, Prufrock gives a clear, one-word answer to his question. What is it, and where is it stated?

7a. What image near the end of the poem suggests that Prufrock would rather stay on the edge of things than plunge into action? **b.** What quality in the mermaids, expressed in lines 126–128, does Prufrock seem to admire?

8. In a sense, Eliot's hero is typical of characters in early twentieth-century literature. He is a self-doubting man who decides not to plunge into a love affair that he thinks would too deeply disturb his trivial life, even though he is fully aware of the dryness of that life. Is Prufrock actually afraid of the possibilities of personal freedom?

Literary Elements

Simile and Metaphor

T. S. Eliot's poems are noted for their startling similes and metaphors. In "Prufrock" these figures of speech are used both to characterize Prufrock and to reveal his state of mind. For example, when Prufrock says that "the evening is spread out against the sky / Like a patient etherized upon a table" (lines 2–3), the simile expresses the stagnant quality of his life and his own sense of spiritual isolation. When he says, "I have measured out my life with coffee spoons" (line 51), he uses a metaphor to suggest his cramped, trivial existence. Explain the simile in lines 8–9. What two things are compared? How does the simile tell us about Prufrock as well as describe the streets? Explain the extended metaphor in lines 15–22. What two things are compared? How do the metaphors in lines 57–58 and 73–74 characterize Prufrock?

Stream of Consciousness

One reason that Eliot's poem may seem difficult at first is that it uses a **stream-of-consciousness** technique. With stream of consciousness, the writer tries to imitate the natural flow of a character's thoughts, memories, and reflections, as the character experiences them. In attempting to capture the random movement of a character's consciousness, this technique disposes of the logical connections and transitions of ordinary prose. Instead, the character's thoughts are organized by a system of associations, in which one thought can suddenly trigger another seemingly unrelated one. Stream of consciousness allows the writer to present an intimate picture of a character's personality.

Reread lines 37–48. How do the lines enclosed in parentheses suggest the random flow of Prufrock's thoughts? What other examples of stream of consciousness do you find in this passage? What important aspect of Prufrock's character is illustrated here?

Writing About Literature

Comparing Speakers

In a composition, compare the speaker of "The Love Song of J. Alfred Prufrock" with the speaker of Robert Frost's "After Apple-Picking" (page 744). Consider the following: How does each speaker seem to regard himself? What does each speaker seem to regret about his life? One speaker lives in a city and the other in the country. How have these different backgrounds shaped their lives, as these lives appear in the two poems?

JOHN CROWE RANSOM
1888–1974

John Crowe Ransom.

Along with Robert Penn Warren and Allen Tate, John Crowe Ransom was a member of a group of poets centered at Vanderbilt University in Nashville, Tennessee. In later years these three Southerners made individual reputations for themselves, but they are often still identified with the Fugitives, a group of Southern literary and social critics to which they belonged. Whereas Warren and Tate were jarred out of traditional poetic ways by the influence of T. S. Eliot and Ezra Pound, Ransom never echoed either of these poets. Instead he arrived at an original style marked by the interaction of open emotion and understated, wry, or merely suggested response to a situation. His poems frequently express both deep feelings and a sense of detachment from those feelings. Often among his subjects are human defeat and death; but through wit and irony he gives readers a balanced perspective on these crushing experiences. His former student and fellow poet Randall Jarrell called Ransom's manner "a way of handling sentiment or emotion without even seeming sentimental or overemotional. . . ."

The son of a minister, Ransom grew up in Pulaski, Tennessee, and was educated at Vanderbilt. As a Rhodes Scholar, he studied at Oxford University in England, and he returned to Vanderbilt as a teacher of English. He published only three small volumes of poetry, all early in his life. In the late 1930s he moved to Kenyon College in Ohio, where he established the *Kenyon Review,* one of the most important literary and critical journals of our time. His book *The New Criticism* (1941) provided the name for the influential critical movement that stresses the close analysis of literary works, especially poems. He advocated the view that poetry is a special way of knowing reality and that, as a way of understanding the world, it is just as important as scientific investigation. Occasionally he has been accused of encouraging an overly intellectual approach to poetry. Many of Ransom's readers, however, feel that he has written a number of poems of great originality.

Janet Waking

Beautifully Janet slept
Till it was deeply morning. She woke then
And thought about her dainty-feathered hen,
To see how it had kept.

One kiss she gave her mother,   5
Only a small one gave she to her daddy
Who would have kissed each curl of his shining baby;
No kiss at all for her brother.

"Old Chucky, Old Chucky!" she cried,
Running on little pink feet upon the grass   10
To Chucky's house, and listening. But alas,
Her Chucky had died.

It was a transmogrifying° bee
Came droning down on Chucky's old bald head
And sat and put the poison. It scarcely bled,   15
But how exceedingly

13. **transmogrifying** (trăns-mŏg′rə-fī′ĭng): transforming, often in a humorous or grotesque way.

John Crowe Ransom   **783**

And purply did the knot
Swell with the venom and communicate
Its rigor! Now the poor comb stood up straight
But Chucky did not.   20

So there was Janet
Kneeling on the wet grass, crying her brown hen
(Translated far beyond the daughters of men)
To rise and walk upon it.

And weeping fast as she had breath   25
Janet implored us, "Wake her from her sleep!"
And would not be instructed in how deep
Was the forgetful kingdom of death.

Bells for John Whiteside's Daughter

There was such speed in her little body,
And such lightness in her footfall,
It is no wonder that her brown study°
Astonishes us all.

Her wars were bruited° in our high window.   5
We looked among orchard trees and beyond.
Where she took arms against her shadow
Or harried unto the pond

The lazy geese, like a snow cloud
Dripping their snow on the green grass,   10
Tricking and stopping, sleepy and proud,
Who cried in goose, Alas,

For the tireless heart within the little
Lady with rod that made them rise
From their noon apple-dreams, and scuttle   15
Goose-fashion under the skies!

But now go the bells, and we are ready;
In one house we are sternly stopped
To say we are vexed at her brown study,
Lying so primly propped.   20

3. **brown study:** the state of being in deep thought.   5. **bruited** (broot′əd): reported.

Analyzing and Interpreting the Poems

Janet Waking

1. This poem gains much of its effect by juxtaposing the innocence of the little girl Janet with her sudden experience of death. **a.** What do such words as *beautifully, dainty-feathered,* and *curl* suggest about the kind of world Janet understands? **b.** How does Janet's character begin to emerge in the second stanza?

2. Toward the end of the poem, Ransom moves away from the two earlier worlds of feeling to an attitude of detached, calm wisdom. **a.** What does Janet think has happened to Chucky? **b.** What do the last two lines tell us about Janet?

3. The poem depicts Janet waking up in the morning. In what other senses may Janet be said to be "waking"?

Bells for John Whiteside's Daughter

1. This poem tells about a little girl who has died suddenly. **a.** How does the phrase "brown study" suggest death? **b.** Why is the speaker "astonished"?

2. The middle three stanzas depict the little girl as she was in life. What kind of "wars" was she engaged in?

3a. What words in the middle three stanzas suggest the movement, warmth, and color of her life? **b.** What phrases in the last stanza recall us abruptly to the subject of death? **c.** What do you think the speaker is "vexed" at when he sees the little girl?

Sentimentality and Pathos

These two poems are good examples of Ransom's way of writing with restraint about highly emotional subjects. The subject of death may easily lead a writer into **sentimentality,** a conscious, insincere appeal to the reader's emotions. In both cases Ransom avoids sentimentality. What he captures, however, is the **pathos** of death, the qualities that arouse pity or sorrow in the reader. Through deliberate restraint in language and detail, Ransom avoids overstatement and indicates precisely what his feelings are.

1. What details in "Janet Waking" show that the speaker does not idealize the little girl? What words and phrases indicate that he himself is not greatly affected by Chucky's death? What is he most affected by?

2. What phrases in "Bells for John Whiteside's Daughter" show a deliberate restraint in describing or referring to the girl's death? What details in the speaker's description of the girl suggest that he is deeply moved by her death?

During the early 1920s Edna St. Vincent Millay became famous as a voice of her generation—the same generation about which F. Scott Fitzgerald wrote many of his stories. She was in many ways a traditional Romantic. She favored traditional English verse forms, especially the lyric and the sonnet. She sang of rebellion against convention and wrote witty poems about romantic love. The poems of her maturity were more somber and chastened. They spoke of life's promises and disappointments, of the importance of love, of nature's seeming indifference to human aspiration, and of her own deep desire for beauty. Later in her life, she was concerned with the political stresses and strains leading to World War II. She wrote in opposition to the brutality of the Nazi regime in Germany and urged the Allies to overcome the forces of fascism.

Millay grew up on the shores of Penobscot Bay in Maine. She began contributing poems to magazines while she was still a child. In 1917, the year she graduated from Vassar College, her first book of poems was published. For the next few years, she joined younger and more rebellious spirits like herself in the Greenwich Village section of New York City, where she supported herself by the sale of verse and stories to magazines. She wrote experimental plays for the Provincetown Players, which also produced Eugene O'Neill's earliest plays. When she became famous, she gave very popular poetry

Edna St. Vincent Millay (1929).
Berenice Abbott (1898–   ), Commerce Graphics Ltd., Inc.,
Courtesy National Portrait Gallery, Smithsonian Institution

readings. In an affectionate essay about her, the critic Edmund Wilson described her reading as "thrilling. She pronounced every syllable distinctly; she gave every sound its value." In 1923 she was awarded the Pulitzer Prize for *The Harp-Weaver.* In the same year she married and, with her husband, moved to a farm in the Berkshire Hills called Steepletop, where she lived most of the rest of her life.

God's World

O world, I cannot hold thee close enough!
  Thy winds, thy wide gray skies!
  Thy mists, that roll and rise!
Thy woods, this autumn day, that ache and sag
And all but cry with color! That gaunt crag   5
To crush! To lift the lean of that black bluff!
World, World, I cannot get thee close enough!

Long have I known a glory in it all,
  But never knew I this:
  Here such a passion is   10
As stretcheth me apart—Lord, I do fear
Thou'st made the world too beautiful this year;
My soul is all but out of me—let fall
No burning leaf; prithee, let no bird call.

On Hearing a Symphony of Beethoven

Sweet sounds, oh, beautiful music, do not cease!
Reject me not into the world again.
With you alone is excellence and peace,
Mankind made plausible, his purpose plain.
Enchanted in your air benign and shrewd,   5
With limbs a-sprawl and empty faces pale,
The spiteful and the stingy and the rude
Sleep like the scullions° in the fairy-tale.
This moment is the best the world can give:
The tranquil blossom on the tortured stem.   10
Reject me not, sweet sounds! oh, let me live,
Till Doom espy my towers and scatter them,
A city spell-bound under the aging sun,
Music my rampart, and my only one.

8. **scullion** (skŭl′yən): a servant hired to do the rough, dirty work in a kitchen.

For Study and Discussion

Analyzing and Interpreting the Poems

God's World
1a. What are the poet's feelings on this autumn day? **b.** Does she experience only pleasure in the natural beauty of the world? Explain.
2. Toward the end of the poem, the poet says the world is "too beautiful this year." **a.** How are both pleasure and pain suggested by the poem's language? **b.** Why does she pray "Let no bird call"?

On Hearing a Symphony of Beethoven
1. Beauty of music figures in this poem. What do lines 2–4 claim that such beauty *can* accomplish?
2. What do lines 9 and 10 suggest are the limits to what music can do? In answering, explain the phrases "tranquil blossom" and "tortured stem."
3. In the last lines of the poem, Millay describes herself metaphorically as a fortified city. A rampart is an especially strong fortification. What function does music serve in this metaphor?

Language and Vocabulary

Analyzing Effect of Archaic Words
Although the language of "God's World" is on the whole simple and straightforward, there are several words in the poem that some dictionaries label *archaic,* meaning "out of general use." What effect do the words *thy, thou'st,* and *prithee* create? How do they indicate the poet's attitude toward God and nature? (If you do not know the meaning of *prithee,* look it up in the dictionary.)

Archibald MacLeish was born in Glencoe, Illinois, near Chicago. He attended Yale University and later graduated at the head of his class at Harvard Law School. As a young writer, he lived for a time in Paris, absorbing much of the influence of Ezra Pound and T. S. Eliot. He was particularly moved by their use of language and by their conception of the modern age as a troubled time. Until the 1930s, however, he essentially believed in the value of poetry for its own sake apart from any social value it might have. In his famous poem "Ars Poetica" (page 790), he wrote, "A poem should not mean/But be." After returning to America, MacLeish wrote one of his most ambitious works, the long poem *Conquistador,* which was awarded the Pulitzer Prize in 1933. This poem showed an important change: although meditative like his earlier work, it dealt with historical and social fact. Gradually his work took a sharp turn toward themes of social justice, and increasingly he wrote poems of an almost propagandistic nature against economic exploitation and the rise of fascism. As World War II grew imminent, his poetry celebrated American values of freedom and individualism. He denounced poetry for its own sake and urged other writers to write poems that would serve the public good.

During the war, MacLeish held several important posts in the government and was an adviser to President Roosevelt. In 1949 he became Boylston Professor of Rhetoric at Harvard, and his writing took on more philosophical overtones. In addition to poetry, he wrote several radio and stage plays. His play *J. B.,* which was awarded the Pulitzer Prize in 1959, is a modern version of the story of Job. It concerns a man who, like Job, faces disaster and seeks to discover why such suffering should fall on him. In

Archibald MacLeish.
© Rollie McKenna

Herakles (1967), MacLeish developed a similar theme around the myth of the ancient Greek hero.

Throughout his work, MacLeish was interested in the idea of human life as a troubled passage through time. Whether his poems stress detached artistic creativity, active involvement, or philosophic thought, they present life as an unpredictable process. However, as his later work insists, the human situation demands that people at least search for meaning in life and an understanding of themselves.

Archibald MacLeish   **789**

Ars Poetica°

A poem should be palpable and mute
As a globed fruit

Dumb
As old medallions to the thumb

Silent as the sleeve-worn stone   5
Of casement ledges where the moss has
    grown—

A poem should be wordless
As the flight of birds

A poem should be motionless in time
As the moon climbs   10

Leaving, as the moon releases
Twig by twig the night-entangled trees.

Leaving, as the moon behind the winter leaves,
Memory by memory the mind—

A poem should be motionless in time   15
As the moon climbs

A poem should be equal to:
Not true

For all the history of grief
An empty doorway and a maple leaf   20

For love
The leaning grasses and two lights above the
    sea—

A poem should not mean
But be.

° **Ars Poetica:** from the Latin, meaning "The Art of Poetry." The Roman poet Horace wrote a famous *Ars Poetica.*

The End of the World

Quite unexpectedly as Vasserot
The armless ambidextrian° was lighting
A match between his great and second toe
And Ralph the lion was engaged in biting
The neck of Madame Sossman while the drum   5
Pointed, and Teeny was about to cough
In waltz-time swinging Jocko by the thumb—
Quite unexpectedly the top blew off:

And there, there overhead, there, there, hung over
Those thousands of white faces, those dazed eyes,   10
There in the starless dark, the poise, the hover,
There with vast wings across the canceled skies,
There in the sudden blackness, the black pall°
Of nothing, nothing, nothing—nothing at all.

2. **ambidextrian** (ăm′bĭ-dĕks′trē-ən): a word normally used to describe a person who can use both hands equally well.   13. **pall:** a dark covering.

Acrobats (1919) by Charles Demuth (1883–1935). Watercolor and pencil. The Museum of Modern Art, New York, gift of Abby Aldrich Rockefeller

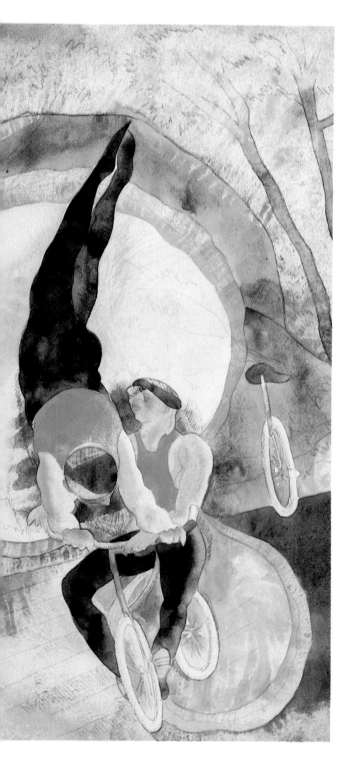

Analyzing and Interpreting the Poems

Ars Poetica

1. Archibald MacLeish was not active in the Imagist movement, but "Ars Poetica" suggests that he was interested in some of its ideas. **a.** To what things does he compare a poem in the first eight lines? **b.** What word in each pair of lines indicates the quality that MacLeish admires in a poem? **c.** How do these four words suggest that the poet is interested more in the idea of a poem as "image" than as "speech"?

2. The poet explores a **paradox** in lines 9–16. Although the moon climbs above the trees, leaving them behind "twig by twig," it appears motionless to the human eye. **a.** In what sense can a poem be motionless? **b.** What does the poet think a poem should leave behind?

3a. What images does MacLeish suggest for "the history of grief"? **b.** For "love"? **c.** In what ways are these images appropriate to grief and to love?

4a. What do lines 17–18 say about the importance of the image in a poem? **b.** In what sense must a poem be "not true"? **c.** If images by themselves can make up a poem, in what sense can a poem be said to "be" rather than "mean"?

The End of the World

1a. What aspects of the circus scene described in the first stanza apply to human life in general? **b.** Why is the circus an appropriate metaphor for life?

2. A familiar name for a circus tent is "the big top." What event is suggested by line 8?

3a. What does the audience see when it looks up at "the canceled skies"? **b.** What is the audience's reaction? **c.** Who might this audience be?

Comparing Views on Poetry

Both Marianne Moore and Archibald MacLeish have definite ideas about what poetry should be. Reread Moore's "Poetry" (page 772). Then, in an essay, compare the two poets' views on poetry. Tell what each requires of a poem. For example, how is MacLeish's insistence that a poem be "palpable and mute" like Moore's demand for "imaginary gardens with real toads in them"? Show how both poets use specific images to communicate their standards.

Archibald MacLeish **791**

E. E. CUMMINGS
1894–1962

A first glance at E. E. Cummings' poems, with their unusual arrangements on the page, may suggest that they are difficult, abstract reading. The reader soon discovers, however, that the subject of the poems is often simple feelings and warm human relationships. Cummings was a painter as well as a poet, and in his attempts to make poetry a refreshing experience for the reader, he used visual as well as verbal devices. The "look" of his poetry is unique, and it contributes to making his lyrics among the most delightful of the twentieth century.

Edward Estlin Cummings was born and raised in Cambridge, Massachusetts. His father was a Harvard professor who later became a Unitarian minister in Boston. Cummings had a lifelong love and admiration for his parents, and his several poems about them are among the most serious and deeply felt of all his work. He graduated from Harvard in 1915 and served in the French ambulance corps in World War I. During the war, he was unjustly imprisoned for treason in a French concentration camp. Later he published a prose work about this misadventure called *The Enormous Room* (1922). After the war, Cummings lived in Paris and took up painting along with writing. After returning to the United States, he settled in New York's Greenwich Village.

Cummings was a prolific writer, producing many collections of poems, as well as several experimental plays and a travel book expressing his outrage at

E. E. Cummings (1962).
UPI / Bettmann Newsphotos

the regimentation of individuals in the Soviet Union. He was a serious and innovative poetic craftsman, though his poems often reveal a mischievous wit and a childlike sense of fun. He stridently opposed war in some poems; in others he poked gentle fun at the world's absurdities. He celebrated his favorite season, spring, and sang about the joys of romantic love. In these lyrics about nature and about love, Cummings is at his best, expressing a passion for beauty and a jubilant intoxication of the senses.

anyone lived in a pretty how town

anyone lived in a pretty how town
(with up so floating many bells down)
spring summer autumn winter
he sang his didn't he danced his did.

Women and men(both little and small)   5
cared for anyone not at all
they sowed their isn't they reaped their same
sun moon stars rain

children guessed(but only a few
and down they forgot as up they grew   10
autumn winter spring summer)
that noone loved him more by more

when by now and tree by leaf
she laughed his joy she cried his grief
bird by snow and stir by still   15
anyone's any was all to her

someones married their everyones
laughed their crying and did their dance
(sleep wake hope and then)they
said their nevers they slept their dream   20

stars rain sun moon
(and only the snow can begin to explain
how children are apt to forget to remember
with up so floating many bells down)

one day anyone died i guess   25
(and noone stooped to kiss his face)
busy folk buried them side by side
little by little and was by was

all by all and deep by deep
and more by more they dream their sleep 30
noone and anyone earth by april
wish by spirit and if by yes.

Women and men(both dong and ding)
summer autumn winter spring
reaped their sowing and went their came 35
sun moon stars rain

E. E. Cummings   **793**

pity this busy monster,manunkind

pity this busy monster,manunkind,

not. Progress is a comfortable disease:
your victim(death and life safely beyond)

plays with the bigness of his littleness
—electrons° deify one razorblade   5
into a mountainrange;lenses extend

unwish through curving wherewhen till unwish
returns on its unself.
                              A world of made
is not a world of born—pity poor flesh

and trees,poor stars and stones,but never this   10
fine specimen of hypermagical

ultraomnipotence. We doctors know

a hopeless case if—listen: there's a hell
of a good universe next door;let's go

5. **electrons:** The reference is to an electron microscope.

For Study and Discussion

Analyzing and Interpreting the Poems

anyone lived in a pretty how town

1. This poem tells of a quiet life lived by a couple in an ordinary town. Considering that the word "know-how" refers to busyness and work, what kind of town is suggested by Cummings' phrase "pretty how"?
2. The hero of our story is "anyone"; "noone" is the heroine. **a.** What do the names *anyone* and *noone* suggest about the kind of people Cummings is concerned with? **b.** What line first indicates that noone loves anyone?
3. The "someones" and "everyones" are the people all around "anyone" and "noone"—all the somebodies doing their important busyness. **a.** What is suggested about the someones and everyones by the phrase "both little and small"? **b.** What is sug-

gested about the meanings of the words *little* and *small* by "*both* little and small"?
4. The people in the town, when they are not lovers, are simply "Women and men." What words in the second and fifth stanzas suggest that their lives are rather negative and monotonous?
5. Everybody in the town experiences the passage of time. **a.** What two lines in the poem refer to this? **b.** How are these lines varied in the poem?
6. The line "with up so floating many bells down" is suggestive but indefinite. **a.** Does the meaning "with so much going on all the time" explain this phrase in the two places it occurs? **b.** In this context, what might the children have forgotten "as up they grew"?
7. In the last stanza the townspeople are referred to as "dong and ding." **a.** What does the poem say children and lovers experience that these other townspeople do not? **b.** Why are the townspeople unable to feel what the children and lovers feel?

pity this busy monster,manunkind

1. Cummings attacks what he calls "progress," which he sees as the problem in much of modern life. **a.** To what condition does he liken progress? **b.** What does the word *manunkind* suggest is the cause of this condition? **c.** What word best explains why we need not pity the victim?

2. The poem holds that "manunkind" suffers from a warped sense of what is real and truly important. Find two comparisons that refer to this distorted sense of reality, and explain the meaning of each.

3. Cummings states that the victim is a specimen of "hypermagical ultraomnipotence." What do the prefixes *hyper* and *ultra* suggest?

4. What might Cummings mean by the "good universe next door"?

Literary Elements

The Look of a Poem

Some modern poets, such as E. E. Cummings, have been fascinated with the way a poem looks on the page. This interest is not new. The seventeenth-century English poet George Herbert wrote one poem in the shape of an altar and another in the shape of wings. Although modern poets do not usually try to suggest particular objects, they have tried to make their poems look new, so that readers will approach them as original creations, not simply as reworkings of traditional forms and subjects. In addition, poets have used visual arrangements to emphasize particular words and to suggest ideas: for example, the stanzaic arrangement of William Carlos Williams' "The Red Wheelbarrow" (page 758) gives special emphasis to three objects—the wheelbarrow, the water, the chickens—and thus urges readers to truly see these simple objects.

Cummings' poems use capitalization (or the lack of it) and punctuation for two purposes: to indicate how pauses and emphases should fall, and to suggest particular feelings and ideas. Sometimes Cummings uses almost no punctuation (as in "anyone lived in a pretty how town") so that what few marks are used indicate special emphasis. Often he uses commas, colons, semicolons, and periods without providing the space after them that is customary in print. Where such spaces do appear, they indicate breaks or pauses. Also, Cummings likes to insert long and often complicated parenthetical expressions into a poem, just as we may do in speaking.

In general, Cummings avoids capital letters, except for emphasis. The small "i" of his poems shows his preference for the idea of the self as a modest, private entity. Sometimes he runs two words together, such as *manunkind* and *noone*. He combines these words for satirical purposes, to express his belief that people tend to be at their worst when they forget kindness and sympathy, and at their best when they love unselfishly.

1. "anyone lived in a pretty how town" has almost no punctuation; and the result is a continuous flow of language. How does such an unbroken flow parallel the life that the poem portrays?

2. In "pity this busy monster,manunkind," the first dash signals a shift from general statement to examples. **a.** How would you describe the effect of the dash in line 13? **b.** What effect is gained by setting the first line apart and beginning the second line with "not"?

Writing About Literature

Comparing Two Poems

In a brief essay compare Cummings' view of the universe in "pity this busy monster,manunkind" with Jeffers' view of the universe and humanity's place in it, as expressed in "Evening Ebb" (page 770). In your comparison, discuss the following points: What do both poems imply about humanity's limitations? Cummings wryly invites readers to a "good universe next door." Does Jeffers take this universe into consideration?

Jazz by Romare Bearden (1914–   ). Silk screen.

The Harlem Renaissance

The 1920s saw a flowering of black writing, art, music, and thought that came to be known as the Harlem Renaissance. The entry of the United States into World War I had created a boom in American industry, and as a result many blacks moved from the South to take jobs in Northern industrial plants. Blacks remained in large Northern cities, notably Chicago and New York. Harlem, a section of New York, became the cosmopolitan center of black life in America. Among the writers living in Harlem were the poets Claude McKay, Jean Toomer, Langston Hughes, and Countee Cullen.

Claude McKay (1890–1948) was the oldest of the Harlem Renaissance writers and the first to publish. He was born in Sunny Ville, Jamaica, in the West Indies. When he was fourteen, he moved to Kingston, where he later became a police officer. In Kingston he began to write poems in the Jamaican dialect. When he was twenty-two, he published two collections of poems and won a medal and an award of money from the Institute of Arts and Letters. The money enabled him to emigrate to the United States, where he attended Tuskegee Institute and Kansas State College. For some years he lived in Harlem, supporting himself with odd jobs, and in 1922 he published his most important collection of poems, *Harlem Shadows*. In addition to poems, McKay wrote several novels, including *Home to Harlem* (1928). Both his poetry and his fiction are marked by strong protest against the injustices done to blacks.

Jean Toomer (1894–1967) was born and raised in Washington, D.C. After high school, he studied at colleges in Wisconsin, Illinois, Massachusetts, and New York, taking courses in physical education, agriculture, medicine, sociology, and history. He taught school in Georgia for several years and then lived for a time in Harlem. During the 1920s, his work began to appear in literary magazines. Toomer's reputation rests chiefly on his novel *Cane*, which was published in 1923; he published there-after. *Cane* is an unusual novel, as it consists of prose sketches, stories, poems, and a one-act play. One theme binds all these disparate elements—that blacks are most free when they recognize and celebrate their heritage. When *Cane* was first published, it sold only about five hundred copies and dropped into obscurity. More recently, literary critics and historians recognized it as one of the most important and accomplished creations of the Harlem Renaissance, a work that continues to influence black writing not only in the United States but also in Africa.

Langston Hughes (1902–1967), more than any other writer, is associated with the life of Harlem. In his writing he depicted the joys, troubles, and hopes of its people. Hughes was born in Joplin, Missouri, and grew up in Joplin, in Lincoln, Illinois, and in Cleveland, Ohio. He attended Central High School in Cleveland, where he first began to write poems for the school magazine. After graduation, he worked at various jobs, and in 1921, he went to New York to attend Columbia University. A year later, he traveled as a seaman and cook's helper on a steamer to Africa and Europe. He took a variety of odd jobs in Paris and Italy and then returned to the United States, where he worked in a Washington, D.C., hotel. He was "discovered" there by the poet Vachel Lindsay, who praised his poetry and encouraged him to continue writing. Hughes settled in Harlem and became part of the Harlem Renaissance. *The Weary Blues,* his first book of poems, was published in 1926; other collections followed, as well as fiction, plays, and autobiographical works.

He is also well known for his series of sketches about a citizen of Harlem named Jess B. Semple, known as "Simple" to his friends, who speaks his mind on a variety of subjects and issues. Hughes was the most influential and the most versatile of all the writers of the Harlem Renaissance. He wrote opera, fiction, journalism, drama, poetry, essays, and he edited other black writers.

Countee Cullen (1903–1946) was born in New York City. He graduated from New York University and received a master's degree in English literature from Harvard. After some travel and study abroad, he became assistant editor of the magazine *Opportunity,* in which many of his poems appeared. During the last eleven years of his life, he taught French in New York schools. *Color,* his first collection of poems, was published in 1925. His other books include *Copper Sun* and *The Ballad of the Brown Girl,* both published in 1927. Cullen wrote of his poems, "Most things I write I do for the sheer love of the music in them." He preferred old-fashioned poetic styles and looked to the English Romantic poet John Keats as a model. He wished to be known as a poet first and a black poet second. Yet he was also drawn to the subject of his race: "Somehow I find my poetry of itself treating of the Negro, of his joys and his sorrows—mostly of the latter—and of the heights and depths of emotion I feel as a Negro."

These writers and others, including Zora Neale Hurston (page 901), were encouraged by Charles S. Johnson, who edited *Opportunity.* Like other American writers during the 1920s, black writers reflected the spirit of the times, a sense of expanded opportunities, and the importance of personal fulfillment.

Claude McKay (1941). Photograph by Carl Van Vechten.

Jean Toomer.

And like others, they reflected wide literary trends, including the struggle between traditional and experimental literature. For example, whereas Countee Cullen favored traditional poetic forms, Langston Hughes incorporated blues and contemporary jazz rhythms into his verse. But the writers of the Harlem Renaissance also had unique aims: to define and renew the black heritage; to protest oppression of blacks; and to make other Americans aware of black life.

Langston Hughes (1939). Photograph by Carl Van Vechten.

Countee Cullen (1941). Photograph by Carl Van Vechten.

The Tropics in New York

CLAUDE MCKAY

Bananas ripe and green, and ginger-root,
  Cocoa in pods and alligator pears,
And tangerines and mangoes and grapefruit,
  Fit for the highest prize at parish fairs,

Set in the window, bringing memories   5
  Of fruit-trees laden by low-singing rills,
And dewy dawns, and mystical blue skies
  In benediction over nun-like hills.

My eyes grew dim, and I could no more gaze;
  A wave of longing through my body swept,   10
And, hungry for the old, familiar ways,
  I turned aside and bowed my head and wept.

November Cotton Flower

JEAN TOOMER

Boll-weevil's coming, and the winter's cold,
Made cotton-stalks look rusty, seasons old,
And cotton, scarce as any southern snow,
Was vanishing; the branch, so pinched and slow,
Failed in its function as the autumn rake;   5
Drouth fighting soil had caused the soil to take
All water from the streams; dead birds were found
In wells a hundred feet below the ground—
Such was the season when the flower bloomed.
Old folks were startled, and it soon assumed   10
Significance. Superstition saw
Something it had never seen before:
Brown eyes that loved without a trace of fear,
Beauty so sudden for that time of year.

The Negro Speaks of Rivers

LANGSTON HUGHES

I've known rivers:
I've known rivers ancient as the world and older than the flow
    of human blood in human veins.

My soul has grown   deep like rivers.

I bathed in the Euphrates when dawns were young.
I built my hut near the Congo and it lulled me to sleep.   5
I looked upon the Nile and raised the pyramids above it.
I heard the singing of the Mississippi when Abe Lincoln went
    down to New Orleans, and I've seen its muddy bosom turn
    all golden in the sunset.

I've known rivers:
Ancient, dusky rivers.

My soul has grown   deep like rivers.   10

As I Grew Older

LANGSTON HUGHES

It was a long time ago.
I have almost forgotten my dream.
But it was there then,
In front of me,
Bright like a sun—   5
My dream.

And then the wall rose,
Rose slowly,
Slowly,
Between me and my dream.   10
Rose slowly, slowly,
Dimming,
Hiding,
The light of my dream.
Rose until it touched the sky—   15
The wall.

Shadow.
I am black.

I lie down in the shadow.
No longer the light of my dream before me,   20
Above me.
Only the thick wall.
Only the shadow.

My hands!
My dark hands!   25
Break through the wall!
Find my dream!
Help me to shatter this darkness,
To smash this night,
To break this shadow   30
Into a thousand lights of sun,
Into a thousand whirling dreams
Of sun!

Building More Stately Mansions (1944)
by Aaron Douglas (1899–1979). Oil
on canvas.
Fisk University Museum of Art, Nashville

Any Human to Another

COUNTEE CULLEN

The ills I sorrow at
Not me alone
Like an arrow,
Pierce to the marrow,
Through the fat   5
And past the bone.

Your grief and mine
Must intertwine
Like sea and river,
Be fused and mingle,   10
Diverse yet single,
Forever and forever.

Let no man be so proud
And confident,
To think he is allowed   15
A little tent

Pitched in a meadow
Of sun and shadow
All his little own.

Joy may be shy, unique,   20
Friendly to a few,
Sorrow never scorned to speak
To any who
Were false or true.

Your very grief   25
Like a blade
Shining and unsheathed
Must strike me down.
Of bitter aloes° wreathed,
My sorrow must be laid   30
On your head like a crown.

29. **aloes** (ăl′ōz): leaves of the aloe plant, whose bitter juice
is used as a drug.

From the Dark Tower

COUNTEE CULLEN

We shall not always plant while others reap
The golden increment of bursting fruit,
Not always countenance, abject and mute,
That lesser men should hold their brothers cheap;
Not everlastingly while others sleep   5
Shall we beguile their limbs with mellow flute,
Not always bend to some more subtle brute;
We were not made eternally to weep.

The night whose sable breast relieves the stark,
White stars is no less lovely being dark,   10
And there are buds that cannot bloom at all
In light, but crumple, piteous, and fall;
So in the dark we hide the heart that bleeds,
And wait, and tend our agonizing seeds.

Her World (c. 1940) by
Philip Evergood (1901–
1973). Oil on canvas.
Metropolitan Museum of Art,
Arthur Hoppock Hearn Fund

For Study and Discussion

Analyzing and Interpreting the Poems

The Tropics in New York
1. In this poem, Claude McKay looks back on his youth in the tropics. **a.** What sights remind him of the tropics? **b.** How do the images in stanza 2 suggest a broader picture of his home?
2. What special quality of his homeland is suggested by the words *mystical* and *benediction?*
3. In the last stanza, the poet says that his eyes "grew dim." **a.** What feelings replace remembering? **b.** How does his feeling of hunger for the old ways grow out of the images in stanza 1?

November Cotton Flower
1. The season in Jean Toomer's poem is late autumn. What besides the season has contributed to the withering of the cotton?
2. The word *branch* in line 4 refers to a stream. **a.** How may a flowing stream be said to function in autumn as a rake? **b.** Where does the speaker say the branch water has gone?
3a. What particular dramatic event does the poem center on? **b.** Why should it arouse superstitious feelings? **c.** What other feelings does it arouse?
4. The last line of the poem refers to the unexpected appearance of beauty. Suppose that the dry and lifeless scene depicted in the poem represents a harsh, sterile world. What might this sudden beauty symbolize? (Consider line 13 in answering this question.)

The Negro Speaks of Rivers
1. What does the poet imply about the durability and dignity of his people when he refers to the great age of rivers?
2. In what way is the "I" in the poem a symbol of something larger?
3. Rivers usually flow quietly, but they cover great distances and become wider and deeper as they progress. What feeling for the fullness of the black experience does Hughes express through the imagery of rivers?
4. Each of the four rivers named is associated with a region that developed into a civilization. **a.** Identify these civilizations and explain the significance of each one. **b.** What is the poet implying about his race in lines 4–7?

As I Grew Older
1. This poem is concerned with growing up. How do the images in lines 5 and 7 express the change from early years to later years?
2. The poem depends on an interplay between brightness and darkness. What two phrases unite the speaker's hopes with brightness?
3. The speaker says that the wall created a shadow. **a.** In what lines does he identify his own dark color with the shadow? **b.** What does the speaker imply by the metaphor of the wall?
4a. In which lines does the speaker change from a passive to an active role? **b.** What, according to the poem's conclusion, will be the result of destroying the wall? **c.** How is the conclusion linked to the poet's dream?

Any Human to Another
1a. In what way are human griefs "diverse yet single"? **b.** What simile is used to suggest both unity and diversity?
2. Why, according to the speaker, is joy more difficult to share than sorrow?
3. What, according to the poem, is the necessary relationship of "any human to another"?

From the Dark Tower
1. Cullen, like Hughes, gives darkness a metaphorical significance. What does the image of the starry sky suggest is the value of darkness?
2. Lines 11–12 refer to a plant like the night-blooming cereus, whose flower appears only in the dark. What are these lines a metaphor for?
3. The poem begins and ends with images of tending seeds. According to the last two lines, what must the speaker do to realize the hope implied in the first two lines?
4. In the organization of its ideas and in its rhyme scheme, what is the form of this poem?

Writing About Literature

Analyzing Traditional Images
Countee Cullen's poems contain images that are particularly forceful because they carry certain traditional associations. For example, "the golden increment of bursting fruit" in "From the Dark Tower" suggests a rich harvest, which for centuries has represented plentitude and a fulfilled life. In a brief composition, analyze another poem you have read in this unit that uses one or more traditional images, such as a wall, night, the seasons, or the sea.

Ogden Nash, a descendant of the family after which Nashville was named, was born in Rye, New York, and grew up in various cities up and down the East Coast. This ex-schoolteacher, ex-bondsalesman, ex-advertising writer became the gentle satirist who is still generally considered to be the dean of American writers of light verse. He once identified his subject matter as "the minor idiocies of humanity."

His first collection of poems, *Hard Lines* (1931), identified his targets: banality, sentimentality, cliché, and the easy, conventional moralizing that comes out of bad verse and shallow minds. He began to appear regularly in *The New Yorker* magazine in the 1920s and developed his materials into hilarious examinations of the foibles of middle-class urban and suburban life. Parents and children furnished a constant theme for Nash's poems ("Children aren't happy with nothing to ignore, / And that's what Parents were created for"), which became identified with outrageous rhymes and metrics ("And if you serve meat balls for dinner they look put upon and say Can't we ever have a sirloin or a porterhouse, / So you get them what they want and then when the bills come in they act as if you were trying to drive them to the slorterhouse").

Nash wrote for Hollywood, for Broadway (he coauthored the musical hit *One Touch of Venus*), and for television, and he was honored by membership in the American Academy of Arts and Letters and the National Institute of Arts and Letters. He earned his fame through his adult, urban view of modern life, concentrating on all the minor harassments of social existence. The titles of some of Nash's many books of verse are indications of his sensibility: *The Face Is Familiar* (1940, 1954), *I'm a*

Ogden Nash.
Henry Groskinsky, *Life Magazine,* © Time Inc.

Stranger Here Myself (1938), *You Can't Get There from Here* (1957), and *There's Always Another Windmill* (1968). Nash's poems reflect the puzzled parent—*Parents Keep Out: Elderly Poems for Youngerly Readers* (1951), *Santa Go Home: A Case History for Parents* (1967)—the bemused ordinary citizen who is beleaguered not only by children but by household appliances, leaky faucets, tax forms, toothpaste tubes, righteous moralists, cocktail parties, reformers, and any kind of red tape. The poems are a kind of happy revenge, delivered with wry and gentle good humor and a keen sense of the absurd.

Very like a Whale

Throughout this poem Nash alludes to well-known works of literature. The title is a phrase taken from William Shakespeare's *Hamlet*. Hamlet, who is feigning madness, pretends to see a cloud in the shape of a whale, and he asks Polonius, the Lord Chamberlain, if he doesn't agree. To humor him, Polonius responds, "Very like a whale." In other words, he will go along with the mad Hamlet's most farfetched comparisons.

One thing that literature would be greatly the better for
Would be a more restricted employment by authors of simile and metaphor.
Authors of all races, be they Greeks, Romans, Teutons or Celts,
Can't seem just to say that anything is the thing it is but have to go out of their way to say
    that it is like something else.
What does it mean when we are told   5
That the Assyrian came down like a wolf on the fold?°
In the first place, George Gordon Byron had had enough experience
To know that it probably wasn't just one Assyrian, it was a lot of Assyrians.
However, as too many arguments are apt to induce apoplexy and thus hinder longevity,
We'll let it pass as one Assyrian for the sake of brevity.   10
Now then, this particular Assyrian, the one whose cohorts were gleaming in purple and
    gold,
Just what does the poet mean when he says he came down like a wolf on the fold?
In heaven and earth more than is dreamed of in our philosophy° there are a great many
    things,
But I don't imagine that among them there is a wolf with purple and gold cohorts or
    purple and gold anythings.
No, no, Lord Byron, before I'll believe that this Assyrian was actually like a wolf I must
    have some kind of proof;   15
Did he run on all fours and did he have a hairy tail and a big red mouth and big white
    teeth and did he say Woof woof?
Frankly I think it very unlikely, and all you were entitled to say, at the very most,
Was that the Assyrian cohorts came down like a lot of Assyrian cohorts about to destroy
    the Hebrew host.
But that wasn't fancy enough for Lord Bryon, oh dear me no, he had to invent a lot of
    figures of speech and then interpolate° them,
With the result that whenever you mention Old Testament soldiers to people they say Oh
    yes, they're the ones that a lot of wolves dressed up in gold and purple ate them.   20

---

6. **Assyrian . . . fold:** an allusion to "The Destruction of Sennacherib," a poem by George Gordon, Lord Byron (1788–1824). The poem is based on a story told in the Bible (II Kings 19:35). The opening lines of the poem are: "The Assyrian came down like the wolf on the fold, / And his cohorts were gleaming in purple and gold."   13. **In heaven . . . philosophy:** a deliberately mangled line from *Hamlet*. After seeing his father's spirit in arms, Hamlet tells his friend, Horatio, "There are more things in Heaven and earth, Horatio, / Than are dreamt of in your philosophy (I, v, 166–167).   19. **interpolate** (ĭn-tûr′pə-lāt′): to insert additional text.

That's the kind of thing that's being done all the time by poets, from Homer to Tennyson;
They're always comparing ladies to lilies and veal to venison,
And they always say things like that the snow is a white blanket after a winter storm.
Oh it is, all right then, you sleep under a six-inch blanket of snow and I'll sleep under a
     half-inch blanket of unpoetical blanket material and we'll see which one keeps warm,
And after that maybe you'll begin to comprehend dimly   25
What I mean by too much metaphor and simile.

For Study and Discussion

Analyzing and Interpreting the Poem

1. In this poem Nash humorously takes the point of view of someone perplexed by figurative language. As the poem progresses we are amused by the speaker's failure to grasp anything but the most literal statements. For example, in lines 7–8, the speaker quibbles with the singular form of Assyrian, claiming that there must have been "a lot of Assyrians." **a.** What other objections does the speaker raise to Bryon's comparison? **b.** What objection does the speaker have to poets in general?

2. Nash's rhymes can be surprising, delightful, and outrageous. **a.** In lines 21–22, he rhymes *Tennyson* with *venison*. What is the effect of coupling these words? **b.** What is the effect of rhyming *dimly* with *simile* in lines 25–26? **c.** What ingenious solution does he find for *interpolate them* (line 19)?

3a. What is your reaction to the speaker? **b.** Do you find his matter-of-fact approach comical? Is it also refreshing?

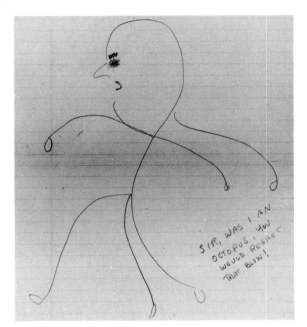

Pencil sketch by Ogden Nash.
Harry Ransom Humanities Research Center,
The University of Texas at Austin

RICHARD EBERHART
1904–

Richard Eberhart.

Richard Eberhart's poems are marked by wit and emotional intensity, though their concerns are often intellectual. They are also characterized by rugged, sometimes abrupt language. Eberhart once defined poetry as "continuously aggravating perception into expressing life," and his own perceptions have been moved to creative activity by such things as war, science, and philosophical and religious ideas.

Eberhart had a varied and extensive educational background. He was born in Austin, Minnesota, and he studied at the University of Minnesota. He received his B.A. from Dartmouth College. With no clear idea of what he wanted to do, he worked as a department store floorwalker, an advertising writer, and a deck hand on tramp steamers. In 1929 he completed a second B.A. degree at Cambridge University in England. He then spent a year in America tutoring the son of the King of Siam. He studied for a while at Harvard but returned to Cambridge University to obtain his M.A. In recent years, Eberhart has taught at various colleges, including Princeton and Dartmouth. He has been a professor of English and poet-in-residence at Dartmouth since 1956. In 1966 his *Selected Poems, 1930–1965* was awarded the Pultizer Prize.

The Horse Chestnut Tree

Boys in sporadic but tenacious droves
Come with sticks, as certainly as Autumn,
To assault the great horse chestnut tree.

There is a law governs their lawlessness.
Desire is in them for a shining amulet   5
And the best are those that are highest up.

They will not pick them easily from the ground.
With shrill arms they fling to the higher branches,
To hurry the work of nature for their pleasure.

I have seen them trooping down the street   10
Their pockets stuffed with chestnuts shucked, unshucked.
It is only evening keeps them from their wish.

Sometimes I run out in a kind of rage
To chase the boys away: I catch an arm,
Maybe, and laugh to think of being the lawgiver.   15

I was once such a young sprout myself
And fingered in my pocket the prize and trophy.
But still I moralize upon the day

And see that we, outlaws on God's property,
Fling out imagination beyond the skies,   20
Wishing a tangible good from the unknown.

And likewise death will drive us from the scene
With the great flowering world unbroken yet,
Which we held in idea, a little handful.

For Study and Discussion

Analyzing and Interpreting the Poem

1. The poem opens with a picture of boys attempting to knock horse chestnuts out of a tree to obtain the beautiful, shiny brown nuts as prizes. **a.** What, according to lines 5–9, is the nature of the "law" that governs the boys' actions? **b.** Why does the speaker laugh at himself for trying to stop the boys?
2. The best chestnuts are those "highest up" and therefore most difficult to obtain. What analogy does the speaker draw between the boys' energetic attempts to gather chestnuts and all humanity's striving in life?
3. What does the phrase "outlaws on God's property" (line 19) imply about the place of human beings in the universe?
4. The poem's final image is of "a little handful." **a.** What does this phrase refer to? **b.** What does the image imply about human attainments?

Richard Eberhart   **809**

ROBERT PENN WARREN
1905–

America's first Poet Laureate, Robert Penn Warren is one of the most highly awarded writers in the history of the United States. He won the Pulitzer Prize three times (once for fiction—*All the King's Men* in 1946—and twice for poetry—*Promises* in 1957 and *Now and Then* in 1979). In the course of his richly productive life he has also been awarded (among many other prestigious honors) the National Book Award, the Chair of Poetry at the Library of Congress, the Bollingen Prize, Guggenheim Fellowships, a MacArthur Fellowship, the National Medal for Literature, and the Presidential Medal of Freedom.

A child with flame-red hair, "Red" Warren was the eldest son of a businessman-schoolteacher in Guthrie, Kentucky. He went to Vanderbilt University, where he was taught by and became a coworker with an intellectual elite called the Fugitives, whose members included the poets John Crowe Ransom and Alan Tate. This group (named for *The Fugitive,* a magazine they worked with) felt themselves fugitives from the urbanism, commercialism, and industrialization of the modern world. These critics introduced "the New Criticism," which has influenced the reading and writing of literature ever since the 1930s. After receiving his degree summa cum laude in 1925, Penn Warren went on to earn a Master's degree two years later at the University of California. Then he attended Yale and Oxford universities for further study, receiving, in 1930, his B. Litt. as a Rhodes Scholar at Oxford. He has taught at Vanderbilt University, at the University of Minnesota, and at Yale.

In 1938 he became an internationally outstanding academic with his publication of *Understanding Poetry,* a textbook he edited with Cleanth Brooks, another Southerner who would be transplanted to Yale. This book, which changed the way poetry was taught and read, was but one of Penn Warren's many works of scholarship and criticism. He has written on authors as diverse as Theodore Dreiser,

Robert Penn Warren.
© Thomas Victor, 1987

Herman Melville, and William Faulkner. Penn Warren is also a distinguished essayist and dramatist, having set some of his fiction to the stage and having written verse dramas. Musical comedy is probably the only literary genre at which this versatile man has not tried his hand.

There are at least three constantly recurring themes in Penn Warren's poetry: time, loss, and the self. From his first pamphlet of poems (*Driftwood Flames,* 1923) to his most recent collection (*New and Selected Poems 1923–1985,* 1985), the poems are meditations on the reality of the self; on the isolation of the self; on the sad differences between expectations and experience, between youth and age; and on the apparently uncaring vastness of time and space that make human concerns, if matters of indifference to the universe, therefore all the more intensely crucial for human beings. In an overview of Penn Warren's poetry, one could say that the mysteries of time, loss, and the self result in speculations about the nature of God; and the ways in which they do so point toward the essential necessity of and hunger for human love.

Why Boy Came to Lonely Place

Limestone and cedar. Indigo shadow
On whiteness. The sky is flawlessly blue.
Only the cicada speaks. No bird. I do not know
Why I have these miles come. Here is only *I*. Not *You*.

Did I clamber these miles of distance   5
Only to quiver now in identity?
You are yourself only by luck, disaster, or chance,
And only alone may believe in your reality.

What drove you forth?—
Age thirteen, ignorant, lost in the world,   10
Canteen now dry and of what worth
With the cheese sandwich crumbling, and lettuce brown-curled?

Under the ragged shadow of cedar
You count the years you have been in the world,
And wonder what heed or   15
Care the world would have had of your absence as it whirled

In the iron groove of its circuit of space.
You say the name they gave you. That's all you are.
You move your fingers down your face,
And wonder how many years you'll be what you are.   20

But what is that? To find out you come to this lonely place.

Commentary

In this poem a young boy confronts death in the problem of his own identity. We do not know what drove the boy forth to contemplate himself all alone. It might have been an argument with his parents, a fight with a friend, a feeling of depression; but the specific cause itself does not matter. What we do know is that he seeks to go as far as he can from the everyday human world around him, far from where he has to bother about his response to others and the response of others to him: "Here is only *I*. Not *You*." We see the boy as though he exists in the recollection of the grown man who reflects upon this incident of his own boyhood. He talks to himself as he was when a boy, re-creating the boy's inner thoughts. The boy seeks the hard, clear sense of his own self, not a self according to "the name they gave you." And he ponders two great questions. One is whether the world knows or cares whether he lives or dies; he thinks to himself about "what heed or/Care the world would have had of your absence as it whirled/In the iron groove of its circuit of space" (lines 15–17). The tone and imagery suggest a hard, harsh answer: we are all tiny, unimportant beings in the whirling of the world, and the universe doesn't care if we live or die. The other question the boy ponders is whether he really has any self apart from the complex of relations the "I" always has with all "you" out there in his life.

The name given by parents, the label one goes by—"That's all you are." The boy touches his face as though to assure himself of his own reality and wonders how long he will have a real identity and how long that identity will last. But what is his identity? The questions that rise in the boy's mind hint at his fear that there might be no essentially real identity in any of us and that whatever our identities might be, they do not last long: we have but brief mortal lives—you wonder "how many years you'll be what you are" (line 20). The questions and answers that the poem hints about are not soft and reassuring and easy: they are given their characteristics in the hard, sharp, flawless, clear, inhuman landscape to which the boy has come in order to be alone with his doubts and fears and questions—to be alone with his self in order to try to find it. Any person, male or female, young or old, who ever has felt alone, lonely, unwanted; who ever has felt angry at the world around him, including those most loved; who ever has felt bewildered about who or what he is, will understand "why boy came to lonely place."

For Study and Discussion

Analyzing and Interpreting the Poem

1. In this poem an adult is remembering an incident in his boyhood and recalling the thoughts and feelings of that time. Speaking to his own self, he remembers clearly the boy's sense of separateness from others. **a.** How do the details of the landscape in stanza 1 suggest the boy's feeling of loneliness and alienation? **b.** What is suggested about the boy's feelings by the sentence structure in stanza 1?

2. The boy asks himself if he has made this journey "Only to quiver now in identity." **a.** What does it mean "to quiver in identity"? **b.** Interpret lines 7–8. Do they mean that the boy is the only person in the world who believes in his identity, or that he believes in his identity only when he is alone? **c.** Consider Penn Warren's purpose in writing the lines so that both meanings are intended. How do both meanings fit the sense of the poem?

3. Sometimes the difference between "You" and "I" in the poem is the difference between the adult speaker and the childhood self. Sometimes it is the difference between the self and other people. In this context consider line 18: "You say the name they gave you." **a.** Who are "they"? **b.** What does the poet evoke by referring to "them" rather than to identified people? **c.** Who says "That's all you are" (line 18)—the adult speaker or the remembered boyhood self? **d.** What is gained by leaving the question open so that *both* the boy and the adult might be saying it?

4. Look at lines 14–17. **a.** What does the boy think and feel? **b.** How do the words "iron groove" help you arrive at an answer?

5. Details of good poems reinforce each other in subtle and complex ways. Consider the relationship between "Limestone and cedar" in the opening line and the cheese sandwich in stanza 3. **a.** What is suggested about the boy's journey by the fact that the canteen is dry, the cheese sandwich is crumbling, and the lettuce is brown-curled? **b.** How do the details of imagery and sentence structure in stanza 1 relate to the details of the boy's provisions in stanza 3?

6a. What do you make of the fact that the adult looking back into the mind of the boy recalls the incident so clearly? **b.** What does this suggest about adult feelings of loneliness and alienation? **c.** How different are they from those of a thirteen-year-old?

W. H. AUDEN
1907–1973

W. H. Auden.
© Rollie McKenna

It is difficult to decide whether W. H. Auden is more properly considered an English or an American poet. He was born in England and spent the first thirty-two years of his life there; during the 1930s he was considered one of the leading English poets. However, after settling in America in 1939 (he became an American citizen in 1946), he showed in many of his poems that he took his new nationality seriously. He became an international literary figure, living in Austria, Italy, and again in England, where he returned to spend the last years of his life, and where he died. His poetry was deeply immersed in the events and problems of the world, indicative of his international identity.

Wystan Hugh Auden was born in York. His father was a doctor and a professor of public health, and as a boy, Auden pursued interests that were entirely scientific. At Oxford University he was the dominant figure in his circle of students, many of whom (such as Stephen Spender) became noted writers. In addition to his literary ability, Auden had a wonderful talent for mimicry and delighted in assuming comic roles. A great walker, he is remembered following his favorite route past the Oxford gas works and the city dump, talking incessantly and moving with large, ungainly strides.

Auden was a prolific and varied poet. From the beginning he showed an original style characterized by technical versatility, elegance of language, and wit. He wrote exquisite love lyrics and superb narrative poems, such as *The Age of Anxiety,* which was awarded the Pulitzer Prize in 1948. In his early poems Auden was concerned with the troubled state of English life after World War I. In the years before his move to America, he developed strong political interests, and his poems dealt with such issues as poverty, bad government, the emergence of Nazism in Germany, and the Spanish Civil War. Around the time he settled in America, his writing began to reflect new religious beliefs; his poems spoke of the value of Christianity in coping with the problems of the twentieth century and focused on the need for renewed love and forbearance. Several of his most famous poems are moving statements of his admiration for such men as W. B. Yeats, Henry James, and Sigmund Freud. Other poems are celebrations of the blessings of a truly civilized life. Generally, his poems recommend art and genuine emotion as humanizing forces.

Auden was a great influence on the poets of his time. In the 1940s and 1950s, many younger writers sought to be poets of mind and wit like Auden. Auden's poetry is a dazzling achievement, the work of a thoughtful, gifted man, deeply involved in both contemporary issues and eternal questions.

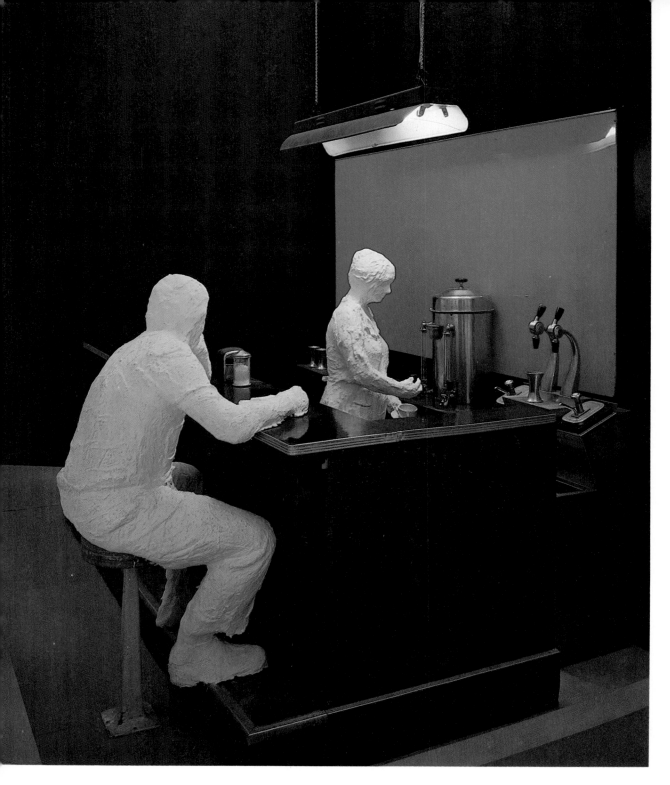

The Unknown Citizen

(To JS/07/M/378
This Marble Monument
Is Erected by the State)

He was found by the Bureau of Statistics to be
One against whom there was no official complaint,
And all the reports of his conduct agree
That, in the modern sense of an old-fashioned word, he was a saint,
For in everything he did he served the Greater Community.   5
Except for the War till the day he retired
He worked in a factory and never got fired,
But satisfied his employers, Fudge Motors Inc.
Yet he wasn't a scab or odd in his views,
For his Union reports that he paid his dues,   10
(Our report on his Union shows it was sound)
And our Social Psychology workers found
That he was popular with his mates and liked a drink.
The Press are convinced that he bought a paper every day
And that his reactions to advertisements were normal in every way.   15
Policies taken out in his name prove that he was fully insured,
And his Health card shows he was once in hospital but left it cured.
Both Producers Research and High-Grade Living declare
He was fully sensible to the advantages of the Installment Plan
And had everything necessary to the Modern Man,   20
A phonograph, a radio, a car, and a frigidaire.
Our researchers into Public Opinion are content
That he held the proper opinions for the time of year;
When there was peace, he was for peace; when there was war, he went.
He was married and added five children to the population,   25
Which our Eugenist° says was the right number for a parent of his generation,
And our teachers report that he never interfered with their education.
Was he free? Was he happy? The question is absurd:
Had anything been wrong, we should certainly have heard.

26. **Eugenist** (yōo-jĕn′ĭst): a specialist concerned with improving the physical and mental characteristics of human beings through heredity.

The Diner (1964–1966) by George Segal
(1924–   ). Plaster, wood, chrome,
formica, masonite, fluorescent light.
Collection Walker Art Center, Minneapolis,
gift of T. B. Walker Foundation

Analyzing and Interpreting the Poem

1. "The Unknown Citizen" is a satirical view of the tendency of modern society to depersonalize its citizens. **a.** What is suggested by the numbers and letters in the dedication? **b.** What well-known monument does the title recall?

2a. What kinds of studies of people are suggested by such names as "Producers Research" and "Social Psychology?" **b.** What kind of information do these groups have on the citizen? **c.** How personal could their knowledge of the citizen be?

3. By capitalizing such phrases as "Modern Man" and "Public Opinion," Auden criticizes the modern tendency to reduce individuals to statistics. **a.** How is this criticism emphasized by referring to the citizen's behavior as "normal," "sensible," and "necessary"? **b.** In line 28, the speaker asks two important questions, "Was he free? Was he happy?" What is ironic about the speaker's response?

Satire

Satire is a kind of writing that holds up to ridicule the vices and follies of human beings. Satire can range in tone from gentle amusement to bitter irony and denunciation. Nash's poem "Very like a Whale" (page 806) might be described as genial satire; its object is good-natured fun. The spirit of Auden's poem is more critical. His obituary exposes the dehumanizing effect of bureaucracy in modern society.

A satirist often adopts a **persona,** or mask, so that the identity of the speaker is different from that of the writer. Who is the speaker in Auden's poem? How do you know? Where does Auden make apparent his own attitude toward the unknown citizen?

Writing a Satire

Write your own satirical tribute to a "perfect" person or thing. If you like, write a brief satire on some aspect of modern society. Your tribute can be in prose, or, like Auden's, in verse.

THEODORE ROETHKE
1908–1963

Theodore Roethke.
© Rollie McKenna

The image of a dancing bear, which Theodore Roethke (rĕt′kē) used in a poem to express his attempts to master the graces of poetry, could well have been applied to the poet in a physical sense. He was a big blond man (six feet two and over two hundred pounds) who was surprisingly agile on the tennis court and who was varsity tennis coach at several of the colleges at which he taught. He once wrote that he had lived "very quietly and then foolishly and violently." His poetry reflects the different aspects of his life, especially the violence and strain and the struggle toward serenity and wisdom. Often his search for fulfillment was reflected in his poetry by an identification with plants, with the green peace of solidly rooted and slowly growing things.

Roethke was born in Saginaw, Michigan, and was educated at the University of Michigan and at Harvard. His early experiences in a "beautiful greenhouse" owned by his father and uncle colored much of his poetry. Roethke began to write poetry seriously at Harvard, where the encouragement of a teacher convinced him that he should follow his talent. For a good part of his life, he made a living by teaching writing at Bennington College, the Pennsylvania State University, and the University of Washington. He wrote slowly, and it took him ten years to write enough poems for his slim first book, *Open House*, published in 1941. In 1954 he received the Pulitzer Prize for *The Waking*, and in 1965 he was posthumously awarded the National Book Award for *The Far Field*.

Roethke wrote many compressed poems in strict stanza forms. These often communicate a sense of violence under powerful control and show the acknowledged influence of the great Irish poet W. B. Yeats. Roethke also wrote many long, highly personal poems in free verse. The poet Stanley Kunitz noted the "ferocity of Roethke's imagination," and W. H. Auden paid tribute to Roethke's rare achievement, "both to remember and to transform his humiliations into something beautiful."

The Pike

The river turns,
Leaving a place for the eye to rest,
A furred, a rocky pool,
A bottom of water.

The crabs tilt and eat, leisurely,   5
And the small fish lie, without shadow, motionless,
Or drift lazily in and out of the weeds.
The bottom-stones shimmer back their irregular striations,
And the half-sunken branch bends away from the gazer's eye.

A scene for the self to abjure!—   10
And I lean, almost into the water,
My eye always beyond the surface reflection;
I lean, and love these manifold shapes,
Until, out from a dark cove,
From beyond the end of a mossy log,   15
With one sinuous ripple, then a rush,
A thrashing-up of the whole pool,
The pike strikes.

Elegy for Jane

My Student, Thrown by a Horse

I remember the neckcurls, limp and damp as tendrils,
And her quick look, a sidelong pickerel smile;
And how, once startled into talk, the light syllables leaped for
    her,
And she balanced in the delight of her thought,
A wren, happy, tail into the wind,   5
Her song trembling the twigs and small branches.
The shade sang with her;
The leaves, their whispers turned to kissing;
And the mold sang in the bleached valleys under the rose.

Oh, when she was sad, she cast herself down into such a pure
    depth,   10
Even a father could not find her:
Scraping her cheek against straw;
Stirring the clearest water.

My sparrow, you are not here,
Waiting like a fern, making a spiny shadow.   15
The sides of wet stones cannot console me,
Nor the moss, wound with the last light.

If only I could nudge you from this sleep,
My maimed darling, my skittery pigeon.
Over this damp grave I speak the words of my love: 20
I, with no rights in this matter,
Neither father nor lover.

For Study and Discussion

Analyzing and Interpreting the Poems

The Pike

1a. Make a list of words in this poem that refer to restfulness and peace. **b.** How does the progression in length of the first nine lines suggest relaxation and the speaker's growing participation in the scene?

2. The poem's mood shifts in line 10. **a.** What is the meaning of the word *abjure*? **b.** The "self" in line 10 may refer either to one's soul or to one's outer, practical side. Which self should "abjure" this almost unreal scene? **c.** How does line 11 indicate that the speaker does not really abjure the scene?

3. What emotional element does the pike, a large predatory fish, introduce into the scene?

4. The first and last lines of the poem are similar in their briefness. Read both lines aloud. **a.** What feeling does the sound of the first line suggest? **b.** What contrasting feeling does the sound of the last line suggest?

Elegy for Jane

1. The first five lines of this poem give a sense of Jane as a person. What do such phrases as "quick look," "light syllables," and "delight of her thought" tell us of her personality?

2a. In what way were Jane's sadder moods like her happy ones? **b.** How does the phrase "a pure depth" suggest this similarity?

3. Roethke often expresses complicated feelings through images drawn from simple aspects of nature. For example, he says he is left with "wet stones" and "moss." How do these images contrast with the images used to describe Jane's happiness?

4. In the poem's last stanza, what element complicates the poet's feelings for Jane?

Literary Elements

The Elegy

The **elegy** has a long history in poetry. In the past, it designated any meditative poem dealing with a serious theme, often death. Now the term applies to any poem dealing with the subject of death or with the death of a particular person. Theodore Roethke uses the term in the latter sense in "Elegy for Jane." Elegies often recall what the deceased person was like and usually express the speaker's sorrow over what has happened. In "Elegy for Jane," what phrase immediately sets the elegiac tone? Which lines in the third part of the poem indicate that the speaker's grief cannot be overcome? Some elegies lament the passing of beauty. In what way does this elegy mourn the passing of something beautiful?

Writing About Literature

Comparing Poems

Compare the treatment of death and mourning in "Elegy for Jane" and John Crowe Ransom's "Bells for John Whiteside's Daughter" (page 784). Which poem is more openly emotional? Would you judge that one poem is a more effective statement of grief than the other, or do you think that the poems are equally effective in their different ways? Cite lines and phrases from the poems to support your general statements.

Elizabeth Bishop.
© Rollie McKenna

Elizabeth Bishop was born in Worcester, Massachusetts, and grew up in New England and Nova Scotia. She was educated at Vassar College. She traveled extensively, living periodically in Key West, Florida, and in Brazil. Many of her poems reflect her fondness for travel and the manifold experiences it makes possible. Bishop's poems recall those of Marianne Moore, whom she met in 1934, the year of her graduation from Vassar. Both poets were attracted to seemingly accidental objects and events that turn up in the course of experience. Both wrote with intense concentration and focus on closely observed details. Neither developed a marked philosophy or set of ideas. With both poets, the attitude varies from poem to poem, and the reader will be rewarded by studying each individual work carefully. There is one important difference between the two poets: whereas Marianne Moore often seems detached and unemotional, Elizabeth Bishop charges her poems with expressions of emotion. Bishop's collections of verse include *Poems: North and South—A Cold Spring*, which won the Pulitzer Prize in 1955, *Questions of Travel* (1965), *Selected Poems* (1967), and *Complete Poems* (1969).

The Fish

I caught a tremendous fish
and held him beside the boat
half out of water, with my hook
fast in a corner of his mouth.
He didn't fight.   5
He hadn't fought at all.
He hung a grunting weight,
battered and venerable°
and homely. Here and there
his brown skin hung in strips   10
like ancient wallpaper,
and its pattern of darker brown
was like wallpaper:
shapes like full-blown roses
stained and lost through age.   15
He was speckled with barnacles,
fine rosettes° of lime,
and infested
with tiny white sea lice,
and underneath two or three   20
rags of green weed hung down.
While his gills were breathing in
the terrible oxygen
—the frightening gills,
fresh and crisp with blood,   25
that can cut so badly—

8. **venerable:** old and respected.

17. **rosettes:** shapes resembling roses.

I thought of the coarse white flesh
packed in like feathers,
the big bones and little bones,
the dramatic reds and blacks   30
of his shiny entrails,°
and the pink swim bladder°
like a big peony.
I looked into his eyes
which were far larger than mine   35
but shallower, and yellowed,
the irises backed and packed
with tarnished tinfoil
seen through the lenses
of old scratched isinglass.°   40
They shifted a little, but not
to return my stare.
—It was more like the tipping
of an object toward the light.
I admired his sullen face,   45
the mechanism of his jaw,
and then I saw
that from his lower lip
—if you could call it a lip—
grim, wet, and weaponlike,   50
hung five old pieces of fish line,
or four and a wire leader
with the swivel still attached,
with all their five big hooks
grown firmly in his mouth.   55
A green line, frayed at the end
where he broke it, two heavier lines,
and a fine black thread
still crimped from the strain and snap
when it broke and got away.   60
Like medals with their ribbons
frayed and wavering,
a five-haired beard of wisdom
trailing from his aching jaw.
I stared and stared   65
and victory filled up
the little rented boat,
from the pool of bilge°
where oil had spread a rainbow

around the rusted engine   70
to the bailer rusted orange,
the sun-cracked thwarts,°
the oarlocks on their strings,
the gunnels°—until everything
was rainbow, rainbow, rainbow!   75
And I let the fish go.

72. **thwarts:** seats of a boat.   74. **gunnels:** upper edges
of a boat's side.

Fish and Flowering Branch by John LaFarge
(1835–1910). Stained glass window.
Museum of Fine Arts, Boston, anonymous gift and
Edwin E. Jack Fund

31. **entrails:** inner organs.   32. **swim bladder:** balloon-
like inner organ.   40. **isinglass** (ī′zĭng-glăs′): mica, a glittering, transparent mineral formed in thin sheets.
68. **bilge:** dirty water gathering at a boat's lower part.

For Study and Discussion

Analyzing and Interpreting the Poem
1. The speaker examines the old fish closely.
a. What is its brown skin compared to in lines 9–
15?   **b.** What details make this comparison effective?
2. How is the inside of the fish described?
3. The old fish is viewed as a kind of war veteran.   **a.** How does the comparison in lines 47–61
reinforce this idea?   **b.** Whose "victory" is the
speaker talking about in lines 66–67?
4. The feeling of "victory" expands until everything is a "rainbow" (line 75). Why do you think the
speaker lets the fish go?

Elizabeth Bishop   **821**

Ā. Douglas '54

Robert Hayden (1954) by Aaron Douglas.
Charcoal sketch.

Robert Hayden was born in Detroit, Michigan. He completed graduate studies at the University of Michigan and was a professor there and at Fisk University in Tennessee. Hayden was an extremely versatile poet. His style ranged from the simple and direct to the elaborate and baroque. He wrote effectively in both free verse and the sonnet form. He was perhaps best known for his narrative and dramatic poems, with their vivid, strong characters. Out of an interest in black history and folklore, Hayden wrote many poems set in the past. But his subjects were as varied as his style; he also wrote about current world events and about personal feelings. His book *A Ballad of Remembrance* was awarded The Grand Prize for Poetry at The First World Festival of Negro Arts held in Dakar, Senegal, in 1966. Other collections of verse include *Heart-Shape in the Dust* (1940), *The Lion and the Archer* (1948), *Figures of Time: Poems* (1955), *Words in the Mourning Time: Poems* (1970), and *The Night-Blooming Cereus* (1972).

The Diver

Sank through easeful	
azure. Flower	
creatures flashed and	
shimmered there—	
lost images	5
fadingly remembered.	
Swiftly descended	
into canyon of cold	
nightgreen emptiness.	
Freefalling, weightless	10
as in dreams of	
wingless flight,	
plunged through infra-	
space and came to	
the dead ship,	15
carcass that swarmed with	
voracious life.	
Angelfish, their	
lively blue and	
yellow prized° from	20
darkness by the	
flashlight's beam,	
thronged her portholes.	
Moss of bryozoans°	
blurred, obscured her	25
metal. Snappers,	
gold groupers explored her,	
fearless of bubbling	
manfish. I entered	
the wreck, awed by her silence,	30
feeling more keenly	
the iron cold.	
With flashlight probing	
fogs of water	
saw the sad slow	35
dance of gilded	
chairs, the ectoplasmic°	
swirl of garments,	
drowned instruments	
of buoyancy,	40

20. **prized:** here, pried.   24. **bryozoans** (brī'ə-zō'-ənz): tiny water animals that form mosslike colonies. 37. **ectoplasmic** (ĕk'tə-plăz'mĭk): vaporous and spiritlike.

drunken shoes. Then
livid gesturings,
eldritch° hide and
seek of laughing
faces. I yearned to   45
find those hidden
ones, to fling aside
the mask and call to them,
yield to rapturous
whisperings, have   50
done with self and
every dinning
vain complexity.
Yet in languid
frenzy strove, as   55
one freezing fights off
sleep desiring sleep;
strove against the
cancelling arms that
suddenly surrounded   60
me, fled the numbing
kisses that I craved.
Reflex of life-wish?
Respirator's brittle
belling? Swam from   65
the ship somehow;
somehow began the
measured rise.

43. **eldritch** (ĕl′drĭch): weird.

For Study and Discussion

Analyzing and Interpreting the Poem

1a. How are the exotic fish under water described? **b.** What is the color of the deep sea?
c. To what does the speaker compare the sensation
of deep-sea diving?
2. What word in line 29 indicates that the speaker
identifies with the creatures around him?
3. As he probes the sunken ship, the speaker finds
traces of human life. **a.** What does the speaker
yearn for? **b.** What reason does he give in lines
50–53 for his feelings?
4. What sudden "reflex" causes the speaker to
change his mind?

Robert Hayden   **823**

KARL SHAPIRO
1913–

Karl Shapiro was born and raised in Baltimore, Maryland. He studied briefly at the University of Virginia, but discovered that he was more interested in writing poetry than in academic study. He began publishing poems in his early twenties, and his first collection, *Poems*, appeared in 1936. *Person, Place, and Thing*, which includes the poem "Auto Wreck," appeared in 1942 and was widely praised. This collection reveals, even in its title, Shapiro's interest in the ordinary events and details of life. While serving in the army in the South Pacific during World War II, Shapiro produced the collection *V-Letter and Other Poems* (1944). This collection, which contains many poems dealing with army life, won the Pulitzer Prize in 1945.

Shapiro has been editor of two distinguished literary magazines, *Poetry* and *The Prairie Schooner*. He has taught at the University of Nebraska and the University of California, and is presently Professor of English at the University of Illinois. For much of his career, Shapiro has opposed formal, intellectual poetry and favored a more spontaneous kind of verse. He has pointed to the example of Walt Whitman, with his direct expression of personal experience and his immersion in the physical world.

Karl Shapiro.
© Rollie McKenna

Shapiro has experimented, in recent years, with Whitmanesque free verse and with prose poems, through which he has sought what he calls a "sense of identification with the universe."

Auto Wreck

Its quick soft silver bell beating, beating
And down the dark one ruby flare
Pulsing out red light like an artery,
The ambulance at top speed floating down
Past beacons and illuminated clocks   5
Wings in a heavy curve, dips down,
And brakes speed, entering the crowd.
The doors leap open, emptying light;

Stretchers are laid out, the mangled lifted
And stowed into the little hospital.
Then the bell, breaking the hush, tolls once,   10
And the ambulance with its terrible cargo
Rocking, slightly rocking, moves away,
As the doors, an afterthought, are closed.

We are deranged, walking among the cops   15
Who sweep glass and are large and composed.
One is still making notes under the light.
One with a bucket douches ponds of blood
Into the street and gutter.
One hangs lanterns on the wrecks that cling,   20
Empty husks of locusts, to iron poles.

Our throats were tight as tourniquets,
Our feet were bound with splints, but now
Like convalescents intimate and gauche,°   **24. gauche** (gōsh): awkward.
We speak through sickly smiles and warn   25
With the stubborn saw of common sense,
The grim joke and the banal resolution.
The traffic moves around with care,
But we remain, touching a wound
That opens to our richest horror.   30
Already old, the question Who shall die?
Becomes unspoken Who is innocent?
For death in war is done by hands;
Suicide has cause; and stillbirth, logic.
But this invites the occult mind,   35
Cancels our physics with a sneer,
And spatters all we know of denouement°   **37. denouement** (dā-nōo-
Across the expedient and wicked stones.   mān′): usually, the outcome
                                                                                or clarification of a plot.

For Study and Discussion

Analyzing and Interpreting the Poem

1. The first two parts of this poem depict the scene of the auto wreck. **a.** What images give the impression of flooding lights and sudden, harsh sounds? **b.** How do the images in lines 2–3, 12–13, and 18–21 contribute to the nightmarish atmosphere?

2. The third part of the poem focuses on the spectators of the wreck, including the speaker. To what physical and emotional states do the medical descriptions in lines 22–25 refer?

3a. What reaction do you have on reading the phrase "touching a wound"? **b.** In what way is this an appropriate description of the spectators' conversation about the wreck?

4a. According to the speaker, how are death by war, suicide, and stillbirth alike? **b.** How are they different from the kind of death presented in this poem?

5a. How would you define *denouement* in the context of the poem? **b.** In what sense might the pavement stones be "expedient and wicked"? **c.** How does this final image suggest a hostile universe?

Karl Shapiro   **825**

RANDALL JARRELL
1914–1965

Randall Jarrell.

Among the poets to emerge after World War II, Randall Jarrell (jə-rĕl′) was one of the most brilliant. The critic R. W. Flint described him as "in many ways the wonder and terror of American poetry during the late 40s and early 50s." He not only wrote some of the best poems about World War II ("The Death of the Ball Turret Gunner" is perhaps the best-known American poem on the war); he was also an outstanding and influential critic who helped revitalize the reputations of Walt Whitman, Robert Frost, and William Carlos Williams in the 1950s. On the literature he disliked, his reviews were devastating—filled with learned allusions, epigrams, and contemptuous wisecracks. He argued passionately for the value of poetry, going so far as to say that without some form of it, human life is "but animal existence."

Jarrell was born in Nashville, Tennessee. A child of the Great Depression, he spent many hours alone in the local public library. He studied at Vanderbilt University in Nashville. Later he taught briefly at Kenyon College in Ohio, where his friends included the poets John Crowe Ransom and Robert Lowell. Jarrell taught at the Women's College of the University of North Carolina from 1947 until his death in 1965 in a road accident. One of his favorite subjects was childhood. He wrote about childhood and children with a magical feeling, often populating his poems with characters from fairy tales—kind animals, lost children, witches, and dragons. Childhood is the theme of his last book of poems, *The Lost World* (1965).

The Death of the Ball Turret Gunner

In some World War II bomber planes, the ball turret was a small space, enclosed in plexiglass, on the underside of the plane's fuselage. The ball turret held a man and two machine guns. During an air fight, the gunner would fire from a cramped and often upside-down position.

From my mother's sleep I fell into the State,
And I hunched in its belly till my wet fur froze.
Six miles from earth, loosed from its dream of life,
I woke to black flak and the nightmare fighters.
When I died they washed me out of the turret with a hose.

For Study and Discussion

Analyzing and Interpreting the Poem

1a. Considering the position of a ball turret gunner, why do you think the poet uses images of an unborn creature still in its mother's womb? **b.** What is the "wet fur"?

2. The word *State* in line 1 is capitalized, suggesting a government or nation. In what sense did the gunner fall "into the State"?

3. As an airplane gunner, the speaker is "loosed" from the earth. **a.** Why does he refer to life on earth as a "dream"? **b.** What is meant by awakening from "dream" to "nightmare"? **c.** What phrase suggests that his experience as a gunner is a kind of bad dream?

4a. What does the last line imply about the condition of the plane and how it landed? **b.** What does it imply about the actualities of war?

JOHN BERRYMAN
1914–1972

John Berryman was born in McAlester, Oklahoma, but grew up in Tampa, Florida. He went to Kent School in Connecticut and to Columbia College, where he won a scholarship to Cambridge University in England. Like several other poets of his generation, Berryman began under the influence of W. H. Auden. Some of his early poems dealt with the unease of the years during and after World War II.

Increasingly, Berryman's poetry expressed his own life and his erratic, usually gloomy feelings. He developed a characteristic rugged style, marked by insistent stresses and unusual, startling syntax. The poem that established him as a major poet was *Homage to Mistress Bradstreet* (1956), a long meditation on the colonial poet Anne Bradstreet and on his relationship to her as a poet. In 1965 Berryman was awarded the Pulitzer Prize for *77 Dream Songs*. This collection later formed the first part of his greatest work, *The Dream Songs*, a series of 385 related lyrics, each consisting of three six-line stanzas with various rhythms and rhyme schemes. They center on an imaginary character named Henry, though they reflect Berryman's own troubled life. Their moods range from the hilarious to the theatrical to the mournful. Berryman saw the present age as a difficult one for poetry, and in *The Dream Songs* he expressed sorrow over the suffering and early deaths of several poets who were his friends. His

John Berryman.
© Rollie McKenna

poems—intense, demanding, comic and despairing by turns—are among the most moving poems written by an American in the twentieth century.

The Ball Poem

What is the boy now, who has lost his ball,
What, what is he to do? I saw it go
Merrily bouncing, down the street, and then
Merrily over—there it is in the water!
No use to say 'O there are other balls':   5
An ultimate shaking grief fixes the boy
As he stands rigid, trembling, staring down
All his young days into the harbor where
His ball went. I would not intrude on him,
A dime, another ball, is worthless. Now   10
He senses first responsibility
In a world of possessions. People will take balls,
Balls will be lost always, little boy,
And no one buys a ball back. Money is external.
He is learning, well behind his desperate eyes,   15
The epistemology° of loss, how to stand up
Knowing what every man must one day know
And most know many days, how to stand up
And gradually light returns to the street,
A whistle blows, the ball is out of sight,   20
Soon part of me will explore the deep and dark
Floor of the harbor . . . I am everywhere,
I suffer and move, my mind and my heart move
With all that move me, under the water
Or whistling, I am not a little boy.   25

16. **epistemology** (ĭ-pĭs′tə-mŏl′ə-jē): the branch of philosophy dealing with the nature and limits of knowledge; it explores what human beings can know and how much they can know.

For Study and Discussion

Analyzing and Interpreting the Poem

1. The speaker in this poem begins by observing a ball lost in the harbor water and gradually identifies with the boy who lost the ball. What sentence in lines 6–10 suggests that the speaker is becoming involved in the boy's plight?

2. The phrase "epistemology of loss" can be rephrased as "how we know what loss is." **a.** Which phrase implies that some losses are final? **b.** What does the speaker say one must do in the face of loss? **c.** What does line 19 suggest will then happen?

3. The speaker is perhaps remembering an experience from his own childhood. At the end of the poem, he says that "part" of him will explore the bottom of the harbor. **a.** What do you think that part of him is looking for? **b.** How do you interpret the last four lines of the poem?

John Berryman   **829**

William Stafford was born in Hutchinson, Kansas, and received his B.A. from the University of Kansas. He did graduate work at Iowa State University, and for many years was a professor of literature at Lewis and Clark College in Portland, Oregon. Stafford worked as the poetry consultant at the Library of Congress. He is a poet much at home in the American Midwest and Far West. Stafford is noted for a plain-spoken and straightforward style. He has commented, "My poetry seems to be direct and communicative, with some oddity and variety. It is usually not formal. It is much like talk, with some enhancement . . . it delivers a sense of place and event; it has narrative impulses." In addition to poetry, Stafford has written critical essays.

William Stafford.

Traveling Through the Dark

Traveling through the dark I found a deer
dead on the edge of the Wilson River road.
It is usually best to roll them into the canyon:
that road is narrow; to swerve might make more dead.

By glow of the tail-light I stumbled back of the car   5
and stood by the heap, a doe, a recent killing;
she had stiffened already, almost cold.
I dragged her off; she was large in the belly.

My fingers touching her side brought me the reason—
her side was warm; her fawn lay there waiting,   10
alive, still, never to be born.
Beside that mountain road I hesitated.

The car aimed ahead its lowering parking lights;
under the hood purred the steady engine.
I stood in the glare of the warm exhaust turning red;   15
around our group I could hear the wilderness listen.

I thought hard for us all—my only swerving—
then pushed her over the edge into the river.

For Study and Discussion

Analyzing and Interpreting the Poem
1. What is the speaker's dilemma?
2a. How is the dilemma made more pointed by the statement that "to swerve might make more dead,"
and by the assertion that "I thought hard for us all"? **b.** What does the poet mean when he calls his hard thinking his "only swerving"?
3. What does the poem's title imply about our ability to make certain decisions?

JOSÉ GARCIA VILLA
1914–

José Garcia Villa (vĭl′ä) was born in the Philippines and emigrated to the United States in 1930. He studied at the University of New Mexico and did graduate work at Columbia University in New York City, where he has lived for many years. Villa was first recognized as a short-story writer. In the 1930s he began to study poetry. He worked slowly, and it was several years before he produced his first collection of poems, *Many Voices,* published in the Philippines in 1939. His first collection published in the United States was *Have Come, Am Here* (1942). Since then he has produced several other books of poems as well as a short-story collection. One critic has said that Villa's poetry "springs with a wild force, straight from the poet's being, from his blood, from his spirit, as a fire breaks from wood, or as a flower grows from its soil."

José Garcia Villa.

Be Beautiful, Noble, like the Antique Ant

Be beautiful, noble, like the antique ant,
Who bore the storms as he bore the sun,
Wearing neither gown nor helmet,
Though he was archbishop and soldier:
Wore only his own flesh.   5

Salute characters with gracious dignity:
Though what these are is left to
Your own terms. Exact: the universe is
Not so small but these will be found
Somewhere. Exact: they will be found.   10

Speak with great moderation: but think
With great fierceness, burning passion:
Though what the ant thought
No annals reveal, not his descendants
Break the seal.   15

Trace the tracelessness of the ant,
Every ant has reached this perfection.
As he comes, so he goes,
Flowing as water flows,
Essential but secret like a rose.   20

For Study and Discussion

Analyzing and Interpreting the Poem

1. The word *antique* in this poem is used in its root meaning of "ancient." **a.** How might the ant be thought of as "antique"? **b.** In what sense are ants "soldiers"? **c.** In lines 1–5, what dignity are ants shown to have?

2. According to the third stanza, how should one think?

3. How does the poem use nature to illustrate the value of modesty?

Of her own poetry Margaret Walker has said simply, "I want to write the songs of my people." In some poems she has done so through the long free-verse lines introduced into poetry by Walt Whitman and carried into the twentieth century by Carl Sandburg. Just as Whitman used free verse to express an expansive vision of America, so Margaret Walker uses it to celebrate the struggles and aspirations of black America. Walker has also helped to revive the ballad tradition, adapting this form to tell of black history and legend. She has also written in the sonnet form, sometimes strictly following its traditional patterns, other times adapting it for more flexible expression.

Margaret Walker was born and grew up in Birmingham, Alabama, where her father earned his living as a tailor and preached in a Methodist church. She graduated from Northwestern University and received her doctorate at the University of Iowa. She has taught for much of her life at Jackson State College in Mississippi, where she has also directed an institute for the advancement of black life and culture.

Margaret Walker.
Reprinted from *Images of the Southern Writer,* photograph by Mark Morrow. © The University of Georgia Press

The Miner (1925) by George Benjamin
Luks (1866–1933). Oil on canvas.
National Gallery of Art, Washington,
gift of Chester Dale

Childhood

When I was a child I knew red miners
dressed raggedly and wearing carbide lamps.
I saw them come down red hills to their camps
dyed with red dust from old Ishkooda mines.
Night after night I met them on the roads,   5
or on the streets in town I caught their glance;
the swing of dinner buckets in their hands,
and grumbling undermining all their words.

I also lived in low cotton country
where moonlight hovered over ripe haystacks,   10
or stumps of trees, and croppers' rotting shacks
with famine, terror, flood, and plague near by,
where sentiment and hatred still held sway
and only bitter land was washed away.

For Study and Discussion

Analyzing and Interpreting the Poem

1a. What two meanings does the word *undermine* have? **b.** In what two senses does "grumbling" undermine the miners' words?
2. The second part of the poem begins with an image of serenity. **a.** What does the speaker seem to remember most vividly? **b.** What is implied in the poem's final line?
3a. What is the poem's rhyme scheme? **b.** A **slant rhyme** is a rhyme that is not quite exact. Which rhymes in the poem are slant rhymes?
4a. What traditional type of poem is "Childhood"? **b.** How does the poet use the form of this poem to structure her ideas?

Américo Paredes (pă-rā′děs) was born the son of a rancher in Brownsville, Texas. He was educated at the University of Texas, where he is now professor of English and anthropology and director of the Mexican-American Studies Program. In addition to poems, Paredes has written short stories and edited several anthologies of Mexican-American writing and Mexican folklore, folk songs, and legends. He is the author of *"With His Pistol in His Hand": A Border Ballad and Its Hero* (1958), which is a biography of Gregorio Cortez, who became a figure in Texas-Mexican folklore.

Américo Paredes.
University of Texas Student Publications, Inc.

Guitarreros°

Black against twisted black
The old mesquite°
Rears up against the stars
Branch bridle hanging,
While the bull comes down from the
    mountain   5
Driven along by your fingers,
Twenty nimble stallions prancing up and
    down the *redil*° of the guitars.
One leaning on the trunk, one facing—
Now the song:
Not cleanly flanked, not pacing,   10
But in a stubborn yielding that unshapes
And shapes itself again,
Hard-mouthed, zigzagged, thrusting,
Thrown, not sung,

One to the other.   15
The old man listens in his cloud
Of white tobacco smoke.
"It was so," he says,
"In the old days it was so."

° **Guitarreros** (gĭt′ə-rĕr′ōs): guitar players. 2. **mesquite** (mĕs-kēt′): a kind of thorny tree or shrub common in the American Southwest and in Mexico. 7. *redil* (rə-dēl′): sheepfold.

For Study and Discussion

Analyzing and Interpreting the Poem

1. In this poem an old man listens to two guitarists playing a song about the capture of a bull. **a.** What is the poem's setting? **b.** How do lines 5–6 indicate that the story is being told through a song, and that the bull is not actually charging down the mountain? **2a.** To what does the poet compare the guitarists' fingers in line 7? **b.** How are the guitarists positioned as they play? **3.** In what way do lines 9–12 also describe the song's content—the story of the bull's capture? **4.** What is the song's effect on the old man?

Robert Lowell was a Boston Lowell, a member of the prominent family descended from early settlers of New England. Amy Lowell was a relative, and James Russell Lowell was his grandfather's brother. Lowell has described his boyhood in Boston in his memoir, "91 Revere Street." For two years he attended Harvard University, where he submitted his poems to Robert Frost for advice, then transferred to Kenyon College in Ohio, where he studied under John Crowe Ransom. His first slim book of poems, *The Land of Unlikeness,* was published in 1944 but received little attention. In 1946, his second collection, *Lord Weary's Castle,* convinced many readers that an important new poet was at work. This volume was awarded the Pulitzer Prize the following year. His third book, *The Mills of the Kavanaughs,* containing a long narrative poem and several shorter dramatic monologues, appeared four years later.

In most of his early poetry, Lowell relied on traditional forms. He wrote sonnets and was highly original in his use of the pentameter couplet. Then, in 1959, with the publication of *Life Studies,* his poetry took a new direction. It became freer and more direct. It dealt openly and frankly with his personal life and with members of his family. *Life Studies,* one of the most influential books of poetry in our time, gave rise to a school of "confessional poetry," whose members later included John Berryman, Anne Sexton, and Sylvia Plath. Lowell's later work expressed a diversity of interests. He did translations of the Latin poet Juvenal and the French playwright Racine. Some of his poems in *Near the Ocean* (1967) were written in tetrameter couplets, recalling the

Robert Lowell.

verse of the eighteenth-century English writer Jonathan Swift. The major work of Lowell's final years was a long series of related fourteen-line poems in which he examined the human experience from ancient times to the present; this long, loosely connected poem was published in 1973 as *History.*

Robert Lowell is regarded by many readers of poetry as the finest American poet of his generation. Most of his poetry is somber; some of it is harsh. Occasionally it is overweighted with literary allusions and a violence of language that seems unjustified. At its best, however, it is strikingly intense, the complex expression of a man of deep feeling and learning who was also a gifted poet.

The Gulls, Monhegan (c. 1913) by George Bellows (1882–1925). Oil on canvas.

Water

It was a Maine lobster town—
each morning boatloads of hands
pushed off for granite
quarries on the islands,

and left dozens of bleak   5
white frame houses stuck
like oyster shells
on a hill of rock,

and below us, the sea lapped
the raw little match-stick   10
mazes of a weir,°
where the fish for bait were trapped.

Remember? We sat on a slab of rock.
From this distance in time,
it seems the color   15
of iris, rotting and turning purpler,

11. **weir** (wîr): a fence placed in water in order to trap
fish.

but it was only
the usual gray rock
turning the usual green
when drenched by the sea.   20

The sea drenched the rock
at our feet all day,
and kept tearing away
flake after flake.

One night you dreamed   25
You were a mermaid clinging to a wharf-pile,
and trying to pull
off the barnacles with your hands.

We wished our two souls
might return like gulls   30
to the rock. In the end,
the water was too cold for us.

Analyzing and Interpreting the Poem

1. In this poem a failed relationship between two people is expressed in terms of a cold natural landscape. How do the images in stanzas 1 and 2 suggest barrenness and harshness?

2. The fourth and fifth stanzas focus on the color of a piece of rock. How does the shifting color of the rock symbolize the connection between the two people?

3a. What effect does the water have on the rock? **b.** How does this effect suggest the breakdown of the relationship?

4. What does the last line add to your understanding of the relationship?

5. Reread the three opening stanzas of the poem. **a.** Why is this poem about a personal relationship introduced by these stanzas? **b.** How do the stanzas suggest a connection between the lives of the town's inhabitants and the bait-fish? **c.** How does the private relationship become wider than just two people in its implications about what happens to people's lives?

Writing About Literature

Explaining How an Image Is Used

Certain images drawn from nature are so expressive that they have been used effectively throughout the history of art. One such image is water, which is the basis of Robert Lowell's poem. In it, water is seen as a hostile, chilling element that colors and erodes rock. Among the other poems in this unit, Langston Hughes's "The Negro Speaks of Rivers" (page 799) uses water as an image. What meanings for water do you find in this poem? Find other poems in this book that use some form of water as an image and, in a brief composition, explain how the image is used.

Hawthorne

Follow its lazy main street lounging
from the alms house° to Gallows Hill°
along a flat, unvaried surface
covered with wooden houses
aged by yellow drain   5
like the unhealthy hair of an old dog.
You'll walk to no purpose
in Hawthorne's Salem.

I cannot resilver the smudged plate.°

I drop to Hawthorne, the customs officer,°   10
measuring coal and mostly trying to keep warm—
to the stunted black schooner,
the dismal South-end dock,
the wharf-piles with their fungus of ice.

2. **alms house:** poorhouse. **Gallows Hill:** a hill in Salem, Massachusetts, where nineteen supposed witches were hanged.   9. **resilver . . . plate:** Early photographs were taken on a metal plate with a silver coating.   10. **customs officer:** Hawthorne served as a customs officer in Boston and in Salem.

On State Street°   15
a steeple with a glowing dial-clock
measures the weary hours,
the merciless march of professional feet.
Even this shy distrustful ego
sometimes walked on top of the blazing roof,   20
and felt those flashes
that char the discharged cells° of the brain.

Look at the faces—
Longfellow, Lowell, Holmes and Whittier!
Study the grizzled silver of their beards.   25
Hawthorne's picture,
however, has a blond mustache
and golden General Custer° scalp.
He looks like a Civil War officer.
He shines in the firelight. His hard   30
survivor's smile is touched with fire.
Leave him alone for a moment or two,
and you'll see him with his head
bent down, brooding, brooding,
eyes fixed on some chip,   35
some stone, some common plant,
the commonest thing,
as if it were the clue.
The disturbed eyes rise,
furtive, foiled, dissatisfied   40
from meditation on the true
and insignificant.

15. **State Street:** the principal street in the business district of Boston.   22. **discharged cells:** a reference to the cells of a battery.   28. **General Custer:** George Armstrong Custer (1839–1876), who served as a general in the Civil War and whose troops were killed by the Sioux at the Battle of the Little Big Horn, had long blond hair.

Commentary

In his day, Hawthorne felt isolated in a society which had not yet acknowledged a respected place for the artist and which was not yet aware of an estimable, native literary tradition. A good many American writers today do not think of themselves as isolated figures striving only to express themselves. They are aware of themselves as part of a tradition which they must face up to and which they can help shape. As a member of an old New England family that produced many distinguished men and women, in-cluding two important poets, Robert Lowell was probably more aware of tradition than most. His elegy "The Quaker Graveyard in Nantucket" shows a detailed knowledge of Herman Melville's *Moby-Dick*. He wrote three poems about Jonathan Edwards and that divine's wrestling with the problems of good and evil. Like the novelist Henry James, who found in Nathaniel Hawthorne a confirmation of his ambition to become a literary artist, Lowell too drew sustenance from Hawthorne's example. The poem "Hawthorne" is an attempt to explain why.

Custom House (1818) in Salem, Massachusetts.
Courtesy, Essex Institute, Salem, Massachusetts

This poem, which shows detailed knowledge of Hawthorne's works, is a good example of how poets can shape to their own purposes what they have found in their reading. The opening portions of the poem draw heavily on Hawthorne's writings, and even the later passages seem to have been developed from hints found in Hawthorne's work. Lowell's description of the meandering main street of Salem is based closely on a sentence in "The Custom-House," the introductory essay to *The Scarlet Letter*. He added the reference to "yellow drain like the unhealthy hair of an old dog," cut out words he considered unnecessary, and subtly altered the rhythm.

The description of the lethargic customs officer at work in Boston is derived from a letter in which Hawthorne wrote to his wife, "Your husband has been measuring coal all day, aboard a black little British schooner, in a dismal dock at the North end of the city. Most of the time he paced the deck to keep himself warm." Later in the letter Hawthorne mentions a church steeple near the Bunker Hill monument "with the dial of clock upon it, whereby I was enabled to measure the march of the weary hours." Lowell sharpened the image of the schooner by making it "stunted" instead of merely "little," and he made the clock more vivid. The image of "wharf-piles with their fungus of ice" was Lowell's own invention. His most notable change was to move the steeple to State Street, the center of Boston's business district, and to transport the dock to the South end. This shift enabled him to include not only Hawthorne's impression of the dreary progress of time, but also a suggestion of the dispiriting routines of those concerned only with material things.

Lowell's lines describing Hawthorne's walking on top of the blazing roof were probably based on the novelist's description of himself pacing the Custom House and developing the plot of *The Scarlet Letter*. Lowell's use of images drawn from photography, which originally required a silvered plate, was perhaps suggested by Hawthorne's describing his imagination at this time as "a tarnished mirror." The images of the flashes which burned into Hawthorne's brain and of the fire which touched "his hard survivor's smile" recall a passage in "The Custom-House" telling how the glow of a coal fire

helped to stimulate his creativity and to convert his imagined characters from pale "snow images into men and women."

Hawthorne's casual reference, in another part of the Custom House essay, to his picking Indian arrowheads from a field near the Old Manse in Concord seems particularly to have impressed Lowell. From this clue he constructed the powerful concluding stanza. Its intensity comes from the use of rhyme, the tightening of the rhythm, and from the force of repetition as we watch Hawthorne with head "bent down, brooding, brooding." It is in this last section of the poem that Hawthorne's significance to Lowell most clearly emerges. It is Hawthorne the seeker, the artist who probes the commonplace objects of life ("some stone, some common plant, the commonest thing") to penetrate to the cosmic mystery behind them, who fascinates Lowell. Yet, as Lowell must admit, Hawthorne registered the mystery of life but not its solution. Al-

ways "the disturbed eyes rise, furtive, foiled, dissatisfied. . . ." What Hawthorne (and with him Lowell) observed—the hill where supposed witches were hanged, the dreary streets of Salem, the "dismal South-end dock" in Boston, and State Street which bears "the merciless march of professional feet"—all the sights that shaped Hawthorne's tragic vision of life, these must remain the pieces of an unresolved puzzle that poets or storytellers may use in their art but which they can never wholly explain.

For Study and Discussion

Analyzing and Interpreting the Poem

1. What details at the beginning of the poem suggest that Salem is in a state of decay? **b.** How does the metaphor in line 9 suggest that the town has no significance for the poet?

2. Where in the poem does the speaker imply that life in contemporary Boston is essentially trivial and unpleasant?

3. Lines 23–31 suggest that Hawthorne was a livelier man than many of his literary contemporaries. **a.** What reason for his liveliness is given in lines 19–22? **b.** How is this related to the activity described in lines 32–38?

4. In his essay "The Custom-House," Hawthorne wrote, "The page of life that was spread out before me seemed dull and commonplace, only because I had not fathomed its deeper import. . . . my brain wanted the insight and my hand the cunning to transcribe it." In what way would Hawthorne have agreed with Lowell's poem about him?

5a. Why does Lowell describe "the true" as insignificant? **b.** Consider the shades of meaning attached to the root meaning of *insignificant*, meaning that derives from the word *sign*. How do those meanings fit into Hawthorne's (and Lowell's) sense of being "foiled, dissatisfied"?

Gwendolyn Brooks was born in Topeka, Kansas, but grew up in Chicago, Illinois, the setting for much of her writing. Her love of poetry began early. At the age of seven, she "began to put rhymes together," and when she was thirteen, one of her poems was published in a children's magazine. During her teens she contributed more than seventy-five poems to a Chicago newspaper. In 1941 she began attending classes in poetry writing at the South Side Community Art Center, and several years later her poems began appearing in *Poetry* and other magazines. Her first collection of poems, *A Street in Bronzeville*, was published in 1945. Four years later, *Annie Allen*, her second collection, appeared. Called "essentially a novel," it is divided into three parts—"Notes from the Childhood and the Girlhood," "The Anniad," and "The Womanhood"—and tells the story of Annie's life. Brooks has also published a novel, *Maud Martha* (1953), about a young black girl growing up in Chicago.

Gwendolyn Brooks is widely regarded as one of America's finest poets. Her poems about ghetto life in Chicago are intense, direct, and superbly crafted. Her terse style often draws on the intonations of black American speech. Her poems encompass a broad spectrum of characters and situations, often dealing with the destructive side of city life. She is a realist in verse and, as such, captures the hard particulars of a world she knows.

In 1950 Brooks was awarded the Pultizer Prize

Gwendolyn Brooks (1983).
Paul Sequeira / Photo Researchers

for *Annie Allen*. She has received a number of other awards and honors, including several Poetry Workshop Awards of the Midwest Writers' Conference, two Guggenheim Fellowships, an award from the American Academy of Arts and Letters, and the Eunice Tietjens Memorial Award given by *Poetry* magazine.

In Honor of
David Anderson Brooks,
My Father

July 30, 1883–November 21, 1959

A dryness is upon the house
My father loved and tended.
Beyond his firm and sculptured door
His light and lease have ended.

He walks the valleys, now—replies   5
To sun and wind forever.
No more the cramping chamber's chill,
No more the hindering fever.

Now out upon the wide clean air
My father's soul revives,   10
All innocent of self-interest
And the fear that strikes and strives.

He who was Goodness, Gentleness,
And Dignity is free,
Translates to public Love   15
Old private Charity.

That Gentleman (1960) by Andrew Wyeth (1917–   ). Tempera on panel.
Dallas Museum of Art, Dallas Art Association Purchase

The Explorer

Somehow to find a still spot in the noise
Was the frayed inner want, the winding, the frayed hope
Whose tatters he kept hunting through the din.
A velvet peace somewhere.
A room of wily hush somewhere within.   5

So tipping down the scrambled halls he set
Vague hands on throbbing knobs. There were behind
Only spiraling, high human voices,
The scream of nervous affairs,
Wee griefs,   10
Grand griefs. And choices.

He feared most of all the choices, that cried to be taken.

There were no bourns.
There were no quiet rooms.

For Study and Discussion

Analyzing and Interpreting the Poems

In Honor of David Anderson Brooks, My Father
1a. Which lines in stanza 1 tell that the poet's father
carefully attended to life's demands? **b.** What is
his "firm and sculptured door" now?
2. In the poem, death is seen as a liberator from
the restrictions of life. In stanza 2, what difference
does the poet imagine between the conditions of
death and those of life?
3. As the father has moved into a larger realm, so
his virtues seem to have grown. **a.** In the last
stanza, what change does the poet say has occurred? **b.** How does this change relate to the
change described in stanza 2? **c.** Where does Charity begin? **d.** How does the last stanza relate back
to the first?

The Explorer
1a. What details indicate that the central figure in
this poem lives in a crowded place? **b.** What is this
figure looking for?
2. We need not confine the poem to a ghetto situation. How might the images of "noise," "scrambled
halls," and "nervous affairs" apply to life in general?
3a. Considering what this figure is looking for, why
do you think he fears making choices most of
all? **b.** What might he be afraid of?
4a. What are *bourns* (line 13) in the context of the
poem? Can the word *bourn* have more than one
meaning? Explain. **b.** At the end of the poem,
what discoveries does this explorer make?

RICHARD WILBUR
1921–

Of all modern American poets, Richard Wilbur is perhaps the most graceful and elegant. In reviewing Wilbur's second collection of poems, Randall Jarrell called him "delicate, charming, and skillful. . . . His poems not only make you use, but make you eager to use, words like *attractive* and *appealing* and *engaging*." The subject of much of his poetry is suggested by the titles of two poems: " 'A World Without Objects Is a Sensible Emptiness' " and "Love Calls Us to the Things of This World."

Wilbur was born in New York City. His father was an artist, and his mother came from a family of journalists. When he was a child, his parents took an old house in rural northern New Jersey, where he developed a love for country things. He edited student newspapers in high school and at Amherst College. He began to write poetry seriously while serving in the army in Italy during World War II. He has commented, "One does not use poetry for its major purposes, as a means of organizing oneself and the world, until one's world somehow gets out of hand." After the war, he was a junior fellow and assistant professor of English at Harvard University. In 1947 he published his first book of poems, *The Beautiful Changes and Other Poems. Ceremony and Other Poems* followed in 1950, and his third collection, *Things of This World* (1956), received both the Pulitzer Prize and the National Book Award. In addition to lyric poetry, Wilbur has written verse translations of Molière's *The Misanthrope* and *Tartuffe,*

Richard Wilbur.
© Thomas Victor, 1987

and with Leonard Bernstein and Lillian Hellman, collaborated on *Candide,* a comic opera based on Voltaire's novel. Since 1957, Wilbur has taught at Wesleyan University in Middletown, Connecticut. In 1987 he succeeded Robert Penn Warren as Poet Laureate.

The Beautiful Changes

One wading a Fall meadow finds on all sides
The Queen Anne's Lace° lying like lilies
On water; it glides
So from the walker, it turns
Dry grass to a lake, as the slightest shade of you   5
Valleys my mind in fabulous blue Lucernes.°

The beautiful changes as a forest is changed
By a chameleon's tuning his skin to it;
As a mantis, arranged
On a green leaf, grows   10
Into it, makes the leaf leafier, and proves
Any greenness is deeper than anyone knows.

Your hands hold roses always in a way that says
They are not only yours; the beautiful changes
In such kind ways,   15
Wishing ever to sunder
Things and things' selves for a second finding, to lose
For a moment all that it touches back to wonder.

2. **Queen Anne's Lace:** a delicate weed with white flowers.   6. **Lucernes** (lōō-sûrnz′):
The Lake of Lucerne is in central Switzerland.

Boy at the Window

Seeing the snowman standing all alone
In dusk and cold is more than he can bear.
The small boy weeps to hear the wind prepare
A night of gnashings and enormous moan.
His tearful sight can hardly reach to where   5
The pale-faced figure with bitumen° eyes
Returns him such a god-forsaken stare
As outcast Adam gave to Paradise.

The man of snow is, nonetheless, content,
Having no wish to go inside and die.   10
Still, he is moved to see the youngster cry.
Though frozen water is his element,
He melts enough to drop from one soft eye
A trickle of the purest rain, a tear
For the child at the bright pane surrounded by   15
Such warmth, such light, such love, and so much fear.

6. **bitumen** (bī-tōō′mən): soft coal.

For Study and Discussion

Analyzing and Interpreting the Poems

The Beautiful Changes

1. Although the speaker is describing a meadow in the first stanza, he uses words, such as "wading," that suggest water. Tell in your own words what comparison is drawn in the first four lines and how that comparison is extended in lines 5–6.
2. Both the chameleon, a small lizard, and the mantis, a large insect, can change color to match their surroundings. Why might such a change make ordinary color seem "deeper" or more mysterious than usual?
3. Is the word *beautiful*, which appears in the title and in lines 7 and 14, a noun or an adjective? How do you know?
4a. What do you think the speaker means by saying that change offers "a second finding" of an object?   **b.** Why does the speaker think that "wonder" may be the result of change?
5. Wilbur skillfully changes "The Beautiful Changes" from a nature poem to a love poem.

a. In which lines does he do so?   **b.** How does the last stanza make the beloved seem like all of beautiful nature?

Boy at the Window

1. What images of bitter winter emphasize the boy's sympathy for the snowman?
2a. What common feeling moves both the boy and the snowman?   **b.** Why does the snowman pity the boy?
3a. What allusion is contained in lines 6–8?
b. Why is the phrase *god-forsaken* appropriate to the subject of this poem?
4. The boy is surrounded by fear as well as warmth and love.   **a.** To what extent is fear a part of childhood?   **b.** In spite of the security of a home and family, can childhood be an unhappy time?

James Dickey.

Reprinted from *Images of the Southern Writer*, photograph by Mark Morrow. © 1985 The University of Georgia Press

JAMES DICKEY
1923–

James Dickey has led an active and athletic life. To this day he is a keen outdoorsman, a lover of the wilderness, and an expert archer. He was born in Atlanta, Georgia, on Ground Hog Day. By the time he was a high school football star, Dickey was already six feet three. After a year in college, he left to become a bomber pilot in World War II, and he flew more than a hundred combat missions in the South Pacific. On his return from the war, he attended Vanderbilt University in Nashville, Tennessee, where he eagerly studied philosophy, anthropology, and foreign languages. He began writing poetry seriously under the encouragement of a professor, and in his senior year he saw one of his poems published in the *Sewanee Review*. For some years Dickey worked for an advertising agency in Atlanta. He resigned from the agency, however, when he decided that poetry was his true calling.

Dickey's poetry is unique among contemporary poets. In his poems, events in nature become dreamlike in a way that is both fantastic and realistic. His is an elemental and brutal world, yet often exhilarating and sometimes even purifying, as if a return to elemental forces could cleanse readers of the humdrum and the everyday. In its concern with ancient dreams, nightmares, and the basic elements of existence, James Dickey's poetry has much in common with the novels of his fellow Southerner William Faulkner. In addition to several volumes of verse, including *Buckdancer's Choice* (1965) and *Poems 1957–1967* (1967), Dickey has written literary criticism and a novel, *Deliverance* (1970), which was made into a film.

The Heaven of Animals

Here they are. The soft eyes open.
If they have lived in a wood
It is a wood.
If they have lived on plains
It is grass rolling   5
Under their feet forever.

Having no souls, they have come,
Anyway, beyond their knowing.
Their instincts wholly bloom
And they rise.   10
The soft eyes open.

To match them, the landscape flowers,
Outdoing, desperately
Outdoing what is required:
The richest wood,   15
The deepest field.

For some of these,
It could not be the place
It is, without blood.
These hunt, as they have done,   20
But with claws and teeth grown perfect,

More deadly than they can believe.
They stalk more silently,
And crouch on the limbs of trees,
And their descent   25
Upon the bright backs of their prey

May take years
In a sovereign floating of joy.
And those that are hunted
Know this as their life,   30
Their reward: to walk

Under such trees in full knowledge
Of what is in glory above them,
And to feel no fear,
But acceptance, compliance.   35
Fulfilling themselves without pain.

At the cycle's center,
They tremble, they walk
Under the tree,
They fall, they are torn,   40
They rise, they walk again.

For Study and Discussion

Analyzing and Interpreting the Poem
1. How does the speaker in this poem conceive of the animals' afterlife?
2a. What happens to the animals' instincts in heaven? **b.** How are the animals' surroundings in heaven different from those on earth?
3a. How are predatory animals different? **b.** How are the animals who are hunted in life rewarded?
4. According to the last line, what is the difference between the animals' heaven and their earth?

Cutout of animals, nineteenth century. Artist unknown. Watercolor and paper.
National Gallery of Art, Washington, gift of Edgar William and Bernice Chrysler Garbisch

Denise Levertov.
© Thomas Victor, 1987

Denise Levertov (lĕv′ər-tŭv) was born in Essex, England. During World War II, while working as a nurse in London hospitals, she wrote most of the poems for her first collection, *The Double Image* (1946). In 1947 she married the American writer Mitchell Goodman and settled in the United States, where she became a citizen in 1956.

Levertov's earliest poems were written in traditional stanza forms, but her admiration for such contemporary poets as Charles Olson, Robert Creeley, and Robert Duncan led her to the freer forms characteristic of modern poetry. One critic has called her poetry "a poetry of secrets." Indeed, many of her poems search for the deeper structures and implications in everyday events and objects. Levertov values the actual and the authentic, which she discovers chiefly by looking at the world as if for the first time, through newly awakened eyes. Appropriately, the titles of her books of poems include *With Eyes at the Back of Our Heads* (1960), *O Taste and See* (1964), and *Relearning the Alphabet* (1970).

Merritt Parkway°

As if it were
forever that they move, that we
keep moving—

    Under a wan sky where
    as the lights went on a star,   5
        pierced the haze & now
    follows steadily
           a constant
    above our six lanes
    the dreamlike continuum . . .   10

And the people—ourselves!
  the humans from inside the
cars, apparent
only at gasoline stops
           unsure,   15
    eyeing each other

      drink coffee hastily at the
    slot machines & hurry
back to the cars
    vanish   20
    into them forever, to
    keep moving—

Houses now & then beyond the
sealed road, the trees / trees, bushes
passing by, passing   25
    the cars that
      keep moving ahead of
us, past us, pressing behind us
           and
      over left, those that come   30
    toward us shining too brightly
moving relentlessly

    in six lanes, gliding
    north & south, speeding with
a slurred sound—   35

° **Merritt Parkway:** a highway in Connecticut.

For Study and Discussion

Analyzing and Interpreting the Poem

1. "Merritt Parkway" depicts a modern highway filled with cars. **a.** Why might the traffic seem to move "forever"? **b.** In what sense is the word *dreamlike* appropriate to this scene?

2. What details in lines 11–21 suggest that the people are more secure in their cars than with other people?

3a. What is described in lines 23–28? **b.** What does the word *sealed* imply about the relationship between the traffic and the rest of the world?

4. Modern poets often experiment with the arrangement of words on the page. How does the shape of this poem reinforce its meaning?

JAMES MERRILL
1926–

James Ingram Merrill is the son of one of the most famous brokers in the history of American finance, Charles Merrill, the founder of Merrill Lynch. Raised in New York in the cosmopolitan atmosphere of wealth and elegance such parentage suggests, James Merrill early was made aware of the multilingual possibilities of speech and composition by his European governess, "Mademoiselle." But at twelve years of age his childhood abruptly ended when his parents were divorced, and much of his poetry is a seeking, a journeying through memories of the past to the meaning of disrupted patterns in human lives. As Merrill's poetry developed, it became increasingly an amalgam of private memory and universal meaning: love brings pain and time brings loss.

After earning his B.A. degree at Amherst College in 1947, Merrill published *First Poems* (1951), a misleading title, for he had published other work previously. Living abroad (mostly in Athens) for half the time each year, Merrill settled at 10 Water Street, in Stonington, Connecticut, the source of the volume of poems *Water Street* (1962). Although some of his plays have been produced and he has published novels (*The Seraglio*, 1957, and *The (Diblos) Notebook*, 1965), Merrill is recognized primarily as a poet. He has won the National Book Award for *Nights and Days* (1966) and *Mirabell: Books of Number* (1978), the prestigious Bollingen Prize (1973), and the Pulitzer Prize for *Divine Comedies* (1976). In 1986 he became the Poet Laureate of Connecticut.

Merrill's early poems attracted attention for their wit and cool elegance and complete mastery of rhyme, meter, and poetic forms, but to many readers they seemed empty of any important human content. However, with the publication of "The Book of Ephraim," which appeared in *Divine Comedies* (1976), commentators began to mention Merrill in conjunction with such immortal poets as Dante and Yeats. "The Book of Ephraim," "Mira-

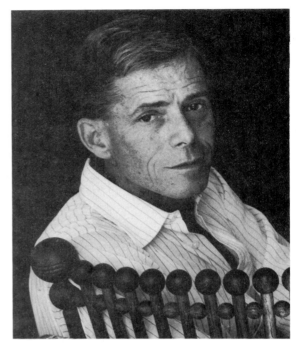

James Merrill.
© Rollie McKenna

bell: Books of Number," "Scripts for the Pageant" (1980), and a coda, "The Higher Keys," comprise a 500-page poem titled *The Changing Light at Sandover* (1982), which has been hailed by some as the greatest poem in English in the twentieth century.

All three major parts of *The Changing Light at Sandover* are based on the letters, numbers, and words on the Ouija (wē′jə) board. The poem itself is a revelation, through the guides from the other world, who communicate with the poet via the Ouija, of the nature of life and death and heaven and hell. In this long work, Merrill presents a vision of a few creative souls who give the race its only real immortality. The rest of the human race, still animalistic, selfish, shortsighted, and crude, mindlessly threatens to bring about annihilation through pollution, atomic weaponry, and all the other technological aspects of the modern world. The struggle between the two levels of human development and the poet's place in that struggle are the Ouija message that is indicative of Merrill's sense of the poet's high calling.

Detail from Inspiration of the Poet by Nicolas Poussin (1594–1665). Oil on canvas.
The Louvre, Paris,
Courtesy Art Resource

Marsyas

In Greek mythology Marsyas (mär′sē-əs) was a satyr who found Athena's discarded flute, an instrument the goddess had invented. Teaching himself to play the divine instrument, Marsyas thought he was as good as any god and he challenged Apollo, the god of music and poetry, to a contest of their art. The Muses were the judges; the stakes were that the winner could do what he wished with the loser. Apollo was pronounced the winner: the true god and his lyre were too much for a mere satyr using an instrument he had not invented and could not master like a god. Apollo, exacting his victor's vengeance on the upstart, skinned Marsyas alive.

I used to write in the café sometimes:
Poems on menus, read all over town
Or talked out before ever written down.
One day a girl brought in his latest book.
I opened it—stiff rhythms, gorgeous rhymes—   5
And made a face. Then crash! my cup upset.
Of twenty upward looks mine only met
His, that gold archaic lion's look

Wherein I saw my wiry person skinned
Of every skill it labored to acquire   10
And heard the plucked nerve's elemental twang.
They found me dangling where his golden wind
Inflicted so much music on the lyre
That no one could have told you what he sang.

Commentary

This is a poem about poetry. The speaker is a poet who suddenly has become aware of his own inadequacy when confronted by a greater poet.

In effect, the poem says that we recognize great art, but that we don't judge it as much as we are evaluated by it. Somehow we sense that it reveals a state of being greater than anything we lesser creatures attain. But so great is the power of true art that we can never quite absorb or understand it—it is too much for us. We hear the superhuman identity, the god, in the art, but we cannot really know it: "no one could have told you what he sang." Literally, the poem is about a poet who gives fashionable readings in all the modish cafés favored by artists: we know that he is in the mode, not above it. Also, he talks away many of his poems, so that they are never written. He is the fashionable artisan, not the true artist. He makes "a face" and an easy summation ("stiff rhythms, gorgeous rhymes") of a book of poems by a great master—and then suddenly is hit by the force of great poetry, the presence of a great artist.

Overwhelmed (he knocks his cup over with a crash), he is suddenly aware of an enormous sense of his own defeat, his own inferiority. He feels that his gifts are mere surface skills and that even those have been stripped from him in his knowledge of his own superficiality: "I saw my wiry person skinned / Of every skill it labored to acquire." The true god (Apollo, associated with both the sun and the moon, is the "golden" god) is merciless in his revelations; he allows only the flaying truth of his own greatness. Truth, art, the divine are one: like the lion they are the remorseless king, being in their very nature the greatness by which our lesser stature is measured. The broken, imitative lesser poet is found "dangling" in what is left of the great poet's song.

For Study and Discussion

Analyzing and Interpreting the Poem

1. The "I" narrating "Marsyas" is recounting something that happened to him. How does Merrill expand this bit of the narrator's autobiography into larger meaning by using mythology?

2. Note the careful crafting of *up* repeated in "my cup *up*set and "twenty *up*ward looks" (lines 6–7). "Twenty upward looks," subtly reinforced by repeated sound pattern, creates a whole scene. What is the physical scene and setting created by these few words?

3. Of the twenty people who look up quickly at the crash of the cup, only one fills the speaker's vision—the "golden" poet. **a.** What sense of the poet is created by the phrase, "that gold archaic lion's look"? **b.** Who is Marsyas in the poem?

4a. Consider the nature of the speaker's "every skill." That is, suppose that Merrill had had the speaker say, "I saw my wiry person *gutted* / Of every skill it labored to acquire." What is the difference between *gutted* and *skinned*? **b.** What does *skinned* suggest about the true depths of the speaker's "skill"? **c.** What is suggested by the fact that now the speaker refers *to his own person* as "it"?

5a. Why does the song of the true poet—the god's "golden wind"—*inflict* "so much music on the lyre"? **b.** Why should the touch of the divine be considered an *infliction*?

Writing About Literature

Comparing Poems

Compare Merrill's "Marsyas" with any two of the following: Marianne Moore's "Poetry" (page 772), William Carlos Williams' "The Red Wheelbarrow" (page 758), Wallace Stevens' "Anecdote of the Jar" (page 761), and Archibald MacLeish's "Ars Poetica" (page 790). Essentially, all these poems are about art, especially poetry. Explain how "Marsyas" and the two other poems agree in their assessment of art and how they differ. Or, perhaps you would rather write the same statement in a slightly different way: name the poems you choose and explain which (including "Marsyas") you like best and why. In making this statement you should explain not only what you like about the poem you choose, but also what you don't like about the poems you reject.

Rodolfo Gonzales was born in Denver, Colorado, the son of a migrant worker. Along with being a poet, he has been active in the civil rights movement for Mexican-Americans. He is the founder and director of the Crusade for Justice, a Denver-based social action group that gives legal and medical help to needy Mexican-Americans. His poem *I Am Joaquín* (1967) depicts the injustices experienced by people of Mexican origin.

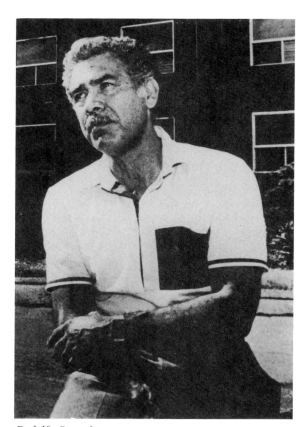

Rodolfo Gonzales.
Steve Groer, *Rocky Mountain News*, Denver

FROM

I Am Joaquín

I am in the eyes of woman,
      sheltered beneath
her shawl of black,
      deep and sorrowful
      eyes   5
that bear the pain of sons long buried
      or dying,
      dead
on the battlefield or on the barbed wire
      of social strife.   10

Her rosary she prays and fingers
endlessly
      like the family
working down a row of beets
      to turn around   15
      and work
      and work.
      There is no end.
Her eyes a mirror of all the warmth
      and all the love for me,   20
and I am her
and she is me.
      We face life together in sorrow,
      anger, joy, faith and wishful
      thoughts.   25

For Study and Discussion

Analyzing and Interpreting the Poem
1. The speaker in this poem expresses his sense of belonging to a people who feel the pressure of poverty and social struggle. What struggles might the mother's sons have endured?
2a. What comparison is drawn in lines 11–18?
b. What two important aspects of the family's life are joined in this simile?
3a. How does the speaker identify with the mother? **b.** If we imagine the woman as an embodiment of the whole people, what strengths do you think the poet finds in these people?

Anne Sexton was born in Newton, Massachusetts, and educated at Garland Junior College. In addition to writing, she worked as a high school teacher in Massachusetts and lectured at several colleges. She once said that poetry "should be a shock to the senses. It should almost hurt." Like John Berryman, Sylvia Plath, and others, she was one of the "confessional" poets, a group strongly influenced by Robert Lowell to turn to the intimacies of their own lives and feelings for their subjects. Among her collections of poetry are *All My Pretty Ones* (1962), *Live or Die* (1967), which won the Pulitzer Prize, *Love Poems* (1969), and *The Book of Folly* (1972). Much of her poetry was colored by the anguish of recurring mental illness and experiences in hospitals. But, in poems like "The Fortress," she also reached out with love to embrace the suffering of others and to protect them from life's "terrible changes."

Anne Sexton.
© Rollie McKenna

The Fortress

(While Taking a Nap with Linda)

Under the pink quilted covers,
I hold the pulse that counts your blood.
I think the woods outdoors
are half asleep,
left over from summer   5
like a stack of books after a flood,
left over like the promises I never keep.
On the right, the scrub pine tree
waits like a fruit store
holding up bunches of tufted broccoli.   10

We watch the wind from our square bed.
I press down my index finger,

half in jest, half in dread,
on the brown mole
under your left eye, inherited   15
from my right cheek—a spot of danger
where a bewitched worm ate its way through our soul
in search of beauty. Child, since July
the leaves have been fed
secretly from a pool of beet-red dye.   20

And sometimes they are battle green
with trunks as wet as hunters' boots,
smacked hard by the wind, clean
as oilskins. No,
the wind's not off the ocean.   25
Yes, it cried in your room like a wolf
and your ponytail hurt you. That was a long time ago.
The wind rolled the tide like a dying
woman. She wouldn't sleep;
she rolled there all night, grunting and sighing.   30

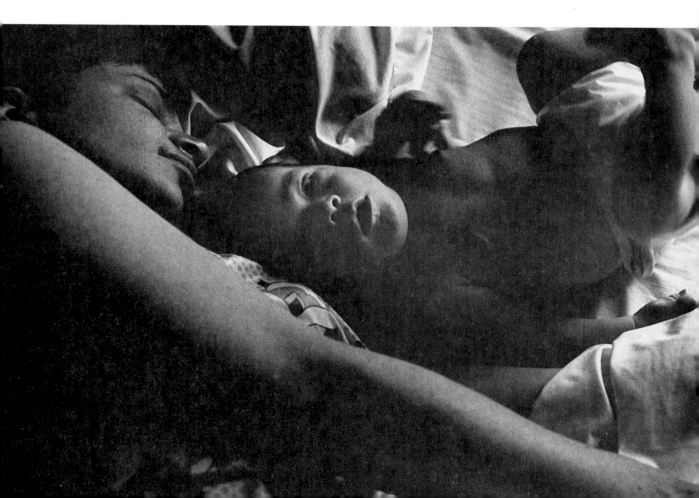

Darling, life is not in my hands;
life with its terrible changes
will take you, bombs or glands,
your own child at
your breast, your own house on your own land.   35
Outside, the bittersweet turns orange.
Before she died, my mother and I picked those fat
branches, finding orange nipples
on the gray wire strands.
We weeded the forest, curing trees like cripples.   40

Your feet thump-thump against my back
and you whisper to yourself. Child,
what are you wishing? What pact
are you making?
What mouse runs between your eyes? What ark   45
can I fill for you when the world goes wild?
The woods are under water, their weeds are shaking
in the tide; birches like zebra fish
flash by in a pack.
Child, I cannot promise that you will get your wish.   50

I cannot promise very much.
I give you the images I know.
Lie still with me and watch.
A pheasant moves
by like a seal, pulled through the mulch   55
by his thick white collar. He's on show
like a clown. He drags a beige feather that he removed,
one time, from an old lady's hat.
We laugh and we touch.
I promise you love. Time will not take away that.   60

For Study and Discussion

Analyzing and Interpreting the Poem

1. The speaker in this poem silently addresses her sleeping daughter. What does the mole under the daughter's eye signify for the speaker?

2a. What feelings are suggested in the third stanza by the descriptions of the trees and the wind? **b.** How is the wind personified?

3. The daughter is clearly very young and innocent. In lines 42–43, the speaker imagines that the child is hopeful. What attitude toward life does the speaker pose against the child's hopefulness?

4. Genesis 6:9–22 tells the story of Noah and the ark. Which lines in this poem contain an allusion to the story of Noah?

5a. In spite of the hardships of life, what can the speaker finally promise her daughter? **b.** What is "the fortress"?

ADRIENNE RICH
1929–

Adrienne Rich's interest in poetry began while she was still a child in Baltimore, Maryland. Her first book, *A Change of World* (1951), was recommended for publication by W. H. Auden the year Rich graduated from Radcliffe College. Her early traditional poems, accomplished as they were, proved to be only the beginning of her poetic development. As time passed, she abandoned formal stanzas for free verse. Her poems took up an issue that has preoccupied many artists: how to reconcile a desire for love and permanent relationships with an active participation in a world of conflicting events. "I think I began at this point," she has said, "to feel that 'struggle' was not something 'out there' but 'in here' and of the essence of my condition." Her poems explore her feelings about being a woman, about the use of intelligence and emotion, and about the significance of struggle.

Adrienne Rich.
© Nancy Crampton

Song

You're wondering if I'm lonely:
OK then, yes, I'm lonely
as a plane rides lonely and level
on its radio beam, aiming
across the Rockies   5
for the blue-strung aisles
of an airfield on the ocean

You want to ask, am I lonely?
Well, of course, lonely
as a woman driving across country   10
day after day, leaving behind
mile after mile
little towns she might have stopped
and lived and died in, lonely

If I'm lonely   15
it must be the loneliness
of waking first, of breathing
dawn's first cold breath on the city
of being the one awake
in a house wrapped in sleep   20

If I'm lonely
it's with the rowboat ice-fast on the shore
in the last red light of the year
that knows what it is, that knows it's neither
ice nor mud nor winter light   25
but wood, with a gift for burning

For Study and Discussion

Analyzing and Interpreting the Poem

1. The speaker in this poem enjoys being alone, though others assume she is lonely. She compares her "loneliness" to that of an airplane. What compensates for the airplane's loneliness?

2a. How does the comparison to the woman driving cross-country suggest the need for self-reliance when one is alone? **b.** According to stanza 3, what special pleasure can one enjoy if alone?

3a. The rowboat at the end of the poem sits alone on the frozen shore, apparently useless and forgotten. Yet what "gift" or value does it have? **b.** How does the example of the rowboat support the view that a person may appear lonely but really be quite happy and secure?

Sylvia Plath.

SYLVIA PLATH
1932–1963

Sylvia Plath was born and grew up in Boston. During her junior year at Smith College, she suffered a nervous breakdown but nevertheless returned to Smith to graduate with high honors. After leaving Smith, she attended Cambridge University in England and there married the English poet Ted Hughes. After returning to America to teach at Smith for a year, she settled in England with her husband. Her first book, *The Colossus*, appeared in 1960. It was the only volume of her poems to be published during her lifetime. The three volumes that were published after her death make it plain that the last years of her short life were deeply troubled. Like Robert Lowell, John Berryman, Anne Sexton, and others, Sylvia Plath has been called a "confessional" poet, because much of her writing deals with personal experiences.

Mushrooms

Overnight, very
Whitely, discreetly,
Very quietly

Our toes, our noses
Take hold on the loam,   5
Acquire the air.

Nobody sees us,
Stops us, betrays us;
The small grains make room.

Soft fists insist on   10
Heaving the needles,
The leafy bedding,

Even the paving.
Our hammers, our rams,
Earless and eyeless,   15

Perfectly voiceless,
Widen the crannies,
Shoulder through holes. We

Diet on water,
On crumbs of shadow,   20
Bland-mannered, asking

Little or nothing.
So many of us!
So many of us!

We are shelves, we are   25
Tables, we are meek,
We are edible,

Nudgers and shovers
In spite of ourselves.
Our kind multiplies: 30

We shall by morning
Inherit the earth.
Our foot's in the door.

For Study and Discussion

Analyzing and Interpreting the Poem

1a. What process is described in this poem? **b.** Do you find the poem humorous? Frightening? Both?
2a. What images in the fourth and fifth stanzas give the mushrooms a sinister quality? **b.** *Take hold, acquire, insist, widen,* and *shoulder* are among the verbs used to describe the activity of the mushrooms. How do these words add to the poem's ominous mood?

3. What view of nature is presented in this poem?
4a. What does the poem—especially in the context of the last stanza—say about the meek in spirit?
b. Does the poem want them to triumph?

Leslie Marmon Silko.

Leslie Marmon Silko was born in Albuquerque, New Mexico, and grew up on the Laguna Pueblo Reservation. She now lives Tucson, Arizona. She was educated at the University of New Mexico and at present teaches literature and creative writing there. In addition to poems, she has published short stories and a novel, *Ceremony* (1977). She has written the following note for her poem "Story from Bear Country": "The Pueblo and Navajo people in the Southwest believe that bears are special animals which should be respected. The people believe that if humans are careful not to trespass, then the bears will not harm them. However, there are stories about people who accidentally wandered into bear territory. Usually this happened to small children who got lost while camping with their parents, but sometimes an adult carelessly stepped into bear country. Contrary to popular culture stereotypes about bears being dangerous killers, the old stories reveal that the bears 'adopted' the children and adults who wandered too close to them. Years later, hunters would come home and report that far off in the distance they had sighted a human being among a group of bears feeding on wild grapes."

Story from Bear Country

You will know
when you walk
in bear country
By the silence
flowing swiftly between the juniper trees   5
by the sundown colors of sandrock
all around you.

You may smell damp earth
scratched away
from yucca roots   10
You may hear snorts and growls
slow and massive sounds
from caves
in the cliffs high above you.

It is difficult to explain   15
how they call you
All but a few who went to them
left behind families
            grandparents
            and sons   20
            a good life.

The problem is
you will never want to return.

Their beauty will overcome your memory
like winter sun   25
melting ice shadows from snow
And you will remain with them

locked forever inside yourself
      your eyes will see you
        dark shaggy and thick.   30

We can send bear priests
loping after you
their medicine bags
bouncing against their chests
Naked legs painted black   35
bear claw necklaces
rattling against
their capes of blue spruce.

They will follow your trail
into the narrow canyon   40
through the blue-gray mountain sage
to the clearing
where you stopped to look back
and saw only bear tracks
behind you.   45

When they call
faint memories
will writhe around your heart
and startle you with their distance.
But the others will listen   50
because bear priests sing
beautiful songs.
They must
if they are ever to call you back.

They will try to bring you   55
step by step
back to the place you stopped
and found only bear prints in the sand
where your feet had been.

Whose voice is this?   60
You may wonder
hearing this story when
after all
you are alone
hiking in these canyons and hills   65
while your wife and sons are waiting
back at the car for you.

But you have been listening to me
for some time now
from the very beginning in fact   70
and you are alone in this canyon of stillness
not even cedar birds flutter.

See, the sun is going down now
the sandrock is washed in its colors
Don't be afraid   75
      we love you
      we've been calling you
      all this time

Go ahead
turn around   80
see the shape
of your footprints
in the sand.

For Study and Discussion

Analyzing and Interpreting the Poem

1. Once a wanderer is enchanted by bear country, what traits of bears does that person assume?
2a. According to lines 46–49, what becomes of wanderers' feelings for the human world once they have found bear country? **b.** How do the bear priests try to bring the lost wanderers back to humanity?
3. At the end of the poem, we learn that the speaker is addressing someone who has been wandering alone in bear country. **a.** Who does the speaker turn out to be? **b.** What has happened to the listener in the course of the poem?

MODERN NONFICTION

The selections in this unit represent three basic nonfiction forms: *essay, speech,* and *biography.*

The word *essay* comes from the French word *essai,* meaning "attempt." This term was first used to distinguish the essay from more formal, elaborate kinds of discourse. Yet while an essay may be a relatively unrestricted kind of writing, it does not lack form. If a writer's tone is humorous, personal, or relaxed, the essay is considered informal and is generally intended to entertain as well as to awaken thought. E. B. White and S. J. Perelman are masters of this style. If a writer's tone is serious or objective, with more rigid adherence to rules of discourse (stating and developing a theme according to principles of unity, coherence, and emphasis), then the essay is considered formal and probably is intended to instruct. One kind of formal essay is the *critical* essay, which deals with literature or any of the arts. James Baldwin's "The Creative Process" is an excellent example of this type of essay.

Speeches are intended primarily for oral presentation, but many, such as the three reprinted here, are meant to be read silently as well. Two of these speeches were delivered upon the writer's acceptance of an award: Faulkner used his platform to address a central question of history; Ellison spoke of his own literary concerns and the forces that helped shape his writing. Hinojosa-Smith, speaking at a conference on the Texas literary tradition, talked about the importance of "place" in his own writing.

In biography (which includes autobiography), authors write about their own lives or the lives of others. As a literary form, biography has recently undergone significant changes. Many nineteenth-century biographies were eulogistic—and often dull. Modern psychological studies, with their emphasis on a person's inner life and on the significant events of childhood, have stimulated a broader and deeper exploration of the personal rather than the public character of a subject. And, with the advent of realism, writers have dared to assess the failings as well as the virtues of their subjects. Many biographers have come to regard themselves as artists who interpret rather than record facts, or as portrait painters who create an impression of their subject's essential personality. They have borrowed the devices of the novelist, avoiding dull stretches, concentrating on revealing incidents, and taking the liberty of entering a subject's mind. An artful example of this approach, in which the biography is "fictionalized" or "impressionistic," is John Dos Passos' sketch of Henry Ford. The remaining selections in this unit are examples of autobiographical writing by celebrated writers: Zora Neale Hurston, Thomas Wolfe, Ernesto Galarza, Richard Wright, N. Scott Momaday, and Richard Rodriguez.

E. B. White as a staff member at *The New Yorker,* 1954.

E. B. WHITE
1899–1985

E. B. White is regarded by many readers as one of our most distinguished essayists and stylists. His friend James Thurber once wrote of White's "silver and crystal sentences which had a ring like the ring of nobody else's sentences in the world." From his own advice to young writers, it is evident that White was above all a careful, patient writer. He counseled, "The approach to style is by way of plainness, simplicity, orderliness, sincerity." In a striking metaphor, he commented that a writer must be as alert, quick, and patient as a hunter: "Writing is, for most, laborious and slow. The mind travels faster than the pen; consequently, writing becomes a question of learning to make occasional wing shots, bringing down the bird of thought as it flashes by. A writer is a gunner, sometimes waiting in his blind for something to come in, sometimes roaming the countryside hoping to scare something up. Like other gunners, he must cultivate patience; he may have to work many covers to bring down one partridge." Like many supremely skillful athletes, White was not a flashy, but a deceptively simple, performer.

Yet he was so sure in his craft that many of his seemingly casual sentences linger in the memory.

The son of an executive in a piano manufacturing company, Elwyn Brooks White grew up in Mount Vernon, New York. While attending Cornell University, he was editor of the Cornell *Daily Sun* and won an Associated Press Award for the best undergraduate editorial of the year. It was at Cornell that White acquired the nickname "Andy." As Thurber explained in an essay on his friend, "He went to Cornell, and it seems that every White who goes there is nicknamed Andy for the simple if rather faraway reason that the first president of the University was named Andrew White." For a number of years White was a staff member of *The New Yorker*, and he played a major part in shaping the distinctive style of that magazine. His essays and stories have been collected in *Quo Vadimus, One Man's Meat, The Second Tree from the Corner, The Points of My Compass*, and *Essays of E. B. White*. In addition to being a fine essayist, White was a very skillful writer of light verse. His verse has been collected in *The Lady Is Cold* and *The Fox of Peapack*. White wrote three popular books for children, *Stuart Little, Charlotte's Web*, and *The Trumpet of the Swan*. With his wife, Katharine S. White, he edited *A Subtreasury of American Humor*. *Letters of E. B. White*, edited by Dorothy Lobrano Guth, was published in 1976. After his retirement from *The New Yorker* staff, White lived on a farm in Maine. Like one of his favorite subjects, Thoreau, he pursued simplicity in his life as well as in his writing.

Walden
(June 1939)

Miss Nims, take a letter to Henry David Thoreau.

Dear Henry: I thought of you the other afternoon as I was approaching Concord, doing fifty on Route 62. That is a high speed at which to hold a philosopher in one's mind, but in this century we are a nimble bunch.

On one of the lawns in the outskirts of the village, a woman was cutting the grass with a motorized lawn mower. What made me think of you was that the machine had rather got away from her, although she was game enough, and in the brief glimpse I had of the scene, it appeared to me that the lawn was mowing the lady. She kept a tight grip on the handles, which throbbed violently with every explosion of the one-cylinder motor, and as she steered around bushes and lurched along at a reluctant trot behind her impetuous servant, she looked like a puppy who had grabbed something that was too much for him. Concord hasn't changed much, Henry; the farm implements and the animals still have the upper hand.

I may as well admit that I was journeying to Concord with the deliberate intention of visiting your woods; for although I have never knelt at the grave of a philosopher nor placed wreaths on moldy poets, and have often gone a mile out of my way to avoid some place of historical interest, I have always wanted to see Walden Pond. The account which you left of your sojourn there is, you will be amused to learn, a document of increasing pertinence; each year it seems to gain a little headway, as the world loses ground. We may all be transcendental yet, whether we like it or not. As our common complexities increase, any tale of individual simplicity (and yours is the best written and the cockiest) acquires a new fascination; as our goods accumulate, but not our well-being, your report of an existence without material adornment takes on a certain awkward credibility.

My purpose in going to Walden Pond, like yours, was not to live cheaply or to live dearly there, but to transact some private business with the fewest obstacles. Approaching Concord, doing forty, doing forty-five, doing fifty, the steering wheel held snug in my palms, the highway held grimly in my vision, the crown of the road now serving me (on the right-hand curves), now defeating me (on the left-hand curves), I began to rouse myself from the stupefaction which a day's motor journey induces. It was a delicious evening, Henry, when the whole body is one sense, and imbibes delight through every pore, if I may coin a phrase. Fields were richly brown where the harrow, drawn by the stripped Ford, had lately sunk its teeth; pastures were green; and overhead the sky had that same everlasting great look which you will find on page 144 of the Oxford pocket edition.[1] I could feel the road entering me, through tire, wheel, spring, and cushion; shall I not have intelligence with earth too? Am I not partly leaves and vegetable mold myself?—a man of infinite horsepower, yet partly leaves.

Stay with me on 62, and it will take you into Concord. As I say, it was a delicious evening. The snake had come forth to die in a bloody S on the highway, the wheel upon its head, its bowels flat now and exposed. The turtle had come up too to cross the road and die in the attempt, its hard shell smashed under the rubber blow, its intestinal yearning (for the other side of the road) forever squashed. There was a sign by the wayside which announced that the road had a "cotton surface." You wouldn't know what that is, but neither, for that matter, did I. There is a cryptic ingredient in many of our modern improvements—we are awed and pleased without knowing quite what we are enjoying. It is something to be traveling on a road with a cotton surface.

The civilization round Concord today is an odd distillation of city, village, farm, and manor. The houses, yards, fields look not quite suburban, not quite rural. Under the bronze beech and the blue spruce of the departed baron grazes the milch[2] goat of the heirs. Under the porte-cochere[3] stands the reconditioned station wagon; under the grape arbor sit the puppies for sale. (But why do men degenerate ever? What makes families run out?)

It was June and everywhere June was publishing her immemorial stanza; in the lilacs, in the syringa,[4] in the freshly edged paths and the sweetness of moist, beloved gardens, and the little wire wickets that preserve the tulips' front. Farmers were already moving the fruits of their toil into their yards, arranging the rhubarb, the asparagus, the strictly fresh eggs on the painted stands under the little shed roofs with the patent shingles. And though it was almost a hundred years since you had taken your ax and started cutting out your home on Walden Pond, I was interested to observe that the philosophical spirit was still alive in Massachusetts: in the center of a vacant lot, some boys were assembling the framework of the rude shelter, their whole mind and skill concentrated in the rather inauspicious helter-skelter of studs and rafters. They too were escaping from town, to live naturally, in a rich blend of savagery and philosophy.

That evening, after supper at the inn, I strolled out into the twilight to dream my shapeless transcendental dreams and see that the car was locked up for the night (first open the right front door, then reach over, straining, and pull up the handles of the left rear and the left front till you hear the click, then the handle of the right rear, then shut the right front but open it again, remembering that the key is still in the ignition switch, remove the key, shut the right front again with a bang, push the tiny keyhole cover to one side, insert

1. **Oxford pocket edition:** an edition of Thoreau's *Walden* published by the Oxford University Press.

2. **milch:** milk-giving.
3. **porte-cochere** (pôrt′kō-shâr′): carport, consisting of an extended roof that provides shelter for a car.
4. **syringa** (sə-rĭng′gə): a large white flower.

key, turn, and withdraw). It is what we all do, Henry. It is called locking the car. It is said to confuse thieves and keep them from making off with the lap robe. Four doors to lock behind one robe. The driver himself never uses a lap robe, the free movement of his legs being vital to the operation of the vehicle; so that when he locks the car, it is a pure and unselfish act. I have in my life gained very little essential heat from lap robes, yet I have ever been at pains to lock them up.

The evening was full of sounds, some of which would have stirred your memory. The robins still love the elms of New England villages at sundown. There is enough of the thrush in them to make song inevitable at the end of day, and enough of the tramp to make them hang round the dwellings of men. A robin, like many another American, dearly loves a white house with green blinds. Concord is still full of them.

Your fellow townsmen were stirring abroad—not many afoot, most of them in their cars; and the sound which they made in Concord at evening was a rustling and a whispering. The sound lacks steadfastness and is wholly unlike that of a train. A train, as you know who lived so near the Fitchburg line, whistles once or twice sadly and is gone, trailing a memory in smoke, soothing to ear and mind. Automobiles, skirting a village green, are like flies that have gained the inner ear—they buzz, cease, pause, start, shift, stop, halt, brake, and the whole effect is a nervous polytone,[5] curiously disturbing.

As I wandered along, the toc-toc of ping-pong balls drifted from an attic window. In front of the Reuben Brown house, a Buick was drawn up. At the wheel, motionless, his hat upon his head, a man sat, listening to Amos and Andy[6] on the radio (it is a drama of many scenes and without an end). The deep voice of Andrew Brown, emerging from the car, al-

though it originated more than two hundred miles away, was unstrained by distance. When you used to sit on the shore of your pond on Sunday morning, listening to the church bells of Acton and Concord, you were aware of the excellent filter of the intervening atmosphere. Science has attended to that, and sound now maintains its intensity without regard for distance. Properly sponsored, it goes on forever.

A fire engine, out for a trial spin, roared past Emerson's house, hot with readiness for public duty. Over the barn roofs the martins dipped and chittered. A swarthy daughter of an asparagus grower, in culottes, shirt, and bandanna, pedaled past on her bicycle. It was indeed a delicious evening, and I returned to the inn (I believe it was your house once) to rock with the old ladies on the concrete veranda.

Next morning early I started afoot for Walden, out Main Street and down Thoreau, past the depot and the Minuteman Chevrolet Company. The morning was fresh, and in a bean field along the way, I flushed an agriculturalist, quietly studying his beans. Thoreau Street soon joined Number 126, an artery of the State. We number our highways nowadays, our speed being so great we can remember little of their quality or character and are lucky to remember their number. (Men have an indistinct notion that if they keep up this activity long enough, all will at length ride somewhere, in next to no time.) Your pond is on 126.

I knew I must be nearing your woodland retreat when the Golden Pheasant lunchroom came into view—Sealtest ice cream, toasted sandwiches, hot frankfurters, waffles, tonics, and lunches. Were I the proprietor, I should add rice, Indian meal, and molasses[7]—just for old time's sake. The Pheasant, incidentally, is for sale: a chance for some nature lover who wishes to set himself up beside a pond in the Concord atmosphere and live deliberately, fronting only the essential facts of life on

5. **polytone:** combination of sounds.
6. **Amos and Andy:** a radio serial popular in the 1930s and 1940s, presenting mostly comic episodes. Andrew Brown was Andy's full name.

7. **rice . . . molasses:** the main ingredients of Thoreau's diet at Walden Pond.

Number 126. Beyond the Pheasant was a place called Walden Breezes, an oasis whose porch pillars were made of old green shutters sawed into lengths. On the porch was a distorting mirror, to give the traveler a comical image of himself, who had miraculously learned to gaze in an ordinary glass without smiling. Behind the Breezes, in a sun-parched clearing, dwelt your philosophical descendants in their trailers, each trailer the size of your hut, but all grouped together for the sake of congeniality. Trailer people leave the city, as you did, to discover solitude and in any weather, at any hour of the day or night, to improve the nick of time; but they soon collect in villages and get bogged deeper in the mud than ever. The camp behind Walden Breezes was just rousing itself to the morning. The ground was packed hard under the heel, and the sun came through the clearing to bake the soil and enlarge the wry smile of cramped housekeeping. Cushman's bakery truck had stopped to deliver an early basket of rolls. A camp dog, seeing me in the road, barked petulantly. A man emerged from one of the trailers and set forth with a bucket to draw water from some forest tap.

Leaving the highway, I turned off into the woods toward the pond, which was apparent through the foliage. The floor of the forest was strewn with dried old oak leaves and *Transcripts*.[8] From beneath the flattened popcorn wrapper (*granum explosum*) peeped the frail violet. I followed a footpath and descended to the water's edge. The pond lay clear and blue in the morning light, as you have seen it so many times. In the shallows a man's waterlogged shirt undulated gently. A few flies came out to greet me and convoy me to your cove, past the No Bathing signs on which the fellows and the girls had scrawled their names. I felt strangely excited suddenly to be snooping around your premises, tiptoeing along watchfully, as though not to tread by mistake upon the intervening century. Before I got to the cove, I heard something which seemed to me quite wonderful: I heard your frog, a full, clear *troonk*, guiding me, still hoarse and solemn, bridging the years as the robins had bridged them in the sweetness of the village evening. But he soon quit, and I came on a couple of young boys throwing stones at him.

Your front yard is marked by a bronze tablet set in a stone. Four small granite posts, a few feet away, show where the house was. On top of the tablet was a pair of faded blue bathing trunks with a white stripe. Back of it is a pile of stones, a sort of cairn, left by your visitors as a tribute, I suppose. It is a rather ugly little heap of stones, Henry. In fact, the hillside itself seems faded, browbeaten; a few tall, skinny pines, bare of lower limbs, a smattering of young maples in suitable green, some birches and oaks, and a number of trees felled by the last big wind. It was from the bole[9] of one of these fallen pines, torn up by the roots, that I extracted the stone which I added to the cairn—a sentimental act in which I was interrupted by a small terrier from a nearby picnic group, who confronted me and wanted to know about the stone.

I sat down for a while on one of the posts of your house to listen to the bluebottles and the dragonflies. The invaded glade sprawled shabby and mean at my feet, but the flies were tuned to the old vibration. There were the remains of a fire in your ruins, but I doubt that it was yours; also two beer bottles trodden into the soil and become part of earth. A young oak had taken root in your house, and two or three ferns, unrolling like the ticklers at a banquet. The only other furnishings were a DuBarry pattern sheet, a page torn from a picture magazine, and some crusts in wax paper.

Before I quit, I walked clear round the pond and found the place where you used to sit on the northeast side to get the sun in the fall, and the beach where you got sand for scrub-

---

8. **Transcripts:** *The Evening Transcript* was a Boston newspaper.

9. **bole:** trunk.

Swimmers at Walden Pond, which is now a recreation area.

bing your floor. On the eastern side of the pond, where the highway borders it, the State has built dressing rooms for swimmers, a float with diving towers, drinking fountains of porcelain, and rowboats for hire. The pond is in fact a State Preserve, and carries a twenty-dollar fine for picking wildflowers, a decree signed in all solemnity by your fellow citizens Walter C. Wardwell, Erson B. Barlow, and Nathaniel I. Bowditch. There was a smell of creosote[10] where they had been building a wide wooden stairway to the road and the

10. **creosote** (krē′ə-sōt′): tar.

parking area. Swimmers and boaters were arriving; bodies plunged vigorously into the water and emerged wet and beautiful in the bright air. As I left, a boatload of town boys were splashing about in mid-pond, kidding and fooling, the young fellows singing at the tops of their lungs in a wild chorus:

"Amer-ica, Amer-ica, God shed his grace on thee,
And crown thy good with brotherhood
From sea to shi-ning sea!"

I walked back to town along the railroad, following your custom. The rails were expand-

E. B. White **871**

ing noisily in the hot sun, and on the slope of the roadbed, the wild grape and the blackberry sent up their creepers to the track.

The expense of my brief sojourn in Concord was:

Canvas shoes	$1.95	
Baseball bat	.25	gifts to
Left-handed fielder's		take back
glove	1.25	to a boy
Hotel and meals	4.25	
In all	$7.70	

As you see, this amount was almost what you spent for food for eight months. I cannot defend the shoes or the expenditure for shelter and food: they reveal a meanness and grossness in my nature which you would find contemptible. The baseball equipment, however, is the kind of impediment with which you were never on even terms. You must remember that the house where you practiced the sort of economy which I respect was haunted only by mice and squirrels. You never had to cope with a shortstop.

Reading Check

1. What does White say is his reason for journeying to Concord?
2. What does White think is missing from the lunchroom's menu?
3. How is the site of Thoreau's house marked?
4. What monument has been left by visitors to the site of Thoreau's house?

For Study and Discussion

Analyzing and Interpreting the Essay

1. At the beginning of the essay, White observes a woman with a motorized lawn mower. What is the significance of the scene he describes?

2a. Why does White feel that Thoreau's book *Walden* each year "seems to gain a little headway, as the world loses ground"? **b.** Throughout the essay there is a contrast between Thoreau's life at Walden Pond and modern life. Referring to details in the essay, tell how life around Walden Pond has changed since Thoreau's time.

3. White observes that "the philosophical spirit [is] still alive in Massachusetts." **a.** How does this observation apply to the group of boys who are "assembling the framework of the rude shelter"? **b.** In what ways are these boys like Thoreau?

4a. What is White's attitude toward the trailer camp? **b.** What irony can you find in the paragraph dealing with the camp (page 870)? **c.** How does White use irony throughout the essay to express his attitudes toward the modern world? Cite specific passages to support your answer.

5a. Why do you think White wrote this essay in the form of a letter addressed to Thoreau instead of addressing himself directly to the reader? **b.** How does the last paragraph of the essay indicate White's position in the modern world?

Creative Writing

Composing a Humorous Letter

Write a humorous letter to some person you admire, living or dead. In your letter, talk about an issue that is important to both of you. If the person is a writer, you may wish to follow E. B. White's example in alluding to or quoting briefly from that person's works.

S. J. Perelman.
© Nancy Crampton

The humorist Sidney Joseph Perelman, whom Eudora Welty called "a living National Treasure," was born in Brooklyn, New York. He graduated from Brown University in 1925 and began supporting himself by writing humorous pieces for various magazines. In 1929 he moved to Hollywood, where he became well known as the scriptwriter for the best Marx Brothers comedies.

Over the years his articles, stories, and comic travel adventures appeared in various magazines, especially *The New Yorker*. Periodically they were collected in book form and issued to his countless readers who delight in what he once termed "weird grammatical flora."

Perelman excelled in writing parody and satire and in depicting the zany misadventures of ordinary people trying to cope with such complexities of modern life as assembling a model truck in the presence of anxious children or safely retrieving a sport coat from the cleaner without resorting to a lawsuit.

Insert Flap "A" and Throw Away

One stifling summer afternoon last August, in the attic of a tiny stone house in Pennsylvania, I made a most interesting discovery: the shortest, cheapest method of inducing a nervous breakdown ever perfected. In this technique, the subject is placed in a sharply sloping attic heated to 340°F. and given a mothproof closet known as the Jiffy-Cloz to assemble. The Jiffy-Cloz, procurable at any department store or neighborhood insane asylum, consists of half a dozen gigantic sheets of red cardboard, two plywood doors, a clothes rack, and a packet of staples. With these is included a set of instructions mimeographed in pale-violet ink, fruity with phrases like "Pass Section F through Slot AA, taking care not to fold tabs behind washers (see Fig. 9)." The cardboard is so processed that as the subject struggles convulsively to force the staple through, it suddenly buckles, plunging the staple deep into his thumb. He

S. J. Perelman   **873**

thereupon springs up with a dolorous cry and smites his knob (Section K) on the rafters (RR). As a final demonic touch, the Jiffy-Cloz people cunningly omit four of the staples necessary to finish the job, so that after indescribable purgatory, the best the subject can possibly achieve is a sleazy, capricious structure which would reduce any self-respecting moth to helpless laughter. The cumulative frustration, the tropical heat, and the soft, ghostly chuckling of the moths are calculated to unseat the strongest mentality.

In a period of rapid technological change, however, it was inevitable that a method as cumbersome as the Jiffy-Cloz would be superseded. It would be superseded at exactly nine-thirty Christmas morning by a device called the Self-Running 10-Inch Scale-Model Delivery-Truck Kit Powered by Magic Motor, costing twenty-nine cents. About nine on that particular morning, I was spread-eagled on my bed, indulging in my favorite sport of mouth-breathing, when a cork fired from a child's air gun mysteriously lodged in my throat. The pellet proved awkward for a while, but I finally ejected it by flailing the little marksman (and his sister, for good measure) until their welkins rang,[1] and sauntered in to breakfast. Before I could choke down a healing fruit juice, my consort, a tall, regal creature indistinguishable from Cornelia, the Mother of the Gracchi,[2] except that her foot was entangled in a roller skate, swept in. She extended a large, unmistakable box covered with diagrams.

"Now don't start making excuses," she whined. "It's just a simple cardboard toy. The directions are on the back——"

"Look, dear," I interrupted, rising hurriedly and pulling on my overcoat, "it clean slipped my mind. I'm supposed to take a lesson in crosshatching[3] at Zim's School of Cartooning today."

"On Christmas?" she asked suspiciously.

"Yes, it's the only time they could fit me in," I countered glibly. "This is the big week for crosshatching, you know, between Christmas and New Year's."

"Do you think you ought to go in your pajamas?" she asked.

"Oh, that's O.K.," I smiled. "We often work in our pajamas up at Zim's. Well, goodbye now. If I'm not home by Thursday, you'll find a cold snack in the safe-deposit box." My subterfuge, unluckily, went for naught, and in a trice I was sprawled on the nursery floor, surrounded by two lambkins and ninety-eight segments of the Self-Running 10-Inch Scale-Model Delivery-Truck Construction Kit.

The theory of the kit was simplicity itself, easily intelligible to Kettering of General Motors, Professor Millikan, or any first-rate physicist. Taking as my starting point the only sentence I could comprehend, "Fold down on all lines marked 'fold down'; fold up on all lines marked 'fold up,'" I set the children to work. In a few moments, my skin was suffused with a delightful tingling sensation and I was ready for the second phase, lightly referred to in the directions as "Preparing the Spring Motor Unit." As nearly as I could determine after twenty minutes of mumbling, the Magic Motor ("No Electricity—No Batteries—Nothing to Wind—Motor Never Wears Out") was an accordion-pleated affair operating by torsion,[4] attached to the axles. "It is necessary," said the text, "to cut a slight notch in each of the axles with a knife (see Fig. C). To find the exact place to cut this notch, lay one of the axles over diagram at bottom of page."

"Well, now we're getting some place!" I boomed, with a false gusto that deceived nobody. "Here, Buster, run in and get Daddy a knife."

"I dowanna," quavered the boy, backing away. "You always cut yourself at this stage." I gave the wee fellow an indulgent pat on the

---

1. **their welkins rang:** *Welkin* is an archaic word for sky; thus, the skies rang with their screams.
2. **the Gracchi** (grăk′ī): the brothers Gaius and Tiberius Gracchus, famous Roman statesmen.
3. **crosshatching:** in drawing, a method of shading with a series of crossing parallel lines.

4. **torsion** (tôr′shən): tension caused by the twisting of a wire or rod, which in turn produces motion.

head that flattened it slightly, to teach him civility, and commandeered a long, serrated bread knife from the kitchen. "Now watch me closely, children," I ordered. "We place the axle on the diagram as in Fig. C, applying a strong downward pressure on the knife handle at all times." The axle must have been a factory second, because an instant later I was in the bathroom grinding my teeth in agony and attempting to stanch the flow of blood. Ultimately, I succeeded in contriving a rough bandage and slipped back into the nursery without awaking the children's suspicions. An agreeable surprise awaited me. Displaying a mechanical aptitude clearly inherited from their sire, the rascals had put together the chassis of the delivery truck.

"Very good indeed," I complimented (naturally, one has to exaggerate praise to develop a child's self-confidence). "Let's see—what's the next step? Ah, yes, 'Lock into box shape by inserting tabs C, D, E, F, G, H, J, K, and L into slots C, D, E, F, G, H, J, K, and L. Ends of front axle should be pushed through holes A and B.' " While marshalling the indicated parts in their proper order, I emphasized to my rapt listeners the necessity of patience and perseverance. "Haste makes waste, you know," I reminded them. "Rome wasn't built in a day. Remember, your daddy isn't always going to be here to show you."

"Where *are* you going to be?" they demanded.

"In the movies, if I can arrange it," I snarled. Poising tabs C, D, E, F, G, H, J, K, and L in one hand and the corresponding slots in the other, I essayed a union of the two, but in vain. The moment I made one set fast and tackled another, tab and slot would part company, thumbing their noses at me. Although the children were too immature to understand, I saw in a flash where the trouble lay. Some idiotic employee at the factory had punched out the wrong design, probably out of sheer spite. So that was the game, eh? I set my lips in a grim line and, throwing one hundred and fifty-

seven pounds of fighting fat into the effort, pounded the component parts into a homogeneous mass.

"There," I said with a gasp, "that's close enough. Now then, who wants candy? One, two, three—everybody off to the candy store!"

"We wanna finish the delivery truck!" they wailed. "Mummy, he won't let us finish the delivery truck!" Threats, cajolery, bribes were of no avail. In their jungle code, a twenty-nine-cent gewgaw bulked larger than a parent's love. Realizing that I was dealing with a pair of monomaniacs, I determined to show them who was master and wildly began locking the cardboard units helter-skelter, without any regard for the directions. When sections refused to fit, I gouged them with my nails and forced them together, cackling shrilly. The side panels collapsed; with a bestial oath, I drove a safety pin through them and lashed them to the roof. I used paper clips, bobby pins, anything I could lay my hands on. My fingers fairly flew and my breath whistled in my throat. "You want a delivery truck, do you?" I panted. "All right, I'll show you!" As merciful blackness closed in, I was on my hands and knees, bunting the infernal thing along with my nose and whinnying, "Roll, confound you, roll!"

"Absolute quiet," a carefully modulated voice was saying, "and fifteen of the white tablets every four hours." I opened my eyes carefully in the darkened room. Dimly I picked out a knifelike character actor in a Vandyke beard[5] and pencil-striped pants folding a stethoscope into his bag. "Yes," he added thoughtfully, "if we play our cards right, this ought to be a long, expensive recovery." From far away, I could hear my wife's voice bravely trying to control her anxiety.

"What if he becomes restless, Doctor?"

"Get him a detective story," returned the leech. "Or better still, a nice, soothing picture puzzle—something he can do with his hands."

---

5. **Vandyke beard:** a trim, pointed beard, such as those found in portraits by the Flemish painter Van Dyck.

S. J. Perelman **875**

Reading Check

1. What is a "Jiffy-Cloz"?
2. What is the cardboard toy the children ask their father to assemble?
3. Why does the son not want to get a knife for his father?
4. What does the doctor recommend to speed the narrator's recovery?

For Study and Discussion

Analyzing and Interpreting the Essay

S. J. Perelman uses several comic devices to develop his essay and to satirize do-it-yourself projects:

1. **Exaggeration.** Locate several examples of situations Perelman has overstated until they go beyond truth or reason. For example, "The cardboard is so processed that . . . the subject struggles convulsively to force the staple through. . . ."

2. **Absurdity.** Locate elements wildly contrary to common sense: " . . . a cork fired from a child's air gun mysteriously lodged in my throat."

3. **Sarcasm.** Using the first sentence as an example, find other examples of sarcastic comments.

4. **Mock-Seriousness.** Find some mock-serious statements, in which Perelman seems to be imitating inflated diction with a kind of sly innocence. For example, "In a period of rapid technological change, however, it was inevitable that a method as cumbersome as the Jiffy-Cloz would be superseded."

5. **Unexpected and Unusual Wording.** Notice the humor in Perelman's phrases: "until their welkins rang," "my rapt listeners," "in their jungle code," "the leech." Find other examples.

Creative Writing

Writing a Humorous Essay

Using one or more of Perelman's comic devices, write an essay in which you tell about a do-it-yourself project, such as hanging wallpaper, putting up a tent, matting and framing a picture, assembling stereo equipment, and the like. If you wish, invent some other characters who add to your comic complications.

As a writer, James Baldwin showed a special talent for working outward from a special situation—his own or that of the characters in his novels—toward a universal moral significance. Although he was a sharp critic of American society, his was essentially (in Robert Frost's phrase) "a lover's quarrel with the world." In his novels, stories, and plays, he was true to the duty of an artist, as he saw it: to expose others to unpleasant realities, to "let us know that there is nothing stable under heaven," and to "drive to the heart of every answer and expose the question the answer hides."

James Baldwin was born in the Harlem section of New York City. After his graduation from De Witt Clinton High School in 1942, he worked for a while in defense plants. Then he moved to Greenwich Village and worked as a handyman, office boy, and waiter by day while writing at night. Eventually he was able to publish book reviews in national magazines. While he was working on a novel, he met the famous writer Richard Wright, who shared his devotion to the concerns of black people. Wright helped Baldwin get a Eugene F. Saxton Memorial Trust Award. In 1948 Baldwin moved to Paris, where he lived on and off for nearly ten years. While he was overseas, his first novel, *Go Tell It on the Mountain* (1953), was published and praised by many critics. In 1955, the publication of a collection of essays, *Notes of a Native Son*, led several reviewers to comment that perhaps Baldwin's true talent was as an essayist rather than as a writer of fiction. The essays ranged from a touching account of the death of Baldwin's father to a discussion of the "protest novel" in America. *Nobody Knows My Name* (1961) and *The Fire Next Time* (1963) added to Baldwin's reputation as an essayist. Baldwin's other works include the novels *Tell Me How Long the Train's Been Gone* (1968), *If Beale Street Could Talk* (1974), and his collected nonfiction, *The Price of the Ticket* (1985).

James Baldwin.
© Nancy Crampton

As Baldwin indicated in several essays, his stay in Europe made him more aware of his identity as an American and of the qualities and attitudes that he shared with other Americans. He determined to return home and to involve himself in the affairs of his country. Upon his return he made a reputation not only as an important writer but as a prominent public figure. A television documentary about his childhood that he wrote and narrated was broadcast nationally. He appeared on a number of public affairs programs. The sociologist and writer Dr. Kenneth Clark described Baldwin as "a little man, physically, with tremendous emotional and intellectual power. He radiates a nervous, sensitive involvement with all aspects of his environment."

The Creative Process

Perhaps the primary distinction of the artist is that he must actively cultivate that state which most men, necessarily, must avoid: the state of being alone. That all men *are*, when the chips are down, alone, is a banality—a banality because it is very frequently stated, but very rarely, on the evidence, believed. Most of us are not compelled to linger with the knowledge of our aloneness, for it is a knowledge that can paralyze all action in the world. There are, forever, swamps to be drained, cities to be created, mines to be exploited, children to be fed. None of these things can be done alone. But the conquest of the physical world is not man's only duty. He is also enjoined to conquer the great wilderness of himself. The precise role of the artist, then, is to illuminate that darkness, blaze roads through that vast forest, so that we will not, in all our doing, lose sight of its purpose, which is, after all, to make the world a more human dwelling place.

The state of being alone is not meant to bring to mind merely a rustic musing beside some silver lake. The aloneness of which I speak is much more like the aloneness of birth or death. It is like the fearful aloneness that one sees in the eyes of someone who is suffering, whom we cannot help. Or it is like the aloneness of love, the force and mystery that so many have extolled and so many have cursed, but which no one has ever understood or ever really been able to control. I put the matter this way, not out of any desire to create pity for the artist—God forbid!—but to suggest how nearly, after all, is his state the state of everyone, and in an attempt to make vivid his endeavor. The states of birth, suffering, love, and death are extreme states—extreme, universal, and inescapable. We all know this, but we would rather not know it. The artist is present to correct the delusions to which we fall prey in our attempts to avoid this knowledge.

It is for this reason that all societies have battled with that incorrigible disturber of the peace—the artist. I doubt that future societies will get on with him any better. The entire purpose of society is to create a bulwark against the inner and the outer chaos, in order to make life bearable and to keep the human race alive. And it is absolutely inevitable that when a tradition has been evolved, whatever the tradition is, the people, in general, will suppose it to have existed from before the beginning of time and will be most unwilling and indeed unable to conceive of any changes in it. They do not know how they will live without those traditions that have given them their identity. Their reaction, when it is suggested that they can or that they must, is panic. And we see this panic, I think, everywhere in the world today, from the streets of New Orleans to the grisly battleground of Algeria.[1] And a higher level of consciousness among the people is the only hope we have, now or in the future, of minimizing human damage.

The artist is distinguished from all other responsible actors in society—the politicians, legislators, educators, and scientists—by the fact that he is his own test tube, his own laboratory, working according to very rigorous rules, however unstated these may be, and cannot allow any consideration to supersede his responsibility to reveal all that he can possibly discover concerning the mystery of the human being. Society must accept some things as real; but he must always know that visible reality hides a deeper one, and that all our action and achievement rests on things unseen. A society must assume that it is stable, but the artist must know, and he must let us know, that there is nothing stable under heaven. One cannot pos-

1. **Algeria:** In its last years as a French colony, Algeria waged a fierce struggle for independence, which it achieved in 1962.

sibly build a school, teach a child, or drive a car without taking some things for granted. The artist cannot and must not take anything for granted, but must drive to the heart of every answer and expose the question the answer hides.

I seem to be making extremely grandiloquent claims for a breed of men and women historically despised while living and acclaimed when safely dead. But, in a way, the belated honor that all societies tender their artists proves the reality of the point I am trying to make. I am really trying to make clear the nature of the artist's responsibility to his society. The peculiar nature of this responsibility is that he must never cease warring with it, for its sake and for his own. For the truth, in spite of appearances and all our hopes, is that everything is always changing and the measure of our maturity as nations and as men is how well prepared we are to meet these changes and, further, to use them for our health.

Now, anyone who has ever been compelled to think about it—anyone, for example, who has ever been in love—knows that the one face that one can never see is one's own face. One's lover—or one's brother, or one's enemy—sees the face you wear, and this face can elicit the most extraordinary reactions. We do the things we do and feel what we feel essentially because we must—we are responsible for our actions, but we rarely understand them. It goes without saying, I believe, that if we understood ourselves better, we would damage ourselves less. But the barrier between oneself and one's knowledge of oneself is high indeed. There are so many things one would rather not know! We become social creatures because we cannot live any other way. But in order to become social, there are a great many other things that we must not become, and we are frightened, all of us, of those forces within us that perpetually menace our precarious security. Yet the forces are there; we cannot will them away. All we can do is learn to live with them. And we cannot learn this unless we are willing to tell the truth about ourselves, and the truth about us is always at variance with what we wish to be. The human effort is to bring these two realities into a relationship resembling reconciliation. The human beings whom we respect the most, after all—and sometimes fear the most—are those who are deeply involved in this delicate and strenuous effort, for they have the unshakable authority that comes only from having looked on and endured and survived the worst. That nation is healthiest which has the least necessity to distrust or ostracize or victimize these people—whom, as I say, we honor, once they are gone, because somewhere in our hearts we know that we cannot live without them.

The dangers of being an American artist are not greater than those of being an artist anywhere else in the world, but they are very particular. These dangers are produced by our history. They rest on the fact that in order to conquer this continent, the particular aloneness of which I speak—the aloneness in which one discovers that life is tragic, and therefore unutterably beautiful—could not be permitted. And that this prohibition is typical of all emergent nations will be proved, I have no doubt, in many ways during the next fifty years. This continent now is conquered, but our habits and our fears remain. And, in the same way that to become a social human being one modifies and suppresses and, ultimately, without great courage, lies to oneself about all one's interior, uncharted chaos, so have we, as a nation, modified and suppressed and lied about all the darker forces in our history. We know, in the case of the person, that whoever cannot tell himself the truth about his past is trapped in it, is immobilized in the prison of his undiscovered self. This is also true of nations. We know how a person, in such a paralysis, is unable to assess either his weaknesses or his strengths, and how frequently indeed he mistakes the one for the other. And this, I think, we do. We are the strongest nation in the Western world, but this is not for the reasons that we think. It is because we have an opportunity that no other nation has of moving beyond the Old World concepts of race and class and caste, to create, finally, what we must have had in mind when we first began speaking of the New World. But the price of this is a long look backward whence we came and an unflinching assessment of the record. For an artist, the record of that journey is most clearly revealed in the personalities of the people the journey produced. Societies never know it, but the war of an artist with his society is a lover's war, and he does, at his best, what lovers do, which is to reveal the beloved to himself and, with that revelation, to make freedom real.

Reading Check

1. According to Baldwin, one of our duties is to conquer the physical world. What is our second duty?
2. What is the "darkness" that the artist must illuminate?
3. How does the artist differ from all other "responsible actors in society"?
4. What is Baldwin's test for a healthy society?

For Study and Discussion

Analyzing and Interpreting the Essay

1a. What does Baldwin mean by "aloneness"? **b.** How is this concept particularly important to his discussion of the artist's situation?
2a. Why does Baldwin say that "all societies have battled with that incorrigible disturber of the peace—the artist"? **b.** In what sense is the artist a "disturber of the peace"?
3a. What claims does Baldwin make for the artist? **b.** Why must an artist "drive to the heart of every answer and expose the question the answer hides"? **c.** What, according to Baldwin, is the artist's responsibility to society?
4. In what ways is this essay an exploration of the basic relationship of all individuals to society?

Language and Vocabulary

Finding Synonyms

Find synonyms for the italicized words below. Discuss whether your synonyms clarify the meaning of Baldwin's sentences or make the meaning less precise.
1. "That all men are, when the chips are down, alone, is a *banality* . . ." (page 878)
2. "He is also *enjoined* to conquer the great wilderness of himself." (page 878)
3. "The state of being alone is not meant to bring to mind merely a *rustic* musing beside some silver lake." (page 878)
4. " . . . the *grisly* battleground of Algeria . . ." (page 878)
5. "I seem to be making extremely *grandiloquent* claims . . ." (page 879)

Writing About Literature

Taking a Position

Baldwin writes, "That nation is healthiest which has the least necessity to distrust or ostracize or victimize these people—whom, as I say, we honor, once they are gone, because somewhere in our hearts we know that we cannot live without them." Referring to the essay, explain who is meant by "these people." Then tell whether you agree or disagree with Baldwin's statement that we cannot live without such people. Be sure to give reasons in support of your position.

During the 1930s and 1940s William Faulkner was generally regarded as an eccentric regional writer. His books, with their oppressive, violent themes, their use of both classical mythology and the author's private mythology, and their extremely complex structure and language, were left to the academics and ignored by the general reader. By 1945 his novels (almost twenty in number) were nearly out of print. Yet, in the late 1940s, a few perceptive critics undertook a reevaluation of Faulkner's profound work. These critics, including Malcolm Cowley and Robert Penn Warren, discovered and wrote about the technical virtuosity and thematic richness of his books. Faulkner's writing seemed Shakespearean in its great expressiveness and in its remarkable range of characters, situations, and tones. By 1951 Faulkner had received, for several of the books that had almost gone permanently out of print, a Pulitzer Prize, a National Book Award, and the Nobel Prize. When he received the Nobel Prize in 1950, he delivered the following classic statement on the role of the writer in society.

Nobel Prize Acceptance Speech

Stockholm, Sweden
December 10, 1950

I feel that this award was not made to me as a man but to my work—a life's work in the agony and sweat of the human spirit, not for glory and least of all for profit, but to create out of the materials of the human spirit something which did not exist before. So this award is only mine in trust. It will not be difficult to find a dedication for the money part of it commensurate with the purpose and significance of its origin. But I would like to do the same with the acclaim too, by using this moment as a pinnacle from which I might be listened to by the young men and women already dedicated to the same anguish and travail, among whom is already that one who will someday stand here where I am standing.

Our tragedy today is a general and universal physical fear so long sustained by now that we can even bear it. There are no longer problems of the spirit. There is only the question: When will I be blown up? Because of this, the young man or woman writing today has forgotten the problems of the human heart in conflict with itself which alone can make good writing because only that is worth writing about, worth the agony and the sweat.

He must learn them again. He must teach himself that the basest of all things is to be afraid; and, teaching himself that, forget it forever, leaving no room in his workshop for anything but the old verities and truths of the heart, the old universal truths lacking which any story is ephemeral and doomed—love and honor and pity and pride and compassion and sacrifice. Until he does so he labors under a curse. He writes not of love but of lust, of defeats in which nobody loses anything of value, of victories without hope and worst of all without pity or compassion. His griefs grieve on no universal bones, leaving no scars. He writes not of the heart but of the glands.

Until he relearns these things he will write as though he stood among and watched the end of man. I decline to accept the end of man. It is easy enough to say that a man is immortal simply because he will endure; that when the last ding-dong of doom has clanged and faded from the last worthless rock hanging tideless in the last red and dying evening, that even then there will still be one more sound: that of his puny inexhaustible voice, still talking. I refuse to accept this. I believe that man will not merely endure: he will prevail. He is immortal, not because he alone among creatures has an inexhaustible voice, but because he has a soul, a spirit capable of compassion and sacrifice and endurance. The poet's, the writer's, duty is to write about these things. It is his privilege to help man endure by lifting his heart, by reminding him of the courage and honor and hope and pride and compassion and pity and sacrifice which have been the glory of his past. The poet's voice need not merely be the record of man, it can be one of the props, the pillars to help him endure and prevail.

For Study and Discussion

Analyzing and Interpreting the Speech

1. What do you think Faulkner means when he says that the award is only his "in trust"?

2a. According to Faulkner, what is the only thing worth writing about? **b.** Why does he consider it the most important subject?
3a. How does Faulkner define humankind? **b.** How, according to Faulkner, can a writer help humanity to prevail?
4. In this address, Faulkner uses certain **rhetorical devices**—techniques that lend a speech clarity and force, and make it memorable. Two rhetorical devices Faulkner uses are repetition and parallelism (the use of sentences, phrases, or words that are the same or similar in meaning and structure). What examples of repetition and parallelism can you find in the address?

For Research

Reporting on the Nobel Prize

Do some research on the background of the Nobel Prize. Find out, for example, when the first prize was awarded, how many prizes are presented each year, and in what categories. Which Americans have won the prize for literature? Has anyone ever rejected the award? After consulting encyclopedias and magazine articles kept on file in your library, discuss in a brief essay the aspect of the Nobel Prize that most interested you.

Faulkner accepting the Nobel Prize from King Gustaf VI in Stockholm.

UPI / Bettmann Newsphotos

RALPH ELLISON
1914—

Ralph Ellison was born and raised in Olkahoma City. In school he developed an interest in jazz and in classical music. In 1933 Ellison entered Tuskegee Institute, the famous black college in Alabama founded by Booker T. Washington. There he studied classical music and discovered an interest in sculpture. After three years at Tuskegee, he moved to New York, where he came to know the pioneer modern black novelist Richard Wright (page 917). With Wright's encouragement Ellison turned to journalistic writing and then to fiction.

Ellison's earliest published writings were short stories. In 1952 he published *Invisible Man,* a powerful novel which, in 1965, a poll of literary critics voted the "most distinguished single work" appearing in America since the end of World War II. Many critics consider *Invisible Man* the greatest piece of black writing produced in America. In addition to his single novel and his short stories, Ellison has published two highly praised collections of essays, *Shadow and Act* (1964) and *Going to the Territory* (1986). In *Shadow and Act* he discusses his literary and intellectual concerns and the forces that helped shape them. "Brave Words for a Startling Occasion," a selection from *Shadow and Act,* was originally presented as a speech in 1953 when Ellison received the National Book Award for *Invisible Man.*

Ralph Ellison.
© Nancy Crampton

Brave Words for a Startling Occasion

First, as I express my gratitude for this honor which you have bestowed on me, let me say that I take it that you are rewarding my efforts rather than my not quite fully achieved attempt at a major novel. Indeed, if I were asked in all seriousness just what I considered to be the chief significance of *Invisible Man* as a fiction, I would reply: Its experimental attitude, and its attempt to return to the mood of personal moral responsibility for democracy which typified the best of our nineteenth-century fiction. That my first novel should win this most coveted prize must certainly indicate that there is a crisis in the American novel. You as critics have told us so, and current fiction sales would indicate that the reading public agrees. Certainly the younger novelists concur. The explosive nature of events mocks our brightest efforts. And the very "facts" which the naturalists assumed would make us free have lost the power to protect us from despair. Controversy now rages over just what aspects of American experience are suitable for novelistic treatment. The prestige of the theorists of the so-called novel of manners has been challenged. Thus after a long period of stability we find our assumptions concerning the novel being called into question. And though I was only vaguely aware, it was this growing crisis which shaped the writing of *Invisible Man*.

After the usual apprenticeship of imitation and seeking with delight to examine my experience through the discipline of the novel, I became gradually aware that the forms of so many of the works which impressed me were too restricted to contain the experience which I knew. The diversity of American life with its extreme fluidity and openness seemed too vital and alive to be caught for more than the briefest instant in the tight well-made Jamesian[1] novel, which was, for all its artistic perfection, too concerned with "good taste" and stable areas. Nor could I safely use the forms of the "hard-boiled" novel, with its dedication to physical violence, social cynicism and understatement. Understatement depends, after all, upon commonly held assumptions and my minority status rendered all such assumptions questionable. There was also a problem of language, and even dialogue, which, with its hard-boiled stance and its monosyllabic utterance, is one of the shining achievements of twentieth-century American writing. For despite the notion that its rhythms were those of everyday speech, I found that when compared with the rich babel of idiomatic expression around me, a language full of imagery and gesture and rhetorical canniness, it was embarrassingly austere. Our speech I found resounding with an alive language swirling with over three hundred years of American living, a mixture of the folk, the Biblical, the scientific and the political. Slangy in one instance, academic in another, loaded poetically with imagery at one moment, mathematically bare of imagery in the next. As for the rather rigid concepts of reality which informed a number of the works which impressed me and to which I owe a great deal, I was forced to conclude that reality was far more mysterious and uncertain, and more exciting, and still, despite its raw violence and capriciousness, more promising. To attempt to express that American experience which has carried one back and forth and up and down the land and across, and across again the great river, from freight train to Pullman car, from contact with slavery

1. **Jamesian:** referring to the American novelist Henry James (1843–1916).

to contact with a world of advanced scholarship, art and science, is simply to burst such neatly understated forms of the novel asunder.

A novel whose range was both broader and deeper was needed. And in my search I found myself turning to our classical nineteenth-century novelists. I felt that except for the work of William Faulkner something vital had gone out of American prose after Mark Twain. I came to believe that the writers of that period took a much greater responsibility for the condition of democracy and, indeed, their works were imaginative projections of the conflicts within the human heart which arose when the sacred principles of the Constitution and the Bill of Rights clashed with the practical exigencies of human greed and fear, hate and love. Naturally I was attracted to these writers as a Negro. Whatever they thought of my people per se,[2] in their imaginative economy the Negro symbolized both the man lowest down and the mysterious, underground aspect of human personality. In a sense the Negro was the gauge of the human condition as it waxed and waned in our democracy. These writers were willing to confront the broad complexities of American life and we are the richer for their having done so.

Thus to see America with an awareness of its rich diversity and its almost magical fluidity and freedom, I was forced to conceive of a novel unburdened by the narrow naturalism which has led, after so many triumphs, to the final and unrelieved despair which marks so much of our current fiction. I was to dream of a prose which was flexible, and swift as American change is swift, confronting the inequalities and brutalities of our society forthrightly, but yet thrusting forth its images of hope, human fraternity and individual self-realization. It would use the richness of our speech, the idiomatic expression and the rhetorical flourishes from past periods which are still alive among us. And despite my personal failures, there must be possible a fiction which, leaving sociology to the scientists, can arrive at the truth about the human condition, here and now, with all the bright magic of a fairy tale.

What has been missing from so much experimental writing has been the passionate will to dominate reality as well as the laws of art. This will is the true source of the experimental attitude. We who struggle with form and with America should remember Eidothea's[3] advice to Menelaus[4] when in the *Odyssey* he and his friends are seeking their way home. She tells him to seize her father, Proteus, and to hold him fast "however he may struggle and fight. He will turn into all sorts of shapes to try you," she says, "into all the creatures that live and move upon the earth, into water, into blazing fire; but you must hold him fast and press him all the harder. When he is himself, and questions you in the same shape that he was when you saw him in his bed, let the old man go; and then, sir, ask which god it is who is angry, and how you shall make your way homewards over the fish-giving sea."

For the novelist, Proteus stands for both America and the inheritance of illusion through which all men must fight to achieve reality; the offended god stands for our sins against those principles we all hold sacred. The way home we seek is that condition of man's being at home in the world, which is called love, and which we term democracy. Our task then is always to challenge the apparent forms of reality—that is, the fixed manners and values of the few, and to struggle with it until it reveals its mad, vari-implicated chaos, its false faces, and on until it surrenders its insight, its truth. We are fortunate as American writers in that with our variety of racial and national traditions, idioms and manners, we are yet one. On its profoundest level American experience is of a whole. Its truth lies in its di-

2. **per se** (pĕr sā′): a Latin phrase meaning "in or by itself."

3. **Eidothea** (ī′dō-thē′ə): the daughter of Proteus, the mythological sea deity who had the power to change shape.
4. **Menelaus** (mĕn′ə-lā′əs): in Greek mythology, the King of Sparta, who journeyed to Troy to obtain his wife, Helen. Kept by the gods from returning home, he was finally aided by Eidothea.

versity and swiftness of change. Through forging forms of the novel worthy of it, we achieve not only the promise of our lives, but we anticipate the resolution of those world problems of humanity which for a moment seem to those who are in awe of statistics completely insoluble.

Whenever we as Americans have faced serious crises we have returned to fundamentals; this, in brief, is what I have tried to do.

Reading Check

1. What, for Ellison, is the "chief significance" of his novel, *Invisible Man*?
2. Which nineteenth-century writer does Ellison admire for confronting "the broad complexities of American life"?
3. Which twentieth-century American writer does Ellison admire for his prose style?
4. What myth does Ellison refer to in order to explain his rejection of realism and naturalism?

For Study and Discussion

Analyzing and Interpreting the Speech

1a. In what way did Ellison find various forms of the novel "too restricted" as a model for his own writing? **b.** What problem did the language common to modern American writing present when Ellison compared it to "the rich babel" around him? **c.** Why does Ellison say "the rich babel" rather than "the rich babble"?

2. In the third paragraph, Ellison praises the nineteenth-century American novel for having represented "the broad complexities" of both American individuals and American society. In what way does Ellison say his newly created prose is a return to nineteenth-century fiction?

3. In seeking the "truth about the human condition," what, in addition to a critical look at society, does Ellison feel must be included in the ideal prose?

4. According to Ellison, what should be the writer's basic task?

Writing About Literature

Analyzing a Statement About Faulkner

Explain why you think Ellison considers William Faulkner an exception in modern American prose writing. Consider the statements both have made regarding the conflicts of the human heart, and especially the importance of writing about hope and compassion in the face of defeat and despair. Refer to Faulkner's speech on page 881.

ROLANDO R. HINOJOSA-SMITH
1929–

Rolando R. Hinojosa (ē-nō-hō′sä)-Smith was born in Mercedes, Texas, a town close to the Mexican border, in 1929. His family on his father's side has been living in this region of Texas, the Rio Grande Valley, since the 1740s. Hinojosa-Smith was raised in a bilingual family, with Spanish usually spoken at home. He received a Ph.D. in Spanish literature from the University of Illinois, and is currently Professor of English at the University of Texas.

Hinojosa-Smith is a prize-winning Chicano writer. (The word *Chicano* refers to Americans of Mexican descent.) Among his many publications are *Estampas del Valle y otras obras*° (*Portraits of the Valley and Other Works*), *Klail City y sus alrededores (Klail City and Its Environs)*, and *The Valley*, which is a reworking and English rewriting of *Estampas del Valle y otras obras*. Hinojosa-Smith's work depicts the Rio Grande Chicano culture coping with the larger American world. In his own words, Chicano literature is about "our presence in our own native land as people who

° *Estampas . . . obras* (ĕs-täm′päs dāl bä′yä ē ō′träs ō′bräs).

Rolando R. Hinojosa-Smith.

continue to maintain an identity that will not disappear anytime soon."

In the following speech, Hinojosa-Smith discusses the importance of place, of an accurate rendering of the Rio Grande Valley, to his writing.

This Writer's Sense of Place

I should like to begin with a quote from a man imprisoned for his participation in the Texas-Santa Fe Expedition of 1841;[1] while in his cell in Mexico City, he spurned Santa Anna's[2] offer

1. **Texas . . . 1841:** Five years after Texan independence, an irregular group of Texans invaded the territory of New Mexico. The effort failed and the Texas contingent was imprisoned.
2. **Santa Anna:** Antonio López de Santa Anna (1795–1876), military leader and politician. He led the Mexican attack on the Alamo in 1836.

of freedom in exchange for renouncing the Republic of Texas.[3] Those words of 1842 were said by a man who had signed the Texas Declaration of Independence and who had served in the Congress of the Republic. Later on, he was to cast a delegate vote for annexation and contribute to the writing of the first state con-

3. **Republic of Texas:** From 1836 to 1845 Texas was an independent republic, not part of Mexico or the United States. In 1845, it became the 28th state.

stitution. He would win election to the state legislature and still later he would support secession.

And this is what he said:

> I have sworn to be a good Texan; and that I will not forswear. I will die for that which I firmly believe, for I know it is just and right. One life is a small price for a cause so great. As I fought, so shall I be willing to die. I will never forsake Texas and her cause. I am her son.

The words were written by José Antonio Navarro, a native-born Texan, for whom a county is named. A Texas historian named James Wilson once wrote that Navarro's name is virtually unknown to Texas school children and, for the most part, unknown to their teachers as well. I believe that Professor Wilson is correct in his assessment of the lack of knowledge of this place in which we were born and in which some of us still live.

The year 1983 marks the one hundredth anniversary of the birth of my father, Manuel Guzmán Hinojosa, in the Campacuás Ranch, some three miles north of Mercedes, down in the Valley;[4] his father was born in that ranch as was his father's father. My mother arrived in the Valley at the age of six weeks in the year 1887 as one of the first Anglo-American settlers enticed to the mid-valley by Jim Wells, one of the early developers on the northern bank. As you may already know, it's no accident that Jim Wells County in South Texas is named for him.

One of the earliest stories I heard about Grandfather Smith was a supposed conversation he had with Lawyer Wells; you are being asked to imagine the month of July in the Valley with no air conditioning, in 1887; Wells was extolling the Valley and said that all it needed was a little water and a few good people; my grandfather replied, "Well, that's all

The Rio Grande near Frontera. Nineteenth-century engraving.

Hell needs, too." The story is apocryphal; it has to be, but living in the Valley, and hearing that type of story, laid the foundation for what I later learned was to give me a sense of place. By that I do not mean that I had a feel for the place; no, not at all. I had a sense of it, and by that I mean that I was not learning about the culture of the Valley, but living it, forming part of it and, thus, contributing to it.

But a place is merely that until it is populated, and once populated, the histories of the place and its people begin. For me and mine, history began in 1749 when the first colonists

---

4. **Campacuás** (käm-pä-kwäs′) . . . **Valley:** the valley of the Rio Grande, the boundary between the United States and Mexico.

led the Borderers to label their fellow Mexicans who came from the interior, as *fuereños*, or foreigners; and later, when the "people from the North" started coming to the Border, these were labeled *gringos*, another word for foreigner and nothing else until the *gringo* himself, from all evidence, took the term as a pejorative label.

For me, then, part of a sense of the border came from sharing: the sharing of names, of places, of a common history, and of belonging to the place; one attended funerals, was taken to cemeteries, and one saw names that correspond to one's own or to one's friends and neighbors—and relatives.

When I first started to write—and being what we call "empapado" which translates as drenched, imbibed, soaked, or drunk, with the place—I had to eschew the romanticism and the sentimentalism that tend to blind the unwary, that get in the way of truth. It's no great revelation when I say that romanticism and sentimentalism tend to corrupt clear thinking. The border wasn't paradise, and it didn't have to be; but it was more than paradise, it was home and (as Frost once wrote) home, when you have to go there, is the place where they have to take you in.[6]

And the Border was home; and it was also the home of the petty officeholder elected by an uninformed citizenry; a home for bossism, and for small-time smuggling as a way of life for some. But it also maintained the remains of a social democracy that cried out for independence, for a desire to be left alone, and for the continuance of a sense of community.

The history one learned there was an oral one and somewhat akin to the oral religion brought by the original colonials of 1749. Many of my generation were raised with the music written and composed by Valley people, and we learned the ballads of the Border, little knowing that they were a true native art form. And one was also raised and steeped in the

began moving onto the southern and northern banks of the Rio Grande. That river was not yet a jurisdictional barrier and was not to be until almost one hundred years later; but, by then, the Border had its own history, its own culture, and its own sense of place: it was Nuevo Santander, named for old Santander[5] in the Spanish Peninsula.

The last names were similar up and down on both banks of the river, and as second and third cousins were allowed to marry, this further promulgated and propagated blood relationships and that sense of belonging that

5. **Santander** (sän-tän′där): a province of Old Castile, on the Bay of Biscay.

6. **Frost . . . take you in:** See "The Death of the Hired Man," lines 118–119, page 750.

Rolando R. Hinojosa-Smith **889**

Juan Cortina.
Barker Texas History Center

stories and exploits of Juan Nepomuceno Cortina,[7] in the nineteenth century, and with stories of the Texas Rangers in that century and of other Ranger stories in this century and then, as always, names, familiar patronymics:[8] Jacinto Treviño, Aniceto Pizaña,[9] the Seditionists of 1915 who had camped in Mercedes, at a place my father would take me and show and

mark for me the spot where the Seditionists had camped and barbecued their meat half a generation before. These were men of flesh and bone who lived and died there in Mercedes, in the Valley. And then there were the stories of the Revolution of 1910,[10] and of the participation in it for the next ten years off and on by Valley *mexicanos* who fought alongside their south bank relatives, and the stories told to me and to those of my generation by exiles, men and women from Mexico, who earned a living by teaching us school on the northern bank while they bided their time to return to Mexico.

But we didn't return to Mexico; we didn't have to; we were Borderers with a living and unifying culture born of conflict with another culture and this, too, helped to cement further still our knowing exactly where we came from and from whom we were descended.

The language, too, was a unifier and as strong an element as there is in fixing one's sense of place; the language of the Border is a derivative of the Spanish language of Northern Mexico; a language whose nouns and other grammatical complements were no longer used in the Spanish Peninsula but which persisted there; and the more the linguistically uninformed went out of their way to denigrate the language, the stiffer the resistance to maintain it and to nurture it on the northern bank. And the uninformed failed, of course, for theirs was a momentary diversion to those committed to its preservation; the price that many Texas-Mexicans paid for keeping the language and the sense of place has been exorbitant.

As a Borderer, the northbank Mexican couldn't, to repeat a popular phrase, "go back to where you came from." The Borderer was there and had been before the interlopers; but what of the indigenous population prior to the

7. **Juan Nepomuceno Cortina:** a Texas-born rancher who shot a Texas ranger for abusing some of his ranch hands. He joined the Mexican army and became a general. He is considered a border hero of the Lower Rio Grande Valley (Brownsville, Texas).
8. **patronymics** (păt′rə-nĭm′ĭks): names showing descent from ancestors.
9. **Jacinto ... Pizaña:** Jacinto Treviño (hä-sēn′tō trä-bē′nyō) and Aniceto Pizaña (ä-nē-sä′tō pē-sä′nyä′) were ranchers who defied Texan authorities at the beginning of this century. They were among the Seditionists of 1915, a loosely organized army of Texas-Mexicans, Texas-Anglos, and blacks. They operated in the Lower Rio Grande Valley and called themselves El Ejercito Libertador Mexico-Texano (The Liberating Texas-Mexican Army). Their uprising was due to racism and other forms of social discrimination.

10. **Revolution of 1910:** a rebellion against the oppressive rule of Porfirio Díaz (1830–1915), president of Mexico. The revolt was led by Francisco I. Madero, who opposed Díaz' dictatorial ways and favored, among other things, agrarian reforms.

1749 settlement?[11] Since Nuevo Santander was never under the presidio[12] system and since its citizens did not build missions that trapped and stultified the indigenous people, they remained there and, in time, settled down or were absorbed by the colonial population and thus the phrase hurled at the Border Mexican "go back to where you came from" was, to use another popular term, "inoperative." And this, too, fostered that sense of place.

For the writer—this writer—a sense of place was not a matter of importance; it became essential. And so much so that my stories are not held together by the *peripeteia,*[13] or the plot, as much as by the *what* the people who populate the stories say and *how* they say it; how they look at the world out and the world in; and the works, then, become studies of perceptions and values and decisions reached by them because of those perceptions and values which in turn were fashioned and forged by the place and its history.

What I am saying here is not to be taken to mean that it is impossible for a writer to write about a place, its history, and its people if the writer is not from that particular place; it can be done, and it has been done. What I *am* saying is that I needed a sense of place, and that this helped me no end in the way that, I would say, Américo Paredes in *With His Pistol in His Hand,* Larry McMurtry in *Horseman, Pass By,* and Fred Gipson in *Hound-Dog Man,* William A. Owens in that fine, strong *This Stubborn Soil,* and Tomás Rivera in . . . *and the earth did not part* were all helped by a sense of place.

11. **the 1749 Settlement:** The Lower Rio Grande Valley (Brownsville to Rio Grande City, Texas) was explored by the Spanish crown in 1747, and opened for settlement in 1749.
12. **presidio** (prĭ-sē′dē-ō′, prä-sē′dē-ō): garrison or military post established in the Southwest by the Spanish.
13. **peripeteia** (pĕr′ə-pə-tē′ə): in Greek tragedy, a sudden change or reversal in the course of events.

United States and Mexican boundary survey, Brownsville, Texas.
Barker Texas History Center

And I say this, because to me these writers and others impart a sense of place and a sense of truth about the place and about the values of that place. Theirs isn't a studied attitude, but rather one of a certain love, to use that phrase, and of an understanding for the place that they captured in print for themselves. A sense of place: as Newark, New Jersey, in the works of Philip Roth; wonderful storyteller that he is, Roth tells us of his Jewish traditions and conflicts, and we note that those traditions and conflicts become the essential background whenever he writes of relationships, which, after all, is what writers usually write about.

I am not making a medieval pitch for the shoemaker to stick to his last here, but if the writer puts a lifetime of living in a work, the writer sometimes finds it difficult to remove the place of provenance[14] from the writings, irrespective of where he situates his stories. That's a strong statement and one which may elicit comment or disagreement, but what spine one has is formed early in life, and it is formed at a specific place; later on when one grows up, one may mythicize, adopt a persona, become an actor, restructure family history, but the original facts of one's formation remain as facts always do.

It's clear, then, that I am not speaking of the formula novel, nor is it my intent to denigrate it or its practitioners; far from it. I consider the formula novel as fine art, if done well, and many of us know that good formula novels do exist. I speak of something else—neither nobler nor better—no, merely different from that genre. It's a personal thing, because I found that after many years of hesitancy, and fits and spurts, and false starts, that despite what education I had acquired, I was still limited in many ways; that whatever I attempted to write came out false and frail. Now, I know I wanted to write, had to write, was burning to write and all of those things that some writers say to garden clubs, but the truth and heart of the matter were that I did not know where

to begin; and there it was again, that adverb of place, the *where;* and then I got lucky: I decided to write whatever it was I had, in Spanish, and I decided to set it on the Border, in the Valley.

As reduced as that space was, it too was Texas with all of its contradictions and its often-repeated, one-sided telling of Texas history. When the characters stayed in the Spanish-speaking milieu or society, the Spanish language worked well, and then it was in the natural order of things that English made its entrance when the characters strayed or found themselves in Anglo institutions; in cases where both cultures came into contact, both languages were used, and I would employ both; and where one and only one would do, I would use that one. What dominated, then, was the place, at first. Later on I discovered that generational and class differences also dictated not only usage but *what* language as well. From this came the *how* they said *what* they said. As the census rolls filled up in the works, so did some distinguishing features, characteristics, viewpoints, values, decisions; and thus I used the Valley and the Border, and the history and the people. The freedom to do this also led me to use the folklore and the anthropology of the Valley, to use whatever literary form I desired and saw fit to use to tell my stories: dialogs, duologs,[15] monologs, imaginary newspaper clippings, and whatever else I felt would be of use. And it *was* the Valley, but it remained forever Texas. At the same time, I could see this Valley, this border, and I drew a map, and this, too, was another key, and this led to more work and to more characters in that place.

It was a matter of luck in some ways, as I said, but mostly it was the proper historical moment; it came along, and I took what had been there for some time, but which I had not been able to see, since I had not fully developed a sense of place; I had left the Valley for the service, for formal university training, and

---

14. **provenance** (prŏv′ə-nəns): origin.

15. **duolog:** dialogue limited to two.

for a series of very odd jobs, only to return to it in my writing.

I have mentioned values and decisions; as I see them, these are matters inculcated by one's elders first, by one's acquaintances later on, and usually under the influence of one's society, which is another way of saying one's place of origin. Genetic structure may enter into holding to certain values and perhaps in the manner of reaching decisions, for all I know. Ortega y Gasset,[16] among others, I suspect, wrote that man makes dozens of decisions every day and the process helps man to make and to reach more serious, deliberate, and even important decisions when the time presents itself. A preparatory stage, as it were. The point of this is that my decision to write what I write and to situate the writing where I do is not based on anything else other than a desire to write about what I know, the place I know, the language used, the values held. When someone mentions universality, I say that what happens to the characters happens to other peoples of the world at given times, and I've no doubt on that score. What has helped me to write has also been a certain amount of questionable self-education, a long and fairly misspent youth in the eyes of some, an acceptance of certain facts, and some misrepresentations of the past which I could not change but which led to a rejection not of those unalterable facts but of hypocrisy and the smugness of the self-satisfied. For this and other personal reasons, humor creeps into my writing once in a while, because it was the use of irony, as many of us know, that allowed the Borderer to survive and thus to maintain a certain measure of dignity.

Serious writing is a deliberate act, a consequence of an arrived-at decision; what one writes may be of value or not, but I believe that one's fidelity to history is the first step to fixing a sense of place, whether that place is a worldwide arena or a corner of it—as is mine.

16. **Ortega y Gasset:** Spanish writer and philosopher (1883–1955).

Reading Check

1. Where is the Valley Hinojosa-Smith writes about located?
2. What is the significance of the year 1749 to Mexican-Americans?
3. According to the author, what is the true native art form of the Border?
4. Name three unifying elements that fixed a sense of place for the author.

For Study and Discussion

Analyzing and Interpreting the Speech

1. Hinojosa-Smith discusses the various elements that have given him a sense of place for his writing. Why does he ascribe so much importance to names?
2. In what way did storytelling help him to develop a sense of place?
3. Hinojosa-Smith says that when he began to write he had to "eschew romanticism and sentimentalism." How would these elements get in the way of truth?
4. How did the language of the Border function as an element in fixing his sense of place?

Creative Writing

Using Setting in Personal Writing

Hinojosa-Smith says that when he first started to write he was "drenched, imbibed, soaked, or drunk" with a sense of place. Agreeing with Hinojosa-Smith that place is indeed of central importance in personal writing, write several paragraphs about an incident from your past and steep your incident in the particulars of the place in which you were raised.

The following selection is from an essay, "The Form of Texas-Mexican Fiction." Ramón Saldívar, who teaches English at the University of Texas, discusses Hinojosa-Smith's technique in *The Valley*. He finds the writer's use of narrative time and his use of place to be inseparably linked.

Hinojosa's novel, *The Valley*, is a rich documentary of fleeting scenes, thoughts, images, dreams, and actions which fuse to create a mosaic of South Texas life. As the narrative cuts from one character to another—he gives us over a hundred of them, without apparent logic or order—it intends to represent the continuing presence, the inter-mingling, of four generations of life. In Hinojosa's novel, however, the normal separations between time past and time present that we would expect to find in a chronicle of life are not present. Narrative time is fluid, as characters from the past seem to coexist with characters from the present. Because of this instability of narrative time, Hinojosa's *The Valley* is less a novel about individual subjects, unique individuals (although it certainly does provide some unique individuals in Texas fiction) than it is a novel about *community*. The collective social life of the Valley Texas-Mexicans becomes a kind of *spiritus loci*,[1] a disembodied consciousness existing in alliance with the scrabble rock reality of that *resaca*-dotted[2] land.

The first sketch of the novel, entitled "Braulio Tapia,"[3] is not a privileged point in history or a necessary origin for the many tales which are to unfold before us in the coming pages. It is simply an arbitrary moment in the history of the lives of these people, as if one moment could serve as well as any other as the "introduction" to that story.

Braulio Tapia

Squat, what the Germans call *dicke* and thus heavy of chest and shoulders, Roque Malacara carries his hat in his hand; this last shouldn't fool the reader, however, since R. M.'s step is firm and resolute.

I'm standing on the doorway on the east porch of a hot Thursday afternoon, and he says: My coming here alone isn't a matter of disrespect, sir, it's just that I've no money for sponsors.

He then asks me for my daughter Tere's hand; I nod and point to the living room. Hat held in a firm hand, he follows with the same and sure unwavering step.

He then reminds me that I gave him permission to call on Tere: it's been over a year and a half, sir. Again I nod and this time we shake hands.

1. *spiritus loci* (spĭr′ĭ-təs lō′sī′, -kī′): Latin for "spirit of the place."
2. *resaca* (rä-sä′kä′)-**dotted:** marked with channels of streams.
3. **Braulio Tapia** (broul′yō tä′pē-ä).

Turning my head slightly to the right, I catch a glimpse, or think I do, of my late father-in-law, don Braulio Tapia: long sideburns and matching black mustache à la Kaiser; don Braulio raises his hand to shake mine as he did years ago when I first came here to this house to ask for Matilde's hand.

By that time, with doña Sóstenes's[4] death, he'd been a widower as I now am and have been since Matti's death years ago. Don Braulio nods, takes my hand, and bids me enter.

Who did don Braulio see when he walked up these steps to ask for his wife's hand?

Notice what is going on here: we watch with the anonymous narrator as his future son-in-law, Roque Malacara,[5] approaches to ask for the hand in marriage of the narrator's daughter, Teresa. All of this is in the present. At the same time, the narrator remembers the day that he too approached his future father-in-law, don Braulio Tapia, to ask for his daughter's hand in marriage. One page into the novel, in other words, we enter a world where the past is starkly visible, as in broad panorama. And that past too serves as a window to still other past moments, even as it implies the future. Don Braulio Tapia, the title character of the first chapter, is not even present, and yet in another sense of course he is present. In this one single moment of multiple presents, the broad context of time which the novel is to dramatize is flashed before our eyes: we see simultaneously five generations of history. Over the coming pages, we will learn that this anonymous first narrator is Jehú Vilches,[6] the grandfather of one of the novel's two main protagonists, Jehú Malacara, the future son of Roque and Teresa.

The unity in this kaleidoscope[7] of time is provided by the stability of place. These very same steps, this same porch and living room have witnessed the rituals of marriage and death and regeneration for generations on end, going back in time through the twentieth century to the nineteenth century and perhaps beyond, and forward into the mid-twentieth century.

4. **doña Sóstenes** (dō′nyä sō′stā-něs).
5. **Roque Malacara** (rō′kä mä-lä-kä′rä).
6. **Jehú Vilches** (yā-hoō′ bēl′chěs).
7. **kaleidoscope** (kə-lī′də-scōp′): something that constantly changes patterns.

For Study and Discussion

Analyzing and Interpreting the Selection

1. For Saldívar, what is the effect of Hinojosa-Smith's "fluid" use of time?

2. According to Saldívar, what is the real subject of *The Valley?*

3. How does place provide an element of unity in the novel?

John Dos Passos' father was a wealthy and successful corporation lawyer, and his mother came from a socially prominent Maryland family. As a boy he traveled widely with his parents and lived in different locations in the United States and abroad. He attended private schools and, after further travel and tutoring, entered Harvard University in 1912.

Shortly after Dos Passos graduated from Harvard, America entered World War I. Dos Passos enlisted first as an ambulance driver and then as an active combatant. He depicted his grueling experiences in two novels, *One Man's Initiation—1917* (1920) and *Three Soldiers* (1921). After the war, he traveled extensively in both the United States and Europe, eagerly observing people and their surroundings. In 1922 he published a collection of essays on the culture of Spain and a book of poems based on his experiences there. In his first novel about contemporary America, *Manhattan Transfer* (1925), he illustrated the complex life of New York City. Then, in an impressive effort to tell the story of the first three decades of the twentieth century in the United States, he published *The 42nd Parallel* (1930), the first novel in a trilogy. The second and third novels of the trilogy were *1919* (1932) and *The Big Money* (1936). Although Dos Passos wrote a great many more novels, biographical sketches, travel writings, and political essays up to the middle 1960s, his reputation rests on his large work which, in 1938, was published in its entirety under the title *U.S.A.*

U.S.A. tells of thirteen characters living between the early years of the century and the end of the

John Dos Passos.
The Bettmann Archive

great business boom of the 1920s. In addition to these major characters, scores of lesser figures appear in a wide variety of public and private events. The trilogy is interspersed with dramatically written biographical sketches of then prominent and influential American figures, such as Henry Ford. Dos Passos' aim in these sketches was to give sharp impressions of an emerging industrialized America, a nation often caught up in the issues surrounding war, commercialism, and rapid technological change.

Henry Ford shown with his first car and his ten-millionth car.

Tin Lizzie

"Mr. Ford the automobileer," the featurewriter wrote in 1900,

"Mr. Ford the automobileer began by giving his steed three or four sharp jerks with the lever at the righthand side of the seat; that is, he pulled the lever up and down sharply in order, as he said, to mix air with gasoline and drive the charge into the exploding cylinder. . . . Mr. Ford slipped a small electric switch handle and there followed a puff, puff, puff. . . . The puffing of the machine assumed a higher key. She was flying along about eight miles an hour. The ruts in the road were deep, but the machine certainly went with a dreamlike smoothness. There was none of the bumping common even to a streetcar. . . . By this time the boulevard had been reached, and the automobileer, letting a lever fall a little, let her out. Whiz! She picked up speed with infinite rapidity. As she ran on there was a clattering behind, the new noise of the automobile.

For twenty years or more,
ever since he'd left his father's farm when he was sixteen to get a job in a Detroit machineshop, Henry Ford had been nuts

about machinery. First it was watches, then he designed a steamtractor, then he built a horseless carriage with an engine adapted from the Otto gasengine he'd read about in *The World of Science,* then a mechanical buggy with a onecylinder fourcycle motor, that would run forward but not back;

at last, in ninetyeight, he felt he was far enough along to risk throwing up his job with the Detroit Edison Company, where he'd worked his way up from night fireman to chief engineer, to put all his time into working on a new gasoline engine,

(in the late eighties he'd met Edison at a meeting of electriclight employees in Atlantic City. He'd gone up to Edison after Edison had delivered an address and asked him if he thought gasoline was practical as a motor fuel. Edison had said yes. If Edison said it, it was true. Edison was the great admiration of Henry Ford's life);

and in driving his mechanical buggy, sitting there at the lever jauntily dressed in a tightbuttoned jacket and a high collar and a derby hat, back and forth over the level illpaved streets of Detroit,

scaring the big brewery horses and the skinny trotting horses and the sleekrumped pacers with the motor's loud explosions,

looking for men scatterbrained enough to invest money in a factory for building automobiles.

He was the eldest son of an Irish immigrant who during the Civil War had married the daughter of a prosperous Pennsylvania Dutch farmer and settled down to farming near Dearborn in Wayne County, Michigan;

like plenty of other Americans, young Henry grew up hating the endless sogging through the mud about the chores, the hauling and pitching manure, the kerosene lamps to clean, the irk and sweat and solitude of the farm.

He was a slender, active youngster, a good skater, clever with his hands; what he liked was to tend the machinery and let the others do the heavy work. His mother had told him not to drink, smoke, gamble, or go into debt, and he never did.

When he was in his early twenties his father tried to get him back from Detroit, where he was working as mechanic and repairman for the Drydock Engine Company that built engines for steamboats, by giving him forty acres of land.

Young Henry built himself an uptodate square white dwellinghouse with a false mansard[1] roof and married and settled down on the farm,

but he let the hired men do the farming;

he bought himself a buzzsaw and rented a stationary engine and cut the timber off the woodlots.

He was a thrifty young man who never drank or smoked or gambled or coveted his neighbor's wife, but he couldn't stand living on the farm.

He moved to Detroit, and in the brick barn behind his house tinkered for years in his spare time with a mechanical buggy that would be light enough to run over the clayey wagonroads of Wayne County, Michigan.

By 1900 he had a practicable car to promote.

He was forty years old before the Ford Motor Company was started and production began to move.

Speed was the first thing the early automobile manufacturers went after. Races advertised the makes of cars.

Henry Ford himself hung up several records at the track at Grosse Pointe and on the ice on Lake St. Clair. In his 999 he did the mile in thirtynine and fourfifths seconds.

But it had always been his custom to hire others to do the heavy work. The speed he was busy with was speed in production, the records records in efficient output. He hired Barney Oldfield, a stunt bicyclerider from Salt Lake City, to do the racing for him.

1. **mansard** (măn'särd): a roof with two slopes on each of four sides; named after the French architect François Mansard (1598–1666).

Henry Ford had ideas about other things than the designing of motors, carburetors, magnetos, jigs and fixtures, punches and dies; he had ideas about sales.

that the big money was in economical quantity production, quick turnover, cheap interchangeable easilyreplaced standardized parts;

it wasn't until 1909, after years of arguing with his partners, that Ford put out the first Model T.

Henry Ford was right.

That season he sold more than ten thousand tin lizzies, ten years later he was selling almost a million a year.

In these years the Taylor Plan was stirring up plantmanagers and manufacturers all over the country. Efficiency was the word. The same ingenuity that went into improving the performance of a machine could go into improving the performance of the workmen producing the machine.

In 1913 they established the assemblyline at Ford's. That season the profits were something like twentyfive million dollars, but they had trouble in keeping the men on the job, machinists didn't seem to like it at Ford's.

Henry Ford had ideas about other things than production.

He was the largest automobile manufacturer in the world; he paid high wages; maybe if the steady workers thought they were getting a cut (a very small cut) in the profits, it would give trained men an inducement to stick to their jobs,

wellpaid workers might save enough money

First assembly line in Highland Park, Michigan, 1913, shown lowering the auto body onto the chassis.
Ford Motor Company, Dearborn, Michigan

to buy a tin lizzie; the first day Ford's announced that cleancut properlymarried American workers who wanted jobs had a chance to make five bucks a day (of course it turned out that there were strings to it; always there were strings to it)

such an enormous crowd waited outside the Highland Park plant

all through the zero January night

that there was a riot when the gates were opened; cops broke heads, jobhunters threw bricks; property, Henry Ford's own property, was destroyed. The company dicks[2] had to turn on the firehose to beat back the crowd.

The American Plan; automotive prosperity seeping down from above; it turned out there were strings to it.

But that five dollars a day

paid to good, clean American workmen

who didn't drink or smoke cigarettes or read or think,

and who didn't commit adultery

and whose wives didn't take in boarders,

made America once more the Yukon[3] of the sweated workers of the world;

made all the tin lizzies and the automotive age, and incidentally,

made Henry Ford the automobileer, the admirer of Edison, the birdlover,

the great American of his time.

2. **company dicks:** armed guards.
3. **Yukon:** a reference to the Alaskan gold rush of 1896–1899.

Reading Check

1. How old was Henry Ford when he left his father's farm to work in Detroit?
2. Which inventor did Ford admire?
3. Why did Ford hire Barney Oldfield?
4. When was the first Model T Ford produced?
5. Why was there a riot at Ford's plant?

For Study and Discussion

Analyzing and Interpreting the Essay

1. "Tin Lizzie" is an **impressionistic** biography of Henry Ford. While Dos Passos presents some basic facts of Ford's life, he is more interested in giving his impressions of Ford's character. How does Dos Passos characterize Ford as a young man?

2. Although Dos Passos seems to devote his essay to Ford's achievements, his selection of detail and his tone suggest that he is actually mocking Ford's contributions to American life. For example, in referring to Ford's early work, Dos Passos might have called him simply an "engineer." What attitude toward Ford does he reveal by using the journalist's grand-sounding but awkward word, *automobileer*?

3. Dos Passos' tone in this essay is sharply ironic. What does his statement "If Edison said it, it was true" imply about Ford's depth of thought?

4. Find three other examples of phrases and sentences used to establish an ironic tone and to undercut the portrayal of Ford as "the great American of his time."

Creative Writing

Writing an Impressionistic Biography

Select a real or invented public figure. In a short essay, present facts about that person's life that give the reader a definite impression of his or her character.

ZORA NEALE HURSTON
1891?–1960

Like Langston Hughes, Jean Toomer, Claude McKay, and Countee Cullen (page 796), Zora Neale Hurston was active in the Harlem Renaissance. The author of such early stories as "Spunk" and "Isis," Hurston was also a prominent Harlem personality who gained a reputation as a wit for both her humorous tales of small-town life and her high spirited nature.

Hurston was born in the all-black town of Eatonville, Florida, probably in 1891. Throughout her life Hurston was deliberately ambiguous about her birthdate, giving various dates in her writings. Arriving in New York in 1925 to pursue a literary career, Hurston became the personal secretary to novelist Fanny Hurst and enrolled in Barnard College to study anthropology (she had previously studied at Howard University in Washington, D.C., at the time the nation's leading black university).

In 1927, after her graduation from Barnard, Hurston returned to Florida, already a published story writer, to study Negro folk traditions. *Mules and Men* (1935), her most popular book, made use of folk materials. Her anthropological research also undoubtedly contributed to her ample supply of stories about small-town life, her commitment to oral narrative, and her ability to suffuse actual speech patterns into her prose.

Hurston's best novel, *Their Eyes Were Watching God* (1937), appeared after the Great Depression had brought an end to the Harlem Renaissance. By the time her autobiography, *Dust Tracks on a Road*, ap-

Zora Neale Hurston, 1935.

peared in 1942, there was no longer an audience for her work. She spent the last decade of her life in Florida, working as a maid and trying unsuccessfully to find a publisher for a long novel about Herod the Great. Only in the 1970s was her work rediscovered, and she is now widely recognized as an important interpreter of the black American experience.

FROM

Dust Tracks on a Road

Perhaps a year before the old man[1] died, I came to know two other white people for myself. They were women.

It came about this way. The whites who came down from the North were often brought by their friends to visit the village school. A Negro school was something strange to them, and while they were always sympathetic and kind, curiosity must have been present, also. They came and went, came and went. Always, the room was hurriedly put in order, and we were threatened with a prompt and bloody death if we cut one caper while the visitors were present. We always sang a spiritual, led by Mr. Calhoun himself. Mrs. Calhoun always stood in the back, with a palmetto switch in her hand as a squelcher. We were all little angels for the duration, because we'd better be. She would cut her eyes and give us a glare that meant trouble, then turn her face towards the visitors and beam as much as to say it was a great privilege and pleasure to teach lovely children like us. They couldn't see that palmetto hickory in her hand behind all those benches, but we knew where our angelic behavior was coming from.

Usually, the visitors gave warning a day ahead and we would be cautioned to put on shoes, comb our heads, and see to ears and fingernails. There was a close inspection of every one of us before we marched in that morning. Knotty heads, dirty ears and fingernails got hauled out of line, strapped and sent home to lick the calf over again.

This particular afternoon, the two young ladies just popped in. Mr. Calhoun was flustered, but he put on the best show he could. He dismissed the class that he was teaching up at the front of the room, then called the fifth grade in reading. That was my class.

So we took our readers and went up front. We stood up in the usual line, and opened to the lesson. It was the story of Pluto and Persephone.[2] It was new and hard to the class in general, and Mr. Calhoun was very uncomfortable as the readers stumbled along, spelling out words with their lips, and in mumbling undertones before they exposed them experimentally to the teacher's ears.

Then it came to me. I was fifth or sixth down the line. The story was not new to me, because I had read my reader through from lid to lid, the first week that Papa had bought it for me.

That is how it was that my eyes were not in the book, working out the paragraph which I knew would be mine by counting the children ahead of me. I was observing our visitors, who held a book between them, following the lesson. They had shiny hair, mostly brownish. One had a looping gold chain around her neck. The other one was dressed all over in black and white with a pretty finger ring on her left hand. But the thing that held my eyes were their fingers. They were long and thin, and very white, except up near the tips. There they were baby pink. I had never seen such hands. It was a fascinating discovery for me. I wondered how they felt. I would have given those hands more attention, but the child before me was almost through. My turn next, so I got on my mark, bringing my eyes back to the book and made sure of my place. Some of the stories I had reread several times, and this Greco-Roman myth was one of my favorites. I

1. **old man:** a white farmer who knew Zora Neale's family well. He had assisted at her birth and afterward took an interest in the girl, taking her fishing, telling her stories, and giving her advice.

2. **Pluto and Persephone** (pər-sĕf′ə-nē): In Roman mythology Pluto is the god of the underworld. He is identified with the Greek Hades. Persephone is the Greek name for Pluto's wife. She is queen of the underworld. Hurston is retelling the well-known classical myth of the origin of the seasons.

Dunbar High School, Quincy, Florida, c. 1910.
Florida State Archives

was exalted by it, and that is the way I read my paragraph.

"Yes, Jupiter[3] had seen her (Persephone). He had seen the maiden picking flowers in the field. He had seen the chariot of the dark monarch pause by the maiden's side. He had seen him when he seized Persephone. He had seen the black horses leap down Mount Aetna's[4] fiery throat. Persephone was now in Pluto's dark realm and he had made her his wife."

The two women looked at each other and then back to me. Mr. Calhoun broke out with a proud smile beneath his bristly moustache, and instead of the next child taking up where I had ended, he nodded to me to go on. So I read the story to the end, where flying Mercury, the messenger of the gods, brought Persephone back to the sunlit earth and restored her to the arms of Dame Ceres,[5] her mother, that the world might have springtime and summer flowers, autumn and harvest. But because she had bitten the pomegranate while in Pluto's kingdom, she must return to him for three months of each year, and be his queen. Then the world had winter, until she returned to earth.

The class was dismissed and the visitors smiled us away and went into a low-voiced conversation with Mr. Calhoun for a few minutes. They glanced my way once or twice and I began to worry. Not only was I barefooted, but my feet and legs were dusty. My hair was

3. **Jupiter:** king of the gods; Pluto's brother. He is also known as Zeus and Jove.
4. **Mount Aetna:** an active volcano in eastern Sicily.

5. **Ceres** (sîr′ēz): Roman goddess of agriculture.

Zora Neale Hurston **903**

more uncombed than usual, and my nails were not shiny clean. Oh, I'm going to catch it now. Those ladies saw me, too. Mr. Calhoun is promising to 'tend to me. So I thought.

Then Mr. Calhoun called me. I went up thinking how awful it was to get a whipping before company. Furthermore, I heard a snicker run over the room. Hennie Clark and Stell Brazzle did it out loud, so I would be sure to hear them. The smart aleck was going to get it. I slipped one hand behind me and switched my dress tail at them, indicating scorn.

"Come here, Zora Neale," Mr. Calhoun cooed as I reached the desk. He put his hand on my shoulder and gave me little pats. The ladies smiled and held out those flower-looking fingers towards me. I seized the opportunity for a good look.

"Shake hands with the ladies, Zora Neale," Mr. Calhoun prompted and they took my hand one after the other and smiled. They asked me if I loved school, and I lied that I did. There was *some* truth in it, because I liked geography and reading, and I liked to play at recess time. Whoever it was invented writing and arithmetic got no thanks from me. Neither did I like the arrangement where the teacher could sit up there with a palmetto stem and lick me whenever he saw fit. I hated things I couldn't do anything about. But I knew better than to bring that up right there, so I said yes, I *loved* school.

"I can tell you do," Brown Taffeta gleamed. She patted my head, and was lucky enough not to get sandspurs in her hand. Children who roll and tumble in the grass in Florida, are apt to get sandspurs in their hair. They shook hands with me again and I went back to my seat.

When school let out at three o'clock, Mr. Calhoun told me to wait. When everybody had gone, he told me I was to go to the Park House, that was the hotel in Maitland, the next afternoon to call upon Mrs. Johnstone and Miss Hurd. I must tell Mama to see that I was clean and brushed from head to feet, and I must

wear shoes and stockings. The ladies liked me, he said, and I must be on my best behavior.

The next day I was let out of school an hour early, and went home to be stood up in a tub of suds and be scrubbed and have my ears dug into. My sandy hair sported a red ribbon to match my red and white checked gingham dress, starched until it could stand alone. Mama saw to it that my shoes were on the right feet, since I was careless about left and right. Last thing, I was given a handkerchief to carry, warned again about my behavior, and sent off, with my big brother John to go as far as the hotel gate with me.

First thing, the ladies gave me strange things, like stuffed dates and preserved ginger, and encouraged me to eat all that I wanted. Then they showed me their Japanese dolls and just talked. I was then handed a copy of *Scribner's Magazine*, and asked to read a place that was pointed out to me. After a paragraph or two, I was told with smiles, that that would do.

I was led out on the grounds and they took my picture under a palm tree. They handed me what was to me then a heavy cylinder done up in fancy paper, tied with a ribbon, and they told me goodbye, asking me not to open it until I got home.

My brother was waiting for me down by the lake, and we hurried home, eager to see what was in the thing. It was too heavy to be candy or anything like that. John insisted on toting it for me.

My mother made John give it back to me and let me open it. Perhaps, I shall never experience such joy again. The nearest thing to that moment was the telegram accepting my first book. One hundred goldy-new pennies rolled out of the cylinder. Their gleam lit up the world. It was not avarice that moved me. It was the beauty of the thing. I stood on the mountain. Mama let me play with my pennies for a while, then put them away for me to keep.

That was only the beginning. The next day I received an Episcopal hymnbook bound in white leather with a golden cross stamped into the front cover, a copy of *The Swiss Family Robinson*,[6] and a book of fairy tales.

I set about to commit the song words to memory. There was no music written there, just the words. But there was to my consciousness music in between them just the same. "When I survey the Wondrous Cross" seemed the most beautiful to me, so I committed that to memory first of all. Some of them seemed dull and without life, and I pretended they were not there. If white people liked trashy singing like that, there must be something funny about them that I had not noticed before. I stuck to the pretty ones where the words marched to a throb I could feel.

A month or so after the two young ladies returned to Minnesota, they sent me a huge box packed with clothes and books. The red coat with a wide circular collar and the red tam pleased me more than any of the other things. My chums pretended not to like anything that I had, but even then I knew that they were jealous. Old Smarty had gotten by them again. The clothes were not new, but they were very good. I shone like the morning sun.

But the books gave me more pleasure than the clothes. I had never been too keen on dressing up. It called for hard scrubbings with Octagon soapsuds getting in my eyes, and none too gentle fingers scrubbing my neck and gouging in my ears.

In that box were *Gulliver's Travels, Grimm's Fairy Tales, Dick Whittington,*[7] *Greek and Roman Myths,* and best of all, *Norse Tales.*[8] Why did the Norse tales strike so deeply into my soul?

I do not know, but they did. I seemed to remember seeing Thor swing his mighty short-handled hammer as he sped across the sky in rumbling thunder, lightning flashing from the tread of his steeds and the wheels of his chariot. The great and good Odin, who went down to the well of knowledge to drink, and was told that the price of a drink from that fountain was an eye. Odin drank deeply, then plucked out one eye without a murmur and handed it to the grizzly keeper, and walked away. That held majesty for me.

Of the Greeks, Hercules moved me most. I followed him eagerly on his tasks. The story of the choice of Hercules as a boy when he met Pleasure and Duty, and put his hand in that of Duty and followed her steep way to the blue hills of fame and glory, which she pointed out at the end, moved me profoundly. I resolved to be like him. The tricks and turns of the other gods and goddesses left me cold. There were other thin books about this and that sweet and gentle little girl who gave up her heart to Christ and good works. Almost always they died from it, preaching as they passed. I was utterly indifferent to their deaths. In the first place I could not conceive of death, and in the next place they never had any funerals that amounted to a hill of beans, so I didn't care how soon they rolled up their big, soulful, blue eyes and kicked the bucket. They had no meat on their bones.

But I also met Hans Andersen[9] and Robert Louis Stevenson.[10] They seemed to know what I wanted to hear and said it in a way that tingled me. Just a little below these friends was Rudyard Kipling in his *Jungle Books.*[11] I loved his talking snakes as much as I did the hero.

---

6. ***The Swiss Family Robinson:*** a story of a family shipwrecked on an uninhabited island, by the Swiss writer Johann David Wyss (1743–1818).
7. ***Gulliver's . . . Whittington:*** *Gulliver's Travels,* by the English satirist Jonathan Swift (1667–1745); *Grimm's Fairy Tales,* German tales collected by the brothers Jakob Ludwig Grimm (1785–1863) and Wilhelm Karl Grimm (1786–1859); *Dick Whittington,* a tale about an actual mayor of London in the early fifteenth century. Dick is a poor orphan who achieves great success.
8. ***Norse Tales:*** the mythology of Scandinavian people. Thor is the god of thunder; Odin, the ruler of the Norse gods, holds a position similar to that of Zeus (Jupiter) in Greek and Roman mythology.

9. **Hans Andersen:** Hans Christian Andersen (1805–1875), Danish author of over 150 fairy tales.
10. **Robert Louis Stevenson:** Scottish author (1850–1894) of such exciting adventure stories as *Treasure Island* and *Kidnapped.*
11. **Rudyard Kipling:** English writer (1865–1936) of such popular children's books as *Kim, Captains Courageous,* and *The Jungle Books,* which recount the adventures of Mowgli, an Indian boy who gets lost in a forest and finds shelter with a family of wolves.

Reading Check

1. What story does Zora's class read for their visitors?
2. What subjects does Zora like at school?
3. During her visit to the hotel, what do the ladies ask Zora to do?
4. At the end of her visit, what do the ladies give Zora?

For Study and Discussion

Analyzing and Interpreting the Selection

1. Hurston has a reputation as a rich and expressive stylist. She makes effective use of idiomatic speech patterns in an attempt to bring the oral voice to her writing. Early in this selection, in talking about the inspection, she says that "Knotty heads, dirty ears and fingernails got hauled out of line, strapped and sent home to lick the calf over again." **a.** What does she mean by "lick the calf over again"? **b.** What does such an unusual expression convey, and why is it an effective means of description?

2a. What opinion does Zora have of the two women? **b.** What evidence is presented that enables you to tell what she thinks?

3. The author mentions "thin books" that left her unmoved. What do you learn about her tastes in reading?

4a. What words would you use to characterize the young Zora? **b.** How does she present herself?

Writing About Literature

Discussing Reading Tastes

In this selection from her autobiography, Hurston reveals that there were books she particularly liked as a child and others to which she was indifferent. Write an essay discussing her reading tastes, citing evidence from the selection.

Thomas Wolfe was a giant of a man (six feet six inches tall) with tremendous emotions and appetites, who acknowledged his own "intemperate excess, an almost insane hunger to devour the body of human experience." He was a feverishly energetic writer, amassing great piles of manuscript that his distinguished editor, Maxwell Perkins, helped him to trim and shape into his first novel, *Look Homeward, Angel.* As a writer, Wolfe has been criticized for his inability to know when to stop the mad rush of words and feelings that tears down all subtleties. Yet despite his failings, Wolfe had considerable talent, even if he sometimes misused it, and it is difficult to read Wolfe's writings without experiencing moments of great power.

Wolfe was born in Asheville, North Carolina, and attended the University of North Carolina. At first, his ambition was to be a dramatist, and after graduation from college he went to Harvard to study playwriting in a famous course conducted by George Pierce Baker, who had been the teacher of Eugene O'Neill. Gradually, Wolfe found the drama too confining for his talent. While teaching in New York, he wrote novels at night. Several publishers rejected Wolfe's enormous manuscripts until Perkins, discerning the talent beneath the wordage, worked with Wolfe for eight months to get a book into shape for publication. *Look Homeward, Angel* (1929), an obviously autobiographical novel, was an enormous success and established Wolfe's reputation. In his thinly disguised depictions of his hometown neighbors he offended a number of people.

Always Wolfe had felt that because of his height and sensitivity, he was different from other men. Now he felt more isolated than ever. With Perkins' help, he published a second novel, *Of Time and the River* (1935). Then, perhaps feeling that Perkins had played too great a role in determining the final shape of his novels, Wolfe went to another publisher

Thomas Wolfe.
Culver Pictures

and editor. The hero of Wolfe's first two novels was Eugene Gant, a character who, in height and ambitions, was very much like Wolfe himself. To demonstrate that he was much more than an autobiographical novelist, Wolfe created a new hero for his later work, George Webber. After Wolfe's death, two novels about George Webber were published: *The Web and the Rock* (1939) and *You Can't Go Home Again* (1940). His other major writings include a fifth novel, *The Hills Beyond* (1941), and a critical work, *The Story of a Novel* (1936). The following piece, from the collection *From Death to Morning* (1935), demonstrates two of Wolfe's gifts as a writer: his terrific energy and his almost perfect memory for sensory details.

Thomas Wolfe **907**

Circus at Night (1960) by Waldo Peirce (1884–1970). Oil on canvas.
Museum of Art of Ogunquit, Maine

Circus at Dawn

There were times in early autumn—in September—when the greater circuses would come to town—the Ringling Brothers, Robinson's, and Barnum and Bailey shows, and when I was a route-boy on the morning paper, on those mornings when the circus would be coming in, I would rush madly through my route in the cool and thrilling darkness that comes just before break of day, and then I would go back home and get my brother out of bed.

Talking in low excited voices we would walk rapidly back toward town under the rustle of September leaves, in cool streets just grayed now with that still, that unearthly and magical first light of day which seems suddenly to rediscover the great earth out of darkness, so that the earth emerges with an awful, glorious sculptural stillness, and one looks out with a feeling of joy and disbelief, as the first men on this earth must have done, for to see this happen is one of the things that men will remember out of life forever and think of as they die.

At the sculptural still square where at one

corner, just emerging into light, my father's shabby little marble shop stood with a ghostly strangeness and familiarity, my brother and I would "catch" the first streetcar of the day bound for the "depot" where the circus was—or sometimes we would meet someone we knew, who would give us a lift in his automobile.

Then, having reached the dingy, grimy, and rickety depot section, we would get out, and walk rapidly across the tracks of the station yard, where we could see great flares and steamings from the engines, and hear the crash and bump of shifting freight cars, the swift sporadic thunders of a shifting engine, the tolling of bells, the sounds of great trains on the rails.

And to all these familiar sounds, filled with their exultant prophecies of flight, the voyage, morning, and the shining cities—to all the sharp and thrilling odors of the trains—the smell of cinders, acrid smoke, of musty, rusty freight cars, the clean pine-board of crated produce, and the smells of fresh stored food—oranges, coffee, tangerines and bacon, ham, and flour and beef—there would be added now, with an unforgettable magic and familiarity, all the strange sounds and smells of the coming circus.

The gay yellow sumptuous-looking cars in which the star performers lived and slept, still dark and silent, heavily and powerfully still, would be drawn up in long strings upon the tracks. And all around them the sounds of the unloading circus would go on furiously in the darkness. The receding gulf of lilac and departing night would be filled with the savage roar of the lions, the murderously sudden snarling of great jungle cats, the trumpeting of the elephants, the stamp of the horses, and with the musty, pungent, unfamiliar odor of the jungle animals: the tawny camel smells, and the smells of panthers, zebras, tigers, elephants, and bears.

Then, along the tracks, beside the circus trains, there would be the sharp cries and oaths of the circus men, the magical swinging dance of lanterns in the darkness, the sudden heavy rumble of the loaded vans and wagons as they were pulled along the flats[1] and gondolas,[2] and down the runways to the ground. And everywhere, in the thrilling mystery of darkness and awakening light, there would be the tremendous conflict of a confused, hurried, and yet orderly movement.

The great iron-gray horses, four and six to a team, would be plodding along the road of thick white dust to a rattling of chains and traces and the harsh cries of their drivers. The men would drive the animals to the river which flowed by beyond the tracks, and water them; and as first light came, one could see the elephants wallowing in the familiar river and the big horses going slowly and carefully down to drink.

Then, on the circus grounds, the tents were going up already with the magic speed of dreams. All over the place (which was near the tracks and the only space of flat land in the town that was big enough to hold a circus) there would be this fierce, savagely hurried, and yet orderly confusion. Great flares of gaseous circus light would blaze down on the seared and battered faces of the circus toughs as, with the rhythmic precision of a single animal—a human riveting machine—they swung their sledges at the stakes, driving a stake into the earth with the incredible instancy of accelerated figures in a motion picture. And everywhere, as light came, and the sun appeared, there would be a scene of magic, order, and of violence. The drivers would curse and talk their special language to their teams, there would be the loud, gasping, and uneven labor of a gasoline engine, the shouts and curses of the bosses, the wooden riveting of driven stakes, and the rattle of heavy chains.

Already in an immense cleared space of dusty beaten earth, the stakes were being driven for the main exhibition tent. And an elephant would lurch ponderously to the field,

1. **flats:** flatcars.
2. **gondolas** (gŏnd′l-əz): railroad cars with sides and ends, but without tops.

slowly lower his great swinging head at the command of a man who sat perched upon his skull, flourish his gray, wrinkled snout a time or two, and then solemnly wrap it around a tent pole big as the mast of a racing schooner. Then the elephant would back slowly away, dragging the great pole with him as if it were a stick of matchwood. . . .

Meanwhile, the circus food tent—a huge canvas top without concealing sides—had already been put up, and now we could see the performers seated at long trestled tables underneath the tent, as they ate breakfast. And the savor of the food they ate—mixed as it was with our strong excitement, with the powerful but wholesome smells of the animals, and with all the joy, sweetness, mystery, jubilant magic and glory of the morning and the coming of the circus—seemed to us to be of the most maddening and appetizing succulence of any food that we had ever known or eaten.

We could see the circus performers eating tremendous breakfasts, with all the savage relish of their power and strength: they ate big fried steaks, pork chops, rashers[3] of bacon, a half-dozen eggs, great slabs of fried ham and great stacks of wheat cakes which a cook kept flipping in the air with the skill of a juggler, and which a husky-looking waitress kept rushing to their tables on loaded trays held high and balanced marvelously on the fingers of a brawny hand. And above all the maddening odors of the wholesome and succulent food, there brooded forever the sultry and delicious fragrance—that somehow seemed to add a zest and sharpness to all the powerful and thrilling life of morning—of strong boiling coffee, which we could see sending off clouds of steam from an enormous polished urn, and which the circus performers gulped down cup after cup.

And the circus men and women themselves—these star performers—were such fine-looking people, strong and handsome, yet speaking and moving with an almost stern dig-

nity and decorum, that their lives seemed to us to be as splendid and wonderful as any lives on earth could be. There was never anything loose, rowdy, or tough in their comportment. . . .

Rather, these people in an astonishing way seemed to have created an established community which lived an ordered existence on wheels, and to observe with a stern fidelity unknown in towns and cities the decencies of family life. There would be a powerful young man, a handsome and magnificent young woman with blond hair and the figure of an Amazon,[4] and a powerfully built, thickset man of middle age, who had a stern, lined, responsible-looking face and a bald head. They were probably the members of a trapeze team—the young man and woman would leap through space like projectiles, meeting the grip of the older man and hurtling back again upon their narrow perches, catching the swing of their trapeze in midair, and whirling thrice before they caught it, in a perilous and beautiful exhibition of human balance and precision.

But when they came into the breakfast tent, they would speak gravely yet courteously to other performers, and seat themselves in a family group at one of the long tables, eating their tremendous breakfast with an earnest concentration, seldom speaking to one another, and then gravely, seriously, and briefly.

And my brother and I would look at them with fascinated eyes; my brother would watch the man with the bald head for a while and then turn toward me, whispering:

"D-d-do you see that f-f-fellow there with the bald head? W-w-well, he's the heavy man," he whispered knowingly. "He's the one that c-c-c-catches them! That f-f-fellow's got to know his business! You know what happens if he m-m-misses, don't you?" said my brother.

"What?" I would say in a fascinated tone.

My brother snapped his fingers in the air.

"Over!" he said. "D-d-done for! W-w-why,

3. **rashers:** thin slices.

4. **Amazon:** a member of a legendary race of women warriors; used generally to describe a woman of great strength or size.

they'd be d-d-d-dead before they knew what happened. Sure!" he said, nodding vigorously. "It's a f-f-f-fact! If he ever m-m-m-misses it's all over! That boy has g-g-g-got to know his s-s-s-stuff!" my brother said. "W-w-w-why," he went on in a low tone of solemn conviction, "it w-w-w-wouldn't surprise me at all if they p-p-p-pay him s-s-seventy-five or a hundred dollars a week! It's a fact!" my brother cried vigorously.

And we would turn our fascinated stares again upon these splendid and romantic creatures, whose lives were so different from our own, and whom we seemed to know with such familiar and affectionate intimacy. And at length, reluctantly, with full light come and the sun up, we would leave the circus grounds and start for home.

And somehow the memory of all we had seen and heard that glorious morning, and the memory of the food tent with its wonderful smells, would waken in us the pangs of such a ravenous hunger that we could not wait until we got home to eat. We would stop off in town at lunchrooms and, seated on tall stools before the counter, we would devour ham-and-egg sandwiches, hot hamburgers, red and pungent at their cores with coarse, spicy, sanguinary beef, coffee, glasses of foaming milk, and doughnuts, and then go home to eat up everything in sight upon the breakfast table.

Analyzing and Interpreting the Selection

1. How does each of the circus scenes convey the special qualities that might be missing during other times of day?

2. To the boys, how does the behavior of the circus people differ from that of ordinary people?

3. Wolfe is sensitive to sights, sounds, and odors. Find descriptive phrases that you think are particularly effective in appealing to the senses.

4. Wolfe wrote this piece from the point of view of an adult re-creating his childhood experiences. Do you think adults or adolescents are more likely to see their childhood in true perspective or to romanticize it and distort the truth? Support your answer with examples from this selection and from your own experience.

Language and Vocabulary

Noting Characteristics of Style

It is interesting to note various characteristics of Wolfe's style. In "Circus at Dawn," find two examples of each of these stylistic devices:

1. the piling up of detail upon detail

2. the joining together of a number of clauses

3. the extravagant use of adjectives and adverbs such as *thrilling*, *magical*, *powerfully*, and *pungent*.

What effect on the reader does Wolfe create?

Reading Check

1. What job must the narrator complete before leaving for the circus?
2. Which animal assists in setting up the circus tent?
3. What are the three circus scenes described?
4. Which performers does the narrator's brother talk about?

ERNESTO GALARZA
1905–1984

Ernesto Galarza was born in the mountain village of Jalcocotán in western Mexico. When he was a boy, he and his family were uprooted by the Mexican Revolution and fled to the United States. *Barrio Boy* (1971) is Galarza's true account of their journey and their settlement in Sacramento, California.

Galarza, a United States citizen, received his Ph.D. from Columbia University. Besides writing, he taught and lectured for many years, and was a Chicano activist. He wrote *Zoo Risa, Merchants of Labor, Spiders in the House and Workers in the Field,* and was coauthor of *Mexican Americans in the Southwest.*

In the following excerpt from *Barrio Boy,* Galarza describes some of the details of his family's daily life in the small Mexican town of Jalcocotán. This scene takes place early in the book, before the family must emigrate from Mexico.

Ernesto Galarza, June, 1972.
Jess Ramirez

FROM

Barrio Boy

Like many other mountain pueblos, Jalcocotán had no school. Once the village had sent a committee to Tepic[1] to petition the government for a teacher. The committee assured the government that the neighbors would be willing to build the school themselves and to provide the teacher with a place to live. Once in a great while, when the *Jefe Político,*[2] who represented the government, visited Jalco he would be asked very discreetly and courteously about the petition. The answer was always the same: "It is under consideration." Many years had passed—how many no one really knew—and Jalco still had neither teacher nor school when we went to live there.

Reading, writing, and arithmetic were held in great esteem by the jalcocotecanos. A few adults in the town had finished the third or fourth grade somewhere else. They taught

1. **Tepic** (tä-pēk'): town in western Mexico.
2. **Jefe Político:** governor of a province.

their own children the *a, b, c's* and simple arithmetic with the abacus. For writing they had the *pizarra* and the *pizarrín*—a small square of slate with a decorated wooden frame and a slate pencil.

Books were rare. My mother had one, which she kept in the cedar box. It had a faded polychrome drawing on the cover with the title *La Cocinera Poblana*,[3] a cookbook which had belonged to Grandmother Isabel. We did not need it for cooking the simple, never-changing meals of the family. It was the first book from which Doña[4] Henriqueta ever read to me. The idea of making printed words sound like the things you already knew about first came through to me from her reading of the recipes. I thought it remarkable that you could find oregano in a book as well as in the herb pot back of our house. I learned to pick out words like *sal* and *frijoles, chile piquín* and *panocha*[5]—things we ate. From hearing my mother repeat the title so often when she read to us, and from staring at the cover drawing, I guessed that the beautiful girl in the colorful costume was the *Cocinera Poblana*. The words above her picture were obviously her name. I memorized them and touched them. I could read.

For me and my cousins until we were six, book learning was limited to a glimpse now and then of my mother's cookbook. Our school was the corral, the main street of Jalco, the arroyo, and the kitchen.

We learned to roast coffee on the *comal*.[6] In the back of the house we kept a large basket of green coffee beans covered with a straw mat. Every few days my aunt scooped a bowl of the beans and spread them on the hot griddle. We took turns stirring them with a long wooden spoon. When the beans were toasted to a shade of rich brown, which my aunt called *el punto*,[7] she took over. Too much brown and

the coffee would taste burnt. Too little and it would taste raw. While this was going on the incense of coffee filled the house.

The toasted beans were then stored in an earthen pot covered with a cloth and a lid. Every afternoon a portion of this supply was measured out and chucked into the coffee grinder with the bronze cast-iron dome, the crooked handle, and the tiny wooden drawer. We took turns at the daily grind to give us enough fresh coffee for the next three meals.

The green coffee and the other staples of corn, beans, and rice were kept in rattan baskets along the back wall where it was always coolest and darkest. From a rafter there usually hung a stem of bananas, the king-sized ones called *plátano grande*. Braids of red peppers hung there also, and white onions. Three boards resting on pegs made a shelf where we kept the bundles of cornhusks and the dried herbs. Stashed somewhere in the larder there was always a jar of raisins and some vanilla pods which appeared in the kitchen only on special occasions. From this storehouse came the foods and aromas of Doña Esther's kitchen.

Watching her, I learned to cook rice. She poured a cup of water into the rice bowl and churned it with a spoon to rinse it. In a clay frying pan the cooking oil was already sputtering, and in it the washed rice was spread and stirred constantly until it turned a light brown. The rice was then covered with boiling water, salted, peppered, seasoned with minced onions and set on a side burner of the *pretil*[8] to simmer. The grains of rice came out of the pan crisp and whole, the mark of proper Mexican rice.

Our cooking lessons included roasting *pinole*, brewing *atole*,[9] steaming tamales, and barbecuing the big bananas.

Pinole was for birthdays, the only production in which my cousins and I had more to do than my aunt or my mother. On the *comal* we

---

3. **La Cocinera Poblana:** *The Cook from Puebla.*
4. **Doña:** a Spanish title of respect used with a lady's given name.
5. **sal . . . panocha:** salt, pinto beans, chili peppers, and coarse sugar.
6. **comal:** a flat, earthenware pan.
7. **el punto:** the moment or precise point.

8. **pretil:** stove.
9. **pinole:** a finely ground, brownish powder; **atole:** a gruel made of brewing corn meal and other ingredients.

Kneading dough for tortillas.
Keith Gunnar / Bruce Coleman, Inc.

As a combination, *atole* with *panocha* was almost in the same class with *pinole*. The *atole* was a thick gruel of plain cornmeal. By itself it was ordinary stuff. But with *panocha* it was delicious. On Sunday evenings or on birthdays, instead of coffee we were served, in the same big earthen cups, steaming *atole*. Between careful nips of it Jesús, Catarino, and I passed around a chunk of the brown sugar cone for a suck and a lick. How you handled your *atole* marked the difference between a man and a boy. A man would gulp the thick, scalding liquid and crunch his own *panocha*. A boy sipped between licks at the sugar cone; a child would be given lukewarm *atole* dipped out of the cup on his mother's finger. For this we had a saying, "I gave him *atole* with my finger," which meant someone was a babe in the woods.

If we were in luck the *atole* and *panocha* were served with tamales. The day special visitors came we had a *tamalada*.[11] It was an all-day affair; getting the cornhusks down from the back shelf; washing them until they bent without cracking; grinding the corn to make the *masa*;[12] boiling the chicken; smearing the husks with moist cornmeal; tucking a bit of chicken into each chunk of *masa*, with a raisin or two; doubling the ends of the corn wrappers back and tying them in the middle of the *tamal* with a strip of husk.

The magic of the *tamalada* was not in all this preparation but in the *olla*—a huge earthen pot made of red baked clay like the rest of our kitchen ware, rough outside, glazed inside, and burnt black on the bottom. Into the belly of the olla went three or four small flat rocks. These were covered with water; on top of them a layer of shredded green banana leaves; on top of the leaves layer after layer, each crosswise to the next, of raw tamales. Some folded cloth napkins were battened down on top of the loaded *olla*. Set on the main burner of our stove, it became a pressure cooker, spitting steam around the edges of the napkins.

roasted a cupful of dried corn, which we passed through the coffee grinder; on the *metate*[10] we ground vanilla pods, lemon leaves, and raisins which had been dried in the sun until they were brittle. My aunt added a few scrapings of chocolate. We tightened the coffee grinder and put the mix through again. It came out *pinole*, a fine brownish powder that we ate a pinch at a time and that required much chewing and a great deal of saliva.

10. *metate:* a flat stone used to grind maize.

11. *tamalada:* The general sense is "a tamale party."
12. *masa:* dough.

Kitchen in rural Mexico.

The visitors were served first, along with the men of the household. They took their *atole* boiling and crunched the *panocha* instead of licking it. When everyone had been served, the corn wrappers were dumped in the corral under the willow. Coronel, the hens, and Nerón[13] soon scattered them, sniffing and pecking for bits of cooked *masa* that had not been scraped from the husks.

Even less frequent than the *tamaladas* were the banana barbecues which we called *tatemas*. Somewhere up on the mountain my Uncle Gus cut down a stem of the *plátanos grandes*. It was hung from the beam in the back of the house. Its long green fingers turned in, tight and solid, with straight brown ridges showing like veins from tip to tip. A cluster of these fingers was called, naturally, a hand.

In the corral the men dug a large round hole. The bottom was covered with rocks, and on top of them we burned *ocote*[14] and charcoal.

13. **Coronel . . . Nerón:** a rooster and a dog, Ernesto's pets.

14. *ocote:* torch pine.

Ernesto Galarza **915**

When the stones were at top heat a thick pad of banana leaves was laid on them, followed by a layer of bananas, another layer of leaves, and so on until the hole was packed. Level with the ground a mattress of leaves and dirt was laid, weighed down by short, heavy poles.

The hard part came next—to wait overnight until one of the men began the unpacking. From between the layers of steaming leaves the huge *plátanos* came forth, dripping in their own syrup. My aunt laid them inside the *olla*, from which she would take them one by one and serve them sliced, with *atole*. As they came out of the pit some of the bananas were wrapped in leaves, and we were sent to take them to the neighbors. This was better than taking cups of rice or beans because we could suck our fingers returning home.

Reading Check

1. What was Ernesto Galarza's first experience with reading?
2. What served as the children's schoolroom?
3. What kind of cookware does Galarza say is responsible for the character of Mexican food?
4. What food was prepared in barbecue pits?

For Study and Discussion

Analyzing and Interpreting the Selection
1. At the opening of the selection, Galarza tells us that his village had no school. What is the relevance of this information to the rest of the chapter?
2. How did the villagers provide for the education of their children?
3. How does Galarza convey the pleasures of preparing and eating Mexican food?

Expository Writing

Explaining the Preparation of a Dish
Every family has its own favorite and holiday dishes. Choose a favorite family dish and, like Galarza, describe both how it is made and the atmosphere surrounding its preparation.

RICHARD WRIGHT
1908–1960

Richard Wright.
Sylvia Beach Collection, Princeton University
Library, courtesy Photo Researchers

Richard Wright was the earliest of twentieth-century authors to examine the social, economic, and moral conditions of the urban black ghetto. He was born on a plantation near Natchez, Mississippi, but grew up in Memphis, Tennessee. His father deserted the family when Wright was five. A few years later, his mother, who was ill, placed her children first in an orphanage and then in the care of various relatives. At the age of nineteen, shortly before the advent of the Great Depression, Wright and one of his aunts made their way to Chicago. They were soon joined there by Wright's mother and brother, and survival became the family's constant worry.

Wright published his first collection of short stories in 1938 but became well known with the publication in 1940 of his first novel, *Native Son*. *Native Son* is significant in American literature for bringing unprecedented attention to black literature and black writers. *Black Boy*, the story of Wright's experiences growing up in the South, appeared in 1945. This autobiographical work brought him the highest literary acclaim. After World War II, Wright moved with his family to Paris, where he lived until his death. He continued to write about the plight of the black American, and his work has served as an example and encouragement to many black writers. The critic Irving Howe attributed Wright's success to his having "kept faith with the experience of the boy who had fought his way out of the depths to speak for those who remained behind."

In addition to *Native Son* and *Black Boy*, which are among his finest contributions to American literature, Wright produced many other volumes, including *The God That Failed* (1950) and *Eight Men* (published posthumously in 1961). In 1977 *American Hunger*, the second part of Wright's autobiography, was published. Written in the 1940s, it continues the story begun in *Black Boy*, which ends with Wright's leaving the South. *American Hunger* begins with his arrival in Chicago in 1927. The following excerpt is from the opening chapter, in which Wright tells about his early days in Chicago and his first attempts at writing.

FROM

American Hunger

My first glimpse of the flat black stretches of Chicago depressed and dismayed me, mocked all my fantasies. Chicago seemed an unreal city whose mythical houses were built of slabs of black coal wreathed in palls of gray smoke, houses whose foundations were sinking slowly into the dank prairie. Flashes of steam showed intermittently on the wide horizon, gleaming translucently in the winter sun. The din of the city entered my consciousness, entered to remain for years to come. The year was 1927.

What would happen to me here? Would I survive? My expectations were modest. I wanted only a job. Hunger had long been my daily companion. Diversion and recreation, with the exception of reading, were unknown. In all my life—though surrounded by many people—I had not had a single satisfying, sustained relationship with another human being and, not having had any, I did not miss it. I made no demands whatever upon others. . . .

Wright visits an aunt living in Chicago and decides to settle temporarily in a rented room. After landing a job in a delicatessen, he takes an examination for a possible job as a postal clerk. He soon leaves the delicatessen and finds a new job as a dishwasher in a North Side café.

I worked at the café all spring and in June I was called for temporary duty in the post office. My confidence soared; if I obtained an appointment as a regular clerk, I could spend at least five hours a day writing.

I reported at the post office and was sworn in as a temporary clerk. I earned seventy cents an hour and I went to bed each night now with a full stomach for the first time in my life. When I worked nights, I wrote during the day; when I worked days, I wrote during the night.

But the happiness of having a job did not keep another worry from rising to plague me. Before I could receive a permanent appointment I would have to take a physical examination. The weight requirement was one hundred and twenty-five pounds and I—with my long years of semistarvation—barely tipped the scales at a hundred and ten. Frantically I turned all my spare money into food and ate. But my skin and flesh would not respond to the food. Perhaps I was not eating the right diet? Perhaps my chronic anxiety kept my weight down. I drank milk, ate steak, but it did not give me an extra ounce of flesh. I visited a doctor who told me that there was nothing wrong with me except malnutrition, that I must eat and sleep long hours. I did and my weight remained the same. I knew now that my job was temporary and that when the time came for my appointment I would have to resume my job hunting again.

At night I read Stein's *Three Lives,* Crane's *The Red Badge of Courage,* and Dostoevski's *The Possessed,*[1] all of which revealed new realms of feeling. But the most important discoveries came when I veered from fiction proper into the field of psychology and sociology. I ran through volumes that bore upon the causes of my conduct and the conduct of my people. I studied tables of figures relating population density to insanity, relating housing to disease, relating school and recreational opportunities to crime, relating various forms of neurotic behavior to environment, relating racial insecurities to the conflicts between whites and blacks. . . .

1. **Stein's *Three Lives* . . . *The Possessed:*** Gertrude Stein (1874–1946) and Stephen Crane (1871–1900), American writers; and Feodor Dostoevski (dôs′tô-yĕf′skē) (1821–1881), Russian writer. Each of the three books named was influential in the boldness of its subject matter and prose style.

I still had no friends, casual or intimate, and felt the need for none. I had developed a self-sufficiency that kept me distant from others, emotionally and psychologically. Occasionally I went to house-rent parties, parties given by working-class families to raise money to pay the landlord, the admission to which was a quarter or a half-dollar. At these affairs I drank home-brewed beer, ate spaghetti and chitterlings, laughed and talked with black, Southern-born girls who worked as domestic servants in white middle-class homes. But with none of them did my relations rest upon my deepest feelings. I discussed what I read with no one, and to none did I confide. Emotionally, I was withdrawn from the objective world; my desires floated loosely within the walls of my consciousness, contained and controlled.

As a protective mechanism, I developed a terse, cynical mode of speech that rebuffed those who sought to get too close to me. Conversation was my way of avoiding expression; my words were reserved for those times when I sat down alone to write. My face was always a deadpan or a mask of general friendliness; no word or event could jar me into a gesture of enthusiasm or despair. A slowly, hestitantly spoken "Yeah" was my general verbal reaction to almost everything I heard. "That's pretty good," said with a slow nod of the head, was my approval. "Aw, naw," muttered with a cold smile, was my rejection. Even though I reacted deeply, my true feelings raced along underground, hidden.

I did not act in this fashion deliberately; I did not prefer this kind of relationship with people. I wanted a life in which there was a constant oneness of feeling with others, in which the basic emotions of life were shared, in which common memory formed a common past, in which collective hope reflected a national future. But I knew that no such thing was possible in my environment. The only ways in which I felt that my feelings could go outward without fear of rude rebuff or searing reprisal was in writing or reading, and to me they were ways of living. . . .

Repeatedly I took stabs at writing, but the results were so poor that I would tear up the sheets. I was striving for a level of expression that matched those of the novels I read. But I always somehow failed to get onto the page what I thought and felt. Failing at sustained narrative, I compromised by playing with single sentences and phrases. Under the influence of Stein's *Three Lives,* I spent hours and days pounding out disconnected sentences for the sheer love of words.

I would write:

"The soft melting hunk of butter trickled in gold down the stringy grooves of the split yam."

Or:

"The child's clumsy fingers fumbled in sleep, feeling vainly for the wish of its dream."

"The old man huddled in the dark doorway, his bony face lit by the burning yellow in the windows of distant skyscrapers."

My purpose was to capture a physical state or movement that carried a strong subjective impression, an accomplishment which seemed supremely worth struggling for. If I could fasten the mind of the reader upon words so firmly that he would forget words and be conscious only of his response, I felt that I would be in sight of knowing how to write narrative. I strove to master words, to make them disappear, to make them important by making them new, to make them melt into a rising spiral of emotional stimuli, each greater than the other, each feeding and reinforcing the other, and all ending in an emotional climax that would drench the reader with a sense of a new world. That was the single aim of my living.

Autumn came and I was called for my physical examination for the position of regular postal clerk. I had not told my mother or brother or aunt that I knew I would fail. On the morning of the examination I drank two quarts of buttermilk, ate six bananas, but it did not hoist the red arrow of the government scales to the required mark of one hundred and twenty-five pounds. I went home and sat disconsolately in my back room, hating myself, wondering where I could find another job. I had almost got my hands upon a decent job and had lost it, had let it slip through my fingers. Waves of self-doubt rose to haunt me. Was I always to hang on the fringes of life? What I wanted was truly modest, and yet my past, my diet, my hunger, had snatched it from before my eyes. But these self-doubts did not last long; I dulled the sense of loss through reading, reading, writing and more writing.

I asked for my job back at the café and the boss lady allowed me to return; again I served breakfast, washed dishes, carted trays of food up into the apartments. Another postal examination was scheduled for spring and to that end I made eating an obsession. I ate when I did not want to eat, drank milk when it sickened me. Slowly my starved body responded to food and overcame the lean years of Mississippi, Arkansas, and Tennessee, counteracting the flesh-sapping anxiety of fear-filled days.

I read Proust's[2] *A Remembrance of Things Past*, admiring the lucid, subtle but strong prose, stupefied by its dazzling magic, awed by the vast, delicate, intricate, and psychological structure of the Frenchman's epic of death and decadence. But it crushed me with hopelessness, for I wanted to write of the people in my environment with an equal thoroughness, and the burning example before my eyes made me feel that I never could.

My ability to endure tension had now grown amazingly. From the accidental pain of Southern years, from anxiety that I had sought to avoid, from fear that had been too painful to bear, I had learned to like my unintermittent burden of feeling, had become habituated to acting with all of my being, had learned to seek those areas of life, those situations, where I knew that events would complement my own inner mood. I was conscious of what was hap-

pening to me; I knew that my attitude of watchful wonder had usurped all other feelings, had become the meaning of my life, an integral part of my personality; that I was striving to live and measure all things by it. Having no claims upon others, I bent the way the wind blew, rendering unto my environment that which was my environment's, and rendering unto myself that which I felt was mine.

It was a dangerous way to live, far more dangerous than violating laws or ethical codes of conduct; but the danger was for me and me alone. Had I not been conscious of what I was doing, I could have easily lost my way in the fogbound regions of compelling fantasy. Even so, I floundered, staggered; but somehow I always groped my way back to that path where I felt a tinge of warmth from an unseen light.

Hungry for insight into my own life and the lives about me, knowing my fiercely indrawn nature, I sought to fulfill more than my share of all obligations and responsibilities, as though offering libations of forgiveness to my environment. Indeed, the more my emotions claimed my attention, the sharper—as though in ultimate self-defense—became my desire to measure accurately the reality of the objective world so that I might more than meet its demands. At twenty years of age the mold of my life was set, was hardening into a pattern, a pattern that was neither good nor evil, neither right nor wrong.

2. **Proust** (pro͞ost): the French novelist Marcel Proust (1871–1922).

Reading Check

1. What did Wright find so appealing about his job as a postal clerk?
2. Why did his job as a postal clerk turn out to be temporary?
3. What job did Wright get after losing his position at the post office?
4. What were "house-rent" parties?
5. How old was Wright at this time?

Analyzing and Interpreting the Selection

1. The critic Lionel Trilling said that Wright "does not wholly identify himself with his painful experience," that he "does not make himself [out to be] a 'sufferer.' " **a.** Why does Trilling put the word *sufferer* in quotation marks? **b.** Consider how Wright presents himself. Although he faced some brutal aspects of his environment, does he appear to have pitied himself?

2. Wright says that he "strove to master words" (page 919), to make writing "the single aim" of his life. **a.** How did writing free him from the restrictions of his environment? **b.** Why did Wright regard his attitudes and life style as "a dangerous way to live"?

3. In the last paragraph, Wright speaks of his "fiercely indrawn nature." Why did Wright avoid involvement with people? Cite several passages from the essay that support his self-description.

Creative Writing

Discussing a Major Influence

Choose a major influence in your life. It might be a person, or it might be books, music, films, or a favorite activity. Tell about a time in your life when that major influence contributed to your understanding of your own character.

N. Scott Momaday.
Courtesy of the author

N. Scott Momaday was born in Lawton, Oklahoma. His father was a Kiowa (kī'ə-wô', -wä', -wə') Indian. His mother, the child of white settlers, had one Cherokee great-grandmother. She adopted an Indian name and chose to attend Indian schools. Both parents taught at Indian reservations. Momaday spent his boyhood on a number of reservations in the Southwest, acquiring a close knowledge of American Indian culture and history. He graduated from the University of New Mexico in 1958 and went on to obtain a Ph.D. in English in 1963 from Stanford University. He is currently a professor of English at Stanford.

Momaday's first book, *House Made of Dawn* (1968), dealing with a young Indian's attempt to reconcile the values of an old way of life with those of the modern world, was awarded the Pulitzer Prize for fiction. Momaday had earlier written a historical study of the Kiowa tribe, and later he enlarged this work to include his impressions of the contemporary history and culture of his people. This expanded book, published under the title *The Way to Rainy Mountain* (1969), is one of the most eloquent and perceptive accounts of American Indian life and culture yet to appear. Momaday, who has said that he considers himself primarily a poet, is the author of two books of poems, *Angle of Geese and Other Poems* (1974) and *The Gourd Dancer* (1976). These volumes reflect his interest in American Indian subjects, but they also contain poems in a philosophical and meditative vein. In 1976 he published

The Names, a memoir about his parents' lives and his boyhood on various reservations, including the Navaho, the San Carlos, the Jicarilla Apache, and the Jemez Pueblo.

Of his storytelling methods, Momaday has said, "When I turn my mind to my early life, it is the imaginative part of it that comes first and irresistibly into reach, and of that part I take hold. This is one way to tell a story . . . it is my way, and it is the way of my people."

The Way to Rainy Mountain

A single knoll rises out of the plain in Oklahoma, north and west of the Wichita Range. For my people, the Kiowas, it is an old landmark, and they gave it the name Rainy Mountain. The hardest weather in the world is there. Winter brings blizzards, hot tornadic winds arise in the spring, and in summer the prairie is an anvil's edge. The grass turns brittle and brown, and it cracks beneath your feet. There are green belts along the rivers and creeks, linear groves of hickory and pecan, willow and witch hazel. At a distance in July or August the steaming foliage seems almost to writhe in fire. Great green and yellow grasshoppers are everywhere in the tall grass, popping up like corn to sting the flesh, and tortoises crawl about on the red earth, going nowhere in the plenty of time. Loneliness is an aspect of the land. All things in the plain are isolate; there is no confusion of objects in the eye, but *one* hill or *one* tree or *one* man. To look upon that landscape in the early morning, with the sun at your back, is to lose the sense of proportion. Your imagination comes to life, and this, you think, is where Creation was begun.

I returned to Rainy Mountain in July. My grandmother had died in the spring, and I wanted to be at her grave. She had lived to be very old and at last infirm. Her only living daughter was with her when she died, and I was told that in death her face was that of a child.

I like to think of her as a child. When she was born, the Kiowas were living the last great moment of their history. For more than a hundred years they had controlled the open range from the Smoky Hill River to the Red, from the headwaters of the Canadian to the fork of the Arkansas and Cimarron. In alliance with the Comanches, they had ruled the whole of the southern Plains. War was their sacred business, and they were among the finest horsemen the world has ever known. But warfare for the Kiowas was preeminently a matter of disposition rather than of survival, and they never understood the grim, unrelenting advance of the U.S. Cavalry. When at last, divided and ill-provisioned, they were driven onto the Staked Plains in the cold rains of autumn, they fell into panic. In Palo Duro Canyon they abandoned their crucial stores to pillage and had nothing then but their lives. In order to save themselves, they surrendered to the soldiers at Fort Sill and were imprisoned in the old stone corral that now stands as a military museum. My grandmother was spared the humiliation of those high gray walls by eight or ten years, but she must have known from birth the affliction of defeat, the dark brooding of old warriors.

Her name was Aho, and she belonged to the last culture to evolve in North America. Her forebears came down from the high country in western Montana nearly three centuries ago. They were a mountain people, a mysterious tribe of hunters whose language has never been positively classified in any major group. In the late seventeenth century they began a long migration to the south and east. It was a journey toward the dawn, and it led to a golden age. Along the way the Kiowas were befriended by the Crows, who gave them the culture and religion of the Plains. They acquired horses, and their ancient nomadic spirit was suddenly free of the ground. They acquired Tai-me, the sacred Sun Dance doll, from that moment the object and symbol of their worship, and so shared in the divinity of the sun. Not least, they acquired the sense of destiny, therefore courage and pride. When they entered upon the southern Plains they had been transformed. No longer were they slaves to the simple necessity of survival; they were a lordly and dangerous society of fighters and thieves, hunters and priests of the sun. According to their origin myth, they entered the world through a hollow log. From one point of view, their migration was the fruit of an old prophecy, for indeed they emerged from a sunless world.

Although my grandmother lived out her long life in the shadow of Rainy Mountain, the immense landscape of the continental interior lay like memory in her blood. She could tell of the Crows, whom she had never seen, and of the Black Hills, where she had never been. I wanted to see in reality what she had seen more perfectly in the mind's eye, and traveled fifteen hundred miles to begin my pilgrimage.

Yellowstone, it seemed to me, was the top of the world, a region of deep lakes and dark timber, canyons and waterfalls. But, beautiful as it is, one might have the sense of confinement there. The skyline in all directions is close at hand, the high wall of the woods and deep cleavages of shade. There is a perfect freedom in the mountains, but it belongs to the eagle and the elk, the badger and the bear. The Kiowas reckoned their stature by the distance they could see, and they were bent and blind in the wilderness.

Descending eastward, the highland meadows are a stairway to the plain. In July the inland slope of the Rockies is luxuriant with flax and buckwheat, stonecrop[1] and larkspur. The earth unfolds and the limit of the land recedes. Clusters of trees, and animals grazing far in the distance, cause the vision to reach away and wonder to build upon the mind. The sun follows a longer course in the day, and the sky is immense beyond all comparison. The great billowing clouds that sail upon it are shadows that move upon the grain like water, dividing light. Farther down, in the land of the Crows and Blackfeet, the plain is yellow. Sweet clover takes hold of the hills and bends upon itself to cover and seal the soil. There the Kio-

was paused on their way; they had come to the place where they must change their lives. The sun is at home on the plains. Precisely there does it have the certain character of a god. When the Kiowas came to the land of the Crows, they could see the dark lees[2] of the hills at dawn across the Bighorn River, the profusion of light on the grain shelves, the oldest deity ranging after the solstices. Not yet would they veer southward to the caldron of the land that lay below; they must wean their blood from the northern winter and hold the mountains a while longer in their view. They bore Tai-me in procession to the east.

A dark mist lay over the Black Hills, and the land was like iron. At the top of a ridge I caught sight of Devil's Tower upthrust against the gray sky as if in the birth of time the core of the earth had broken through its crust and the motion of the world was begun. There are things in nature that engender an awful quiet in the heart of man; Devil's Tower is one of them. Two centuries ago, because they could not do otherwise, the Kiowas made a legend at the base of the rock. My grandmother said:

Eight children were there at play, seven sisters and their brother. Suddenly the boy was struck dumb; he trembled and began to run upon his hands and feet. His fingers became claws, and his body was covered with fur. Directly there was a bear where the boy had been. The sisters were terrified; they ran, and the bear after them. They came to the stump of a great tree, and the tree spoke to them. It bade them climb upon it, and as they did so it began to rise into the air. The bear came to kill them, but they were just beyond its reach. It reared against the tree and scored the bark all around with its claws. The seven sisters were borne into the sky, and they became the stars of the Big Dipper.

From that moment, and so long as the legend lives, the Kiowas have kinsmen in the night sky. Whatever they were in the mountains, they could be no more. However tenuous their

---

1. **stonecrop:** a plant found on rocks and walls.

2. **lees:** sheltered sides, protected from the wind.

Devils Tower, Wyoming.

N. Scott Momaday   **925**

well-being, however much they had suffered and would suffer again, they had found a way out of the wilderness.

My grandmother had a reverence for the sun, a holy regard that now is all but gone out of mankind. There was a wariness in her, and an ancient awe. She was a Christian in her later years, but she had come a long way about, and she never forgot her birthright. As a child she had been to the Sun Dances; she had taken part in those annual rites, and by them she had learned the restoration of her people in the presence of Tai-me. She was about seven when the last Kiowa Sun Dance was held in 1887 on the Washita River above Rainy Mountain Creek. The buffalo were gone. In order to consummate the ancient sacrifice—to impale the head of a buffalo bull upon the medicine tree—a delegation of old men journeyed into Texas, there to beg and barter for an animal from the Goodnight herd. She was ten when the Kiowas came together for the last time as a living Sun Dance culture. They could find no buffalo; they had to hang an old hide from the sacred tree. Before the dance could begin, a company of soldiers rode out from Fort Sill under orders to disperse the tribe. Forbidden without cause the essential act of their faith, having seen the wild herds slaughtered and left to rot upon the ground, the Kiowas backed away forever from the medicine tree. That was July 20, 1890, at the great bend of the Washita. My grandmother was there. Without bitterness, and for as long as she lived, she bore a vision of deicide.[3]

Now that I can have her only in memory, I see my grandmother in the several postures that were peculiar to her: standing at the wood stove on a winter morning and turning meat in a great iron skillet; sitting at the south window, bent above her beadwork, and afterwards, when her vision failed, looking down for a long time into the fold of her hands; going out upon a cane, very slowly as she did when the weight of age came upon her; pray-

3. **deicide** (dē′ə-sīd′): the killing of a god.

ing. I remember her most often at prayer. She made long, rambling prayers out of suffering and hope, having seen many things. I was never sure that I had the right to hear, so exclusive were they of all mere custom and company. The last time I saw her she prayed standing by the side of her bed at night, naked to the waist, the light of a kerosene lamp moving upon her dark skin. Her long, black hair, always drawn and braided in the day, lay upon her shoulders and against her breasts like a shawl. I do not speak Kiowa, and I never understood her prayers, but there was something inherently sad in the sound, some merest hesitation upon the syllables of sorrow. She began in a high descending pitch, exhausting her breath to silence; then again and again— and always the same intensity of effort, of something that is, and is not, like urgency in the human voice. Transported so in the dancing light among the shadows of her room, she seemed beyond the reach of time. But that was illusion; I think I knew then that I should not see her again.

Houses are like sentinels in the plain, old keepers of the weather watch. There, in a very little while, wood takes on the appearance of great age. All colors wear soon away in the wind and rain, and then the wood is burned gray and the grain appears and the nails turn red with rust. The windowpanes are black and opaque; you imagine there is nothing within, and indeed there are many ghosts, bones given up to the land. They stand here and there against the sky, and you approach them for a longer time than you expect. They belong in the distance; it is their domain.

Once there was a lot of sound in my grandmother's house, a lot of coming and going, feasting and talk. The summers there were full of excitement and reunion. The Kiowas are a summer people; they abide the cold and keep to themselves, but when the season turns and the land becomes warm and vital they cannot hold still; an old love of going returns upon them. The aged visitors who came to my grandmother's house when I was a child were made of lean and leather, and they bore themselves upright. They wore great black hats and bright ample shirts that shook in the wind. They rubbed fat upon their hair and wound their braids with strips of colored cloth. Some of them painted their faces and carried the scars of old and cherished enmities. They were an old council of warlords, come to remind and be reminded of who they were. Their wives and daughters served them well. The women might indulge themselves; gossip was at once the mark and compensation of their servitude. They made loud and elaborate talk among themselves, full of jest and gesture, fright and false alarm. They went abroad in fringed and flowered shawls, bright beadwork and German silver. They were at home in the kitchen, and they prepared meals that were banquets.

There were frequent prayer meetings and great nocturnal feasts. When I was a child I played with my cousins outside, where the lamplight fell upon the ground and the singing of the old people rose up around us and carried away into the darkness. There were a lot of good things to eat, a lot of laughter and surprise. And afterwards, when the quiet returned, I lay down with my grandmother and could hear the frogs away by the river and feel the motion of the air.

Now there is a funeral silence in the rooms, the endless wake of some final word. The walls have closed in upon my grandmother's house. When I returned to it in mourning, I saw for the first time in my life how small it was. It was late at night, and there was a white moon, nearly full. I sat for a long time on the stone steps by the kitchen door. From there I could see out across the land; I could see the long rows of trees by the creek, the low light upon the rolling plains, and the stars of the Big Dipper. Once I looked at the moon and caught sight of a strange thing. A cricket had perched upon the handrail, only a few inches away from me. My line of vision was such that the creature filled the moon like a fossil. It had gone there, I thought, to live and die, for

Wichita Mountains in Oklahoma.

there, of all places, was its small definition made whole and eternal. A warm wind rose up and purled like the longing within me.

The next morning I awoke at dawn and went out on the dirt road to Rainy Mountain. It was already hot, and the grasshoppers began to fill the air. Still, it was early in the morning, and the birds sang out of the shadows. The long yellow grass on the mountain shone in the bright light, and a scissortail hied above the land. There, where it ought to be, at the end of a long and legendary way, was my grandmother's grave. Here and there on the dark stones were ancestral names. Looking back once, I saw the mountain and came away.

N. Scott Momaday **927**

Reading Check

1. What, and where, is Rainy Mountain?
2. What, in the past, was the "sacred business" of the Kiowa Indians?
3. What was Tai-me?
4. According to their origin myth, how did Kiowa Indians enter the world?
5. Why did the Kiowas have to discontinue their ancient sacrifice?

For Study and Discussion

Analyzing and Interpreting the Selection

1. Momaday's reflections about his grandmother lead him to thoughts of the Kiowa Indians. What event that occurred eight or ten years before his grandmother's birth put an end to the traditional life of her people?

2. Originally a mountain people, the Kiowas moved to the southern Plains where they entered "a golden age." In what ways were their lives transformed?

3. As a child, Momaday's grandmother witnessed the destruction of the Kiowas' symbol of worship. What does Momaday tell about his grandmother to show that the old Kiowa religious spirit survived in her?

4a. In what ways did the Kiowas relive their past at their summer reunions? **b.** Although Momaday realizes that the Kiowas' days of glory are gone forever, what does seeing the cricket "whole and eternal" suggest to him about the human spirit?

Descriptive Writing

Describing a Special Place

In the first paragraph, Momaday describes Rainy Mountain: the weather, the grass, the "steaming foliage," the grasshoppers, the tortoises going nowhere, the loneliness. He makes it clear that this special place has influenced people who have lived there. Describe a place that is special to you. Through your selection of details, indicate how the place has influenced you.

RICHARD RODRIGUEZ
1946–

Richard Rodriguez was born in San Francisco, California, to Mexican parents. When he entered his first classroom, he knew about fifty English words. Today he holds a Ph.D. in English literature. Rodriguez is currently a lecturer and writer with an interest in Mexico and Mexican-American subjects. His work has appeared in such magazines as *Harper's*, *U.S. News and World Report*, and *American Scholar*.

Hunger of Memory, like Richard Wright's *American Hunger* (page 918), is an autobiographical essay in which the Mexican-American author examines his emotional and intellectual development. The book, which appeared in 1982, has been highly praised for both its subject and style. The excerpt included here is a frank appraisal of the author's ambitions for academic success and his achievements.

Richard Rodriguez.

FROM

Hunger of Memory

In fourth grade I embarked upon a grandiose reading program. "Give me the names of important books," I would say to startled teachers. They soon found out that I had in mind "adult books." I ignored their suggestion of anything I suspected was written for children. (Not until I was in college, as a result, did I read *Huckleberry Finn* or *Alice's Adventures in Wonderland*.) Instead, I read *The Scarlet Letter* and Franklin's *Autobiography*. And whatever I read I read for extra credit. Each time I finished a book, I reported the achievement to a teacher and basked in the praise my effort

earned. Despite my best efforts, however, there seemed to be more and more books I needed to read. At the library I would literally tremble as I came upon whole shelves of books I hadn't read. So I read and I read and I read: *Great Expectations;* all the short stories of Kipling; *The Babe Ruth Story;* the entire first volume of the *Encyclopaedia Britannica* (A-AN-STEY); the *Iliad; Moby Dick; Gone with the Wind; The Good Earth; Ramona; Forever Amber; The Lives of the Saints; Crime and Punishment; The Pearl.* . . . Librarians who initially frowned when I checked out the maximum ten books at a time started saving books they thought I might like. Teachers would say to the rest of the class, "I only wish the rest of you took reading as seriously as Richard obviously does."

But at home I would hear my mother wondering, "What do you see in your books?" (Was reading a hobby like her knitting? Was so much reading even healthy for a boy? Was it the sign of "brains"? Or was it just a convenient excuse for not helping around the house on Saturday mornings?) Always, "What do you see . . . ?"

What *did* I see in my books? I had the idea that they were crucial for my academic success, though I couldn't have said exactly how or why. In the sixth grade I simply concluded that what gave a book its value was some major idea or theme it contained. If that core essence could be mined and memorized, I would become learned like my teachers. I decided to record in a notebook the themes of the books that I read. After reading *Robinson Crusoe*, I wrote that its theme was "the value of learning to live by oneself." When I completed *Wuthering Heights*, I noted the danger of "letting emotions get out of control." Rereading these brief moralistic appraisals usually left me disheartened. I couldn't believe that they were really the source of reading's value. But for many more years, they constituted the only means I had of describing to myself the educational value of books.

In spite of my earnestness, I found reading a pleasurable activity. I came to enjoy the lonely good company of books. Early on weekday mornings, I'd read in my bed. I'd feel a mysterious comfort then, reading in the dawn quiet—the blue-gray silence interrupted by the occasional churning of the refrigerator motor a few rooms away or the more distant sounds of a city bus beginning its run. On weekends I'd go to the public library to read, surrounded by old men and women. Or, if the weather was fine, I would take my books to the park and read in the shade of a tree. A warm summer evening was my favorite reading time. Neigh-bors would leave for vacation and I would water their lawns. I would sit through the twilight on the front porches or in backyards, reading to the cool, whirling sounds of the sprinklers.

I also had favorite writers. But often those writers I enjoyed most I was least able to value. When I read William Saroyan's *The Human Comedy,* I was immediately pleased by the narrator's warmth and the charm of his story. But as quickly I became suspicious. A book so enjoyable to read couldn't be very "important." Another summer I determined to read all the novels of Dickens. Reading his fat novels, I loved the feeling I got—after the first hundred pages—of being at home in a fictional world where I knew the names of the characters and cared about what was going to happen to them. And it bothered me that I was forced away at the conclusion, when the fiction closed tight, like a fortune-teller's fist—the futures of all the major characters neatly resolved. I never knew how to take such feelings seriously, however. Nor did I suspect that these experiences could be part of a novel's meaning. Still, there were pleasures to sustain me after I'd finish my books. Carrying a volume back to the library, I would be pleased by its weight. I'd run my fingers along the edge of the pages and marvel at the breadth of my achievement. Around my room, growing stacks of paperback books reenforced my assurance.

I entered high school having read hundreds of books. My habit of reading made me a confident speaker and writer of English. Reading also enabled me to sense something of the shape, the major concerns, of Western thought. (I was able to say something about Dante and Descartes and Engels and James Baldwin[1] in my high school term papers.) In these various ways, books brought me aca-

1. **Dante . . . Baldwin:** Dante Alighieri (dän′tä ä′lē-gyä′rē), Italian poet (1265–1321) author of *The Divine Comedy;* René Descartes (dā-kärt′), French philosopher and mathematician (1596–1650); Friedrich Engels (ĕng′əls), German writer and socialist leader (1820–1895); James Baldwin, American writer (1924–1987), author of fiction, essays, and plays. See page 877.

demic success as I hoped that they would. But I was not a good reader. Merely bookish, I lacked a point of view when I read. Rather, I read in order to acquire a point of view. I vacuumed books for epigrams, scraps of information, ideas, themes—anything to fill the hollow within me and make me feel educated. When one of my teachers suggested to his drowsy tenth-grade English class that a person could not have a "complicated idea" until he had read at least two thousand books, I heard the remark without detecting either its irony or its very complicated truth. I merely determined to compile a list of all the books I had ever read. Harsh with myself, I included only once a title I might have read several times. (How, after all, could one read a book more than once?) And I included only those books over a hundred pages in length. (Could anything shorter be a book?)

There was yet another high school list I compiled. One day I came across a newspaper article about the retirement of an English professor at a nearby state college. The article was accompanied by a list of the "hundred most important books of Western Civilization." "More than anything else in my life," the professor told the reporter with finality, "these books have made me all that I am." That was the kind of remark I couldn't ignore. I clipped out the list and kept it for the several months it took me to read all the titles. Most books, of course, I barely understood. While reading Plato's *Republic,* for instance, I needed to keep looking at the book jacket comments to remind myself what the text was about. Nevertheless, with the special patience and superstition of a scholarship boy, I looked at every word of the text. And by the time I reached the last word, relieved, I convinced myself that I had read *The Republic.* In a ceremony of great pride, I solemnly crossed Plato off my list.

Reading Check

1. Who are the two writers Rodriguez says were favorites even before he entered high school?
2. How did his reading habits affect his speaking?
3. When Rodriguez compiled a list of the books he had read, which books did he *not* include?
4. What other list did he keep?

For Study and Discussion

Analyzing and Interpreting the Selection

1. In this section of his autobiographical essay, Richard Rodriguez writes about his early efforts to discover the value of reading. In fourth grade he "embarked upon a grandiose reading program." What appears to have motivated this project?

2a. What scheme did Rodriguez hit upon in sixth grade? **b.** Why does he feel his efforts were not completely satisfying?

3. How did Rodriguez' earnestness and academic ambitions interfere with his pleasure in reading books?

4. Rodriguez says that although he did very well in school he was not a good reader. How does the anecdote about Plato's *Republic* illustrate his limitations as a reader?

5. Rodriguez says that he lacked a point of view when he read. What does this comment imply about the abilities of a "good reader"?

Writing About Literature

Discussing Two Kinds of Readers

How do you think Rodriguez would distinguish the "merely bookish" individual from the well-educated individual? Write a paragraph discussing the distinction, using evidence from the essay to support your thesis.

Mexican-American Literature
ROLANDO HINOJOSA-SMITH

American literature has always enjoyed a wide-ranging variety of contributions from individuals of different ethnic and cultural backgrounds. The literature written by Americans of Mexican descent presents one more addition to the general body of American literature. Mexican-American writing is unique in the respect that some authors write in English while others write in Spanish, and to a lesser degree, some write in a mixture of both languages.

Most scholars agree that the Mexican-American literary contribution begins after the end of The Mexican War in 1848. That year, the United States acquired additional territory in the Southwest. Part of the peace treaty stated that the people in the new territory could resettle in Mexico and thus retain their Mexican citizenship. However, they would be accorded American citizenship if they chose to remain in the territory. The majority did remain and became United States citizens. Their early literary contributions were in Spanish and reflected their background since that was the predominant language at the time. Subsequent historical processes saw that Spanish was retained, but as years passed, English also formed an additional part of the literature. That English language contributions have become the majority form of expression is also part of our country's historical process. To be sure, though, the Spanish Southwest flavor remains and this adds significantly to our country's highly interesting literary contribution to world literature. One example of the Hispanic influence may be seen in Rodolfo Gonzales' *I Am Joaquín* (page 855).

Among the older Hispanic forms that survive, the most important are the *corridos* and the *coplas*. The corrido, briefly, is a ballad form that recounts historical and personal events in a particular region. The most widely known corrido of the twentieth century was written in Texas, *El Corrido de Gregorio Cortez*. The corrido tells of Cortez, a cowman, who takes a stand for justice when wrongly accused of a crime. There are many versions of this corrido, and the best compilation of it appears in *With His Pistol in His Hand* by Américo Paredes, an internationally recognized scholar in this field of study. Other corridos describe the Mexican-American experience as railroad workers as in *El Corrido de la Pensilvania,* among others. The copla is also a poetic form, and it was devised in Spain and brought to the New World as early as the sixteenth century. The themes for the copla are multiple and they include honor, love, death, loyalty, as well as Mexican-American folk humor. The corrido is set to music while the copla is usually recited. Contemporary corridos and coplas address social and political themes affecting Mexican-Americans in the United States. Among the issues addressed have been the Great

Depression of the thirties, World War II, the Korean War, the assassination of President John F. Kennedy, the Vietnam War, and the like. The two forms, in their way, continue the Spanish-language tradition.

The best known and most widely distributed Mexican-American contributions to the body of United States literature, however, date from 1970 with the publication of Tomás Rivera's . . . *y no se lo tragó la tierra*. Written in Spanish, it was also published with an accompanying text in English. A new English rendition, *This Migrant Earth*, was published in 1987. The brief novel presents twenty-seven gripping scenes of the lives and deaths of Mexican-American migrant farm laborers in the nineteen-fifties and has been praised here and abroad for its stark realism.

Rivera's work is also important because it inspired many Americans of Mexican descent to write and this again widened the body of United States literature. Various works by Mexican-American writers have received worldwide recognition, and annual conferences studying the literature have been held in Europe, Mexico, and South America to discuss what has been termed "a dynamic contribution" to American literature. Aside from Tomás Rivera, the following have also received international acclaim: Rudolfo A. Anaya, Ron Arias, Rolando Hinojosa, and Miguel Mendez. Most recently, Pat Mora has also had her work read and analyzed in national conferences.

Other interesting aspects of this addition to American literature show that women writers figure just as prominently as the men. Books by Angela de Hoyos, Evangelina Vigil, and Carmen Tafolla are currently enjoying international acknowledgement. Too, the Modern Language Association of America, the oldest and most influential linguistic and literary organization in the United States, includes this newer American literature in its yearly national and regional conferences. In addition, with an increase of university and high-school courses devoted to this literature since the seventies, Mexican-American men and women continue to invigorate our country's literature. In many ways, then, they resemble the early literary pioneers during this country's westward movement in the early part of the nineteenth century.

For Study and Discussion

1. What historical events are associated with the emergence of Mexican-American literature?

2a. What distinction is there between the **corrido** and the **copla**? **b.** What subjects have been treated in these forms? **c.** How do contemporary corridos and coplas continue the older traditions?

3. According to the author, what has been the significance of Tomás Rivera's work?

MODERN DRAMA

The word *drama* comes from the Greek word *dran*, which means "to do" or "to act." Besides being traditionally literary, the drama is a theatrical form. Dramatists do not usually write with the purpose of communicating directly to the reader, as do fiction writers, poets, and essayists. Instead, dramatists ask people of the theater—actors and actresses, directors, set designers, and others—to assist them in communicating to the audience. Good dramatists are aware of the resources and limitations of their medium. They recognize that they must tell their stories in a different way from novelists. Yet like other literary artists, dramatists attempt to construct meaningful works in two ways: by the precise and evocative use of words, and by careful attention to basic structure.

The Structure of Drama

The Greek philosopher Aristotle, in writing a treatise based on the plays of his time (the fifth century B.C.), defined drama as "an imitation of an action," a definition which has become the basis for most subsequent dramatic criticism. Aristotle's definition is more complicated than may at first appear, and it should be considered carefully.

To take the last word first, by *action* Aristotle meant not merely activity or exertion, but rather the direction the play moves in, the closely related series of events that give the play its momentum. A play, in Aristotle's terms, must have a *plot* with a beginning, middle, and end. Almost always, a plot involves *conflict*, either an outer conflict between the main character and other characters or an inner conflict in the mind of the main character, or both. Also, the plot must involve some kind of decision; the main character must choose to perform or not to perform some morally meaningful act that will lead to the play's resolution.

Imitation, the first term in Aristotle's definition, does not necessarily mean a close copying of real life. To imitate something is not always to reproduce it exactly. Even a photograph, which most people would call more lifelike than a painting of the same subject, is seldom life-size and always two- rather than three-dimensional. A photograph can freeze a subject at a particular moment in a particular place, but a painter, after long acquaintance and careful study, can frequently create a truer likeness: not "this is how the subject looked at that moment in that place," but "this is how the subject looks over and over again; this captures the spirit." Like any other work of art, a play arranges the substance of life in some significant, meaningful

Detail from *The School of Athens* (1509–1511) by Raphael (1483–1520).
Fresco. Aristotle is shown holding a copy of the *Ethics*.
Stanza della Signatura, The Vatican, Courtesy Art Resource

pattern. All of us go to plays (or read them) so that we can, in some way, see reenacted the impulses, fears, or aspirations that we share with others. These are often embedded in our society, and usually we respond to plays collectively, as an audience, rather than as individuals. It is this collective sense that we must bear in mind when we speak of a play as an *imitation*. A great modern writer said that in one classic French play, a parent talks to a child in a way no parent ever spoke to any child, but all parents and all children could see themselves in the same situation. This is close to what Aristotle probably meant by *imitation*.

Types of Drama

Drama has been traditionally categorized under two main types: *tragedy* and *comedy.* The most obvious difference between them is that comedies end happily and tragedies do not. A more profound difference is in the perspective that each has on human life. Tragedy focuses on the individual rather than on the group. The central characters of tragedy encounter forces larger than themselves, often hostile or alien: fate, chance, nature, the gods, the irrational, evil. The struggle in tragedy, therefore, is that of the individual against impossible odds. The main character, or *protagonist,* of tragedy decides upon a course of action (in itself heroic, considering the odds), suffers as a result of the decision, and ultimately perceives the discrepancy between a single personal choice and vast uncontrollable forces. While this description hardly does justice to the sweeping implications of tragedy, it may suggest the sense of aspiration, agony, and comprehension at the heart of it. Tragedy involves a net that tightens around the protagonists in spite of, and perhaps even because of their efforts to escape it. Because of this focus on the individual challenging unbreakable cosmic laws, watching a great tragedy (or reading it perceptively) can be a profoundly moving experience.

Comedy, on the other hand, is more interested in the group. It focuses on the welfare of society and of the human race itself. The *antagonists* of comedy are filled with the vices and follies of human nature, and the plot of comedy involves their reformation, so that they become fit company for others. The comic protagonists are typically a young couple who are in love, intent upon furthering the race by establishing a family and forming a new human society. Opposing them is a group of powerful older people who have silly or malicious reasons for keeping the young apart. In the end, the foolish are reformed, and good sense, flexibility, and wit prevail. Comedies frequently end with a celebration—a wedding, a feast, or a dance—which symbolizes the new social agreement that has been arrived at. Whereas tragedy ends with death, comedy ends with an affirmation of life.

Dialogue and Staging

As readers, we are forced to rely principally on a play's *dialogue* to learn what it is all about. But in order to visualize the play in our minds, we must pay attention to the other language of drama, *staging* or stagecraft. This is what Aristotle called *spectacle.* Here are some of the aspects of staging we should keep in mind.

1. *Scenery.* The setting of a play is normally indicated by painted scenery that provides a visual frame for the action. Many modern

plays use very detailed scenery to make the audience feel it is watching something that is actually taking place. Thornton Wilder's *Our Town* makes a dramatic point in just the opposite way, by using practically no scenery at all.

2. *Costume.* What a character wears, too, has particular significance in the theater. Since much information about a character must be communicated in a short time, costume becomes an essential statement of drama. For example, when the heroine of *Our Town* appears in a white dress (page 998), the costume tells us a good deal about the play's attitude toward death.

3. *Gesture and movement.* Greek dramatists had their choruses dance out their speeches in a series of highly stylized steps. Today a shrug or even a raised eyebrow, executed by a skillful performer, can convey a world of feeling.

4. *Lighting.* In the modern theater, much is done to convey a mood or an atmosphere with lights. A comic scene may not seem half so funny if it is dimly lit, while a serious one can lose its emotional intensity if the lights are too bright. Lights can suggest a time or season, pinpoint an action, or isolate a character.

All these aspects of staging, the visual tools of the theater, allow the dramatist to underscore the action of a play and to help the audience understand its structure and meaning. In written versions of a play, the stage directions help readers to re-create the staging in their minds.

Scene from a Roman comedy. Relief from Pompeii.
The Bettmann Archive

A scene from the original production of *Death of a Salesman* (1949).
The Bettmann Archive

The Development of American Drama

Modern drama began by turning toward *realism* and away from the fantasy of nineteenth-century melodrama and farce. Realism gave rise to various innovations that served to express the dramatist's vision of what reality is. These attempts to show psychological reality can be called *expressionism*. Realism and expressionism are the two dominant modes of drama in the twentieth century. One focuses on the external details of everyday life, while the other focuses on the life of the mind and feelings and tries to show how human beings perceive the world.

Two Scandinavian playwrights were chiefly responsible for these innovations: the Norwegian Henrik Ibsen (1828–1906) and the Swede August Strindberg (1849–1912). Theatrical realism is exemplified by the plays of Ibsen. He tries to present ordinary life as it appears to most people. He asks the audience to assume that the play is a "slice of life." The stage is assumed to be an ordinary room with one wall removed to permit the audience to eavesdrop on the action. The scenery and furniture are accurately representational, and the dialogue tries to imitate what people would actually say. Like most realistic playwrights, Ibsen asks us to scrutinize the world as it is and, frequently, to reform it. Ibsen's plays are called *problem* plays, and they deal with problems common to modern society: corruption, hypocrisy, and greed.

Strindberg's plays typify the theater of expressionism. The real world with its problems is less important to him than the mind and feelings. He has been called the explorer of inner geography. The titles of his plays, *A Dream Play* and *The Ghost Sonata,* suggest a turning away from reality to the psychological and spiritual aspects of our perception of reality. These two impulses, realism and expressionism, helped shape a truly international dramatic movement.

The American theater began responding to these impulses around the time of World War I. Eugene O'Neill was the foremost American playwright of the next few decades. In such plays as *Beyond the Horizon,* he stayed within the conventions of the realistic play. But in such plays as *The Great God Brown, Strange Interlude, and Mourning Becomes Electra,* he experimented with ways of expanding the theater beyond the realistic frame. He had his characters wear masks; he reintroduced the Greek device of the *chorus,* a person or persons who comment on the action; and he showed, through *asides,* what a character was thinking. O'Neill's efforts opened the door for further experimentation in such plays as Elmer Rice's *The Adding Machine* and William Saroyan's *My Heart's in the Highlands.* Maxwell Anderson brought dramatic verse back to the stage in works such as *Elizabeth the Queen* and *Winterset.* In *Our Town* and *The Skin of Our Teeth,* Thornton Wilder confronted audiences with the fact that a play is, after all, a work to be performed by actors and actresses on a stage. Yet other important playwrights—S. N. Behrman, Robert Sherwood, Clifford Odets, Sidney Kingsley, Lillian Hellman, and Philip Barry among them—worked most effectively within the limits of realistic drama.

Tennessee Williams and Arthur Miller—two prominent playwrights to emerge since World War II—have made effective use of both realistic and nonrealistic techniques. In *The Glass Menagerie,* a "memory play," Williams uses suggestive visual effects and poetic dialogue to convey the narrator's perceptions of the past. Miller's *Death of a Salesman,* a searching examination of contemporary values, lies within the realistic tradition, yet makes extensive use of expressionistic techniques. Other contemporary playwrights working in both conventional and experimental modes include Edward Albee, David Rabe, Sam Shepard, Arthur Kopit, David Mamet, Ntozake Shange, and Elizabeth Swados.

SUSAN GLASPELL
1882–1948

Susan Glaspell.

Susan Glaspell was born and raised in the Middle West. Before she met and married George Cram Cook, in 1913, she worked as a newspaper reporter. In 1915 she and her husband helped organize the Provincetown Players, a "little theater" group for which O'Neill wrote his early plays (see page 950).

Before writing *Trifles*, in 1916, Glaspell had never studied dramatic writing. In *The Road to the Temple*, the biography of her husband, she reveals that the play was written in ten days. The story was based on an experience she had had while working as a journalist in the Middle West. The play was first performed by the Provincetown Players at the Wharf Theatre in Provincetown, Massachusetts, on August 8, 1916. In that performance Glaspell played the role of Mrs. Hale. In *Trifles* Glaspell introduced a dramatic technique she was to use again: leaving the central character off stage and allowing her to be revealed through the dialogue and action of on-stage figures. She later turned the play into a short story called "A Jury of Her Peers."

Glaspell wrote or coauthored nearly a dozen plays for the Provincetown Players. She also wrote full-length drama. *Alison's House*, a play about Emily Dickinson, won the Pulitzer Prize in 1931. In addition to plays she wrote novels. Some critics think that *Trifles*, her best-known play, is also the best one-act play of the American theater.

Trifles

Characters

George Henderson, County Attorney
Henry Peters, Sheriff
Lewis Hale, a neighboring farmer
Mrs. Peters
Mrs. Hale

Scene: *The kitchen in the now abandoned farm-house of* John Wright, *a gloomy kitchen, and left without having been put in order—unwashed pans under the sink, a loaf of bread outside the breadbox, a dish towel on the table—other signs of incompleted work. At the rear the outer door opens and the* Sheriff *comes in followed by the* County Attorney *and* Hale. *The* Sheriff *and* Hale *are men in middle life, the* County Attorney *is a young man; all are much bundled up and go at once to the stove. They are followed by the two women—the* Sheriff's *wife first; she is a slight wiry woman, a thin nervous face.*

Mrs. Hale *is larger and would ordinarily be called more comfortable looking, but she is disturbed now and looks fearfully about as she enters. The women have come in slowly, and stand close together near the door.*

County Attorney (*rubbing his hands*). This feels good. Come up to the fire, ladies.
Mrs. Peters (*after taking a step forward*). I'm not—cold.
Sheriff (*unbuttoning his overcoat and stepping away from the stove as if to mark the beginning of official business*). Now, Mr. Hale, before we move things about, you explain to Mr. Henderson just what you saw when you came here yesterday morning.
County Attorney. By the way, has anything been moved? Are things just as you left them yesterday?
Sheriff (*looking about*). It's just the same. When

A scene from *Trifles,* performed in 1917 by the Washington Square Players.
The New York Public Library at Lincoln Center

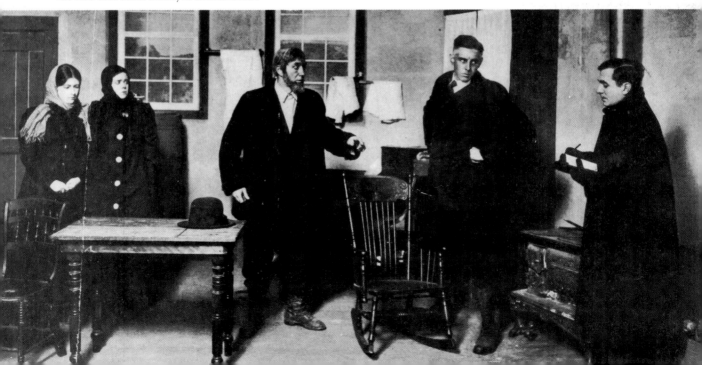

it dropped below zero last night I thought I'd better send Frank out this morning to make a fire for us—no use getting pneumonia with a big case on, but I told him not to touch anything except the stove—and you know Frank.

County Attorney. Somebody should have been left here yesterday.

Sheriff. Oh—yesterday. When I had to send Frank to Morris Center for that man who went crazy—I want you to know I had my hands full yesterday. I knew you could get back from Omaha by today and as long as I went over everything here myself——

County Attorney. Well, Mr. Hale, tell just what happened when you came here yesterday morning.

Hale. Harry and I had started to town with a load of potatoes. We came along the road from my place and as I got here I said, "I'm going to see if I can't get John Wright to go in with me on a party telephone." I spoke to Wright about it once before and he put me off, saying folks talked too much anyway, and all he asked was peace and quiet—I guess you know about how much he talked himself; but I thought maybe if I went to the house and talked about it before his wife, though I said to Harry that I didn't know as what his wife wanted made much difference to John——

County Attorney. Let's talk about that later, Mr. Hale. I do want to talk about that, but tell now just what happened when you got to the house.

Hale. I didn't hear or see anything; I knocked at the door, and still it was all quiet inside. I knew they must be up, it was past eight o'clock. So I knocked again, and I thought I heard somebody say, "Come in." I wasn't sure. I'm not sure yet, but I opened the door—this door (*indicating the door by which the two women are still standing*) and there in that rocker—(*pointing to it*) sat Mrs. Wright.

[*They all look at the rocker.*]

County Attorney. What—what was she doing?

Hale. She was rockin' back and forth. She had her apron in her hand and was kind of—pleating it.

County Attorney. And how did she—look?

Hale. Well, she looked queer.

County Attorney. How do you mean—queer?

Hale. Well, as if she didn't know what she was going to do next. And kind of done up.[1]

County Attorney. How did she seem to feel about your coming?

Hale. Why, I don't think she minded—one way or other. She didn't pay much attention. I said, "How do, Mrs. Wright, it's cold, ain't it?" And she said, "Is it?"—and went on kind of pleating at her apron. Well, I was surprised; she didn't ask me to come up to the stove, or to set down, but just sat there, not even looking at me, so I said, "I want to see John." And then she—laughed. I guess you would call it a laugh. I thought of Harry and the team outside, so I said a little sharp: "Can't I see John?" "No," she says, kind o' dull like. "Ain't he home?" says I. "Yes," says she, "he's home." "Then why can't I see him?" I asked her, out of patience. "'Cause he's dead," says she. "*Dead?*" says I. She just nodded her head, not getting a bit excited, but rockin' back and forth. "Why—where is he?" says I, not knowing what to say. She just pointed upstairs—like that (*himself pointing to the room above*). I got up, with the idea of going up there. I walked from there to here—then I says, "Why, what did he die of?" "He died of a rope round his neck," says she, and just went on pleatin' at her apron. Well, I went out and called Harry. I thought I might—need help. We went upstairs and there he was lyin'——

County Attorney. I think I'd rather have you go into that upstairs, where you can point it all out. Just go on now with the rest of the story.

Hale. Well, my first thought was to get that rope off. It looked . . . (*stops, his face twitches*) . . . but Harry, he went up to him, and he said, "No, he's dead all right, and we'd better not touch anything." So we went back downstairs. She was still sitting that same way. "Has any-

---

1. **done up:** exhausted.

body been notified?" I asked. "No," says she, unconcerned. "Who did this, Mrs. Wright?" said Harry. He said it businesslike—and she stopped pleatin' of her apron. "I don't know," she says. "You don't *know*?" says Harry. "No," says she. "Weren't you sleepin' in the bed with him?" says Harry. "Yes," says she, "but I was on the inside." "Somebody slipped a rope round his neck and strangled him and you didn't wake up?" says Harry. "I didn't wake up," she said after him. We must 'a' looked as if we didn't see how that could be, for after a minute she said, "I sleep sound." Harry was going to ask her more questions but I said maybe we ought to let her tell her story first to the coroner, or the sheriff, so Harry went fast as he could to Rivers' place, where there's a telephone.

County Attorney. And what did Mrs. Wright do when she knew that you had gone for the coroner?

Hale. She moved from that chair to this one over here (*pointing to a small chair in the corner*) and just sat there with her hands held together and looking down. I got a feeling that I ought to make some conversation, so I said I had come in to see if John wanted to put in a telephone, and at that she started to laugh, and then she stopped and looked at me— scared. (*The* County Attorney, *who has had his notebook out, makes a note.*) I dunno, maybe it wasn't scared. I wouldn't like to say it was. Soon Harry got back, and then Dr. Lloyd came, and you, Mr. Peters, and so I guess that's all I know that you don't.

County Attorney (*looking around*). I guess we'll go upstairs first—and then out to the barn and around there. (*To the* Sheriff) You're convinced that there was nothing important here—nothing that would point to any motive?

Sheriff. Nothing here but kitchen things.

[*The* County Attorney, *after again looking around the kitchen, opens the door of a cupboard closet. He gets up on a chair and looks on a shelf. Pulls his hand away, sticky.*]

County Attorney. Here's a nice mess.

[*The women draw nearer.*]

Mrs. Peters (*to the other woman*). Oh, her fruit; it did freeze. (*To the* County Attorney) She worried about that when it turned so cold. She said the fire'd go out and her jars would break.

Sheriff. Well, can you beat the women! Held for murder and worryin' about her preserves.

County Attorney. I guess before we're through she may have something more serious than preserves to worry about.

Hale. Well, women are used to worrying over trifles.

[*The two women move a little closer together.*]

County Attorney (*with the gallantry of a young politician*). And yet, for all their worries, what would we do without the ladies? (*The women do not unbend. He goes to the sink, takes a dipperful of water from the pail and pouring it into a basin, washes his hands. Starts to wipe them on the roller towel, turns it for a cleaner place.*) Dirty towels! (*Kicks his foot against the pans under the sink*) Not much of a housekeeper, would you say, ladies?

Mrs. Hale (*stiffly*). There's a great deal of work to be done on a farm.

County Attorney. To be sure. And yet (*with a little bow to her*) I know there are some Dickson county farmhouses which do not have such roller towels. (*He gives it a pull to expose its full length again.*)

Mrs. Hale. Those towels get dirty awfully quick. Men's hands aren't always as clean as they might be.

County Attorney. Ah, loyal to your sex, I see. But you and Mrs. Wright were neighbors. I suppose you were friends, too.

Mrs. Hale (*shaking her head*). I've not seen much of her of late years. I've not been in this house—it's more than a year.

County Attorney. And why was that? You didn't like her?

Mrs. Hale. I liked her all well enough. Farmers' wives have their hands full, Mr. Henderson. And then——

County Attorney. Yes——?

Mrs. Hale (*looking about*). It never seemed a very cheerful place.

County Attorney. No—it's not cheerful. I shouldn't say she had the homemaking instinct.

Mrs. Hale. Well, I don't know as Wright had, either.

County Attorney. You mean that they didn't get on very well?

Mrs. Hale. No, I don't mean anything. But I don't think a place'd be any cheerfuller for John Wright's being in it.

County Attorney. I'd like to talk more of that a little later. I want to get the lay of things upstairs now. (*He goes to the left, where three steps lead to a stair door.*)

Sheriff. I suppose anything Mrs. Peters does'll be all right. She was to take in some clothes for her, you know, and a few little things. We left in such a hurry yesterday.

County Attorney. Yes, but I would like to see what you take, Mrs. Peters, and keep an eye out for anything that might be of use to us.

Mrs. Peters. Yes, Mr. Henderson.

[*The women listen to the men's steps on the stairs, then look about the kitchen.*]

Mrs. Hale. I'd hate to have men coming into my kitchen, snooping around and criticizing. (*She arranges the pans under sink which the* County Attorney *had shoved out of place.*)

Mrs. Peters. Of course it's no more than their duty.

Mrs. Hale. Duty's all right, but I guess that deputy sheriff that came out to make the fire might have got a little of this on. (*Gives the roller towel a pull*) Wish I'd thought of that sooner. Seems mean to talk about her for not having things slicked up when she had to come away in such a hurry.

Mrs. Peters (*who has gone to a small table in the left rear corner of the room, and lifted one end of a towel that covers a pan*). She had bread set. (*Stands still*)

Mrs. Hale (*eyes fixed on a loaf of bread beside the breadbox, which is on a low shelf at the other side of the room. Moves slowly toward it*). She was going to put this in there. (*Picks up loaf, then abruptly drops it. In a manner of returning to familiar things*) It's a shame about her fruit. I wonder if it's all gone. (*Gets up on the chair and looks*) I think there's some here that's all right, Mrs. Peters. Yes—here; (*holding it toward the window*) this is cherries, too. (*Looking again*) I declare I believe that's the only one. (*Gets down, bottle in her hand. Goes to the sink and wipes it off on the outside*) She'll feel awful bad after all her hard work in the hot weather. I remember the afternoon I put up my cherries last summer.

[*She puts the bottle on the big kitchen table, center of the room. With a sigh, is about to sit down in the rocking chair. Before she is seated realizes what chair it is; with a slow look at it, steps back. The chair which she has touched rocks back and forth.*]

Mrs. Peters. Well, I must get those things from the front room closet. (*She goes to the door at the right, but after looking into the other room, steps back.*) You coming with me, Mrs. Hale? You could help me carry them.

[*They go in the other room; reappear, Mrs. Peters carrying a dress and skirt,* Mrs. Hale *following with a pair of shoes.*]

Mrs. Peters. My, it's cold in there. (*She puts the clothes on the big table, and hurries to the stove.*)

Mrs. Hale (*examining the skirt*). Wright was close. I think maybe that's why she kept so much to herself. She didn't even belong to the Ladies' Aid. I suppose she felt she couldn't do her part, and then you don't enjoy things when you feel shabby. She used to wear pretty clothes and be lively, when she was Minnie Foster, one of the town girls singing in the choir. But that—oh, that was thirty years ago. This all you was to take in?

Mrs. Peters. She said she wanted an apron. Funny thing to want, for there isn't much to get you dirty in jail, goodness knows. But I suppose just to make her feel more natural. She said they was in the top drawer in this cupboard. Yes, here. And then her little shawl that always hung behind the door. (*Opens stair door and looks*) Yes, here it is. (*Quickly shuts door leading upstairs*)

Mrs. Hale (*abruptly moving toward her*). Mrs. Peters?

Mrs. Peters. Yes, Mrs. Hale?

Mrs. Hale. Do you think she did it?

Mrs. Peters (*in a frightened voice*). Oh, I don't know.

Mrs. Hale. Well, I don't think she did. Asking for an apron and her little shawl. Worrying about her fruit.

Mrs. Peters (*starts to speak, glances up, where footsteps are heard in the room above. In a low voice*). Mr. Peters says it looks bad for her. Mr. Henderson is awful sarcastic in a speech and he'll make fun of her sayin' she didn't wake up.

Mrs. Hale. Well, I guess John Wright didn't wake when they was slipping that rope under his neck.

Mrs. Peters. No, it's strange. It must have been done awful crafty and still. They say it was such a—funny way to kill a man, rigging it all up like that.

Mrs. Hale. That's just what Mr. Hale said. There was a gun in the house. He says that's what he can't understand.

Mrs. Peters. Mr. Henderson said coming out that what was needed for the case was a motive; something to show anger, or—sudden feeling.

Mrs. Hale (*who is standing by the table*). Well, I don't see any signs of anger around here. (*She puts her hand on the dish towel which lies on the table, stands looking down at table, one half of which is clean, the other half messy.*) It's wiped to here. (*Makes a move as if to finish work, then turns and looks at loaf of bread outside the breadbox. Drops towel. In that voice of coming back to familiar things*) Wonder how they are finding things upstairs. (*Crossing below table to downstage right*) I hope she had it a little more redd-up[2] up there. You know, it seems kind of *sneaking*.

2. **redd-up:** put in order.

Locking her up in town and then coming out here and trying to get her own house to turn against her!

Mrs. Peters. But, Mrs. Hale, the law is the law.

Mrs. Hale. I s'pose 'tis. (*Unbuttoning her coat*) Better loosen up your things, Mrs. Peters. You won't feel them when you go out.

[Mrs. Peters *takes off her fur tippet, goes to hang it on hook at back of room, stands looking at the under part of the small corner table.*]

Mrs. Peters. She was piecing a quilt.

[*She brings the large sewing basket to the center table and they look at the bright pieces.*]

Mrs. Hale. It's a log-cabin pattern. Pretty, isn't it? I wonder if she was goin' to quilt it or just knot it?

[*Footsteps have been heard coming down the stairs. The* Sheriff *enters followed by* Hale *and the* County Attorney.]

Sheriff. They wonder if she was going to quilt it or just knot it!

[*The men laugh, the women look abashed.*]

County Attorney (*rubbing his hands over the stove*). Frank's fire didn't do much up there, did it? Well, let's go out to the barn and get that cleared up.

[*The men go outside.*]

Mrs. Hale (*resentfully*). I don't know as there's anything so strange, our takin' up our time with little things while we're waiting for them to get the evidence. (*She sits down at the big table smoothing out a block with decision.*) I don't see as it's anything to laugh about.

Mrs. Peters (*apologetically*). Of course they've got awful important things on their minds. (*Pulls up a chair and joins* Mrs. Hale *at the table*)

Mrs. Hale (*examining another block*). Mrs. Peters,

look at this one. Here, this is the one she was working on, and look at the sewing! All the rest of it has been so nice and even. And look at this! It's all over the place! Why, it looks as if she didn't know what she was about!

[*After she has said this they look at each other, then start to glance back at the door. After an instant* Mrs. Hale *has pulled at a knot and ripped the sewing.*]

Mrs. Peters. Oh, what are you doing, Mrs. Hale?

Mrs. Hale (*mildly*). Just pulling out a stitch or two that's not sewed very good. (*Threading a needle*) Bad sewing always made me fidgety.

Mrs. Peters (*nervously*). I don't think we ought to touch things.

Mrs. Hale. I'll just finish up this end. (*Suddenly stopping and leaning forward*) Mrs. Peters?

Mrs. Peters. Yes, Mrs. Hale?

Mrs. Hale. What do you suppose she was so nervous about?

Mrs. Peters. Oh—I don't know. I don't know as she was nervous. I sometimes sew awful queer when I'm just tired. (Mrs. Hale *starts to say something, looks at* Mrs. Peters, *then goes on sewing.*) Well, I must get these things wrapped up. They may be through sooner than we think. (*Putting apron and other things together*) I wonder where I can find a piece of paper, and string.

Mrs. Hale. In that cupboard, maybe.

Mrs. Peters (*looking in cupboard*). Why, here's a birdcage. (*Holds it up*) Did she have a bird, Mrs. Hale?

Mrs. Hale. Why, I don't know whether she did or not—I've not been here for so long. There was a man around last year selling canaries cheap, but I don't know as she took one; maybe she did. She used to sing real pretty herself.

Mrs. Peters (*glancing around*). Seems funny to think of a bird here. But she must have had one, or why would she have a cage? I wonder what happened to it?

Mrs. Hale. I s'pose maybe the cat got it.

Mrs. Peters. No, she didn't have a cat. She's got that feeling some people have about cats—being afraid of them. My cat got in her room and she was real upset and asked me to take it out.

Mrs. Hale. My sister Bessie was like that. Queer, ain't it?

Mrs. Peters (*examining the cage*). Why, look at this door. It's broke. One hinge is pulled apart.

Mrs. Hale (*looking too*). Looks as if someone must have been rough with it.

Mrs. Peters. Why, yes. (*She brings the cage forward and puts it on the table.*)

Mrs. Hale. I wish if they're going to find any evidence they'd be about it. I don't like this place.

Mrs. Peters. But I'm awful glad you came with me, Mrs. Hale. It would be lonesome for me sitting here alone.

Mrs. Hale. It would, wouldn't it? (*Dropping her sewing*) But I tell you what I do wish, Mrs. Peters. I wish I had come over sometimes when *she* was here. I—(*looking around the room*)—wish I had.

Mrs. Peters. But of course you were awful busy, Mrs. Hale—your house and your children.

Mrs. Hale. I could've come. I stayed away because it weren't cheerful—and that's why I ought to have come. I—I've never liked this place. Maybe because it's down in a hollow and you don't see the road. I dunno what it is, but it's a lonesome place and always was. I wish I had come over to see Minnie Foster sometimes. I can see now——(*Shakes her head*)

Mrs. Peters. Well, you mustn't reproach yourself, Mrs. Hale. Somehow we just don't see how it is with other folks until—something turns up.

Mrs. Hale. Not having children makes less work—but it makes a quiet house, and Wright out to work all day, and no company when he did come in. Did you know John Wright, Mrs. Peters?

Mrs. Peters. Not to know him; I've seen him in town. They say he was a good man.

Mrs. Hale. Yes—good; he didn't drink, and kept his word as well as most, I guess, and paid his debts. But he was a hard man, Mrs. Peters. Just to pass the time of day with him—— (*Shivers*) Like a raw wind that gets to the bone. (*Pauses, her eye falling on the cage*) I should think she would 'a' wanted a bird. But what do you suppose went with it?

Mrs. Peters. I don't know, unless it got sick and died.

[*She reaches over and swings the broken door, swings it again, both women watch it.*]

Mrs. Hale. You weren't raised round here, were you? (Mrs. Peters *shakes her head.*) You didn't know—her?

Mrs. Peters. Not till they brought her yesterday.

Mrs. Hale. She—come to think of it, she was kind of like a bird herself—real sweet and pretty, but kind of timid and—fluttery. How—she—did—change. (*Silence; then as if struck by a happy thought and relieved to get back to everyday things.*) Tell you what, Mrs. Peters, why don't you take the quilt in with you? It might take up her mind.

Mrs. Peters. Why, I think that's a real nice idea, Mrs. Hale. There couldn't possibly be any objection to it, could there? Now, just what would I take? I wonder if her patches are in here—and her things.

[*They look in the sewing basket.*]

Mrs. Hale. Here's some red. I expect this has got sewing things in it. (*Brings out a fancy box*) What a pretty box. Looks like something somebody would give you. Maybe her scissors are in here. (*Opens box. Suddenly puts her hand to her nose*) Why—— (Mrs. Peters *bends nearer, then turns her face away.*) There's something wrapped up in this piece of silk.

Mrs. Peters. Why, this isn't her scissors.

Mrs. Hale. (*lifting the silk*). Oh, Mrs. Peters—it's——

[Mrs. Peters *bends closer.*]

Mrs. Peters. It's the bird.

Mrs. Hale (*jumping up*). But, Mrs. Peters—look at it! Its neck! Look at its neck! It's all—other side *to*.

Mrs. Peters. Somebody—wrung—its—neck.

[*Their eyes meet. A look of growing comprehension, of horror. Steps are heard outside. Mrs. Hale slips box under quilt pieces, and sinks into her chair. Enter Sheriff and County Attorney. Mrs. Peters rises.*]

County Attorney (*as one turning from serious things to little pleasantries*). Well, ladies, have you decided whether she was going to quilt it or knot it?

Mrs. Peters. We think she was going to—knot it.

County Attorney. Well, that's interesting, I'm sure. (*Seeing the birdcage*) Has the bird flown?

Mrs. Hale (*putting more quilt pieces over the box*). We think the—cat got it.

County Attorney (*preoccupied*). Is there a cat?

[Mrs. Hale *glances in a quick covert way at* Mrs. Peters.]

Mrs. Peters. Well, not *now*. They're superstitious, you know. They leave.

County Attorney (*to Sheriff Peters, continuing an interrupted conversation*). No sign at all of anyone having come from the outside. Their own rope. Now let's go up again and go over it piece by piece. (*They start upstairs.*) It would have to have been someone who knew just the——

[Mrs. Peters *sits down. The two women sit there not looking at one another, but as if peering into something and at the same time holding back. When they talk now it is in the manner of feeling their way over strange ground, as if afraid of what they are saying, but as if they cannot help saying it.*]

Mrs. Hale. She liked the bird. She was going to bury it in that pretty box.

Mrs. Peters (*in a whisper*). When I was a girl—my kitten—there was a boy took a hatchet, and before my eyes—and before I could get there——(*Covers her face an instant*) If they hadn't held me back I would have—(*catches herself, looks upstairs where steps are heard, falters weakly*)—hurt him.

Mrs. Hale (*with a slow look around her*). I wonder how it would seem never to have had any children around. (*Pause*) No, Wright wouldn't like the bird—a thing that sang. She used to sing. He killed that, too.

Mrs. Peters (*moving uneasily*). We don't know who killed the bird.

Mrs. Hale. I knew John Wright.

Mrs. Peters. It was an awful thing was done in this house that night, Mrs. Hale. Killing a man while he slept, slipping a rope around his neck that choked the life out of him.

Mrs. Hale. His neck. Choked the life out of him. (*Her hand goes out and rests on the birdcage.*)

Mrs. Peters (*with rising voice*). We don't know who killed him. We don't know.

Mrs. Hale (*her own feeling not interrupted*). If there'd been years and years of nothing, then a bird to sing to you, it would be awful—still, after the bird was still.

Mrs. Peters (*something within her speaking*). I know what stillness is. When we homesteaded in Dakota, and my first baby died—after he was two years old, and me with no other then——

Mrs. Hale (*moving*). How soon do you suppose they'll be through looking for the evidence?

Mrs. Peters. I know what stillness is. (*Pulling herself back*) The law has got to punish crime, Mrs. Hale.

Mrs. Hale (*not as if answering that*). I wish you'd seen Minnie Foster when she wore a white dress with blue ribbons and stood up there in the choir and sang. (*A look around the room*) Oh, I *wish* I'd come over here once in a while! That was a crime! That was a crime! Who's going to punish that?

Mrs. Peters (*looking upstairs*). We mustn't—take on.

Mrs. Hale. I might have known she needed help! I know how things can be—for women. I tell you, it's queer, Mrs. Peters. We live close together and we live far apart. We all go through the same things—it's all just a differ- ent kind of the same thing. (*Brushes her eyes; noticing the bottle of fruit, reaches out for it*) If I was you I wouldn't tell her her fruit was gone. Tell her it *ain't*. Tell her it's all right. Take this in to prove it to her. She—she may never know whether it was broke or not.

Mrs. Peters (*takes the bottle, looks about for something to wrap it in; takes petticoat from the clothes brought from the other room, very nervously begins winding this around the bottle. In a false voice*). My, it's a good thing the men couldn't hear us. Wouldn't they just laugh! Getting all stirred up over a little thing like a—dead canary. As if that could have anything to do with—with— wouldn't they *laugh*!

[*The men are heard coming downstairs.*]

Mrs. Hale (*under her breath*). Maybe they would—maybe they wouldn't.

County Attorney. No, Peters, it's all perfectly clear except a reason for doing it. But you know juries when it comes to women. If there was some definite thing. Something to show— something to make a story about—a thing that would connect up with this strange way of doing it——

[*The women's eyes meet for an instant. Enter* Hale *from outer door.*]

Hale. Well, I've got the team around. Pretty cold out there.

County Attorney. I'm going to stay here awhile by myself. (*To the* Sheriff) You can send Frank out for me, can't you? I want to go over every- thing. I'm not satisfied that we can't do better.

Sheriff. Do you want to see what Mrs. Peters is going to take in?

[*The* County Attorney *goes to the table, picks up the apron, laughs.*]

County Attorney. Oh, I guess they're not very dangerous things the ladies have picked out. (*Moves a few things about, disturbing the quilt pieces which cover the box. Steps back*) No, Mrs. Peters doesn't need supervising. For that matter, a sheriff's wife is married to the law. Ever think of it that way, Mrs. Peters?

Mrs. Peters. Not—just that way.

Sheriff (*chuckling*). Married to the law. (*Moves toward the other room*) I just want you to come in here a minute, George. We ought to take a look at these windows.

County Attorney (*scoffingly*). Oh, windows!

Sheriff. We'll be right out, Mr. Hale.

[Hale *goes outside. The* Sheriff *follows the* County Attorney *into the other room. Then* Mrs. Hale *rises, hands tight together, looking intensely at* Mrs. Peters, *whose eyes make a slow turn, finally meeting* Mrs. Hale's. *A moment* Mrs. Hale *holds her, then her own eyes point the way to where the box is concealed. Suddenly* Mrs. Peters *throws back quilt pieces and tries to put the box in the bag she is carrying. It is too big. She opens box, starts to take bird out, cannot touch it, goes to pieces, stands there helpless. Sound of a knob turning in the other room.* Mrs. Hale *snatches the box and puts it in the pocket of her big coat. Enter* County Attorney *and* Sheriff.]

County Attorney (*facetiously*). Well, Henry, at least we found out that she was not going to quilt it. She was going to—what is it you call it, ladies?

Mrs. Hale (*her hands against her pocket*). We call it—knot it, Mr. Henderson.

[*Curtain*]

Reading Check

1. What was Hale's reason for stopping at the farmhouse?
2. Why have Mrs. Hale and Mrs. Peters accompanied the men to the farmhouse?
3. Why do the women decide to take the quilt with them?
4. At the end of the play, what happens to the box containing the dead bird?

For Study and Discussion

Analyzing and Interpreting the Play

1. At one point Hale says that "women are used to worrying over trifles." Why is this statement ironic?

2a. Why does the County Attorney's gallantry irk Mrs. Hale and Mrs. Peters? **b.** How would you describe his attitude toward women?

3. Trace the steps by which Mrs. Hale and Mrs. Peters discover the motive for the murder.

4. Why does Mrs. Hale feel guilty of a crime?

5. After they find the dead bird, Mrs. Peters recalls a violent incident in her childhood, involving a kitten. How does the introduction of this memory gain sympathy for Mrs. Wright?

6. Why do the women suppress the evidence they have found?

7. Explain the closing line of the play.

8. Susan Glaspell turned *Trifles* into a short story called "A Jury of Her Peers." In what sense is Mrs. Wright tried by her peers?

9. Do you condemn the actions of Mrs. Hale and Mrs. Peters? Why or why not?

Writing About Literature

Analyzing Character

Two important characters in the play—Mr. and Mrs. Wright—do not appear, but a great deal is revealed about them and their relationship in the course of the play. Write an analysis of *one* of these characters, citing evidence to support your impression.

Discussing Moral Conflict of Characters

Mrs. Peters says, "The law has got to punish crime" (page 948). Discuss the moral dilemma that Mrs. Peters and Mrs. Hale face.

UPI/Bettmann Newsphotos

Eugene O'Neill (1926).

Eugene O'Neill, more than any other playwright, introduced modern drama into the American theater. His singular achievement was recognized by his contemporaries. The novelist Sinclair Lewis, in his Nobel Prize speech of 1930, said of O'Neill that he had "done nothing much for the American drama save transform it utterly in ten or twelve years from a false world of neat and competent trickery to a world of splendor, fear and greatness." Six years later O'Neill himself received the Nobel Prize in recognition of his trailblazing efforts.

O'Neill was born in a hotel on Broadway in New York City. His father, James O'Neill, was a famous popular actor, performing in the very world of neat and competent trickery his son was to abolish. The elder O'Neill played the title role in *The Count of Monte Cristo,* a lavish romance based on Alexander Dumas' novel, over six thousand times. He toured with this and other sentimental melodramas for most of his life. As a young man, O'Neill toured with his father and played minor roles in his company. In 1910, inspired by the sea novels of Joseph Conrad, he signed on a Norwegian ship bound for Buenos Aires.

O'Neill returned to his parents' home in 1912 determined to be a writer. The plays that he began to write, however, were very different from the ones that he had acted in with his father. He looked to his own experiences for subject matter rather than to the contrived plots of older melodrama. In this he was following the expressionism of the European dramatists, particularly Strindberg. "I have never written anything that did not come directly or indirectly from some event or impression of my own," he later wrote. His experience at sea provided material for his first short plays. His own experience of family life provided plots for several of his later great plays.

His first play, *Bound East for Cardiff,* was produced by the Provincetown Players in 1916. It was an immediate success. His first full-length play, *Beyond the Horizon,* was produced on Broadway in 1920. For this play he was awarded the first of four Pulitzer Prizes.

O'Neill called his first plays "novel plays." In them he wanted to develop realistic characters such as those found in the novels of Stephen Crane and Theodore Dreiser. At the same time he was writing realistic plays such as *Anna Christie* (1921) and *Desire Under the Elms* (1924), he was also experimenting with ways to present "inner" reality. In this he continued to follow the example of his mentor Strindberg. He was struck by the effect of dreams on people's lives and especially by their waking dreams—their illusions. He introduced dreams and illusions into his plays to represent the psychological reality of his characters. He also used masks, asides, and monologues in such plays as *The Emperor Jones* (1920), *The Great God Brown* (1926), and *Strange Interlude* (1928).

By the early thirties, O'Neill was a literary figure of international importance. In 1936, the year he was awarded the Nobel Prize, he was stricken with an odd nervous disorder, which made him retire from public life. However, he continued to write and produced his two greatest works, *The Ice Man Cometh* (1946) and *Long Day's Journey into Night* (1956). O'Neill died in 1953, leaving the latter play unproduced. It has since been produced many times and, like several of his other plays, adapted to film. In *Long Day's Journey into Night,* now widely considered his masterpiece, he explores most deeply the tangled family relationships that are the theme of many of his dramas.

Where the Cross Is Made (1918) is one of O'Neill's short plays that combine the elements of realism and expressionism. It involves familiar themes: the relationship between father and son and the tension between reality and illusion.

Where the Cross Is Made

Characters

Captain Isaiah Bartlett
Nat Bartlett, his son
Sue Bartlett, his daughter
Doctor Higgins
Silas Horne, mate ⎫ of the schooner
Cates, bosun ⎭ *Mary Allen*
Jimmy Kanaka,[1] harpooner

Scene: Captain Bartlett's *"cabin"—a room erected as a lookout post at the top of his house situated on a high point of land on the California coast. The inside of the compartment is fitted up like the captain's cabin of a deep-sea sailing vessel. On the left, forward, a porthole. Farther back, the stairs of the companionway. Still farther, two more portholes. In the rear, left, a marble-topped sideboard with a ship's lantern on it. In the rear, center, a door opening on stairs which lead to the lower house. A cot with a blanket is placed against the wall to the right of the door. In the right wall, five portholes. Directly under them, a wooden bench. In front of the bench, a long table with two straight-backed chairs, one in front, the other to the left of it. A cheap, dark-colored rug is on the floor. In the ceiling, midway from front to rear, a skylight extending from opposite the door to above the left edge of the table. In the right extremity of the skylight is placed a floating ship's compass. The light from the binnacle[2] sheds over this from above and seeps down into the room, casting a vague globular shadow of the compass on the floor.*

The time is an early hour of a clear windy night in the fall of the year 1900. Moonlight, winnowed by the wind which moans in the stubborn angles of the old house, creeps wearily through the portholes and rests like tired dust in circular patches upon the floor and table. An insistent monotone of thundering surf, muffled and far-off, is borne upward from the beach below.

After the curtain rises the door in the rear is opened slowly and the head and shoulders of Nat Bartlett *appear over the sill. He casts a quick glance about the room, and seeing no one there, ascends the remaining steps and enters. He makes a sign to someone in the darkness beneath:* "All right, Doctor." Doctor Higgins *follows him into the room and, closing the door, stands looking with great curiosity around him. He is a slight, medium-sized, professional-looking man of about thirty-five.* Nat Bartlett *is very tall, gaunt, and loose-framed. His right arm has been amputated at the shoulder and the sleeve on that side of the heavy mackinaw he wears hangs flabbily or flaps against his body as he moves. He appears much older than his thirty years. His shoulders have a weary stoop as if worn down by the burden of his massive head with its heavy shock of*

---

1. **Kanaka:** South Sea Islander.

2. **binnacle** (bĭn′ə-kəl): the case that holds the compass.

tangled black hair. His face is long, bony, and sallow, with deep-set black eyes, a large aquiline[3] nose, a wide thin-lipped mouth shadowed by an unkempt bristle of mustache. His voice is low and deep with a penetrating, hollow, metallic quality. In addition to the mackinaw, he wears corduroy trousers stuffed down into high laced boots.

Nat. Can you see, Doctor?

Higgins (*in the too-casual tones which betray an inward uneasiness*). Yes—perfectly—don't trouble. The moonlight is so bright——

Nat. Luckily. (*Walking slowly toward the table*) He doesn't want any light—lately—only the one from the binnacle there.

Higgins. He? Ah—you mean your father?

Nat (*impatiently*). Who else?

Higgins (*a bit startled—gazing around him in embarrassment*). I suppose this is all meant to be like a ship's cabin?

Nat. Yes—as I warned you.

Higgins (*in surprise*). Warned me? Why warned? I think it's very natural—and interesting—this whim of his.

Nat (*meaningly*). Interesting, it may be.

Higgins. And he lives up here, you said—never comes down?

Nat. Never—for the past three years. My sister brings his food up to him. (*He sits down in the chair to the left of the table.*) There's a lantern on the sideboard there, Doctor. Bring it over and sit down. We'll make a light, I'll ask your pardon for bringing you to this room on the roof—but—no one'll hear us here; and by seeing for yourself the mad way he lives—— Understand that I want you to get all the facts—just that, facts!—and for that light is necessary. Without that—they become dreams up here—dreams, Doctor.

Higgins (*with a relieved smile carries over the lantern*). It is a trifle spooky.

Nat (*not seeming to notice this remark*). He won't take any note of this light. His eyes are too busy—out there. (*He flings his left arm in a wide gesture seaward.*) And if he does notice—well,

let him come down. You're bound to see him sooner or later. (*He scratches a match and lights the lantern.*)

Higgins. Where is—he?

Nat (*pointing upward*). Up on the poop. Sit down, man! He'll not come—yet awhile.

Higgins (*sitting gingerly on the chair in front of table*). Then he has the roof too rigged up like a ship?

Nat. I told you he had. Like a deck, yes. A wheel, compass, binnacle light, the companionway there (*he points*), a bridge to pace up and down on—*and keep watch.* If the wind wasn't so high you'd hear him now—back and forth—all the livelong night. (*With a sudden harshness*) Didn't I tell you he's mad?

Higgins (*with a professional air*). That was nothing new. I've heard that about him from all sides since I first came to the asylum yonder. You say he only walks at night—up there?

Nat. Only at night, yes. (*Grimly*) The things he wants to see can't be made out in daylight—dreams and such.

Higgins. But just what is he trying to see? Does anyone know? Does he tell?

Nat (*impatiently*). Why, everyone knows what Father looks for, man! The ship, of course.

Higgins. What ship?

Nat. His ship—the *Mary Allen*—named for my dead mother.

Higgins. But—I don't understand—— Is the ship long overdue—or what?

Nat. Lost in a hurricane off the Celebes[4] with all on board—three years ago!

Higgins (*wonderingly*). Ah. (*After a pause*) But your father still clings to a doubt——

Nat. There is no doubt for him or anyone else to cling to. She was sighted bottom up, a complete wreck, by the whaler *John Slocum.* That was two weeks after the storm. They sent a boat out to read her name.

Higgins. And hasn't your father ever heard——

Nat. He was the first to hear, naturally. Oh, he knows right enough, if that's what you're driv-

---

3. **aquiline** (ăk′wə-līn′): curved or hooked.

4. **Celebes** (sĕl′ə-bēz): an island, together with smaller nearby islands, of Indonesia.

ing at. (*He bends toward the doctor—intensely.*) He *knows*, Doctor, he *knows*—but he won't *believe.* He can't—and keep living.

Higgins (*impatiently*). Come, Mr. Bartlett, let's get down to brass tacks. You didn't drag me up here to make things more obscure, did you? Let's have the facts you spoke of. I'll need them to give sympathetic treatment to his case when we get him to the asylum.

Nat (*anxiously—lowering his voice*). And you'll come to take him away tonight—for sure?

Higgins. Twenty minutes after I leave here I'll be back in the car. That's positive.

Nat. And you know your way through the house?

Higgins. Certainly, I remember—but I don't see——

Nat. The outside door will be left open for you. You must come right up. My sister and I will be here—with him. And you understand —— Neither of us knows anything about this. The authorities have been complained to—not by us, mind—but by someone. He must never know——

Higgins. Yes, yes—but still I don't—— Is he liable to prove violent?

Nat. No—no. He's quiet always—too quiet; but he might do something—anything—if he knows——

Higgins. Rely on me not to tell him, then; but I'll bring along two attendants in case—— (*He breaks off and continues in matter-of-fact tones.*) And now for the facts in this case, if you don't mind, Mr. Bartlett.

Nat (*shaking his head—moodily*). There are cases where facts—— Well, here goes—the brass tacks. My father was a whaling captain as his father before him. The last trip he made was seven years ago. He expected to be gone two years. It was four before we saw him again. His ship had been wrecked in the Indian Ocean. He and six others managed to reach a small island on the fringe of the Archipelago[5]—an island barren as hell, Doctor—after seven days in an open boat. The rest

of the whaling crew never were heard from again—gone to the sharks. Of the six who reached the island with my father only three were alive when a fleet of Malay canoes picked them up, mad from thirst and starvation, the four of them. These four men finally reached Frisco. (*With great emphasis*) They were my father; Silas Horne, the mate; Cates, the bo-sun; and Jimmy Kanaka, a Hawaiian har-pooner. Those four! (*With a forced laugh*) There are facts for you. It was all in the papers at the time—my father's story.

Higgins. But what of the other three who were on the island?

Nat (*harshly*). Died of exposure, perhaps. Mad and jumped into the sea, perhaps. That was the told story. Another was whispered—killed and eaten, perhaps! But gone—vanished—that, undeniably. That was the fact. For the rest—who knows? And what does it matter?

Higgins (*with a shudder*). I should think it would matter—a lot.

Nat (*fiercely*). We're dealing with facts, Doctor! (*With a laugh*) And here are some more for you. My father brought the three down to this house with him—Horne and Cates and Jimmy Kanaka. We hardly recognized my father. He had been through hell and looked it. His hair was white. But you'll see for yourself—soon. And the others—they were all a bit queer, too—mad, if you will. (*He laughs again.*) So much for the facts, Doctor. They leave off there and the dreams begin.

Higgins (*doubtfully*). It would seem—the facts are enough.

Nat. Wait. (*He resumes deliberately.*) One day my father sent for me and in the presence of the others told me the dream. I was to be heir to the secret. Their second day on the island, he said, they discovered in a sheltered inlet the rotten, water logged hulk of a Malay prau[6]— a proper war prau such as the pirates used to use. She had been there rotting—God knows how long. The crew had vanished—God knows

5. **Archipelago** (är′kə-pĕl′ə-gō′): a group of islands.

6. **prau** (prou): a Malayan boat having one sail and an outrigger (also called *proa*).

where, for there was no sign on the island that man had ever touched there. The Kanakas went over the prau—they're devils for staying underwater, you know—and they found—in two chests—— (*He leans back in his chair and smiles ironically.*) Guess what, Doctor?

Higgins (*with an answering smile*). Treasure, of course.

Nat (*leaning forward and pointing his finger accusingly at the other*). You see! The root of belief is in you, too! (*Then he leans back with a hollow chuckle.*) Why, yes. Treasure, to be sure. What else? They landed it and—you can guess the rest, too—diamonds, emeralds, gold ornaments—innumerable, of course. Why limit the stuff of dreams? Ha-ha! (*He laughs sardonically as if mocking himself.*)

Higgins (*deeply interested*). And then?

Nat. They began to go mad—hunger, thirst, and the rest—and they began to forget. Oh, they forgot a lot, and lucky for them they did, probably. But my father realizing, as he told me, what was happening to them, insisted that while they still knew what they were doing they should—guess again now, Doctor. Ha-ha!

Higgins. Bury the treasure?

Nat (*ironically*). Simple, isn't it? Ha-ha. And then they made a map—the same old dream, you see—with a charred stick, and my father had care of it. They were picked up soon after, mad as hatters, as I have told you, by some Malays. (*He drops his mocking and adopts a calm, deliberate tone again.*) But the map isn't a dream, Doctor. We're coming back to facts again. (*He reaches into the pocket of his mackinaw and pulls out a crumpled paper.*) Here. (*He spreads it out on the table.*)

Higgins (*craning his neck eagerly*). Dammit! This is interesting. The treasure, I suppose, is where——

Nat. Where the cross is made.

Higgins. And here are the signatures, I see. And that sign?

Nat. Jimmy Kanaka's. He couldn't write.

Higgins. And below? That's yours, isn't it?

Nat. As heir to the secret, yes. We all signed it here the morning the *Mary Allen,* the schooner my father had mortgaged this house to fit out, set sail to bring back the treasure. Ha-ha.

Higgins. The ship he's still looking for—that was lost three years ago?

Nat. The *Mary Allen,* yes. The other three men sailed away on her. Only father and the mate knew the approximate location of the island—and I—as heir. It's—— (*He hesitates, frowning.*) No matter. I'll keep the mad secret. My father wanted to go with them—but my mother was dying. I dared not go, either.

Higgins. Then you wanted to go? You believed in the treasure then?

Nat. Of course. Ha-ha. How could I help it? I believed until my mother's death. Then *he* became mad, entirely mad. He built this cabin—to wait in—and he suspected my growing doubt as time went on. So, as final proof, he gave me a thing he had kept hidden from them all—a sample of the richest of the treasure. Ha-ha. Behold! (*He takes from his pocket a heavy bracelet thickly studded with stones and throws it on the table near the lantern.*)

Higgins (*picking it up with eager curiosity—as if in spite of himself*). Real jewels?

Nat. Ha-ha. You want to believe, too. No—paste and brass—Malay ornaments.

Higgins. You had it looked over?

Nat. Like a fool, yes. (*He puts it back in his pocket and shakes his head as if throwing off a burden.*) Now you know why he's mad—waiting for that ship—and why in the end I had to ask you to take him away where he'll be safe. The mortgage—the price of that ship—is to be foreclosed. We have to move, my sister and I. We can't take him with us. She is to be married soon. Perhaps away from the sight of the sea he may——

Higgins (*perfunctorily*). Let's hope for the best. And I fully appreciate your position. (*He gets up, smiling.*) And thank you for the interesting story. I'll know how to humor him when he raves about treasure.

Nat (*somberly*). He is quiet always—too quiet. He only walks to and fro—watching——

Higgins. Well, I must go. You think it's best to take him tonight?

Nat (*persuasively*). Yes, Doctor. The neighbors—they're far away but—for my sister's sake—you understand.

Higgins. I see. It must be hard on her—this sort of thing—— Well—— (*He goes to the door, which Nat opens for him.*) I'll return presently. (*He starts to descend.*)

Nat (*urgently*). Don't fail us, Doctor. And come right up. He'll be here. (*He closes the door and tiptoes carefully to the companionway. He ascends it a few steps and remains for a moment listening for some sound from above. Then he goes over to the table, turning the lantern very low, and sits down, resting his elbow, his chin on his hand, staring somberly before him. The door in the rear is slowly opened. It creaks slightly and* Nat *jumps to his feet—in a thick voice of terror.*) Who's there?

[*The door swings wide open, revealing* Sue Bartlett. *She ascends into the room and shuts the door behind her. She is a tall, slender woman of twenty-five, with a pale, sad face framed in a mass of dark red hair. This hair furnishes the only touch of color about her. Her full lips are pale; the blue of her wistful wide eyes is fading into a twilight gray. Her voice is low and melancholy. She wears a dark wrapper and slippers.*]

Sue (*stands and looks at her brother accusingly*). It's only I. What are you afraid of?

Nat (*averts his eyes and sinks back on the chair again*). Nothing. I didn't know—I thought you were in your room.

Sue (*comes to the table*). I was reading. Then I heard some one come down the stairs and go out. Who was it? (*With sudden terror*) It wasn't—Father?

Nat. No. He's up there—watching—as he always is.

Sue (*sitting down—insistently*). Who was it?

Nat (*evasively*). A man—I know.

Sue. What man? What is he? You're holding something back. Tell me.

Nat (*raising his eyes defiantly*). A doctor.

Sue (*alarmed*). Oh! (*With quick intuition*) You brought him up here—so that I wouldn't know!

Nat (*doggedly*). No. I took him up here to see how things were—to ask him about Father.

Sue (*as if afraid of the answer she will get*). Is he one of them—from the asylum? Oh, Nat, you haven't——

Nat (*interrupting her—hoarsely*). No, no! Be still.

Sue. That would be—the last horror.

Nat (*defiantly*). Why? You always say that. What could be more horrible than things as they are? I believe—it would be better for him—away—where he couldn't see the sea. He'll forget his mad idea of waiting for a lost ship and a treasure that never was. (*As if trying to convince himself—vehemently*) I believe this!

Sue (*reproachfully*). You don't, Nat. You know he'd die if he hadn't the sea to live with.

Nat (*bitterly*). And you know old Smith will foreclose the mortgage. Is that nothing? We cannot pay. He came yesterday and talked with me. He knows the place is his—to all purposes. He talked as if we were merely his tenants, curse him! And he swore he'd foreclose immediately unless——

Sue (*eagerly*). What?

Nat (*in a hard voice*). Unless we have—Father—taken away.

Sue (*in anguish*). Oh! But why, why? What is Father to him?

Nat. The value of the property—our home which is his, Smith's. The neighbors are afraid. They pass by on the road at nights coming back to their farms from the town. They see *him* up there walking back and forth—waving his arms against the sky. They're afraid. They talk of a complaint. They say for his own good he must be taken away. They even whisper the house is haunted. Old Smith is afraid of his property. He thinks that *he* may set fire to the house—do anything——

Sue (*despairingly*). But you told him how foolish that was, didn't you? That Father is quiet, always quiet.

Nat. What's the use of telling—when they believe—when they're afraid? (Sue *hides her face in her hands—a pause—*Nat *whispers hoarsely.*) I've been afraid myself—at times.

Sue. Oh, Nat! Of what?

Nat (*violently*). Oh, him and the sea he calls to! Of the damned sea he forced me on as a boy—the sea that robbed me of my arm and made me the broken thing I am!

Sue (*pleadingly*). You can't blame Father—for your misfortune.

Nat. He took me from school and forced me on his ship, didn't he? What would I have been now but an ignorant sailor like him if he had had his way? No. It's the sea I should not blame, that foiled him by taking my arm and then throwing me ashore—another one of *his* wrecks!

Sue (*with a sob*). You're bitter, Nat—and hard. It was so long ago. Why can't you forget?

Nat (*bitterly*). Forget! You can talk! When Tom comes home from this voyage you'll be married and out of this life before you—a captain's wife as our mother was. I wish you joy.

Sue (*supplicatingly*). And you'll come with us, Nat—and Father, too—and then——

Nat. Would you saddle your young husband with a madman and a cripple? (*Fiercely*) No, no, not I! (*Vindictively*) And not him, either! (*With sudden meaning—deliberately*) I've got to stay here. My book is three-fourths done—my book that will set me free! But I know, I feel, as sure as I stand here living before you, that I must finish it here. It could not live for me outside of this house where it was born. (*Staring at her fixedly*) So I will stay—in spite of hell! (*Sue sobs hopelessly. After a pause he continues.*) Old Smith told me I could live here indefinitely without paying—as a caretaker—if——

Sue (*fearfully—like a whispered echo*). If?

Nat (*staring at her—in a hard voice*). If I have *him* sent—where he'll no longer harm himself—nor others.

Sue (*with horrified dread*). No—no, Nat! For our dead mother's sake.

Nat (*struggling*). Did I say I had? Why do you look at me—like that?

Sue. Nat! Nat! For our mother's sake!

Nat (*in terror*). Stop! Stop! She's dead—and at peace. Would you bring her tired soul back to him again to be bruised and wounded?

Sue. Nat!

Nat (*clutching at his throat as though to strangle something within him—hoarsely*). Sue! Have mercy! (*His sister stares at him with dread foreboding.* Nat *calms himself with an effort and continues deliberately.*) Smith said he would give two thousand cash if I would sell the place to him—and he would let me stay, rent-free, as a caretaker.

Sue (*scornfully*). Two thousand! Why, over and over the mortgage it's worth——

Nat. It's not what it's worth. It's what one can get, cash—for my book—for freedom!

Sue. So that's why he wants Father sent away, the wretch! He must know the will Father made——

Nat. Gives the place to me. Yes, he knows. I told him.

Sue (*dully*). Ah, how vile men are!

Nat (*persuasively*). If it were to be done—if it were, I say—there'd be half for you for your wedding portion. That's fair.

Sue (*horrified*). Blood money! Do you think I could touch it?

Nat (*persuasively*). It would be only fair. I'd give it to you.

Sue. My God, Nat, are you trying to bribe me?

Nat. No. It's yours in all fairness. (*With a twisted smile*) You forget I'm heir to the treasure, too, and can afford to be generous. Ha-ha.

Sue (*alarmed*). Nat! You're so strange. You're sick, Nat. You couldn't talk this way if you were yourself. Oh, we must go away from here—you and Father and I! Let Smith foreclose. There'll be something over the mortgage; and we'll move to some little house—by the sea so that Father——

Nat (*fiercely*). Can keep up his mad game with me—whispering dreams in my ear—pointing out to sea—mocking me with stuff like this! (*He takes the bracelet from his pocket. The sight of it infuriates him and he hurls it into a corner, exclaiming in a terrible voice.*) No! No! It's too late for dreams now. It's too late! I've put them behind me tonight—forever!

Sue (*looks at him and suddenly understands that what she dreads has come to pass—letting her head fall on her outstretched arms with a long moan*). Then—you've done it! You've sold him! Oh,

Northern Seascape, Off the Banks (1936–1937) by Marsden Hartley (1877–1943).
Oil on cardboard.
Milwaukee Art Museum, Bequest of Max E. Friedmann

Nat, you're cursed!

Nat (*with a terrified glance at the roof above*). Ssshh! What are you saying? He'll be better off—away from the sea.

Sue (*dully*). You've sold him.

Nat (*wildly*). No! No! (*He takes the map from his pocket.*) Listen, Sue! For God's sake, listen to me! See! The map of the island. (*He spreads it out on the table.*) And the treasure—where the cross is made. (*He gulps and his words pour out incoherently.*) I've carried it about for years. Is that nothing? You don't know what it means.

It stands between me and my book. It's stood between me and life—driving me mad. *He* taught me to wait and hope with him—wait and hope—day after day. He made me doubt my brain and give the lie to my eyes—when hope was dead—when I knew it was all a dream—I couldn't kill it! (*His eyes starting from his head*) God forgive me, I still believe! And that's mad—mad, do you hear?

Sue (*looking at him with horror*). And that is why—you hate him!

Nat. No, I don't—— (*Then in a sudden frenzy*)

Yes! I do hate him! He's stolen my brain! I've got to free myself, can't you see, from him—and his madness.

Sue (*terrified—appealingly*). Nat! Don't! You talk as if——

Nat (*with a wild laugh*). As if I were mad? You're right—but I'll be mad no more! See! (*He opens the lantern and sets fire to the map in his hand. When he shuts the lantern again it flickers and goes out. They watch the paper burn with fascinated eyes as he talks.*) See how I free myself and become sane. And now for facts, as the doctor said. I lied to you about him. He was a doctor from the asylum. See how it burns! It must be destroyed—this poisonous madness. Yes, I lied to you—see—it's gone—the last speck—and the only other map is the one Silas Horne took to the bottom of the sea with him. (*He lets the ash fall to the floor and crushes it with his foot.*) Gone! I'm free of it—at last! (*His face is very pale, but he goes on calmly.*) Yes, I sold him, if you will—to save my soul. They're coming from the asylum to get him——

[*There is a loud, muffled cry from above, which sounds like "Sail-ho," and a stamping of feet. The slide to the companionway above is slid back with a bang. A gust of air tears down into the room. Nat and Sue have jumped to their feet and stand petrified. Captain Bartlett tramps down the stair.*]

Nat (*with a shudder*). God! Did he hear?
Sue. Ssshh.

[Captain Bartlett *comes into the room. He bears a striking resemblance to his son, but his face is more stern and formidable, his form more robust, erect and muscular. His mass of hair is pure white, his bristly mustache the same, contrasting with the weatherbeaten leather color of his furrowed face. Bushy gray brows overhang the obsessed glare of his fierce dark eyes. He wears a heavy, double-breasted blue coat, pants of the same material, and rubber boots turned down from the knee.*]

Bartlett (*in a state of mad exultation strides toward his son and points an accusing finger at him. Nat shrinks backward a step.*) Bin thinkin' me mad, did ye? Thinkin' it for the past three years, ye bin—ever since them fools on the *Slocum* tattled their damn lie o' the *Mary Allen* bein' a wreck.

Nat (*swallowing hard—chokingly*). No—Father—I——

Bartlett. Don't lie, ye whelp! You that I'd made my heir—aimin' to git me out o' the way! Aimin' to put me behind the bars o' the jail for mad folk!

Sue. Father—no!

Bartlett (*waving his hand for her to be silent*). Not you, girl, not you. You're your mother.

Nat (*very pale*). Father—do you think—I——

Bartlett (*fiercely*). A lie in your eyes! I bin a-readin' 'em. My curse on you!

Sue. Father! Don't!

Bartlett. Leave me be, girl. He believed, didn't he? And ain't he turned traitor—mockin' at me and sayin' it's all a lie—mockin' at himself, too, for bein' a fool to believe in dreams, as he calls 'em.

Nat (*placatingly*). You're wrong, Father. I do believe.

Bartlett (*triumphantly*). Aye, now ye do! Who wouldn't credit their own eyes?

Nat (*mystified*). Eyes?

Bartlett. Have ye not seen her, then? Did ye not hear me hail?

Nat (*confusedly*). Hail? I heard a shout. But—hail what?—seen what?

Bartlett (*grimly*). Aye, now's your punishment, Judas. (*Explosively*) The *Mary Allen*, ye blind fool, come back from the Southern Seas—come back as I swore she must!

Sue (*trying to soothe him*). Father! Be quiet. It's nothing.

Bartlett (*not heeding her—his eyes fixed hypnotically on his son's*). Turned the pint a half-hour back—the *Mary Allen*—loaded with gold as I swore she would be—carryin' her lowers—not a reef in 'em—makin' port, boy, as I swore she must—too late for traitors, boy, too late!—droppin' her anchor just when I hailed her.

Nat (*a haunted, fascinated look in his eyes, which are fixed immovably on his father's*). The *Mary*

Allen! But how do you know?

Bartlett. Not know my own ship! 'Tis you're mad!

Nat. But at night—some other schooner—

Bartlett. No other, I say! The *Mary Allen*—clear in the moonlight. And heed this: d'you call to mind the signal I gave to Silas Horne if he made this port o' a night?

Nat (*slowly*). A red and green light at the mainmasthead.

Bartlett (*triumphantly*). Then look out if ye dare! (*He goes to the porthole, left forward.*) Ye can see it plain from here. (*Commandingly*) Will ye believe your eyes? Look—and then call me mad!

[Nat *peers through the porthole and starts back, a dumbfounded expression on his face.*]

Nat (*slowly*). A red and a green at the mainmasthead. Yes—clear as day.

Sue (*with a worried look at him*). Let me see. (*She goes to the porthole.*)

Bartlett (*to his son with fierce satisfaction*). Aye, ye see now clear enough—too late for you. (Nat *stares at him spellbound.*) And from above I saw Horne and Cates and Jimmy Kanaka plain on the deck in the moonlight lookin' up at me. Come!

[*He strides to the companionway, followed by* Nat. *The two of them ascend.* Sue *turns from the porthole, an expression of frightened bewilderment on her face. She shakes her head sadly. A loud "Mary Allen, ahoy!" comes from above in* Bartlett's *voice, followed like an echo by the same hail from* Nat. Sue *covers her face with her hands, shuddering.* Nat *comes down the companionway, his eyes wild and exulting.*]

Sue (*brokenly*). He's bad tonight, Nat. You're right to humor him. It's the best thing.

Nat (*savagely*). Humor him? What in hell do you mean?

Sue (*pointing to the porthole*). There's nothing there, Nat. There's not a ship in harbor.

Nat. You're a fool—or blind! The *Mary Allen*'s

there in plain sight of anyone, with the red and green signal lights. Those fools lied about her being wrecked. And I've been a fool, too.

Sue. But, Nat, there's nothing. (*She goes over to the porthole again.*) Not a ship. See.

Nat. I saw, I tell you! From above it's all plain.

[*He turns from her and goes back to his seat by the table.* Sue *follows him, pleading frightenedly.*]

Sue. Nat! You musn't let this—— You're all excited and trembling, Nat. (*She puts a soothing hand on his forehead.*)

Nat (*pushing her away from him roughly*). You blind fool!

[Bartlett *comes down the steps of the companionway. His face is transfigured with the ecstasy of a dream come true.*]

Bartlett. They've lowered a boat—the three—Horne and Cates and Jimmy Kanaka. They're a-rowin' ashore. I heard the oars in the locks. Listen! (*A pause*)

Nat (*excitedly*). I hear!

Sue (*who has taken the chair by her brother—in a warning whisper*). It's the wind and sea you hear, Nat. Please!

Bartlett (*suddenly*). Hark! They've landed. They're back on earth again as I swore they'd come back. They'll be a-comin' up the path now.

[*He stands in an attitude of rigid attention.* Nat *strains forward in his chair. The sound of the wind and sea suddenly ceases and there is a heavy silence. A dense green glow floods slowly in rhythmic waves like a liquid into the room—as of great depths of the sea fairly penetrated by light.*]

Nat (*catching at his sister's hand—chokingly*). See how the light changes! Green and gold! (*He shivers.*) Deep under the sea! I've been drowned for years! (*Hysterically*) Save me! Save me!

Sue (*patting his hand comfortingly*). Only the moonlight, Nat. It hasn't changed. Be quiet, dear, it's nothing.

[*The green light grows deeper and deeper.*]

Bartlett (*in a crooning, monotonous tone*). They move slowly—slowly. They're heavy, I know, heavy—the two chests. Hark! They're below at the door. You hear?

Nat (*starting to his feet*). I hear! I left the door open.

Bartlett. For them?

Nat. For them.

Sue (*shuddering*). Ssshh!

[*The sound of a door being heavily slammed is heard from way down in the house.*]

Nat (*to his sister—excitedly*). There! You hear?

Sue. A shutter in the wind.

Nat. There is no wind.

Bartlett. Up they come! Up, bullies! They're heavy—heavy!

[*The paddling of bare feet sounds from the floor below—then comes up the stairs.*]

Nat. You hear them now?

Sue. Only the rats running about. It's nothing, Nat.

Bartlett (*rushing to the door and throwing it open*). Come in, lads, come in!—and welcome home!

[*The forms of* Silas Horne, Cates, *and* Jimmy Kanaka *rise noiselessly into the room from the stairs. The last two carry heavy inlaid chests.* Horne *is a parrot-nosed, angular old man dressed in gray cotton trousers and a singlet torn open across his hairy chest.* Jimmy *is a tall, sinewy, bronzed young Kanaka. He wears only a breechcloth.* Cates *is squat and stout and is dressed in dungaree pants and a shredded white sailor's blouse, stained with iron rust. All are in their bare feet. Water drips from their soaked and rotten clothes. Their hair is matted, intertwined with slimy strands of seaweed. Their eyes, as they glide silently into the room, stare frightfully wide at nothing. Their flesh in the green light has the suggestion of decomposition. Their bodies sway limply, nervelessly, rhythmically as if to the pulse of long swells of the deep sea.*]

Nat (*taking a step toward them*). See! (*Frenziedly*) Welcome home, boys!

Sue (*grabbing his arm*). Sit down, Nat. It's nothing. There's no one there. Father—sit down!

Bartlett (*grinning at the three and putting his finger to his lips*). Not here, boys, not here—not before him. (*He points to his son.*) He has no right, now. Come. The treasure is ours only. We'll go away with it together. Come. (*He goes to the companionway. The three follow. At the foot of it* Horne *puts a swaying hand on his shoulder and with the other holds out a piece of paper to him.* Bartlett *takes it and chuckles exultantly.*) That's right—for him—that's right!

[*He ascends. The figures sway up after him.*]

Nat (*frenziedly*). Wait! (*He struggles toward the companionway.*)

Sue (*trying to hold him back*). Nat—don't! Father—come back!

Nat. Father! (*He flings her away from him and rushes up the companionway. He pounds against the slide, which seems to have been shut down on him.*)

Sue (*hysterically—runs wildly to the door in rear*). Help! Help! (*As she gets to the door* Doctor Higgins *appears, hurrying up the stairs.*)

Higgins (*excitedly*). Just a moment, Miss. What's the matter?

Sue (*with a gasp*). My father—up there!

Higgins. I can't see—where's my flash? Ah. (*He flashes it on her terror-stricken face, then quickly around the room. The green glow disappears. The wind and sea are heard again. Clear moonlight floods through the portholes.* Higgins *springs to the companionway.* Nat *is still pounding.*) Here, Bartlett. Let me try.

Nat (*coming down—looking dully at the doctor*). They've locked it. I can't get up.

Higgins (*looks up—in an astonished voice*). What's the matter, Bartlett? It's all open. (*He starts to ascend.*)

Nat (*In a voice of warning*). Look out, man! Look out for them!

Higgins (*calls down from above*). Them? Who? There's no one here. (*Suddenly—in alarm*) Come up! Lend a hand here! He's fainted!

[*Nat goes up slowly.* Sue *goes over and lights the*

lantern, then hurries back to the foot of the companionway with it. There is a scuffling noise from above. They reappear, carrying Captain Bartlett's *body.*]

Higgins. Easy now! (*They lay him on the couch in rear.* Sue *sets the lantern down by the couch.* Higgins *bends and listens for a heartbeat. Then he rises, shaking his head.*) I'm sorry——
Sue (*dully*). Dead?
Higgins (*nodding*). Heart failure, I should judge. (*With an attempt at consolation*) Perhaps it's better so, if——
Nat (*as in a trance*) There was something Horne handed him. Did you see?
Sue (*wringing her hands*). Oh, Nat, be still! He's dead. (*To* Higgins *with pitiful appeal*) Please go—go——
Higgins. There's nothing I can do?
Sue. Go—please——

[Higgins *bows stiffly and goes out.* Nat *moves slowly to his father's body, as if attracted by some irresistible fascination.*]

Nat. Didn't you see? Horne handed him something.
Sue (*sobbing*). Nat! Nat! Come away! Don't touch him, Nat! Come away.

[*But her brother does not heed her. His gaze is fixed on his father's right hand, which hangs downward over the side of the couch. He pounces on it and, forcing the clenched fingers open with a great effort, secures a crumpled ball of paper.*]

Nat (*flourishing it above his head with a shout of triumph*). See! (*He bends down and spreads it out in the light of the lantern.*) The map of the island! Look! It isn't lost for me after all! There's still a chance—*my* chance! (*With mad, solemn decision*) When the house is sold I'll go—and I'll find it! Look! It's written here in his handwriting: "The treasure is buried where the cross is made."
Sue (*covering her face with her hands—brokenly*). Oh, God! Come away, Nat! Come away!

[*The curtain falls.*]

Reading Check

1. Why does Nat Bartlett bring Doctor Higgins to his home?
2. Identify the *Mary Allen.*
3. What is the significance of the cross on the map?
4. Why are Nat and his sister about to lose their home?
5. What arrangement has Nat made with Smith?

Commentary

Where the Cross Is Made was produced in 1918, very early in O'Neill's career. It is interesting for its combination of a surface realism with an underlying expressionism that attempts to uncover psychological motives. It is especially interesting because its expressionistic qualities are achieved through an innovative use of the stock devices of melodrama.

The play's setting is an isolated house on the wind-swept California coast. The design and lighting seem to make the sea and land merge, blurring the distinction between them. Its action takes place on a dark and windy night. Its characters are maimed, gaunt, weary, hunted, pale, wistful, melancholy, or mad. The plot involves shipwreck, double-dealing, buried treasure, secret oaths, phantom ships, and a suggestion of cannibalism. All of these are elements O'Neill could have learned from the popular theater of his time. (*The Count of Monte Cristo* involves the finding of buried treasure.) What makes this play original is O'Neill's use of these creaking devices to reflect the psychological reality of his characters' thoughts and feelings. The highly theatrical situations and devices highlight the unreality of the world his characters inhabit, a world distorted by their dreams and illusions.

The play's melodramatic devices lead to an almost tragic sense of the power of consuming passion. Captain Bartlett has put not only his wealth and energy into recovering his lost treasure, but his human feelings as well. His withdrawal from all human contact is symbolized by the "cabin" and "deck" that he has built for himself at the top of his house and that he never leaves. He lives in his own mad, self-centered world, which is based on a delusion. His son in turn has allowed his resentment of his father to become the controlling passion of his life. He feels that he must sell his father in order to be free. O'Neill suggests that such resentment only repeats the alienation from human feelings to which the father has fallen victim. The son, ironically, is condemned to follow his father's path into self-centered madness.

Such extreme situations are common in O'Neill's later work. They reflect his conviction that what we call insanity or neurosis—life lost in consuming delusions—is a severe or twisted form of feeling known to us all. O'Neill seldom produced pure melodrama, because his central interest was the emotional relationships between people, often members of the same family. He was a serious, and at his best, a tragic dramatist who sounded the darker regions of human emotions for psychological truths.

For Study and Discussion

Analyzing and Interpreting the Play

1. Captain Bartlett's shiplike tower is called a natural, interesting whim by the doctor and a proof of madness by his son. **a.** How are the lantern and the poop deck used to suggest madness? **b.** How does the setting suggest that what the audience is going to see will be a blend of realism and fantasy?

2. Nat Bartlett divides his story to the doctor into two parts he calls *fact* and *dream*. **a.** What particular object does he suggest forms the center of the dream? **b.** What proof does he offer of its dreamlike character?

3. The sea is a pervading presence throughout this play, but it means different things to different characters. What does it mean to the Captain? to Nat? to Sue? to the Captain's crew?

4. The climax of the play's action comes with the apparition of the three sailors carrying the treasure. Explain how the playwright uses Sue Bartlett to make the nature of their appearance apparent to the audience.

5. O'Neill wrote frequently about the power of illusion and the necessity of it. Referring to particular speeches, tell how this is illustrated in the play.

6a. Cite two or three speeches from the play to show that Nat Bartlett has in fact taken on his father's willfulness in the plans he makes against his father. **b.** How does his willfulness explain his behavior at the end of the play?

7. The title of the play suggests not only X's marking the spot, but also crossroads and crossovers. In what ways are these meanings touched upon in the play?

Writing About Literature

Discussing the Meaning of the Title

Consider the various meanings of the word *cross* in the title of O'Neill's play. What is its literal meaning? What symbolic meaning or meanings does it have? Might the word also refer to some change that occurs?

Thornton Wilder was one of the few American writers to gain distinction both as a novelist and as a dramatist. A novel, *The Bridge of San Luis Rey* (1927), and two plays, *Our Town* (1938) and *The Skin of Our Teeth* (1942), were awarded Pulitzer Prizes. In most of his work, Wilder sought to go beneath situations and circumstances peculiar to a specific time, to touch the universal. Often the underlying ideas are only hinted at, and the emotions that propel a novel or play find open expression only in a few terse, crucial passages. Wilder's style has been praised for its poetic grace, a grace that lends much of his work a deceptively placid surface. The reader must go beneath this surface, just as Wilder goes beneath the surface of everyday life, to discover what he once called "the All . . . the Everywhere . . . the Always."

Thornton Wilder was born in Madison, Wisconsin. His father was a newspaper publisher who was active in politics and was appointed consul general in China when his son was nine years old. Much of Wilder's boyhood was spent in China. After graduation from high school in Berkeley, California (where his family had settled after returning from China), Wilder attended Oberlin College for two years and then Yale University, from which he was graduated in 1920. He spent the next year studying archaeology at the American Academy in Rome. For seven years he was a housemaster and teacher of French at the Lawrenceville School in New Jersey. Later he taught at the University of Chicago and at Harvard University.

Wilder's first novel, *The Cabala* (1926), grew out of notebooks he had kept during his year in Rome. It received little attention. His second novel, *The Bridge of San Luis Rey*, was published a year later, and, somewhat to his surprise, it was hailed as a masterpiece, became a best seller, and is still generally considered his finest novel. Wilder's full-length plays are *Our Town, The Merchant of Yonkers, The Skin of Our Teeth,* and *The Matchmaker.* The

Thornton Wilder.

Matchmaker, a revised version of *The Merchant of Yonkers,* was successfully produced on Broadway and later adapted as an enormously popular musical comedy, *Hello, Dolly.*

Wilder was not as prolific as other major writers, but he consistently created work of polish and intelligence. His plays show an innovative use of the stage. *Our Town,* a recognized classic of the American theater, may seem disarmingly easy to read. The language is simple and straightforward, the characters uncomplicated, and the plot immediately comprehensible. The play's subtlety and irony lie not so much in what happens but rather in how it is presented onstage.

As you read the play, try to imagine yourself in a theater, as part of the audience, watching *Our Town* as it unfolds on a stage. Read the opening stage directions carefully, and consider how an audience would react to a play that opens with "no curtain" and "no scenery." Consider that the first character you meet is called the "Stage Manager"—someone who ordinarily never appears before an audience.

Thornton Wilder **963**

Consider that he begins the play in a most unusual way—by talking directly to the audience, announcing the cast and setting the scene. Later, when two trellises are pushed onstage, the Stage Manager casually remarks, "There's some scenery for those who think they have to have scenery." Apparently, scenery is not very important to this play. There seem to be good reasons for the bareness of the stage and for the unconvincing bits of scenery that are occasionally used. As you read, be attentive to all the unusual characteristics of the staging and ask yourself what reasons might lie behind them. Only then will you fully respond to this carefully conceived play.

Our Town

Characters

Stage Manager	Woman in the Balcony
Dr. Gibbs	Man in the Auditorium
Joe Crowell	Lady in the Box
Howie Newsome	Simon Stimson
Mrs. Gibbs	Mrs. Soames
Mrs. Webb	Constable Warren
George Gibbs	Si Crowell
Rebecca Gibbs	Stagehands
Wally Webb	Three Baseball Players
Emily Webb	Sam Craig
Professor Willard	Joe Stoddard
Mr. Webb	Men and Women Among the Dead

The entire play takes place in Grover's Corners, New Hampshire.

Act One

No curtain.

No scenery.

The audience, arriving, sees an empty stage in half-light.

Presently the Stage Manager, *hat on and pipe in mouth, enters and begins placing a table and three chairs downstage left, and a table and three chairs downstage right. He also places a low bench at the corner of what will be the Webb house, left.*

"Left" and "right" are from the point of view of the actor facing the audience. "Up" is toward the back wall.

As the house lights go down he has finished setting the stage and leaning against the right proscenium[1] pillar watches the late arrivals in the audience.

When the auditorium is in complete darkness he speaks.

1. **proscenium** (prō-sē′nē-əm): the small area of the stage in front of the curtain, where action takes place when the curtain is closed.

JED HARRIS

presents

OUR TOWN

A PLAY BY
THORNTON WILDER

with

FRANK CRAVEN

Title page of playbill for the original production of *Our Town*.

Stage Manager. This play is called *Our Town*. It was written by Thornton Wilder; produced and directed by A_____ (or: produced by A_____; directed by B_____). In it you will see Miss C_____; Miss D_____; Miss E_____; and Mr. F_____; Mr. G_____; Mr. H_____; and many others. The name of the town is Grover's Corners, New Hampshire—just across the Massachusetts line: latitude 42 degrees 40 minutes; longitude 70 degrees 37 minutes. The first act shows a day in our town. The day is May 7, 1901. The time is just before dawn.

[*A rooster crows.*]

The sky is beginning to show some streaks of light over in the East there, behind our mount'in.

The morning star always gets wonderful bright the minute before it has to go—doesn't it? (*He stares at it for a moment, then goes upstage.*)

Well, I'd better show you how our town lies. Up here—(*That is, parallel with the back wall*) is Main Street. Way back there is the railway station; tracks go that way. Polish Town's across the tracks, and some Canuck[2] families. (*Toward the left*) Over there is the Congregational Church; across the street's the Presbyterian.

Methodist and Unitarian are over there.

Baptist is down in the holla' by the river.

Catholic Church is over beyond the tracks.

Here's the Town Hall and Post Office combined; jail's in the basement.

Bryan[3] once made a speech from these very steps here.

Along here's a row of stores. Hitching posts and horse blocks in front of them. First automobile's going to come along in about five years—belonged to Banker Cartwright, our richest citizen . . . lives in the big white house up on the hill.

2. **Canuck:** French-Canadian.
3. **Bryan:** William Jennings Bryan (1860–1925), a famous American lawyer, statesman, and orator, and three-time Democratic Presidential candidate, in 1896, 1900, and 1908.

Here's the grocery store and here's Mr. Morgan's drugstore. Most everybody in town manages to look into those two stores once a day.

Public school's over yonder. High school's still farther over. Quarter of nine mornings, noontimes, and three o'clock afternoons, the hull town can hear the yelling and screaming from those schoolyards. (*He approaches the table and chairs downstage right.*)

This is our doctor's house—Doc Gibbs's. This is the back door.

[*Two arched trellises, covered with vines and flowers, are pushed out, one by each proscenium pillar.*]

There's some scenery for those who think they have to have scenery.

This is Mrs. Gibbs's garden. Corn . . . peas . . . beans . . . hollyhocks . . . heliotrope . . . and a lot of burdock. (*Crosses the stage*)

In those days our newspaper come out twice a week—the Grover's Corners *Sentinel*—and this is Editor Webb's house.

And this is Mrs. Webb's garden.

Just like Mrs. Gibbs's, only it's got a lot of sunflowers, too. (*He looks upward, center stage.*)

Right here . . . 's a big butternut tree. (*He returns to his place by the right proscenium pillar and looks at the audience for a minute.*)

Nice town, y'know what I mean?

Nobody very remarkable ever come out of it, s'far as we know.

The earliest tombstones in the cemetery up there on the mountain say 1670, 1680—they're Grovers and Cartwrights and Gibbses and Herseys—same names as are here now.

Well, as I said: it's about dawn.

The only lights on in town are in a cottage over by the tracks where a Polish mother's just had twins. And in the Joe Crowell house, where Joe Junior's getting up so as to deliver the paper. And in the depot, where Shorty Hawkins is gettin' ready to flag the 5:45 for Boston.

[*A train whistle is heard. The* Stage Manager *takes out his watch and nods.*]

Naturally, out in the country—all around—there've been lights on for some time, what with milkin's and so on. But town people sleep late.

So—another day's begun.

There's Doc Gibbs comin' down Main Street now, comin' back from that baby case. And here's his wife comin' downstairs to get breakfast.

[Mrs. Gibbs, *a plump, pleasant woman in the middle thirties, comes "downstairs" right. She pulls up an imaginary window shade in her kitchen and starts to make a fire in her stove.*]

Doc Gibbs died in 1930. The new hospital's named after him.

Mrs. Gibbs died first—long time ago, in fact. She went out to visit her daughter, Rebecca, who married an insurance man in Canton, Ohio, and died there—pneumonia—but her body was brought back here. She's up in the cemetery there now—in with a whole mess of Gibbses and Herseys—she was Julia Hersey 'fore she married Doc Gibbs in the Congregational Church over there.

In our town we like to know the facts about everybody.

There's Mrs. Webb, coming downstairs to get her breakfast, too.—That's Doc Gibbs. Got that call at half past one this morning. And there comes Joe Crowell, Jr., delivering Mr. Webb's *Sentinel*.

[Dr. Gibbs *has been coming along Main Street from the left. At the point where he would turn to approach his house, he stops, sets down his—imaginary—black bag, takes off his hat, and rubs his face with fatigue, using an enormous handkerchief.*

Mrs. Webb, *a thin, serious, crisp woman, has entered her kitchen, left, tying on an apron. She goes through the motions of putting wood into a stove, lighting it, and preparing breakfast.*

Suddenly, Joe Crowell, Jr., *eleven, starts down Main Street from the right, hurling imaginary newspapers into doorways.*]

Joe Crowell, Jr. Morning, Doc Gibbs.
Dr. Gibbs. Morning, Joe.
Joe Crowell, Jr. Somebody been sick, Doc?
Dr. Gibbs. No. Just some twins born over in Polish Town.
Joe Crowell, Jr. Do you want your paper now?
Dr. Gibbs. Yes, I'll take it.—Anything serious goin' on in the world since Wednesday?
Joe Crowell, Jr. Yessir. My schoolteacher, Miss Foster, 's getting married to a fella over in Concord.
Dr. Gibbs. I declare—How do you boys feel about that?
Joe Crowell, Jr. Well, of course, it's none of my business—but I think if a person starts out to be a teacher, she ought to stay one.
Dr. Gibbs. How's your knee, Joe?
Joe Crowell, Jr. Fine, Doc, I never think about it at all. Only like you said, it always tells me when it's going to rain.
Dr. Gibbs. What's it telling you today? Goin' to rain?
Joe Crowell, Jr. No, sir.
Dr. Gibbs. Sure?
Joe Crowell, Jr. Yessir.
Dr. Gibbs. Knee ever make a mistake?
Joe Crowell, Jr. No, sir.

[Joe *goes off.* Dr. Gibbs *stands reading his paper.*]

Stage Manager. Want to tell you something about that boy Joe Crowell there. Joe was awful bright—graduated from high school here, head of his class. So he got a scholarship to Massachusetts Tech. Graduated head of his class there, too. It was all wrote up in the Boston paper at the time. Goin' to be a great engineer, Joe was. But the war broke out and he died in France—All that education for nothing.
Howie Newsome (*off left*). Giddap, Bessie! What's the matter with you today?
Stage Manager. Here comes Howie Newsome, deliverin' the milk.

[Howie Newsome, *about thirty, in overalls, comes along Main Street from the left, walking beside an invisible horse and wagon and carrying an imaginary rack with milk bottles. The sound of clinking milk bottles is heard. He leaves some bottles at* Mrs. Webb's *trellis, then, crossing the stage to* Mrs. Gibbs's, *he stops center to talk to* Dr. Gibbs.]

Howie Newsome. Morning, Doc.
Dr. Gibbs. Morning, Howie.
Howie Newsome. Somebody sick?
Dr. Gibbs. Pair of twins over to Mrs. Goruslawski's.
Howie Newsome. Twins, eh? This town's gettin' bigger every year.
Dr. Gibbs. Goin' to rain, Howie?
Howie Newsome. No, no. Fine day—that'll burn through. Come on, Bessie.
Dr. Gibbs. Hello Bessie. (*He strokes the horse, which has remained up center.*) How old is she, Howie?
Howie Newsome. Going on seventeen. Bessie's all mixed up about the route ever since the Lockharts stopped takin' their quart of milk every day. She wants to leave 'em a quart just the same—keeps scolding me the hull trip.

[*He reaches* Mrs. Gibbs's *back door. She is waiting for him.*]

Mrs. Gibbs. Good morning, Howie.
Howie Newsome. Morning, Mrs. Gibbs. Doc's just comin' down the street.
Mrs. Gibbs. Is he? Seems like you're late today.
Howie Newsome. Yes. Somep'n went wrong with the separator.[4] Don't know what 'twas. (*He passes* Dr. Gibbs *up center.*) Doc!
Dr. Gibbs. Howie!
Mrs. Gibbs (*calling upstairs*). Children! Children! Time to get up.
Howie Newsome. Come on Bessie! (*He goes off right.*)
Mrs. Gibbs. George! Rebecca!

[Dr. Gibbs *arrives at his back door and passes through the trellis into his house.*]

Mrs. Gibbs. Everything all right, Frank?
Dr. Gibbs. Yes. I declare—easy as kittens.

4. **separator:** a machine that separates cream from milk.

Mrs. Gibbs. Bacon'll be ready in a minute. Set down and drink your coffee. You can catch a couple hours' sleep this morning, can't you?
Dr. Gibbs. Hm! . . . Mrs. Wentworth's coming at eleven. Guess I know what it's about, too. Her stummick ain't what it ought to be.
Mrs. Gibbs. All told, you won't get more'n three hours' sleep. Frank Gibbs, I don't know what's goin' to become of you. I do wish I could get you to go away someplace and take a rest. I think it would do you good.
Mrs. Webb. Emileeee! Time to get up! Wally! Seven o'clock!
Mrs. Gibbs. I declare, you got to speak to George. Seems like something's come over him lately. He's no help to me at all. I can't even get him to cut me some wood.
Dr. Gibbs (*washing and drying his hands at the sink.* Mrs. Gibbs *is busy at the stove*). Is he sassy to you?
Mrs. Gibbs. No. He just whines! All he thinks about is that baseball——George! Rebecca! You'll be late for school.
Dr. Gibbs. M-m-m . . .
Mrs. Gibbs. George!
Dr. Gibbs. George, look sharp!
George's Voice. Yes, Pa!
Dr. Gibbs (*as he goes off the stage*). Don't you hear your mother calling you? I guess I'll go upstairs and get forty winks.
Mrs. Webb. Walleee! Emileee! You'll be late for school! Walleee! You wash yourself good or I'll come up and do it myself.
Rebecca Gibbs's Voice. Ma! What dress shall I wear?
Mrs. Gibbs. Don't make a noise. Your father's been out all night and needs his sleep. I washed and ironed the blue gingham for you special.
Rebecca. Ma, I hate that dress.
Mrs. Gibbs. Oh, hush-up-with-you.
Rebecca. Every day I go to school dressed like a sick turkey.
Mrs. Gibbs. Now, Rebecca, you always look *very* nice.
Rebecca. Mama, George's throwing soap at me.

Mrs. Gibbs. I'll come and slap the both of you—that's what I'll do.

[*A factory whistle sounds.*

The children *dash in and take their places at the tables. Right,* George, *about sixteen, and* Rebecca, *eleven. Left,* Emily *and* Wally, *same ages. They carry strapped schoolbooks.*]

Stage Manager. We've got a factory in our town too—hear it? Makes blankets. Cartwrights own it and it brung 'em a fortune.

Mrs. Webb. Children! Now I won't have it. Breakfast is just as good as any other meal and I won't have you gobbling like wolves. It'll stunt your growth—that's a fact. Put away your book, Wally.

Wally. Aw, Ma! By ten o'clock I got to know all about Canada.

Mrs. Webb. You know the rule's well as I do —no books at table. As for me, I'd rather have my children healthy than bright.

Emily. I'm both, Mama: you know I am. I'm the brightest girl in school for my age. I have a wonderful memory.

Mrs. Webb. Eat your breakfast.

Wally. I'm bright, too, when I'm looking at my stamp collection.

Mrs. Gibbs. I'll speak to your father about it when he's rested. Seems to me twenty-five cents a week's enough for a boy your age. I declare I don't know how you spend it all.

George. Aw, Ma—I gotta lotta things to buy.

Mrs. Gibbs. Strawberry phosphates[5]—that's what you spend it on.

George. I don't see how Rebecca comes to have so much money. She has more'n a dollar.

Rebecca (*spoon in mouth, dreamily*). I've been saving it up gradual.

Mrs. Gibbs. Well, dear, I think it's a good thing to spend some every now and then.

Rebecca. Mama, do you know what I love most in the world—do you?—Money.

Mrs. Gibbs. Eat your breakfast.

The Children. Mama, there's first bell.—I

---

5. **phosphate:** a soft drink made with soda and syrup.

gotta hurry.—I don't want any more.—I gotta hurry.

[*The* children *rise, seize their books and dash out through the trellises. They meet down center, and chattering, walk to Main Street, then turn left.*

The Stage Manager *goes off, unobtrusively, right.*]

Mrs. Webb. Walk fast, but you don't have to run. Wally, pull up your pants at the knee. Stand up straight, Emily.

Mrs. Gibbs. Tell Miss Foster I send her my best congratulations—can you remember that?

Rebecca. Yes, Ma.

Mrs. Gibbs. You look real nice, Rebecca. Pick up your feet.

All. Goodbye.

[Mrs. Gibbs *fills her apron with food for the chickens and comes down to the footlights.*]

Mrs. Gibbs. Here, chick, chick, chick.

No, go away, you. Go away.

Here, chick, chick, chick.

What's the matter with *you?* Fight, fight, fight—that's all you do.

Hm . . . *you* don't belong to me. Where'd you come from? (*She shakes her apron.*) Oh, don't be so scared. Nobody's going to hurt you.

[Mrs. Webb *is sitting on the bench by her trellis, stringing beans.*]

Good morning, Myrtle. How's your cold?

Mrs. Webb. Well, I still get that tickling feeling in my throat. I told Charles I didn't know as I'd go to choir practice tonight. Wouldn't be any use.

Mrs. Gibbs. Have you tried singing over your voice?

Mrs. Webb. Yes, but somehow I can't do that and stay on the key. While I'm resting myself I thought I'd string some of these beans.

Mrs. Gibbs (*rolling up her sleeves as she crosses the stage for a chat*). Let me help you. Beans have been good this year.

Photographs for *Our Town* are from a 1975 production at the American
Shakespeare Theater, Stratford, Connecticut.

Mrs. Webb. I've decided to put up forty quarts if it kills me. The children say they hate 'em, but I notice they're able to get 'em down all winter.

[*Pause. Brief sound of chickens cackling.*]

Mrs. Gibbs. Now, Myrtle. I've got to tell you something, because if I don't tell somebody I'll burst.

Mrs. Webb. Why, Julia Gibbs!

Mrs. Gibbs. Here, give me some more of those beans. Myrtle, did one of those secondhand-furniture men from Boston come to see you last Friday?

Mrs. Webb. No-o.

Mrs. Gibbs. Well, he called on me. First I thought he was a patient wantin' to see Dr.

Gibbs. 'N he wormed his way into my parlor, and, Myrtle Webb, he offered me three hundred and fifty dollars for Grandmother Wentworth's highboy, as I'm sitting here!

Mrs. Webb. Why, Julia Gibbs!

Mrs. Gibbs. He did! That old thing! Why, it was so big I didn't know where to put it and I almost give it to Cousin Hester Wilcox.

Mrs. Webb. Well, you're going to take it, aren't you?

Mrs. Gibbs. I don't know.

Mrs. Webb. You don't know—three hundred and fifty dollars! What's come over you?

Mrs. Gibbs. Well, if I could get the Doctor to take the money and go away someplace on a real trip, I'd sell it like that.—Y'know, Myrtle, it's been the dream of my life to see Paris, France.—Oh, I don't know. It sounds crazy, I

suppose, but for years I've been promising myself that if we ever had the chance——
Mrs. Webb. How does the Doctor feel about it?
Mrs. Gibbs. Well, I did beat about the bush a little and said if I got a legacy—that's the way I put it—I'd make him take me somewhere.
Mrs. Webb. M-m-m . . . What did he say?
Mrs. Gibbs. You know how he is. I haven't heard a serious word out of him since I've known him. No, he said, it might make him discontented with Grover's Corners to go traipsin' about Europe; better let well enough alone, he says. Every two years he makes a trip to the battlefields of the Civil War and that's enough treat for anybody, he says.
Mrs. Webb. Well, Mr. Webb just *admires* the way Dr. Gibbs knows everything about the Civil War. Mr. Webb's a good mind to give up Napoleon and move over to the Civil War, only Dr. Gibbs being one of the greatest experts in the country just makes him despair.
Mrs. Gibbs. It's a fact! Dr. Gibbs is never so happy as when he's at Antietam or Gettysburg. The times I've walked over those hills, Myrtle, stopping at every bush and pacing it all out, like we were going to buy it.
Mrs. Webb. Well, if that secondhand man's really serious about buyin' it, Julia, you sell it. And then you'll get to see Paris, all right. Just keep droppin' hints from time to time—that's how I got to see the Atlantic Ocean, y'know.
Mrs. Gibbs. Oh, I'm sorry I mentioned it. Only it seems to me that once in your life before you die you ought to see a country where they don't talk in English and don't even want to.

[*The* Stage Manager *enters briskly from the right. He tips his hat to the ladies, who nod their heads.*]

Stage Manager. Thank you, ladies. Thank you very much.

[Mrs. Gibbs *and* Mrs. Webb *gather up their things, return into their homes and disappear.*]

Now we're going to skip a few hours.

But first we want a little more information about the town, kind of a scientific account, you might say.
So I've asked Professor Willard of our State University to sketch in a few details of our past history here.
Is Professor Willard here?

[Professor Willard, *a rural savant,*[6] *pince-nez*[7] *on a wide satin ribbon, enters from the right with some notes in his hand.*]

May I introduce Professor Willard of our State University.
A few brief notes, thank you, Professor—unfortunately our time is limited.
Professor Willard. Grover's Corners . . . let me see . . . Grover's Corners lies on the old Pleistocene[8] granite of the Appalachian range. I may say it's some of the oldest land in the world. We're very proud of that. A shelf of Devonian basalt crosses it with vestiges of Mesozoic shale, and some sandstone outcroppings; but that's all more recent: two hundred, three hundred million years old.
Some highly interesting fossils have been found . . . I may say: unique fossils . . . two miles out of town, in Silas Peckham's cow pasture. They can be seen at the museum in our University at any time—that is, any reasonable time. Shall I read some of Professor Gruber's notes on the meteorological situation—mean precipitation, et cetera?
Stage Manager. Afraid we won't have time for that, Professor. We might have a few words on the history of man here.
Professor Willard. Yes . . . anthropological data: Early Amerindian[9] stock. Cotahatchee[10] tribes . . . no evidence before the tenth century of this era . . . hm . . . now entirely disappeared

---

6. *savant* (sə-vänt′): scholar.
7. *pince-nez* (păns′nā′): old fashioned eyeglasses that are clipped to the nose with a spring.
8. **Pleistocene** (plī′stə-sēn′) . . . **Mesozoic** (mĕz′ə-zō′ĭk): geological eras when the granite, basalt, and shale, respectively, were formed.
9. **Amerindian** (ăm′ə-rĭn′dē-ən): here, American Indian.
10. **Cotahatchee** (kō′-tə-hă′chē).

. . . possible traces in three families. Migration toward the end of the seventeenth century of English brachycephalic[11] blue-eyed stock . . . for the most part. Since then some Slav and Mediterranean——

Stage Manager. And the population, Professor Willard?

Professor Willard. Within the town limits: 2,640.

Stage Manager. Just a moment, Professor. (*He whispers into the professor's ear.*)

Professor Willard. Oh, yes, indeed?—The population, *at the moment,* is 2,642. The postal district brings in 507 more, making a total of 3,149.—Mortality and birth rates: constant.—By MacPherson's gauge: 6,032.

Stage Manager. Thank you very much, Professor. We're all very much obliged to you, I'm sure.

Professor Willard. Not at all, sir; not at all.

Stage Manager. This way, Professor, and thank you again.

[*Exit* Professor Willard.]

Now the political and social report: Editor Webb—Oh, Mr. Webb?

[Mrs. Webb *appears at her back door.*]

Mrs. Webb. He'll be here in a minute. . . . He just cut his hand while he was eatin' an apple.

Stage Manager. Thank you, Mrs. Webb.

Mrs. Webb. Charles! Everybody's waitin'. (*Exit* Mrs. Webb.)

Stage Manager. Mr. Webb is publisher and editor of the Grover's Corners *Sentinel.* That's our local paper, y'know.

[Mr. Webb *enters from his house, pulling on his coat. His finger is bound in a handkerchief.*]

Mr. Webb. Well . . . I don't have to tell you that we're run here by a board of selectmen.[12]—All males vote at the age of twenty-

11. **brachycephalic** (brăk′ē-sə-făl′ĭk): short-headed or broad-headed.
12. **board of selectmen:** a board of municipal officers elected annually.

one. Women vote indirect. We're a lower-middle class: sprinkling of professional men . . . ten percent illiterate laborers. Politically, we're eighty-six percent Republicans; six percent Democrats; four percent Socialists; rest, indifferent.

Religiously, we're eighty-five percent Protestants; twelve percent Catholics; rest, indifferent.

Stage Manager. Have you any comments, Mr. Webb?

Mr. Webb. Very ordinary town, if you ask me. Little better behaved than most. Probably a lot duller.

But our young people here seem to like it well enough. Ninety percent of 'em graduating from high school settle down right here to live—even when they've been away to college.

Stage Manager. Now, is there anyone in the audience who would like to ask Editor Webb anything about the town?

Woman in the Balcony. Is there much drinking in Grover's Corners?

Mr. Webb. Well, ma'am, I wouldn't know what you'd call *much.* Satiddy nights the farmhands meet down in Ellery Greenough's stable and holler some. We've got one or two town drunks, but they're always having remorses every time an evangelist comes to town. No, ma'am, I'd say likker ain't a regular thing in the home here, except in the medicine chest. Right good for snakebite, y'know—always was.

Belligerent Man at Back of Auditorium. Is there no one in town aware of——

Stage Manager. Come forward, will you, where we can all hear you——What were you saying?

Belligerent Man. Is there no one in town aware of social injustice and industrial inequality?

Mr. Webb. Oh, yes, everybody is—somethin' terrible. Seems like they spend most of their time talking about who's rich and who's poor.

Belligerent Man. Then why don't they do something about it? (*He withdraws without waiting for an answer.*)

Mr. Webb. Well, I dunno. . . . I guess we're all hunting like everybody else for a way the diligent and sensible can rise to the top and the lazy and quarrelsome can sink to the bottom. But it ain't easy to find. Meanwhile, we do all we can to help those that can't help themselves and those that can we leave alone.—Are there any other questions?

Lady in a Box. Oh, Mr. Webb? Mr. Webb, is there any culture or love of beauty in Grover's Corners?

Mr. Webb. Well, ma'am, there ain't much—not in the sense you mean. Come to think of it, there's some girls that play the piano at high school commencement; but they ain't happy about it. No, ma'am, there isn't much culture; but maybe this is the place to tell you that we've got a lot of pleasures of a kind here: we like the sun comin' up over the mountain in the morning, and we all notice a good deal about the birds. We pay a lot of attention to them. And we watch the change of the seasons; yes, everybody knows about them. But those other things—you're right, ma'am—there ain't much.—*Robinson Crusoe* and the Bible; and Handel's "Largo," we all know that; and Whistler's *Mother*—those are just about as far as we go.

Lady in a Box. So I thought. Thank you, Mr. Webb.

Stage Manager. Thank you, Mr. Webb.

[Mr. Webb *retires.*]

Now, we'll go back to the town. It's early afternoon. All 2,642 have had their dinners and all the dishes have been washed.

[Mr. Webb, *having removed his coat, returns and starts pushing a lawn mower to and fro beside his house.*]

There's an early-afternoon calm in our town: a buzzin' and a hummin' from the school buildings; only a few buggies on Main Street— the horses dozing at the hitching posts; you all remember what it's like. Doc Gibbs is in his office, tapping people and making them say "ah." Mr. Webb's cuttin' his lawn over there;

one man in ten thinks it's a privilege to push his own lawn mower.

No, sir. It's later than I thought. There are the children coming home from school already.

[*Shrill girls' voices are heard, off left.* Emily *comes along Main Street, carrying some books. There are some signs that she is imagining herself to be a lady of startling elegance.*]

Emily. I *can't,* Lois, I've got to go home and help my mother. I *promised.*

Mr. Webb. Emily, walk simply. Who do you think you are today?

Emily. Papa, you're terrible. One minute you tell me to stand up straight and the next minute you call me names. I just don't listen to you. (*She gives him an abrupt kiss.*)

Mr. Webb. Golly, I never got a kiss from such a great lady before.

[*He goes out of sight.* Emily *leans over and picks some flowers by the gate of her house.*

George Gibbs *comes careening down Main Street. He is throwing a ball up to dizzying heights, and waiting to catch it again. This sometimes requires his taking six steps backward. He bumps into an* Old Lady *invisible to us.*]

George. Excuse me, Mrs. Forrest.

Stage Manager (*as Mrs. Forrest*). Go out and play in the fields, young man. You got no business playing baseball on Main Street.

George. Awfully sorry, Mrs. Forrest.—Hello, Emily.

Emily. H'lo.

George. You made a fine speech in class.

Emily. Well . . . I was really ready to make a speech about the Monroe Doctrine, but at the last minute Miss Corcoran made me talk about the Louisiana Purchase instead. I worked an awful long time on both of them.

George. Gee, it's funny, Emily. From my window up there I can just see your head nights when you're doing your homework over in your room.

Emily. Why, can you?

George. You certainly do stick to it, Emily. I don't see how you can sit still that long. I guess you like school.

Emily. Well, I always feel it's something you have to go through.

George. Yeah.

Emily. I don't mind it really. It passes the time.

George. Yeah.—Emily, what do you think? We might work out a kinda telegraph from your window to mine; and once in a while you could give me a kinda hint or two about one of those algebra problems. I don't mean the answers, Emily, of course not . . . just some little hint . . .

Emily. Oh, I think *hints* are allowed.—So—ah—if you get stuck, George, you whistle to me; and I'll give you some hints.

George. Emily, you're just naturally bright, I guess.

Emily. I figure that it's just the way a person's born.

George. Yeah. But, you see, I want to be a farmer, and my Uncle Luke says whenever I'm ready I can come over and work on his farm and if I'm any good I can just gradually have it.

Emily. You mean the house and everything?

[*Enter* Mrs. Webb *with a large bowl and sits on the bench by her trellis.*]

George. Yeah. Well, thanks . . . I better be getting out to the baseball field. Thanks for the talk, Emily.—Good afternoon, Mrs. Webb.

Mrs. Webb. Good afternoon, George.

George. So long, Emily.

Emily. So long, George.

Mrs. Webb. Emily, come and help me string these beans for the winter. George Gibbs let himself have a real conversation, didn't he? Why, he's growing up. How old would George be?

Emily. I don't know.

Mrs. Webb. Let's see. He must be almost sixteen.

Emily. Mama, I made a speech in class today and I was very good.

Mrs. Webb. You must recite it to your father at supper. What was it about?

Emily. The Louisiana Purchase. It was like silk off a spool. I'm going to make speeches all my life.—Mama, are these big enough?

Mrs. Webb. Try and get them a little bigger if you can.

Emily. Mama, will you answer me a question, serious?

Mrs. Webb. Seriously, dear—not serious.

Emily. Seriously—will you?

Mrs. Webb. Of course, I will.

Emily. Mama, am I good-looking?

Mrs. Webb. Yes, of course you are. All my children have got good features; I'd be ashamed if they hadn't.

Emily. Oh, Mama, that's not what I mean. What I mean is: am I *pretty*?

Mrs. Webb. I've already told you, yes. Now that's enough of that. You have a nice young pretty face. I never heard of such foolishness.

Emily. Oh, Mama, you never tell us the truth about anything.

Mrs. Webb. I *am* telling the truth.

Emily. Mama, were *you* pretty?

Mrs. Webb. Yes, I was, if I do say so. I was the prettiest girl in town next to Mamie Cartwright.

Emily. But, Mama, you've got to say *some*thing about me. Am I pretty enough . . . to get anybody . . . to get people interested in me?

Mrs. Webb. Emily, you make me tired. Now stop it. You're pretty enough for all normal purposes.—Come along now and bring that bowl with you.

Emily. Oh, Mama, you're no help at all.

Stage Manager. Thank you, Thank you! That'll do. We'll have to interrupt again here. Thank you, Mrs. Webb; thank you, Emily.

[Mrs. Webb *and* Emily *withdraw.*]

There are some more things we want to explore about this town.

[*He comes to the center of the stage. During the following speech the lights gradually dim to darkness, leaving only a spot on him.*]

I think this is a good time to tell you that the Cartwright interests have just begun building a new bank in Grover's Corners—had to go to Vermont for the marble, sorry to say. And they've asked a friend of mine what they should put in the cornerstone for people to dig up . . . a thousand years from now. . . . Of course, they've put in a copy of the *New York Times* and a copy of Mr. Webb's *Sentinel*. . . . We're kind of interested in this because some scientific fellas have found a way of painting all that reading matter with a glue—a silicate glue—that'll make it keep a thousand—two thousand years.

We're putting in a Bible . . . and the Constitution of the United States—and a copy of William Shakespeare's plays. What do you say, folks? What do you think?

Y'know—Babylon once had two million people in it, and all we know about 'em is the names of the kings and some copies of wheat contracts . . . and contracts for the sales of slaves. Yet every night all those families sat down to supper, and the father came home from his work, and the smoke went up the chimney—same as here. And even in Greece and Rome, all we know about the *real* life of the people is what we can piece together out of the joking poems and the comedies they wrote for the theater back then.

So I'm going to have a copy of this play put in the cornerstone and the people a thousand years from now'll know a few simple facts about us—more than the Treaty of Versailles[13] and the Lindbergh flight.

See what I mean?

So—people a thousand years from now— this is the way we were in the provinces north of New York at the beginning of the twentieth century.—This is the way we were: in our growing up and in our marrying and in our living and in our dying.

[*A choir partially concealed in the orchestra pit has begun singing "Blessed Be the Tie That Binds."*

Simon Stimson *stands directing them.*

Two ladders have been pushed onto the stage; they serve as indication of the second story in the Gibbs and Webb houses. George *and* Emily *mount them, and apply themselves to their schoolwork.*

Dr. Gibbs *has entered and is seated in his kitchen reading.*]

Well!—good deal of time's gone by. It's evening.

You can hear choir practice going on in the Congregational Church.

The children are at home doing their schoolwork.

13. **Treaty of Versailles** (vər-sī′): the treaty signed at the end of World War I (1919).

The day's running down like a tired clock.

Simon Stimson. Now look here, everybody. Music come into the world to give pleasure.— Softer! Softer! Get it out of your heads that music's only good when it's loud. You leave loudness to the Methodists. You couldn't beat 'em, even if you wanted to. Now again. Tenors!

George. Hssst! Emily!

Emily. Hello.

George. Hello!

Emily. I can't work at all. The moonlight's so *terrible.*

George. Emily, did you get the third problem?

Emily. Which?

George. The *third?*

Emily. Why, yes, George—that's the easiest of them all.

George. I don't see it. Emily, can you give me a hint?

Emily. I'll tell you one thing: the answer's in yards.

George. !!! In yards? How do you mean?

Emily. In *square* yards.

George. Oh . . . in square yards.

Emily. Yes, George, don't you see?

George. Yeah.

Emily. In square yards of *wallpaper.*

George. Wallpaper—oh, I see. Thanks a lot, Emily.

Emily. You're welcome. My, isn't the moonlight *terrible?* And choir practice going on.—I think if you hold your breath you can hear the train all the way to Contoocook. Hear it?

George. M-m-m——What do you know!

Emily. Well, I guess I better go back and try to work.

George. Good night, Emily. And thanks.

Emily. Good night, George.

Simon Stimson. Before I forget it: how many of you will be able to come in Tuesday afternoon and sing at Fred Hersey's wedding?— show your hands. That'll be fine; that'll be right nice. We'll do the same music we did for Jane Trowbridge's last month.

—Now we'll do: "Art Thou Weary, Art Thou Languid?" It's a question, ladies and gentlemen, make it talk. Ready.

Dr. Gibbs. Oh, George, can you come down a minute?

George. Yes, Pa. (*He descends the ladder.*)

Dr. Gibbs. Make yourself comfortable, George; I'll only keep you a minute. George, how old are you?

George. I? I'm sixteen, almost seventeen.

Dr. Gibbs. What do you want to do after school's over?

George. Why, you know, Pa. I want to be a farmer on Uncle Luke's farm.

Dr. Gibbs. You'll be willing, will you, to get up early and milk and feed the stock . . . and you'll be able to hoe and hay all day.

George. Sure, I will. What are you . . . what do you mean, Pa?

Dr. Gibbs. Well, George, while I was in my office today I heard a funny sound . . . and what do you think it was? It was your mother chopping wood. There you see your mother—getting up early; cooking meals all day long; washing and ironing—and still she has to go out in the backyard and chop wood. I suppose she just got tired of asking you. She just gave up and decided it was easier to do it herself. And you eat her meals, and put on the clothes she keeps nice for you, and you run off and play baseball—like she's some hired girl we keep around the house but that we don't like very much. Well, I knew all I had to do was call your attention to it. Here's a handkerchief, son. George, I've decided to raise your spending money twenty-five cents a week. Not, of course, for chopping wood for your mother, because that's a present you give her, but because you're getting older—and I imagine there are lots of things you must find to do with it.

George. Thanks, Pa.

Dr. Gibbs. Let's see—tomorrow's your payday. You can count on it——Hmm. Probably Rebecca'll feel she ought to have some more too. Wonder what could have happened to your mother. Choir practice never was as late as this before.

George. It's only half past eight, Pa.

Dr. Gibbs. I don't know why she's in that old choir. She hasn't any more voice than an old crow. . . . Traipsin' around the streets at this hour of the night . . . Just about time you retired, don't you think?

George. Yes, Pa.

[George *mounts to his place on the ladder.*

Laughter and good-nights can be heard on stage left and presently Mrs. Gibbs, Mrs. Soames *and* Mrs. Webb *come down Main Street. When they arrive at the corner of the stage they stop.*]

Mrs. Soames. Good night, Martha. Good night, Mr. Foster.

Mrs. Webb. I'll tell Mr. Webb; I *know* he'll want to put it in his paper.

Mrs. Gibbs. My, it's late!

Mrs. Soames. Good night, Irma.

Mrs. Gibbs. Real nice choir practice, wa'n't it? Myrtle Webb! Look at that moon, will you! Tsk-tsk-tsk. Potato weather, for sure.

[*They are silent a moment, gazing up at the moon.*]

Mrs. Soames. Naturally I didn't want to say a word about it in front of those others, but now we're alone—really, it's the worst scandal that ever was in this town!

Mrs. Gibbs. What?

Mrs. Soames. Simon Stimson!

Mrs. Gibbs. Now, Louella!

Mrs. Soames. But, Julia! To have the organist of a church *drink* and *drunk* year after year. You know he was drunk tonight.

Mrs. Gibbs. Now, Louella! We all know about Mr. Stimson and we all know about the trouble he's been through, and Dr. Ferguson knows too, and if Dr. Ferguson keeps him on there in his job the only thing the rest of us can do is just not to notice it.

Mrs. Soames. *Not to notice it!* But it's getting worse.

Mrs. Webb. No, it isn't, Louella. It's getting better. I've been in that choir twice as long as you have. It doesn't happen anywhere near so often. . . . My, I hate to go to bed on a night like this.—I better hurry. Those children'll be sitting up till all hours. Good night, Louella.

[*They all exchange good-nights. She hurries downstage, enters her house and disappears.*]

Mrs. Gibbs. Can you get home safe, Louella?

Mrs. Soames. It's as bright as day. I can see Mr. Soames scowling at the window now. You'd think we'd been to a dance the way the menfolk carry on.

[*More good-nights.* Mrs. Gibbs *arrives at her home and passes through the trellis into the kitchen.*]

Mrs. Gibbs. Well, we had a real good time.

Dr. Gibbs. You're late enough.

Mrs. Gibbs. Why, Frank, it ain't any later 'n usual.

Dr. Gibbs. And you stopping at the corner to gossip with a lot of hens.

Mrs. Gibbs. Now, Frank, don't be grouchy. Come out and smell the heliotrope in the moonlight. (*They stroll out arm in arm along the footlights.*) Isn't that wonderful? What did you do all the time I was away?

Dr. Gibbs. Oh, I read—as usual. What were the girls gossiping about tonight?

Mrs. Gibbs. Well, believe me, Frank—there is something to gossip about.

Dr. Gibbs. Hmm! Simon Stimson far gone, was he?

Mrs. Gibbs. Worst I've ever seen him. How'll that end, Frank? Dr. Ferguson can't forgive him forever.

Dr. Gibbs. I quess I know more about Simon Stimson's affairs than anybody in this town. Some people ain't made for small-town life. I don't know how that'll end; but there's nothing we can do but just leave it alone. Come, get in.

Mrs. Gibbs. No, not yet . . . Frank, I'm worried about you.

Dr. Gibbs. What are you worried about?

Mrs. Gibbs. I think it's my duty to make plans for you to get a real rest and change. And if I get that legacy, well, I'm going to insist on it.

Dr. Gibbs. Now, Julia, there's no sense in going over that again.

Mrs. Gibbs. Frank, you're just *unreasonable!*

Dr. Gibbs (*starting into the house*). Come on, Julia, it's getting late. First thing you know you'll catch cold. I gave George a piece of my mind tonight. I reckon you'll have your wood chopped for a while anyway. No, no, start getting upstairs.

Mrs. Gibbs. Oh, dear. There's always so many things to pick up, seems like. You know, Frank, Mrs. Fairchild always locks her front door every night. All those people up that part of town do.

Dr. Gibbs (*blowing out the lamp*). They're all getting citified, that's the trouble with them.

They haven't got nothing fit to burgle and everybody knows it.

[*They disappear.*
Rebecca *climbs up the ladder beside* George.]

George. Get out, Rebecca. There's only room for one at this window. You're always spoiling everything.
Rebecca. Well, let me look just a minute.
George. Use your own window.
Rebecca. I did, but there's no moon there. . . . George, do you know what I think, do you? I think maybe the moon's getting nearer and nearer and there'll be a big 'splosion.
George. Rebecca, you don't know anything. If the moon were getting nearer, the guys that sit up all night with telescopes would see it first and they'd tell about it, and it'd be in all the newspapers.
Rebecca. George, is the moon shining on South America, Canada and half the whole world?
George. Well—prob'ly is.

[*The* Stage Manager *strolls on.*
Pause. The sound of crickets is heard.]

Stage Manager. Nine thirty. Most of the lights are out. No, there's Constable Warren trying a few doors on Main Street. And here comes Editor Webb, after putting his newspaper to bed.

[Mr. Warren, *an elderly policeman, comes along Main Street from the right,* Mr. Webb *from the left.*]

Mr. Webb. Good evening, Bill.
Constable Warren. Evenin', Mr. Webb.
Mr. Webb. Quite a moon!
Constable Warren. Yepp.
Mr. Webb. All quiet tonight?
Constable Warren. Simon Stimson is rollin' around a little. Just saw his wife movin' out to hunt for him so I looked the other way—there he is now.

[Simon Stimson *comes down Main Street from the left, only a trace of unsteadiness in his walk.*]

Mr. Webb. Good evening, Simon. . . . Town seems to have settled down for the night pretty well. . . .

[Simon Stimson *comes up to him and pauses a moment and stares at him, swaying slightly.*]

Good evening. . . . Yes, most of the town's settled down for the night, Simon. . . . I guess we better do the same. Can I walk along a ways with you?

[Simon Stimson *continues on his way without a word and disappears at the right.*]

Good night.
Constable Warren. I don't know how that's goin' to end, Mr. Webb.
Mr. Webb. Well, he's seen a peck of trouble, one thing after another. . . . Oh, Bill . . . if you see my boy smoking cigarettes, just give him a word, will you? He thinks a lot of you, Bill.
Constable Warren. I don't think he smokes no cigarettes, Mr. Webb. Leastways, not more'n two or three a year.
Mr. Webb. Hm . . . I hope not.—Well, good night, Bill.
Constable Warren. Good night, Mr. Webb. (*Exit.*)
Mr. Webb. Who's that up there? Is that you, Myrtle?
Emily. No, it's me, Papa.
Mr. Webb. Why aren't you in bed?
Emily. I don't know. I just can't sleep yet, Papa. The moonlight's so *won*-derful. And the smell of Mrs. Gibbs's heliotrope. Can you smell it?
Mr. Webb. Hm . . . Yes. Haven't any troubles on your mind, have you, Emily?
Emily. *Troubles,* Papa? No.
Mr. Webb. Well, enjoy yourself, but don't let your mother catch you. Good night, Emily.
Emily. Good night, Papa.

[Mr. Webb *crosses into the house, whistling "Blessed Be the Tie That Binds," and disappears.*]

Rebecca. I never told you about that letter Jane Crofut got from her minister when she was sick. He wrote Jane a letter and on the envelope the address was like this. It said: Jane Crofut; the Crofut Farm; Grover's Corners; Sutton County; New Hampshire; United States of America.

George. What's funny about that?

Rebecca. But listen, it's not finished: the United States of America; Continent of North America; Western Hemisphere; the Earth; the Solar System; the Universe; the Mind of God— that's what it said on the envelope.

George. What do you know!

Rebecca. And the postman brought it just the same.

George. What do you know!

Stage Manager. That's the end of the first act, friends. You can go and smoke now, those that smoke.

Reading Check

1. Why is Dr. Gibbs unwilling to travel to Europe?
2. According to Editor Webb, what do the people of Grover's Corners have instead of culture?
3. What are George Gibbs's plans for the future?
4. What keeps distracting Emily from her homework?

Commentary

By now you are probably aware of the tension between the commonplace simplicity of the events of *Our Town* and the unusually sophisticated way in which these events are presented on the stage. As far as the events of the play are concerned, Thornton Wilder seems to stress the ordinary over the extraordinary, the typical over the unusual. He concentrates on two families, the Gibbses and the Webbs, both of whom seem to live routine and conventional lives. Even the minor characters in the play are shown in everyday circumstances. The first act of *Our Town* is permeated with a sense of the ever-occurring, predictable, circular patterns of daily life.

True, there are a few hints of unusual events in the play. For instance, Mrs. Gibbs says she may sell an antique and take a trip abroad; and Simon Stimson, the church organist, apparently has been drinking. But when we consider these details, we realize that the playwright introduces them only to emphasize the idea of orderly routine. Mrs. Gibbs, we feel, will forego her trip to Paris and settle for the usual trip to Gettysburg. A prospective change in routine will be defeated by the routine itself. Simon Stimson drinks, we learn, because "some people ain't made for small-town life." His drinking is a protest against commonplace routines, and yet, ironically, his drinking has become a routine itself, a commonplace part of the life in Grover's Corners.

Routine, then, seems to be the word that best describes the events of Act One of *Our Town*. Behind these events there are reminders of other routines. A rooster crows at daybreak; a schoolbell calls children to school; a whistle calls workers to the factory. The whole act, in fact, is bracketed by two cosmically continual events: the rising of the sun in the morning and the rising of the moon in the evening.

Yet if the events of the play are consistently and constantly commonplace, they are presented to us in a theatrically unusual way. The playwright always attempts to make the ordinary *seem* extraordinary by throwing a very different sort of light upon it. The staging of the play constantly reminds us that these events are being presented before an audience. Normally, plays use curtains, scenery, lighting, every effect they can, to draw us into an imaginary world. But here, the playwright does the very opposite: there is no curtain at the beginning, very little scenery throughout, and the actors use imaginary or crudely representative props. George and Emily converse not from windowsills but from stepladders, and behind them is the dull brick backstage wall. Apparently, in *Our Town*, we are not supposed to lose ourselves in the story, but rather remain detached from it because of the obvious artificiality of its staging. The constant presence of the Stage Manager contributes to this effect of detachment. He pulls the strings of the play before our eyes, bringing characters on and off, tampering with time, commenting on what is happening. We are asked to think about what we see and hear, rather than to respond emotionally to it. The humdrum life of a small New Hampshire town is put under a cool, intellectual light so that this life—as it unfolds during the course of this play—will gain new meaning, new significance.

Thus there is an odd contrast between the events themselves and the attitude we are encouraged to take toward these events. The characters respond with great feeling to what is happening, but we the audience are supposed to remain distant and thoughtful. Emily finds the moonlight "terrible" and emotes about algebra, but the audience sees the more general issue of two young people falling in love; George apparently cries when he is reprimanded by his father, but we probably don't cry with him, knowing that the scene is really about all boys growing up. The characters respond to specific things; the audience understands the general implications. The characters are involved; the audience is presumably detached.

Perhaps the whole effect can best be summarized in the address on Jane Crofut's letter:

Jane Crofut; The Crofut Farm; Grover's Corners; Sutton County; New Hampshire; United States of America; . . . Continent of North America; Western Hemisphere; the Earth; the Solar System; the Universe; the Mind of God . . .

From Jane Crofut's point of view, the address is particularly exciting because she is linked with a vast cosmic concept. To us the audience, however, the address also emphasizes the unimportance of Jane when she is viewed against such a sweeping backdrop. The address, like the play itself, connects both viewpoints: the intense concern of the individual and the cosmic detachment of a deity. And the letter is delivered: "the postman brought it just the same"—a wonderful line, suggesting that the routines of life go on no matter what the point of view.

For Study and Discussion

Analyzing and Interpreting the Play

1. Toward the end of his first speech, the Stage Manager says that in Grover's Corners, everybody likes "to know the facts about everybody." What details in his speech indicate that he is talking about an ordinary small town and its people?

2. Professor Willard describes Grover's Corners scientifically: Emily and George are of "brachycephalic" stock; the New Hamshire countryside rests upon "a shelf of Devonian basalt." **a.** What is the effect of this information on the audience? **b.** How does it contribute to what appears to be the playwright's purpose?

3. In his speech on page 975, the Stage Manager speaks of leaving a time capsule for people living a thousand years from now. He remarks on how little we know about the lives of people in ancient Babylon, Greece, and Rome. What do these and future civilizations have to do with Grover's Corners in the early years of the twentieth century?

4a. What seems to set the Stage Manager apart from the other characters? **b.** What does the Stage Manager have in common with the other characters?

Act Two

The tables and chairs of the two kitchens are still on the stage.

The ladders and the small bench have been withdrawn.

The Stage Manager *has been at his accustomed place watching the audience return to its seats.*

Stage Manager. Three years have gone by.

Yes, the sun's come up over a thousand times.

Summers and winters have cracked the mountains a little bit more and the rains have brought down some of the dirt.

Some babies that weren't even born before have begun talking regular sentences already; and a number of people who thought they were right young and spry have noticed that they can't bound up a flight of stairs like they used to, without their heart fluttering a little.

All that can happen in a thousand days.

Nature's been pushing and contriving in other ways, too: a number of young people fell in love and got married.

Yes, the mountain got bit away a few fractions of an inch; millions of gallons of water went by the mill; and here and there a new home was set up under a roof.

Almost everybody in the world gets married—you know what I mean? In our town there aren't hardly any exceptions. Most everybody in the world climbs into their graves married.

The first act was called the Daily Life. This act is called Love and Marriage. There's another act coming after this: I reckon you can guess what that's about.

So:

It's three years later. It's 1904.

It's July 7th, just after high school commencement.

That's the time most of our young people jump up and get married.

Soon as they've passed their last examinations in solid geometry and Cicero's[1] orations, looks like they suddenly feel themselves fit to be married.

It's early morning. Only this time it's been raining. It's been pouring and thundering.

Mrs. Gibbs's garden, and Mrs. Webb's here: drenched.

All those bean poles and pea vines: drenched.

All yesterday over there on Main Street, the rain looked like curtains being blown along.

Hm . . . it may begin any minute.

There! You can hear the 5:45 for Boston.

[Mrs. Gibbs *and* Mrs. Webb *enter their kitchens and start the day as in the first act.*]

And there's Mrs. Gibbs and Mrs. Webb come down to make breakfast, just as though it were an ordinary day. I don't have to point out to the women in my audience that those ladies they see before them, both of those ladies cooked three meals a day—one of 'em for twenty years, the other for forty—and no summer vacation. They brought up two children apiece, washed, cleaned the house—and *never a nervous breakdown.*

It's like what one of those Middle West poets said: You've got to love life to have life, and you've got to have life to love life.[2] . . .

It's what they call a vicious circle.

Howie Newsome (*off stage left*). Giddap, Bessie!

Stage Manager. Here comes Howie Newsome delivering the milk. And there's Si Crowell delivering the papers like his brother before him.

[Si Crowell *has entered hurling imaginary newspapers into doorways;* Howie Newsome *has come along Main Street with Bessie.*]

Si Crowell. Morning, Howie.

---

1. **Cicero:** a Roman statesman and orator, 106–43 B.C. His speeches are often studied in advanced Latin classes.
2. **You've . . . life:** an approximate quotation from the poem "Lucinda Matlock" in Edgar Lee Masters' *Spoon River Anthology.* The actual line from the poem reads, "It takes life to love life." See page 503.

Howie Newsome. Morning, Si.—Anything in the papers I ought to know?

Si Crowell. Nothing much, except we're losing about the best baseball pitcher Grover's Corners ever had—George Gibbs.

Howie Newsome. Reckon he is.

Si Crowell. He could hit and run bases, too.

Howie Newsome. Yep. Mighty fine ball player.—Whoa! Bessie! I guess I can stop and talk if I've a mind to!

Si Crowell. I don't see how he could give up a thing like that just to get married. Would you, Howie?

Howie Newsome. Can't tell, Si. Never had no talent that way.

[Constable Warren *enters. They exchange good-mornings.*]

You're up early, Bill.

Constable Warren. Seein' if there's anything I can do to prevent a flood. River's been risin' all night.

Howie Newsome. Si Crowell's all worked up here about George Gibbs's retiring from baseball.

Constable Warren. Yes, sir; that's the way it goes. Back in '84 we had a player, Si—even George Gibbs couldn't touch him. Name of Hank Todd. Went down to Maine and become a parson. Wonderful ball player.—Howie, how does the weather look to you?

Howie Newsome. Oh, 'tain't bad. Think maybe it'll clear up for good.

[Constable Warren *and* Si Crowell *continue on their way.*
   Howie Newsome *brings the milk first to* Mrs. Gibbs's *house. She meets him by the trellis.*]

Mrs. Gibbs. Good morning, Howie. Do you think it's going to rain again?

Howie Newsome. Morning, Mrs. Gibbs. It rained so heavy, I think maybe it'll clear up.

Mrs. Gibbs. Certainly hope it will.

Howie Newsome. How much did you want today?

Mrs. Gibbs. I'm going to have a houseful of relations, Howie. Looks to me like I'll need three-a-milk and two-a-cream.

Howie Newsome. My wife says to tell you we both hope they'll be very happy, Mrs. Gibbs. Know they *will.*

Mrs. Gibbs. Thanks a lot, Howie. Tell your wife I hope she gits there to the wedding.

Howie Newsome. Yes, she'll be there; she'll be there if she kin. (Howie Newsome *crosses to* Mrs. Webb's *house.*) Morning, Mrs. Webb.

Mrs. Webb. Oh, good morning, Mr. Newsome. I told you four quarts of milk, but I hope you can spare me another.

Howie Newsome. Yes'm . . . and the two of cream.

Mrs. Webb. Will it start raining again, Mr. Newsome?

Howie Newsome. Well. Just sayin' to Mrs. Gibbs as how it may lighten up. Mrs. Newsome told me to tell you as how we hope they'll both be very happy, Mrs. Webb. Know they *will.*

Mrs. Webb. Thank you and thank Mrs. Newsome and we're counting on seeing you at the wedding.

Howie Newsome. Yes, Mrs. Webb. We hope to git there. Couldn't miss that. Come on, Bessie.

[*Exit* Howie Newsome.
   Dr. Gibbs *descends in shirt sleeves, and sits down at his breakfast table.*]

Dr. Gibbs. Well, Ma, the day has come. You're losin' one of your chicks.

Mrs. Gibbs. Frank Gibbs, don't you say another word. I feel like crying every minute. Sit down and drink your coffee.

Dr. Gibbs. The groom's up shaving himself— only there ain't an awful lot to shave. Whistling and singing, like he's glad to leave us.—Every now and then he says "I do" to the mirror, but it don't sound convincing to me.

Mrs. Gibbs. I declare Frank, I don't know how he'll get along. I've arranged his clothes and seen to it he's put warm things on—Frank! they're too *young*. Emily won't think of such things. He'll catch his death of cold within a week.

Dr. Gibbs. I was remembering my wedding morning, Julia.

Mrs. Gibbs. Now don't start that, Frank Gibbs.

Dr. Gibbs. I was the scaredest young fella in the state of New Hampshire. I thought I'd made a mistake for sure. And when I saw you comin' down that aisle I thought you were the prettiest girl I'd ever seen, but the only trouble was that I'd never seen you before. There I was in the Congregational Church marryin' a total stranger.

Mrs. Gibbs. And how do you think I felt!— Frank, weddings are perfectly awful things. Farces—that's what they are! (*She puts a plate before him.*) Here, I've made something for you.

Dr. Gibbs. Why, Julia Hersey—French toast!

Mrs. Gibbs. 'Tain't hard to make and I had to do *some*thing.

[*Pause. Dr. Gibbs pours on the syrup.*]

Dr. Gibbs. How'd you sleep last night, Julia?

Mrs. Gibbs. Well, I heard a lot of the hours struck off.

Dr. Gibbs. Ye-e-s! I get a shock every time I think of George setting out to be a family man—that great gangling thing!—I tell you Julia, there's nothing so terrifying in the world as a *son*. The relation of father and son is the darndest, awkwardest——

Mrs. Gibbs. Well, mother and daughter's no picnic, let me tell you.

Dr. Gibbs. They'll have a lot of troubles, I suppose, but that's none of our business. Everybody has a right to their own troubles.

Mrs. Gibbs (*at the table, drinking her coffee, meditatively*). Yes . . . people are meant to go through life two by two. 'Tain't natural to be lonesome.

[*Pause. Dr. Gibbs starts laughing.*]

Dr. Gibbs. Julia, do you know one of the things I was scared of when I married you?

Mrs. Gibbs. Oh, go along with you!

Dr. Gibbs. I was afraid we wouldn't have material for conversation more'n'd last us a few weeks. (*Both laugh.*) I was afraid we'd run out and eat our meals in silence, that's a fact.— Well, you and I been conversing for twenty years now without any noticeable barren spells.

Mrs. Gibbs. Well—good weather, bad weather —'tain't very choice, but I always find something to say. (*She goes to the foot of the stairs.*) Did you hear Rebecca stirring around upstairs?

Dr. Gibbs. No. Only day of the year Rebecca hasn't been managing everybody's business up there. She's hiding in her room.—I got the impression she's crying.

Mrs. Gibbs. Lord's sakes!—This has got to stop.—Rebecca! Rebecca! Come and get your breakfast.

[George *comes rattling down the stairs, very brisk.*]

George. Good morning, everybody. Only five more hours to live. (*Makes the gesture of cutting his throat, and a loud "k-k-k," and starts through the trellis.*)

Mrs. Gibbs. George Gibbs, where are you going?

George. Just stepping across the grass to see my girl.

Mrs. Gibbs. Now, George! You put on your overshoes. It's raining torrents. You don't go out of this house without you're prepared for it.

George. Aw, Ma. It's just a *step*!

Mrs. Gibbs. George! You'll catch your death of cold and cough all through the service.

Dr. Gibbs. George, do as your mother tells you!

[Dr. Gibbs *goes upstairs.*

George *returns reluctantly to the kitchen and pantomimes putting on overshoes.*]

Mrs. Gibbs. From tomorrow on you can kill yourself in all weathers, but while you're in my house you'll live wisely, thank you.—Maybe Mrs. Webb isn't used to callers at seven in the morning.—Here, take a cup of coffee first.

George. Be back in a minute. (*He crosses the stage, leaping over the puddles.*) Good morning, Mother Webb.

Mrs. Webb. Goodness! You frightened me!— Now, George, You can come in a minute out of the wet, but you know I can't ask you in.

George. Why not—?

Mrs. Webb. George, you know's well as I do: the groom can't see his bride on his wedding day, not until he sees her in church.

George. Aw!—that's just a superstition.—Good morning, Mr. Webb.

[*Enter* Mr. Webb.]

Mr. Webb. Good morning, George.

George. Mr. Webb, you don't believe in that superstition, do you?

Mr. Webb. There's a lot of common sense in some superstitions, George. (*He sits at the table, facing right.*)

Mrs. Webb. Millions have folla'd it, George, and you don't want to be the first to fly in the face of custom.

George. How is Emily?

Mrs. Webb. She hasn't waked up yet. I haven't heard a sound out of her.

George. Emily's *asleep*!!!

Mrs. Webb. No wonder! We were up 'til all hours, sewing and packing. Now I'll tell you what I'll do; you set down here a minute with Mr. Webb and drink this cup of coffee; and I'll go upstairs and see she doesn't come down and surprise you. There's some bacon, too; but don't be long about it.

[*Exit* Mrs. Webb.
Embarrassed silence.
Mr. Webb *dunks doughnuts in his coffee.*
More silence.]

Mr. Webb (*suddenly and loudly*). Well, George, how are you?

George (*startled, choking over his coffee*). Oh, fine, I'm fine. (*Pause*) Mr. Webb, what sense could there be in a superstition like that?

Mr. Webb. Well, you see—on her wedding morning a girl's head's apt to be full of . . .

clothes and one thing and another. Don't you think that's probably it?

George. Ye-e-s. I never thought of that.

Mr. Webb. A girl's apt to be a mite nervous on her wedding day. (*Pause*)

George. I wish a fellow could get married without all that marching up and down.

Mr. Webb. Every man that's ever lived has felt that way about it, George; but it hasn't been any use. It's the womenfolk who've built up weddings, my boy. For a while now the women have it all their own. A man looks pretty at a wedding, George. All those good women standing shoulder to shoulder making sure that the knot's tied in a mighty public way.

George. But . . . you *believe* in it, don't you, Mr. Webb?

Mr. Webb (*with alacrity*). Oh, yes; *oh, yes*. Don't you misunderstand me, my boy. Marriage is a wonderful thing—wonderful thing. And don't you forget that, George.

George. No, sir—Mr. Webb, how old were you when you got married?

Mr. Webb. Well, you see: I'd been to college and I'd taken a little time to get settled. But Mrs. Webb—she wasn't much older than what Emily is. Oh, age hasn't much to do with it, George—not compared with . . . uh . . . other things.

George. What were you going to say, Mr. Webb?

Mr. Webb. Oh, I don't know.—Was I going to say something? (*Pause*) George, I was thinking the other night of some advice my father gave me when I got married. Charles, he said, Charles, start out early showing who's boss, he said. Best thing to do is to give an order, even if it don't make sense; just so she'll learn to obey. And he said: If anything about your wife irritates you—her conversation, or anything— just get up and leave the house. That'll make it clear to her, he said. And, oh, yes! he said never, *never* let your wife know how much money you have, never.

George. Well, Mr. Webb . . . I don't think I could . . .

Mr. Webb. So I took the opposite of my father's

advice and I've been happy ever since. And let that be a lesson to you, George, never to ask advice on personal matters.—George, are you going to raise chickens on your farm?

George. What?

Mr. Webb. Are you going to raise chickens on your farm?

George. Uncle Luke's never been much interested, but I thought——

Mr. Webb. A book came into my office the other day, George, on the Philo System of raising chickens. I want you to read it. I'm thinking of beginning in a small way in the backyard, and I'm going to put an incubator in the cellar——

[*Enter* Mrs. Webb.]

Mrs. Webb. Charles, are you talking about that old incubator again? I thought you two'd be talking about things worthwhile.

Mr. Webb (*bitingly*). Well, Myrtle, if you want to give the boy some good advice, I'll go upstairs and leave you alone with him.

Mrs. Webb (*pulling* George *up*). George, Emily's got to come downstairs and eat her breakfast. She sends you her love but she doesn't want to lay eyes on you. Goodbye.

George. Goodbye. (George *crosses the stage to his own home, bewildered and crestfallen. He slowly dodges a puddle and disappears into his house.*)

Mr. Webb. Myrtle, I guess you don't know about that older superstition.

Mrs. Webb. What do you mean, Charles?

Mr. Webb. Since the cave men: no bridegroom should see his father-in-law on the day of the wedding, or near it. Now remember that. (*Both leave the stage.*)

Stage Manager. Thank you very much, Mr. and Mrs. Webb.—Now I have to interrupt again here. You see, we want to know how all this began—this wedding, this plan to spend a lifetime together. I'm awfully interested in how big things like that begin.

You know how it is: you're twenty-one or twenty-two and you make some decisions; then whisssh! you're seventy: you've been a lawyer for fifty years, and that white-haired lady at your side has eaten over fifty thousand meals with you.

How do such things begin?

George and Emily are going to show you now the conversation they had when they first knew that . . . that . . . as the saying goes . . . they were meant for one another.

But before they do I want you to try and remember what it was like to have been very young.

And particularly the days when you were first in love; when you were like a person sleep-walking, and you didn't quite see the street you were in, and didn't quite hear everything that was said to you.

You're just a little bit crazy. Will you remember that, please?

Now they'll be coming out of high school at three o'clock. George has just been elected president of the junior class, and as it's June, that means he'll be president of the senior class all next year. And Emily's just been elected secretary and treasurer. I don't have to tell you how important that is. (*He places a board across the backs of two chairs, which he takes from those at the Gibbs family's table. He brings two high stools from the wings and places them behind the board. Persons sitting on the stools will be facing the audience. This is the counter of Mr. Morgan's drugstore. The sounds of young people's voices are heard off left.*) Yepp—there they are coming down Main Street now.

[Emily, *carrying an armful of—imaginary—schoolbooks, comes along Main Street from the left.*]

Emily. I can't, Louise. I've got to go home. Goodbye. Oh, Ernestine! Ernestine! Can you come over tonight and do Latin? Isn't that Cicero the worst thing—! Tell your mother you *have* to. G'bye. G'bye, Helen. G'bye, Fred.

[George, *also carrying books, catches up with her.*]

George. Can I carry your books home for you, Emily?

Emily (*coolly*). Why . . . uh . . . Thank you. It isn't far. (*She gives them to him.*)

George. Excuse me a minute, Emily.—Say, Bob, if I'm a little late, start practice anyway. And give Herb some long high ones.

Emily. Goodbye, Lizzy.

George. Goodbye, Lizzy.—I'm awfully glad you were elected, too, Emily.

Emily. Thank you.

[*They have been standing on Main Street, almost against the back wall. They take the first steps toward the audience when* George *stops and says:*]

George. Emily, why are you mad at me?

Emily. I'm not mad at you.

George. You've been treating me so funny lately.

Emily. Well, since you ask me, I might as well say it right out, George——(*She catches sight of a teacher passing.*) Goodbye, Miss Corcoran.

George. Goodbye, Miss Corcoran.—Wha—what is it?

Emily (*not scoldingly; finding it difficult to say*). I don't like the whole change that's come over you in the last year. I'm sorry if that hurts your feelings, but I've got to—tell the truth and shame the devil.

George. A *change?*—Wha—what do you mean?

Emily. Well, up to a year ago I used to like you a lot. And I used to watch you as you did everything . . . because we'd been friends so long . . . and then you began spending all your time at *baseball* . . . and you never stopped to speak to anybody any more. Not even to your own family you didn't . . . and, George, it's a fact, you've got awful conceited and stuck-up, and all the girls say so. They may not say so to your face, but that's what they say about you behind your back, and it hurts me to hear them say it, but I've got to agree with them a little. I'm sorry if it hurts your feelings . . . but I can't be sorry I said it.

George. I . . . I'm glad you said it, Emily. I never thought that such a thing was happening to me. I guess it's hard for a fella not to have faults creep into his character.

[*They take a step or two in silence, then stand still in misery.*]

Emily. I always expect a man to be perfect and I think he should be.

George. Oh . . . I don't think it's possible to be perfect, Emily.

Emily. Well, my *father* is, and as far as I can see *your* father is. There's no reason on earth why you shouldn't be, too.

George. Well, I feel it's the other way round. That men aren't naturally good; but girls are.

Emily. Well, you might as well know right now that I'm not perfect. It's not as easy for a girl to be perfect as a man, because we girls are more—more—nervous.—Now I'm sorry I said all that about you. I don't know what made me say it.

George. Emily——

Emily. Now I can see it's not the truth at all. And I suddenly feel that it isn't important, anyway.

George. Emily . . . would you like an ice-cream soda, or something, before you go home?

Emily. Well, thank you. . . . I would.

[*They advance toward the audience and make an abrupt right turn, opening the door of Morgan's drugstore. Under strong emotion,* Emily *keeps her face down.* George *speaks to some passers-by.*]

George. Hello, Stew—how are you?—Good afternoon, Mrs. Slocum.

[*The* Stage Manager, *wearing spectacles and assuming the role of Mr. Morgan, enters abruptly from the right and stands between the audience and the counter of his soda fountain.*]

Stage Manager. Hello, George. Hello, Emily.—What'll you have?—Why, Emily Webb—what you been crying about?

George (*He gropes for an explanation.*) She . . .

she just got an awful scare, Mr. Morgan. She almost got run over by that hardware-store wagon. Everybody says that Tom Huckins drives like a crazy man.

Stage Manager (*drawing a drink of water*). Well, now! You take a drink of water, Emily. You look all shook up. I tell you, you've got to look both ways before you cross Main Street these days. Gets worse every year.—What'll you have?

Emily. I'll have a strawberry phosphate, thank you, Mr. Morgan.

George. No, no, Emily. Have an ice-cream soda with me. Two strawberry ice-cream sodas, Mr. Morgan.

Stage Manager (*working the faucets*). Two strawberry ice-cream sodas, yes sir. Yes, sir. There are a hundred and twenty-five horses in Grover's Corners this minute I'm talking to you. State inspector was in here yesterday. And now they're bringing in these auto-mobiles, the best thing to do is to just stay home. Why, I can remember when a dog could go to sleep all day in the middle of Main Street and nothing come along to disturb him. (*He sets the imaginary glasses before them.*) There they are. Enjoy 'em. (*He sees a customer, right.*) Yes, Mrs. Ellis. What can I do for you? (*He goes out right.*)

Emily. They're so expensive.

George. No, no—don't you think of that. We're celebrating our election. And then do you know what else I'm celebrating?

Emily. N-no.

George. I'm celebrating because I've got a friend who tells me all the things that ought to be told me.

Emily. George, *please* don't think of that. I don't know why I said it. It's not true. You're——

George. No, Emily, you stick to it. I'm glad you spoke to me like you did. But you'll *see:* I'm going to change so quick—you bet I'm going to change. And, Emily, I want to ask you a favor.

Emily. What?

George. Emily, if I go away to State Agriculture College next year, will you write me a letter once in a while?

Emily. I certainly will. I certaintly will, George. . . .

[*Pause. They start sipping the sodas through the straws.*]

It certainly seems like being away three years you'd get out of touch with things. Maybe letters from Grover's Corners wouldn't be so interesting after a while. Grover's Corners isn't a very important place when you think of all—New Hampshire; but I think it's a very nice town.

George. The day wouldn't come when I wouldn't want to know everything that's happening here. I know *that's* true, Emily.

Emily. Well, I'll try to make my letters interesting.

[*Pause*]

George. Y'know, Emily, whenever I meet a farmer I ask him if he thinks it's important to go to agriculture school to be a good farmer.

Emily. Why, George——

George. Yeah, and some of them say that it's even a waste of time. You can get all those things, anyway, out of the pamphlets the government sends out. And Uncle Luke's getting old—he's about ready for me to start in taking over his farm tomorrow, if I could.

Emily. My!

George. And, like you say, being gone all that time . . . in other places and meeting other people . . . Gosh, if anything like that can happen I don't want to go away. I guess new people aren't any better than old ones. I'll bet they almost never are. Emily . . . I feel that you're as good a friend as I've got. I don't need to go and meet the people in other towns.

Emily. But, George, maybe it's important for you to go and learn all that about—cattle judging and soils and those things. . . . Of course, I don't know.

George (*after a pause, very seriously*). Emily, I'm going to make up my mind right now. I won't go. I'll tell Pa about it tonight.

Emily. Why, George, I don't see why you have to decide right now. It's a whole year away.

George. Emily, I'm glad you spoke to me about that . . . that fault in my character. What you said was right; but there was *one* thing wrong in it, and that was when you said that for a year I wasn't noticing people, and . . . you, for instance. Why, you say you were watching me when I did everything . . . I was doing the same about you all the time. Why, sure—I always thought about you as one of the chief people I thought about. I always made sure where you were sitting on the bleachers, and who you were with, and for three days now I've been trying to walk home with you; but something's always got in the way. Yesterday I was standing over against the wall waiting for you, and you walked home with *Miss Corcoran.*

Emily. George! . . . Life's awful funny! How could I have known that? Why, I thought——

George. Listen, Emily, I'm going to tell you why I'm not going to agriculture school. I think that once you've found a person that you're very fond of . . . I mean a person who's fond of you, too, and likes you enough to be interested in your character . . . Well, I think that's just as important as college is, and even more so. That's what I think.

Emily. I think it's awfully important, too.

George. Emily.

Emily. Y-yes, George.

George. Emily, if I *do* improve and make a big change . . . would you be . . . I mean: *could* you be . . .

Emily. I . . . I am now; I always have been.

George (*pause*). So I guess this is an important talk we've been having.

Emily. Yes . . . yes.

George (*takes a deep breath and straightens his back*). Wait just a minute and I'll walk you home.

[*With mounting alarm he digs into his pockets for the money.*

The Stage Manager *enters, right.*

George, *deeply embarrassed, but direct, says to him:*]

Mr. Morgan, I'll have to go home and get the money to pay you for this. It'll only take me a minute.

Stage Manager (*pretending to be affronted*). What's that? George Gibbs, do you mean to tell me—!

George. Yes, but I had reasons, Mr. Morgan.— Look, here's my gold watch to keep until I come back with the money.

Stage Manager. That's all right. Keep your watch. I'll trust you.

George. I'll be back in five minutes.

Stage Manager. I'll trust you ten years, George—not a day over.—Got all over your shock, Emily?

Emily. Yes, thank you, Mr. Morgan. It was nothing.

George (*taking up the books from the counter*). I'm ready.

[*They walk in grave silence across the stage and pass through the trellis at the Webbs' back door and disappear.*

The Stage Manager *watches them go out, then turns to the audience, removing his spectacles.*]

Stage Manager. Well——(*He claps his hands as a signal.*) Now we're ready to get on with the wedding.

[*He stands waiting while the set is prepared for the next scene.*

Stagehands *remove the chairs, tables and trellises from the Gibbs and Webb houses.*

They arrange the pews for church in the center of the stage. The congregation will sit facing the back wall. The aisle of the church starts at the center of the back wall and comes toward the audience.

A small platform is placed against the back wall on which the Stage Manager *will stand later, playing the minister. The image of a stained-glass window is cast from a lantern slide upon the back wall.*

When all is ready the Stage Manager *strolls to the center of the stage, down front, and, musingly, addresses the audience.*]

There are a lot of things to be said about a wedding; there are a lot of thoughts that go on during a wedding.

We can't get them all into one wedding, naturally, and especially not into a wedding at Grover's Corners, where they're awfully plain and short.

In this wedding I play the minister. That gives me the right to say a few more things about it.

For a while now, the play gets pretty serious.

Y'see, some churches say that marriage is a sacrament. I don't quite know what that means, but I can guess. Like Mrs. Gibbs said a few minutes ago: People were made to live two by two.

This is a good wedding, but people are so put together that even at a good wedding there's a lot of confusion way down deep in people's minds and we thought that that ought to be our play, too.

The real hero of this scene isn't on the stage at all, and you know who that is. It's like what one of those European fellas said: Every child born into the world is nature's attempt to make a perfect human being. Well, we've seen nature pushing and contriving for some time now. We all know that nature's interested in quantity; but I think she's interested in quality, too— that's why I'm in the ministry.

And don't forget all the other witnesses at this wedding—the ancestors. Millions of them. Most of them set out to live two by two, also. Millions of them.

Well, that's all my sermon. 'Twan't very long, anyway.

[*The organ starts playing Handel's "Largo."*

The congregation streams into the church and sits in silence.

Church bells are heard.

Mrs. Gibbs *sits in the front row, the first seat on the aisle, the right section; next to her are* Rebecca *and* Dr. Gibbs.

Across the aisle Mrs. Webb, Wally *and* Mr. Webb. *A small choir takes its place, facing the audience under the stained-glass window.*

Mrs. Webb, *on the way to her place, turns back and speaks to the audience.*]

Mrs. Webb. I don't why on earth I should be crying. I suppose there's nothing to cry about. It came over me at breakfast this morning; there was Emily eating her breakfast as she's done for seventeen years and now she's going off to eat it in someone else's house. I suppose that's it.

And Emily! She suddenly said: I can't eat another mouthful, and she put her head down on the table and *she* cried. (*She starts toward her seat in the church, but turns back and adds:*) Oh, I've got to say it: you know, there's something downright cruel about sending our girls out into marriage this way.

I hope some of her girlfriends have told her a thing or two. It's cruel, I know, but I couldn't bring myself to say anything. I went into it blind as a bat myself. (*In half-amused exasperation*) The whole world's wrong, that's what's the matter.

There they come. (*She hurries to her place in the pew.*)

[George *starts to come down the right aisle of the theater, through the audience.*

Suddenly Three Members *of his baseball team appear by the right proscenium pillar and start whis-*

tling and catcalling to him. They are dressed for the ball field.]

The Baseball Players. Eh, George, George! Hast-yaow! Look at him, fellas—he looks scared to death. Yaow! George, don't look so innocent, you old geezer. We know what you're thinking. Don't disgrace the team, big boy. Whoo-oo-oo.

Stage Manager. All right! All right! That'll do. That's enough of that.

[*Smiling, he pushes them off the stage. They lean back to shout a few more catcalls.*]

There used to be an awful lot of that kind of thing at weddings in the old days—Rome, and later. We're more civilized now—so they say.

[*The choir starts singing "Love Divine, All Love Excelling." George has reached the stage. He stares at the congregation a moment, then takes a few steps of withdrawal, toward the right proscenium pillar. His mother, from the front row, seems to have felt his confusion. She leaves her seat and comes down the aisle quickly to him.*]

Mrs. Gibbs. George! George! What's the matter?

George. Ma, I don't want to grow old. Why's everybody pushing me so?

Mrs. Gibbs. Why, George . . . you wanted it.

George. No, Ma, listen to me——

Mrs. Gibbs. No, no, George—you're a man now.

George. Listen, Ma—for the last time I ask you . . . All I want to do is to be a fella——

Mrs. Gibbs. George! If anyone should hear you! Now, stop. Why, I'm ashamed of you!

George (*He comes to himself and looks over the scene.*) What? Where's Emily?

Mrs. Gibbs (*relieved*). George! You gave me such a turn.

George. Cheer up, Ma. I'm getting married.

Mrs. Gibbs. Let me catch my breath a minute.

George (*comforting her*). Now, Ma, you save Thursday nights. Emily and I are coming over to dinner every Thursday night . . . you'll see. Ma, what are you crying for? Come on; we've got to get ready for this.

[*Mrs. Gibbs, mastering her emotion, fixes his tie and whispers to him.*

In the meantime, Emily, in white and wearing her wedding veil, has come through the audience and mounted onto the stage. She too draws back, frightened, when she sees the congregation in the church. The choir begins: "Blessed Be the Tie That Binds."]

Emily. I never felt so alone in my whole life. And George over there, looking so . . . ! I *hate* him. I wish I were dead. Papa! Papa!

Mr. Webb (*leaves his seat in the pews and comes toward her anxiously*). Emily! Emily! Now don't get upset. . . .

Emily. But, Papa—I don't want to get married. . . .

Mr. Webb. Sh-sh—Emily. Everything's all right.

Emily. Why can't I stay for a while just as I am? Let's go away——

Mr. Webb. No, no, Emily. Now stop and think a minute.

Emily. Don't you remember that you used to say—all the time you used to say—all the time: that I was *your* girl! There must be lots of places we can go to. I'll work for you. I could keep house.

Mr. Webb. Sh . . . You mustn't think of such things. You're just nervous, Emily. (*He turns and calls:*) George! George! Will you come here a minute? (*He leads her toward* George.) Why, you're marrying the best young fellow in the world. George is a fine fellow.

Emily. But Papa——

[*Mrs. Gibbs returns unobtrusively to her seat.*

Mr. Webb has one arm around his daughter. He places his hand on George's shoulder.]

Mr. Webb. I'm giving away my daughter, George. Do you think you can take care of her?

George. Mr. Webb, I want to . . . I want to try.

Emily, I'm going to do my best. I love you, Emily. I need you.

Emily. Well, if you love me, help me. All I want is someone to love me.

George. I will, Emily. Emily, I'll try.

Emily. And I mean for*ever*. Do you hear me? Forever and ever.

[*They fall into each other's arms.*
The "March" from Lohengrin *is heard.*
The Stage Manager, as Clergyman, *stands on the box, up center.*]

Mr. Webb. Come, they're waiting for us. Now you know it'll be all right. Come, quick.

[George *slips away and takes his place beside the Stage Manager-Clergyman.*
Emily *proceeds up the aisle on her father's arm.*]

Stage Manager. Do you, George, take this woman, Emily, to be your wedded wife, to have . . .

[Mrs. Soames *has been sitting in the last row of the congregation.*
She now turns to her neighbors and speaks in a shrill voice. Her chatter drowns out the rest of the clergyman's words.]

Mrs. Soames. Perfectly lovely wedding! Loveliest wedding I ever saw. Oh, I do love a good wedding, don't you? Doesn't she make a lovely bride?

George. I do.

Stage Manager. Do you, Emily, take this man, George, to be your wedded husband——

[*Again, his further words are covered by those of* Mrs. Soames.]

Mrs. Soames. Don't know *when* I've seen such a lovely wedding. But I always cry. Don't know why it is, but I always cry. I just like to see young people happy, don't you? Oh, I think it's lovely.

[*The ring.*
The kiss.
The stage is suddenly arrested into silent tableau.

The Stage Manager, *his eyes on the distance, as though to himself:*]

Stage Manager. I've married over two hundred couples in my day.

Do I believe in it?

I don't know.

M____ marries N____ millions of them.

The cottage, the go-cart, the Sunday-afternoon drives in the Ford, the first rheumatism, the grandchildren, the second rheumatism, the deathbed, the reading of the will——(*He now looks at the audience for the first time, with a warm smile that removes any sense of cynicism from the next line.*) Once in a thousand times it's interesting.

—Well, let's have Mendelssohn's "Wedding March"!

[*The organ picks up the "March."*
The Bride *and* Groom *come down the aisle, radiant, but trying to be very dignified.*]

Mrs. Soames. Aren't they a lovely couple? Oh, I've never been to such a nice wedding. I'm sure they'll be happy. I always say: *happiness,* that's the great thing! The important thing is to be happy.

[*The* Bride *and* Groom *reach the steps leading into the audience. A bright light is thrown upon them. They descend into the auditorium and run up the aisle joyously.*]

Stage Manager. That's all the second act, folks. Ten minutes' intermission.

Reading Check

1. What does Dr. Gibbs admit he was most afraid of when he got married?
2. According to Emily, what happened to spoil her friendship with George?
3. Why does George decide against going to agriculture school?
4. What role does the Stage Manager play during the wedding?

Early in Act Two the Stage Manager tells us, "The first act was called the Daily Life. This act is called Love and Marriage." He assumes that we expect the last act to be entitled "Death." We realize more and more, as we read on in Act Two, that Thornton Wilder intends to give a panoramic picture of the human experience, as exemplified by the events in Grover's Corners, particularly by what happens to George Gibbs and Emily Webb. The Stage Manager tells us what he thinks is behind the whole experience: "Nature's been pushing and contriving," he says, implying that marriage is as natural a process as erosion or gravity. "Most everybody in the world climbs into their graves married," he goes on, and by associating marriage with death (the grave), he again stresses the inevitability of both events.

In Act Two, as in Act One, the Stage Manager maintains his slightly bemused, calmly detached attitude toward the events of the play, and he invites the audience to share his point of view. But the other characters are intensely concerned with their own issues of love and marriage. George says jokingly that he has "only five more hours to live," and later he momentarily panics at the whole idea. Emily also becomes frightened, and even their parents, who have been through it before, become awkward and confused. Marriage, to those involved, is clearly an important event.

In Act Two the clash continues between the particular and the general. For example, notice how the Stage Manager uses time. He shows us the morning of the marriage before we see George and Emily become engaged. As we watch the scenes in which they fall in love, we already know the outcome and can concentrate on the broader implications of the particular moment. Thus we are made aware of the slow "contriving" of nature as it "pushes" two people toward a new stage in life.

The Stage Manager finally suggests who "the real hero" of the wedding scene is: "Every child born into the world is nature's attempt to make a perfect human being." Nature's purpose becomes clearer: the eventual perfection of the human race. Behind all the events of Act One and Act Two, there is a universal process, even if the characters on the stage are unaware of it. The Stage Manager's remark about the millions of ancestors witnessing the wedding makes sense when we recall that they, too, were part of nature's ongoing movement toward a perfect human being. The address on Jane Crofut's letter now gains additional meaning. It expresses a continuity between the individual and the Mind of God, which universal forces work to join through events such as marriage and birth.

Yet the process of nature can be painful for those who live through it. We sympathize with George and Emily as they hesitate on the brink of a new stage of life. We respond also to the confusion of their parents. "There's a lot of confusion way down deep in people's minds," we are told, and this confusion seems to be at the heart of the human predicament. Living under the influence of such a powerful impetus toward perfection, yet sad that the present moment must be left behind, the characters in this play experience the transitory pleasures of life without comprehending the purpose behind them.

For Study and Discussion

Analyzing and Interpreting the Play

1. As in Act One, the Stage Manager opens with a speech that sets the tone for much of what follows. **a.** What details suggest that he regards George and Emily's marriage as part of the natural order of things? **b.** Toward what state of affairs does he suggest the natural order tends?

2a. Find a speech on pages 983–984 in which Mrs. Gibbs summarizes her objections to George's marriage and compare it to one in which she accepts the idea. **b.** Why does she change her mind?

3a. What in Act One has prepared us for the unusual treatment of time in Act Two? **b.** What is the effect of this treatment?

4. In the scene in the drugstore, how important do all the details about the cost of sodas and letter writing eventually become for George and Emily?

5. On page 993, the Stage Manager remarks that a wedding is interesting only once in a thousand times. **a.** Why then does he show us a wedding? **b.** What is the significance of his remark about the "real hero of this scene"?

6. Both George and Emily panic at the altar. **a.** How does this reflect people's occasional feelings about being caught up in the flow of life? **b.** How do Dr. Gibbs's reminiscences about his wedding day place this scene in perspective?

7. "Sentiment" is genuine feeling; "sentimentality" is false and exaggerated feeling. Which word best describes the wedding scene? Explain.

Act Three

During the intermission the audience has seen the Stage Hands *arranging the stage. On the right-hand side, a little right of the center, ten or twelve ordinary chairs have been placed in three openly spaced rows facing the audience.*

These are graves in the cemetery.

Toward the end of the intermission the actors enter and take their places. The front row contains: toward the center of the stage, an empty chair; then Mrs. Gibbs*; Simon Stimson.*

The second row contains, among others, Mrs. Soames.

The third row has Wally Webb.

The dead do not turn their heads or their eyes to right or left, but they sit in a quiet without stiffness. When they speak their tone is matter-of-fact, without sentimentality and, above all, without lugubriousness.

The Stage Manager *takes his accustomed place and waits for the house lights to go down.*

Stage Manager. This time nine years have gone by, friends—summer, 1913.

Gradual changes in Grover's Corners. Horses are getting rarer. Farmers coming into town in Fords.

Everybody locks their house doors now at night. Ain't been any burglars in town yet, but everybody's heard about 'em.

You'd be surprised, though—on the whole, things don't change much around here.

This is certainly an important part of Grover's Corners. It's on a hilltop—a windy hilltop—lots of sky, lots of clouds—often lots of sun and moon and stars.

You come up here, on a fine afternoon and you can see range on range of hills—awful blue they are—up there by Lake Sunapee and Lake Winnipesaukee . . . and way up, if you've got a glass, you can see the White Mountains and Mt. Washington—where North Conway and Conway is. And, of course, our favorite mountain, Mt. Monadnock, 's right here—and all these towns that lie around it: Jaffrey, 'n East Jaffrey, 'n Peterborough, n' Dublin; and (*Then pointing down in the audience*) there, quite a ways down, is Grover's Corners.

Yes, beautiful spot up here. Mountain laurel and li-lacks. I often wonder why people like to be buried in Woodlawn and Brooklyn when they might pass the same time up here in New Hampshire. Over there—(*Pointing to stage left*) are the old stones—1670, 1680. Strong-minded people that come a long way to be independent. Summer people walk around there laughing at the funny words on the tombstones . . . it don't do any harm. And genealogists come up from Boston—get paid by city people for looking up their ancestors. They want to make sure they're Daughters of the American Revolution and of the *Mayflower*. . . . Well, I guess that don't do any harm, either. Wherever you come near the human race, there's layers and layers of nonsense. . . .

Over there are some Civil War veterans. Iron flags on their graves . . . New Hampshire boys . . . had a notion that the Union ought to be kept together, though they'd never seen more than fifty miles of it themselves. All they knew was the name, friends—the United States of America. The United States of America. And they went and died about it.

This here is the new part of the cemetery. Here's your friend Mrs. Gibbs. 'N let me see——Here's Mr. Stimson, organist at the Congregational Church. And Mrs. Soames, who enjoyed the wedding so—you remember? Oh, and a lot of others. And Editor Webb's boy, Wallace, whose appendix burst while he was on a Boy Scout trip to Crawford Notch.

Yes, an awful lot of sorrow has sort of quieted down up here. People just wild with grief have brought their relatives up to this hill. We all know how it is . . . and then time . . . and sunny days . . . and rainy days . . . 'n snow . . . We're all glad they're in a beautiful place and we're coming up here ourselves when our fit's over.

Now there are some things we all know, but we don't take 'm out and look at 'm very often.

We all know that *something* is eternal. And it ain't houses and it ain't names, and it ain't earth, and it ain't even the stars . . . everybody knows in their bones that *something* is eternal, and that something has to do with human beings. All the greatest people ever lived have been telling us that for five thousand years and yet you'd be surprised how people are always losing hold of it. There's something way down deep that's eternal about every human being. (*Pause*)

You know as well as I do that the dead don't stay interested in us living people for very long. Gradually, gradually, they lose hold of the earth . . . and the ambitions they had . . . and the pleasures they had . . . and the things they suffered . . . and the people they loved.

They get weaned away from the earth—that's the way I put it—weaned away.

And they stay here while the earth part of 'em burns away, burns out; and all that time they slowly get indifferent to what's goin' on in Grover's Corners.

They're waitin'. They're waitin' for something that they feel is comin'. Something important, and great. Aren't they waitin' for the eternal part in them to come out clear?

Some of the things they're going to say maybe'll hurt your feelings—but that's the way it is: mother 'n daughter . . . husband 'n wife . . . enemy 'n enemy . . . money 'n miser . . . all those terribly important things kind of grow pale around here. And what's left when memory's gone, and your identity, Mrs. Smith? (*He looks at the audience a minute, then turns to the stage.*)

Well! There are some *living* people. There's Joe Stoddard, our undertaker, supervising a new-made grave. And here comes a Grover's Corners boy, that left town to go out West.

[Joe Stoddard *has hovered about in the background.* Sam Craig *enters left, wiping his forehead from the exertion. He carries an umbrella and strolls front.*]

Sam Craig. Good afternoon, Joe Stoddard.

Joe Stoddard. Good afternoon, good afternoon. Let me see now: do I know you?

Sam Craig. I'm Sam Craig.

Joe Stoddard. Gracious sakes' alive! Of all people! I should'a knowed you'd be back for the funeral. You've been away a long time, Sam.

Sam Craig. Yes, I've been away over twelve years. I'm in business out in Buffalo now, Joe. But I was in the East when I got news of my cousin's death, so I thought I'd combine things a little and come and see the old home. You look well.

Joe Stoddard. Yes, yes, can't complain. Very sad, our journey today, Samuel.

Sam Craig. Yes.

Joe Stoddard. Yes, yes. I always say I hate to supervise when a young person is taken. They'll be here in a few minutes now. I had to come here early today—my son's supervisin' at the home.

Sam Craig (*reading stones*). Old Farmer Mc-Carty, I used to do chores for him—after school. He had the lumbago.

Joe Stoddard. Yes, we brought Farmer Mc-Carty here a number of years ago now.

Sam Craig (*staring at* Mrs. Gibbs's *knees*). Why, this is my Aunt Julia . . . I'd forgotten that she'd . . . of course, of course.

Joe Stoddard. Yes, Doc Gibbs lost his wife two, three years ago . . . about this time. And today's another pretty bad blow for him, too.

Mrs Gibbs (*to* Simon Stimson: *in an even voice*). That's my sister Carey's boy, Sam . . . Sam Craig.

Simon Stimson. I'm always uncomfortable when *they're* around.

Mrs. Gibbs. Simon.

Sam Craig. Do they choose their own verses much, Joe?

Joe Stoddard. No . . . not usual. Mostly the bereaved pick a verse.

Sam Craig. Doesn't sound like Aunt Julia. There aren't many of those Hersey sisters left now. Let me see: where are . . . I wanted to look at my father's and mother's . . .

Joe Stoddard. Over there with the Craigs . . . Avenue F.

Sam Craig (*reading* Simon Stimson's *epitaph*). He was organist at church, wasn't he?—Hm, drank a lot, we used to say.

Joe Stoddard. Nobody was supposed to know about it. He'd seen a peck of trouble. (*Behind his hands*) Took his own life, y' know?

Sam Craig. Oh, did he?

Joe Stoddard. Hung himself in the attic. They tried to hush it up, but of course it got around. He chose his own epy-taph. You can see it there. It ain't a verse exactly.

Sam Craig. Why, it's just some notes of music—what is it?

Joe Stoddard. Oh, I wouldn't know. It was wrote up in the Boston papers at the time.

Sam Craig. Joe, what did she die of?

Joe Stoddard. Who?

Sam Craig. My cousin.

Joe Stoddard. Oh, didn't you know? Had some trouble bringing a baby into the world. 'Twas her second, though. There's a little boy 'bout four years old.

Sam Craig (*opening his umbrella*). The grave's going to be over there?

Joe Stoddard. Yes, there ain't much more room over here among the Gibbses, so they're opening up a whole new Gibbs section over by Avenue B. You'll excuse me now. I see they're comin'.

[*From left to center, at the back of the stage, comes a procession.* Four men *carry a casket, invisible to us. All the rest are under umbrellas. One can vaguely see:* Dr. Gibbs, George, *the* Webbs, *etc. They gather about a grave in the back center of the stage, a little to the left of center.*]

A scene from a Canadian production of *Our Town* in Ottawa in 1980.
F. R. Leclair, Ottawa

Mrs. Soames. Who is it, Julia?

Mrs. Gibbs (*without raising her eyes*). My daughter-in-law, Emily Webb.

Mrs. Soames (*a little surprised, but no emotion*). Well, I declare! The road up here must have been awfully muddy. What did she die of, Julia?

Mrs. Gibbs. In childbirth.

Mrs. Soames. Childbirth. (*Almost with a laugh*) I'd forgotten all about that. My, wasn't life awful—(*with a sigh*) and wonderful.

Simon Stimson (*with a sideways glance*). Wonderful, was it?

Mrs. Gibbs. Simon! Now, remember!

Mrs. Soames. I remember Emily's wedding. Wasn't it a lovely wedding! And I remember her reading the class poem at graduation exercises. Emily was one of the brightest girls ever graduated from high school. I've heard Principal Wilkins say so time after time. I called on them at their new farm, just before I died. Perfectly beautiful farm.

A Woman from Among the Dead. It's on the same road we lived on.

A Man Among the Dead. Yepp, right smart farm.

[*They subside. The group by the grave starts singing "Blessed Be the Tie That Binds."*]

A Woman Among the Dead. I always liked that hymn. I was hopin' they'd sing a hymn.

[*Pause. Suddenly* Emily *appears from among the umbrellas. She is wearing a white dress. Her hair is down her back and tied by a white ribbon like a little girl. She comes slowly, gazing wonderingly at the dead, a little dazed. She stops halfway and smiles faintly. After looking at the mourners for a moment, she walks slowly to the vacant chair beside* Mrs. Gibbs *and sits down.*]

Emily (*to them all, quietly, smiling*). Hello.

Mrs. Soames. Hello, Emily.

A Man Among the Dead. Hello, M's Gibbs.

Emily (*warmly*). Hello, Mother Gibbs.

Mrs. Gibbs. Emily.

Emily. Hello. (*With surprise*) It's raining. (*Her eyes drift back to the funeral company.*)

Mrs. Gibbs. Yes . . . They'll be gone soon, dear. Just rest yourself.

Emily. It seems thousands and thousands of years since I . . . Papa remembered that that was my favorite hymn.

Oh, I wish I'd been here a long time. I don't like being new here.—How do you do, Mr. Stimson?

Simon Stimson. How do you do, Emily.

[Emily *continues to look about her with a wondering smile; as though to shut out from her mind the thought of the funeral company she starts speaking to* Mrs. Gibbs *with a touch of nervousness.*]

Emily. Mother Gibbs, George and I have made that farm into just the best place you ever saw. We thought of you all the time. We wanted to show you the new barn and a great long cement drinking fountain for the stock. We bought that out of the money you left us.

Mrs. Gibbs. I did?

Emily. Don't you remember, Mother Gibbs— the legacy you left us? Why, it was over three hundred and fifty dollars.

Mrs. Gibbs. Yes, yes, Emily.

Emily. Well, there's a patent device on the drinking fountain so that it never overflows, Mother Gibbs, and it never sinks below a certain mark they have there. It's fine. (*Her voice trails off and her eyes return to the funeral group.*) It won't be the same to George without me, but it's a lovely farm. (*Suddenly she looks directly at* Mrs. Gibbs.) Live people don't understand, do they?

Mrs. Gibbs. No, dear—not very much.

Emily. They're sort of shut up in little boxes, aren't they? I feel as though I knew them last a thousand years ago . . . My boy is spending the day at Mrs. Carter's. (*She sees* Mr. Carter, *among the dead.*) Oh, Mr. Carter, my little boy is spending the day at your house.

Mr. Carter. Is he?

Emily. Yes, he loves it there.—Mother Gibbs, we have a Ford, too. Never gives any trouble. I don't drive, though. Mother Gibbs, when does this feeling go away?—Of being . . . one of *them*? How long does it . . . ?

Mrs. Gibbs. Sh! dear. Just wait and be patient.

Emily (*with a sigh*). I know.—Look, they're finished. They're going.

Mrs. Gibbs. Sh—.

[*The umbrellas leave the stage.* Dr. Gibbs *has come over to his wife's grave and stands before it a moment.* Emily *looks up at his face.* Mrs. Gibbs *does not raise her eyes.*]

Emily. Look! Father Gibbs is bringing some of my flowers to you. He looks just like George, doesn't he? Oh, Mother Gibbs, I never realized before how troubled and how . . . how in the dark live persons are. Look at him. I loved him so. From morning till night, that's all they are—troubled.

[Dr. Gibbs *goes off.*]

The Dead. Little cooler than it was.—Yes, that rain's cooled it off a little. Those northeast winds always do the same thing, don't they? If it isn't a rain, it's a three-day blow.—

[*A patient calm falls on the stage. The* Stage Manager *appears at his proscenium pillar, smoking.* Emily *sits up abruptly with an idea.*]

Emily. But, Mother Gibbs, one can go back; one can go back there again . . . into living. I feel it, I know it. Why, then just for a moment I was thinking about . . . about the farm . . . and for a minute I *was* there, and my baby was on my lap as plain as day.

Mrs. Gibbs. Yes, of course you can.

Emily. I can go back there and live all those days over again . . . why not?

Mrs. Gibbs. All I can say is, Emily, don't.

Emily. (*She appeals urgently to the* Stage Manager.) But it's true, isn't it? I can go and live . . . back there . . . again.

Stage Manager. Yes, some have tried—but they soon come back here.

Mrs. Gibbs. Don't do it, Emily.

Mrs. Soames. Emily, don't. It's not what you think it'd be.

Emily. But I won't live over a sad day. I'll choose a happy one—I'll choose the day I first knew that I loved George. Why should that be painful?

[*They are silent. Her question turns to the* Stage Manager.]

Stage Manager. You not only live it; but you watch yourself living it.

Emily. Yes?

Stage Manager. And as you watch it, you see the thing that they—down there—never know. You see the future. You know what's going to happen afterwards.

Emily. But is that—painful? Why?

Mrs. Gibbs. That's not the only reason why you shouldn't do it, Emily. When you've been here longer you'll see that our life here is to forget all that, and think only of what's ahead, and be ready for what's ahead. When you've been here longer, you'll understand.

Emily (*softly*). But, Mother Gibbs, how can I *ever* forget that life? It's all I know. It's all I had.

Mrs. Soames. Oh, Emily. It isn't wise. Really, it isn't.

Emily. But it's a thing I must know for myself. I'll choose a happy day, anyway.

Mrs. Gibbs. *No!*—at least, choose an unimportant day. Choose the least important day in your life. It will be important enough.

Emily (*to herself*). Then it can't be since I was married; or since the baby was born. (*To the* Stage Manager, *eagerly.*) I can choose a birthday at least, can't I?—I choose my twelfth birthday.

Stage Manager. All right. February 11th, 1899. A Tuesday.—Do you want any special time of day?

Emily. Oh, I want the whole day.

Stage Manager. We'll begin at dawn. You remember it had been snowing for several days; but it had stopped the night before, and they had begun clearing the roads. The sun's coming up.

Emily (*with a cry; rising*). There's Main Street . . . why, that's Mr. Morgan's drugstore before he changed it! . . . And there's the livery stable.

[*The stage at no time in this act has been very dark; but now the left half of the stage gradually becomes very bright—the brightness of a crisp winter morning.* Emily *walks toward Main Street.*]

Stage Manager. Yes, it's 1899. This is fourteen years ago.

Emily. Oh, that's the town I knew as a little girl. And *look,* there's the old white fence that used to be around our house. Oh, I'd forgotten that! Oh, I love it so! Are they inside?

Stage Manager. Yes, your mother'll be coming downstairs in a minute to make breakfast.

Emily (*softly*). Will she?

Stage Manager. And you remember: your father had been away for several days; he came back on the early-morning train.

Emily. No . . . ?

Stage Manager. He'd been back to his college to make a speech—in western New York, at Clinton.

Emily. Look! There's Howie Newsome. There's our policeman. But he's *dead; he died.*

[*The voices of* Howie Newsome, Constable Warren *and* Joe Crowell, Jr., *are heard at the left of the stage.* Emily *listens in delight.*]

Howie Newsome. Whoa, Bessie!—Bessie! 'Morning, Bill.

Constable Warren. Morning, Howie.

Howie Newsome. You're up early.

Constable Warren. Been rescuin' a party; darn near froze to death, down by Polish Town thar. Got drunk and lay out in the snowdrifts. Thought he was in bed when I shook'm.

Emily. Why, there's Joe Crowell. . . .

Joe Crowell, Jr. Good morning, Mr. Warren. 'Morning, Howie.

[Mrs. Webb *has appeared in her kitchen, but* Emily *does not see her until she calls.*]

Mrs. Webb. Chil-*dren!* Wally! Emily! . . . Time to get up.

Emily. Mama, I'm here! Oh! how young Mama looks! I didn't know Mama was ever that young.

Mrs. Webb. You can come and dress by the kitchen fire, if you like; but hurry.

[Howie Newsome *has entered along Main Street and brings the milk to* Mrs. Webb's *door.*]

Good morning, Mr. Newsome. Whhhh—it's cold.

Howie Newsome. Ten below by my barn, Mrs. Webb.

Mrs. Webb. Think of it! Keep yourself wrapped up. (*She takes her bottles in, shuddering.*)

Emily (*with an effort*). Mama, I can't find my blue hair ribbon anywhere.

Mrs. Webb. Just open your eyes, dear, that's all. I laid it out for you special—on the dresser, there. If it were a snake it would bite you.

Emily. Yes, yes . . .

[*She puts her hand on her heart.* Mr. Webb *comes along Main Street, where he meets Constable Warren. Their movements and voices are increasingly lively in the sharp air.*]

Mr. Webb. Good morning, Bill.

Constable Warren. Good morning, Mr. Webb. You're up early.

Mr. Webb. Yes, just been back to my old college in New York State. Been any trouble here?

Constable Warren. Well, I was called up this

mornin' to rescue a Polish fella—darn near froze to death he was.

Mr. Webb. We must get it in the paper.

Constable Warren. 'Twan't much.

Emily (*whispers*). Papa.

[Mr. Webb *shakes the snow off his feet and enters his house.* Constable Warren *goes off, right.*]

Mr. Webb. Good morning, Mother.

Mrs. Webb. How did it go, Charles?

Mr. Webb. Oh, fine, I guess. I told'm a few things.—Everything all right here?

Mrs. Webb. Yes—can't think of anything that's happened, special. Been right cold. Howie Newsome says it's ten below over to his barn.

Mr. Webb. Yes, well, it's colder than that at Hamilton College. Students' ears are falling off. It ain't Christian.—Paper have any mistakes in it?

Mrs. Webb. None that I noticed. Coffee's ready when you want it. (*He starts upstairs.*) Charles! Don't forget; it's Emily's birthday. Did you remember to get her something?

Mr. Webb (*patting his pocket*). Yes, I've got something here. (*Calling up the stairs*) Where's my girl? Where's my birthday girl? (*He goes off left.*)

Mrs. Webb. Don't interrupt her now, Charles. You can see her at breakfast. She's slow enough as it is. Hurry up, children! It's seven o'clock. Now, I don't want to call you again.

Emily (*softly, more in wonder than in grief*). I can't bear it. They're so young and beautiful. Why did they ever have to get old? Mama, I'm here. I'm grown up. I love you all, everything.—I can't look at everything hard enough.

[She *looks questioningly at the* Stage Manager, *saying or suggesting: "Can I go in?" He nods briefly. She crosses to the inner door to the kitchen, left of her mother, and as though entering the room, says, suggesting the voice of a girl of twelve:*]

Good morning, Mama.

Mrs. Webb (*crossing to embrace and kiss her; in her characteristic matter-of-fact manner*). Well, now, dear, a very happy birthday to my girl and many happy returns. There are some surprises waiting for you on the kitchen table.

Emily. Oh, Mama, you *shouldn't* have. (*She throws an anguished glance at the* Stage Manager.) I can't—I can't.

Mrs. Webb (*facing the audience, over her stove*). But birthday or no birthday, I want you to eat your breakfast good and slow. I want you to grow up and be a good strong girl.

That in the blue paper is from your Aunt Carrie; and I reckon you can guess who brought the postcard album. I found it on the doorstep when I brought in the milk—George Gibbs . . . must have come over in the cold pretty early . . . right nice of him.

Emily (*to herself*). Oh, George! I'd forgotten that. . . .

Mrs. Webb. Chew that bacon good and slow. It'll help keep you warm on a cold day.

Emily (*with mounting urgency*). Oh, Mama, just look at me one minute as though you really saw me. Mama, fourteen years have gone by. I'm dead. You're a grandmother, Mama. I married George Gibbs, Mama. Wally's dead, too. Mama, his appendix burst on a camping trip to North Conway. We felt just terrible about it—don't you remember? But, just for a moment now we're all together. Mama, just for a moment we're happy. *Let's look at one another.*

Mrs. Webb. That in the yellow paper is something I found in the attic among your grandmother's things. You're old enough to wear it now, and I thought you'd like it.

Emily. And this is from you. Why, Mama, it's just lovely and it's just what I wanted. It's beautiful!

[She *flings her arms around her mother's neck. Her* Mother *goes on with her cooking, but is pleased.*]

Mrs. Webb. Well, I hoped you'd like it. Hunted all over. Your Aunt Norah couldn't find one in Concord, so I had to send all the way to Boston. (*Laughing*) Wally has something for you, too. He made it at manual-training class and he's very proud of it. Be sure you make a big fuss about it.—Your father had a surprise for you, too; don't know what it is myself. Sh— here he comes.

Mr. Webb (*off stage*). Where's my girl? Where's my birthday girl?

Emily (*in a loud voice to the* Stage Manager.) I can't. I can't go on. It goes so fast. We don't have time to look at one another.

[*She breaks down sobbing.*
The lights dim on the left half of the stage. Mrs. Webb *disappears.*]

I didn't realize. So all that was going on and we never noticed. Take me back—up the hill— to my grave. But first: Wait! One more look.

Goodbye. Goodbye, world. Goodbye, Grover's Corners . . . Mama and Papa. Goodbye to clocks ticking . . . and Mama's sunflowers. And food and coffee. And new-ironed dresses and hot baths . . . and sleeping and waking up. Oh, earth, you're too wonderful for anybody to realize you. (*She looks toward the* Stage Manager *and asks abruptly, through her tears:*) Do any human beings ever realize life while they live it?— every, every minute?

Stage Manager. No. (*Pause*) The saints and poets, maybe—they do some.

Emily. I'm ready to go back. (*She returns to her chair beside* Mrs. Gibbs. *Pause.*)

Mrs. Gibbs. Were you happy?

Emily. No . . . I should have listened to you. That's all human beings are! Just blind people.

Mrs. Gibbs. Look, it's clearing up. The stars are coming out.

Emily. Oh, Mr. Stimson, I should have listened to them.

Simon Stimson (*with mounting violence; bitingly*). Yes, now you know. Now you know! That's what it was to be alive. To move about in a cloud of ignorance; to go up and down trampling on the feelings of those . . . of those about you. To spend and waste time as though you had a million years. To be always at the mercy of one self-centered passion, or another. Now you know—that's the happy existence you wanted to go back to. Ignorance and blindness.

Mrs. Gibbs (*spiritedly*). Simon Stimson, that ain't the whole truth and you know it. Emily, look at that star. I forget its name.

A Man Among the Dead. My boy Joel was a sailor—knew 'em all. He'd set on the porch evenings and tell 'em all by name. Yes, sir, wonderful!

Another Man Among the Dead. A star's mighty good company.

A Woman Among the Dead. Yes. Yes, 'tis.

Simon Stimson. Here's one of *them* coming.

The Dead. That's funny. 'Tain't no time for one of them to be here.—Goodness sakes.

Emily. Mother Gibbs, it's George.

Mrs. Gibbs. Sh, dear. Just rest yourself.

Emily. It's George.

[George *enters from the left, and slowly comes toward them.*]

A Man from Among the Dead. And my boy, Joel, who knew the stars—he used to say it took millions of years for that speck o' light to git to the earth. Don't seem like a body could believe it, but that's what he used to say— millions of years.

[George *sinks to his knees, then falls full length at* Emily's *feet.*]

A Woman Among the Dead. Goodness! That ain't no way to behave!

Mrs. Soames. He ought to be home.

Emily. Mother Gibbs?

Mrs. Gibbs. Yes, Emily?

Emily. They don't understand, do they?

Mrs. Gibbs. No, dear. They don't understand.

[*The* Stage Manager *appears at the right, one hand on a dark curtain which he slowly draws across the scene.*
In the distance a clock is heard striking the hour very faintly.]

Stage Manager. Most everybody's asleep in Grover's Corners. There are a few lights on:

Shorty Hawkins, down at the depot, has just watched the Albany train go by. And at the livery stable somebody's setting up late and talking.—Yes, it's clearing up. There are the stars—doing their old, old crisscross journeys in the sky. Scholars haven't settled the matter yet, but they seem to think there are no living beings up there. Just chalk . . . or fire. Only this one is straining away, straining away all the time to make something of itself. The strain's so bad that every sixteen hours everybody lies down and gets a rest. (*He winds his watch.*)

Hm. . . . Eleven o'clock in Grover's Corners.—You get a good rest, too. Good night.

Reading Check

1. What happened to the money Mrs. Gibbs received for her highboy?
2. What day does Emily choose to relive?
3. Why is Emily startled by her parents' appearance?
4. Who is the last living person Emily sees?

Commentary

As the Stage Manager suggests at the beginning of Act Two, we may well be tempted to call Act Three "Death." But perhaps the Stage Manager's opening speech in Act Three gives a more apt suggestion in the repetition of the word *eternal*, a word suggestive of the universal, recurrent patterns in life that are a central theme in *Our Town*. The individual lives of people in Grover's Corners may lose importance with burials and the passage of time, but the town's collective life, beyond the immediate present, is meaningful to all later viewers like ourselves.

In one sense life certainly ends with death. Emily Gibbs, disregarding the Stage Manager's warning, tries for a moment to reenter the world of the living but discovers that the living really have time only for themselves. Her mother sees her and talks to her, but only as the little girl Emily used to be and not as the grown woman she has become. The insight seems a true one: certainly we remember the dead as the living persons they were and we find it difficult if not impossible to conceive of them in any other way.

However, Wilder suggests that death, like birth, love, and marriage, is further participation in a kind of process. The Stage Manager tells us that "there's something way down deep that's eternal about every human being," though no one alive can say exactly what that is. He says (and we observe) that the dead lose interest in the living, and that their existence is one in which they are "weaned away" from the earth, waiting for the eternal in them to "come out clear."

What is perhaps more important to us, however, is what we learn about life itself. The dead Simon Stimson speaks about the living with contempt when he notes how much of life most people waste. Mrs. Soames has more mixed feelings as she declares that life was both "awful—and wonderful." Near the end of the play, when the sorrowful George Gibbs throws himself on his wife's grave, Emily herself comments that the living "don't understand, do they?" George cannot yet grasp the eternal aspect of life—the recurrent patterns—with which Emily is becoming acquainted.

Thus Wilder completes his treatment of the American small town, moving from a survey of its daily doings to hints of an ongoing process, and to the suggestion that in such a process "our town" is always and everywhere. The village contains in itself all the elements of domestic life. Beyond these elements, however, the forces of time and of nature, driving toward life, nurturing it in the town, and pursuing it finally into death, provide a clue to all human existence. However trivial or dated the affairs of the town may seem at any moment, they are all instances of a universal and timeless cycle of things.

For Study and Discussion

Analyzing and Interpreting the Play

1. At the beginning of Act Three, the Stage Manager observes that in spite of gradual outward change in Grover's Corners, "on the whole, things don't change much. . . ." **a.** In what details of his opening speech does he point out the universality of death? **b.** How does he suggest that death is a natural part of life?

2a. Select speeches from among those made by the dead to show that they are still somewhat governed by the attitudes they had in life. **b.** How do these speeches support the Stage Manager's conviction that death is a process of learning to forget about life?

3a. When Emily returns to the living, what does she experience that makes her wish to return to the dead? **b.** What does she realize about life and human nature that makes her exclaim, "Oh, earth, you're too wonderful for anybody to realize you"?

4. Just after Emily returns from the living, Mrs. Gibbs makes a seemingly irrelevant observation: "The stars are coming out." **a.** Why do you think she points out the stars to Emily? **b.** What significance do you find in the Stage Manager's closing comparison of the Earth and the distant stars?

5. In *Our Town* the characters' concerns are generally distanced from the audience by the Stage Manager's detached point of view. But at several points in Act Three, we feel the grief of those who have lost loved ones. **a.** How does the Stage Manager's concluding remark about sleep in Grover's Corners represent a serene, hopeful attitude toward life and death? **b.** How does it suggest that everyone is caught up in an endless, perhaps hopeless strain? **c.** Do you think that Wilder wants both overtones at once?

Writing About Literature

Responding to the Author's Ideas

Write a composition in which you agree or disagree with the author's ideas about nature, as these ideas are expressed in the play. Use incidents from the play and from your own knowledge and experience to support your point of view.

Comparing Themes

The seemingly insignificant details of life that people tend to overlook is an important theme in *Trifles* (page 941) and in *Our Town*. Show how the idea is developed in both plays, pointing out significant similarities and differences of presentation.

Creative Writing

Presenting a Cross-Section of People

Our Town presents a cross-section of life in Grover's Corners. Present a cross-section of life in your town, either in the form of an essay describing various people in your town or in the form of a dramatic sketch in which the people speak for themselves. (You might have a stage manager introduce them.) Choose your characters carefully and be sure they are significant and representative figures in the life of your town.

Literature in Modern America

Discuss one of the following statements in terms of the literature you have studied in this unit.

1. The British scholar Marcus Cunliffe has noted that a central theme in American writing is that of "secession from society." Each of the following selections in part portrays a *secession*, or separation, from society: "In Another Country," "Flight," "Lost," "The Life You Save May Be Your Own." In an essay, show how one of these stories develops this theme. Which character secedes? What is the nature of his or her secession? In what way is the story critical of society, either explicitly or implicitly? Be sure to refer to specific passages in the selection you choose.

2. Modern fiction writers have been working away from the neatly plotted, "well-made" short story. For example, Sherwood Anderson experimented with the "open form" of the short story, aiming more at the expression of character and mood than at plot development. Which stories in this unit have tightly constructed, compelling plots? Which stories have little or no plot and emphasize mood and character? Choose a selection from this unit as an example of the kind of story you prefer. Then, in an essay, defend your choice by answering the following questions: (1) How does the author make use of either the "open" or the "tight" form? (2) What are the advantages and limitations of either form? Be sure to make specific references to the story.

3. In this unit you have studied the work of some of the important "experimental" poets of the modern period. Their work introduced new ideas and techniques that helped broaden the scope of poetry. Reread the selections by one of the following poets: T. S. Eliot, William Carlos Williams, E. E. Cummings, Marianne Moore, Denise Levertov. In an essay, discuss his or her use of such devices as the arrangement of words on the page, "unpoetic" language, sudden leaps in thought, and unusual quotations.

4. In a work of nonfiction, the author's style—his or her characteristic way of writing—is almost as important as the subject. The critic Alfred Kazin has written,

> . . . it is not the "subject" that counts with us, for this subject might have been arrived at by anyone—it is the subject as arrived at by the writer, as it has grown in his thought, as it has been done justice to by himself alone.

(from *The Open Form*)

In an essay, discuss the style of one of the works in this unit. How would you characterize the author's style? What devices does the author use to give the piece its distinctive style? In what way is the style appropriate to the subject? Be sure to refer to specific passages in the selection.

5. Any successful essay, speech, or memoir—no matter how informal in style—maintains the thread of its argument. Choose one of the following selections and, in an essay of your own, (1) state its principal argument; and (2) show how the argument is sustained throughout the piece: "Walden," "The Creative Process," Faulkner's Nobel Prize Acceptance Speech, "Brave Words for a Startling Occasion," "Tin Lizzie."

6. Read the following statement and consider how it may be applied to one of the plays in this unit:

> [The] essence of drama is *crisis*. A play is a more or less rapidly developing crisis in destiny or circumstance, and a dramatic scene is a crisis within a crisis, clearly furthering the ultimate event. The drama may be called the art of crises, as fiction is the art of gradual developments.
>
> William Archer
> (from *Play-Making*)

Write an essay in which you show how one of the plays you have studied presents and resolves a crisis or series of crises. How does the crisis illuminate some aspect of human nature or circumstance? Be sure to refer to specific passages in the play.

7. Discuss one of the plays in this unit in the light of the following statement:

> [The] "serious" modern playwright is, or should be, engaged, along with other modern writers, in the search for the human essence. If it is possible to state in a word what moral quality the artist engaged in this quest needs above all others, I should say that it is audacity.
>
> Eric Bentley
> (from *The Theatre of Commitment*)

In what way does the play represent a quest for human essence? What elements of the play (for example, its subject, staging, or technique) strike you as audacious, or bold? Why? In your essay, make specific references to the work.

For Further Reading

Short Stories

Anderson, Sherwood, *Sherwood Anderson: Short Stories* (Random House, 1956, 1977)

Faulkner, William, *Collected Stories* (Random House, 1956, 1977)

Hemingway, Ernest, *Short Stories of Ernest Hemingway* (Scribner, 1938)

Malamud, Bernard, *The Magic Barrel* (Farrar, Straus & Giroux, 1958; paperback, Avon, 1980)

O'Connor, Flannery, *The Complete Stories* (Farrar, Straus & Giroux, 1971)

Porter, Katherine Anne, *The Collected Stories* (Harcourt Brace Jovanovich, 1979)

Singer, Isaac B., *The Collected Stories of Isaac Bashevis Singer* (Farrar, Straus & Giroux, 1982)

Steinbeck, John, *The Long Valley* (Viking; 1938; paperback, Penguin, 1986)

Stuart, Jesse, *A Jesse Stuart Reader* (McGraw-Hill, 1963)

Thurber, James, *My World—and Welcome to It* (Harcourt Brace Jovanovich, 1969, 1983)

Updike, John, *Pigeon Feathers and Other Stories* (Knopf, 1962)

Walker, Alice, *In Love & Trouble* (Harcourt Brace Jovanovich, 1974)

Welty, Eudora, *The Bride of the Innisfallen and Other Stories* (Harcourt Brace Jovanovich, 1972)

Nonfiction

Galarza, Ernesto, *Barrio Boy* (University of Notre Dame Press, 1971)

Hurston, Zora Neale, *Dust Tracks on a Road: An Autobiography* (University of Illinois Press, 1984)

Momaday, N. Scott, *The Way to Rainy Mountain* (University of Mexico Press, 1976)

Perelman, S. J., *The Most of S. J. Perelman* (Simon and Schuster, 1962)

Rodriguez, Richard, *Hunger of Memory: The Education of Richard Rodriguez* (Godine, 1981)

White, E. B., *Essays of E. B. White* (Harper & Row, 1979)

Wright, Richard, *American Hunger* (Harper & Row, 1983)

Poetry

Auden, W. H., *Selected Poems* (Random House, 1979)

Bishop, Elizabeth, *The Complete Poems* (Farrar, Straus & Giroux, 1969, 1983)

Brooks, Gwendolyn, *Selected Poems* (Harper & Row, 1963)

Cullen, Countee, *On These I Stand* (Harper & Row, 1947)

Cummings, E. E., *Complete Poems* (Harcourt Brace Jovanovich, 1972, 1980)

Eliot, T. S., *The Collected Poems* (Harcourt Brace Jovanovich, 1963)

Frost, Robert, *The Poetry of Robert Frost*, edited by Edward Connery Lathem (H. Holt, 1979)

Gonzales, Rodolfo, *I Am Joaquín* (Bantam, 1972)

Hayden, Robert, *Collected Poems* (Liveright, 1985)

Hughes, Langston, *Selected Poems* (Knopf, 1959)

Lowell, Robert, *Selected Poems* (Farrar, Straus & Giroux, 1976)

MacLeish Archibald, *New and Collected Poems* (Houghton Mifflin, 1985)

McKay, Claude, *Selected Poems of Claude McKay* (Harcourt Brace Jovanovich, 1969)

Millay, Edna St. Vincent, *Collected Poems* (Harper & Row, 1981)

Moore, Marianne, *The Complete Poems* (Penguin, 1982)

Ransom, John Crowe, *Selected Poems* (Ecco, 1978)

Rich, Adrienne, *Diving into the Wreck* (Norton, 1973)

Roethke, Theodore, *The Collected Poems* (Doubleday, 1975)

Sandburg, Carl, *Complete Poems* (Harcourt Brace Jovanovich, 1970)

Sexton, Anne, *Complete Poems* (Houghton Mifflin, 1982)

Stevens, Wallace, *The Collected Poems of Wallace Stevens* (Knopf, 1954)

Walker, Margaret, *For My People* (Yale University Press, 1942)

Warren, Robert Penn, *Selected Poems* (Random House, 1976)

Wilbur, Richard, *The Poems of Richard Wilbur* (Harcourt Brace Jovanovich, 1963)

Williams, William Carlos, *Selected Poems* (New Directions, 1985)

Drama

Anderson, Robert, *I Never Sang for My Father*

Miller, Arthur, *Death of a Salesman*

O'Neill, Eugene, *Long Day's Journey into Night*

Wilder, Thornton, *The Long Christmas Dinner*

Williams, Tennessee, *The Glass Menagerie*

READING AND WRITING ABOUT LITERATURE

Developing Skills in Critical Thinking

In your high school English classes, you have been asked to write essays about literature in response to homework assignments, examination questions, or research projects. At times you may have been given topics such as the following to work on: show how plot is developed in a selection; compare two characters; analyze the imagery in a poem; agree or disagree with an interpretation of some work. At other times you may have been instructed to choose your own topic for a paper. Such writing assignments are an important part of literary study, which aims at greater understanding and appreciation of the works you read.

Writing about a literary work is a way of getting to know it better, of experiencing it more fully. When you write about a literary work, you become involved in clarifying your own responses to what you have read. You must sort out your thoughts, weigh evidence, and reach conclusions.

Throughout your studies you have acquired a substantial body of information and skills that you can use in writing about literature. You have learned a special language of terms and techniques that is useful in analyzing literary works. You can safely assume that your readers will understand what you mean when you refer to such elements of fiction as **plot** and **conflict,** or to such terms as **metaphor** and **symbol.**

These words are part of a common vocabulary used in writing about literature. (See the *Guide to Literary Terms and Techniques, page 1043.*)

There are, as well, certain topics or approaches that are considered appropriate in writing about literature. It is quite acceptable, for example, to examine one part of a literary work in order to make clear its relationship to the whole. Thus, you might isolate the **setting** or **point of view** in order to explain its function in a story. You might take a short passage in a long work and *explicate* it (analyze it line by line) in order to focus on its significance in the entire work. Or you might approach a work in broader terms, choosing to comment on its structure or its relationship to other works by the same author. (A fuller discussion of sample topics appears on page 1032.) The object of all such literary inquiry is to discover the meaning of a work (or group of works) and to transmit your insights and conclusions to other readers who share your interest.

The material on the following pages offers help in planning and writing papers about literature. Here you will find suggestions for reading and analyzing literature, answering examination questions, choosing topics, gathering evidence, organizing essays, and writing, evaluating, and revising papers. Also included are several model essays.

How well you write about literature depends in large measure on how well you read literature. Reading well is more than a matter of understanding what all the words mean and getting all the facts straight. To read for explicit meaning alone is not sufficient. Often an author does not tell you everything directly, but leads you to make discoveries by drawing *inferences* about the characters, the situation, or the meaning of a work. To read literature well, you have to be an active reader, aware of *what* the author is doing, *how* the author is doing it, and *why*. A good reader probes beneath the surface of a work, asking the right questions at the right time.

When you are asked to write about a literary work, be sure you read it carefully before you begin writing. Read actively, asking yourself questions as you work through the selection.

Close Reading of a Short Story

Here is a brief story that has been read carefully by an experienced reader. The notes and questions in the margin show how this reader thinks in working through a story. Read the story at least twice before proceeding to the analysis on page 1013. You may wish to make notes of your own on a separate sheet of paper as you read.

A Game of Catch

RICHARD WILBUR

Thinking Model

Monk and Glennie were playing catch on the side lawn of the firehouse when Scho caught sight of them. They were good at it, for seventh-graders, as anyone could see right away. Monk, wearing a catcher's mitt, would lean easily sidewise and back, with one leg lifted and his throwing hand almost down to the grass, and then lob the white ball straight up into the sunlight. Glennie would shield his eyes with his left hand and, just as the ball fell past him, snag it with a little dart of his glove. Then he would burn the ball straight toward Monk, and it would spank into the round mitt and sit, like a still-life apple[1] on a plate, until Monk flipped it over into his right hand and, with a negligent flick of his hanging arm, gave Glennie a fast grounder.

They were going on and on like that, in a kind of slow, mannered,[2] luxurious dance in the sun, their faces perfectly blank and entranced,

Wilbur shows how good the boys are in simulating fielding situations an outfielder, a catcher, or a shortstop might face in a baseball game.
Note precise use of baseball jargon.

Emphasizes boys' skill and confidence.

Monk and Glennie are like partners in a dance.

1. **still-life apple:** an apple in a still-life painting.
2. **mannered:** conforming to a set pattern; highly stylized.

when Glennie noticed Scho dawdling along the other side of the street and called hello to him. Scho crossed over and stood at the front edge of the lawn, near an apple tree, watching.

"Got your glove?" asked Glennie after a time. Scho obviously hadn't.

"You could give me some easy grounders," said Scho. "But don't burn 'em."

"All right," Glennie said. He moved off a little, so the three of them formed a triangle, and they passed the ball around for about five minutes, Monk tossing easy grounders to Scho, Scho throwing to Glennie, and Glennie burning them in to Monk. After a while, Monk began to throw them back to Glennie once or twice before he let Scho have his grounder, and finally Monk gave Scho a fast, bumpy grounder that hopped over his shoulder and went into the brake on the other side of the street.

"Not so hard," called Scho as he ran across to get it.

"You should've had it," Monk shouted.

It took Scho a little while to find the ball among the ferns and dead leaves, and when he saw it, he grabbed it up and threw it toward Glennie. It struck the trunk of the apple tree, bounced back at an angle, and rolled steadily and stupidly onto the cement apron in front of the firehouse, where one of the trucks was parked. Scho ran hard and stopped it just before it rolled under the truck, and this time he carried it back to his former position on the lawn and threw it carefully to Glennie.

"I got an idea," said Glennie. "Why don't Monk and I catch for five minutes more, and then you can borrow one of our gloves?"

"That's all right with me," said Monk. He socked his fist into his mitt, and Glennie burned one in.

"All right," Scho said, and went over and sat under the tree. There in the shade he watched them resume their skillful play. They threw lazily fast or lazily slow—high, low, or wide—and always handsomely, their expressions serene, changeless and forgetful. When Monk missed a low backhand catch, he walked indolently after the ball and, hardly even looking, flung it sidearm for an imaginary put-out.[3] After a good while of this, Scho said, "Isn't it five minutes yet?"

"One minute to go," said Monk, with a fraction of a grin.

Scho stood up and watched the ball slap back and forth for several minutes more, and then he turned and pulled himself up into the crotch of the tree.

"Where you going?" Monk asked.

"Just up the tree," Scho said.

"I guess he doesn't want to catch," said Monk.

Scho went up and up through the fat light-gray branches until they grew slender and bright and gave under him. He found a place where several supple branches were knit to make a dangerous chair, and sat

---

3. **put-out:** in baseball, a fielding play that causes a runner to be out.

Scho is the outsider watching the game.

Why the unnecessary question?
Note lifelike dialogue.

Is Monk beginning to ease Scho out of the game?

Is Monk's grounder deliberate?

Is Monk impatient with Scho's lack of skill?

Scho misjudges and throws the ball inaccurately.

Glennie suggests a new game.

Compare the way Monk goes after a ball with the way Scho chased the grounder earlier.

Monk's grin makes it evident that they are using a ruse to keep Scho out of the game.

Why does Scho climb the tree?

Note that this perch is dangerous.

there with his head coming out of the leaves into the sunlight. He could see the two other boys down below, the ball going back and forth between them as if they were bowling on the grass, and Glennie's crewcut head looking like a sea-urchin.

"I found a wonderful seat up here," Scho said loudly. "If I don't fall out." Monk and Glennie didn't look up or comment, and so he began jouncing gently in his chair of branches and singing "Yo-ho, heave ho" in an exaggerated way.

Scho tries to get attention by making a nuisance of himself.

"Do you know what, Monk?" he announced in a few moments. "I can make you two guys do anything I want. Catch that ball, Monk! Now you catch it, Glennie!"

Scho is playing a game of his own, with words.

"I was going to catch it anyway," Monk suddenly said. "You're not making anybody do anything when they're already going to do it anyway."

"I made you say what you just said," Scho replied joyfully.

"No, you didn't," said Monk, still throwing and catching but now less serenely absorbed in the game.

Scho is pleased that he can irritate Monk.

"That's what I wanted you to say," Scho said.

Scho succeeds in destroying the peaceful mood of the game.

The ball bounded off the rim of Monk's mitt and plowed into a gladiolus bed beside the firehouse, and Monk ran to get it while Scho jounced in his treetop and sang, "I wanted you to miss that. Anything you do is what I wanted you to do."

"Let's quit for a minute," Glennie suggested.

"We might as well, until the peanut gallery[4] shuts up," Monk said.

By making a pest of himself, Scho succeeds in stopping the game.

They went over and sat cross-legged in the shade of the tree. Scho looked down between his legs and saw them on the dim, spotty ground, saying nothing to one another. Glennie soon began abstractedly spinning his glove between his palms; Monk pulled his nose and stared out across the lawn.

"I want you to mess around with your nose, Monk," said Scho, giggling. Monk withdrew his hand from his face.

Scho enjoys this new game — getting even by being obnoxious.

"Do that with your glove, Glennie," Scho persisted. "Monk, I want you to pull up hunks of grass and chew on it."

Glennie looked up and saw a self-delighted, intense face staring down at him through the leaves. "Stop being a dope and come down and we'll catch for a few minutes," he said.

Glennie offers a way out, by beginning a new game of catch.

Scho hesitated, and then said, in a tentatively mocking voice, "That's what I wanted you to say."

"All right then, nuts to you," said Glennie.

"Why don't you keep quiet and stop bothering people?" Monk asked.

Why does Scho refuse? Does he feel unable to compete as an athlete? Does he enjoy asserting his power through words?

"I made you say that," Scho replied, softly.

"Shut up," Monk said.

Scho is testing this new power, varying his tone.

4. **peanut gallery:** slang for the topmost part of a theater balcony, where the seats are cheapest.

"I made you say that, and I want you to be standing there looking sore. And I want you to climb up the tree. I'm making you do it!"

Monk was scrambling up through the branches, awkward in his haste, and getting snagged on twigs. His face was furious and foolish, and he kept telling Scho to shut up, shut up, shut up, while the other's exuberant and panicky voice poured down upon his head.

"*Now* you shut up or you'll be sorry," Monk said, breathing hard as he reached up and threatened to shake the cradle of slight branches in which Scho was sitting.

"I *want* ——" Scho screamed as he fell. Two lower branches broke his rustling, crackling fall, but he landed on his back with a deep thud and lay still, with a strangled look on his face and his eyes clenched. Glennie knelt down and asked breathlessly, "Are you O.K., Scho? Are you O.K.?" while Monk swung down through the leaves crying that honestly he hadn't even touched him, the crazy guy just let go. Scho doubled up and turned over on his right side, and now both the other boys knelt beside him, pawing at his shoulder and begging to know how he was.

Then Scho rolled away from them and sat partly up, still struggling to get his wind but forcing a species of smile onto his face.

"I'm sorry, Scho," Monk said. "I didn't mean to make you fall."

Scho's voice came out weak and gravelly, in gasps. "I meant—you to do it. You—had to. You can't do—anything—unless I want—you to."

Glennie and Monk looked helplessly at him as he sat there, breathing a bit more easily and smiling fixedly, with tears in his eyes. Then they picked up their gloves and the ball, walked over to the street, and went slowly away down the sidewalk, Monk punching his fist into the mitt, Glennie juggling the ball between glove and hand.

From under the apple tree, Scho, still bent over a little for lack of breath, croaked after them in triumph and misery, "I want you to do whatever you're going to do for the whole rest of your life!"

Marginal notes:

Scho's need to assert himself takes the form of claiming he can control their thoughts and actions by sheer will.

Scho provokes Monk until he threatens violence.

Boys' anger turns to fear and guilt.

Scho tries to cover up his humiliation.

Scho refuses to accept sympathy or apology.

Boys feel confusion. They withdraw.

The story ends without a resolution of the conflict.

Nobody wins.

Analysis

"A Game of Catch" is about a common experience of youth. The outsider—Scho—wants to join the insiders—Monk and Glennie. Lacking their playing skills, he is rejected and finds a way to get even by teasing and annoying them. A game that begins serenely ends with a near tragedy.

At the opening of the story, Monk and Glennie are enjoying a game of catch. They handle the ball skillfully and confidently. The words "blank and entranced" suggest that they are in a world of their own, almost under a hypnotic spell. The boys are like partners in a dance, each one doing the specified (mannered) steps or movements in slow, steady, rhythmic fashion. They are serenely happy.

A third boy, Scho, watches them for a time until he is noticed and acknowledged. Scho uses Glennie's offhand question about the glove to gain entrance into the game. He suggests that they throw him some easy grounders. It is apparent that Scho isn't welcome. For a short while, his intrusion into the game is tolerated, but then Monk begins to ease Scho out of the game by passing the ball to Glennie when it is Scho's turn to catch. Monk then throws Scho a fast grounder, which he misses.

Scho is not at a disadvantage merely because he does not have a baseball glove. It becomes evident that he is not as good at the game as Monk and Glennie, glove or no glove. After he permits the ball to hop over his shoulder (Monk claims that Scho should have caught it), he retrieves it and throws it to Glennie. His throw is inaccurate, and the ball bounces off a tree. He then carefully returns to "his former position on the lawn" before tossing again to Glennie. He has none of the other boys' confidence or skill.

Glennie and Monk now hit upon the idea of taking turns playing with the gloves. This becomes a ruse to exclude Scho from the game. We witness a kind of game within a game—the object of which seems to be keeping Scho at bay. Scho realizes that he is being toyed with after Monk announces that there is one minute to go but plays on indefinitely. There is also a flicker of a grin on Monk's face, which indicates that he has no intention of changing partners.

Scho now climbs a tree, possibly out of boredom. Here he discovers a game of his own. He realizes that he can intrude upon the game of catch by heckling Monk and Glennie. Knowing that he is not as good an athlete as they, he uses his game to give him a feeling of superiority and power over the others. His need to assert himself takes the form of claiming he can control their thoughts and actions by sheer will.

Scho manages to divert their attention from their game and to destroy their idyllic mood. Once he discovers that he can irritate them, he will not or cannot stop. When Glennie offers to include him in the game of catch, a kind of peace offering, Scho hesitates, then mocks him. He succeeds in provoking Monk's anger, and inadvertently causes his own fall from the tree.

After his humiliating accident, Scho feels that his dignity is at stake and refuses to accept the apology of the other boys. As they leave in confusion, he continues to rage at them, refusing to call off his game.

What makes the story so effective is the objectivity with which the characters and the situation are handled. Wilbur tells the story almost as if he were a witness passing by and stopping to watch the three boys. For the most part, he tells only what a witness would see and hear. He records the dialogue and action impeccably, limiting himself to reporting what the boys say and do and how they appear.

An objective point of view tends to keep readers at an equal distance from all characters and thus avoids sentimentality. Wilbur is not taking sides. None of the boys is hero or villain or more to blame than another. All three are simply boys, caught in an unpleasant situation.

To appreciate the honesty and artistry of Wilbur's story, we need only compare it with the formula stories written for teen-agers, in which it is customary for the rejected youngster to win recognition for some praiseworthy act and to be accepted by the peer group. In such a story, Scho would earn the respect of the other boys by demonstrating that he is their equal in skill. But Wilbur is not writing about adolescent wish fulfillment. He is writing about isolation and frustration. That these sources of human pain should take place against the background of such a trivial incident and in such a peaceful setting makes the point obvious.

This reader has arrived at an interpretation of the story by actively questioning the author's intent. The commentary accounts for the significant details of description and action; it comes to grips with the "point" of the story—its overall meaning or theme.

With practice, you can develop skill in reading and analyzing a literary work. Here are some guidelines for reading a story.

Guidelines for Reading a Short Story

1. *Look up unfamiliar words and references.* Wilbur uses a number of baseball terms in "A Game of Catch." A careful reader would be sure to check such words in a standard dictionary or other reference book.

2. *Learn to probe beneath the surface.* Wilbur does not tell you directly that Scho is less skillful than Monk and Glennie in playing catch. However, you can draw this inference from several clues: Scho misses a fast grounder; when he throws the ball to Glennie, it strikes the apple tree; he has to return to his position on the lawn in order to control his aim.

3. *Actively question the author's purpose and method.* Ask yourself what significance there might be to details that the author gives you. Wilbur opens his story on an idyllic note. This mood gives ironic force to the conflicts that shortly erupt.

4. *Be alert to the author's emphasis.* The opening passage of "A Game of Catch" gives a detailed description of the game, emphasizing the skill and grace of the players. Their accomplished movements, noted at several points in the story, serve as a contrast to Scho's inept playing.

5. *Account for all significant elements of the work.* In addition to understanding the characters and events, the reader must understand Wilbur's strategy in choosing an objective point of view for the story.

6. *Probe for the central idea or point—the underlying meaning of the work.* Try to state this idea in one or two sentences in the following manner: *In his presentation of the conflict in "A Game of Catch," Wilbur gives the reader insight into the motives behind exclusion and into the effect of rejection on outsiders.*

Close Reading of a Poem

It is a good idea to read a selection more than once. A poem ought to be read several times, and aloud at least once. You may find it helpful to write a prose paraphrase of a poem, restating all its ideas in plain language. A paraphrase is no substitute for the "meaning" of a poem, but it helps you clarify and simplify the author's text.

The more information and experience you bring to a poem, the greater will be your understanding and appreciation of what you read. The reader who understands the conventions of the sonnet (see page 304) will take added pleasure in reading the following sonnet by the American poet Elinor Wylie (1886–1928). Read the poem several times, using the notes to guide you in interpreting the poem. When you are satisfied that you have understood the poem, turn to the explication that follows.

Puritan Sonnet

ELINOR WYLIE

(11)	*a*	Down to the Puritan marrow of my bones	*irregular line, with emphasis on first word*
	b	There's something in this richness that I hate.	
	b	I love the look, austere, immaculate,	*contrast of love/hate*
	a	Of landscapes drawn in pearly monotones.	
	a	There's something in my very blood that owns 5	*language stresses austerity language contracts into monosyllables*
	b	Bare hills, cold silver on a sky of slate,	
	b	A thread of water, churned to milky spate°	
	a	Streaming through slanted pastures fenced with stones.	
	c	I love those skies, thin blue or snowy gray,	*sestet is one sentence with 6 end-stopped lines*
(11)	*d*	Those fields sparse-planted, rendering meager sheaves; 10	
	e	That spring, briefer than apple-blossom's breath,	*last 4 lines—characteristics of seasons*
	c	Summer, so much too beautiful to stay,	
(9)	*d*	Swift autumn, like a bonfire of leaves,	
Italian sonnet	*e*	And sleepy winter, like the sleep of death.	

7. **spate:** a sudden overflow of a stream.

Explication

The word *Puritan* in the first line of the poem aligns the speaker with the Puritans who settled in New England. The Puritans valued simplicity in all aspects of their life, including language. Wylie deliberately adopts a plain style for her sonnet. She uses simple words, monosyllabic words, straightforward syntax, and familiar comparisons to render a landscape that is beautiful in its austerity.

The speaker asserts her tastes dramatically in the opening lines of the poem. She does not tell us what scene she is viewing, only that she hates its *richness*—presumably the abundance of vegetation, or even the variety of her surroundings. She emphasizes her strong feelings by throwing the stress on the opening syllable of the poem—*down*—presenting us at the outset with a variation from the predominant iambic meter. She has, she tells us, an affinity for a stark, unsoftened environment. She identifies imaginatively with a landscape that is "austere" and "immaculate." It is a landscape with a gray sameness ("pearly monotones"). The words and images she uses connote severity and denial: "bare hills"; "cold silver on a sky of slate"; "a thread of water"; "fenced with stones"; "thin blue"; "fields sparse-planted"; "meager sheaves." In this harsh, unyielding land, nothing seems full-blooded or alive; winter reigns "like the sleep of death."

The poet's style is admirably suited to her subject. Her language is spare and unadorned; several lines are predominantly monosyllabic (6, 7, 9, 14). Within the strict confines of the Italian sonnet form, Wylie achieves considerable variety, by subtle changes in the meter (lines 1, 10, 13); by using run-on lines (1, 5, 7); and by coupling monosyllabic and polysyllabic words in end rhyme (*bones/monotones; hate/immaculate*).

There is an interesting tension in the poem between the intensity of the speaker's emotions and the austere character of the land she prefers. References to the marrow of her bones (line 1) and her blood (line 5), as well as the direct statements of hate (line 2) and love (lines 3, 9), are somewhat at odds with the "pearly monotones," "bare hills," and "cold silver" that she feels are suited to her nature.

Guidelines for Reading a Poem

1. *Read the poem aloud at least once, following the author's clues for phrasing.* Punctuation is one clue to the author's intentions. Wylie does not expect her reader to pause at the end of each line. Some lines run over (see lines 1, 5, 7). In some lines she signals more than one pause (see lines 3, 6, 9–14).

2. *Be alert to key words and references.* In poetry, the connotative meaning of a word is frequently more telling than its denotative meaning. The word *Puritan,* for example, is a key word that conveys emotional associations. Look up any unfamiliar words.

3. *Write a paraphrase of any lines that need clarification or simplification.* A paraphrase helps a reader understand imagery, figurative language, and unusual syntax by presenting the author's ideas in straightforward prose. A paraphrase of line 7 might read: A thin stream, agitated to produce a whitish foam.

4. *Look for the relationship of content and technique.* The plain style that Wylie chooses for her poem supports the austere effect of the New England scene she depicts.

5. *Arrive at the central idea or meaning of the poem.* Try to state this idea in one or two sentences: *The lyric "Puritan Sonnet" is a highly personal statement in which the speaker identifies her own temperament with the austere, unembellished aspects of nature.*

Close Reading of a Play

While many of the elements studied in connection with short stories and poetry are relevant to the study of drama, there are several additional elements that need to be taken into account. Dramatists frequently make use of stage directions to create setting and to give players instructions for acting. A playwright may decide to use a character to comment on the action. Sometimes a character will step out of the play to address the audience, as the Stage Manager does in *Our Town* (page 964). Gener-ally, however, dialogue is the dramatist's most important device for presenting character and for moving the action along.

The following scene is from the second act of Arthur Miller's *Death of a Salesman*, which was first produced in 1949. Willy Loman, a traveling salesman, has come into the New York office of his firm to have a talk with his boss, Howard Wagner. As you read, be alert not only to the content of the speeches, but to the dramatist's tone, that is, Miller's attitude toward his subject. For example, does Miller seem to be sympathetic? mocking? solemn?

After you have read the passage several times, and aloud at least once, turn to the analysis on page 1021.

FROM

Death of a Salesman

ARTHUR MILLER

Thinking Model

Howard. Say, aren't you supposed to be in Boston?

Willy. That's what I want to talk to you about, Howard. You got a minute? (*He draws a chair in from the wing.*)

Howard. What happened? What're you doing here?

Willy. Well . . .

Howard. You didn't crack up again, did you?

Willy. Oh, no. No . . .

Howard. Geez, you had me worried there for a minute. What's the trouble?

Willy. Well, tell you the truth, Howard. I've come to the decision that I'd rather not travel any more.

Dialogue reveals that Willy has become a liability to his employer.

Situation is established—Willy wants to change his job.

Howard. Not travel! Well, what'll you do?

Willy. Remember, Christmas time, when you had the party here? You said you'd try to think of some spot for me here in town.

Howard. With us?

Willy. Well, sure.

Howard. Oh, yeah, yeah. I remember. Well, I couldn't think of any-thing for you, Willy.

Howard doesn't seem eager to accommodate Willy.

Willy. I tell ya, Howard. The kids are all grown up, y'know. I don't need much any more. If I could take home—well, sixty-five dollars a week,[1] I could swing it.

Howard. Yeah, but Willy, see I——

Willy. I tell ya why, Howard. Speaking frankly and between the two of us, y'know—I'm just a little tired.

Howard. Oh, I could understand that, Willy. But you're a road man, Willy, and we do a road business. We've only got a half-dozen salesmen on the floor here.

Willy. God knows, Howard, I never asked a favor of any man. But I was with the firm when your father used to carry you in here in his arms.

Howard. I know that, Willy, but——

Willy. Your father came to me the day you were born and asked me what I thought of the name of Howard, may he rest in peace.

Howard. I appreciate that, Willy, but there just is no spot here for you. If I had a spot I'd slam you right in, but I just don't have a single solitary spot.

[*He looks for his lighter.* Willy *has picked it up and gives it to him. Pause.*]

Willy (*with increasing anger*). Howard, all I need to set my table is fifty dollars a week.

Howard. But where am I going to put you, kid?

Willy. Look, it isn't a question of whether I can sell merchandise, is it?

Howard. No, but it's a business, kid, and everybody's gotta pull his own weight.

Willy (*desperately*). Just let me tell you a story, Howard——

Howard. 'Cause you gotta admit, business is business.

Willy (*angrily*). Business is definitely business, but just listen for a minute. You don't understand this. When I was a boy—eighteen, nineteen—I was already on the road. And there was a question in my mind as to whether selling had a future for me. Because in those days I had a yearning to go to Alaska. See, there were three gold strikes in one month in Alaska, and I felt like going out. Just for the ride, you might say.

Howard (*barely interested*). Don't say.

Willy. Oh, yeah, my father lived many years in Alaska. He was an adventurous man. We've got quite a little streak of self-reliance in our family. I thought I'd go out with my older brother and try to locate him, and maybe settle in the North with the old man. And I was almost decided to go, when I met a salesman in the Parker House. His name was Dave Singleman. And he was eighty-four years old, and he'd drummed merchandise in thirty-one states. And old Dave, he'd go up to his room, y'understand, put on his green velvet slippers—I'll never

---

1. sixty-five . . . week: In 1949, when this play was first produced, this would have been a modest but reasonable income.

Language captures rhythm of colloquial speech.

Willy admits to being worn out.

Setting is a showroom.

Willy reminds Howard of his long service to the company.

Howard seems unmoved by considerations of gratitude or loyalty.

Willy offers to settle for less money.

Word kid *is patronizing.*

Note Howard's use of clichés.

Howard relies on stock phrases.

Willy is concerned in justifying his position.

Story of Dave Singleman illuminates Willy's idea of success.

forget—and pick up his phone and call the buyers, and without ever leaving his room, at the age of eighty-four, he made his living. And when I saw that, I realized that selling was the greatest career a man could want. 'Cause what could be more satisfying than to be able to go, at the age of eighty-four, into twenty or thirty different cities, and pick up a phone, and be remembered and loved and helped by so many different people? Do you know? when he died—and by the way he died the death of a salesman, in his green velvet slippers in the smoker of the New York, New Haven and Hartford, going into Boston—when he died, hundreds of salesmen and buyers were at his funeral. Things were sad on a lotta trains for months after that. (*He stands up. Howard has not looked at him.*) In those days there was personality in it, Howard. There was respect, and comradeship, and gratitude in it. Today, it's all cut and dried, and there's no chance for bringing friendship to bear—or personality. You see what I mean? They don't know me any more.

Willy has naive faith in the magic of personality.

He believes in using friends for material success.

Willy acknowledges his disillusionment.

Howard (*moving away to the right*). That's just the thing, Willy.

Willy. If I had forty dollars a week—that's all I'd need. Forty dollars, Howard.

Howard. Kid, I can't take blood from a stone, I——

Willy (*desperation is on him now*). Howard, the year Al Smith[2] was nominated, your father came to me and——

Howard (*starting to go off*). I've got to see some people, kid.

Howard is evasive. Willy's plight becomes more desperate.

Willy (*stopping him*). I'm talking about your father! There were promises made across this desk! You mustn't tell me you've got people to see—I put thirty-four years into this firm, Howard, and now I can't pay my insurance! You can't eat the orange and throw the peel away—a man is not a piece of fruit! (*After a pause*) Now pay attention. Your father—in 1928 I had a big year. I averaged a hundred and seventy dollars a week in commissions.

Willy reproaches Howard for being indifferent.

He feels cast off.

Is Willy distorting the past?

Howard (*impatiently*). Now, Willy, you never averaged——

Willy (*banging his hand on the desk*). I averaged a hundred and seventy dollars a week in the year of 1928! And your father came to me—or rather, I was in the office here—it was right over this desk—and he put his hand on my shoulder——

Willy begins to ramble.

Howard (*getting up*). You'll have to excuse me, Willy, I gotta see some people. Pull yourself together. (*Going out*) I'll be back in a little while.

Willy has mishandled the situation. Howard is exasperated and cuts him off.

2. Al Smith: Alfred E. Smith (1873–1944), governor of New York, who received the Democratic nomination for President in the 1928 election. He ran against Herbert Hoover and lost.

Analysis

In this scene Miller presents Willy Loman as a man whose hopes of success have foundered. After thirty-four years as a salesman with the same firm, he can't pay his insurance. He is no longer dependable on the road, for he has had accidents, and he is not needed or wanted in the company showroom. His boss, Howard, is a younger man who patronizes him and tries to put him off with clichés. Willy seems unable to understand the position he is in. He tries to exert pressure on Howard by recalling his friendship with Howard's father and reminding him of his obligations. By the end of the scene, he has made things worse: Howard loses patience and leaves.

The dream of material success clearly has been the driving force in Willy's life. His ambition, he reveals, has been to emulate Dave Singleman, a salesman who achieved great success through personal charm. Willy admires Dave's facility at using friendships to advance his career. Willy does not perceive that there is anything false in exploiting relationships for material success. He feels that success has eluded him because times have changed. The work is routine and lifeless; no one knows him anymore. We see Willy as a man who has succumbed to an illusory dream; we are moved by his inability to understand the failure of that dream and its shallow values.

Unpretentious, colloquial speech is a natural vehicle for Miller's characters. They speak in banal, hackneyed phrases. Howard's speeches are filled with clichés and stale slogans: "Business is business"; "I can't take blood from a stone"; "everybody's gotta pull his own weight." Willy speaks of himself being cast off like an orange peel. In addition to sounding authentic, the language is particularly effective in helping to create the emotional climate of Willy's life.

Guidelines for Reading a Play

1. *Note any information that establishes the setting or explains the situation.* Exposition may be provided throughout a play. Although this scene occurs in the second act of the play, it reveals some important things about Willy Loman's past. It illuminates Willy's dream of material success and shows that his dream is in conflict with reality.

2. *Note clues that tell what the players are doing or how the lines are spoken.* Miller provides some information in stage directions. Other instructions are built into the dialogue. As this scene progresses, the talk between Howard and Willy turns into an overt conflict. Willy shows his growing desperation in his angry tone and reproaches. Howard shows his indifference in his impatience and evasiveness.

3. *Anticipate the action that will develop out of each scene.* This scene leads to the conclusion that Howard will not help Willy out of his desperate situation, thereby raising suspense about what Willy will do.

4. *Be alert to the mood of the play.* Note how Miller evokes a range of moods in this scene revealing Willy's psychological state: his faith in the magic of success, touchingly recounted in the story of Dave Singleman; his mounting apprehension as his hopes clash with reality.

5. *Examine the relationship between style and subject matter.* Miller uses a straightforward, vernacular style. His realistic portrayal of the characters is underscored by the dialogue, which captures the rhythm of colloquial speech, with its contractions, slang, broken thoughts, and repetitions.

WRITING ABOUT LITERATURE
The Writing Process

We often refer to writing an essay as a *process*, which consists of six key stages or phases: **prewriting, writing, evaluating, revising, proofreading,** and **writing the final version.** In this process, much of the critical work—the thinking and planning—precedes the actual writing of the paper.

In the **prewriting** stage, the writer makes decisions about what to say and how to say it. Prewriting activities include choosing and limiting a subject; considering purpose and audience; deciding on an attitude toward the topic, expressed through the language in the paper; gathering ideas; organizing ideas into a plan; and arriving at a *thesis*—the controlling idea for the paper. In the **writing** stage, the writer uses the working plan to write a first draft of the essay. In the **evaluating** stage, the writer judges the first draft to identify its strengths and weaknesses in content, organization, and style. **Revising,** the fourth stage, involves making changes to improve the weaknesses identified through evaluating. The writer can revise by adding, cutting, reordering, or replacing ideas and details. In the **proofreading** stage, the writer checks the revised draft to correct errors in grammar, usage, and mechanics. The last stage, **writing the final version,** involves preparing a clean copy and then proofreading it to catch any omissions or errors.

The stages of the writing process are interdependent, usually resulting in a "back and forth" movement among the stages. Rarely does a writer complete one stage entirely before moving to another, nor does he or she progress in a straight line from one stage to the next. For example, as ideas are developed on paper in the writing stage, the writer may discover that additional evidence is needed to support a point or that some parts of the paper need to be reorganized. Gathering additional evidence leads "back" to prewriting while reorganizing moves "ahead" to revising. This interplay among stages is a natural part of writing—for all writers.

The amount of time devoted to each stage will vary with individual assignments. During a classroom examination, you will have limited time to plan your essay and to proofread your paper. For a term paper, you may have weeks or even months to prepare your essay.

On the following pages the steps in this process are illustrated through the development of several model papers.

Answering Examination Questions

From time to time you will be asked to demonstrate your understanding of a literary work or a topic by writing a short essay in class. Usually, your teacher will designate the subject of the essay. How well you respond will depend not only on how carefully you have prepared for the examination but also on how carefully you read and interpret the question. Remember too that length alone is not satisfactory. Your answer must be relevant, and it must be presented in correct English.

Before you begin to answer an examination question, be sure you understand what the question calls for. If a question requires that you give *three* reasons and you supply only *two,* you will not have fulfilled the requirements of the question. Always take some time to read the essay question carefully.

Remember that you are expected to demonstrate specific knowledge of the literature. Any general statement should be supported by evidence. If you wish to show that a character changes, for example, you should refer to specific actions, dialogue, thoughts and feelings, or direct comments by the author in order to illustrate your point. If you are allowed to use your textbook during the examination, you may occasionally quote short passages or refer to a specific page in order to provide supporting evidence.

The key word in examination questions is the *verb.* Let us look briefly at some common instructions used in examinations.

Analysis. You may be asked to *analyze* some aspect of a literary work or topic. When you analyze something, you take it apart to see how each part works. On an examination, you will generally be directed to focus on some limited but essential aspect of a work in order to demonstrate your knowledge and understanding. A common type of exercise is *character analysis,* in which you draw on the most significant details of characterization in order to reach conclusions about a specific figure. For example, you might be asked to analyze the character of Judy Jones in "Winter Dreams" (page 610), taking into account the methods used to characterize her. You might be asked to analyze the structure of a sonnet such as "Douglass" (page 507). Analysis may be applied to form, technique, or ideas.

Comparison/Contrast. A question may ask that you *compare* (or *contrast*) two things, such as techniques, ideas, characters, or works. When you *compare,* you point out likenesses; when you *contrast,* you point out differences. At times you will be asked to *compare and contrast.* In that event, you will be expected to deal with similarities and differences. You might be asked to compare the ideas of Ralph Waldo Emerson and Walt Whitman in order to find similarities in their philosophies. Or you might be asked to contrast the free-verse techniques of Walt Whitman and Stephen Crane. Sometimes the instruction to *compare* implies both comparison and contrast. Always check with your teacher to make sure how inclusive the term *compare* is intended to be.

Definition. A question may ask you to *define* a literary term—to answer the question "What is it?" Defining a term involves first classifying it, or assigning it to a class or group, and then discussing the specific features that make it different from other members of the same class or group. You should also provide specific examples that illustrate your statement of definition. For example, if asked to define the term *realism,* you could identify it as a literary movement (general class) that aimed to depict the everyday life and speech of ordinary people without sentimentalizing or idealizing their lives (special features). You might then use Willa Cather's "The Sculptor's Funeral" (page 471) as a specific example of this kind of writing.

Description. If a question asks you to *describe* a setting or a character, you are expected to give a picture in words. In describing a setting, include details that establish the historical period as well as the locale. You might be asked to describe the setting of William Faulkner's "The Bear" (page 628) in order to clarify the role of the wilderness in that story. You might be asked to describe the elements of setting that contribute to the atmosphere of Stephen Vincent Benét's "The Devil and Daniel Webster" (page 641). You might be asked to focus on those characteristics that portray the dignity and strength of Phoenix Jackson in Eudora Welty's "A Worn Path" (page 691).

Discussion. The word *discuss* in a question is much more general than the other words we've looked at. When you are asked to discuss a subject, you are expected to examine the subject thoroughly and to treat it in all significant aspects. A question might direct you to discuss the relevance of Thoreau's ideas to our own time. You might be asked to discuss the influence of Ezra Pound's ideas on the Imagist poets.

Evaluation. If a question asks you to *evaluate* a literary work or some aspect of one or more works, you are expected to determine if a writer has successfully achieved his or her purpose, and how important that purpose is. To evaluate, you must apply criteria, or standards of judgment, which may relate to both literary content and form. You must also supply evidence from the literary work or works to support your judgment. You might be asked to evaluate Twain's use of vernacular speech in "The Notorious Jumping Frog of Calaveras County" (page 391) and "Baker's Bluejay Yarn" (page 398). Your object would be to determine how effectively Twain handles dialect as a literary language.

Explanation. A question may ask you to *explain* something. When you explain, you give reasons for something being the way it is. You make clear a character's actions, or you show how something has come about. You might, for example, be asked to explain the Romantic attitude toward nature as illustrated in poems by William Cullen Bryant. You might be asked to explain why Eugene O'Neill's play *Where the Cross Is Made* (page 951) is said to blend elements of realism and expressionism.

Illustration. The word *illustrate, demonstrate,* or *show* asks that you provide examples to support a point. You might be asked to illustrate Walt Whitman's use of homely diction. You might be asked to demonstrate Mark Twain's use of the colloquial style. Or you might be asked to show that *Our Town* (page 964) presents a cross-section of life in small-town America.

Interpretation. The word *interpret* in a question asks that you give the meaning or significance of something. You might, for example, be asked to provide an interpretation for a symbol, such as the road in Robert Frost's poem "The Road Not Taken" (page 741). You might be asked to offer an interpretation of the poetry that the father quotes in Faulkner's "The Bear" (page 628). You might be asked to interpret the meaning of a work such as Poe's "The Raven" (page 184). Sometimes you will be asked to agree or disagree with a stated interpretation of a work, giving specific evidence to support your position.

You will find that there is frequent overlapping of approaches. In discussing a subject, you may draw upon illustration, explanation, analysis, or any other approach that is useful. In comparing or contrasting two works, you may rely on description or interpretation. However, an examination question generally will have a central purpose, and it is important that you focus on this purpose in preparing your answer.

Using the Writing Process to Answer an Essay Question

Even if you are well prepared for an examination, you may not develop your essay effectively unless you manage your time well. Although you may have to work quickly, you should nevertheless allocate some time for each stage of the writing process. Once you become familiar with this pattern, you will have a plan that enables you to work quickly and efficiently.

Prewriting. The examination question itself often establishes the topic and, through its key verb (*analyze, compare, interpret,* etc.) suggests an approach for developing an answer. Several prewriting steps remain:

1. *Formulate a thesis statement.* A *thesis statement* is a sentence that represents the main point of your paper. It generally appears at the beginning of an essay and establishes the position you are going to support.

2. *Develop points that support the thesis statement.* There should always be at least two supporting points. In a short essay all the points may be presented in a single paragraph. In a longer paper each point may be stated as the topic sentence of a separate paragraph. Each point should clearly support the idea expressed in the thesis.

3. *Locate supporting evidence in the literary work(s).* Evidence can include specific details, direct quotations, incidents, or images that support each point.

4. *Organize the major points and evidence.* Arrange your ideas and details logically so that your plan includes an introduction, a body, and a conclusion.

Writing. Using your prewriting plan as a guide, write your essay. In the **introduction,** identify the work(s) under study and state your thesis. In the **body** present your major points with supporting evidence. In the **conclusion** restate your thesis and summarize what you have demonstrated. As you write, adopt a tone appropriate for your purpose (to convey ideas) and for your audience (your teacher, in most cases). Use straightforward language that is serious without being affected, and include transitional expressions (connecting words or phrases, such as *nevertheless, finally,* and *by contrast*) to make clear the relationships among ideas.

Evaluating. Quickly evaluate, or judge, your answer by asking the following questions:

Purpose	**1.** Have I addressed the assignment or question?
Introduction	**2.** Have I included a thesis statement which specifies what the answer will discuss?
Body	**3.** Have I developed at least two major points which support the thesis statement?
	4. Have I included enough evidence from the literary work to support each major point?
	5. Is the order of ideas in the essay clear and logical?
Conclusion	**6.** Have I included a conclusion that summarizes findings or restates the main idea?

Revising. Using your evaluation, improve your essay by adding, cutting, reordering, or replacing ideas and details.

Proofreading. Review your answer to locate and correct errors in grammar, usage, and mechanics. If your teacher indicates that you have time to do so, prepare a clean copy of your answer and proofread it again to catch any errors or omissions.

Sample Examination Questions and Answers

On the following pages you will find some sample examination questions and answers for study and discussion. Note that the questions or assignments (shown in italics) may be phrased as essay topics.

I

QUESTION

Puritan writing is pervaded by a belief in grace, the standard of plainness in language, and conviction of a divine mission in the New World. How are these three aspects of Puritanism illustrated in the works of William Bradford, Anne Bradstreet, Edward Taylor, and Jonathan Edwards?

DEVELOPING AN ANSWER

This is an exercise in *illustration*. In naming the three aspects of Puritan writing, the question provides you with a thesis statement. Still, you must decide how to proceed.

There are two possible approaches: 1) Treat each of the authors independently, citing examples from various works; 2) Treat each aspect, citing relevant examples from various authors.

If you choose the first method, you are required to demonstrate each of the aspects in each author's work. That will result in a long-winded and repetitive essay. If you choose the second approach, you can cite the most effective examples of each aspect for your presentation.

Once you have chosen an approach, you can jot down some prewriting notes to guide you in writing. These notes can be arranged under the three subheads of the assignment:

Grace

Edward Taylor's "Huswifery" expresses the gift of grace as a miraculous transformation.

Jonathan Edwards' portrait of Sarah Pierrepont describes someone who is in a state of grace.

Edwards' sermon presents a horrifying picture of the torments in store for sinners who have not experienced grace.

Plainness

William Bradford's *Of Plymouth Plantation* illustrates plain style in prose: simple, homely words in clear order.
Cite passage introducing Samoset.

Anne Bradstreet's poem "Upon the Burning of Our House" shows plain style in poetry: short, homely words from domestic life; direct statement.

Divine Mission

Bradford's history gives clear statement of the Puritan vision of America as divinely appointed.
He cites several examples showing God's intervention.
He calls Squanto an instrument of God.

You now have a scheme for writing the essay.

Puritan writing in colonial America was pervaded by a belief in grace, the standard of plainness in language, and the conviction of a divine mission in the New World. We can appreciate how central these three aspects were to the Puritan experience by examining the work of four authors: the historian William Bradford, the poets Anne Bradstreet and Edward Taylor, and the Puritan minister Jonathan Edwards.

BODY
In topic sentence show
grasp of concept.

In supporting statements
identify each work by
title and author.

Puritans believed strongly in the possibility of self-transformation, of purifying human nature by achieving grace. In "Huswifery," Edward Taylor explains the gift of grace by comparing the miraculous transformation of the soul—God's handiwork—to the transformation of raw wool into beautiful robes. In his portrait of Sarah Pierrepont, Jonathan Edwards gives us a picture of someone who is under the influence of grace. Free of sin, she enjoys the benevolence of God. Her life is filled with joy and sweetness. Edwards is also capable of describing vividly the torments of those who are not elect and who must suffer everlasting damnation. In his sermon "Sinners in the Hands of an Angry God," he depicts the sinner as a loathsome insect hanging by a slender thread over the pit of Hell.

Puritans valued clarity and simplicity in language and aimed for a style that would be intelligible to every reader. William Bradford's history, *Of Plymouth Plantation*, illustrates characteristics of this style in prose. Bradford tends to use simple words in clear order. He does not use many polysyllabic words, and he avoids elegant phrasing. The passage in which he introduces Samoset is a model of the plain style. In "Upon the Burning of Our House," Anne Bradstreet illustrates the plain style in poetry. She chooses short, homely words from domestic life, such as *roof, table,* and *chest.* She relies on direct statement rather than on metaphor.

The Puritans had a sense of being God's appointed people, and they envisioned America as the Promised Land. Bradford's history gives us a clear statement of the Puritan vision of the New World as a land under divine guidance. He frequently points to God's intervention on behalf of the Puritan settlers. He cites the "just hand of God" in punishing a cruel and profane sailor. He tells how God's providence saved a man from drowning. He attributes the survival of the Puritans during their terrible first winter to the benevolence of God, and he refers to Squanto, the Indian who helped the settlers, as a "special instrument" of God.

As these examples indicate, the spiritual values that are characteristic of the Puritans are reflected in early American literature.

Length: 430 words

QUESTION *Compare and contrast the title characters in "Miniver Cheevy" (page 497) and "Mr. Flood's Party" (page 498). In your essay, consider Robinson's attitude toward these figures.*

DEVELOPING AN ANSWER This is an exercise in *comparison and contrast.* The question requires that you supply your own thesis statement. Your thesis statement should be formulated *after* you have sifted your ideas and come to a conclusion about the subject.

You might begin by jotting down notes under the headings of *Similarities* and *Differences:*

Similarities	*Differences*
Both characters are misfits.	Robinson treats Miniver ironically.
Both drink to escape.	Miniver's dreams are absurd.
Both mourn the past.	He is filled with self-pity.
	He blames fate for his failures.
	Robinson treats Flood with pathos and humor.
	Flood's disappointed hopes are treated with sympathy.
	He is compared to a noble, heroic figure.

WRITING AN ANSWER You might then arrive at your thesis statement. The thesis statement should appear at the opening of your essay and should be supported by evidence in the body of the essay.

INTRODUCTION

Thesis Statement

In Miniver Cheevy and Eben Flood, E. A. Robinson depicts two lonely misfits who find refuge from their problems in drinking. *Although both characters are studies of failed lives, Robinson presents them with a difference: his view of Miniver is consistently ironic and mocking, while his view of Eben blends pathos with humor.*

BODY

Topic Sentence

Supporting Statements

Both Miniver and Eben mourn the past and drink to escape the dreariness of their lives. Miniver is out of step in the present. He longs for the Romantic past, for the days of chivalry and heroic actions. He blames fate for his failure and drinks to escape his disappointments. Eben, too, has no place in the present. An old man who has known better days, he is now alone among strangers, and homeless. He has nothing to look forward to; he can only look back into the past for memories of friends now gone. He holds a drinking party with himself, for a time relieving the misery of his loneliness and disappointed hopes.

| | While both figures are regarded with a degree of wry amusement, there are significant differences in tone in the two poems. **Robinson's attitude toward Miniver is one of ironic detachment.** Miniver professes to love the Romantic past, but he has no real understanding or knowledge of the things he admires. He misses "the medieval grace/Of iron clothing"; yet no one could have moved gracefully in a suit of armor. The Medici is just a name to him. While he claims to scorn money, he is "sore annoyed" without it. Through the skillful use of anticlimax, Robinson exposes Miniver's self-deception and reduces his beliefs to absurdity. |

Transition Sentence

Topic Sentence

Direct Quotations

Topic Sentence

Supporting Statements

Eben Flood, on the other hand, is treated sympathetically. There are comic elements in his presentation, in the way he greets himself cordially, offers himself a drink, and declines a refill, and in the way he enjoys singing while under the influence. Blending with the humor is a strong element of pathos. Robinson emphasizes Eben's isolation. We feel keenly the love that is missing from his life. Robinson refers to his disappointed hopes as "valiant armor" and suggests that like the legendary hero Roland, who sounded a horn for help, old Eben is calling for help that will never come. Robinson's compassionate view is conveyed by gentle images, such as that of the mother's tenderness for her child and that of the silver moon.

CONCLUSION

In his portraits of these two "losers," Robinson manifests a keen understanding of human beings out of harmony with their times.

Length: 418 words

III

QUESTION

The conflict between European and American social attitudes is an important theme in Henry James's Daisy Miller. *With this theme in mind, analyze Winterbourne's attitude toward Daisy. How does his attitude reflect that conflict?*

DEVELOPING AN ANSWER

To develop an answer to this question, you might proceed chronologically, noting Winterbourne's responses to Daisy throughout the narrative. The following notes about Winterbourne's attitude at various points in the story could guide the development of a thesis statement and the writing of an essay answer.

On meeting Daisy in Switzerland:

Is struck by Daisy's prettiness and decides to speak to her, even though he knows it's not entirely proper to do so.

Notes Daisy's freshness and innocence, and asks himself: "Was she simply a pretty girl from New York State. . . . Or was she also a designing, an audacious, an unscrupulous young person?" (page 525)

Comforts himself that Daisy is only a flirt and recognizes that he wants to see her again.

Knows that it is scandalous to go alone with Daisy to the Château de Chillon, but enjoys the trip—although he is surprised by her boldness.

Agrees to visit Daisy in Rome in the winter.

On seeing Daisy in Rome:

Is disappointed and annoyed to hear from his aunt that Daisy has several male companions in Rome.

Meets Daisy at Mrs. Walker's home—she scolds him for not seeing her sooner and refers to her friend, Giovanelli.

Is shocked that Daisy would go to meet Giovanelli at the Pincio without proper companions and decides to go with her.

Comments about Daisy: "It was impossible to regard her as a perfectly well-conducted young lady; she was wanting in a certain indispensable delicacy" (page 542); and, "But Daisy, on this occasion, continued to present herself as an inscrutable combination of audacity and innocence" (page 542).

Is stunned by Daisy's refusal to ride in Mrs. Walker's carriage to save her reputation.

Urges Daisy to conform to social customs and not flirt and observes Mrs. Walker snubbing Daisy at her party.

Doesn't see Daisy often after Mrs. Walker's party, yet wonders how she feels at being excluded from the "right" circles.

Is surprised by his conversation with Daisy at the Palace of the Caesars, when she says she is engaged and then says she is not.

Is concerned about Daisy's health when he sees her with Giovanelli at the Forum.

Hears about Daisy's illness and learns from Mrs. Miller that Daisy was never engaged.

Learns of Daisy's death and tells his aunt that he did Daisy an injustice: "I was booked to make a mistake. I have lived too long in foreign parts" (page 558).

Drawing on these prewriting notes, you might develop the following thesis statement: *Throughout* Daisy Miller, *Winterbourne's attitude toward Daisy shifts between two poles, as he wavers between regarding her as a careless, irresponsible flirt and an innocent, free-spirited young woman.*

WRITING AN ANSWER   Using the prewriting notes and thesis statement as a guide, you might write the following essay:

INTRODUCTION   In his novels, Henry James often explored the conflict between European and American social attitudes. This conflict is a theme in *Daisy Miller,* James's study of how Winterbourne, a young American living abroad, reacts to the brash and lovely American tourist Daisy

Thesis Statement	Miller. *Throughout* Daisy Miller, *Winterbourne's attitude toward Daisy shifts between two poles, as he wavers between regarding her as a careless, irresponsible flirt and an innocent, free-spirited young woman.*
Topic Sentence	**From their first meeting, Winterbourne is uncertain about how to regard Daisy.** Lounging in the garden of his Swiss hotel, Winter-
Supporting Statements	bourne happens to meet Daisy Miller. Struck by her beauty and charm, Winterbourne also recognizes that it is not proper for them to speak without formal introductions in the presence of chaperones. Nevertheless, they speak and, because of this, Winterbourne first questions Daisy's character. He asks himself, "Was she simply a pretty girl from
Direct quotation used as evidence	New York State. . . . Or was she also a designing, an audacious, an unscrupulous young person?" (page 525). Wanting to see Daisy again, Winterbourne comforts himself that Daisy is a harmless and innocent flirt. At the same time, he senses that his idea of how a young woman should behave may prevent him from understanding and accepting Daisy. On their trip to the Château de Chillon, Winterbourne is again surprised by Daisy's boldness and flaunting of social rules. Nevertheless, he agrees to visit Daisy in Rome in the winter.
Topic Sentence	**In Rome, Daisy continues to baffle Winterbourne.** When he first sees Daisy at Mrs. Walker's home, he is disappointed and annoyed to
Supporting Statements	hear that Daisy has several companions. While Daisy playfully scolds him for not calling upon her sooner, Winterbourne continues to wonder about the impression she is creating. Later, despite Mrs. Walker's protests about proper behavior, Daisy persists in planning to meet Giovanelli on the Pincio. Winterbourne accompanies her, saying it
Direct quotation used as evidence	"was impossible to regard her as a perfectly well-conducted young lady; she was wanting in a certain indispensable delicacy" (page 542). But Winterbourne still seems indecisive about Daisy, noting that she
Direct quotation used as evidence	"continued to present herself as an inscrutable combination of audacity and innocence" (page 542). Even when Daisy refuses to save her reputation by riding in Mrs. Walker's carriage, Winterbourne tells Mrs. Walker that he likes Daisy very much. Despite Daisy's improper behavior, Winterbourne cannot dismiss her entirely.
Transition Sentence **Topic Sentence** **Supporting Statements**	After the carriage incident, however, Daisy's reputation worsens. **Still, Winterbourne continues to be concerned about Daisy, although he remains confused by her reckless actions.** At the party where Mrs. Walker snubs Daisy, Winterbourne again warns Daisy not to flirt, for people will not understand. After the party, he sees Daisy infrequently and wonders how she feels "about all the cold shoulders that were turned toward her" (page 551), if, indeed, she is even aware of being excluded. As their meeting at the Palace of the Caesars shows, Winterbourne still cares for Daisy deeply, being disappointed and surprised when she first asserts and then denies her engagement to Giovanelli. His conflicting feelings are also evident at their last encounter at the Colosseum. Although Winterbourne is shocked that Daisy would be there at midnight with Giovanelli, he warns her about the *perniciosa*, or malaria. Only days later, Winterbourne learns of Daisy's illness and

Direct quotation used as evidence

CONCLUSION

calls on her mother, who gives him Daisy's urgent message about not being engaged. When Daisy dies, Winterbourne is at last struck by how he misjudged her, telling his aunt that "it was on his conscience that he had done her injustice" (page 557).

Throughout *Daisy Miller,* Winterbourne is uncertain about his feelings for Daisy. He seems to sense that Daisy is merely a free-spirited young woman, yet his ideas about propriety force him to doubt her. Only with Daisy's death does Winterbourne realize that he saw her not through American eyes, but through the eyes of a young man who has "lived too long in foreign parts" (page 558).

Length: 443 words

Writing on a Topic of Your Own

Choosing a Topic

At times you may be asked to write an essay on a topic of your own choosing. Often you may need to read a work or group of works more than once before you find a suitable topic.

The object of literary analysis is to say something meaningful about the work under consideration. Some topics lend themselves to more useful investigation than others. A catalog of the devices of sound in Poe's "The Raven" (page 184) is not likely to add to greater understanding and appreciation of the poem. A study of the relationship between sound and sense, however, might yield insight into the hypnotic character of the verse. Choosing a topic is, in the first place, a matter of pursuing a worthwhile line of inquiry.

Choosing a topic is also a matter of making use of special abilities, experiences, and background. A writer with a strong interest in music might profitably study the influence of music on the poetry of Sidney Lanier.

The choice of a topic, moreover, depends on the amount of time and space available. A writer who is asked for a 500-word paper would not choose a topic that calls for exhaustive treatment. A three-paragraph essay might be just room enough to say something about the theme of illusion in O'Neill's *Where the Cross Is Made* (page 951). A 1500-word essay might give a writer enough room to discuss the play's melodramatic devices. What the writer must often do is to limit a broad subject to a narrow topic— one that can be discussed in the time and space available. You might have to divide a subject into several parts and select only one part as the focus of your essay.

Sometimes a topic will suggest itself while you are reading a work. You may be puzzled or fascinated by some idea or technique. While you were reading "A Game of Catch" (page 1010), you noted that the author chose an objective point of view for the narrative. A good topic for study might be the function of point of view in Wilbur's story.

A topic may focus on one element or technique in a work. If you are writing about fiction, you might concentrate on some aspect of plot, such as conflict. Or you might concentrate on character, setting, or theme. If you are writing about poetry, you might choose to explore imagery or figurative language. A topic may deal with more than one aspect of a work. You might, for example, discuss several elements of a short story in order to show how an idea or theme is developed. And a topic may deal with some aspect of two or more works.

You may find it helpful to phrase the problem or topic as a question. For example, if you have decided to compare the free-verse techniques of Whitman and Sandburg, you might phrase your assignment as: "How are their styles alike, and how are they different?"

A topic provides you with a focus for analysis. It is a point of departure for further study.

Once you have a topic in mind, your object is to form it into a *thesis*, a controlling idea that represents the conclusion of your findings. Often a paper is unsatisfactory because it does not present a thesis clearly or forcefully. A paper that rambles on about nature imagery in Thoreau's *Walden* (page 235) may contain a great deal of information, but without a controlling idea, it will remain inclusive. A paper that sets out to show the superiority of nature to civilization in *Walden* has a clear purpose and focus.

You may have to read a work several times before you can formulate a thesis. Do not be overly concerned if an idea comes slowly. This is a common experience. You would then need to present the evidence supporting your position. Here are some examples showing how a thesis differs from a topic:

Topic	Conflict in Willa Cather's "The Sculptor's Funeral" (page 471)
Thesis	The central conflict is one of values—the materialistic, crass values of the townspeople in opposition to the aesthetic values of the sculptor.
Topic	The Relationship of Sound and Sense in Poe's Poetry
Works Selected	"The Raven" (page 184) "The Bells" (page 190)
Thesis	In these two poems the sound is of such overwhelming power that it has an existence independent of meaning.
Topic	The Influence of the American Wilderness on Early Romantic Writers
Works Selected	Washington Irving, "The Devil and Tom Walker" (page 128) James Fenimore Cooper, *The Deerslayer* (page 139)
Thesis	For Irving, the American landscape was a picturesque setting for fanciful and legendary events; for Cooper, the wilderness was a moral force that shaped human character.

Gathering Evidence/Formulating Major Points

It is a good idea to take notes as you read, even if you do not yet have a topic in mind. Later on, when you have settled on a topic, you can discard any notes that are not relevant. Some people prefer a worksheet, others index cards. In the beginning, you should record all your reactions. A topic may emerge during this early stage. As you continue to read, you will shape your topic into a rough thesis. With a rough thesis in mind, you can begin to formulate major points and to gather evidence that supports the thesis statement.

When you take notes, make an effort to state ideas in your own words. If a specific phrase or line is so important that it deserves to be quoted directly, be sure to enclose the words in quotation marks. When you transfer your notes to your final paper, be sure to copy quotations exactly.

If you cite lines in a poem, you should enclose the line numbers in parentheses following the quotation. The following note, which is for Bryant's poem "Thanatopsis" (page 153), shows you how to incorporate two lines of a poem into your own text:

Bryant concludes with an image of a person sustained by trust, who approaches the grave "Like one who wraps the drapery of his couch/About him, and lies down to pleasant dreams" (lines 80–81).

The slash (/) shows the reader where line 80 ends and line 81 begins. If you cite three or more lines, you should separate the quotation from your own text.

Suppose that you have just concluded the unit on modern American poetry in this textbook and are instructed to write an essay of approximately 500 words on a topic of your own choice. You realize that you must choose a relatively limited topic if you are to treat it thoroughly.

You haven't any ideas at the outset so you skim through the unit, refreshing your memory of poems studied in class and reading additional poems that interest you. You reread introductions and headnotes, sifting through this material for approaches and ideas. You become aware that two poems in the unit deal with a similar subject: Robert Frost's "Fire and Ice" (page 742) and Archibald MacLeish's "The End of the World" (page 790). You wonder whether a comparison would help to illuminate both works. You decide to investigate.

You read each poem several times, paraphrasing lines for clarity wherever necessary. You might work out a chart of this kind for recording your notes:

POINTS OF COMPARISON	"Fire and Ice"	"The End of the World"
IDEAS	Opening lines allude to scientific predictions about the way the world will end.	Central metaphor presents the world as a circus. It is a place filled with absurd and grotesque performers: an armless ambidextrian; a lion biting a woman's neck; one creature swinging another by the thumb.
	Fire a symbol for desire; ice a symbol for hate.	
	Knowing what he does about his own nature, the speaker believes desire and hate would be equally effective agents of destruction.	In the midst of this chaos, the top blows off, a metaphor for annihilation of the world.
	Poem suggests that human beings will be the vehicle for the destruction of the world.	Poem suggests that some cosmic force indifferent to the spectacle of human life will destroy the world.
LANGUAGE	Language is simple: Frost uses diction of everyday speech.	Images of bewildering activity in lines 1–7 suggest lack of cohesion.
	Symbols of fire and ice are highly evocative: fire suggests power, greed, corruption; ice suggests bigotry, war.	Word play on *top* (line 8) prompts double meaning of a circus "big top" and the "top of the world."
	Compression of language lends intensity to poem.	Images and repetition in lines 9–14 convey emptiness of infinite space: "sudden blackness" and the "black pall/Of nothing."
	Poem is organized on principle of contrasts—fire/ice; desire/hate.	Juxtaposition of imagery creates dramatic shock.
TONE	Ambiguous: both light and serious. There is dry humor in the notion of choice—either will do.	Tone is a curious blend of humor and grimness.
	Use of understatement in last line undercuts gravity.	Levity is produced by the circus performers, the pun on *top,* and the irony of spectators paying to see the "greatest show on earth" and getting to see the show to end all shows.
	Calm surface of poem may be a disguise for anxiety.	

You might find at this point that a focused and specific thesis statement has begun to emerge: *Although the poems present quite different visions of doomsday, both convey immense terror with grim irony.* You would continue to study the poems, developing major points and gathering additional evidence to support your thesis statement. The next step is organizing the material.

Organizing Ideas

Before you begin writing, organize your main ideas to provide for an introduction, a body, and a conclusion. The introduction should identify the authors and works. It should contain a statement of your thesis as well. The body of your paper should present the evidence supporting your thesis. The conclusion should bring together your main ideas.

The plan will grow out of the notes you have compiled. Remember that you need not use *all* the evidence you have collected. You should include material that has bearing on your topic.

Planning is the last important stage before writing your paper. A plan shows your major ideas and the order in which you will present them. If you plan carefully, you will have a valuable guide to writing a coherent and effective essay.

To organize your ideas and evidence, you may use an informal plan or an outline (topic or sentence). Although many writers use the topic outline with success, you may prefer to use the sentence outline, which is more detailed. By phrasing your main ideas as complete sentences, you may arrive at the key statements of your paper.

Here is one kind of plan you might use for a short paper. It indicates the main idea of each paragraph and identifies the major points of the essay.

INTRODUCTION

Paragraph 1   *Thesis Statement* Although the poems present quite different visions of the end, both temper their terrifying visions with a tone of grim irony.

BODY

Paragraph 2   Frost's poem suggests that the destruction of the world will be caused by unchecked human emotions.

Paragraph 3   MacLeish's poem envisions some cosmic force unexpectedly obliterating everything.

Paragraph 4   Both poets adopt an ironic tone that subtly mixes elements of humor with deadly seriousness.

CONCLUSION

Paragraph 5   The ambiguous tone in both poems is deliberately unsettling.

Writing the Essay

Use your prewriting plan as a guide in writing your paper. Focus on expressing clearly the major points and evidence supporting your thesis statement. Include a topic sentence and supporting sentences in each paragraph. As you write, use language that is appropriate in tone. Include transitional expressions to make clear the relationships among your ideas.

Here is a model essay of comparison on Frost's "Fire and Ice" and MacLeish's "The End of the World." For an earlier draft of this essay, see pages 1039–1041.

TITLE

INTRODUCTION
Identify works and authors.

Thesis Statement

BODY
Topic Sentence

Restate ideas in your own words.

Supporting Statements

Topic Sentence

Supporting Statements

Topic Sentence

Supporting Statements

Transition

Supporting Statements

CONCLUSION
Topic Sentence

A COMPARISON OF "FIRE AND ICE" AND "THE END OF THE WORLD"

Robert Frost, in "Fire and Ice," and Archibald MacLeish, in "The End of the World," address themselves to a horrifying subject—the physical destruction of our world. *Although the poems present quite different visions of the end, both temper their terrifying visions with a tone of grim irony.*

Frost's poem suggests that the destruction of the world will be caused by unchecked human emotions. Scientific authorities (the "Some" referred to in the opening lines) predict that the world will end either by fire (possibly by the sun becoming a nova) or by ice (entering a new ice age), but the speaker has an idea that human beings will not have to wait for either of these predictions to come true. His own experiences, alluded to in lines 3 and 6, have taught him the destructive power of human emotions. Taking fire as a symbol for desire, or passion, and ice as a symbol for hate, the speaker concludes that either of these impulses has the potential for terminating civilization.

MacLeish's poem envisions some cosmic force unexpectedly obliterating everything. The central metaphor of the poem depicts life as a three-ring circus, filled with main attractions that are grotesque and absurd. As the performers become increasingly frantic, quite unexpectedly the "top" blows off. It is as if no lid can any longer contain and hold together such chaos. In one ghastly moment, creation is swallowed up by an abyss of blackness and nothingness.

Both poets adopt an ironic tone that subtly mixes elements of humor with deadly seriousness. Frost's poem has a deceptively calm surface. The speaker sounds like a cracker-barrel philosopher who is speculating about the future. The simplicity of language disguises the intensity and implication of what he is saying. The symbols of fire and ice are powerfully evocative. The fire of desire suggests power, greed, corruption; the ice of hate suggests bigotry, war. There is dry humor in the notion that either destructive agent will do. The use of understatement in the last line—the word *suffice* rather than a stronger word— also undercuts the gravity of his theme. **MacLeish's poem, too, blends humor and grimness.** There is a zaniness in the spectacle of the circus performers: an armless ambidextrian lighting a match between his toes; a lion biting a woman's neck; a creature—presumably a chimpanzee or a monkey—being swung by its thumb. The word play on *top* (line 8), with its double meaning of the "big top" of the circus tent and the "top of the world," also contributes to the levity of tone. Moreover there is the irony of spectators who have come to see the "greatest show on earth" getting to see the show to end all shows—cosmic annihilation.

The ambiguous tone in both poems is deliberately unsettling. The irony creates a distance between us and the subject matter of the poems. Perhaps the contemplation of the destruction of the world is so horrifying that our anxiety must be shielded behind some form of humor.

Length: 502 words

Evaluating and Revising Papers

When you write an essay in class, you have a limited amount of time to plan and develop your essay. Nevertheless, you should save a few minutes to read over your work and make necessary improvements. When an essay is assigned as homework, you have more time to prepare it carefully. Get into the habit of evaluating and revising your work. A first draft of an essay should be treated as a rough copy of your manuscript. Chances are that thinking about reworking your first draft will result in a clearer and stronger paper.

To evaluate an essay, you judge its content, organization, and style by applying a set of criteria, or standards. Your goal in evaluating is to identify the strengths and weaknesses of the paper. Knowing this, you will be able make the changes that will improve the essay. To evaluate an essay about literature, ask yourself the following questions:

Guidelines for Evaluating an Essay

Introduction   1. Have I included an introduction that identifies the subject of the paper? Have I identified the author(s) and literary work(s) the paper will deal with?

Thesis Statement   2. Have I included a thesis statement that clearly expresses the controlling idea for the paper?

Thesis Development 3. Have I included convincing main points that develop the thesis in the body of the paper?

4. Have I included sufficient evidence from the work to support each main point?

Conclusion   5. Have I included a conclusion that synthesizes the main ideas or that suggests additional ideas for study?

Coherence   6. Have I arranged ideas logically and related them clearly to one another?

Style   7. Have I varied sentence beginnings and sentence structure? Have I defined any unfamiliar words or unusual terms? Have I used vivid and specific words?

Tone   8. Have I used language that is appropriate for my purpose and audience?

Having identified the strengths and weaknesses of your essay, you can then revise it. Writers usually revise by using any one of four basic techniques: *adding, cutting, reordering,* and *replacing.* For example, if the relationship of ideas is unclear, you can *add* transitional expressions (such as *first, finally,* and *by contrast).* If your language is not appropriate, you can *replace* slang, contractions, and informal expressions with more formal language. You can *cut* unrelated evidence, and you can *reorder,* or rearrange, ideas that are difficult to follow.

On the following pages you will find a revised draft of the essay that appears on page 1037. The annotations in the margins indicate which revising techniques were used to make the changes. Compare the two versions of this paper, noting where the writer has made vague or general statements more specific, clear, and concise.

replace; add   ~~In their respective poems,~~ Of Robert Frost, in "Fire and Ice" and Archibald MacLeish, in "The End

cut   of the World," ~~the poets Robert Frost and Archibald MacLeish~~

address themselves to a horrifying subject –– the physical

destruction of our world. Although the poems present quite different

replace; add   visions of the end, both ~~convey immense terror~~ temper their terrifying visions with a tone of grim irony.

Frost's poem suggests that the destruction of the world

add   will be caused by unchecked human emotions. (The "Some" referred Scientific authorities

cut   to in the opening lines) ~~are scientific authorities who~~ predict

replace   that the world will end either by fire (~~by the expansion of the~~ possibly by the sun becoming

replace; add   ~~sun~~ a nova) or by ice (entering a new ice age). The speaker has an idea but

that human beings will not have to wait for either of these

replace   predictions to come true. His own experiences, ~~which he refers~~ alluded

replace   to in lines 3 and 6, have taught him ~~that human nature can be~~ the destructive power of human

replace   ~~destructive~~ emotions. Taking fire as a symbol for desire, or passion,

and ice as a symbol for hate, the speaker concludes that either

replace   of these ~~emotional extremes~~ impulses has the potential for terminating

civilization.

MacLeish's poem envisions some cosmic force unexpectedly

cut   obliterating everything. ~~In~~ the central metaphor of the poem,

<del>MacLeish</del> depicts life as a three-ring circus, filled with main

replace; cut attractions that <del>create a</del> *are* grotesque and absurd <del>spectacle.</del> As

cut the performers become increasingly frantic, <del>and their actions</del>

cut; replace <del>make one giddy,</del> quite unexpectedly the "top" blows off. *It is as if* <del>Such</del>

replace *no lid can any longer contain and hold together such chaos.* <del>chaos can no longer be contained and held together by a lid.</del>

Creation is swallowed up by an abyss of blackness and

reorder nothingness in one ghastly moment.

Both poets adopt an ironic tone that subtly mixes elements

add of humor with deadly seriousness. Frost's poem has a *deceptively* calm

surface. The speaker sounds like a cracker-barrel philosopher

replace; cut who is <del>predicting</del> *speculating about* the future. <del>He muses on scientific theories</del>

cut <del>and casually suggests that human impulses are sufficiently</del>

cut <del>powerful to destroy the world.</del> The simplicity of language

replace <del>belies</del> *disguises* the intensity and implication of what he is saying.

replace The symbols of fire and ice are <del>richly suggestive.</del> *powerfully evocative* The fire of

replace desire <del>stands for</del> *suggests* power, greed, corruption; the ice of hate

replace; reorder <del>means</del> *suggests* bigotry, war. The use of understatement in the last

add line also undercuts the gravity of his theme. *—the word suffice rather than a stronger word—* There is

<del>wryness</del> *dry humor* in the notion that either destructive agent will do.

MacLeish's poem, too, blends humor and grimness. There is a

zaniness in the spectacle of the circus performers: an

[replace; replace] armless ambidextrian ~~is trying to light~~ *lighting* a match between ~~two~~ *his*

[cut] toes; a lion ~~is~~ biting a woman's neck; a creature -- presumably

[cut; cut] a chimpanzee or a monkey -- ~~is~~ being swung ~~around~~ by its thumb.

[replace] ~~The double meaning of the word top also contributes to the~~ *The word play on top (line 8), with its double meaning of the "big top" of the circus tent and the "top of the world," also contributes to the*

[add] levity of tone. *Moreover* There is the irony of spectators who have come

[replace] to see the "~~biggest~~ *greatest* show on earth" getting to see the show to

end all shows -- cosmic annihilation.

The ambiguous tone in both poems is deliberately unsettling.

[replace] ~~To create~~ *The irony creates a* distance between us and the subject matter of the poems.

[cut; replace] ~~the poets use irony.~~ ~~The poems seem to be saying that~~ *Perhaps* the

[replace] contemplation of the destruction of the world is so ~~horrific~~ *horrifying* that

our anxiety must be shielded behind some form of humor.

Proofreading and Writing
a Final Version

After you have revised your draft, proofread your essay to locate and correct any errors in grammar, usage, and mechanics. Pay particular attention to the correct capitalization and punc-tuation of any direct quotations you cite as evidence. Then prepare a final version of your essay by following correct manuscript form or your teacher's instructions for the assignment. After writing this clean copy, proofread once more to catch any errors or omissions in copying.

GUIDE TO LITERARY TERMS AND TECHNIQUES

ALLEGORY *A tale in prose or verse in which characters, actions, or settings represent abstract ideas or moral qualities.* Thus, an allegory has two meanings, a literal meaning and a symbolic meaning. The most famous allegory in English is John Bunyan's *The Pilgrim's Progress* (1678). A well-known American allegory is Nathaniel Hawthorne's "Dr. Heidegger's Experiment."

A related form is the **parable,** a short, simple tale from which a moral lesson is drawn. Probably the most famous of all parables are those told by Jesus in the New Testament.

See pages 174, 180, 255.

ALLITERATION *The repetition of similiar sounds, usually consonants, in a group of words.* Sometimes the term is limited to the repetition of initial consonant sounds. Alliteration serves several purposes: it is pleasing to the ear, it emphasizes the words in which

it occurs, and it links and emphasizes the ideas these words express. Edgar Allan Poe frequently used alliteration, as in this line from "The Raven":

Doubting, dreaming dreams no mortal ever dared to dream before.

Here, alliteration links the ideas of dreaming, doubting, and daring.

See **Assonance, Consonance.**
See also pages 96, 189, 195, 386.

ALLUSION *A reference to a person, a place, an event, or a literary work that a writer expects a reader to recognize.* Allusions may be drawn from literature, mythology, religion, history, or geography. An allusion to Greek mythology is found in this line from Oliver Wendell Holmes's "The Chambered Nautilus":

In gulfs enchanted, where the Siren sings

Here, Holmes alludes to the Sirens, sea nymphs who enchanted sailors with their songs and lured them to their deaths. This allusion helps to evoke the mystery of the sea. The title of Archibald MacLeish's poem "Ars Poetica" alludes to a famous long poem of the same name by the Roman poet Horace.

See pages 93, 183.

ALMANAC *A book of months and days for one year, containing weather predictions, a wide variety of miscellaneous information, and, often, proverbs.* Benjamin Franklin's *Poor Richard* almanacs (1732 – 1757) were among the earliest American almanacs.

See page 87.

ANALOGY *A comparison made between two things to show the similarities between them.* Analogies can be used for illustration (to explain something unfamiliar by comparing it to something familiar) or for argument (to persuade that what holds true for one thing holds true for the thing to which it is compared). Henry Wadsworth Longfellow draws an analogy for the sake of illustration in "The Tide Rises, the Tide Falls," where he compares the repeated rise and fall of the tide to the passage of time and human life.

See pages 96, 303.

ANAPEST *A poetic foot consisting of two unstressed syllables followed by a stressed syllable (˘ ˘ ´).*

ANECDOTE *A very short story that is told to make a point.* Many anecdotes are humorous; some are serious. In his *Autobiography,* Benjamin Franklin tells a humorous anecdote about a man who prefers a speckled ax to a spotless one. The point of the anecdote is to explain his own flagging pursuit of virtue.

See page 761.

ANTAGONIST *A person or force opposing the protagonist in a drama or a narrative.* The word *antagonist* comes from a Greek word meaning "to struggle against." In Herman Melville's novel *Moby-Dick,* the white whale is Captain Ahab's antagonist. Another famous antagonist is Professor Moriarty, Sherlock Holmes's rival in Arthur Conan Doyle's detective stories.

See **Protagonist.**
See also page 936.

APHORISM *A terse, pointed statement expressing some wise or clever observation about life.* Here is an example:

He that lives upon hope will die fasting.
—Benjamin Franklin

Some writers, especially essayists, are known for their **aphoristic style;** that is, their writing incorporates many aphorisms, or memorable statements. The essays of the English writer Francis Bacon are noted for their aphoristic style, as are the essays of Ralph Waldo Emerson. Emerson's "Self-Reliance" abounds in famous aphorisms. Here are two well-known examples:

Trust thyself: every heart vibrates to that iron string.

A foolish consistency is the hobgoblin of little minds . . .

See pages 87, 96.

APOSTROPHE *A figure of speech in which an absent or dead person, an abstract quality, or something inanimate or nonhuman is addressed directly.* Apostrophe is a common device in poetry. William Cullen Bryant uses an apostrophe when he addresses a bird in "To a Waterfowl":

Whither, midst falling dew,
While glow the heavens with the last steps of day,
Far, through their rosy depths, dost thou pursue
Thy solitary way?

See page 232.

ASIDE *In drama, a short speech spoken by a character in an undertone or directly to the audience.* An aside is meant to be heard by the audience but not by the other characters onstage. Occasionally in fiction, a character speaks in an aside. In Herman Melville's *Moby-Dick,* Captain Ahab tries to persuade Starbuck, his first mate, to join in hunting the white whale. Ahab's aside expresses his belief that he has won the reluctant Starbuck over:

"Speak, but speak!—Aye, aye! thy silence, then, *that* voices thee. (*Aside*) Something shot from my dilated nostrils, he has inhaled it in his lungs. Starbuck now is mine; cannot oppose me now without rebellion."

See page 281.

ASSONANCE *The repetition of similar vowel sounds, especially in poetry.* Assonance creates a musical effect and emphasizes certain sounds to create a mood. Here is an example of assonance from Edgar Allan Poe's "The Bells":

From the molten-golden notes.

See page 195.

AUTOBIOGRAPHY   *A person's account of his or her own life.* An autobiography is generally written in narrative form and includes some introspection. Autobiographies are distinct from diaries, journals, and letters, which are not unified life stories written for publication. Autobiographies are also different from memoirs, which often deal, at least in part, with public events and important persons other than the author. Notable autobiographies in American literature include Benjamin Franklin's *Autobiography* and *The Education of Henry Adams.* Autobiographies are sometimes written in the guise of fiction. For example, Thomas Wolfe's novels *Look Homeward, Angel* and *Of Time and the River* are based on persons and events from Wolfe's life and are therefore autobiographical; but these persons and events have been thinly disguised by the author and made to appear fictional.

See page 85.

BALLAD   *A story told in verse and usually meant to be sung.* Ballads are generally classified as **folk ballads** or **literary ballads.** Folk ballads have no known authors. They are composed anonymously and transmitted orally. Literary ballads are composed by known writers who are imitating folk ballads. A well-known American folk ballad is "John Henry." Henry Wadsworth Longfellow wrote several literary ballads, among them "The Skeleton in Armor."

Many English and Scottish folk ballads have survived from the Middle Ages. They were transmitted by word-of-mouth from generation to generation and were not set down in writing until centuries after they were first sung. In America a folk-ballad tradition has flourished in the Appalachian Mountains, among cowhands, and within labor movements. The subject matter of folk ballads stems from the everyday life of the common people. The most popular themes, often tragic ones, are disappointed love, jealousy, revenge, sudden disaster, and deeds of adventure and daring. Generally, the language is simple, the rhythm pronounced, and the story told through dialogue and action. A **refrain,** or chorus, is a common element.

The traditional **ballad stanza** consists of four lines. The first and third lines of the stanza each have four stressed words or syllables. The second and fourth lines have three stresses. The number of unstressed syllables in a line may vary. The second and fourth lines rhyme. Here is a ballad stanza from an American folk ballad, "The Lover's Lament":

My dearest dear, the time draws near

When you and I must part;

But little do you know the grief or woe

Of my poor troubled heart.

BIOGRAPHY   *A detailed account of a person's life written by another person.* Many modern biographers strive to convey the historical and social background as well as the central events of a subject's life. An **impressionistic biography** does not aim to give a clear account of someone's life but rather to create an impression of that person by conveying his or her essence. John Dos Passos' novel *U.S.A.* contains many impressionistic biographies, including one of Henry Ford.

See pages 865, 900.

BLANK VERSE   *Verse written in unrhymed iambic pentameter.* Blank verse is used in some of the greatest English and American poetry. Here are some blank verse lines from William Cullen Bryant's "Thanatopsis":

Like one who wraps the drapery of his couch

About him, and lies down to pleasant dreams.

See pages 157, 751.

BRAG   See **Tall Tale.**

CAESURA   *A break or pause in a line of poetry, which contributes to the rhythm of the poem.* The caesuras in these lines from William Cullen Bryant's "Thanatopsis" are indicated by double lines (‖):

Go forth,‖under the open sky,‖and list
To Nature's teachings,‖while from all around—
Earth and her waters,‖and the depths of air—
Comes a still voice—

See page 157.

CATALOG   *A long list of things, people, or events.* Poets often use catalogs to suggest largeness and inclusiveness. For example, in "Song of the Broad-Axe," Walt Whitman uses a catalog to suggest America's rapid industrial growth:

The shapes arise!
Shapes of factories, arsenals, foundries, markets,
Shapes of two-threaded tracks of railroads,
Shapes of the sleepers of bridges, vast frameworks,
    girders, arches,
Shapes of the fleets of barges, tows, lake and canal
    craft, river craft . . .

CHARACTER *A person—or an animal, a thing, or a natural force presented as a person—appearing in a literary work.* To make the actions of a character believable, a writer must provide **motivation,** the stated or implied reason behind the character's behavior. Characters may be motivated by external events or by inner needs or fears. In discussing fictional characters, critics distinguish between **round characters** and **flat characters.** A round character is well developed, usually with many traits. Readers feel that a round character might exist in life. A flat character has only one or two distinguishing traits. Mark Twain's Huckleberry Finn is a round character. Tom Walker and his wife, in Washington Irving's "The Devil and Tom Walker," are flat characters. **Stock** or **stereotyped characters** are character types that appear so often their nature is immediately familiar to a reader or to an audience. Examples are the harassed husband, the absent-minded professor, the stalwart cowboy, the villain with a waxed mustache, and the temperamental movie star.

See pages 135, 607, 625.

CHARACTERIZATION *The means by which a writer reveals a character's personality.* Generally, a writer develops a character in one or more of the following ways: (1) through the character's actions; (2) through the character's speeches and thoughts; (3) through a physical description of the character; (4) through showing what other characters think or say about the character; (5) through a direct statement revealing the writer's idea of the character.

CHORUS *In drama, one or more characters who comment on the action.* In classical Greek tragedy, the chorus was a group of people who commented on the downfall of the protagonist. In Thornton Wilder's *Our Town,* the Stage Manager functions as a chorus.

See page 939.

CLASSICISM *A movement or tendency in art, literature, and music reflecting the principles manifested in the art of ancient Greece and Rome.* Classicism emphasizes the traditional and the universal, placing value on reason, clarity, balance, and order. Much English and American writing of the eighteenth century reflects the classical influence; the Declaration of Independence is a model of classical prose. Classicism is traditionally opposed to Romanticism, which is concerned with emotions and personal themes.

See **Romanticism.**
See also page 119.

CLIMAX *The decisive point in a narrative or drama; the point of greatest intensity or interest.* The climax is usually the turning point in the protagonist's fortunes or point of view. In Bernard Malamud's "The First Seven Years," the climax occurs when the shoemaker Feld confronts his assistant Sobel, who confesses his love for Feld's daughter Miriam. Surprised and resentful at first out of concern for Miriam's future, Feld finally overcomes his reservations when he recognizes the depth and sincerity of Sobel's feelings.

See **Plot.**

COMEDY *In general, a literary work that ends happily.* Comedy is distinct from **tragedy,** which is generally concerned with a protagonist who meets an unhappy end. Two American dramatists well-known for their comedies are S. N. Behrman and Neil Simon. Eugene O'Neill, although better known for his tragic plays, wrote one notable comedy, *Ah, Wilderness!*

See **Tragedy.**
See also page 936.

CONCEIT *A kind of metaphor that makes a comparison between two startlingly different things.* A conceit may be brief or it may provide the basis for an entire poem.

See page 40.

CONCRETE POETRY *Poetry that uses the appearance of the verse lines on the page to suggest or imitate the poem's subject.* The arrangement of lines in Denise Levertov's "Merritt Parkway" suggests the flow of traffic on a highway.

See page 851.

CONFESSIONAL POETRY *Poetry that makes frank, explicit use of incidents in the poet's life.* Confessional poetry has been an important movement in modern American poetry since the publication in 1959 of Robert Lowell's *Life Studies.* Other important confessional poets are Anne Sexton, Sylvia Plath, John Berryman, and W. D. Snodgrass.

See page 836.

CONFLICT *A struggle between two opposing forces or characters in a short story, novel, play, or narrative poem.* The struggle may be an **external conflict** (between two persons, between a person and society, between a person and nature), or it may be an **internal conflict** (between two elements struggling for mastery within a person). Many works present more than one kind of conflict. For example, in F. Scott Fitzgerald's story "Winter Dreams," there is an external conflict between Dexter Greene and Judy Jones, but there is also an internal conflict within Dexter between his romantic longings and his practical nature.

See **Plot.**
See also pages 589, 934.

CONSONANCE *The repetition of similar consonant sounds in a group of words.* The term is often used for a form of partial rhyme in which the consonants are the same but the vowels are different: *took/tack; bitter/butter.* Sometimes the term is limited to the repetition of final consonant sounds.

See **Alliteration, Assonance.**

COUPLET *Two consecutive lines of poetry that rhyme.* An *iambic couplet* is a couplet written in iambic feet. Here are two couplets from John Greenleaf Whittier's "Snowbound":

The sun that brief December *day*
Rose cheerless over hills of *gray,*
And, darkly circled, gave at *noon*
A sadder light than waning *moon.*

See pages 37, 157, 304.

DACTYL *A poetic foot consisting of a stressed syllable followed by two unstressed syllables (´ ˘ ˘).*

DÉNOUEMENT (dā-nōō-män´) *The outcome of a plot.* The dénouement (from the French word for "unknotting") is that part of a story, novel, play, or narrative poem in which conflicts are resolved and the fortunes of the protagonist are decided.

See **Plot.**

DESCRIPTION *The type of writing that deals with the appearance of a person, an object, or a place.* Description is one of the major **forms of discourse.** Description works through images that appeal to the senses. In short stories and novels, description is often used to characterize or to create mood. In the following passage from "The Devil and Tom Walker," Washington Irving indicates the miserliness and mean style of living of Tom Walker and his wife through a description of their dwelling place:

They lived in a forlorn-looking house that stood alone and had an air of starvation. A few straggling savin trees, emblems of sterility, grew near it; no smoke ever curled from its chimney; no traveler stopped at its door. A miserable horse, whose ribs were as articulate as the bars of a gridiron, stalked

about a field, where a thin carpet of moss, scarcely covering the ragged beds of puddingstone, tantalized and balked his hunger . . .

See **Exposition, Narration, Persuasion.**
See also page 22.

DIALECT *The characteristic speech of a particular region or social group.* Dialect differs from standard English in sentence structure, vocabulary, and pronunciation. Writers often use dialect to establish local color. Here is a humorous example of dialect from "Baker's Bluejay Yarn" by Mark Twain:

"So he flew off and fetched another acorn and dropped it in, and tried to flirt his eye to the hole quick enough to see what become of it, but he was too late. He held his eye there as much as a minute; then he raised up and sighed, 'Confound it, I don't seem to understand this thing, no way; however, I'll tackle her again.'"

See **Vernacular.**
See also pages 317, 347 – 348.

DICTION *A writer's choice of words, particularly for clarity, effectiveness, and precision.* Diction can be formal or informal, abstract or concrete. One aspect of a writer's style, diction must be appropriate to a writer's subject and audience. Words that are appropriate in informal dialogue might not be appropriate in a formal essay. The elevated, formal diction of the following passage from Ralph Waldo Emerson's *Nature* is appropriate to its subject:

In the woods, we return to reason and faith. There I feel that nothing can befall me in life—no disgrace, no calamity (leaving me my eyes), which nature cannot repair. Standing on the bare ground—my head bathed by the blithe air and uplifted into infinite space—all mean egotism vanishes.

See pages 36, 353.

DRAMATIC IRONY See **Irony.**

DRAMATIC MONOLOGUE *A narrative poem in which one character speaks to one or more listeners whose replies are not given in the poem.* The occasion is usually a crucial one in the speaker's life, and the speaker's words serve to reveal that character's personality. The English poet Robert Browning is the most notable writer of dramatic monologues. Among American poets, Edwin Arlington Robinson and Robert Frost have written dramatic monologues.

DRAMATIC POEM *A narrative poem in which one or more characters speak.* Each speaker always addresses a specific listener. This listener may be silent but identifiable, as in a dramatic monologue, or the listener may be another character who carries on a dialogue with the first speaker, as in Robert Frost's "The Death of the Hired Man."

ELEGY *A poem of mourning, usually over the death of an individual.* It may also be a lament over the passing of life and beauty or a meditation on the nature of death. An elegy is a type of **lyric** poem, usually formal in language and structure, and solemn or even melancholy in tone. Walt Whitman's "When Lilacs Last in the Dooryard Bloom'd" is an elegy that mourns the death of President Lincoln. An example of a modern elegy is Theodore Roethke's "Elegy for Jane."

See page 819.

END RHYME See **Rhyme.**

END-STOPPED LINE *A line of verse with a pause at the end, often signaled by a comma, dash, or period.* The opening lines of Henry Wadsworth Longfellow's "The Tide Rises, the Tide Falls" are end-stopped:

The tide rises, the tide falls,
The twilight darkens, the curlew calls;

See **Run-On Line.**

EPIC *A long narrative poem describing the deeds of a great hero and reflecting the values of the culture from which it originated.* Many epics were drawn from an oral tradition and transmitted by song and recitation before they were written down. Two of the most famous epics of Western civilization are Homer's *Iliad* and *Odyssey.* In the seventeenth century, the English poet John Milton wrote two great Christian epics, *Paradise Lost* and *Paradise Regained.* In American literature, Henry Wadsworth Longfellow's *Song of Hiawatha* is an epic.

EPIGRAM *A short, witty statement in prose or verse.* Here are two examples:

A man being (is) sometimes more generous when he has but a little money than when he has plenty, perhaps through fear of being thought to have but little.

—Benjamin Franklin

Nature fits all her children with something to do,
He who would write and can't write, can surely review.

—James Russell Lowell

EPIGRAPH *A quotation or motto at the beginning of a chapter, book, short story, or poem that makes some point about the work.* T. S. Eliot uses a quotation from Dante's *Divine Comedy* as the epigraph to "The Love Song of J. Alfred Prufrock." In the passage, one of the damned consents to tell his story, believing it will never be repeated. Eliot suggests through this epigraph that Prufrock, the poem's central character, is also making a shameful confession.

See page 775.

EPITAPH *An inscription on a gravestone or a short poem written in memory of someone who has died.* Many epitaphs, such as Benjamin Franklin's "A Printer's Epitaph," are actually **epigrams,** or short, witty statements, and are not intended for serious use as monument inscriptions.

See pages 88, 501.

EPITHET *A descriptive name or phrase used to characterize someone or something, such as "fair-weather friend" or "Catherine the Great."* Homer's *Odyssey* is filled with epithets, such as "wine-dark sea" and "keen-edged sword." In "The Crisis, Number 1," Thomas Paine uses the epithets "the summer soldier" and "the sunshine patriot" to characterize those who fail to serve their country in time of crisis.

ESSAY *A prose work, usually short, that deals with a subject in a limited way and expresses a particular point of view.* An essay is never a comprehensive treatment of a subject (the word comes from a French word, *essai,* meaning "attempt" or "try"). An essay may be serious or humorous, tightly organized or rambling, restrained or emotional.

The two general classifications of essay are the **informal essay** (also called the **familiar** or **personal essay**) and the **formal essay.** An informal essay is usually brief and is written as if the writer is talking informally to the reader about some topic, using a conversational style and a personal or humorous tone. In an informal essay, the writer might digress from the topic at hand, or express some amusing, startling, or absurd opinions. In general, an informal essay reveals as much about the personality of its author as it does about its subject. An example of the informal essay is E. B. White's "Walden (June 1939)." By contrast, a formal essay is tightly organized, dignified in style, and serious in tone. Ralph Waldo Emerson's "Self-Reliance" is an example of a formal essay. A **critical essay,** one kind of formal essay, deals with a particular work of art, a particular artist, or some issue concerning the arts. An example of the critical essay is James Baldwin's "The Creative Process."

See page 865.

EXPOSITION *The kind of writing that is intended primarily to present information.* Exposition is one of the major **forms of discourse.** The introductions to the units in this book are examples of exposition.

The term **exposition** also refers to that part of a short story, a novel, a narrative poem, or a play which gives the reader or audience essential background information. In Thornton Wilder's *Our Town,* the Stage Manager provides exposition throughout the play.

See Description, Narration, Persuasion.
See also page 22.

EXPRESSIONISM *A movement in literature and art that emphasized the life of the mind and feelings rather than the realistic, external details of everyday life.* The expressionistic plays of August Strindberg, the Swedish dramatist, have had an important influence on modern American drama.

See page 938.

FABLE *A brief story that is told to present a moral, or practical lesson.* The best-known fables are those attributed to Aesop. In the seventeenth century, the French writer La Fontaine wrote elegant, witty fables in verse. The American writer James Thurber wrote modern fables, which he called "fables for our time," that often give ironic twists to the morals of older fables.

FALLING ACTION See **Plot.**

FARCE *A type of comedy based on a farfetched humorous situation, often with ridiculous or stereotyped characters.* The humor in a farce is largely slapstick.

See Character.

FIGURATIVE LANGUAGE *Language that is not intended to be interpreted in a literal sense.* Figurative language consists of **figures of speech.** Emily Dickinson uses figurative language when she compares an abstract idea—hope—to a living creature—a bird:

> "Hope" is the thing with feathers—
> That perches in the soul—
> And sings the tune without the words—
> And never stops—at all—

This implied comparison is a **metaphor,** one kind of figurative language. Figurative language appeals to the imagination, as this poem shows, and thus provides new ways of looking at the world.

See Hyperbole, Metonymy, Oxymoron,
Personification, Simile, Synecdoche.

FIGURE OF SPEECH *A word or expression that is not meant to be interpreted in a literal sense.* More than two hundred different kinds of figures of speech have been classified, but the ones used most frequently in literature are **hyperbole, metaphor, metonymy, oxymoron, personification, simile,** and **synecdoche.**

See terms noted above.
See also pages 333, 781.

FLASHBACK *A scene in a short story, a novel, a narrative poem, or a play that interrupts the action to show an event that happened earlier.* Many narratives present events as they occur in time—that is, in chronological order. Sometimes, however, a writer interrupts this natural sequence of events and "flashes back" to tell the reader or audience what happened earlier in the story or in a character's life. Often a flashback takes the form of a reminiscence by one of the characters. In Sherwood Anderson's story "Sophistication," there is a flashback when Helen White recalls what happened when she and George Willard took a summer evening's walk.

See page 598.

FOIL *A character who sets off another character by contrast.* In John Updike's story "The Lucid Eye in Silver Town," the narrator's father and uncle serve as foils to each other. The father is passive but cleareyed and wise while the uncle is confident and compelling but a bit shallow.

FOLKLORE *Traditional songs, myths, legends, fables, fairy tales, proverbs, and riddles composed anonymously and either written down or passed on by word-of-mouth from generation to generation.* Folklore reveals a great deal about the culture in which it originated. Traditional **ballads** are a kind of folklore as are Indian songs and **spirituals.**

FOOT *A unit used to measure the meter, or rhythmic pattern, of a line of poetry.* A foot is made up of one stressed syllable and, usually, one or more unstressed syllables. A line of poetry has as many feet as it has stressed syllables. Four kinds of feet are common in English and American poetry:

The **iamb.** The iamb is the most common foot in English and American poetry. It consists of an unstressed syllable followed by a stressed syllable. The following line from Henry Wadsworth Longfellow's "Divina Commedia I" consists of five iambic feet:

The loud | voci|fera|tions of | the street

The **trochee.** The trochee is the reverse of the iamb. It consists of a stressed syllable followed by an unstressed syllable. This line from Edgar Allan Poe's "The Raven" is in trochaic meter:

Once up | on a | midnight | dreary, | while I |
pondered, | weak and | weary

The **anapest.** The anapest is a foot of three syllables, two unstressed syllables followed by a stressed syllable. This line from James Russell Lowell's *A Fable for Critics* is in anapestic meter:

There is Haw|thorne with ge|nius so shrink-|
ing and rare

The **dactyl.** The dactyl is the opposite of the anapest. It consists of a stressed syllable followed by two unstressed syllables. The following line by the English poet Thomas Hood is in dactylic meter:

Take her up | tenderly

See **Scansion.**
See also pages 157, 318.

FORESHADOWING *The use of hints or clues in a narrative to suggest what action is to come.* Writers use foreshadowing to create interest and build **suspense.** Sometimes foreshadowing also prepares the reader for the ending of a story.

FORM *The structure and organization of a literary work, as distinct from its content, which is what the work is about.*

FORMS OF DISCOURSE *A classification of writing into types, according to the writer's main purpose.* Four forms of discourse are **description, exposition, narration,** and **persuasion.**

See page 22.

FREE VERSE *Unrhymed verse that has either no metrical pattern or an irregular pattern.* Walt Whitman was the first poet in English to use free verse extensively. The following lines of free verse are from his poem "Song of Myself":

The last scud of the day holds back for me.
It flings my likeness after the rest and true as any
    on the shadow'd wilds,
It coaxes me to the vapor and the dusk.

See pages 157, 353, 756.

GOTHIC *A term that describes the use in fiction of grotesque, gloomy settings (often castles) and mysterious, violent, and supernatural occurrences to create suspense and awe.* The term is most often used in reference to **Gothic novels,** which became popular in England in the eighteenth century. Many of Edgar Allan Poe's short stories contain Gothic elements.

See page 510.

HAIKU *A Japanese verse form consisting of three lines and seventeen syllables.* The first line of a haiku contains five syllables; the second line, seven; and the third, five. A haiku usually focuses on an image that suggests a thought or emotion, as in the following example:

A bead of water
Clinging to a willow branch:
The first drop of rain!

The Imagist poets were influenced by Oriental verse forms, particularly by the haiku and a related Japanese form, the **tanka.**

See page 759.

HARLEM RENAISSANCE *A flowering of black writing, art, and music in the 1920s.* Harlem, New York, was the center of this movement. The writers of the movement had several aims: to define and preserve the black heritage; to protest oppression of blacks; and to make other Americans aware of black life and culture. Among the best-known writers of the Harlem Renaissance are Langston Hughes, Countee Cullen, Claude McKay, Jean Toomer, and Arna Bontemps.

See page 796.

HYPERBOLE *A figure of speech using exaggeration, or overstatement, for special effect.* Walt Whitman uses hyperbole for dramatic emphasis in this line from "Song of Myself":

And a mouse is miracle enough to stagger sextillions of infidels. . . .

IAMB   *A poetic foot consisting of an unstressed syllable
followed by a stressed syllable (◡ ◠).*

IAMBIC PENTAMETER   *The most common verse
line in English and American poetry.* It consists of five
verse *feet* (*penta-* is from a Greek word meaning
"five"), with each foot an *iamb*—that is, an unstressed
syllable followed by a stressed syllable. The following
lines from William Cullen Bryant's "Thanatopsis"
are written in iambic pentameter:

Thou go not, like the quarry-slave at night;
Scourged to this dungeon, but, sustained and
    soothed

William Shakespeare's plays are written almost
entirely in iambic pentameter. Unrhymed iambic
pentameter is called **blank verse.**

See **Meter, Scansion.**
See also pages 157, 318.

IMAGERY   *Words or phrases that create pictures, or
images, in the reader's mind.* Images are primarily visual; that is, they usually appeal to the reader's sense of
sight, as in these lines from Oliver Wendell Holmes's
poem "The Chambered Nautilus":

This is the ship of pearl, which, poets feign,
    Sails the unshadowed main—
The venturous bark that flings
On the sweet summer wind its purpled wings
In gulfs enchanted, where the Siren sings,
    And coral reefs lie bare,
Where the cold sea-maids rise to sun their
    streaming hair.

Images can also appeal to senses other than sight:
touch, taste, smell, hearing. For example, the following passage from John Greenleaf Whittier's poem
Snowbound appeals to the senses of hearing and
touch:

. . . we heard the roar
Of Ocean on his wintry shore,
And felt the strong pulse throbbing there
Beat with low rhythm our inland air.

See page 309.

IMAGISM   *A movement in American and English poetry
begun in 1912 by the American poet Ezra Pound.* Seeking
to free poetry from stale conventions and vague
high-flown language, Pound set forth the basic prin-

ciples of Imagism: (1) direct concentration on the
precise image; (2) use of precise words and the language of common speech; (3) creation of new
rhythms (and the use of free verse); (4) complete
freedom in choice of subject. Other notable American Imagists were Amy Lowell, H. D. (Hilda Doolittle), John Gould Fletcher, and William Carlos
Williams.

See page 757.

INCONGRUITY   *The joining of opposites to create an
unexpected situation.* Incongruity is often used for
comic effect, as in Mark Twain's "The Notorious
Jumping Frog" and S. J. Perelman's essay "Insert
Flap 'A' and Throw Away."

See pages 397, 607.

INTERNAL RHYME   See **Rhyme.**

INVERSION   *The reversal of usual word order.* Inversion may be used to secure some kind of emphasis. In
poetry inversion may be used for the sake of meter or
rhyme. In the following line from Robert Frost's
"Mending Wall," inversion emphasizes the first and
last words in the line:

Something there is that doesn't love a *wall*

IRONY   *A contrast or an incongruity between what is
stated and what is meant, or between what is expected to
happen and what actually happens.* Three kinds of irony
are (1) **verbal irony,** in which a writer or speaker says
one thing and means something entirely different;
(2) **dramatic irony,** in which a reader or an audience
perceives something that a character in the story or
play does not know; (3) **irony of situation,** in which
the writer shows a discrepancy between the expected
result of some action or situation and its actual result.

An example of verbal irony occurs in W. H. Auden's
"The Unknown Citizen," when the poet says that his
subject "had everything neccessary to the Modern
Man." Auden intends for us to understand that he is
critical of the values of modern society. Edwin
Arlington Robinson uses dramatic irony in "Miniver
Cheevy." Miniver deludes himself into believing that
he is the victim of fate, but the reader knows that
Miniver's failure is of his own making. An example of
irony of situation is found in Robinson's "Richard
Cory." Cory, who seems to have every reason for
living, inexplicably kills himself.

See page 718.

JOURNAL *A kind of autobiographical writing, generally a day-by-day record of events in a person's life and of that person's reflections.* William Byrd kept a journal of a surveying expedition, which he used in writing *The History of the Dividing Line.* Ralph Waldo Emerson, Henry David Thoreau, and Nathaniel Hawthorne kept journals in which they recorded ideas that became the basis of published works.

See page 52.

LITERARY LETTER *A letter that is deliberately written to be read by a wide audience.* Michel-Guillaume Jean de Crèvecoeur's *Letters from an American Farmer* is a collection of literary letters. They are supposedly written by a farmer named James to an English friend named Mr. F. B., but they actually express Crèvecoeur's impressions of America.

See page 107.

LOCAL COLOR *The use of specific details describing the dialect, dress, customs, and scenery associated with a particular region or section of the country.* The purpose of local color is to suggest the unique flavor of a particular locale. In the years following the Civil War, stories of local color flourished in the United States. Bret Harte used the local color of the West in such stories as "The Outcasts of Poker Flat." Mark Twain re-created the local color of a small town along the Mississippi River in many writings.

See page 341.

LYRIC *A poem, usually a short one, that expresses a speaker's personal thoughts and feelings.* As its Greek name indicates, a lyric was originally a poem sung to the accompaniment of a lyre, and lyrics to this day have retained a melodic quality. The **elegy,** the **ode,** and the **sonnet** are all forms of the lyric. Another kind of lyric is the **dramatic lyric,** in which emotions are attributed to an imaginary character, as in Ezra Pound's "The River-Merchant's Wife: a Letter."

See page 767.

MELODRAMA *A drama that has stereotyped characters, exaggerated emotions, and a conflict that pits an all-good hero or heroine against an all-evil villain.* The good characters always win and the evil ones are always punished. Originally, melodramas were so called because melodies accompanied certain actions (*melos* means "song" in Greek). Also, each character in a melodrama had a theme melody, which was played each time he or she made an appearance on stage.

METAPHOR *A figure of speech that makes a comparison between two things which are basically dissimilar.* "Life is a dream," "Life is a vale of tears," and "Life is a hard road" are all examples of metaphor. Unlike a **simile,** a metaphor does not use a connective word such as *like, as,* or *than* in making the comparison.

Many metaphors are implied, or suggested. An **implied metaphor** does not directly state that one thing is another, different thing. In her poem "Upon the Burning of Our House," Anne Bradstreet uses an implied metaphor when, in referring to heaven, she speaks of the beautiful "house" above built by the mightiest "architect."

An **extended metaphor** is a metaphor that is extended throughout a poem. In Emily Dickinson's "'Hope' Is the Thing with Feathers," the metaphor is stated in the title and the first line of the poem. The comparison of hope to a bird is then continued throughout the poem.

A **dead metaphor** is a metaphor which has become so commonplace that it seems literal rather than figurative. Some examples are the *foot* of a hill, the *head* of the class, a *point* in time, and the *leg* of a chair.

A **mixed metaphor** is the use of two or more inconsistent metaphors in one expression. When they are examined, mixed metaphors make no sense. Mixed metaphors are often unintentionally humorous: "The storm of protest was nipped in the bud" or "To hold the fort, he'd have to shake a leg."

See **Figurative Language.**
See also pages 333, 781.

METER *A generally regular pattern of stressed and unstressed syllables in poetry.* The basic unit of meter is the **foot,** and the most commonly used feet in English and American poetry are the **iamb,** the **trochee,** the **anapest,** and the **dactyl.** In these lines from Oliver Wendell Holmes's "Old Ironsides," the stressed syllables are marked (´) and the unstressed syllables are marked (˘):

Nail to the mast her holy flag,

Set every threadbare sail,

And give her to the god of storms,

The lightning and the gale!

See **Foot, Scansion.**
See also pages 157, 299, 318.

METONYMY (mə-tŏn′ə-mē) *A figure of speech in which something very closely associated with a thing is used to stand for or suggest the thing itself.* "Three sails came into the harbor" is an example of metonymy; the word *sails* stands for the ships themselves. Other common examples of metonymy are *crown* to mean a king, *hardhat* to mean a construction worker, and *White House* to mean the President.

MONOLOGUE *An extended speech by a character in a play, short story, novel, or narrative poem.* The speech may be made to other characters or, as in a **soliloquy,** represent the character thinking aloud. In Herman Melville's novel *Moby Dick,* Ahab's speech on the quarter-deck to his crew is virtually a monologue, although it is interrupted by the crew's comments. One form of monologue is the **dramatic monologue.**

MOOD *The prevailing feeling or emotional climate of a literary work, often developed, at least in part, through descriptions of* **setting.** Edgar Allan Poe often establishes an atmosphere of gloom at the very opening of a work, as in "The Fall of the House of Usher."

See page 160.

MOTIF *A recurring feature (such as a name, an image, or a phrase) in a work of literature.* A motif generally contributes in some way to the theme of a short story, novel, poem, or play. For example, Stephen Crane uses the following pattern of thought as a motif in "The Open Boat" to reinforce the theme of nature's indifference to humanity:

> If I am going to be drowned—if I am going to be drowned—if I am going to be drowned, why, in the name of the seven mad gods who rule the sea, was I allowed to come thus far and contemplate sand and trees?

At times, motif is used to refer to some commonly used plot or character type in literature. The "ugly duckling motif" refers to a plot that involves the transformation of a plain-looking person into a beauty. Two other commonly used motifs are the "Romeo and Juliet motif" (about doomed lovers) and the "Horatio Alger motif" (about the office clerk who becomes the corporation president).

MOTIVATION See **Character.**

MYTH *A story, often about immortals and sometimes connected with religious rituals, that attempts to give meanings to the mysteries of the world.* In myths, gods and goddesses are usually identified with the immense powers of the universe: in Greek myths, Zeus is associated with the sky, Hades with the underworld, Poseidon with the sea, Apollo with the sun, Athena with wisdom, Ares with war. But the gods are also given the forms and feelings of human beings. Thus, myths make it possible for people to understand and deal with things that they cannot control and often cannot see.

The body of related myths that is accepted by a people is known as its **mythology** . A mythology tells a people what it is most concerned about: where it came from, who its gods are, what its most sacred rituals are, and what its destiny is.

NARRATION *The kind of writing or speaking that tells a story.* Narration is one of the major **forms of discourse.** A narrative may be book length, such as a novel, or it may be paragraph length, such as an ancedote. The short stories, narrative poems, and plays in this book are all examples of narration.

See **Description, Exposition, Persuasion.**
See also page 22.

NARRATIVE POEM *A poem that tells a story.* One kind of narrative poem is the **epic,** a long poem which sets forth the heroic ideals of a particular people. The **ballad** is another kind of narrative poem. Examples of narrative poems in American literature are Edgar Allan Poe's "The Raven," Henry Wadsworth Longfellow's *Evangeline,* and Robert Frost's "The Death of the Hired Man."

NARRATOR *One who narrates, or tells, a story.* A story may be told by a **first-person narrator,** someone who is either a major or a minor character in the story. Edgar Allan Poe uses a first-person narrator in "The Fall of the House of Usher." A story may also be told by a **third-person narrator,** who is not in the story at all. F. Scott Fitzgerald's "Winter Dreams" is told by a third-person narrator.

The word *narrator* can also refer to a character in a drama who guides the audience through the play, often commenting on the action and sometimes participating in it. In Thornton Wilder's play *Our Town,* the Stage Manager serves as a narrator.

See **Point of View.**

NATURALISM *An extreme form of realism.* Naturalistic writers usually depict the sordid side of life and show characters who are severely, if not hopelessly, limited by their environment or heredity. The most highly regarded American naturalistic writers are Theodore Dreiser, Frank Norris, and Stephen Crane. John Steinbeck sometimes used naturalistic techniques. His novel *The Grapes of Wrath* shows a poor migrant family ruthlessly crushed by natural and social forces over which they have no control.

See page 447.

NOVEL *A book-length fictional prose narrative, having many characters and, often, a complex plot.* Famous American novels include Nathaniel Hawthorne's *The Scarlet Letter,* Herman Melville's *Moby-Dick,* Mark Twain's *Adventures of Huckleberry Finn,* Willa Cather's *My Ántonia,* F. Scott Fitzgerald's *The Great Gatsby,* and Ralph Ellison's *Invisible Man.* A related form is the **novella,** a prose work longer than a short story but shorter and less complex than a novel. Distinguished American novellas include *The Turn of the Screw,* by Henry James, and *Noon Wine,* by Katherine Anne Porter.

See page 509.

OCTAVE *An eight-line poem or stanza.* Usually the term **octave** refers to the first eight lines of an **Italian sonnet.** The remaining six lines form a **sestet.**

See **Sonnet.**
See also page 304.

ODE *A complex and often lengthy lyric poem, written in a dignified formal style on some lofty or serious subject.* Odes are often written for a special occasion, to honor a person or a season, or to commemorate an event. Some famous odes by English poets are Percy Bysshe Shelley's "Ode to the West Wind," John Keats's "Ode on a Grecian Urn," and William Wordsworth's "Ode: Intimations of Immortality." Henry Timrod wrote "Ode on the Confederate Dead" to be sung at a ceremony in 1867 in which the graves of the Confederate dead at Magnolia Cemetery in Charleston, South Carolina, were decorated.

See page 382.

ONOMATOPOEIA *The use of a word whose sound in some degree imitates or suggests its meaning.* The names of some birds are onomatopoetic, imitating the cries of the birds named: *cuckoo, whippoorwill, owl, crow, towhee, bob-white.* Some onomatopoetic words are *hiss, clang, rustle,* and *snap.* In these lines from Edgar Allan Poe's poem "The Bells," the word *tintinnabulation* is onomatopoetic:

Keeping time, time, time
In sort of Runic rhyme,
To the *tintinnabulation* that so musically wells
From the bells, bells, bells, bells

See page 195.

ORAL HUMOR *A type of humor achieved in writing through representing the actual speech of a character, often including mispronunciations, grammatical errors, and colorful expressions.*

See **Dialect.**

ORAL LITERATURE *Literature not written down but passed from generation to generation through performance or word-of-mouth.* Indian songs and **spirituals** are oral literature, as are traditonal **ballads.**

See page 371.

ORATORY *Formal public speaking and literature that grows out of public speeches.* Two famous **orations** are Patrick Henry's "Speech in the Virginia Convention" and Abraham Lincoln's "Gettysburg Address."

See page 368.

ORNATE STYLE *A highly elaborate style of writing popular in England and America in the seventeenth and eighteenth centuries.* Ornate style is characterized by difficult vocabulary, intricate sentence structure, complex figures of speech, and obscure allusions. Ornate style is usually contrasted with **plain style.**

See page 32.

OXYMORON *A figure of speech that combines opposite or contradictory ideas or terms, as in "sweet sorrow," "wise fool," "living death," and "honest thief."* An oxymoron suggests a **paradox,** but it does so very briefly, usually in two or three words.

PARABLE See **Allegory.**

PARADOX *A statement that reveals a kind of truth, although it seems at first to be self-contradictory and untrue.* Emily Dickinson uses a paradox in the title of one of her poems: "Much Madness Is Divinest Sense."

See page 232.

PARALLELISM *The use of phrases, clauses, or sentences that are similar or complementary in structure or in meaning.* These lines from Walt Whitman's "Beat! Beat! Drums!" include parallel phrases, sentence structures, and meanings:

Beat! beat! drums!—blow! bugles! blow!
Make no parley—stop for no expostulation,
Mind not the timid—mind not the weeper
or prayer,
Mind not the old man beseeching the young man.

See pages 104, 756, 882.

PARODY *The humorous imitation of a work of literature, art, or music.* A parody often achieves its humorous effect through the use of exaggeration or mockery. In literature, parody can be made of a plot, a character, a writing style, or a sentiment or theme.

Certain writers with distinctive styles are often the subjects of parody. In American literature, Walt Whitman, Ernest Hemingway, and Edgar Allan Poe have been parodied.

PATHOS *The quality in a work of literature that arouses a feeling of pity, or sorrow, or compassion in the reader.* The term is usually used to refer to situations in which innocent characters suffer through no fault of their own. Pathos is distinct from **sentimentality,** artificial or superficial emotion in a work of literature or art. Pathos is genuine, whereas sentimentality is false.

See pages 500, 785.

PERSONA *The person who speaks in a literary work, from the Latin word for* mask. In *A Modest Proposal,* a famous satire by the English writer Jonathan Swift, Swift adopts the persona of a "projector," a character who sounds like a modern economic planner.

PERSONIFICATION *A figure of speech in which something nonhuman is given human qualities.* In "Because I Could Not Stop for Death," Emily Dickinson personifies death by depicting it as a person who drives a carriage and makes stops for passengers.

See pages 110, 232, 756.

PERSUASION *The type of speaking or writing that is intended to make its audience adopt a certain opinion, or perform an action, or do both.* Persuasion is one of the major **forms of discourse.** Modern examples of persuasion include political speeches, television commercials, and newspaper editorials. Patrick Henry's "Speech in the Virginia Convention" and Thomas Paine's "The Crisis, Number 1" are major persuasive pieces from the American Revolutionary period.

See **Description, Narration, Exposition.**
See also pages 22, 59, 93, 96, 104.

PLAIN STYLE *A simple and clear style of writing which began as a revolt against ornate style.* The Puritans were the first advocates of plain style, which was in keeping with their plain way of life. The chief features of plain style are common vocabulary, simple sentence structure, clear and vivid images, and direct and precise statement. Plain style is exemplified in the writings of William Bradford and Benjamin Franklin, and it influenced such later American writers as Mark Twain, Sherwood Anderson, and Ernest Hemingway.

See page 32.

PLOT *The sequence of events or actions in a short story, novel, play, or narrative poem.* Plots may be simple or complicated, loosely constructed or close-knit. But every plot is made up of a series of incidents that are related to one another.

Conflict, a struggle of some kind, is the most important element of plot. Conflict may be **external** or **internal,** and there may be more than one form of conflict in a work. As the plot advances, we learn how the conflict is resolved, either through the action or through major changes in the attitudes or personalities of the characters.

Action is generally introduced by the **exposition,** information essential to understanding the situation. The action rises to a *crisis,* or **climax.** This movement is called the **rising action.** The **falling action,** which follows the crisis, shows a reversal of fortune for the protagonist. In a tragedy, this reversal leads to disaster; in a comedy, it leads to a happy ending.

The **dénouement,** or **resolution,** is the moment when the conflict ends and the outcome of the action is clear.

See pages 589, 934.

POINT OF VIEW *The vantage point from which a narrative is told.* There are two basic points of view. (1) In the **first-person point of view,** the story is told by one of the characters in his or her own words, and the reader is told only what this character knows and observes. An example is found in John Updike's "The Lucid Eye in Silver Town," which is narrated by an adult who recalls an incident from his youth. (2) In the **third-person point of view,** the narrator is not a character in the story at all. The third-person narrator might tell a story from a **limited point of view,** focusing on only one character in the story. Eudora Welty's "A Worn Path" is told by a third-person narrator, but it focuses on the thoughts and experiences of only one character, Phoenix Jackson. The third-person narrator might, on the other hand, be an all-knowing, or **omniscient,** observer who describes and comments on *all* the characters and actions in a story. Stephen Crane tells "The Open Boat" from this third-person omniscient point of view.

See pages 85, 727.

PROTAGONIST *The central character of a drama, novel, short story, or narrative poem.* The protagonist is the character on whom the action centers and with whom the reader sympathizes most. Often, the protagonist strives against an opponent, or **antagonist.** The protagonist may strive against other characters, as Daniel Webster strives to outwit the devil in a courtroom in "The Devil and Daniel Webster."

See page 936.

PUN *The use of a word or phrase to suggest two or more meanings at the same time, or the use of two different words or phrases that sound alike.* Puns are generally humorous. An example of the second type of pun is this statement by the nineteenth-century English poet and humorist Thomas Hood: "They went and told the sexton and the sexton tolled the bell."

QUATRAIN *Usually a stanza or poem of four lines.* However, a quatrain may also be any group of four lines unified by a rhyme scheme. Quatrains usually follow an *abab, abba,* or *abcb* rhyme scheme. Here is a quatrain from James Russell Lowell's "The Courtin'":

a God makes sech nights, all white an' *still*
b Fur 'z you can look or *listen,*
a Moonshine an' snow on field an' *hill,*
b All silence an' all *glisten.*

See page 304.

REALISM *The attempt in literature and art to represent life as it really is, without sentimentalizing or idealizing it.* Realistic writing often depicts the everyday life and speech of ordinary people.

See **Naturalism.**
See also pages 340, 447, 938.

REFRAIN *A word, phrase, line, or group of lines repeated regularly in a poem, usually at the end of each stanza.* Refrains are often used in **ballads** and other **narrative poems** to create a songlike effect and to help build suspense. Refrains can also serve to

emphasize a particular idea. Perhaps the most famous refrain in American literature is the line repeated at the end of several stanzas of Edgar Allan Poe's "The Raven":

Quoth the Raven, "Nevermore."

See pages 189, 386.

REQUIEM *A prayer, poem, or song for the repose of the dead.* An example of a requiem is Herman Melville's poem "Shiloh: A Requiem."

See page 294.

REVELATION *The focal point of many narratives.* In such narratives, all the details are organized to provide a moment of insight into a character or a situation. For example, in William Faulkner's "The Bear," the revelation occurs at the end of the story, when the boy begins to comprehend the true meaning of his experience hunting the great bear.

See page 708.

RHETORIC *The art of using language for persuasion.* Scholars have noted many rhetorical devices—elements of logic or of style that help persuade. One of the most common is the **rhetorical question,** a question suggesting its own answer or not requiring an answer. Patrick Henry uses rhetorical questions in his "Speech in the Virginia Convention":

They tell us, sir, that we are weak—unable to cope with so formidable an adversary. But when shall we be stronger? Will it be the next week, or the next year? Will it be when we are totally disarmed, and when a British guard shall be stationed in every house?

See pages 93, 882.

RHYME *The repetition of sounds in two or more words or phrases that appear close to each other in a poem.* Examples are *river-shiver, song-long,* and *leap-deep.* If the rhyme occurs at the ends of lines, it is called **end rhyme.** Here is an example from John Greenleaf Whittier's *Snowbound:*

All day the gusty north wind *bore*
The loosening drift its breath *before;*
Low circling round its southern *zone,*
The sun through dazzling snow-mist *shone.*

If rhyme occurs within a line, it is called **internal rhyme.** Here is an example of internal rhyme from Edgar Allan Poe's "The Bells":

To the *rhyming* and the *chiming* of the bells!

Approximate rhyme, also called **slant rhyme** or **off rhyme,** is rhyme in which the final sounds of the words are similar but not identical (as opposed to *exact rhyme*). *Cook-look* is an exact rhyme; *cook-lack* is an approximate rhyme. Ralph Waldo Emerson uses approximate rhyme in his poem "Concord Hymn":

> On this green bank, by this soft stream,
> > We set today a votive *stone;*
> That memory may their deed redeem,
> > When, like our sires, our sons are *gone.*

The pattern of end rhymes in a poem is called **rhyme scheme.** A poem's rhyme scheme may be identified by assigning the letter *a* to the first rhyme, the letter *b* to the second rhyme, and so forth. For example, the first stanza of Poe's "To Helen" has an *ababb* rhyme scheme:

a	Helen, thy beauty is to *me*
b	Like those Nicéan barks of *yore,*
a	That gently, o'er a perfumed *sea,*
b	The weary, way-worn wanderer *bore*
b	To his own native *shore.*

See pages 189, 232, 386, 834.

RHYTHM *The arrangement of stressed and unstressed syllables into a pattern.* Rhythm is most apparent in poetry, though it is part of all good writing. Rhythm often gives a poem a distinct musical quality, as in Sidney Lanier's "The Marshes of Glynn":

> Vanishing, swerving, evermore curving again
> > into sight,
> Softly the sand beach wavers away to a dim gray
> > looping of light.

Poets also use rhythm to echo meaning. In these lines from Edgar Allan Poe's "The Bells," a pounding rhythm suggests the persistent clanging of bells:

> Bells, bells, bells—
> In the clamor and the clangor of the bells!

Some poets who compose **free verse** use a kind of **organic rhythm,** which grows naturally out of the thoughts and feelings expressed in the poem.

See pages 157, 764.

RISING ACTION See **Plot.**

ROMANTICISM *A movement that flourished in literature, philosophy, music, and art in Western culture during most of the nineteenth century, beginning as a revolt against classicism.* There have been different varieties of Romanticism in different times and places. Romanticism essentially upholds feeling and the imagination over reason and fact. Whereas **realism** attempts to show life as it really is, Romanticism attempts to show life as we might imagine it to be, or think it should be. Romanticism favors the picturesque, the emotional, the exotic, and the mysterious. One kind of Romanticism glorifies nature and upholds the notion that people are basically good and perfectible, as in the **transcendentalism** of Ralph Waldo Emerson and Henry David Thoreau. Another kind investigates the dark side of the human soul, as in the short stories of Edgar Allan Poe.

See pages 119, 340.

RUN-ON LINE *A line of poetry that has no pause at its end but "runs on" naturally to the next line.* Run-on lines serve to vary the rhythm in a poem and to prevent a sing-song effect. In the following lines from Henry Wadsworth Longfellow's "The Tide Rises, the Tide Falls," the first is a run-on line:

> The morning breaks; the steeds in their stalls
> Stamp and neigh as the hostler calls

See **End-Stopped Line.**

SARCASM See **Irony.**

SATIRE *A kind of writing that holds up to ridicule or contempt the weaknesses and wrongdoings of individuals, groups, institutions, or humanity in general.* The aim of satirists is to set a moral standard for society, and they attempt to persuade the reader to see their point of view through the force of laughter. The most famous satirical work in English is Jonathan Swift's *Gulliver's Travels,* published in 1726, which satirizes the English people, and people in general, in the course of describing Gulliver's fantastic adventures. For an example of American satire, see John Dos Passos' "Tin Lizzie."

See page 816.

SCANSION *The analysis of verse in terms of meter.* Meter is measured in units called **feet.** A foot consists of one stressed syllable and, usually, one or two unstressed syllables. A line of poetry is scanned by dividing it into feet and marking the stressed and unstressed syllables. Here is a scanned line from William Cullen Bryant's "Thanatopsis":

> So live, | that when | thy sum | mons comes | to join

There are five feet in this line, and the rhythm is

iambic (**iambic pentameter**). The other principal kinds of feet are the **trochee, the anapest,** and the **dactyl.** In addition to **pentameter,** the terms describing the number of feet in a line are **monometer** (one foot), **dimeter** (two feet), **trimeter** (three feet), **tetrameter** (four feet), and **hexameter** (six feet).

See **Foot, Meter.**
See also page 319.

SESTET   *A six-line poem or stanza.* Usually the term **sestet** refers to the last six lines of an **Italian sonnet.** The first eight lines of an Italian sonnet form an **octave.**

See **Sonnet.**
See also page 304.

SETTING   *The time and place in which events in a short story, novel, play, or narrative poem occur.* A setting may simply serve as a physical background, but a skillful writer may use the setting to establish a particular atmosphere in a work. For example, both Stephen Crane in "The Open Boat" and Jack London in "To Build a Fire" establish settings in their opening paragraphs; in both stories, the setting creates an appropriate atmosphere of bleakness and isolation.

See page 673.

SIMILE   *A figure of speech comparing two essentially unlike things through the use of a specific word of comparison, such as* like, as, than, *or* resembles. Henry Wadsworth Longfellow uses a simile in the following lines from his poem "The Arsenal at Springfield" to convey the look of stacked weapons in an arsenal:

This is the Arsenal. From floor to ceiling,
Like a huge organ, rise the burnished arms.

See pages 88, 333, 781.

SLICE OF LIFE   See **Realism.**

SOLILOQUY   *An extended speech, usually in a drama, delivered by a character alone onstage.* The character reveals his or her innermost thoughts and feelings directly to the audience, as if thinking aloud. Soliloquies are used occasionally by prose writers. For example, Captain Ahab delivers several soliloquies in Herman Melville's novel *Moby-Dick.*

SONNET   *A lyric poem of fourteen lines, usually written in rhymed iambic pentameter.* Sonnets vary in structure and rhyme scheme, but are generally of two types: the **Petrarchan,** or **Italian, sonnet** and the

Shakespearean, or **English, sonnet.** A sonnet usually expresses a single idea or theme.

The Italian sonnet is a form that originated in Italy in the thirteenth century. The Italian sonnet has two parts, an **octave** (eight lines) and a **sestet** (six lines). It is usually rhymed *abbaabba cdecde.* The two parts of the Italian sonnet play off each other in a variety of ways. Sometimes the octave raises a question which the sestet answers. Sometimes the sestet opposes what the octave says or extends it.

The Italian sonnet is often called the Petrarchan sonnet because the Italian poet Francesco Petrarch used it so extensively. Petrarch dedicated more than three hundred sonnets to a woman named Laura.

The Shakespearean sonnet, a form made famous by William Shakespeare, consists of three **quatrains** (four-line stanzas) and a concluding **couplet** (two rhyming lines), with the rhyme scheme *abab cdcd efef gg.* In a typical Shakespearean sonnet, each quatrain is a variant of the basic idea and the couplet draws a conclusion about it.

See page 304.

SPIRITUAL   *A folk song, usually on a religious theme.* Many moving spirituals were written by black slaves. These spirituals have two levels of meaning; they express a yearning for both spiritual salvation and deliverance from slavery.

See page 361.

STAGING (or STAGECRAFT)   *All the devices except dialogue which a dramatist uses to communicate to an audience.* Important elements of staging include *scenery, costume, gesture* and *movement,* and *lighting.*

See page 936.

STANZA   *A unit of a poem that is longer than a single line.* Many stanzas have a fixed pattern—that is, the same number of lines and the same rhyme scheme. "The Beautiful Changes" by Richard Wilbur has a regular pattern. Each of the three stanzas has three lines with the rhyme scheme *abacdc.* Some poems do not repeat the same pattern in each stanza. Yet, each group of lines is still referred to as a stanza. "Song" by Adrienne Rich has four stanzas, but there is no regular pattern of line length or rhyme scheme.

A stanza may be as short as the **couplet,** two rhyming lines. The **tercet,** or triplet, is a stanza of three lines, often with one rhyme.

The **quatrain** is a four-line stanza with many patterns of rhyme and rhythm. Emily Dickinson excelled in this form. The typical ballad stanza is a quatrain in which only the second and fourth lines rhyme.

STEREOTYPE See **Character.**

STREAM OF CONSCIOUSNESS *The style of writing that attempts to imitate the natural flow of a character's thoughts, feelings, reflections, memories, and mental images, as the character experiences them.* The stream-of-consciousness technique enables a writer to delve deeply into a character's psychology and to record fully a character's consciousness—not only *what* the character thinks, but also *how* the character thinks. As a record of the spontaneous flow of a character's consciousness, this technique makes no attempt to be logical or even clear. It simply attempts to follow the mind wherever it goes. Katherine Anne Porter uses the stream-of-consciousness technique to present Granny Weatherall's thoughts in "The Jilting of Granny Weatherall."

See pages 598, 781.

STYLE *A writer's characteristic way of writing, determined by the choice of words, the arrangement of words in sentences, and the relationship of the sentences to one another.* Thus, one writer, such as Abraham Lincoln, may write long, complex sentences, while another, such as Ernest Hemingway, writes terse ones. One writer may use few adjectives, while another uses many. Style also refers to the particular way in which a writer uses **imagery, figurative language,** and **rhythm.** Style is the sum total of qualities and characteristics that distinguish the works of one writer from those of another.

See **Ornate Style, Plain Style, Vernacular.**
See also pages 32, 96, 347, 625.

SUSPENSE *The quality of a short story, novel, play, or narrative poem that makes the reader or audience uncertain or tense about the outcome of events.* Suspense makes readers ask, "What will happen next?" or "How will this work out?" and impels them to read on. Suspense is greatest when it focuses attention on a sympathetic character. Thus, the most familiar kind of suspense involves a character in mortal danger: hanging from the ledge of a tall building; tied to railroad tracks as a train approaches; or alone in an old house, ascending a staircase to open the attic door. But suspense may simply arise from curiosity, as when a character must make a decision, or seek an explanation for something.

SYMBOL *Any object, person, place, or action that has a meaning in itself and that also stands for something larger than itself, such as a quality, an attitude, a belief, or a value.* A rose is often a symbol of love or beauty; a skull is often a symbol of death; spring and winter often symbolize youth and old age; a dove usually symbolizes peace. In Nathaniel Hawthorne's story "The Minister's Black Veil," the black veil of the title is a symbol of secret sin.

See pages 181, 255, 293, 589.

SYMBOLISM *A literary movement that arose in France in the last half of the nineteenth century and that greatly influenced many English writers, particularly poets, of the twentieth century.* To the Symbolist poets, an emotion is indefinite and therefore difficult to communicate. Symbolist poets tend to avoid any direct statement of meaning. Instead, they work through emotionally powerful symbols that suggest meaning and mood.

SYNECDOCHE (sĭ-nĕk′də-kē) *A figure of speech in which part of a thing is used to stand for or suggest the whole.* An example is T. S. Eliot's use of "faces" to stand for "people" in "The Love Song of J. Alfred Prufrock."

TALL TALE *A humorous story that is outlandishly exaggerated.* Many tall tales are a part of folk literature, and many are associated with the American frontier of the early nineteenth century. Tall tales relate superhuman feats of strength, stamina, and cunning. One special form of the tall tale is the **brag,** in which the person bragging makes incredible claims.

See pages 52, 398.

TANKA *A Japanese verse form consisting of five lines and thirty-one syllables.* The first line contains five syllables; the second line, seven; the third line, five; the fourth line, seven; and the fifth line, seven. Like a related form, the **haiku,** the tanka often focuses on an image that suggests a thought or emotion, as in the following example:

The grass sends agents,
Their heads barely raised, to scout
The ground. Then it strikes!
Green spears march from lawn to lawn
Seizing the pliable sod.

See page 759.

TERCET   See **Stanza.**

THEME   *The general idea or insight about life that a writer wishes to convey in a literary work.* Not all literary works can be said to express a theme. Theme generally is not a concern in those works that are told primarily for entertainment; it is of importance in those literary works that comment on or present some insight about the meaning of life.

In some literary works the theme is expressed directly, but more often theme is *implicit*—that is, it must be dug out and thought about. A simple theme can often be stated in a single sentence. But sometimes a literary work is rich and complex, and a paragraph or even an essay is needed to state the theme.

See page 639.

TONE   *The attitude a writer takes toward his or her subject, characters, and readers.* Abraham Lincoln, in "The Gettysburg Address," writes about war in a solemn tone. Mark Twain, in *Life on the Mississippi,* writes of his personal experiences in a humorous, affectionate tone. Through tone, a writer can amuse, anger, or shock the reader. Often the reader must figure out a writer's tone in order to understand a literary work.

See page 173.

TRAGEDY   *In general, a literary work in which the protagonist meets an unhappy or disastrous end.* Unlike **comedy,** tragedy often depicts the problems of a central character who is of significant or dignified stature. Through a series of events, this main character, the **tragic hero** or **heroine,** is brought to a final downfall. The causes of this downfall vary. In traditional dramas, the cause can be fate, a flaw in character, or an error in judgment. In modern dramas, the causes range from a moral or psychological weakness to the evils of society. The tragic protagonist, though defeated, usually gains a measure of wisdom or self-awareness.

See **Comedy.**
See also page 936.

TRANSCENDENTALISM   *A philosophy which holds that basic truths can be reached through intuition rather than through reason.* To arrive at such truths, according to transcendentalist philosophy, people must go beyond, or *transcend,* what their reason and their senses tell them. Transcendentalist thinkers, influenced by European **Romanticism,** stress the beauty of nature, the essential divinity of all people, and the primary importance of the human spirit. Transcendentalism was developed in the 1830s and 1840s by Ralph Waldo Emerson, Henry David Thoreau, and the thinkers who met with them in Concord, Massachusetts.

See page 208.

TROCHEE   *A poetic foot consisting of a stressed syllable followed by an unstressed syllable (, ⌣).*

UNDERSTATEMENT   *A restrained statement in which less is said than is meant.* If it is ten degrees below zero and someone says, "It's a bit cool out today," that person is making an understatement.

UTOPIAN NOVEL   *A type of novel which arose from the technological revolution preceding World War I, depicting a perfect future society achieved through science.*

VERNACULAR   *The everyday spoken language of people in a particular locality, and writing that imitates or suggests such language.*

See pages 347, 396, 403.

VOICE   *A language style adopted by an author to create the effect of a particular speaker.*

GLOSSARY

Strictly speaking, the word *glossary* means a collection of technical, obscure, or foreign words found in a certain field of work. Of course, the words in this glossary are not "technical, obscure, or foreign," but are those that might present difficulty as you read the selections in this textbook.

Many words in the English language have several meanings. In this glossary, the meanings given are the ones that apply to the words as they are used in the selections in the textbook. Words closely related in form and meaning are generally listed together in one entry (**capricious** and **capriciousness**), and the definition is given for the first form. Related words that generally appear as separate entries in dictionaries are listed separately (**contrivance** and **contrive**). Regular adverbs (ending in *-ly*) are defined in their adjective form, with the adverb form shown at the end of the definition.

The following abbreviations are used:

adj. adjective	*n.* noun
adv. adverb	*v.* verb

A

abash (ə-băsh′) *v.* To disconcert.—**abashed** *adj.*

abate (ə-bāt′) *v.* To reduce in amount or degree.

abdicate (ăb′dĭ-kāt′) *v.* To give up officially.

aberration (ăb′ə-rā′shən) *n.* A deviation from the proper or ordinary.

abeyance (ə-bā′əns) *n.* A temporary discontinuance.

abhor (ăb-hôr′) *v.* To despise.—**abhorrence** *n.*

abide (ə-bīd′) *v.* **1.** To tolerate. **2.** To remain.

abject (ăb′jĕkt′, ăb-jĕkt′) *adj.* Miserable; wretched.—**abjectness** *n.*

abjure (ăb-jōōr′) *v.* To reject.

abominable (ə-bŏm′ə-nə-bəl) *adj.* Loathsome.

aboriginal (ab′ə-rĭj′ə-nəl) *adj.* Native; from earliest times.

aborigine (ăb′ə-rĭj′ə-nē′) *n.* The native inhabitant of a region.

abound (ə-bound′) *v.* To be large in number.

abrasion (ə-brā′zhən) *n.* A rubbing or scraping.

absolute (ab′sə-lōot) *adj.* Not to be doubted.

absolve (ăb-zŏlv′,-sŏlv′) *v.* To free from responsibilities.

abyss (ə-bĭs′) *n.* An infinite void.

acclivity (ə-klĭv′ə-tē) *n.* An upward slope.

accolade (ăk′ə-lād′, ăk′ə-läd′) *n.* A ceremony or symbol of achievement or approval.

accommodate (ə-kom′ə-dāt′) *v.* To provide.

accouterment (ə-kōō′tər-mənt) *n.* Equipment.

accredit (ə-krĕd′ĭt) *v.* To acknowledge.—**accredited** *adj.*

acquiesce (ăk′wē-ĕs′) *v.* To comply without protest.

acquiescence (ăk′wē-ĕs′əns) *n.* Agreement without protest.

adduce (ə-dōōs′, ə-dyōōs′, ă-) *v.* To present for consideration.

admonish (ăd-mŏn′ĭsh) *v.* To warn.

admonition (ăd′mə-nĭsh′ən) *n.* Warning.

adversity (ăd-vûr′sə-tē) *n.* Misfortune.

advert (ăd-vûrt′) *v.* To refer; call attention.

affable (af′ə-bəl) *adj.* Friendly; agreeable.

affinity (ə-fĭn′ə-tē) *n.* **1.** Close connection. **2.** Sympathy.

affluence (ăf′lōō-əns) *n.* Wealth.

affront (ə-frŭnt′) *v.* To offend openly.—**affronted** *adj.*

aforesaid (ə-fôr′sĕd′, ə-fōr′-) *adj.* Previously mentioned.

agate (ăg′ĭt) *n.* A type of quartz with clouded or striped coloring.

aggregate (ăg′rə-gĭt) *n.* Total.

agile (ăj′əl, ăj′īl) *adj.* Able to move quickly and carefully.—**agilely** *adv.*

ague (ā′gyōō) *n.* A feverish condition, marked by severe, recurring chills.

alacrity (ə-lăk′rə-tē) *n.* Eagerness.

alarum (ə-lär′əm, ə-lăr′-) *v. Archaic or poetic.* To sound a warning.

alleviate (ə-lē′vē-āt′) *v.* To relieve or reduce.

alleviation (ə-lē′vē-ā′shən) *n.* Relief.

allure (ə-lōōr′) *v.* To tempt.—**allurement** *n.*

amber (ăm′bər) *n.* An extremely hard, brownish-yellow, glasslike substance often used to make jewelry.

ambiguity (ăm′bĭ-gyōō′ə-tē) *n.* Uncertainty; that which has more than one possible meaning.

amethyst (ăm′ə-thĭst) *n.* A purple variety of transparent quartz used in jewelry.

amiss (ə-mĭs′) *adj.* Not in proper order.—*Take amiss.* To resent.

amity (ăm′ə-tē) *n.* Friendship.

ample (ăm′pəl) *adj.* Abundant.

amply (ăm′plē) *adv.* Sufficiently.

amulet (ăm′yə-lĭt) *n.* An object worn for its supposed magic powers to ward off harm or evil.

anarchy (ăn′ər-kē) *n.* Total absence of political authority and order.

anathema (ə-năth′ə-mə) *n.* A curse.

andiron (ănd′ī′ərn) *n.* One of two metal supports used to hold logs in a fireplace.

anesthetic (ăn′ĭs-thĕt′ĭk) *n.* A drug that induces loss of feeling or unconsciousness.

annals (ăn′əlz) *n. pl.* Historical records.

ă pat/ā pay/âr care/ä father/b, **bib**/ch **church**/d **deed**/ĕ **pet**/ē be/f **fife**/g **gag**/h **hat**/hw **which**/ĭ **pit**/ī **pie**/îr **pier**/j **judge**/k **kick**/l **lid**, needle/m **mum**/n no, sudden/ng **thing**/ŏ **pot**/ō **toe**/ô **paw**, for/oi **noise**/ou **out**/ōō **took**/ōō **boot**/p **pop**/r **roar**/s **sauce**/sh **ship**, dish/t **tight**/th **thin**, path/*th* **this**, bathe/ū **cut**/ûr **urge**/v **valve**/w **with**/y **yes**/z **zebra**, size/zh **vision**/ə **about**, item, edible, gallop, circus/à *Fr.* **ami**/œ *Fr.* **feu**, *Ger.* **schön**/ü *Fr.* **tu**, *Ger.* **über**/кн *Ger.* **ich**, *Scot.* **loch**/N *Fr.* **bon**.

annex (ə-nĕks′, ăn′ĕks′) v. To attach.

annuity (ə-nōō′ə-tē, ə-nyōō′-) n. An investment that guarantees regular payments for a specified period of time, often the holder's lifetime.

annul (ə-nŭl′) v. To cancel.

anomalous (ə-nŏm′ə-ləs) adj. Abnormal.

anomaly (ə-nŏm′ə-lē) n. An irregularity.

antagonize (ăn-tăg′ə-nīz′) v. To counteract; make an enemy of.

ante (ăn′tē) v. To pay one's share.—used with *up*.

anthracite (ăn′thrə-sīt′) n. A type of hard coal that burns cleanly and gives much heat.

anthropology (ăn′thrə-pŏl′ə-jē) n. Study of development and behavior of human beings.

antipathy (ăn-tĭp′ə-thē) n. A deep dislike.

apace (ə-pās′) adv. Quickly.

apathetic (ăp′ə-thĕt′ĭk) adj. Indifferent.—**apathetically** adv.

apocryphal (ə-pŏk′rə-fəl) adj. Fictitious; questionable.

apoplexy (ăp′ə-plĕk′sē) n. A stroke; sudden paralysis.

apparition (ăp′ə-rĭsh′ən) n. A sudden, extraordinary appearance.

appease (ə-pēz′) v. To calm.—**appeasingly** adv. Rare.

appellation (ăp′ə-lā′shən) n. A name.

append (ə-pĕnd′) v. To add.

appendage (ə-pĕn′dĭj) n. An attached object.

appraisal (ə-prā′səl) n. Judgment of value.

apprehension (ăp′rĭ-hĕn′shən) n. 1. Fear; dread. 2. Understanding.

apprise (ə-prīz′) v. To inform.

approbation (ăp′rə-bā′shən) n. Approval.

appropriation (ə-prō′prē-ā′shən) n. Taking possession for a specific purpose.

arabesque (ăr′ə-bĕsk′) adj. Fanciful; elaborate.

arbitrary (är′bə-trĕr′ē) adj. Without design or apparent reason.

arbor (är′bər) n. A shaded area, usually in a garden.

arduous (är′jōō-əs) adj. Difficult; strenuous.

aromatic (ăr′ə-măt′ĭk) adj. Fragrant.

array (ə-rā′) n. An impressive military grouping.

arroyo (ə-roi′ō) n. A dry gully cut by a stream.

articulate (är-tĭk′yə-lĭt) adj. Distinct.

artifice (är′tə-fĭs) n. An ingenious or artful trick.

ascertain (ăs′ər-tān′) v. To find out; discover.

ascribe (ə-skrīb′) v. To attribute to a particular cause.

ashen (ăsh′ən) adj. The color of ashes; pale.

askance (ə-skăns′) adv.—**1.** With suspicion.—**2.** With a side glance.

asperity (ăs-pĕr′ə-tē) n. Sharpness.

aspiration (ăs′pə-rā′shən) n. Ambition.

assail (ə-sāl′) v. To attack.

assiduous (ə-sĭj′ōō-əs) adj. Diligent.—**assiduously** adv.

assimilate (əsĭm′ə-lāt′) v. To make similar.

asunder (ə-sŭn′dər) adv. Into pieces.

attribute (ăt′rə-byōōt′) n. Distinctive quality or feature.

audacious (ô-dā′shəs) adj. Bold; insolent.

audacity (ô-dăs′ə-tē) n. Boldness; impudence.

aught (ôt) n. Anything.

august (ô-gŭst′) adj. Impressive.

austere (ô-stîr′) adj. Plain; barren.

automaton (ô-tŏm′ə-tən, -tŏn′) n. Robot.

avail (ə-vāl′) v. To be of use.

avarice (ăv′ə-rĭs) n. Desire for wealth.

averse (ə-vûrs′) adj. Opposed.

aversion (ə-vûr′zhən, -shən) n. An intensely disliked person or thing.

avert (ə-vûrt′) v. To prevent.

axiom (ăk′sē-əm) n. A self-evident truth; a statement accepted as true.

azure (ăzh′ər) adj. Light blue; the color of the sky.

B

babel (bā′bəl, băb′əl) n. A mixture of languages, voices, or sounds.

balk (bôk) v. To frustrate.

balmy (bä′mē) adj. Pleasant and mild.

banal (bə-năl′, nä′, bā′nəl) adj. Trite; predictable.

bask (băsk, bäsk) v. To enjoy warm or pleasant feelings.

bayou (bī′ōō, bī′ō) n. A slow, marshy body of water that is a tributary to a lake or river.

becoming (bĭ-kŭm′ĭng) adj. Suitable; proper.

bedraggle (bĭ-drăg′əl) v. To make limp.—**bedraggled** adj.

beguile (bĭ-gīl′) v. 1. To deceive. 2. To pass effortlessly and pleasantly.

beholden (bĭ-hōl′dən) adj. Obliged.

behoof (bĭ-hōōf′) n. Benefit.

belated (bĭ-lā′tĭd) adj. Late.

bellicose (bĕl′ĭ-kōs′) adj. Hostile.

belligerent (bə-lĭj′ər-ənt) adj. Anxious to quarrel or fight.

benediction (bĕn′ə-dĭk′shən) n. A blessing.

beneficent (bə-nĕf′ə-sənt) adj. Kind; charitable.

benevolence (bə-nĕv′ə-ləns) n. Kindliness.

benign (bĭ-nīn′) adj. Gentle.

bequeath (bĭ-kwēth′, -kwēth′) v. To hand down.

bereave (bĭ-rēv′) v. 1. To deprive. 2. To leave in a mournful state, especially by death.—**bereaved** or **bereft** adj.

beseech (bĭ-sēch′) v. To request earnestly.

betimes (bĭ-tīmz′) adv. Early.

bittern (bĭt′ərn) n. A wading bird, noted for its deep, resounding cry.

blasphemous (blăs′fə-məs) adj. Disrespectful to God; irreverent.

blasphemy (blăs′fə-mē) n. Disrespectful speech or action concerning God.

blatant (blā′tənt) adj. Obvious.—**blatantly** adv.

blithe (blīth, blīth) adj. Cheerful; carefree.

bode (bōd) v. To predict.

boding (bō′dĭng) adj. Ominous.

boisterous (boi′stər-əs, -strəs) adj. Unrestrained; turbulent.

bookish (bōōk′ĭsh) adj. Studious; dull and pedantic.

boon (bōōn) adj. Merry; fun-loving.

bower (bou′ər) n. Private dwelling.

bracing (brā′sĭng) adj. Refreshing; stimulating.

bray (brā) v. To make a loud, unpleasant sound.—**braying** adj.

brazier (brā′zhər) n. An open pan used to hold burning coals.

brethren (brĕth′rən) n. pl. Archaic. Brothers.

brogue (brōg) n. A heavy Irish accent.

brood (brōōd) n. Children.

bullock (bōōl′ək) n. A young bull.

bullyrag (bōōl′ē-răg′) v. To mistreat; bully.

bulwark (bōōl′wərk, bŭl′-, -wôrk′) n. A strong defense.

buoyant (boi′ənt, boo′yənt) *adj.* Lighthearted; cheerful.
burly (bûr′lē) *adj.* Heavy; muscular.
buxom (bŭk′səm) *adj.* Healthy; shapely.

C

cache (kăsh) *v.* To hide for future use.
cadaverous (kə-dăv′ər-əs) *adj.* Resembling a corpse.—**cadaverousness** *n.*—**cadaverously** *adv.*
cajole (kə-jōl′) *v.* To coax by flattering.—**cajolery** *n.*
calculable (kăl′kyə-lə-bəl) *adj.* Capable of being estimated or calculated.
calico (kăl′ĭ-kō) *n.* A plain, coarse cotton cloth.
canny (kăn′ē) *adj.* Shrewd and cautious.—**canniness** *n.*
canonize (kăn′ə-nīz′) *v.* To formally pronounce a saint.
caper (kā′pər) *n.* An escapade.
caprice (kə-prēs′) *n.* Impulse; unexpected or willful behavior.
capricious (kə-prĭsh′əs, -prē′shəs) *adj.* Tending to change suddenly for no apparent reason.—**capriciousness** *n.*
carbuncle (kär′bŭng′kəl) *n.* Boil.
careen (kə-rĭn′) *v.* To rush at high speed.
carmine (kär′mĭn, -mīn′) *n.* A purplish-red or crimson color.
carrion (kăr′ē-ən) *n.* Dead and decomposing flesh.—*adj.* Carrion-eating.
casement (kās′mənt) *n.* A window that opens on side hinges.
catamount (kăt′ə-mount′) *n.* Any wild cat.
cataract (kăt′ə-răkt′) *n.* A downpour or deluge.
caulk (kôk) *v.* To make waterproof by filling cracks with tar or a tarlike substance.
cavort (kə-vôrt′) *v.* To frolic.
celestial (sə-lĕs′chəl) *adj.* Divine.
celibacy (sĕl′ə-bə-sē) *n.* Condition of being unmarried.
censer (sĕn′sər) *n.* A vessel in which incense is burned.
censure (sĕn′shər) *v.* To criticize severely; scold.
cerements (sîr′ə-məntz) *n.* Burial clothes; shroud.
ceremonial (sĕr′ə-mō′nē-əl) *adj.* Formal; appropriate to a ceremony.
certitude (sûr′tə-tood′, -tyood′) *n.* Absolute sureness.
cessation (sĕ-sā′shən) *n.* A termination.
chafe (chāf) *v.* To warm by rubbing.
chaff (chăf) *n.* Grain husks separated in threshing.
chaplet (chăp′lĭt) *n.* A wreath or garland.
chasten (chā′sən) *v.* To refine.—**chastened** *adj.*
chastise (chăs-tīz′) *v.* To scold or punish.
chide (chīd) *v.* To scold.
cinch (sĭnch) *v.* To tighten the saddle.
circumspect (sur′kəm-spekt′) *adj.* Heedful; careful.
civility (sə-vĭl′ə-tē) *n.* Politeness.
clandestine (klăn-dĕs′tən) *adj.* Secret.
clerical (klĕr′ĭ-kəl) *adj.* Characteristic of the clergy.
cloven (klō′vən) *adj.* Split, as by an ax.
cloy (kloi) *v.* To fill to excess.
coalesce (kō′ə-lĕs′) *v.* To merge into a whole.

coffer (kô′fər, kŏf′ər) *n.* Strongbox.
cohere (kō-hîr′) *v.* To form a united whole.
cohort (kō′hôrt′) *n.* Group of soldiers.
collocation (kŏl′ō-kā′shən) *n.* An arrangement.
comely (kŭm′lē) *adj.* Attractive.—**comeliness** *n.*
commendable (kə-mĕnd′ə-bəl) *adj.* Deserving approval.
commendation (kŏm′ən-dā′shən) *n.* Praise.
commensurate (kə-mĕn′sə-rĭt, -shə-rĭt) *adj.* Equal to.
commingle (kə-mĭng′gəl) *v.* To mix together.
commiserate (kə-mĭz′ə-rāt′) *v.* To express pity for.—**commiseratingly** *adv.*
commiseration (kə-mĭz′ə-rā′shən) *n.* Expression of sympathy.
commodious (kə-mō′dē-əs) *adj.* Convenient.
communion (kə-myoon′yən) *n.* A profound understanding of and involvement with another person or thing.
compacted (kəm-păkt′əd) *adj.* Closely arranged; compressed.
complacent (kəm-plā′sənt) *adj.* Obliging; calm.—**complacently** *adv.*
complaisant (kəm-plā′sənt, -zənt, kom′plā-zănt′) *adj.* Agreeable; wishing to please.
complement (kŏm′plə-mənt) *v.* To add the part needed to complete a whole.
compliance (kəm-plī′əns) *n.* Giving in to others.
complicity (kəm-plĭs′ə-tē) *n.* Involvement in wrongdoing.
comport (kəm-pôrt′) *v.* To agree.
comprise (kəm-prīz′) *v.* To include.
compromise (kŏm′prə-mīz′) *v.* To endanger one's reputation.
concentric (kən-sĕn′trĭk) *adj.* Having a common center.
concert (kŏn′sûrt) *n.* Agreement.
concision (kən-sĭzh′ən) *n.* Pointedness.
concourse (kŏn′kôrs, -kōrs, kŏng′-) *n.* Crowd; throng.
condescend (kŏn′dĭ-sĕnd′) *v.* To deal with people as if they were inferior.—**condescending** *adj.*
condescension (kŏn′dĭ-sĕn′shən) *n.* Coming down to the level of one's inferiors.
congenial (kən-jēn′yəl) *adj.* Friendly.—**congeniality** *n.*
conjectural (kən-jĕk′chər-əl) *adj.* Characterized by theorizing or guesswork.
conjecture (kən-jĕk′chər) *n.* Guesswork. *v.* To guess.
conjurer (kŏn′jər-ər, kŭn′-) *n.* A magician.
connivance (kə-nī′vəns) *n.* A scheme.
consecrate (kŏn′sə-krāt′) *v.* To declare as sacred.
consign (kən-sīn′) *v.* To hand over; entrust.
consolation (kŏn′sə-lā′shən) *n.* Giving of comfort.
constitute (kŏn′stə-toot′, -tyoot′) *v.* To make up; compose.
constrain (kən-strān′) *v.* To compel or force.
consummate (kŏn′sə-māt′) *v.* To complete.
consumptive (kən-sŭmp-tĭv) *adj.* **1.** Wasteful. **2.** Thin, as though afflicted with consumption, or tuberculosis.
contemn (kən-tĕm′) *v.* To treat with contempt.
contemporaneous (kən-tĕm′pə-rā′nē-əs) *adj.* Occurring at the same time.
contention (kən-tĕn′shən) *n.* Discord; controversy.

ă pat/ā pay/âr care/ä father/b, bib/ch church/d deed/ē pet/ē be/f fife/g gag/h hat/hw which/ĭ pit/ī pie/îr pier/j judge/k kick/l lid, needle/ m mum/n no, sudden/ng thing/ŏ pot/ō toe/ô paw, for/oi noise/ou out/oo took/oo boot/p pop/r roar/s sauce/sh ship, dish/t tight/th thin, path/th this, bathe/ū cut/ûr urge/v valve/w with/y yes/z zebra, size/zh vision/ə about, item, edible, gallop, circus/à *Fr.* ami/œ *Fr.* feu, *Ger.* schön/ü *Fr.* tu, *Ger.* über/кн *Ger.* ich, *Scot.* loch/ɴ *Fr.* bon.

contingency (kən-tĭn′jən-sē) *n.* A possibility.

continuum (kən-tĭn′yōō -əm) *n.* A continuous, unbroken whole.

contrivance (kən-trī′vəns) *n.* Device or plan.

contrive (kən-trīv′) *v.* To manage cleverly.

convalescent (kŏn′və-lĕs′ənt) *n.* A person recovering from an illness.

convex (kŏn′vĕks, kən-vĕks′) *adj.* Curving outward.

conviction (kən-vĭk′shən) *n.* Belief.

convivial (kən-vĭv′ē-əl) *adj.* Festive.—**convivially** *adv.*

convulse (kən-vŭls′) *v.* To agitate; cause to shake.

coquetry (kō′kə-trē, kō-kĕt′rē) *n.* Flirting.

cordial (kôr′jəl) *n.* A stimulating substance.

cornice (kôr′nĭs) *n.* A projecting, decorative molding along the top of a wall or building.

corpulent (kôr′pyə-lĕnt) *adj.* Fat.

corrode (kə-rōd′) *v.* To consume; gnaw.

cosmopolitan (kŏz′mə-pŏl′ə-tən) *adj.* Familiar with a wide variety of people and places.

countenance (koun′tə-nəns) *n.* **1.** Approval. **2.** The face. *v.* To give approval to.

covet (kŭv′ĭt) *v.* To desire keenly.

craven (crā′vən) *adj.* Extremely cowardly.

credence (krē′dəns) *n.* Belief.

credulity (krĭ-dōō′lə-tē, -dyōō′lə-tē) *n.* A tendency to believe easily.

crimp (krĭmp) *v.* To make wrinkled or wavy.—**crimped** *adj.*

crypt (krĭpt) *n.* An underground vault, often used as a burial place.

cryptic (krĭp′tĭk) *adj.* Mysterious.

crystalline (krĭs′tə-lĭn) *adj.* Clear and dazzling, like crystal.

cumulative (kyōōm′yə-lā′tĭv, -yə-lə-tĭv) *adj.* Accumulated.

cursory (kûr′sə-rē) *adj.* Hasty; done rapidly with little attention to detail.

cynical (sĭn′ĭ-kəl) *adj.* Distrustful of people's motives, actions, or statements.

D

damask (dăm′əsk) *adj.* Made from damask, a woven, patterned fabric used for draperies and furniture covering.

daunt (dônt, dänt) *v.* To frighten or intimidate.

dauntless (dônt′lĭs, dänt′-) *adj.* Fearless; bold.

debauchee (dĕb′ô-chē′, -shē, dĭ-bô′chē) *n.* One who pursues pleasure excessively.

decadence (dĭ-kā′dəns, dĕk′ə-dəns) *n.* Moral deterioration.

decompose (dē′kəm-pōz′) *v.* To cause to break down.

decorous (dĕk′ər-əs, dĭ-kôr′əs) *adj.* Proper.

decorum (dĭ-kôr′əm, dĭ-kōr′əm) *n.* **1.** Appropriate social behavior. **2.** Stiff formality.

decrepit (dĭ-krĕp′ĭt) *adj.* Broken down by old age, disease, or overuse.

decrepitude (dĭ-krĕp′ĭ-tōōd′, -tyōōd′) *n.* Broken-down condition.

deem (dēm) *v.* To consider.

deference (dĕf′ər-əns) *n.* Respect.

deferential (dĕf′ə-rĕn′shəl) *adj.* Very respectful.

degradation (dĕg′rə-dā′shən) *n.* Disgrace.

deify (dē′ə-fī′) *v.* To exalt.

delude (dĭ-lōōd′) *v.* To deceive; mislead.

delusive (dĭ-lōō′sĭv) *adj.* False.

demean (dĭ-mēn′) *v.* To degrade.

demeanor (dĭ-mē′nər) *n.* Manner.

demijohn (dĕm′ē-jŏn′) *n.* A large bottle with a handle and a narrow neck, usually encased in wicker.

demur (dĭ-mûr′) *v.* To object.

denigrate (dĕn′ĭ-grāte′) *v.* To defame.

denunciation (dĭ-nŭn′sē-ā′shən, -shē-ā′shən) *n.* Condemnation.

depend (dĭ-pĕnd′) *v.* To hang down.

deportment (dĭ-pôrt′mənt, dĭ-pōrt′-) *n.* Behavior.

deprecate (dĕp′rĭ-kāt′) *v.* To express disapproval of.

deputation (dĕp′yə-tā′shən) *n.* A group of people chosen to represent others.

derange (dĭ-rānj′) *v.* To disturb mentally.—**deranged** *adj.*

dereliction (dĕr′ə-lĭk′shən) *n.* Neglect.

derivative (dĭ-rĭv′ə-tĭv) *adj.* Adapted from something else.

descry (dĭ-skrī′) *v.* To observe something far away or difficult to see.

despotic (dĭ-spŏt′ĭk) *adj.* Exercising absolute power.

despotism (dĕs′pə-tĭz′əm) *n.* Tyranny.

destitute (dĕs′tə-tōōt′, -tyōōt′) *adj.* Impoverished.

desultory (dĕs′əl-tôr′ē, -tōr′ē) *adj.* Disconnected.

devious (dē′vē-əs) *adj.* Cleverly roundabout.

diabolic (dī′ə-bŏl′ĭk) *adj.* Also **diabolical** (-ĭ-kəl). Characteristic of the devil; fiendish.

diffuse (dĭ-fyōōz′) *v.* To spread throughout an area.

digress (dī-grĕs′, dĭ-) *v.* To depart from the main topic.

dilapidation (dĭ-lăp′ə-dā′shən) *n.* A state of disrepair.

dilate (dī-lāt′, dī′lāt′, dĭ-lāt′) *v.* To expand in size.

disapprobation (dĭs-ăp′rə-ba′shən) *n.* Disapproval.

disavow (dĭs′ə-vou′) *v.* To refuse to support.

discern (dĭ-sûrn′, -zûrn′) *v.* To perceive clearly.

discernible (dĭ-sûr′nə-bəl, dĭ-zûr′-) *adj.* Noticeable.

disclosure (dĭs-klō′zhər) *n.* Something that is revealed.

disconcert (dĭs-kən′sûrt′) *v.* Upset; disturbance.

disconsolate (dĭs-kŏn′sə-lĭt) *adj.* Hopelessly dejected.—**disconsolately** *adv.*

discordant (dĭs-kôr′dənt) *adj.* Not harmonious.

discreet (dĭs-krēt′) *adj.* Respectful.—**discreetly** *adv.*

disembodied (dĭs′ĭm-bŏd′ēd) *adj.* Without a body; freed from physical existence.

dishearten (dĭs-härt′n) *v.* To discourage; dispirit.

disheveled (dĭ-shĕv′əld) *adj.* Untidy.

disparage (dĭs-păr′ĭj) *v.* To belittle.

dispassionate (dĭs-păsh′ən-ĭt) *adj.* Calm; impartial.

dispossess (dĭs′pə-zĕs′) *v.* To deprive of some possession.

disposition (dĭs′pə-zĭsh′ən) *n.* Inclination or tendency.

disquisition (dĭs′kwə-zĭsh′ən) *n.* A formal treatise.

dissension (dĭ-sĕn′shən) *n.* Disagreement.

dissipate (dĭs′ə-pāt′) *v.* To drive away.

dissipation (dĭs′ə-pā′shən) *n.* **1.** A scattering. **2.** Excessive and harmful pursuit of pleasure.

dissolution (dĭs′ə-lōō′shən) *n.* Disintegration.

dissuade (dĭ-swād′) *v.* To persuade against an action.

distend (dĭs-tĕnd′) *v.* To swell or bulge.

distillation (dĭs′tə-lā′shən) *n.* **1.** The process of refining to an essence. **2.** A refined essence.

distraught (dĭs-trôt′) *adj.* Troubled; distracted.

divers (dī′vərz) *adj.* Several.

divest (dĭ-vĕst′, dī-) *v.* To strip.

divination (dĭv′ə-nā′shən) *n.* Intuitive understanding.

doleful (dōl′fəl) *adj.* Mournful, melancholy.

dolesome (dōl′səm) *adj.* Sad or mournful.

dolorous (dō'lə-rəs, dŏl'-) *adj.* Painful.
dominion (də-mĭn'yən) *n.* Control.
dormant (dôr'mənt) *adj.* Inactive.
dotage (dō'tĭj) *n.* A childlike state due to old age.
dotard (dō'tərd) *n.* A feeble, senile person.
douche (dōōsh) *v.* To wash away with streams of water.
doughty (dou'tē) *adj.* Brave.
ductile (dŭk'tĭl) *adj.* Flexible; pliable.
dun (dŭn) *n.* A demand for payment.
dyspepsia (dĭs-pĕp'shə, -sē-ə) *n.* Indigestion.

E

ebon (ĕb'ən) *adj.* Black like ebony, a durable, dark wood.
ebony (ĕb'ə-nē) *adj.* Made of or like ebony, a hard, dark-colored wood.
eccentric (ĕk-sĕn'trĭk, ĭk-) *adj.* Strange; odd.
edify (ĕd'ə-fī') *v.* To instruct; enlighten.
educe (ĭ-dōōs', ĭ-dyōōs') *v.* To draw out; deduce.
efface (ĭ-fās') *v.* To erase or rub out.
effectual (ĭ-fĕk'chōō-əl) *adj.* Effective.—**effectually** *adv.*
effervesce (ĕf'ər-vĕs') *v.* To bubble out.
effervescent (ĕf'ər-vĕs'ənt) *adj.* Bubbling.
effulgence (ĭ-fŭl'jəns) *n.* Radiance.
egress (ē'grĕs) *n.* A way out; exit.
ejaculate (ĭ-jăk'yə-lāt') *v.* To exclaim.
ejaculation (ĭ-jăk'yə-lā'shən) *n.* A sudden exclamation.
elation (ĭ-lā'shən) *n.* A feeling of terrific joy or triumph.
elemental (ĕl'ə-mĕnt'l) *adj.* Fundamental.
elusive (ĭ-lōō'sĭv) *adj.* Difficult to grasp.
emaciate (ĭ-mā'shē-āt') *v.* To make abnormally thin, as by illness or starvation.—**emaciated** *adj.*
emanate (ĕm'ə-nāt') *v.* To flow out.
embellishment (ĕm-bĕl'ĭsh-mənt) *v.* An ornament.
embrasure (ĕm-brā'zhər, ĭm-) *n.* A wall opening for a gun.
eminent (ĕm'ə-nənt) *adj.* Prominent.
emphatic (ĕm-făt'ĭk) *adj.* Forceful; done with emphasis.
encompass (ĕn-kŭm'pəs, ĭn-) *v.* To surround.
encrust (ĕn-krŭst', ĭn-) *v.* To cover with a hard dry layer.
endowment (ĕn-dou'mənt, ĭn-) *n.* A natural gift, ability, or quality.
engender (ĕn-jĕn'dər, ĭn-) *v.* To produce.
enjoin (ĕn-join', ĭn-) *v.* To command.
enmity (ĕn'mə-tē) *n.* Hatred.
enterprising (ĕn'tər-prī'zĭng) *adj.* Showing initiative and imagination.
entreaty (ĕn-trē'tē, ĭn-) *n.* Pleading.
enumerable (ĭ-nōō'mə-rə-bəl) *adj.* Capable of being counted.
enumeration (ĭ-nōō'mə-rā'shən, ĭ-nyōō'-) *n.* List.—**enumerate** *v.*
environ (ĕn-vī'rən, ĭn-) *v.* To surround.
ephemeral (ĭ-fĕm'ər-əl) *adj.* Short-lived.
epigram (ĕp'ĭ-grăm') *n.* A cleverly worded statement.
epithet (ĕp'ə-thĕt') *n.* A characterizing word or phrase, often derogatory.
equanimity (ē'kwə-nĭm'ə-tē, ĕk'wə-) *n.* Composure.

equilibrium (ē'kwə-lĭb'rē-əm) *n.* Balance.
equivocal (ĭ-kwĭv'ə-kəl) *adj.* Puzzling; ambiguous.
eradicate (ĭ-răd'ĭ-kāt') *v.* To uproot; remove completely.
eschew (ĕs-chōō') *v.* To avoid.
espy (ĕ-spī', ĭ-spī') *v.* To see.
essay (ĕ-sā') *v.* To try out; attempt.
ether (ē'thər) *n.* Space beyond the earth's atmosphere; the heavens.
ethereal (ĭ-thîr'ē-əl) *adj.* Celestial; heavenly.
etherize (ē'thə-rīz') *v.* To put to sleep by an anesthetic.—**etherized** *adj.*
etiquette (ĕt'ə-kĕt,' -kĭt) *n.* Any special code of behavior.
evanescent (ĕv'ə-nĕs'ənt) *adj.* Fleeting; impermanent.—**evanescently** *adv.*
evince (ĭ-vĭns') *v.* To demonstrate plainly.
exacting (ĕg-zăk'tĭng, ĭg-) *adj.* Demanding; not easily satisfied.
exalt (ĕg'zôlt', ĭg-) *v.* To glorify or heighten feeling.
excruciating (ĕk-skrōō'shē-ā'ting, ĭk-) *adj.* Unbearably painful.
execration (ĕk'sĭ-krā'shən) *n.* A curse.
exemplary (ĕg-zĕm'plə-rē, ĭg-) *adj.* Worthy of imitation.
exhalation (ĕks'hə-lā'shən, ĕk'sə-) *n.* That which is given off or emitted.
exigency (ĕk'sə-jən-sē) *n.* A demand.
exorbitant (ĕg-zôr'bə-tənt, ĭg-) *adj.* Extravagant; excessive.
expatriate (ĕks-pā'trē-at') *v.* To exile.—**expatriated** *adj.*
expediency (ĕk-spē'dē-ən-sē) *n.* Appropriateness for the given situation.
expedient (ĕk-spē'dē-ənt) *adj.* Practical for the purpose at hand.
expletive (ĕks'plə-tĭv) *n.* An oath.
exploit (ĕks'ploit') *n.* Bold or brilliant deed.
expostulation (ĕk-spŏs'chōō lā'shən, ĭk-) *n.* An earnest objection.
expunge (ĕk-spŭnj', ĭk-) *v.* To erase.
extemporize (ĕk-stĕm'pə-rīz', ĭk-) *v.* To improvise.
extenuate (ĕk-stĕn'yōō-āt', ĭk-) *v.* To minimize the seriousness of.
extol (ĕk-stōl', ĭk-) *v.* To praise.
exude (ĕg-zōōd', ĭg-, ĕk-sōōd', ĭk-) *v.* To ooze out.

F

facilitate (fə-sĭl'ə-tāt') *v.* To make easier.
fain (fān) *adj.* 1. Willing. 2. Obliged; required. *adv.* Gladly.
fallible (făl'ə-bəl) *adj.* Capable of error.
fallow (făl'o) *adj.* Unused.—**fallowness** *n.*
falsetto (fôl-sĕt'o) *n.* A voice register much higher than the normal male voice.
fastidious (fă-stĭd'ē-əs, fə-) *adj.* Extremely careful about details; precise.
fatuous (făch'ōō-əs) *adj.* Foolish.
feasible (fē'zə-bəl) *adj.* Possible or likely.
felicitate (fĭ-lĭs'ə-tāt') *v.* To congratulate.
felicitous (fĭ-lĭs'ə-təs) *adj.* Well-chosen.
felicity (fĭ-lĭs'ə-tē) *n.* Happiness.

ă **pat**/ā **pay**/âr **care**/ä **father**/b, **bib**/ch **church**/d **deed**/ĕ **pet**/ē **be**/f **fife**/g **gag**/h **hat**/hw **which**/ĭ **pit**/ī **pie**/îr **pier**/j **judge**/k **kick**/l **lid**, **needle**/ m **mum**/n **no**, **sudden**/ng **thing**/ŏ **pot**/ō **toe**/ô **paw**, **for**/oi **noise**/ou **out**/ŏŏ **took**/ōō **boot**/p **pop**/r **roar**/s **sauce**/sh **ship**, **dish**/t **tight**/th **thin**, **path**/th **this**, **bathe**/ŭ **cut**/ûr **urge**/v **valve**/w **with**/y **yes**/z **zebra**, **size**/zh **vision**/ə **about**, item, edible, gallop, circus/à *Fr.* **ami**/œ *Fr.* **feu**, *Ger.* **schön**/ü *Fr.* **tu**, *Ger.* **über**/кн *Ger.* **ich**, *Scot.* **loch**/N *Fr.* **bon**.

felonious (fə-lō′nē-əs) *adj.* Treacherous.

fen (fĕn) *n.* A bog; swampland.

fervid (fûr′vĭd) *adj.* Intensely emotional.

festoon (fĕs-tōon′) *v.* To hang in loops or curves.

fête (fāt, fĕt) *n.* Entertainment; party.

fidelity (fĭ-dĕl′ə-tē, fī-) *n.* Faithfulness.

firmament (fûr′mə-mənt) *n.* Sky.

flail (flāl) *v.* To strike freely and wildly.

flippant (flĭp′ənt) *adj.* Casual; lacking seriousness.

florid (flôr′ĭd, flŏr′-) *adj.* **1.** Flushed; ruddy. **2.** Heavily decorated or flowery.

flotsam (flŏt′səm) *n.* Miscellaneous small plants and twigs floating on a body of water.

fluctuate (flŭk′chōo-āt′) *v.* To change irregularly.

fluke (flōok) *n.* One of the two flattened, horizontal sections of a whale's tail.

fluster (flŭs′tər) *v.* To make nervous; upset.

flux (flŭks) *n.* Any unnatural discharge of body fluid.

foliage (fō′lē-ĭj) *n.* Masses of leaves.

foment (fō-mĕnt′) *v.* To stir up; promote.

forbear (fôr-bâr′) *v.* To refrain from.—**forbore** *past tense.*

foresaid (fôr′sĕd′, fōr′-) *adj.* Previously stated.

forfeiture (fôr′fĭ-chōor′) *n.* Giving up something as a penalty or fine.

forlorn (fôr-lôrn′, fər-) *adj.* Deserted.

formidable (fôr′mə-də-bəl) *adj.* Causing fear or alarm.

fortuitous (fôr-tōo′ə-təs, fôr-tyōo′-) *adj.* Lucky.

foster (fôs′tər, fŏs′-) *v.* To promote.

fray (frā) *v.* To tatter or make threadbare from wear.—**frayed** *adj.*

freshet (frĕs′ĭt) *n.* An overflow of a stream.

frigidity (frĭ-jĭd′ə-tē) *n.* Extreme coldness.

frippery (frĭp′ə-rē) *n.* A useless decoration.

frivolous (frĭv′ə-ləs) *adj.* Playful.

frond (frŏnd) *n.* A leaflike structure, or shoot, of seaweed.

functionary (fŭngk′shə-nĕr′ē) *n.* An official.

furbelow (fûr′bə-lō′) *n.* Ruffle or flounce.

furlough (fûr′lō) *n.* A leave from duty; an absence with permission.

furrow (fûr′ō) *n.* A long, narrow groove in the earth, usually made by a plough.

furtive (fûr′tĭv) *adj.* Stealthy; secretive.—**furtively** *adv.*

futility (fyōo-tĭl′ə-tē) *n.* Uselessness.

G

gall (gôl) *v.* To bruise and scratch.

gambit (găm′bĭt) *n.* An opening strategy calculated to gain an advantage.

garrulity (gə-rōo′lə-tē) *n.* Talkativeness.

garrulous (găr′ə-ləs,-yə-ləs) *adj.* Talkative.

gauche (gōsh) *adj.* Lacking social grace.

gaunt (gônt) *adj.* **1.** Thin and bony. **2.** Bleak; barren.

genealogist (jē′nē-ăl′ə-jĭst) *n.* One who investigates family histories.

generic (jĭ-nĕr′ĭk) *adj.* Characteristic of a whole group.

genial (jēn′yəl, jē′ne-əl) *adj.* Cheerful.

gentry (jĕn′trē) *n.* People of high social position.

gild (gĭld) *v.* To cover with a layer of gold.—**gilded** *adj.*

glib (glĭb) *adj.* Easy and smooth.—**glibly** *adv.*

glimmering (glĭm′ər-ĭng) *n.* A faint light.

gloaming (glō′mĭng) *n.* Twilight.

gossamer (gŏs′ə-mər) *n.* **1.** A very light, thin cloth. **2.** Anything that resembles gossamer in lightness and softness.

grandiloquent (grăn-dĭl′ə-kwənt) *adj.* Grandiose; high-flown.

grandiose (grăn′dē-ōs′) *adj.* Impressive; showy.

grotesque (grō-tĕsk′) *adj.* Bizarre; fantastic.

gruel (grōo′əl) *n.* A thin broth or porridge.

guileless (gīl′lĭs) *adj.* Naive and sincere.

guttural (gŭt′ər-əl) *adj.* Spoken from the throat.

gyration (jī-rā-shən) *n.* Circling or spinning.

gyre (jīr) *n.* A spiral or circular motion.

H

habiliments (hə-bĭl′ə-mənts) *n.* Clothing and accessories suitable to a particular occasion.

habitude (hăb′ə-tōod′, -tyōod′) *n.* Habit.

hallow (hăl′ō) *v.* To establish as sacred.

hallow (hə-lō′) *v.* To shout.

harrow (hăr′ō) *n.* A farming implement consisting of a heavy metal frame with sharp disks or spikes, drawn by a tractor or horse and used to even out plowed land, to uproot weeds, or to cover seeds.

harry (hăr′ē) *v.* To push along.

haughty (hô′tē) *adj.* Vain; smug.

heft (hĕft) *n.* Heaviness.

heifer (hĕf′ər) *n.* A young cow.

heinous (hā′nəs) *adj.* Vile; wicked.

heretofore (hîr′tə-fôr′) *adv.* Up to this time.

highboy (hī′boi′) *n.* A tall bureau divided into two sections and standing on four legs.

hitherto (hĭth′ər-tōo′) *adv.* Until this time.

hoary (hôr′ē, hōr′ē) *adj.* Old and white-haired.

host (hōst) *n.* A great number.

hostler (hŏs′lər) *n.* The person who takes care of horses at a tavern or other public place.

hypochondria (hī′pə-kŏn′drē-ə) *n.* Neurotic belief that one is sick although there is no evidence of illness.

I

ideality (ī′dē-ăl′ə-tē) *n.* The condition or quality of existing only as an ideal, not physically.

idiomatic (ĭd′ē-ə-măt′ĭk) *adj.* Typical of a particular language or dialect.

ignominious (ĭg′nō-mĭn′ē-əs) *adj.* Shameful.

illimitable (ĭ-lĭm′ĭ-tə-bəl) *adj.* Infinite.

illiterate (ĭ-lĭt′ər-ĭt) *adj.* Without the ability to read or write; uneducated.

imbibe (ĭm-bīb′) *v.* To absorb.

imbue (ĭm-byōo′) *v.* To fill completely.—**imbued** *adj.*

immemorial (ĭm′ə-môr′ē-əl, -mōr′ē-əl) *adj.* Ancient; timeless.

imminent (ĭm′ə-nənt) *adj.* About to happen; impending.

immitigable (ĭ-mĭt′ĭ-gə-bəl) *adj.* Not able to be moderated.

immodest (ĭ-mŏd′ĭst) *adj.* Without reserve; forward.

impale (ĭm-pāl′) *v.* To fix on a sharp stake.

impart (ĭm-pärt′) *v.* To grant or bestow; give.

impending (ĭm-pĕn′dĭng) *adj.* **1.** About to occur; imminent. **2.** Overhanging.

imperative (ĭm-pĕr′ə-tĭv) *adj.* Extremely necessary.

imperceptible (ĭm′pər-sĕp′tə-bəl) *adj.* Not capable of being detected by the senses.

imperial (ĭm-pîr′ē-əl) *adj.* Majestic.

imperious (ĭm-pîr′ē-əs) *adj.* **1.** Urgent. **2.** Overbearing; domineering.

impertinent (ĭm-pûrt′n-ənt) *adj.* Rude; excessively forward.

imperturbable (ĭm′pər-tûr′bə-bəl) *adj.* Cool.

impetuous (ĭm-pĕch′ōō-əs) *adj.* **1.** Wildly energetic or violent. **2.** Impulsive or sudden.—**impetuosity** (ĭm-pĕch′ōō-ŏs′ə-tē) *n.*

impiety (ĭm-pī′ə-tē) *n.* Disrespect; undutifulness; lack of reverence.

impinge (ĭm-pĭnj′) *v.* To strike.

impious (ĭm′pē-əs, ĭm-pī′-) *adj.* Disrespectful toward God.

implacable (ĭm-plā′kə-bəl, -plăk′ə-bəl) *adj.* Unstoppable.

importunate (ĭm-pôr′chōō-nĭt) *adj.* Urgent.

imposing (ĭm-pō′zĭng) *adj.* Grand; impressive.

impound (ĭm-pound′) *v.* To gather (water), as into a reservoir.

impracticable (ĭm-prăk′tĭ-kə-bəl) *adj.* Unmanageable.

imprecation (ĭm′prə-kā′shən) *n.* A curse.

impregnable (ĭm-prĕg′nə-bəl) *adj.* Impossible to capture or invade; impenetrable.

impregnate (ĭm-prĕg′nāt′) *v.* To fill throughout.

impromptu (ĭm-prŏmp′tōō, -tyōō) *adj.* Unrehearsed.— *n.* Something that has not been rehearsed.

impropriety (ĭm′prə-prī′ə-tē) *n.* Improper behavior.

improvisation (ĭm-prŏv′ə-zā′shən, ĭm′prə-və-) *n.* Something created or composed spontaneously, on the spur of the moment.

imputation (ĭm′pyōō-tā′shən) *n.* The attribution or accusation of something, generally unpleasant.

impute (ĭm-pyōōt′) *v.* To attribute to a source.

inalienable (ĭn-āl′yə-nə-bəl) *adj.* Unable to be removed or transferred.

inane (ĭn-ān′) *adj.* Silly; meaningless.

inanimate (ĭn-ăn′ə-mĭt) *adj.* Lifeless.

inauspicious (ĭn′ô-spĭsh′əs) *adj.* Not boding well for the future.

incantation (ĭn′kăn-tā′shən) *n.* A ritual chant supposed to raise spirits or cast a spell.

incarnate (ĭn-kär′nāt′) *v.* To give human form to.

incense (ĭn-sĕns′) *v.* To inflame or enrage.

incessant (ĭn-sĕs′ənt) *adj.* Unceasing.—**incessantly** *adv.*

incommode (ĭn′kə-mōd′) *v.* To bother or inconvenience.

inconceivable (ĭn′kən-sē′və-bəl) *adj.* Unimaginable.

inconsequent (ĭn-kŏn′sə-kwənt) *adj.* Not logical or consistent.

incorrigible (ĭn-kôr′ə-jə-bəl, ĭn-kŏr′-) *adj.* Incapable of reform.

incredulous (ĭn-krĕj′ə-ləs) *adj.* Disbelieving.—**incredulously** *adv.*

increment (ĭn′krə-mənt) *n.* Increase.

incur (ĭn-kûr′) *v.* To cause to happen to oneself.

incursion (ĭn′kûr′zhən, -shən) *n.* A raid.

indebtedness (ĭn-dĕt′ĭd-nĭs) *n.* Gratitude for favors; something owed.

indecorous (ĭn-dĕk′ər-əs) *adj.* Improper; contrary to custom.

indelicate (ĭn-dĕl′ĭ-kĭt) *adj.* Offensive; coarse.

indenture (ĭn-dĕn′chər) *n.* A contract in which one person is bound to work for another for a specified period of time.

indigenous (ĭn-dĭj′ə-nəs) *adj.* Native.

indiscretion (ĭn′dĭs-krĕsh′ən) *n.* An imprudent action.

indispensable (ĭn′dĭs-pĕn′sə-bəl) *adj.* Essential.

indisposed (ĭn′dĭs-pōzd′) *adj.* Not well.

indomitable (ĭn-dŏm′ə-tə-bəl) *adj.* Unconquerable.—**indomitably** *adv.*

inducement (ĭn-dōōs′mənt, ĭn-dyōōs′-) *n.* An incentive.

indulgence (ĭn-dŭl′jəns) *n.* **1.** Gentle treatment. **2.** Tolerance.

inebriate (ĭn-ē′brē-ĭt) *n.* An intoxicated person.

ineffable (ĭn-ĕf′ə-bəl) *adj.* Indescribable.

ineffaceable (ĭn′ĭ-fā′sə-bəl) *adj.* Incapable of being erased; indelible.

ineffectual (ĭn′ĭ-fĕk′chōō-əl) *adj.* Powerless.

inestimable (ĭn-ĕs′tə-mə-bəl) *adj.* Too great to be measured.

inevitable (ĭn-ĕv′ə-tə-bəl) *adj.* Unavoidable.

inexplicable (ĭn-ĕk′splĭ-kə-bəl, ĭn′ĭk-splĭk′ə-bəl) *adj.* Not explainable.—**inexplicably** *adv.*

inextricable (ĭn-ĕk′strĭ-kə-bəl) *adj.* Hopelessly involved or complicated.

infamous (ĭn′fə-məs) *adj.* Of bad reputation.

inferential (ĭn′fə-rĕn′shəl) *adj.* Concluded on the basis of existing knowledge or belief.—**inferentially** *adv.*

infest (ĭn-fĕst′) *v.* To exist in unpleasantly and dangerously large numbers.

infidel (ĭn′fə-dəl′, -dĕl′) *n.* A person who has no religious beliefs.

infinitude (ĭn-fĭn′ə-tōōd′, tyōōd′) *n.* Unlimited or infinite quantity.

influx (ĭn′flŭks′) *n.* A flowing in.

ingenuous (ĭn-jĕn′yōō-əs) *adj.* Honest; without pretense. —**ingenuously** *adv.*

ingratiate (ĭn-grā′shē-āt′) *v.* To gain favor by calculated effort.—**ingratiating** *adj.*

ingress (ĭn′grĕs′) *n.* A way in; entrance.

inherent (ĭn-hî′ənt, -hĕr′ənt) *adj.* Existing as a characteristic quality; inborn.

iniquity (ĭ-nĭk′wə-tē) *n.* Wickedness.

innate (ĭ-nāt′, ĭn′āt′) *adj.* Basic or inborn.

inoperative (ĭn-ŏp′ər-ə-tĭv) *adj.* Not working.

inordinate (ĭn-ôrd′n-ĭt) *adj.* Unusual; excessive.

inscrutable (ĭn-skrōō′tə-bəl) *adj.* Incomprehensible; perplexing.

insensible (ĭn-sĕn′sə-bəl) *adj.* Unfeeling.

insidious (ĭn-sĭd′ē-əs) *adj.* Treacherous; deceptive.

insinuate (ĭn-sĭn′yōō-āt′) *v.* To suggest or imply.

insinuating (ĭn-sĭn′yōō-ā′tĭng) *adj.* Calculated to win favor.

insipid (ĭn-sĭp′ĭd) *adj.* **1.** Flavorless. **2.** Dull; lacking spirit.

insolence (ĭn′sə-ləns) *n.* Rudeness.

insufferable (ĭn-sŭf′ər-ə-bəl) *adj.* Intolerable.

ă pat/ā **pay**/âr care/ä father/b, **bib**/ch **church**/d deed/ĕ pet/ē be/f fife/g **gag**/h **h**at/hw **wh**ich/ĭ pit/ī pie/îr pier/j **judge**/k **kick**/l lid, needle/ m **mum**/n no, sudden/ng thing/ŏ pot/ō toe/ô paw, for/oi noise/ou **out**/ŏŏ took/ōō boot/p **pop**/r roar/s sauce/sh ship, dish/t tight/th thin, path/*th* this, bathe/ŭ cut/ûr urge/v valve/w with/y yes/z zebra, size/zh vision/ə about, item, edible, gallop, circus/à *Fr.* ami/œ *Fr.* feu, *Ger.* schön/ü *Fr.* tu, *Ger.* über/κн *Ger.* ich, *Scot.* loch/N *Fr.* bon.

insulate (ĭn′sə-lāt′, ĭns′yə-) v. To isolate.
insurrection (ĭn′sə-rĕk′shən) n. Rebellion.
integral (ĭn′tə-grəl) adj. Essential.
integrity (ĭn-tĕg′rə-tē) n. Completeness and honesty.
interlocutor (ĭn′tər-lŏk′yə-tər) n. A partner in a conversation.
interloper (ĭn-tər-lop′ər) n. Intruder.
interment (ĭn-tûr′mənt) n. Burial.
interminable (ĭn-tûr′mə-nə-bəl) adj. Endless; tiresomely long.
intermittent (ĭn′tər-mit′ənt) adj. Occurring periodically.
internecine (ĭn′tər-nĕs′ēn′, -ən, -nē′sīn′) adj. Mutually destructive.
interpose (ĭn′tər-pōz′) v. 1. To come between. 2. To insert something during a conversation.
intervene (ĭn′tər-vēn′) v. To lie or come between.—**intervening** adj.
intimate (ĭn′tə-māt′) v. To imply or suggest.
invidious (ĭn-vĭd′ē-əs) adj. Giving offense.
inviolable (ĭn-vī′ə-lə-bəl) adj. Secure against attack.
inviolate (ĭn-vī′ə-lĭt) adj. Not violated; whole.
invocation (ĭn′və-kā′shən) n. Prayer.
involution (ĭn′və-loō′shən) n. A tangling.
iridescent (ĭr′ĭ-dĕs′ənt) adj. Shimmering with a wide range of colors.
irreclaimable (ĭr′ĭ-klā′mə-bəl) adj. Incapable of reform.
irredeemable (ĭr′ĭ-dē′mə-bəl) adj. Hopeless.
irrepressible (ĭr′ĭ-prĕs′ə-bəl) adj. Uncontrollable.
irreproachable (ĭr′ĭ-prō′chə-bəl) adj. Faultless.
irresolute (ĭ-rĕz′ə-loōt′) adj. Indecisive.—**irresolution** n.
irrupt (ĭ-rŭpt′) v. To burst forth.—**irruption** n.

J

jargon (jär′gən) n. Incoherent or meaningless language; gibberish.
jocose (jō-kōs′) adj. Humorous; playful.—**jocosely** adv.
jocular (jŏk′yə-lər) adj. Humorous.
judicious (joō-dĭsh′əs) adj. Showing good judgment.
jurisdictional (joōr′-əs-dĭk′shən-əl) adj. Having to do with the territorial extent of authority.

K

khaki (kăk′ē, kä′kē) adj. Made of khaki, a drab yellowish-brown cloth.
kinetic (kĭ-nĕt′ĭk) adj. Energetic.

L

lacquer (lăk′ər) n. A substance applied to surfaces for a protective, glossy finish.—**lacquered** adj.
lamentable (lăm′ən-tə-bel, lə-mĕn′-) adj. Mournful.
languid (lăng′gwĭd) adj. Sluggish.
latent (lā′tənt) adj. Present but hidden.
lattice (lăt′ĭs) n. A framework often used to support or decorate windows, consisting of crossed strips of wood or metal.
laxity (lăk′sə-tē) n. Without strictness.
legacy (lĕg′ə-sē) n. A gift of money or property handed down.

legation (lē-gā′shən) n. A diplomatic mission.
lethargic (lə-thär′jĭk) adj. Sluggish.
libation (lī-bā′shən) n. A ritual in which wine or oil is poured on the ground (as a sacrifice to a god); any sacrifice.
libel (lī-bəl) v. To make damaging statements about others.—**libeling** n.
license (lī′səns) n. Excessive and undisciplined freedom.
lineament (lĭn′ē-ə-mənt) n. A distinctive feature or line, especially of the face.
livid (lĭv′ĭd) adj. Deathly pale.—**lividly** adv.
loathsome (lōth′səm, lōth′) adj. Repulsive.
longevity (lŏn-jĕv′ə-tē) n. Long life.
lucid (loō′sĭd) adj. Clear; rational.
lugubrious (loō-goō′brē-əs, loō-gyoō′-) adj. Excessively mournful.—**lugubriousness** n.
luminous (loō′mə-nəs) adj. Radiant.
lupin (loō′pən) n. A kind of plant with clusters of multi-colored flowers.
lurid (loōr′ĭd) adj. Ghastly.
lustrous (lŭs′trəs) adj. Shining; bright.

M

magnanimity (măg′nə-nĭm′ĭ-tē) n. Nobility of spirit.
maim (mām) v. To injure so as to disable.—**maimed** adj.
malediction (măl′ə-dĭk′shən) n. Curse.
malevolence (mə-lĕv′ə-ləns) n. Ill will.
malevolent (mə-lĕv′ə-lənt) adj. Evil.
malign (mə-līn′) adj. Sinister.
mandate (măn′dāt′) n. Command.
manifest (măn′ə-fĕst′) adj. Evident. v. To appear.
manifestation (măn′ə-fĕs-tā′shən) n. Demonstration.
manifold (măn′ə-fōld) adj. 1. Many and various. 2. In many ways.
marauder (mə-rôd′ər) n. A plunderer.
marly (mär′lē) adj. Scotch and dialect. Spotted.
martial (mär′shəl) adj. Warlike.
mastiff (măs′tĭf) n. A large, strong dog with hanging lips and drooping ears.
matted (măt′ĭd) adj. Densely tangled.
maudlin (môd′lĭn) adj. Overly sentimental.
mediator (mē′dē-ā′tər) n. Someone who intervenes in your behalf.
mendicant (mĕn′dĭ-kənt) n. A beggar.
meridian (mə-rĭd′ē-ən) n. The highest point.
metaphysician (mĕt′ə-fə-zĭsh′ən) n. Someone who specializes in a form of philosophy dealing with the nature of reality.
metaphysics (mĕt′ə-fĭz′ĭks) n. 1. A branch of philosophy that deals with the nature of reality. 2. Subtle or difficult reasoning.
meteorological (mē′tē-ôr′ə-lŏj′ĭ-kəl, -ôr′ə-lŏj′ĭ-kəl) adj. Of weather.
mien (mēn) n. Bearing.
milieu (mē-lyœ′) n. Surroundings.
mimicry (mĭm′ĭk-rē) Imitation.
mincing (mĭn′sĭng) adj. Moving with short steps.—**mincingly** adv.
misanthropic (mĭs′ən-thrŏp′ĭc, mĭz′-) adj. Hating people.
mitigate (mĭt′ĭ-gāt′) v. To reduce in intensity.
molder (mōl′dər) v. To decay.—**moldering** adj.
mollify (mŏl′ə-fī′) v. To pacify.

monitory (mŏn'ə-tôr'ē, -tōr'ē) *adj.* Warning.

morass (mə-răs', mô-) *n.* Swamp.

mortification (môr'tə-fĭ-kā'shən) *n.* Disappointment.

mosaic (mō-zā'ĭk) *n.* Anything that seems made up of small pieces.

motley (mŏt'lē) *adj.* Diverse.

mottle (mŏt'l) *v.* To spot or streak with various colors.—**mottled** *adj.*

mulch (mŭlch) *n.* A covering of leaves or peat moss, spread on the ground around plants to preserve moisture.

multiform (mŭl'tə-fôrm') *adj.* In many forms.

munificent (myōō-nĭf'ə-sənt) *adj.* Extremely generous.

musing (myōō'zĭng) *n.* A reflection.

musky (mŭsk'ē) *adj.* Having the odor of musk, a strong-smelling substance secreted by certain animals.

myriad (mĭr'ē-əd) *adj.* Countless.

mythicize (mĭth'ə-sīz') *v.* To turn into a myth.

N

nabob (nā'bŏb') *n.* A wealthy and prominent man.

nary (nâr'ē) *adj. Dialect.* Not one.

natty (năt'ē) *adj.* Stylish and neat in appearance.

naught (nôt) *n.* Nothing.

nimble (nĭm'bəl) *adj.* Agile.

nimbus (nĭm'bəs) *n.* A surrounding radiance; halo.

nocturnal (nŏk-tûr'nəl) *adj.* Occurring at night.

noisome (noi'səm) *adj.* Dirty and foul-smelling.

nomadic (nō-măd'ĭk) *adj.* Wandering.

nomenclature (nō'mən-klā'chər, nō-mĕn'klə-chər) *n.* System of naming.

nonchalant (nŏn'shə-länt') *adj.* Cooly unconcerned.—**nonchalantly** *adv.*

noncommittal (nŏn'kə-mĭt'l) *adj.* Unrevealing; indefinite.

noxious (nŏk'shəs) *adj.* Harmful.

O

oasis (ō-ā'sĭs) *n.* Any place that offers relief from difficulty or unpleasantness.

obdurate (ŏb'dyōō-rĭt, ŏb'dōō-) *adj.* Rigidly unyielding.

obeisance (ō-bā'səns, ō-bē'-) *n.* A sign of respect.

oblique (ō-blēk', ə-) *adj.* On a slant or at an angle.—**obliquely** *adv.*

obliterate (ə-blĭt'ə-rāt') *v.* To destroy so that no trace is left.

oblivious (ə-blĭv'ē-əs) *adj.* Unmindful.

obsequious (ŏb-sē'kwē-əs, əb-) *adj.* **1.** Excessively agreeable. **2.** Servile; overly submissive.

obstinate (ŏb'stə-nĭt) *adj.* **1.** Stubborn. **2.** Resisting cure.

obstreperous (ŏb-strĕp'ər-əs, -əb) *adj.* Unruly.

obtrude (ŏb-trōōd', əb-) *v.* To thrust upon others; intrude.

obtuse (ŏb-tōōs', -tyōōs', əb-) *adj.* Slow to comprehend.

occult (ə-kŭlt', ō-kŭlt', ŏk'ŭlt') *adj.* Mysterious.

odious (ō-dē'əs) *adj.* Hateful.

ominous (ŏm'ə-nəs) *adj.* Sinister.

omnipotent (ŏm-nĭp'ə-tənt) *adj.* All-powerful.

opaque (ō-pāk') *adj.* Not allowing light through.

opiate (ō'pē-ĭt, āt') *n.* Something that dulls the senses.

oppressive (ə-prĕs'ĭv) *adj.* **1.** Heavy; depressing. **2.** Burdensome.—**oppressively** *adv.*

opulence (ŏp'yə-ləns) *n.* Wealth.

oracle (ôr'ə-kəl, ŏr'-) *n.* A prophet or wise person.

orb (ôrb) *n.* A sphere.

oscillation (ŏs'ə-lā'shən) *n.* Wavering.

ostentation (ŏs'tĕn-tā'shən, ŏs'tən-) *n.* Conceited showiness.

ostentatious (ŏs'tĕn-tā'shəs, ŏs'tən-) *adj.* Showy.

ostracize (ŏs'trə-sīz') *v.* To reject or exclude.—**ostracism** *n.*

P

pacific (pə-sĭf'ĭk) *adj.* Serene; calming.

palatial (pə-lā'shəl) *adj.* Resembling a palace.

pall (pôl) *n.* A coffin.

pallid (păl'ĭd) *adj.* Pale.

pallor (păl'ər) *n.* Paleness.

palpable (păl'pə-bəl) *Adj.* Touchable; tangible.

palpitate (păl'pə-tāt') *v.* To tremble.—**palpitating** *adj.*

panorama (păn'ə-răm'ə, -rä'mə) *n.* A wide view.

pantomime (păn'tə-mīm') *v.* To perform silently with gestures only.

paradoxical (păr'ə-dŏks'ĭ-kəl) *adj.* Apparently contradictory or absurd.

paraphernalia (păr'ə-fər-nāl'yə, -fə-nāl'yə) *n.* The articles related to a particular activity.

pariah (pə-rī'ə) *n.* An outcast.—*adj.* Socially rejected.

parsimony (pär'sə-mō'nē) *n.* Excessive thrift; stinginess.

partisan (pär'tə-zən) *n.* A supporter.

pathological (păth'ə-lŏj'ĭ-kəl) *adj.* Concerned with disease.

patriarch (pā'trē-ärk') *n.* A respected, elderly male leader.

pedantic (pə-dăn'tĭk) *adj.* Placing disproportionate emphasis on trivial information or bits of knowledge.

pedestrian (pə-dĕs'trē-ən) *adj.* Ordinary.

peevish (pē'vĭsh) *adj.* Bad-tempered.

pejorative (pĭ-jôr'ə-tĭv, jŏr'ə-tĭv, pĕj'ə-rā'tĭv, pē'jə-) *adj.* Downgrading.

pendent (pĕn'dənt) *adj.* Hanging.

pensive (pĕn'sĭv) *adj.* Deeply thoughtful.

penury (pĕn'yə-rē) *n.* Poverty.

perceptible (pər-sĕp'tə-bəl) *adj.* Noticeable.

perennial (pə-rĕn'ē-əl) *adj.* Perpetual.

perfidy (pûr'fə-dē) *n.* Treachery.

perfunctory (pər-fŭngk'tə-rē) *adj.* Done carelessly or as a routine.—**perfunctorily** *adv.*

periodicity (pîr'ē-ə-dĭs'ə-tē) *n.* Recurrence at regular intervals.

per se (pûr sā', sē') *adv.* In or by itself.

persevere (pûr'sə-vîr') *v.* To continue undaunted.

persona (pər-sō'nə, -nä') *n.* A role or mask.

pertinacious (pûr'tə-nā'shəs) *adj.* Stubbornly persistent.—**pertinaciously** *adv.*

pertinacity (pûr'tə-nas'ə-tē) *n.* Stubbornness.

pertinence (pûr'tə-nəns) *n.* Appropriateness.

perturbation (pûr'tər-bā'shən) *n.* Alarm; confusion.

ă pat/ā pay/âr care/ä father/b, bib/ch church/d deed/ĕ pet/ē be/f fife/g gag/h hat/hw which/ĭ pit/ī pie/îr pier/j judge/k kick/l lid, needle/ m mum/n no, sudden/ng thing/ŏ pot/ō toe/ô paw, for/oi noise/ou out/ŏŏ took/ōŏ boot/p pop/r roar/s sauce/sh ship, dish/t tight/th thin/ path/th this, bathe/ŭ cut/ûr urge/v valve/w with/y yes/z zebra, size/zh vision/ə about, item, edible, gallop, circus/à *Fr.* ami/œ *Fr.* feu, *Ger.* schön/ü *Fr.* tu, *Ger.* über/кн *Ger.* ich, *Scot.* loch/N *Fr.* bon.

perusal (pə-roō′zəl) *n.* Careful reading or study.

pervade (pər-vād′) *v.* To spread throughout.

pervasive (pər-vā′sĭv, -zĭv) *adj.* Widespread.

perverse (pər-vûrs′) *adj.* Contrary; given to contradiction. —**perversely** *adv.*

perverted (pər-vûr′tĭd) *adj.* **1.** Varying markedly from what is considered right or true. **2.** Misguided.

pestilence (pĕs′tə-ləns) *n.* An epidemic; a contagious deadly disease; plague.

pestilent (pĕs′tə-lənt) *adj.* Dangerously unhealthy.

petulant (pĕch′oō-lənt) *adj.* Irritable.—**petulantly** *adv.*— **petulance** *n.*

phantasm (făn′tăz′əm) *n.* Something imagined but having no physical reality.

phlegmatic (flĕg-măt′ĭk) *adj.* Sluggish; dull-witted.

physiognomy (fĭz′ē-ŏg′nə-mē, -ŏn′ə-mē) *n.* Physical appearance, especially of the face.

physiology (fĭz′ē-ŏl′ə-jē) *n.* The total life processes and functions of an organism.

pickerel (pĭk′ər-əl, pĭk′rəl) *n.* A type of North American freshwater fish.

pillage (pĭl′ĭj) *n.* Violent robbery.

pine (pīn) *v.* To waste away through grief or longing.

pinion (pĭn′yən) *n.* A wing.

pinnacle (pĭn′ə-kəl) *n.* A culmination or high point.

piquancy (pē′kən-sē) *n.* Stimulation; excitement.

pique (pēk) *v.* To irritate.

pirouette (pĭr′oō-ĕt′) *n.* In ballet, a full turn of the body on either the ball of the foot or the point of the toe.

piteous (pĭt′ē-əs) *adj.* Evoking sympathy or pity.—**piteously** *adv.*

pittance (pĭt′əns) *n.* A very small amount of money.

placate (plā′kāt′, plăk′āt′) *v.* To pacify.—**placatingly** *adv.*

placid (plăs′ĭd) *adj.* Calm.—**placidity** *n.*

plaintive (plān′tĭv) *adj.* Mournful; sad.

plashy (plăsh′ē) *adj.* Marshy.

plastic (plăs′tĭk) *adj.* Pliable; capable of being molded.

plausible (plô′zə-bəl) *adj.* Acceptable.

plight (plīt) *v.* To become engaged to marry.—**plighted** *adj.*

poignant (poin′yənt, poi′nənt) *adj.* Sharp; keen.

politic (pŏl′ə-tĭk) *adj.* Shrewd; prudent.

polychrome (pŏl′ē-krōm′) *adj.* Having many colors.

pommel (pŭm′əl, pŏm′-) *n.* The raised front section of a saddle.

pompous (pŏm′pəs) *adj.* Self-important.

ponderous (pŏn′dər-əs) *adj.* Huge.

portent (pôr′tĕnt′, pōr′-) *n.* An omen.

posterity (pŏ-stĕr′ə-tē) *n.* A person's descendants.

poultice (pōl′tĭs) *n.* A soft, damp mass of bread, flour or clay, applied to an aching or infected part of the body.

practicable (prăk′tĭ-kə-bəl) *adj.* Possible.

prattle (prăt′l) *v.* To babble like a child.

precarious (prĭ-kâr′ē-əs) *adj.* Dangerously uncertain or unstable.

precept (prē′sĕpt′) *n.* Rule or principle.

precincts (prē′sĭngkts) *n. pl.* Neighborhood.

precipice (prĕs′ə-pĭs) *n.* An extremely steep cliff.

precipitate (prĭ-sĭp′ə-tāt′) *v.* To cause to happen suddenly. *adj.* Moving rapidly.

precipitation (prĭ-sĭp′ə-tā′shən) *n.* Rain, snow, sleet, or hail.

precipitous (prĭ-sĭp′ə-təs) *adj.* Very steep.

preclude (prĭ-kloōd′) *v.* To prevent.

predispose (prē′dĭs-pōz′) *v.* To influence beforehand.— **predisposing** *adj.*

preeminent (pre-ĕm′ə-nənt) *adj.* Superior to all others.— **preeminently** *adv.*

pregnant (prĕg′nənt) *adj.* Full of significance.—**pregnantly** *adv.*

prerogative (prĭ-rŏg′ə-tĭv) *n.* Right or privilege.

presage (prĭ-sāj′) *v.* To foresee.—**presaging** *adj.*

prescient (prē′shē-ənt, prĕsh′ē) *adj.* Able to know beforehand.

presentiment (prĭ-zĕn′tə-mənt) *n.* A feeling that something is about to occur.

pretension (prĭ-tĕn′shən) *n.* An unjustifiable claim.

preternatural (prē′tər-năch′ər-əl) *adj.* Abnormal; outside nature.

pretext (prē′tĕkst) *n.* An excuse or motive to hide one's real purpose.

prevalent (prĕv′ə-lənt) *adj.* Frequent and widespread.

priggish (prĭg′ĭsh) *adj.* Overly proper.

prim (prĭm) *adj.* Precise and neat.

primeval (prī-mē′vəl) *adj.* Original; earliest.

prismatic (prĭz-măt′ĭk) *adj.* Rainbow-colored.—**prismatically** *adv.*

pristine (prĭs′tēn′, prĭ-stēn′) *adj.* Pure; unblemished.

prize (prīz) *v.* To pry.

procure (prō-kyoōr′, prə-) *v.* To obtain.—**procurable** *adj.*

prodigious (prə-dĭj′əs) *adj.* **1.** Marvelous. **2.** Enormous and awesome.

profane (prō-fān′, prə-) *adj.* Coarse; vulgar.

profane (prō-fān′, prə-) *v.* To treat disrespectfully.

profanity (prō-făn′ə-tē, prə-) *n.* Vulgar language; swearing.

profound (prə-found′, prō′) *adj.* Deep or far-reaching.— **profoundly** *adv.*

profundity (prə-fŭn′də-tē, prō-) *n.* Depth.

profuse (prə-fyoōs′, prō-) *adj.* Abundant.

profusion (prə-fyoō′zhən, prō-) *n.* Abundance.

projectile (prə-jek′təl, tīl′) *adj.* Thrusting forward.

prolix (prō-lĭks′, prō′lĭks) *adj.* Wordy.—**prolixity** *n.*

promontory (prŏm′ən-tôr′ē, -tōr′ē) *n.* A peak of land projecting into a body of water.

promulgate (prŏm′əl-gāt′, prō-mŭl′gāt′) *v.* To make known publicly.

propagate (prŏp′ə-gāt′) *v.* To multiply.

propitiate (prō-pĭsh′ē-āt′) *v.* To gain by pacifying.

propitiatory (prō-pĭsh′ē-ə-tôr′ē, -tōr′ē) *adj.* Friendly; peaceful.

propitious (prə-pĭsh′əs) *adj.* Favorable.

propriety (prə-prī′ə-tē) *n.* What is generally considered appropriate in behavior and taste.

prospect (prŏs′pĕkt′) *n.* Scene or view.

prostrate (prŏs′trāt′) *adj.* Fallen; lying flat.

prostrate (prŏs′trāt′) *v.* To kneel in humility.

protract (prō-trăkt′) *v.* To draw out; extend.

protrude (prō-troōd′) *v.* To jut out.

protuberance (prō-toō′bər-əns, prō-tyoō′-) *n.* Something that bulges or sticks out.

provincial (prə-vĭn′shəl) *adj.* Limited; unsophisticated.

provoke (prə-vōk′) *v.* To anger.

prowess (prou′ĭs) *n.* Great strength and skill.

proximity (prŏk-sĭm′ə-tē) *n.* Closeness.

prudence (proōd′əns) *n.* Good judgment.

prudent (proōd′ənt) *adj.* Wise.

pueblo (pwĕb′lō) *n.* Indian village in the southwestern United States.

puerility (pyōō′rĭl′ə-tē) *n.* Childishness.

pugilist (pyōō′jə-lĭst) *n.* One who fights with his fists; a boxer.—**pugilistic** *adj.*

pullet (pŏŏl′ĭt) *n.* A young hen.

punctilious (pŭngk-tĭl′ē-əs) *adj.* Very careful; exact.—**punctiliously** *adv.*

pungent (pŭn′jənt) *adj.* Sharp; penetrating.

purgatory (pûr-gə-tôr′ē, -tōr′ē) *n.* A condition of temporary punishment.

purl (pûrl) *v.* To move with a murmuring sound.

Q

quadruped (kwŏd′rŏŏ-pĕd′) *n.* A four-footed animal.

quaff (kwŏf, kwăf, kwôf) *v.* To drink enthusiastically.

quagmire (kwăg′mīr′, kwŏg′-) *n.* Marshy ground.

quail (kwāl) *v.* To weaken and lose courage.

quarry (kwôr′ē, kwŏr′ē) *n.* A hunted animal.

quaver (kwā′vər) *n.* A trembling voice.

queasy (kwē′zē) *adj.* Easily nauseated.

querulous (kwĕr′ə-ləs, kwĕr′yə-) *adj.* Complaining; grumbling.

quiescent (kwī-ĕs′ənt, kwē-) *adj.* Motionless; quiet.

R

raiment (rā′mənt) *n.* Clothing.

rakish (rā′kĭsh) *adj.* Jaunty; playful.—**rakishly** *adv.*

ramification (răm′ə-fə-kā′shən) *n.* An arrangement of branches and offshoots.

ratchet (răch′ĭt) *v.* Rare. To make use of a ratchet, a device consisting of a toothed wheel and a bar that allows the wheel to turn in only one direction.

ratify (răt′ə-fī′) *v.* To approve or sanction.

ravening (răv′ən-ĭng) *adj.* Hungrily looking for prey.

ravenous (răv′ən-əs) *adj.* Extremely hungry.

reciprocate (rĭ-sĭp′rə-kāt) *v.* To return.

recompense (rĕk′əm-pĕns′) *n.* Reward.

reconcile (rĕk′ən-sīl′) *v.* To bring to agreement or friendship.—**reconciliation** (rĕk′ən-sĭl′ē-ā′shən) *n.*

rectitude (rĕk′tə-tōōd′, -tyōōd′) *n.* Moral rightness.

redeem (rĭ-dēm′) *v.* To rescue.

redress (rĭ-drĕs′) *n.* Compensation for an injustice.

regale (rĭ-gāl′) *v.* To feast.

regalia (rĭ-gāl′yə, -gā′lē-ə) *n. pl.* Symbols of rank or general status in society.

regenerate (rĭ-jĕn′ə-rāt′) *v.* To renew or give new life to.

reimburse (rē′ĭm-bûrs′) *v.* To repay.

reiterate (rē-ĭt′ə-rāt′) *v.* To repeat.

rejoin (rĭ-join′) *v.* To respond.

rejuvenescent (rĭ-jōō′və-nĕs′ənt) *adj.* Able to restore youth.

reminiscent (rĕm′ə-nĭs′ənt) *adj.* Recalling past events.—**reminiscently** *adv.*

remonstrance (rĭ-mŏn′strəns) *n.* Criticism.

remonstrate (rĭ-mŏn′strāt′) *v.* To argue or plead in protest; object.

repine (rĭ-pīn′) *v.* To complain.

repose (rĭ-pōz′) *v.* To rest.

reprieve (rĭ-prēv′) *v.* To relieve or save from affliction.

reprisal (rĭ-prī′zəl) *n.* Retaliation.

reprobate (rĕp′rə-bāt′) *n.* Unprincipled or dissolute person.

reprove (rĭ-prōōv′) *v.* To scold.

repudiate (rĭ-pyōō′dē-āt′) *v.* To reject.

repugnant (rĭ-pŭg′nənt) *adj.* Repulsive.

requisite (rĕk′wə-zīt) *n.* Necessity.

resolute (rĕz′ə-lōōt′) *adj.* Firm; determined.—**resolutely** *adv.*

resolve (rĭ-zŏlv′) *v.* To come to a decision.

respite (rĕs′pĭt) *n.* A period of relief.

reticent (rĕt′ə-sənt) *adj.* Shy and withdrawn.

retinue (rĕt′n-ōō, rĕt′n-yōō′) *n.* A group of attendants or companions.

retrospective (rĕt′rə-spĕk′tĭv) *adj.* Looking backward.

revel (rĕv′əl) *v.* To enjoy deeply.—**reveler** *n.*

revile (rĭ-vīl′) *v.* To scorn or attack verbally.

rift (rĭft) *n.* A narrow crack, as in a rock.

rivulet (rĭv′yə-lĭt) *n.* A small stream.

robust (rō-bŭst′, rō′bŭst) *adj.* Strong; healthy.

roseate (rō′zē-ĭt, -āt′) *adj.* Rose-colored.

rueful (rōō′fəl) *adj.* Regretful.—**ruefully** *adv.*

S

sable (sā′bəl) *adj.* Black.

sacrament (săk′rə-mənt) *n.* In Christianity, one of the seven rites established by Jesus and considered as means to grace.

sadistic (sə-dĭs′tĭk) *adj.* Able to derive pleasure from inflicting pain on others.

saffron (săf′rən) *n.* An orange-yellow color.

sagacious (sə-gā′shəs) *adj.* Knowing; wise.

sagacity (sə-găs′ə-tē) *n.* Shrewdness.

sallow (săl′ō) *adj.* Pale yellow and sickly in complexion.

sanctified (săngk′tə-fīd′) *n.* Sacred.

sanctity (săngk′tə-tē) *n.* Sacredness.

sapling (săp′lĭng) *n.* A young tree.

sardonic (sär-dŏn′ĭk) *adj.* Scornfully sarcastic.—**sardonically** *adv.*

saunter (sôn′tər) *v.* To walk at a relaxed, leisurely pace.

scatheless (skāth′lĕs) *adj.* Unharmed.

scourge (skûrj) *v.* To whip.—**scourged** *adj.*

scut (skŭt) *n.* A stumpy tail, as that of a rabbit or deer.

sectarian (sĕk-târ′ē-ən) *adj.* Belonging to a particular sect.

sedate (sĭ-dāt′) *adj.* Calm; unemotional.

semblance (sĕm′bləns) *n.* Appearance or exterior form.

sensibility (sĕn′sə-bĭl′ə-tē) *n.* **1.** Refinement; sharp sensitivity to artistic and moral values. **2.** Receptiveness; responsiveness.

ă pat/ā pay/âr care/ä father/b, bib/ch church/d deed/ē pet/ē be/f fife/g gag/h hat/hw which/ī pit/ī pie/îr pier/j judge/k kick/l lid, needle/ m mum/n no, sudden/ng thing/ŏ pot/ō toe/ô paw, for/oi noise/ou out/ōō took/ōō boot/p pop/r roar/s sauce/sh ship, dish/t tight/th thin, path/*th* this, bathe/ŭ cut/ûr urge/v valve/w with/y yes/z zebra, size/zh vision/ə about, item, edible, gallop, circus/à *Fr.* ami/œ *Fr.* feu, *Ger.* schön/ü *Fr.* tu, *Ger.* über/кн *Ger.* ich, *Scot.* loch/ɴ *Fr.* bon.

sepulcher (sĕp′əl-kər) *n.* A chamber for burial.

sepulchral (sə-pŭl′krəl) *adj.* Suggestive of burial; gloomy.

seraph (sĕr′əf) *n.* In Christian theology, an angel of the highest order.

serene (sĭ-rēn′) *adj.* Calm.—**serenely** *adv.*

serrated (sĕr′ā′tĭd) *adj.* With sawlike notches on the edge.

servile (sûr′vəl, -vīl′) *adj.* Slavish.

sexton (sĕks′tən) *n.* The caretaker of a church.

shew (shō) *v.* Archaic form of *show.*

shoal (shōl) *n.* In a body of water, a dangerously shallow place.

shote (shōt) *n.* (*Also spelled* **shoat.**) A young pig.

shroud (shroud) *n.* A sheet used to cover a corpse.

sidle (sīd′l) *v.* To move sideways in a cautious manner.

signet (sĭg′nĭt) *n.* Impression.

silicate (sĭl′ĭ-kāt′, -kĭt) *n.* A compound found in most rocks and used as the basis for glass and brick.

simper (sĭm′pər) *v.* To smile foolishly.

sinewy (sĭn′yoo-ē) *adj.* Thin and muscular.

singe (sĭnj) *v.* To burn slightly.

singular (sĭng′gyə-lər) *adj.* Individual; unusual or strange.

sinuous (sĭn′yoo-əs) *adj.* Winding or wavy.

siren (sī′rən) *n.* In classical mythology, a creature, part woman and part bird, whose beautiful singing lured sailors to their destruction on rocky shores.

skeptic (skĕp′tĭk) *n.* One who doubts or questions persistently.

skitter (skĭt′ər) *v.* To move quickly and lightly.

skulk (skŭlk) *v.* To move about stealthily.

slough (slŭf) *n.* A snake's dead, outer skin which is shed periodically.

slovenly (slŭv′ən-lē) *adj.* Unkempt; sloppy.

smite (smīt) *v.* To afflict suddenly and powerfully.

sog (sŏg) *v.* To become soaked.

sojourn (sō′jûrn, sō-jûrn′) *n.* A brief stay.

solace (sŏl′ĭs) *v.* To comfort.

solicit (sə-lĭs′ĭt) *v.* To appeal to or attract.

solicitation (sə-lĭs′ə-tā′shən) *n.* Earnest request; petition.

solicitous (sə-lĭs′ə-təs) *adj.* Concerned.

solicitude (sə-lĭs′ə-tōōd′, -tyōōd′) *n.* The state of being concerned and attentive.

solstice (sŏl′stəs, sôl′-) *n.* Either the winter or the summer solstice, respectively the shortest and longest days of the year.

somnolent (sŏm′nə-lənt) *adj.* Sleepy.

sonorous (sə-nôr′əs, sə-nōr′-, sŏn′ər-) *adj.* Having a loud, deep sound.—**sonorously** *adv.*

sooth (sōōth) *n. Archaic.* Truth.

soothsayer (sōōth′sā′ər) *n.* One who claims to be able to predict the future.

sovereign (sŏv′ər-ən) *adj.* Supreme.

specious (spē′shəs) *adj.* Artificial; giving a false impression of truth, rightness, or goodness.

speckled (spĕk′əld) *adj.* Marked with small dots of contrasting colors.

spectral (spĕk′trəl) *adj.* Ghostly.

speculative (spĕk′yə-lə-tĭv, -lā′tĭv) *adj.* Based on guesswork.

sporadic (spô-rād′ĭk, spō-) *adj.* Occurring irregularly.

spurious (spyoor′ē-əs) *adj.* False; counterfeit.

squelch (skwĕlch) *v.* To crush; surpress.

squelchy (skwĕlch′ē) *adj.* Making a wet, sucking sound, as of liquid being pressed.

stagnant (stăg′nənt) *adj.* Stale and unclean from lack of motion.

stanch (stänch, stănch) *v.* To stop or decrease the flow of something.

stark (stärk) *adj.* Bare; stripped.—**starkly** *adv.*

stationary (stā′shə-nĕr′ē) *adj.* Not moving; in a fixed position.

staunch (stônch, stänch) *adj.* Watertight.

stealthy (stĕl′thē) *adj.* Secretive.

stigma (stĭg′mə) *n.* A mark or sign indicating a flaw in a person's reputation or character.

striation (strī-ā′shən) *n.* A narrow band or groove, usually parallel.

stultify (stŭl′tə-fī′) *v.* To make dull.

stupefaction (stōō′pə-făk′shən, styōō′-) *n.* A state in which the mind and senses are dulled.

stupendous (stōō-pĕn′dəs, styōō′) *adj.* Immense.

suave (swäv, swāv) *adj.* Polished and sophisticated.

subjection (səb-jĕk′shən) *n.* The condition of being dominated or controlled.

subjoin (səb-join′) *v.* To add; append.

subjugate (sŭb′jə-gāt′) *v.* To make a slave of.—**subjugation** *n.*

sublime (sə-blīm′) *adj.* **1.** Beautiful; majestic. **2.** Awe-inspiring.

sublimity (sə-blĭm′ə-tē) *n.* Loftiness; majesty.

subterfuge (sŭb′tər-fyōōj′) *n.* Deception.

succor (sŭk′ər) *n.* Assistance.

sufferable (sŭf′ər-ə-bəl, sŭf′rə-) *adj.* Bearable.

sufferance (sŭf′ər-əns, sŭf′rəns) *n.* Endurance.

suffice (sə-fīs′) *v.* To be adequate.

suffuse (sə-fyōōz′) *v.* To disperse color, liquid, or light.—**suffusion** *n.* Blush.

sullen (sŭl′ən) *adj.* Ill-humored; gloomy.

sumptuous (sŭmp′chōō-əs) *adj.* Splendid; rich.

sunder (sŭn′dər) *v.* To separate.

sundry (sŭn′drē) *adj.* Several.

superficial (sōō′pər-fĭsh′əl) *adj.* Insignificant.

superfluity (sōō′pər-flōō′ə-tē) *n.* Something that is unnecessary or inessential.

superfluous (sōō-pûr′flōō-əs) *adj.* More than what is needed; unnecessary.

supernal (sōō-pûr′nəl) *adj.* Magical; divine.

supersede (sōō′pər-sēd′) *v.* To replace as an improvement.

supine (sōō′pīn′, sōō-pīn′) *adj.* Lying down; passive.—**supinely** *adv.*

supplicant (sŭp′lĭ-kənt) *n.* One who begs or pleads.

supplicate (sŭp′lĭ-kāt′) *v.* To humbly request.—**supplication** *n.*—**supplicatingly** *adv.*

surcease (sûr′sēs′, sər-sēs′) *n.* End.

surfeit (sûr′fĭt) *n.* Excess.

surly (sûr′lē) *adj.* Ill-tempered.

surmise (sər-mīz′) *v.* To guess.

surmount (sər-mount′) *v.* To overcome.

surplice (sûr′plĭs) *n.* A loose white gown, usually worn by clergy.

surreptitious (sûr′əp-tĭsh′əs) *adj.* Secretive.—**surreptitiously** *adv.*

surveillance (sər-vā′ləns) *n.* Supervision; close watch.

sward (swôrd) *n.* Land thickly covered with grass.

swarthy (swôr′*th*ē) *adj.* Of dark complexion.

sylvan (sĭl′vən) *adj.* Living in the woods.

T

tableau (tăb′lō′, tă-blō′) *n.* An interval during a dramatic scene, in which actors hold a striking pose without speaking or moving.

tacit (tăs′ĭt) *adj.* Unspoken but understood.

taciturn (tăs′ə-tərn) *adj.* Untalkative; uncommunicative.

tangible (tăn′jə-bəl) *adj.* Real; capable of being touched or felt.

tantalize (tăn′tə-līz′) *v.* To tease by keeping something out of reach.

tantrum (tăn′trəm) *n.* A display of childish ill temper.

tawdry (tô′drē) *adj.* Gaudy; showy and cheap.

tawny (tô′nē) *adj.* Brownish-yellow or brownish-orange.

tedious (tē′dē-əs) *adj.* Tiresome; boring.

temerity (tə-mĕr′ə-tē) *n.* Reckless boldness.

temperamental (tĕm′prə-mənt′l, tĕm′pər-ə-) *adj.* Unpredictable; moody.

temporal (tĕm′pər-əl, tĕm′prəl) *adj.* Earthly.

tenacious (tə-nā′shəs) *adj.* Persistent.

tendril (tĕn′drəl) *n.* A long, thin, spiral extension of a climbing plant.

tenuity (tə-nōō′ə-tē, tə-nyōō′-) *n.* Fineness; fragility.

tenuous (tĕn′yōō-əs) *adj.* Slight; indefinite.

termagant (tûr′mə-gənt) *n.* A scolding woman.

terrestrial (tə-rĕs′trē-əl) *adj.* Earthly.

thitherward (thĭth′ər-wərd, thĭth′-) *adv.* There; in that direction.

tincture (tĭngk′chər) *n.* A trace.

torpid (tôr′pĭd) *adj.* Numb; unresponsive.

torpor (tôr′pər) *n.* The state of dullness and inactivity.

torrid (tôr′ĭd, tŏr′-) *adj.* Passionate.

tourniquet (tōōr′nĭ-kĭt, -kā′, tûr′-) *n.* A band tightened around an injured limb to control bleeding.

transcendent (trăn-sĕn′dənt) *adj.* Outstanding; superior to others.

transcendental (trăn′sĕn-dĕnt′l) *adj.* Following the philosophy of transcendentalism in which truth is sought through spiritual intuition.

transfigure (trăns-fĭg′yər) *v.* To change the appearance or shape of.

transient (trăn′shənt, -zhənt, -zē-ənt) *adj.* Impermanent; temporary.

transmute (trăns-myōōt′, trănz-) *v.* To transform.

travail (trə-vāl′, trăv′āl′) *n.* Struggle.

traverse (trăv′ərs, trə-vûrs′) *v.* To cross; travel across.

trellis (trĕl′ĭs) *n.* A frame made of crossed strips of wood or metal, used to train vines or creeping plants.—**trellised** *adj.*

tremulous (trĕm′yə-ləs) *adj.* Trembling.—**tremulousness** *n.*

trepidancy (trĕp′ə-dən-sē) *n.* Trembling from fear.

trepidation (trĕp′ə-dā′shən) *n.* Fear.

troubadour (trōō′bə-dôr′, -dōr′, -dōōr′) *n.* A minstrel who writes and sings lyrics about love and chivalry.

trowel (trou′əl) *n.* A small, pointed, flat, hand tool used in gardening or bricklaying, for digging, smoothing, or spreading.

trustee (trŭs′tē.) *n.* Someone or some institution that is entrusted with responsibility or safekeeping, but not ownership, of another's property.

tumultuous (tə-mŭl′chōō-əs) *adj.* Violently active.

U

unalloyed (ŭn′ăl′oid, ŭn′ə-loid′) *adj.* Not debased or lowered in value.

unconstrained (ŭn′kən-strānd′) *adj.* Natural; unforced.

uncouth (ŭn′kōōth′) *adj.* Crude.—**uncouthness** *n.*

undulate (ŭn′jōō-lāt′, ŭn′dyə-, ŭn′də-) *v.* To move like waves.

undulation (ŭn′jōō-lā′shən, ŭn′dyə-, ŭn′də-) *n.* Wavelike motion.

ungainly (ŭn′gān′lē) *adj.* Homely; awkward.

unkempt (ŭn′kĕmpt′) *adj.* Not combed; untidy.

unobtrusive (ŭn′əb-trōō′sĭv) *adj.* Not easily noticed.—**unobtrusively** *adv.*

unprecedented (ŭn′prĕs′ə-dĕn′tĭd) *adj.* Without precedent or example.

unpremeditated (ŭn′prī-mĕd′ə-tā′tĭd) *adj.* Not thought out beforehand.

unrecking (ŭn-rĕk′ĭng) *adj.* Neglectful; careless.

unremitting (ŭn′rĭ-mĭt′ĭng) *adj.* Unending; incessant.—**unremittingly** *adv.*

unscrupulous (ŭn′skrōō′pyə-ləs) *adj.* Lacking principles or conscience.

unwary (ŭn′wâr′ē) *adj.* Unguarded.

unwieldy (ŭn′wēl′dē) *adj.* Difficult to manage because of awkward size, shape, or weight.

unwonted (ŭn′wôn′tĭd, -wŏn′tĭd, -wŭn′tĭd) *adj.* Unusual.

upbraid (ŭp′brād′) *v.* To scold or criticize sharply.

urbane (ûr′bān′) *adj.* Polished; elegant in manner.

urchin (ûr′chĭn) *n.* A mischievous child.

usurer (yōō′zhər-ər) *n.* A moneylender who charges extreme or unlawfully high interest rates.

usurious (yōō-zhōōr′ē-əs) *adj.* Characteristic of a usurer; charging excessive interest rates on a loan.

usurp (yōō-sûrp′, zûrp′) *v.* To take over by force.

usurpation (yōō′sər-pā′shən, yōō′zər-) *n.* The act of taking possession by force.

utilitarian (yōō-tĭl′ə-târ′ē-ən) *adj.* Practical.

V

vagary (vā′gə-rē, və-gâr′ē) *n.* Oddity; whimsical notion.

vagrant (vā′grənt) *n.* An aimless wanderer.

vainglory (vān′glôr′ē, -glōr′ē) *n.* Excessive pride.

variegated (vâr′ē-ə-gā′tĭd) *adj.* Having several colors.

venerable (vĕn′ər-ə-bəl) *adj.* Worthy of respect for its dignity, character, or age.

veracious (və-rā′shəs) *adj.* Truthful.

veracity (və-răs′ə-tē) *n.* Truth; accuracy.

verdant (vûr′dənt) *adj.* Green.

verdure (vûr′jər) *n.* Green vegetation.

ă pat/ā pay/âr care/ä father/b, bib/ch church/d deed/ē pet/ē be/f fife/g gag/h hat/hw which/ĭ pit/ī pie/îr pier/j judge/k kick/l lid, needle/ m mum/n no, sudden/ng thing/ŏ pot/ō toe/ô paw, for/oi noise/ou out/ōō took/ōō boot/p pop/r roar/s sauce/sh ship, dish/t tight/th thin, path/*th* this, bathe/ŭ cut/ûr urge/v valve/w with/y yes/z zebra, size/zh vision/ə about, item, edible, gallop, circus/à *Fr.* ami/œ *Fr.* feu, *Ger.* schön/ü *Fr.* tu, *Ger.* über/ᴋʜ *Ger.* ich, *Scot.* loch/ɴ *Fr.* bon.

verification (vĕr'ə-fə-kā'shən) *n.* Confirmation of the truth of something.

veritable (vĕr'ə-tə-bəl) *adj.* Real; actual.

verity (vĕr'ə-tē) *n.* Truth.

vernacular (vər-năk'yə-lər) *n.* The everyday speech of a country or particular locale.

vestibule (vĕs'tə-byōōl') *n.* A small entrance hall.

vesture (vĕs'chər) *n.* Clothing.

vexation (vĕk-sā'shən) *n.* Irritation.

vicissitude (vĭ-sĭs'ə-tōōd', -tyōōd') *n.* Alteration.

victual (vĭt'l) *n.* Food.

vigilant (vĭj'ə-lənt) *adj.* Watchful; alert.

vindictive (vĭn-dĭk'tĭv) *adj.* Vengeful; bitter.—**vindictively** *adv.*—**vindictiveness** *n.*

visage (vĭz'ĭj) *n.* Face.

visionary (vĭzh'ən-ĕr'ē) *adj.* Having foresight.

vituperative (vī-tōō'pər-ə-tĭv, vī-tyōō'-, vĭ-) *adj.* Characterized by harsh, abusive language.

vivacious (vĭ-vā'shəs, vī-) *adj.* Energetic; spirited.

vociferate (vō-sĭf'ə-rāt') *v.* To clamor or cry out.—**vociferation** *n.*

volition (və-lĭsh'ən) *n.* The act of willing.

voluminous (və-lōō'mə-nəs) *adj.* Having tremendous volume.—**voluminously** *adv.*

voluptuous (və-lŭp'chōō-əs) *adj.* Luxurious.

voracious (vô-rā'shəs, vō-, və-) *adj.* Greedy; extremely eager in some activity or endeavor.

W

waif (wāf) *n.* An abandoned person.

wanton (wŏn'tən) *adj.* **1.** Immoral. **2.** Reckless.—**wantonness** *n.*

warp (wôrp) *n.* In weaving, the threads that run lengthwise on the loom.

warrant (wôr'ənt, wŏr'-) *n.* Authorization.

wean (wēn) *v.* To separate gradually.

weft (wĕft) *n.* In weaving, the threads carried horizontally across the warp on the loom.

winnow (wĭn'ō) *v.* To scatter.

wistful (wĭst'fəl) *adj.* Sadly wishful.—**wistfully** *adv.*

withal (wĭth-ôl') *adv.* Additionally; also.

wont (wônt, wōnt, wŭnt) *n.* Inclination or habit.

wry (rī) *adj.* Humorous in a dry or ironic way.

Y

yawp (yôp) *n.* A loud, sharp cry.

OUTLINE OF CONCEPTS AND SKILLS

Page numbers in italics refer to entries in the Guide to Literary Terms and Techniques.

LANGUAGE AND VOCABULARY

Finding origins of words, 22
Noting characteristics of plain style and ornate style, 32
Using context clues to derive meanings of words, 53
Finding examples of naturalized words, 62
Identifying examples of specialization, 62
Finding definitions of *temperance* in dictionary and explaining meanings of several related words, 85
Distinguishing meanings of synonyms, 93
Comparing words used in original and revised versions of the Declaration, 104
Locating archaic words, 152
Noting connotative meanings of words in selection, 175
Explaining words in context of excerpts, 255

Evaluating Faulkner's treatment of "old universal truths" in "The Bear," 639
Discussing "The Devil and Daniel Webster" in terms of the tall-tale tradition of American humor, 650
Comparing "The Devil and Daniel Webster" with a selection by Twain or Thurber, 650
Analyzing Hemingway's style, 659
Evaluating a critical statement about Isaac Bashevis Singer's work with specific reference to "Lost," 682
Discussing similarities of theme, character, or situation among short stories, 689
Supporting an opinion on the ending of "A Worn Path," 699
Analyzing plot and theme in "The First Seven Years," 708
Discussing the relation of irony to the theme of a short story, 718
Analyzing the believability of a character, 727
Comparing characters from two different stories, 737
Examining the claim that Frost's poetry has a dark, pessimistic side, with specific reference to poems in the textbook, 751
Comparing Sandburg's technique in the use of free verse with Whitman's, 756
Comparing speakers in "The Love Song of J. Alfred Prufrock" and "After Apple-Picking," 781
Comparing views on poetry of Marianne Moore and Archibald MacLeish, 791
Comparing views of the universe in "Evening Ebb" and "pity this busy monster,manunkind," 795
Analyzing traditional images in a poem, 804
Comparing the treatment of death and mourning in "Elegy for Jane" and "Bells for John Whiteside's Daughter," 819
Explaining how the image of water is used in several poems, 838
Comparing "Marsyas" with other poems about art, 854
Taking a position on Baldwin's statement in "The Creative Process" and giving reasons for position, 880
Writing an essay based on research about the Nobel Prize, 882
Analyzing Ellison's statement about Faulkner's writing, 886
Writing a personal essay with emphasis on setting, 893
Discussing Zora Neale Hurston's reading tastes, citing evidence from her essay, 906
Discussing the distinction between two kinds of readers in *Hunger of Memory,* 931
Analyzing a character in *Trifles,* 949
Discussing the moral dilemma faced by two characters in *Trifles,* 949
Discussing the meaning of the title *Where the Cross Is Made,* 962
Agreeing or disagreeing with ideas about nature expressed in *Our Town,* 1004
Showing how a theme is developed in *Trifles* and *Our Town,* 1004
Writing a critical essay on the selections in "Literature in Modern America," 1005

OTHER WRITING EXERCISES

Writing descriptive, narrative, and expository entries in a diary, 22
Developing an intricate comparison in the manner of a conceit, 40
Describing a trip or a place visited, 48
Analyzing a modern example of persuasion, considering the speaker, the audience, the occasion, and the means of persuasion, 59
Writing an autobiographical essay, 85
Writing aphorisms for today, 87
Writing an epitaph for some well-known person, 88
Writing a persuasive speech, making use of repetition, rhetorical questions, and allusions, 93
Composing a literary letter contrasting modern America with eighteenth-century America, 107
Writing a paragraph that creates a single emotional effect, 175
Writing an imaginary account of the composition of a Poe poem, 189
Considering the importance of "possibility" in Emerson's view of life, 228
Drawing an analogy between an object and some aspect of human life, following Holmes's example in "The Chambered Nautilus," 314
Describing a house or room, using details that suggest the nature of its occupants, 481
Describing a real or imagined experience, using stream-of-consciousness technique, 599
Describing a setting appropriate for the opening paragraph of a story, 673
Describing a place, choosing language and details that reveal the writer's attitude toward the place, 689
Describing an action, selecting words and details that characterize the person performing the action, 699
Writing a character sketch, 737
Writing a satirical tribute to a person or thing, or a satire on modern society, 816
Writing a humorous letter in the manner of E. B. White's "Walden (June 1939)," 872
Writing a humorous essay, 876
Writing an impressionistic biography about a real or invented figure, 900
Explaining the preparation of a favorite family dish, 916
Writing about a major influence that contributed to self-insight, 921
Describing a place and its influence, 928
Presenting a cross-section of life in the form of an essay or dramatic sketch, 1004

CLOSE READING

Paraphrasing a passage from John Smith's *General History* so that the content is clear, 21

Rewriting Bradford's sentences in Modern English, 33

Paraphrasing a passage from *The Journal of Madam Knight* so that the content is clear, 48

Paraphrasing a passage from Franklin's *The Autobiography* so that the content is clear, 85

Rewriting a passage from Paine's *The Crisis* in Modern English and analyzing changes in expression, 96

Analyzing one of Poe's long sentences from "The Fall of the House of Usher," 174

Analyzing style and purpose in Thoreau's *Walden*, 245

Analyzing Twain's vernacular style, 403

EXTENDING YOUR STUDY
First Harvest—page 196

1. Researching the Hudson River School of Painters, checking the availability of reproductions of their landscapes, and sharing findings with the class.
2. Determining how *The Architect's Dream* (page 122) by Thomas Cole expresses classical principles and how *The Moonlit Landscape* (page 123) by Washington Allston expresses Romantic principles.
3. Discussing the distinctive style of Delaware Indian dress as represented in the details of the painting by George Catlin on page 142.
4. Discussing the meditative, foreboding quality conveyed by Asher Durand's *Thanatopsis* on pages 154–155.
5. Evaluating Poe's short stories according to the criteria of his own literary theories.

The Flowering of New England—page 334

1. Discussing Thomas Doughty's use of light to create a particular romantic effect in the painting *In Nature's Wonderland* (page 209).
2. Finding evidence in the writings of Emerson to explain why William James Stillman in *The Philosophers' Camp* (page 222) portrayed him standing apart from his companions.
3. Comparing two very different renderings of Thoreau's cabin at Walden pond.
4. Studying *The Harbor of Papeete* (page 272) and discussing the kinds of changes Melville would expect to come from Western intrusion into Typee life.

5. Relating Henry Lovie's drawing (page 294) and Melville's poem as two responses to the event of the Battle of Shiloh which capture the same mood.
6. Comparing Joseph Meeker's *Land of Evangeline* (page 300) with the passage from Longfellow's poem which it illustrates.
7. Relating Holmes's poem "The Chambered Nautilus" to Edward Weston's photograph, *Shell, 1927*, on page 313.
8. Discussing the details in Edwin Elmer's *Mourning Picture* (pages 328–329) which suggest the typical atmosphere created by nineteenth-century people at the time of loss.

A House Divided and Restored—page 432

1. Reading Chapter XVI of Mark Twain's *Life on the Mississippi* and discussing the details of steamboat racing.
2. Discussing the mood of Conrad Wise Chapman's painting of Fort Sumter on page 338.
3. Researching the biography of the legendary flatboatman Mike Fink and explaining how frontier skills are celebrated in the story of his life.
4. Identifying the distinctive dress styles of American Indian tribes as portrayed by George Catlin (page 376) and Edward Curtis (page 378).
5. Discussing the intent of the humorist who drew the poster (page 391) for a lecture by Mark Twain.

INDEX OF TITLES BY THEMES

Humor and Satire

Generations

COMMENTARIES AND SPECIAL ESSAYS

INDEX OF FINE ART

PHOTO CREDITS

GENERAL INDEX

Titles of selections presented in the textbook are shown in italics. Numbers in italics refer to the pages on which author biographies appear. Names of authors represented in the textbook and other references are shown in regular type.